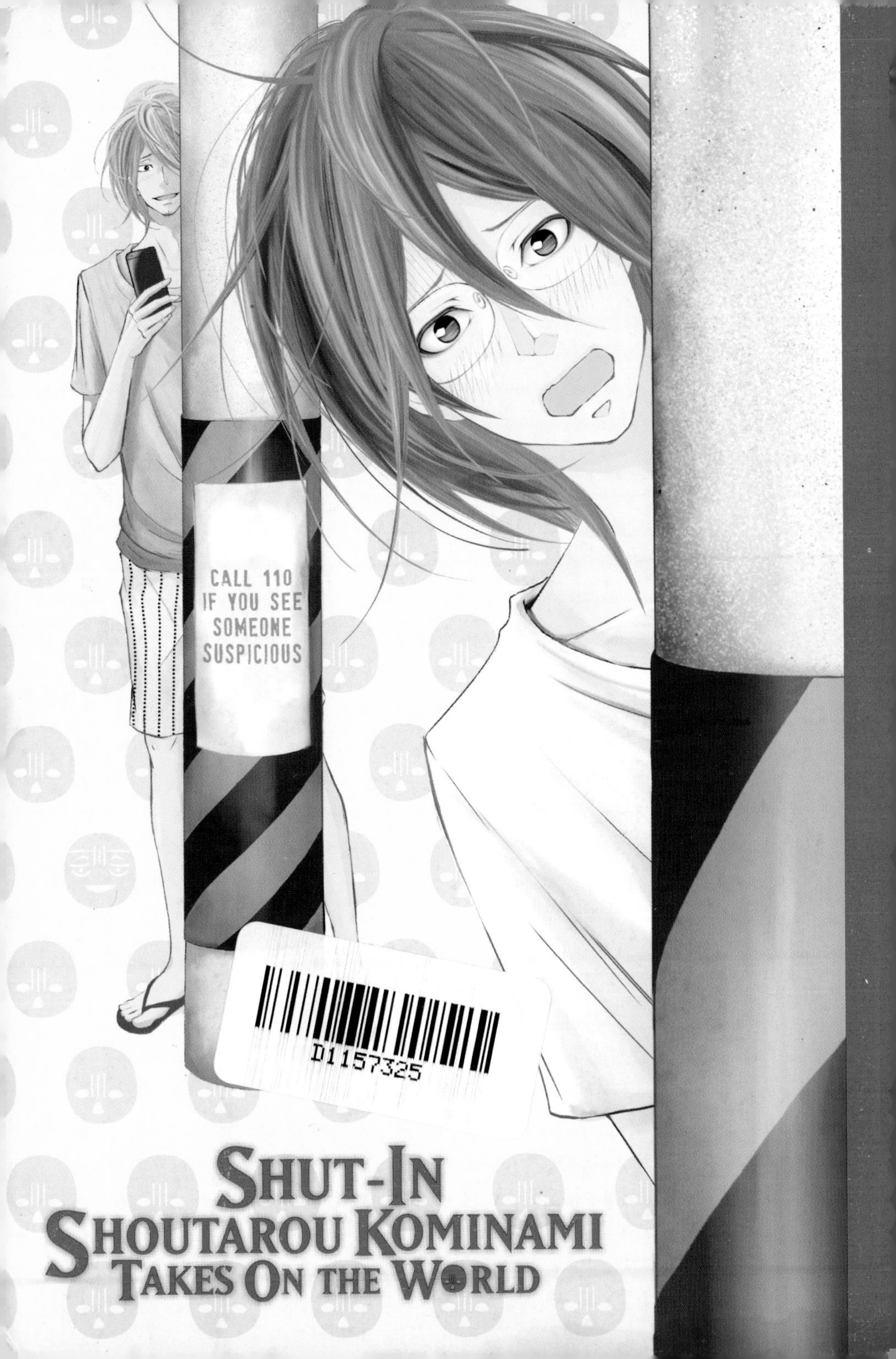
CALL 110
IF YOU SEE
SOMEONE
SUSPICIOUS

Shut-In Shoutarou Kominami Takes On the World

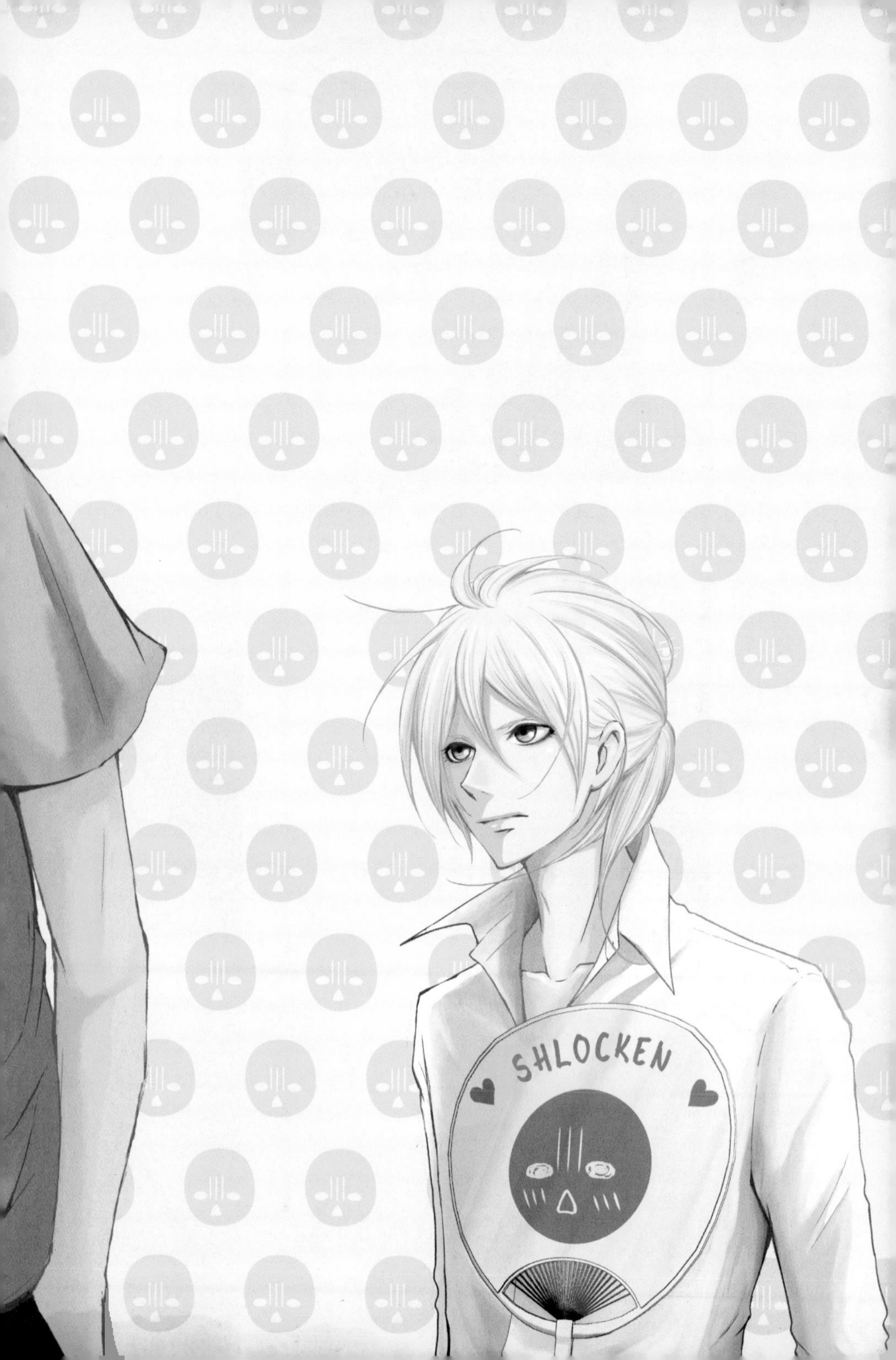
SHLOCKEN

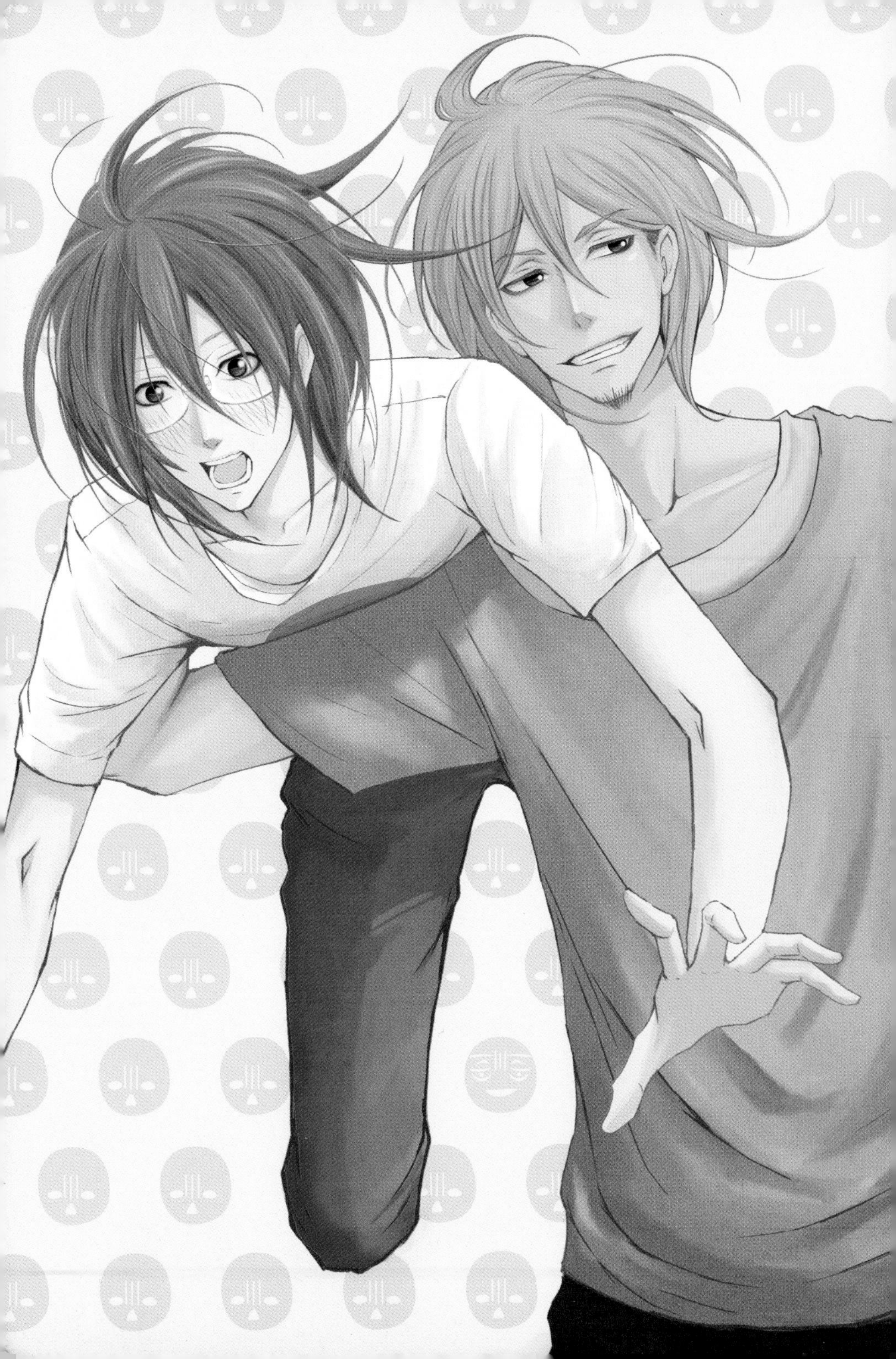

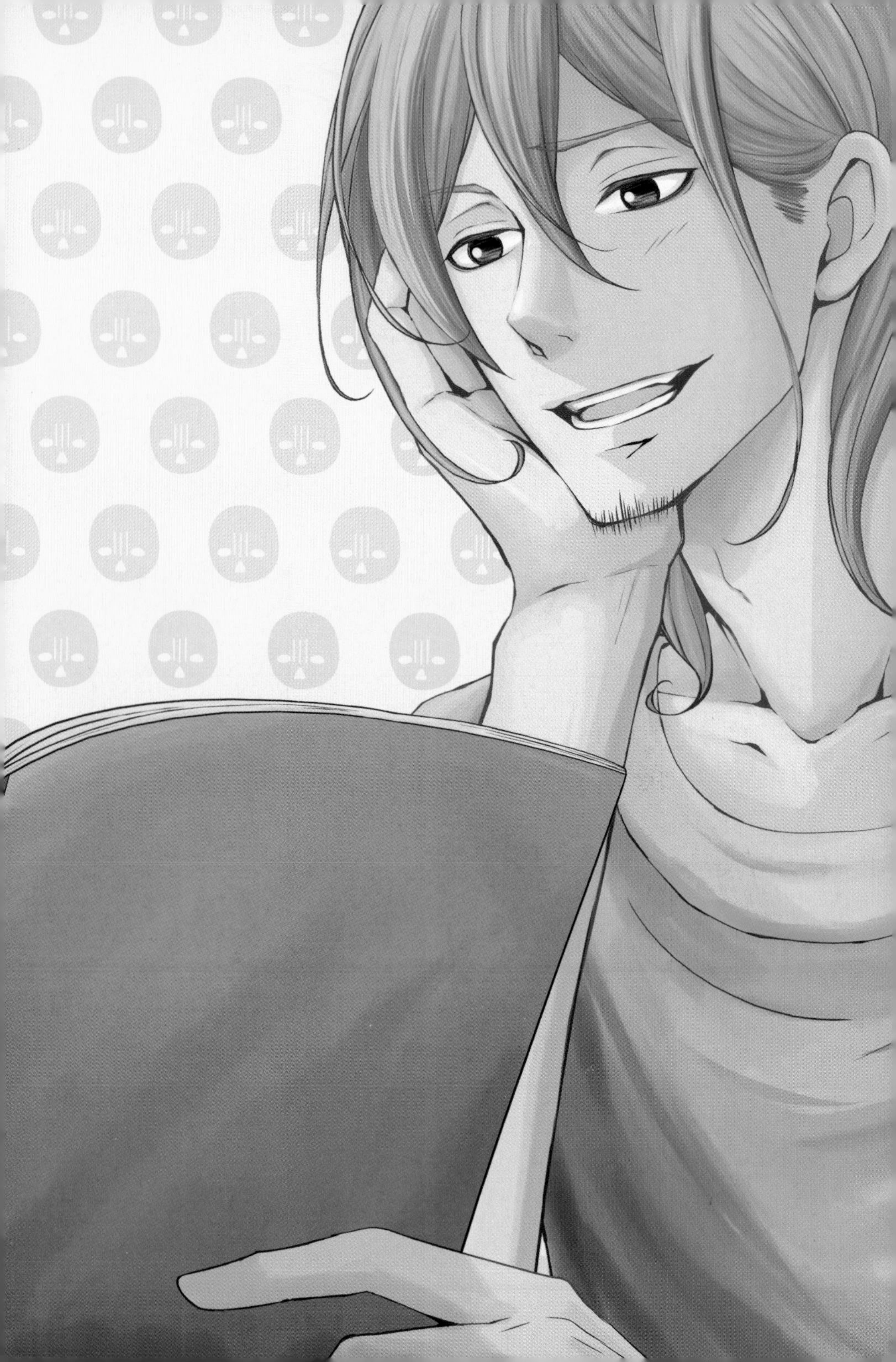

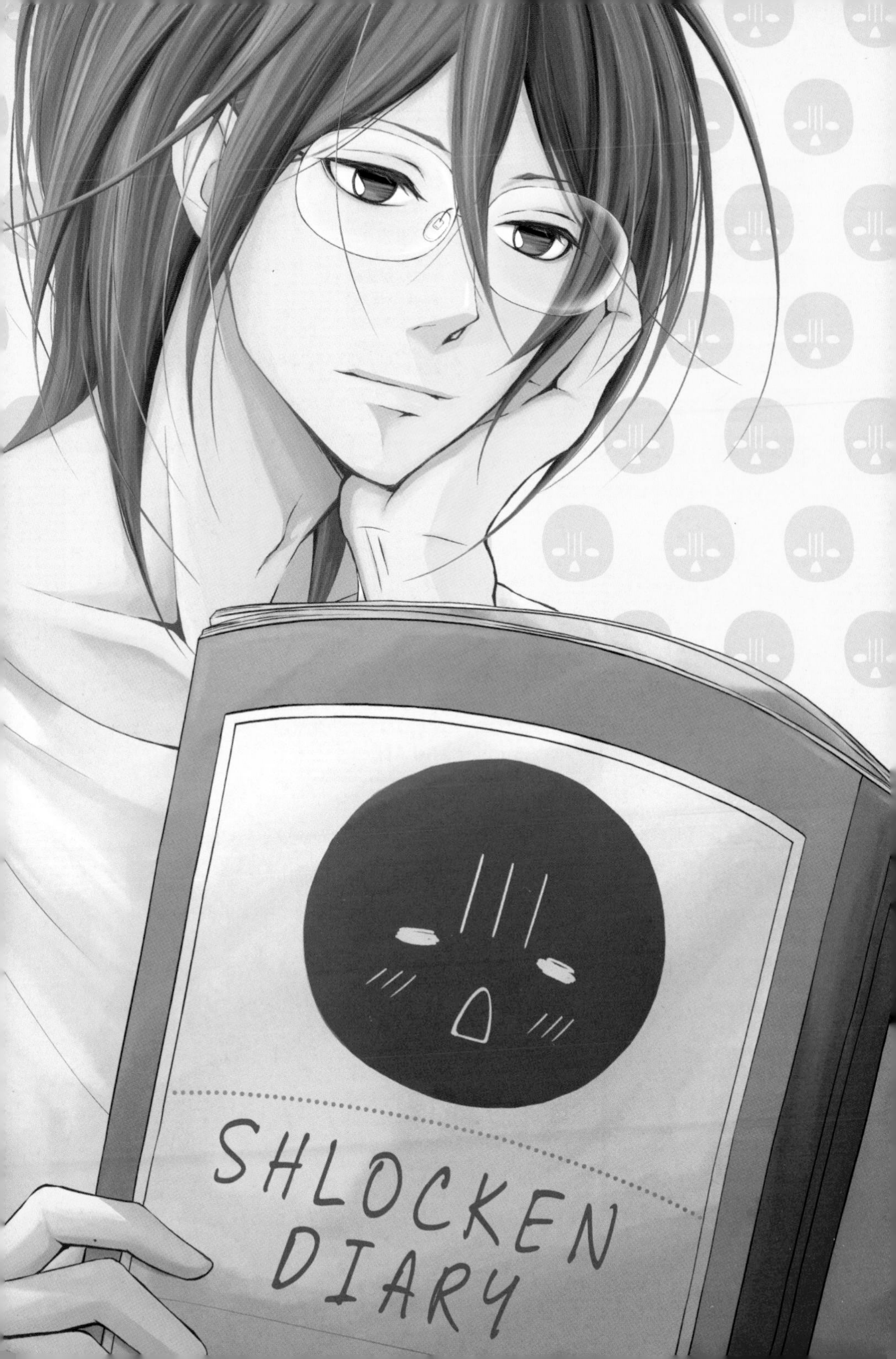
SHLOCKEN DIARY

Contents

Sensei and Me

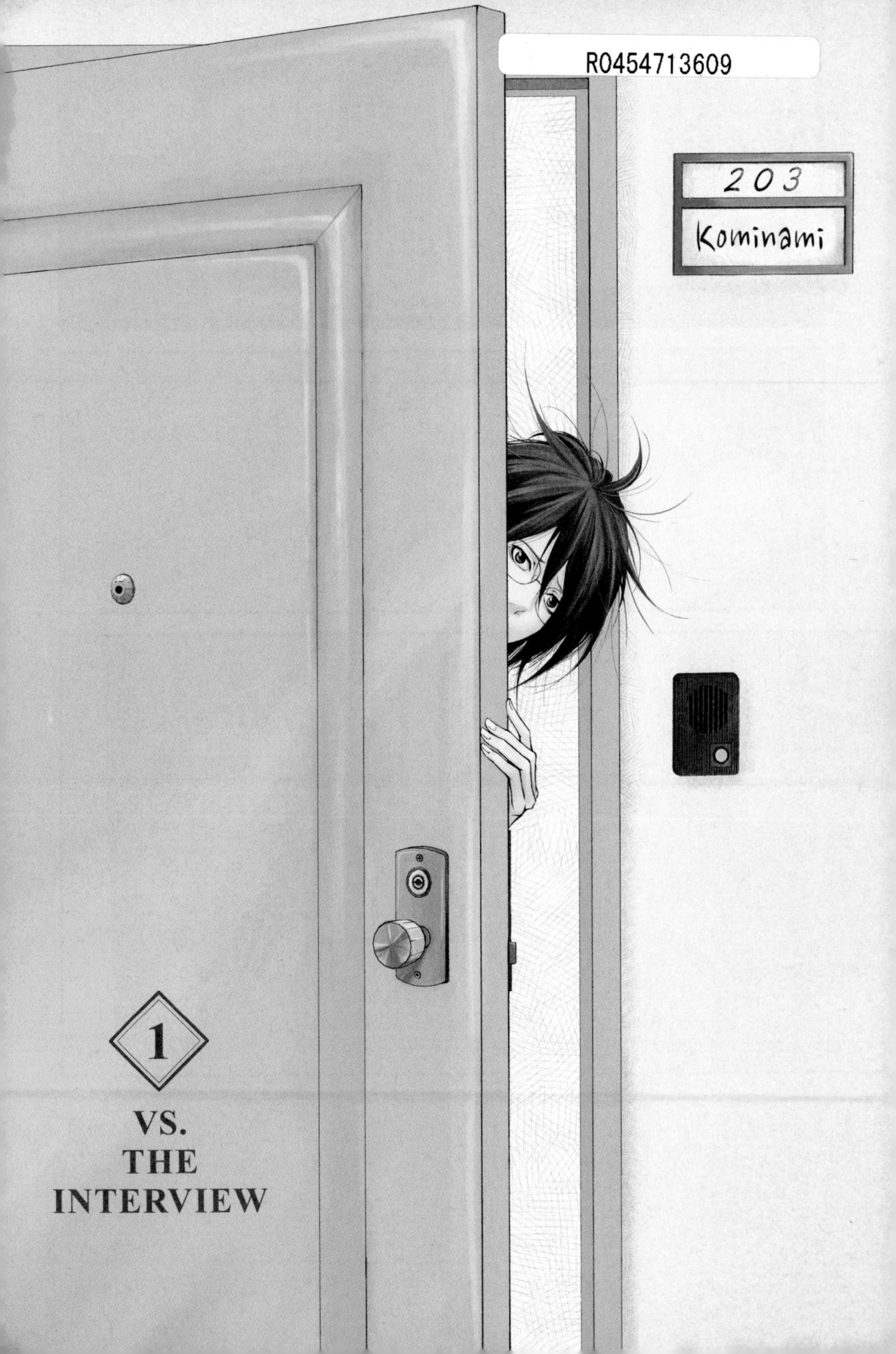
203
Kominami

1 VS. THE INTERVIEW

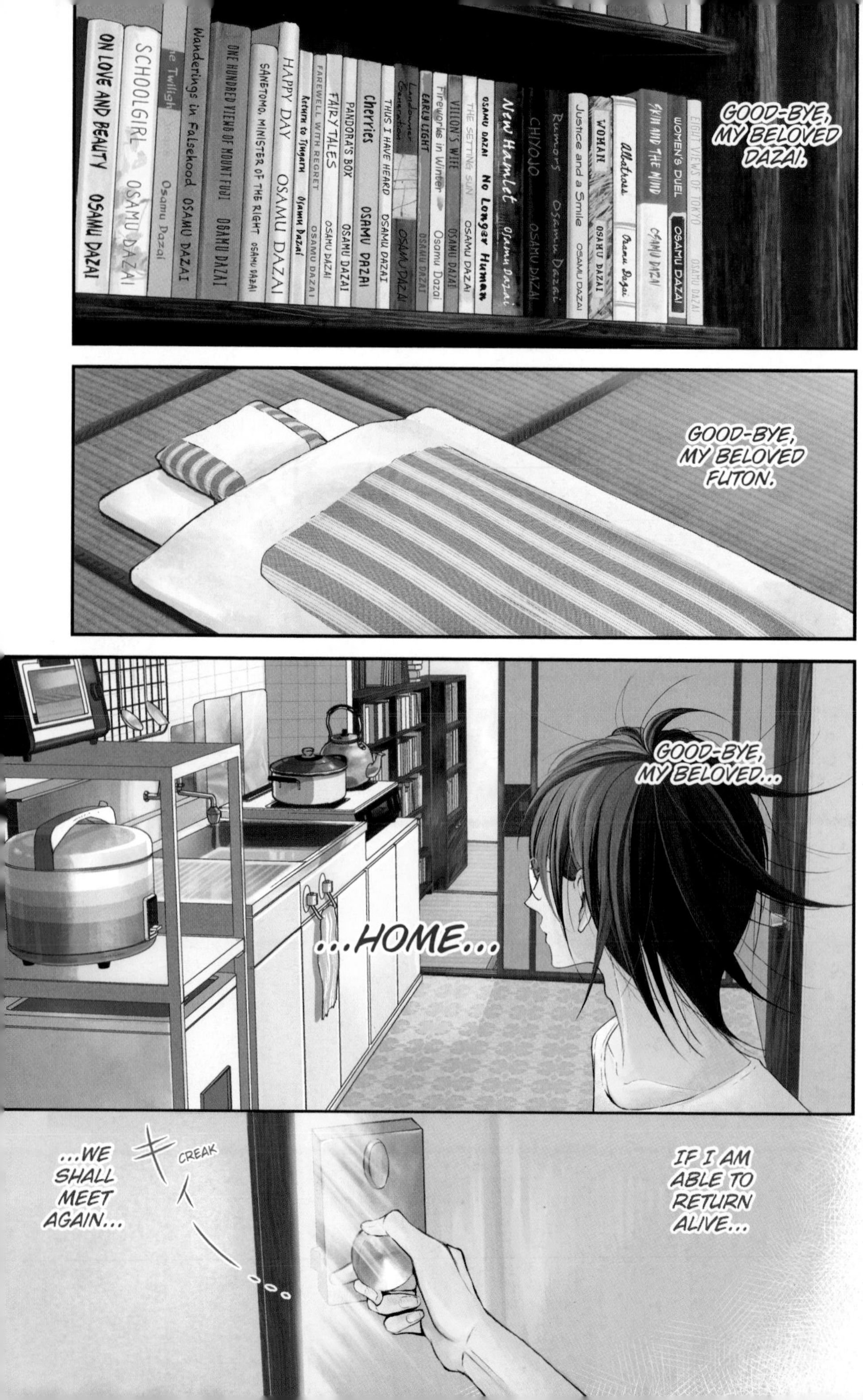
GOOD-BYE, MY BELOVED DAZAI.
ON LOVE AND BEAUTY OSAMU DAZAI
SCHOOLGIRL OSAMU DAZAI
Osamu Dazai
Wanderings in Falsehood OSAMU DAZAI
ONE HUNDRED VIEWS OF MOUNT FUJI OSAMU DAZAI
SANETOMO, MINISTER OF THE RIGHT OSAMU DAZAI
HAPPY DAY OSAMU DAZAI
Return to Tsugaru Osamu Dazai
FAREWELL WITH REGRET OSAMU DAZAI
FAIRY TALES OSAMU DAZAI
PANDORA'S BOX OSAMU DAZAI
Cherries OSAMU DAZAI
THUS I HAVE HEARD OSAMU DAZAI
OSAMU DAZAI
EARLY LIGHT OSAMU DAZAI
Fireworks in Winter Osamu Dazai
VILLON'S WIFE OSAMU DAZAI
THE SETTING SUN OSAMU DAZAI
OSAMU DAZAI No Longer Human
New Hamlet Osamu Dazai
CHIYOJO OSAMU DAZAI
Rumors Osamu Dazai
Justice and a Smile OSAMU DAZAI
WOMAN OSAMU DAZAI
Albatross Osamu Dazai
SKIN AND THE MIND OSAMU DAZAI
WOMEN'S DUEL OSAMU DAZAI
EIGHT VIEWS OF TOKYO OSAMU DAZAI
GOOD-BYE, MY BELOVED FUTON.
GOOD-BYE, MY BELOVED...
...HOME...
IF I AM ABLE TO RETURN ALIVE...
CREAK
...WE SHALL MEET AGAIN...

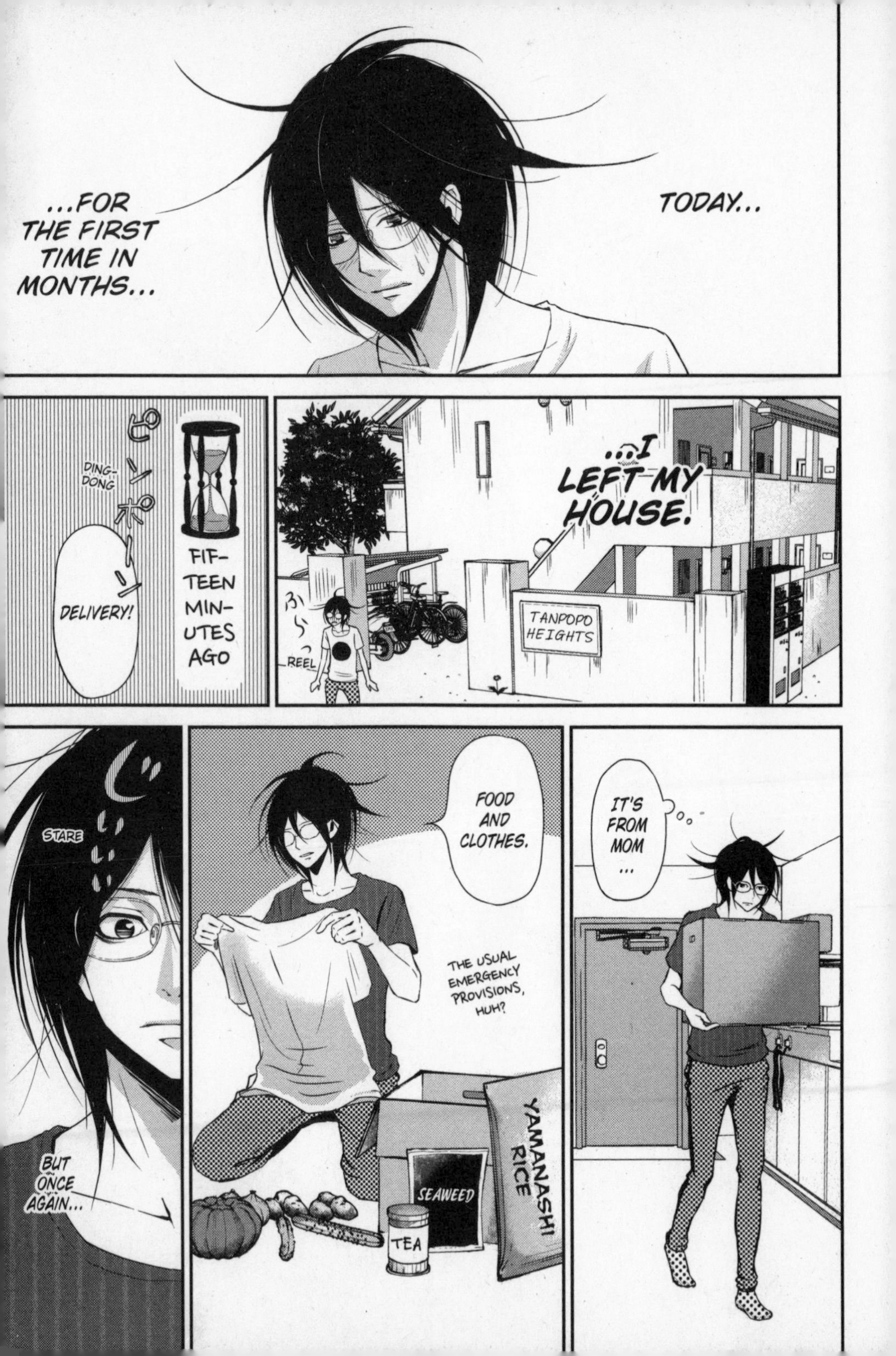
TODAY...
...FOR THE FIRST TIME IN MONTHS...
...I LEFT MY HOUSE.
TANPOPO HEIGHTS
REEL
FIF-TEEN MIN-UTES AGO
DING-DONG
DELIVERY!
IT'S FROM MOM ...
FOOD AND CLOTHES.
THE USUAL EMERGENCY PROVISIONS, HUH?
YAMANASHI RICE
SEAWEED
TEA
STARE
BUT ONCE AGAIN...

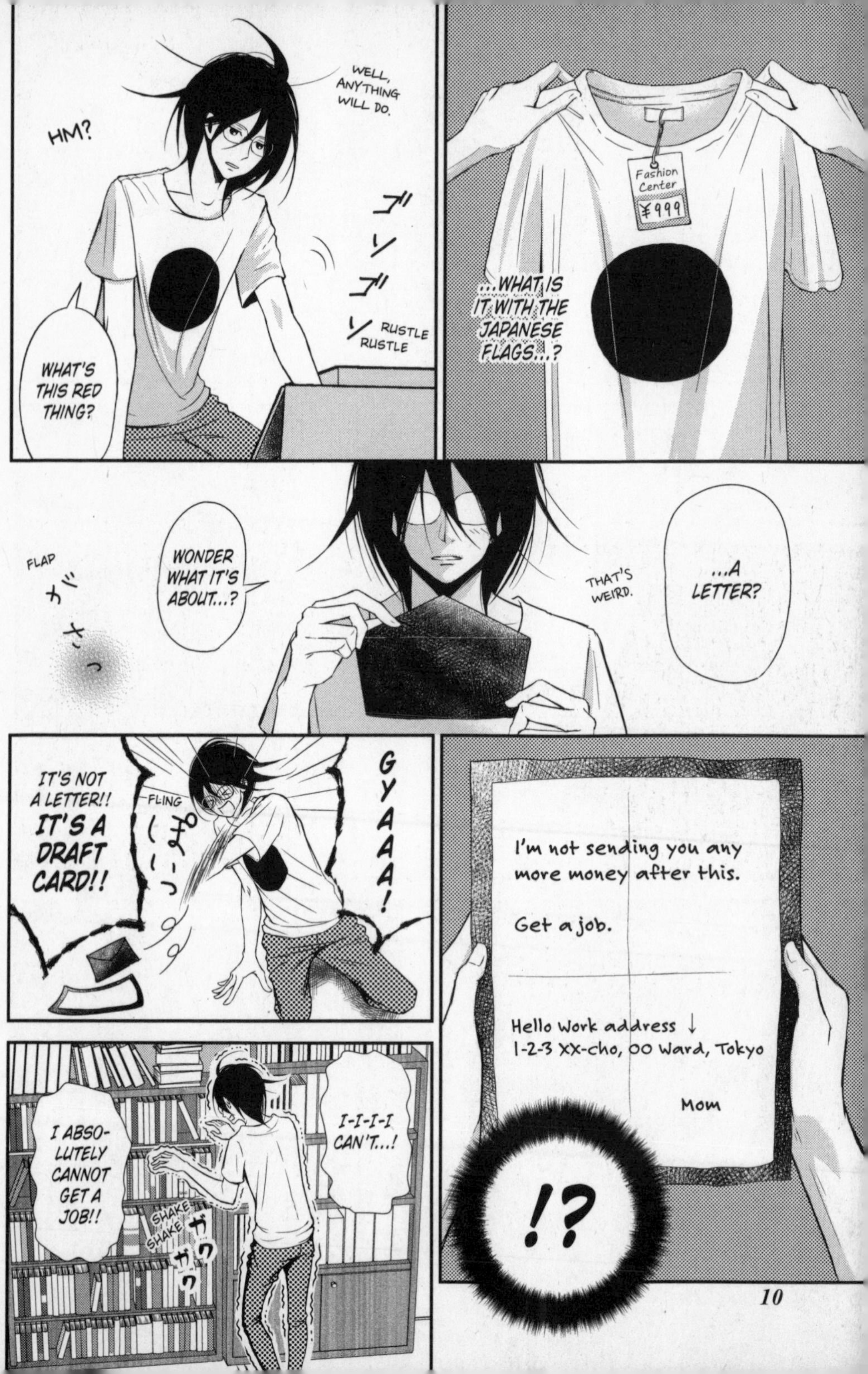
Fashion Center
¥999
...WHAT IS IT WITH THE JAPANESE FLAGS...?
WELL, ANYTHING WILL DO.
HM?
ゴソゴソ
RUSTLE RUSTLE
WHAT'S THIS RED THING?
...A LETTER?
THAT'S WEIRD.
WONDER WHAT IT'S ABOUT...?
FLAP
ガサッ
I'm not sending you any more money after this.
Get a job.
Hello Work address ↓
1-2-3 XX-cho, OO Ward, Tokyo
Mom
!?
GYAAAA!
IT'S NOT A LETTER!! IT'S A DRAFT CARD!!
FLING
ぽーい
I-I-I-I CAN'T...!
SHAKE SHAKE
ガクガク
I ABSO-LUTELY CANNOT GET A JOB!!

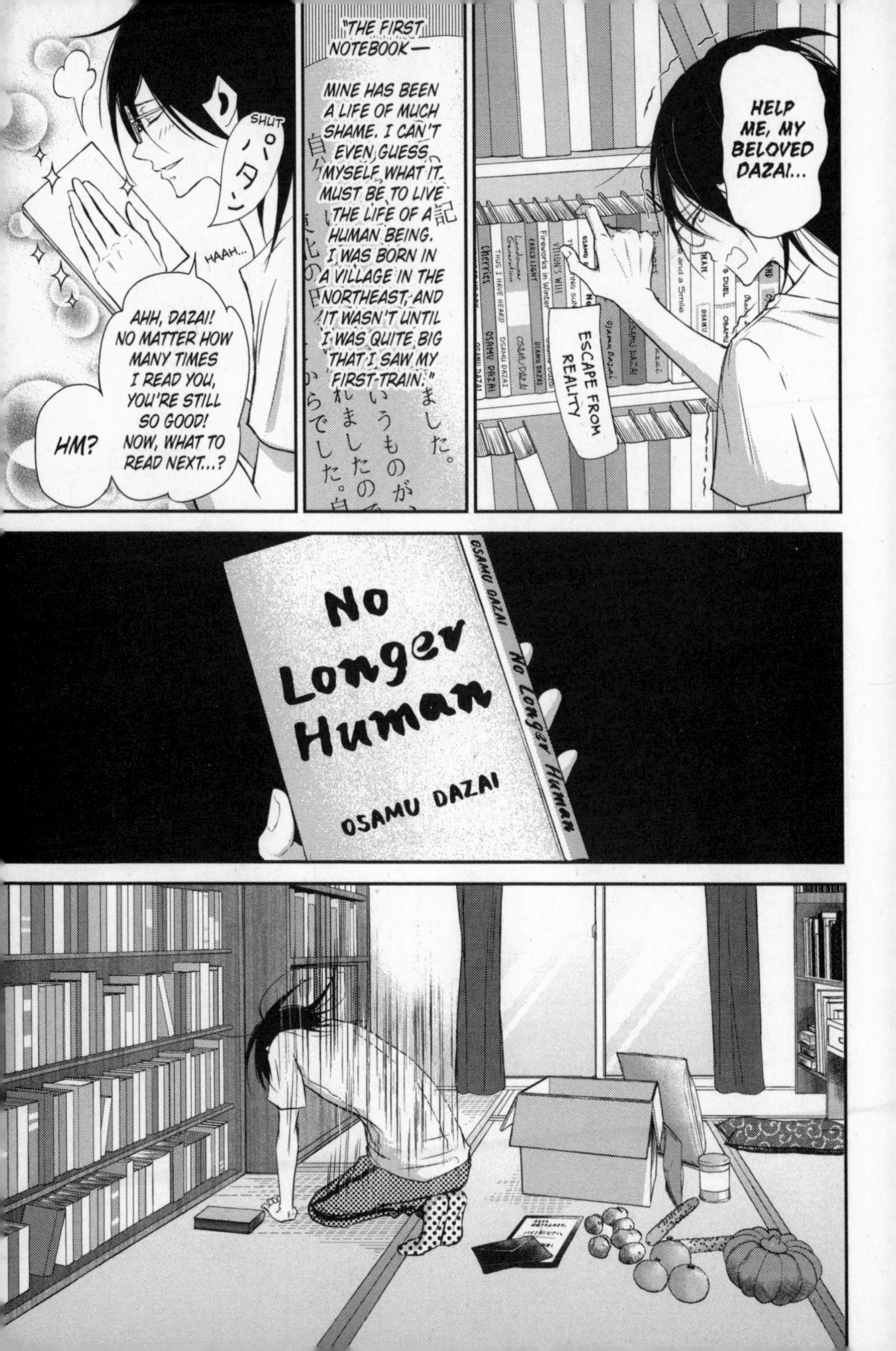
HELP ME, MY BELOVED DAZAI...
ESCAPE FROM REALITY
"THE FIRST NOTEBOOK—
MINE HAS BEEN A LIFE OF MUCH SHAME. I CAN'T EVEN GUESS MYSELF WHAT IT MUST BE TO LIVE THE LIFE OF A HUMAN BEING. I WAS BORN IN A VILLAGE IN THE NORTHEAST, AND IT WASN'T UNTIL I WAS QUITE BIG THAT I SAW MY FIRST TRAIN."
SHUT
HAAH...
AHH, DAZAI! NO MATTER HOW MANY TIMES I READ YOU, YOU'RE STILL SO GOOD! NOW, WHAT TO READ NEXT...?
HM?
No Longer Human
OSAMU DAZAI
OSAMU DAZAI
No Longer Human

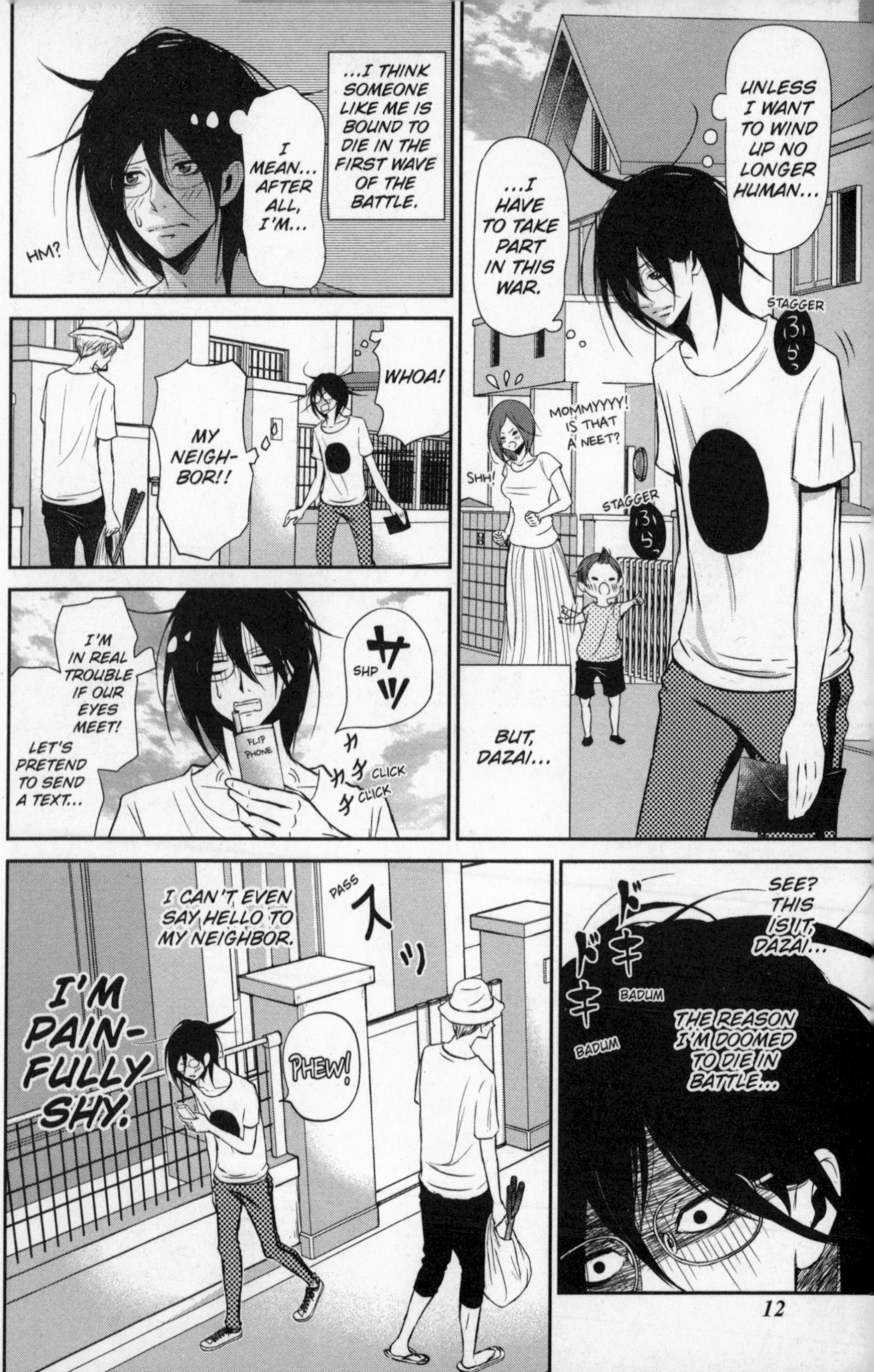
UNLESS I WANT TO WIND UP NO LONGER HUMAN...
...I HAVE TO TAKE PART IN THIS WAR.
STAGGER
MOMMYYYY! IS THAT A NEET?
SHH!
STAGGER
BUT, DAZAI...
...I THINK SOMEONE LIKE ME IS BOUND TO DIE IN THE FIRST WAVE OF THE BATTLE.
I MEAN... AFTER ALL, I'M...
HM?
WHOA!
MY NEIGHBOR!!
I'M IN REAL TROUBLE IF OUR EYES MEET!
SHP
LET'S PRETEND TO SEND A TEXT...
FLIP PHONE
CLICK
CLICK
SEE? THIS IS IT, DAZAI...
BADUM
BADUM
THE REASON I'M DOOMED TO DIE IN BATTLE...
I CAN'T EVEN SAY HELLO TO MY NEIGHBOR.
PASS
PHEW!
I'M PAINFULLY SHY.

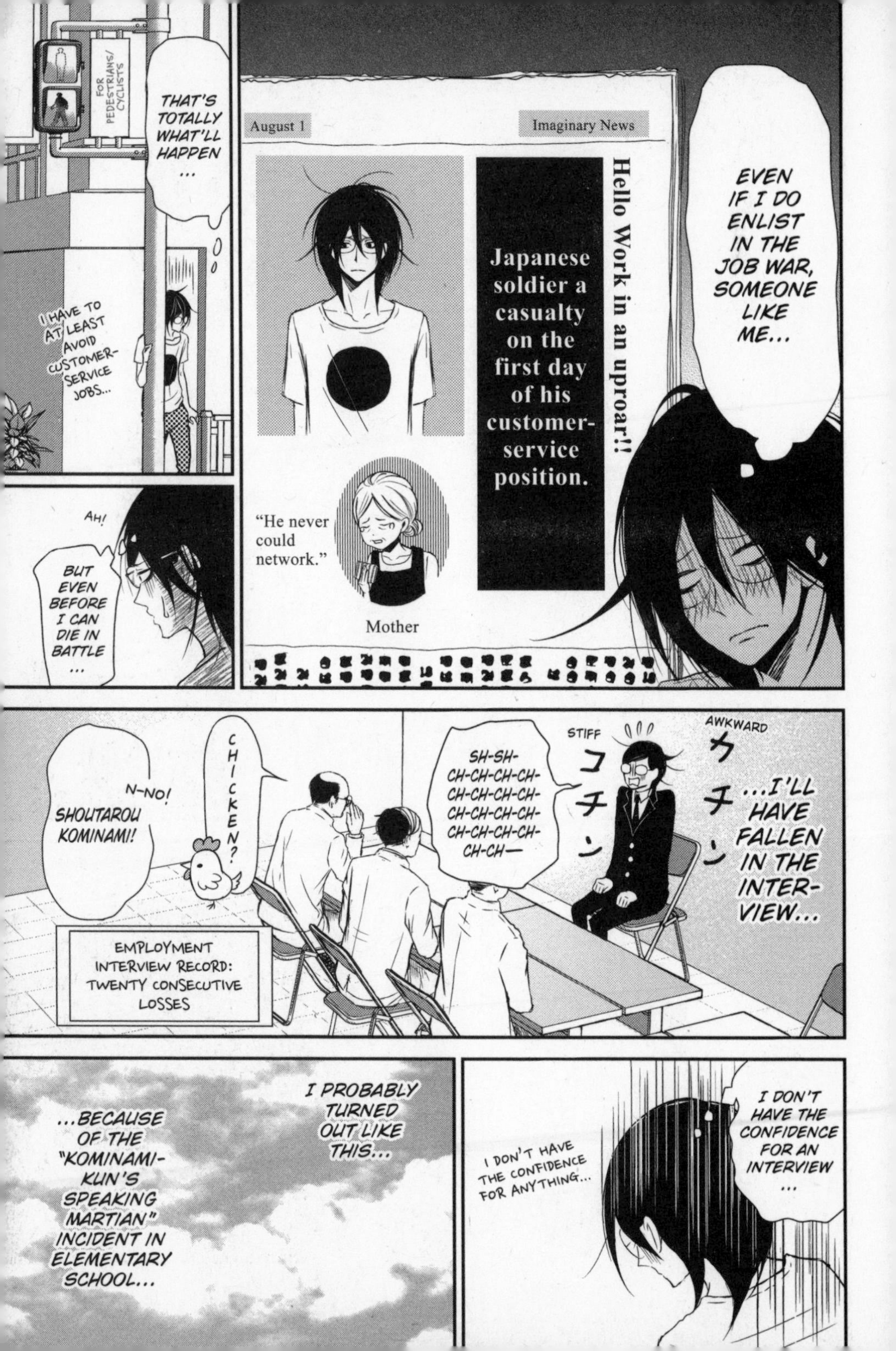
EVEN IF I DO ENLIST IN THE JOB WAR, SOMEONE LIKE ME...
August 1
Imaginary News
Hello Work in an uproar!!
Japanese soldier a casualty on the first day of his customer-service position.
"He never could network."
Mother
THAT'S TOTALLY WHAT'LL HAPPEN...
FOR PEDESTRIANS/ CYCLISTS
I HAVE TO AT LEAST AVOID CUSTOMER-SERVICE JOBS...
AH!
BUT EVEN BEFORE I CAN DIE IN BATTLE...
...I'LL HAVE FALLEN IN THE INTERVIEW...
AWKWARD
カチン
STIFF
コチン
SH-SH-CH-CH-CH-CH-CH-CH-CH-CH-CH-CH-CH-CH-CH-CH-CH-CH-CH-CH—
CHICKEN?
N-NO! SHOUTAROU KOMINAMI!
EMPLOYMENT INTERVIEW RECORD: TWENTY CONSECUTIVE LOSSES
I DON'T HAVE THE CONFIDENCE FOR AN INTERVIEW...
I DON'T HAVE THE CONFIDENCE FOR ANYTHING...
I PROBABLY TURNED OUT LIKE THIS...
...BECAUSE OF THE "KOMINAMI-KUN'S SPEAKING MARTIAN" INCIDENT IN ELEMENTARY SCHOOL...

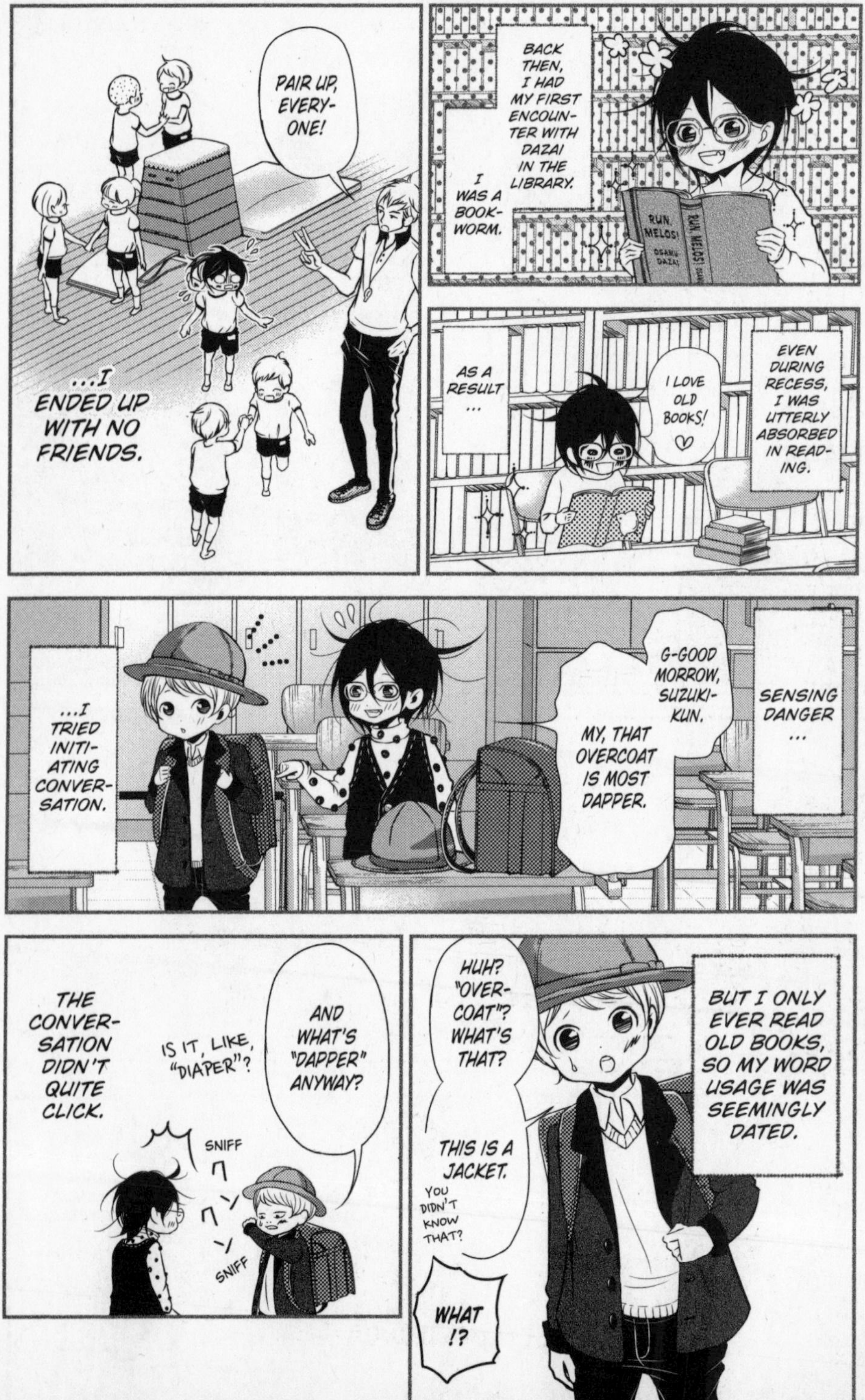
BACK THEN, I HAD MY FIRST ENCOUNTER WITH DAZAI IN THE LIBRARY.
I WAS A BOOKWORM.
RUN, MELOS! OSAMU DAZAI
EVEN DURING RECESS, I WAS UTTERLY ABSORBED IN READING.
I LOVE OLD BOOKS!
AS A RESULT...
PAIR UP, EVERYONE!
...I ENDED UP WITH NO FRIENDS.
SENSING DANGER...
G-GOOD MORROW, SUZUKI-KUN.
MY, THAT OVERCOAT IS MOST DAPPER.
...I TRIED INITIATING CONVERSATION.
BUT I ONLY EVER READ OLD BOOKS, SO MY WORD USAGE WAS SEEMINGLY DATED.
HUH? "OVERCOAT"? WHAT'S THAT?
THIS IS A JACKET.
YOU DIDN'T KNOW THAT?
WHAT!?
AND WHAT'S "DAPPER" ANYWAY?
IS IT, LIKE, "DIAPER"?
THE CONVERSATION DIDN'T QUITE CLICK.
SNIFF
SNIFF

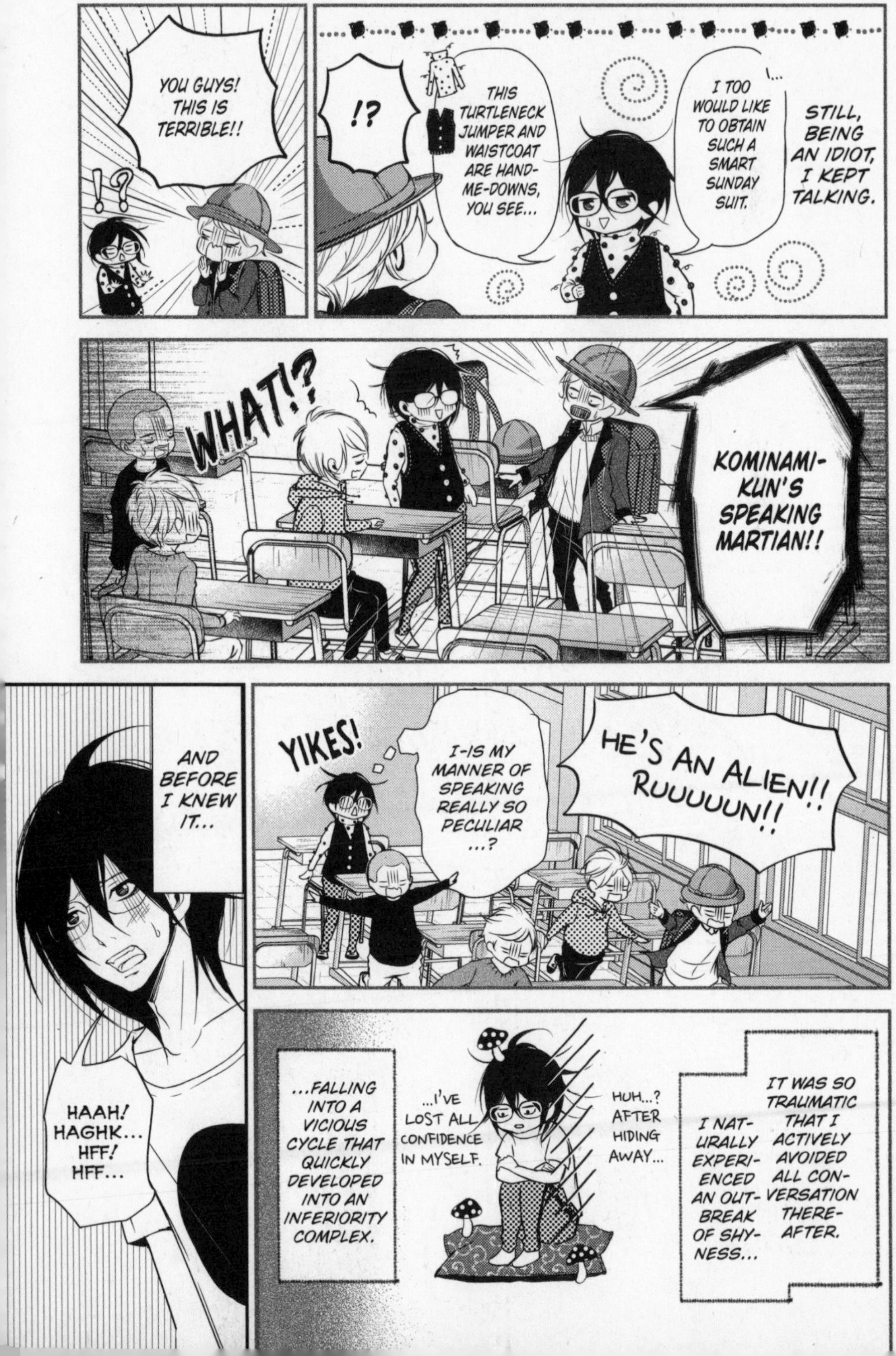
STILL, BEING AN IDIOT, I KEPT TALKING.
I TOO WOULD LIKE TO OBTAIN SUCH A SMART SUNDAY SUIT.
…
THIS TURTLENECK JUMPER AND WAISTCOAT ARE HAND-ME-DOWNS, YOU SEE…
!?
YOU GUYS! THIS IS TERRIBLE!!
!?
KOMINAMI-KUN'S SPEAKING MARTIAN!!
WHAT!?
HE'S AN ALIEN!! RUUUUUN!!
I-IS MY MANNER OF SPEAKING REALLY SO PECULIAR …?
YIKES!
IT WAS SO TRAUMATIC THAT I ACTIVELY AVOIDED ALL CONVERSATION THEREAFTER.
I NATURALLY EXPERIENCED AN OUTBREAK OF SHYNESS…
HUH…? AFTER HIDING AWAY…
…I'VE LOST ALL CONFIDENCE IN MYSELF.
…FALLING INTO A VICIOUS CYCLE THAT QUICKLY DEVELOPED INTO AN INFERIORITY COMPLEX.
AND BEFORE I KNEW IT…
HAAH! HAGHK… HFF! HFF…

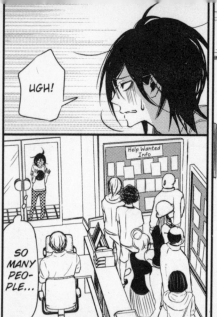

Hello Work
...I WAS OUT OF SHAPE AND UNEMPLOYED.
HFF! I MADE IT... HFF!
UGH!
SO MANY PEOPLE...
WHAT AM I GOING TO DO ...?
WITH THIS MANY PEOPLE LOOKING FOR A JOB...
...I CAN'T IMAGINE ANYONE HIRING A GUY LIKE ME...
EEK!
A COCKROACH!
SHOVE
ゴッ
BONK
OH! I'M SORRY!!
UUURGH...

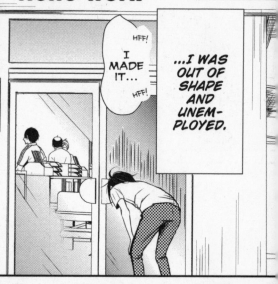

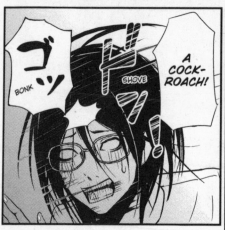

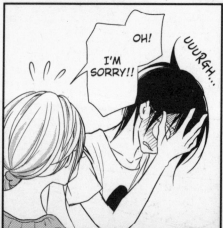

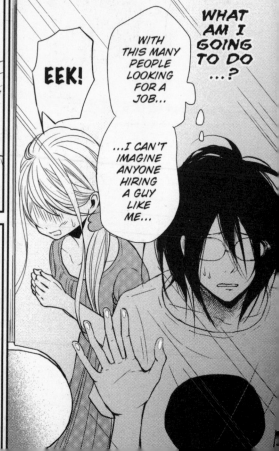

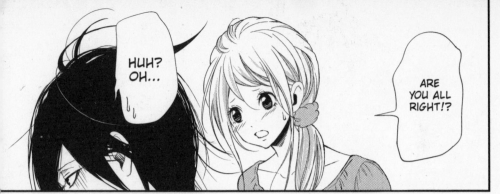

ARE YOU ALL RIGHT!?
HUH? OH...
ACK!
SHE'S SO PRETTY! SHE'S DAZ-ZLING!
LOOKING AT HER IMAGE IN THE WINDOW
AND WHAT'S THAT FILTH REFLECTED NEXT TO HER!?
GARBAGE?
OH. IT'S ME...
I WANT TO DIE...
OH NO! TEARS...
ARE YOU HURT!?
N—
N-N-N-N-N-N-NO!
I-I-I-I-I-I-I'M FINE!
I'M SORRY! I'M SORRY!
I-I-I-I-I-I'M SORRY FOR LIVING!
HUH? LIVING...?
WAAAH!
E-E-E-EXCUSE ME!
......!

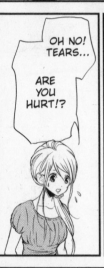

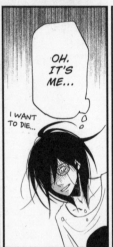

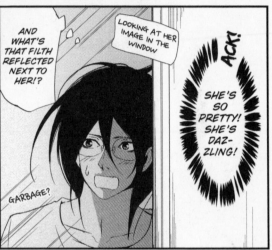

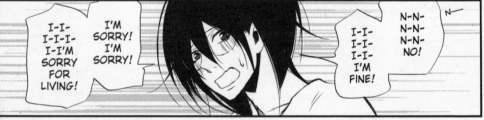

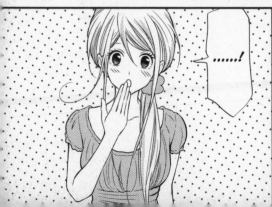

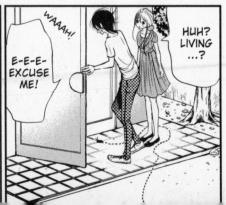

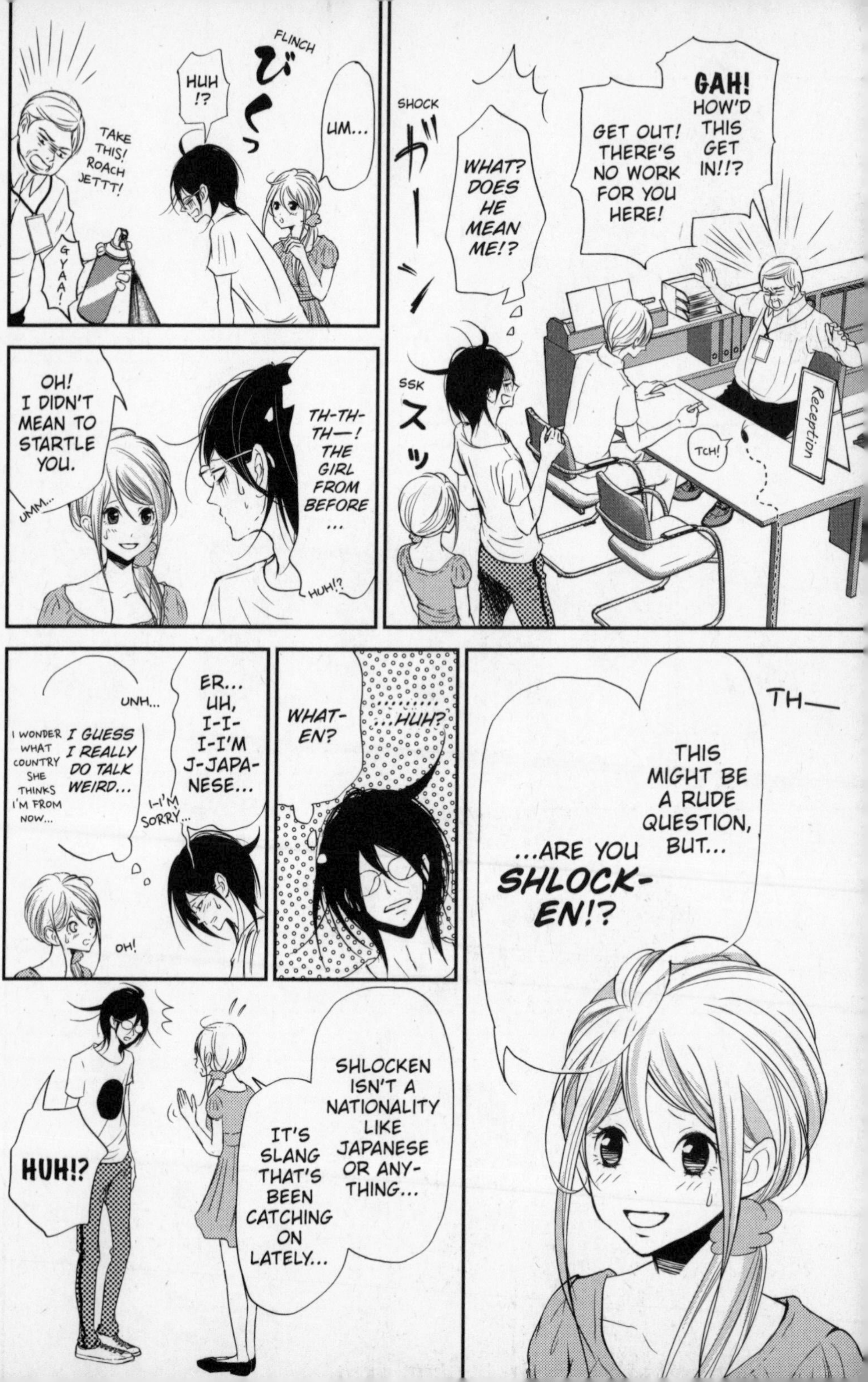
GAH! HOW'D THIS GET IN!!?
GET OUT! THERE'S NO WORK FOR YOU HERE!
SHOCK
ガー
WHAT? DOES HE MEAN ME!?
SSK
スッ
TCH!
Reception
UM...
FLINCH
びくっ
HUH !?
TAKE THIS! ROACH JETTT!
GYAA!
TH-TH-TH—! THE GIRL FROM BEFORE...
HUH!?
OH! I DIDN'T MEAN TO STARTLE YOU.
UMM...
TH—
THIS MIGHT BE A RUDE QUESTION, BUT...
...ARE YOU SHLOCKEN!?
.........HUH?
WHAT-EN?
ER... UH, I-I-I-I'M J-JAPANESE...
I-I'M SORRY...
UNH...
I GUESS I REALLY DO TALK WEIRD...
I WONDER WHAT COUNTRY SHE THINKS I'M FROM NOW...
OH!
SHLOCKEN ISN'T A NATIONALITY LIKE JAPANESE OR ANYTHING...
IT'S SLANG THAT'S BEEN CATCHING ON LATELY...
HUH!?

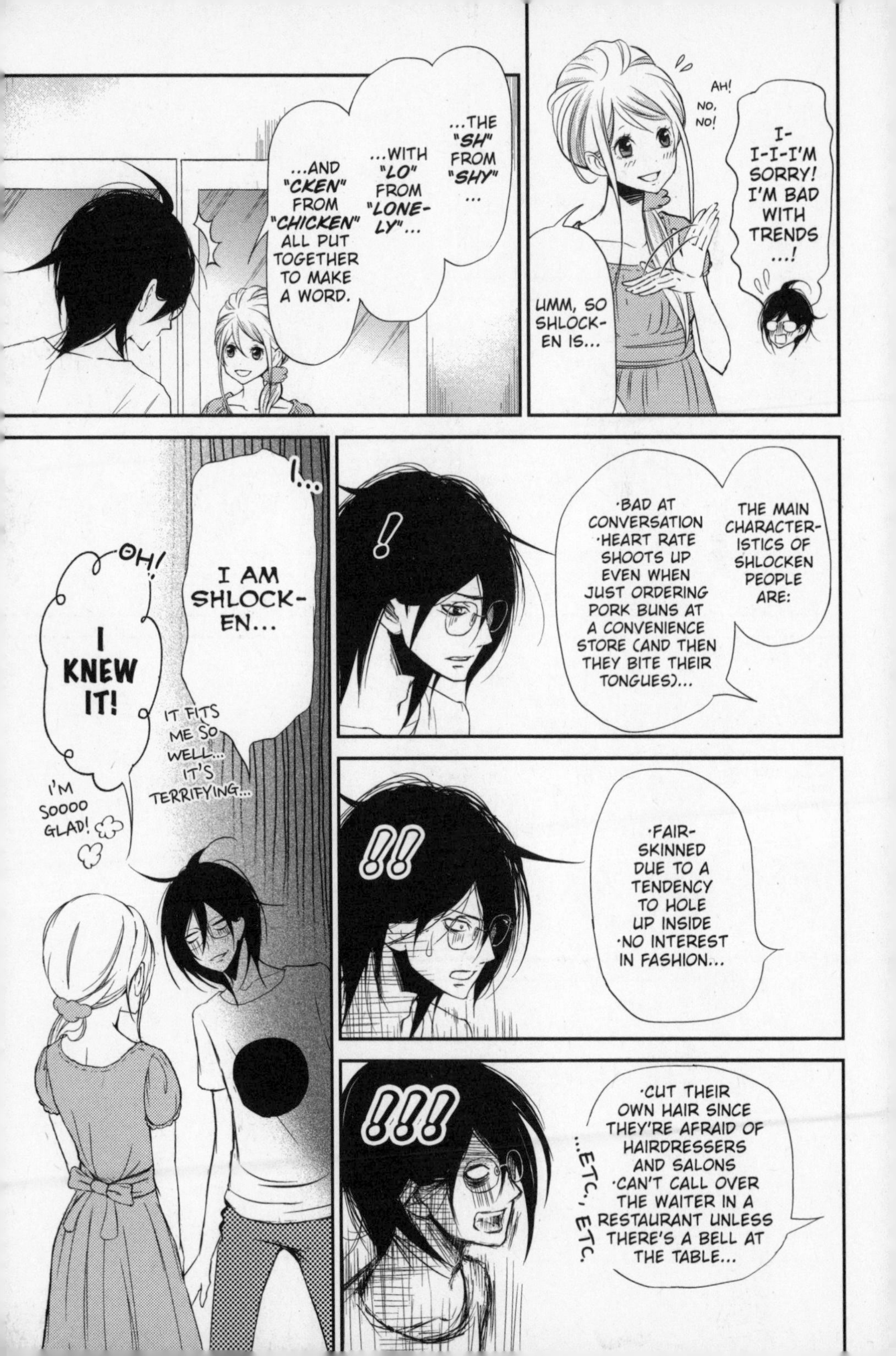
AH! NO, NO!
I-I-I-I'M SORRY! I'M BAD WITH TRENDS...!
UMM, SO SHLOCKEN IS...
..."THE "SH" FROM "SHY"...
...WITH "LO" FROM "LONELY"...
...AND "CKEN" FROM "CHICKEN" ALL PUT TOGETHER TO MAKE A WORD.
THE MAIN CHARACTERISTICS OF SHLOCKEN PEOPLE ARE:
·BAD AT CONVERSATION ·HEART RATE SHOOTS UP EVEN WHEN JUST ORDERING PORK BUNS AT A CONVENIENCE STORE (AND THEN THEY BITE THEIR TONGUES)...
!
·FAIR-SKINNED DUE TO A TENDENCY TO HOLE UP INSIDE ·NO INTEREST IN FASHION...
!!
·CUT THEIR OWN HAIR SINCE THEY'RE AFRAID OF HAIRDRESSERS AND SALONS ·CAN'T CALL OVER THE WAITER IN A RESTAURANT UNLESS THERE'S A BELL AT THE TABLE...
...ETC., ETC.
!!!
I...
I AM SHLOCKEN...
IT FITS ME SO WELL... IT'S TERRIFYING...
OH!
I KNEW IT!
I'M SOOOO GLAD!

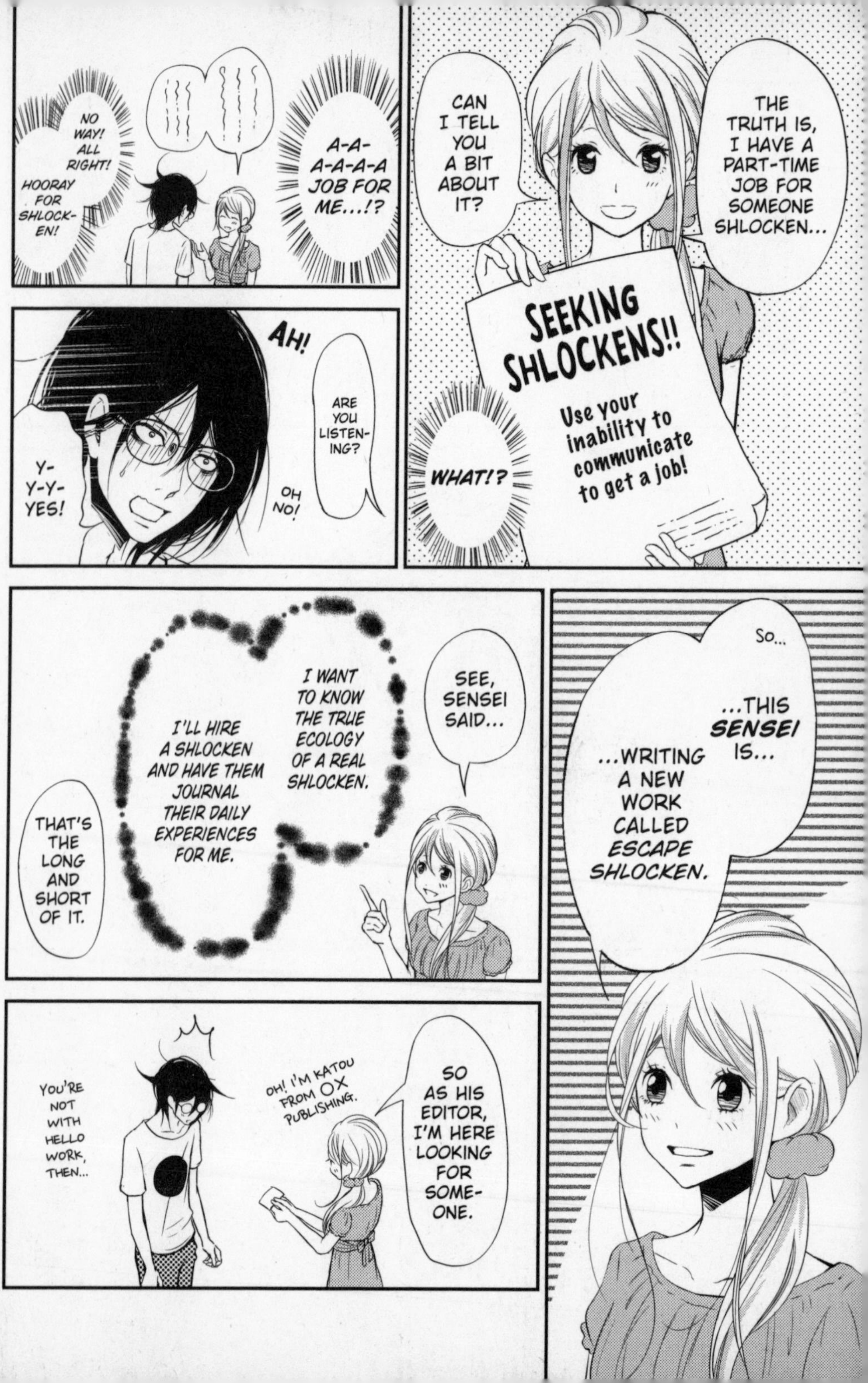
THE TRUTH IS, I HAVE A PART-TIME JOB FOR SOMEONE SHLOCKEN...
CAN I TELL YOU A BIT ABOUT IT?
SEEKING SHLOCKENS!!
Use your inability to communicate to get a job!
WHAT!?
A-A-A-A-A-A JOB FOR ME...!?
NO WAY! ALL RIGHT!
HOORAY FOR SHLOCK-EN!
AH!
ARE YOU LISTEN-ING?
OH NO!
Y-Y-Y-YES!
So...
...THIS SENSEI IS...
...WRITING A NEW WORK CALLED ESCAPE SHLOCKEN.
SEE, SENSEI SAID...
I WANT TO KNOW THE TRUE ECOLOGY OF A REAL SHLOCKEN.
I'LL HIRE A SHLOCKEN AND HAVE THEM JOURNAL THEIR DAILY EXPERIENCES FOR ME.
THAT'S THE LONG AND SHORT OF IT.
SO AS HIS EDITOR, I'M HERE LOOKING FOR SOME-ONE.
OH! I'M KATOU FROM OX PUBLISHING.
YOU'RE NOT WITH HELLO WORK, THEN...

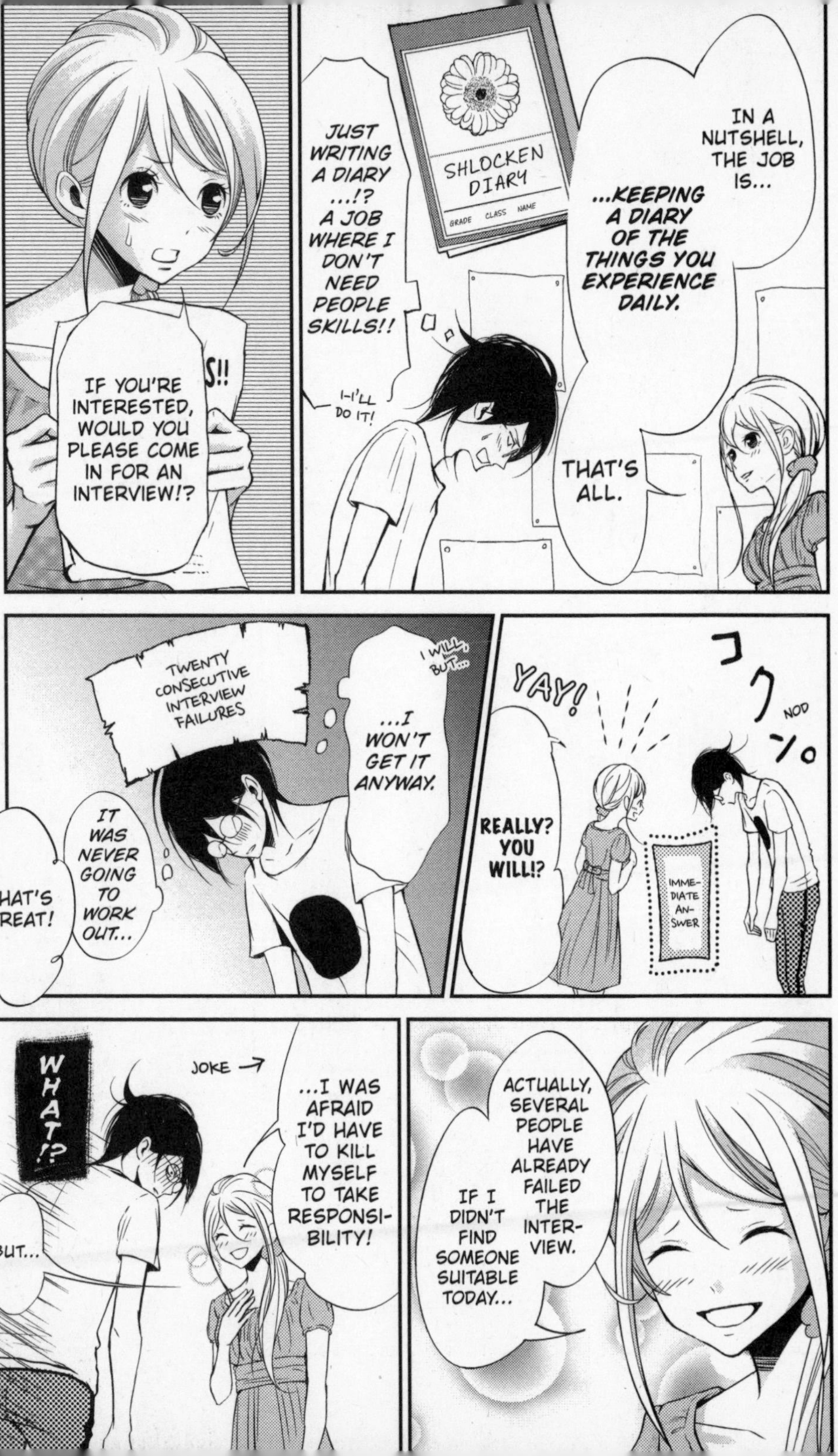
IN A NUTSHELL, THE JOB IS...
...KEEPING A DIARY OF THE THINGS YOU EXPERIENCE DAILY.
THAT'S ALL.
SHLOCKEN DIARY
GRADE CLASS NAME
JUST WRITING A DIARY ...!? A JOB WHERE I DON'T NEED PEOPLE SKILLS!!
I-I'LL DO IT!
IF YOU'RE INTERESTED, WOULD YOU PLEASE COME IN FOR AN INTERVIEW!?
コクッ
NOD
YAY!
REALLY? YOU WILL!?
IMME-DIATE AN-SWER
I WILL, BUT...
...I WON'T GET IT ANYWAY.
TWENTY CONSECUTIVE INTERVIEW FAILURES
IT WAS NEVER GOING TO WORK OUT...
THAT'S GREAT!
ACTUALLY, SEVERAL PEOPLE HAVE ALREADY FAILED THE INTER-VIEW.
IF I DIDN'T FIND SOMEONE SUITABLE TODAY...
...I WAS AFRAID I'D HAVE TO KILL MYSELF TO TAKE RESPONSI-BILITY!
JOKE →
WHAT!?
BUT...

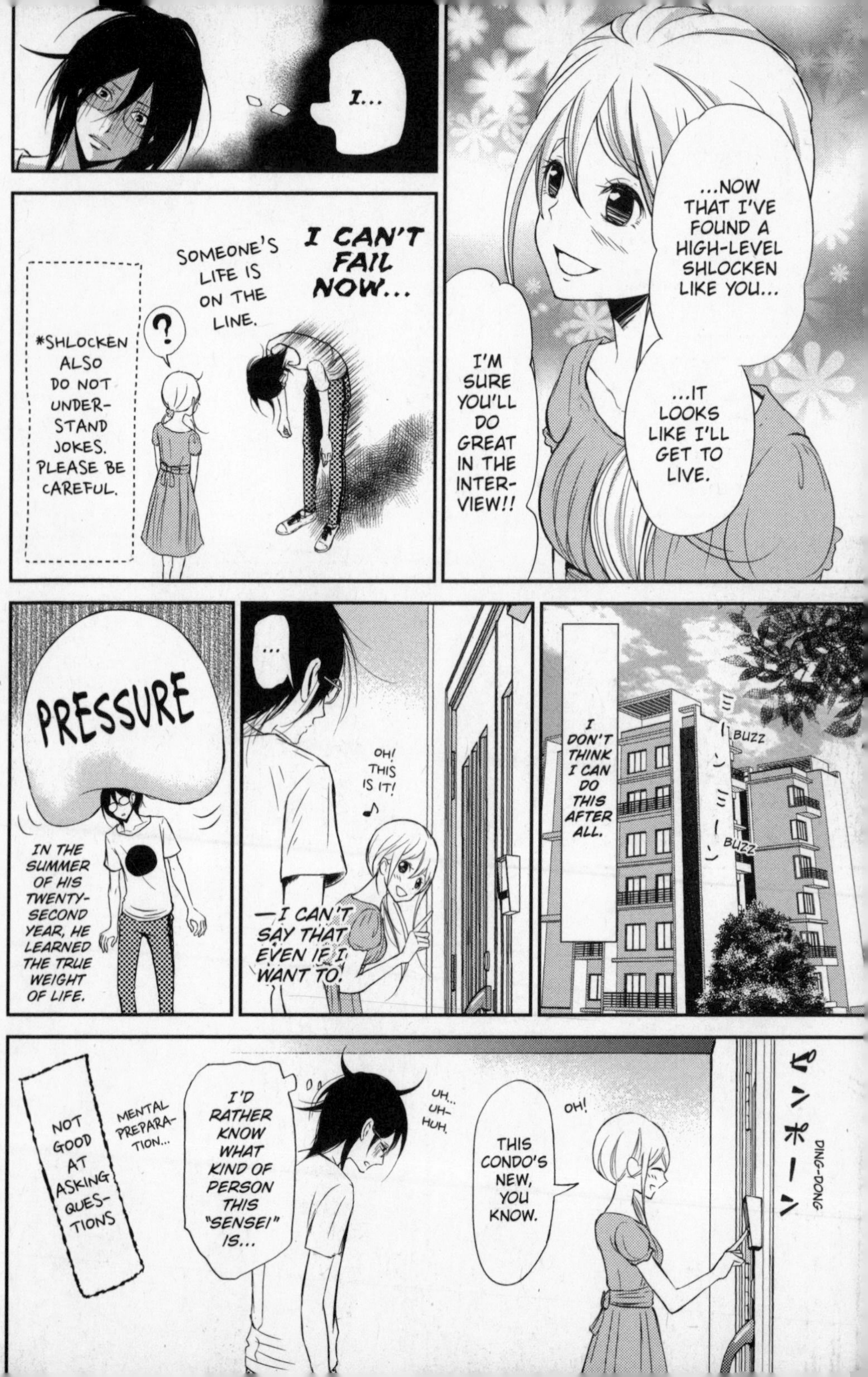
...NOW THAT I'VE FOUND A HIGH-LEVEL SHLOCKEN LIKE YOU...
...IT LOOKS LIKE I'LL GET TO LIVE.
I'M SURE YOU'LL DO GREAT IN THE INTERVIEW!!
I...
I CAN'T FAIL NOW...
SOMEONE'S LIFE IS ON THE LINE.
?
*SHLOCKEN ALSO DO NOT UNDER-STAND JOKES. PLEASE BE CAREFUL.
I DON'T THINK I CAN DO THIS AFTER ALL.
BUZZ
BUZZ
...
OH! THIS IS IT! ♪
—I CAN'T SAY THAT EVEN IF I WANT TO.
PRESSURE
IN THE SUMMER OF HIS TWENTY-SECOND YEAR, HE LEARNED THE TRUE WEIGHT OF LIFE.
ピンポーン
DING-DONG
OH!
THIS CONDO'S NEW, YOU KNOW.
UH... UH-HUH.
I'D RATHER KNOW WHAT KIND OF PERSON THIS "SENSEI" IS...
MENTAL PREPARA-TION...
NOT GOOD AT ASKING QUES-TIONS

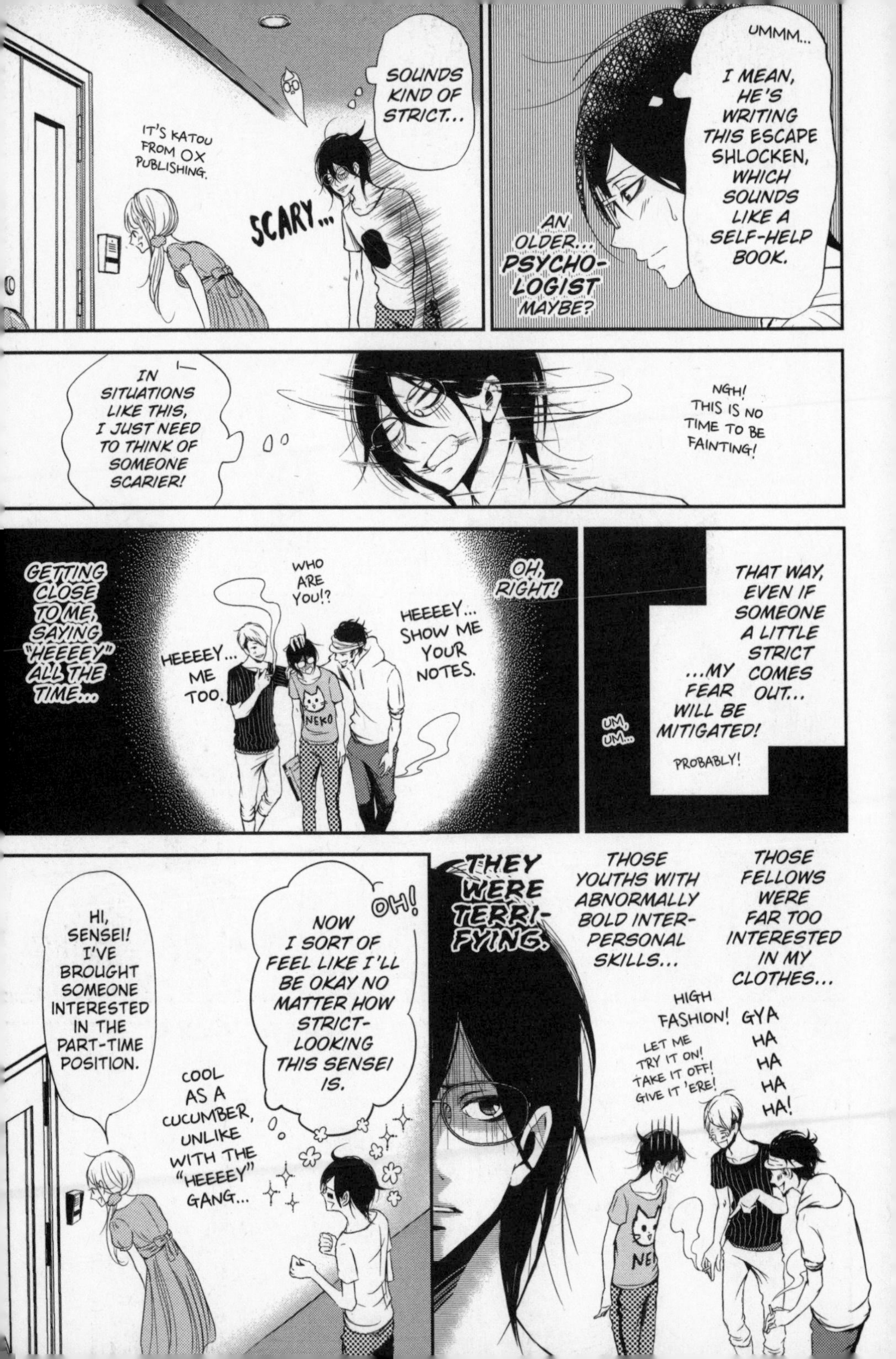

UMMM...
I MEAN, HE'S WRITING THIS ESCAPE SHLOCKEN, WHICH SOUNDS LIKE A SELF-HELP BOOK.
AN OLDER... PSYCHO-LOGIST MAYBE?
SOUNDS KIND OF STRICT...
IT'S KATOU FROM OX PUBLISHING.
SCARY...
NGH! THIS IS NO TIME TO BE FAINTING!
I— IN SITUATIONS LIKE THIS, I JUST NEED TO THINK OF SOMEONE SCARIER!
THAT WAY, EVEN IF SOMEONE A LITTLE STRICT COMES OUT...
...MY FEAR WILL BE MITIGATED!
PROBABLY!
UM, UM...
OH, RIGHT!
HEEEEY... SHOW ME YOUR NOTES.
WHO ARE YOU!?
HEEEEY... ME TOO.
GETTING CLOSE TO ME, SAYING "HEEEEY" ALL THE TIME...
NEKO
THOSE FELLOWS WERE FAR TOO INTERESTED IN MY CLOTHES...
THOSE YOUTHS WITH ABNORMALLY BOLD INTER-PERSONAL SKILLS...
THEY WERE TERRI-FYING.
GYA HA HA HA HA!
HIGH FASHION!
LET ME TRY IT ON! TAKE IT OFF! GIVE IT 'ERE!
OH!
NOW I SORT OF FEEL LIKE I'LL BE OKAY NO MATTER HOW STRICT-LOOKING THIS SENSEI IS.
COOL AS A CUCUMBER, UNLIKE WITH THE "HEEEEY" GANG...
HI, SENSEI! I'VE BROUGHT SOMEONE INTERESTED IN THE PART-TIME POSITION.

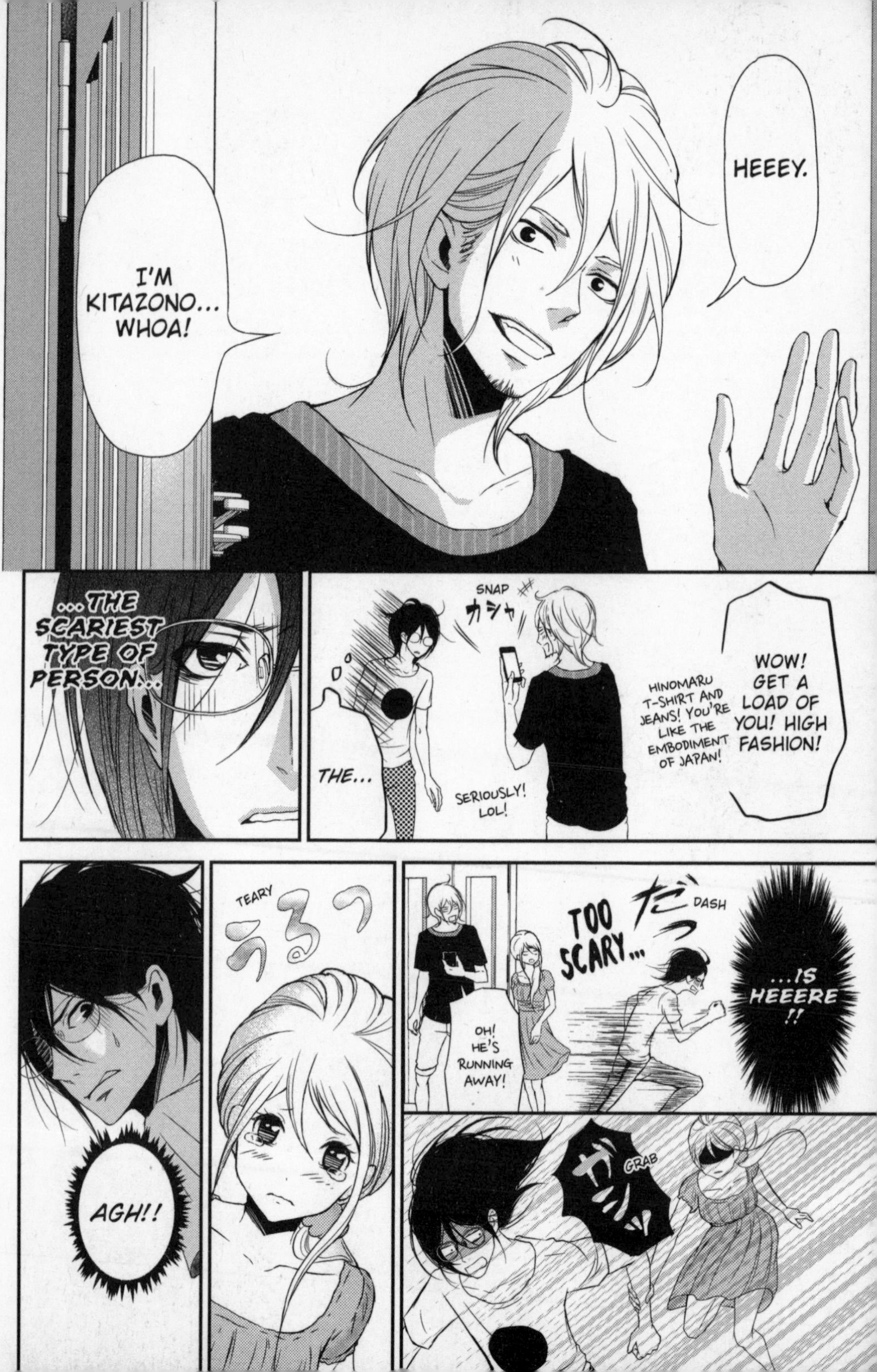
HEEEY.
I'M KITAZONO... WHOA!
WOW! GET A LOAD OF YOU! HIGH FASHION!
HINOMARU T-SHIRT AND JEANS! YOU'RE LIKE THE EMBODIMENT OF JAPAN!
SNAP
カシャ
SERIOUSLY! LOL!
THE...
...THE SCARIEST TYPE OF PERSON...
...IS HEEERE!!
だっ
DASH
TOO SCARY...
OH! HE'S RUNNING AWAY!
GRAB
TEARY
うるっ
AGH!!

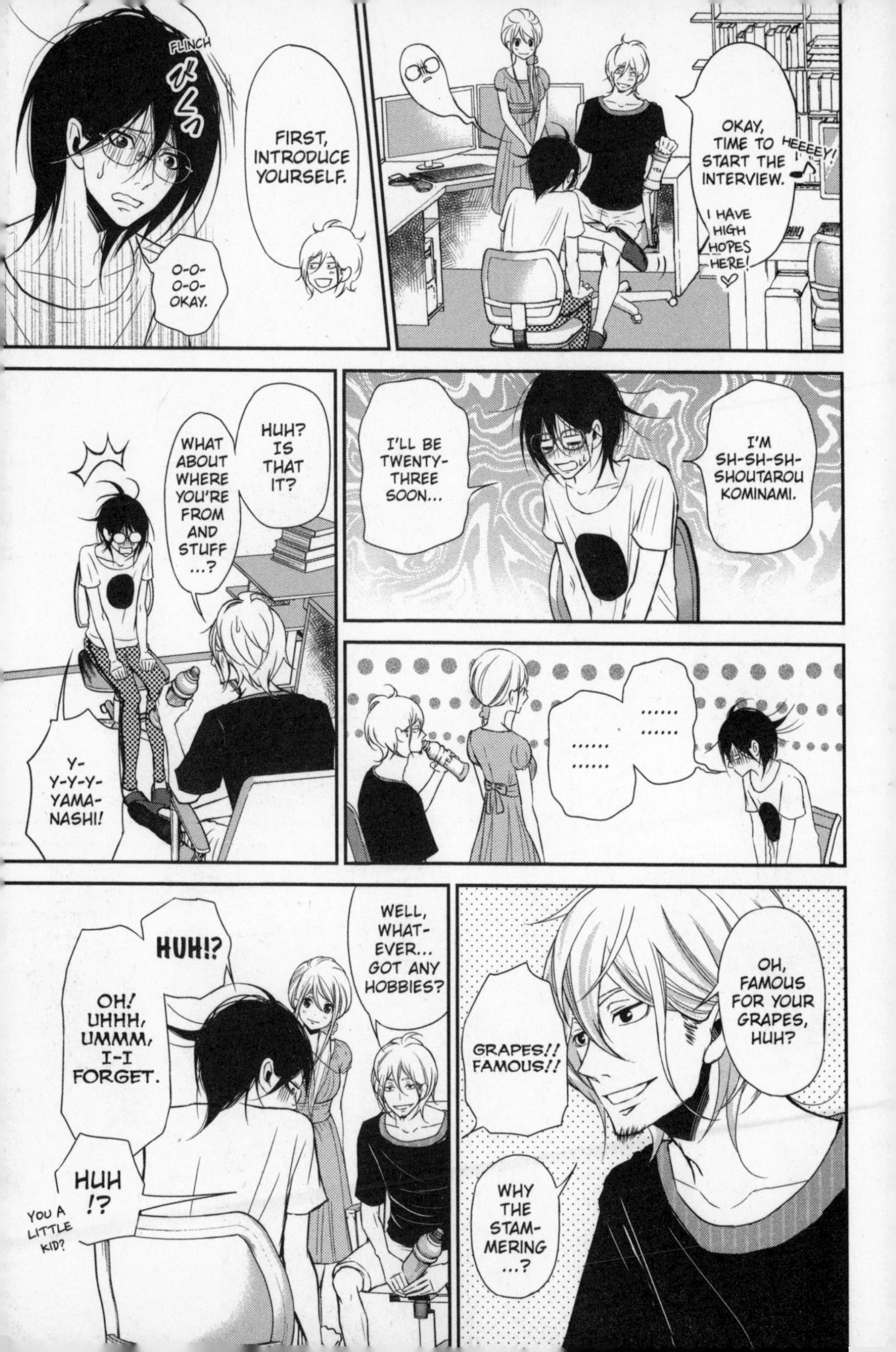
OKAY, TIME TO START THE INTERVIEW.
HEEEEY!
I HAVE HIGH HOPES HERE!
FIRST, INTRODUCE YOURSELF.
FLINCH
O-O-O-O-OKAY.
I'M SH-SH-SH-SHOUTAROU KOMINAMI.
I'LL BE TWENTY-THREE SOON...
....
....
HUH? IS THAT IT?
WHAT ABOUT WHERE YOU'RE FROM AND STUFF ...?
Y-Y-Y-Y-YAMANASHI!
OH, FAMOUS FOR YOUR GRAPES, HUH?
GRAPES!! FAMOUS!!
WHY THE STAMMERING ...?
WELL, WHATEVER... GOT ANY HOBBIES?
HUH!?
OH! UHHH, UMMM, I-I FORGET.
HUH !?
YOU A LITTLE KID?

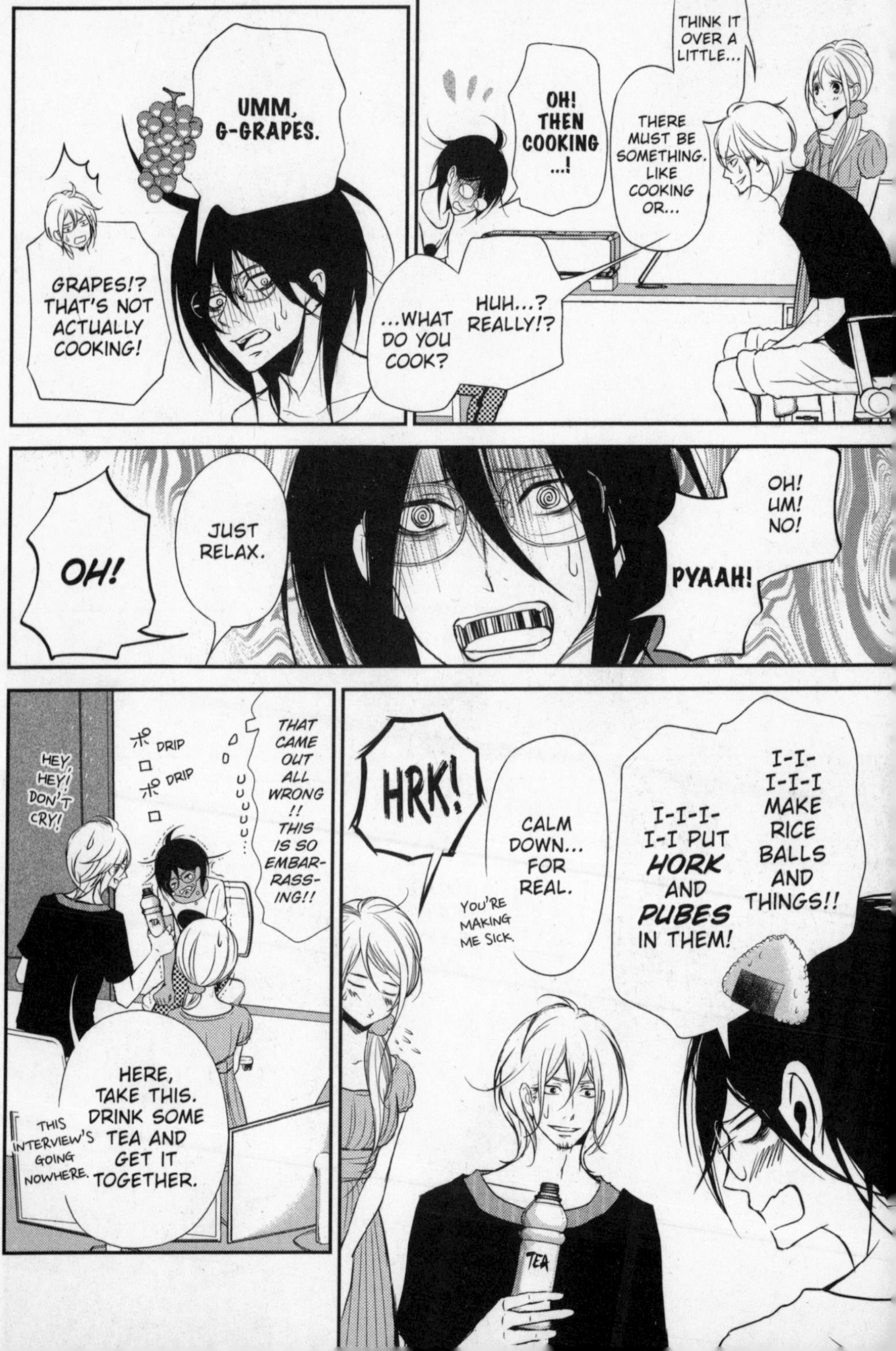
THINK IT OVER A LITTLE...
THERE MUST BE SOMETHING. LIKE COOKING OR...
OH! THEN COOKING ...!
HUH...? REALLY!?
...WHAT DO YOU COOK?
UMM, G-GRAPES.
GRAPES!? THAT'S NOT ACTUALLY COOKING!
OH! UM! NO!
PYAAH!
JUST RELAX.
OH!
I-I- I-I-I MAKE RICE BALLS AND THINGS!!
I-I-I- I-I PUT HORK AND PUBES IN THEM!
HRK!
CALM DOWN... FOR REAL.
YOU'RE MAKING ME SICK.
TEA
THAT CAME OUT ALL WRONG!! THIS IS SO EMBARRASSING!!
UUUUU...
ポ DRIP
ロ
ポ DRIP
ロ
HEY, HEY! DON'T CRY!
TEA
HERE, TAKE THIS. DRINK SOME TEA AND GET IT TOGETHER.
THIS INTERVIEW'S GOING NOWHERE.

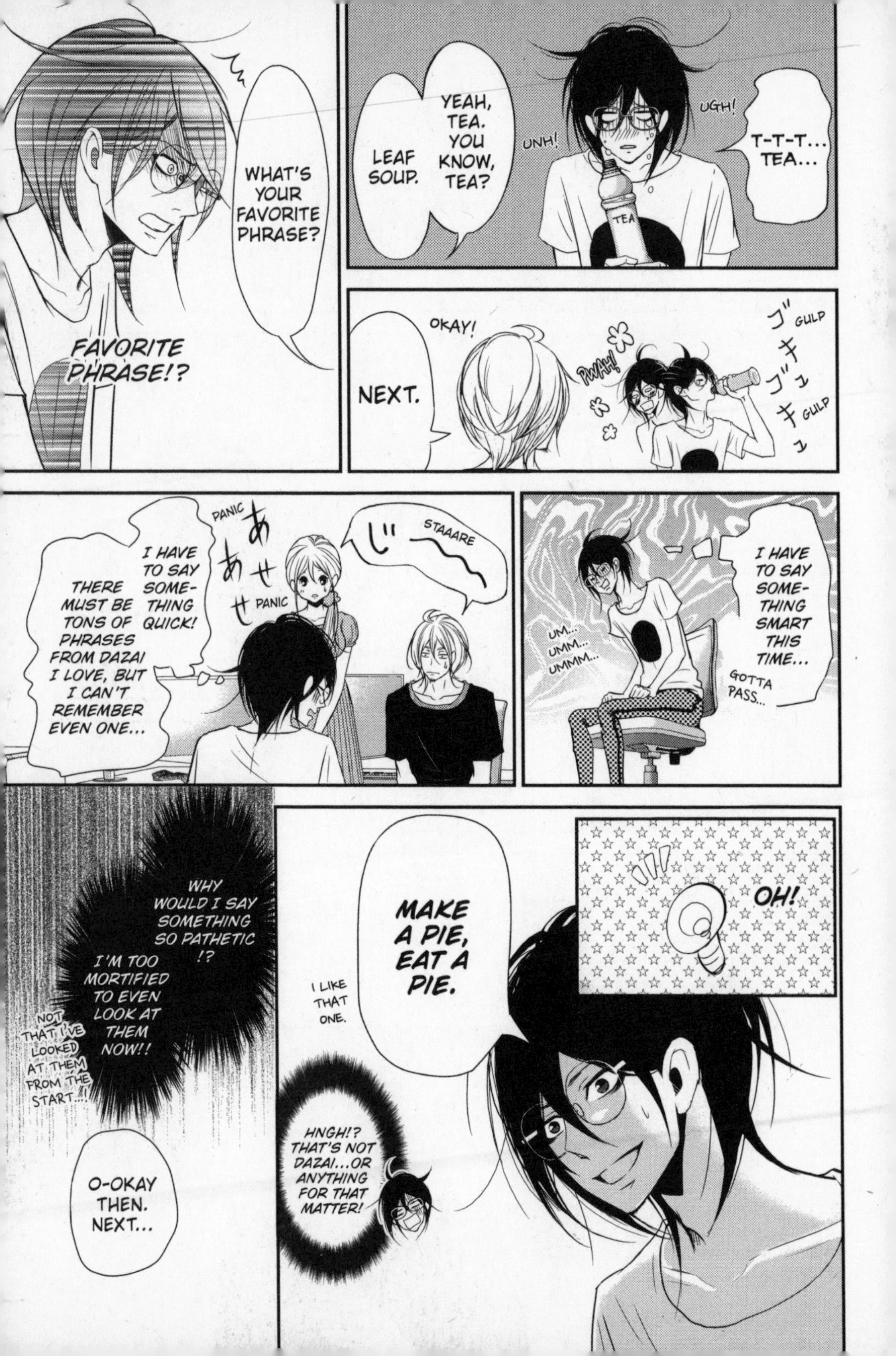

T-T-T... TEA...
UGH!
UNH!
TEA
YEAH, TEA. YOU KNOW, TEA?
LEAF SOUP.
ゴキュゴキュ GULP GULP
PWAH!
OKAY!
NEXT.
WHAT'S YOUR FAVORITE PHRASE?
FAVORITE PHRASE!?
I HAVE TO SAY SOMETHING SMART THIS TIME...
GOTTA PASS...
UM... UMM... UMMM...
じ〜 STAAARE
あせあせ PANIC PANIC
I HAVE TO SAY SOMETHING QUICK!
THERE MUST BE TONS OF PHRASES FROM DAZAI I LOVE, BUT I CAN'T REMEMBER EVEN ONE...
!!
OH!
MAKE A PIE, EAT A PIE.
I LIKE THAT ONE.
HNGH!? THAT'S NOT DAZAI...OR ANYTHING FOR THAT MATTER!
WHY WOULD I SAY SOMETHING SO PATHETIC!?
I'M TOO MORTIFIED TO EVEN LOOK AT THEM NOW!!
NOT THAT I'VE LOOKED AT THEM FROM THE START...
O-OKAY THEN. NEXT...

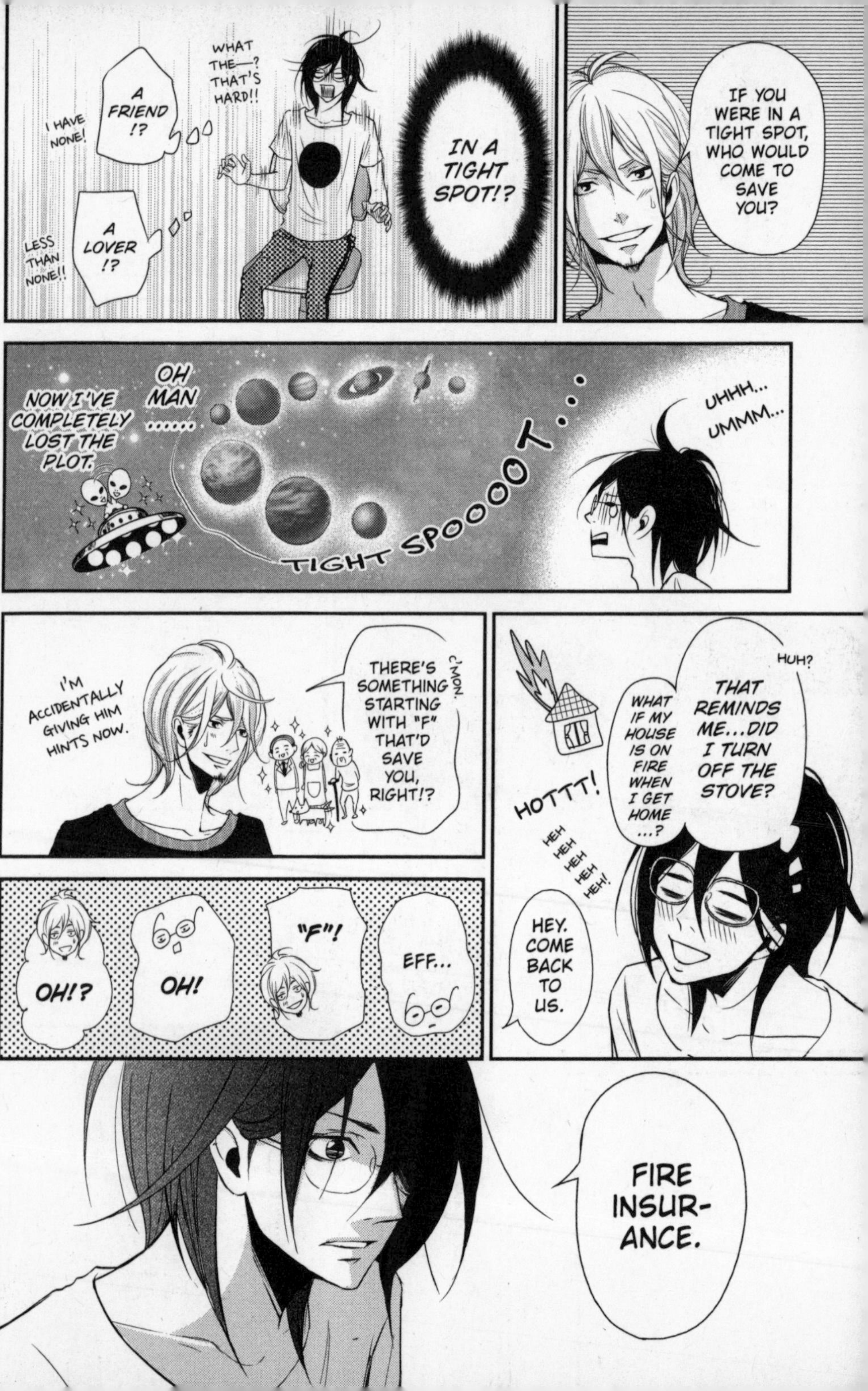
IF YOU WERE IN A TIGHT SPOT, WHO WOULD COME TO SAVE YOU?
IN A TIGHT SPOT!?
WHAT THE—? THAT'S HARD!!
A FRIEND!?
I HAVE NONE!
A LOVER!?
LESS THAN NONE!!
UHHH... UMMM...
TIGHT SPOOOOT...
OH MAN......
NOW I'VE COMPLETELY LOST THE PLOT.
HUH?
THAT REMINDS ME...DID I TURN OFF THE STOVE?
WHAT IF MY HOUSE IS ON FIRE WHEN I GET HOME...?
HOTTT!
HEH HEH HEH HEH HEH!
HEY. COME BACK TO US.
C'MON.
THERE'S SOMETHING STARTING WITH "F" THAT'D SAVE YOU, RIGHT!?
I'M ACCIDENTALLY GIVING HIM HINTS NOW.
EFF...
"F"!
OH!
OH!?
FIRE INSURANCE.

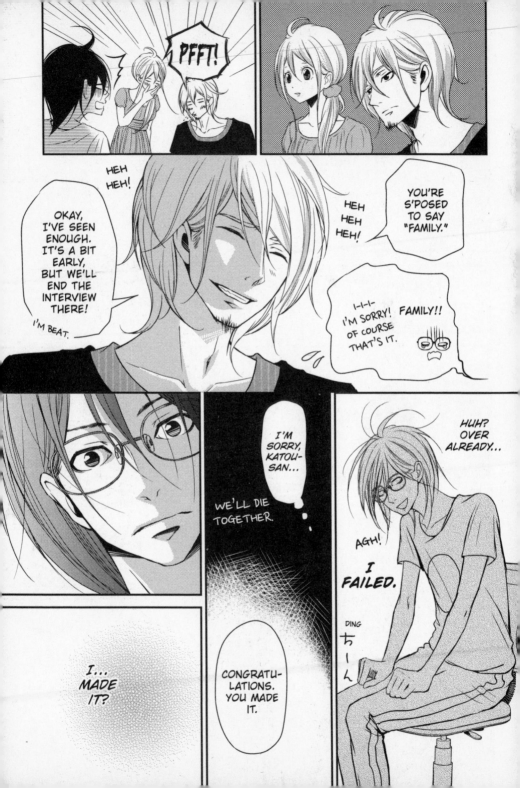

PFFT!
YOU'RE S'POSED TO SAY "FAMILY."
HEH HEH HEH!
HEH HEH!
OKAY, I'VE SEEN ENOUGH. IT'S A BIT EARLY, BUT WE'LL END THE INTERVIEW THERE!
I'M BEAT.
I-I-I- I'M SORRY! OF COURSE THAT'S IT.
FAMILY!!
HUH? OVER ALREADY...
AGH!
I FAILED.
DING
ちーん
I'M SORRY, KATOU-SAN...
WE'LL DIE TOGETHER.
CONGRATU-LATIONS. YOU MADE IT.
I... MADE IT?

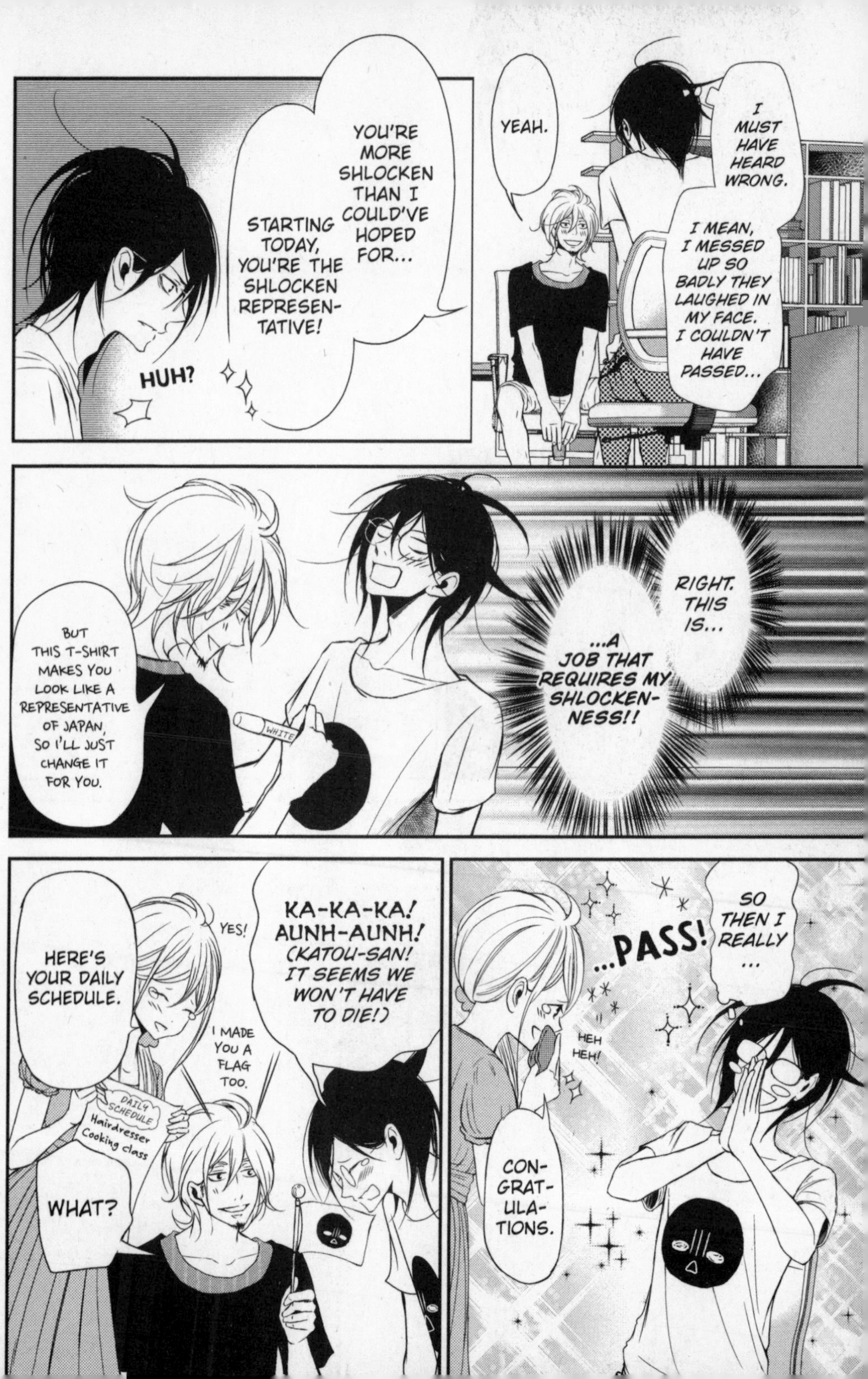
I MUST HAVE HEARD WRONG.
YEAH.
I MEAN, I MESSED UP SO BADLY THEY LAUGHED IN MY FACE. I COULDN'T HAVE PASSED...
YOU'RE MORE SHLOCKEN THAN I COULD'VE HOPED FOR...
STARTING TODAY, YOU'RE THE SHLOCKEN REPRESEN-TATIVE!
HUH?
RIGHT. THIS IS...
...A JOB THAT REQUIRES MY SHLOCKEN-NESS!!
BUT THIS T-SHIRT MAKES YOU LOOK LIKE A REPRESENTATIVE OF JAPAN, SO I'LL JUST CHANGE IT FOR YOU.
WHITE
SO THEN I REALLY ...
...PASS!
HEH HEH!
CON-GRAT-ULA-TIONS.
KA-KA-KA! AUNH-AUNH! (KATOU-SAN! IT SEEMS WE WON'T HAVE TO DIE!)
YES!
HERE'S YOUR DAILY SCHEDULE.
I MADE YOU A FLAG TOO.
DAILY SCHEDULE
Hairdresser
Cooking class
WHAT?

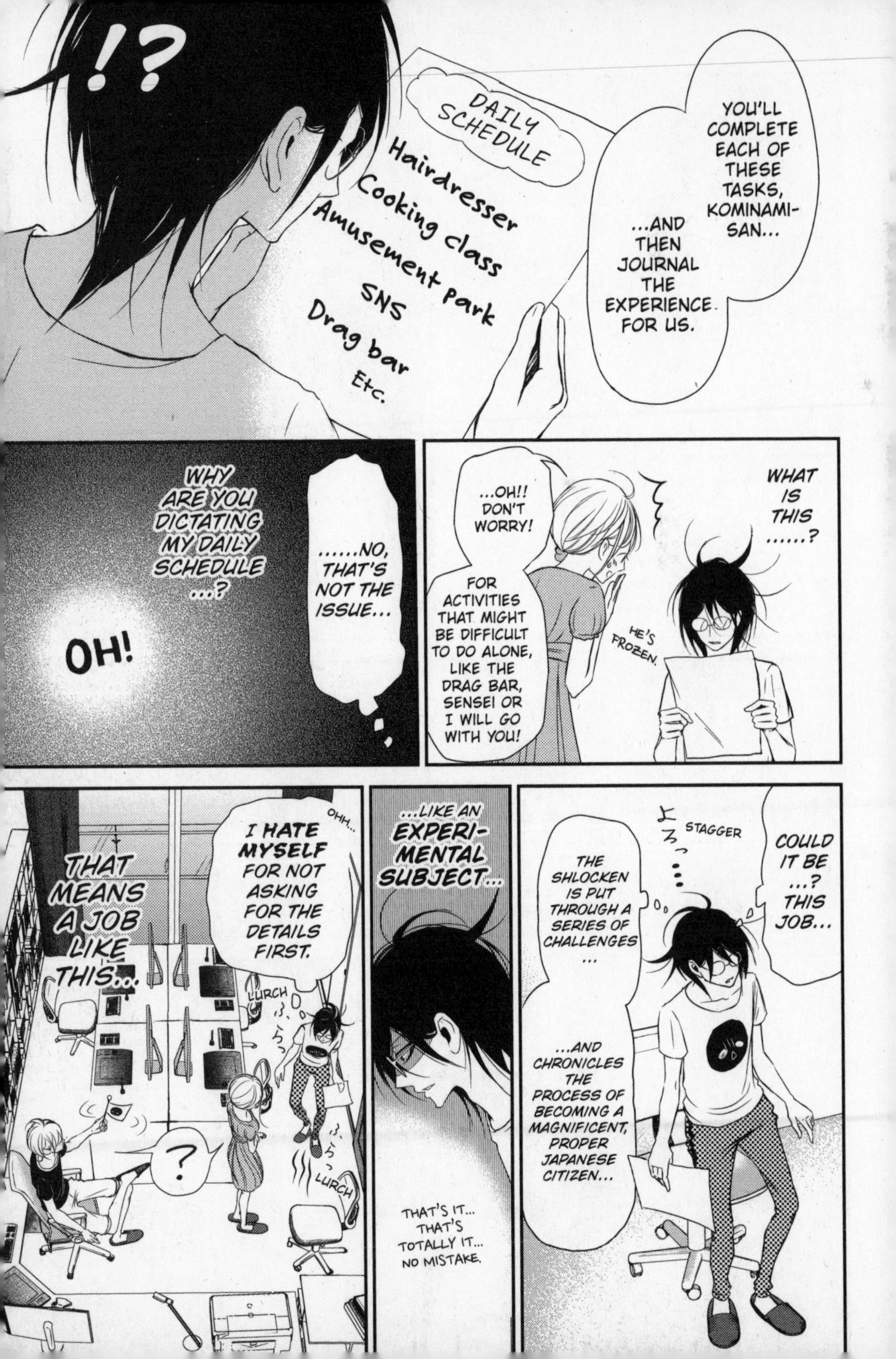
YOU'LL COMPLETE EACH OF THESE TASKS, KOMINAMI-SAN...
...AND THEN JOURNAL THE EXPERIENCE FOR US.
DAILY SCHEDULE
Hairdresser
Cooking class
Amusement park
SNS
Drag bar
Etc.
!?
WHAT IS THIS ......?
...OH!! DON'T WORRY!
FOR ACTIVITIES THAT MIGHT BE DIFFICULT TO DO ALONE, LIKE THE DRAG BAR, SENSEI OR I WILL GO WITH YOU!
HE'S FROZEN.
......NO, THAT'S NOT THE ISSUE...
WHY ARE YOU DICTATING MY DAILY SCHEDULE ...?
OH!
COULD IT BE ...? THIS JOB...
STAGGER
THE SHLOCKEN IS PUT THROUGH A SERIES OF CHALLENGES ...
...AND CHRONICLES THE PROCESS OF BECOMING A MAGNIFICENT, PROPER JAPANESE CITIZEN...
...LIKE AN EXPERIMENTAL SUBJECT...
THAT'S IT... THAT'S TOTALLY IT... NO MISTAKE.
OHH...
I HATE MYSELF FOR NOT ASKING FOR THE DETAILS FIRST.
THAT MEANS A JOB LIKE THIS...
LURCH
?
LURCH

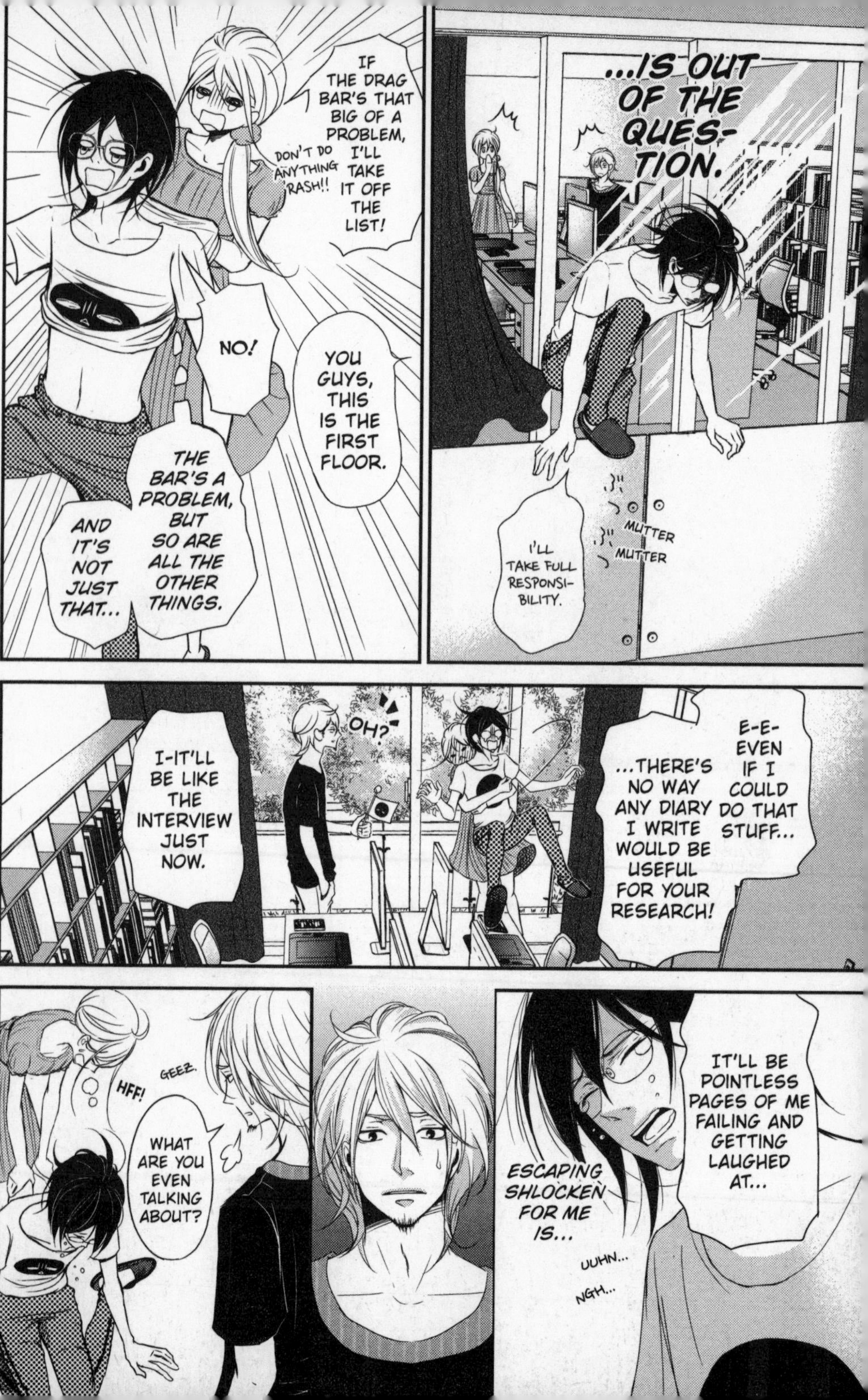
...IS OUT OF THE QUES-TION.
I'LL TAKE FULL RESPONSI-BILITY.
MUTTER
MUTTER
IF THE DRAG BAR'S THAT BIG OF A PROBLEM, I'LL TAKE IT OFF THE LIST!
DON'T DO ANYTHING RASH!!
YOU GUYS, THIS IS THE FIRST FLOOR.
NO!
THE BAR'S A PROBLEM, BUT SO ARE ALL THE OTHER THINGS.
AND IT'S NOT JUST THAT...
E-E-EVEN IF I COULD DO THAT STUFF...
...THERE'S NO WAY ANY DIARY I WRITE WOULD BE USEFUL FOR YOUR RESEARCH!
OH?
I-IT'LL BE LIKE THE INTERVIEW JUST NOW.
IT'LL BE POINTLESS PAGES OF ME FAILING AND GETTING LAUGHED AT...
ESCAPING SHLOCKEN FOR ME IS...
UUHN...
NGH...
GEEZ.
HFF!
WHAT ARE YOU EVEN TALKING ABOUT?

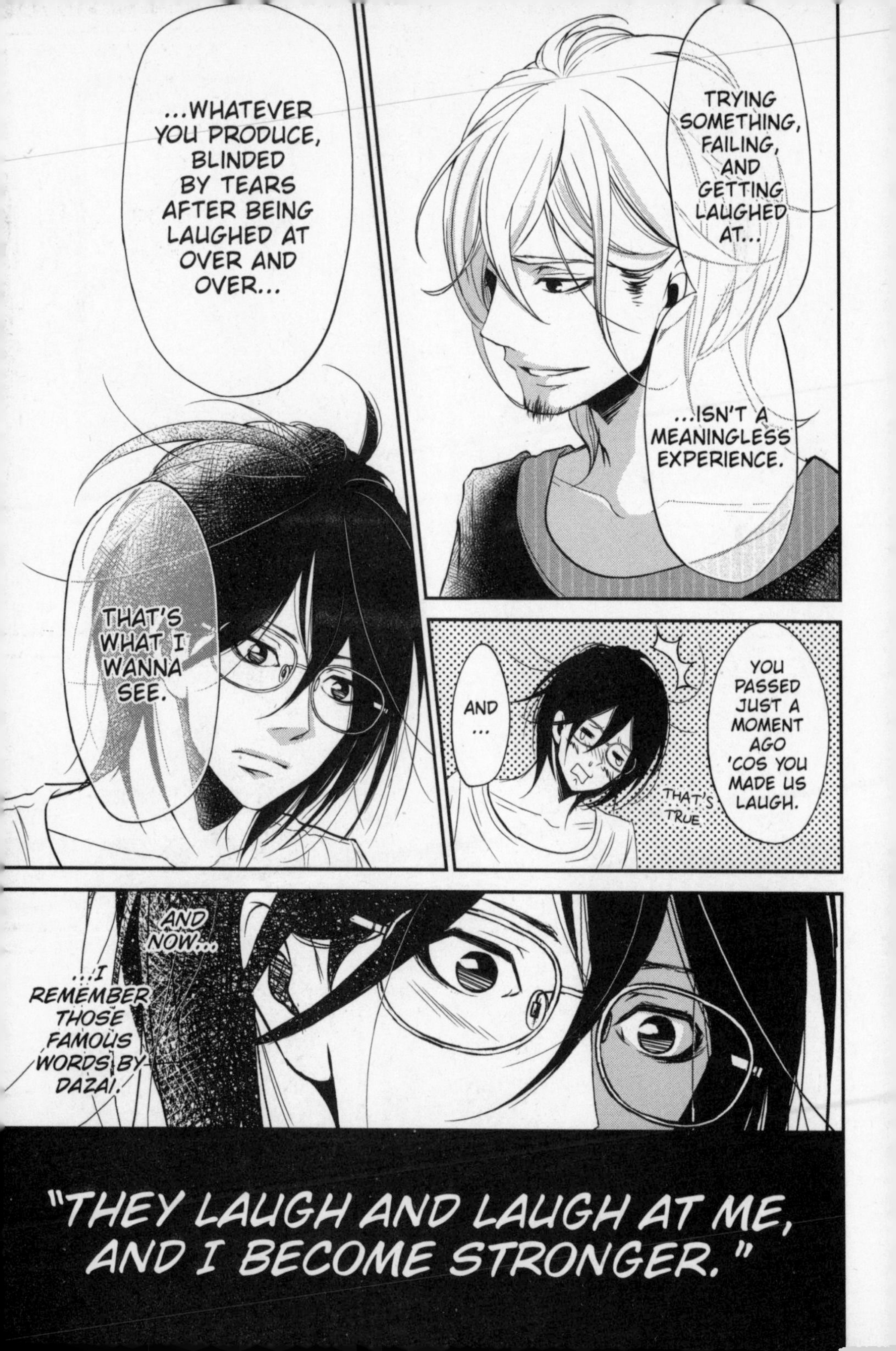
TRYING SOMETHING, FAILING, AND GETTING LAUGHED AT...
...ISN'T A MEANINGLESS EXPERIENCE.
YOU PASSED JUST A MOMENT AGO 'COS YOU MADE US LAUGH.
THAT'S TRUE
AND ...
...WHATEVER YOU PRODUCE, BLINDED BY TEARS AFTER BEING LAUGHED AT OVER AND OVER...
THAT'S WHAT I WANNA SEE.
AND NOW...
...I REMEMBER THOSE FAMOUS WORDS BY DAZAI.
"THEY LAUGH AND LAUGH AT ME, AND I BECOME STRONGER."

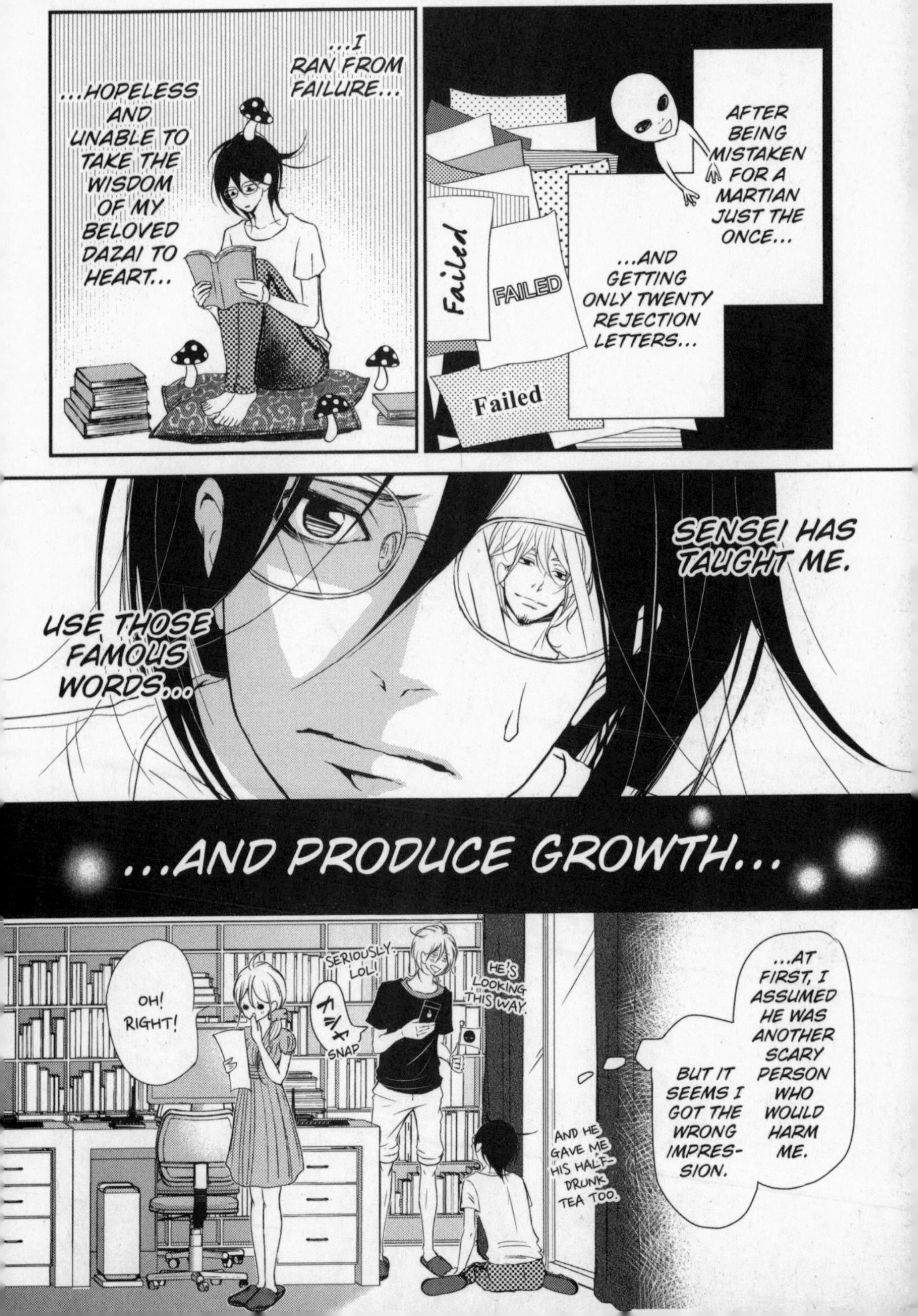
AFTER BEING MISTAKEN FOR A MARTIAN JUST THE ONCE...
...AND GETTING ONLY TWENTY REJECTION LETTERS...
Failed
FAILED
Failed
...I RAN FROM FAILURE...
...HOPELESS AND UNABLE TO TAKE THE WISDOM OF MY BELOVED DAZAI TO HEART...
SENSEI HAS TAUGHT ME.
USE THOSE FAMOUS WORDS...
...AND PRODUCE GROWTH...
...AT FIRST, I ASSUMED HE WAS ANOTHER SCARY PERSON WHO WOULD HARM ME.
BUT IT SEEMS I GOT THE WRONG IMPRES-SION.
AND HE GAVE ME HIS HALF-DRUNK TEA TOO.
HE'S LOOKING THIS WAY.
SERIOUSLY. LOL!
SNAP
OH! RIGHT!

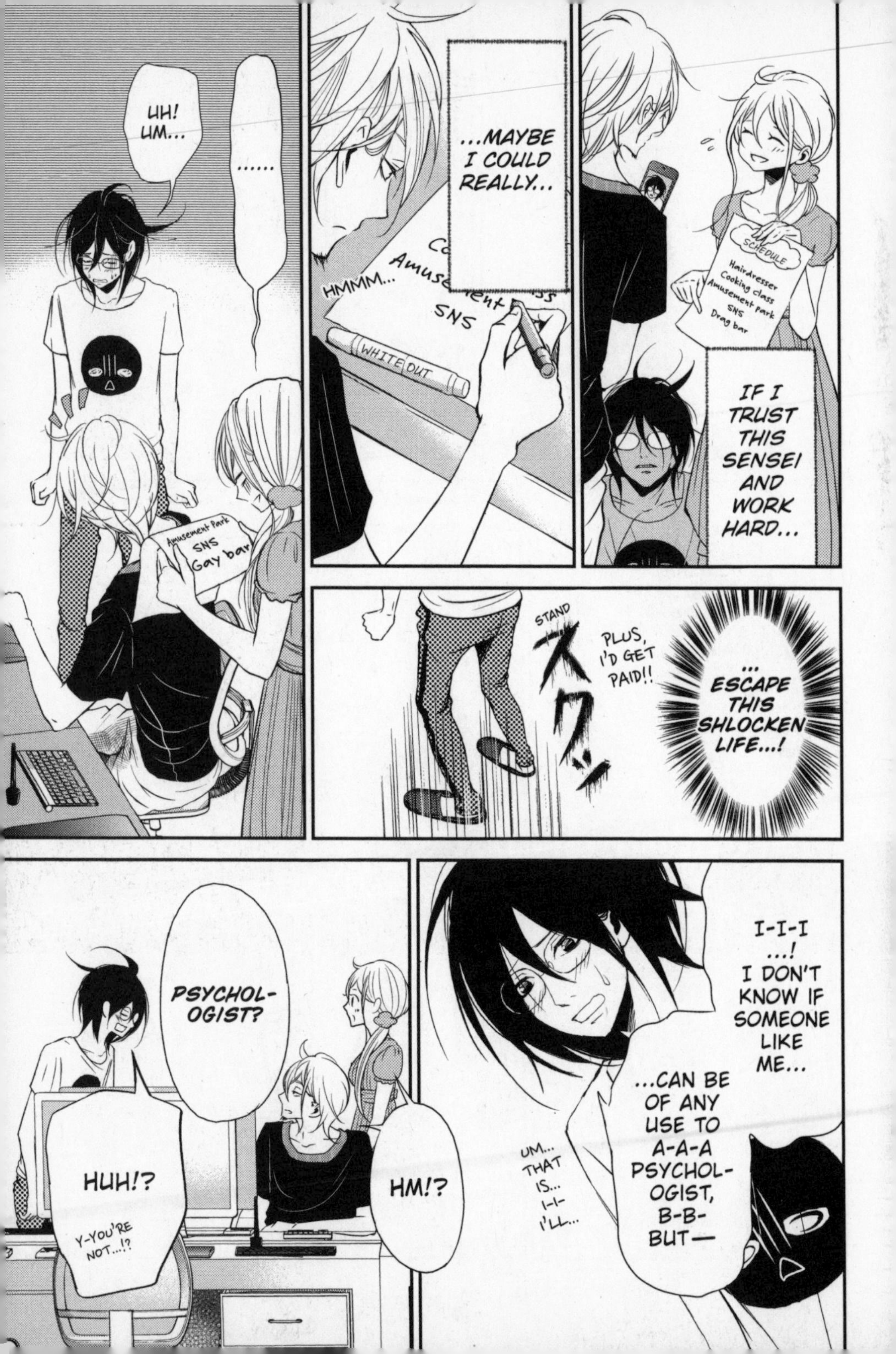
SCHEDULE
Hairdresser
Cooking class
Amusement Park
SNS
Drag bar
IF I TRUST THIS SENSEI AND WORK HARD...
...MAYBE I COULD REALLY...
HMMM...
SNS
WHITE OUT
STAND
PLUS, I'D GET PAID!!
...ESCAPE THIS SHLOCKEN LIFE...!
UH! UM...
......
Amusement Park
SNS
Gay bar
I-I-I ...! I DON'T KNOW IF SOMEONE LIKE ME...
...CAN BE OF ANY USE TO A-A-A PSYCHOL-OGIST, B-B-BUT—
UM... THAT IS... I-I-I'LL...
PSYCHOL-OGIST?
HM!?
HUH!?
Y-YOU'RE NOT...!?

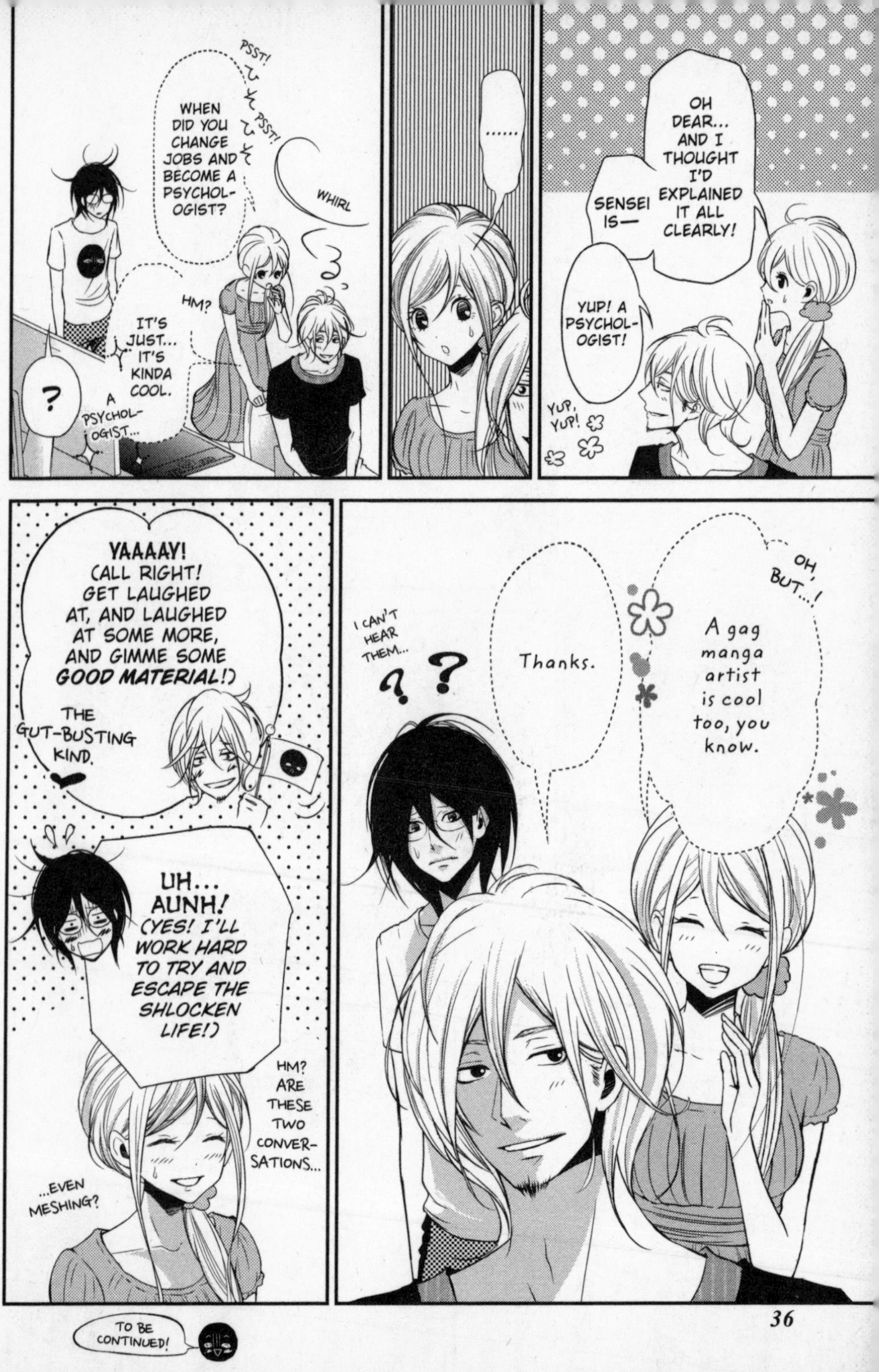
OH DEAR... AND I THOUGHT I'D EXPLAINED IT ALL CLEARLY!
SENSEI IS—
YUP! A PSYCHOLOGIST!
YUP, YUP!
......
WHEN DID YOU CHANGE JOBS AND BECOME A PSYCHOLOGIST?
PSST! ひそ PSST! ひそ
WHIRL
HM?
IT'S JUST... IT'S KINDA COOL.
A PSYCHOLOGIST...
?
OH, BUT...!
A gag manga artist is cool too, you know.
Thanks.
I CAN'T HEAR THEM...
??
YAAAAY! (ALL RIGHT! GET LAUGHED AT, AND LAUGHED AT SOME MORE, AND GIMME SOME GOOD MATERIAL!)
THE GUT-BUSTING KIND.
UH... AUNH! (YES! I'LL WORK HARD TO TRY AND ESCAPE THE SHLOCKEN LIFE!)
HM? ARE THESE TWO CONVERSATIONS...
...EVEN MESHING?
TO BE CONTINUED!

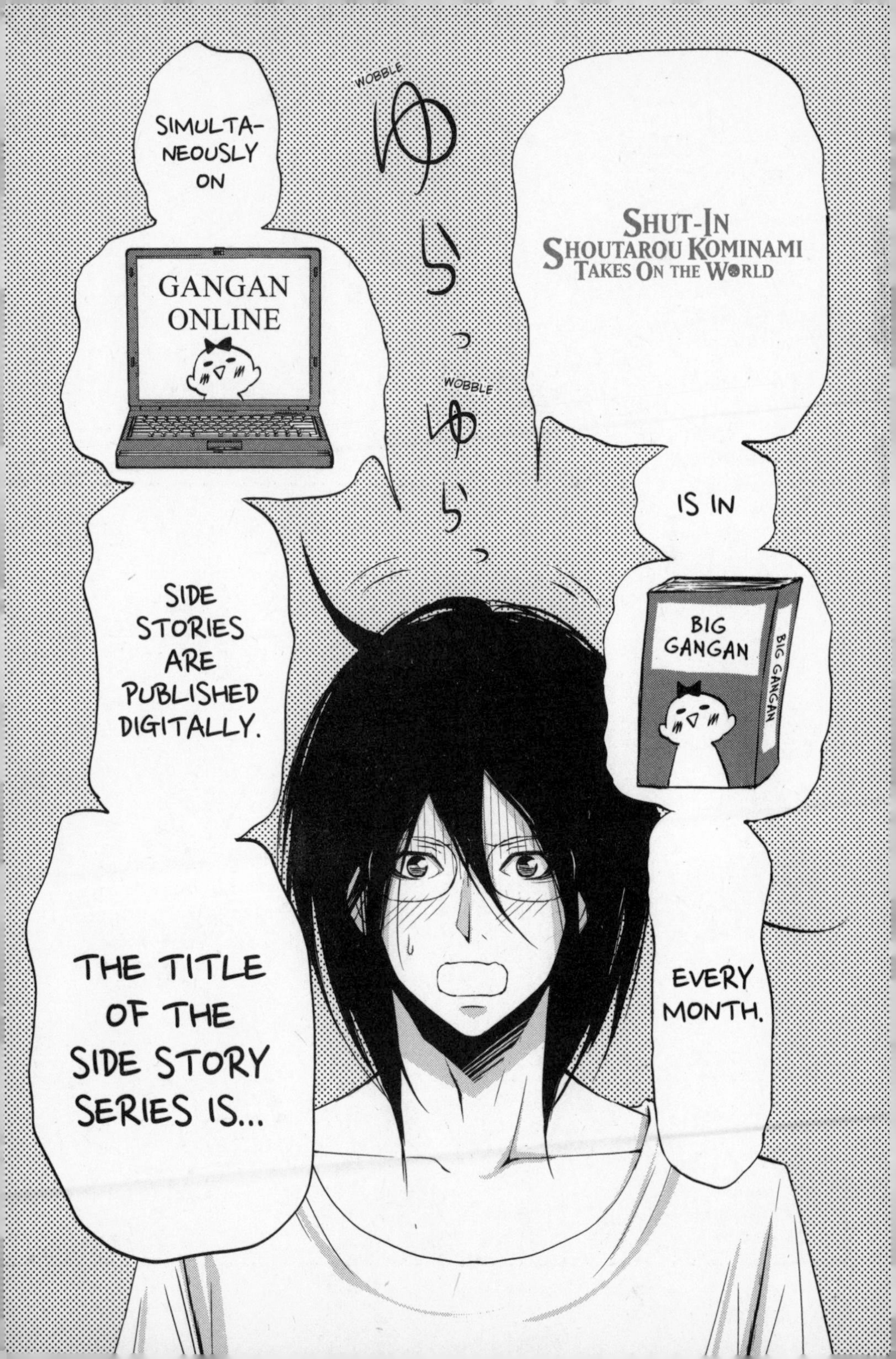

SHUT-IN SHOUTAROU KOMINAMI TAKES ON THE WORLD
IS IN
BIG GANGAN
BIG GANGAN
EVERY MONTH.
ゆらっ
WOBBLE
ゆらっ
WOBBLE
SIMULTA-NEOUSLY ON
GANGAN ONLINE
SIDE STORIES ARE PUBLISHED DIGITALLY.
THE TITLE OF THE SIDE STORY SERIES IS...

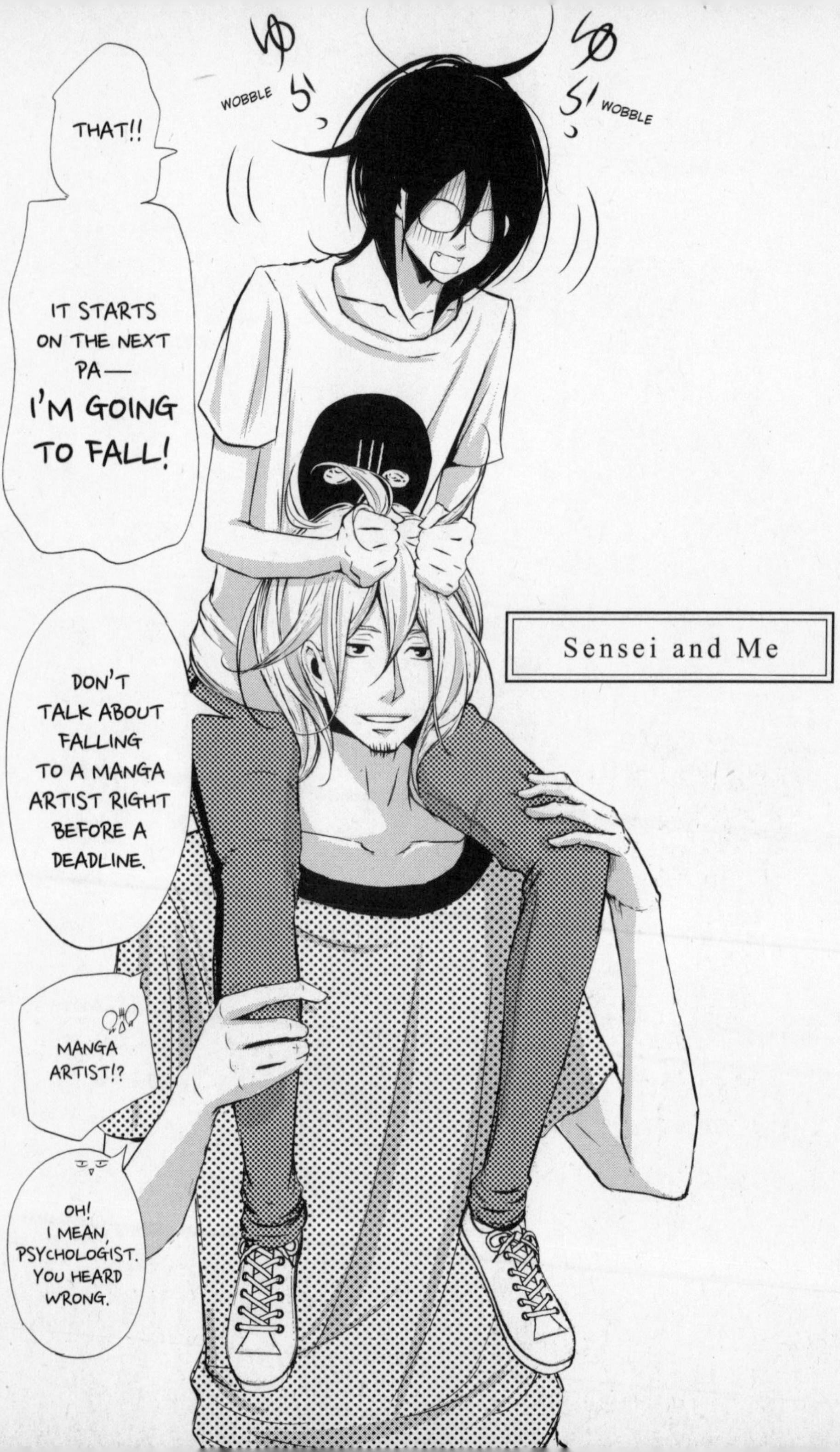
WOBBLE
WOBBLE
THAT!!
IT STARTS ON THE NEXT PA— I'M GOING TO FALL!
Sensei and Me
DON'T TALK ABOUT FALLING TO A MANGA ARTIST RIGHT BEFORE A DEADLINE.
MANGA ARTIST!?
OH! I MEAN, PSYCHOLOGIST. YOU HEARD WRONG.

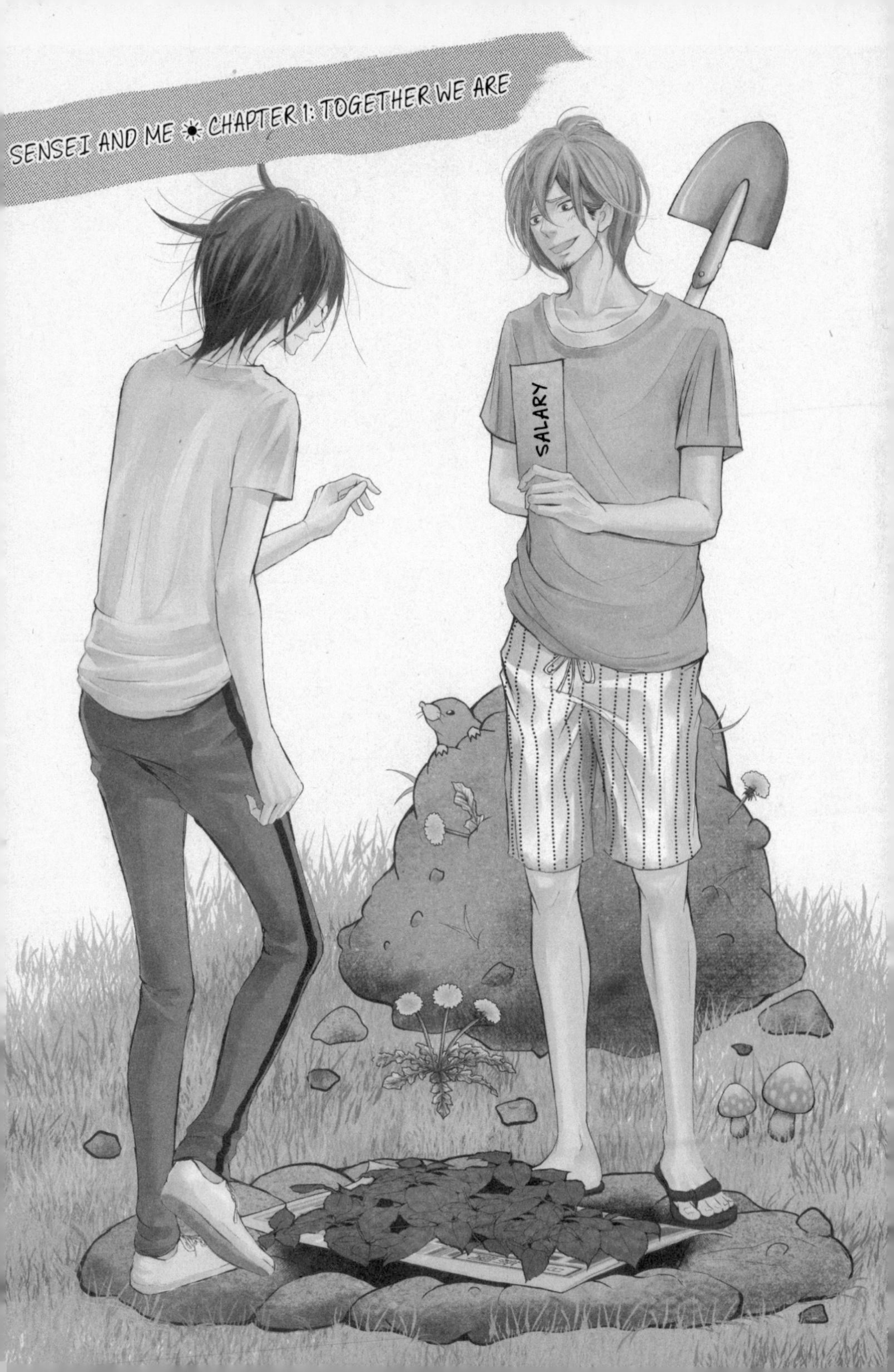
SENSEI AND ME ✹ CHAPTER 1: TOGETHER WE ARE
SALARY

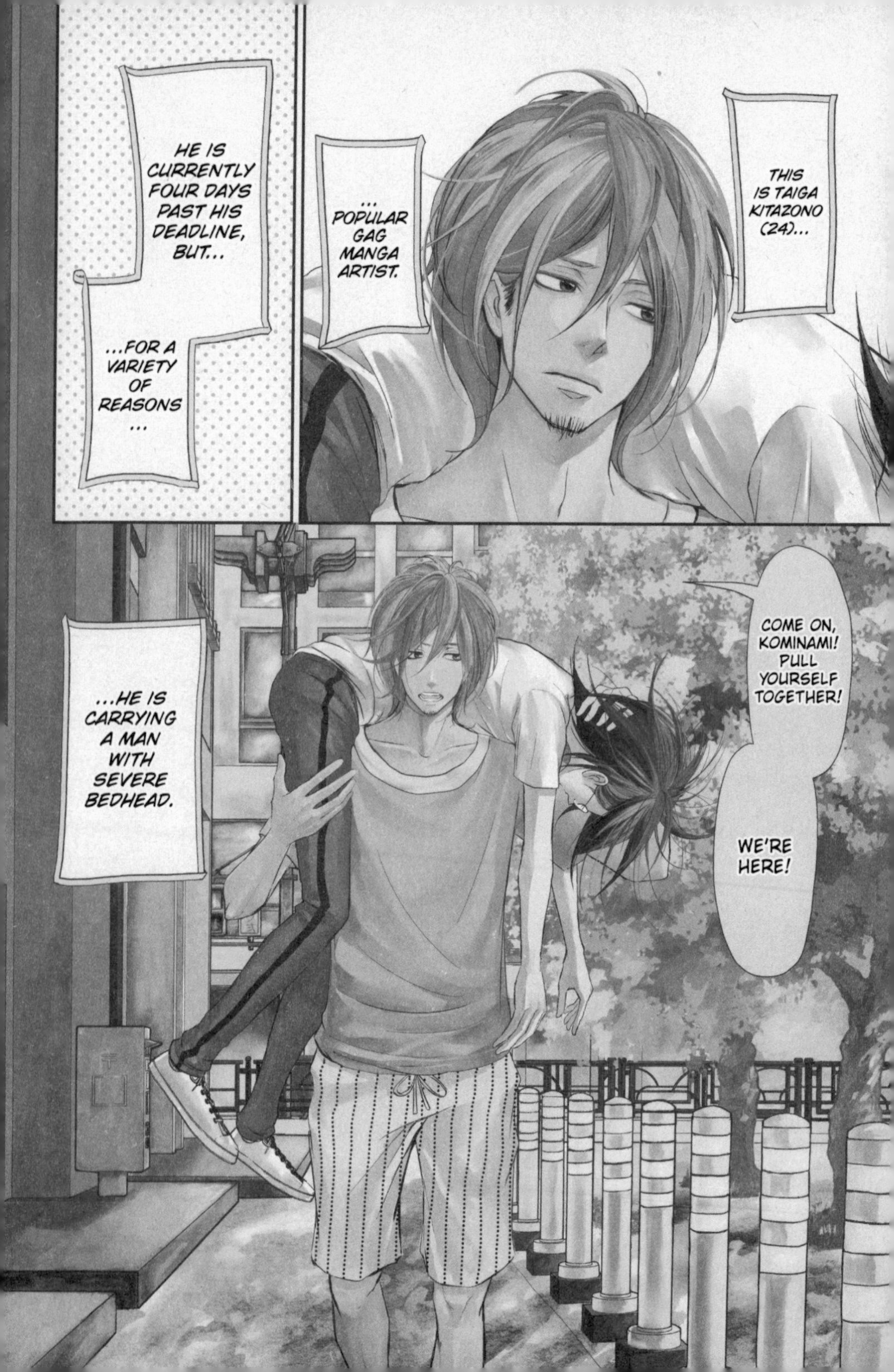
THIS IS TAIGA KITAZONO (24)...
... POPULAR GAG MANGA ARTIST.
HE IS CURRENTLY FOUR DAYS PAST HIS DEADLINE, BUT...
...FOR A VARIETY OF REASONS ...
COME ON, KOMINAMI! PULL YOURSELF TOGETHER!
WE'RE HERE!
...HE IS CARRYING A MAN WITH SEVERE BEDHEAD.

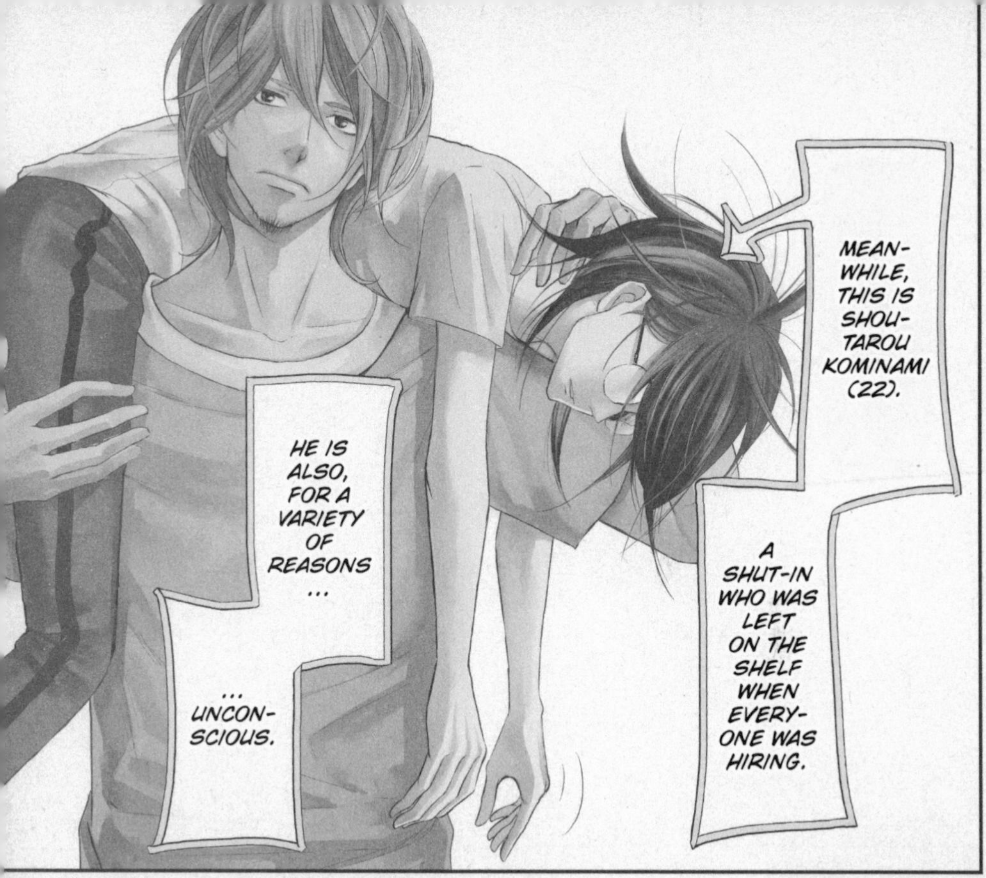
MEANWHILE, THIS IS SHOUTAROU KOMINAMI (22).
A SHUT-IN WHO WAS LEFT ON THE SHELF WHEN EVERYONE WAS HIRING.
HE IS ALSO, FOR A VARIETY OF REASONS...
...UNCONSCIOUS.
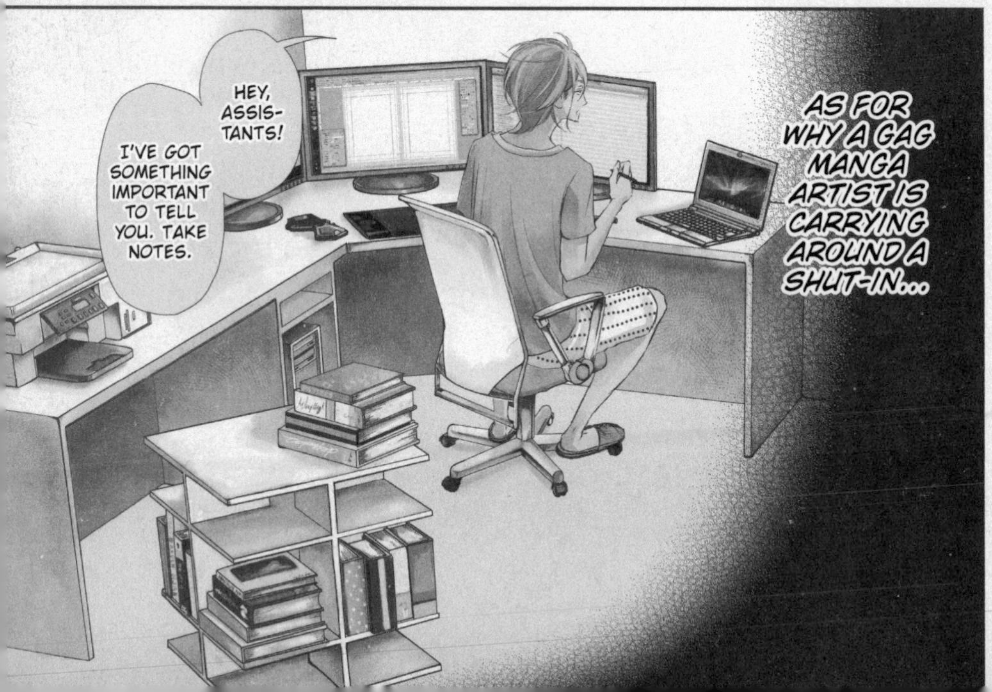
AS FOR WHY A GAG MANGA ARTIST IS CARRYING AROUND A SHUT-IN...
HEY, ASSISTANTS! I'VE GOT SOMETHING IMPORTANT TO TELL YOU. TAKE NOTES.

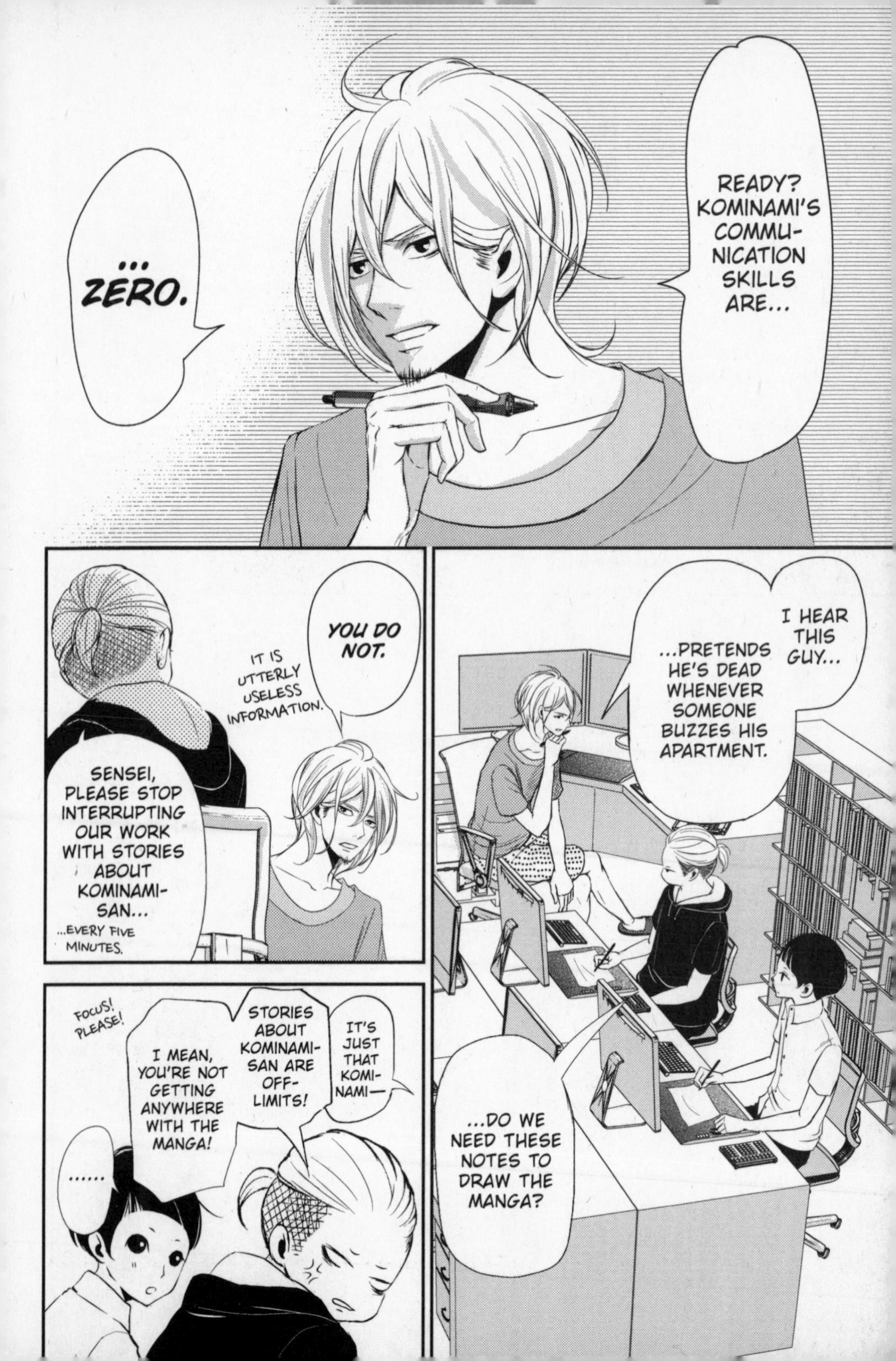
READY? KOMINAMI'S COMMUNICATION SKILLS ARE...
...ZERO.
I HEAR THIS GUY...
...PRETENDS HE'S DEAD WHENEVER SOMEONE BUZZES HIS APARTMENT.
...DO WE NEED THESE NOTES TO DRAW THE MANGA?
YOU DO NOT.
IT IS UTTERLY USELESS INFORMATION.
SENSEI, PLEASE STOP INTERRUPTING OUR WORK WITH STORIES ABOUT KOMINAMI-SAN...
...EVERY FIVE MINUTES.
IT'S JUST THAT KOMINAMI—
STORIES ABOUT KOMINAMI-SAN ARE OFF-LIMITS!
FOCUS! PLEASE!
I MEAN, YOU'RE NOT GETTING ANYWHERE WITH THE MANGA!
......

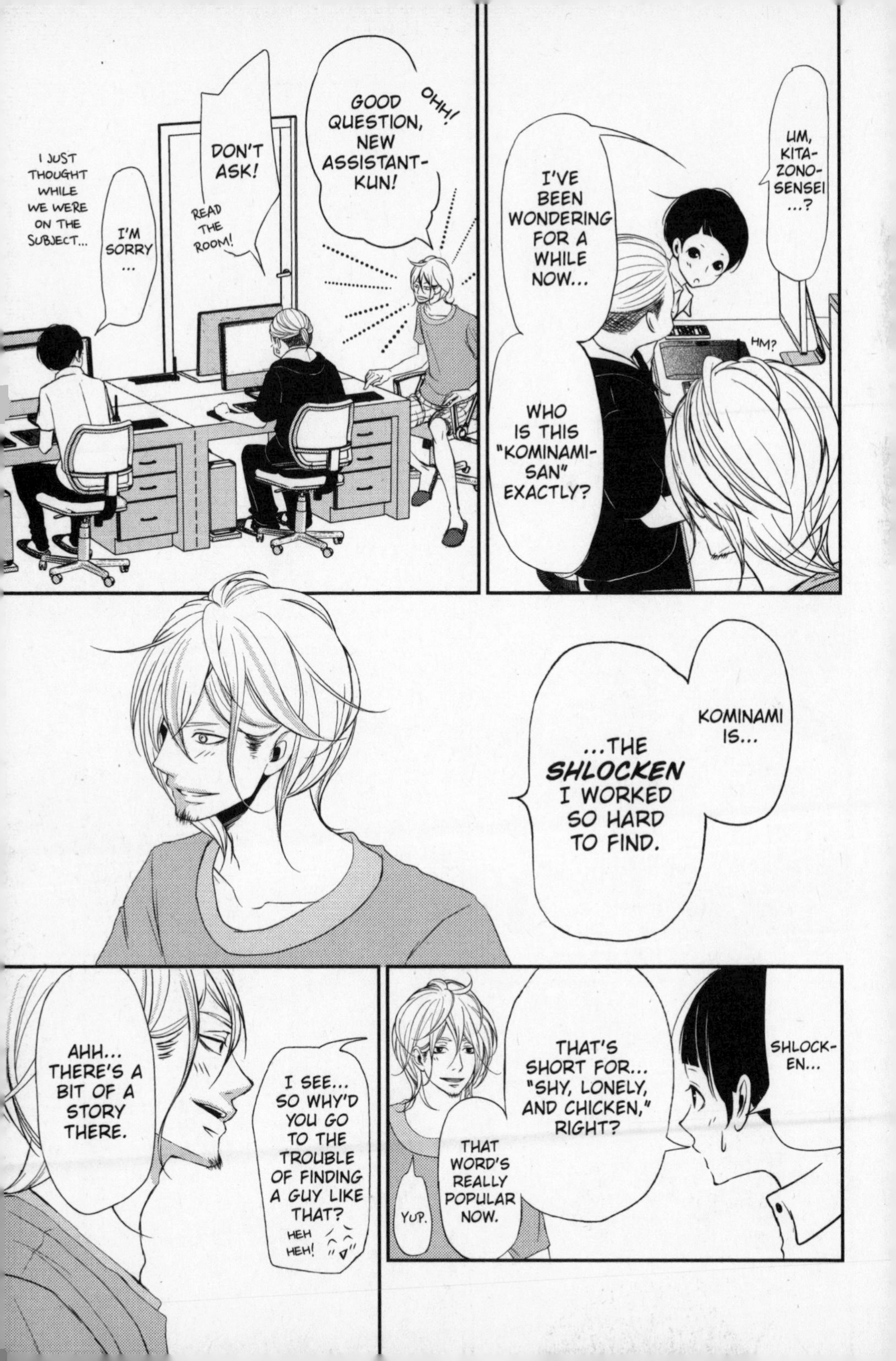
UM, KITAZONO-SENSEI...?
HM?
I'VE BEEN WONDERING FOR A WHILE NOW...
WHO IS THIS "KOMINAMI-SAN" EXACTLY?
OHH!
GOOD QUESTION, NEW ASSISTANT-KUN!
DON'T ASK!
READ THE ROOM!
I'M SORRY...
I JUST THOUGHT WHILE WE WERE ON THE SUBJECT...
KOMINAMI IS...
...THE SHLOCKEN I WORKED SO HARD TO FIND.
SHLOCK-EN...
THAT'S SHORT FOR... "SHY, LONELY, AND CHICKEN," RIGHT?
THAT WORD'S REALLY POPULAR NOW.
YUP.
I SEE... SO WHY'D YOU GO TO THE TROUBLE OF FINDING A GUY LIKE THAT?
HEH HEH!
AHH... THERE'S A BIT OF A STORY THERE.

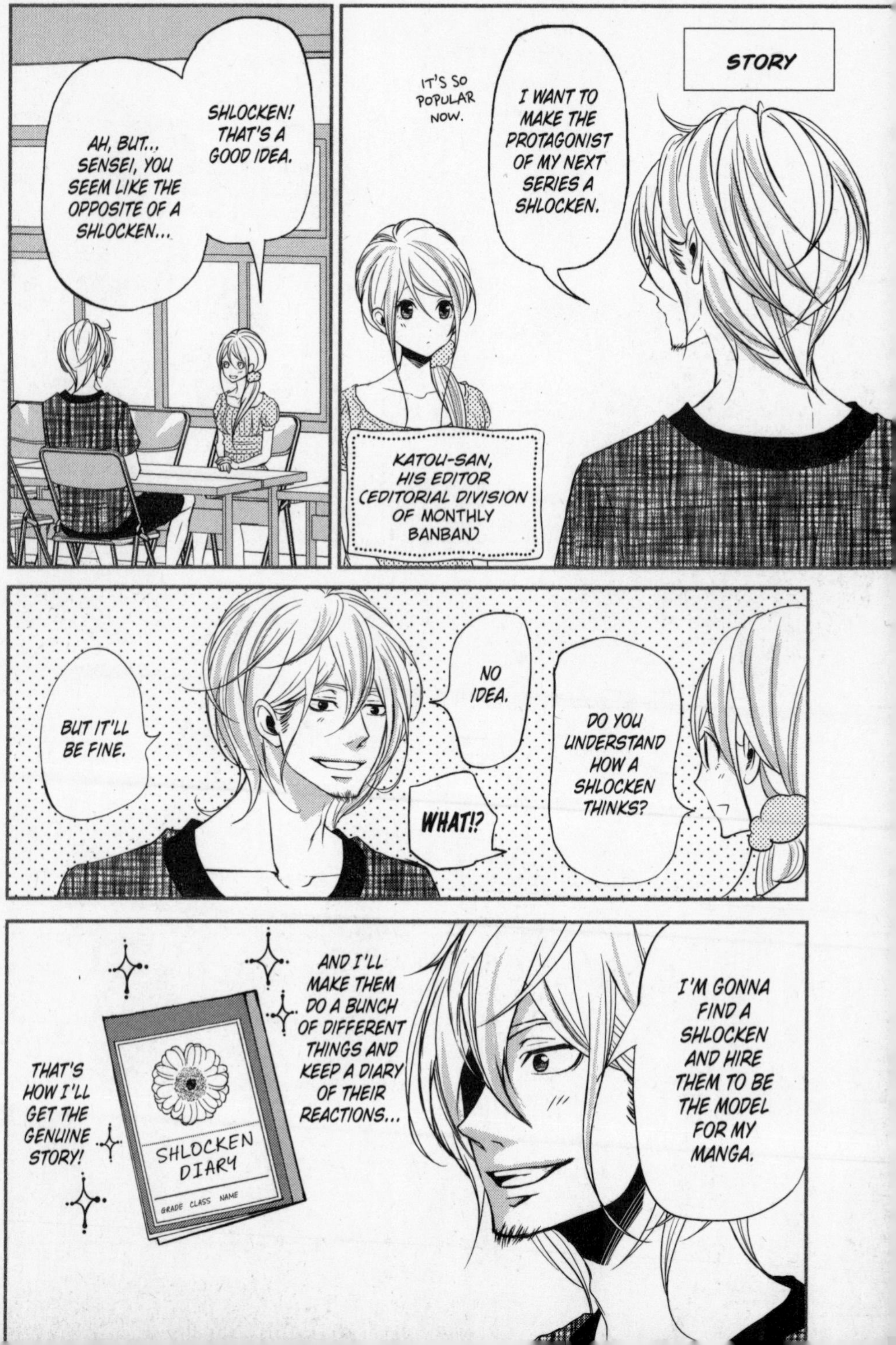
STORY
I WANT TO MAKE THE PROTAGONIST OF MY NEXT SERIES A SHLOCKEN.
IT'S SO POPULAR NOW.
KATOU-SAN, HIS EDITOR (EDITORIAL DIVISION OF MONTHLY BANBAN)
SHLOCKEN! THAT'S A GOOD IDEA.
AH, BUT... SENSEI, YOU SEEM LIKE THE OPPOSITE OF A SHLOCKEN...
DO YOU UNDERSTAND HOW A SHLOCKEN THINKS?
NO IDEA.
WHAT!?
BUT IT'LL BE FINE.
I'M GONNA FIND A SHLOCKEN AND HIRE THEM TO BE THE MODEL FOR MY MANGA.
AND I'LL MAKE THEM DO A BUNCH OF DIFFERENT THINGS AND KEEP A DIARY OF THEIR REACTIONS...
SHLOCKEN DIARY
GRADE CLASS NAME
THAT'S HOW I'LL GET THE GENUINE STORY!

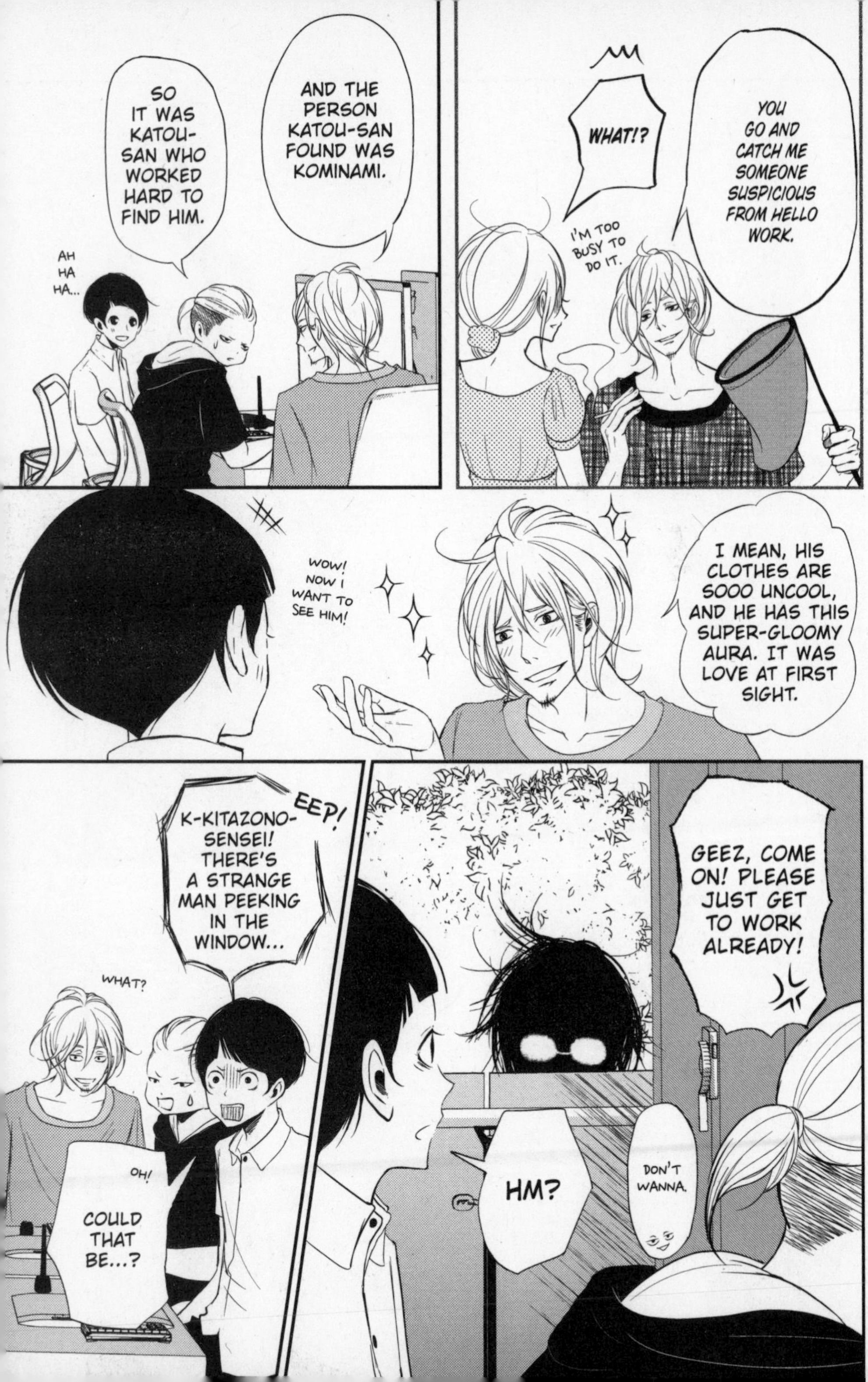
YOU GO AND CATCH ME SOMEONE SUSPICIOUS FROM HELLO WORK.
WHAT!?
I'M TOO BUSY TO DO IT.
AND THE PERSON KATOU-SAN FOUND WAS KOMINAMI.
SO IT WAS KATOU-SAN WHO WORKED HARD TO FIND HIM.
AH HA HA...
I MEAN, HIS CLOTHES ARE SOOO UNCOOL, AND HE HAS THIS SUPER-GLOOMY AURA. IT WAS LOVE AT FIRST SIGHT.
WOW! NOW I WANT TO SEE HIM!
GEEZ, COME ON! PLEASE JUST GET TO WORK ALREADY!
DON'T WANNA.
HM?
EEP!
K-KITAZONO-SENSEI! THERE'S A STRANGE MAN PEEKING IN THE WINDOW...
WHAT?
OH!
COULD THAT BE...?

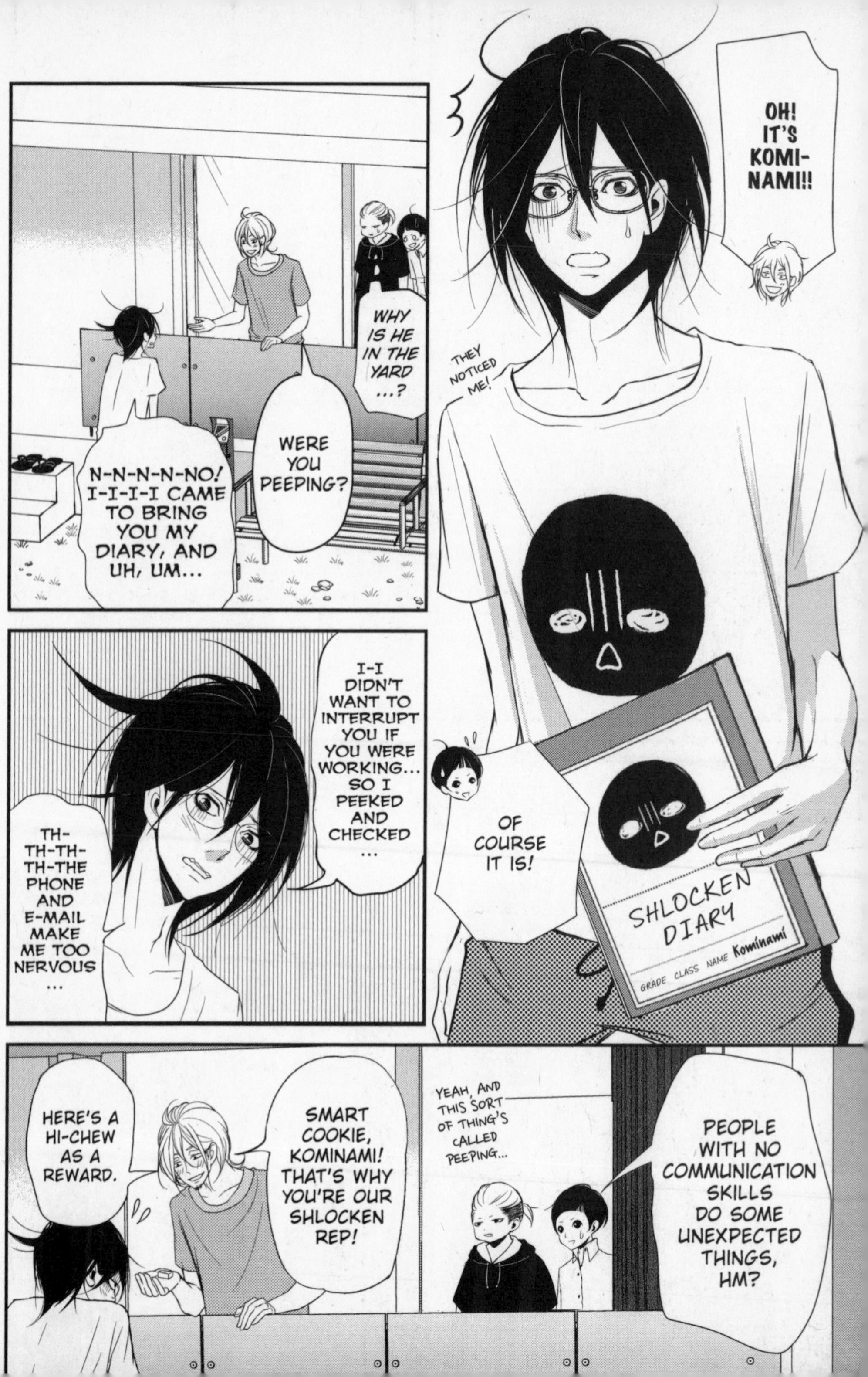
OH! IT'S KOMI-NAMI!!
THEY NOTICED ME!
OF COURSE IT IS!
SHLOCKEN DIARY
GRADE CLASS NAME Kominami
WHY IS HE IN THE YARD ...?
WERE YOU PEEPING?
N-N-N-N-NO! I-I-I-I CAME TO BRING YOU MY DIARY, AND UH, UM...
I-I DIDN'T WANT TO INTERRUPT YOU IF YOU WERE WORKING... SO I PEEKED AND CHECKED ...
TH-TH-TH-TH-THE PHONE AND E-MAIL MAKE ME TOO NERVOUS ...
PEOPLE WITH NO COMMUNICATION SKILLS DO SOME UNEXPECTED THINGS, HM?
YEAH, AND THIS SORT OF THING'S CALLED PEEPING...
SMART COOKIE, KOMINAMI! THAT'S WHY YOU'RE OUR SHLOCKEN REP!
HERE'S A HI-CHEW AS A REWARD.

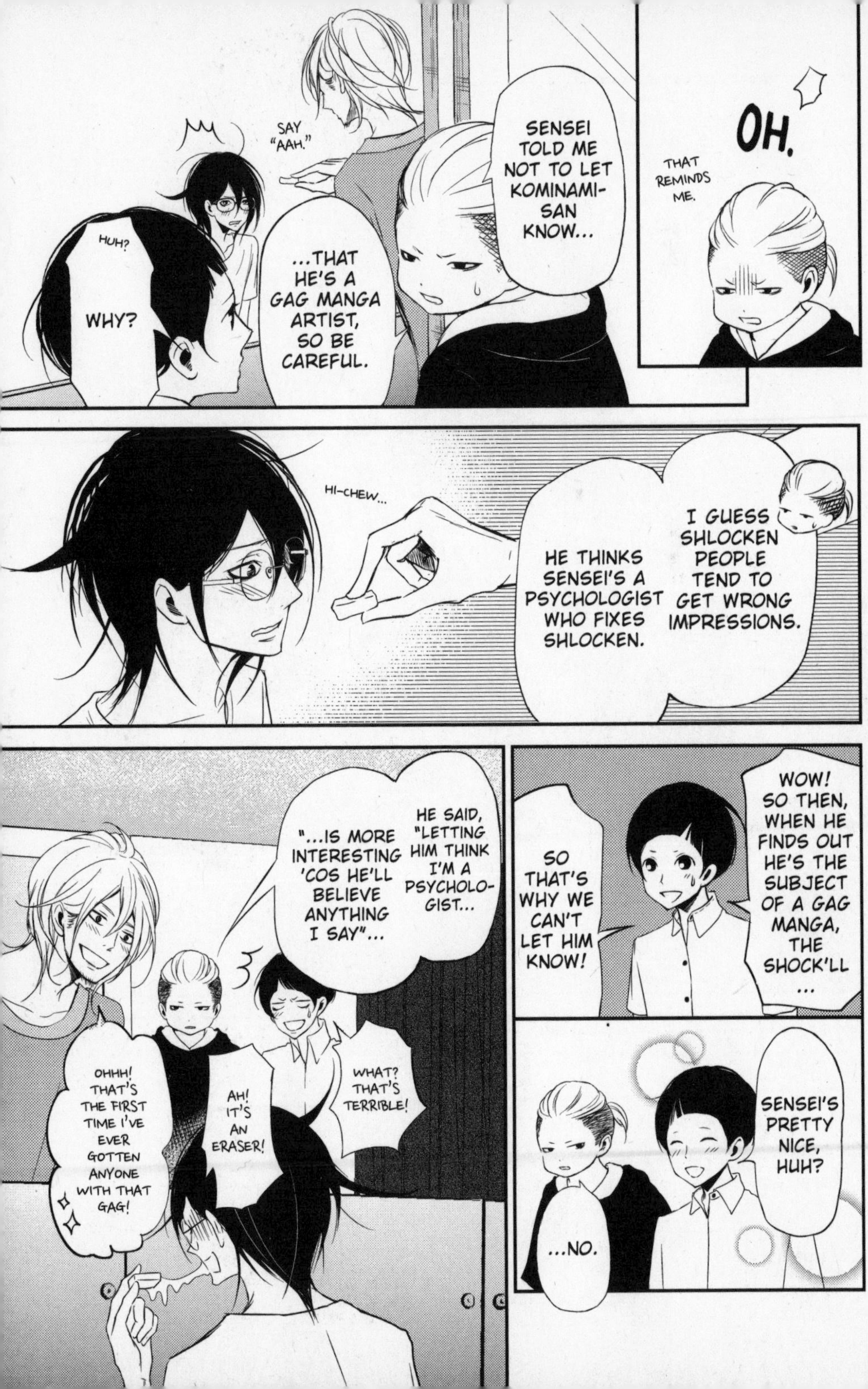
OH.
THAT REMINDS ME.
SENSEI TOLD ME NOT TO LET KOMINAMI-SAN KNOW...
...THAT HE'S A GAG MANGA ARTIST, SO BE CAREFUL.
SAY "AAH."
HUH?
WHY?
I GUESS SHLOCKEN PEOPLE TEND TO GET WRONG IMPRESSIONS.
HE THINKS SENSEI'S A PSYCHOLOGIST WHO FIXES SHLOCKEN.
HI-CHEW...
WOW! SO THEN, WHEN HE FINDS OUT HE'S THE SUBJECT OF A GAG MANGA, THE SHOCK'LL ...
SO THAT'S WHY WE CAN'T LET HIM KNOW!
SENSEI'S PRETTY NICE, HUH?
...NO.
HE SAID, "LETTING HIM THINK I'M A PSYCHOLOGIST...
"...IS MORE INTERESTING 'COS HE'LL BELIEVE ANYTHING I SAY"...
WHAT? THAT'S TERRIBLE!
AH! IT'S AN ERASER!
OHHH! THAT'S THE FIRST TIME I'VE EVER GOTTEN ANYONE WITH THAT GAG!

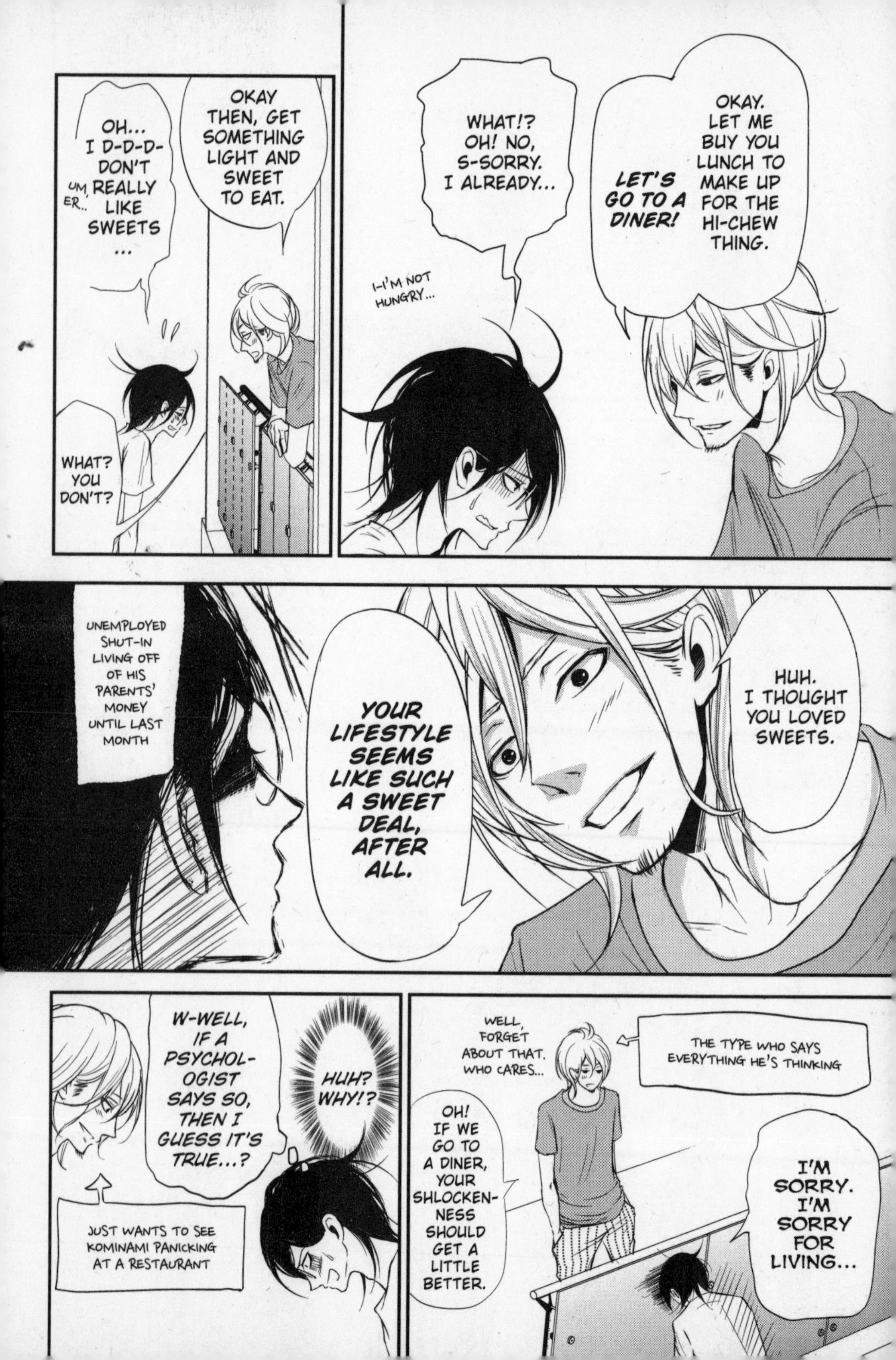
OKAY. LET ME BUY YOU LUNCH TO MAKE UP FOR THE HI-CHEW THING.
LET'S GO TO A DINER!
WHAT!? OH! NO, S-SORRY. I ALREADY...
I-I'M NOT HUNGRY...
OKAY THEN, GET SOMETHING LIGHT AND SWEET TO EAT.
OH... I D-D-D-DON'T REALLY LIKE SWEETS ...
UM, ER..
WHAT? YOU DON'T?
HUH. I THOUGHT YOU LOVED SWEETS.
YOUR LIFESTYLE SEEMS LIKE SUCH A SWEET DEAL, AFTER ALL.
UNEMPLOYED SHUT-IN LIVING OFF OF HIS PARENTS' MONEY UNTIL LAST MONTH
I'M SORRY. I'M SORRY FOR LIVING...
THE TYPE WHO SAYS EVERYTHING HE'S THINKING
WELL, FORGET ABOUT THAT. WHO CARES...
OH! IF WE GO TO A DINER, YOUR SHLOCKENNESS SHOULD GET A LITTLE BETTER.
HUH? WHY!?
W-WELL, IF A PSYCHOLOGIST SAYS SO, THEN I GUESS IT'S TRUE...?
JUST WANTS TO SEE KOMINAMI PANICKING AT A RESTAURANT

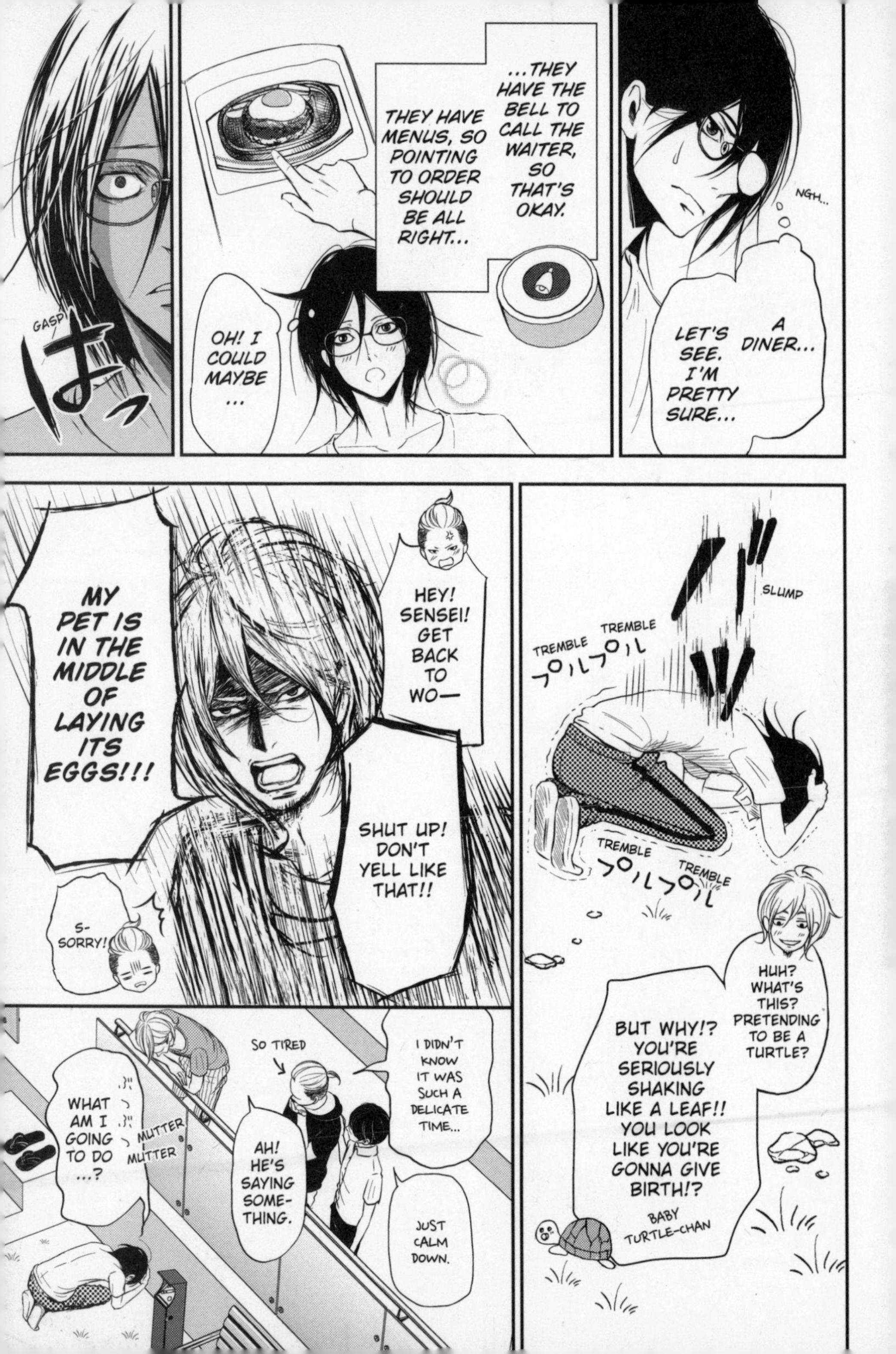
A DINER...
LET'S SEE. I'M PRETTY SURE...
NGH...
...THEY HAVE THE BELL TO CALL THE WAITER, SO THAT'S OKAY.
THEY HAVE MENUS, SO POINTING TO ORDER SHOULD BE ALL RIGHT...
OH! I COULD MAYBE ...
GASP
SLUMP
TREMBLE
TREMBLE
TREMBLE
TREMBLE
HUH? WHAT'S THIS? PRETENDING TO BE A TURTLE?
BUT WHY!? YOU'RE SERIOUSLY SHAKING LIKE A LEAF!! YOU LOOK LIKE YOU'RE GONNA GIVE BIRTH!?
BABY TURTLE-CHAN
HEY! SENSEI! GET BACK TO WO—
MY PET IS IN THE MIDDLE OF LAYING ITS EGGS!!!
SHUT UP! DON'T YELL LIKE THAT!!
S-SORRY!
I DIDN'T KNOW IT WAS SUCH A DELICATE TIME...
SO TIRED
AH! HE'S SAYING SOME-THING.
JUST CALM DOWN.
WHAT AM I GOING TO DO ...?
MUTTER
MUTTER

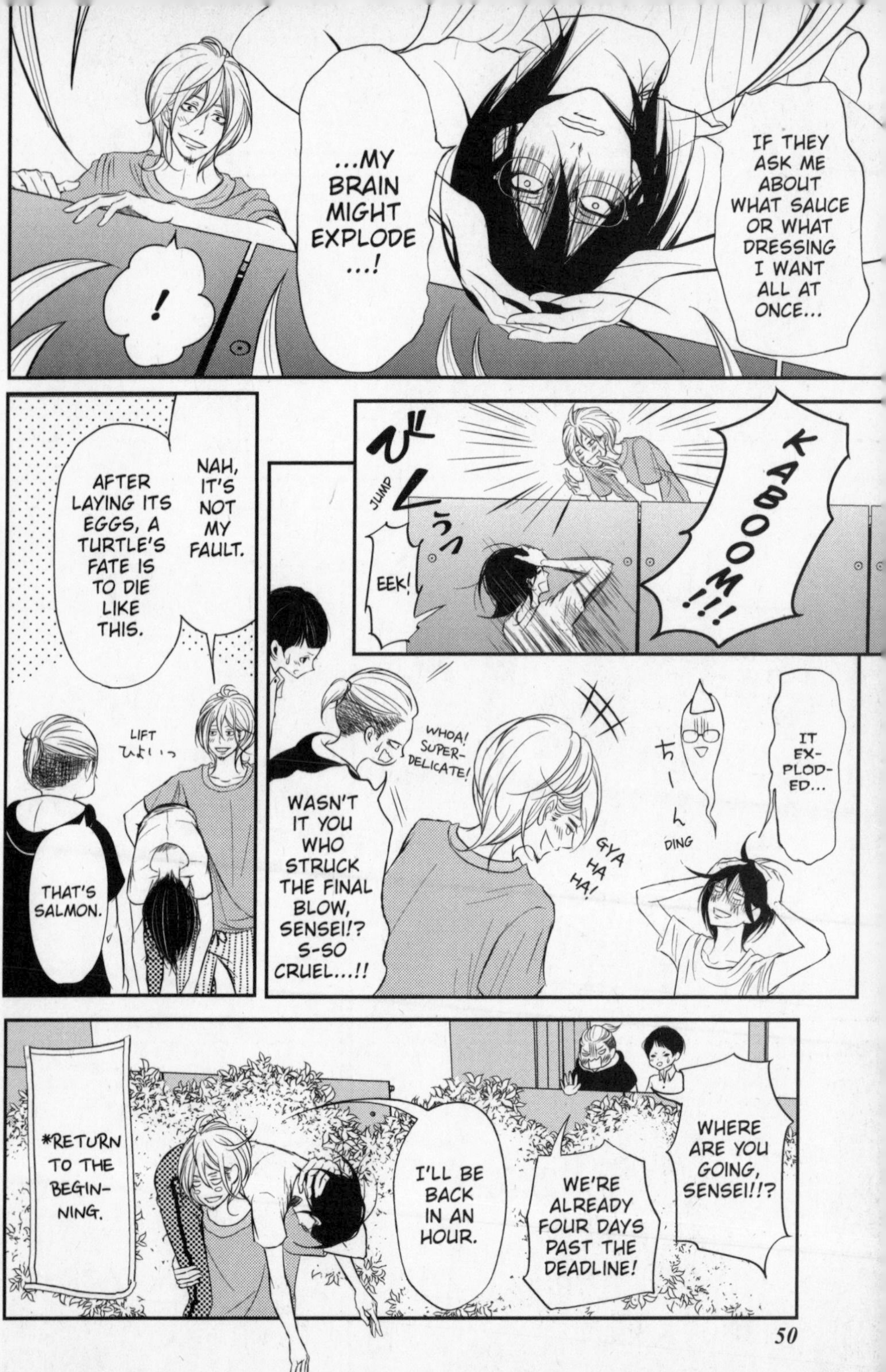
IF THEY ASK ME ABOUT WHAT SAUCE OR WHAT DRESSING I WANT ALL AT ONCE...
...MY BRAIN MIGHT EXPLODE ...!
!
KABOOOM!!!!
EEK!
JUMP
びくっっ
NAH, IT'S NOT MY FAULT.
AFTER LAYING ITS EGGS, A TURTLE'S FATE IS TO DIE LIKE THIS.
IT EXPLODED...
ち～ん
DING
GYA HA HA!
WHOA! SUPER-DELICATE!
WASN'T IT YOU WHO STRUCK THE FINAL BLOW, SENSEI!? S-SO CRUEL...!!
LIFT
ひょいっ
THAT'S SALMON.
WHERE ARE YOU GOING, SENSEI!!?
WE'RE ALREADY FOUR DAYS PAST THE DEADLINE!
I'LL BE BACK IN AN HOUR.
*RETURN TO THE BEGIN-NING.

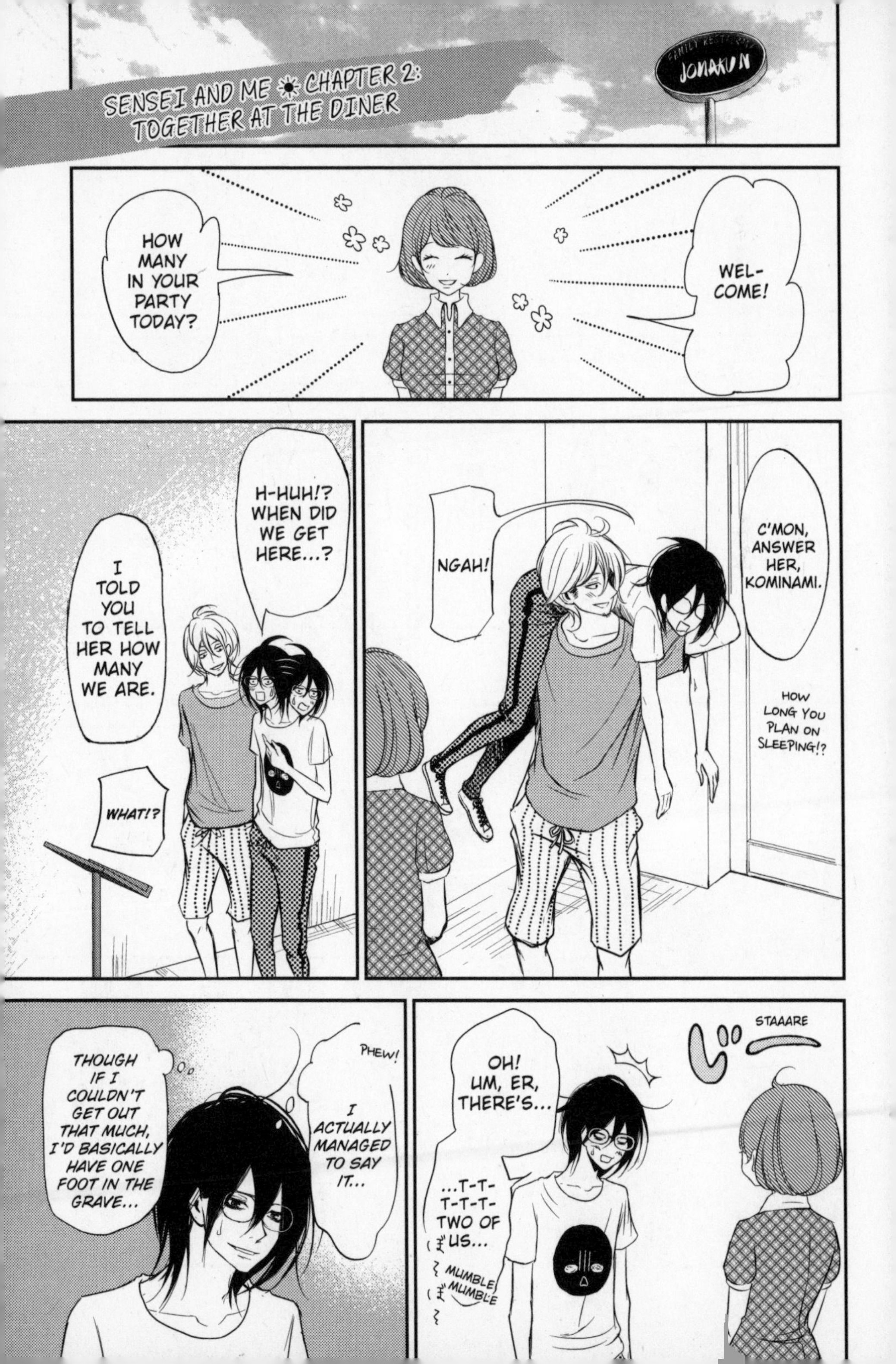
SENSEI AND ME ☀ CHAPTER 2: TOGETHER AT THE DINER
JONAKUN
WEL-COME!
HOW MANY IN YOUR PARTY TODAY?
C'MON, ANSWER HER, KOMINAMI.
HOW LONG YOU PLAN ON SLEEPING!?
NGAH!
H-HUH!? WHEN DID WE GET HERE...?
I TOLD YOU TO TELL HER HOW MANY WE ARE.
WHAT!?
STAAARE
OH! UM, ER, THERE'S...
...T-T-T-T-T-TWO OF US...
MUMBLE MUMBLE
PHEW!
I ACTUALLY MANAGED TO SAY IT...
THOUGH IF I COULDN'T GET OUT THAT MUCH, I'D BASICALLY HAVE ONE FOOT IN THE GRAVE...

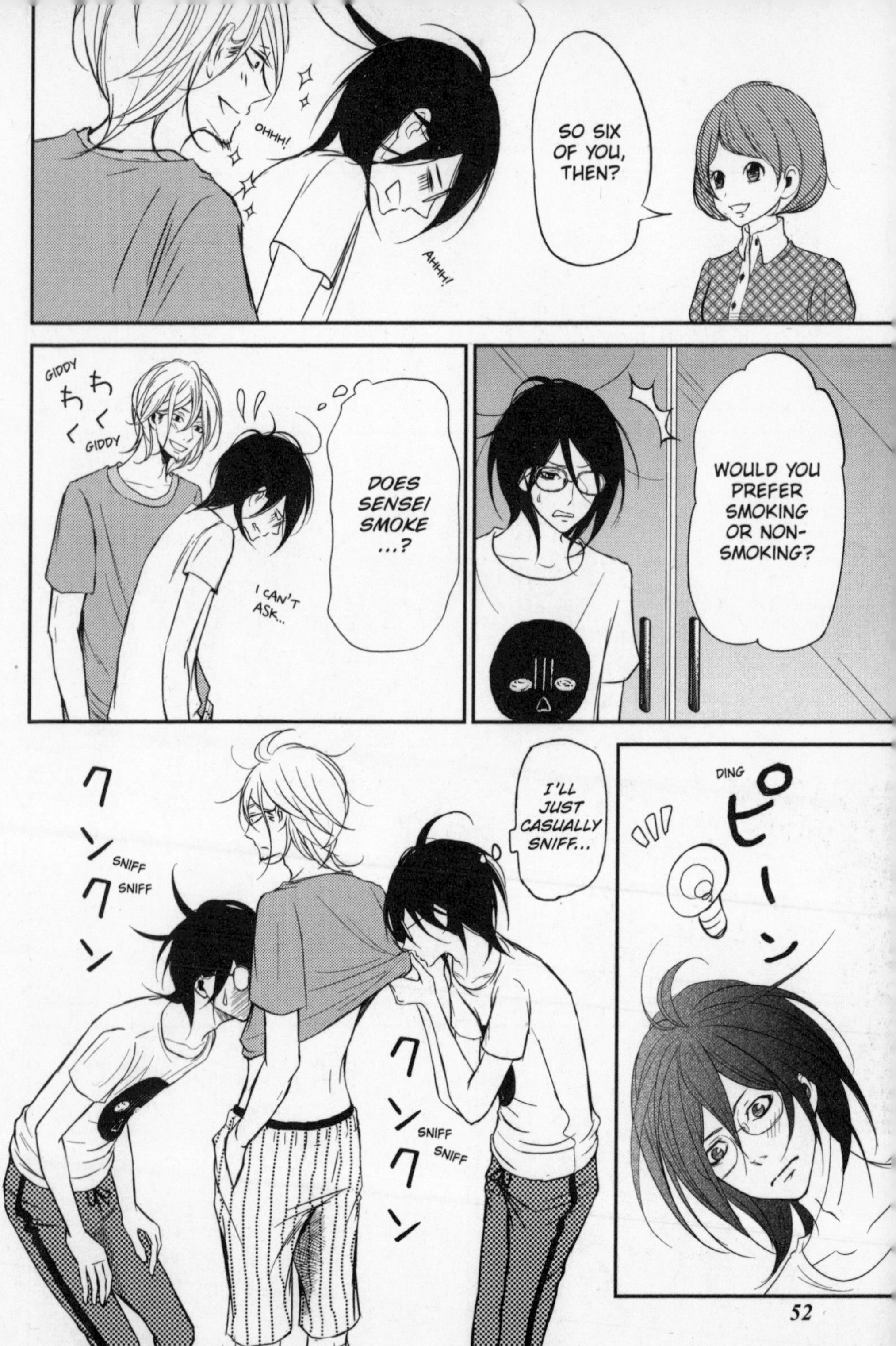
SO SIX OF YOU, THEN?
OHHH!
AHHH!
WOULD YOU PREFER SMOKING OR NON-SMOKING?
DOES SENSEI SMOKE ...?
I CAN'T ASK...
わくわく
GIDDY GIDDY
ピーン
DING
I'LL JUST CASUALLY SNIFF...
クンクン
SNIFF SNIFF
クンクン
SNIFF SNIFF

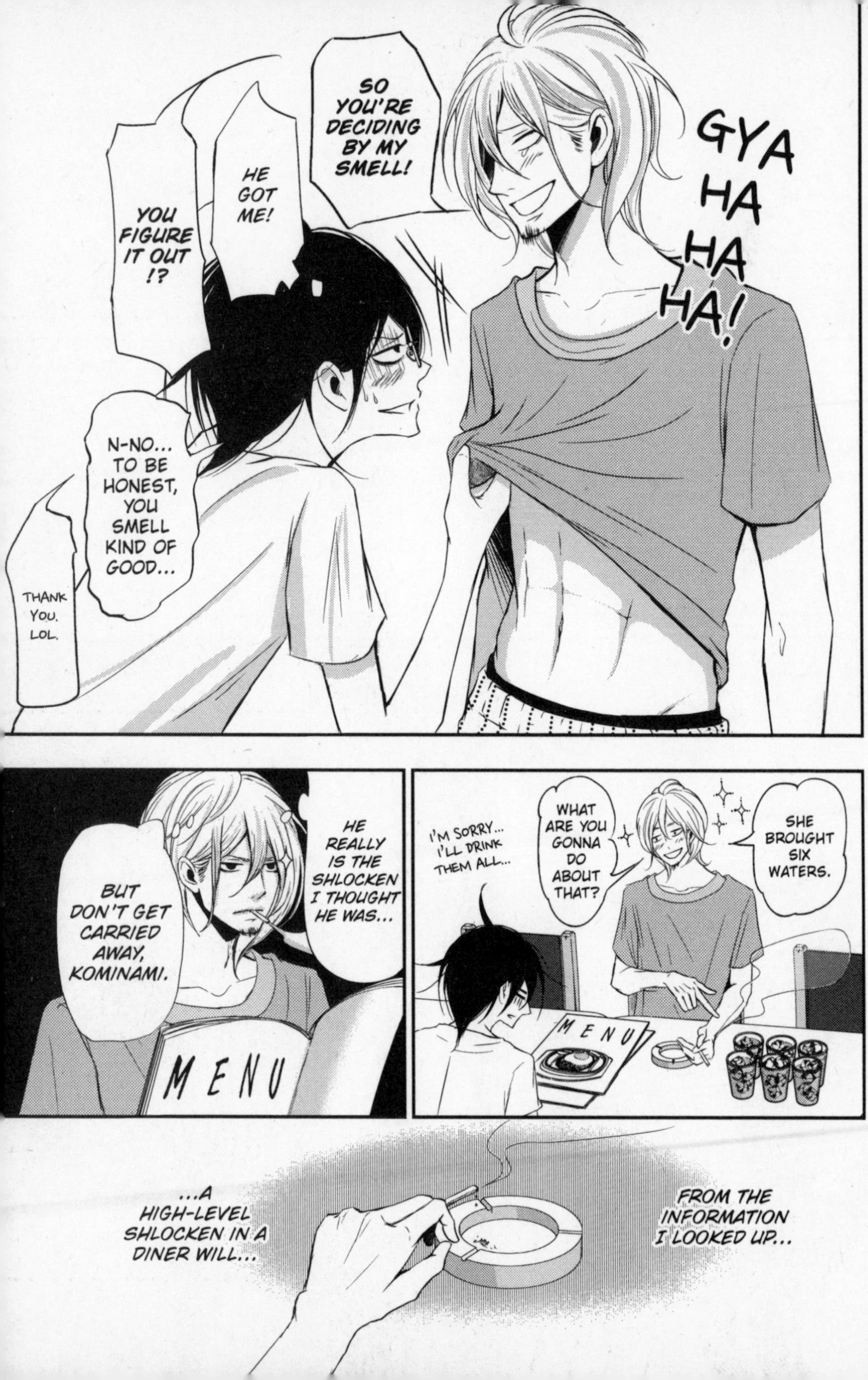
GYA HA HA HA!
SO YOU'RE DECIDING BY MY SMELL!
HE GOT ME!
YOU FIGURE IT OUT !?
N-NO... TO BE HONEST, YOU SMELL KIND OF GOOD...
THANK YOU. LOL.
SHE BROUGHT SIX WATERS.
WHAT ARE YOU GONNA DO ABOUT THAT?
I'M SORRY... I'LL DRINK THEM ALL...
MENU
HE REALLY IS THE SHLOCKEN I THOUGHT HE WAS...
BUT DON'T GET CARRIED AWAY, KOMINAMI.
MENU
FROM THE INFORMATION I LOOKED UP...
...A HIGH-LEVEL SHLOCKEN IN A DINER WILL...

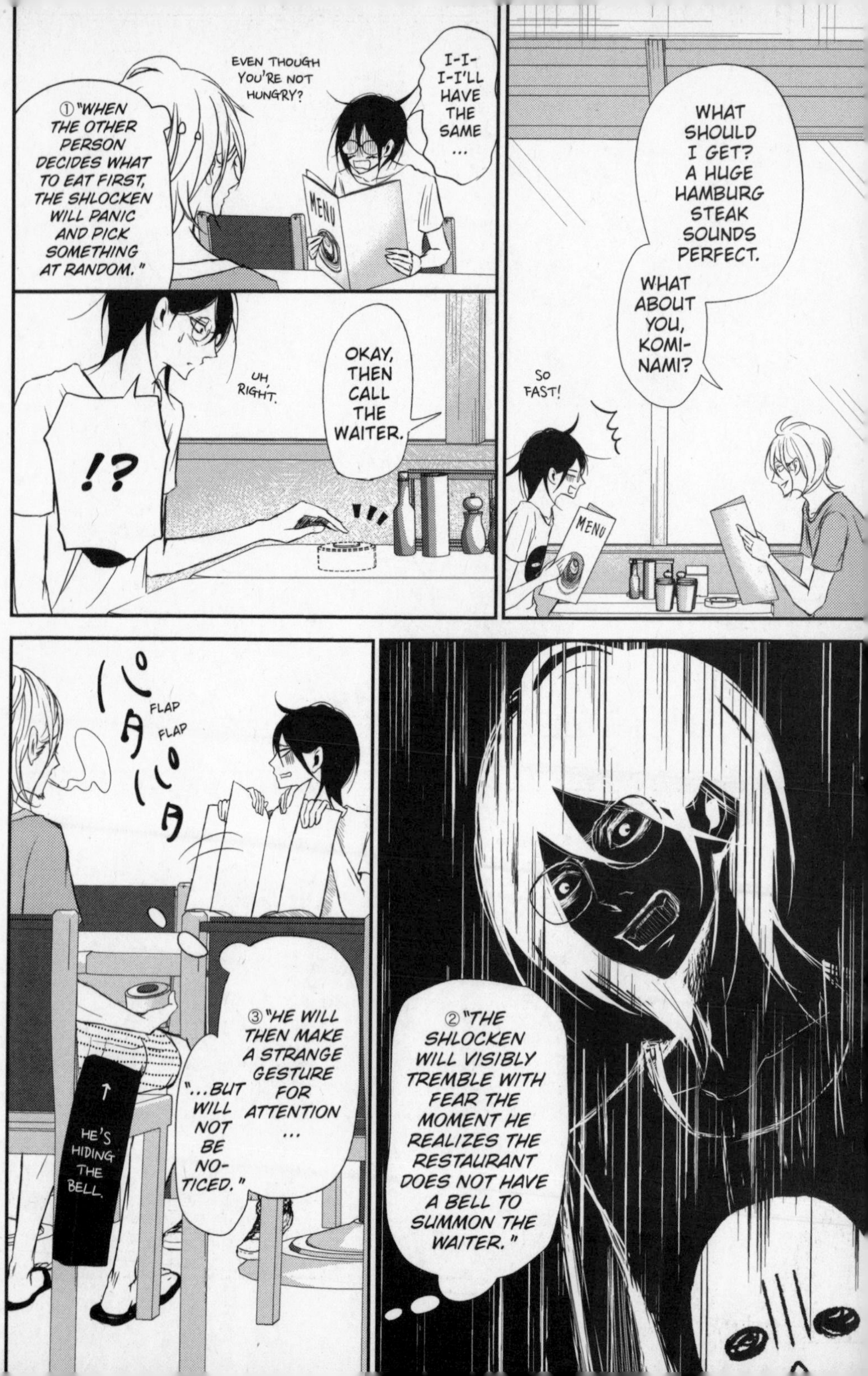
WHAT SHOULD I GET? A HUGE HAMBURG STEAK SOUNDS PERFECT.
WHAT ABOUT YOU, KOMI-NAMI?
SO FAST!
I-I-I-I'LL HAVE THE SAME...
EVEN THOUGH YOU'RE NOT HUNGRY?
①"WHEN THE OTHER PERSON DECIDES WHAT TO EAT FIRST, THE SHLOCKEN WILL PANIC AND PICK SOMETHING AT RANDOM."
OKAY, THEN CALL THE WAITER.
UH RIGHT.
!?
②"THE SHLOCKEN WILL VISIBLY TREMBLE WITH FEAR THE MOMENT HE REALIZES THE RESTAURANT DOES NOT HAVE A BELL TO SUMMON THE WAITER."
パタパタ
FLAP FLAP
③"HE WILL THEN MAKE A STRANGE GESTURE FOR ATTENTION...
"...BUT WILL NOT BE NO-TICED."
↑ HE'S HIDING THE BELL.

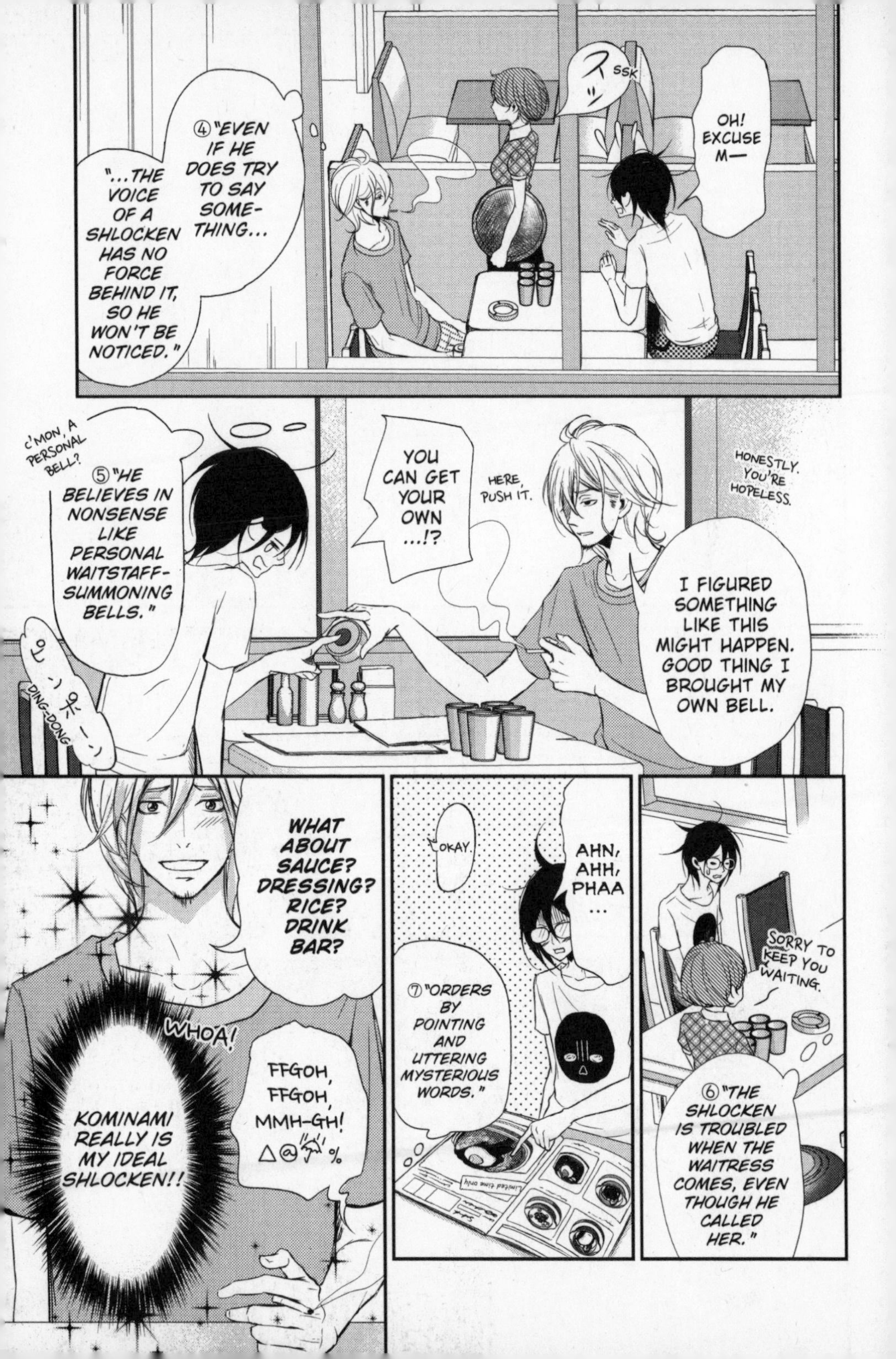

OH! EXCUSE M—
SSK
④ "EVEN IF HE DOES TRY TO SAY SOME-THING...
"...THE VOICE OF A SHLOCKEN HAS NO FORCE BEHIND IT, SO HE WON'T BE NOTICED."
HONESTLY. YOU'RE HOPELESS.
I FIGURED SOMETHING LIKE THIS MIGHT HAPPEN. GOOD THING I BROUGHT MY OWN BELL.
HERE, PUSH IT.
YOU CAN GET YOUR OWN ...!?
C'MON, A PERSONAL BELL?
⑤ "HE BELIEVES IN NONSENSE LIKE PERSONAL WAITSTAFF-SUMMONING BELLS."
DING-DONG
SORRY TO KEEP YOU WAITING.
⑥ "THE SHLOCKEN IS TROUBLED WHEN THE WAITRESS COMES, EVEN THOUGH HE CALLED HER."
AHN, AHH, PHAA ...
OKAY.
⑦ "ORDERS BY POINTING AND UTTERING MYSTERIOUS WORDS."
Limited time only
WHAT ABOUT SAUCE? DRESSING? RICE? DRINK BAR?
FFGOH, FFGOH, MMH-GH! △@☂%
WHOA!
KOMINAMI REALLY IS MY IDEAL SHLOCKEN!!

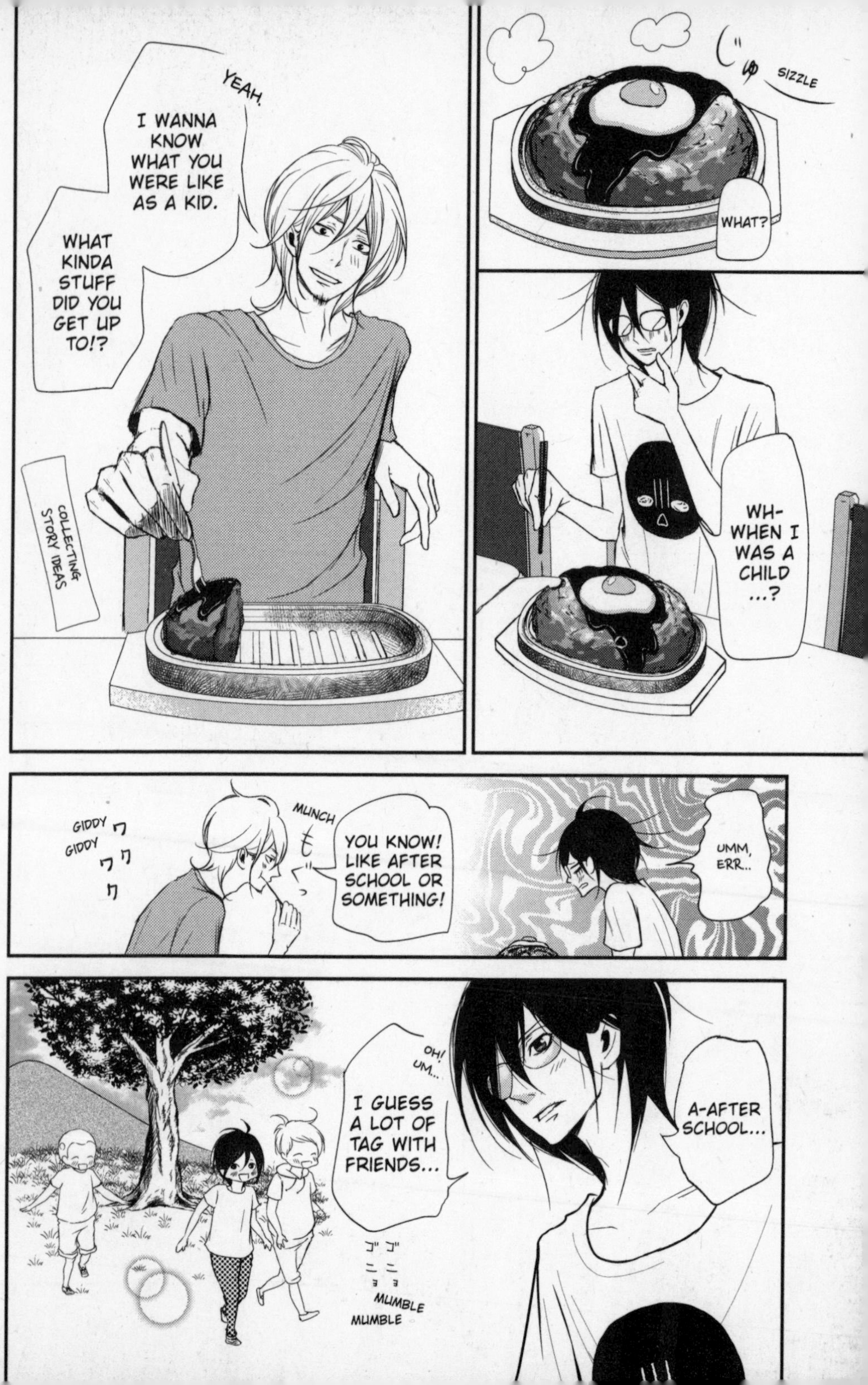
じゅ
SIZZLE
WHAT?
WH- WHEN I WAS A CHILD ...?
YEAH.
I WANNA KNOW WHAT YOU WERE LIKE AS A KID.
WHAT KINDA STUFF DID YOU GET UP TO!?
COLLECTING STORY IDEAS
UMM, ERR...
GIDDY GIDDY
MUNCH
YOU KNOW! LIKE AFTER SCHOOL OR SOMETHING!
A-AFTER SCHOOL...
OH! UM...
I GUESS A LOT OF TAG WITH FRIENDS...
MUMBLE MUMBLE

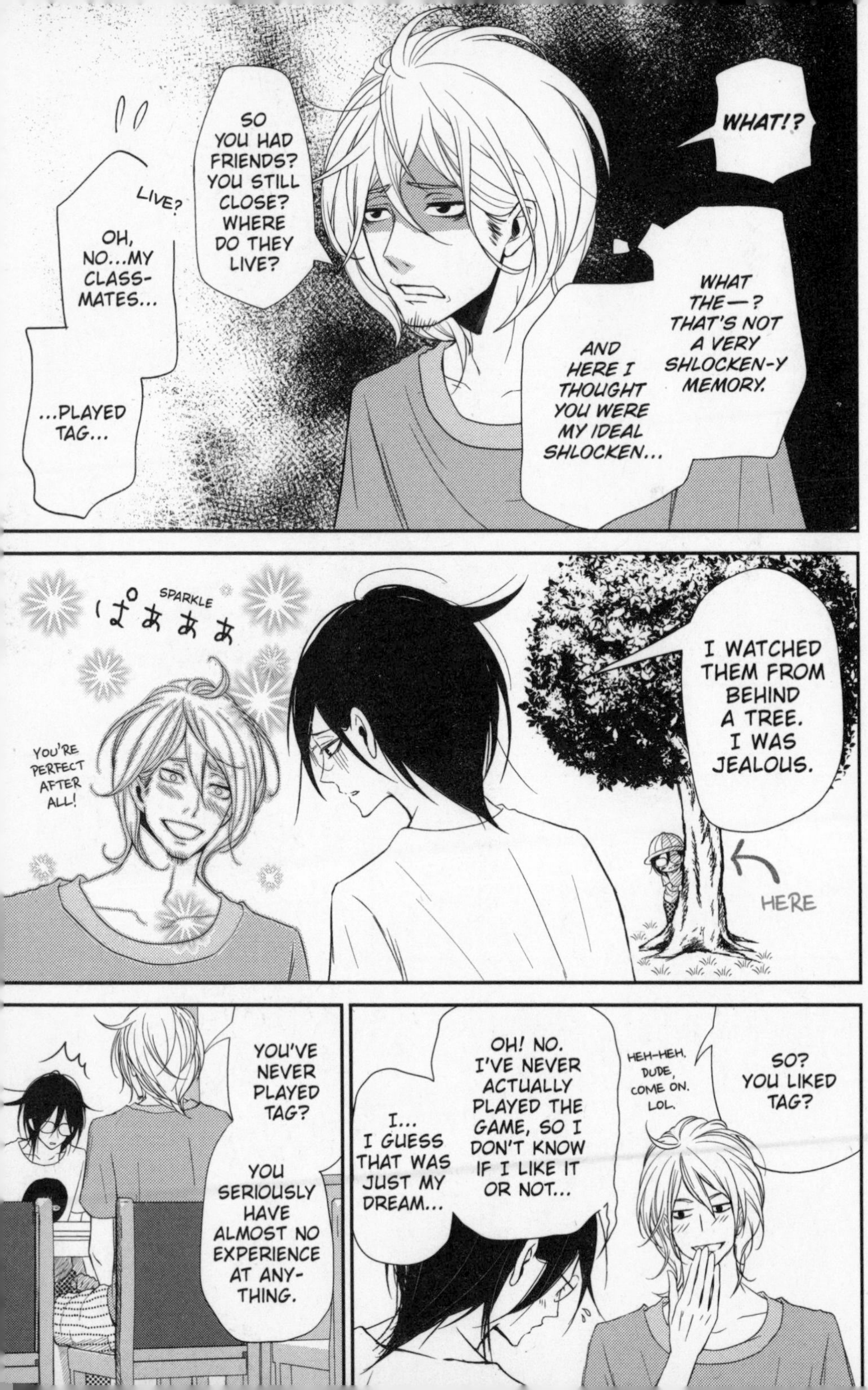
WHAT!?
WHAT THE—? THAT'S NOT A VERY SHLOCKEN-Y MEMORY.
AND HERE I THOUGHT YOU WERE MY IDEAL SHLOCKEN...
SO YOU HAD FRIENDS? YOU STILL CLOSE? WHERE DO THEY LIVE?
LIVE?
OH, NO...MY CLASSMATES...
...PLAYED TAG...
I WATCHED THEM FROM BEHIND A TREE. I WAS JEALOUS.
HERE
SPARKLE
ぱあああ
YOU'RE PERFECT AFTER ALL!
SO? YOU LIKED TAG?
HEH-HEH, DUDE, COME ON. LOL.
OH! NO. I'VE NEVER ACTUALLY PLAYED THE GAME, SO I DON'T KNOW IF I LIKE IT OR NOT...
I... I GUESS THAT WAS JUST MY DREAM...
YOU'VE NEVER PLAYED TAG?
YOU SERIOUSLY HAVE ALMOST NO EXPERIENCE AT ANYTHING.

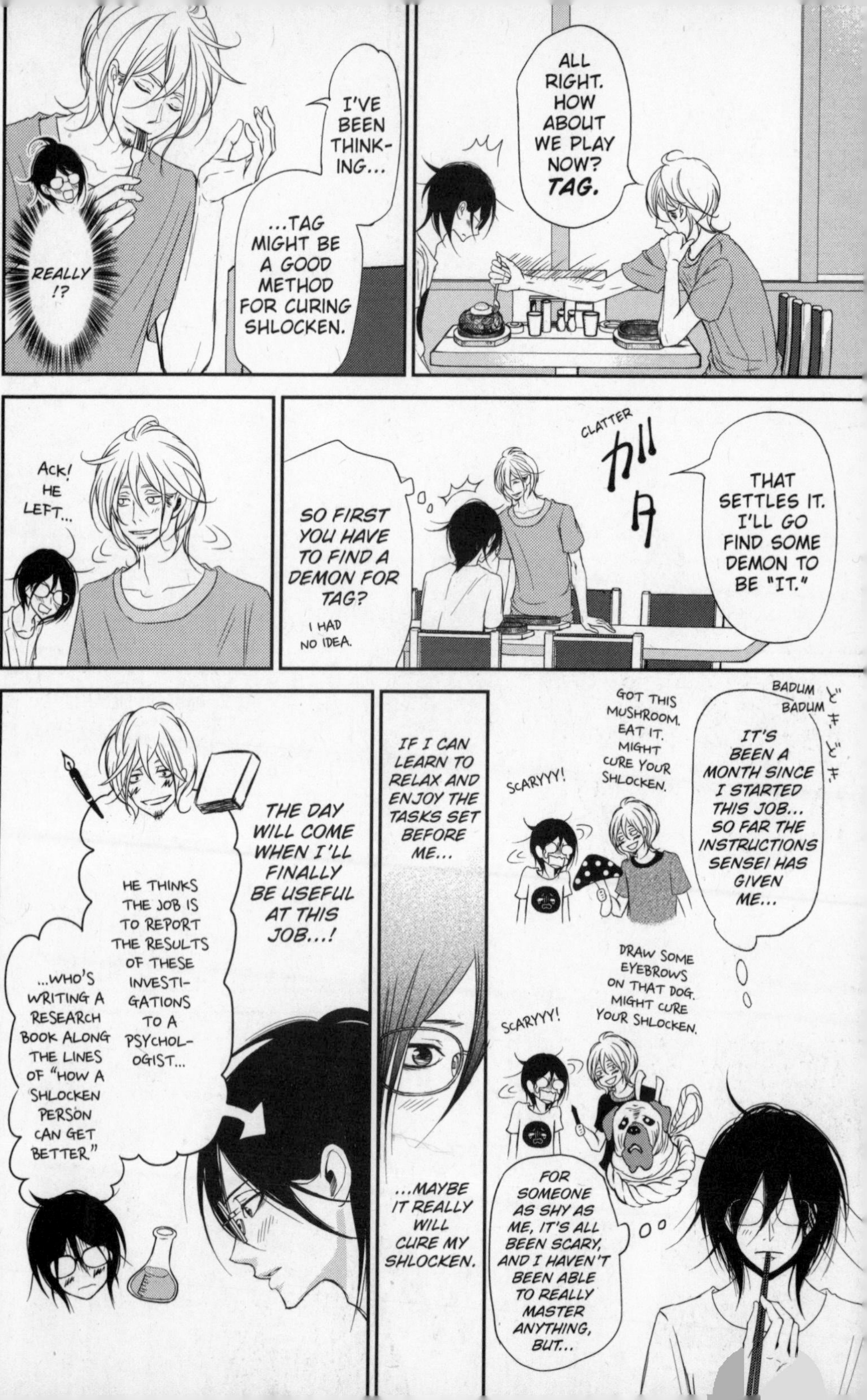
ALL RIGHT. HOW ABOUT WE PLAY NOW? TAG.
I'VE BEEN THINKING...
...TAG MIGHT BE A GOOD METHOD FOR CURING SHLOCKEN.
REALLY!?
CLATTER
THAT SETTLES IT. I'LL GO FIND SOME DEMON TO BE "IT."
SO FIRST YOU HAVE TO FIND A DEMON FOR TAG?
I HAD NO IDEA.
ACK! HE LEFT...
BADUM BADUM
IT'S BEEN A MONTH SINCE I STARTED THIS JOB... SO FAR THE INSTRUCTIONS SENSEI HAS GIVEN ME...
GOT THIS MUSHROOM. EAT IT. MIGHT CURE YOUR SHLOCKEN.
SCARYYY!
DRAW SOME EYEBROWS ON THAT DOG. MIGHT CURE YOUR SHLOCKEN.
SCARYYY!
FOR SOMEONE AS SHY AS ME, IT'S ALL BEEN SCARY, AND I HAVEN'T BEEN ABLE TO REALLY MASTER ANYTHING, BUT...
IF I CAN LEARN TO RELAX AND ENJOY THE TASKS SET BEFORE ME...
...MAYBE IT REALLY WILL CURE MY SHLOCKEN.
THE DAY WILL COME WHEN I'LL FINALLY BE USEFUL AT THIS JOB...!
HE THINKS THE JOB IS TO REPORT THE RESULTS OF THESE INVESTIGATIONS TO A PSYCHOLOGIST...
...WHO'S WRITING A RESEARCH BOOK ALONG THE LINES OF "HOW A SHLOCKEN PERSON CAN GET BETTER"

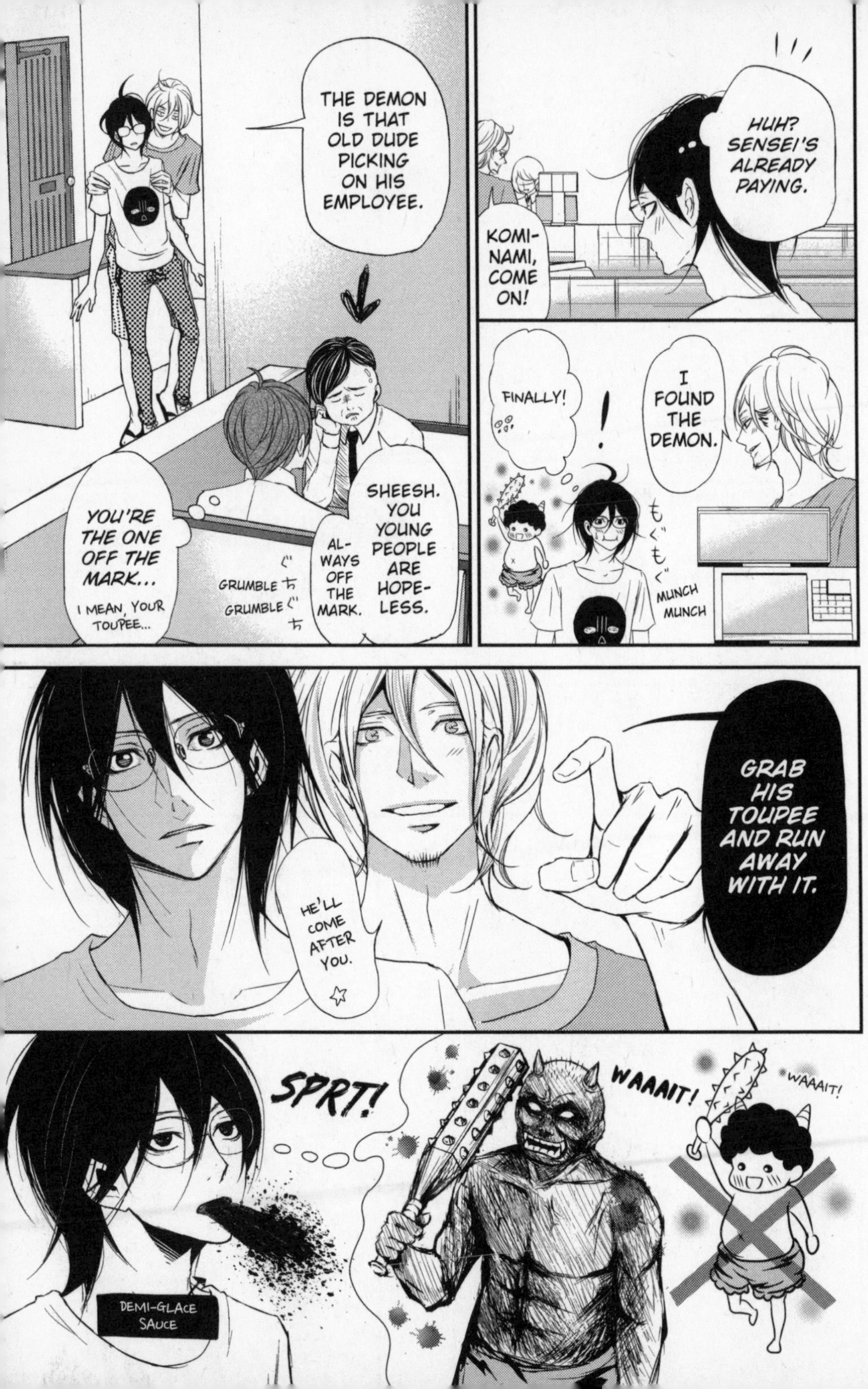
HUH? SENSEI'S ALREADY PAYING.
KOMI-NAMI, COME ON!
I FOUND THE DEMON.
FINALLY!
!
もぐもぐ
MUNCH MUNCH
THE DEMON IS THAT OLD DUDE PICKING ON HIS EMPLOYEE.
SHEESH. YOU YOUNG PEOPLE ARE HOPE-LESS.
AL-WAYS OFF THE MARK.
ぐちぐち
GRUMBLE GRUMBLE
YOU'RE THE ONE OFF THE MARK...
I MEAN, YOUR TOUPEE...
GRAB HIS TOUPEE AND RUN AWAY WITH IT.
HE'LL COME AFTER YOU.
*WAAAIT!
WAAAIT!
SPRT!
DEMI-GLACE SAUCE

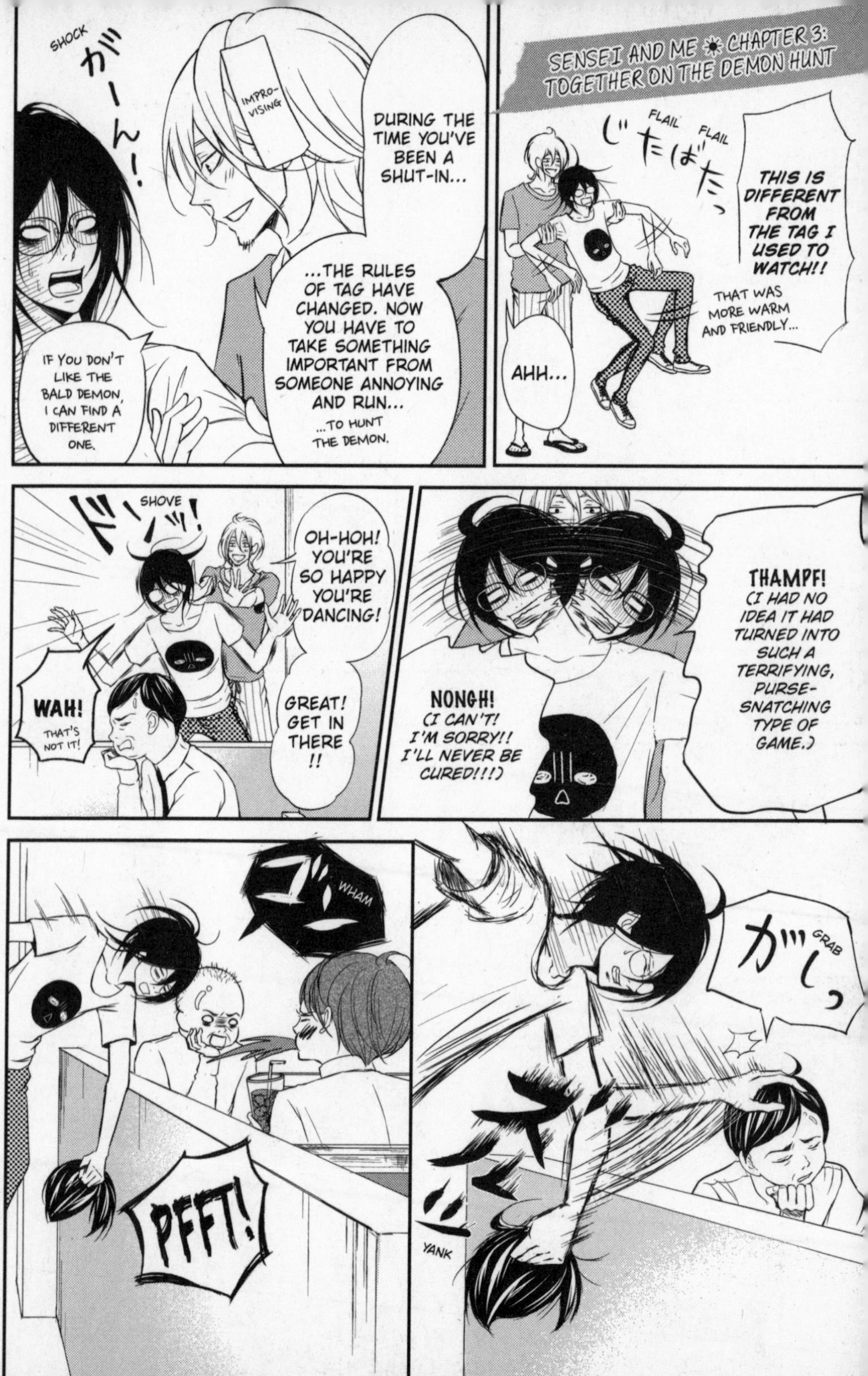
SENSEI AND ME ☀ CHAPTER 3: TOGETHER ON THE DEMON HUNT
じたばたっ
FLAIL FLAIL
THIS IS DIFFERENT FROM THE TAG I USED TO WATCH!!
THAT WAS MORE WARM AND FRIENDLY...
AHH...
DURING THE TIME YOU'VE BEEN A SHUT-IN...
IMPRO-VISING
がーん!
SHOCK
...THE RULES OF TAG HAVE CHANGED. NOW YOU HAVE TO TAKE SOMETHING IMPORTANT FROM SOMEONE ANNOYING AND RUN...
...TO HUNT THE DEMON.
IF YOU DON'T LIKE THE BALD DEMON, I CAN FIND A DIFFERENT ONE.
THAMPF! (I HAD NO IDEA IT HAD TURNED INTO SUCH A TERRIFYING, PURSE-SNATCHING TYPE OF GAME.)
NONGH! (I CAN'T! I'M SORRY!! I'LL NEVER BE CURED!!!)
OH-HOH! YOU'RE SO HAPPY YOU'RE DANCING!
ドンッ!
SHOVE
GREAT! GET IN THERE!!
WAH!
THAT'S NOT IT!
がしっ
GRAB
YANK
WHAM
PFFT!

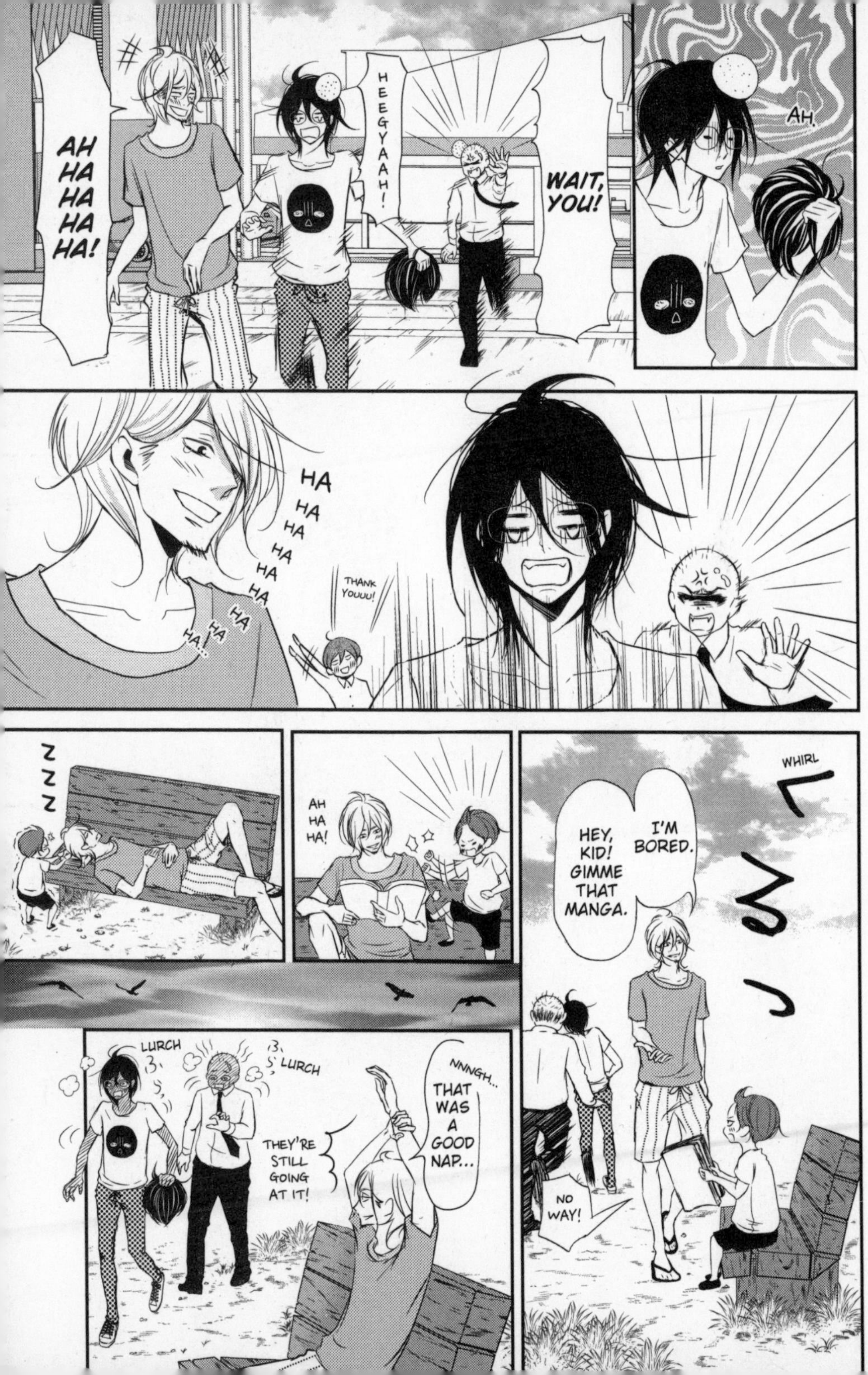
AH.
WAIT, YOU!
HEEGYAAAH!
AH HA HA HA HA HA!
HA HA HA HA HA HA HA HA HA...
THANK YOUUU!
WHIRL
I'M BORED.
HEY, KID! GIMME THAT MANGA.
NO WAY!
AH HA HA!
Z Z Z
NNNGH... THAT WAS A GOOD NAP...
THEY'RE STILL GOING AT IT!
LURCH
LURCH

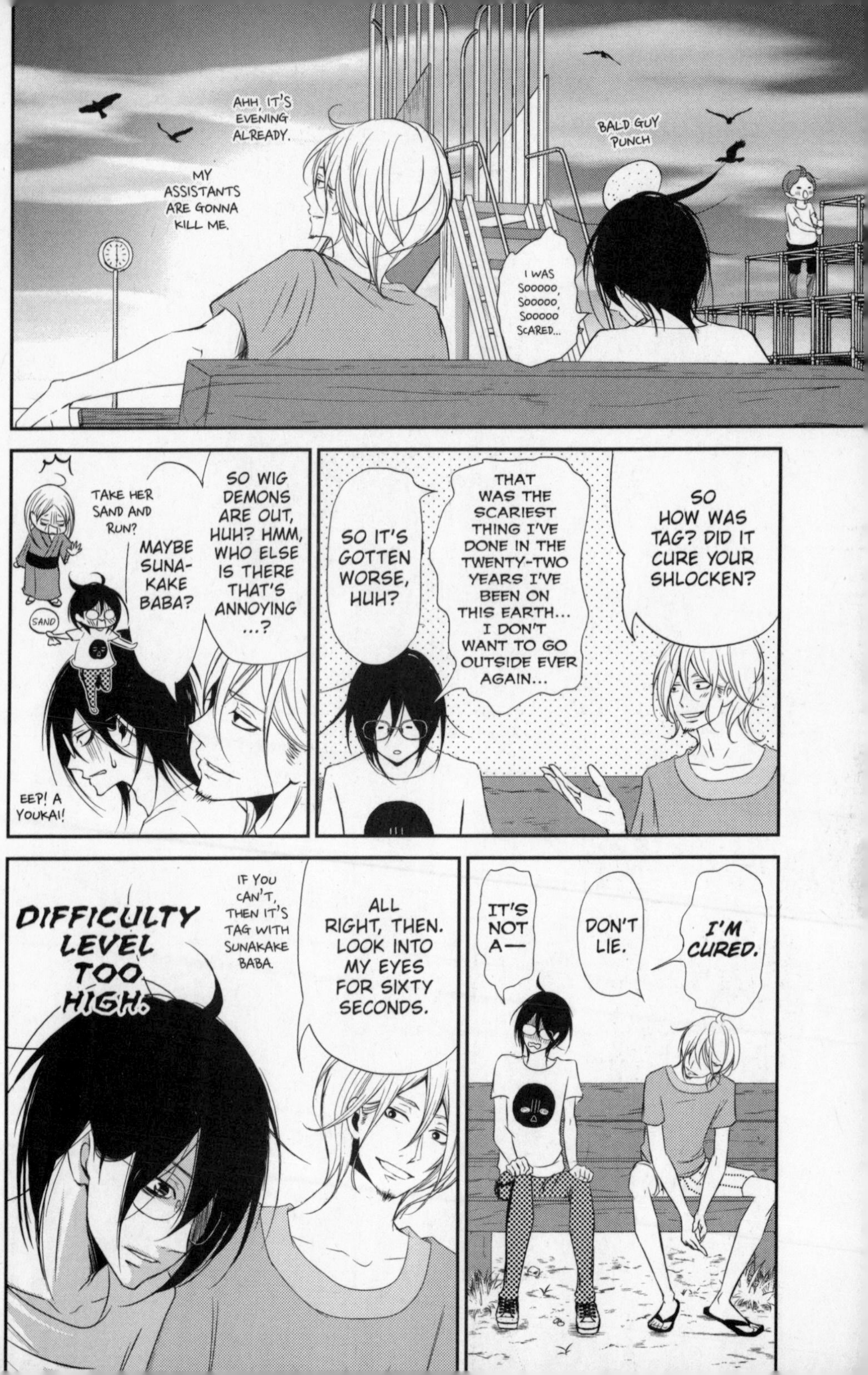
BALD GUY PUNCH
I WAS SOOOOO, SOOOOO, SOOOOO SCARED...
AHH, IT'S EVENING ALREADY.
MY ASSISTANTS ARE GONNA KILL ME.
SO HOW WAS TAG? DID IT CURE YOUR SHLOCKEN?
THAT WAS THE SCARIEST THING I'VE DONE IN THE TWENTY-TWO YEARS I'VE BEEN ON THIS EARTH... I DON'T WANT TO GO OUTSIDE EVER AGAIN...
SO IT'S GOTTEN WORSE, HUH?
SO WIG DEMONS ARE OUT, HUH? HMM, WHO ELSE IS THERE THAT'S ANNOYING ...?
MAYBE SUNA-KAKE BABA?
TAKE HER SAND AND RUN?
SAND
EEP! A YOUKAI!
I'M CURED.
DON'T LIE.
IT'S NOT A—
ALL RIGHT, THEN. LOOK INTO MY EYES FOR SIXTY SECONDS.
IF YOU CAN'T, THEN IT'S TAG WITH SUNAKAKE BABA.
DIFFICULTY LEVEL TOO HIGH.

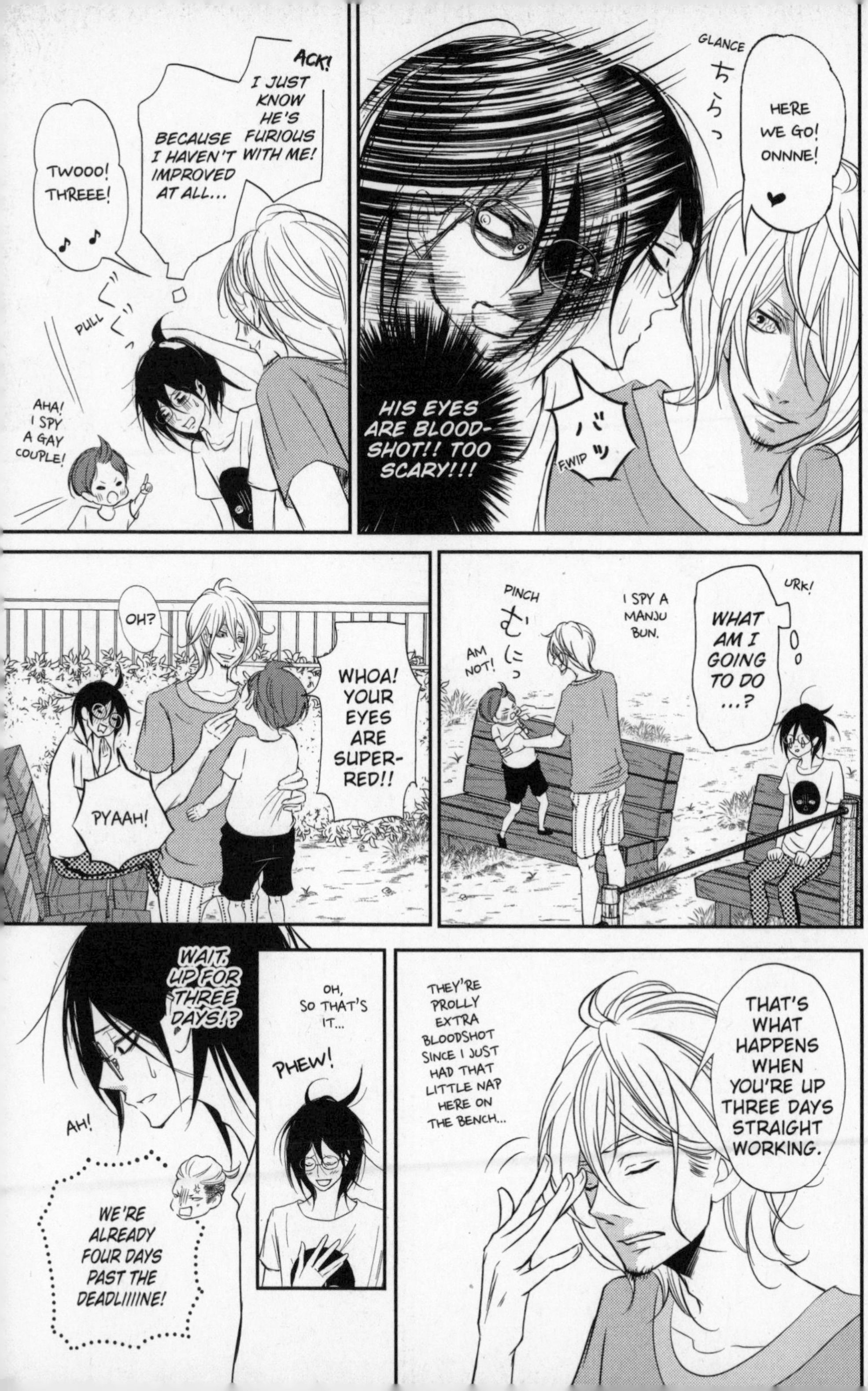
GLANCE
ちらっ
HERE WE GO! ONNNE! ♥
FWIP
バッ
HIS EYES ARE BLOODSHOT!! TOO SCARY!!!
ACK!
I JUST KNOW HE'S FURIOUS WITH ME!
BECAUSE I HAVEN'T IMPROVED AT ALL...
TWOOO! THREEE! ♪ ♪
PULL
ぐぐっ
AHA! I SPY A GAY COUPLE!
URK!
WHAT AM I GOING TO DO ...?
I SPY A MANJU BUN.
PINCH
むにっ
AM NOT!
WHOA! YOUR EYES ARE SUPER-RED!!
OH?
PYAAH!
THAT'S WHAT HAPPENS WHEN YOU'RE UP THREE DAYS STRAIGHT WORKING.
THEY'RE PROLLY EXTRA BLOODSHOT SINCE I JUST HAD THAT LITTLE NAP HERE ON THE BENCH...
OH, SO THAT'S IT...
PHEW!
WAIT. UP FOR THREE DAYS!?
AH!
WE'RE ALREADY FOUR DAYS PAST THE DEADLIIIINE!

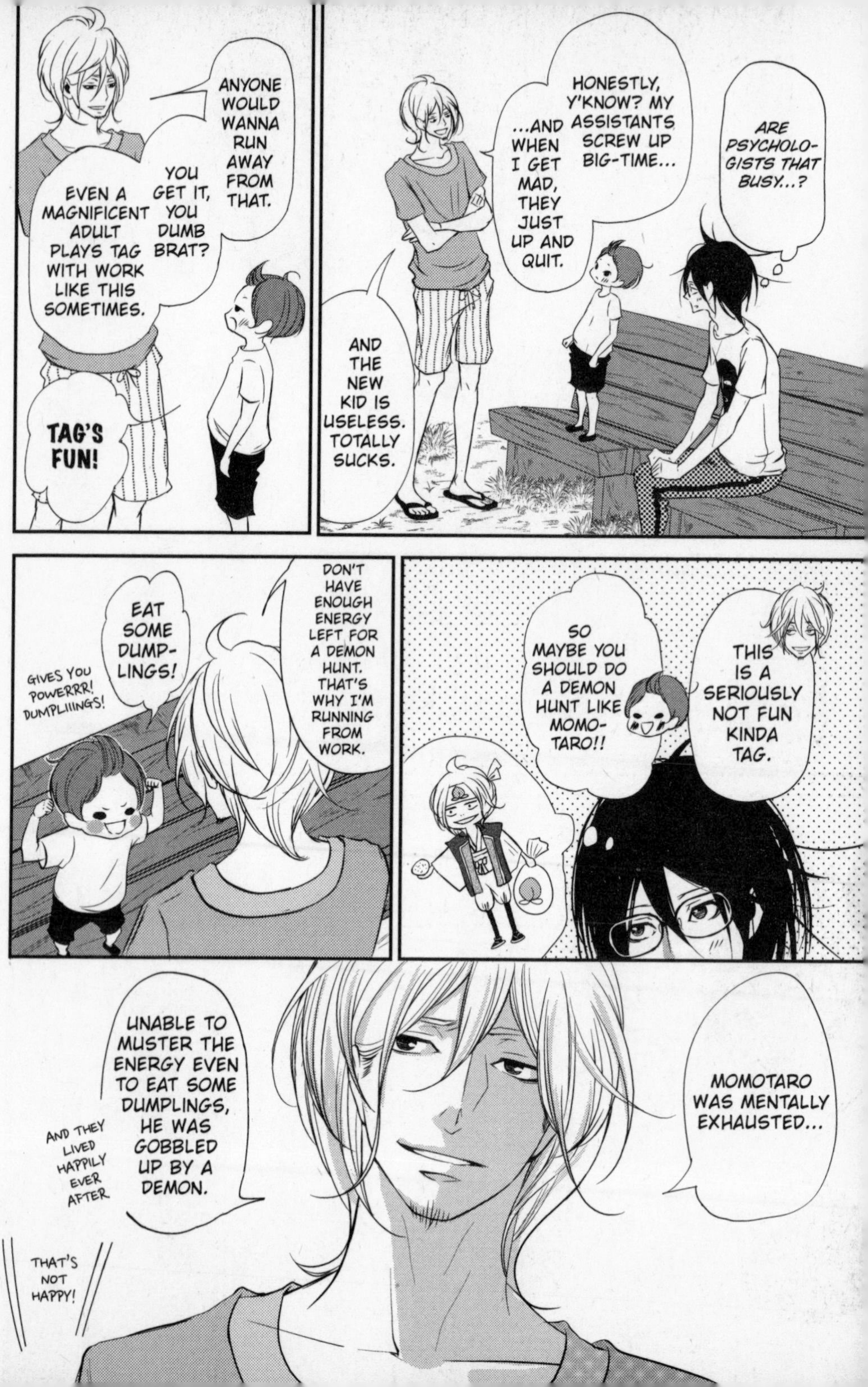
ARE PSYCHOLOGISTS THAT BUSY...?
HONESTLY, Y'KNOW? MY ASSISTANTS SCREW UP BIG-TIME...
...AND WHEN I GET MAD, THEY JUST UP AND QUIT.
AND THE NEW KID IS USELESS. TOTALLY SUCKS.
ANYONE WOULD WANNA RUN AWAY FROM THAT.
YOU GET IT, YOU DUMB BRAT?
EVEN A MAGNIFICENT ADULT PLAYS TAG WITH WORK LIKE THIS SOMETIMES.
TAG'S FUN!
THIS IS A SERIOUSLY NOT FUN KINDA TAG.
SO MAYBE YOU SHOULD DO A DEMON HUNT LIKE MOMOTARO!!
DON'T HAVE ENOUGH ENERGY LEFT FOR A DEMON HUNT. THAT'S WHY I'M RUNNING FROM WORK.
EAT SOME DUMPLINGS!
GIVES YOU POWERRR! DUMPLIIINGS!
MOMOTARO WAS MENTALLY EXHAUSTED...
UNABLE TO MUSTER THE ENERGY EVEN TO EAT SOME DUMPLINGS, HE WAS GOBBLED UP BY A DEMON.
AND THEY LIVED HAPPILY EVER AFTER
THAT'S NOT HAPPY!

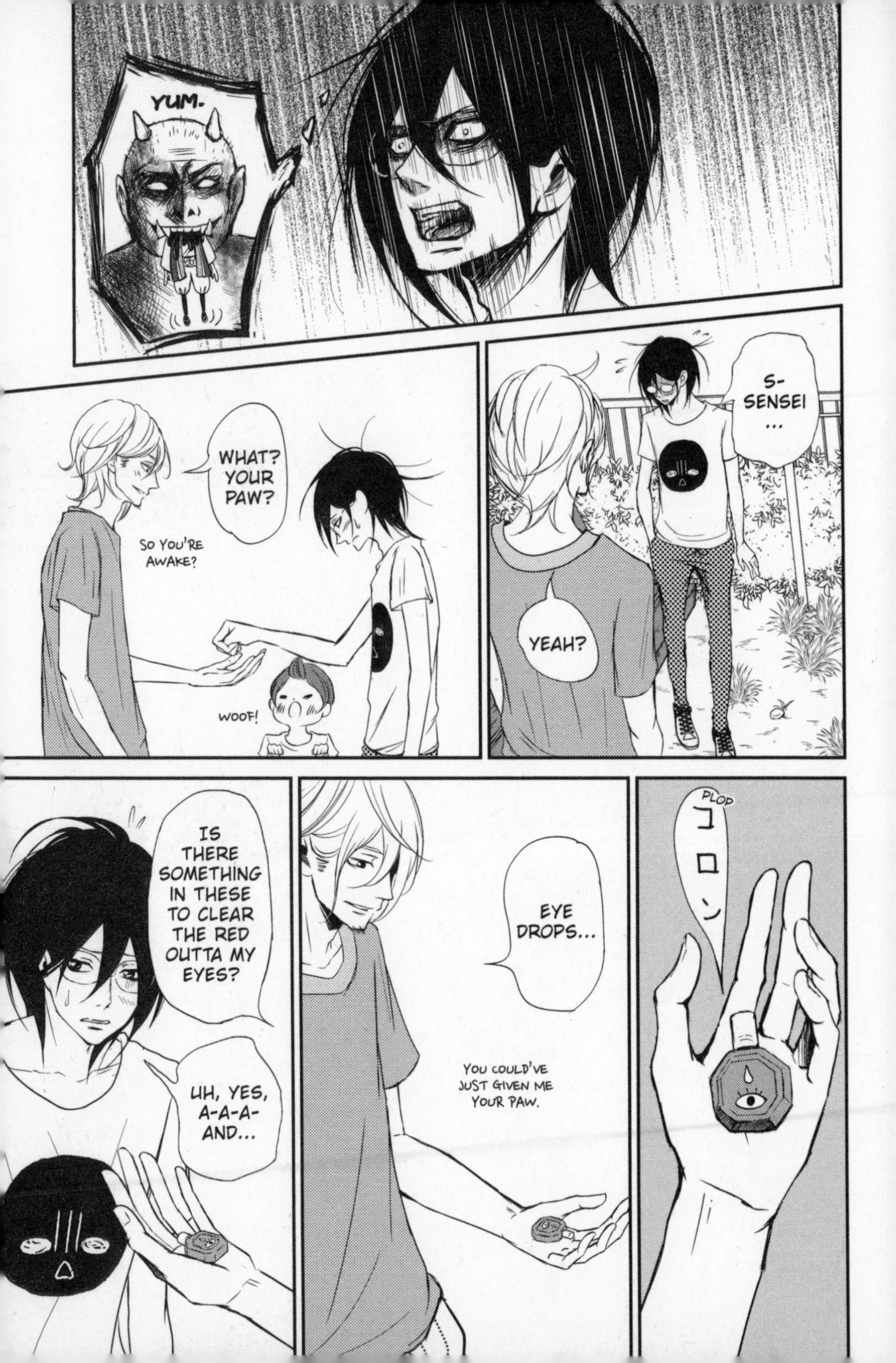
YUM.
S-SENSEI ...
YEAH?
WHAT? YOUR PAW?
SO YOU'RE AWAKE?
WOOF!
PLOP
コロン
EYE DROPS...
YOU COULD'VE JUST GIVEN ME YOUR PAW.
IS THERE SOMETHING IN THESE TO CLEAR THE RED OUTTA MY EYES?
UH, YES, A-A-A-AND...

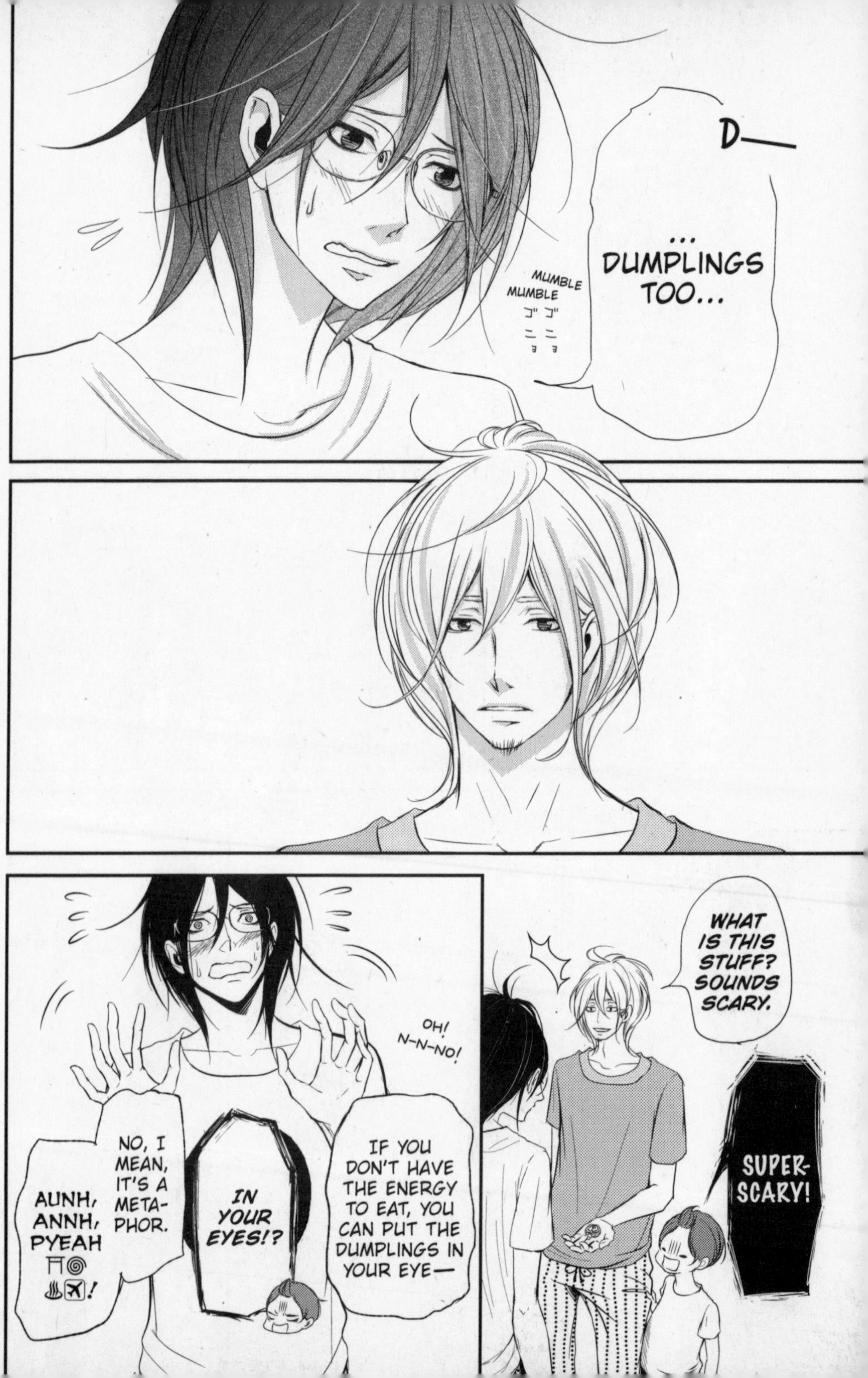
D—
...DUMPLINGS TOO...
MUMBLE MUMBLE
ゴニョゴニョ
WHAT IS THIS STUFF? SOUNDS SCARY.
SUPER-SCARY!
OH! N-N-NO!
IF YOU DON'T HAVE THE ENERGY TO EAT, YOU CAN PUT THE DUMPLINGS IN YOUR EYE—
IN YOUR EYES!?
NO, I MEAN, IT'S A META-PHOR.
AUNH, ANNH, PYEAH

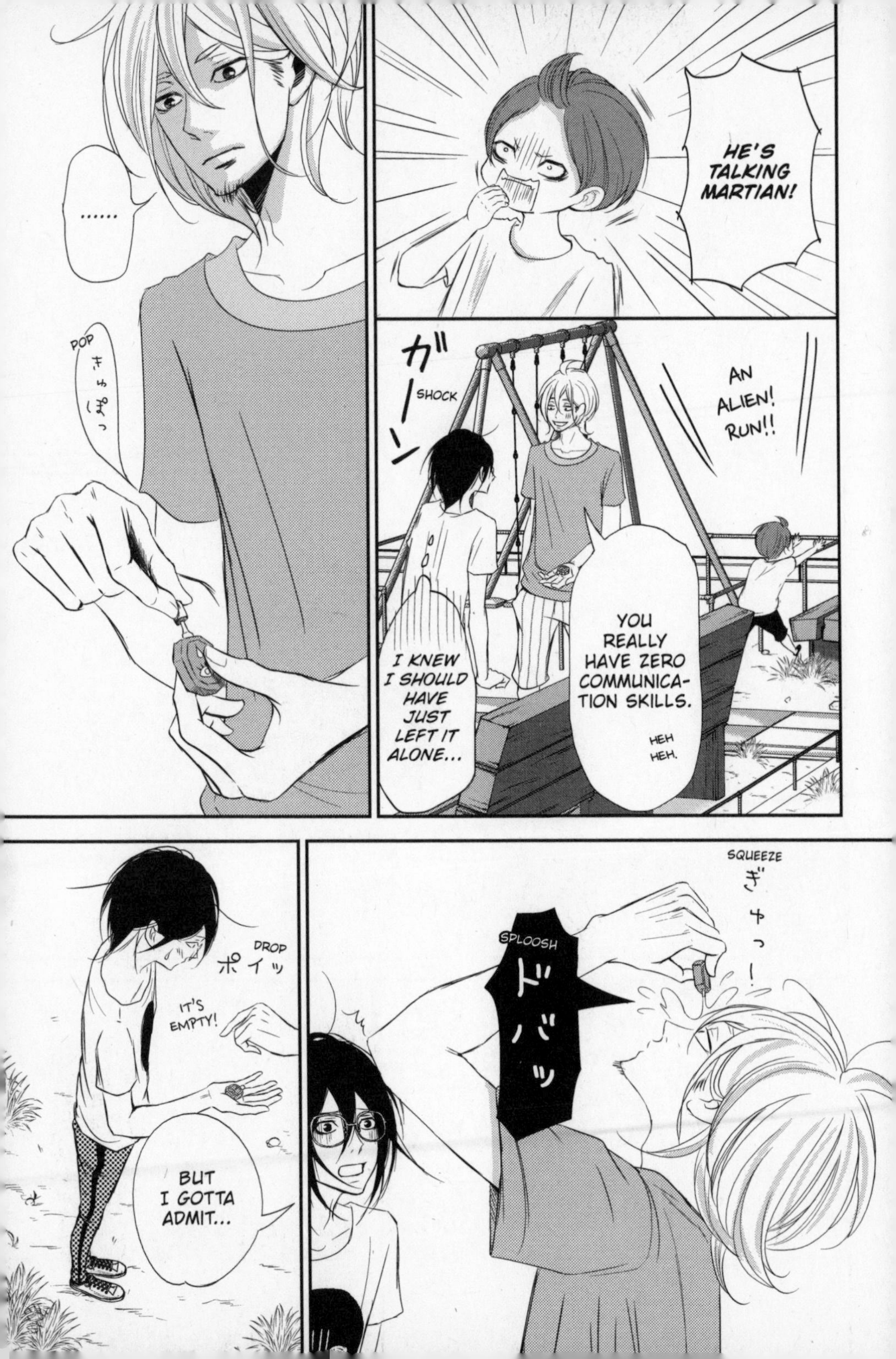
HE'S TALKING MARTIAN!
AN ALIEN! RUN!!
ガーン
SHOCK
YOU REALLY HAVE ZERO COMMUNICATION SKILLS.
HEH HEH.
I KNEW I SHOULD HAVE JUST LEFT IT ALONE...
......
きゅぽっ
POP
ぎゅっ!
SQUEEZE
ドバッ
SPLOOSH
ポイッ
DROP
IT'S EMPTY!
BUT I GOTTA ADMIT...

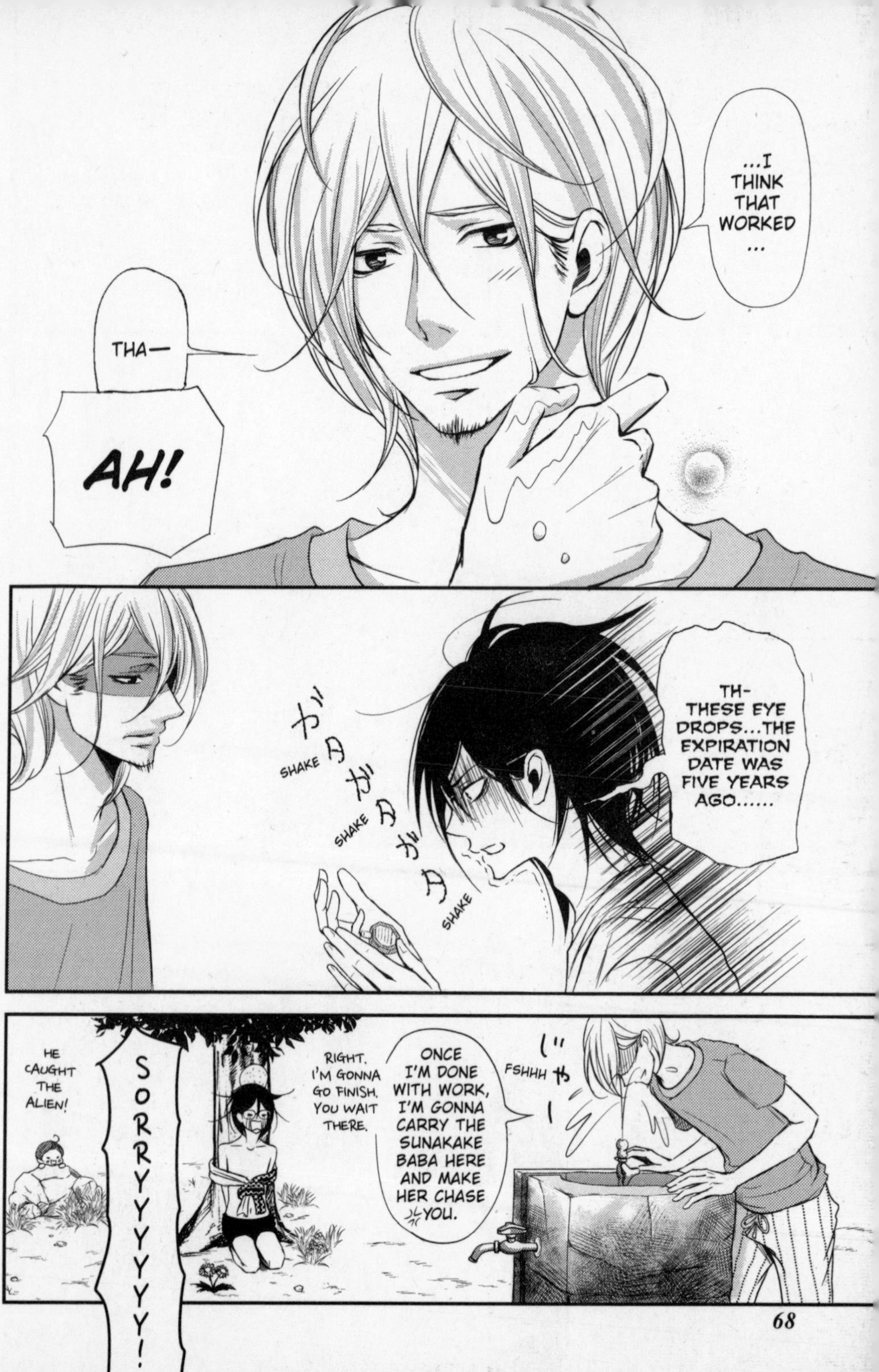

...I THINK THAT WORKED ...
THA—
AH!
TH- THESE EYE DROPS...THE EXPIRATION DATE WAS FIVE YEARS AGO......
SHAKE
SHAKE
SHAKE
FSHHH
ONCE I'M DONE WITH WORK, I'M GONNA CARRY THE SUNAKAKE BABA HERE AND MAKE HER CHASE YOU.
RIGHT. I'M GONNA GO FINISH. YOU WAIT THERE.
SORRYYYYY!
HE CAUGHT THE ALIEN!

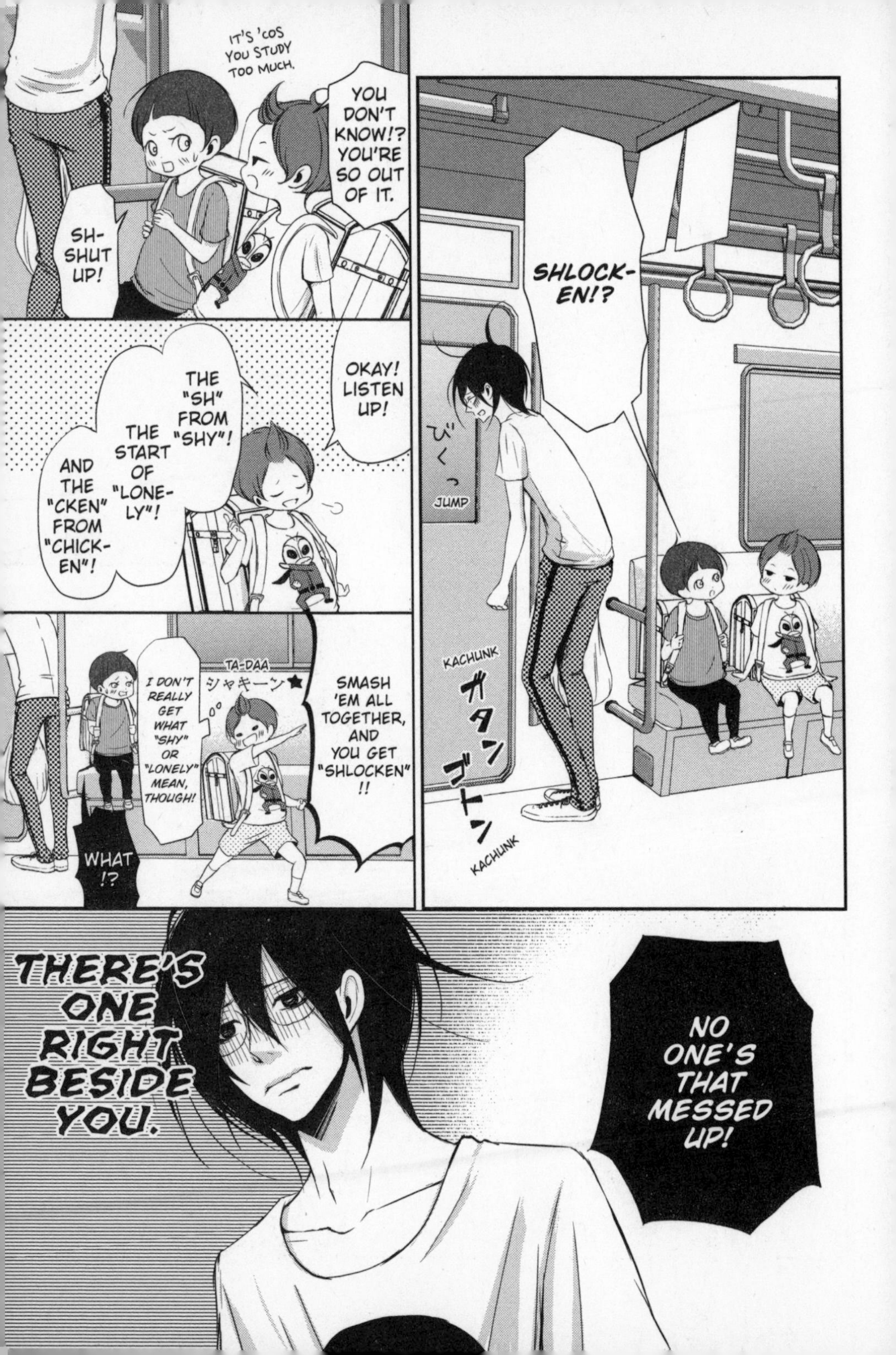
SHLOCK-EN!?
びくっ
JUMP
KACHUNK
ガタン
ゴトン
KACHUNK
YOU DON'T KNOW!? YOU'RE SO OUT OF IT.
IT'S 'COS YOU STUDY TOO MUCH.
SH-SHUT UP!
OKAY! LISTEN UP!
THE "SH" FROM "SHY"!
THE START OF "LONE-LY"!
AND THE "CKEN" FROM "CHICK-EN"!
SMASH 'EM ALL TOGETHER, AND YOU GET "SHLOCKEN" !!
TA-DAA
シャキーン★
I DON'T REALLY GET WHAT "SHY" OR "LONELY" MEAN, THOUGH!
WHAT !?
NO ONE'S THAT MESSED UP!
THERE'S ONE RIGHT BESIDE YOU.

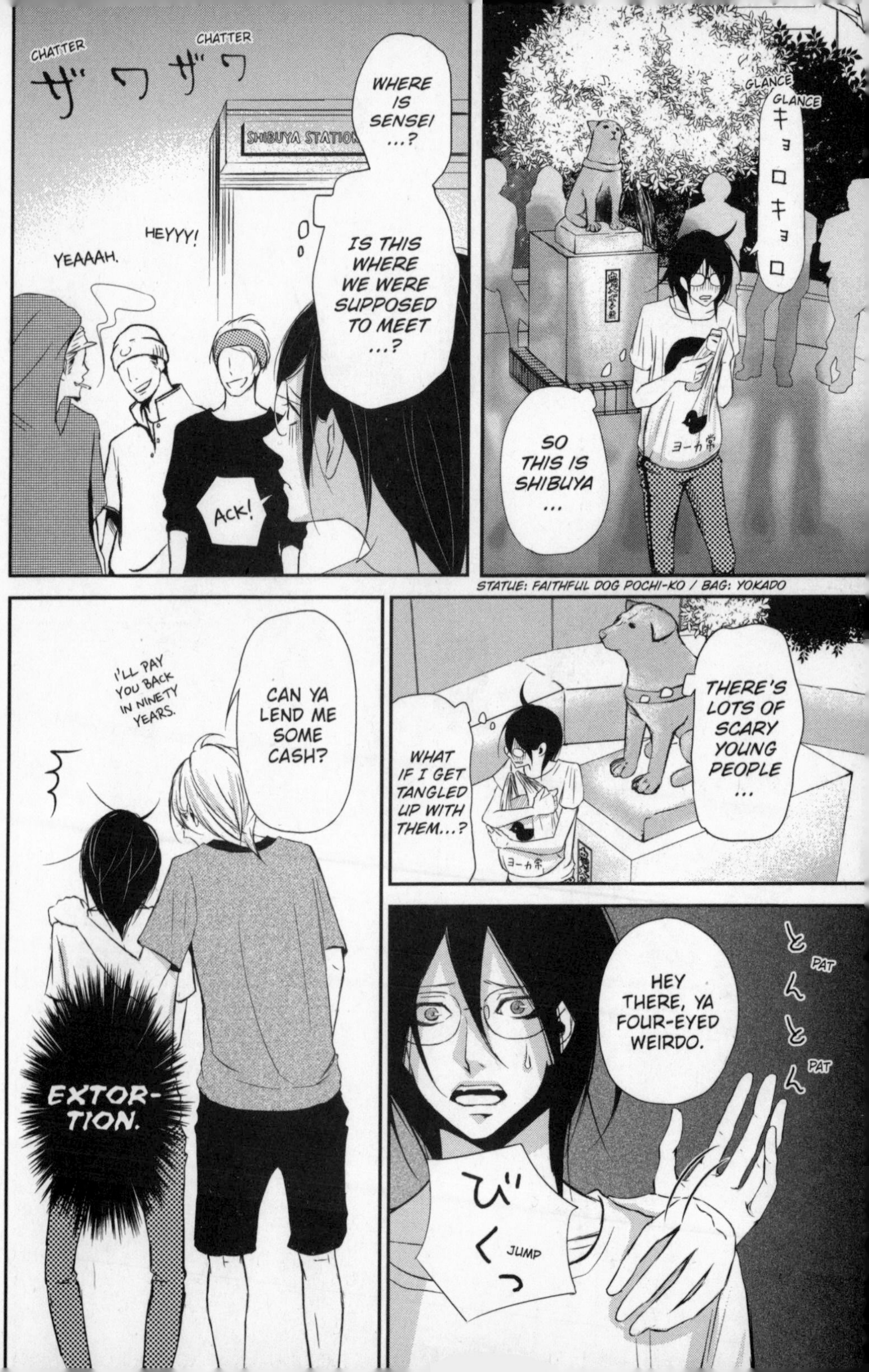
GLANCE GLANCE
キョロキョロ
SO THIS IS SHIBUYA...
STATUE: FAITHFUL DOG POCHI-KO / BAG: YOKADO
CHATTER CHATTER
ザワザワ
SHIBUYA STATION
WHERE IS SENSEI...?
IS THIS WHERE WE WERE SUPPOSED TO MEET...?
HEYYY!
YEAAAH.
ACK!
THERE'S LOTS OF SCARY YOUNG PEOPLE...
WHAT IF I GET TANGLED UP WITH THEM...?
とんとん
PAT PAT
HEY THERE, YA FOUR-EYED WEIRDO.
びくっ
JUMP
CAN YA LEND ME SOME CASH?
I'LL PAY YOU BACK IN NINETY YEARS.
EXTORTION.

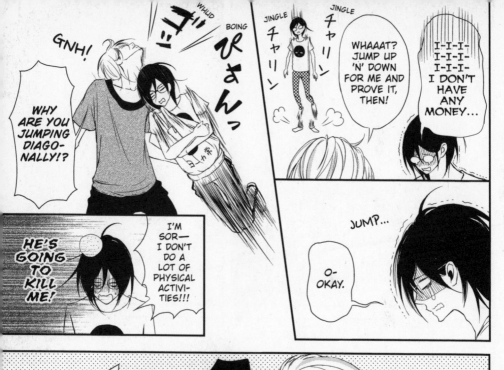

I-I-I-
I-I-I-
I-I-I-
I DON'T HAVE ANY MONEY...
JINGLE
チャリン
JINGLE
チャリン
WHAAAT? JUMP UP 'N' DOWN FOR ME AND PROVE IT, THEN!
WHUD
ゴッ
BOING
ぴょんっ
GNH!
WHY ARE YOU JUMPING DIAGO-NALLY!?
JUMP...
O-OKAY.
I'M SOR— I DON'T DO A LOT OF PHYSICAL ACTIVI-TIES!!!
HE'S GOING TO KILL ME!
AH. NOSE-BLEED.
HUH!?
NOW THAT I LOOK, IT'S SENSEI!!
GOTCHA, HUH, KOMINAMI?
YOU FOOLED ME!
BUT I'M THE VICTIM HERE...
...SOME-HOW.
I-I'M SORRY.

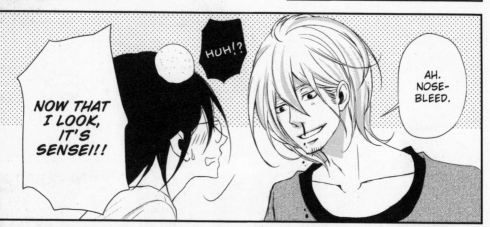

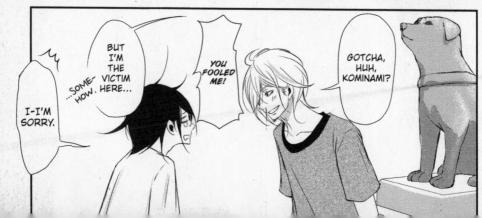

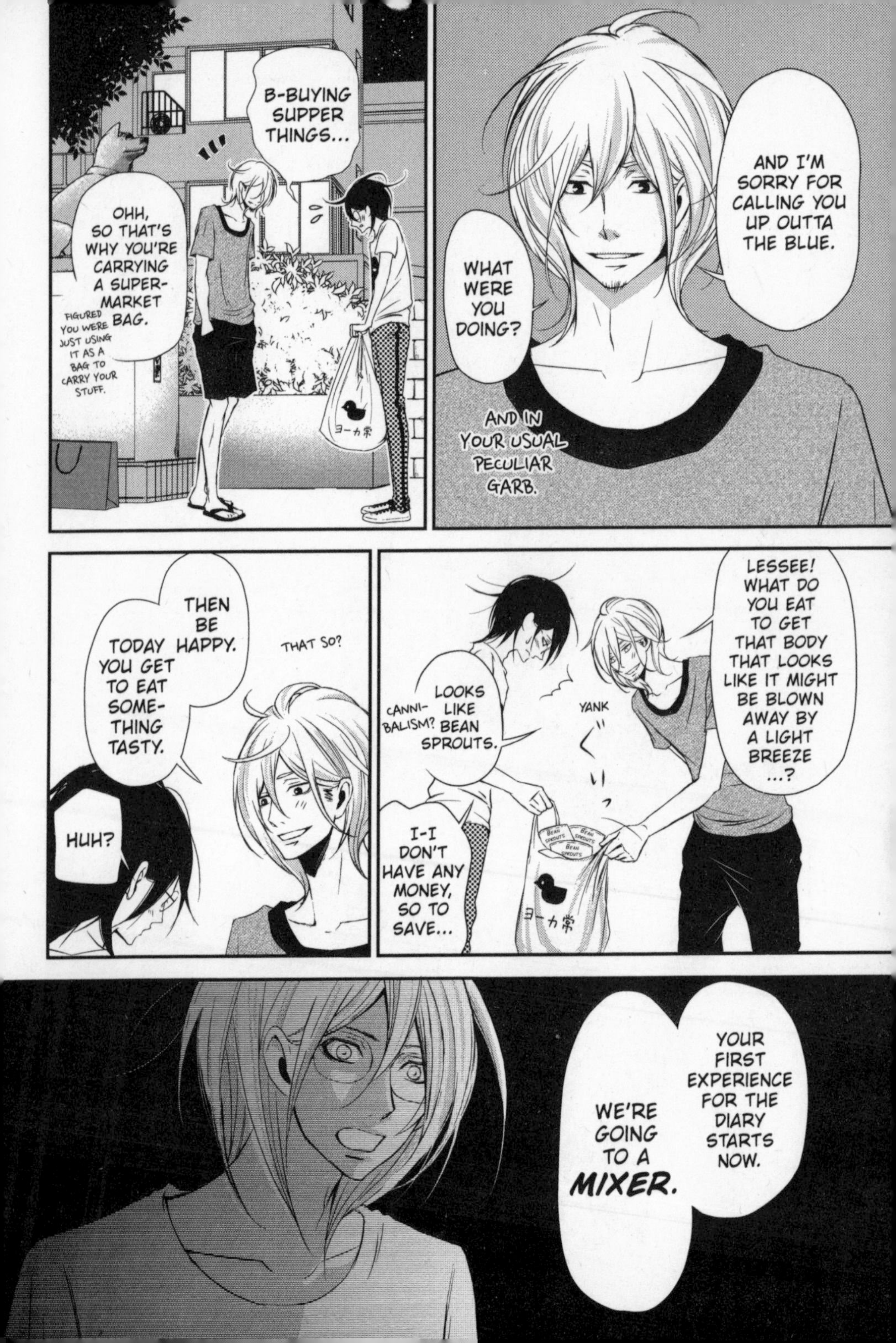
AND I'M SORRY FOR CALLING YOU UP OUTTA THE BLUE.
WHAT WERE YOU DOING?
AND IN YOUR USUAL PECULIAR GARB.
B-BUYING SUPPER THINGS...
OHH, SO THAT'S WHY YOU'RE CARRYING A SUPER-MARKET BAG.
FIGURED YOU WERE JUST USING IT AS A BAG TO CARRY YOUR STUFF.
ヨーカ堂
LESSEE! WHAT DO YOU EAT TO GET THAT BODY THAT LOOKS LIKE IT MIGHT BE BLOWN AWAY BY A LIGHT BREEZE ...?
YANK
LOOKS LIKE BEAN SPROUTS.
CANNI-BALISM?
BEAN SPROUTS
BEAN SPROUTS
BEAN SPROUTS
I-I DON'T HAVE ANY MONEY, SO TO SAVE...
ヨーカ堂
THEN BE HAPPY.
THAT SO?
TODAY YOU GET TO EAT SOME-THING TASTY.
HUH?
YOUR FIRST EXPERIENCE FOR THE DIARY STARTS NOW.
WE'RE GOING TO A *MIXER*.

2 VS. THE MIXER

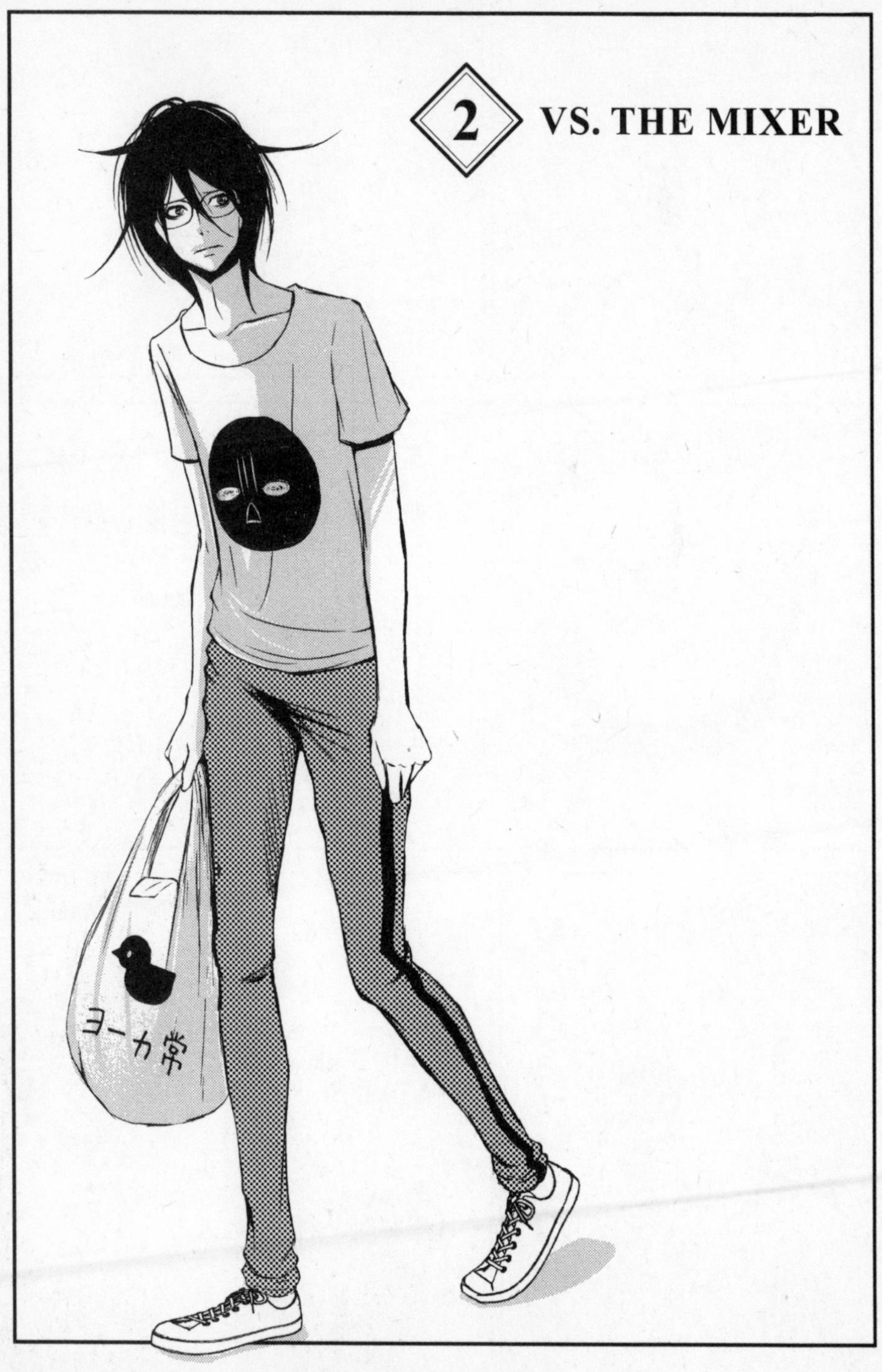
ヨーカ堂

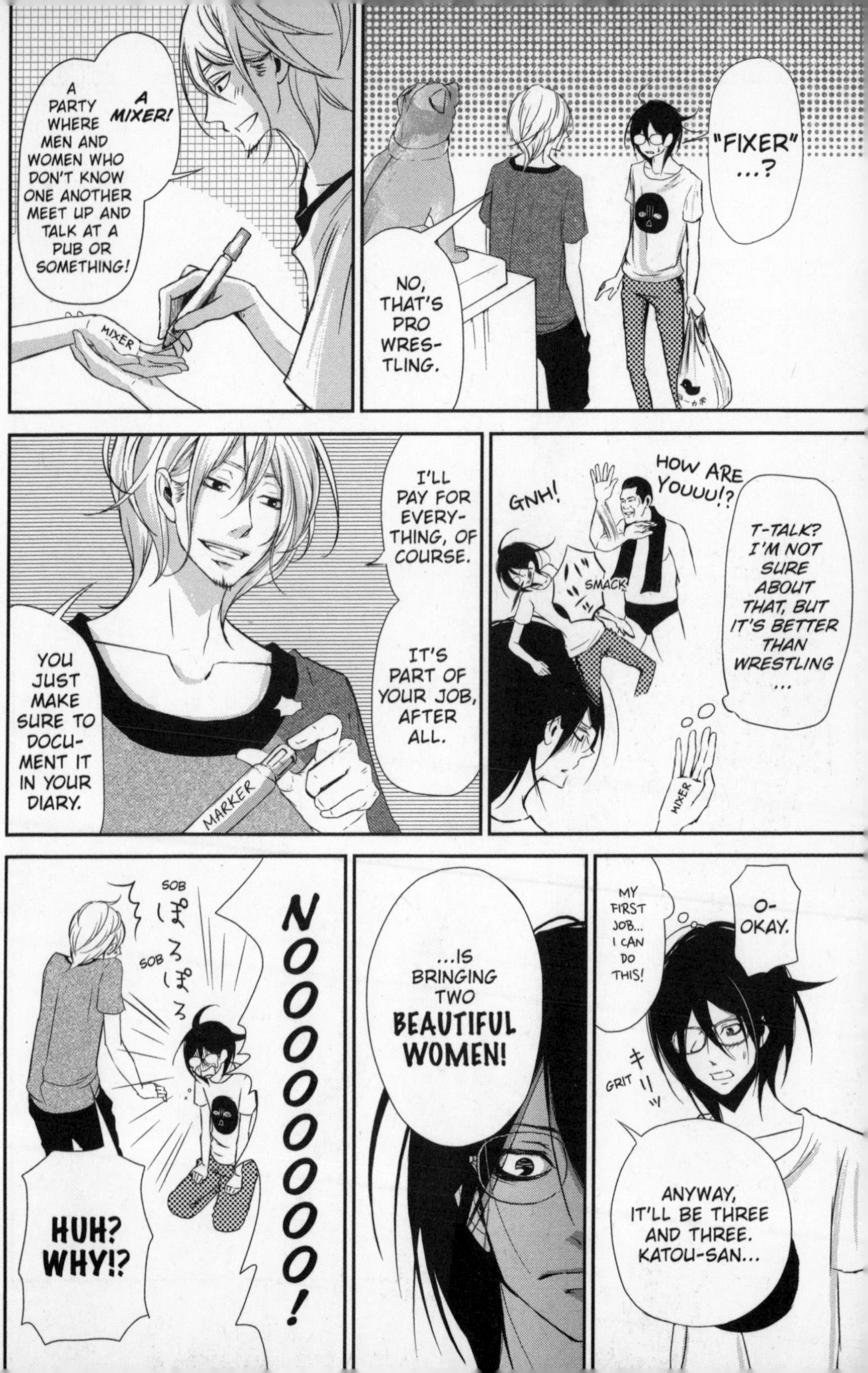
"FIXER" ...?
NO, THAT'S PRO WRES-TLING.
A MIXER!
A PARTY WHERE MEN AND WOMEN WHO DON'T KNOW ONE ANOTHER MEET UP AND TALK AT A PUB OR SOMETHING!
MIXER
HOW ARE YOUUU!?
GNH!
SMACK
T-TALK? I'M NOT SURE ABOUT THAT, BUT IT'S BETTER THAN WRESTLING...
MIXER
I'LL PAY FOR EVERY-THING, OF COURSE.
IT'S PART OF YOUR JOB, AFTER ALL.
YOU JUST MAKE SURE TO DOCU-MENT IT IN YOUR DIARY.
MARKER
O-OKAY.
MY FIRST JOB... I CAN DO THIS!
GRIT
キリッ
ANYWAY, IT'LL BE THREE AND THREE. KATOU-SAN...
...IS BRINGING TWO BEAUTIFUL WOMEN!
NOOOOOOOOOOOO!
SOB
ぽろぽろ
SOB
HUH? WHY!?

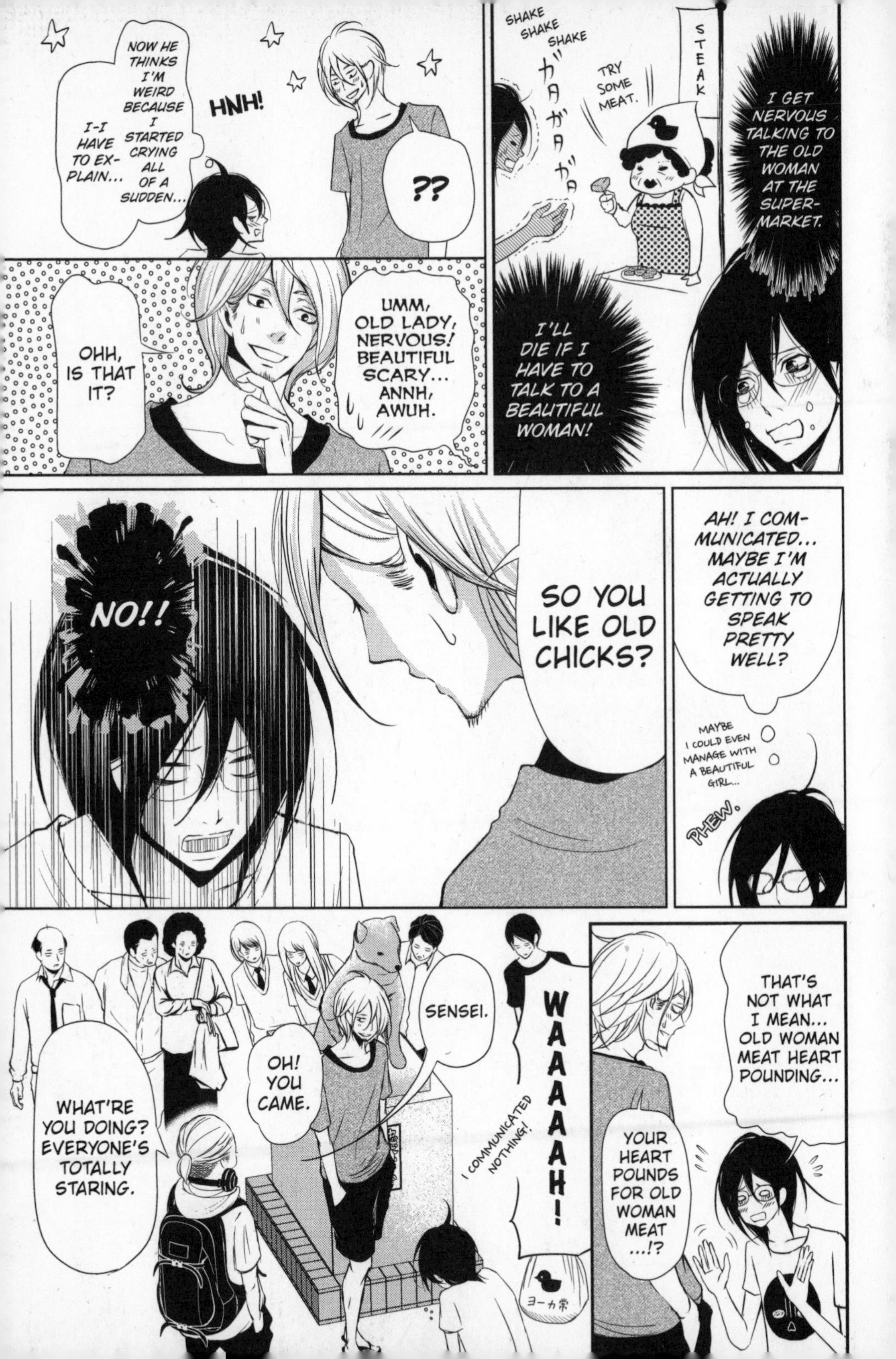
SHAKE SHAKE SHAKE
ガタガタガタ
TRY SOME MEAT.
STEAK
I GET NERVOUS TALKING TO THE OLD WOMAN AT THE SUPER-MARKET.
NOW HE THINKS I'M WEIRD BECAUSE I STARTED CRYING ALL OF A SUDDEN...
I-I HAVE TO EX-PLAIN...
HNH!
??
I'LL DIE IF I HAVE TO TALK TO A BEAUTIFUL WOMAN!
UMM, OLD LADY, NERVOUS! BEAUTIFUL SCARY... ANNH, AWUH.
OHH, IS THAT IT?
AH! I COM-MUNICATED... MAYBE I'M ACTUALLY GETTING TO SPEAK PRETTY WELL?
MAYBE I COULD EVEN MANAGE WITH A BEAUTIFUL GIRL...
PHEW.
SO YOU LIKE OLD CHICKS?
NO!!
THAT'S NOT WHAT I MEAN... OLD WOMAN MEAT HEART POUNDING...
YOUR HEART POUNDS FOR OLD WOMAN MEAT ...!?
WAAAAAAH!
I COMMUNICATED NOTHING!
ヨーカ堂
SENSEI.
OH! YOU CAME.
WHAT'RE YOU DOING? EVERYONE'S TOTALLY STARING.

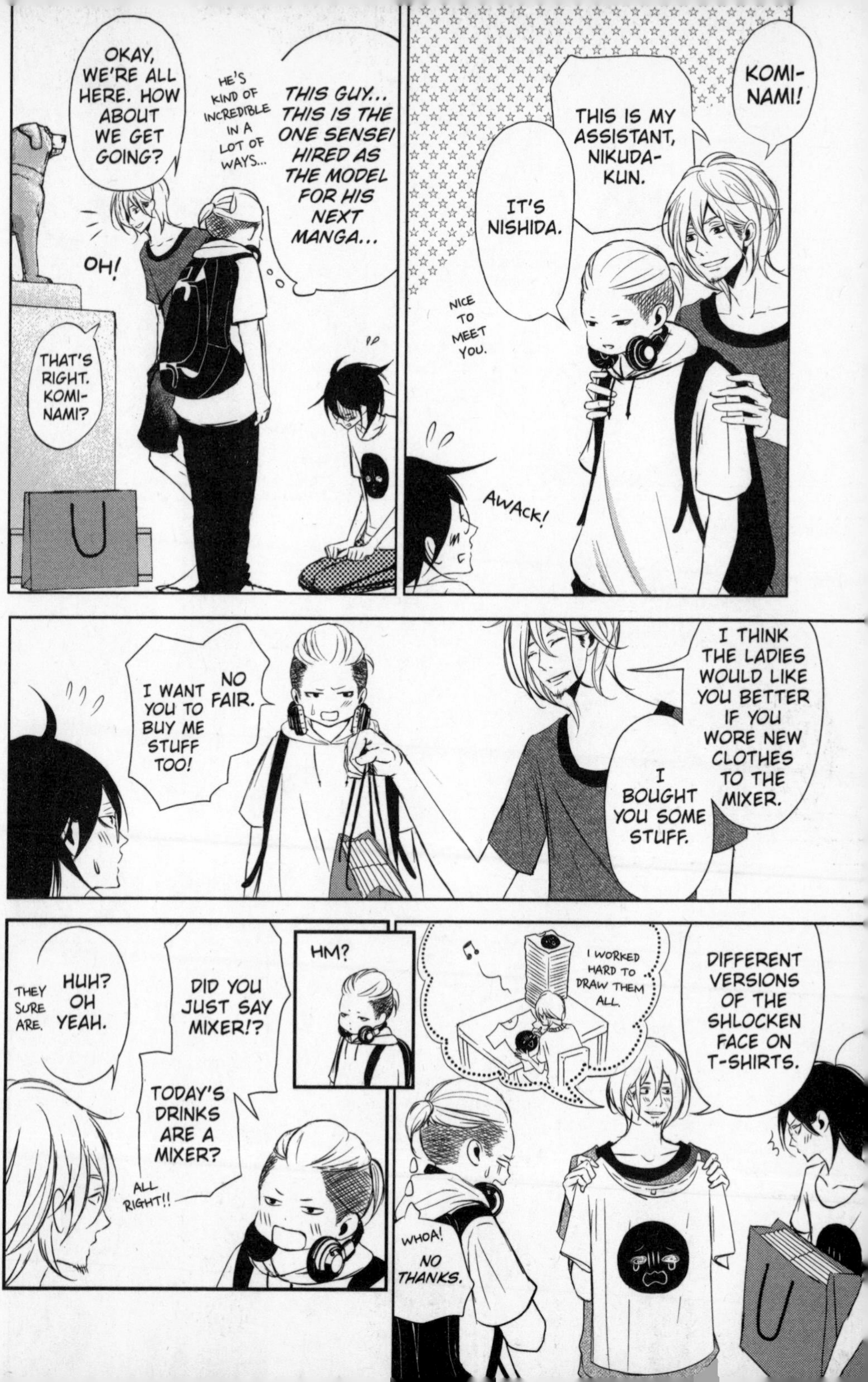
KOMI-NAMI!
THIS IS MY ASSISTANT, NIKUDA-KUN.
IT'S NISHIDA.
NICE TO MEET YOU.
AWACK!
THIS GUY... THIS IS THE ONE SENSEI HIRED AS THE MODEL FOR HIS NEXT MANGA...
HE'S KIND OF INCREDIBLE IN A LOT OF WAYS...
OKAY, WE'RE ALL HERE. HOW ABOUT WE GET GOING?
OH!
THAT'S RIGHT. KOMI-NAMI?
I THINK THE LADIES WOULD LIKE YOU BETTER IF YOU WORE NEW CLOTHES TO THE MIXER.
I BOUGHT YOU SOME STUFF.
NO FAIR.
I WANT YOU TO BUY ME STUFF TOO!
DIFFERENT VERSIONS OF THE SHLOCKEN FACE ON T-SHIRTS.
I WORKED HARD TO DRAW THEM ALL.
WHOA!
NO THANKS.
HM?
DID YOU JUST SAY MIXER!?
HUH? OH YEAH.
THEY SURE ARE.
TODAY'S DRINKS ARE A MIXER?
ALL RIGHT!!

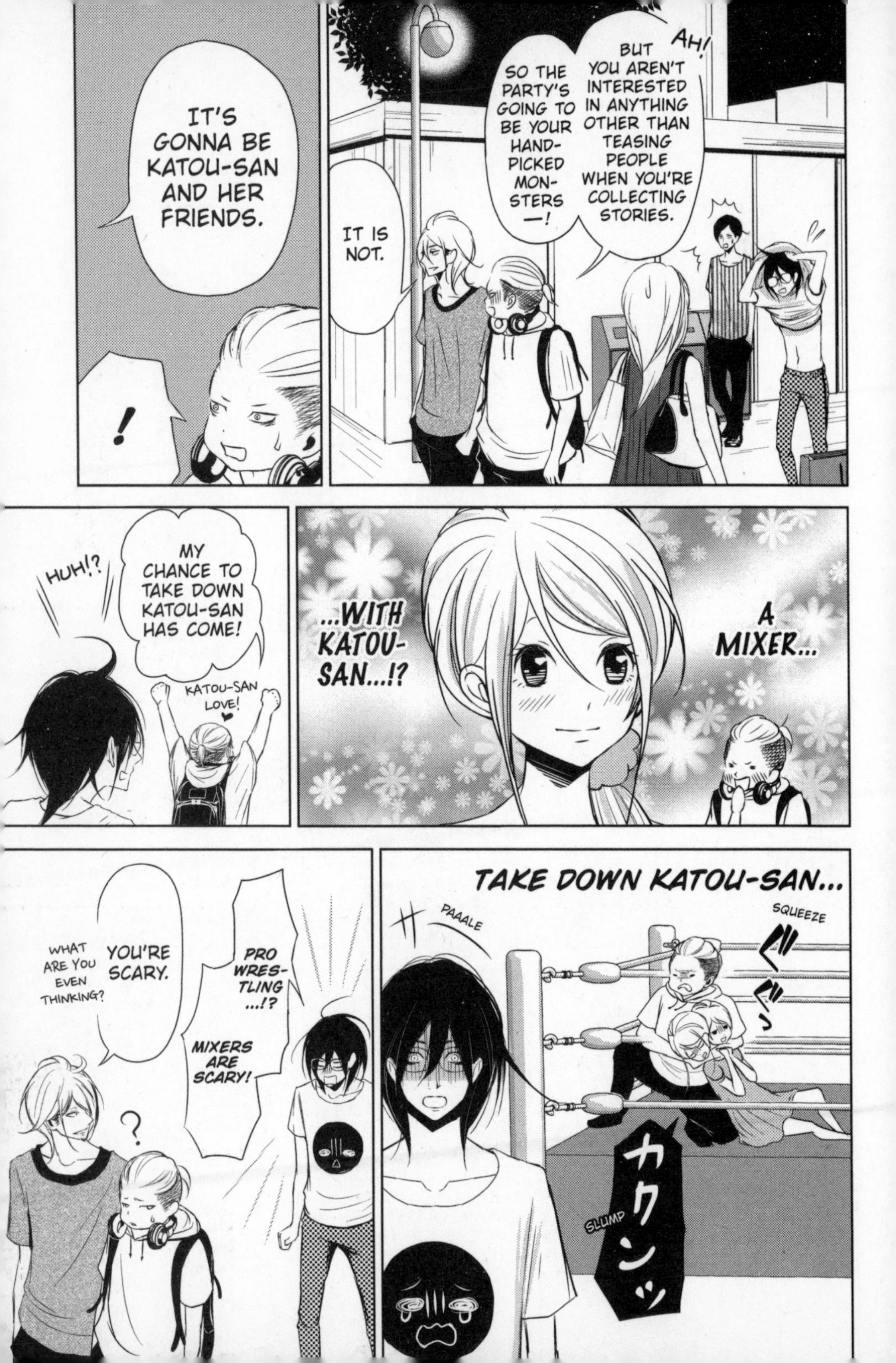
AH!
BUT YOU AREN'T INTERESTED IN ANYTHING OTHER THAN TEASING PEOPLE WHEN YOU'RE COLLECTING STORIES.
SO THE PARTY'S GOING TO BE YOUR HAND-PICKED MON-STERS—!
IT IS NOT.
IT'S GONNA BE KATOU-SAN AND HER FRIENDS.
!
A MIXER...
...WITH KATOU-SAN...!?
MY CHANCE TO TAKE DOWN KATOU-SAN HAS COME!
HUH!?
KATOU-SAN LOVE!
TAKE DOWN KATOU-SAN...
ぐぐっ
SQUEEZE
PAAALE
カクンッ
SLUMP
PRO WRES-TLING ...!?
MIXERS ARE SCARY!
YOU'RE SCARY.
WHAT ARE YOU EVEN THINKING?
?

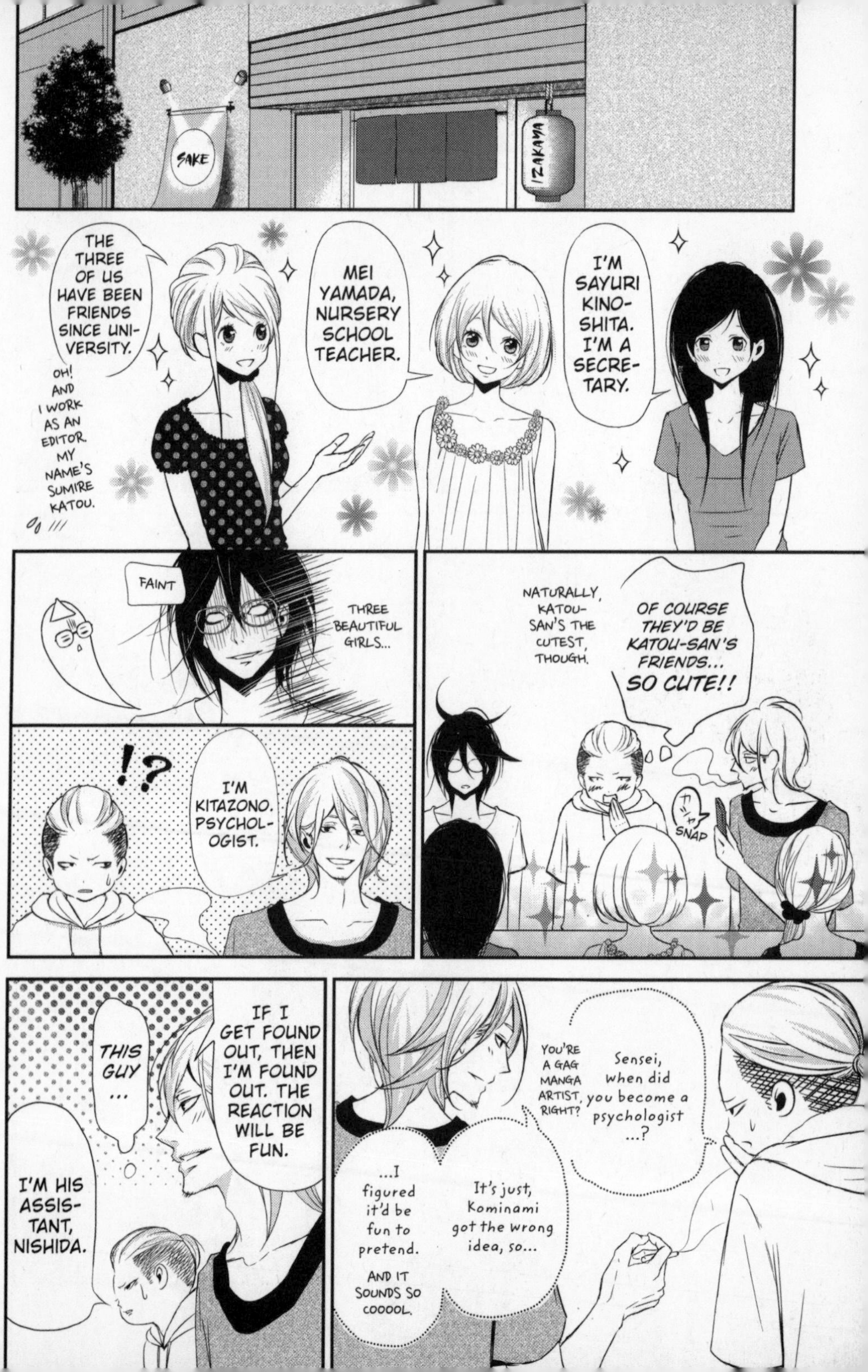
SAKE
IZAKAYA
I'M SAYURI KINO-SHITA. I'M A SECRE-TARY.
MEI YAMADA, NURSERY SCHOOL TEACHER.
THE THREE OF US HAVE BEEN FRIENDS SINCE UNI-VERSITY.
OH! AND I WORK AS AN EDITOR. MY NAME'S SUMIRE KATOU.
OF COURSE THEY'D BE KATOU-SAN'S FRIENDS... SO CUTE!!
NATURALLY, KATOU-SAN'S THE CUTEST, THOUGH.
SNAP
THREE BEAUTIFUL GIRLS...
FAINT
I'M KITAZONO. PSYCHOL-OGIST.
!?
Sensei, when did you become a psychologist ...?
YOU'RE A GAG MANGA ARTIST, RIGHT?
It's just, Kominami got the wrong idea, so...
...I figured it'd be fun to pretend.
AND IT SOUNDS SO COOOOL.
IF I GET FOUND OUT, THEN I'M FOUND OUT. THE REACTION WILL BE FUN.
THIS GUY ...
I'M HIS ASSIS-TANT, NISHIDA.

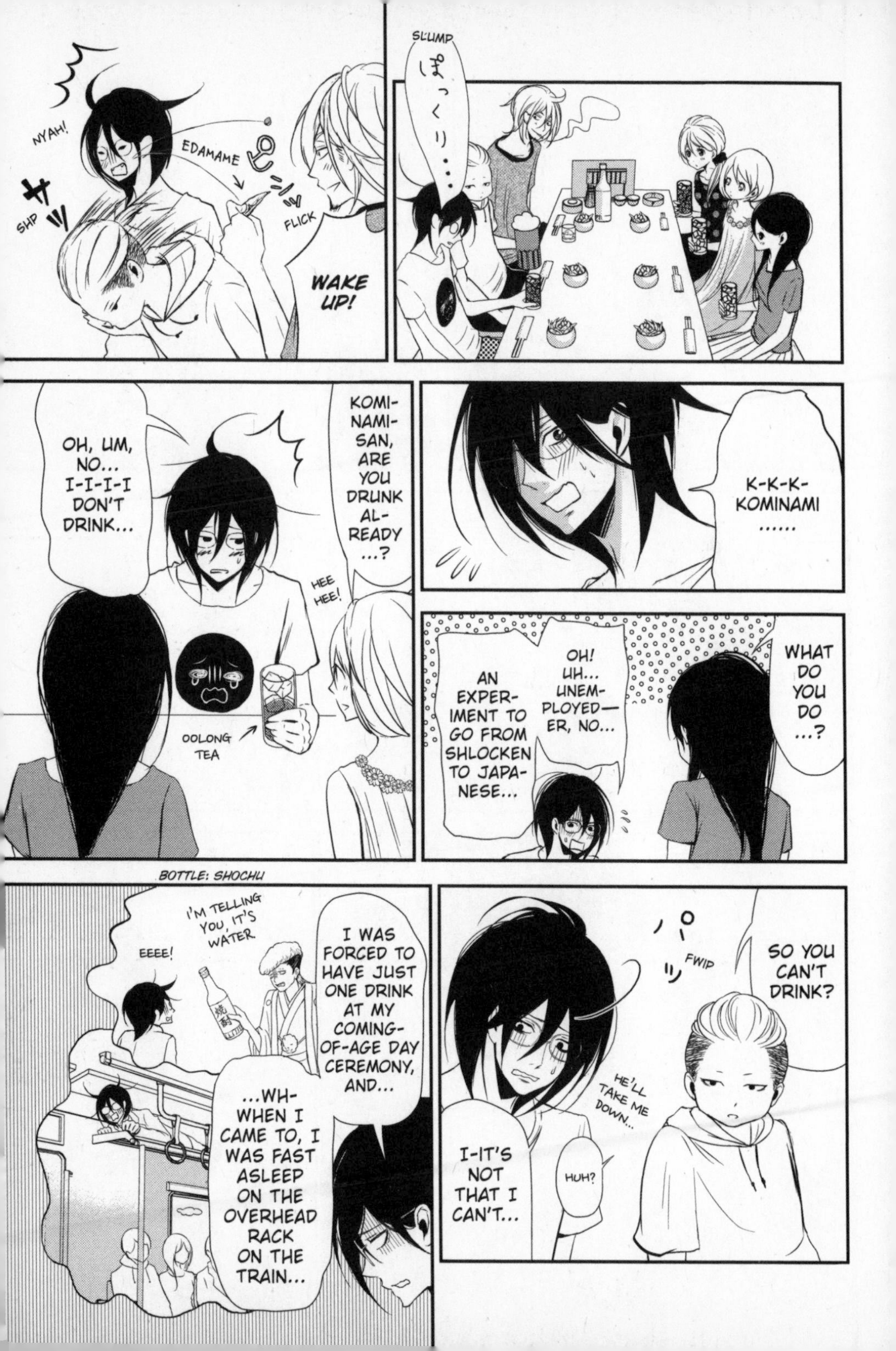
SLUMP
ぽっくり…
NYAH!
EDAMAME
ピ
FLICK
SHP
ヤ
WAKE UP!
K-K-K-KOMINAMI ......
WHAT DO YOU DO...?
OH! UH... UNEMPLOYED—ER, NO...
AN EXPERIMENT TO GO FROM SHLOCKEN TO JAPANESE...
KOMINAMI-SAN, ARE YOU DRUNK ALREADY...?
HEE HEE!
OH, UM, NO... I-I-I-I DON'T DRINK...
OOLONG TEA
BOTTLE: SHOCHU
SO YOU CAN'T DRINK?
パ
FWIP
ッ
HE'LL TAKE ME DOWN...
HUH?
I-IT'S NOT THAT I CAN'T...
I WAS FORCED TO HAVE JUST ONE DRINK AT MY COMING-OF-AGE DAY CEREMONY, AND...
I'M TELLING YOU, IT'S WATER
EEEE!
焼酎
...WH-WHEN I CAME TO, I WAS FAST ASLEEP ON THE OVERHEAD RACK ON THE TRAIN...

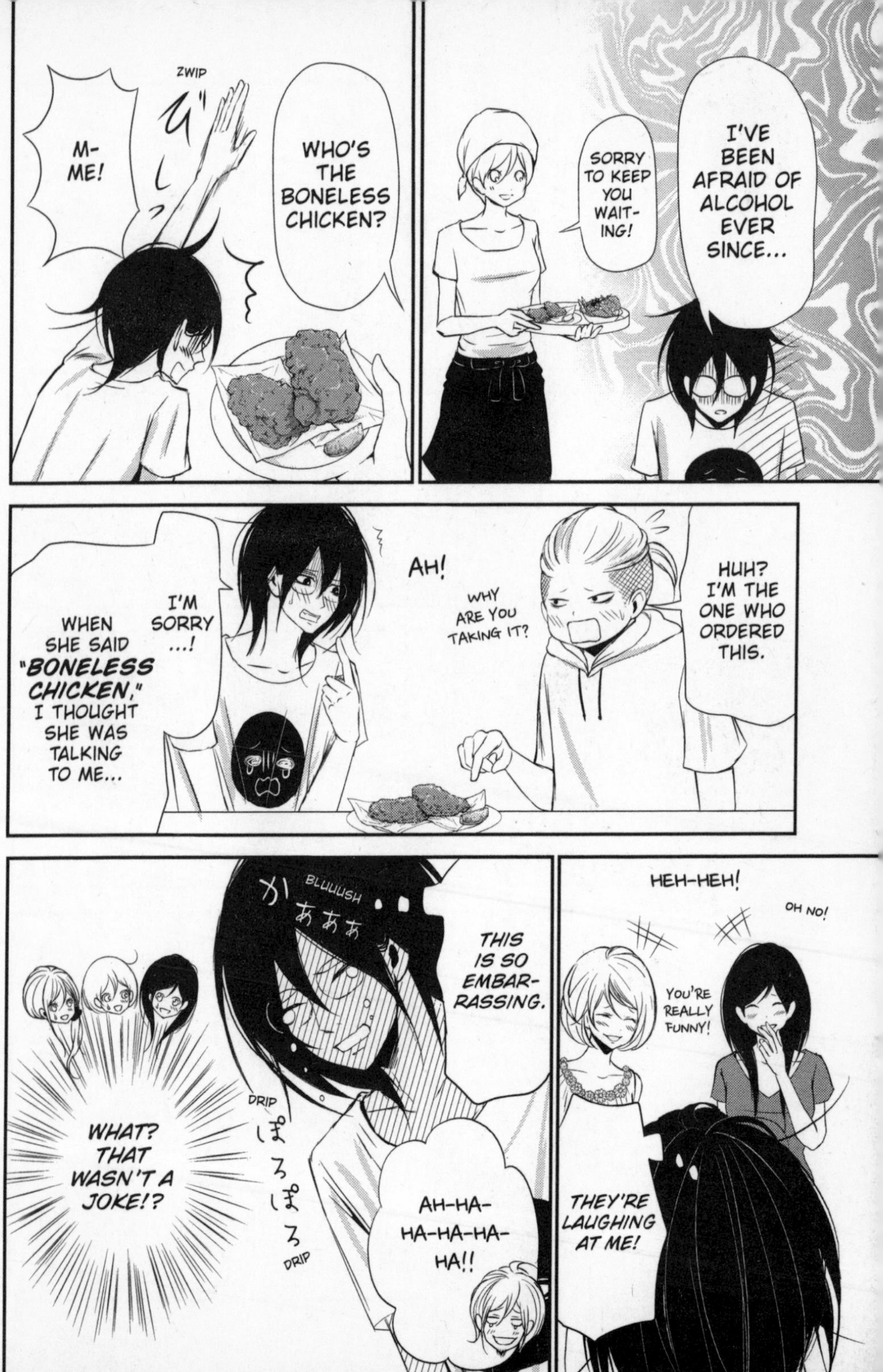
I'VE BEEN AFRAID OF ALCOHOL EVER SINCE...
SORRY TO KEEP YOU WAIT-ING!
WHO'S THE BONELESS CHICKEN?
ZWIP
びしっ
M-ME!
HUH? I'M THE ONE WHO ORDERED THIS.
WHY ARE YOU TAKING IT?
AH!
I'M SORRY ...!
WHEN SHE SAID "BONELESS CHICKEN," I THOUGHT SHE WAS TALKING TO ME...
HEH-HEH!
OH NO!
YOU'RE REALLY FUNNY!
THEY'RE LAUGHING AT ME!
THIS IS SO EMBAR-RASSING.
BLUUUSH
かあああ
AH-HA-HA-HA-HA-HA!!
DRIP
ぽろぽろ
DRIP
WHAT? THAT WASN'T A JOKE!?

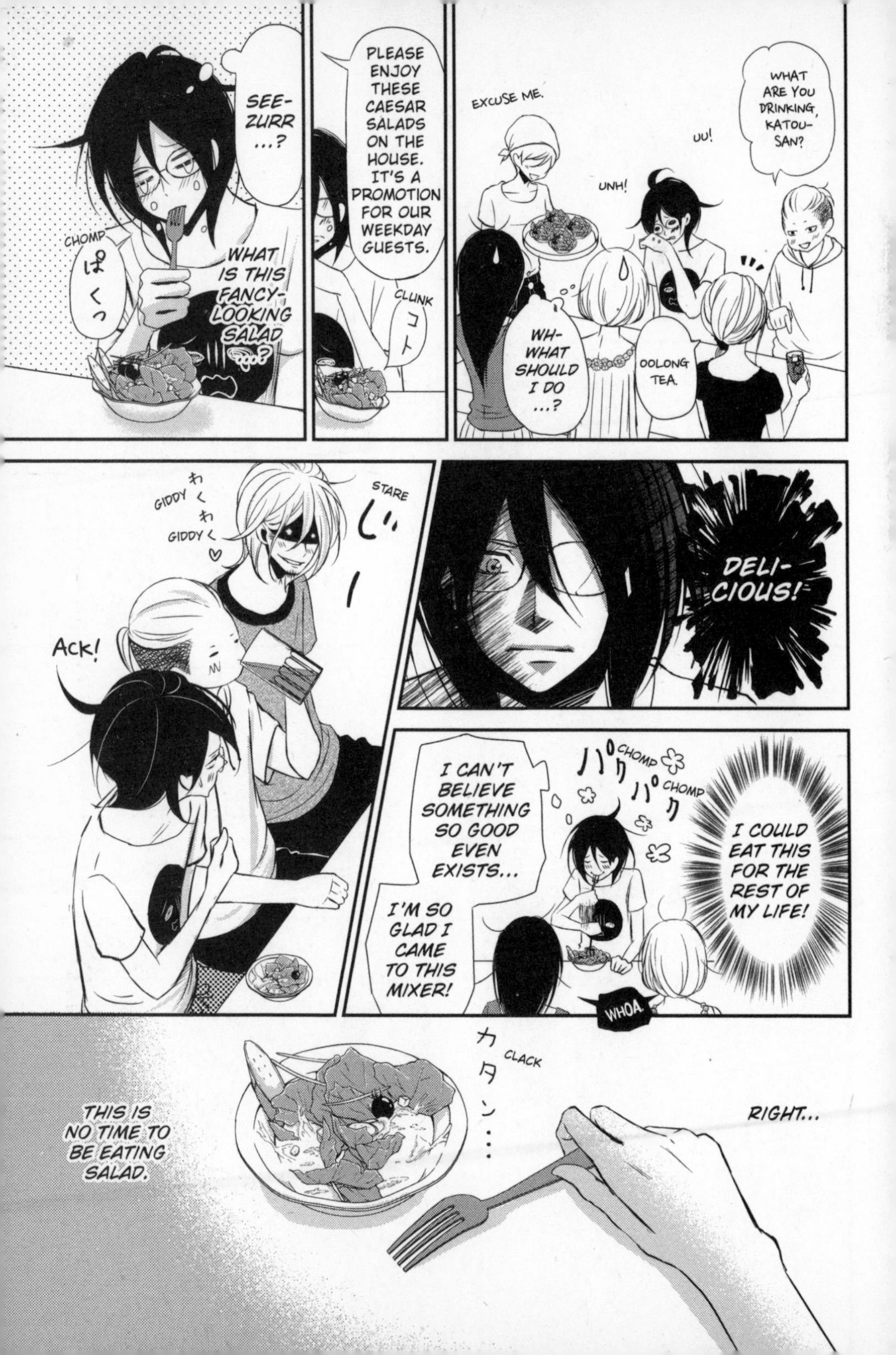
WHAT ARE YOU DRINKING, KATOU-SAN?
UU!
EXCUSE ME.
UNH!
OOLONG TEA.
WH-WHAT SHOULD I DO ...?
PLEASE ENJOY THESE CAESAR SALADS ON THE HOUSE. IT'S A PROMOTION FOR OUR WEEKDAY GUESTS.
CLUNK
コト
SEE-ZURR ...?
WHAT IS THIS FANCY-LOOKING SALAD?
CHOMP
ぱくっ
DELICIOUS!
I COULD EAT THIS FOR THE REST OF MY LIFE!
CHOMP
パク
CHOMP
パク
I CAN'T BELIEVE SOMETHING SO GOOD EVEN EXISTS...
I'M SO GLAD I CAME TO THIS MIXER!
WHOA.
STARE
じー
GIDDY
わくわく
GIDDY
ACK!
RIGHT...
CLACK
カタン…
THIS IS NO TIME TO BE EATING SALAD.

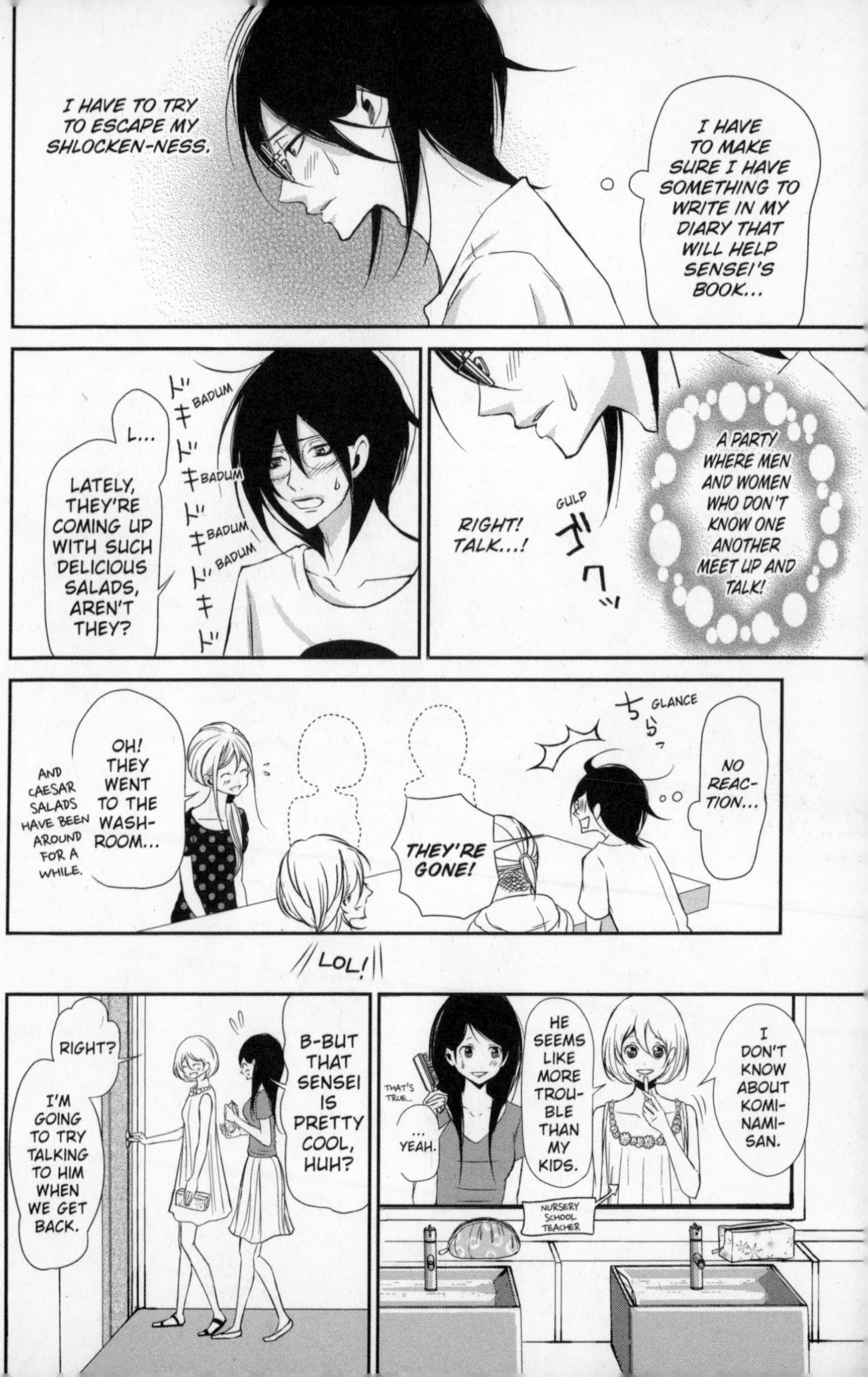
I HAVE TO MAKE SURE I HAVE SOMETHING TO WRITE IN MY DIARY THAT WILL HELP SENSEI'S BOOK...
I HAVE TO TRY TO ESCAPE MY SHLOCKEN-NESS.
A PARTY WHERE MEN AND WOMEN WHO DON'T KNOW ONE ANOTHER MEET UP AND TALK!
ゴクッ GULP
RIGHT! TALK...!
ドキドキドキドキ BADUM BADUM BADUM BADUM
L... LATELY, THEY'RE COMING UP WITH SUCH DELICIOUS SALADS, AREN'T THEY?
NO REACTION...
ちらっ GLANCE
THEY'RE GONE!
OH! THEY WENT TO THE WASHROOM...
AND CAESAR SALADS HAVE BEEN AROUND FOR A WHILE.
LOL!
I DON'T KNOW ABOUT KOMINAMI-SAN.
NURSERY SCHOOL TEACHER
HE SEEMS LIKE MORE TROUBLE THAN MY KIDS.
THAT'S TRUE...
...YEAH.
B-BUT THAT SENSEI IS PRETTY COOL, HUH?
RIGHT?
I'M GOING TO TRY TALKING TO HIM WHEN WE GET BACK.

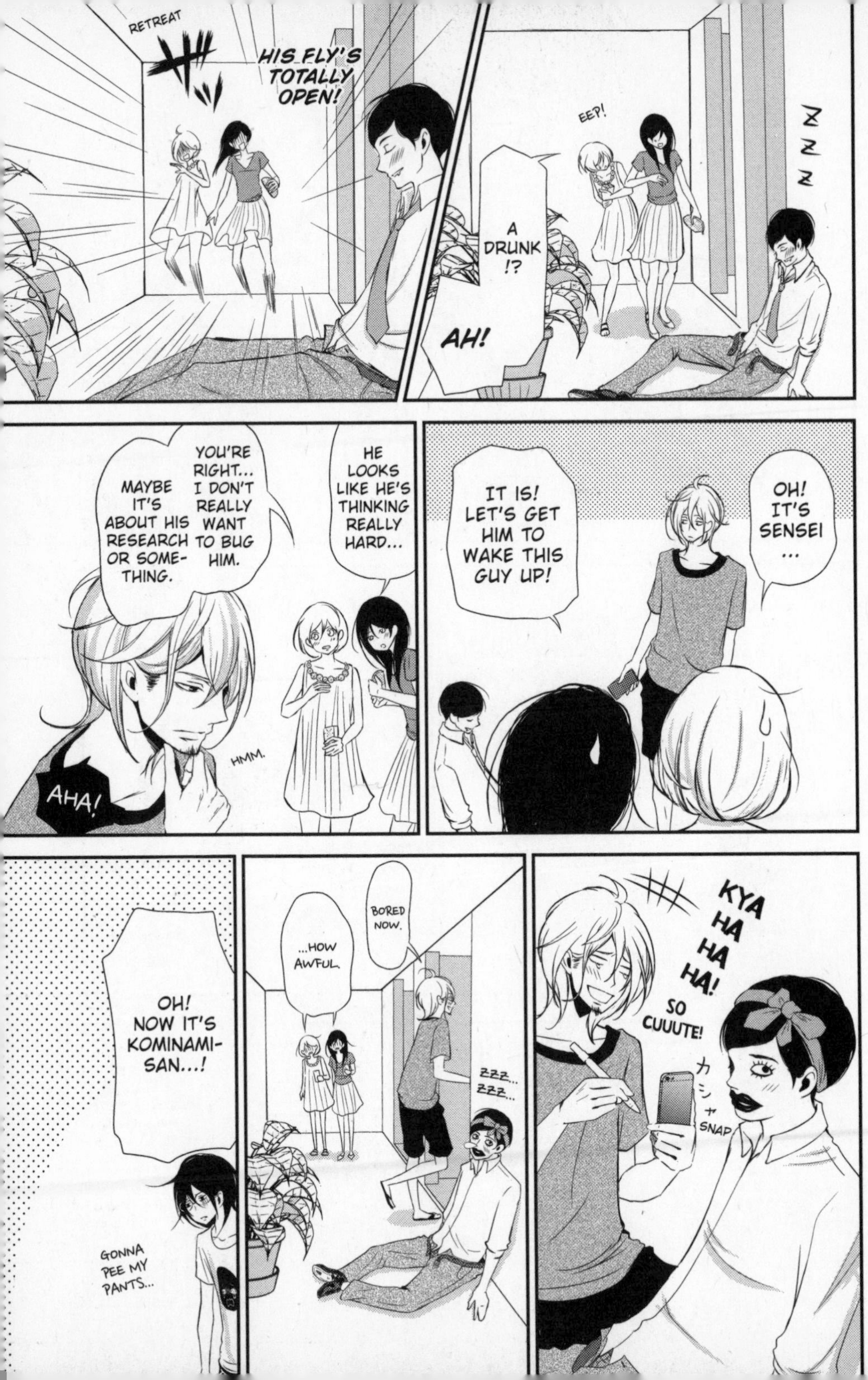
Z Z Z
EEP!
A DRUNK !?
AH!
HIS FLY'S TOTALLY OPEN!
RETREAT
OH! IT'S SENSEI...
IT IS! LET'S GET HIM TO WAKE THIS GUY UP!
HE LOOKS LIKE HE'S THINKING REALLY HARD...
YOU'RE RIGHT... I DON'T REALLY WANT TO BUG HIM.
MAYBE IT'S ABOUT HIS RESEARCH OR SOME-THING.
HMM.
AHA!
KYA HA HA HA!
SO CUUUTE!
カシャ
SNAP
BORED NOW.
...HOW AWFUL.
zzz...
zzz...
OH! NOW IT'S KOMINAMI-SAN...!
GONNA PEE MY PANTS...

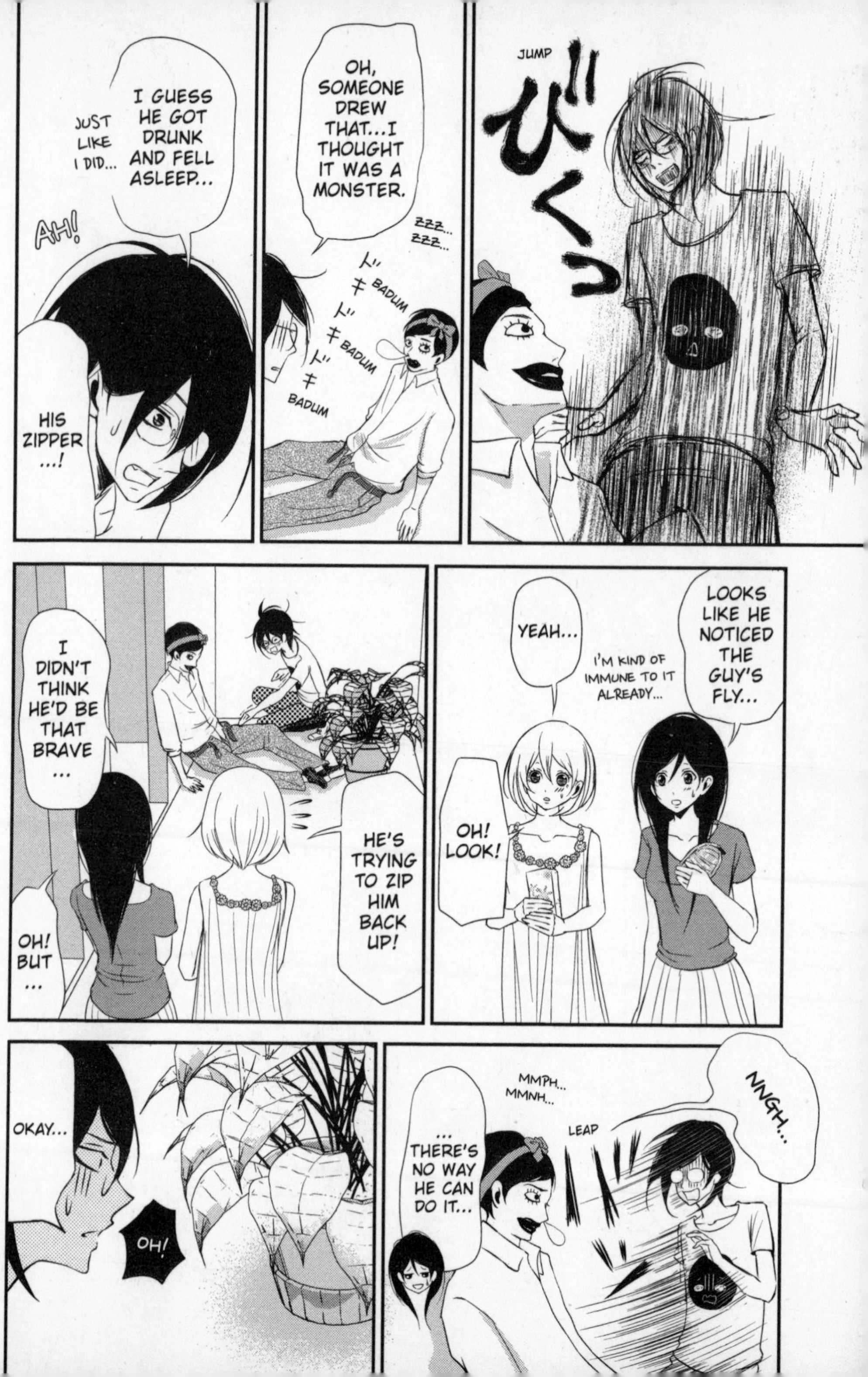
JUMP
びくっ
OH, SOMEONE DREW THAT...I THOUGHT IT WAS A MONSTER.
ZZZ... ZZZ...
ドキ BADUM
ドキ BADUM
ドキ BADUM
I GUESS HE GOT DRUNK AND FELL ASLEEP...
JUST LIKE I DID...
AH!
HIS ZIPPER...!
LOOKS LIKE HE NOTICED THE GUY'S FLY...
YEAH...
I'M KIND OF IMMUNE TO IT ALREADY...
OH! LOOK!
HE'S TRYING TO ZIP HIM BACK UP!
I DIDN'T THINK HE'D BE THAT BRAVE...
OH! BUT...
NNGH...
MMPH... MMNH...
LEAP
...THERE'S NO WAY HE CAN DO IT...
OKAY...
OH!

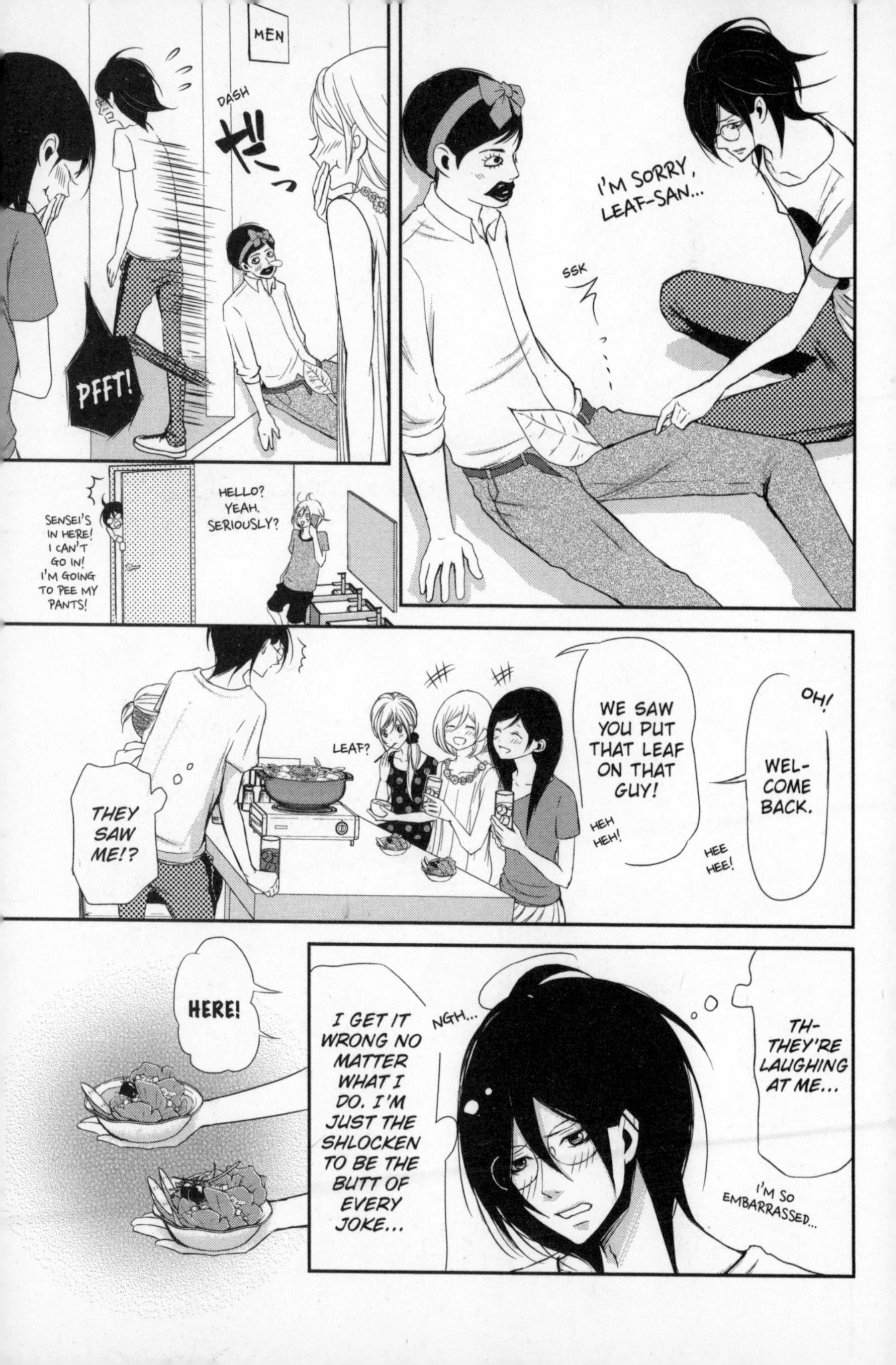
I'M SORRY, LEAF-SAN...
SSK
MEN
DASH
PFFT!
HELLO? YEAH. SERIOUSLY?
SENSEI'S IN HERE! I CAN'T GO IN! I'M GOING TO PEE MY PANTS!
OH! WEL-COME BACK.
WE SAW YOU PUT THAT LEAF ON THAT GUY!
HEE HEE!
HEH HEH!
LEAF?
THEY SAW ME!?
TH-THEY'RE LAUGHING AT ME...
I'M SO EMBARRASSED...
NGH...
I GET IT WRONG NO MATTER WHAT I DO. I'M JUST THE SHLOCKEN TO BE THE BUTT OF EVERY JOKE...
HERE!

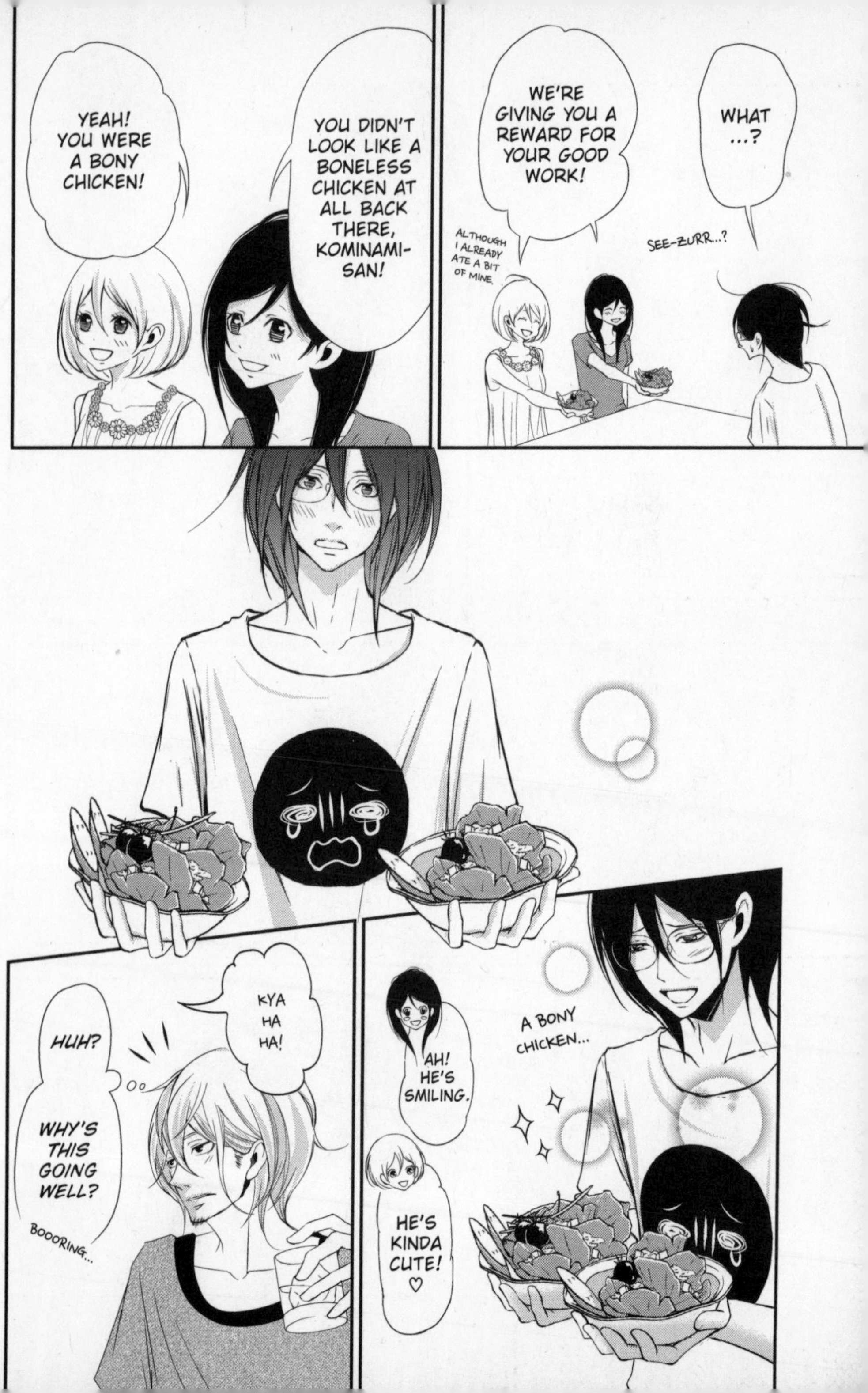
WHAT ...?
SEE-ZURR...?
WE'RE GIVING YOU A REWARD FOR YOUR GOOD WORK!
ALTHOUGH I ALREADY ATE A BIT OF MINE.
YOU DIDN'T LOOK LIKE A BONELESS CHICKEN AT ALL BACK THERE, KOMINAMI-SAN!
YEAH! YOU WERE A BONY CHICKEN!
A BONY CHICKEN...
AH! HE'S SMILING.
HE'S KINDA CUTE! ♡
KYA HA HA!
HUH?
WHY'S THIS GOING WELL?
BOOORING...

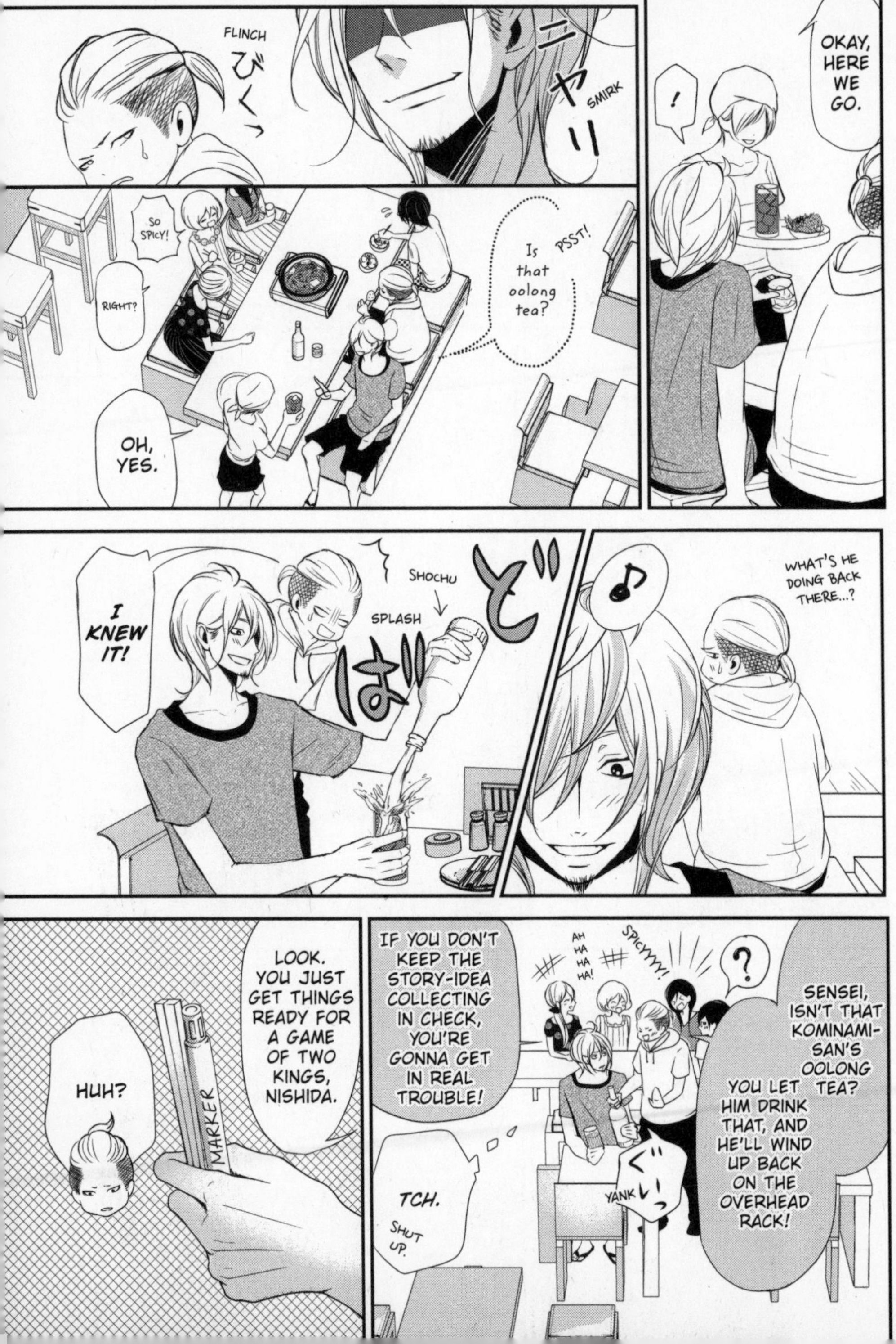
OKAY, HERE WE GO.
!
ニヤリ
SMIRK
FLINCH
びくっ
PSST!
Is that oolong tea?
SO SPICY!
RIGHT?
OH, YES.
♪
WHAT'S HE DOING BACK THERE...?
どぼ
SHOCHU
SPLASH
ばっ
I KNEW IT!
SENSEI, ISN'T THAT KOMINAMI-SAN'S OOLONG TEA?
YOU LET HIM DRINK THAT, AND HE'LL WIND UP BACK ON THE OVERHEAD RACK!
?
SPICYYYY!
AH HA HA HA!
IF YOU DON'T KEEP THE STORY-IDEA COLLECTING IN CHECK, YOU'RE GONNA GET IN REAL TROUBLE!
YANK
ぐいっ
TCH.
SHUT UP.
LOOK. YOU JUST GET THINGS READY FOR A GAME OF TWO KINGS, NISHIDA.
HUH?
MARKER

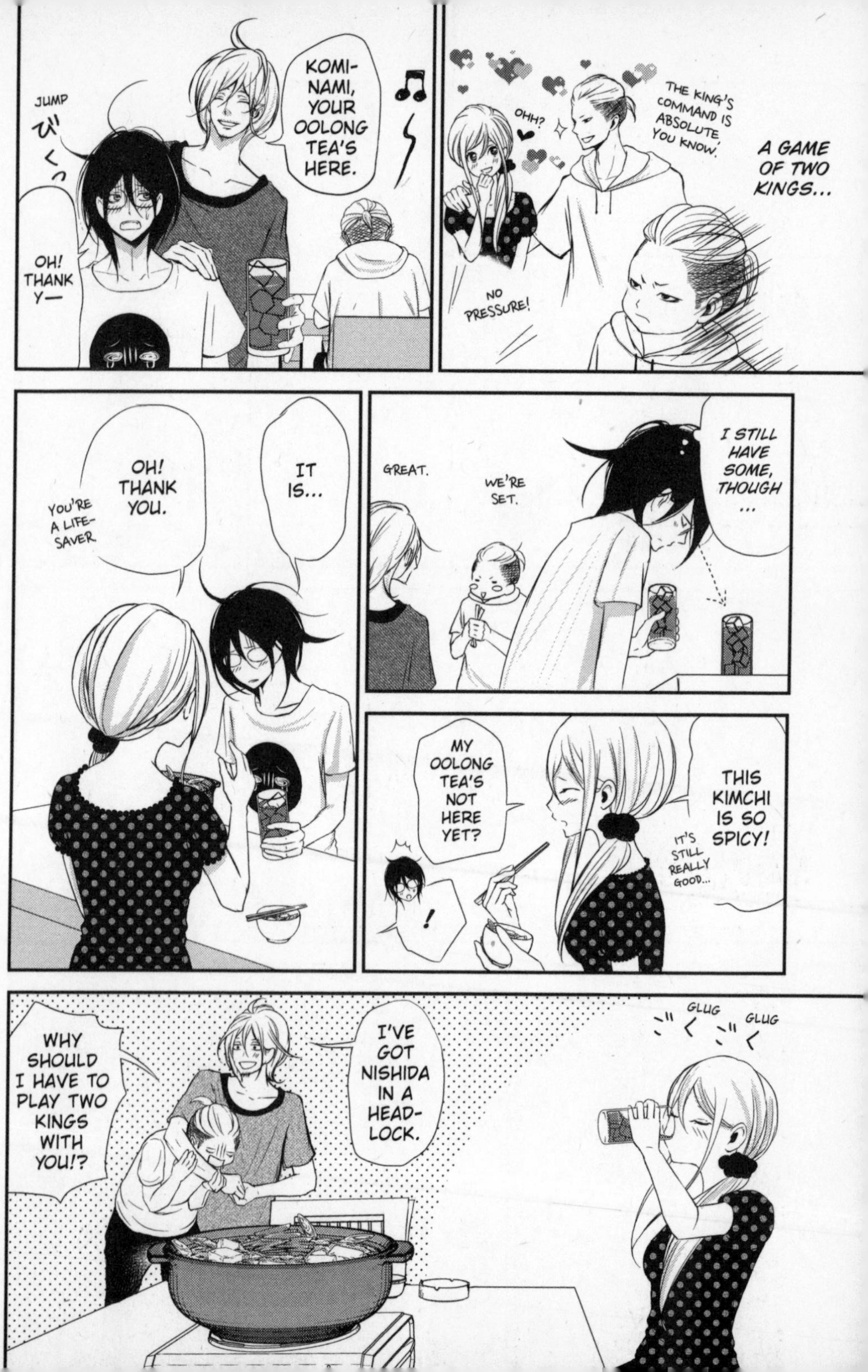
THE KING'S COMMAND IS ABSOLUTE, YOU KNOW.
OHH?
A GAME OF TWO KINGS...
NO PRESSURE!
KOMI-NAMI, YOUR OOLONG TEA'S HERE.
JUMP
びくっ
OH! THANK Y—
I STILL HAVE SOME, THOUGH...
WE'RE SET.
GREAT.
THIS KIMCHI IS SO SPICY!
IT'S STILL REALLY GOOD...
MY OOLONG TEA'S NOT HERE YET?
!
IT IS...
OH! THANK YOU.
YOU'RE A LIFE-SAVER.
GLUG GLUG
ごくごく
I'VE GOT NISHIDA IN A HEAD-LOCK.
WHY SHOULD I HAVE TO PLAY TWO KINGS WITH YOU!?

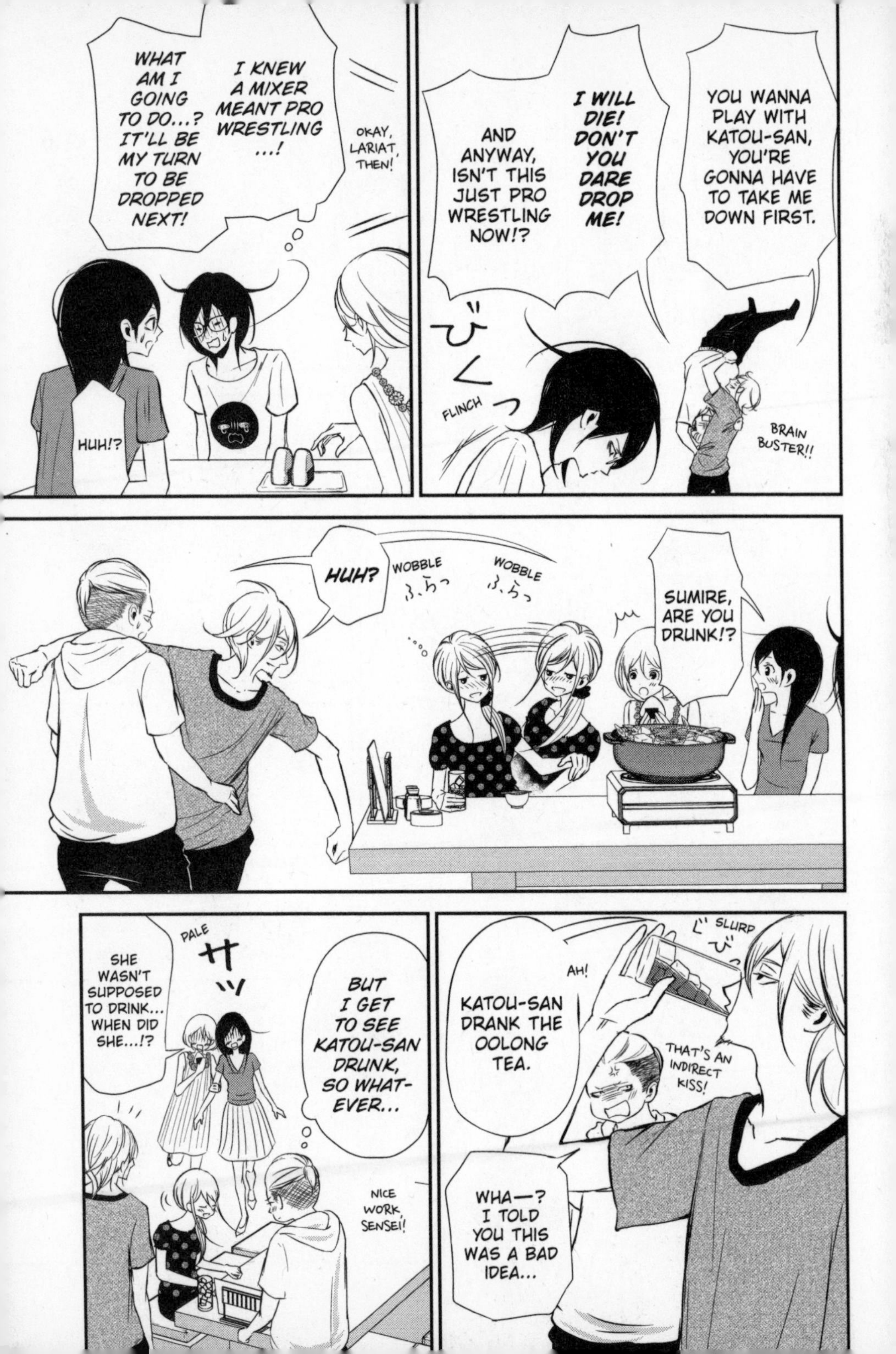

YOU WANNA PLAY WITH KATOU-SAN, YOU'RE GONNA HAVE TO TAKE ME DOWN FIRST.
BRAIN BUSTER!!
I WILL DIE! DON'T YOU DARE DROP ME!
AND ANYWAY, ISN'T THIS JUST PRO WRESTLING NOW!?
びくっ
FLINCH
OKAY, LARIAT, THEN!
I KNEW A MIXER MEANT PRO WRESTLING ...!
WHAT AM I GOING TO DO...? IT'LL BE MY TURN TO BE DROPPED NEXT!
HUH!?
SUMIRE, ARE YOU DRUNK!?
WOBBLE
ふらっ
WOBBLE
ふらっ
HUH?
SLURP
AH!
KATOU-SAN DRANK THE OOLONG TEA.
THAT'S AN INDIRECT KISS!
WHA—? I TOLD YOU THIS WAS A BAD IDEA...
BUT I GET TO SEE KATOU-SAN DRUNK, SO WHATEVER...
PALE
サッ
SHE WASN'T SUPPOSED TO DRINK... WHEN DID SHE...!?
NICE WORK, SENSEI!

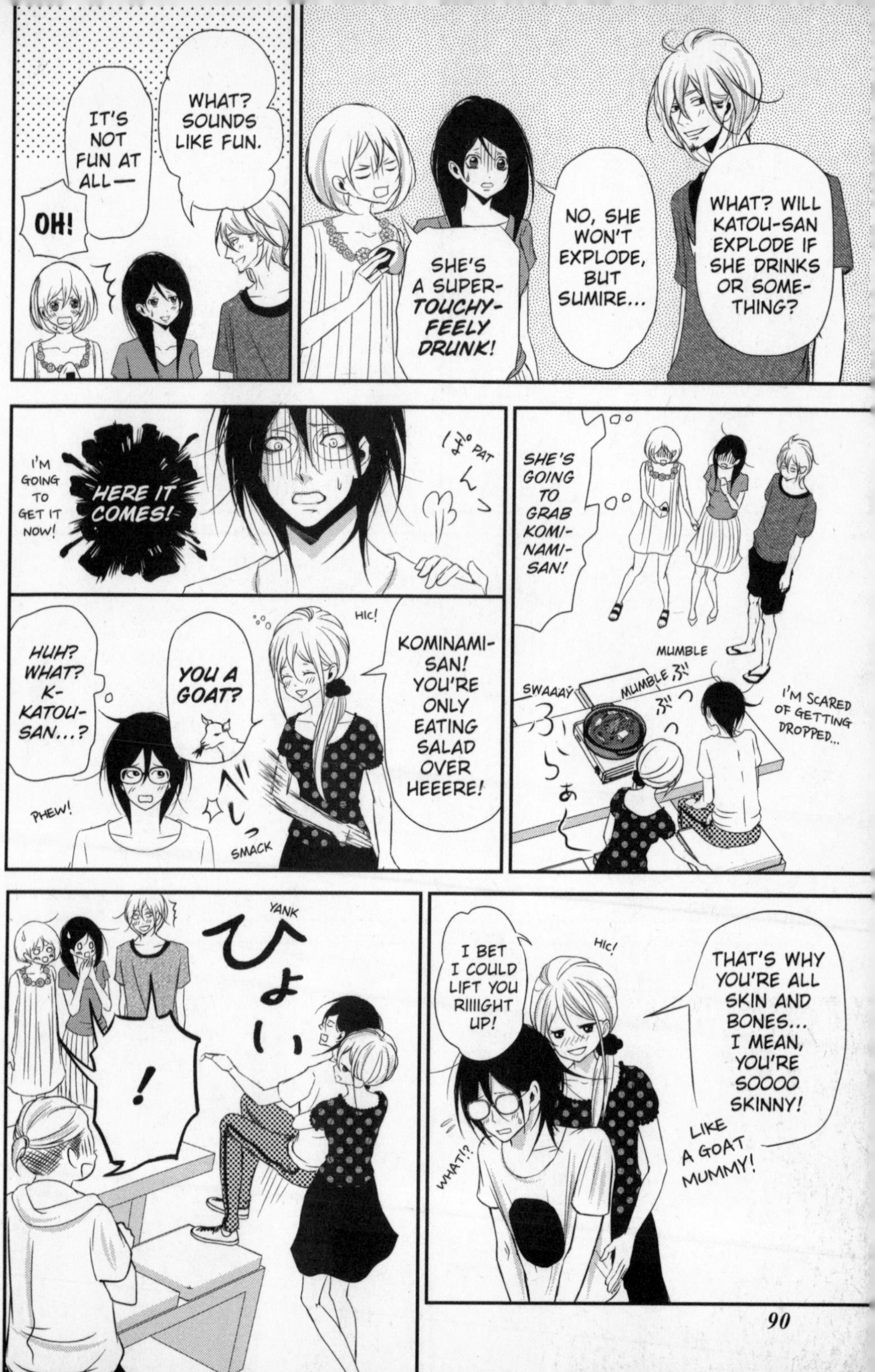

WHAT? WILL KATOU-SAN EXPLODE IF SHE DRINKS OR SOME-THING?
NO, SHE WON'T EXPLODE, BUT SUMIRE...
SHE'S A SUPER-TOUCHY-FEELY DRUNK!
WHAT? SOUNDS LIKE FUN.
IT'S NOT FUN AT ALL—
OH!
SHE'S GOING TO GRAB KOMI-NAMI-SAN!
MUMBLE
MUMBLE
I'M SCARED OF GETTING DROPPED...
SWAAAY
PAT
HERE IT COMES!
I'M GOING TO GET IT NOW!
HIC!
KOMINAMI-SAN! YOU'RE ONLY EATING SALAD OVER HEEERE!
YOU A GOAT?
HUH? WHAT? K-KATOU-SAN...?
SMACK
PHEW!
HIC!
THAT'S WHY YOU'RE ALL SKIN AND BONES... I MEAN, YOU'RE SOOOO SKINNY!
I BET I COULD LIFT YOU RIIIIGHT UP!
LIKE A GOAT MUMMY!
WHAT!?
YANK
!

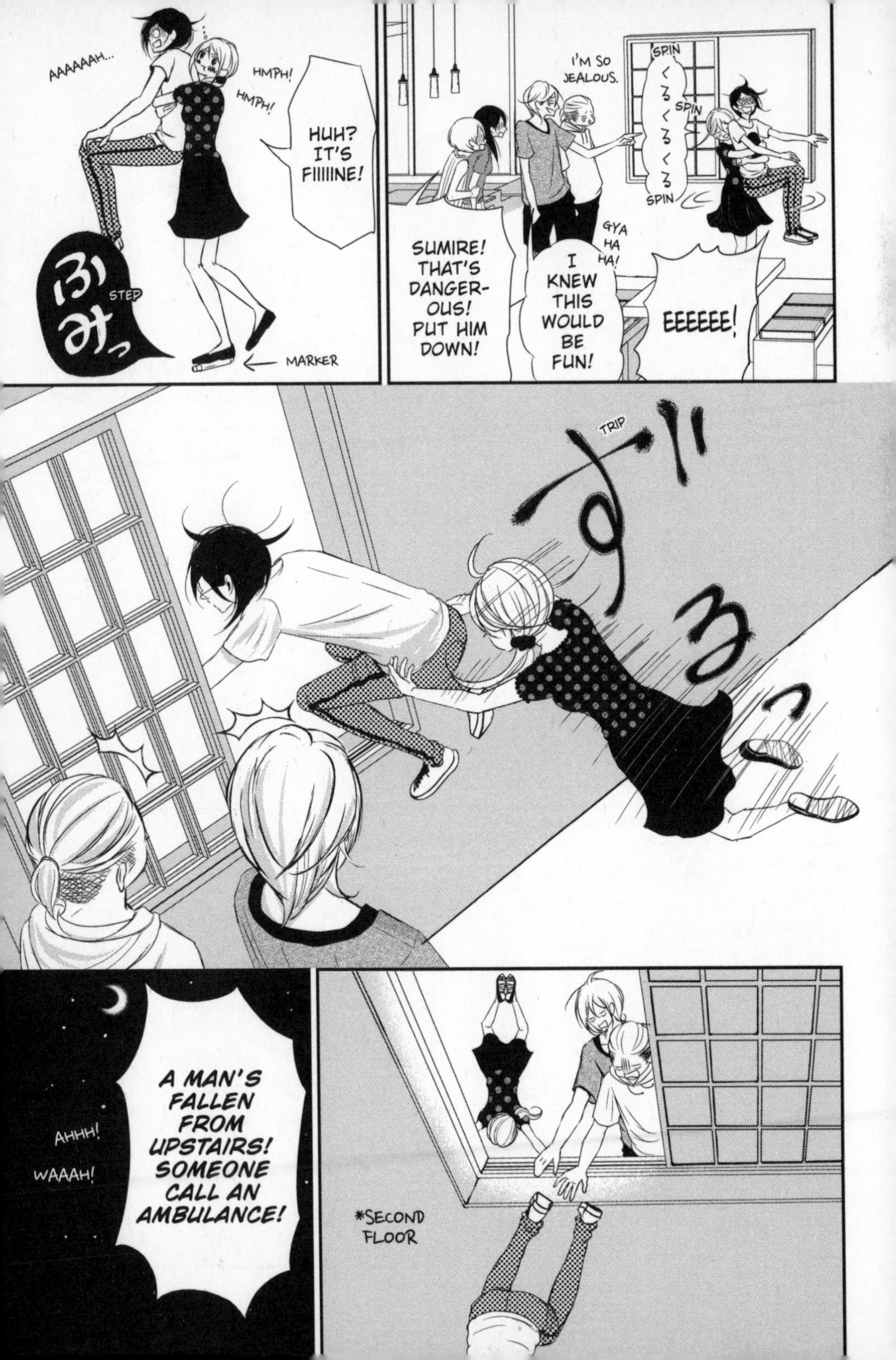
SPIN
くるくるくる
SPIN
SPIN
I'M SO JEALOUS.
EEEEEE!
GYA HA HA!
I KNEW THIS WOULD BE FUN!
SUMIRE! THAT'S DANGER-OUS! PUT HIM DOWN!
HUH? IT'S FIIIIINE!
HMPH!
HMPH!
AAAAAAH...
ふみっ
STEP
MARKER
ずるっ
TRIP
*SECOND FLOOR
A MAN'S FALLEN FROM UPSTAIRS! SOMEONE CALL AN AMBULANCE!
AHHH!
WAAAH!

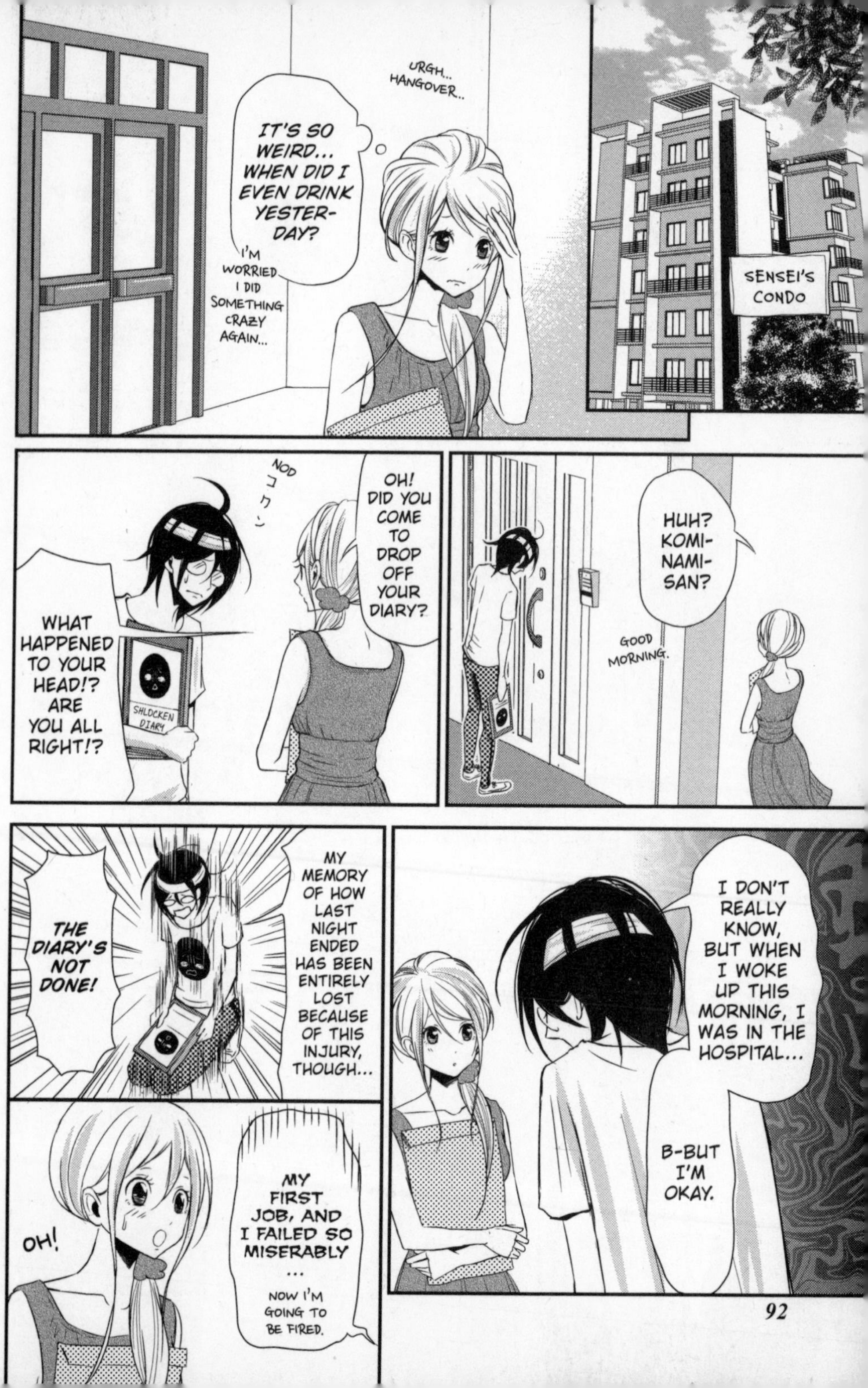
SENSEI'S CONDO
URGH... HANGOVER...
IT'S SO WEIRD... WHEN DID I EVEN DRINK YESTERDAY?
I'M WORRIED I DID SOMETHING CRAZY AGAIN...
HUH? KOMINAMI-SAN?
GOOD MORNING.
NOD
コクン
OH! DID YOU COME TO DROP OFF YOUR DIARY?
WHAT HAPPENED TO YOUR HEAD!? ARE YOU ALL RIGHT!?
SHLOCKEN DIARY
I DON'T REALLY KNOW, BUT WHEN I WOKE UP THIS MORNING, I WAS IN THE HOSPITAL...
B-BUT I'M OKAY.
MY MEMORY OF HOW LAST NIGHT ENDED HAS BEEN ENTIRELY LOST BECAUSE OF THIS INJURY, THOUGH...
THE DIARY'S NOT DONE!
MY FIRST JOB, AND I FAILED SO MISERABLY...
NOW I'M GOING TO BE FIRED.
OH!

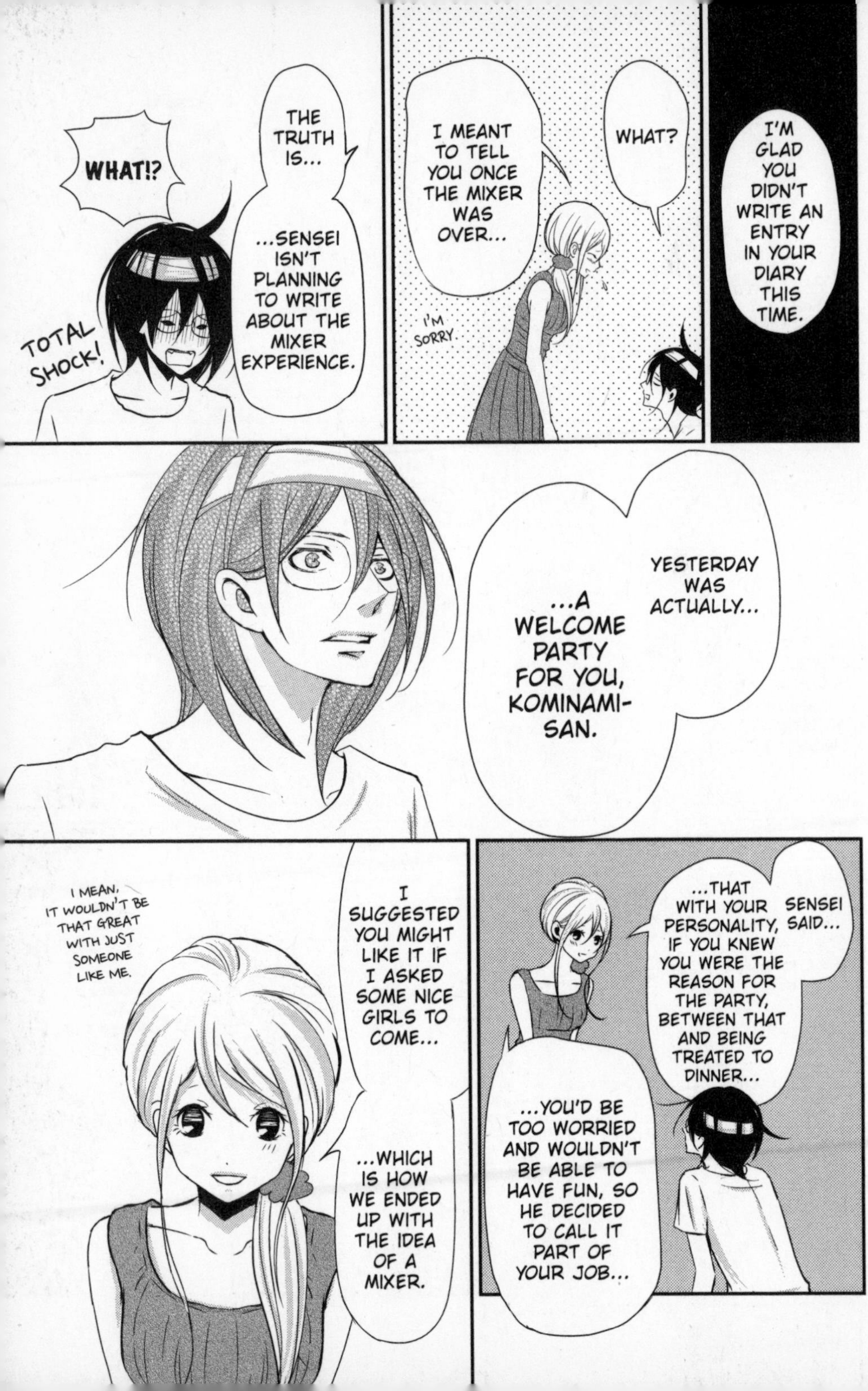
I'M GLAD YOU DIDN'T WRITE AN ENTRY IN YOUR DIARY THIS TIME.
WHAT?
I MEANT TO TELL YOU ONCE THE MIXER WAS OVER...
I'M SORRY.
THE TRUTH IS...
...SENSEI ISN'T PLANNING TO WRITE ABOUT THE MIXER EXPERIENCE.
WHAT!?
TOTAL SHOCK!
YESTERDAY WAS ACTUALLY...
...A WELCOME PARTY FOR YOU, KOMINAMI-SAN.
SENSEI SAID...
...THAT WITH YOUR PERSONALITY, IF YOU KNEW YOU WERE THE REASON FOR THE PARTY, BETWEEN THAT AND BEING TREATED TO DINNER...
...YOU'D BE TOO WORRIED AND WOULDN'T BE ABLE TO HAVE FUN, SO HE DECIDED TO CALL IT PART OF YOUR JOB...
I SUGGESTED YOU MIGHT LIKE IT IF I ASKED SOME NICE GIRLS TO COME...
...WHICH IS HOW WE ENDED UP WITH THE IDEA OF A MIXER.
I MEAN, IT WOULDN'T BE THAT GREAT WITH JUST SOMEONE LIKE ME.

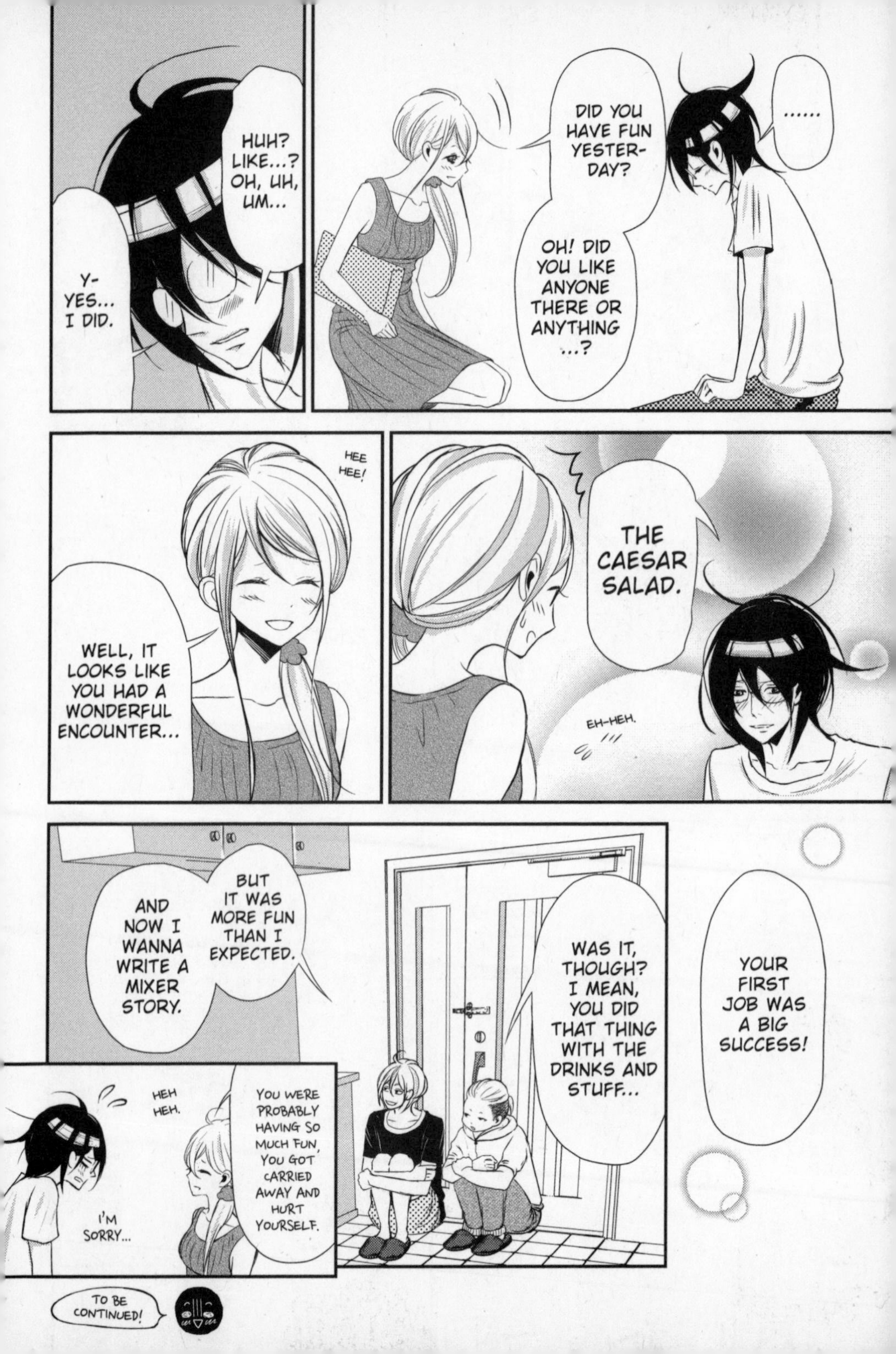
......
DID YOU HAVE FUN YESTER-DAY?
OH! DID YOU LIKE ANYONE THERE OR ANYTHING ...?
HUH? LIKE...? OH, UH, UM...
Y-YES... I DID.
THE CAESAR SALAD.
EH-HEH.
HEE HEE!
WELL, IT LOOKS LIKE YOU HAD A WONDERFUL ENCOUNTER...
YOUR FIRST JOB WAS A BIG SUCCESS!
WAS IT, THOUGH? I MEAN, YOU DID THAT THING WITH THE DRINKS AND STUFF...
BUT IT WAS MORE FUN THAN I EXPECTED.
AND NOW I WANNA WRITE A MIXER STORY.
YOU WERE PROBABLY HAVING SO MUCH FUN, YOU GOT CARRIED AWAY AND HURT YOURSELF.
HEH HEH.
I'M SORRY...
TO BE CONTINUED!

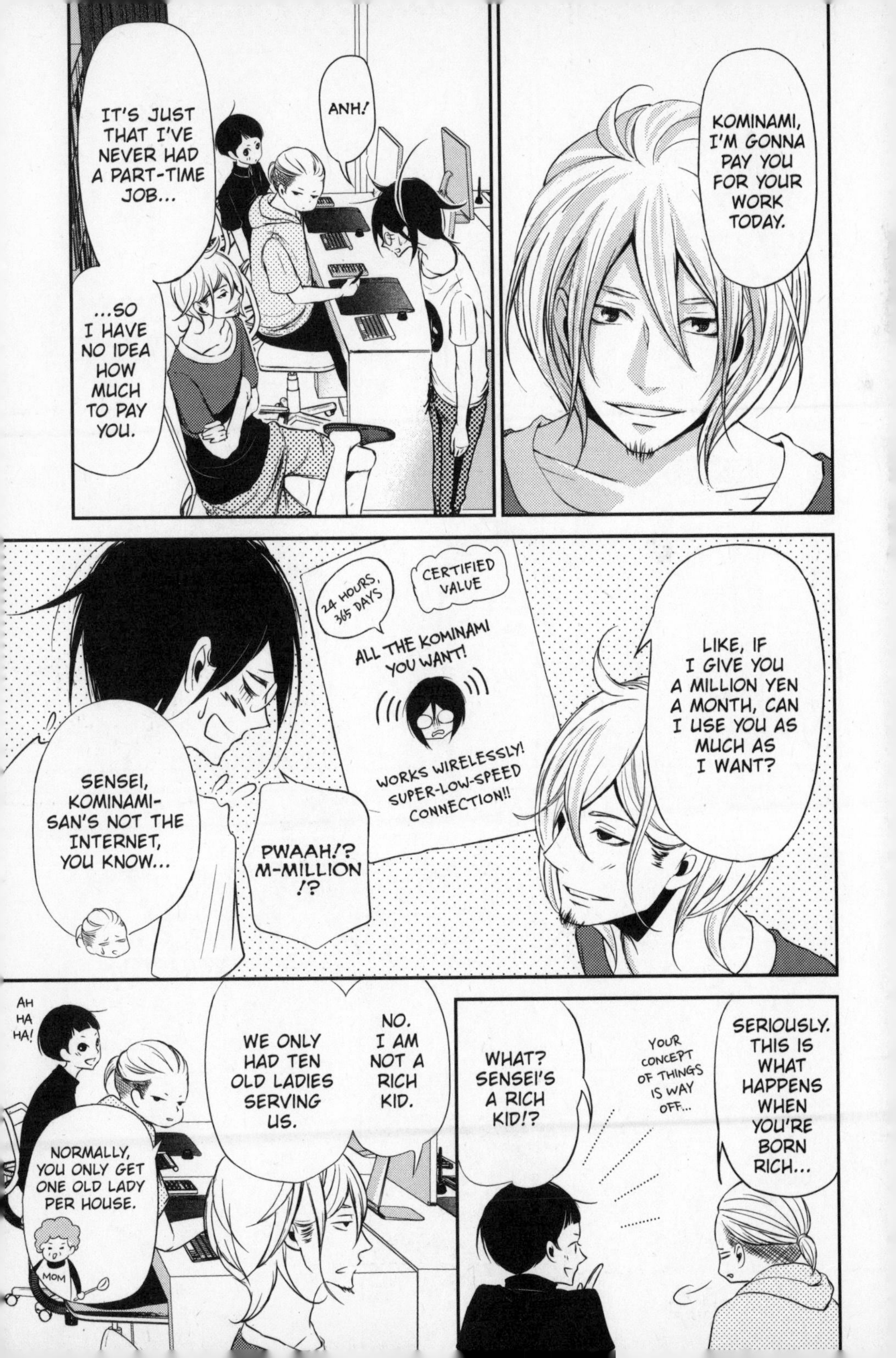

KOMINAMI, I'M GONNA PAY YOU FOR YOUR WORK TODAY.
ANH!
IT'S JUST THAT I'VE NEVER HAD A PART-TIME JOB...
...SO I HAVE NO IDEA HOW MUCH TO PAY YOU.
LIKE, IF I GIVE YOU A MILLION YEN A MONTH, CAN I USE YOU AS MUCH AS I WANT?
CERTIFIED VALUE
24 HOURS, 365 DAYS
ALL THE KOMINAMI YOU WANT!
WORKS WIRELESSLY! SUPER-LOW-SPEED CONNECTION!!
PWAAH!? M-MILLION!?
SENSEI, KOMINAMI-SAN'S NOT THE INTERNET, YOU KNOW...
SERIOUSLY. THIS IS WHAT HAPPENS WHEN YOU'RE BORN RICH...
YOUR CONCEPT OF THINGS IS WAY OFF...
WHAT? SENSEI'S A RICH KID!?
NO. I AM NOT A RICH KID.
WE ONLY HAD TEN OLD LADIES SERVING US.
AH HA HA!
NORMALLY, YOU ONLY GET ONE OLD LADY PER HOUSE.
MOM

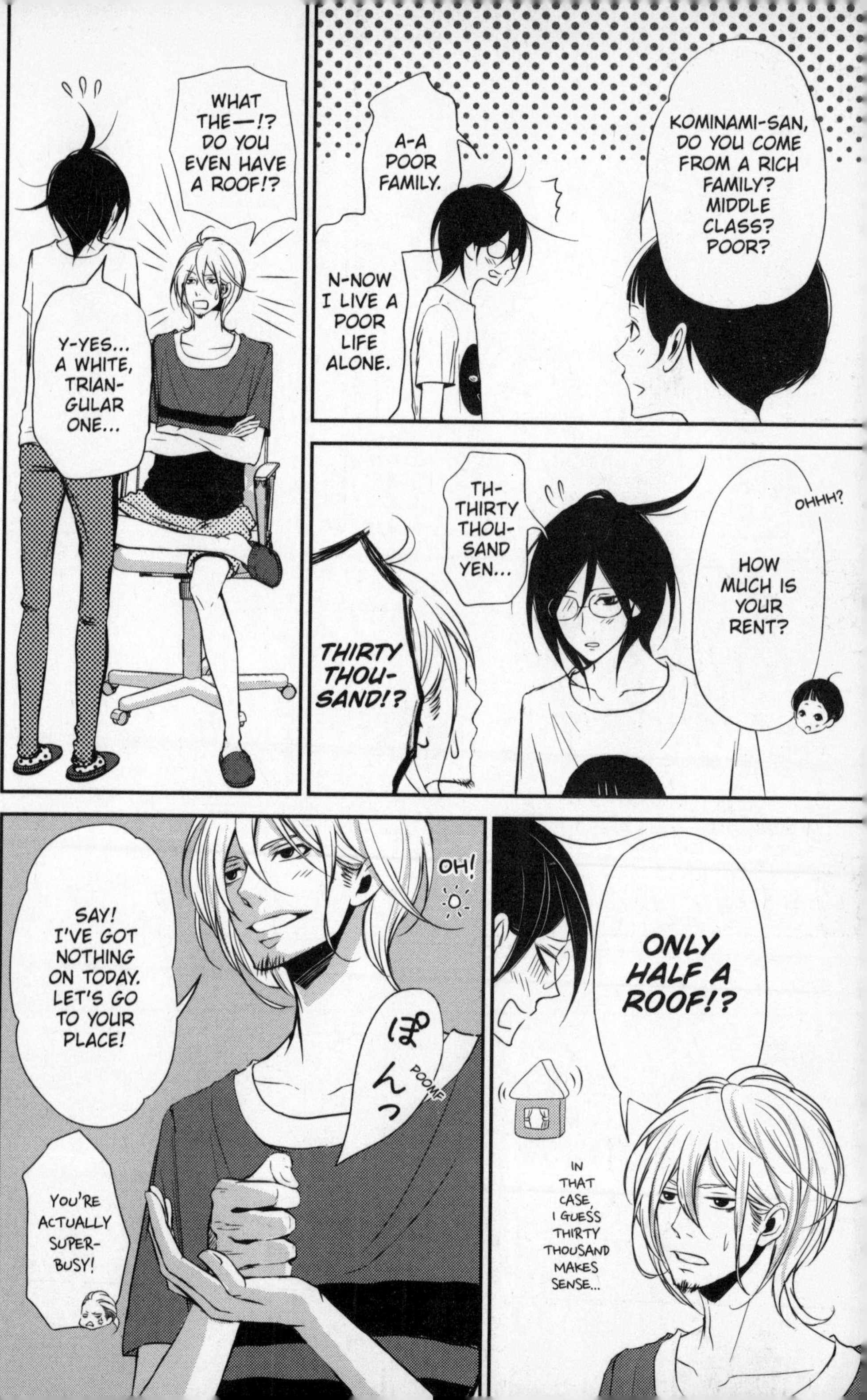
KOMINAMI-SAN, DO YOU COME FROM A RICH FAMILY? MIDDLE CLASS? POOR?
A-A POOR FAMILY.
N-NOW I LIVE A POOR LIFE ALONE.
OHHH?
HOW MUCH IS YOUR RENT?
TH-THIRTY THOUSAND YEN...
THIRTY THOUSAND!?
WHAT THE—!? DO YOU EVEN HAVE A ROOF!?
Y-YES... A WHITE, TRIANGULAR ONE...
ONLY HALF A ROOF!?
IN THAT CASE, I GUESS THIRTY THOUSAND MAKES SENSE...
OH!
SAY! I'VE GOT NOTHING ON TODAY. LET'S GO TO YOUR PLACE!
ぽんっ
POOMF
YOU'RE ACTUALLY SUPER-BUSY!

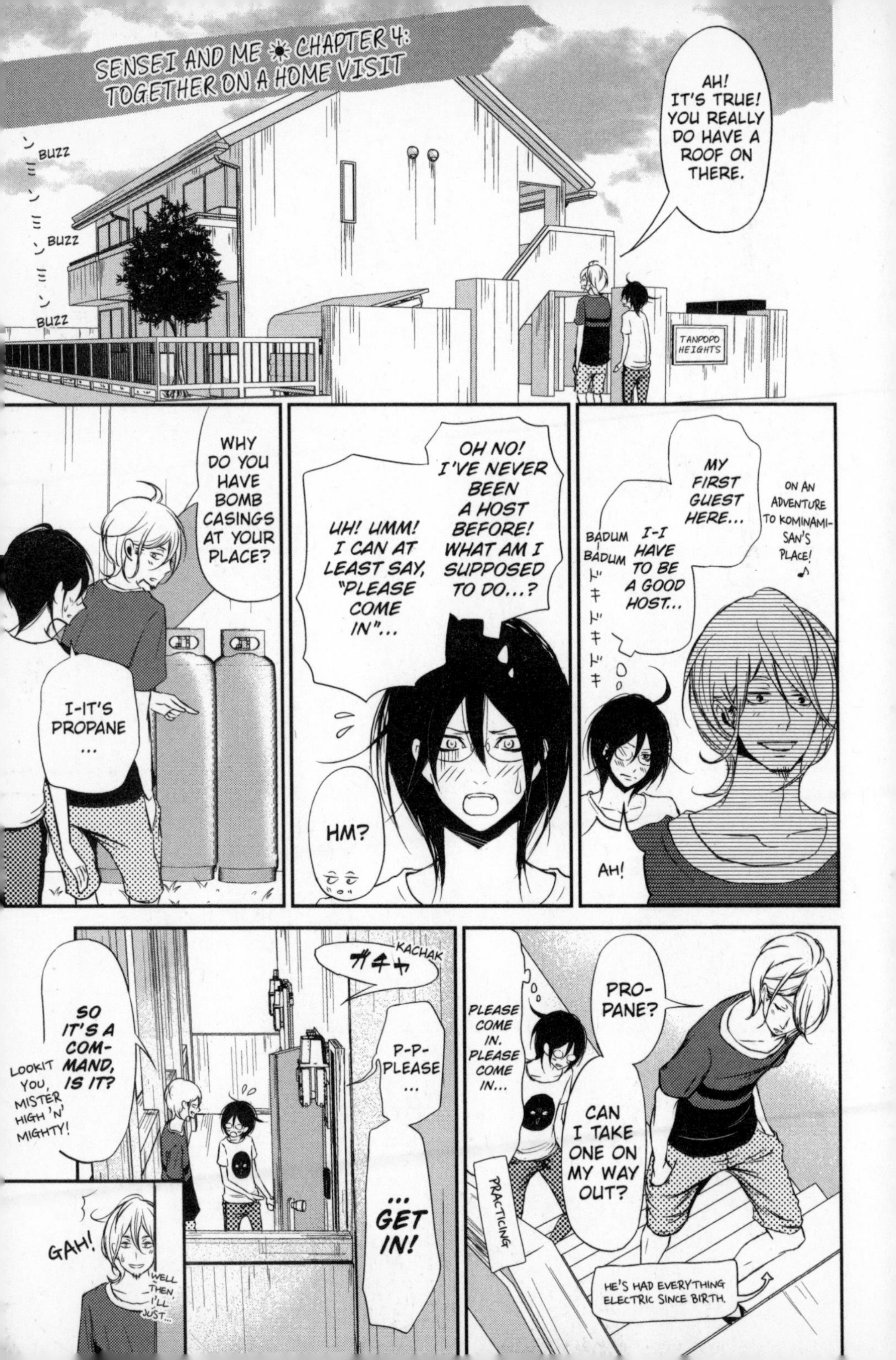
SENSEI AND ME ☀ CHAPTER 4: TOGETHER ON A HOME VISIT
AH! IT'S TRUE! YOU REALLY DO HAVE A ROOF ON THERE.
BUZZ
BUZZ
BUZZ
TANPOPO HEIGHTS
ON AN ADVENTURE TO KOMINAMI-SAN'S PLACE! ♪
MY FIRST GUEST HERE...
I-I HAVE TO BE A GOOD HOST...
BADUM BADUM
ドキドキドキ
AH!
OH NO! I'VE NEVER BEEN A HOST BEFORE! WHAT AM I SUPPOSED TO DO...?
UH! UMM! I CAN AT LEAST SAY, "PLEASE COME IN"...
HM?
WHY DO YOU HAVE BOMB CASINGS AT YOUR PLACE?
I-IT'S PROPANE ...
PRO-PANE?
PLEASE COME IN. PLEASE COME IN...
CAN I TAKE ONE ON MY WAY OUT?
PRACTICING
HE'S HAD EVERYTHING ELECTRIC SINCE BIRTH.
ガチャ
KACHAK
P-P-PLEASE ...
... GET IN!
SO IT'S A COMMAND, IS IT?
LOOKIT YOU, MISTER HIGH 'N' MIGHTY!
GAH!
WELL THEN, I'LL JUST...

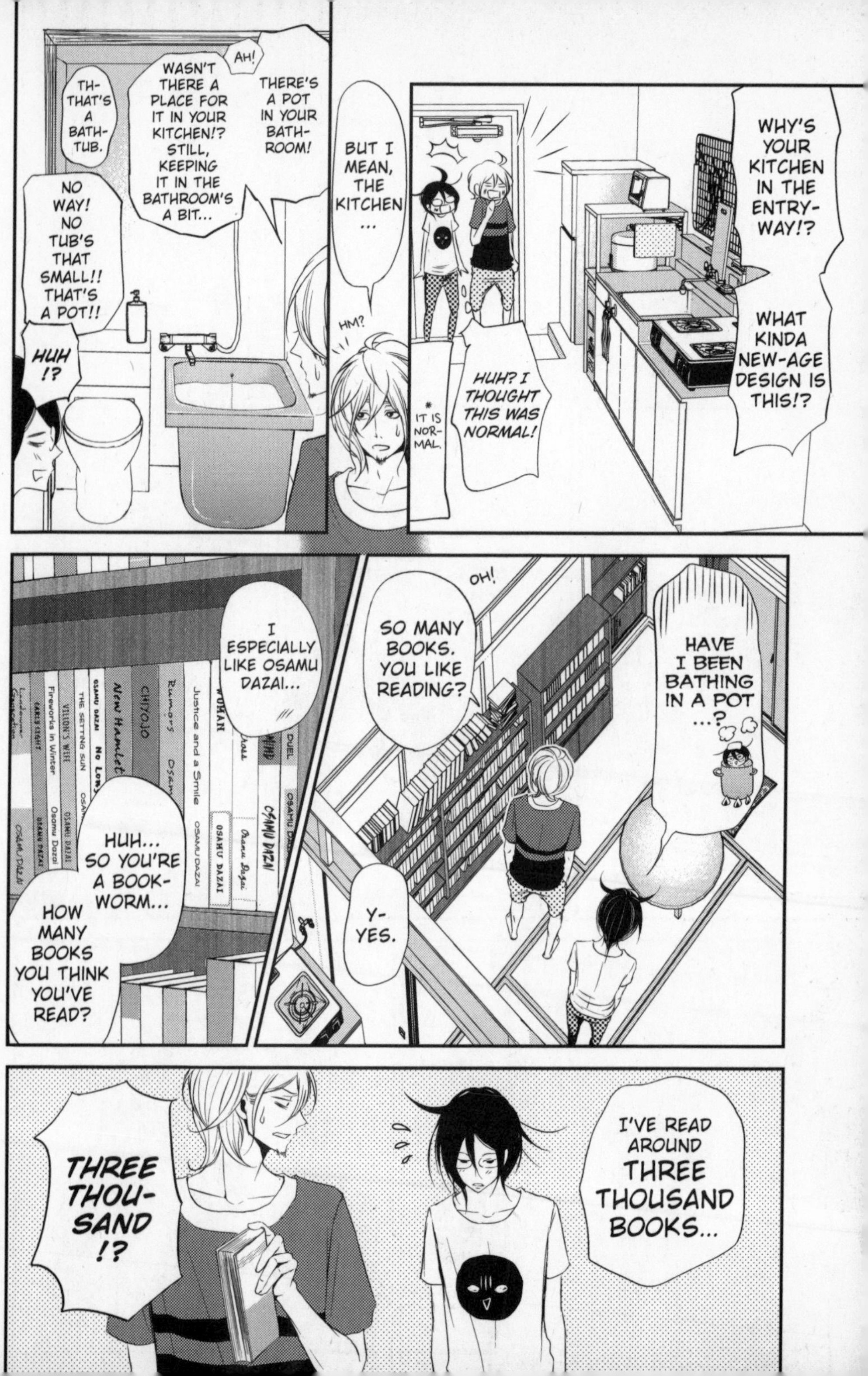
WHY'S YOUR KITCHEN IN THE ENTRY-WAY!?
WHAT KINDA NEW-AGE DESIGN IS THIS!?
HUH? I THOUGHT THIS WAS NORMAL!
* IT IS NORMAL.
BUT I MEAN, THE KITCHEN...
HM?
THERE'S A POT IN YOUR BATHROOM!
AH!
WASN'T THERE A PLACE FOR IT IN YOUR KITCHEN!? STILL, KEEPING IT IN THE BATHROOM'S A BIT...
TH-THAT'S A BATHTUB.
NO WAY! NO TUB'S THAT SMALL!! THAT'S A POT!!
HUH!?
HAVE I BEEN BATHING IN A POT...?
OH!
SO MANY BOOKS. YOU LIKE READING?
Y-YES.
I ESPECIALLY LIKE OSAMU DAZAI...
HUH... SO YOU'RE A BOOK-WORM...
HOW MANY BOOKS YOU THINK YOU'VE READ?
I'VE READ AROUND THREE THOUSAND BOOKS...
THREE THOU-SAND!?

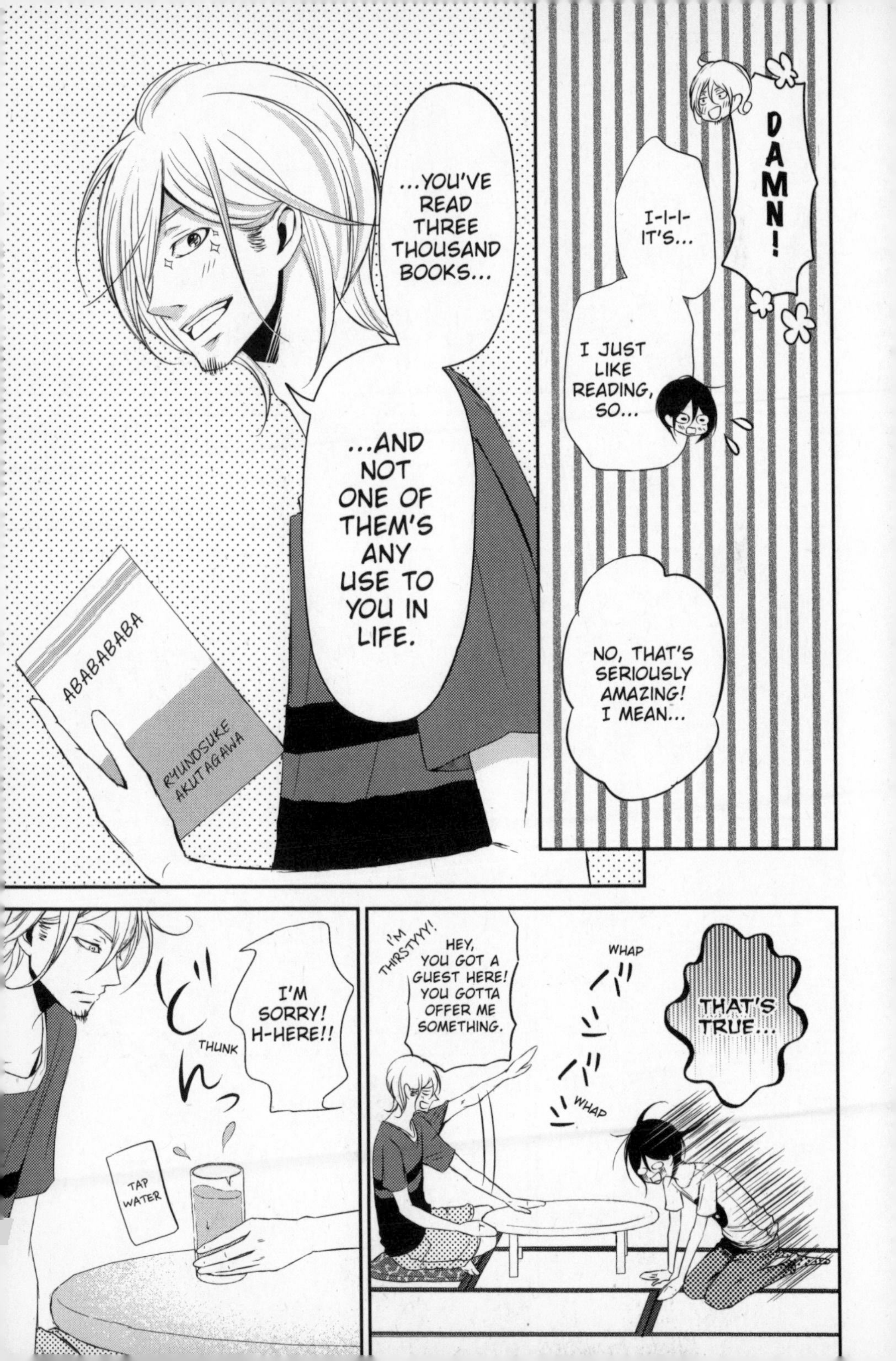
DAMN!
I-I-I-IT'S...
I JUST LIKE READING, SO...
NO, THAT'S SERIOUSLY AMAZING! I MEAN...
...YOU'VE READ THREE THOUSAND BOOKS...
...AND NOT ONE OF THEM'S ANY USE TO YOU IN LIFE.
ABABABABA
RYUNOSUKE AKUTAGAWA
THAT'S TRUE...
WHAP
WHAP
I'M THIRSTYYY!
HEY, YOU GOT A GUEST HERE! YOU GOTTA OFFER ME SOMETHING.
I'M SORRY! H-HERE!!
THUNK
TAP WATER

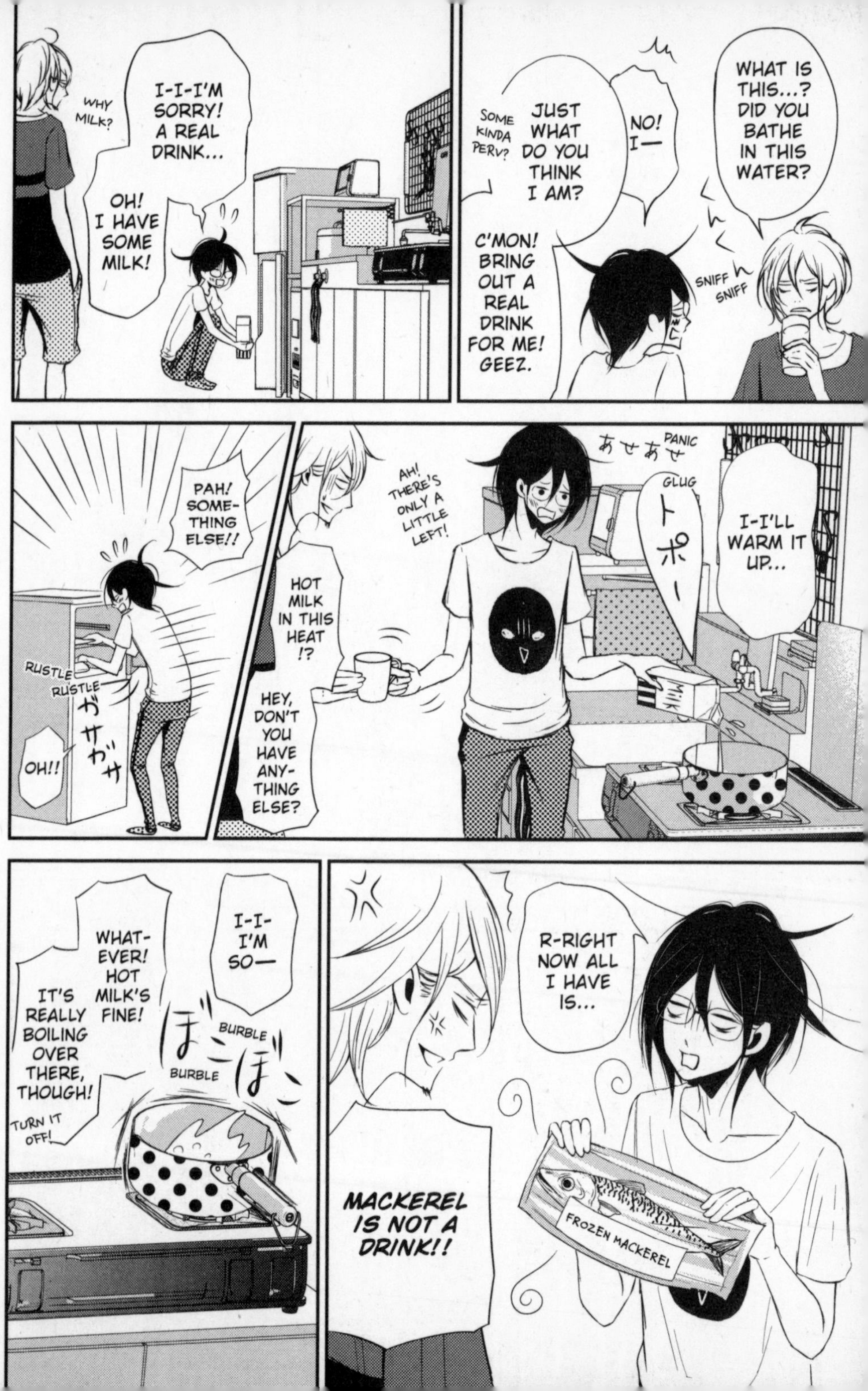
WHAT IS THIS...? DID YOU BATHE IN THIS WATER?
SNIFF SNIFF
NO! I—
JUST WHAT DO YOU THINK I AM?
SOME KINDA PERV?
C'MON! BRING OUT A REAL DRINK FOR ME! GEEZ.
I-I-I'M SORRY! A REAL DRINK...
WHY MILK?
OH! I HAVE SOME MILK!
I-I'LL WARM IT UP...
トポー
GLUG
あせあせ
PANIC
AH! THERE'S ONLY A LITTLE LEFT!
HOT MILK IN THIS HEAT!?
HEY, DON'T YOU HAVE ANYTHING ELSE?
PAH! SOMETHING ELSE!!
ガサガサ
RUSTLE RUSTLE
OH!!
R-RIGHT NOW ALL I HAVE IS...
FROZEN MACKEREL
MACKEREL IS NOT A DRINK!!
I-I-I'M SO—
WHATEVER! HOT MILK'S FINE!
ぼこぼこ
BURBLE BURBLE
IT'S REALLY BOILING OVER THERE, THOUGH!
TURN IT OFF!

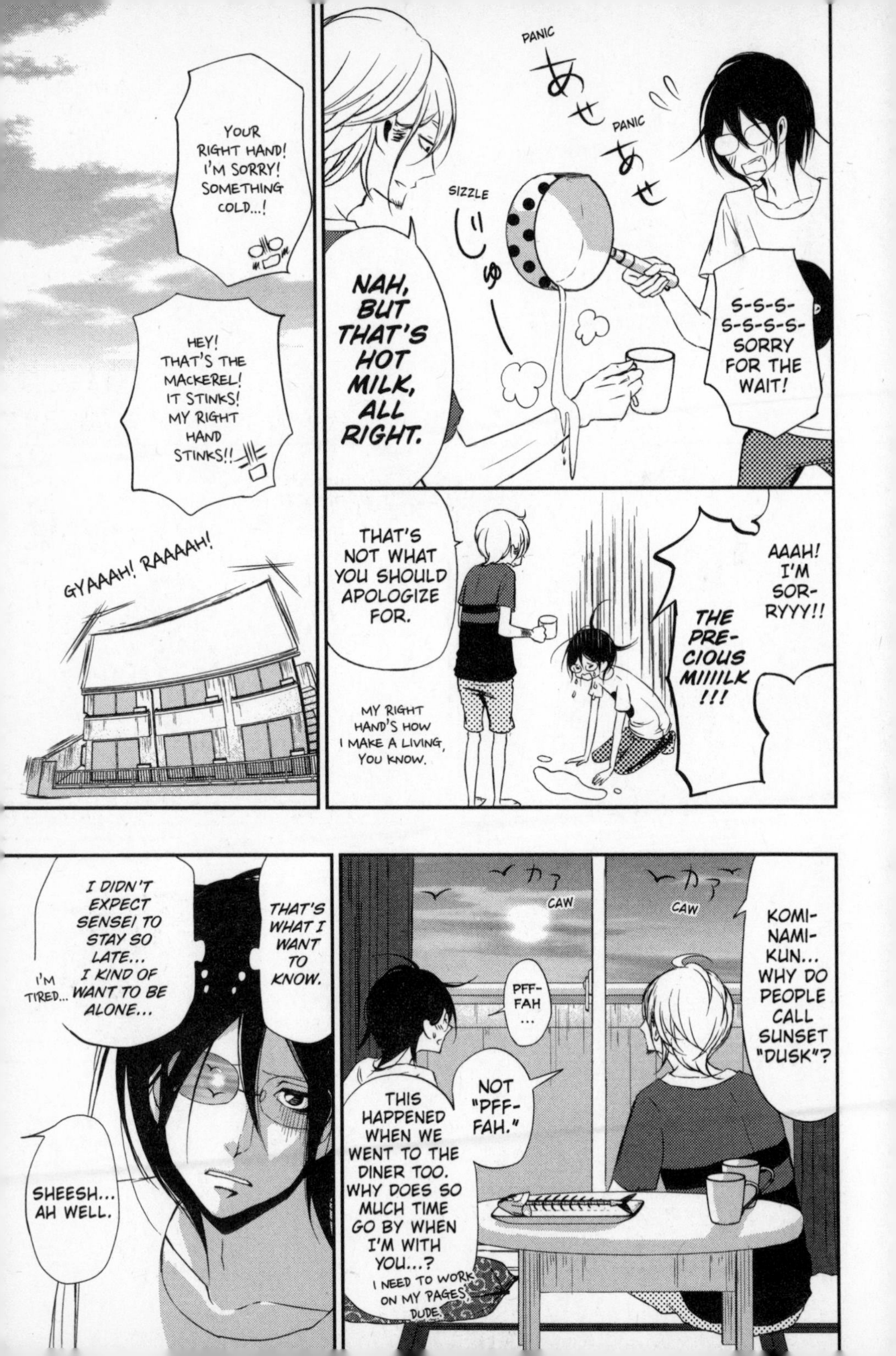
PANIC
あせ
PANIC
あせ
SIZZLE
じゅー
S-S-S-S-S-S-S-SORRY FOR THE WAIT!
NAH, BUT THAT'S HOT MILK, ALL RIGHT.
AAAH! I'M SORRYYY!!
THE PRECIOUS MIIIILK!!!
THAT'S NOT WHAT YOU SHOULD APOLOGIZE FOR.
MY RIGHT HAND'S HOW I MAKE A LIVING, YOU KNOW.
YOUR RIGHT HAND! I'M SORRY! SOMETHING COLD...!
HEY! THAT'S THE MACKEREL! IT STINKS! MY RIGHT HAND STINKS!!
GYAAAH! RAAAAH!
カァ
CAW
カァ
CAW
KOMINAMI-KUN... WHY DO PEOPLE CALL SUNSET "DUSK"?
PFF-FAH...
NOT "PFF-FAH."
THIS HAPPENED WHEN WE WENT TO THE DINER TOO. WHY DOES SO MUCH TIME GO BY WHEN I'M WITH YOU...?
I NEED TO WORK ON MY PAGES, DUDE.
THAT'S WHAT I WANT TO KNOW.
I DIDN'T EXPECT SENSEI TO STAY SO LATE... I KIND OF WANT TO BE ALONE...
I'M TIRED...
SHEESH... AH WELL.

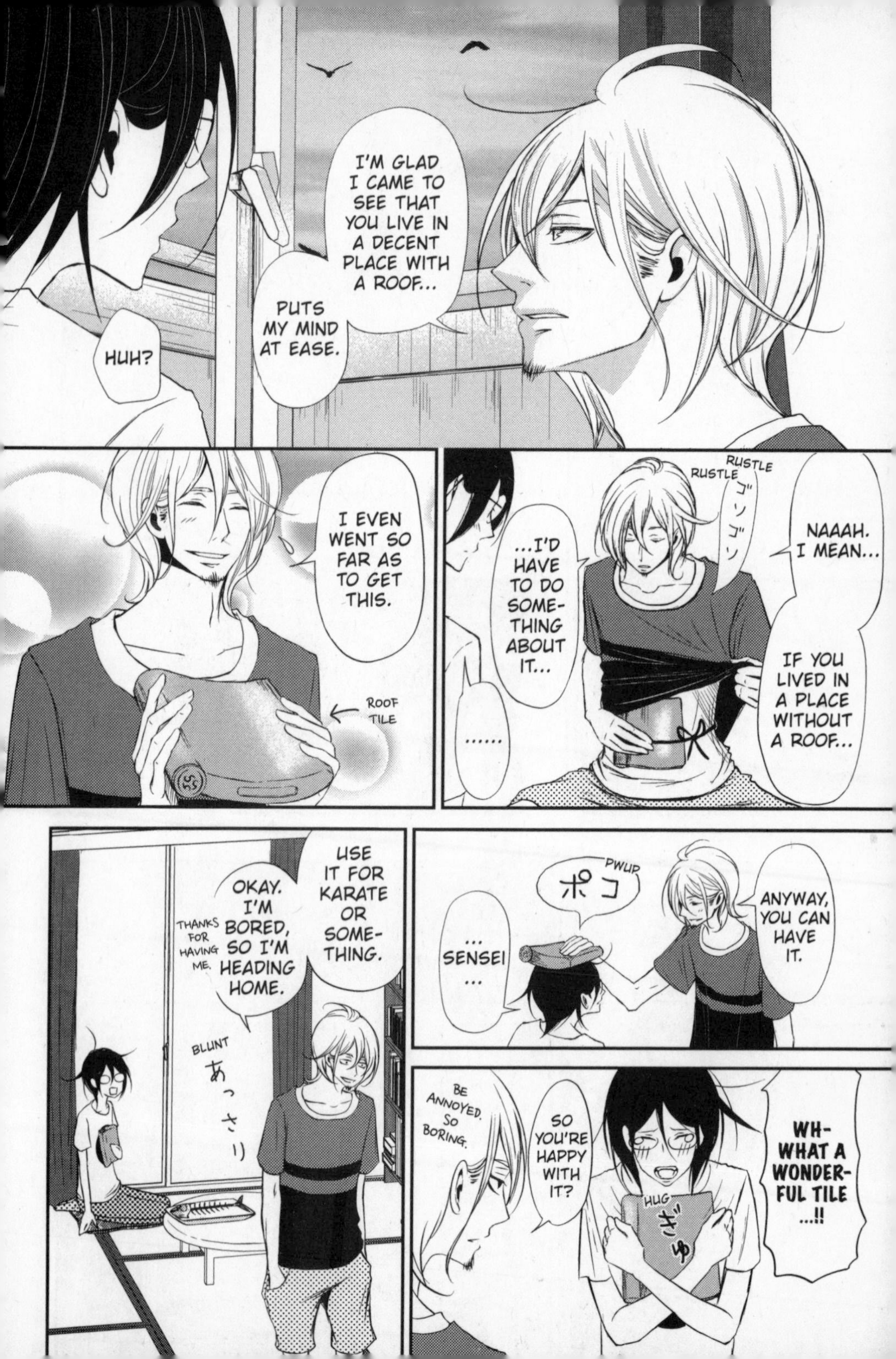
I'M GLAD I CAME TO SEE THAT YOU LIVE IN A DECENT PLACE WITH A ROOF...
PUTS MY MIND AT EASE.
HUH?
NAAAH. I MEAN...
RUSTLE RUSTLE
ゴソゴソ
IF YOU LIVED IN A PLACE WITHOUT A ROOF...
...I'D HAVE TO DO SOME-THING ABOUT IT...
......
I EVEN WENT SO FAR AS TO GET THIS.
ROOF TILE
ANYWAY, YOU CAN HAVE IT.
PWUP
ポコ
... SENSEI ...
WH-WHAT A WONDER-FUL TILE ...!!
HUG
ぎゅ
SO YOU'RE HAPPY WITH IT?
BE ANNOYED. SO BORING.
USE IT FOR KARATE OR SOME-THING.
OKAY. I'M BORED, SO I'M HEADING HOME.
THANKS FOR HAVING ME.
BLUNT
あっさり

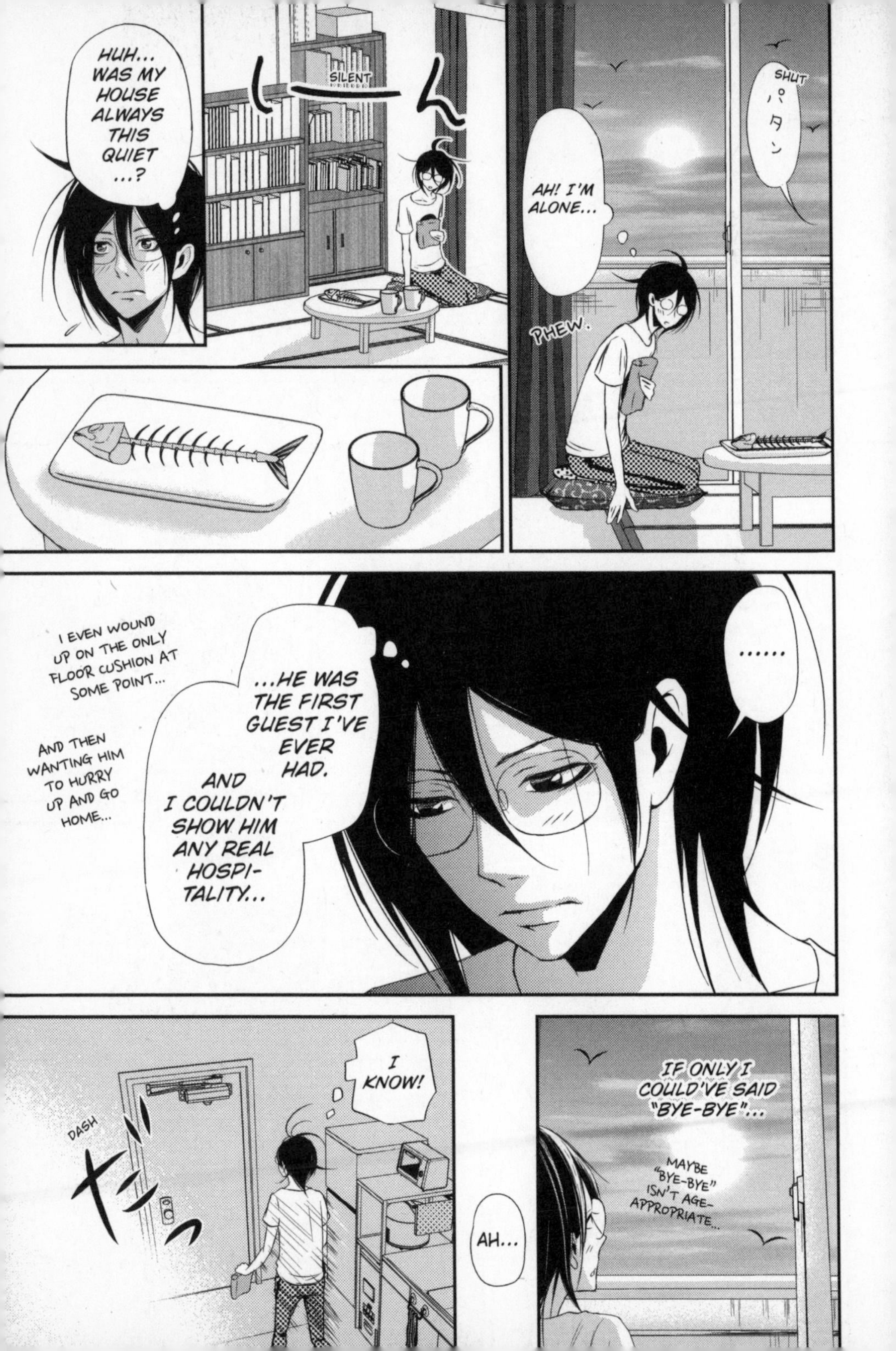
SHUT
パタン
AH! I'M ALONE...
PHEW.
SILENT
しーん
HUH... WAS MY HOUSE ALWAYS THIS QUIET ...?
......
...HE WAS THE FIRST GUEST I'VE EVER HAD.
AND I COULDN'T SHOW HIM ANY REAL HOSPI-TALITY...
I EVEN WOUND UP ON THE ONLY FLOOR CUSHION AT SOME POINT...
AND THEN WANTING HIM TO HURRY UP AND GO HOME...
IF ONLY I COULD'VE SAID "BYE-BYE"...
MAYBE "BYE-BYE" ISN'T AGE-APPROPRIATE...
AH...
I KNOW!
DASH

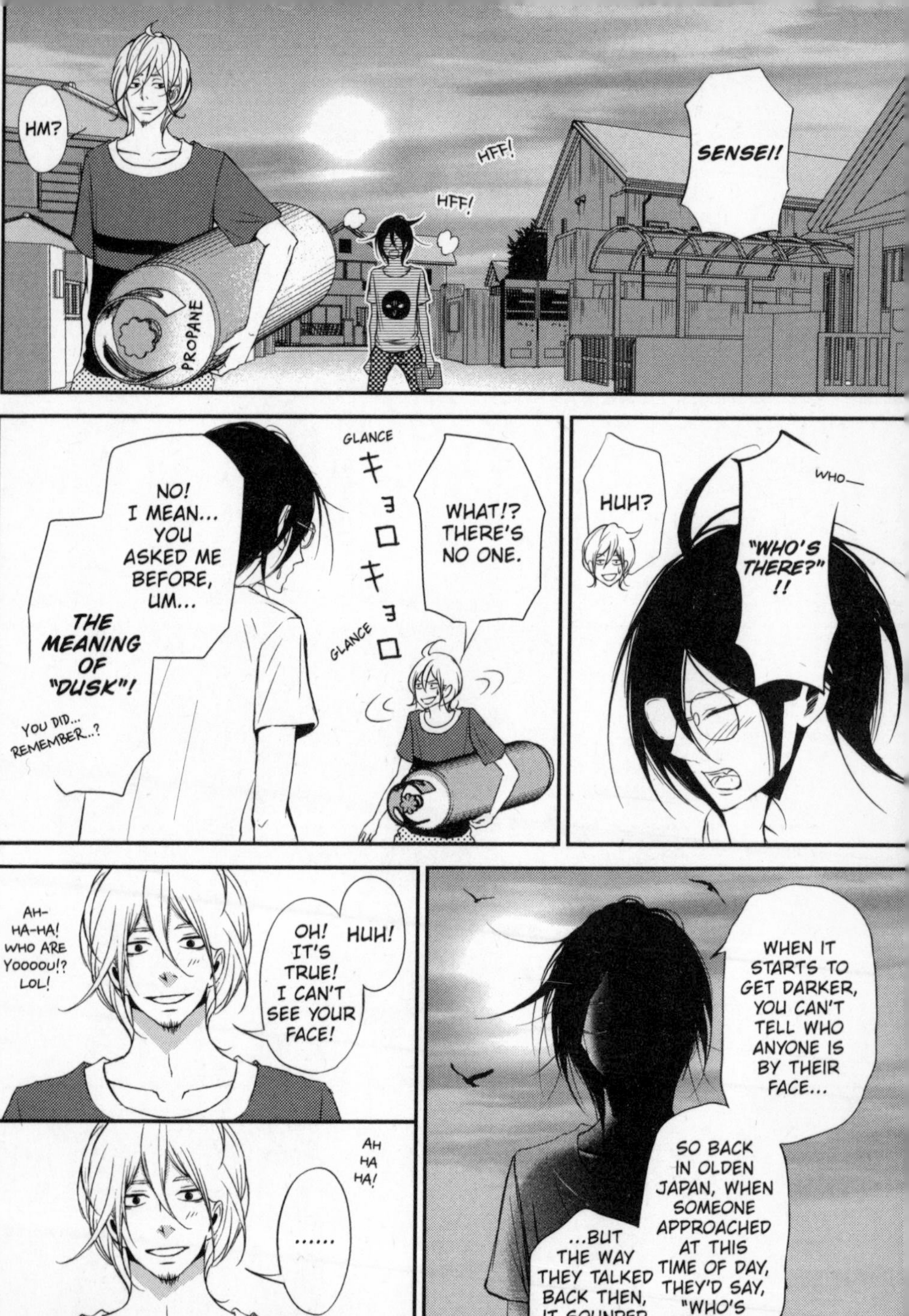
SENSEI!
HFF!
HFF!
HM?
PROPANE
WHO—
"WHO'S THERE?" !!
HUH?
WHAT!? THERE'S NO ONE.
GLANCE
キョロキョロ
GLANCE
NO! I MEAN... YOU ASKED ME BEFORE, UM... THE MEANING OF "DUSK"!
YOU DID... REMEMBER...?
WHEN IT STARTS TO GET DARKER, YOU CAN'T TELL WHO ANYONE IS BY THEIR FACE...
SO BACK IN OLDEN JAPAN, WHEN SOMEONE APPROACHED AT THIS TIME OF DAY, THEY'D SAY, "WHO'S THERE?"...
...BUT THE WAY THEY TALKED BACK THEN, IT SOUNDED LIKE THE WORD "DUSK," SO... I READ IT IN A BOOK...
HUH!
OH! IT'S TRUE! I CAN'T SEE YOUR FACE!
AH-HA-HA! WHO ARE YOOOOU!? LOL!
AH HA HA!
......

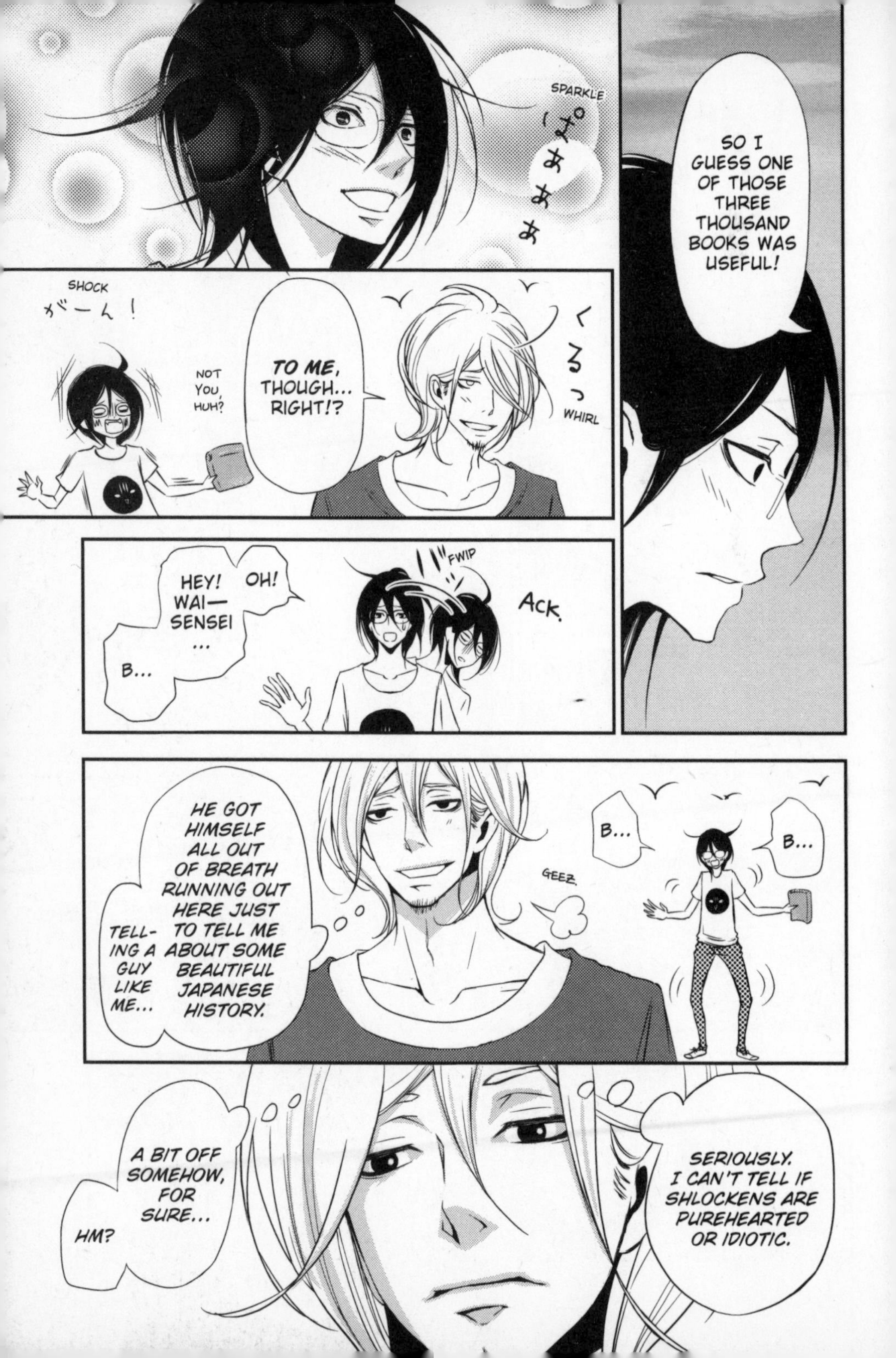
SO I GUESS ONE OF THOSE THREE THOUSAND BOOKS WAS USEFUL!
ぱあああ
SPARKLE
くるっ
WHIRL
TO ME, THOUGH... RIGHT!?
がーん!
SHOCK
NOT YOU, HUH?
FWIP
ACK.
OH!
HEY! WAI— SENSEI ...
B...
B...
B...
GEEZ.
HE GOT HIMSELF ALL OUT OF BREATH RUNNING OUT HERE JUST TO TELL ME ABOUT SOME BEAUTIFUL JAPANESE HISTORY.
TELL-ING A GUY LIKE ME...
SERIOUSLY. I CAN'T TELL IF SHLOCKENS ARE PUREHEARTED OR IDIOTIC.
A BIT OFF SOMEHOW, FOR SURE...
HM?

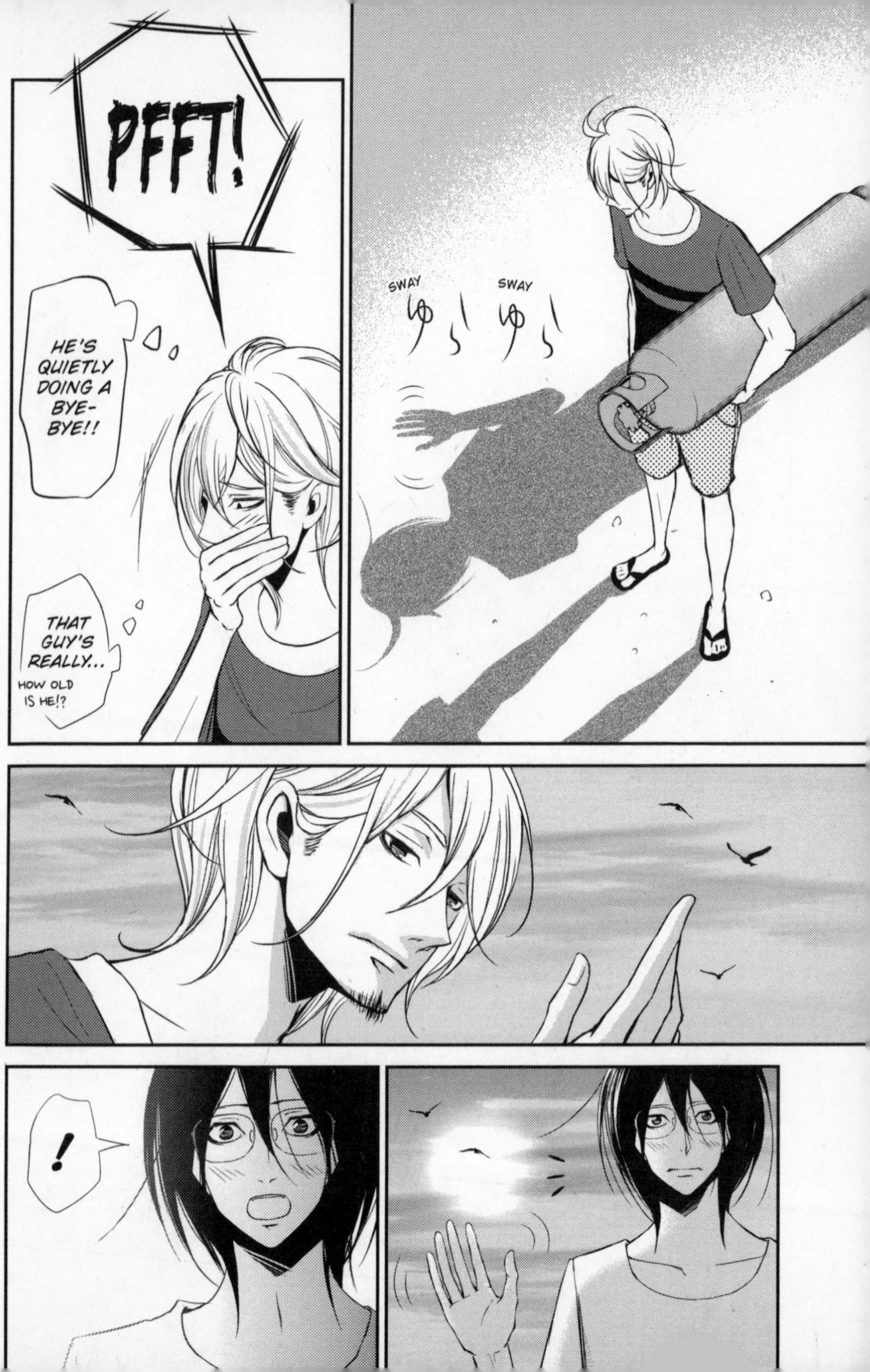
SWAY
ゆら
SWAY
ゆら
PFFT!
HE'S QUIETLY DOING A BYE-BYE!!
THAT GUY'S REALLY...
HOW OLD IS HE!?
!

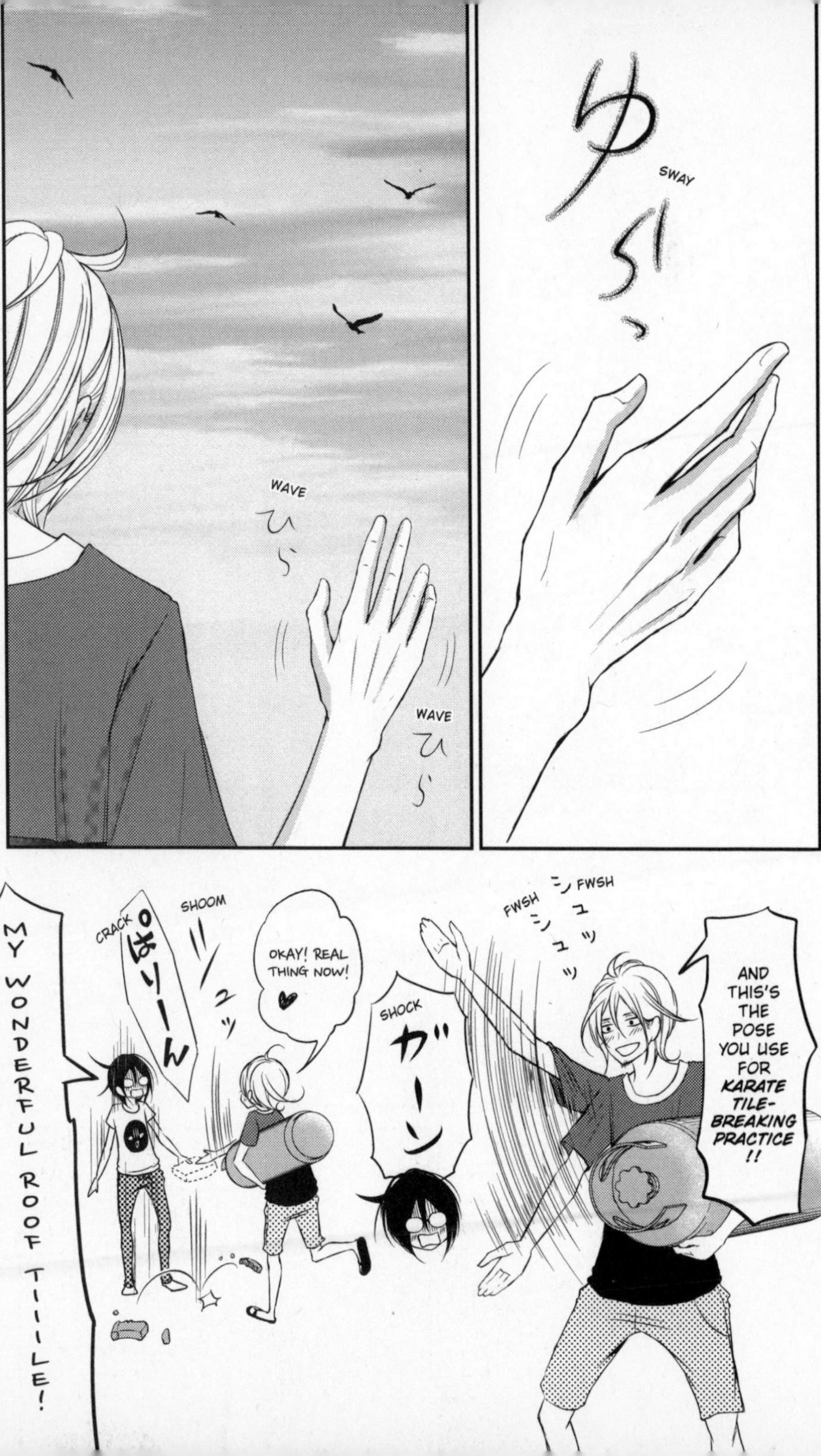
ゆらっ
SWAY
WAVE
ひら
WAVE
ひら
FWSH
シュッ
FWSH
シュッ
AND THIS'S THE POSE YOU USE FOR *KARATE TILE-BREAKING PRACTICE* !!
SHOCK
ガーン
OKAY! REAL THING NOW! ♥
SHOOM
CRACK
ぱりーん
MY WONDERFUL ROOF TIIIILE!

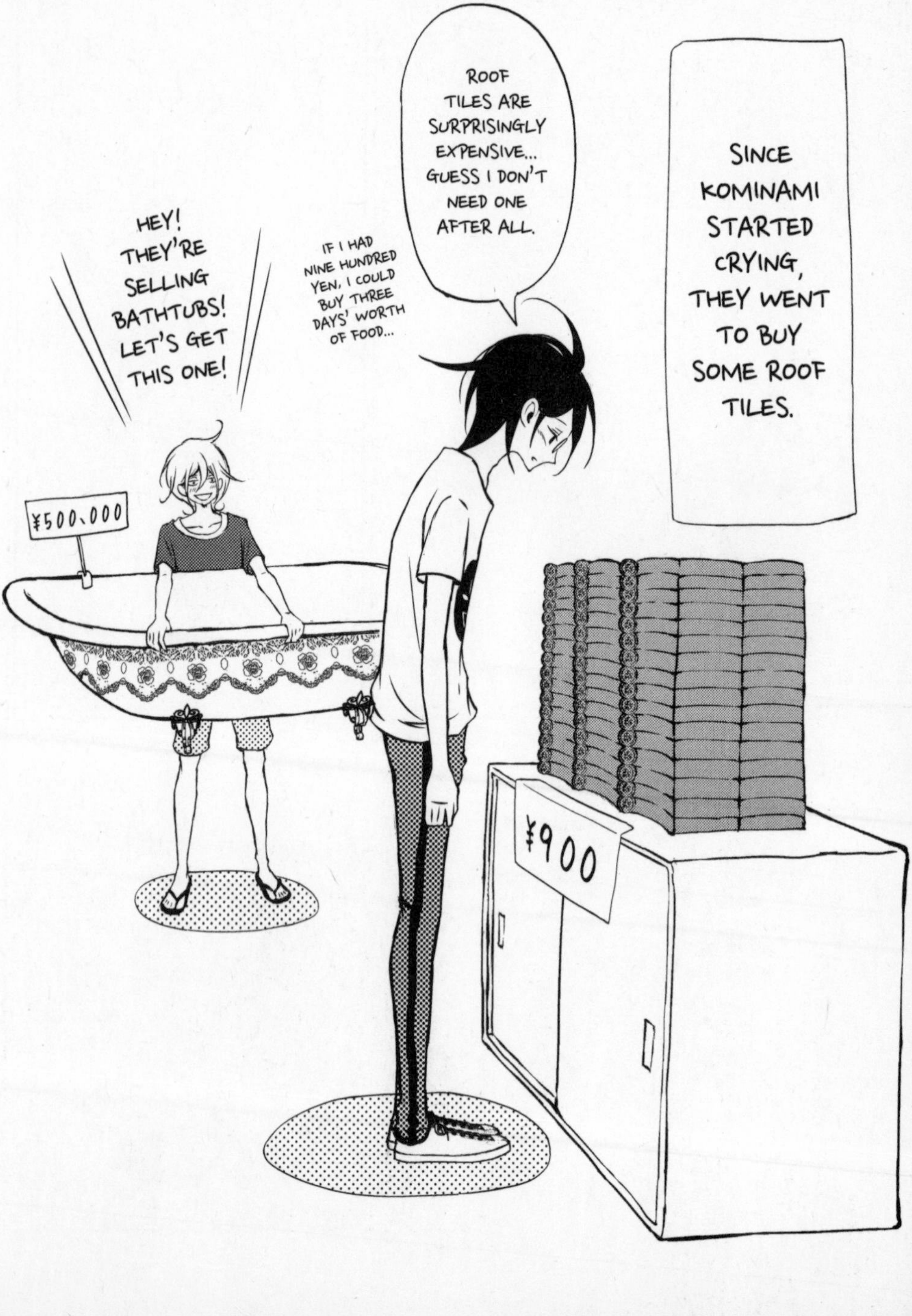
SINCE KOMINAMI STARTED CRYING, THEY WENT TO BUY SOME ROOF TILES.
ROOF TILES ARE SURPRISINGLY EXPENSIVE... GUESS I DON'T NEED ONE AFTER ALL.
¥900
IF I HAD NINE HUNDRED YEN, I COULD BUY THREE DAYS' WORTH OF FOOD...
HEY! THEY'RE SELLING BATHTUBS! LET'S GET THIS ONE!
¥500,000

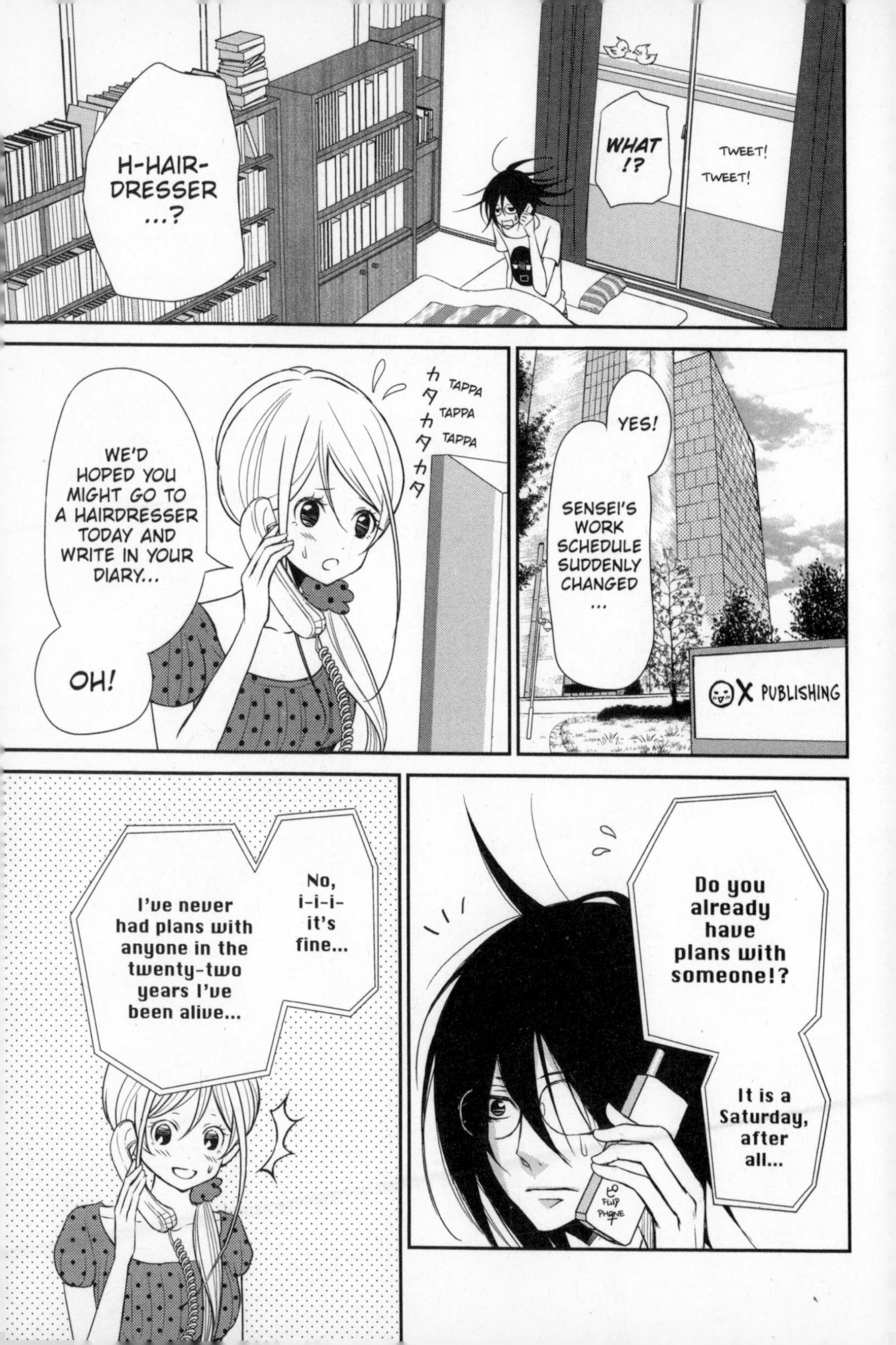
WHAT!?
TWEET!
TWEET!
H-HAIR-DRESSER ...?
YES!
SENSEI'S WORK SCHEDULE SUDDENLY CHANGED ...
PUBLISHING
カタカタカタ
TAPPA
TAPPA
TAPPA
WE'D HOPED YOU MIGHT GO TO A HAIRDRESSER TODAY AND WRITE IN YOUR DIARY...
OH!
Do you already have plans with someone!?
It is a Saturday, after all...
FLIP PHONE
No, i-i-i-it's fine...
I've never had plans with anyone in the twenty-two years I've been alive...

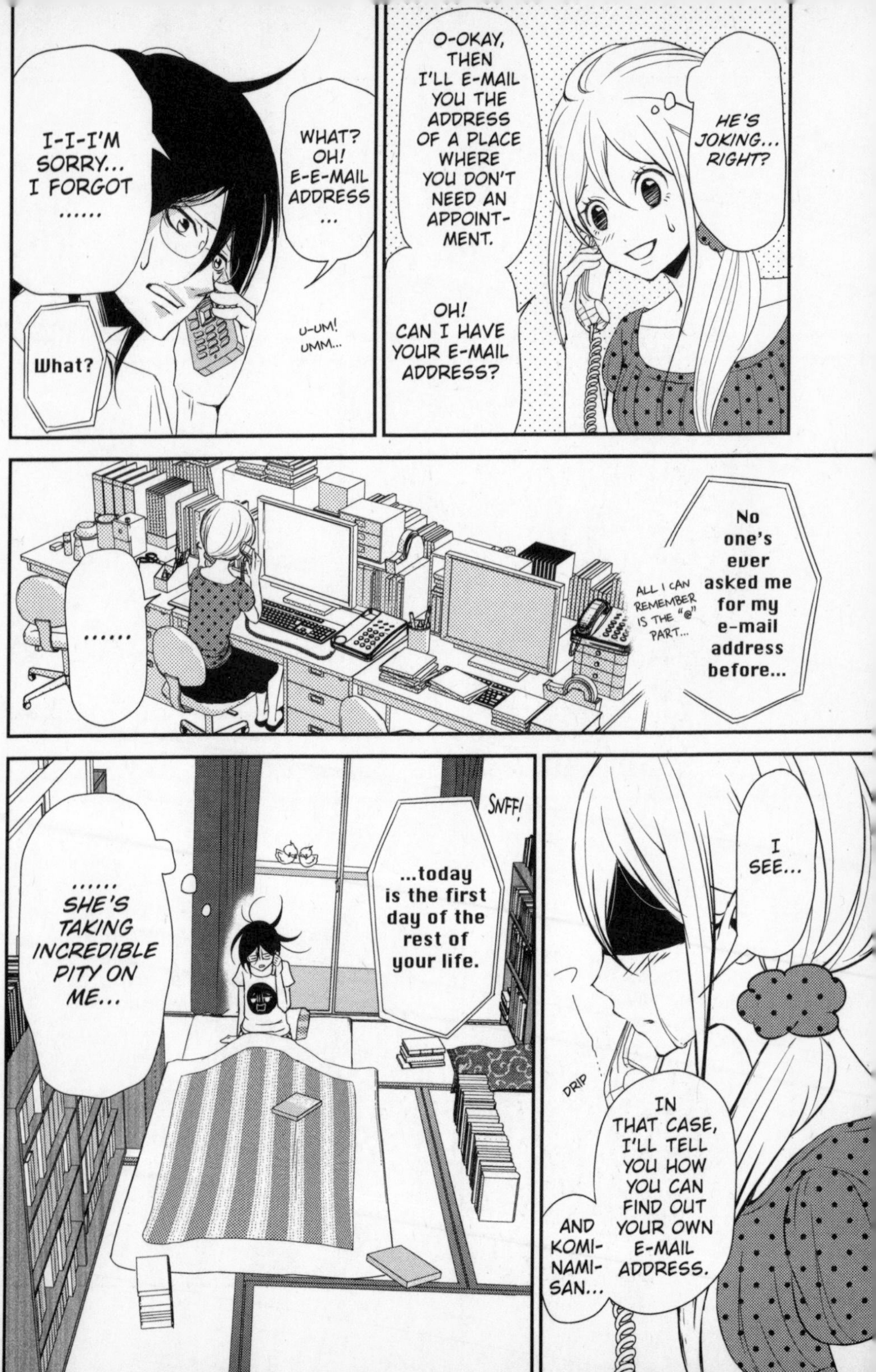
HE'S JOKING... RIGHT?
O-OKAY, THEN I'LL E-MAIL YOU THE ADDRESS OF A PLACE WHERE YOU DON'T NEED AN APPOINTMENT.
OH! CAN I HAVE YOUR E-MAIL ADDRESS?
WHAT? OH! E-E-MAIL ADDRESS ...
I-I-I'M SORRY... I FORGOT ......
U-UM! UMM...
What?
No one's ever asked me for my e-mail address before...
ALL I CAN REMEMBER IS THE "@" PART...
......
I SEE...
DRIP
IN THAT CASE, I'LL TELL YOU HOW YOU CAN FIND OUT YOUR OWN E-MAIL ADDRESS.
AND KOMI-NAMI-SAN...
SNFF!
...today is the first day of the rest of your life.
...... SHE'S TAKING INCREDIBLE PITY ON ME...

3 VS. THE HAIRDRESSER

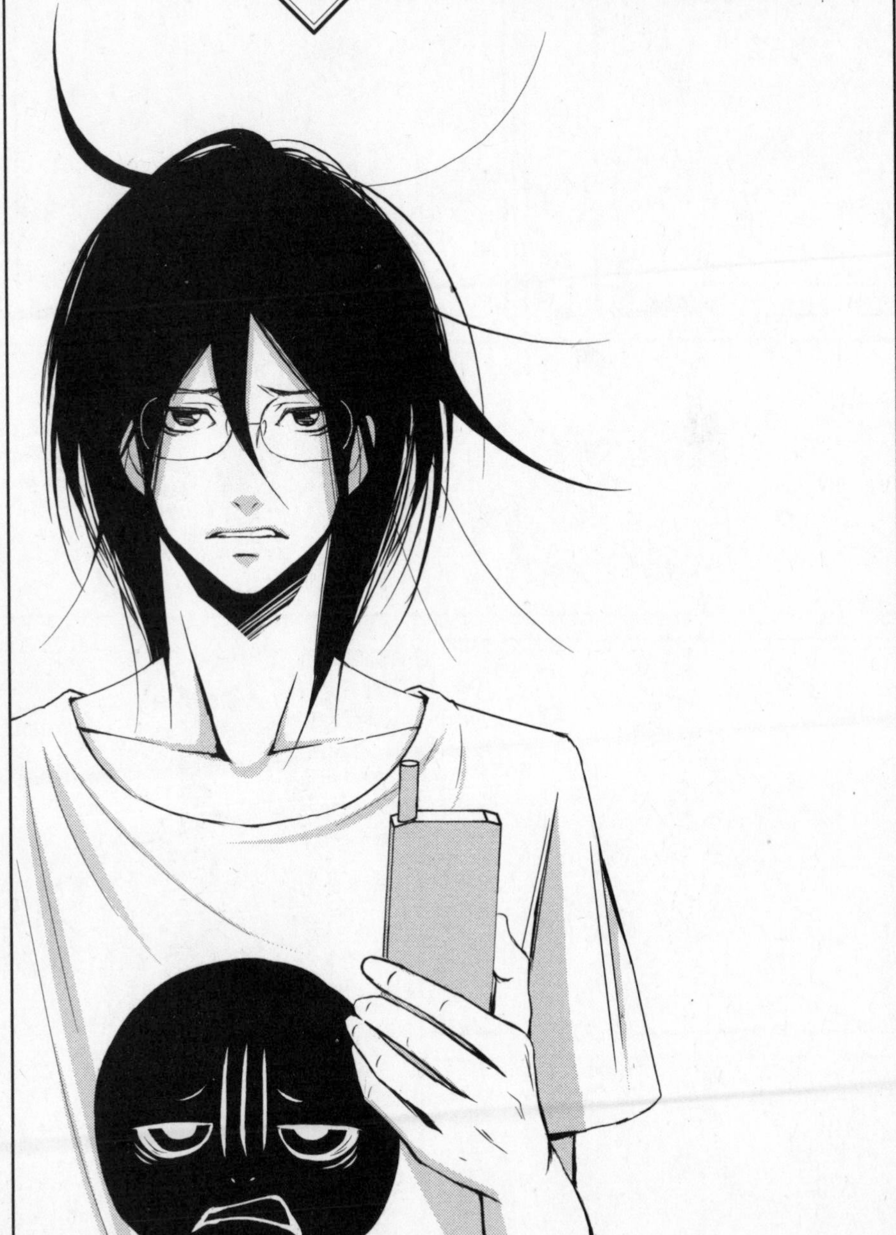

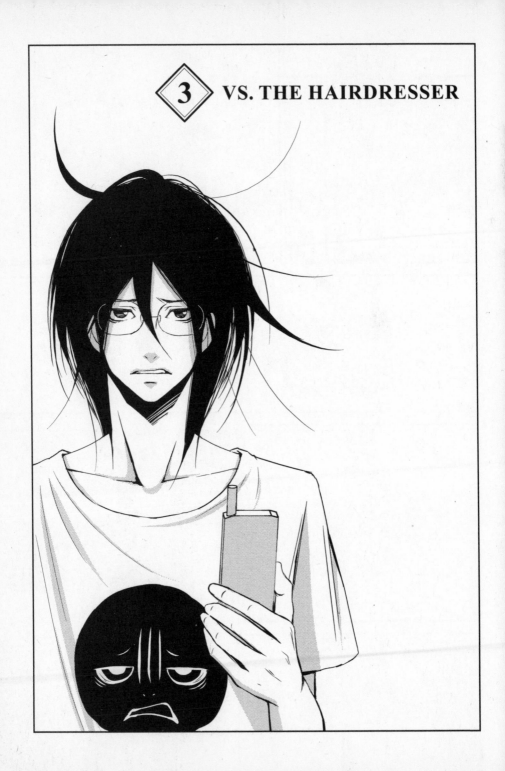

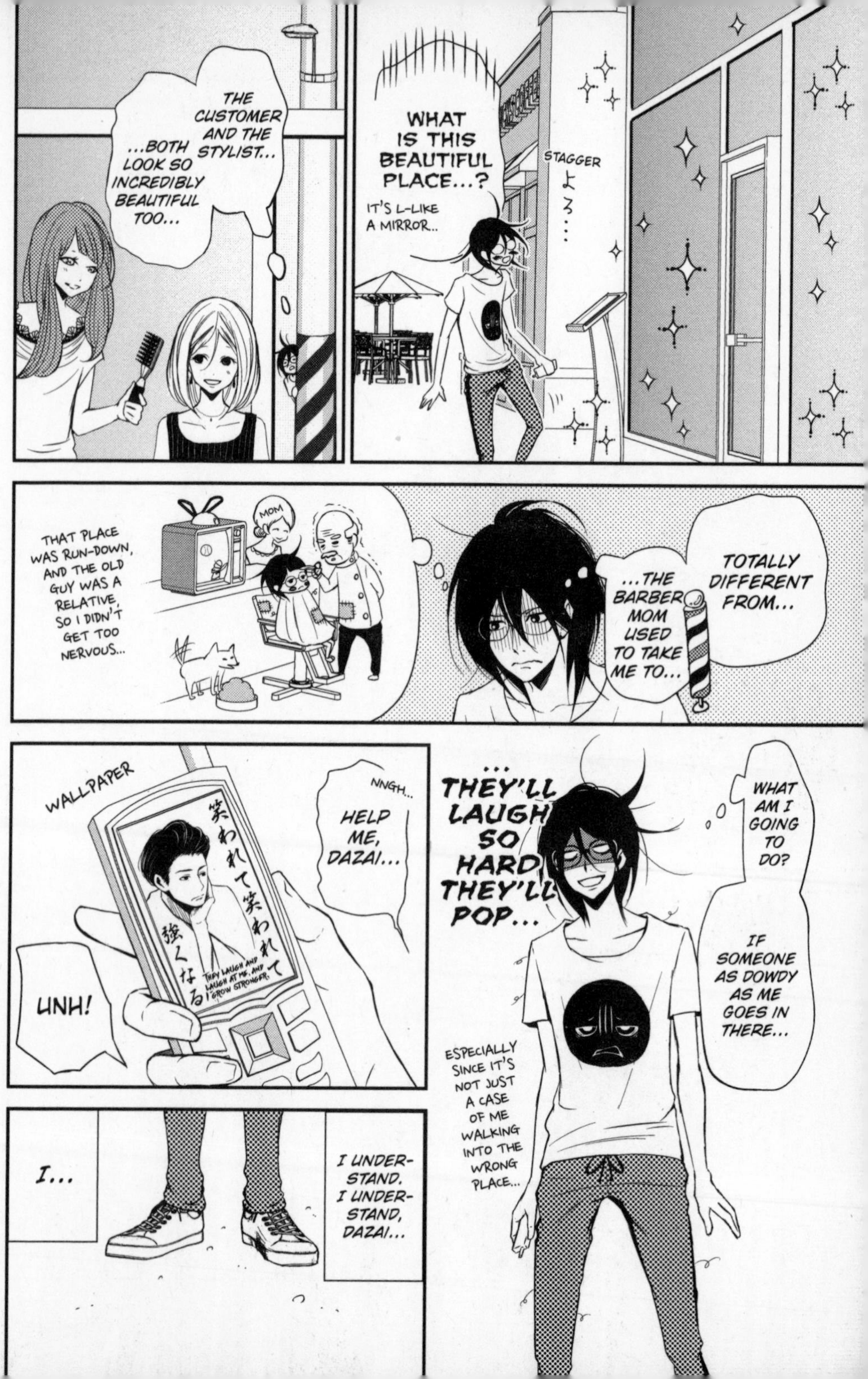
WHAT IS THIS BEAUTIFUL PLACE...?
STAGGER
よろ…
IT'S L-LIKE A MIRROR..
THE CUSTOMER AND THE STYLIST...
...BOTH LOOK SO INCREDIBLY BEAUTIFUL TOO...
TOTALLY DIFFERENT FROM...
...THE BARBER MOM USED TO TAKE ME TO...
MOM
THAT PLACE WAS RUN-DOWN, AND THE OLD GUY WAS A RELATIVE, SO I DIDN'T GET TOO NERVOUS...
WHAT AM I GOING TO DO?
IF SOMEONE AS DOWDY AS ME GOES IN THERE...
...THEY'LL LAUGH SO HARD THEY'LL POP...
ESPECIALLY SINCE IT'S NOT JUST A CASE OF ME WALKING INTO THE WRONG PLACE...
NNGH...
HELP ME, DAZAI...
WALLPAPER
笑われて笑われて強くなる
They laugh and laugh at me, and I grow stronger.
UNH!
I UNDERSTAND. I UNDERSTAND, DAZAI...
I...

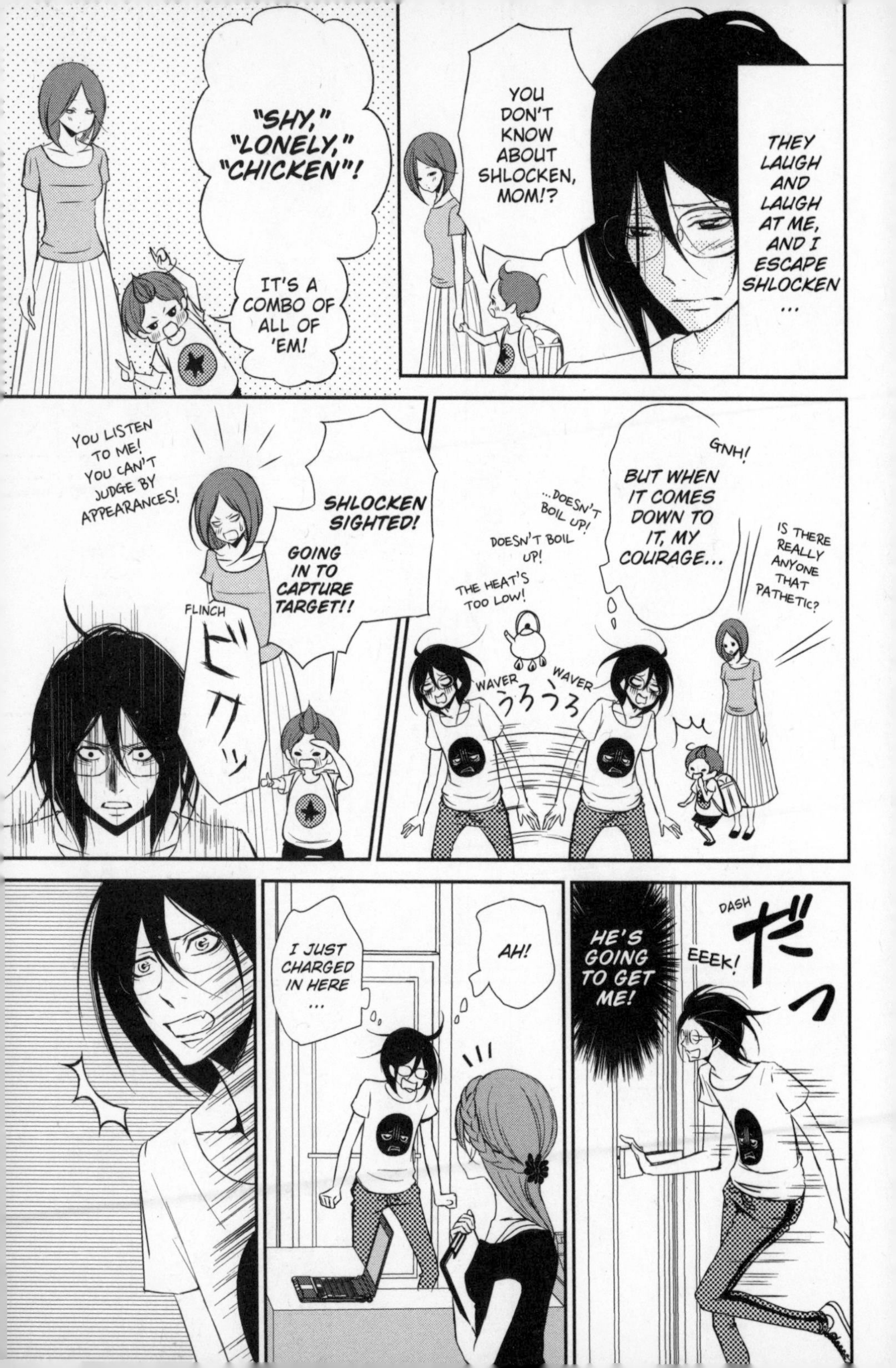

THEY LAUGH AND LAUGH AT ME, AND I ESCAPE SHLOCKEN...
YOU DON'T KNOW ABOUT SHLOCKEN, MOM!?
"SHY," "LONELY," "CHICKEN"!
IT'S A COMBO OF ALL OF 'EM!
GNH!
BUT WHEN IT COMES DOWN TO IT, MY COURAGE...
IS THERE REALLY ANYONE THAT PATHETIC?
...DOESN'T BOIL UP!
DOESN'T BOIL UP!
THE HEAT'S TOO LOW!
WAVER WAVER
うろうろ
SHLOCKEN SIGHTED!
GOING IN TO CAPTURE TARGET!!
YOU LISTEN TO ME! YOU CAN'T JUDGE BY APPEARANCES!
FLINCH
ビクッ
DASH
だっ
EEEK!
HE'S GOING TO GET ME!
AH!
I JUST CHARGED IN HERE...

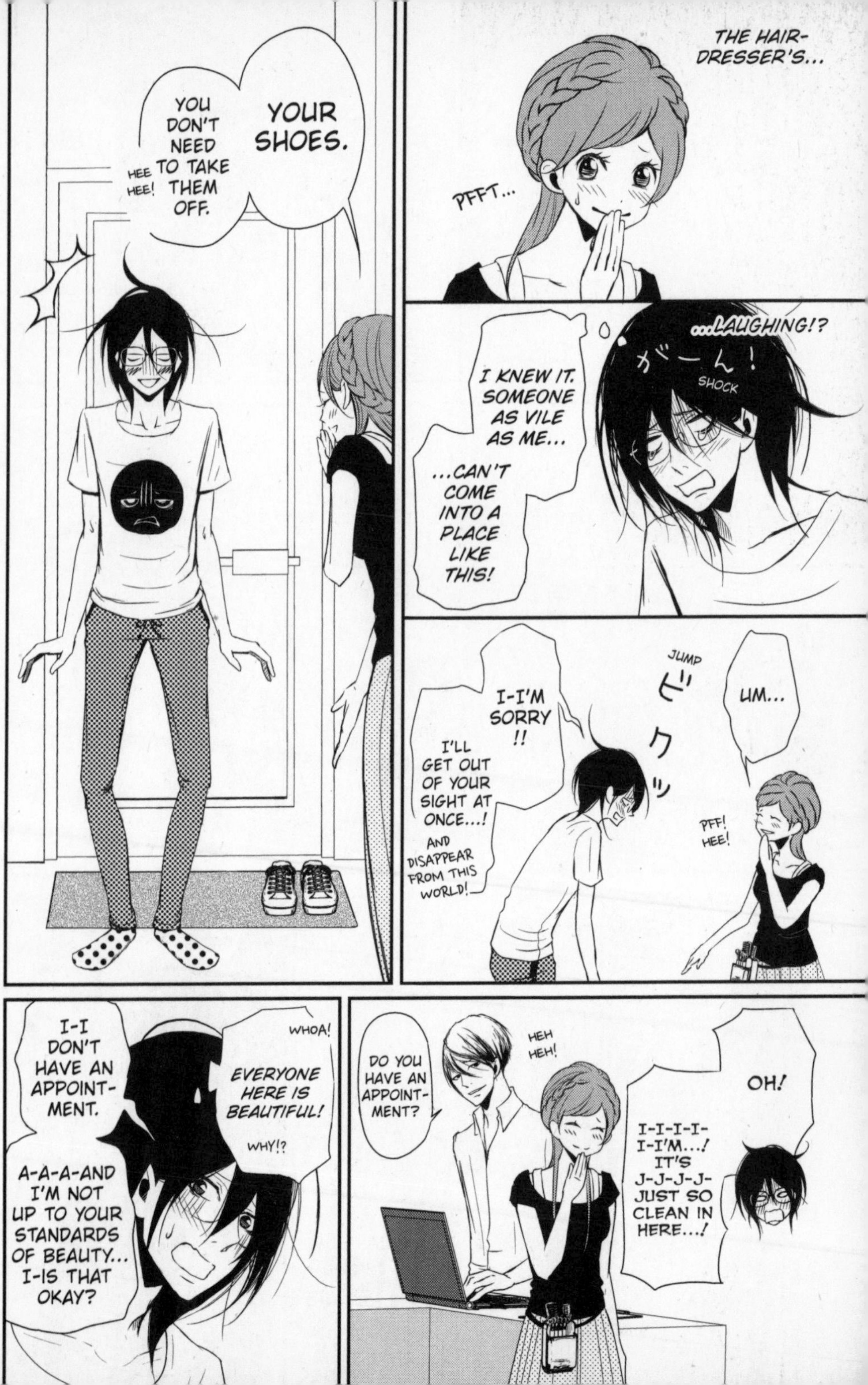
THE HAIR-DRESSER'S...
PFFT...
...LAUGHING!?
がーん！
SHOCK
I KNEW IT. SOMEONE AS VILE AS ME...
...CAN'T COME INTO A PLACE LIKE THIS!
UM...
JUMP
ビクッ
PFF! HEE!
I-I'M SORRY !!
I'LL GET OUT OF YOUR SIGHT AT ONCE...!
AND DISAPPEAR FROM THIS WORLD!
YOUR SHOES.
YOU DON'T NEED TO TAKE THEM OFF.
HEE HEE!
OH!
I-I-I-I-I'M...! IT'S J-J-J-JUST SO CLEAN IN HERE...!
HEH HEH!
DO YOU HAVE AN APPOINT-MENT?
WHOA!
EVERYONE HERE IS BEAUTIFUL!
WHY!?
I-I DON'T HAVE AN APPOINT-MENT.
A-A-A-AND I'M NOT UP TO YOUR STANDARDS OF BEAUTY... I-IS THAT OKAY?

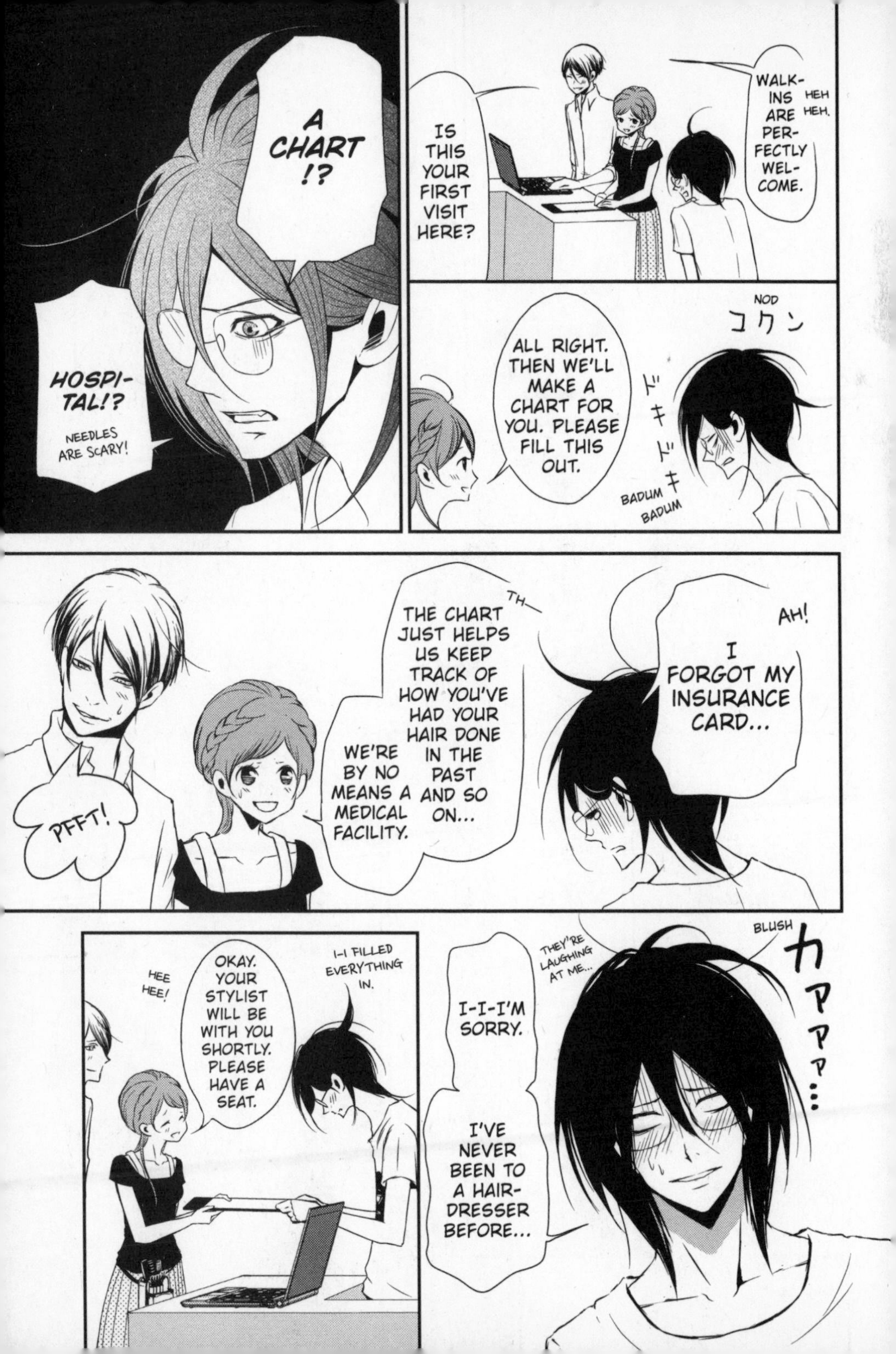
WALK-INS ARE PERFECTLY WELCOME.
HEH HEH.
IS THIS YOUR FIRST VISIT HERE?
NOD
コクン
ALL RIGHT. THEN WE'LL MAKE A CHART FOR YOU. PLEASE FILL THIS OUT.
ドキドキ
BADUM BADUM
A CHART!?
HOSPITAL!?
NEEDLES ARE SCARY!
AH!
I FORGOT MY INSURANCE CARD...
TH—
THE CHART JUST HELPS US KEEP TRACK OF HOW YOU'VE HAD YOUR HAIR DONE IN THE PAST AND SO ON...
WE'RE BY NO MEANS A MEDICAL FACILITY.
PFFT!
BLUSH
カァァ...
THEY'RE LAUGHING AT ME...
I-I-I'M SORRY.
I'VE NEVER BEEN TO A HAIR-DRESSER BEFORE...
I-I FILLED EVERYTHING IN.
OKAY. YOUR STYLIST WILL BE WITH YOU SHORTLY. PLEASE HAVE A SEAT.
HEE HEE!

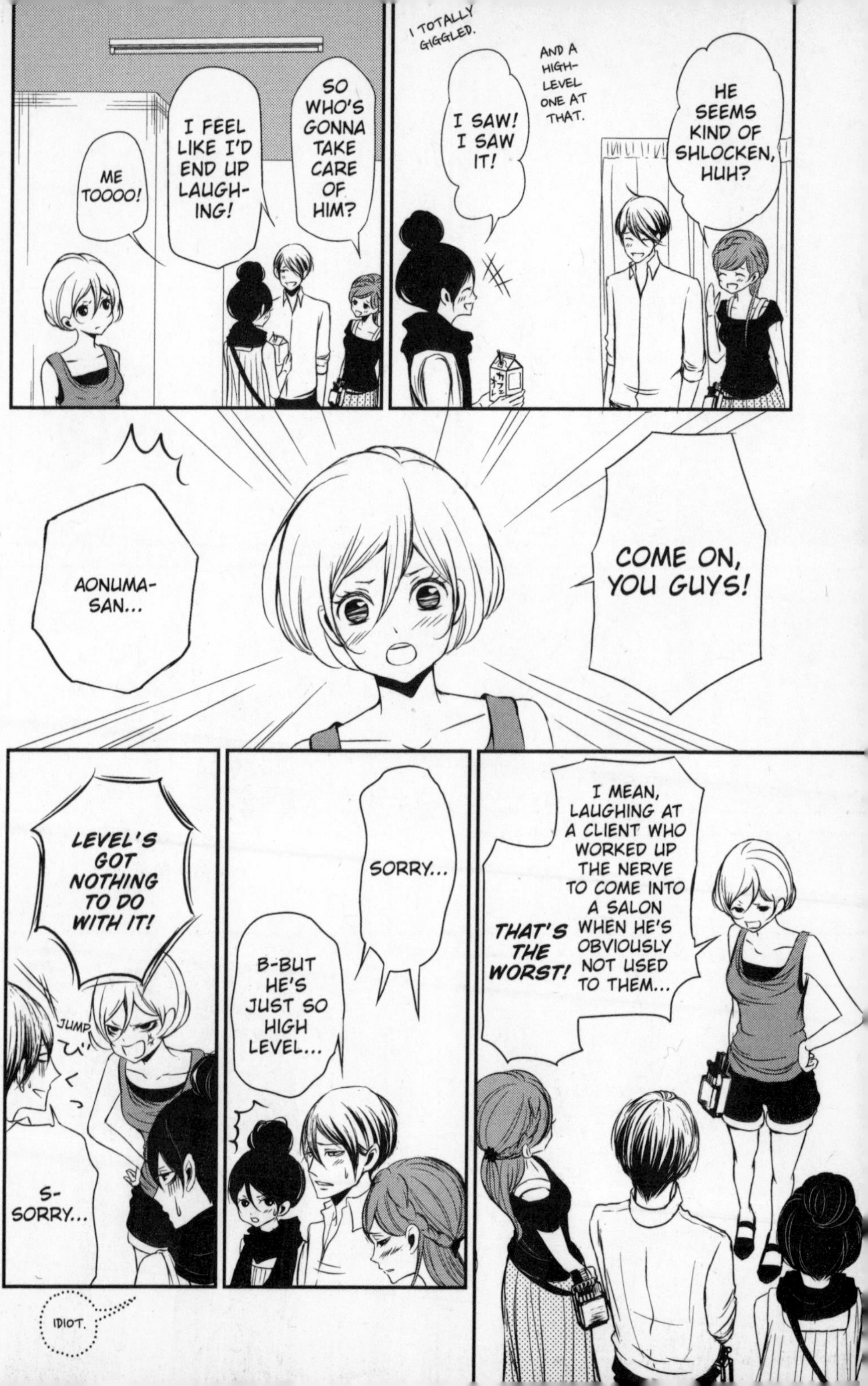

HE SEEMS KIND OF SHLOCKEN, HUH?
AND A HIGH-LEVEL ONE AT THAT.
I SAW! I SAW IT!
I TOTALLY GIGGLED.
SO WHO'S GONNA TAKE CARE OF HIM?
I FEEL LIKE I'D END UP LAUGHING!
ME TOOOO!
COME ON, YOU GUYS!
AONUMA-SAN...
I MEAN, LAUGHING AT A CLIENT WHO WORKED UP THE NERVE TO COME INTO A SALON WHEN HE'S OBVIOUSLY NOT USED TO THEM...
THAT'S THE WORST!
SORRY...
B-BUT HE'S JUST SO HIGH LEVEL...
LEVEL'S GOT NOTHING TO DO WITH IT!
JUMP
S-SORRY...
IDIOT.

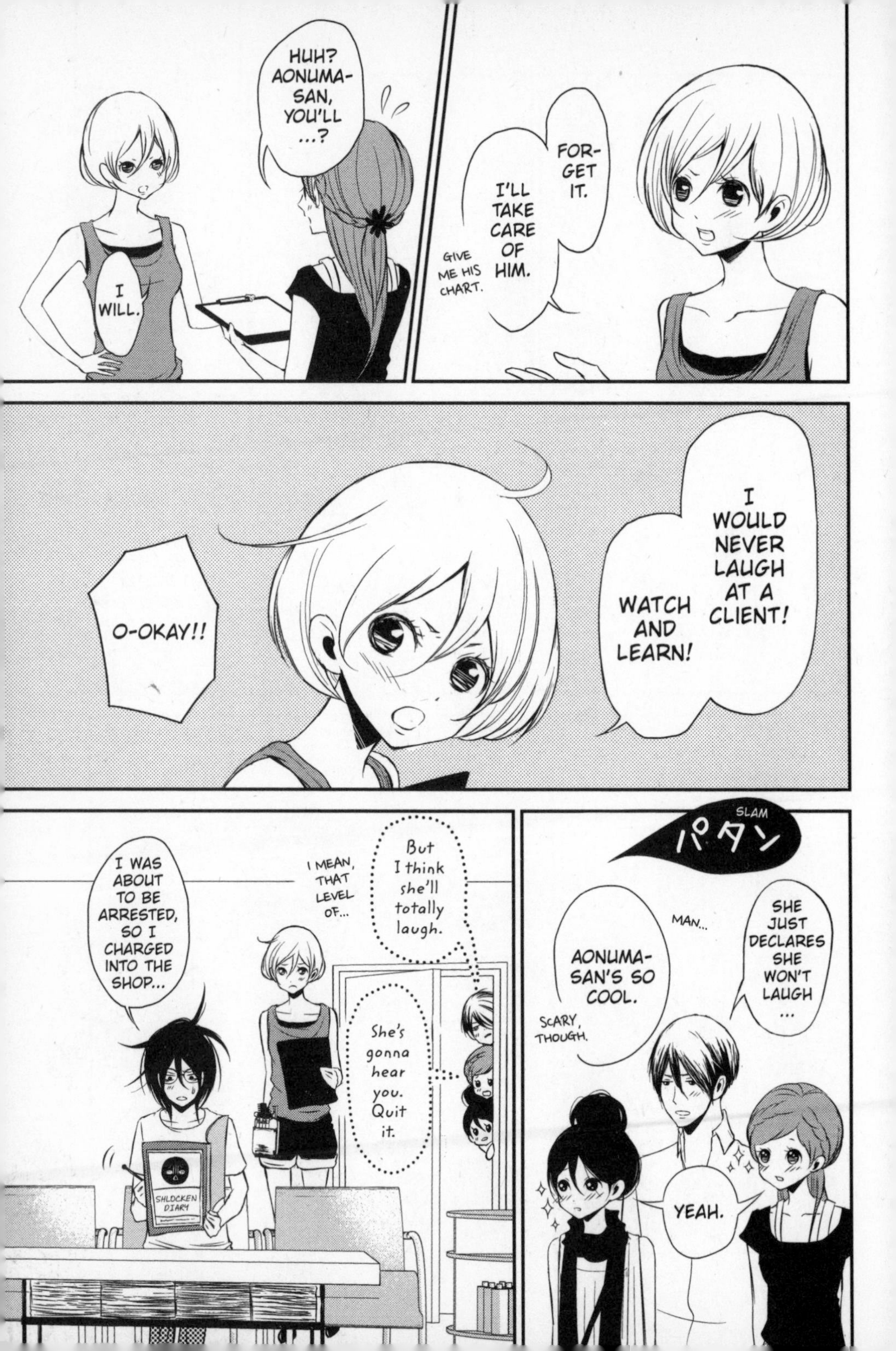
FOR-GET IT.
I'LL TAKE CARE OF HIM.
GIVE ME HIS CHART.
HUH? AONUMA-SAN, YOU'LL ...?
I WILL.
I WOULD NEVER LAUGH AT A CLIENT!
WATCH AND LEARN!
O-OKAY!!
SLAM
パタン
SHE JUST DECLARES SHE WON'T LAUGH ...
MAN...
AONUMA-SAN'S SO COOL.
SCARY, THOUGH.
YEAH.
But I think she'll totally laugh.
I MEAN, THAT LEVEL OF...
She's gonna hear you. Quit it.
I WAS ABOUT TO BE ARRESTED, SO I CHARGED INTO THE SHOP...
SHLOCKEN DIARY

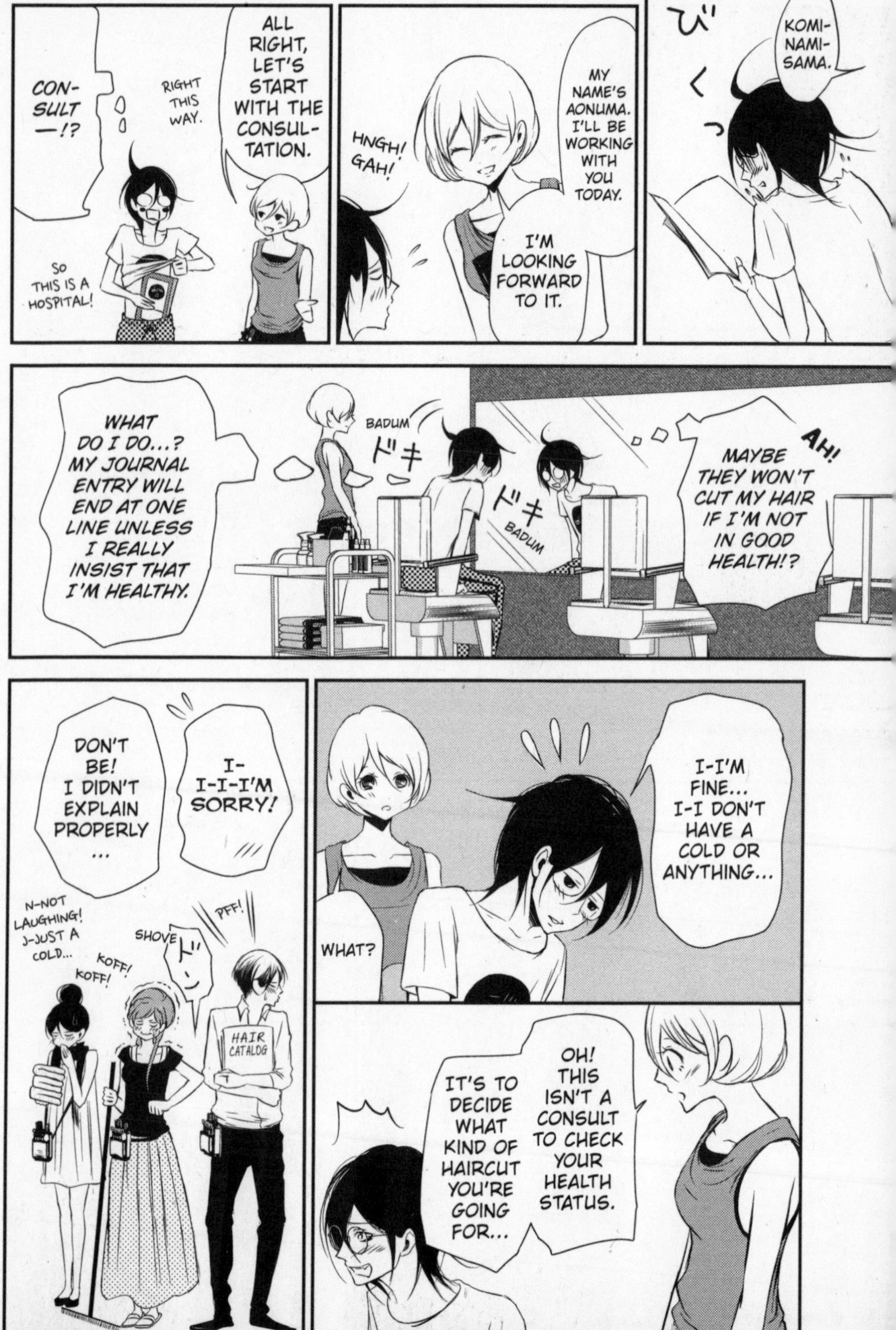
JUMP
びくっ
KOMI-NAMI-SAMA.
MY NAME'S AONUMA. I'LL BE WORKING WITH YOU TODAY.
HNGH! GAH!
I'M LOOKING FORWARD TO IT.
ALL RIGHT, LET'S START WITH THE CONSULTATION.
RIGHT THIS WAY.
CON-SULT—!?
SO THIS IS A HOSPITAL!
AH!
MAYBE THEY WON'T CUT MY HAIR IF I'M NOT IN GOOD HEALTH!?
BADUM
ドキ
BADUM
ドキ
WHAT DO I DO...? MY JOURNAL ENTRY WILL END AT ONE LINE UNLESS I REALLY INSIST THAT I'M HEALTHY.
I-I'M FINE... I-I DON'T HAVE A COLD OR ANYTHING...
WHAT?
OH! THIS ISN'T A CONSULT TO CHECK YOUR HEALTH STATUS.
IT'S TO DECIDE WHAT KIND OF HAIRCUT YOU'RE GOING FOR...
I-I-I-I'M SORRY!
DON'T BE! I DIDN'T EXPLAIN PROPERLY...
PFF!
SHOVE
ドン
N-NOT LAUGHING! J-JUST A COLD...
KOFF! KOFF!
HAIR CATALOG

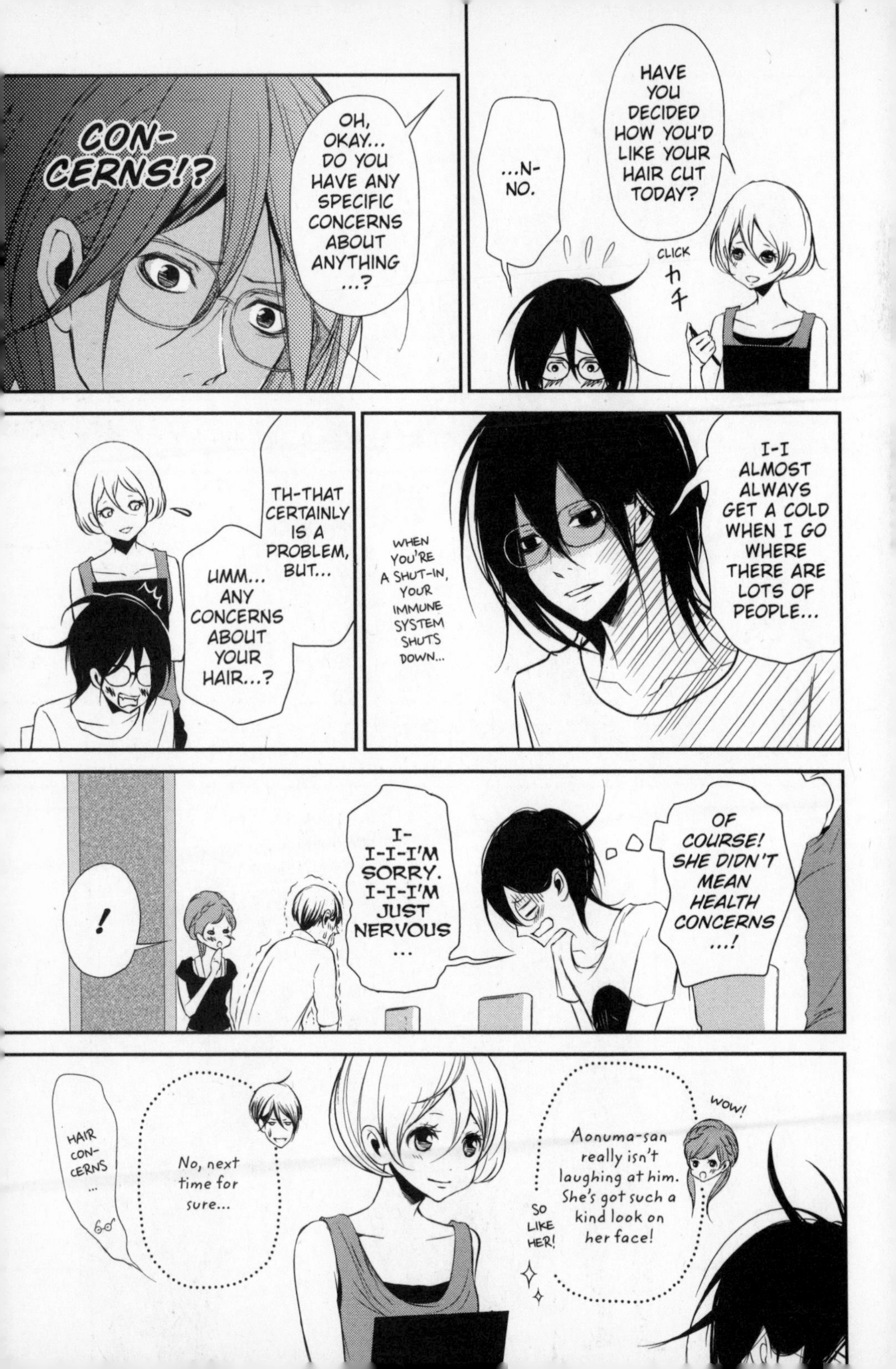
HAVE YOU DECIDED HOW YOU'D LIKE YOUR HAIR CUT TODAY?
CLICK
カチ
...N-NO.
OH, OKAY... DO YOU HAVE ANY SPECIFIC CONCERNS ABOUT ANYTHING ...?
CON-CERNS!?
I-I ALMOST ALWAYS GET A COLD WHEN I GO WHERE THERE ARE LOTS OF PEOPLE...
WHEN YOU'RE A SHUT-IN, YOUR IMMUNE SYSTEM SHUTS DOWN...
TH-THAT CERTAINLY IS A PROBLEM, BUT...
UMM... ANY CONCERNS ABOUT YOUR HAIR...?
OF COURSE! SHE DIDN'T MEAN HEALTH CONCERNS ...!
I- I-I-I'M SORRY. I-I-I'M JUST NERVOUS ...
!
WOW!
Aonuma-san really isn't laughing at him. She's got such a kind look on her face!
SO LIKE HER!
No, next time for sure...
HAIR CON-CERNS ...

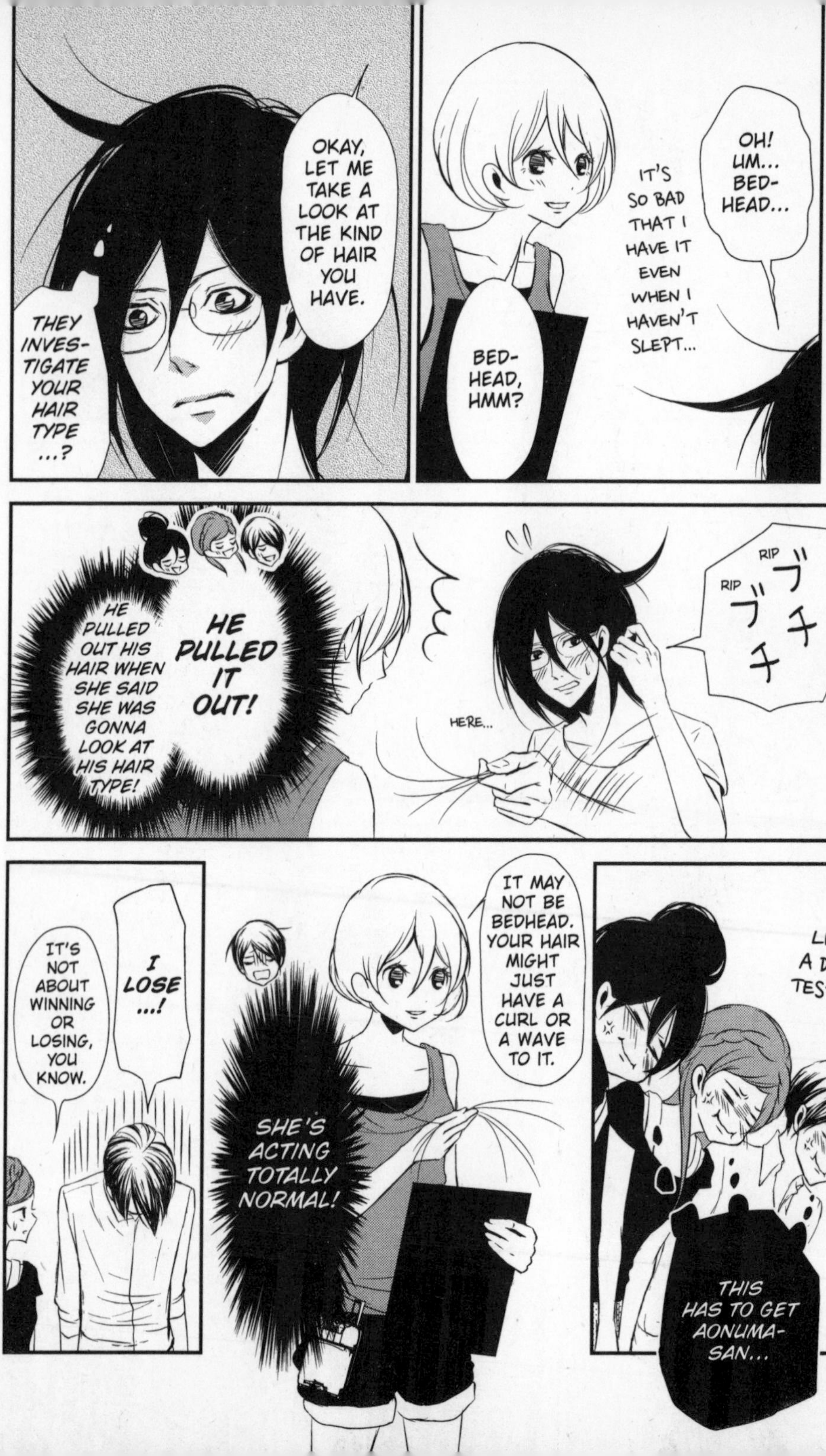
OH! UM... BED-HEAD...
IT'S SO BAD THAT I HAVE IT EVEN WHEN I HAVEN'T SLEPT...
BED-HEAD, HMM?
OKAY, LET ME TAKE A LOOK AT THE KIND OF HAIR YOU HAVE.
THEY INVESTIGATE YOUR HAIR TYPE ...?
ブチ RIP
ブチ RIP
HERE...
HE PULLED IT OUT!
HE PULLED OUT HIS HAIR WHEN SHE SAID SHE WAS GONNA LOOK AT HIS HAIR TYPE!
LIKE A DNA TEST!?
THIS HAS TO GET AONUMA-SAN...
IT MAY NOT BE BEDHEAD. YOUR HAIR MIGHT JUST HAVE A CURL OR A WAVE TO IT.
SHE'S ACTING TOTALLY NORMAL!
I LOSE ...!
IT'S NOT ABOUT WINNING OR LOSING, YOU KNOW.

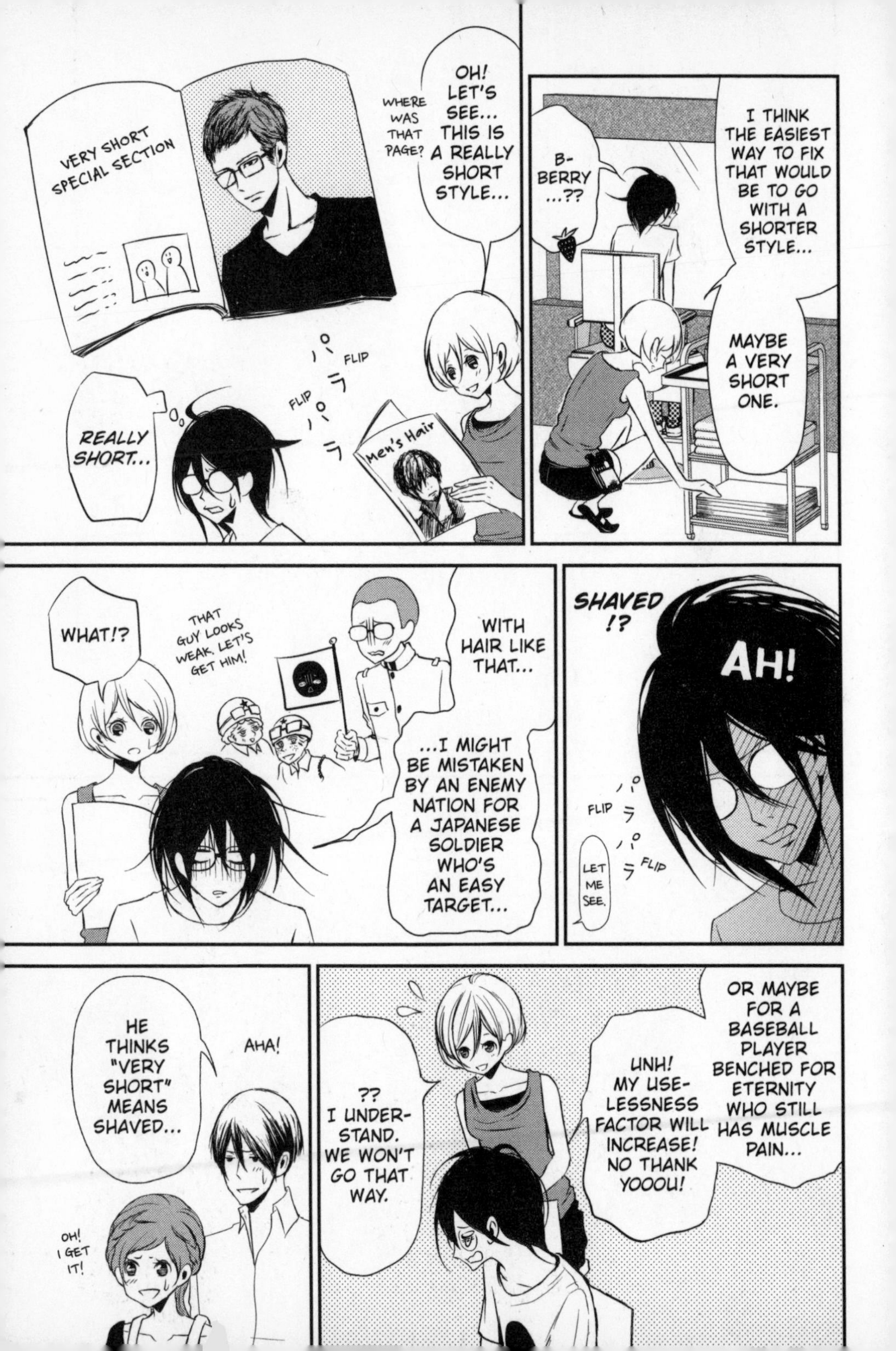
I THINK THE EASIEST WAY TO FIX THAT WOULD BE TO GO WITH A SHORTER STYLE...
MAYBE A VERY SHORT ONE.
B-BERRY...??
OH! LET'S SEE... THIS IS A REALLY SHORT STYLE...
WHERE WAS THAT PAGE?
VERY SHORT SPECIAL SECTION
Men's Hair
パラ FLIP
パラ FLIP
REALLY SHORT...
SHAVED!?
AH!
パラ FLIP
パラ FLIP
LET ME SEE.
WITH HAIR LIKE THAT...
...I MIGHT BE MISTAKEN BY AN ENEMY NATION FOR A JAPANESE SOLDIER WHO'S AN EASY TARGET...
THAT GUY LOOKS WEAK. LET'S GET HIM!
WHAT!?
OR MAYBE FOR A BASEBALL PLAYER BENCHED FOR ETERNITY WHO STILL HAS MUSCLE PAIN...
UNH! MY USELESSNESS FACTOR WILL INCREASE! NO THANK YOOOU!
?? I UNDERSTAND. WE WON'T GO THAT WAY.
HE THINKS "VERY SHORT" MEANS SHAVED...
AHA!
OH! I GET IT!

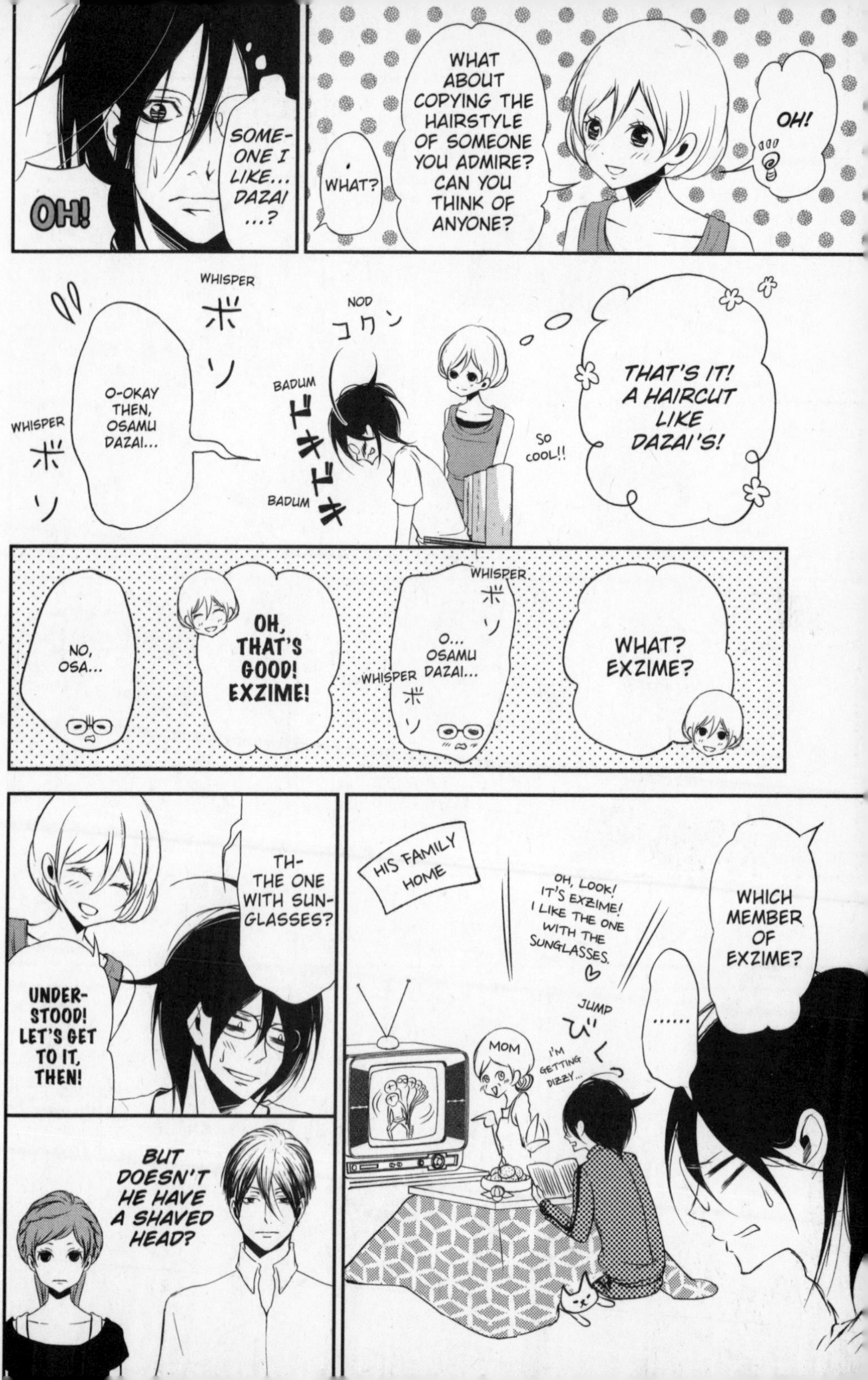
OH!
WHAT ABOUT COPYING THE HAIRSTYLE OF SOMEONE YOU ADMIRE? CAN YOU THINK OF ANYONE?
WHAT?
SOME-ONE I LIKE... DAZAI ...?
OH!
THAT'S IT! A HAIRCUT LIKE DAZAI'S!
SO COOL!!
NOD コクン
BADUM ドキドキ BADUM
WHISPER ボソ
O-OKAY THEN, OSAMU DAZAI...
WHISPER ボソ
WHAT? EXZIME?
WHISPER ボソ
O... OSAMU DAZAI...
WHISPER ボソ
OH, THAT'S GOOD! EXZIME!
NO, OSA...
WHICH MEMBER OF EXZIME?
......
HIS FAMILY HOME
OH, LOOK! IT'S EXZIME! I LIKE THE ONE WITH THE SUNGLASSES.
JUMP びく
MOM
I'M GETTING DIZZY...
TH-THE ONE WITH SUN-GLASSES?
UNDER-STOOD! LET'S GET TO IT, THEN!
BUT DOESN'T HE HAVE A SHAVED HEAD?

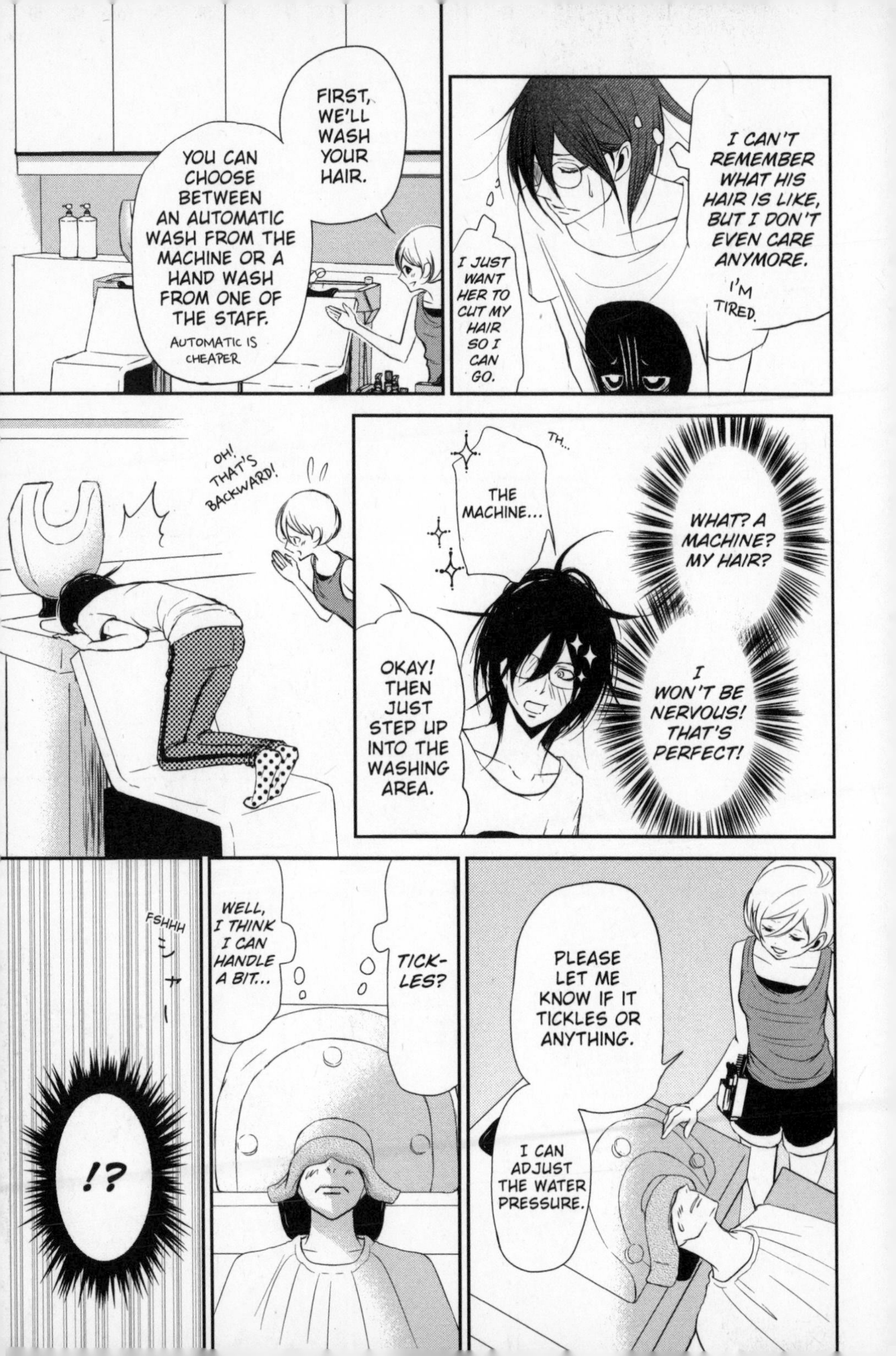
I CAN'T REMEMBER WHAT HIS HAIR IS LIKE, BUT I DON'T EVEN CARE ANYMORE.
I'M TIRED.
I JUST WANT HER TO CUT MY HAIR SO I CAN GO.
FIRST, WE'LL WASH YOUR HAIR.
YOU CAN CHOOSE BETWEEN AN AUTOMATIC WASH FROM THE MACHINE OR A HAND WASH FROM ONE OF THE STAFF.
AUTOMATIC IS CHEAPER
TH...
THE MACHINE...
WHAT? A MACHINE? MY HAIR?
I WON'T BE NERVOUS! THAT'S PERFECT!
OKAY! THEN JUST STEP UP INTO THE WASHING AREA.
OH! THAT'S BACKWARD!
PLEASE LET ME KNOW IF IT TICKLES OR ANYTHING.
I CAN ADJUST THE WATER PRESSURE.
TICKLES?
WELL, I THINK I CAN HANDLE A BIT...
FSHHH
!?

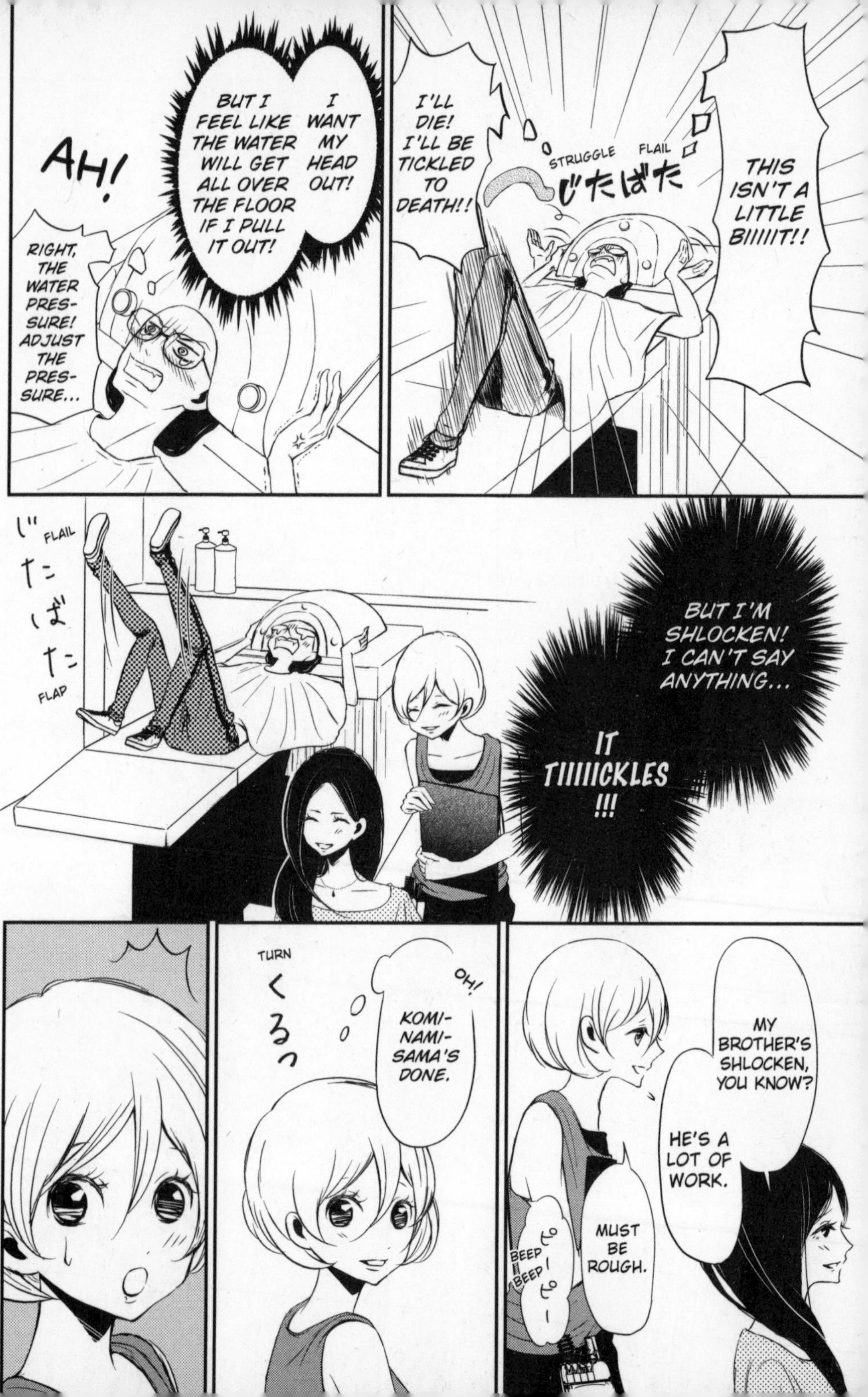
THIS ISN'T A LITTLE BIIIIIT!!
STRUGGLE FLAIL
じたばた
I'LL DIE! I'LL BE TICKLED TO DEATH!!
I WANT MY HEAD OUT!
BUT I FEEL LIKE THE WATER WILL GET ALL OVER THE FLOOR IF I PULL IT OUT!
AH!
RIGHT, THE WATER PRESSURE! ADJUST THE PRESSURE...
BUT I'M SHLOCKEN! I CAN'T SAY ANYTHING...
IT TIIIIICKLES!!!
FLAIL FLAP
じたばた
MY BROTHER'S SHLOCKEN, YOU KNOW?
HE'S A LOT OF WORK.
MUST BE ROUGH.
BEEP BEEP
ピーピー
OH!
KOMINAMI-SAMA'S DONE.
TURN
くるっ

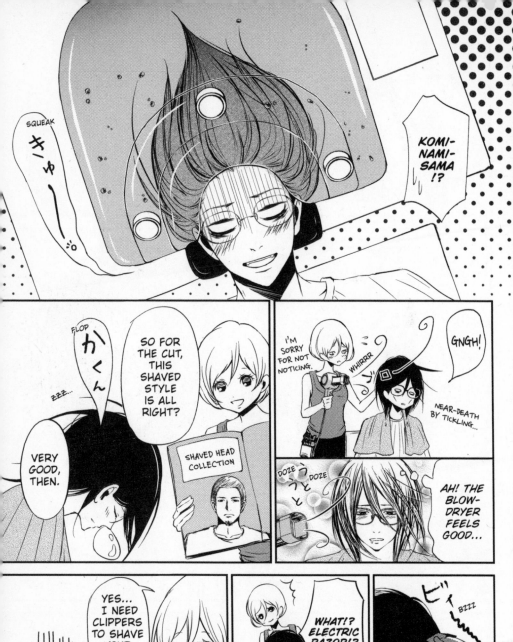

KOMI-NAMI-SAMA!?
SQUEAK
きゅー。
GNGH!
I'M SORRY FOR NOT NOTICING.
WHIRRR
NEAR-DEATH BY TICKLING...
SO FOR THE CUT, THIS SHAVED STYLE IS ALL RIGHT?
FLOP
かくん
ZZZ...
VERY GOOD, THEN.
SHAVED HEAD COLLECTION
AH! THE BLOW-DRYER FEELS GOOD...
DOZE
DOZE
BZZZ
BLINK
パチッ
AH!
WHAT!? ELECTRIC RAZOR!?
SKSH
YES... I NEED CLIPPERS TO SHAVE YOUR HEAD...
SHAVE MY HEAD!?

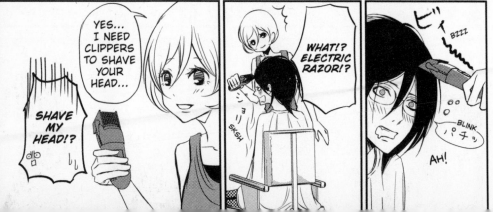

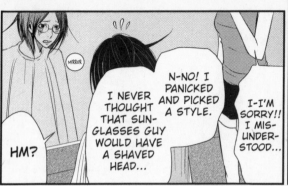

HUH? YOU WANTED A SHAVED HEAD...
SHAKE SHAKE
ぶんぶん！
!?
I-I'M SORRY!! I MISUNDERSTOOD...
N-NO! I PANICKED AND PICKED A STYLE.
I NEVER THOUGHT THAT SUNGLASSES GUY WOULD HAVE A SHAVED HEAD...
MIRROR
HM?
AAAAH!
THERE'S A DESERTER SAMURAI HERE!!
JUMP
びくっ
!?
BUT NO... IT'S ME!
......
WAAAH! SCARYYY! THIS IS GOING TO HAUNT MY DREAMS!

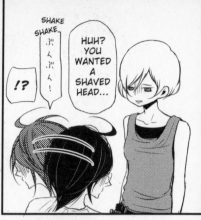

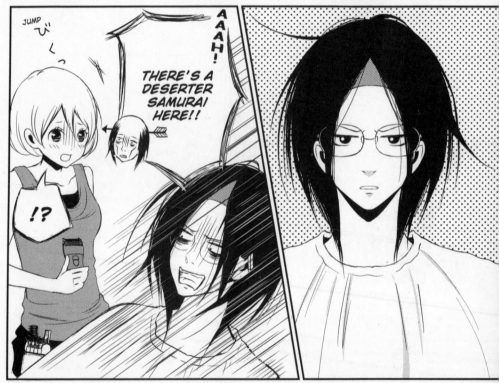

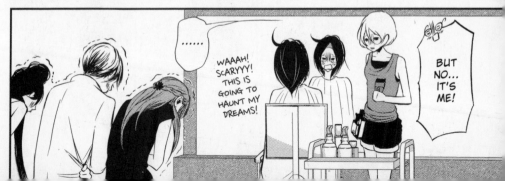

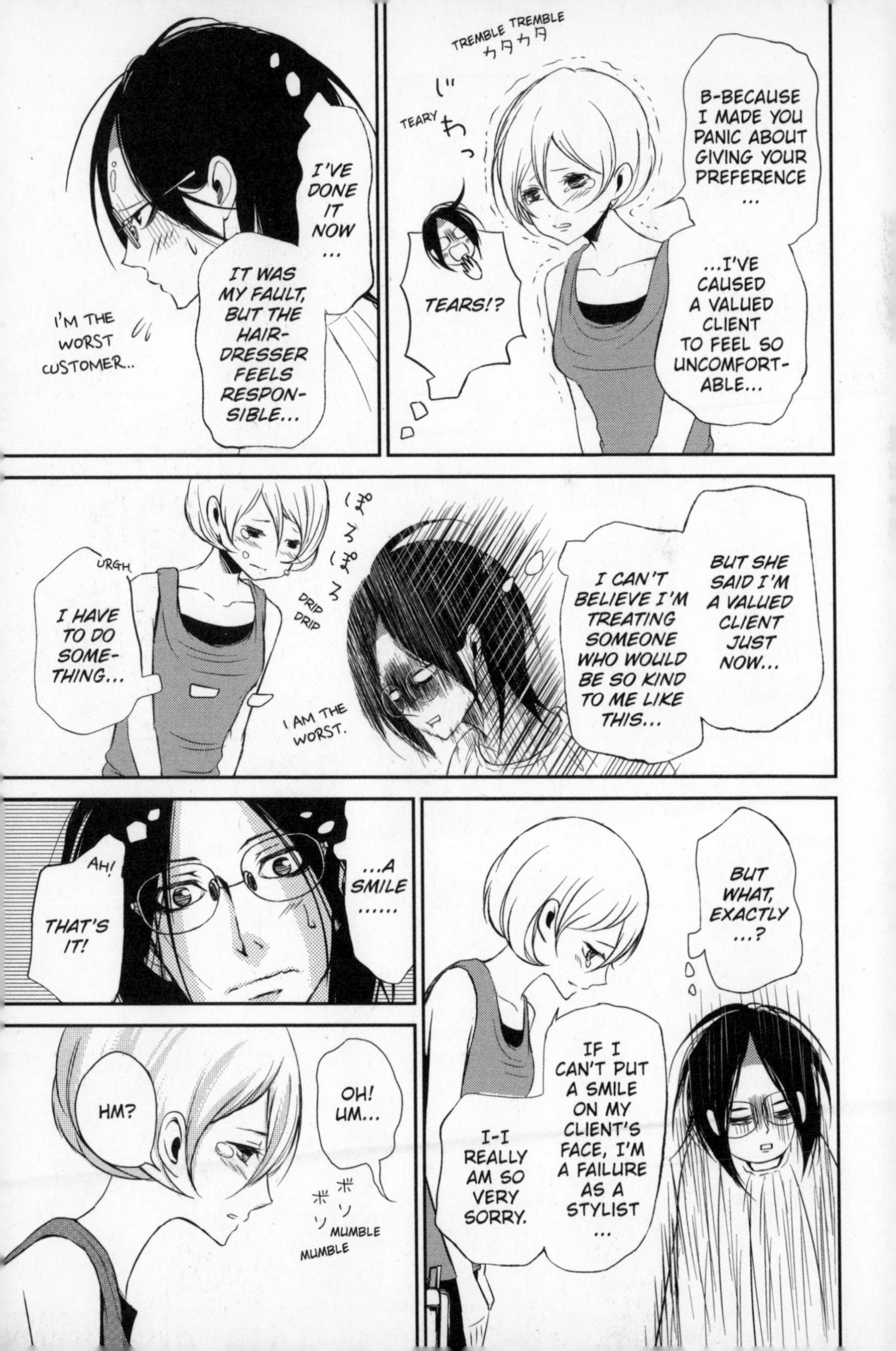
TREMBLE TREMBLE カタカタ
じわっ TEARY
B-BECAUSE I MADE YOU PANIC ABOUT GIVING YOUR PREFERENCE ...
...I'VE CAUSED A VALUED CLIENT TO FEEL SO UNCOMFORTABLE...
TEARS!?
I'VE DONE IT NOW ...
IT WAS MY FAULT, BUT THE HAIRDRESSER FEELS RESPONSIBLE...
I'M THE WORST CUSTOMER...
BUT SHE SAID I'M A VALUED CLIENT JUST NOW...
I CAN'T BELIEVE I'M TREATING SOMEONE WHO WOULD BE SO KIND TO ME LIKE THIS...
I AM THE WORST.
ぽろぽろ DRIP DRIP
URGH.
I HAVE TO DO SOMETHING...
BUT WHAT, EXACTLY ...?
IF I CAN'T PUT A SMILE ON MY CLIENT'S FACE, I'M A FAILURE AS A STYLIST ...
I-I REALLY AM SO VERY SORRY.
...A SMILE ......
AH!
THAT'S IT!
OH! UM...
ボソボソ MUMBLE MUMBLE
HM?

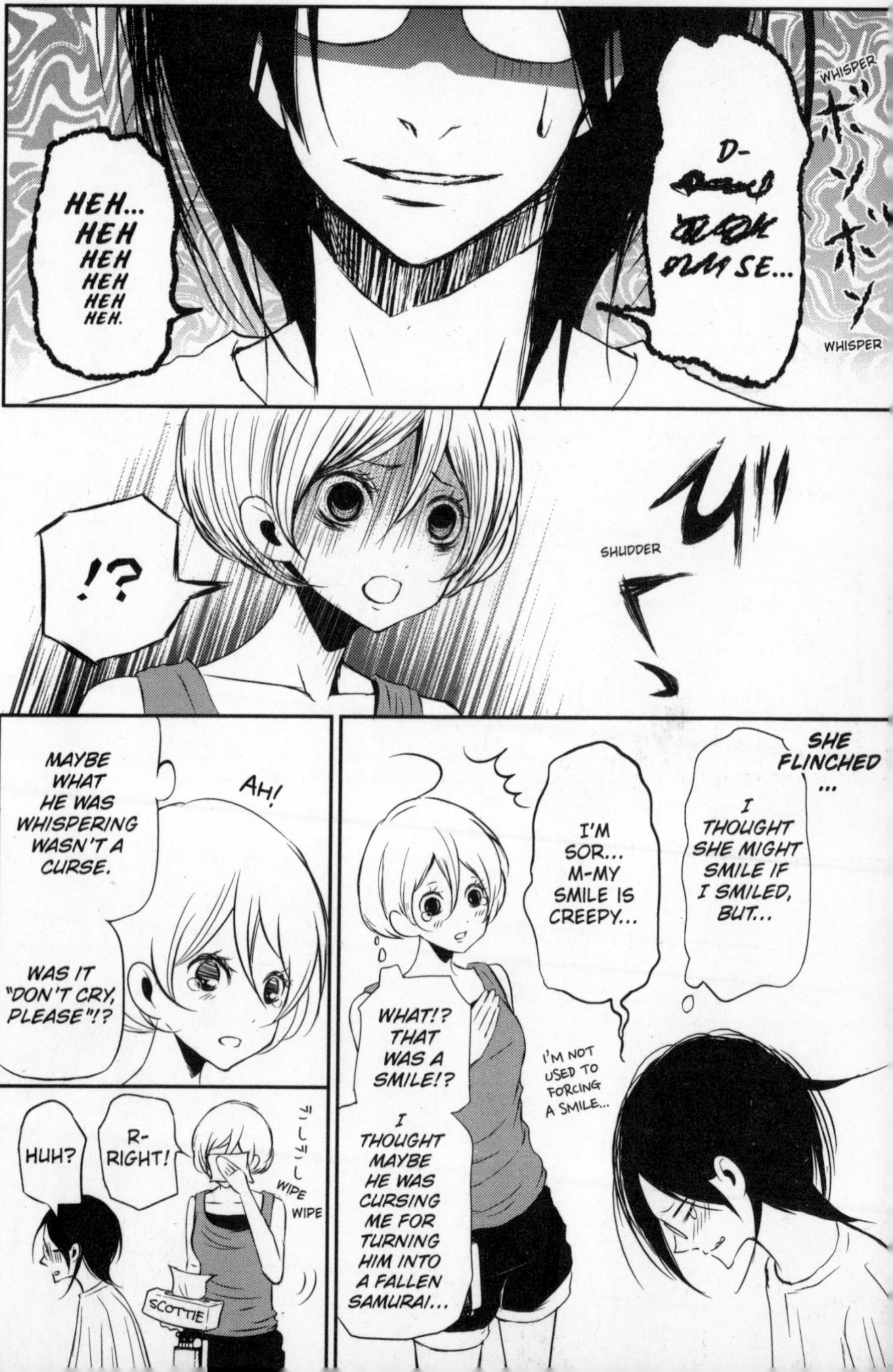
D- SE...
WHISPER
WHISPER
HEH... HEH HEH HEH HEH HEH.
SHUDDER
!?
SHE FLINCHED...
I THOUGHT SHE MIGHT SMILE IF I SMILED, BUT...
I'M SOR... M-MY SMILE IS CREEPY...
I'M NOT USED TO FORCING A SMILE...
WHAT!? THAT WAS A SMILE!?
I THOUGHT MAYBE HE WAS CURSING ME FOR TURNING HIM INTO A FALLEN SAMURAI...
AH!
MAYBE WHAT HE WAS WHISPERING WASN'T A CURSE.
WAS IT "DON'T CRY, PLEASE"!?
R-RIGHT!
HUH?
WIPE WIPE
SCOTTIE

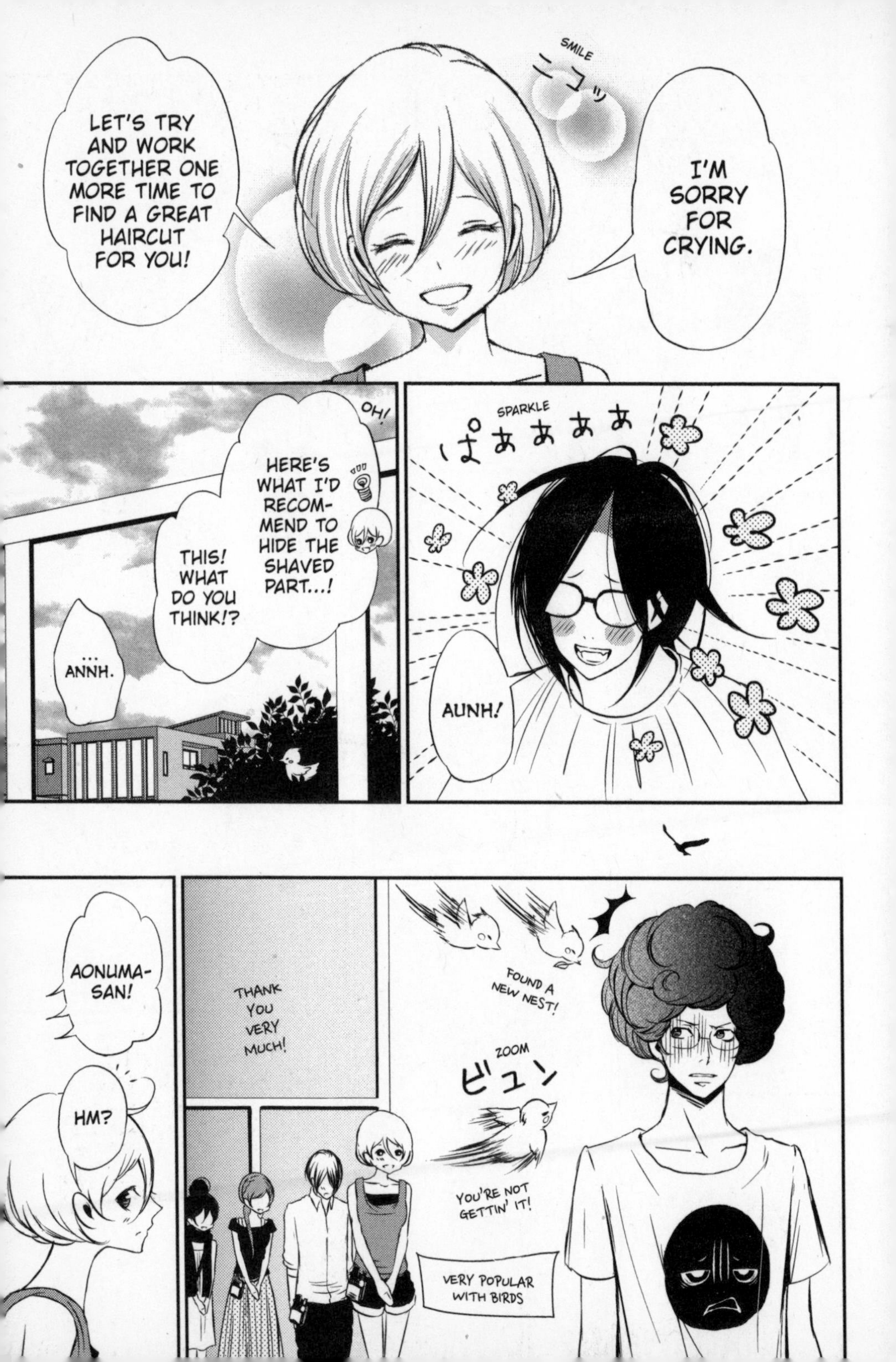
I'M SORRY FOR CRYING.
SMILE
ニコッ
LET'S TRY AND WORK TOGETHER ONE MORE TIME TO FIND A GREAT HAIRCUT FOR YOU!
SPARKLE
ぱぁぁぁぁ
AUNH!
OH!
HERE'S WHAT I'D RECOM-MEND TO HIDE THE SHAVED PART...!
THIS! WHAT DO YOU THINK!?
... ANNH.
FOUND A NEW NEST!
ZOOM
ビュン
YOU'RE NOT GETTIN' IT!
VERY POPULAR WITH BIRDS
THANK YOU VERY MUCH!
AONUMA-SAN!
HM?

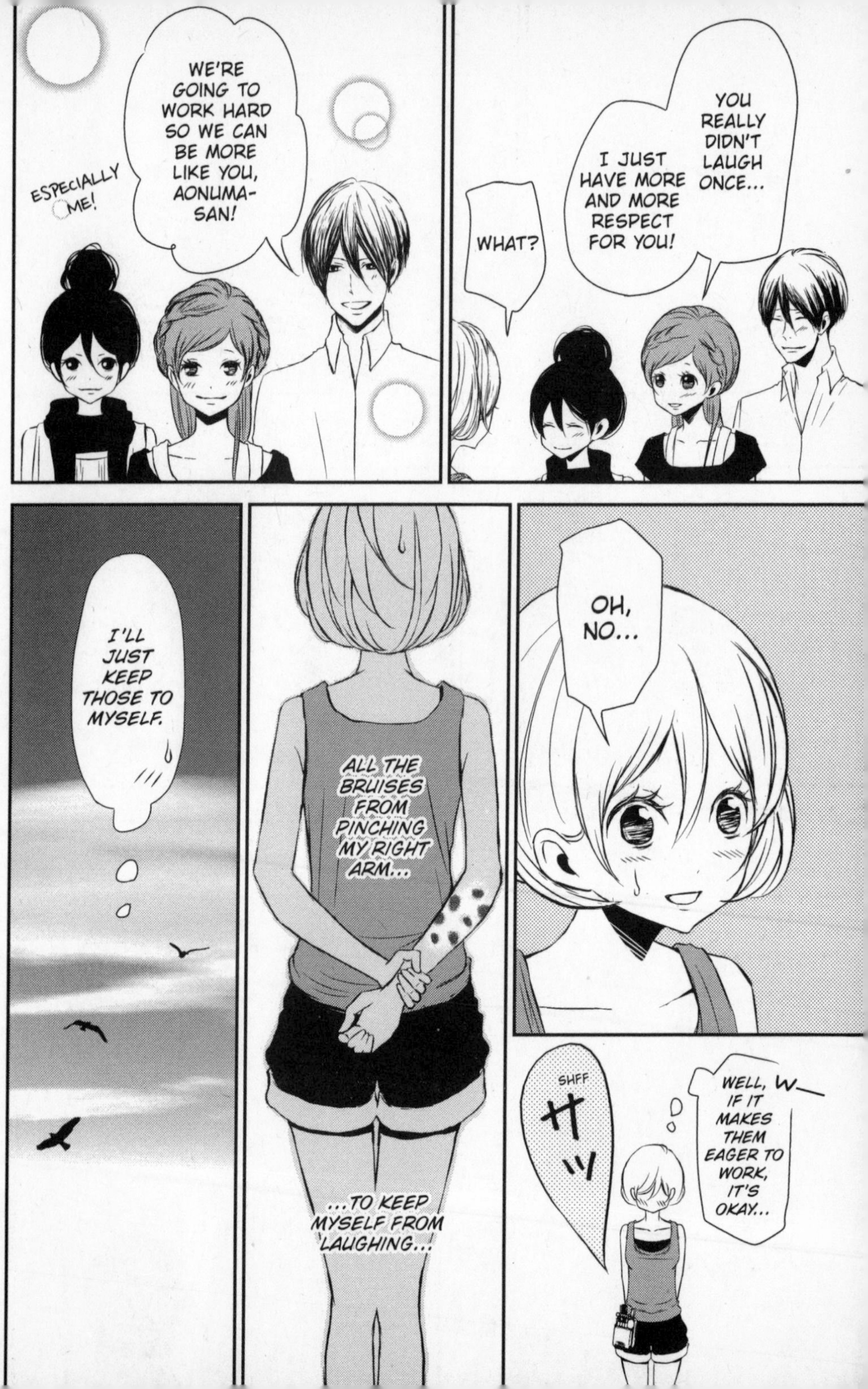
YOU REALLY DIDN'T LAUGH ONCE...
I JUST HAVE MORE AND MORE RESPECT FOR YOU!
WHAT?
WE'RE GOING TO WORK HARD SO WE CAN BE MORE LIKE YOU, AONUMA-SAN!
ESPECIALLY ME!
OH, NO...
WELL, W— IF IT MAKES THEM EAGER TO WORK, IT'S OKAY...
SHFF
サッ
ALL THE BRUISES FROM PINCHING MY RIGHT ARM...
...TO KEEP MYSELF FROM LAUGHING...
I'LL JUST KEEP THOSE TO MYSELF.

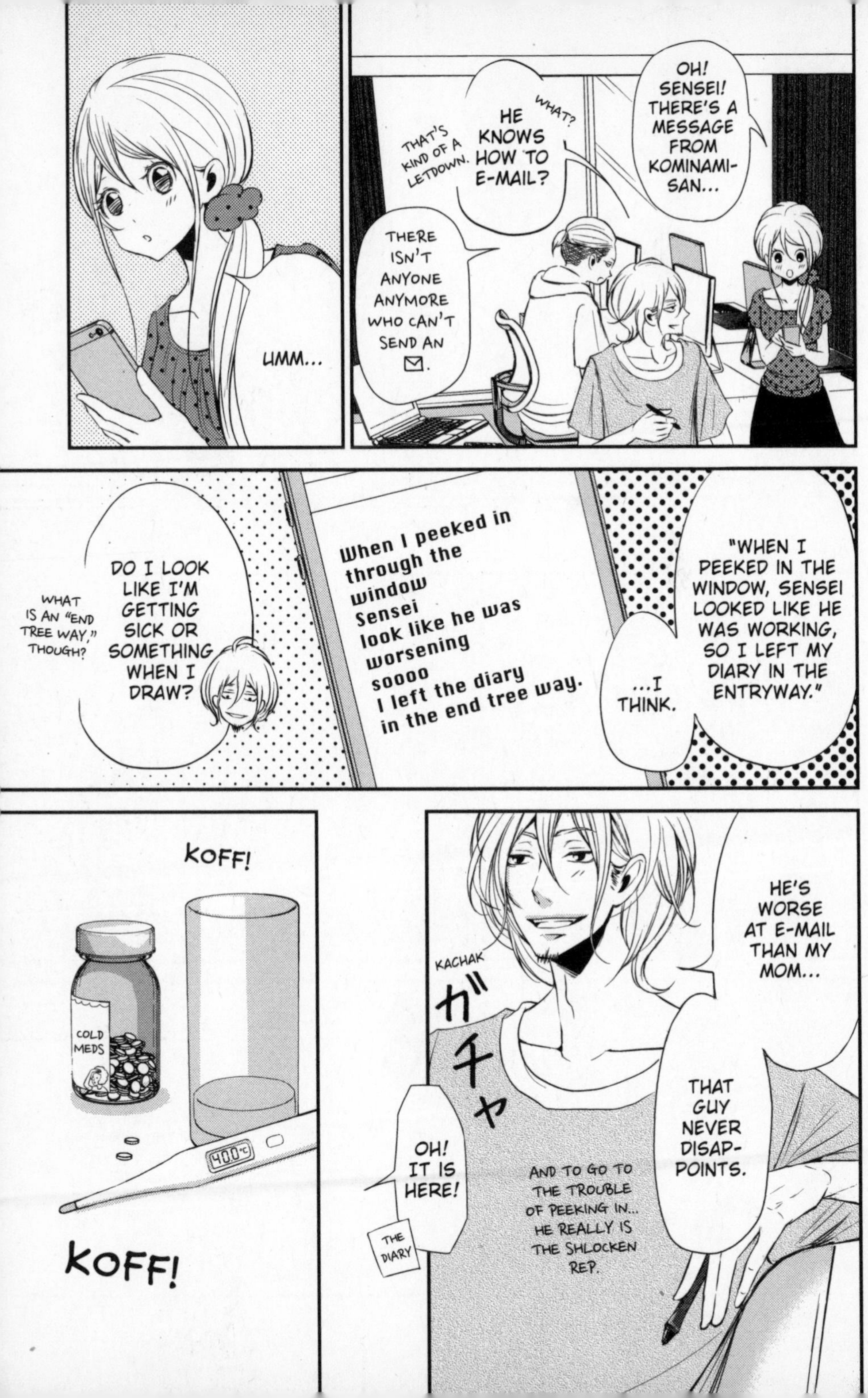
OH! SENSEI! THERE'S A MESSAGE FROM KOMINAMI-SAN...
WHAT?
HE KNOWS HOW TO E-MAIL?
THAT'S KIND OF A LETDOWN.
THERE ISN'T ANYONE ANYMORE WHO CAN'T SEND AN ✉.
UMM...
"WHEN I PEEKED IN THE WINDOW, SENSEI LOOKED LIKE HE WAS WORKING, SO I LEFT MY DIARY IN THE ENTRYWAY."
...I THINK.
When I peeked in through the window Sensei look like he was worsening soooo I left the diary in the end tree way.
DO I LOOK LIKE I'M GETTING SICK OR SOMETHING WHEN I DRAW?
WHAT IS AN "END TREE WAY," THOUGH?
HE'S WORSE AT E-MAIL THAN MY MOM...
THAT GUY NEVER DISAP-POINTS.
AND TO GO TO THE TROUBLE OF PEEKING IN... HE REALLY IS THE SHLOCKEN REP.
KACHAK
ガチャ
OH! IT IS HERE!
THE DIARY
KOFF!
COLD MEDS
40.0°C
KOFF!

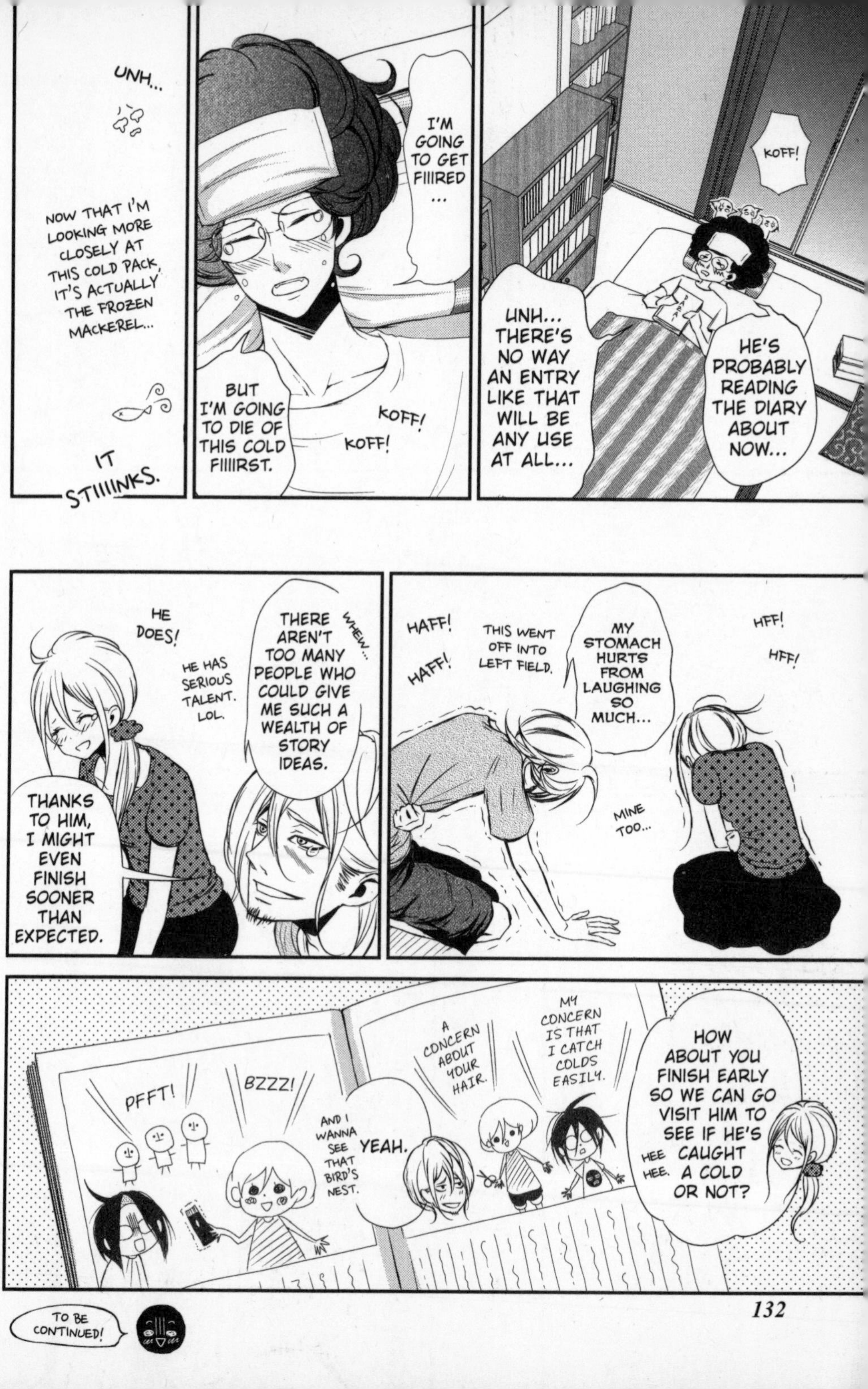
KOFF!
HE'S PROBABLY READING THE DIARY ABOUT NOW...
UNH... THERE'S NO WAY AN ENTRY LIKE THAT WILL BE ANY USE AT ALL...
I'M GOING TO GET FIIIRED ...
BUT I'M GOING TO DIE OF THIS COLD FIIIRST.
KOFF!
KOFF!
UNH...
NOW THAT I'M LOOKING MORE CLOSELY AT THIS COLD PACK, IT'S ACTUALLY THE FROZEN MACKEREL...
IT STIIIINKS.
HFF!
HFF!
MY STOMACH HURTS FROM LAUGHING SO MUCH...
MINE TOO...
THIS WENT OFF INTO LEFT FIELD.
HAFF!
HAFF!
THERE AREN'T TOO MANY PEOPLE WHO COULD GIVE ME SUCH A WEALTH OF STORY IDEAS.
WHEW...
HE HAS SERIOUS TALENT. LOL.
HE DOES!
THANKS TO HIM, I MIGHT EVEN FINISH SOONER THAN EXPECTED.
HOW ABOUT YOU FINISH EARLY SO WE CAN GO VISIT HIM TO SEE IF HE'S CAUGHT A COLD OR NOT?
HEE HEE.
MY CONCERN IS THAT I CATCH COLDS EASILY.
A CONCERN ABOUT YOUR HAIR.
YEAH.
AND I WANNA SEE THAT BIRD'S NEST.
BZZZ!
PFFT!
TO BE CONTINUED!

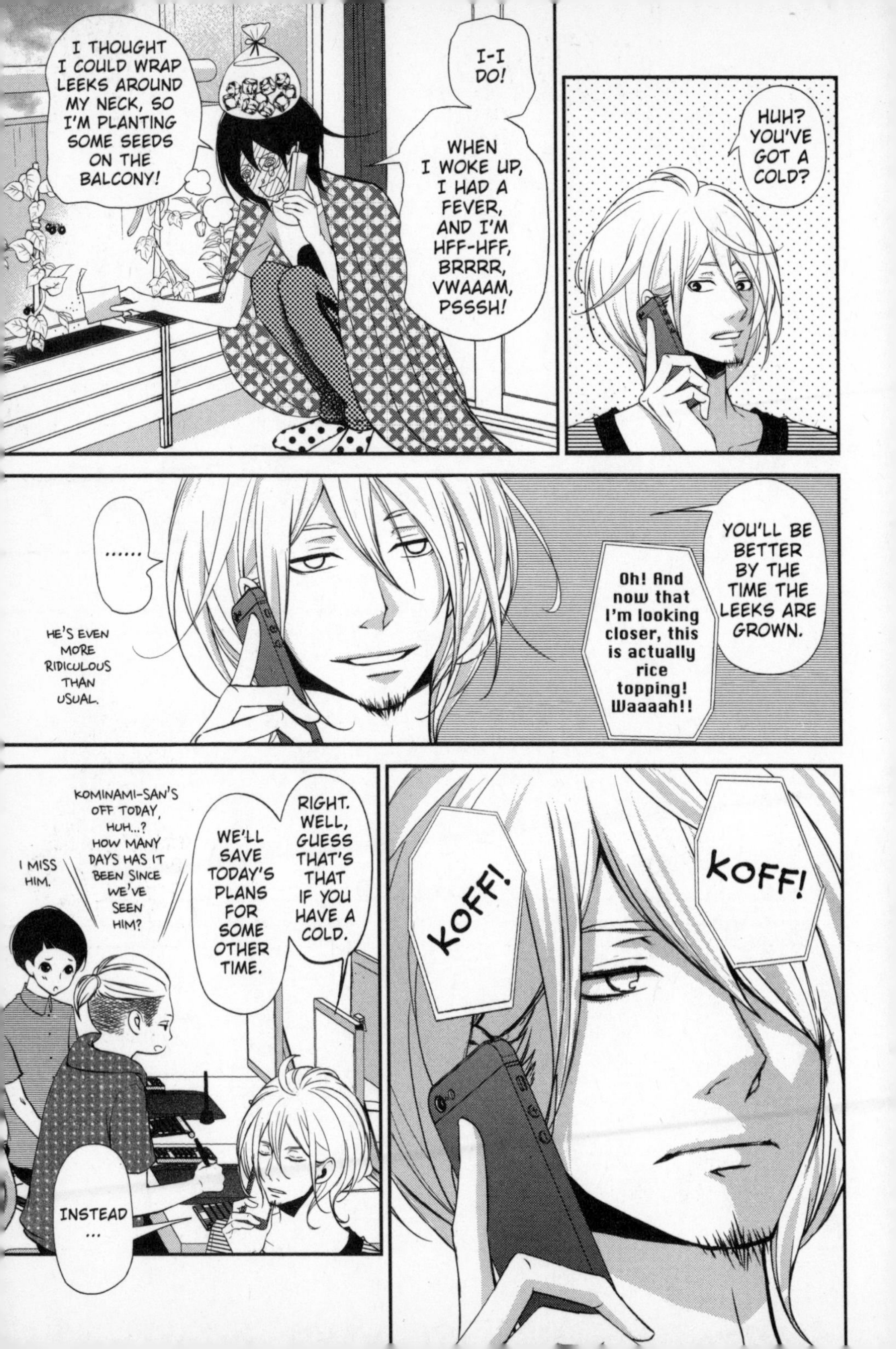
HUH? YOU'VE GOT A COLD?
I-I DO!
WHEN I WOKE UP, I HAD A FEVER, AND I'M HFF-HFF, BRRRR, VWAAAM, PSSSH!
I THOUGHT I COULD WRAP LEEKS AROUND MY NECK, SO I'M PLANTING SOME SEEDS ON THE BALCONY!
YOU'LL BE BETTER BY THE TIME THE LEEKS ARE GROWN.
Oh! And now that I'm looking closer, this is actually rice topping! Waaaah!!
......
HE'S EVEN MORE RIDICULOUS THAN USUAL.
KOFF!
KOFF!
RIGHT. WELL, GUESS THAT'S THAT IF YOU HAVE A COLD.
WE'LL SAVE TODAY'S PLANS FOR SOME OTHER TIME.
KOMINAMI-SAN'S OFF TODAY, HUH...? HOW MANY DAYS HAS IT BEEN SINCE WE'VE SEEN HIM?
I MISS HIM.
INSTEAD ...

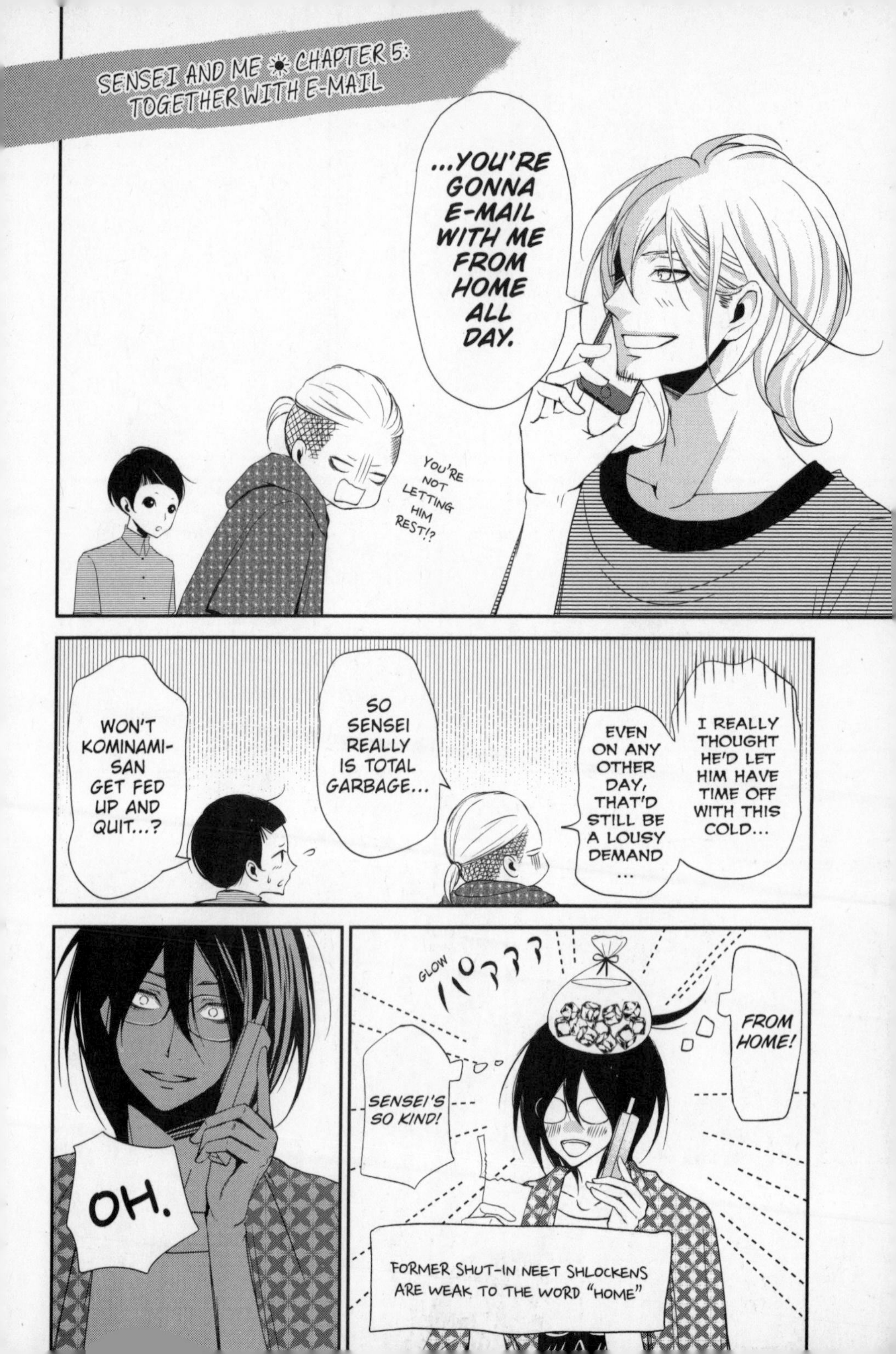
SENSEI AND ME ☀ CHAPTER 5: TOGETHER WITH E-MAIL
...YOU'RE GONNA E-MAIL WITH ME FROM HOME ALL DAY.
YOU'RE NOT LETTING HIM REST!?
I REALLY THOUGHT HE'D LET HIM HAVE TIME OFF WITH THIS COLD...
EVEN ON ANY OTHER DAY, THAT'D STILL BE A LOUSY DEMAND...
SO SENSEI REALLY IS TOTAL GARBAGE...
WON'T KOMINAMI-SAN GET FED UP AND QUIT...?
FROM HOME!
GLOW
SENSEI'S SO KIND!
FORMER SHUT-IN NEET SHLOCKENS ARE WEAK TO THE WORD "HOME"
OH.

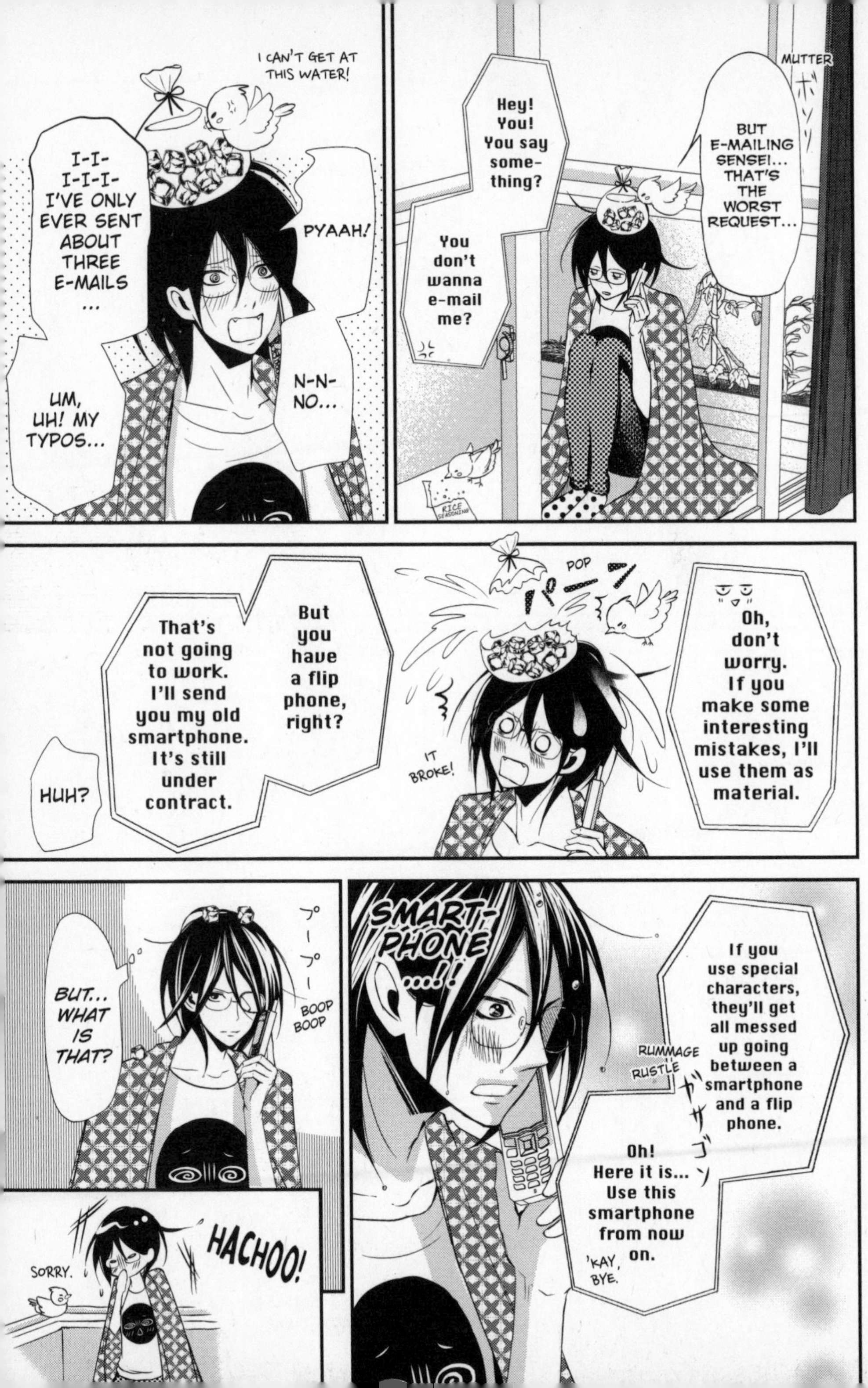
MUTTER
BUT E-MAILING SENSEI... THAT'S THE WORST REQUEST...
Hey! You! You say some-thing?
You don't wanna e-mail me?
RICE SEASONING
I CAN'T GET AT THIS WATER!
I-I-I-I-I- I'VE ONLY EVER SENT ABOUT THREE E-MAILS ...
PYAAH!
N-N-NO...
UM, UH! MY TYPOS...
Oh, don't worry. If you make some interesting mistakes, I'll use them as material.
POP
IT BROKE!
But you have a flip phone, right?
That's not going to work. I'll send you my old smartphone. It's still under contract.
HUH?
If you use special characters, they'll get all messed up going between a smartphone and a flip phone.
RUMMAGE RUSTLE
Oh! Here it is... Use this smartphone from now on.
'KAY, BYE.
SMART-PHONE ...!!
BUT... WHAT IS THAT?
BOOP BOOP
HACHOO!
SORRY.

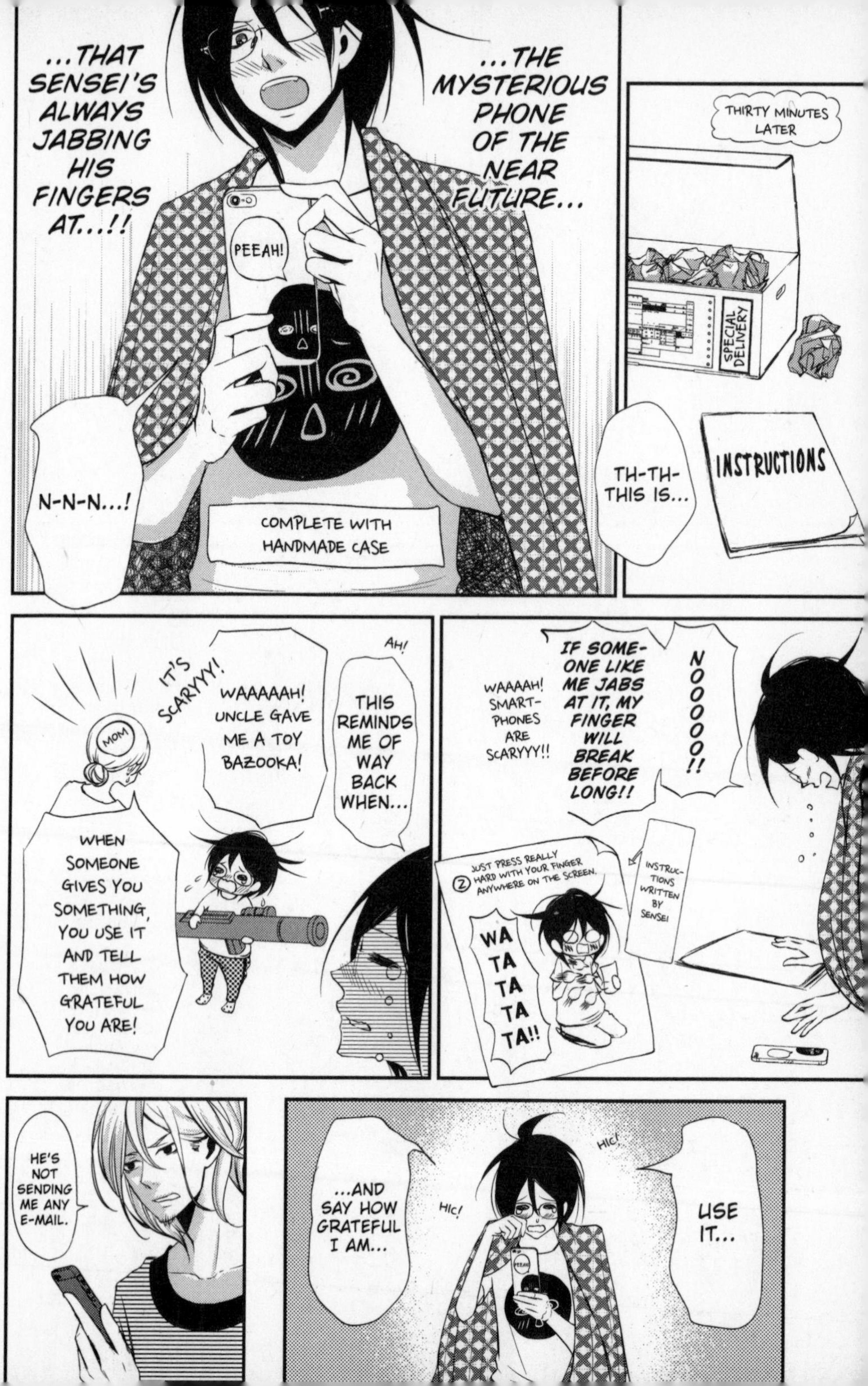
THIRTY MINUTES LATER
SPECIAL DELIVERY
INSTRUCTIONS
TH-TH-THIS IS...
...THE MYSTERIOUS PHONE OF THE NEAR FUTURE...
...THAT SENSEI'S ALWAYS JABBING HIS FINGERS AT...!!
PEEAH!
N-N-N...!
COMPLETE WITH HANDMADE CASE
NOOOOOO!!
IF SOMEONE LIKE ME JABS AT IT, MY FINGER WILL BREAK BEFORE LONG!!
WAAAAH! SMARTPHONES ARE SCARYYY!!
INSTRUCTIONS WRITTEN BY SENSEI
② JUST PRESS REALLY HARD WITH YOUR FINGER ANYWHERE ON THE SCREEN.
WA TA TA TA TA!!
AH!
THIS REMINDS ME OF WAY BACK WHEN...
WAAAAAH! UNCLE GAVE ME A TOY BAZOOKA!
IT'S SCARYYY!
MOM
WHEN SOMEONE GIVES YOU SOMETHING, YOU USE IT AND TELL THEM HOW GRATEFUL YOU ARE!
USE IT...
HIC!
...AND SAY HOW GRATEFUL I AM...
HIC!
HE'S NOT SENDING ME ANY E-MAIL.

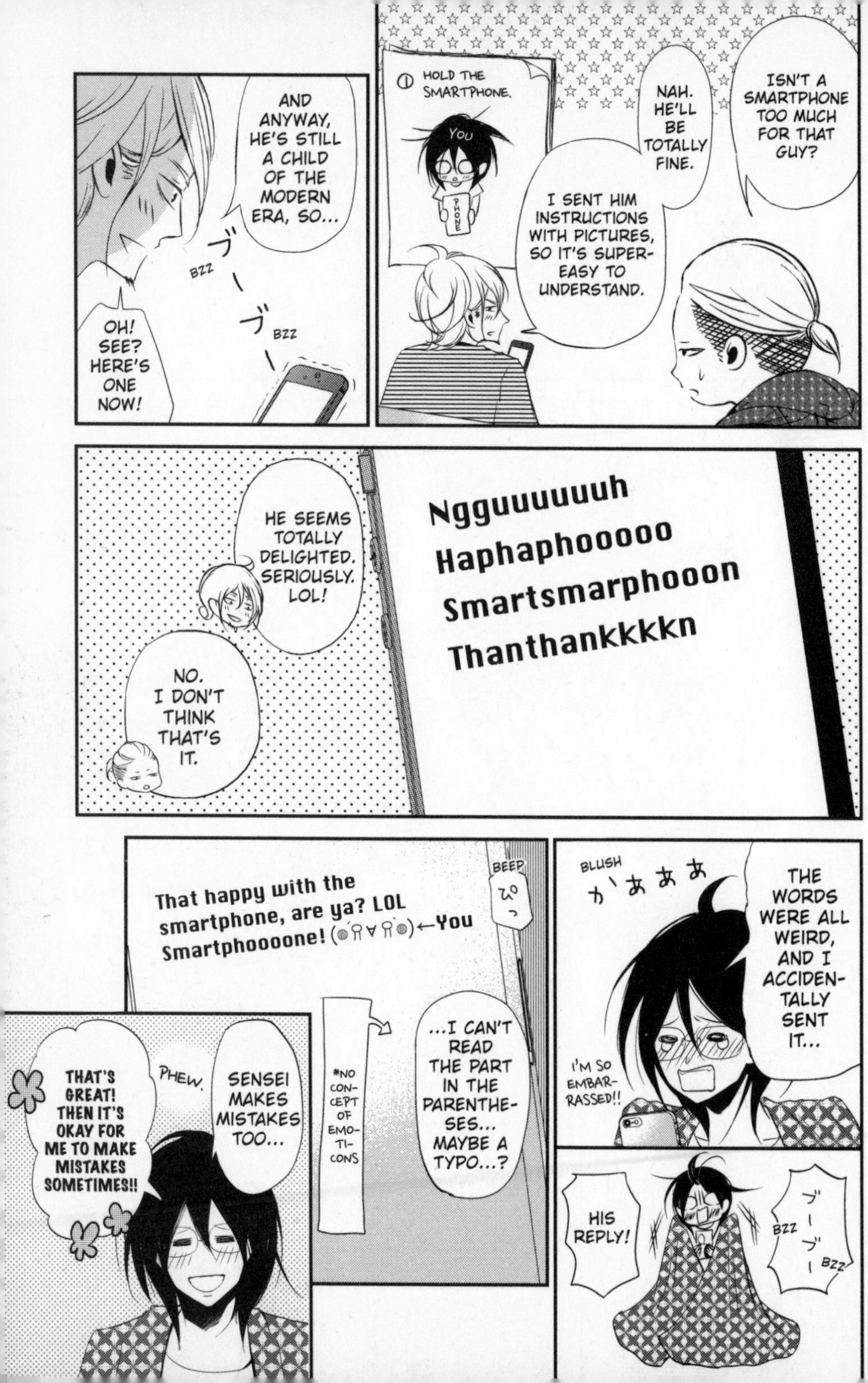
ISN'T A SMARTPHONE TOO MUCH FOR THAT GUY?
NAH. HE'LL BE TOTALLY FINE.
I SENT HIM INSTRUCTIONS WITH PICTURES, SO IT'S SUPER-EASY TO UNDERSTAND.
① HOLD THE SMARTPHONE.
You
PHONE
AND ANYWAY, HE'S STILL A CHILD OF THE MODERN ERA, SO...
BZZ ブー
BZZ ブー
OH! SEE? HERE'S ONE NOW!
Ngguuuuuuh
Haphaphooooo
Smartsmarphooon
Thanthankkkkn
HE SEEMS TOTALLY DELIGHTED. SERIOUSLY. LOL!
NO. I DON'T THINK THAT'S IT.
BLUSH かあああ
THE WORDS WERE ALL WEIRD, AND I ACCIDENTALLY SENT IT...
I'M SO EMBARRASSED!!
HIS REPLY!
BZZ ブー BZZ ブー
BEEP ぴっ
That happy with the smartphone, are ya? LOL
Smartphoooone! (◍ȏ∀ȏ◍)←You
...I CAN'T READ THE PART IN THE PARENTHESES... MAYBE A TYPO...?
*NO CONCEPT OF EMOTICONS
SENSEI MAKES MISTAKES TOO...
PHEW.
THAT'S GREAT! THEN IT'S OKAY FOR ME TO MAKE MISTAKES SOMETIMES!!

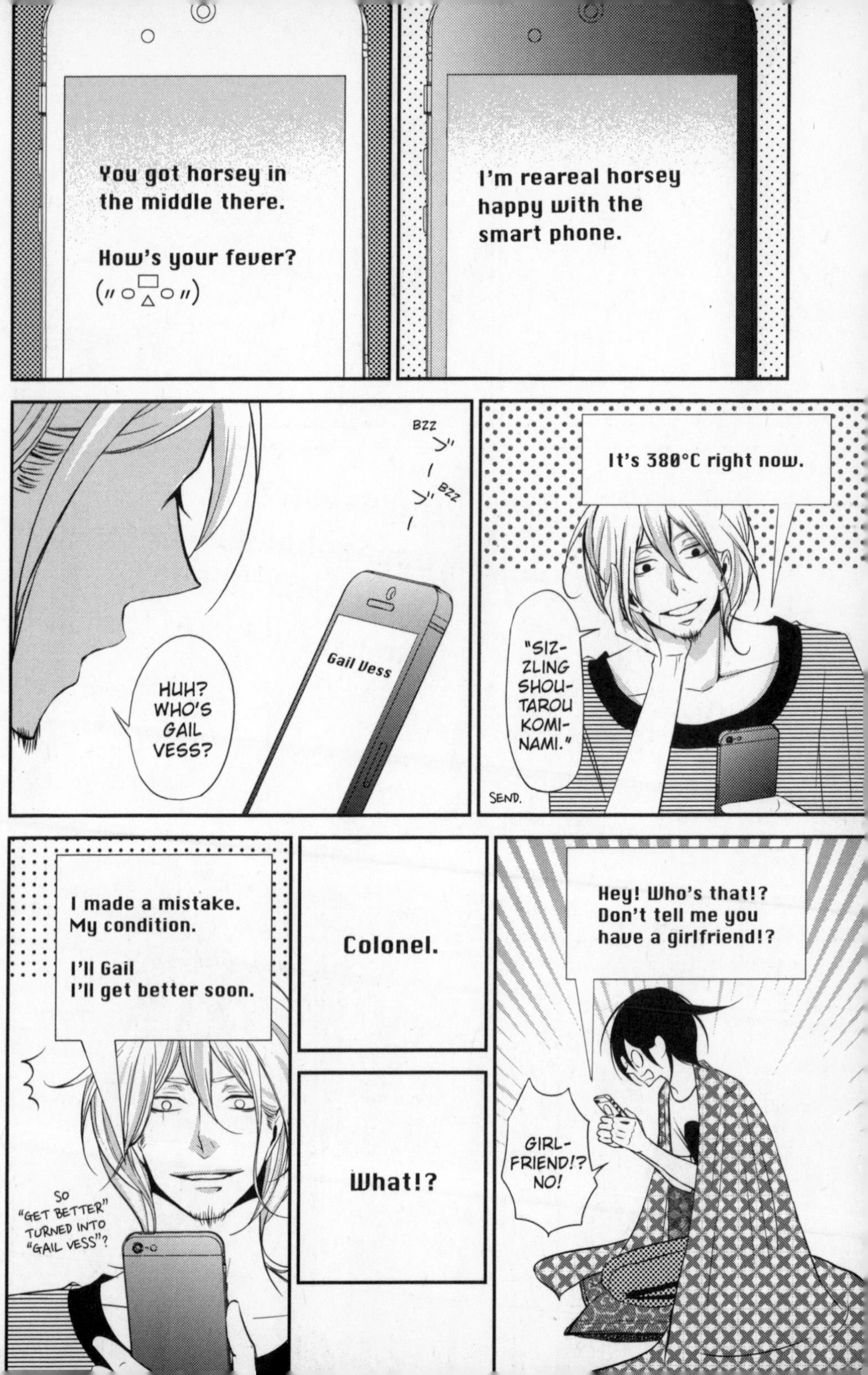
I'm reareal horsey happy with the smart phone.
You got horsey in the middle there.
How's your fever?
It's 380°C right now.
"SIZZLING SHOUTAROU KOMINAMI."
SEND.
BZZ
BZZ
Gail Vess
HUH? WHO'S GAIL VESS?
Hey! Who's that!? Don't tell me you have a girlfriend!?
GIRLFRIEND!? NO!
Colonel.
What!?
I made a mistake. My condition.
I'll Gail
I'll get better soon.
SO "GET BETTER" TURNED INTO "GAIL VESS"?

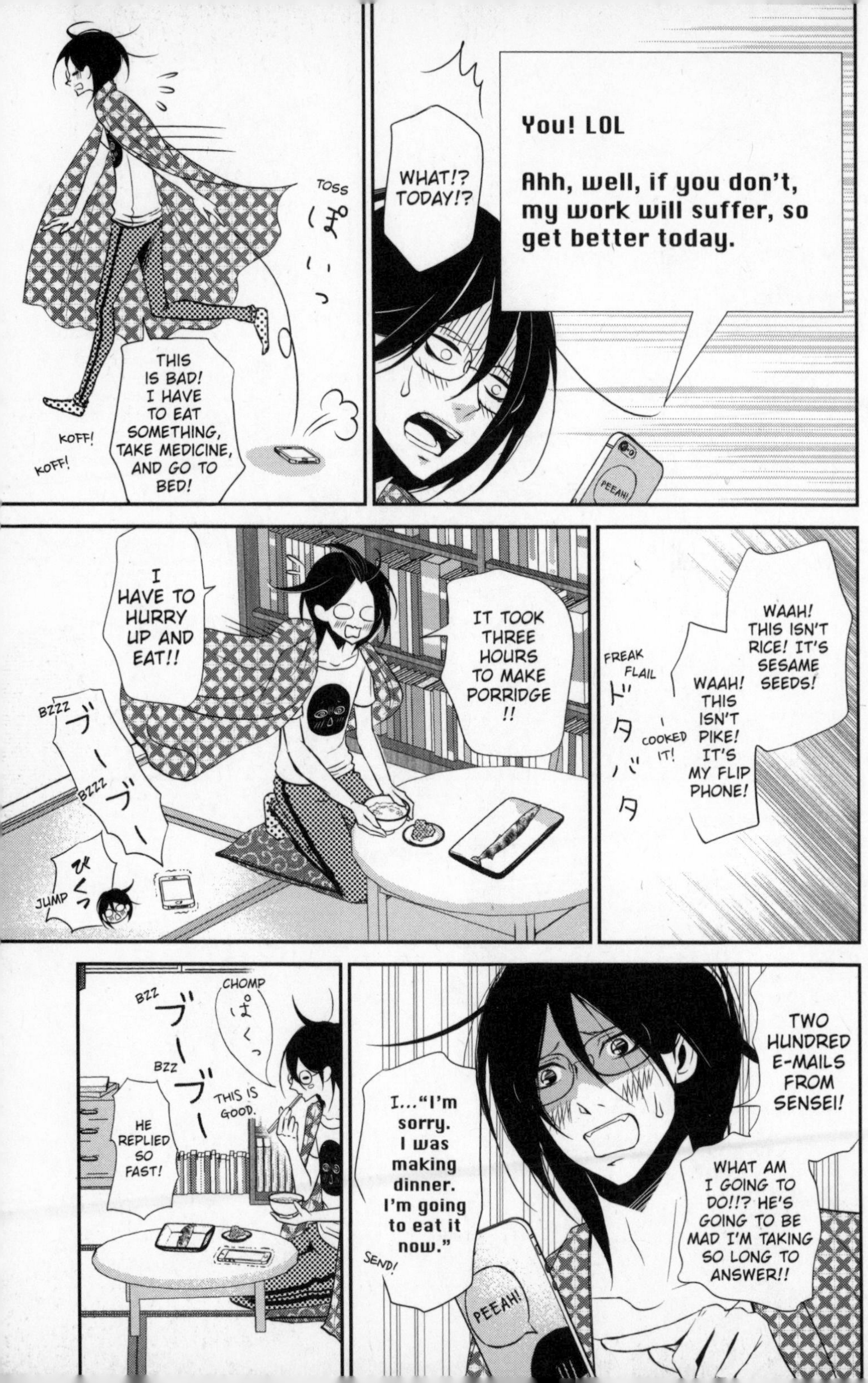
You! LOL
Ahh, well, if you don't, my work will suffer, so get better today.
WHAT!? TODAY!?
PEEAH!
TOSS
ぽいっ
THIS IS BAD! I HAVE TO EAT SOMETHING, TAKE MEDICINE, AND GO TO BED!
KOFF!
KOFF!
WAAH! THIS ISN'T RICE! IT'S SESAME SEEDS!
WAAH! THIS ISN'T PIKE! IT'S MY FLIP PHONE!
FREAK FLAIL
ドタバタ
COOKED IT!
IT TOOK THREE HOURS TO MAKE PORRIDGE!!
I HAVE TO HURRY UP AND EAT!!
BZZZ
BZZZ
ブーブー
JUMP
びくっ
TWO HUNDRED E-MAILS FROM SENSEI!
WHAT AM I GOING TO DO!!? HE'S GOING TO BE MAD I'M TAKING SO LONG TO ANSWER!!
I..."I'm sorry. I was making dinner. I'm going to eat it now."
SEND!
PEEAH!
CHOMP
ぱくっ
BZZ
BZZ
ブーブー
THIS IS GOOD.
HE REPLIED SO FAST!

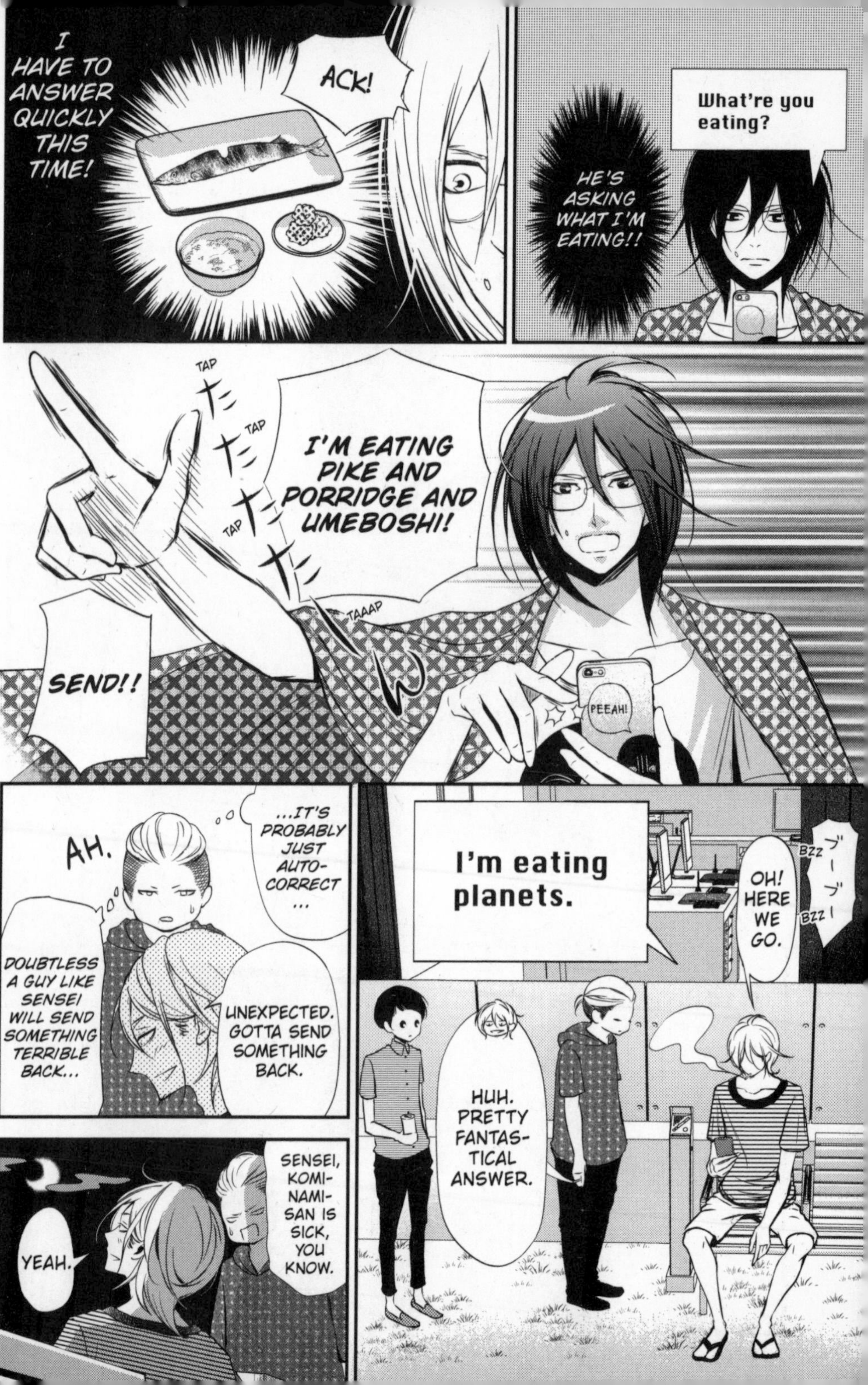
What're you eating?
HE'S ASKING WHAT I'M EATING!!
ACK!
I HAVE TO ANSWER QUICKLY THIS TIME!
TAP
TAP
TAP
TAAAP
I'M EATING PIKE AND PORRIDGE AND UMEBOSHI!
SEND!!
PEEAH!
I'm eating planets.
BZZ
BZZ
OH! HERE WE GO.
HUH. PRETTY FANTASTICAL ANSWER.
...IT'S PROBABLY JUST AUTO-CORRECT...
AH.
UNEXPECTED. GOTTA SEND SOMETHING BACK.
DOUBTLESS A GUY LIKE SENSEI WILL SEND SOMETHING TERRIBLE BACK...
SENSEI, KOMINAMI-SAN IS SICK, YOU KNOW.
YEAH.

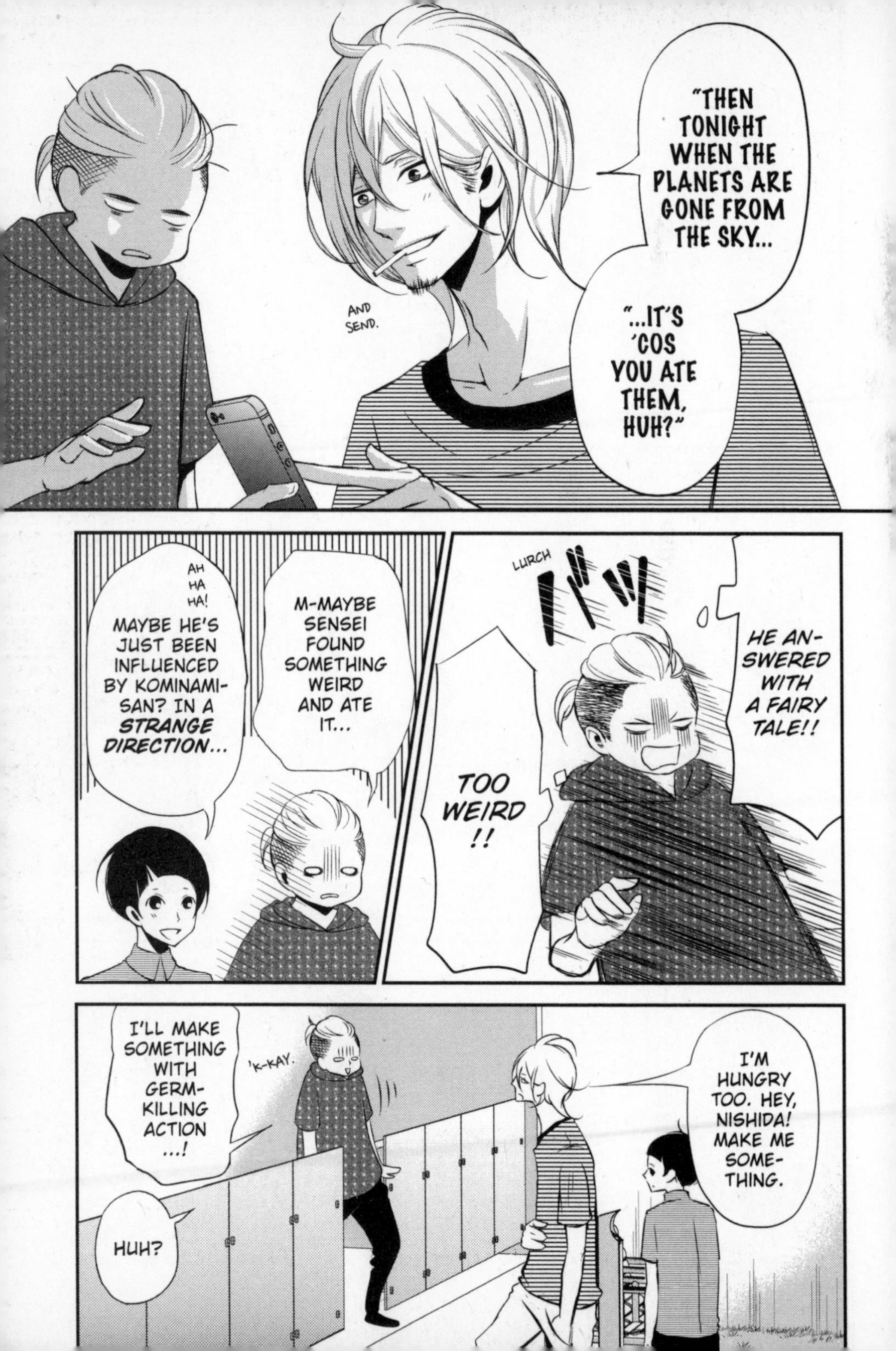
"THEN TONIGHT WHEN THE PLANETS ARE GONE FROM THE SKY...
"...IT'S 'COS YOU ATE THEM, HUH?"
AND SEND.
LURCH
HE AN-SWERED WITH A FAIRY TALE!!
TOO WEIRD!!
M-MAYBE SENSEI FOUND SOMETHING WEIRD AND ATE IT...
AH HA HA! MAYBE HE'S JUST BEEN INFLUENCED BY KOMINAMI-SAN? IN A STRANGE DIRECTION...
I'M HUNGRY TOO. HEY, NISHIDA! MAKE ME SOME-THING.
HUH?
I'LL MAKE SOMETHING WITH GERM-KILLING ACTION...!
'K-KAY.

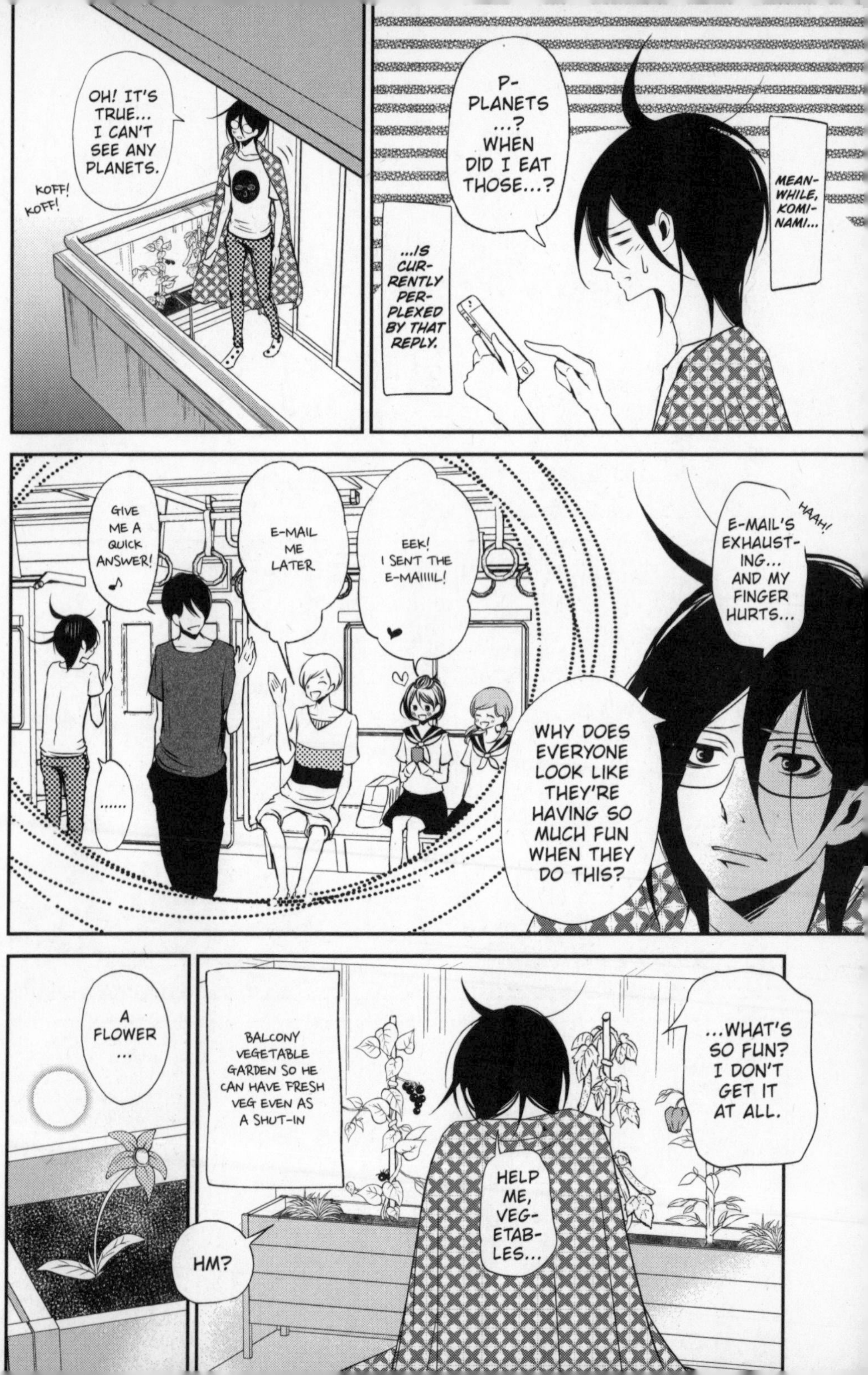
MEANWHILE, KOMINAMI...
P-PLANETS...? WHEN DID I EAT THOSE...?
...IS CURRENTLY PERPLEXED BY THAT REPLY.
OH! IT'S TRUE... I CAN'T SEE ANY PLANETS.
KOFF! KOFF!
HAAH!
E-MAIL'S EXHAUSTING... AND MY FINGER HURTS...
WHY DOES EVERYONE LOOK LIKE THEY'RE HAVING SO MUCH FUN WHEN THEY DO THIS?
EEK! I SENT THE E-MAIIIIL!
E-MAIL ME LATER
GIVE ME A QUICK ANSWER! ♪
......
...WHAT'S SO FUN? I DON'T GET IT AT ALL.
BALCONY VEGETABLE GARDEN SO HE CAN HAVE FRESH VEG EVEN AS A SHUT-IN
HELP ME, VEGETABLES...
HM?
A FLOWER...

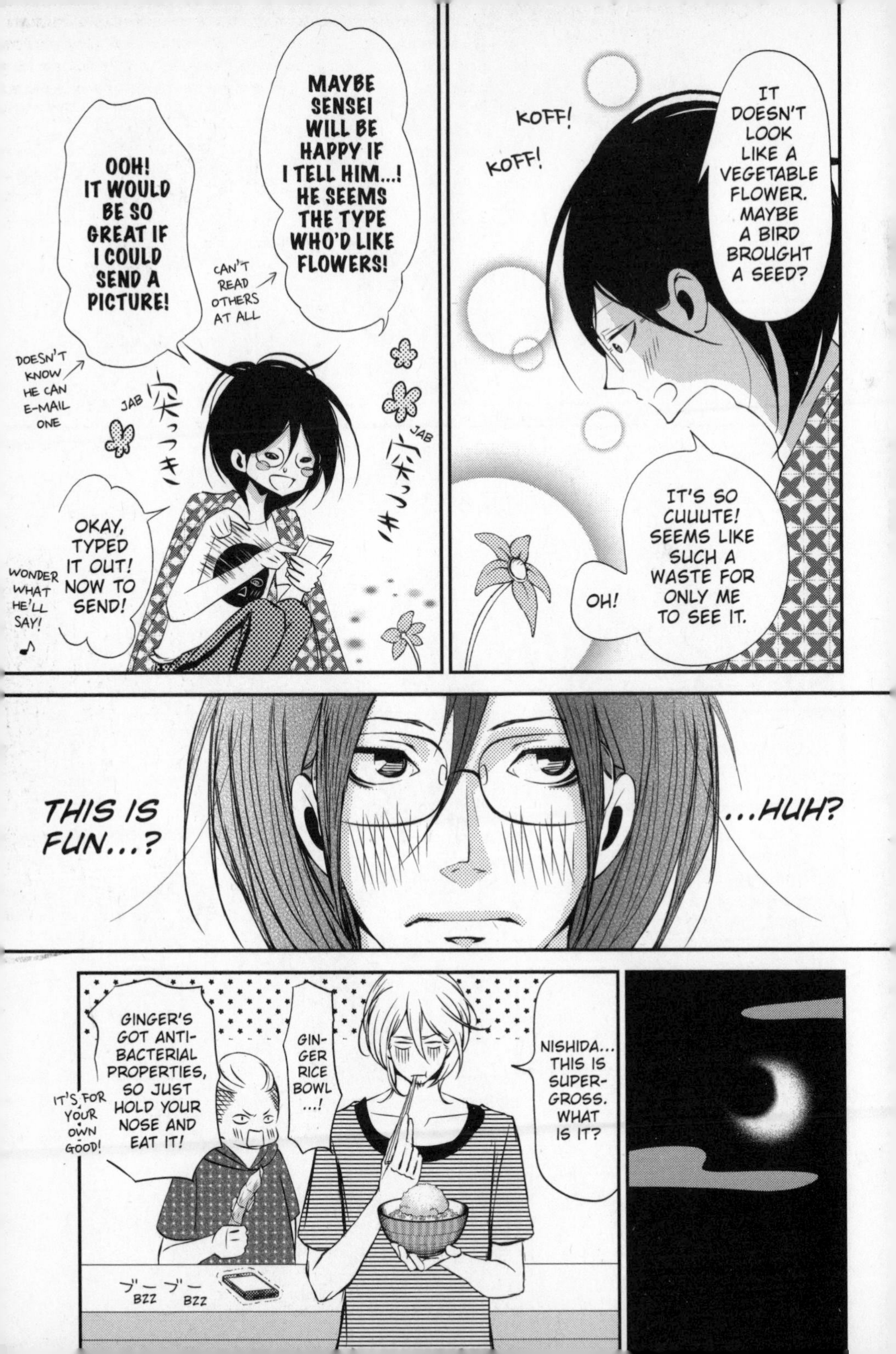
KOFF!
KOFF!
IT DOESN'T LOOK LIKE A VEGETABLE FLOWER. MAYBE A BIRD BROUGHT A SEED?
OH!
IT'S SO CUUUTE! SEEMS LIKE SUCH A WASTE FOR ONLY ME TO SEE IT.
MAYBE SENSEI WILL BE HAPPY IF I TELL HIM...! HE SEEMS THE TYPE WHO'D LIKE FLOWERS!
CAN'T READ OTHERS AT ALL
OOH! IT WOULD BE SO GREAT IF I COULD SEND A PICTURE!
DOESN'T KNOW HE CAN E-MAIL ONE
突っつき JAB
突っつき JAB
OKAY, TYPED IT OUT! NOW TO SEND!
WONDER WHAT HE'LL SAY! ♪
...HUH?
THIS IS FUN...?
NISHIDA... THIS IS SUPER-GROSS. WHAT IS IT?
GINGER RICE BOWL...!
GINGER'S GOT ANTI-BACTERIAL PROPERTIES, SO JUST HOLD YOUR NOSE AND EAT IT!
IT'S FOR YOUR OWN GOOD!
ブーブー BZZ BZZ

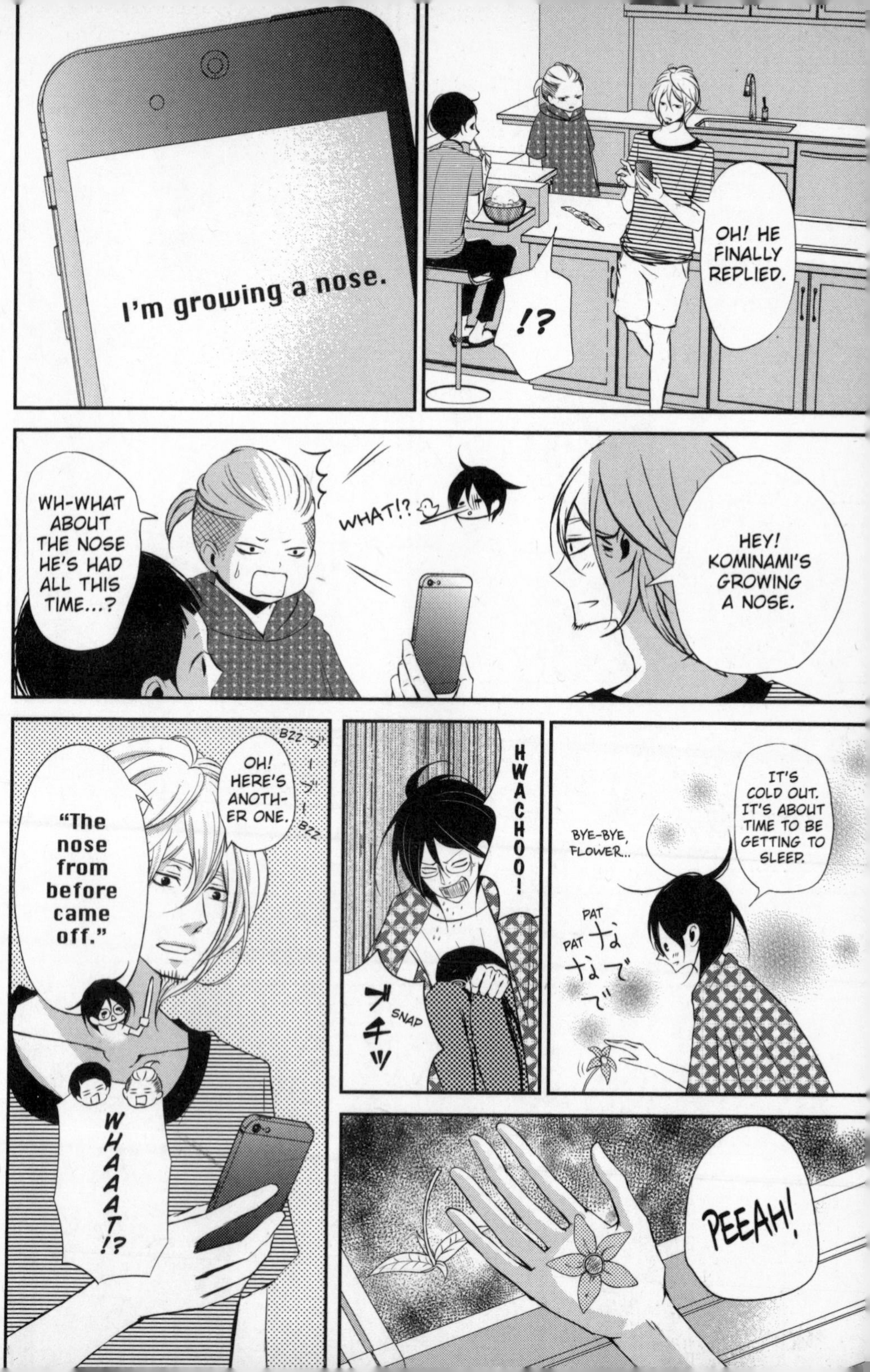
OH! HE FINALLY REPLIED.
!?
I'm growing a nose.
HEY! KOMINAMI'S GROWING A NOSE.
WHAT!?
WH-WHAT ABOUT THE NOSE HE'S HAD ALL THIS TIME...?
IT'S COLD OUT. IT'S ABOUT TIME TO BE GETTING TO SLEEP.
BYE-BYE, FLOWER...
PAT PAT
なでなで
HWACHOO!
SNAP
ブチッ
PEEAH!
BZZ BZZ
OH! HERE'S ANOTHER ONE.
"The nose from before came off."
WHAAAAT!?

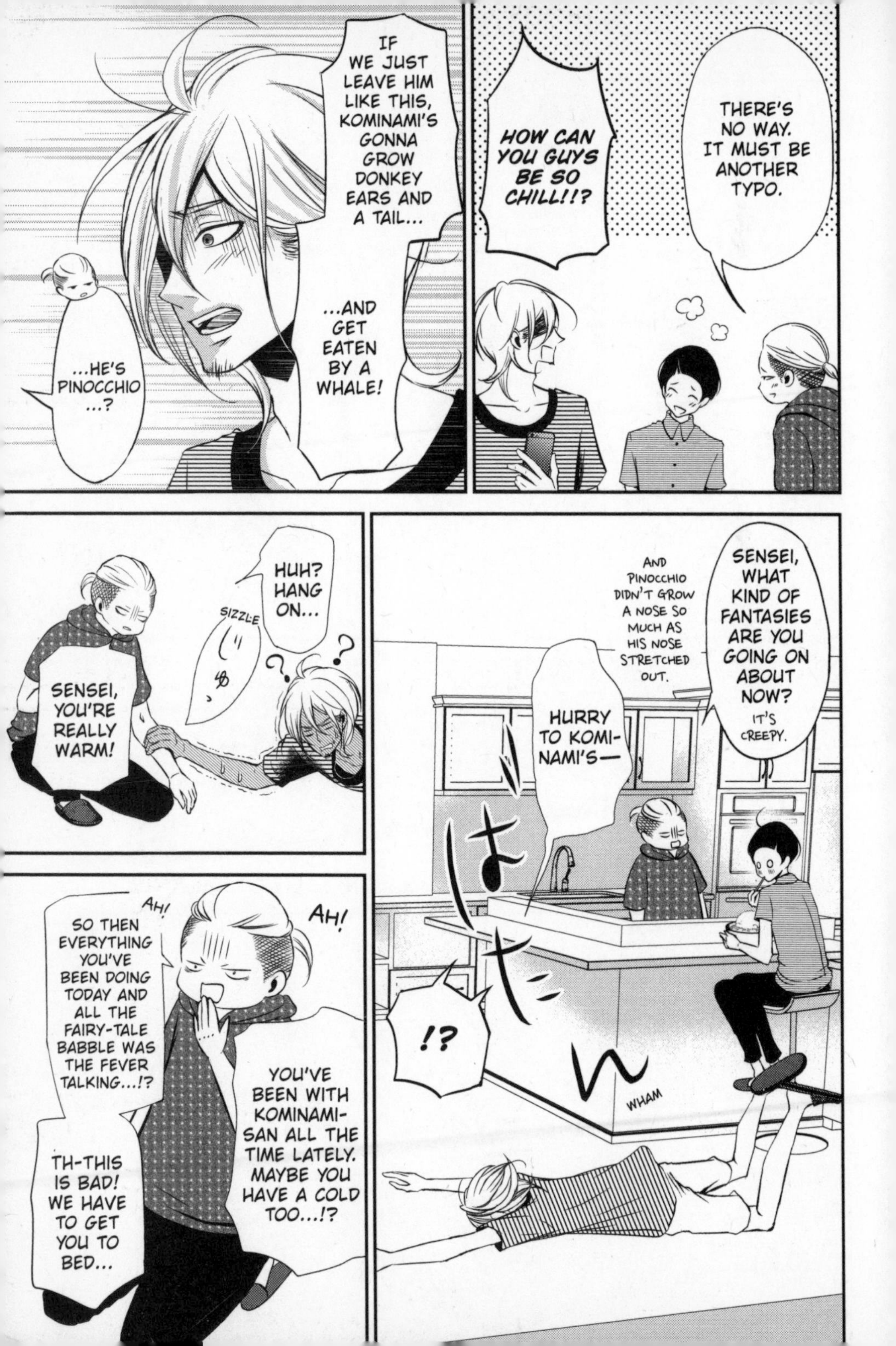

THERE'S NO WAY. IT MUST BE ANOTHER TYPO.
HOW CAN YOU GUYS BE SO CHILL!!?
IF WE JUST LEAVE HIM LIKE THIS, KOMINAMI'S GONNA GROW DONKEY EARS AND A TAIL...
...AND GET EATEN BY A WHALE!
...HE'S PINOCCHIO...?
SENSEI, WHAT KIND OF FANTASIES ARE YOU GOING ON ABOUT NOW?
IT'S CREEPY.
AND PINOCCHIO DIDN'T GROW A NOSE SO MUCH AS HIS NOSE STRETCHED OUT.
HURRY TO KOMINAMI'S—
!?
WHAM
HUH? HANG ON...
SIZZLE
SENSEI, YOU'RE REALLY WARM!
AH!
AH!
SO THEN EVERYTHING YOU'VE BEEN DOING TODAY AND ALL THE FAIRY-TALE BABBLE WAS THE FEVER TALKING...!?
YOU'VE BEEN WITH KOMINAMI-SAN ALL THE TIME LATELY. MAYBE YOU HAVE A COLD TOO...!?
TH-THIS IS BAD! WE HAVE TO GET YOU TO BED...

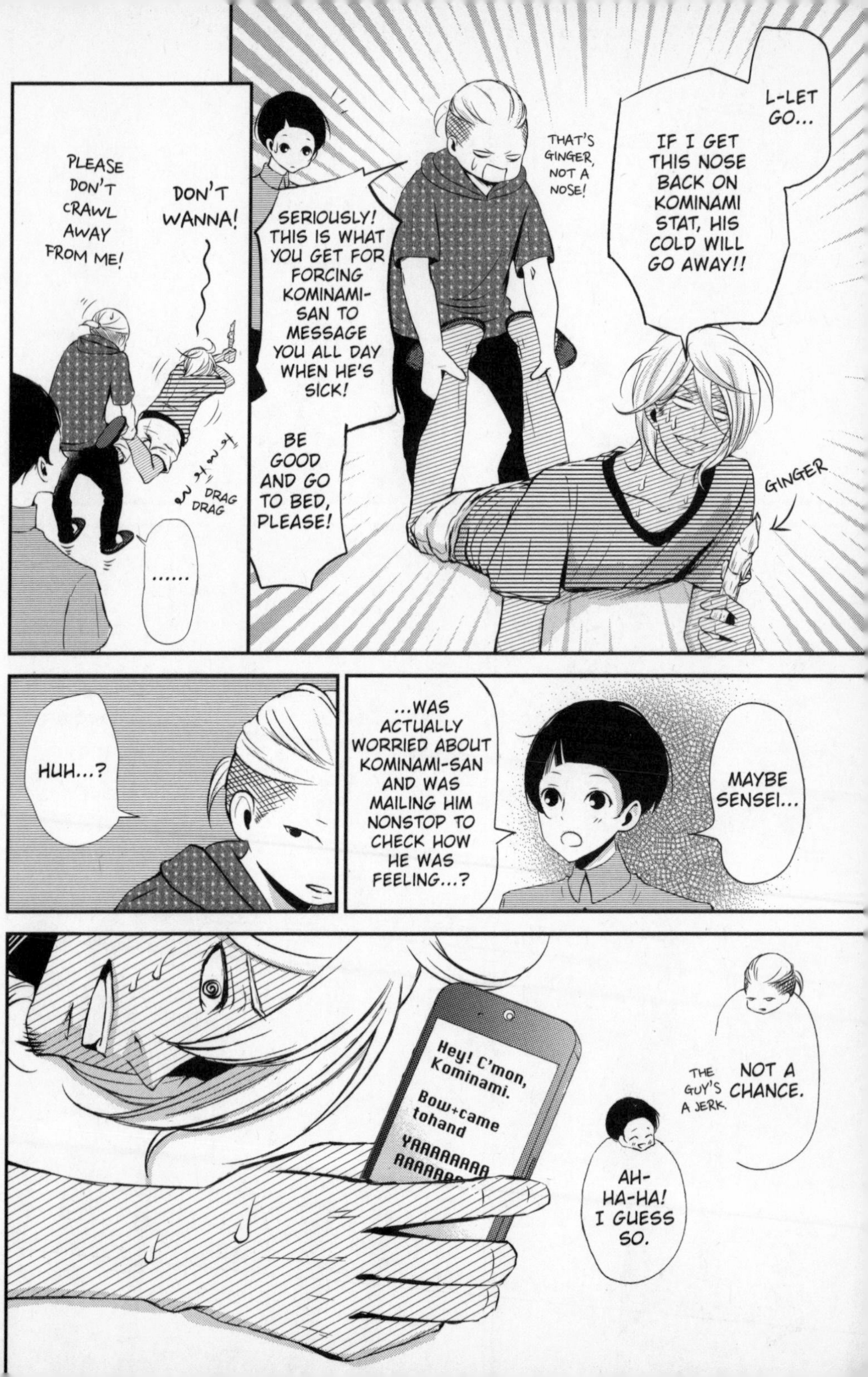
L-LET GO...
IF I GET THIS NOSE BACK ON KOMINAMI STAT, HIS COLD WILL GO AWAY!!
THAT'S GINGER, NOT A NOSE!
SERIOUSLY! THIS IS WHAT YOU GET FOR FORCING KOMINAMI-SAN TO MESSAGE YOU ALL DAY WHEN HE'S SICK!
BE GOOD AND GO TO BED, PLEASE!
GINGER
DON'T WANNA!
PLEASE DON'T CRAWL AWAY FROM ME!
DRAG DRAG
......
MAYBE SENSEI...
...WAS ACTUALLY WORRIED ABOUT KOMINAMI-SAN AND WAS MAILING HIM NONSTOP TO CHECK HOW HE WAS FEELING...?
HUH...?
Hey! C'mon, Kominami.
Bow+came tohand
YAAAAAAAA
NOT A CHANCE.
THE GUY'S A JERK.
AH-HA-HA! I GUESS SO.

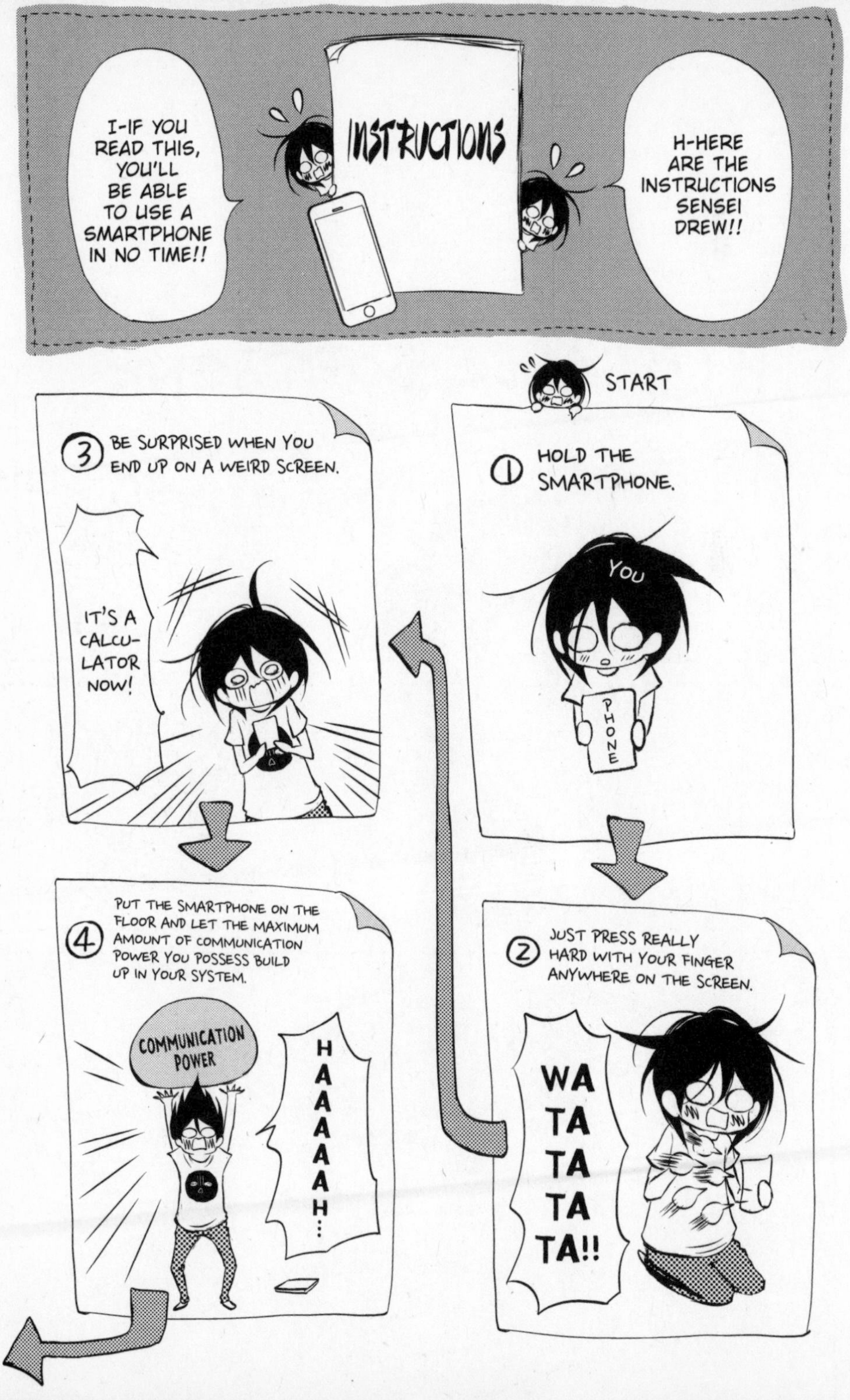
H-HERE ARE THE INSTRUCTIONS SENSEI DREW!!
INSTRUCTIONS
I-IF YOU READ THIS, YOU'LL BE ABLE TO USE A SMARTPHONE IN NO TIME!!
START
① HOLD THE SMARTPHONE.
YOU
PHONE
② JUST PRESS REALLY HARD WITH YOUR FINGER ANYWHERE ON THE SCREEN.
WA TA TA TA TA!!
③ BE SURPRISED WHEN YOU END UP ON A WEIRD SCREEN.
IT'S A CALCU-LATOR NOW!
④ PUT THE SMARTPHONE ON THE FLOOR AND LET THE MAXIMUM AMOUNT OF COMMUNICATION POWER YOU POSSESS BUILD UP IN YOUR SYSTEM.
HAAAAAAH...
COMMUNICATION POWER

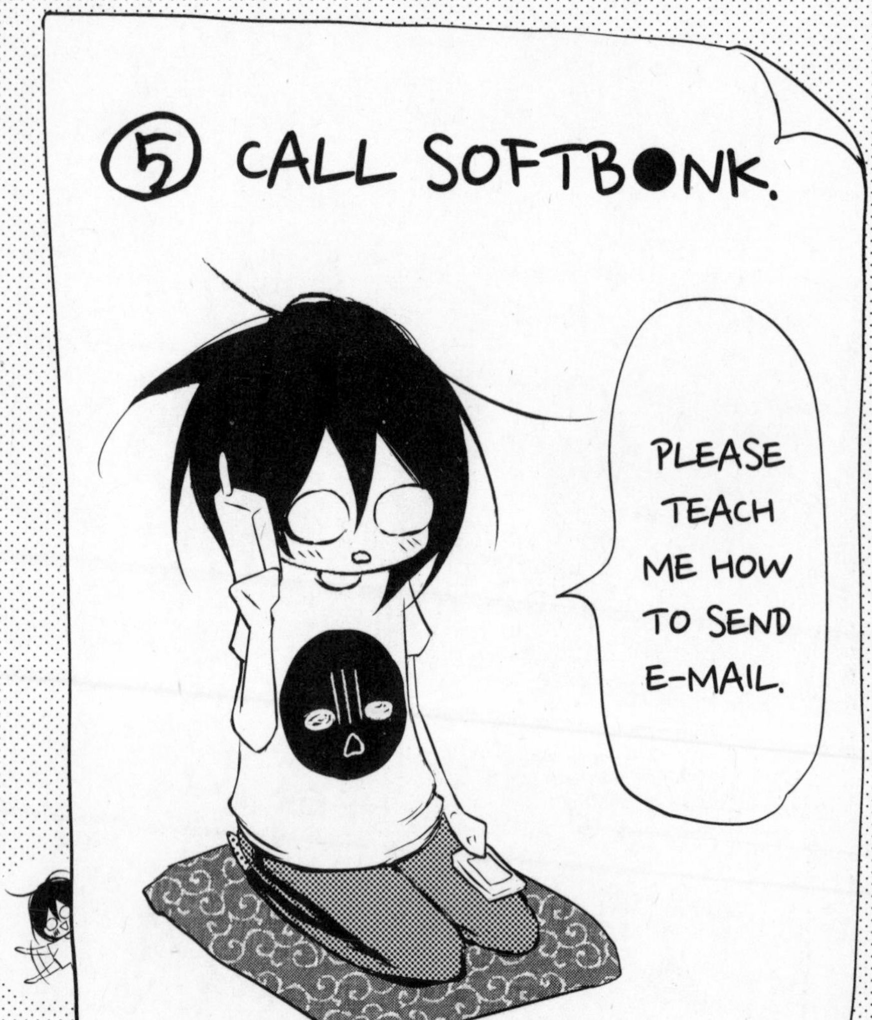
⑤ CALL SOFTB●NK.
PLEASE TEACH ME HOW TO SEND E-MAIL.

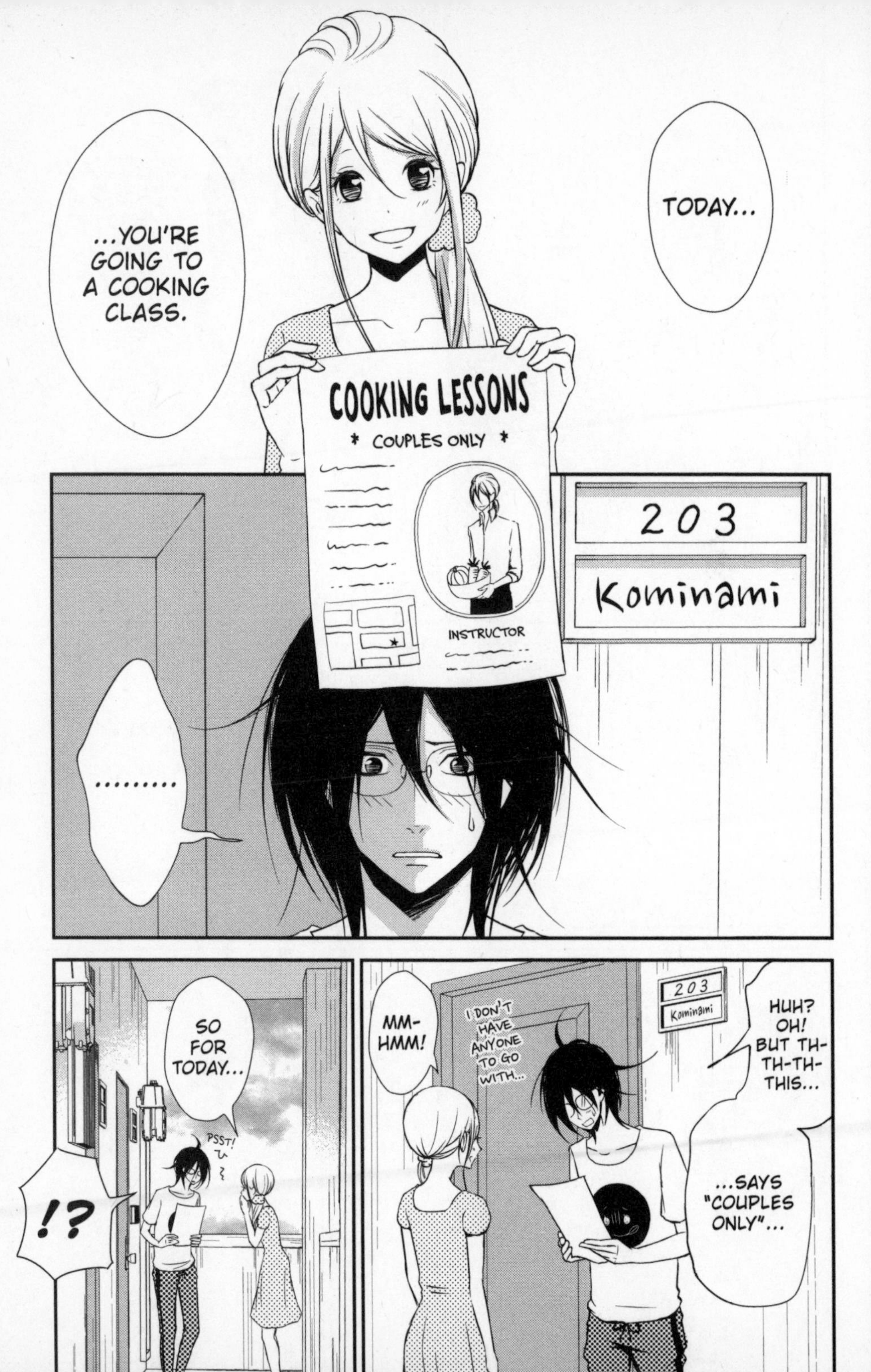
TODAY...
...YOU'RE GOING TO A COOKING CLASS.
COOKING LESSONS
* COUPLES ONLY *
INSTRUCTOR
203
Kominami
....
HUH? OH! BUT TH-TH-TH-THIS...
...SAYS "COUPLES ONLY"...
203
Kominami
I DON'T HAVE ANYONE TO GO WITH...
MM-HMM!
SO FOR TODAY...
PSST!
!?

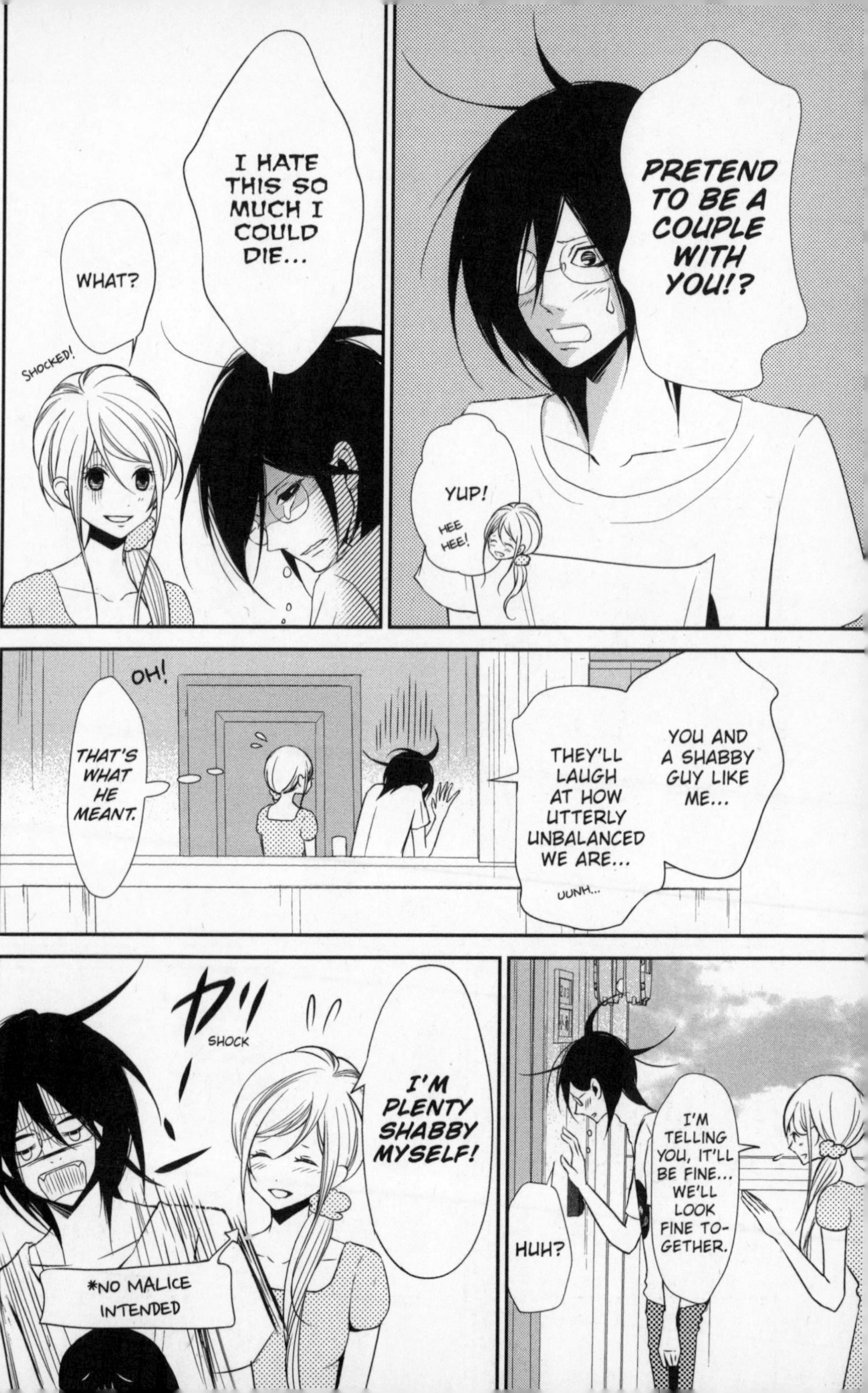
PRETEND TO BE A COUPLE WITH YOU!?
YUP!
HEE HEE!
I HATE THIS SO MUCH I COULD DIE...
WHAT?
SHOCKED!
YOU AND A SHABBY GUY LIKE ME...
THEY'LL LAUGH AT HOW UTTERLY UNBALANCED WE ARE...
UUNH...
OH!
THAT'S WHAT HE MEANT.
I'M TELLING YOU, IT'LL BE FINE... WE'LL LOOK FINE TOGETHER.
HUH?
I'M PLENTY SHABBY MYSELF!
SHOCK
*NO MALICE INTENDED

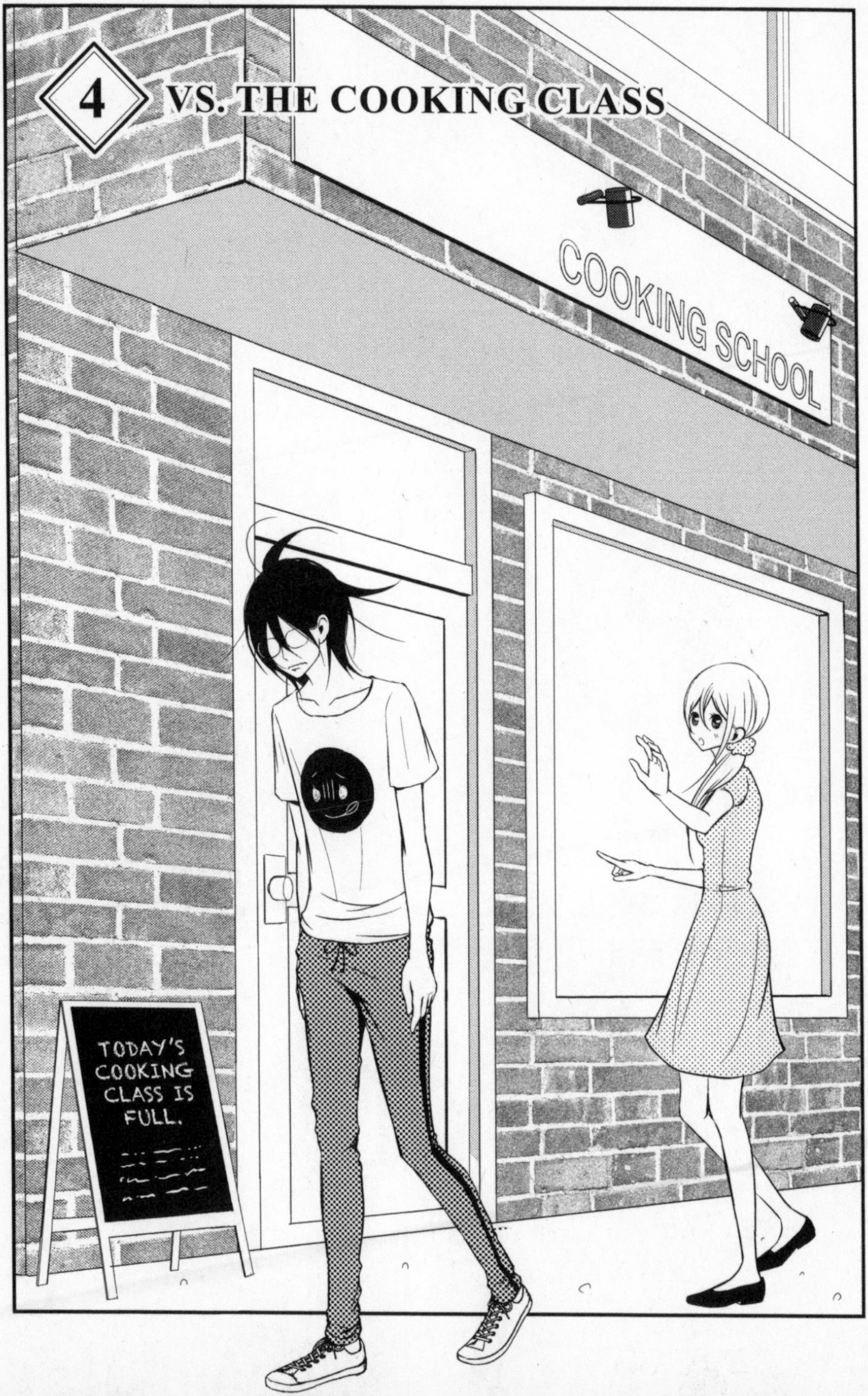
4 VS. THE COOKING CLASS
COOKING SCHOOL
TODAY'S COOKING CLASS IS FULL.

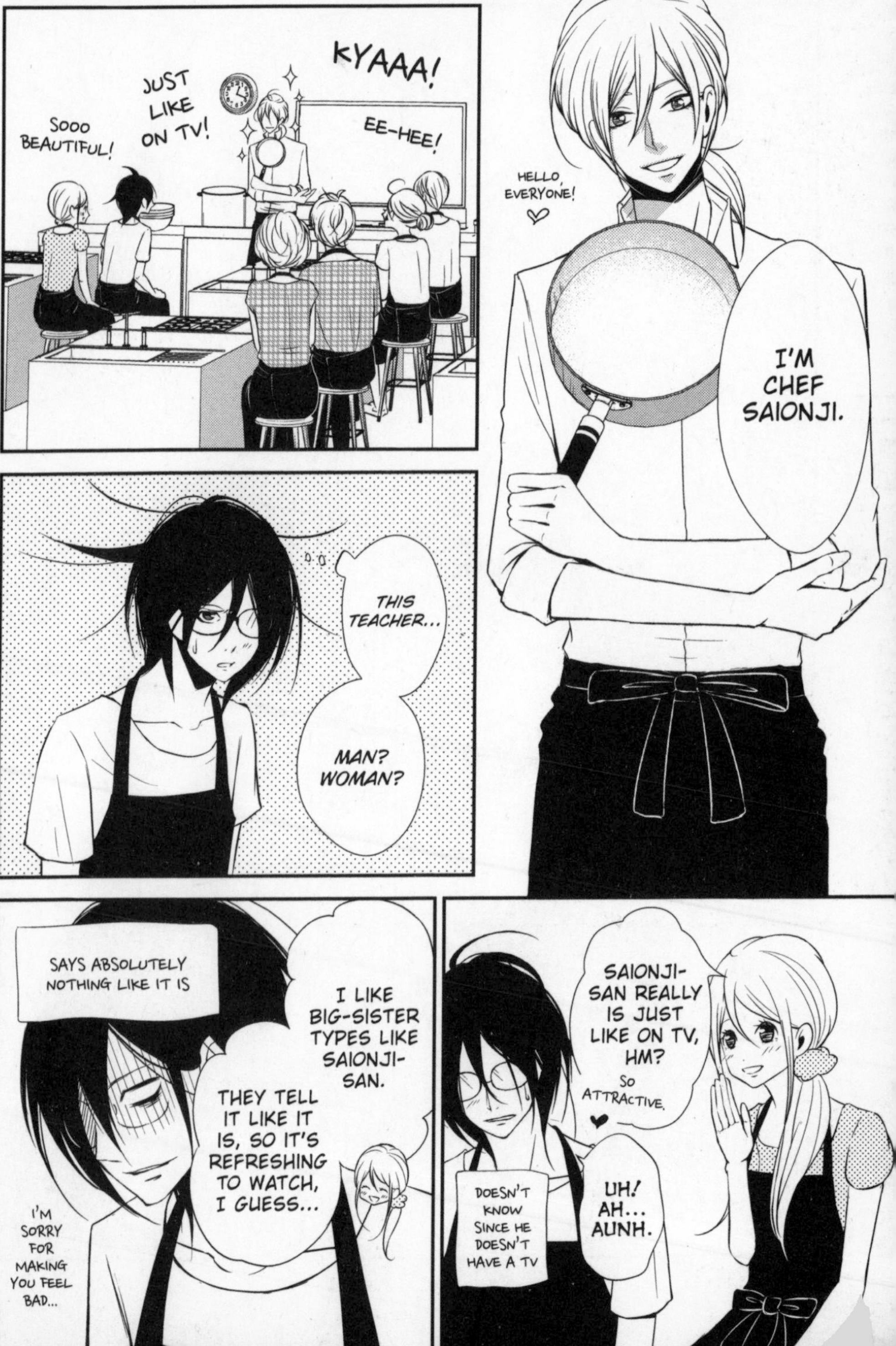
HELLO, EVERYONE! ♥
I'M CHEF SAIONJI.
KYAAA!
EE-HEE!
JUST LIKE ON TV!
SOOO BEAUTIFUL!
THIS TEACHER...
MAN? WOMAN?
SAIONJI-SAN REALLY IS JUST LIKE ON TV, HM?
SO ATTRACTIVE. ♥
UH! AH... AUNH.
DOESN'T KNOW SINCE HE DOESN'T HAVE A TV
I LIKE BIG-SISTER TYPES LIKE SAIONJI-SAN.
THEY TELL IT LIKE IT IS, SO IT'S REFRESHING TO WATCH, I GUESS...
SAYS ABSOLUTELY NOTHING LIKE IT IS
I'M SORRY FOR MAKING YOU FEEL BAD...

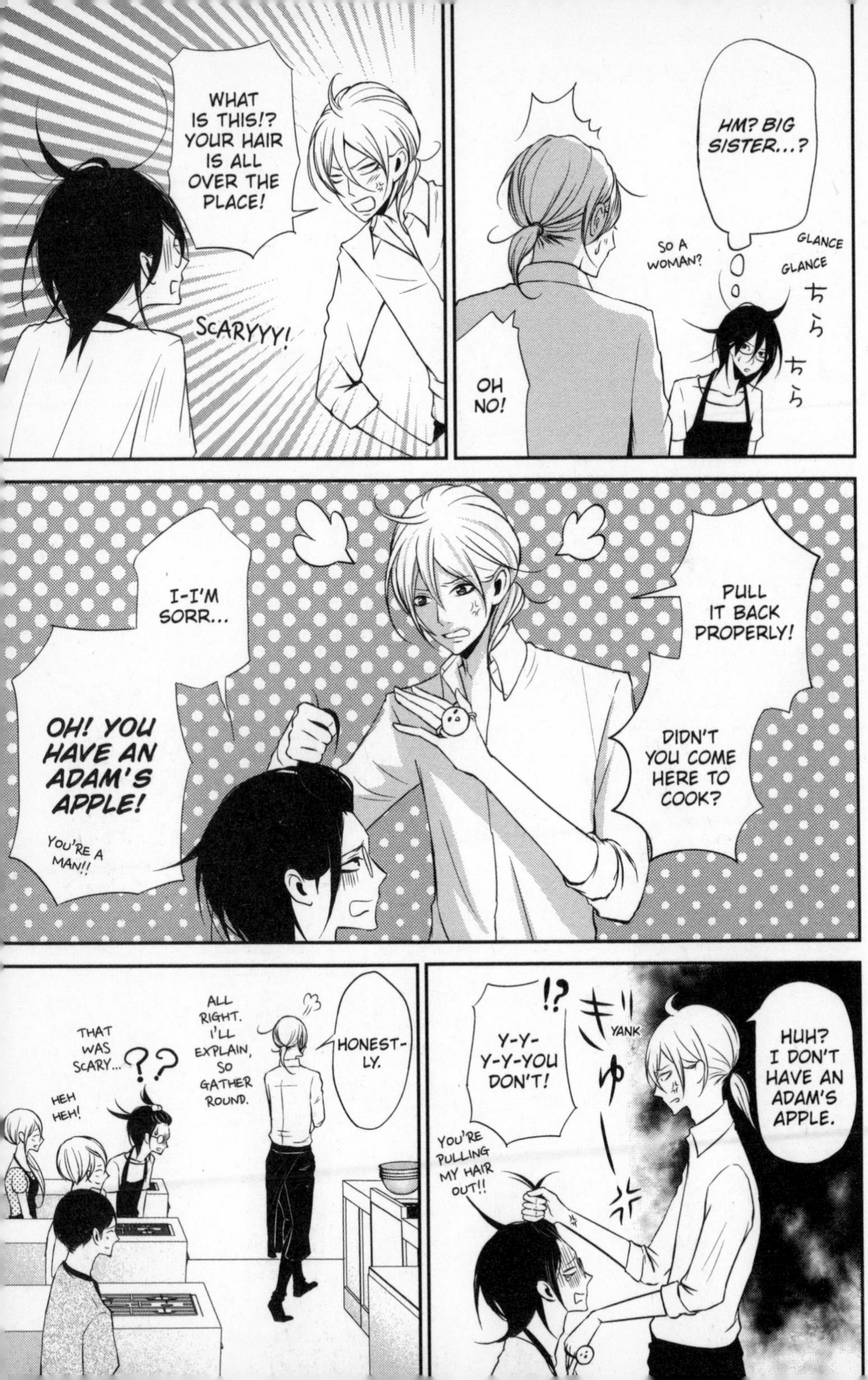
HM? BIG SISTER...?
SO A WOMAN?
GLANCE
GLANCE
ちら
ちら
OH NO!
WHAT IS THIS!? YOUR HAIR IS ALL OVER THE PLACE!
SCARYYY!
PULL IT BACK PROPERLY!
DIDN'T YOU COME HERE TO COOK?
I-I'M SORR...
OH! YOU HAVE AN ADAM'S APPLE!
YOU'RE A MAN!!
HUH? I DON'T HAVE AN ADAM'S APPLE.
ぎゅー
YANK
!?
Y-Y-Y-Y-YOU DON'T!
YOU'RE PULLING MY HAIR OUT!!
HONEST-LY.
ALL RIGHT. I'LL EXPLAIN, SO GATHER ROUND.
THAT WAS SCARY...
??
HEH HEH!

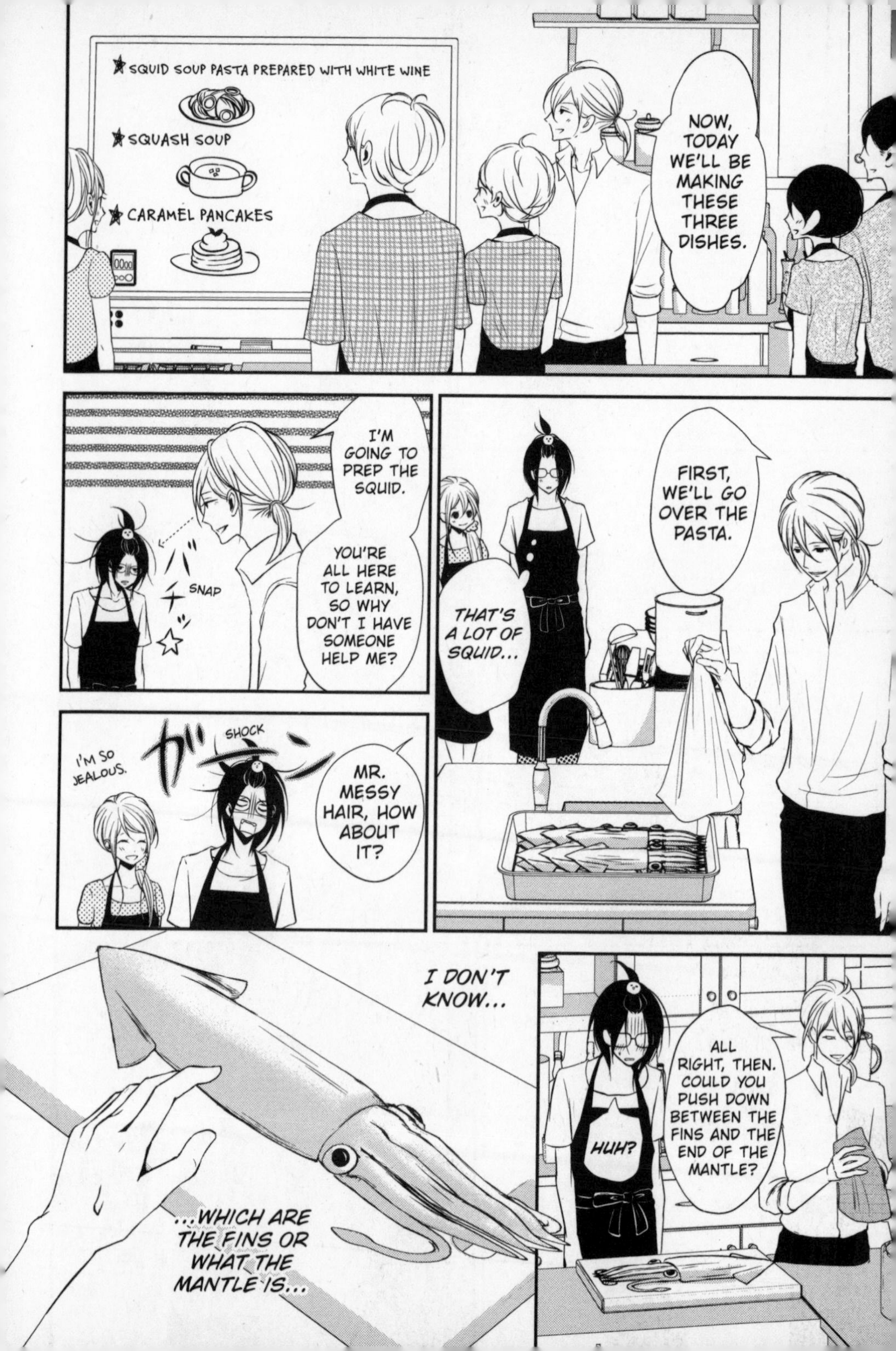
NOW, TODAY WE'LL BE MAKING THESE THREE DISHES.
SQUID SOUP PASTA PREPARED WITH WHITE WINE
SQUASH SOUP
CARAMEL PANCAKES
FIRST, WE'LL GO OVER THE PASTA.
THAT'S A LOT OF SQUID...
I'M GOING TO PREP THE SQUID.
SNAP
YOU'RE ALL HERE TO LEARN, SO WHY DON'T I HAVE SOMEONE HELP ME?
MR. MESSY HAIR, HOW ABOUT IT?
SHOCK
I'M SO JEALOUS.
ALL RIGHT, THEN. COULD YOU PUSH DOWN BETWEEN THE FINS AND THE END OF THE MANTLE?
HUH?
I DON'T KNOW...
...WHICH ARE THE FINS OR WHAT THE MANTLE IS...

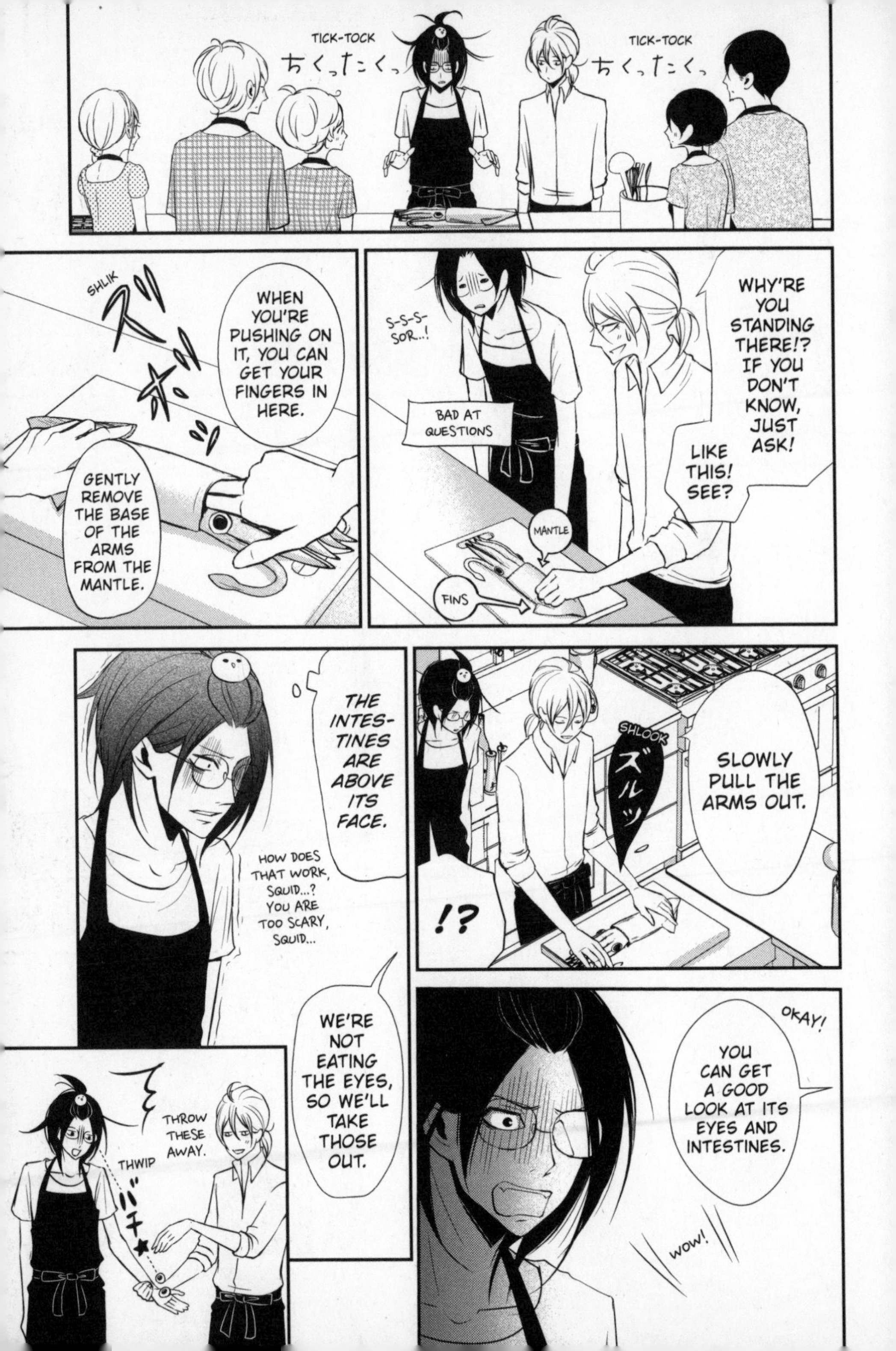
TICK-TOCK
ちくったくっ
TICK-TOCK
ちくったくっ
WHY'RE YOU STANDING THERE!? IF YOU DON'T KNOW, JUST ASK!
S-S-S-SOR...!
LIKE THIS! SEE?
BAD AT QUESTIONS
MANTLE
FINS
WHEN YOU'RE PUSHING ON IT, YOU CAN GET YOUR FINGERS IN HERE.
SHLIK
GENTLY REMOVE THE BASE OF THE ARMS FROM THE MANTLE.
SLOWLY PULL THE ARMS OUT.
SHLOOK
ズルッ
!?
THE INTESTINES ARE ABOVE ITS FACE.
HOW DOES THAT WORK, SQUID...? YOU ARE TOO SCARY, SQUID...
OKAY!
YOU CAN GET A GOOD LOOK AT ITS EYES AND INTESTINES.
WOW!
WE'RE NOT EATING THE EYES, SO WE'LL TAKE THOSE OUT.
THROW THESE AWAY.
THWIP
バチ

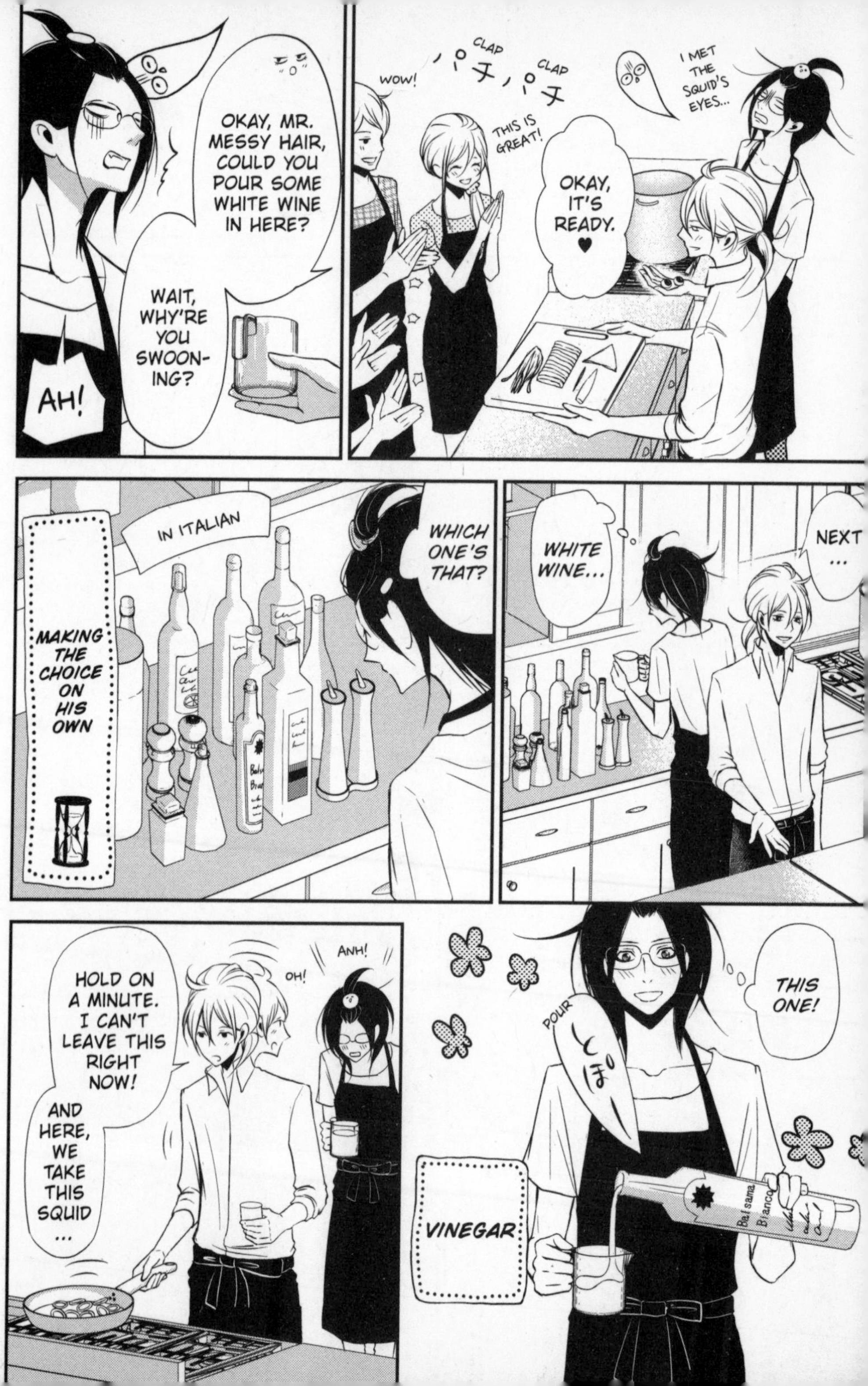
I MET THE SQUID'S EYES...
CLAP パチパチ CLAP
WOW!
THIS IS GREAT!
OKAY, IT'S READY. ♥
OKAY, MR. MESSY HAIR, COULD YOU POUR SOME WHITE WINE IN HERE?
WAIT, WHY'RE YOU SWOONING?
AH!
NEXT ...
WHITE WINE...
WHICH ONE'S THAT?
IN ITALIAN
MAKING THE CHOICE ON HIS OWN
THIS ONE!
POUR とぽ
Balsama Bianco
VINEGAR
ANH!
OH!
HOLD ON A MINUTE. I CAN'T LEAVE THIS RIGHT NOW!
AND HERE, WE TAKE THIS SQUID ...

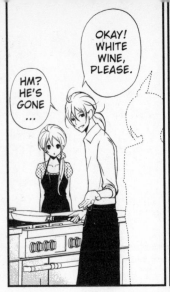

ボーー!!
FWOOM
...AND FLAMBÉ IT.
OOOOH!
OKAY! WHITE WINE, PLEASE.
HM? HE'S GONE...
ぷるぷる
TREMBLE TREMBLE
OH! HE'S HERE...
WHAT!?
I GUESS HE WAS SCARED BY THE FLAMBÉ.
I-I'VE HAD THE VAGUEST SENSE OF IT SINCE YOU GOT HERE, BUT...
...COULD IT BE YOU'RE...
...A COMPLETE WRECK OF A MAN!?
I-I AM...
I-I'M SORRY. I'M AN EYESORE...
NO WAY... A TOTAL DISASTER OF A MAN LIKE YOU...
YOU ADMIT IT, HUH...?

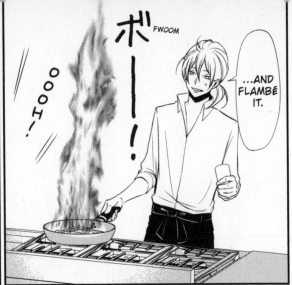

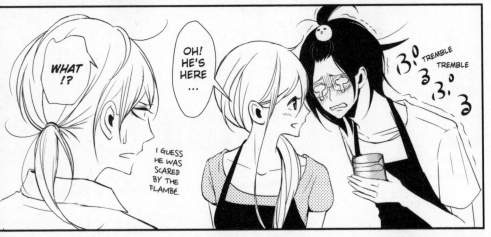

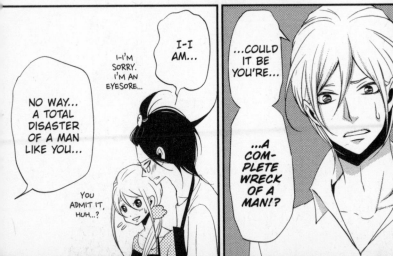

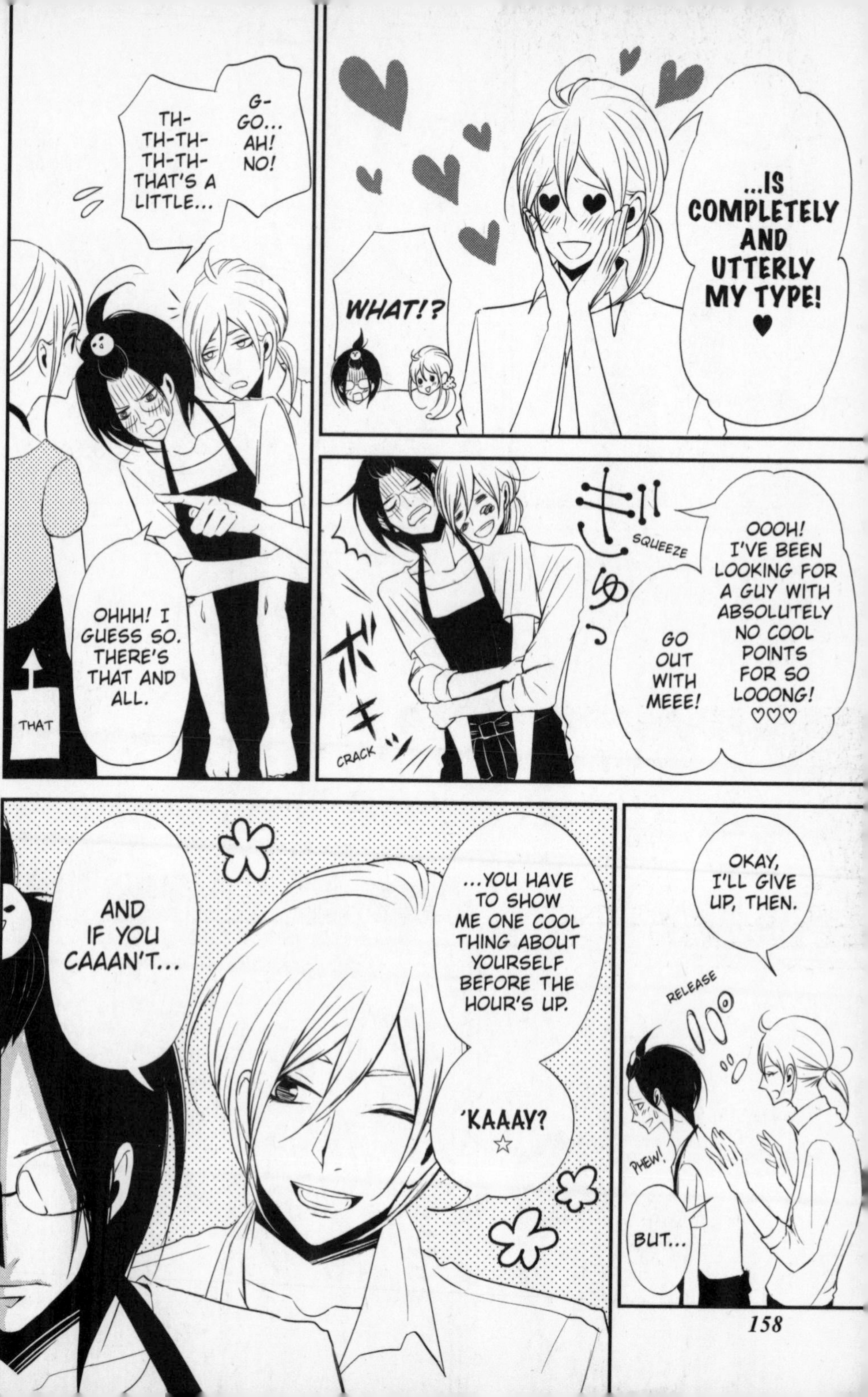
...IS COMPLETELY AND UTTERLY MY TYPE! ♥
WHAT!?
SQUEEZE
OOOH! I'VE BEEN LOOKING FOR A GUY WITH ABSOLUTELY NO COOL POINTS FOR SO LOOONG! ♡♡♡
GO OUT WITH MEEE!
CRACK
G-GO... AH! NO!
TH-TH-TH-TH-TH-THAT'S A LITTLE...
OHHH! I GUESS SO. THERE'S THAT AND ALL.
THAT
OKAY, I'LL GIVE UP, THEN.
RELEASE
PHEW!
BUT...
...YOU HAVE TO SHOW ME ONE COOL THING ABOUT YOURSELF BEFORE THE HOUR'S UP.
'KAAAY? ☆
AND IF YOU CAAAN'T...

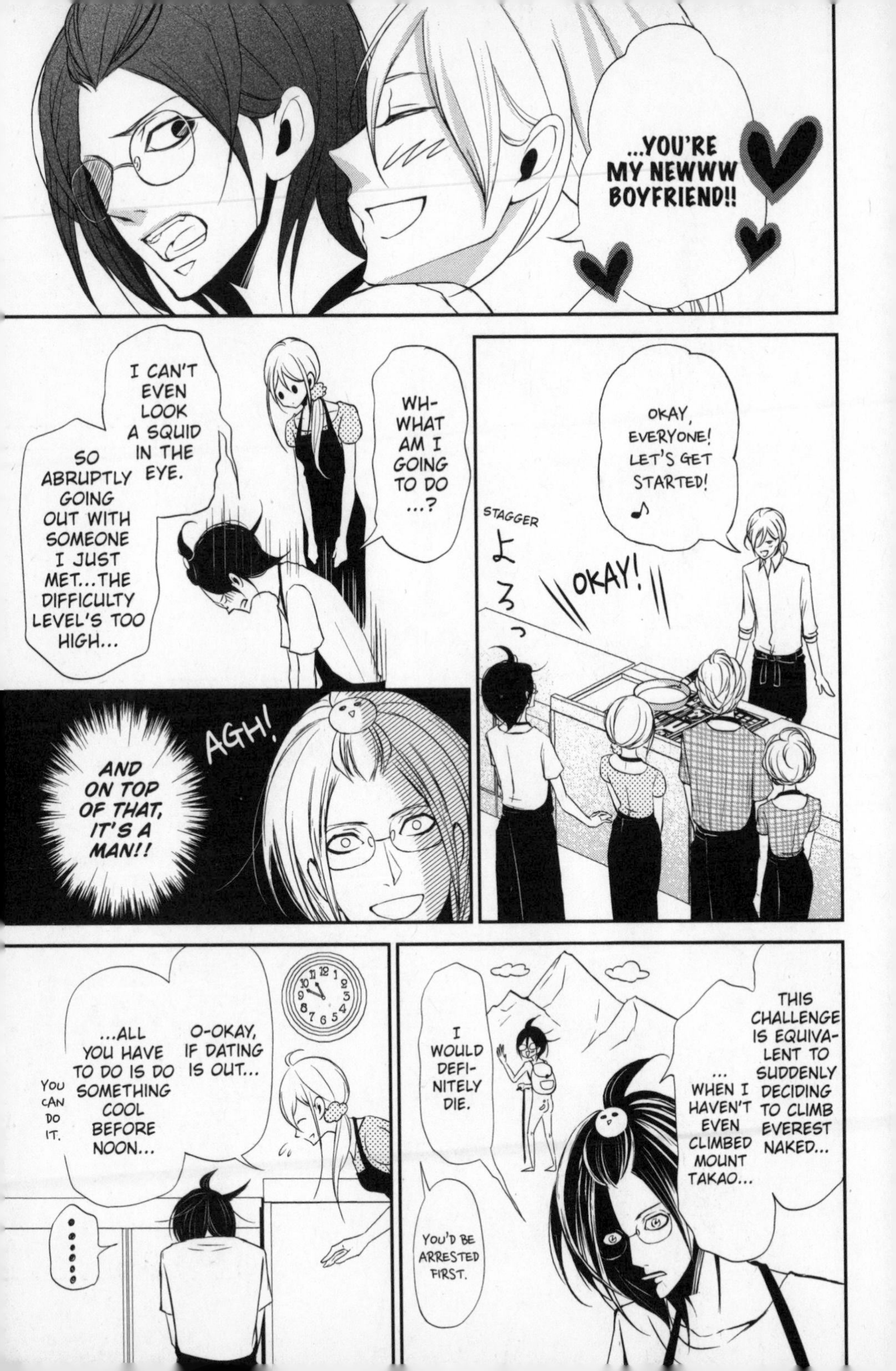
...YOU'RE MY NEWWW BOYFRIEND!!
OKAY, EVERYONE! LET'S GET STARTED! ♪
OKAY!
STAGGER
よろっ
WH-WHAT AM I GOING TO DO ...?
I CAN'T EVEN LOOK A SQUID IN THE EYE.
SO ABRUPTLY GOING OUT WITH SOMEONE I JUST MET...THE DIFFICULTY LEVEL'S TOO HIGH...
AGH!
AND ON TOP OF THAT, IT'S A MAN!!
THIS CHALLENGE IS EQUIVALENT TO SUDDENLY DECIDING TO CLIMB EVEREST NAKED...
...WHEN I HAVEN'T EVEN CLIMBED MOUNT TAKAO...
I WOULD DEFINITELY DIE.
YOU'D BE ARRESTED FIRST.
O-OKAY, IF DATING IS OUT...
...ALL YOU HAVE TO DO IS DO SOMETHING COOL BEFORE NOON...
YOU CAN DO IT.
......

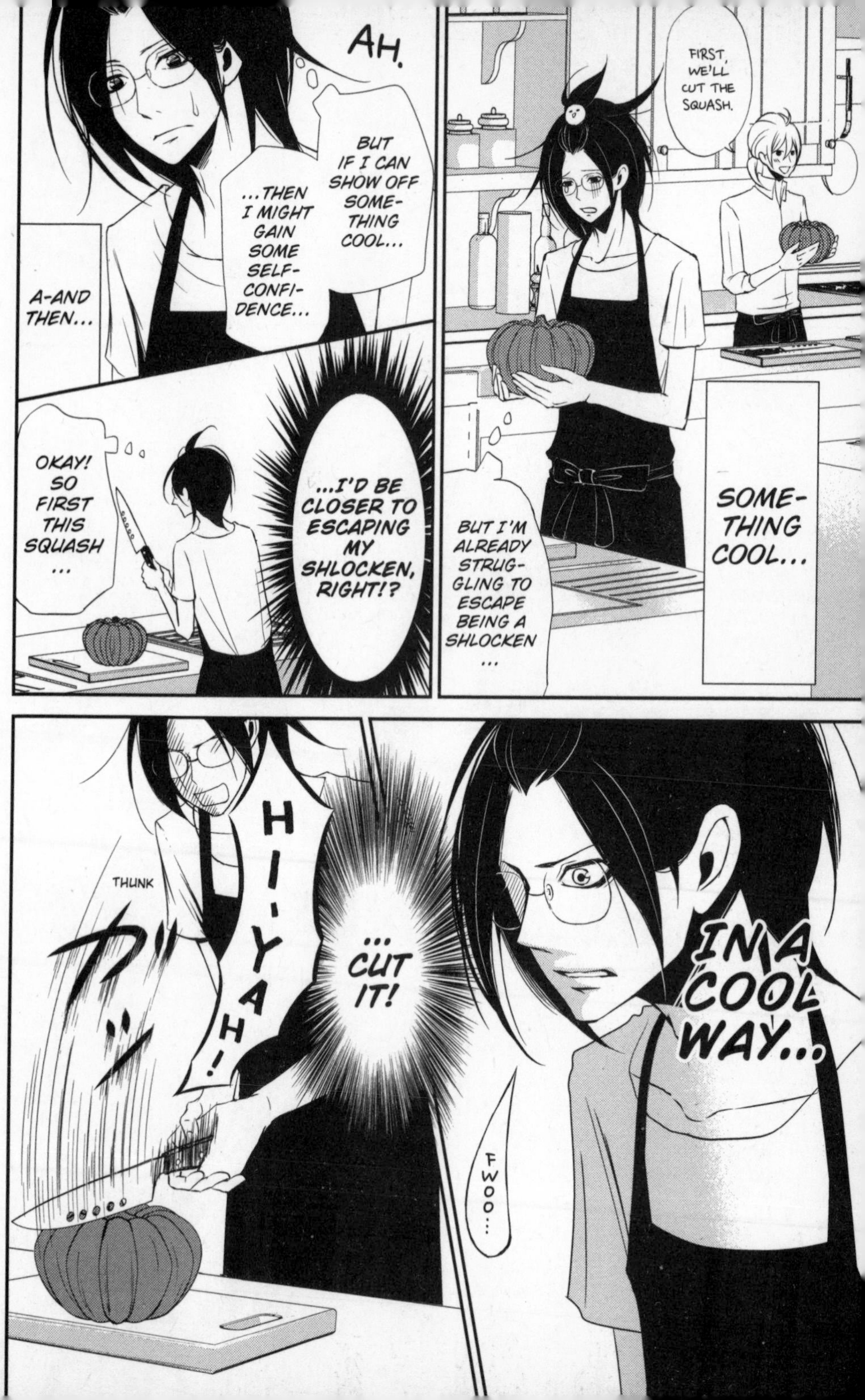
FIRST, WE'LL CUT THE SQUASH.
SOME-THING COOL...
BUT I'M ALREADY STRUG-GLING TO ESCAPE BEING A SHLOCKEN...
AH.
BUT IF I CAN SHOW OFF SOME-THING COOL...
...THEN I MIGHT GAIN SOME SELF-CONFI-DENCE...
A-AND THEN...
...I'D BE CLOSER TO ESCAPING MY SHLOCKEN, RIGHT!?
OKAY! SO FIRST THIS SQUASH...
IN A COOL WAY...
FWOO...
...CUT IT!
HI-YAH!
THUNK

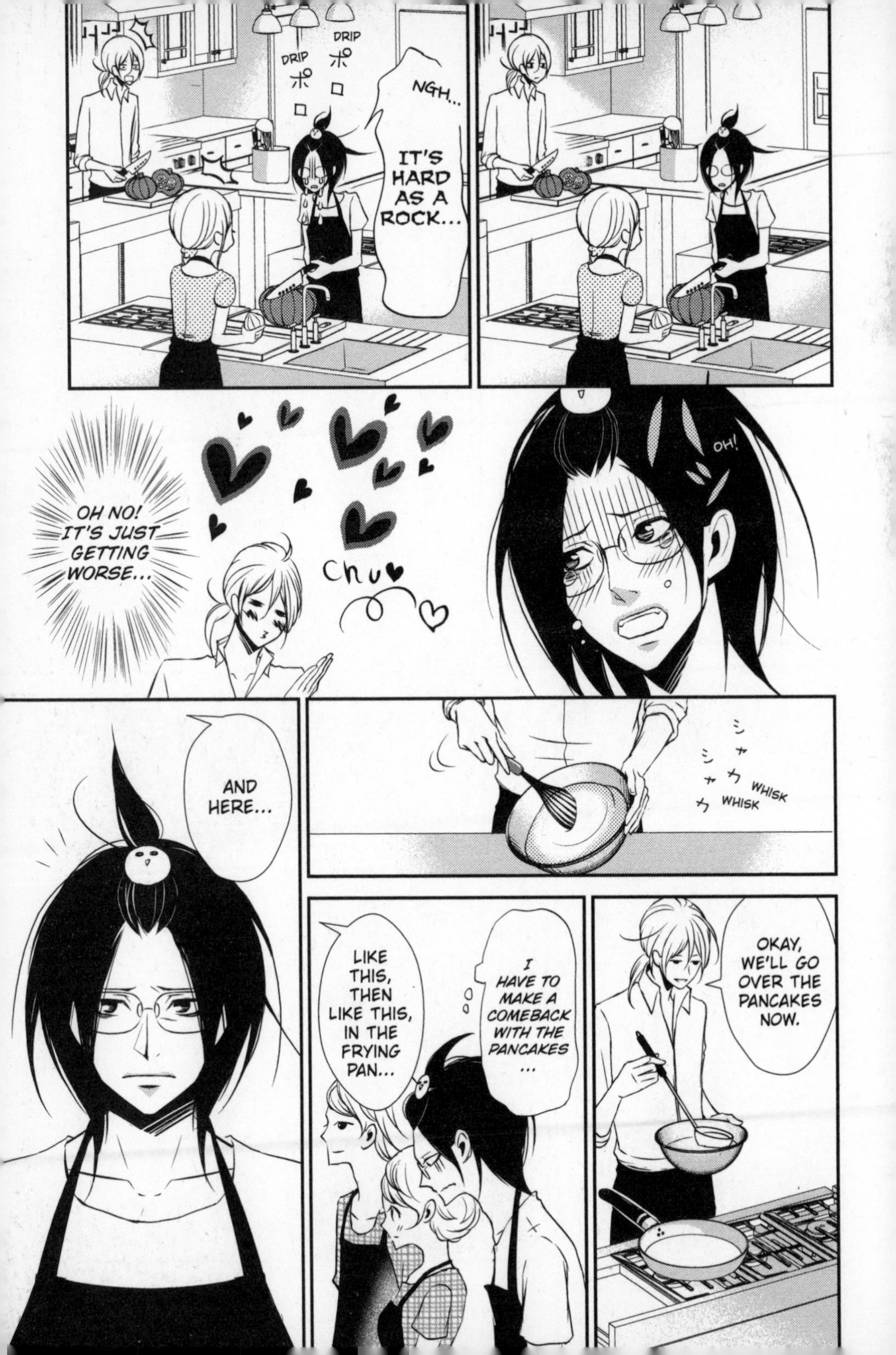
DRIP
ポ
ロ
DRIP
ポ
ロ
NGH...
IT'S HARD AS A ROCK...
OH!
OH NO! IT'S JUST GETTING WORSE...
Chu
シャカ
シャカ
WHISK
WHISK
OKAY, WE'LL GO OVER THE PANCAKES NOW.
I HAVE TO MAKE A COMEBACK WITH THE PANCAKES...
LIKE THIS, THEN LIKE THIS, IN THE FRYING PAN...
AND HERE...

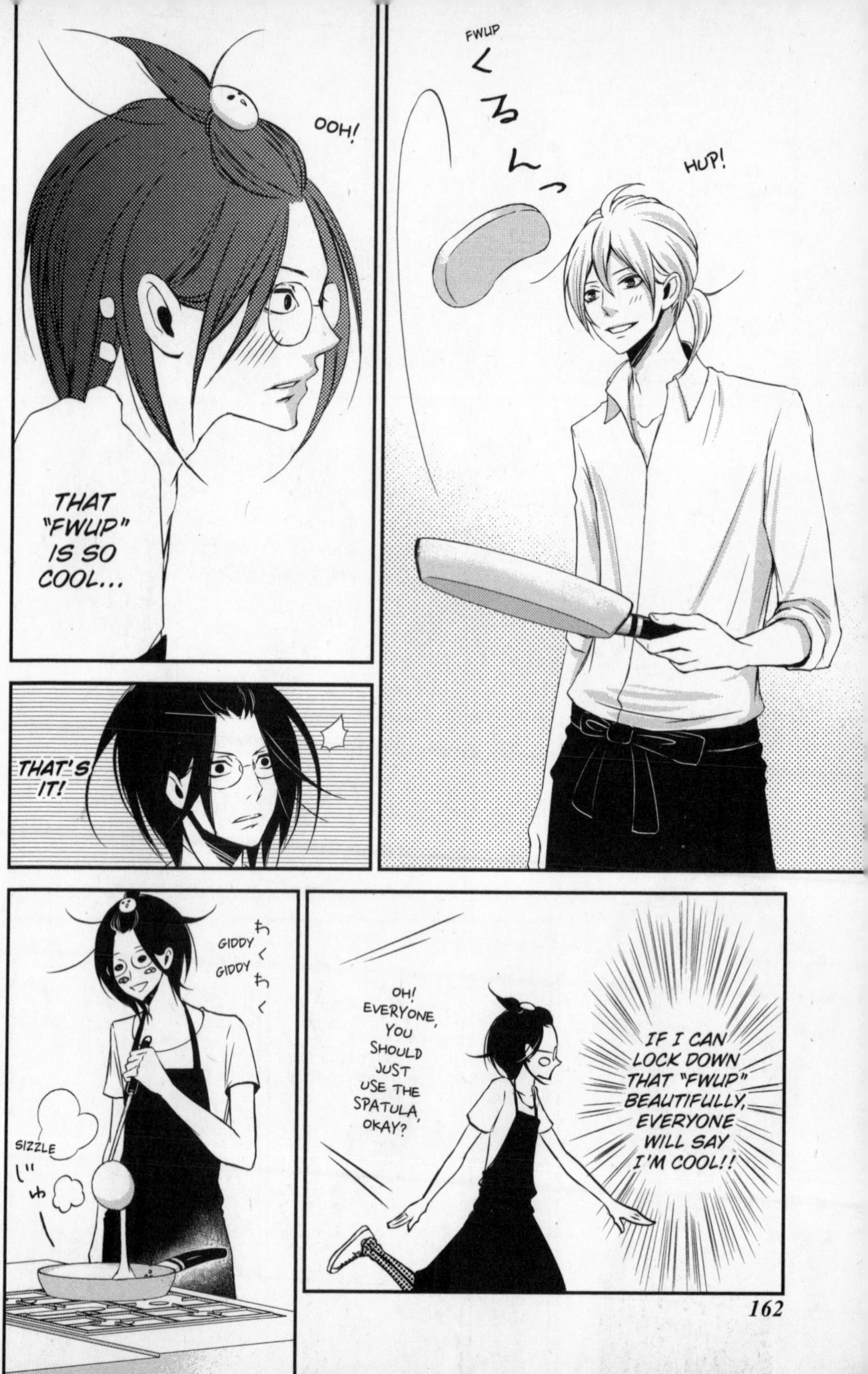
FWUP
くるんっ
HUP!
OOH!
THAT "FWUP" IS SO COOL...
THAT'S IT!
IF I CAN LOCK DOWN THAT "FWUP" BEAUTIFULLY, EVERYONE WILL SAY I'M COOL!!
OH! EVERYONE, YOU SHOULD JUST USE THE SPATULA, OKAY?
GIDDY GIDDY
わくわく
SIZZLE
じゅー

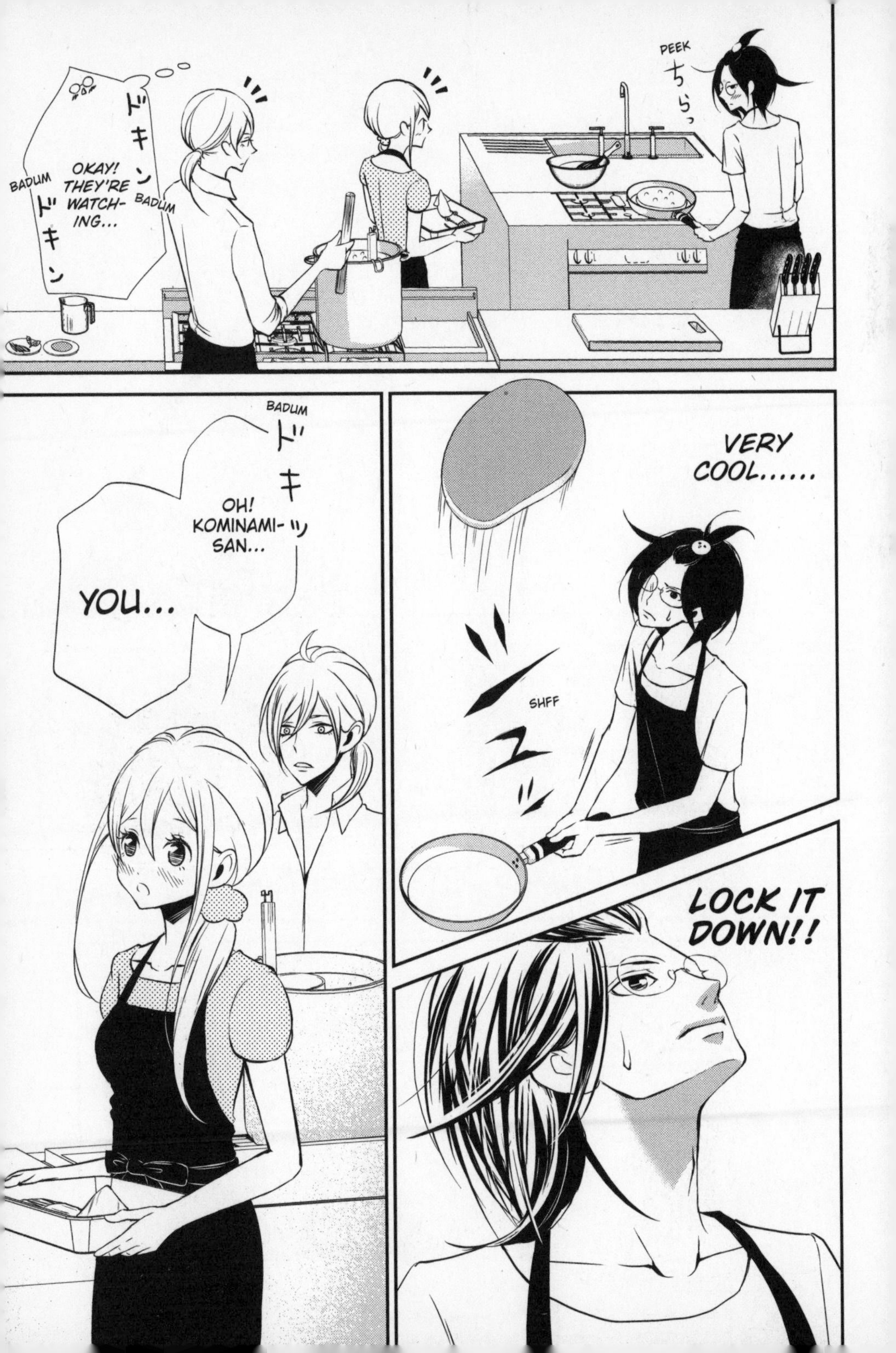
PEEK
ちらっ
BADUM
ドキン
BADUM
ドキン
OKAY! THEY'RE WATCHING...
VERY COOL......
SHFF
LOCK IT DOWN!!
BADUM
ドキッ
OH! KOMINAMI-SAN...
YOU...

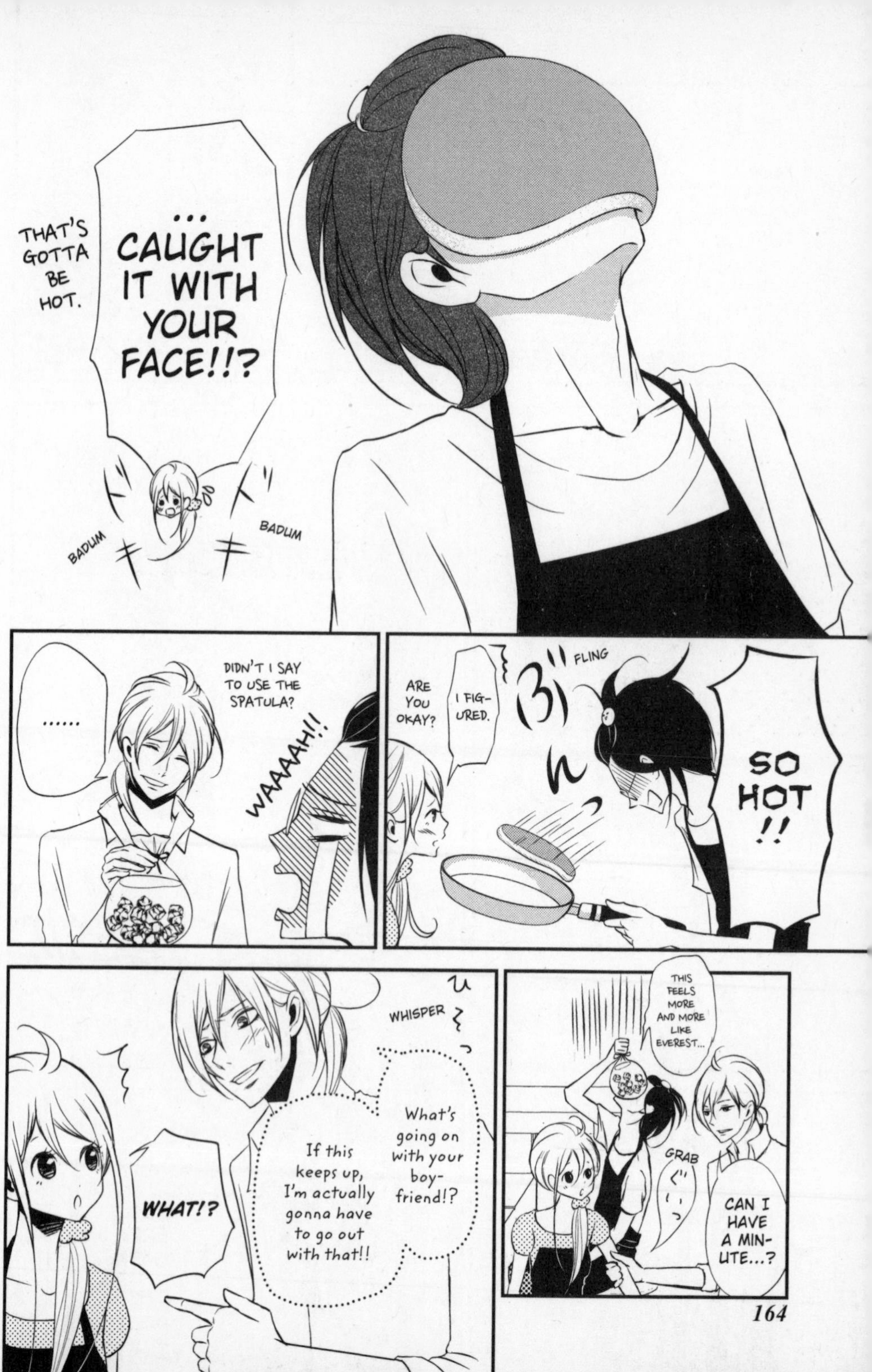
... CAUGHT IT WITH YOUR FACE!!?
THAT'S GOTTA BE HOT.
BADUM
BADUM
SO HOT!!
FLING
I FIG-URED.
ARE YOU OKAY?
WAAAAH!!
DIDN'T I SAY TO USE THE SPATULA?
......
THIS FEELS MORE AND MORE LIKE EVEREST...
GRAB
CAN I HAVE A MIN-UTE...?
WHISPER
What's going on with your boy-friend!?
If this keeps up, I'm actually gonna have to go out with that!!
WHAT!?

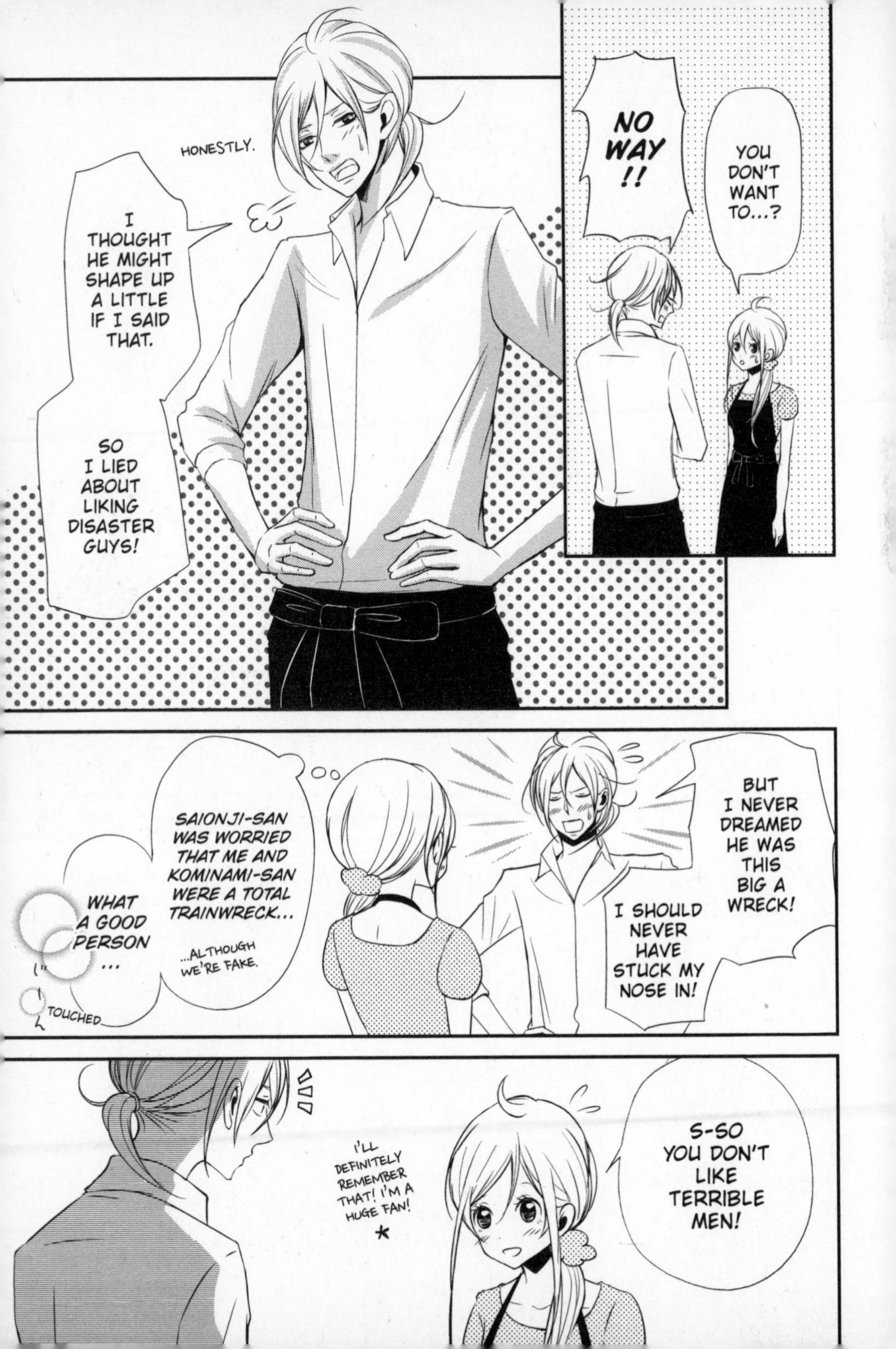

YOU DON'T WANT TO...?
NO WAY!!
HONESTLY.
I THOUGHT HE MIGHT SHAPE UP A LITTLE IF I SAID THAT.
SO I LIED ABOUT LIKING DISASTER GUYS!
BUT I NEVER DREAMED HE WAS THIS BIG A WRECK!
I SHOULD NEVER HAVE STUCK MY NOSE IN!
SAIONJI-SAN WAS WORRIED THAT ME AND KOMINAMI-SAN WERE A TOTAL TRAINWRECK...
...ALTHOUGH WE'RE FAKE.
WHAT A GOOD PERSON...
TOUCHED
S-SO YOU DON'T LIKE TERRIBLE MEN!
I'LL DEFINITELY REMEMBER THAT! I'M A HUGE FAN!

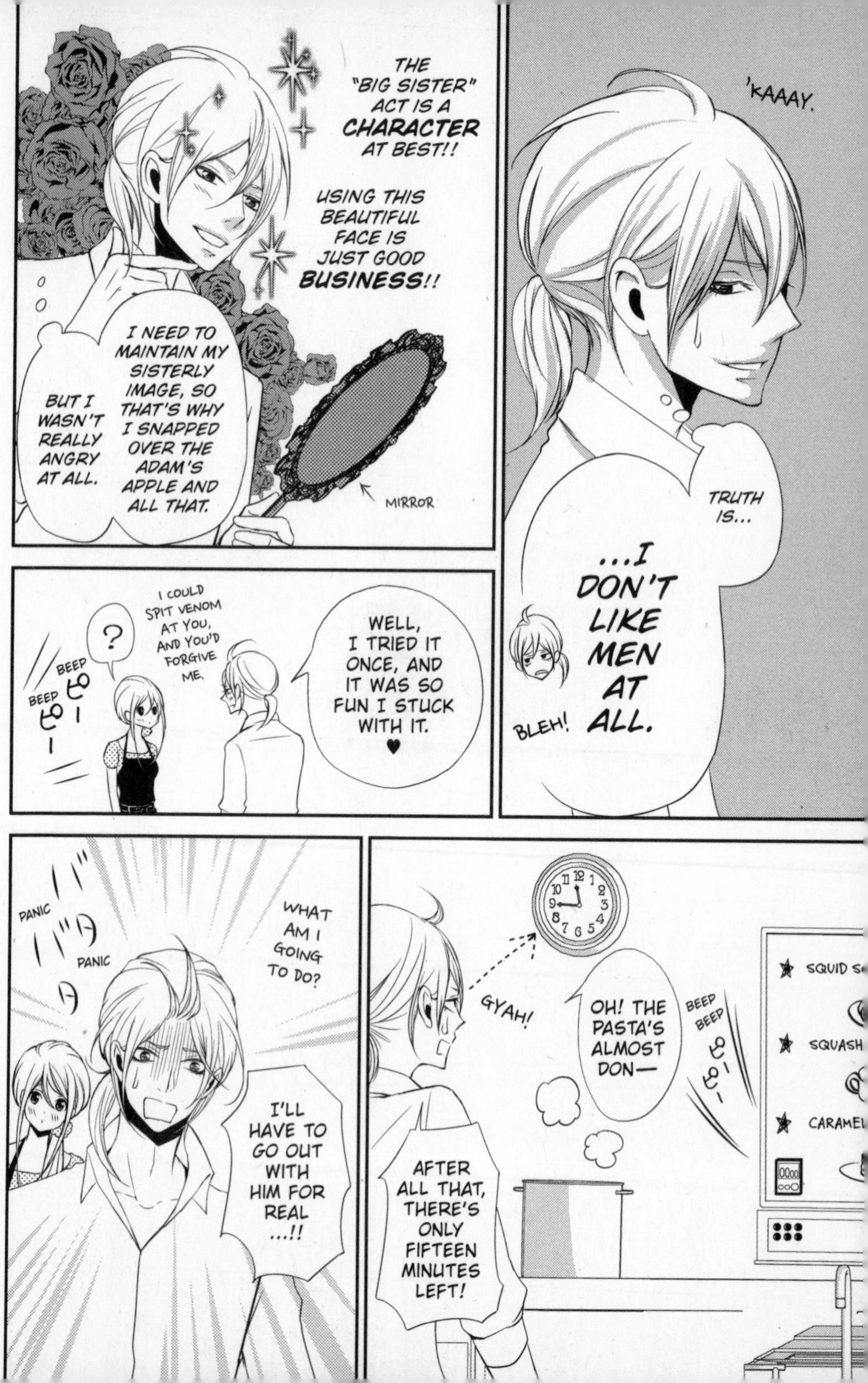
'KAAAY.
TRUTH IS...
...I DON'T LIKE MEN AT ALL.
BLEH!
THE "BIG SISTER" ACT IS A CHARACTER AT BEST!!
USING THIS BEAUTIFUL FACE IS JUST GOOD BUSINESS!!
I NEED TO MAINTAIN MY SISTERLY IMAGE, SO THAT'S WHY I SNAPPED OVER THE ADAM'S APPLE AND ALL THAT.
BUT I WASN'T REALLY ANGRY AT ALL.
MIRROR
WELL, I TRIED IT ONCE, AND IT WAS SO FUN I STUCK WITH IT. ♥
I COULD SPIT VENOM AT YOU, AND YOU'D FORGIVE ME.
?
BEEP
BEEP
SQUASH
BEEP BEEP
OH! THE PASTA'S ALMOST DON—
GYAH!
AFTER ALL THAT, THERE'S ONLY FIFTEEN MINUTES LEFT!
WHAT AM I GOING TO DO?
PANIC
PANIC
I'LL HAVE TO GO OUT WITH HIM FOR REAL ...!!

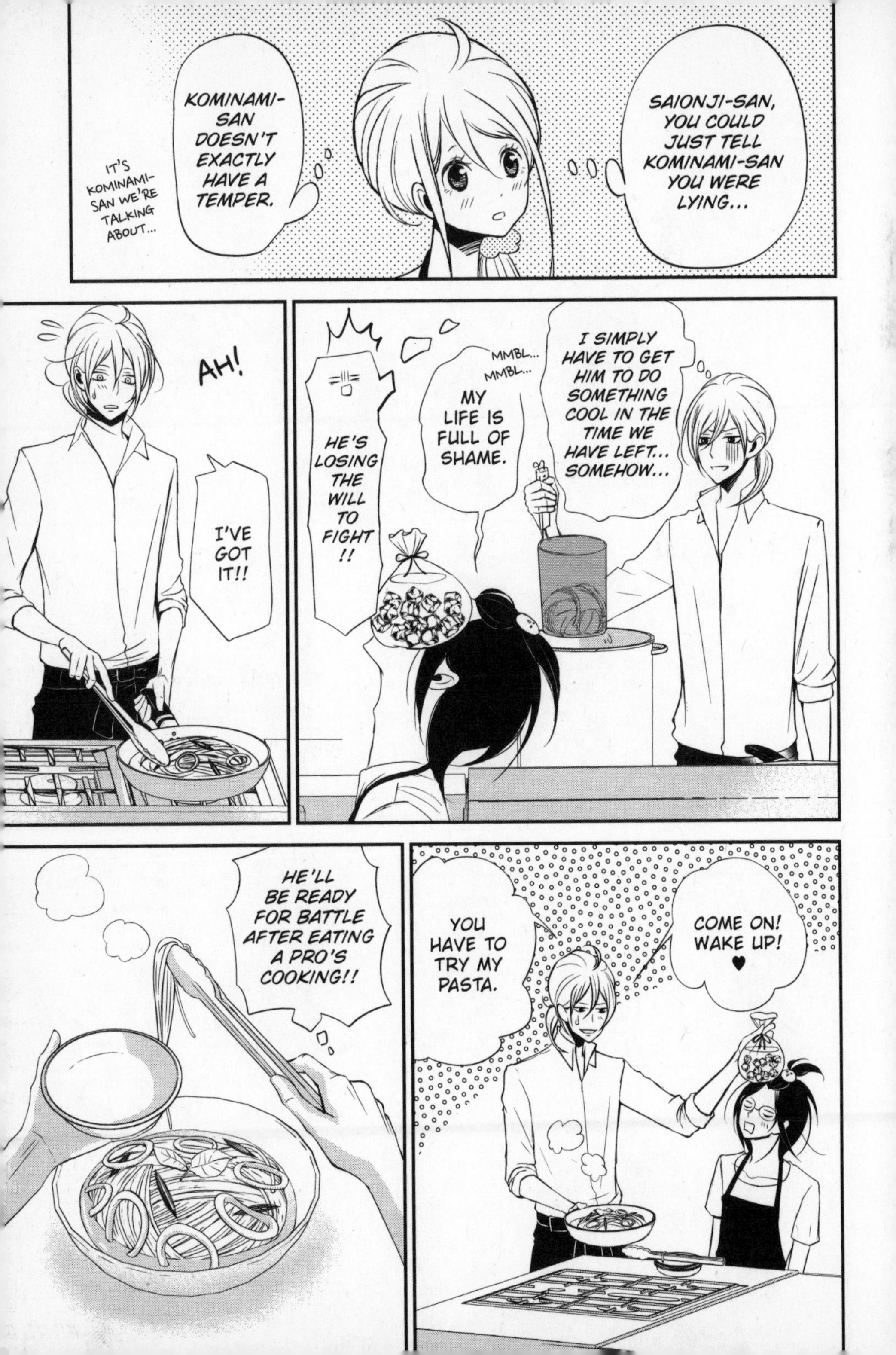
SAIONJI-SAN, YOU COULD JUST TELL KOMINAMI-SAN YOU WERE LYING...
KOMINAMI-SAN DOESN'T EXACTLY HAVE A TEMPER.
IT'S KOMINAMI-SAN WE'RE TALKING ABOUT...
I SIMPLY HAVE TO GET HIM TO DO SOMETHING COOL IN THE TIME WE HAVE LEFT... SOMEHOW...
MMBL... MMBL...
MY LIFE IS FULL OF SHAME.
HE'S LOSING THE WILL TO FIGHT!!
AH!
I'VE GOT IT!!
COME ON! WAKE UP! ♥
YOU HAVE TO TRY MY PASTA.
HE'LL BE READY FOR BATTLE AFTER EATING A PRO'S COOKING!!

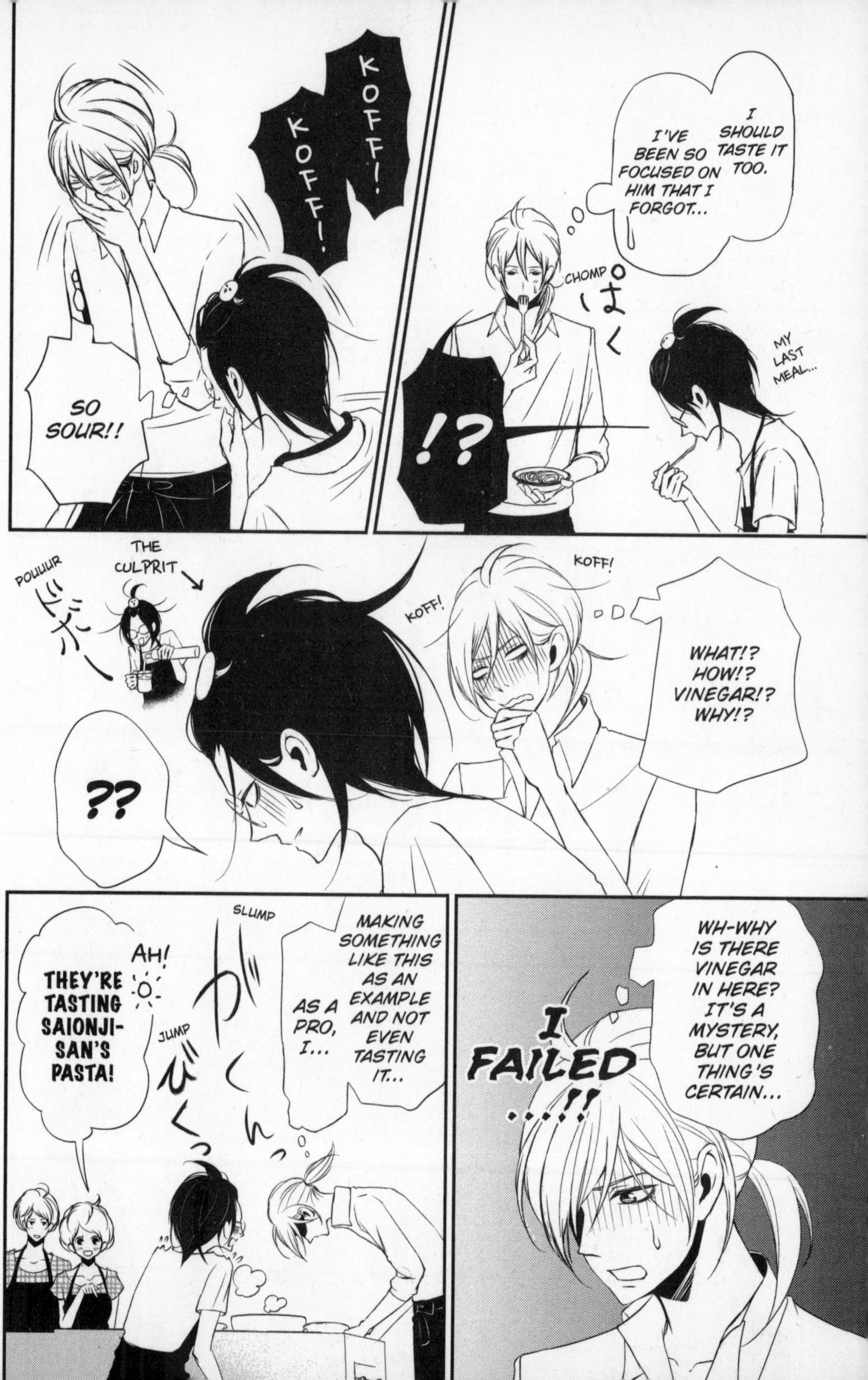
I SHOULD TASTE IT TOO. I'VE BEEN SO FOCUSED ON HIM THAT I FORGOT...
CHOMP
ぱく
MY LAST MEAL...
!?
KOFF! KOFF!
SO SOUR!!
KOFF!
WHAT!? HOW!? VINEGAR!? WHY!?
KOFF!
??
THE CULPRIT
POUUUR
ドボー
WH-WHY IS THERE VINEGAR IN HERE? IT'S A MYSTERY, BUT ONE THING'S CERTAIN...
I FAILED ...!!
MAKING SOMETHING LIKE THIS AS AN EXAMPLE AND NOT EVEN TASTING IT...
AS A PRO, I...
SLUMP
がくん
AH!
THEY'RE TASTING SAIONJI-SAN'S PASTA!
JUMP
びくっ

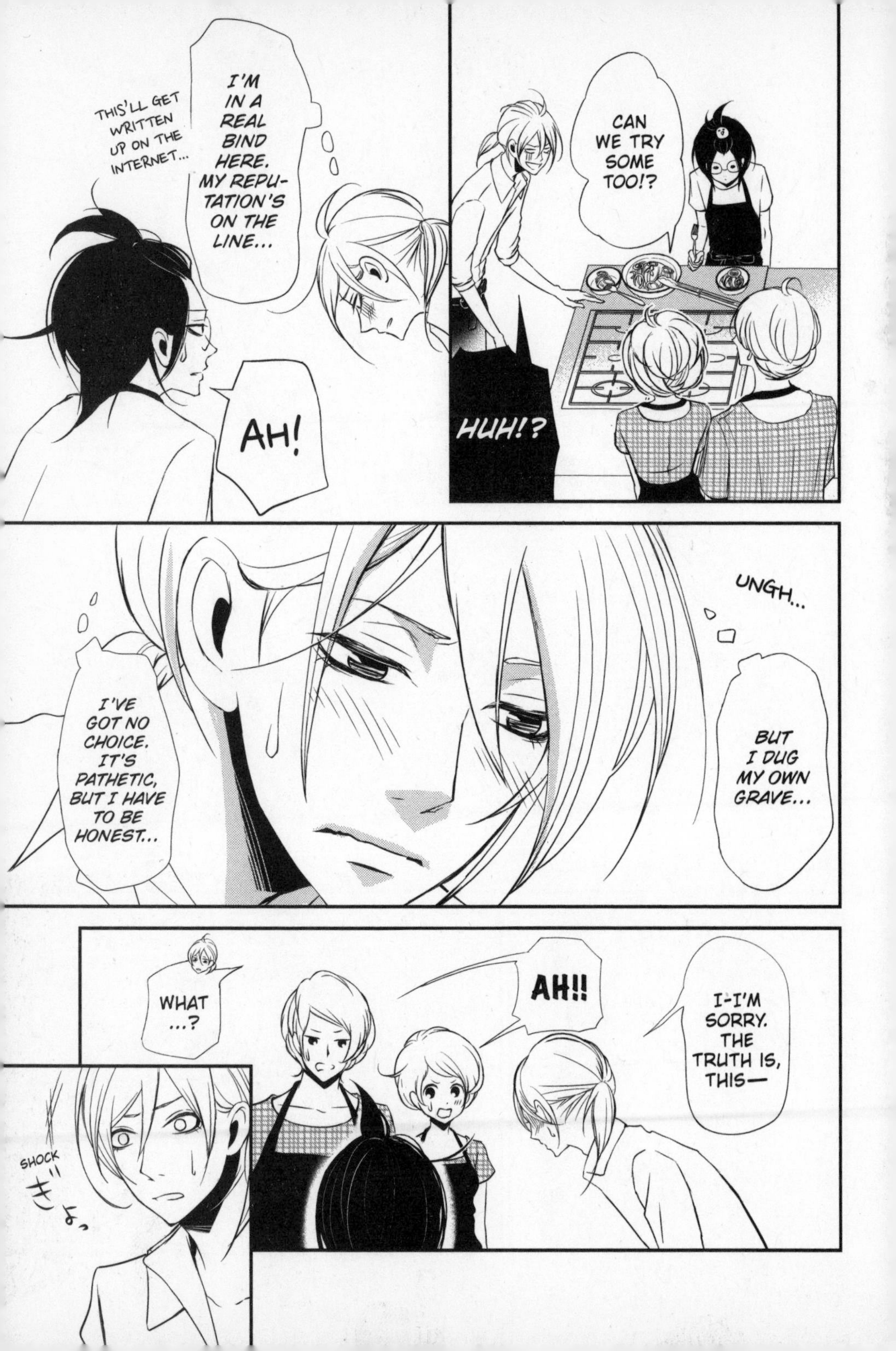
CAN WE TRY SOME TOO!?
HUH!?
I'M IN A REAL BIND HERE. MY REPUTATION'S ON THE LINE...
THIS'LL GET WRITTEN UP ON THE INTERNET...
AH!
UNGH...
BUT I DUG MY OWN GRAVE...
I'VE GOT NO CHOICE. IT'S PATHETIC, BUT I HAVE TO BE HONEST...
I-I'M SORRY. THE TRUTH IS, THIS—
AH!!
WHAT ...?
SHOCK

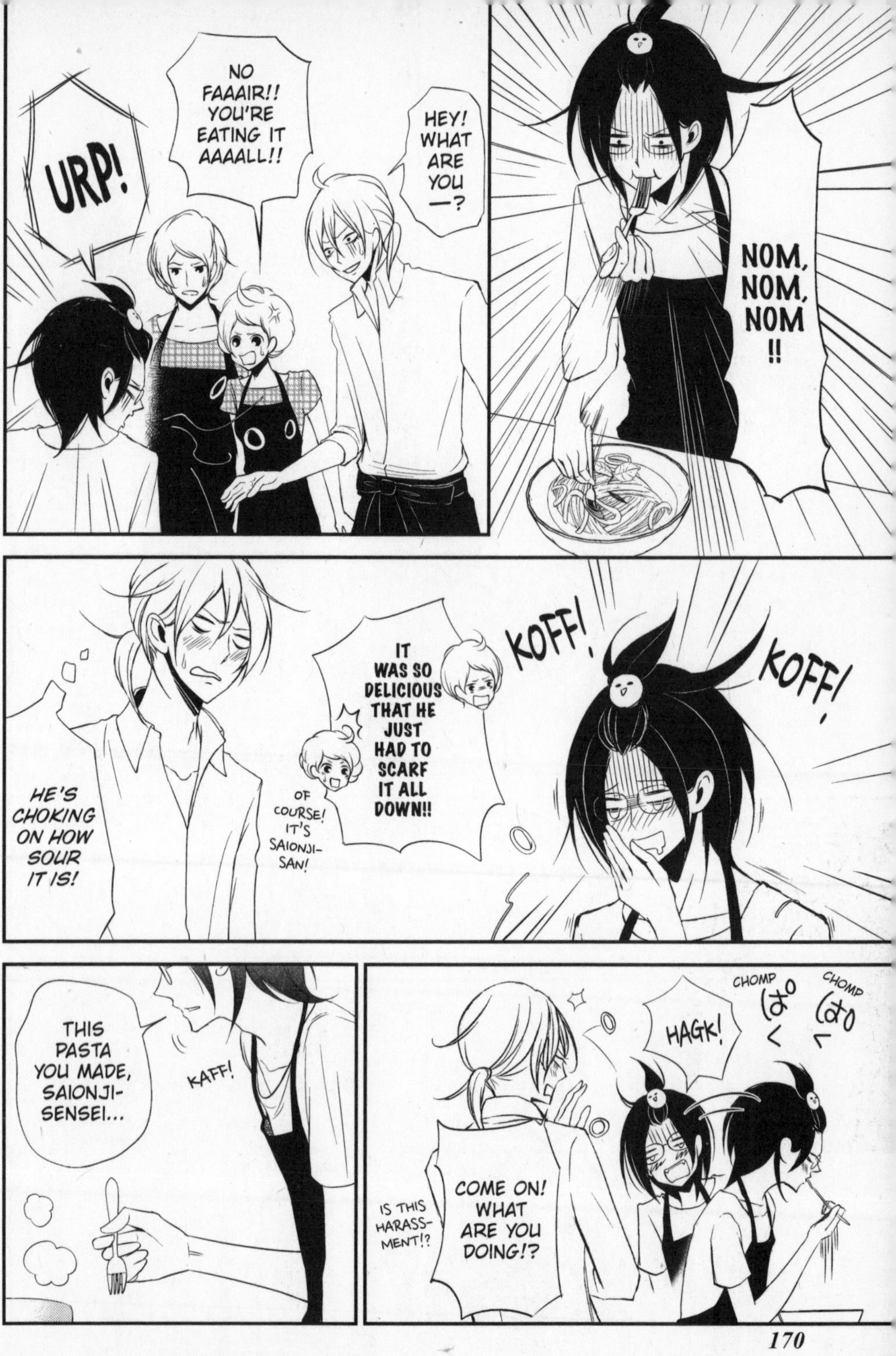
NOM, NOM, NOM!!
HEY! WHAT ARE YOU—?
NO FAAAIR!! YOU'RE EATING IT AAAALL!!
URP!
KOFF! KOFF!
IT WAS SO DELICIOUS THAT HE JUST HAD TO SCARF IT ALL DOWN!!
OF COURSE! IT'S SAIONJI-SAN!
HE'S CHOKING ON HOW SOUR IT IS!
CHOMP ぱく
CHOMP ぱく
HAGK!
COME ON! WHAT ARE YOU DOING!?
IS THIS HARASS-MENT!?
KAFF!
THIS PASTA YOU MADE, SAIONJI-SENSEI...

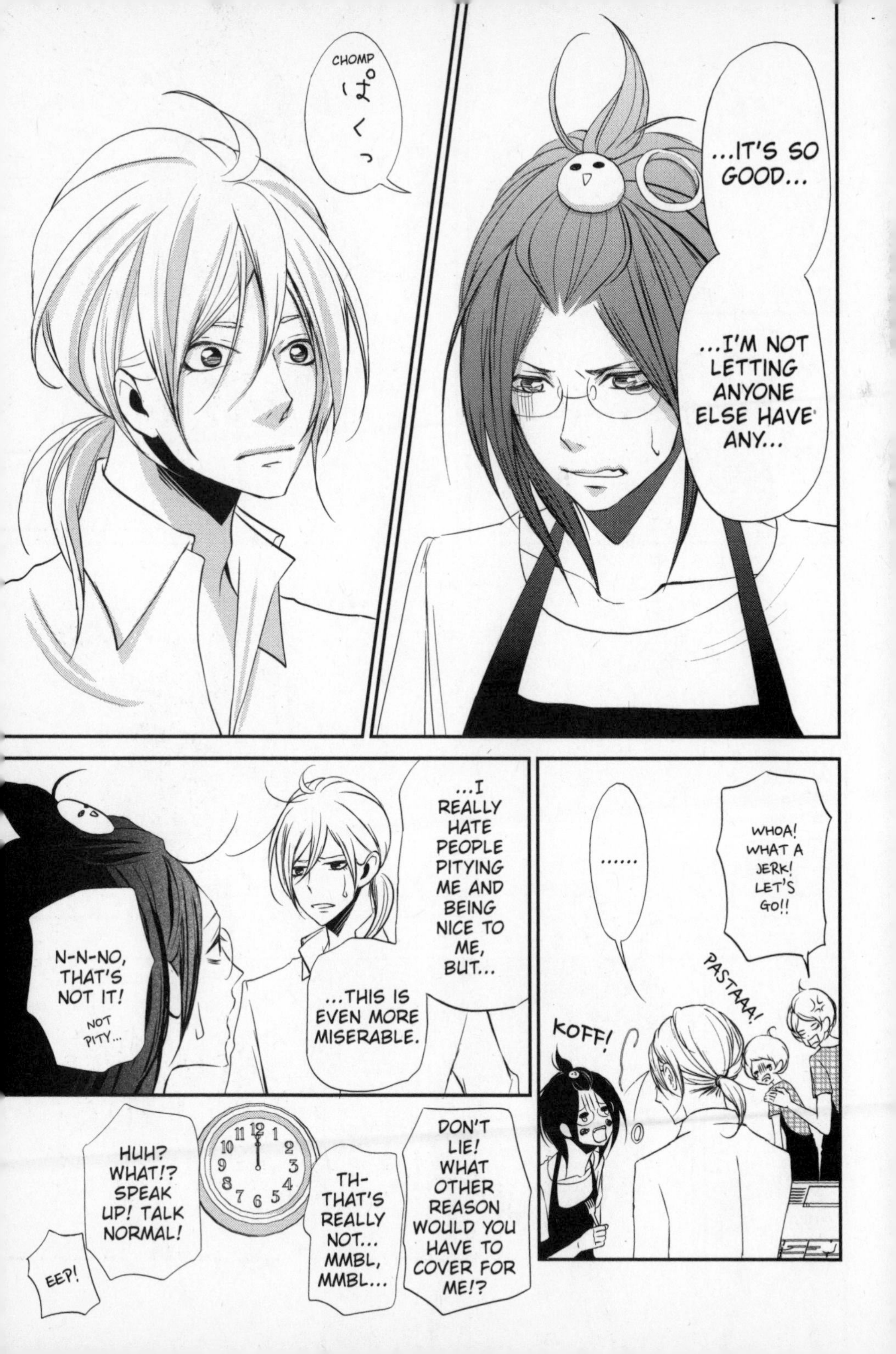
...IT'S SO GOOD...
...I'M NOT LETTING ANYONE ELSE HAVE ANY...
CHOMP
ぱくっ
WHOA! WHAT A JERK! LET'S GO!!
PASTAAA!
......
KOFF!
...I REALLY HATE PEOPLE PITYING ME AND BEING NICE TO ME, BUT...
...THIS IS EVEN MORE MISERABLE.
N-N-NO, THAT'S NOT IT!
NOT PITY...
DON'T LIE! WHAT OTHER REASON WOULD YOU HAVE TO COVER FOR ME!?
TH-THAT'S REALLY NOT... MMBL, MMBL...
HUH? WHAT!? SPEAK UP! TALK NORMAL!
EEP!

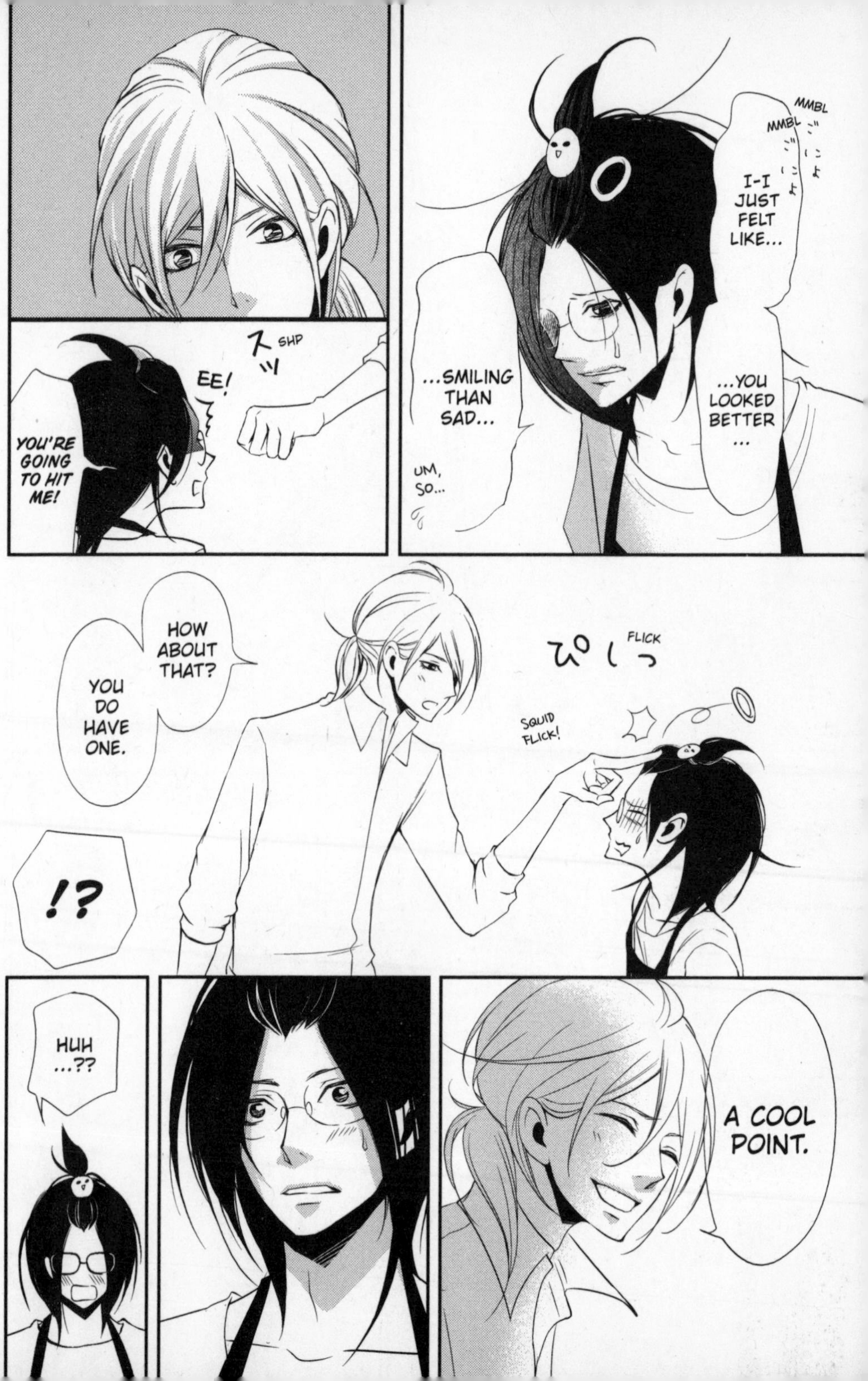
MMBL MMBL
ごにょごにょ
I-I JUST FELT LIKE...
...YOU LOOKED BETTER...
...SMILING THAN SAD...
UM, SO...
スッ SHP
EE!
YOU'RE GOING TO HIT ME!
ぴしっ FLICK
SQUID FLICK!
HOW ABOUT THAT?
YOU DO HAVE ONE.
!?
A COOL POINT.
HUH ...??

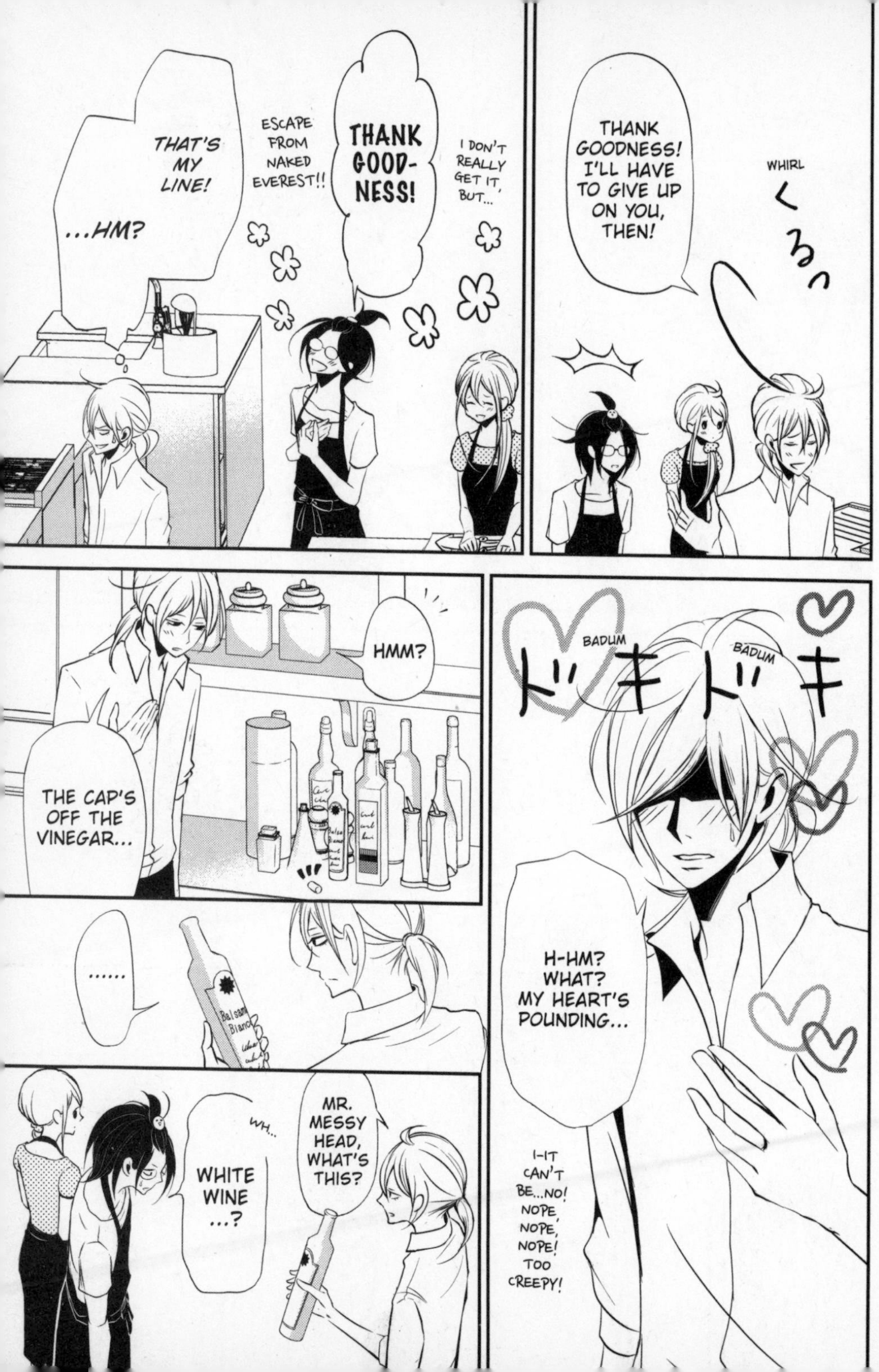
THANK GOODNESS! I'LL HAVE TO GIVE UP ON YOU, THEN!
WHIRL
くるっ
I DON'T REALLY GET IT, BUT...
THANK GOOD-NESS!
ESCAPE FROM NAKED EVEREST!!
THAT'S MY LINE!
...HM?
BADUM
BADUM
ドキドキ
H-HM? WHAT? MY HEART'S POUNDING...
I-IT CAN'T BE...NO! NOPE, NOPE, NOPE! TOO CREEPY!
HMM?
THE CAP'S OFF THE VINEGAR...
......
MR. MESSY HEAD, WHAT'S THIS?
WH...
WHITE WINE ...?

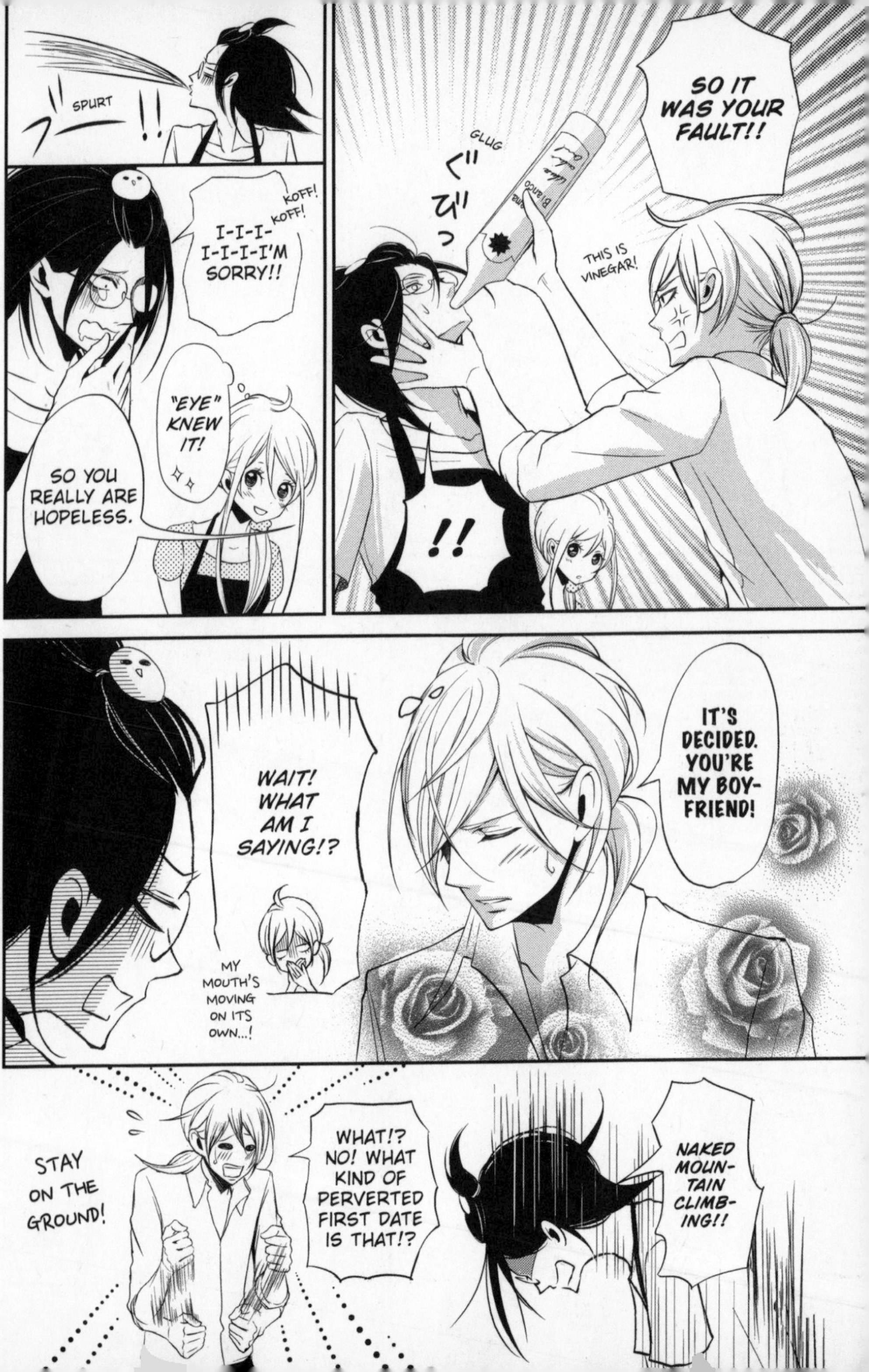
SO IT WAS YOUR FAULT!!
GLUG
THIS IS VINEGAR!
!!
SPURT
!!
KOFF! KOFF!
I-I-I- I-I-I-I'M SORRY!!
"EYE" KNEW IT!
SO YOU REALLY ARE HOPELESS.
IT'S DECIDED. YOU'RE MY BOY-FRIEND!
WAIT! WHAT AM I SAYING!?
MY MOUTH'S MOVING ON ITS OWN...!
NAKED MOUN-TAIN CLIMB-ING!!
WHAT!? NO! WHAT KIND OF PERVERTED FIRST DATE IS THAT!?
STAY ON THE GROUND!

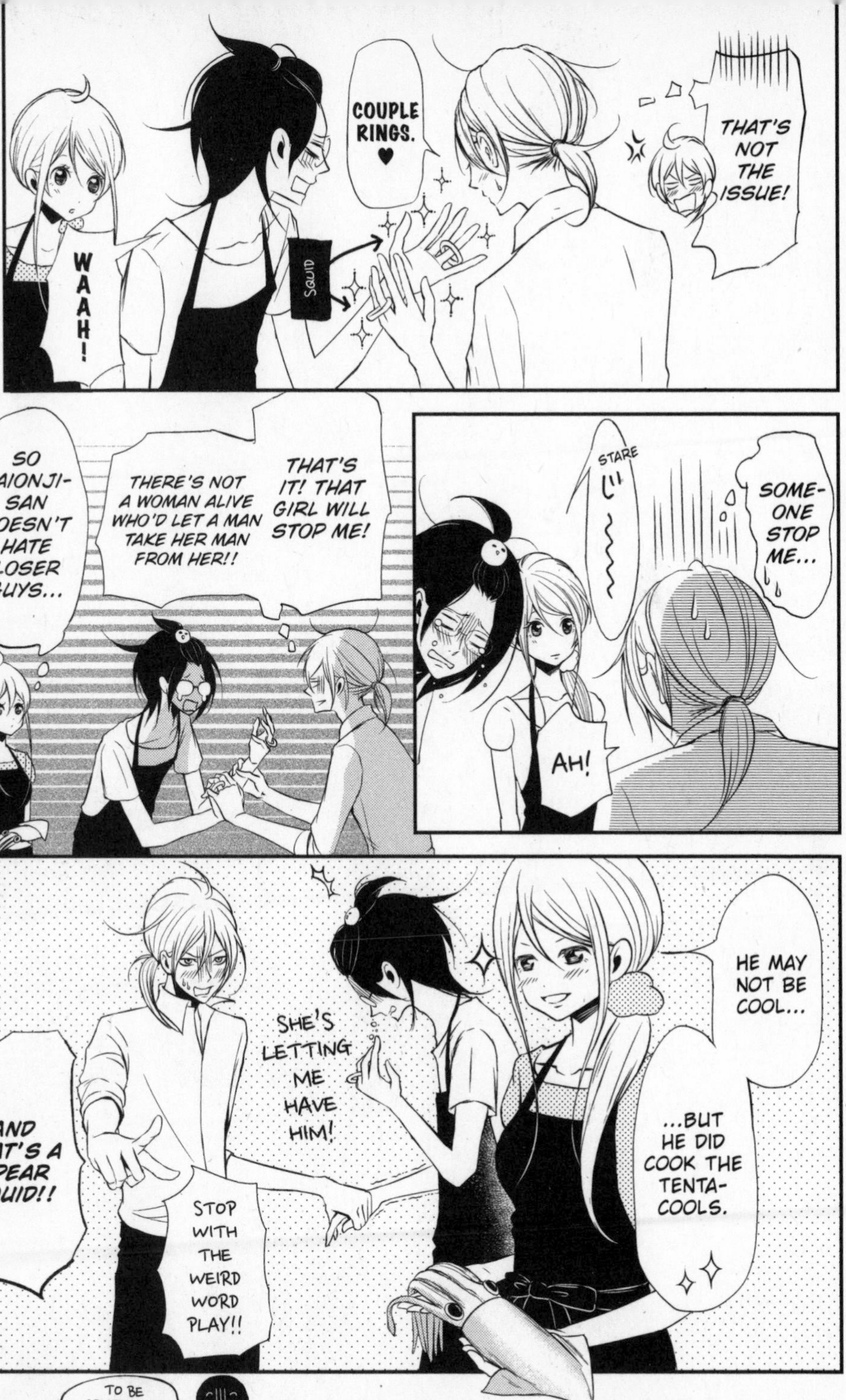
THAT'S NOT THE ISSUE!
COUPLE RINGS. ♥
SQUID
WAAH!
SOME-ONE STOP ME...
STARE
じー
AH!
THAT'S IT! THAT GIRL WILL STOP ME!
THERE'S NOT A WOMAN ALIVE WHO'D LET A MAN TAKE HER MAN FROM HER!!
SO SAIONJI-SAN DOESN'T HATE LOSER GUYS...
HE MAY NOT BE COOL...
...BUT HE DID COOK THE TENTA-COOLS.
SHE'S LETTING ME HAVE HIM!
AND THAT'S A SPEAR SQUID!!
STOP WITH THE WEIRD WORD PLAY!!
TO BE CONTINUED!

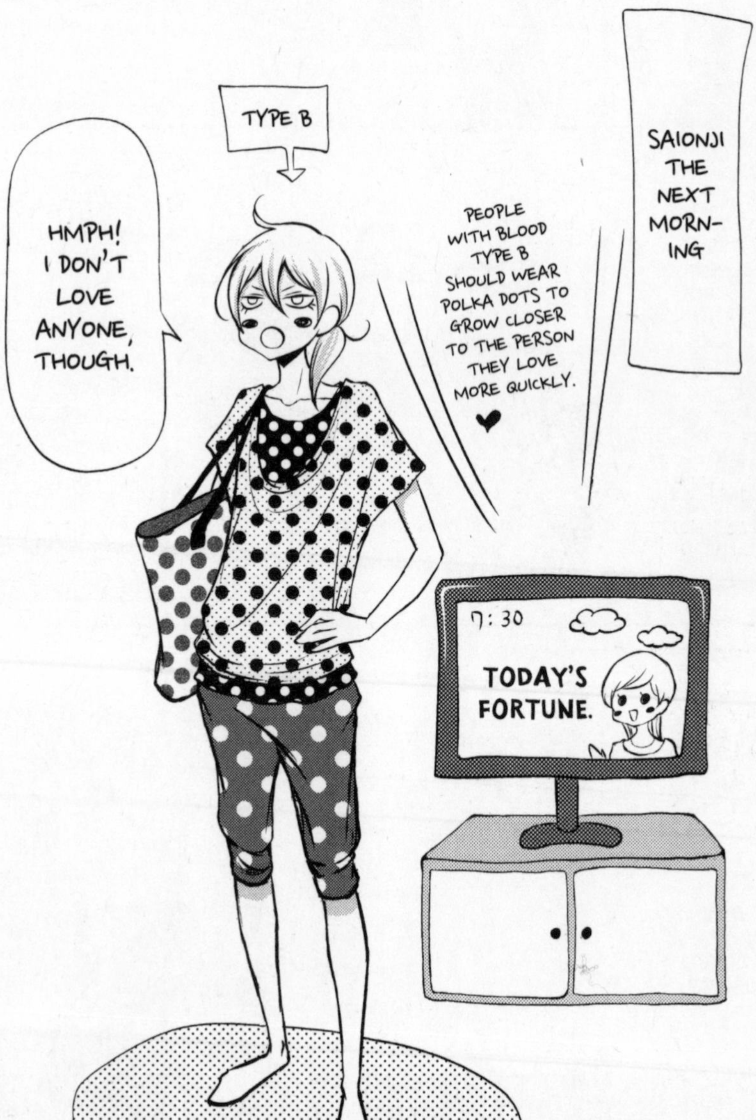
SAIONJI THE NEXT MORN-ING
PEOPLE WITH BLOOD TYPE B SHOULD WEAR POLKA DOTS TO GROW CLOSER TO THE PERSON THEY LOVE MORE QUICKLY. ❤
TYPE B
HMPH! I DON'T LOVE ANYONE, THOUGH.
7:30
TODAY'S FORTUNE.

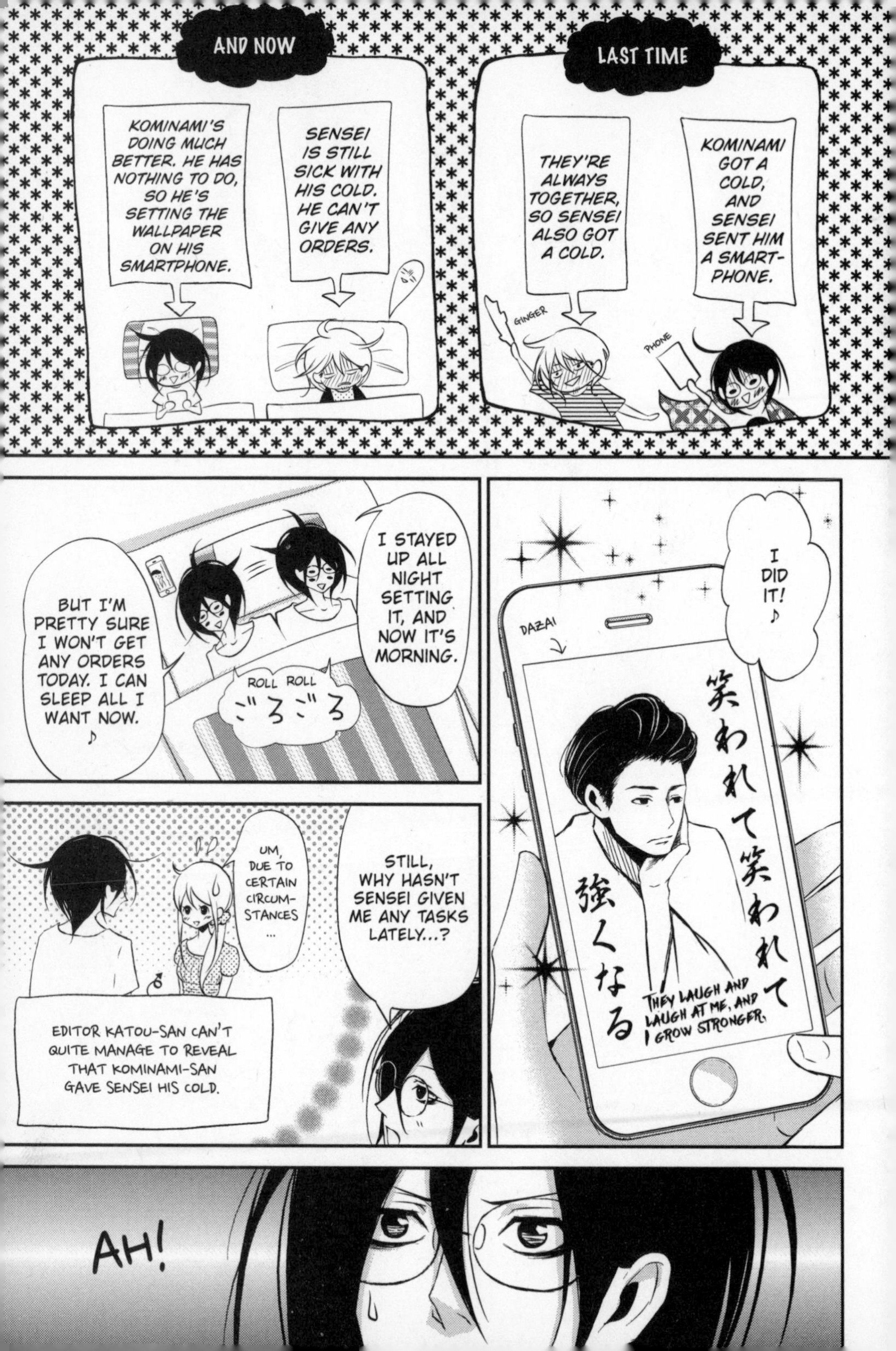
LAST TIME
KOMINAMI GOT A COLD, AND SENSEI SENT HIM A SMART-PHONE.
PHONE
THEY'RE ALWAYS TOGETHER, SO SENSEI ALSO GOT A COLD.
GINGER
AND NOW
SENSEI IS STILL SICK WITH HIS COLD. HE CAN'T GIVE ANY ORDERS.
KOMINAMI'S DOING MUCH BETTER. HE HAS NOTHING TO DO, SO HE'S SETTING THE WALLPAPER ON HIS SMARTPHONE.
I DID IT! ♪
DAZAI
笑われて笑われて強くなる
THEY LAUGH AND LAUGH AT ME, AND I GROW STRONGER.
I STAYED UP ALL NIGHT SETTING IT, AND NOW IT'S MORNING.
ROLL ROLL
ごろごろ
BUT I'M PRETTY SURE I WON'T GET ANY ORDERS TODAY. I CAN SLEEP ALL I WANT NOW. ♪
STILL, WHY HASN'T SENSEI GIVEN ME ANY TASKS LATELY...?
UM, DUE TO CERTAIN CIRCUM-STANCES ...
EDITOR KATOU-SAN CAN'T QUITE MANAGE TO REVEAL THAT KOMINAMI-SAN GAVE SENSEI HIS COLD.
AH!

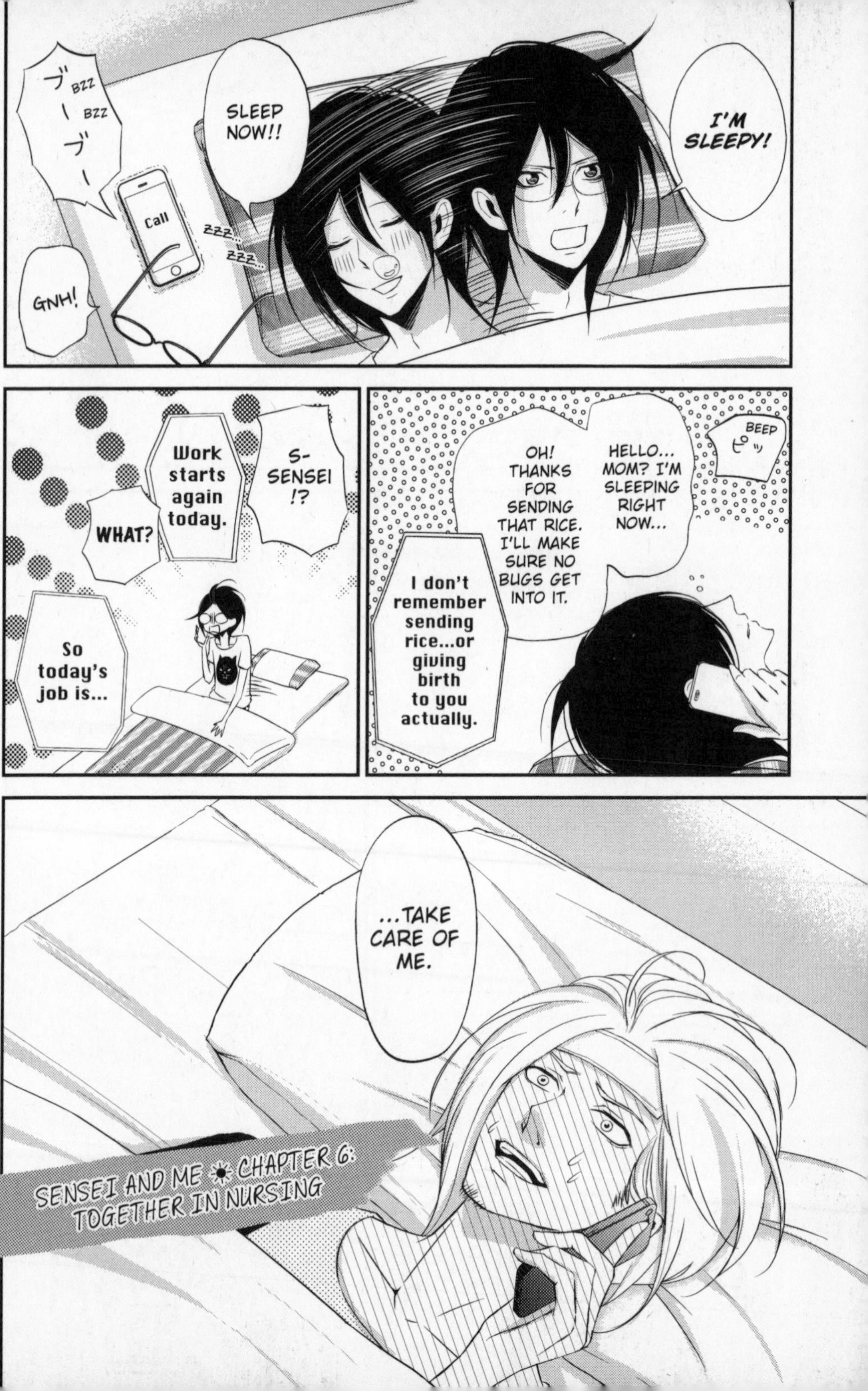
I'M SLEEPY!
SLEEP NOW!!
ZZZ... ZZZ...
ブ BZZ ー ブ BZZ ー
Call
GNH!
ピッ BEEP
HELLO... MOM? I'M SLEEPING RIGHT NOW...
OH! THANKS FOR SENDING THAT RICE. I'LL MAKE SURE NO BUGS GET INTO IT.
I don't remember sending rice...or giving birth to you actually.
S-SENSEI !?
Work starts again today.
WHAT?
So today's job is...
...TAKE CARE OF ME.
SENSEI AND ME ☀ CHAPTER 6: TOGETHER IN NURSING

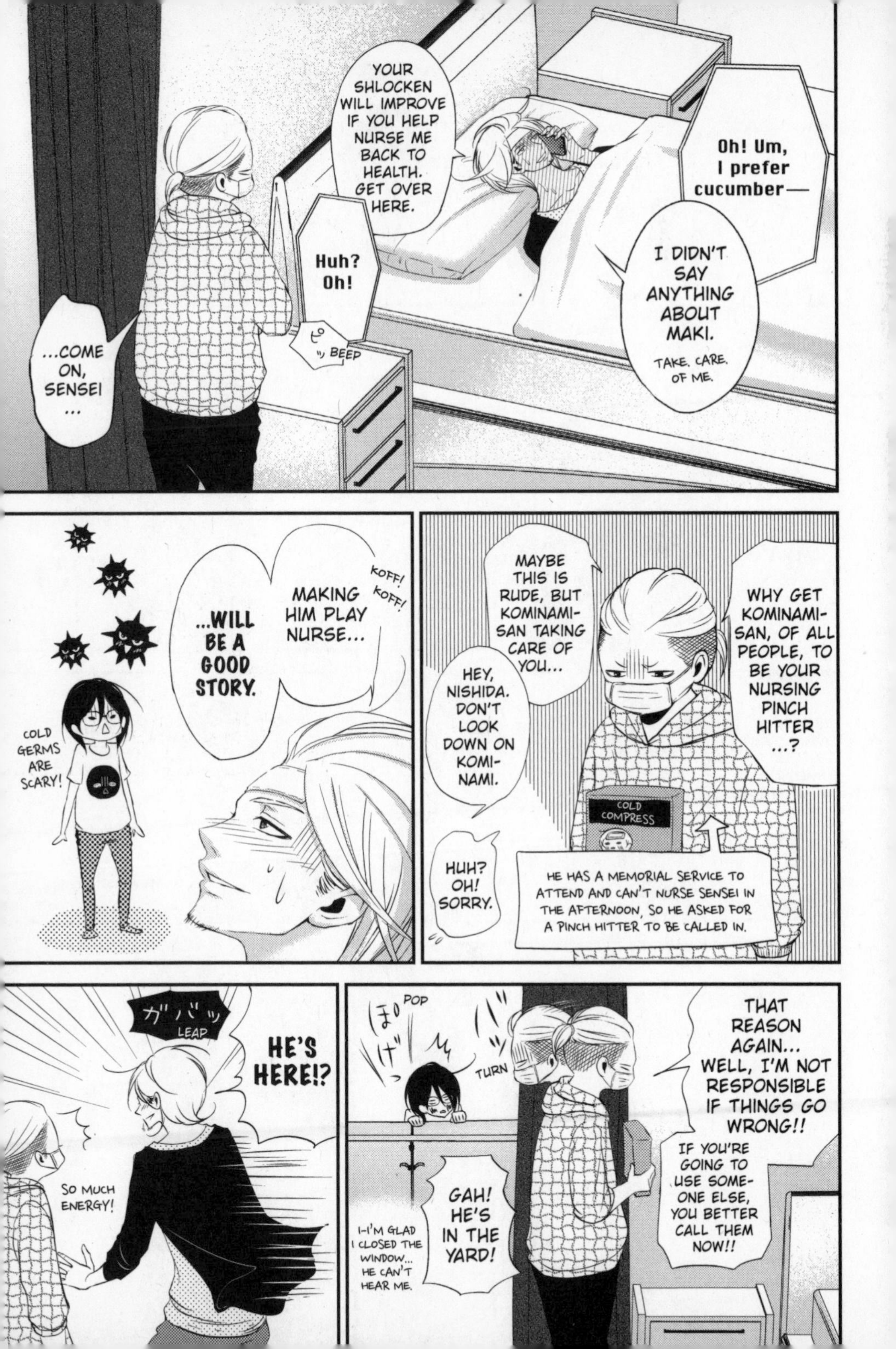
Oh! Um, I prefer cucumber—
I DIDN'T SAY ANYTHING ABOUT MAKI.
TAKE. CARE. OF ME.
YOUR SHLOCKEN WILL IMPROVE IF YOU HELP NURSE ME BACK TO HEALTH. GET OVER HERE.
Huh? Oh!
ピッ BEEP
...COME ON, SENSEI ...
WHY GET KOMINAMI-SAN, OF ALL PEOPLE, TO BE YOUR NURSING PINCH HITTER ...?
MAYBE THIS IS RUDE, BUT KOMINAMI-SAN TAKING CARE OF YOU...
HEY, NISHIDA. DON'T LOOK DOWN ON KOMI-NAMI.
COLD COMPRESS
HE HAS A MEMORIAL SERVICE TO ATTEND AND CAN'T NURSE SENSEI IN THE AFTERNOON, SO HE ASKED FOR A PINCH HITTER TO BE CALLED IN.
HUH? OH! SORRY.
KOFF! KOFF!
MAKING HIM PLAY NURSE...
...WILL BE A GOOD STORY.
COLD GERMS ARE SCARY!
THAT REASON AGAIN... WELL, I'M NOT RESPONSIBLE IF THINGS GO WRONG!!
IF YOU'RE GOING TO USE SOME-ONE ELSE, YOU BETTER CALL THEM NOW!!
バッ TURN
ほげっ POP
GAH! HE'S IN THE YARD!
I-I'M GLAD I CLOSED THE WINDOW... HE CAN'T HEAR ME.
HE'S HERE!?
ガバッ LEAP
SO MUCH ENERGY!

SWOON

HUH?

COLD GERMS ARE SCARY!

KOMINAMI, MY INSIDES ARE RIDDLED WITH COLD GERMS.

AH!

YOU GOT ALL EXCITED AND MADE YOUR FEVER GO UP...

I GUESS HE JUST REALLY WANTED TO TEASE KOMINAMI-SAN SINCE HE HASN'T SEEN HIM IN A WHILE...

I'M SORRY! MY EYES ARE BAD, SO I CAN'T SEE THEM!

AAAAH!

SENSEI'S SERIOUSLY GOING OVER THE TOP HERE...

RIGHT!? SEE!? TONS IN MY THROAT!! CAN YOU SEE THEM!?

SENSEI'S ASKING ME FOR HELP! I HAVE TO TAKE DOWN THOSE COLD GERMS ...!!

THE COLD GERMS ARE RUNNING WILD IN MY THROOOOAT! YOU! IDIOT-FACED FOUR-EYES! HELP MEEE!

KOFF! KOFF!

HONESTLY, THIS GUY ...!!

JUST WHEN YOU WERE FINALLY STARTING TO GET BETTER ...

AH HA HA HA HA HA!

THAT'S A SEA URCHIN.

KOFF! KOFF! KOFF!

DING

HERE! FOR YOU! ♥

KOFF!

OH! A COLD GERM CAME OUT.

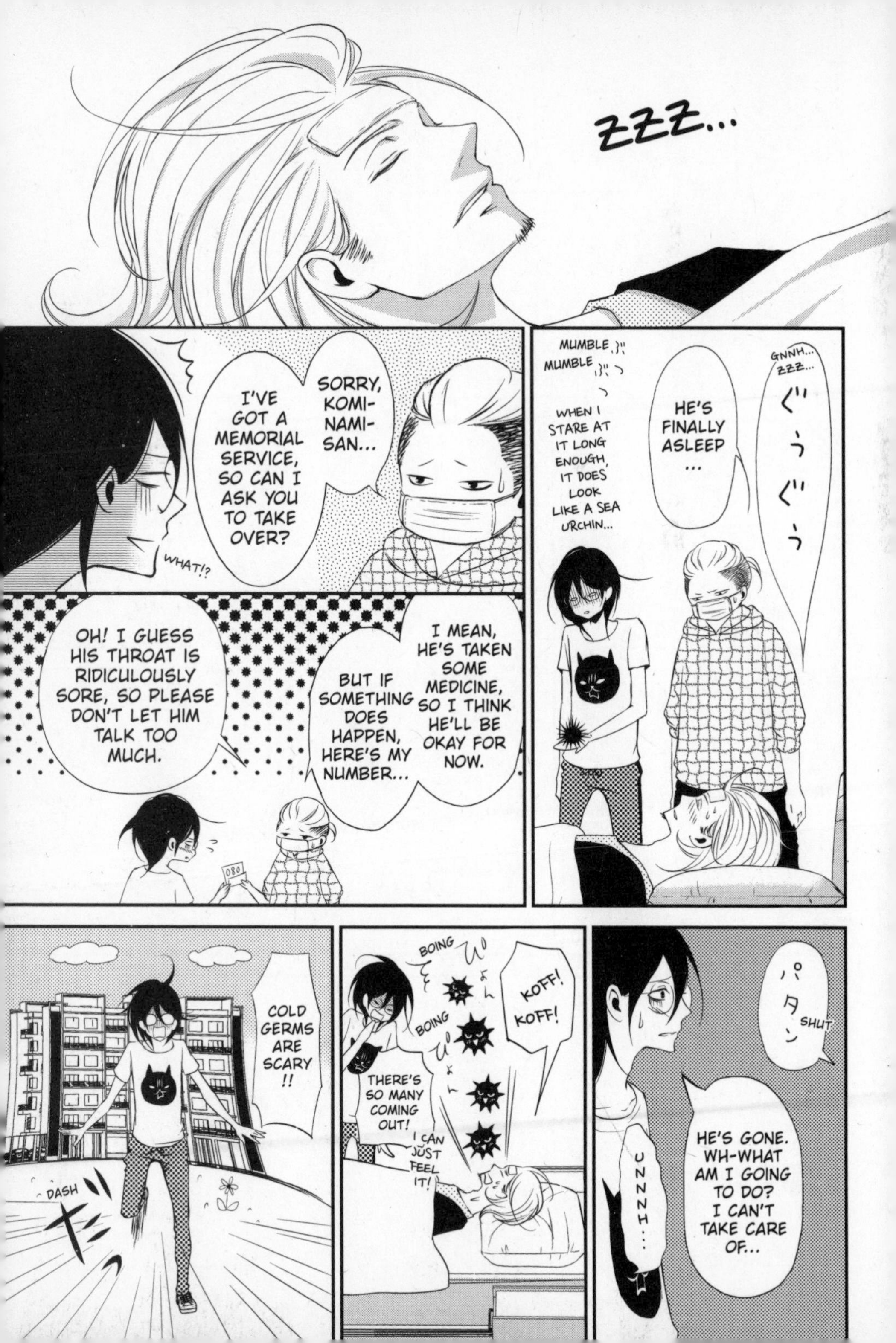
ZZZ...
GNNH... ZZZ...
ぐうぐう
HE'S FINALLY ASLEEP...
MUMBLE ぶつ
MUMBLE ぶつ
WHEN I STARE AT IT LONG ENOUGH, IT DOES LOOK LIKE A SEA URCHIN...
SORRY, KOMI-NAMI-SAN...
I'VE GOT A MEMORIAL SERVICE, SO CAN I ASK YOU TO TAKE OVER?
WHAT!?
I MEAN, HE'S TAKEN SOME MEDICINE, SO I THINK HE'LL BE OKAY FOR NOW.
BUT IF SOMETHING DOES HAPPEN, HERE'S MY NUMBER...
OH! I GUESS HIS THROAT IS RIDICULOUSLY SORE, SO PLEASE DON'T LET HIM TALK TOO MUCH.
080
パタン
SHUT
HE'S GONE. WH-WHAT AM I GOING TO DO? I CAN'T TAKE CARE OF...
UNNNH...
KOFF! KOFF!
BOING
ぴょん
BOING
ぴょん
THERE'S SO MANY COMING OUT!
I CAN JUST FEEL IT!
COLD GERMS ARE SCARY!!
DASH

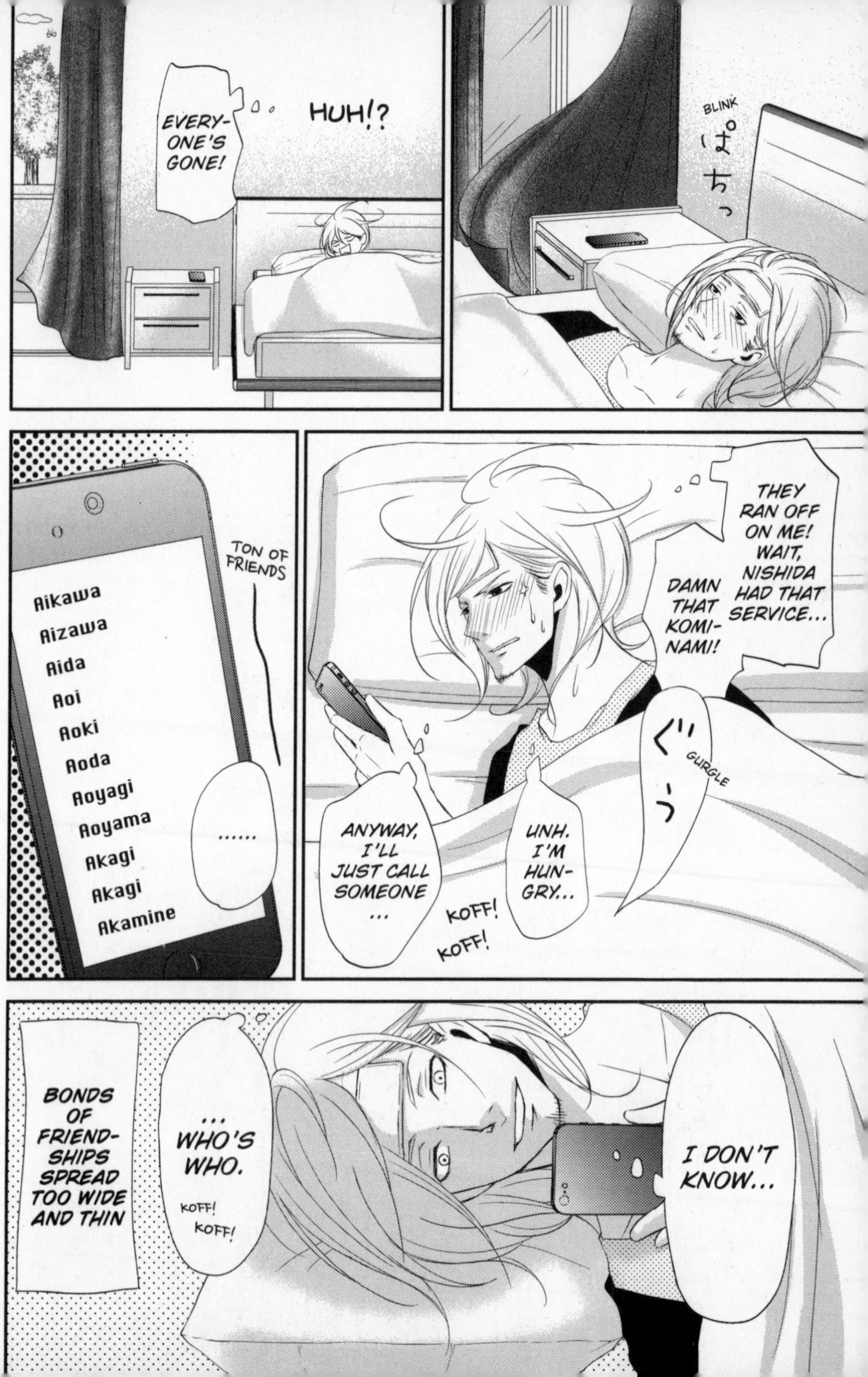
BLINK
ぱちっ
HUH!?
EVERY-ONE'S GONE!
THEY RAN OFF ON ME! WAIT, NISHIDA HAD THAT SERVICE...
DAMN THAT KOMI-NAMI!
ぐぅ
GURGLE
UNH. I'M HUN-GRY...
ANYWAY, I'LL JUST CALL SOMEONE ...
KOFF! KOFF!
TON OF FRIENDS
Aikawa
Aizawa
Aida
Aoi
Aoki
Aoda
Aoyagi
Aoyama
Akagi
Akagi
Akamine
......
I DON'T KNOW...
... WHO'S WHO.
KOFF! KOFF!
BONDS OF FRIEND-SHIPS SPREAD TOO WIDE AND THIN

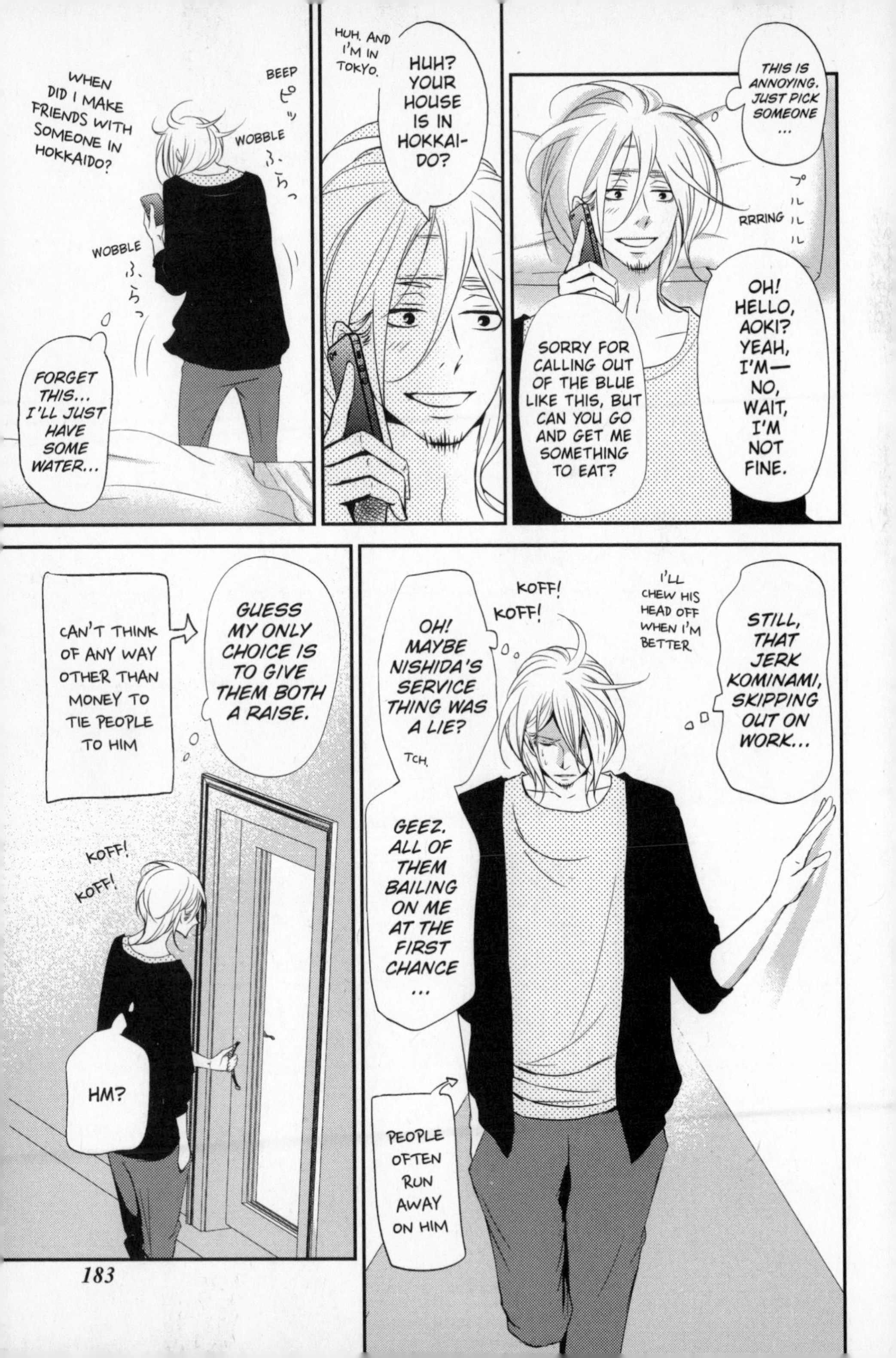
THIS IS ANNOYING. JUST PICK SOMEONE...
プルルル
RRRING
OH! HELLO, AOKI? YEAH, I'M— NO, WAIT, I'M NOT FINE.
SORRY FOR CALLING OUT OF THE BLUE LIKE THIS, BUT CAN YOU GO AND GET ME SOMETHING TO EAT?
HUH? YOUR HOUSE IS IN HOKKAIDO?
HUH. AND I'M IN TOKYO.
ピッ
BEEP
WHEN DID I MAKE FRIENDS WITH SOMEONE IN HOKKAIDO?
ふらっ
WOBBLE
ふらっ
WOBBLE
FORGET THIS... I'LL JUST HAVE SOME WATER...
STILL, THAT JERK KOMINAMI, SKIPPING OUT ON WORK...
I'LL CHEW HIS HEAD OFF WHEN I'M BETTER
KOFF! KOFF!
OH! MAYBE NISHIDA'S SERVICE THING WAS A LIE?
TCH.
GEEZ. ALL OF THEM BAILING ON ME AT THE FIRST CHANCE...
PEOPLE OFTEN RUN AWAY ON HIM
GUESS MY ONLY CHOICE IS TO GIVE THEM BOTH A RAISE.
CAN'T THINK OF ANY WAY OTHER THAN MONEY TO TIE PEOPLE TO HIM
KOFF! KOFF!
HM?

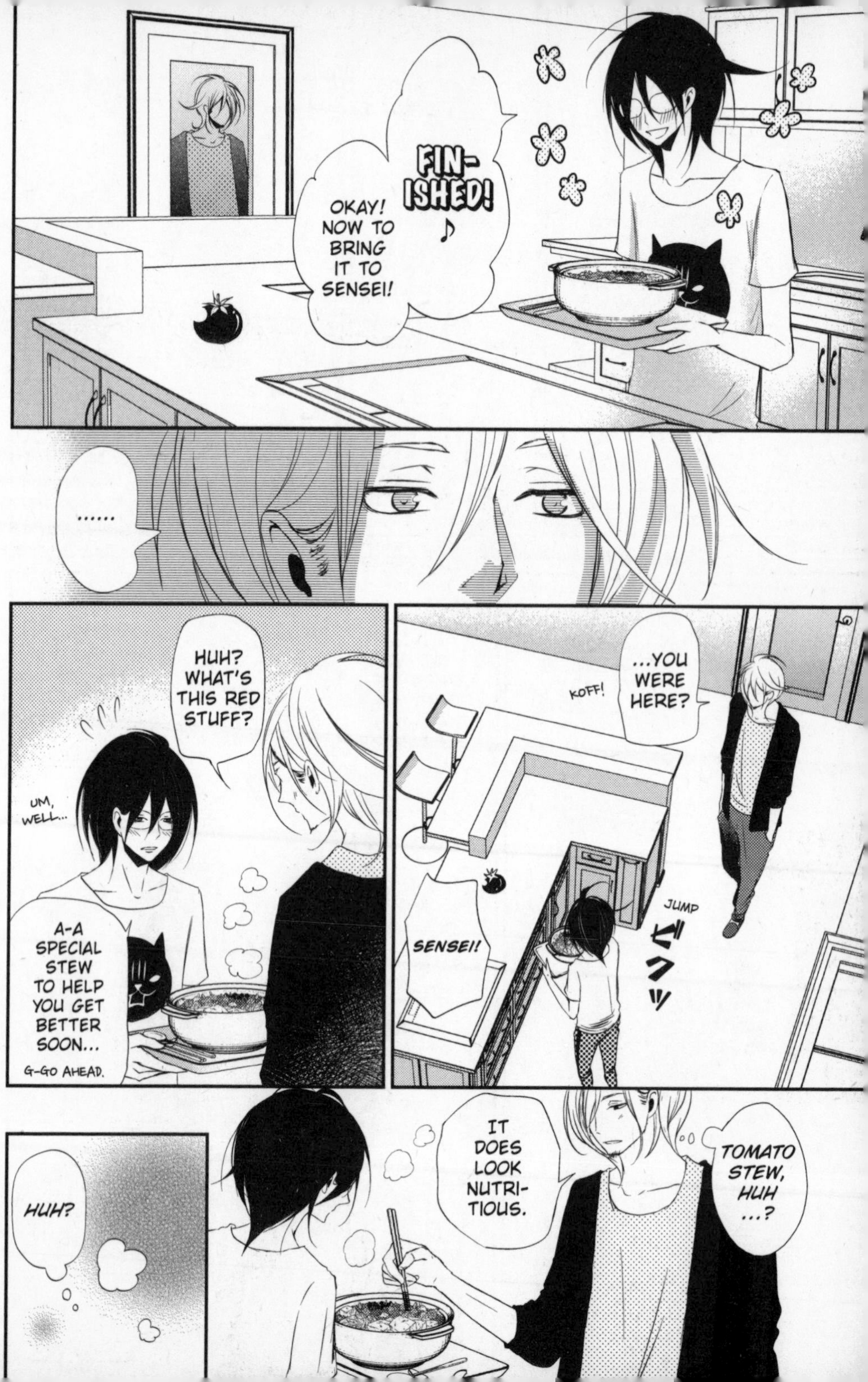
FIN-ISHED! ♪
OKAY! NOW TO BRING IT TO SENSEI!
......
...YOU WERE HERE?
KOFF!
JUMP
ビクッ
SENSEI!
HUH? WHAT'S THIS RED STUFF?
UM, WELL...
A-A SPECIAL STEW TO HELP YOU GET BETTER SOON...
G-GO AHEAD.
TOMATO STEW, HUH ...?
IT DOES LOOK NUTRITIOUS.
HUH?

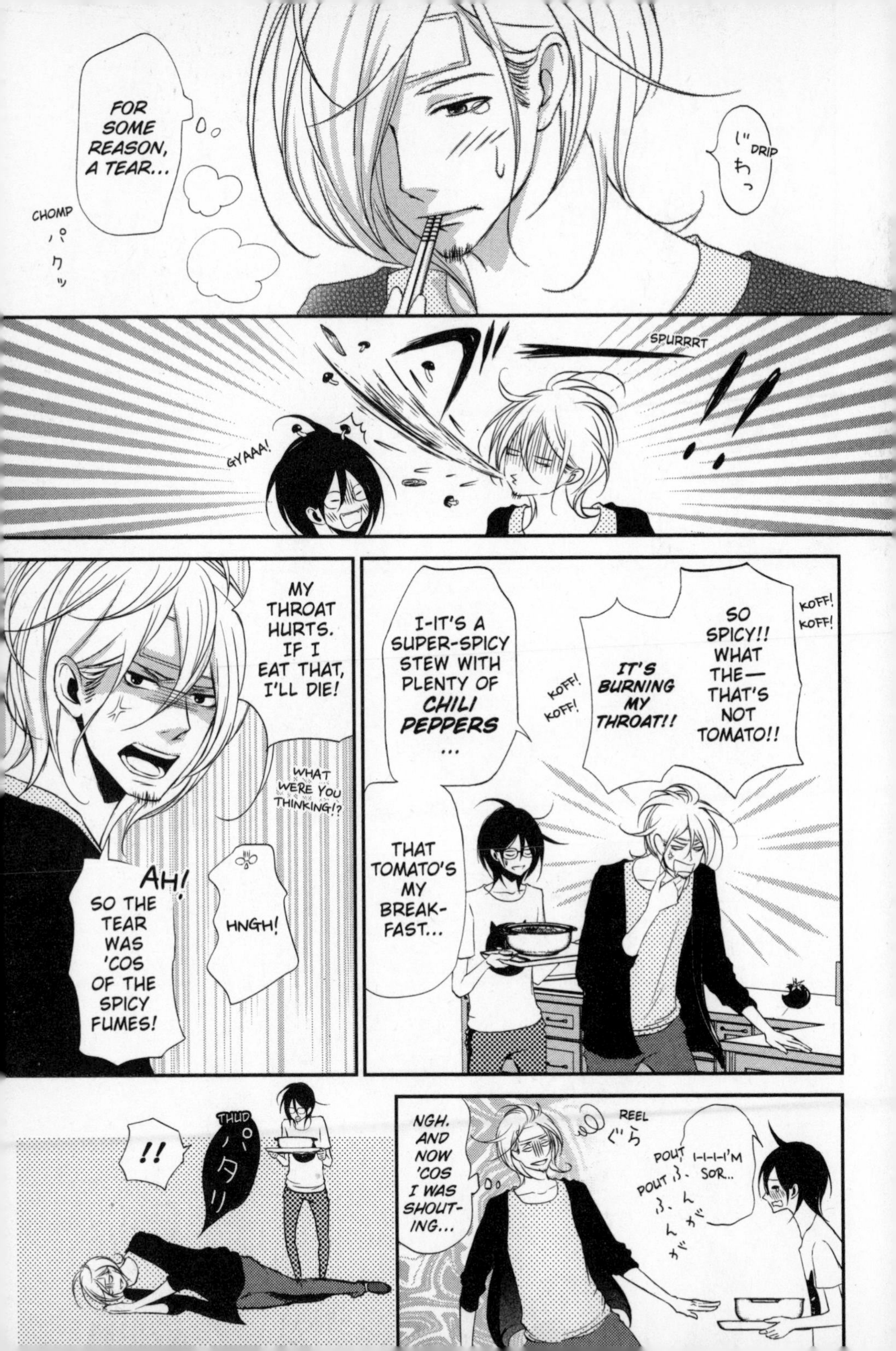
DRIP
じわっ
FOR SOME REASON, A TEAR...
CHOMP
パクッ
SPURRRT
ブーーー
!!
GYAAA!
KOFF! KOFF!
SO SPICY!! WHAT THE— THAT'S NOT TOMATO!!
IT'S BURNING MY THROAT!!
KOFF! KOFF!
I-IT'S A SUPER-SPICY STEW WITH PLENTY OF CHILI PEPPERS...
THAT TOMATO'S MY BREAK-FAST...
MY THROAT HURTS. IF I EAT THAT, I'LL DIE!
WHAT WERE YOU THINKING!?
HNGH!
AH! SO THE TEAR WAS 'COS OF THE SPICY FUMES!
REEL
ぐら
I-I-I-I'M SOR..
POUT POUT
ふんがふんが
NGH. AND NOW 'COS I WAS SHOUT-ING...
THUD
パタリ
!!

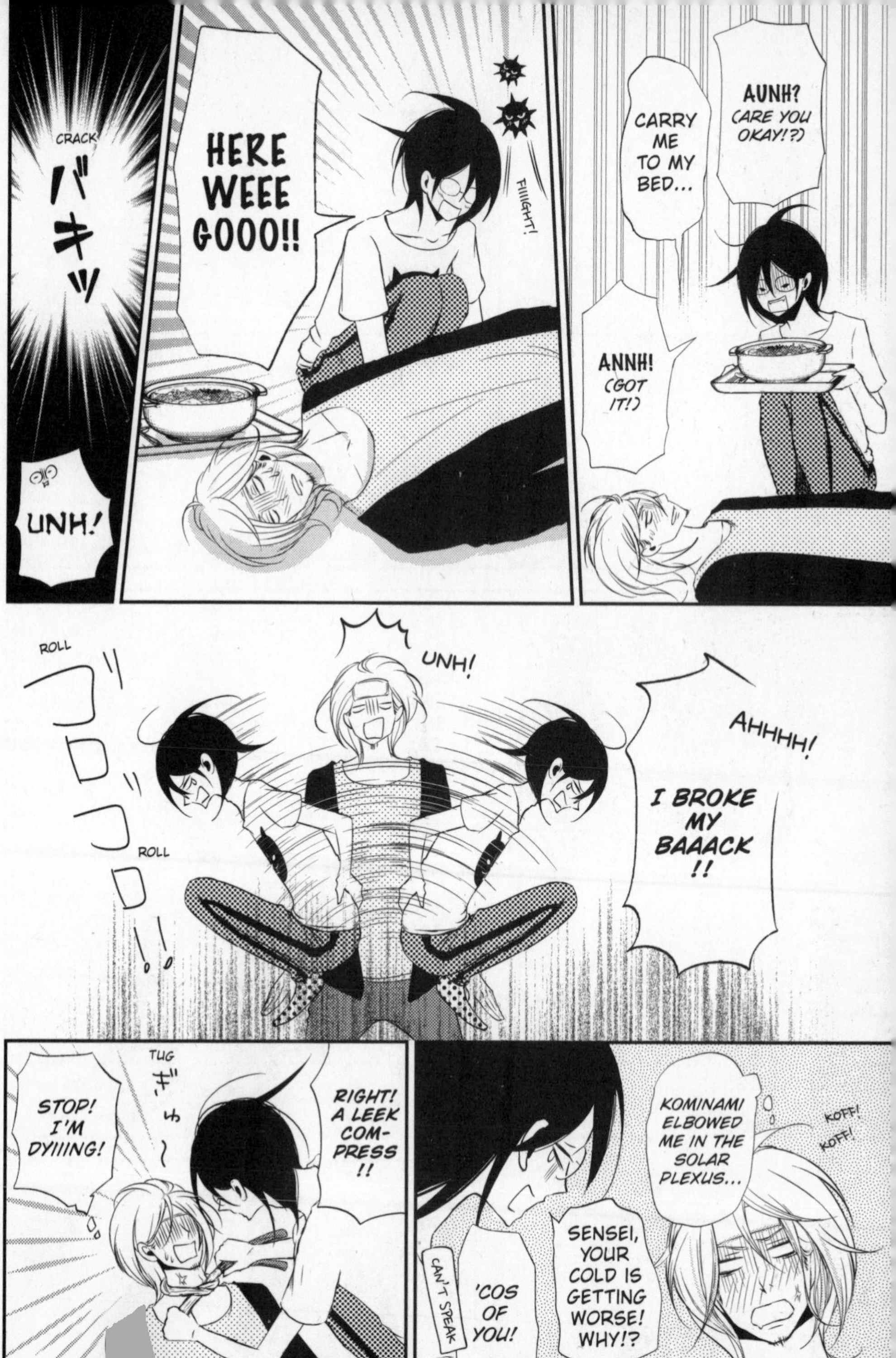
AUNH? (ARE YOU OKAY!?)
CARRY ME TO MY BED...
ANNH! (GOT IT!)
HERE WEEE GOOO!!
FIIIGHT!
CRACK
バキッ
UNH!
AHHHH!
I BROKE MY BAAACK !!
UNH!
ROLL
ROLL
KOMINAMI ELBOWED ME IN THE SOLAR PLEXUS...
KOFF! KOFF!
SENSEI, YOUR COLD IS GETTING WORSE! WHY!?
'COS OF YOU!
CAN'T SPEAK
RIGHT! A LEEK COMPRESS!!
TUG
ぎゅ~
STOP! I'M DYIIING!

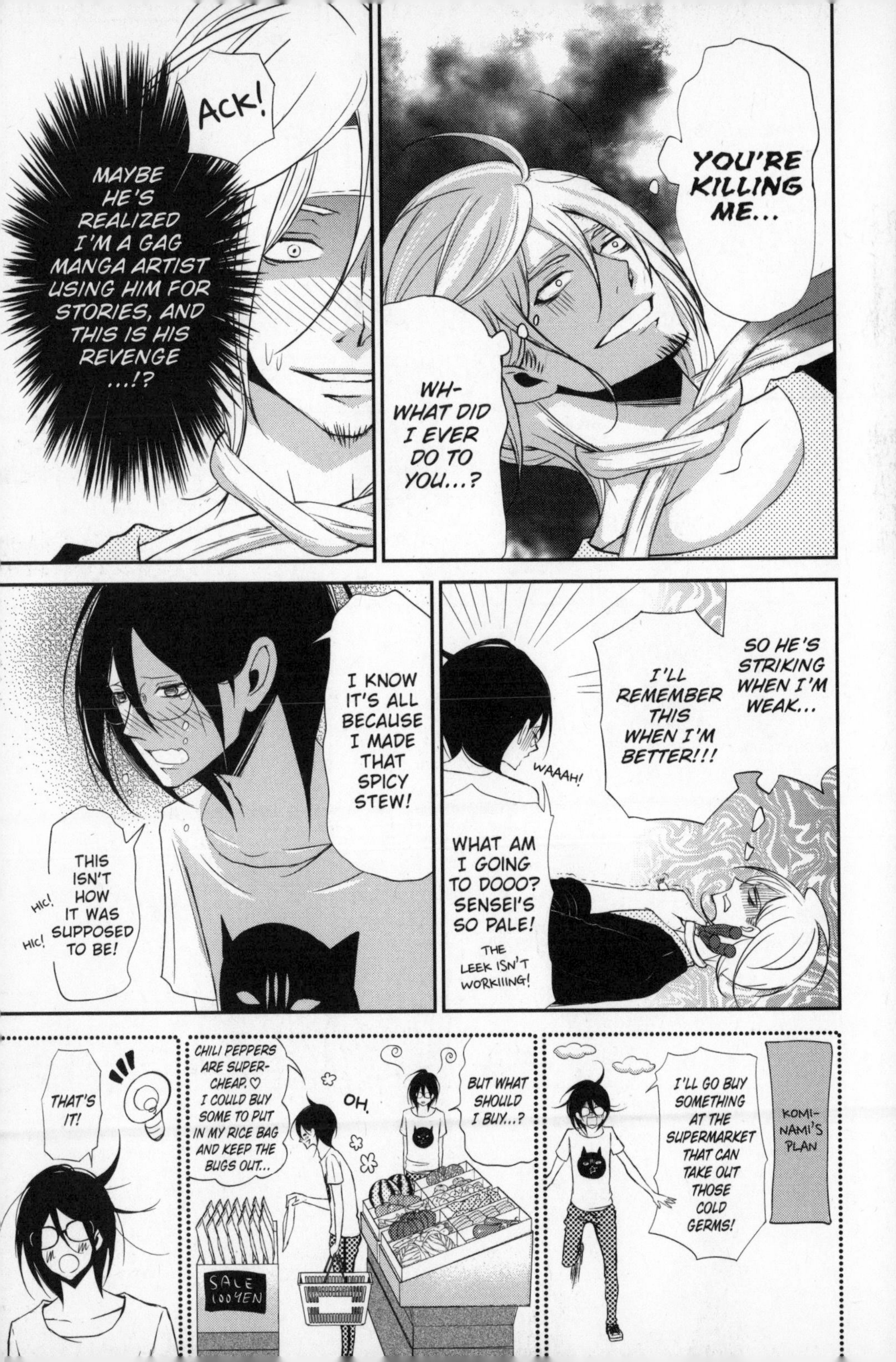
YOU'RE KILLING ME...
WH- WHAT DID I EVER DO TO YOU...?
ACK!
MAYBE HE'S REALIZED I'M A GAG MANGA ARTIST USING HIM FOR STORIES, AND THIS IS HIS REVENGE ...!?
SO HE'S STRIKING WHEN I'M WEAK...
I'LL REMEMBER THIS WHEN I'M BETTER!!!
WAAAH!
WHAT AM I GOING TO DOOO? SENSEI'S SO PALE!
THE LEEK ISN'T WORKIIING!
I KNOW IT'S ALL BECAUSE I MADE THAT SPICY STEW!
THIS ISN'T HOW IT WAS SUPPOSED TO BE!
HIC!
HIC!
KOMI-NAMI'S PLAN
I'LL GO BUY SOMETHING AT THE SUPERMARKET THAT CAN TAKE OUT THOSE COLD GERMS!
BUT WHAT SHOULD I BUY...?
OH.
CHILI PEPPERS ARE SUPER-CHEAP.♡ I COULD BUY SOME TO PUT IN MY RICE BAG AND KEEP THE BUGS OUT...
SALE 100YEN
THAT'S IT!

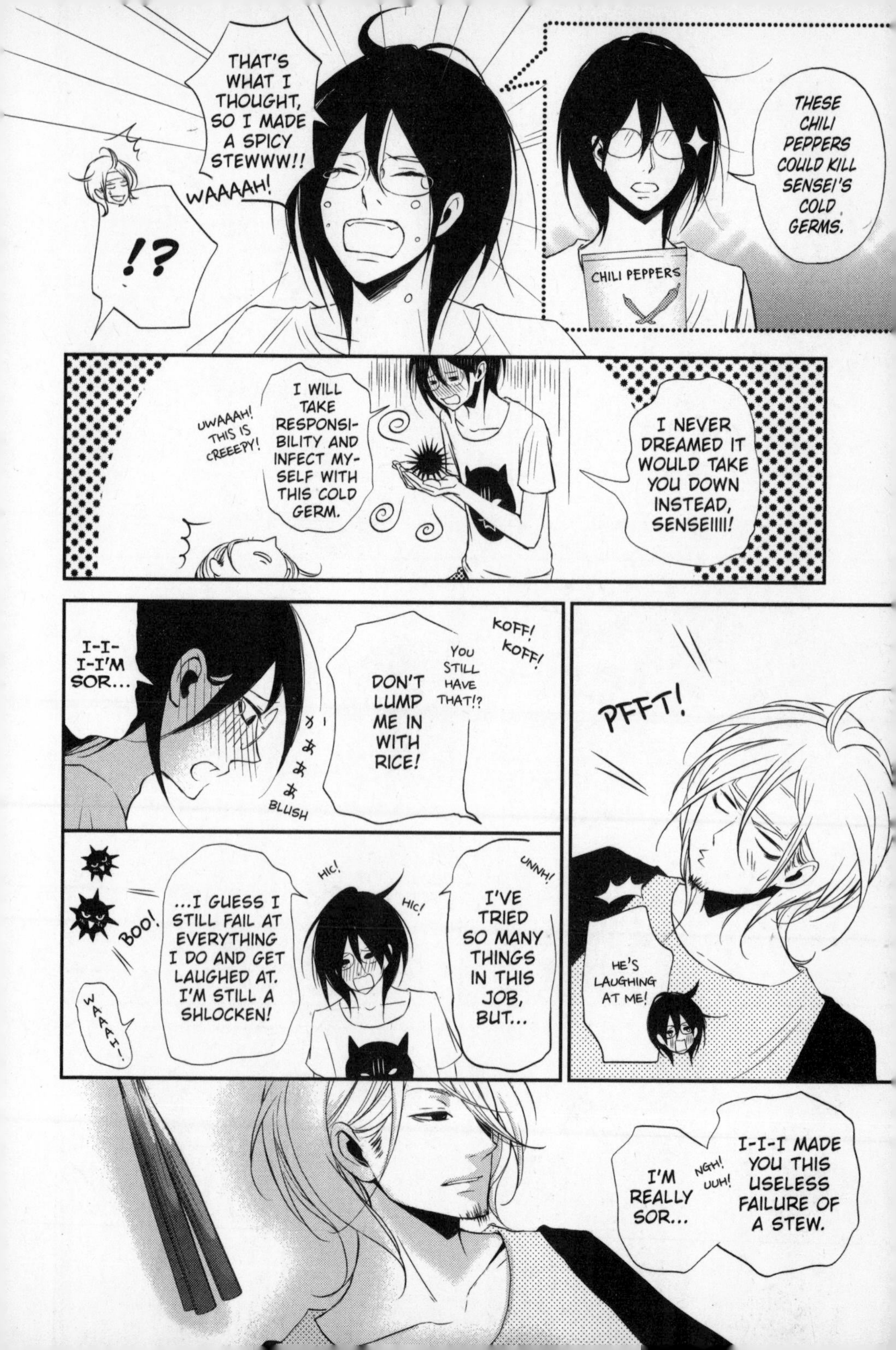
THESE CHILI PEPPERS COULD KILL SENSEI'S COLD GERMS.
CHILI PEPPERS
THAT'S WHAT I THOUGHT, SO I MADE A SPICY STEWWW!!
WAAAAH!
!?
I NEVER DREAMED IT WOULD TAKE YOU DOWN INSTEAD, SENSEIIII!
I WILL TAKE RESPONSI-BILITY AND INFECT MY-SELF WITH THIS COLD GERM.
UWAAAH! THIS IS CREEEPY!
PFFT!
HE'S LAUGHING AT ME!
KOFF! KOFF!
YOU STILL HAVE THAT!?
DON'T LUMP ME IN WITH RICE!
BLUSH
I-I-I-I'M SOR...
UNNH!
I'VE TRIED SO MANY THINGS IN THIS JOB, BUT...
HIC!
HIC!
...I GUESS I STILL FAIL AT EVERYTHING I DO AND GET LAUGHED AT. I'M STILL A SHLOCKEN!
BOO!
WAAAH!
I-I-I MADE YOU THIS USELESS FAILURE OF A STEW.
NGH! UUH!
I'M REALLY SOR...

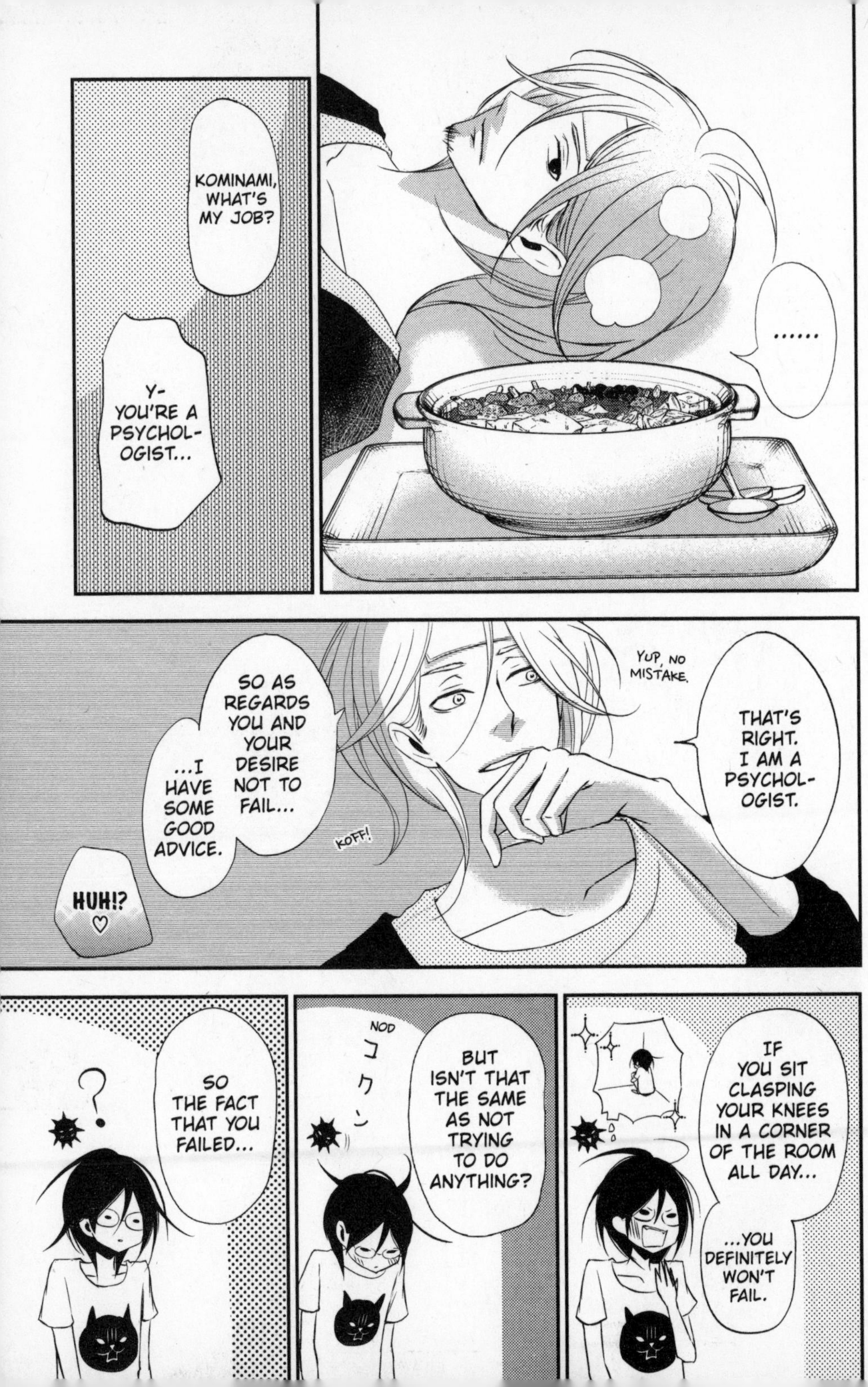
......
KOMINAMI, WHAT'S MY JOB?
Y- YOU'RE A PSYCHOL- OGIST...
YUP, NO MISTAKE.
THAT'S RIGHT. I AM A PSYCHOL- OGIST.
KOFF!
SO AS REGARDS YOU AND YOUR DESIRE NOT TO FAIL...
...I HAVE SOME GOOD ADVICE.
HUH!? ♡
IF YOU SIT CLASPING YOUR KNEES IN A CORNER OF THE ROOM ALL DAY...
...YOU DEFINITELY WON'T FAIL.
NOD
コクン
BUT ISN'T THAT THE SAME AS NOT TRYING TO DO ANYTHING?
SO THE FACT THAT YOU FAILED...

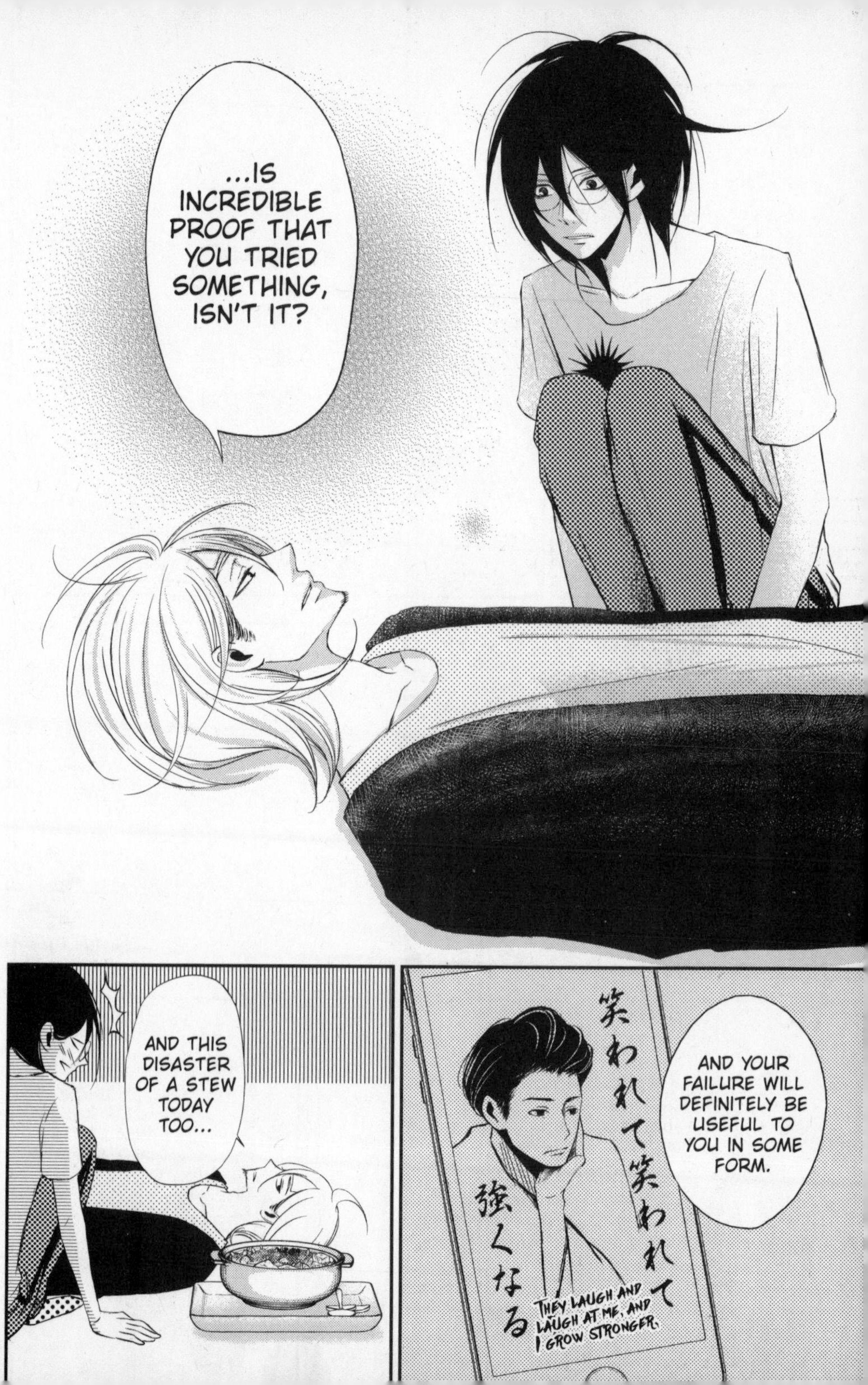
...IS INCREDIBLE PROOF THAT YOU TRIED SOMETHING, ISN'T IT?
AND YOUR FAILURE WILL DEFINITELY BE USEFUL TO YOU IN SOME FORM.
笑われて笑われて強くなる
THEY LAUGH AND LAUGH AT ME, AND I GROW STRONGER.
AND THIS DISASTER OF A STEW TODAY TOO...

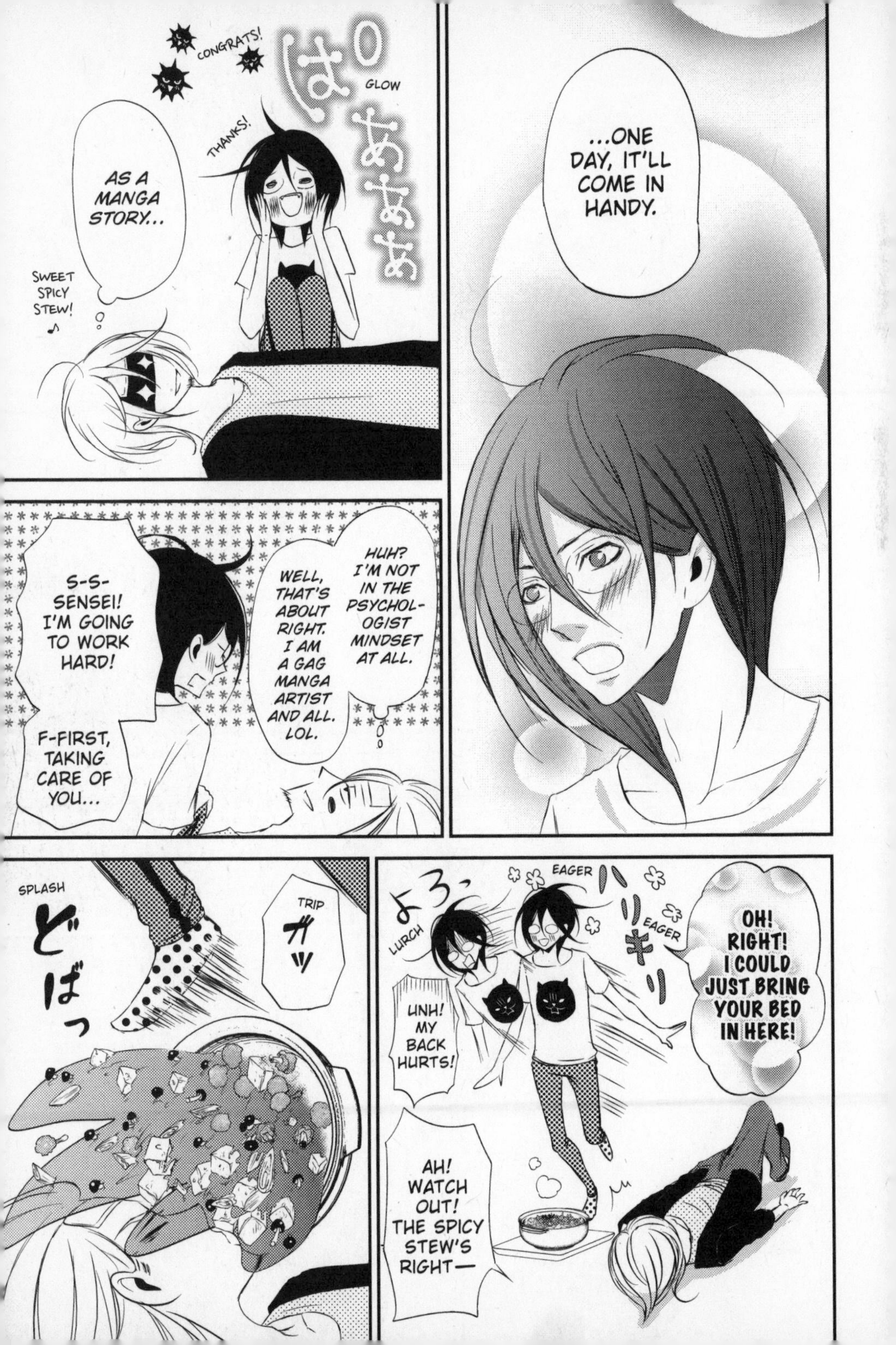
...ONE DAY, IT'LL COME IN HANDY.
CONGRATS!
はああああ
GLOW
THANKS!
AS A MANGA STORY...
SWEET SPICY STEW! ♪
HUH? I'M NOT IN THE PSYCHOL-OGIST MINDSET AT ALL.
WELL, THAT'S ABOUT RIGHT. I AM A GAG MANGA ARTIST AND ALL. LOL.
S-S-SENSEI! I'M GOING TO WORK HARD!
F-FIRST, TAKING CARE OF YOU...
OH! RIGHT! I COULD JUST BRING YOUR BED IN HERE!
ハリキリ
EAGER
EAGER
よろ
LURCH
UNH! MY BACK HURTS!
AH! WATCH OUT! THE SPICY STEW'S RIGHT—
TRIP
ガッ
SPLASH
どばっ

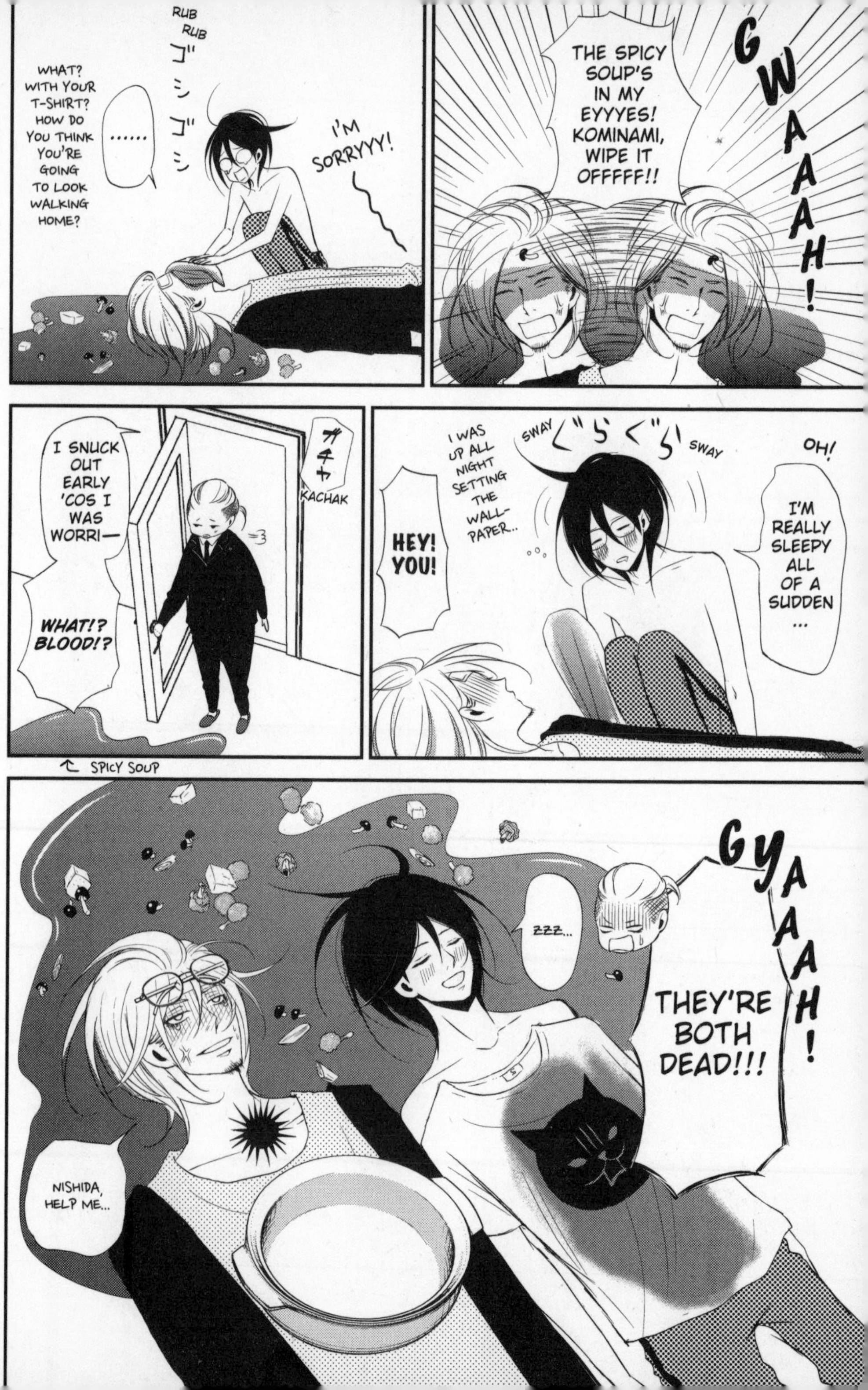
GWAAAH!
THE SPICY SOUP'S IN MY EYYYES! KOMINAMI, WIPE IT OFFFFF!!
RUB RUB
ゴシゴシ
I'M SORRYYY!
......
WHAT? WITH YOUR T-SHIRT? HOW DO YOU THINK YOU'RE GOING TO LOOK WALKING HOME?
OH!
I'M REALLY SLEEPY ALL OF A SUDDEN...
SWAY ぐらぐら SWAY
I WAS UP ALL NIGHT SETTING THE WALL-PAPER...
HEY! YOU!
ガチャ
KACHAK
I SNUCK OUT EARLY 'COS I WAS WORRI—
WHAT!? BLOOD!?
SPICY SOUP
GYAAAAH!
THEY'RE BOTH DEAD!!!
zzz...
NISHIDA, HELP ME...

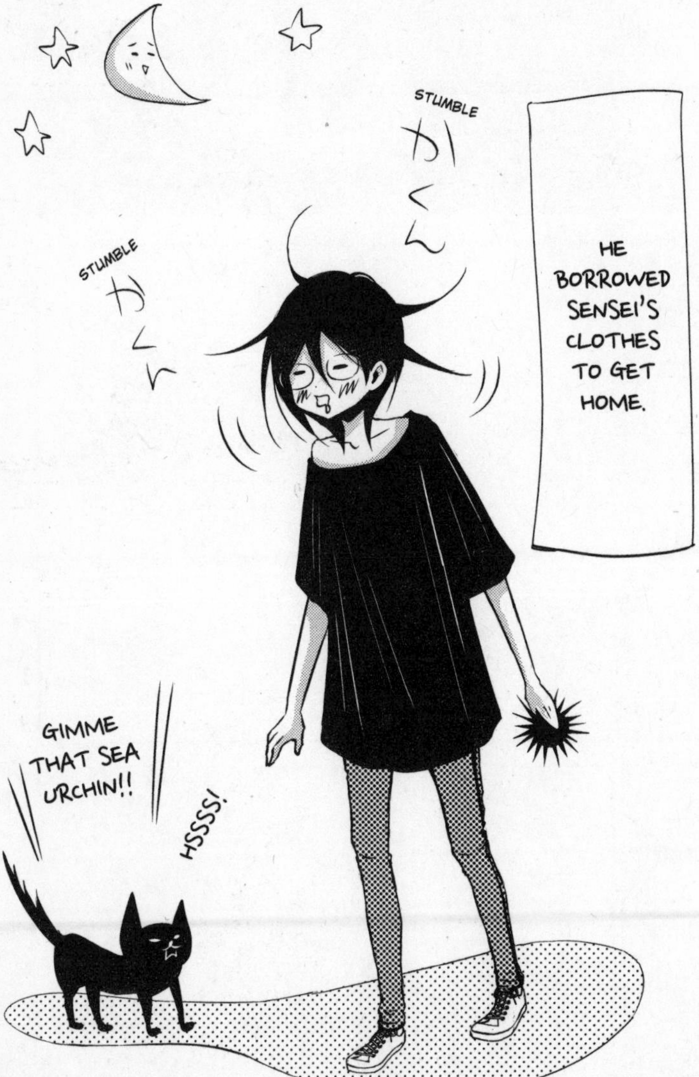
HE BORROWED SENSEI'S CLOTHES TO GET HOME.
STUMBLE
STUMBLE
HSSSS!
GIMME THAT SEA URCHIN!!

BONUS COMIC YOU CAN DO IT, NISHIDA!

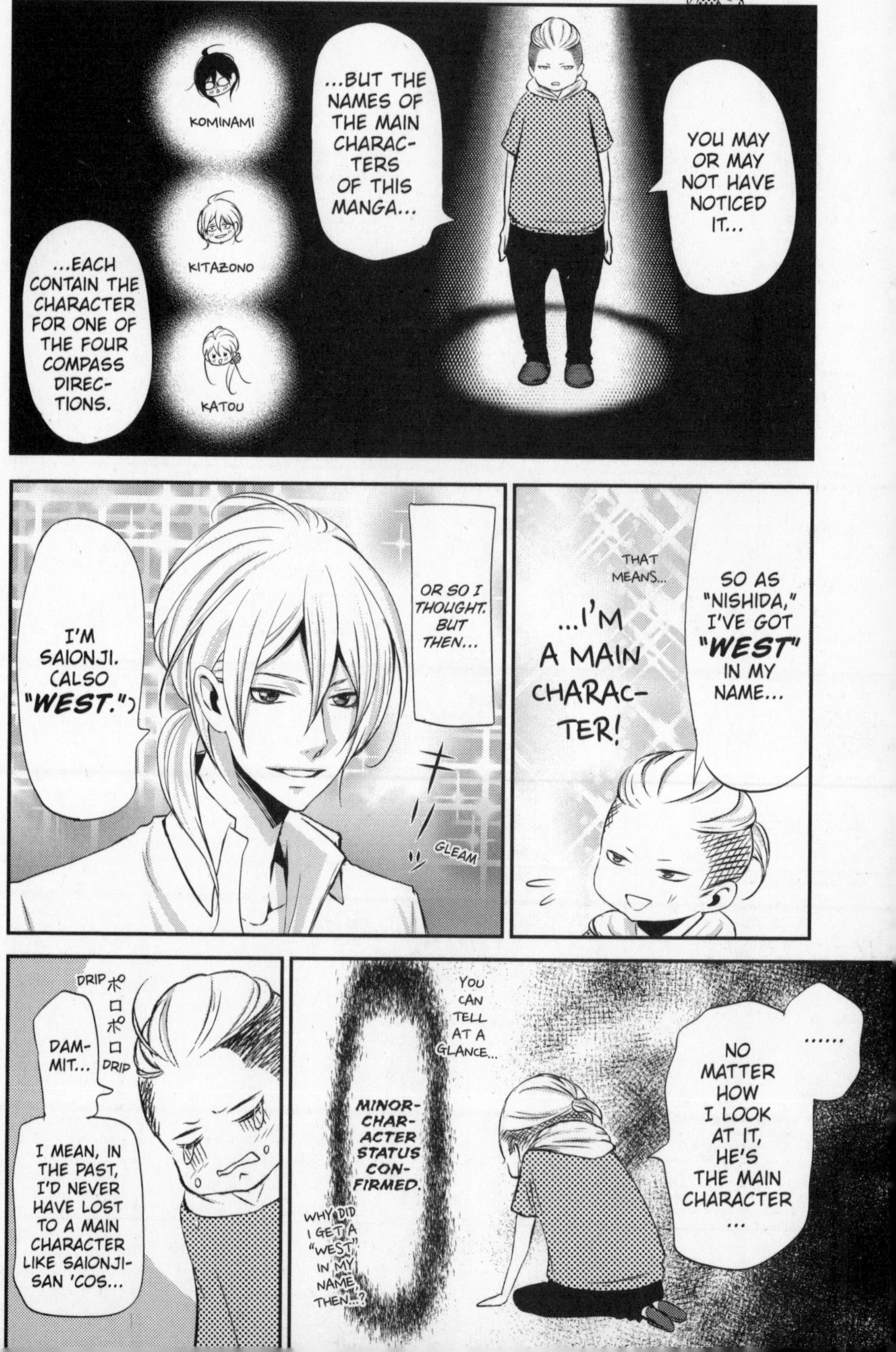
YOU MAY OR MAY NOT HAVE NOTICED IT...
...BUT THE NAMES OF THE MAIN CHARACTERS OF THIS MANGA...
KOMINAMI
KITAZONO
KATOU
...EACH CONTAIN THE CHARACTER FOR ONE OF THE FOUR COMPASS DIRECTIONS.
SO AS "NISHIDA," I'VE GOT "WEST" IN MY NAME...
THAT MEANS...
...I'M A MAIN CHARACTER!
OR SO I THOUGHT. BUT THEN...
GLEAM
I'M SAIONJI. (ALSO "WEST.")
......
NO MATTER HOW I LOOK AT IT, HE'S THE MAIN CHARACTER...
YOU CAN TELL AT A GLANCE...
MINOR-CHARACTER STATUS CONFIRMED.
WHY DID I GET A "WEST" IN MY NAME THEN...?
DRIP
DRIP
DAMMIT...
I MEAN, IN THE PAST, I'D NEVER HAVE LOST TO A MAIN CHARACTER LIKE SAIONJI-SAN 'COS...

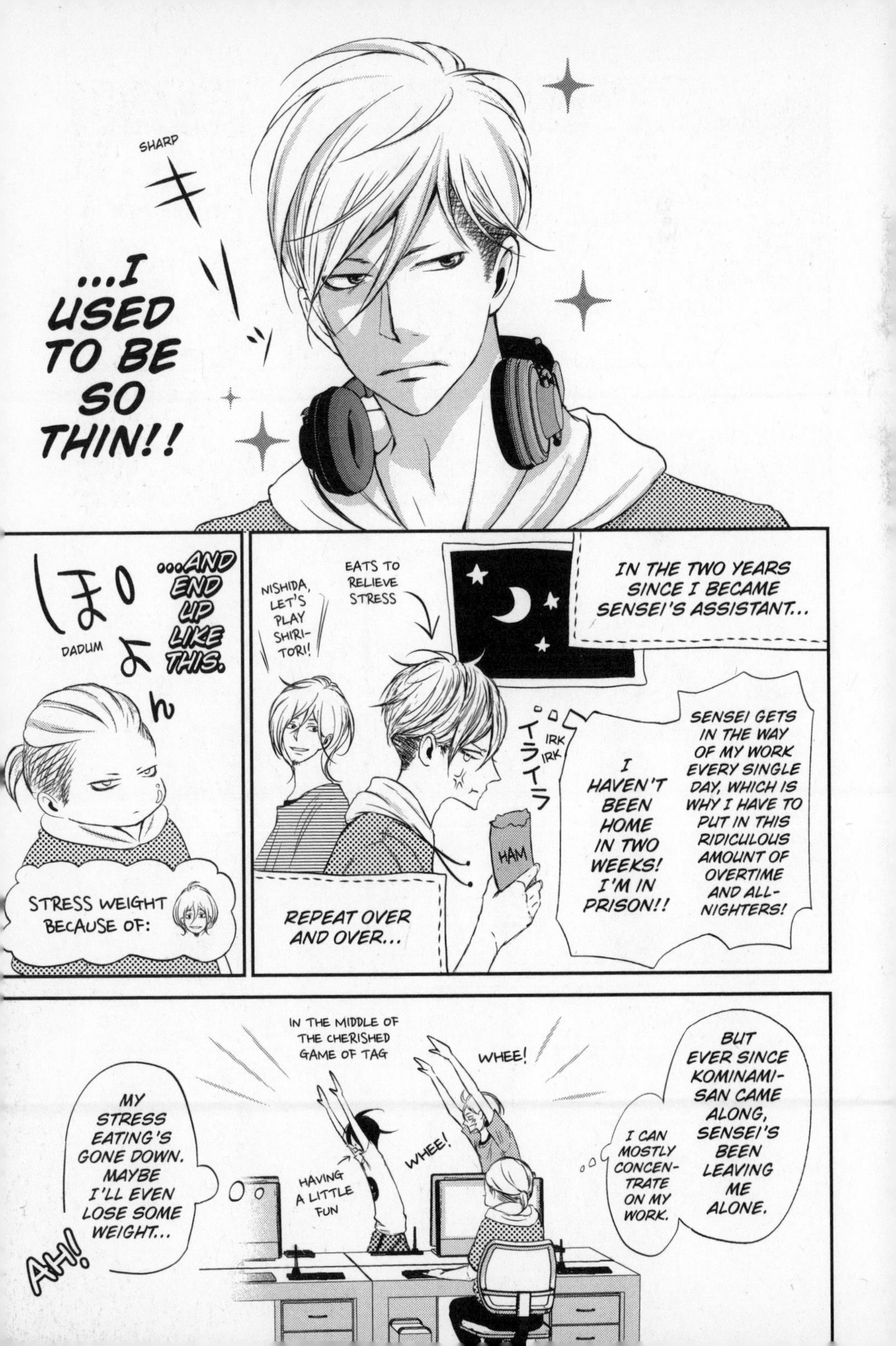

SHARP
キ
...I USED TO BE SO THIN!!
IN THE TWO YEARS SINCE I BECAME SENSEI'S ASSISTANT...
SENSEI GETS IN THE WAY OF MY WORK EVERY SINGLE DAY, WHICH IS WHY I HAVE TO PUT IN THIS RIDICULOUS AMOUNT OF OVERTIME AND ALL-NIGHTERS!
I HAVEN'T BEEN HOME IN TWO WEEKS! I'M IN PRISON!!
イライラ
IRK IRK
EATS TO RELIEVE STRESS
NISHIDA, LET'S PLAY SHIRI-TORI!
HAM
REPEAT OVER AND OVER...
...AND END UP LIKE THIS.
ほよん
DADUM
STRESS WEIGHT BECAUSE OF:
BUT EVER SINCE KOMINAMI-SAN CAME ALONG, SENSEI'S BEEN LEAVING ME ALONE.
I CAN MOSTLY CONCEN-TRATE ON MY WORK.
WHEE!
IN THE MIDDLE OF THE CHERISHED GAME OF TAG
WHEE!
HAVING A LITTLE FUN
MY STRESS EATING'S GONE DOWN. MAYBE I'LL EVEN LOSE SOME WEIGHT...
AH!

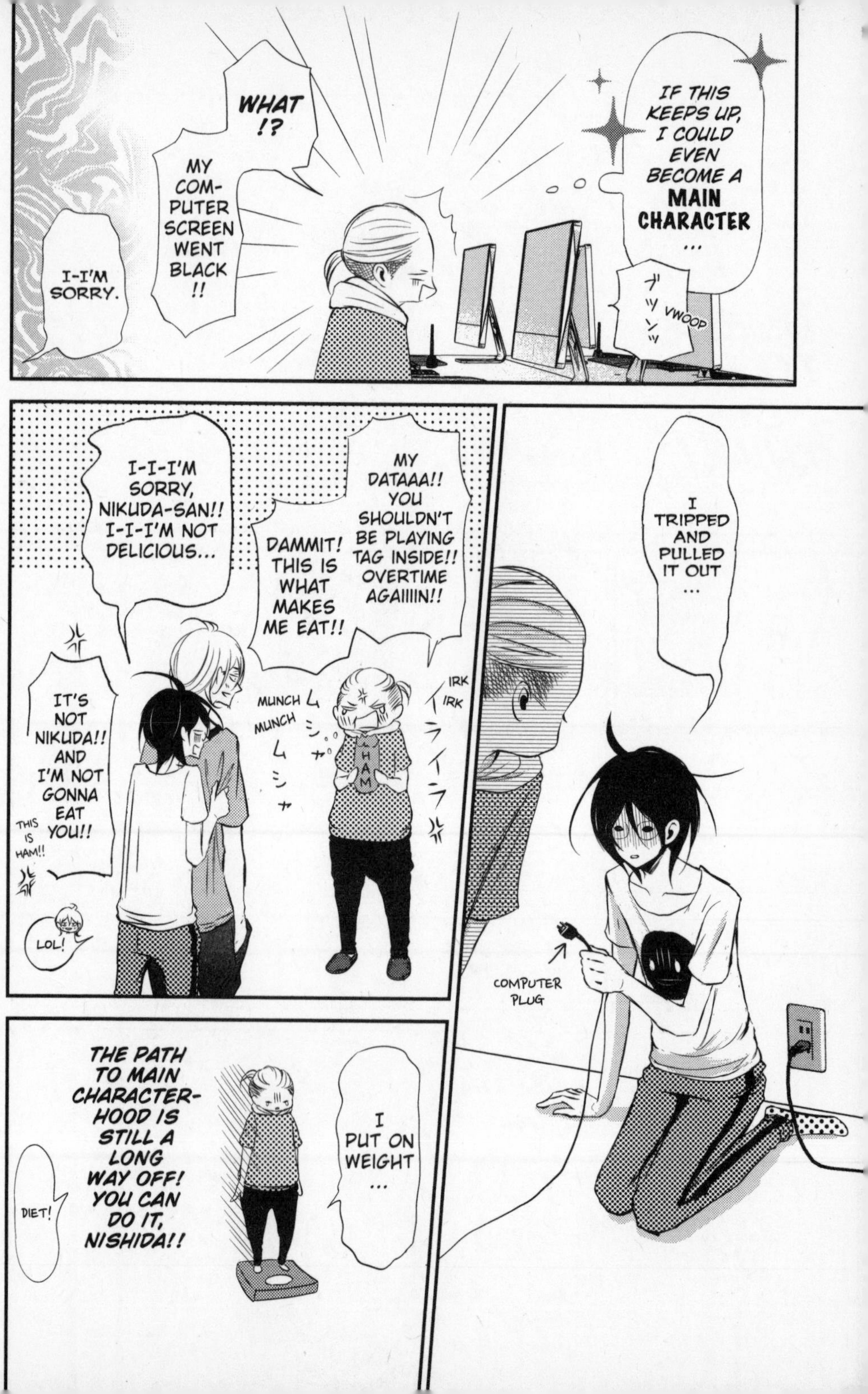
IF THIS KEEPS UP, I COULD EVEN BECOME A MAIN CHARACTER…
ブツッ VWOOP
WHAT!?
MY COMPUTER SCREEN WENT BLACK!!
I-I'M SORRY.
I TRIPPED AND PULLED IT OUT…
COMPUTER PLUG
MY DATAAA!! YOU SHOULDN'T BE PLAYING TAG INSIDE!! OVERTIME AGAIIIIN!!
IRK IRK イライラ
DAMMIT! THIS IS WHAT MAKES ME EAT!!
MUNCH MUNCH ムシャムシャ
HAM
I-I-I'M SORRY, NIKUDA-SAN!! I-I-I'M NOT DELICIOUS…
IT'S NOT NIKUDA!! AND I'M NOT GONNA EAT YOU!!
THIS IS HAM!!
LOL!
I PUT ON WEIGHT…
THE PATH TO MAIN CHARACTER-HOOD IS STILL A LONG WAY OFF! YOU CAN DO IT, NISHIDA!!
DIET!

SHUT-IN
SHOUTAROU KOMINAMI
TAKES ON THE WORLD

TRANSLATION NOTES

COMMON HONORIFICS

no honorific: Indicates familiarity or closeness; if used without permission or reason, addressing someone in this manner would constitute an insult.

-san: The Japanese equivalent of Mr./Mrs./Miss. If a situation calls for politeness, this is the fail-safe honorific.

-sama: Conveys great respect; may also indicate that the social status of the speaker is lower than that of the addressee.

-kun: Used most often when referring to boys, this indicates affection or familiarity. Occasionally used by older men among their peers, but it may also be used by anyone referring to a person of lower standing.

-chan: An affectionate honorific indicating familiarity used mostly in reference to girls; also used in reference to cute persons or animals of either gender.

-sensei: A respectful term for teachers, artists, or high-level professionals.

Yen conversion: While exchange rates fluctuate daily, a convenient conversion estimation is about ¥100 to 1 USD.

Page 10
Hello Work is a government program to help young people find employment.

Page 11
The **excerpt** Shoutarou reads is from the first chapter of Osamu Dazai's *No Longer Human*. The 1973 Donald Keene translation is used here.

Page 12
NEET stands for a young person "not in education, employment, or training" and is similar to the term *freeter*, meaning someone who is not part of the normal full-time employment system in Japan.

Page 21
The **diary** looks just like a grade school notebook.

Page 24
The Hinomaru is the Japanese flag, a large red circle on a white background.

Page 26
In the Japanese, Shoutarou says "*shaka*" and "*okeke.*" Shaka seems to be the mispronounced word for salmon (*sake*). Okeke, which is slang for "pubic hair," seems to be a mispronunciation of *okaka*—bonito flakes.

Page 27
Translated here as "**Make a pie, eat a pie,**" the original saying means that when going somewhere as a group, everyone meets at the intended place and then says their good-byes at that same place, instead of traveling to and fro together. It makes no sense for him to say that there, which he himself notes.

Page 44
Monthly Banban seems to be a parody of *Monthly Gangan*, the magazine in which *Shut-In Shoutarou Kominami Takes On the World* ran.

Page 46
Hi-Chew is a popular chewy candy similar to Starburst.

Page 51
Jona-kun, the diner to which Sensei brings Shoutarou, is a take on the popular diner chain Jonathan, which is spelled Jonasan in Japanese. Since -san is a common honorific, the artist is making a little wordplay with honorific suffixes by using -kun instead.

Page 58
The game we know as **tag** is called *onigokko* in Japanese, which means "demon make-believe." As indicated in the story, the person who is "It" is the "demon" who must hunt down the other players.

Page 62
Sunakake Baba is a youkai (supernatural creature) that takes the form of an old woman who flings sand at people.

Page 64
Momotaro is a hero from an old folktale who goes on a quest to defeat a group of demons. He sets out on his quest with a sack of dumplings.

Page 70
The statue, Faithful Dog Pochi-ko, is a reference to a famous dog in Japan known as "Faithful Dog Hachiko," remembered and honored with a statue at Shibuya station for his incredible loyalty to his owner even after his owner's death. Pochi is a common dog name, and -ko is a suffix meaning "lord."

Page 70
Ito-Yokado is a Japanese department store with a bird logo like the one on Shoutarou's bag.

Page 76
When introducing Nishida, Sensei uses the character for "meat" (niku) instead of the character for "west" (nishi) for Nishida's name. The second character makes this into a slight play on words since da is also the verb "to be," so it could be heard as "niku da" ("he is meat").

Page 79
Shochu is a type of alcohol generally distilled from barley or rice.

Page 104
Some say the story Shoutarou tells is how the word tasogare, which means "dusk," originated. Thus "Tasogare," a phrase which means "who's there?" also took on the meaning of the time of day itself, dusk.

Page 133
A leek compress on the neck is a traditional cold remedy in Japan.

Page 140
Umeboshi is pickled plum.

Page 144
The words for "nose" and "flower" are homonyms in Japanese (hana) but are spelled with different Chinese characters. Kominami accidentally uses the wrong character here.

Page 148
A reference to the Japanese cell phone provider SoftBank.

Page 152
The big-sister type of character on Japanese TV, typically played by gay men, is known as onee (short for onee-san or "older sister"). They use feminine language and generally behave like flirty young women.

Page 159
Mount Takao is a relatively low and climbable mountain just outside of Tokyo.

Page 174
Katou tries to make another terrible pun to herself. In Japanese, Shoutarou says "S-s-s-s-s-sumimasen," and Kato takes the su syllable and attaches the character for "vinegar" to make the pun "precisely because of the vinegar."

Page 175
The original pun is on the phrase ma ii ka which means "well, whatever," but which also sounds like maika, meaning "common squid."

Page 179
Sensei says at the bottom of the previous page "ore no kanbyou" ("nurse/take care of me"), but Shoutarou hears kanpyou (dried gourd used in sushi rolls), so he declines, saying he prefers cucumber rolls.

Page 194
Each of the main characters' names uses a Chinese character for one of the cardinal directions. The minami in Kominami is "south," the kita in Kitazono is "north," the tou in Katou is "east," and the nishi in Nishida is "west." The sai in Saionji is also "west."

Page 195
Shiritori is a word game in which players take turns saying a word that begins with the last syllable of the previous word. For example, sayonara might be followed by rabu ("love"). If one player says a word that ends with n (in the example above, ramen), the game is over because no Japanese words begin with the syllabic "n."

THANK YOU SO MUCH FOR
PICKING UP THIS BOOK.

THE SERIALIZATION OF *SHUT-IN
SHOUTAROU KOMINAMI TAKES ON
THE WORLD* BEGAN AND...

I STOPPED LEAVING MY HOUSE.

I DON'T LOOK VERY HEALTHY...

—DAN ICHIKAWA
BIRTHDAY: MAY 16
BLOOD TYPE: AB

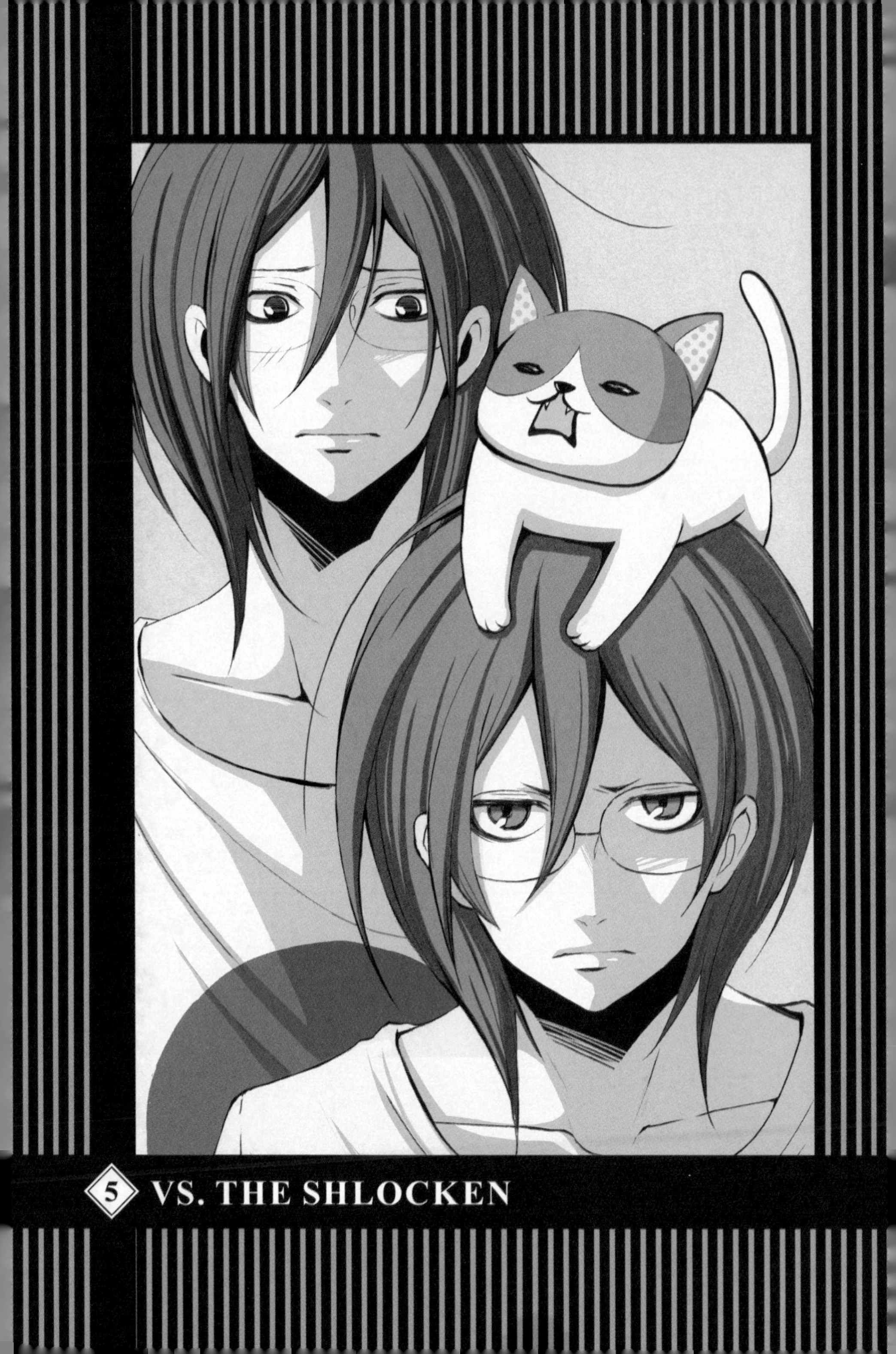

5 VS. THE SHLOCKEN

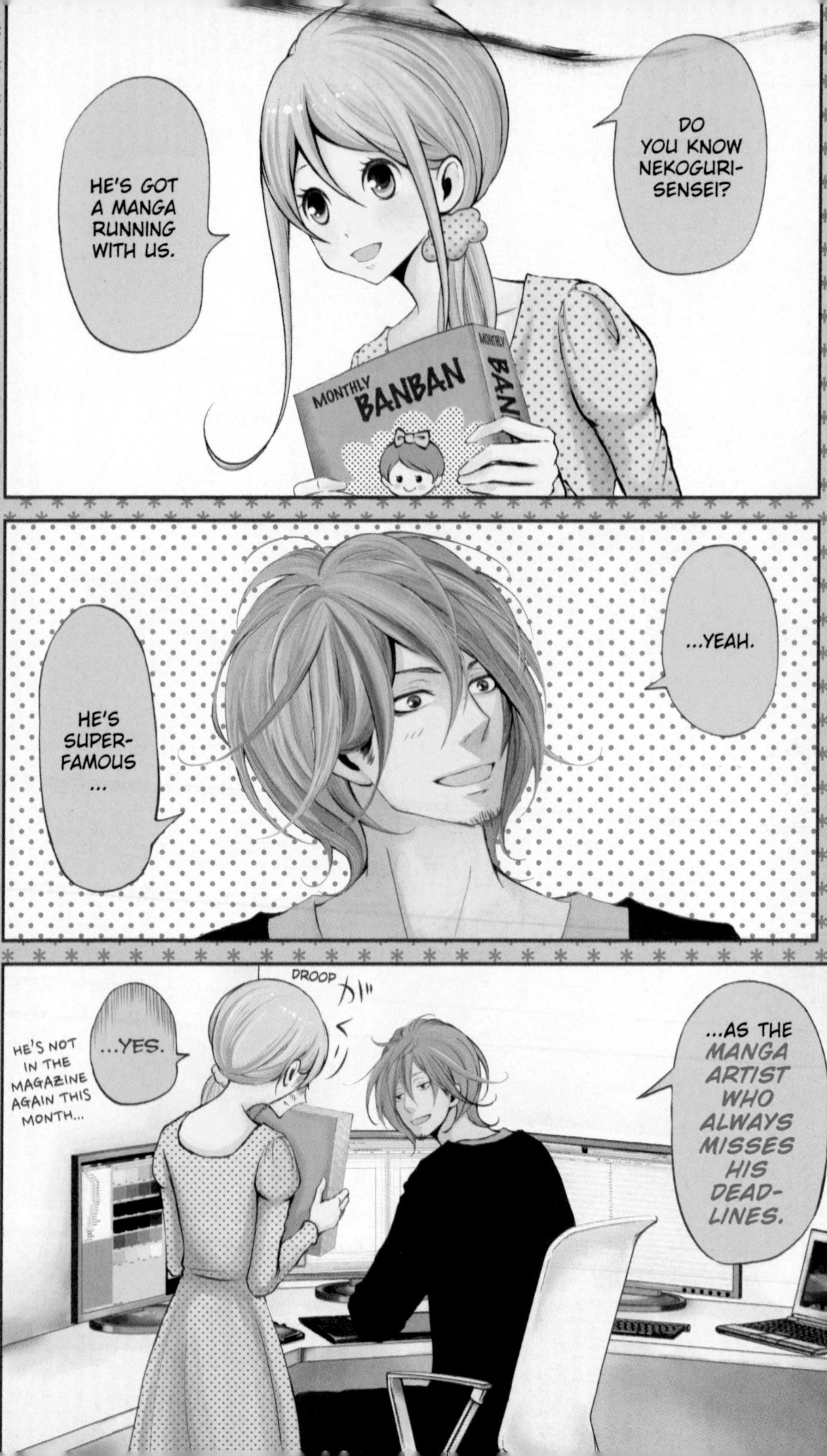
DO YOU KNOW NEKOGURI-SENSEI?
HE'S GOT A MANGA RUNNING WITH US.
MONTHLY BANBAN
MONTHLY BAN
...YEAH.
HE'S SUPER-FAMOUS ...
...AS THE MANGA ARTIST WHO ALWAYS MISSES HIS DEADLINES.
DROOP
...YES.
HE'S NOT IN THE MAGAZINE AGAIN THIS MONTH...

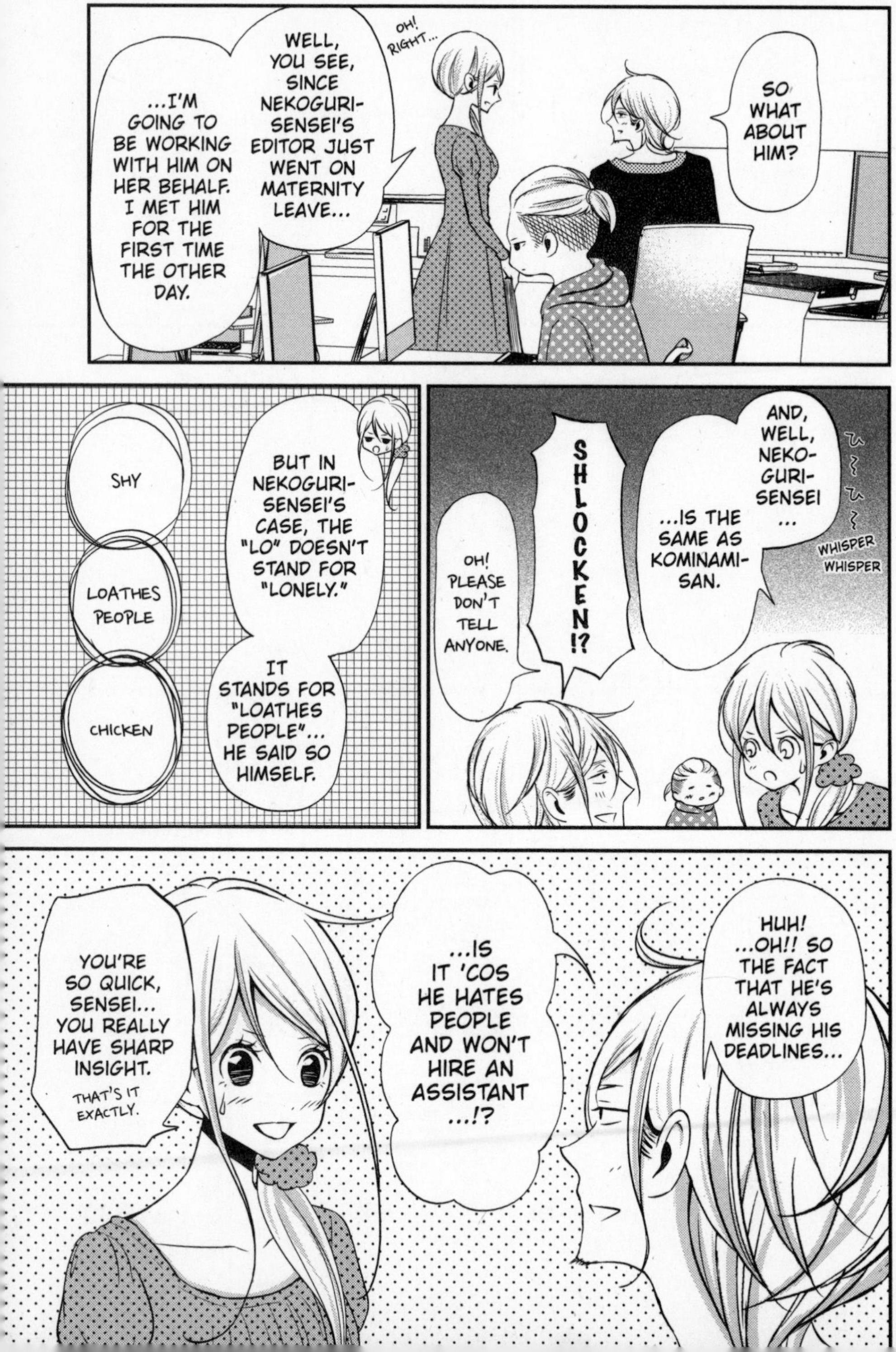
SO WHAT ABOUT HIM?
OH! RIGHT...
WELL, YOU SEE, SINCE NEKOGURI-SENSEI'S EDITOR JUST WENT ON MATERNITY LEAVE...
...I'M GOING TO BE WORKING WITH HIM ON HER BEHALF. I MET HIM FOR THE FIRST TIME THE OTHER DAY.
AND, WELL, NEKOGURI-SENSEI ...
WHISPER WHISPER
...IS THE SAME AS KOMINAMI-SAN.
SHLOCKEN!?
OH! PLEASE DON'T TELL ANYONE.
BUT IN NEKOGURI-SENSEI'S CASE, THE "LO" DOESN'T STAND FOR "LONELY."
IT STANDS FOR "LOATHES PEOPLE"... HE SAID SO HIMSELF.
SHY
LOATHES PEOPLE
CHICKEN
HUH! ...OH!! SO THE FACT THAT HE'S ALWAYS MISSING HIS DEADLINES...
...IS IT 'COS HE HATES PEOPLE AND WON'T HIRE AN ASSISTANT ...!?
YOU'RE SO QUICK, SENSEI... YOU REALLY HAVE SHARP INSIGHT.
THAT'S IT EXACTLY.

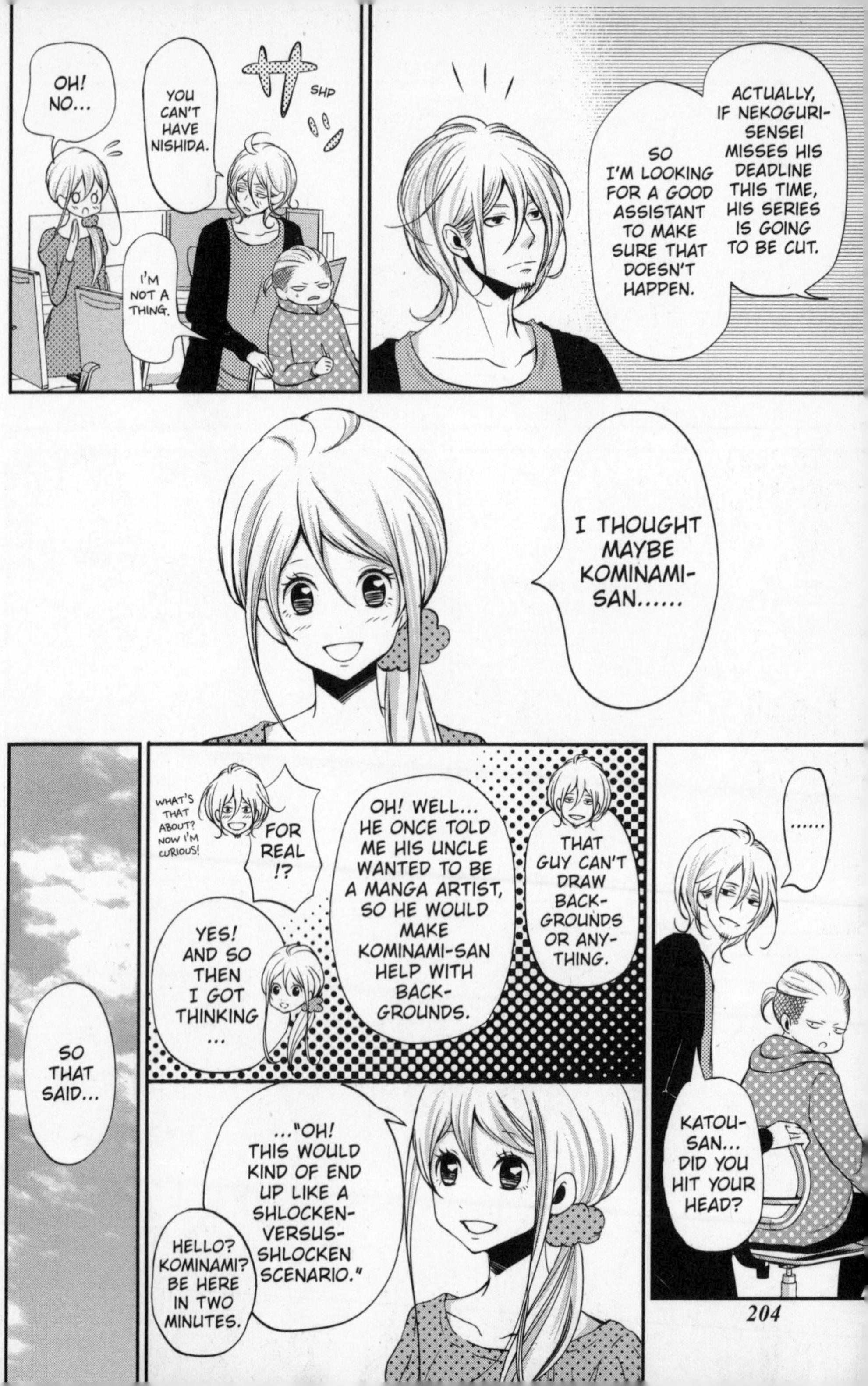
ACTUALLY, IF NEKOGURI-SENSEI MISSES HIS DEADLINE THIS TIME, HIS SERIES IS GOING TO BE CUT.
SO I'M LOOKING FOR A GOOD ASSISTANT TO MAKE SURE THAT DOESN'T HAPPEN.
SHP
YOU CAN'T HAVE NISHIDA.
OH! NO...
I'M NOT A THING.
I THOUGHT MAYBE KOMINAMI-SAN......
......
KATOU-SAN... DID YOU HIT YOUR HEAD?
THAT GUY CAN'T DRAW BACK-GROUNDS OR ANY-THING.
OH! WELL... HE ONCE TOLD ME HIS UNCLE WANTED TO BE A MANGA ARTIST, SO HE WOULD MAKE KOMINAMI-SAN HELP WITH BACK-GROUNDS.
FOR REAL!?
WHAT'S THAT ABOUT? NOW I'M CURIOUS!
YES! AND SO THEN I GOT THINKING...
..."OH! THIS WOULD KIND OF END UP LIKE A SHLOCKEN-VERSUS-SHLOCKEN SCENARIO."
HELLO? KOMINAMI? BE HERE IN TWO MINUTES.
SO THAT SAID...

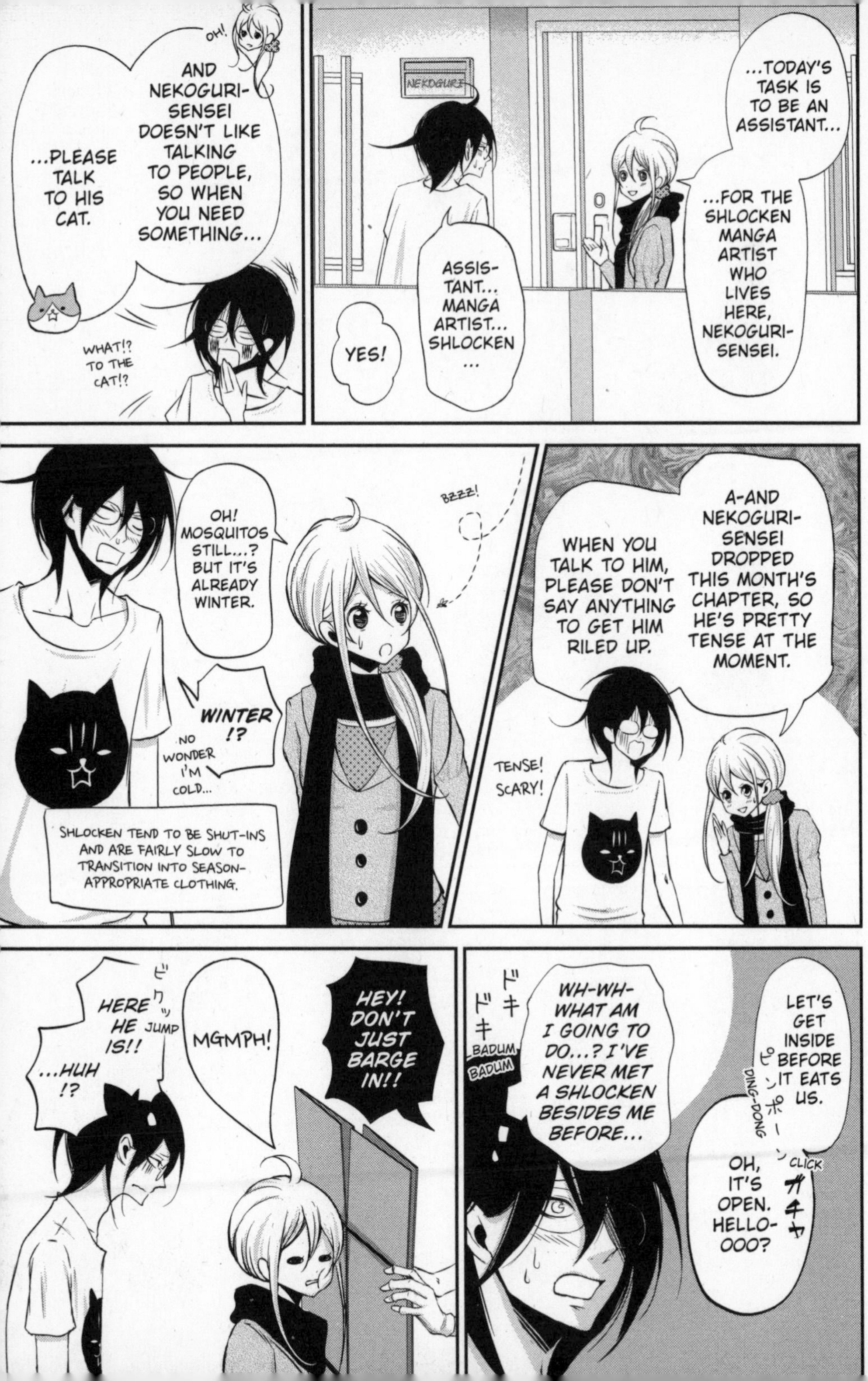
NEKOGURI
...TODAY'S TASK IS TO BE AN ASSISTANT...
...FOR THE SHLOCKEN MANGA ARTIST WHO LIVES HERE, NEKOGURI-SENSEI.
ASSIS-TANT... MANGA ARTIST... SHLOCKEN ...
YES!
OH!
AND NEKOGURI-SENSEI DOESN'T LIKE TALKING TO PEOPLE, SO WHEN YOU NEED SOMETHING...
...PLEASE TALK TO HIS CAT.
WHAT!? TO THE CAT!?
A-AND NEKOGURI-SENSEI DROPPED THIS MONTH'S CHAPTER, SO HE'S PRETTY TENSE AT THE MOMENT.
WHEN YOU TALK TO HIM, PLEASE DON'T SAY ANYTHING TO GET HIM RILED UP.
TENSE! SCARY!
BZZZ!
OH! MOSQUITOS STILL...? BUT IT'S ALREADY WINTER.
WINTER!?
NO WONDER I'M COLD...
SHLOCKEN TEND TO BE SHUT-INS AND ARE FAIRLY SLOW TO TRANSITION INTO SEASON-APPROPRIATE CLOTHING.
LET'S GET INSIDE BEFORE IT EATS US.
ピンポーン
DING-DONG
OH, IT'S OPEN. HELLO-OOO?
ガチャ
CLICK
ドキドキ
BADUM BADUM
WH-WH-WHAT AM I GOING TO DO...? I'VE NEVER MET A SHLOCKEN BESIDES ME BEFORE...
HEY! DON'T JUST BARGE IN!!
MGMPH!
ビクッ
JUMP
HERE HE IS!!
...HUH!?

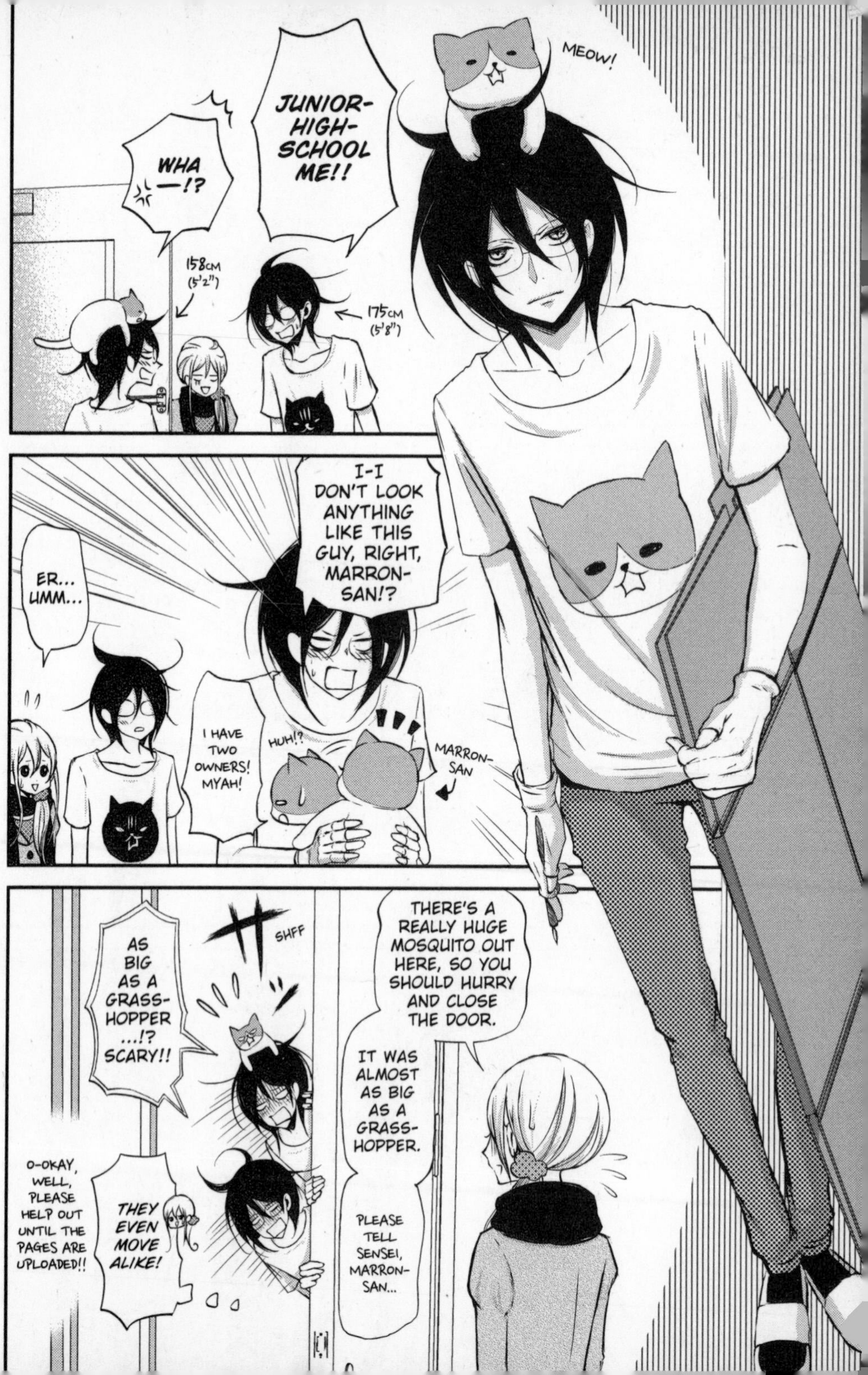
MEOW!
JUNIOR-HIGH-SCHOOL ME!!
WHA—!?
175cm (5'8")
158cm (5'2")
I-I DON'T LOOK ANYTHING LIKE THIS GUY, RIGHT, MARRON-SAN!?
MARRON-SAN
HUH!?
I HAVE TWO OWNERS! MYAH!
ER... UMM...
THERE'S A REALLY HUGE MOSQUITO OUT HERE, SO YOU SHOULD HURRY AND CLOSE THE DOOR.
IT WAS ALMOST AS BIG AS A GRASSHOPPER.
PLEASE TELL SENSEI, MARRON-SAN...
SHFF
AS BIG AS A GRASSHOPPER ...!? SCARY!!
THEY EVEN MOVE ALIKE!
O-OKAY, WELL, PLEASE HELP OUT UNTIL THE PAGES ARE UPLOADED!!

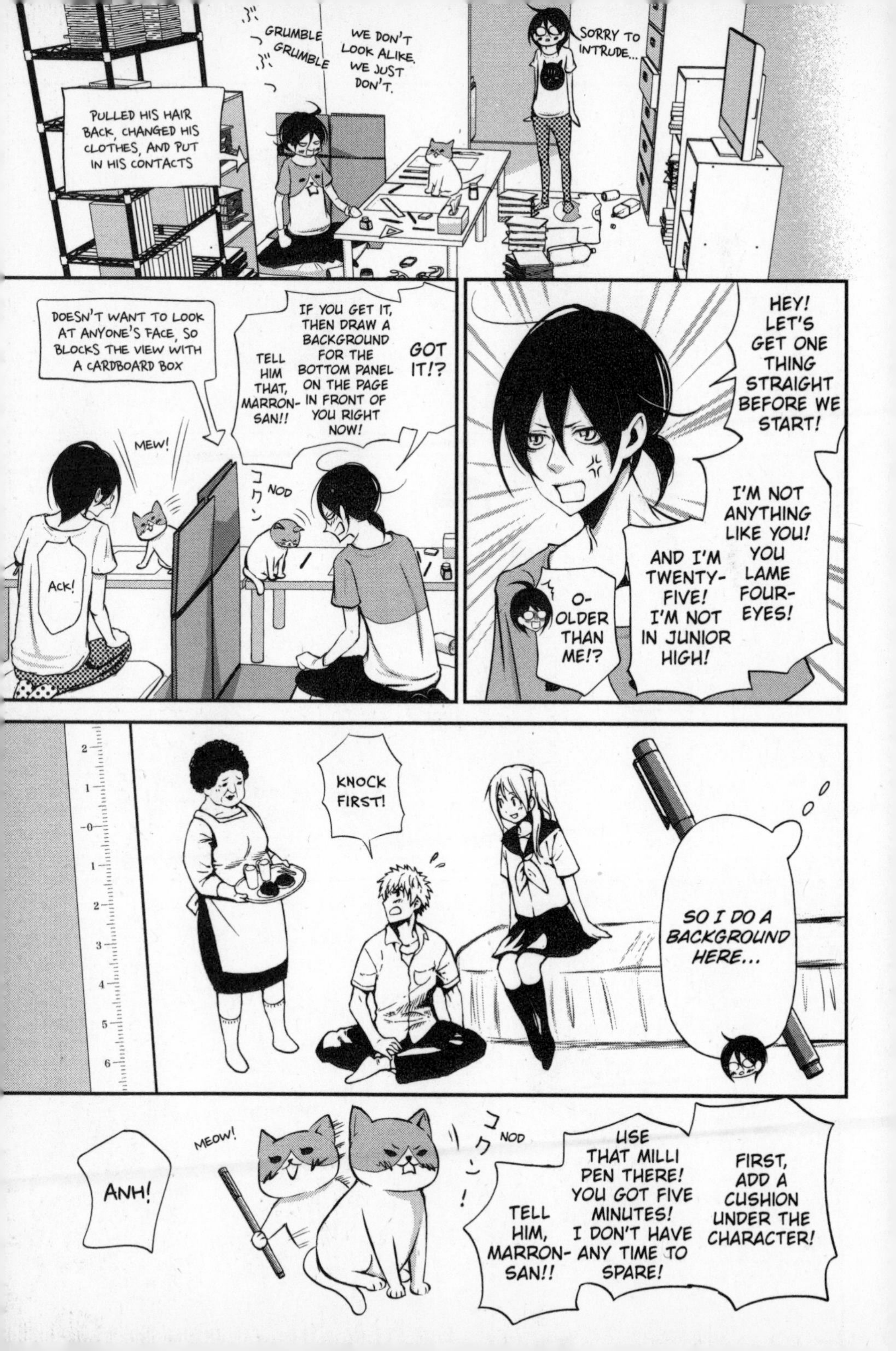

SORRY TO INTRUDE...
WE DON'T LOOK ALIKE. WE JUST DON'T.
GRUMBLE GRUMBLE
PULLED HIS HAIR BACK, CHANGED HIS CLOTHES, AND PUT IN HIS CONTACTS
HEY! LET'S GET ONE THING STRAIGHT BEFORE WE START!
I'M NOT ANYTHING LIKE YOU! YOU LAME FOUR-EYES!
AND I'M TWENTY-FIVE! I'M NOT IN JUNIOR HIGH!
O-OLDER THAN ME!?
GOT IT!?
IF YOU GET IT, THEN DRAW A BACKGROUND FOR THE BOTTOM PANEL ON THE PAGE IN FRONT OF YOU RIGHT NOW!
TELL HIM THAT, MARRON-SAN!!
DOESN'T WANT TO LOOK AT ANYONE'S FACE, SO BLOCKS THE VIEW WITH A CARDBOARD BOX
NOD
MEW!
Ack!
SO I DO A BACKGROUND HERE...
KNOCK FIRST!
FIRST, ADD A CUSHION UNDER THE CHARACTER!
USE THAT MILLI PEN THERE! YOU GOT FIVE MINUTES! I DON'T HAVE ANY TIME TO SPARE!
TELL HIM, MARRON-SAN!!
NOD
MEOW!
ANH!

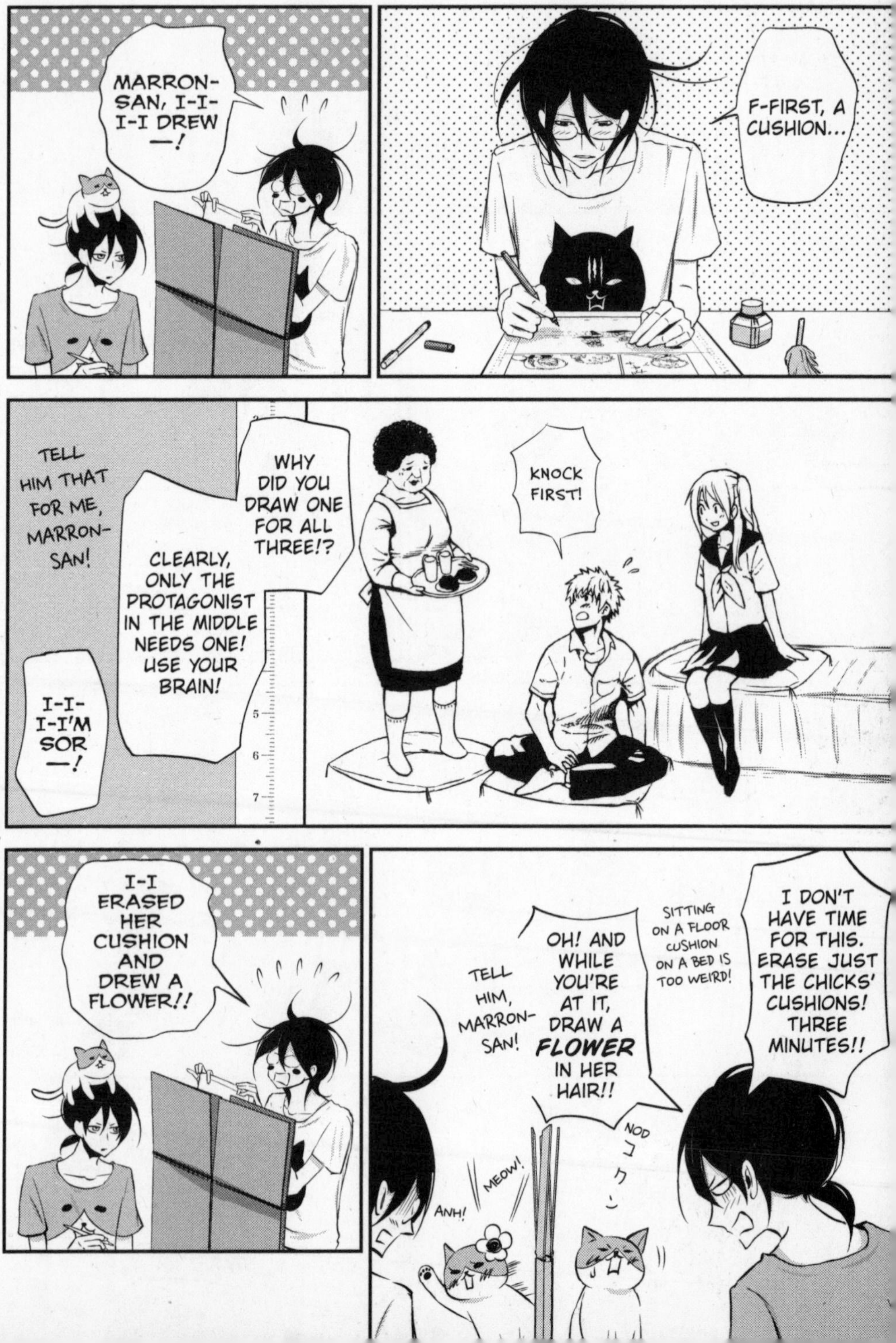
F-FIRST, A CUSHION...
MARRON-SAN, I-I-I-I DREW—!
KNOCK FIRST!
WHY DID YOU DRAW ONE FOR ALL THREE!?
CLEARLY, ONLY THE PROTAGONIST IN THE MIDDLE NEEDS ONE! USE YOUR BRAIN!
TELL HIM THAT FOR ME, MARRON-SAN!
I-I-I-I'M SOR—!
I DON'T HAVE TIME FOR THIS. ERASE JUST THE CHICKS' CUSHIONS! THREE MINUTES!!
SITTING ON A FLOOR CUSHION ON A BED IS TOO WEIRD!
OH! AND WHILE YOU'RE AT IT, DRAW A **FLOWER** IN HER HAIR!!
TELL HIM, MARRON-SAN!
NOD
コク
MEOW!
ANH!
I-I ERASED HER CUSHION AND DREW A FLOWER!!

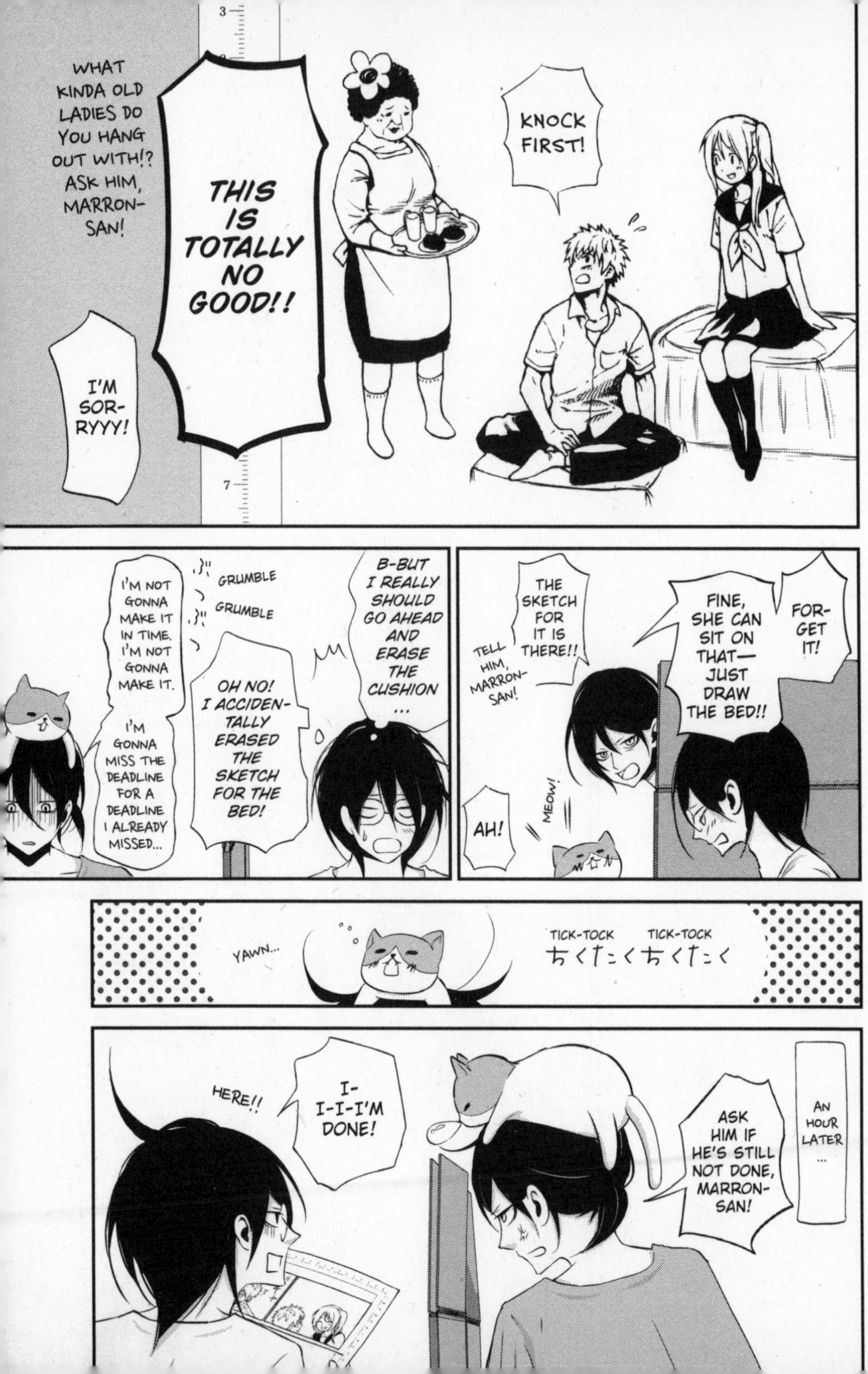
KNOCK FIRST!
THIS IS TOTALLY NO GOOD!!
WHAT KINDA OLD LADIES DO YOU HANG OUT WITH!? ASK HIM, MARRON-SAN!
I'M SORRYYY!
FOR-GET IT!
FINE, SHE CAN SIT ON THAT— JUST DRAW THE BED!!
THE SKETCH FOR IT IS THERE!!
TELL HIM, MARRON-SAN!
MEOW!
AH!
B-BUT I REALLY SHOULD GO AHEAD AND ERASE THE CUSHION...
OH NO! I ACCIDENTALLY ERASED THE SKETCH FOR THE BED!
GRUMBLE
GRUMBLE
I'M NOT GONNA MAKE IT IN TIME. I'M NOT GONNA MAKE IT.
I'M GONNA MISS THE DEADLINE FOR A DEADLINE I ALREADY MISSED...
TICK-TOCK TICK-TOCK
ちくたくちくたく
YAWN...
AN HOUR LATER...
ASK HIM IF HE'S STILL NOT DONE, MARRON-SAN!
I-I-I-I'M DONE!
HERE!!

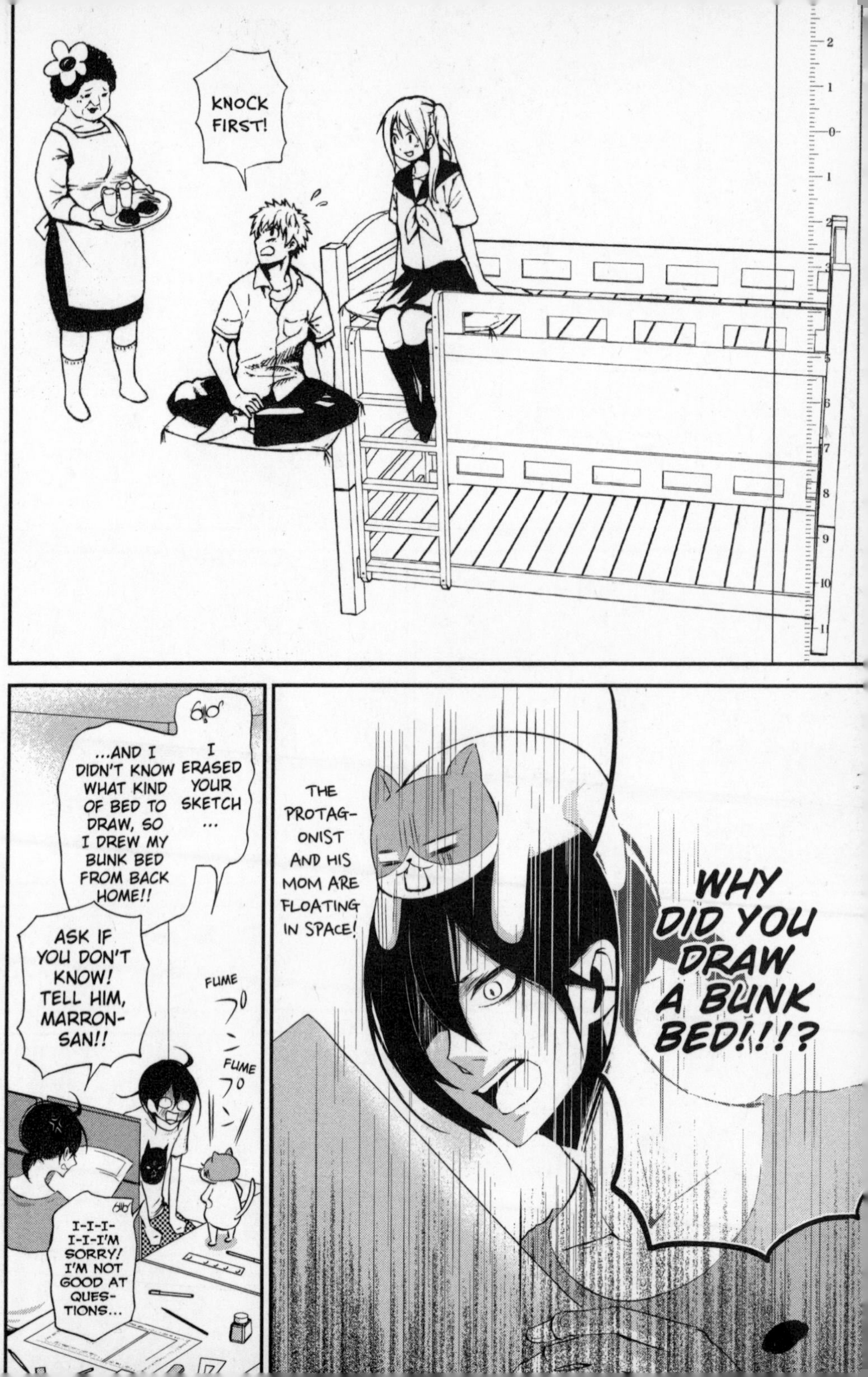
KNOCK FIRST!
WHY DID YOU DRAW A BUNK BED!!!?
THE PROTAGONIST AND HIS MOM ARE FLOATING IN SPACE!
I ERASED YOUR SKETCH...
...AND I DIDN'T KNOW WHAT KIND OF BED TO DRAW, SO I DREW MY BUNK BED FROM BACK HOME!!
ASK IF YOU DON'T KNOW! TELL HIM, MARRON-SAN!!
FUME
FUME
I-I-I-I-I-I'M SORRY! I'M NOT GOOD AT QUESTIONS...

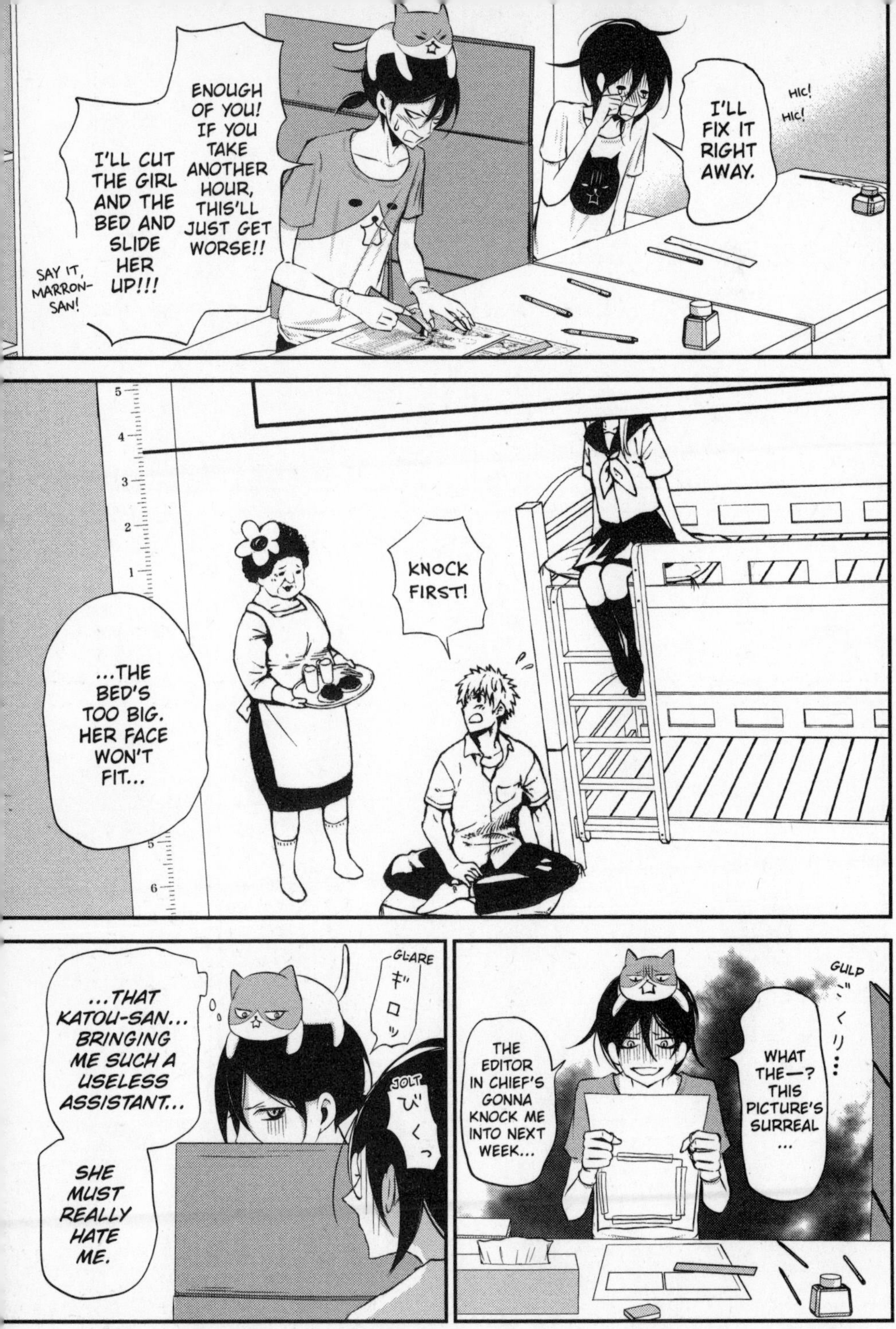
HIC!
HIC!
I'LL FIX IT RIGHT AWAY.
ENOUGH OF YOU! IF YOU TAKE ANOTHER HOUR, THIS'LL JUST GET WORSE!!
I'LL CUT THE GIRL AND THE BED AND SLIDE HER UP!!!
SAY IT, MARRON-SAN!
KNOCK FIRST!
...THE BED'S TOO BIG. HER FACE WON'T FIT...
GULP
ごくり…
WHAT THE—? THIS PICTURE'S SURREAL...
THE EDITOR IN CHIEF'S GONNA KNOCK ME INTO NEXT WEEK...
GLARE
ギロッ
JOLT
びくっ
...THAT KATOU-SAN... BRINGING ME SUCH A USELESS ASSISTANT...
SHE MUST REALLY HATE ME.

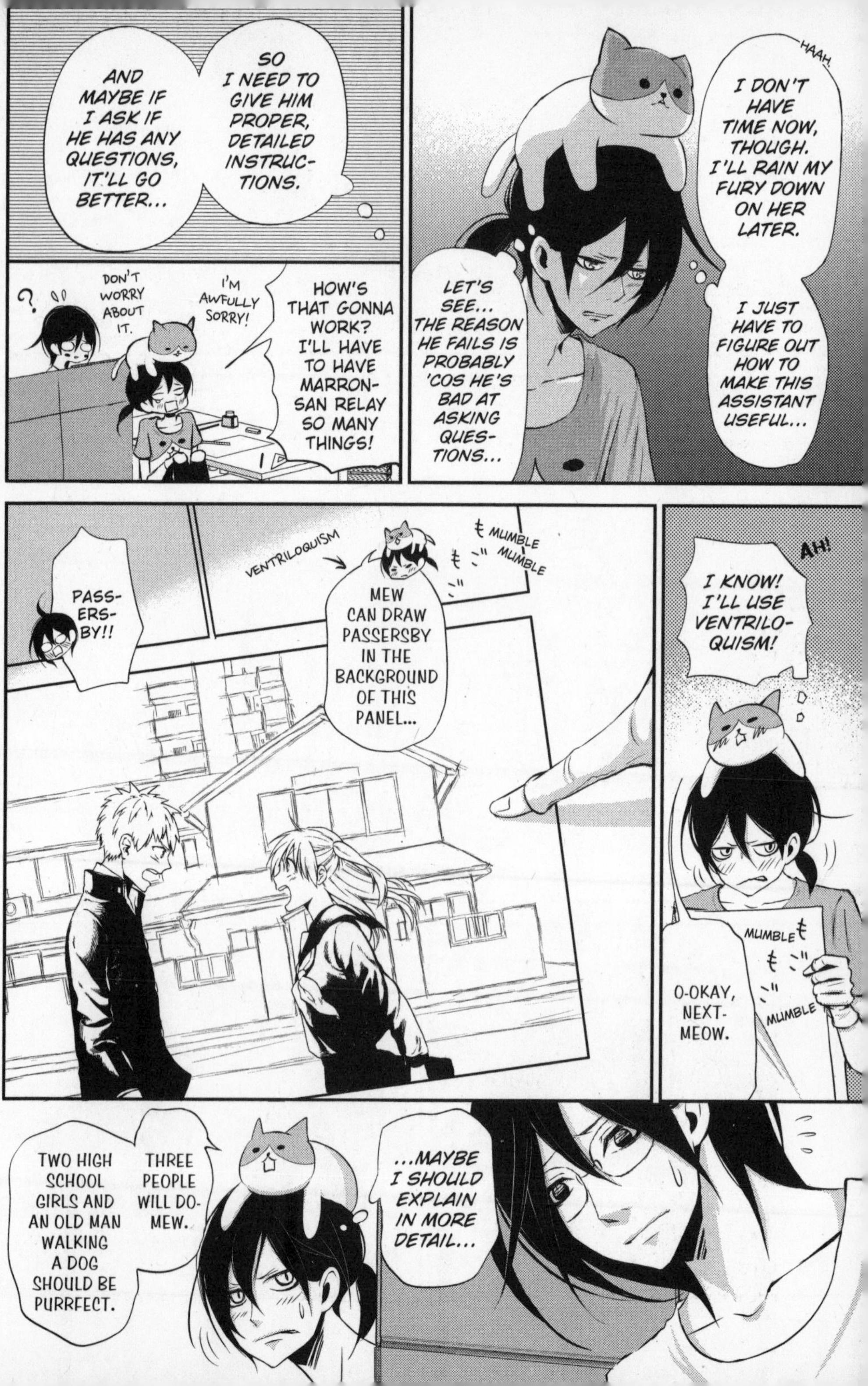
HAAH.
I DON'T HAVE TIME NOW, THOUGH. I'LL RAIN MY FURY DOWN ON HER LATER.
I JUST HAVE TO FIGURE OUT HOW TO MAKE THIS ASSISTANT USEFUL...
LET'S SEE... THE REASON HE FAILS IS PROBABLY 'COS HE'S BAD AT ASKING QUESTIONS...
SO I NEED TO GIVE HIM PROPER, DETAILED INSTRUCTIONS.
AND MAYBE IF I ASK IF HE HAS ANY QUESTIONS, IT'LL GO BETTER...
HOW'S THAT GONNA WORK? I'LL HAVE TO HAVE MARRON-SAN RELAY SO MANY THINGS!
I'M AWFULLY SORRY!
DON'T WORRY ABOUT IT.
AH!
I KNOW! I'LL USE VENTRILOQUISM!
MUMBLE MUMBLE
O-OKAY, NEXT-MEOW.
MUMBLE MUMBLE
MEW CAN DRAW PASSERSBY IN THE BACKGROUND OF THIS PANEL...
VENTRILOQUISM
PASS-ERSBY!!
...MAYBE I SHOULD EXPLAIN IN MORE DETAIL...
THREE PEOPLE WILL DO-MEW.
TWO HIGH SCHOOL GIRLS AND AN OLD MAN WALKING A DOG SHOULD BE PURRFECT.

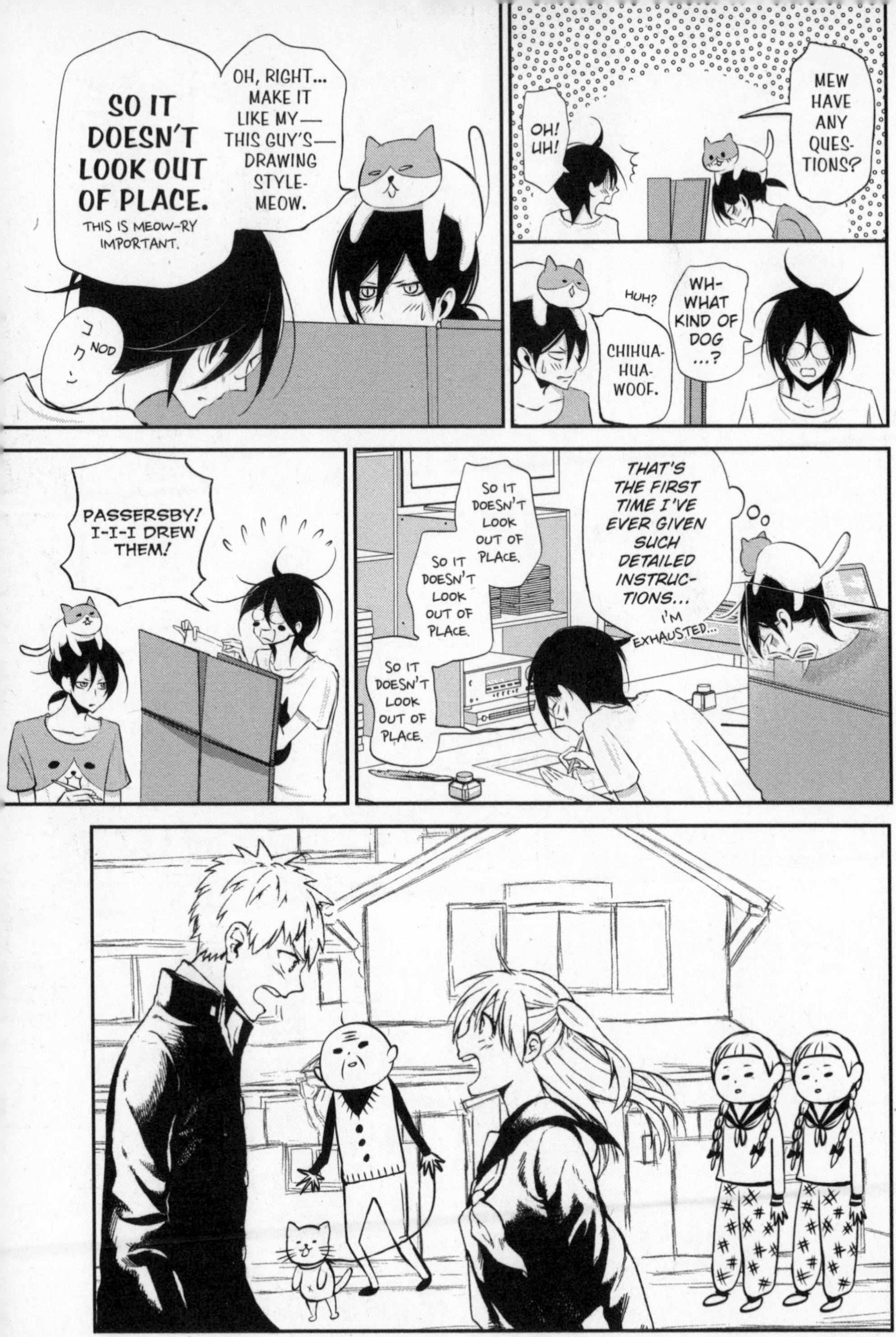
MEW HAVE ANY QUESTIONS?
OH! UH!
WH-WHAT KIND OF DOG ...?
HUH?
CHIHUAHUA-WOOF.
OH, RIGHT... MAKE IT LIKE MY— THIS GUY'S— DRAWING STYLE-MEOW.
SO IT DOESN'T LOOK OUT OF PLACE.
THIS IS MEOW-RY IMPORTANT.
NOD
THAT'S THE FIRST TIME I'VE EVER GIVEN SUCH DETAILED INSTRUCTIONS...
I'M EXHAUSTED...
SO IT DOESN'T LOOK OUT OF PLACE.
SO IT DOESN'T LOOK OUT OF PLACE.
SO IT DOESN'T LOOK OUT OF PLACE.
PASSERSBY! I-I-I DREW THEM!

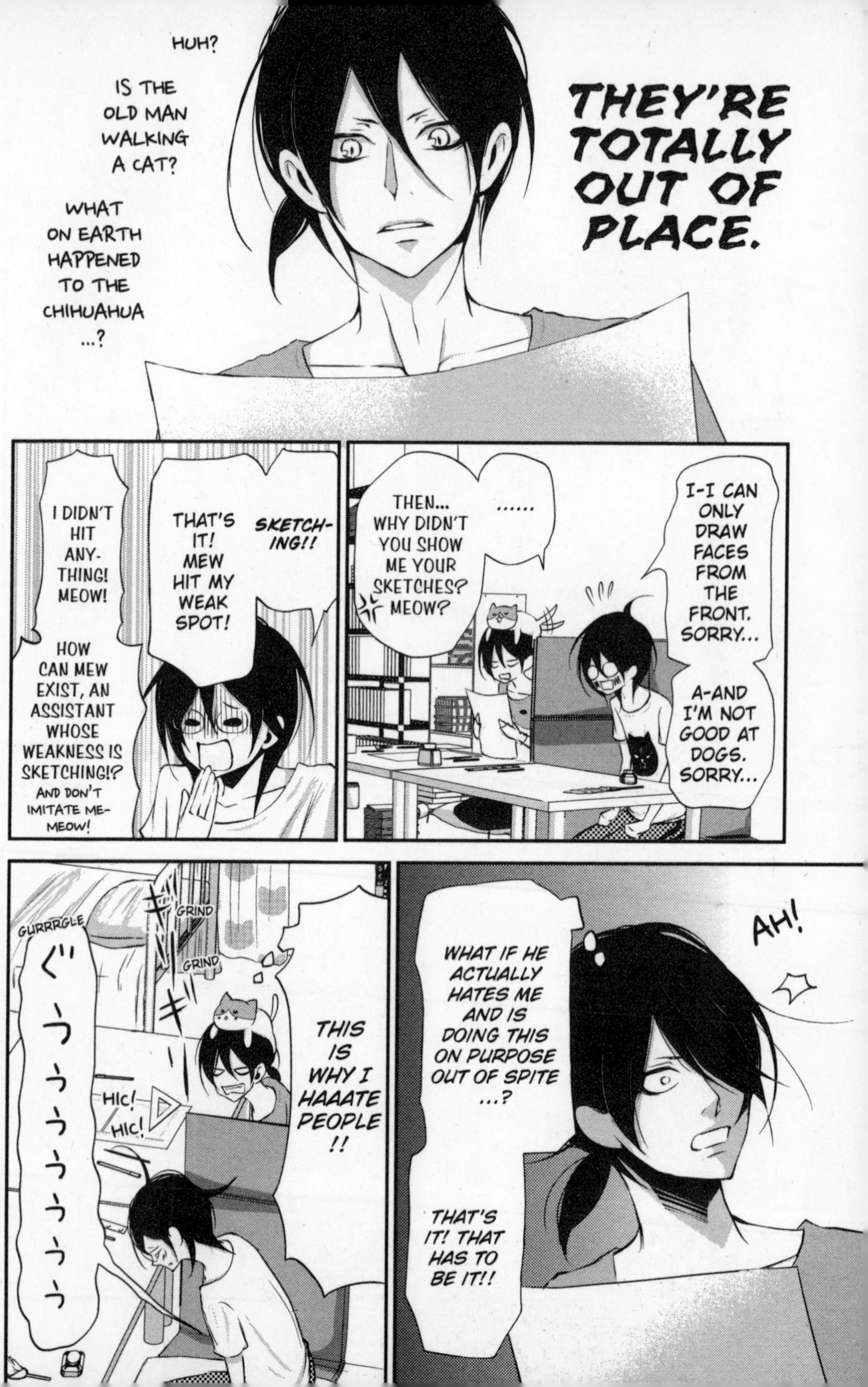
THEY'RE TOTALLY OUT OF PLACE.
HUH?
IS THE OLD MAN WALKING A CAT?
WHAT ON EARTH HAPPENED TO THE CHIHUAHUA ...?
I-I CAN ONLY DRAW FACES FROM THE FRONT. SORRY...
A-AND I'M NOT GOOD AT DOGS. SORRY...
......
THEN... WHY DIDN'T YOU SHOW ME YOUR SKETCHES? MEOW?
SKETCHING!!
THAT'S IT! MEW HIT MY WEAK SPOT!
I DIDN'T HIT ANYTHING! MEOW!
HOW CAN MEW EXIST, AN ASSISTANT WHOSE WEAKNESS IS SKETCHING!?
AND DON'T IMITATE ME-MEOW!
AH!
WHAT IF HE ACTUALLY HATES ME AND IS DOING THIS ON PURPOSE OUT OF SPITE ...?
THAT'S IT! THAT HAS TO BE IT!!
THIS IS WHY I HAAATE PEOPLE !!
GRIND
GRIND
GURRRGLE
ぐううううううう
HIC!
HIC!

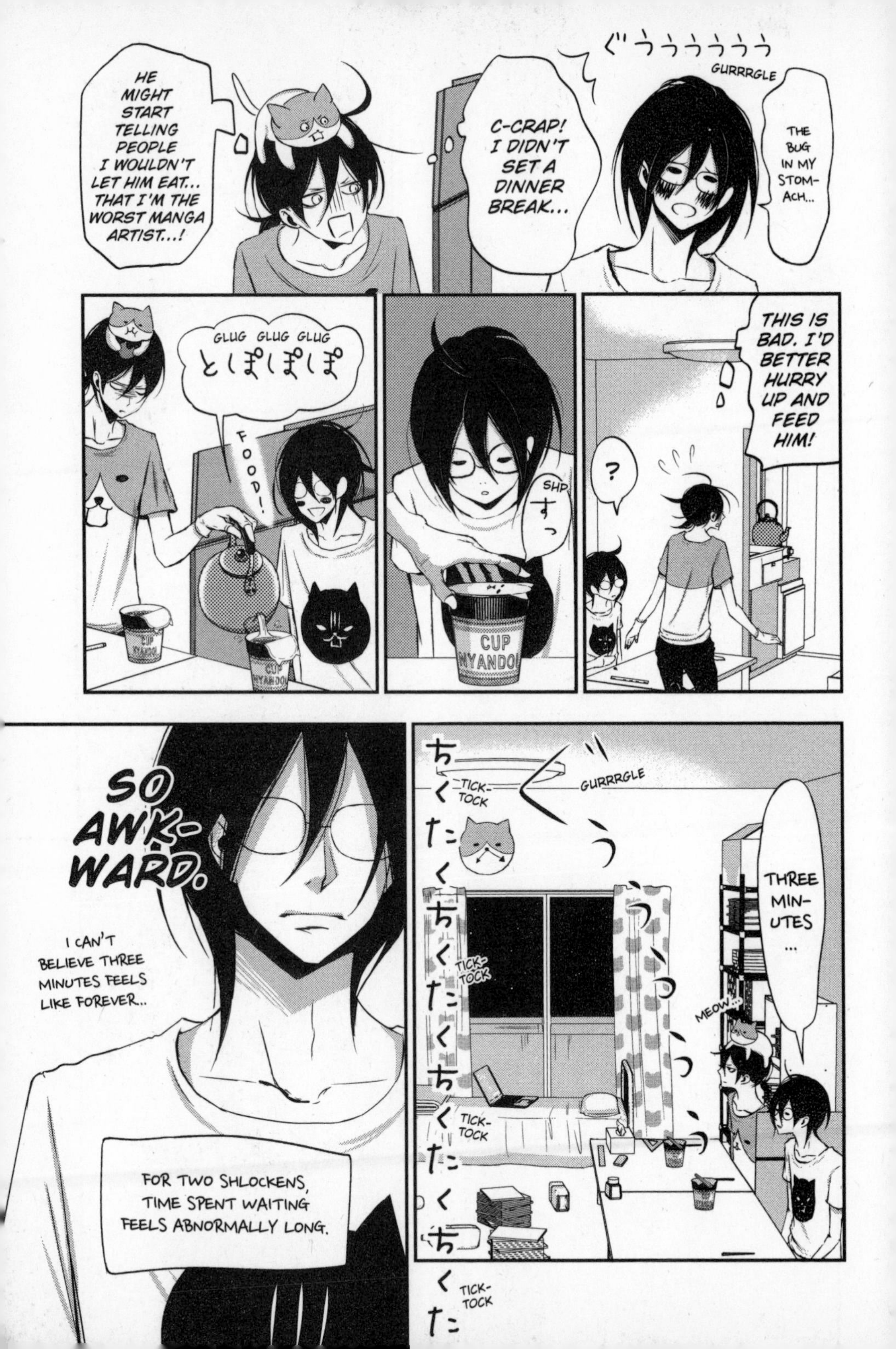
ぐうううううう
GURRRGLE
THE BUG IN MY STOMACH...
C-CRAP! I DIDN'T SET A DINNER BREAK...
HE MIGHT START TELLING PEOPLE I WOULDN'T LET HIM EAT... THAT I'M THE WORST MANGA ARTIST...!
THIS IS BAD. I'D BETTER HURRY UP AND FEED HIM!
?
SHP
すっ
GLUG GLUG GLUG
とぽぽぽ
FOOD!
CUP NYANDOL
ちくたくちくたくちくたくちくたくちくた
TICK-TOCK
TICK-TOCK
TICK-TOCK
TICK-TOCK
GURRRGLE
ぐううううう
THREE MINUTES...
MEOW...
SO AWKWARD.
I CAN'T BELIEVE THREE MINUTES FEELS LIKE FOREVER...
FOR TWO SHLOCKENS, TIME SPENT WAITING FEELS ABNORMALLY LONG.

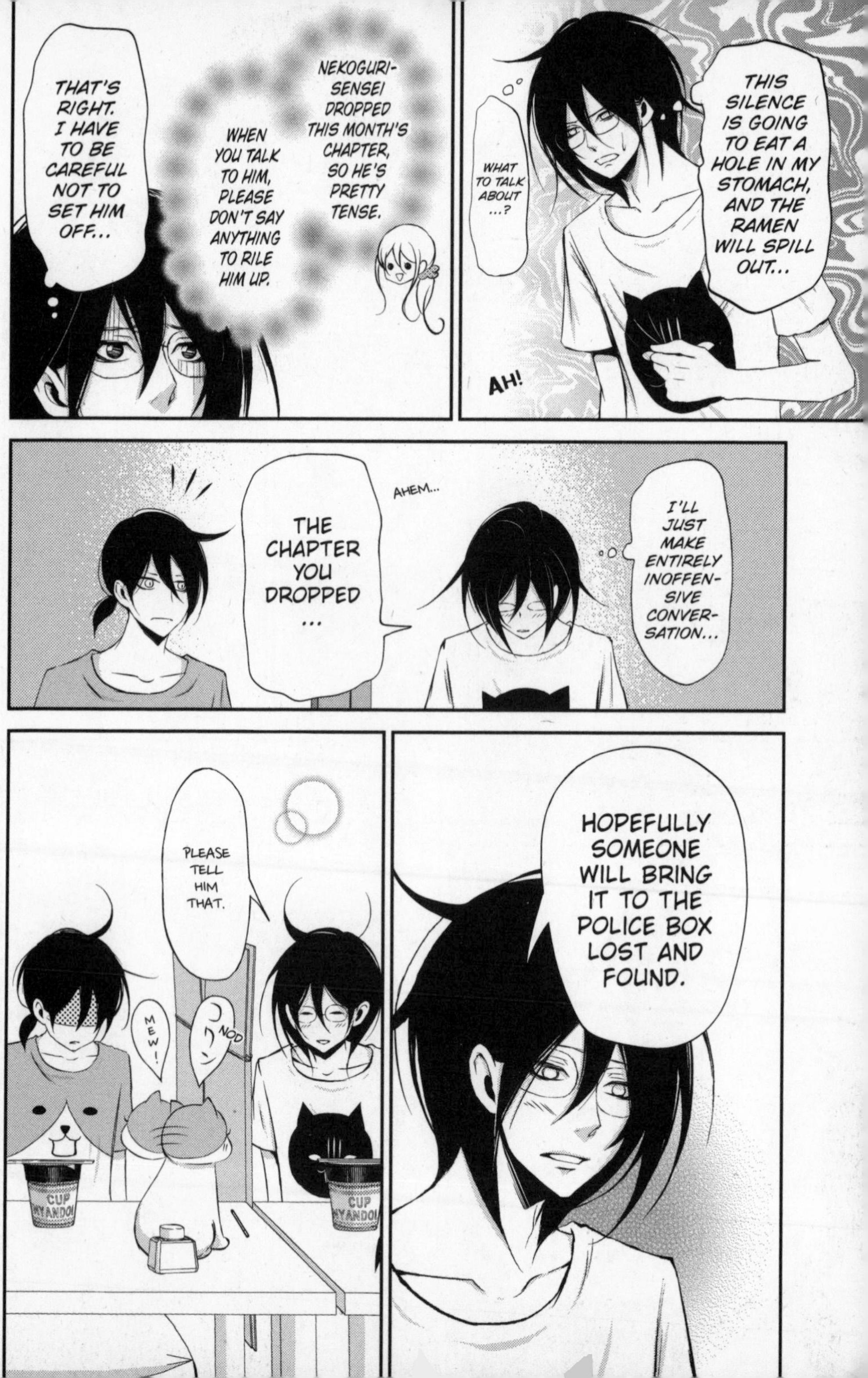
THIS SILENCE IS GOING TO EAT A HOLE IN MY STOMACH, AND THE RAMEN WILL SPILL OUT...
WHAT TO TALK ABOUT ...?
AH!
NEKOGURI-SENSEI DROPPED THIS MONTH'S CHAPTER, SO HE'S PRETTY TENSE.
WHEN YOU TALK TO HIM, PLEASE DON'T SAY ANYTHING TO RILE HIM UP.
THAT'S RIGHT. I HAVE TO BE CAREFUL NOT TO SET HIM OFF...
I'LL JUST MAKE ENTIRELY INOFFENSIVE CONVERSATION...
AHEM...
THE CHAPTER YOU DROPPED ...
HOPEFULLY SOMEONE WILL BRING IT TO THE POLICE BOX LOST AND FOUND.
PLEASE TELL HIM THAT.
NOD
MEW!
CUP NYANDO!
CUP NYANDO!

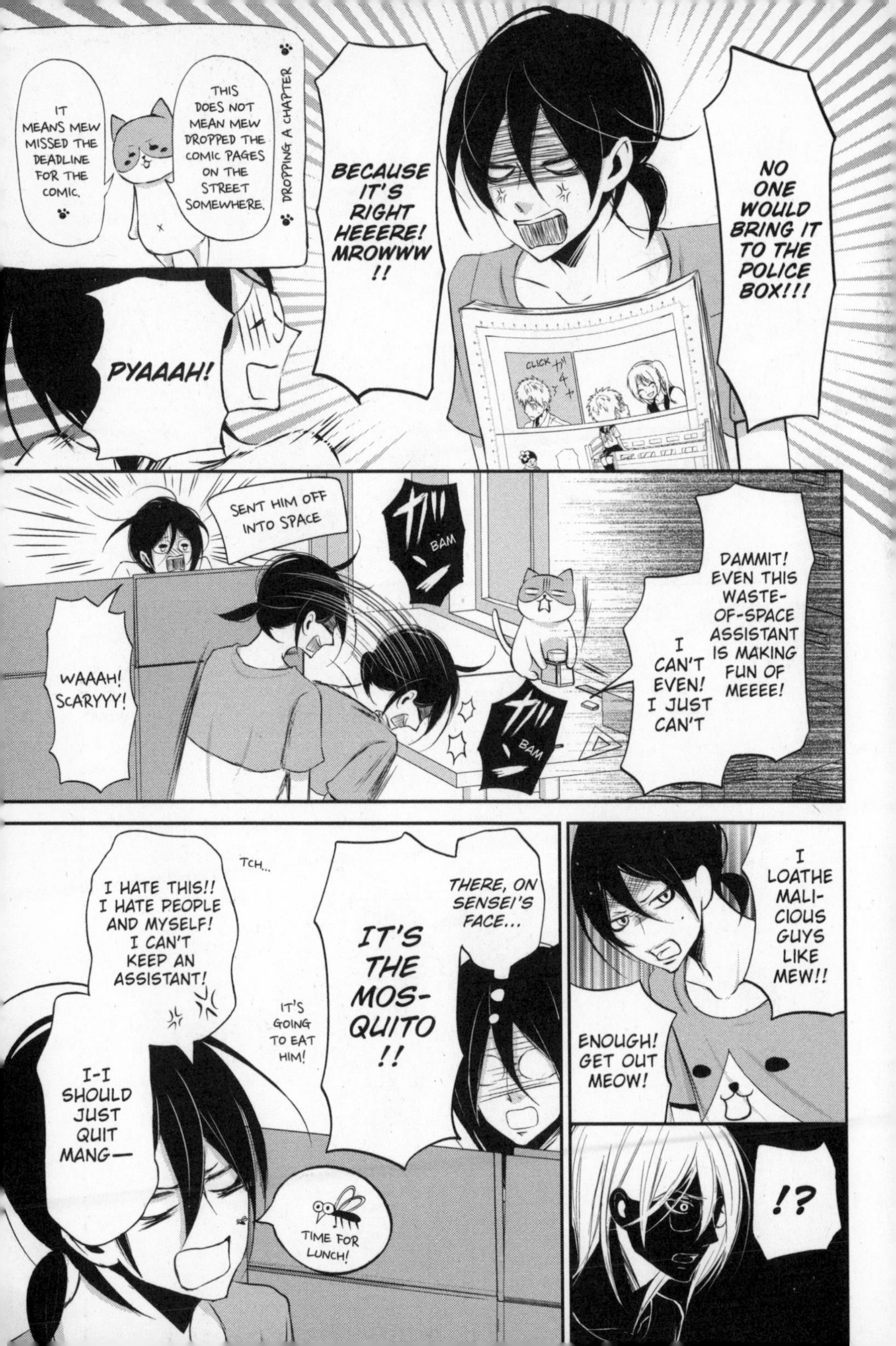
NO ONE WOULD BRING IT TO THE POLICE BOX!!!
BECAUSE IT'S RIGHT HEEERE! MROWWW!!
PYAAAH!
CLICK
DROPPING A CHAPTER
THIS DOES NOT MEAN MEW DROPPED THE COMIC PAGES ON THE STREET SOMEWHERE.
IT MEANS MEW MISSED THE DEADLINE FOR THE COMIC.
DAMMIT! EVEN THIS WASTE-OF-SPACE ASSISTANT IS MAKING FUN OF MEEEE!
I CAN'T EVEN! I JUST CAN'T
BAM
BAM
SENT HIM OFF INTO SPACE
WAAAH! SCARYYY!
I LOATHE MALI-CIOUS GUYS LIKE MEW!!
ENOUGH! GET OUT MEOW!
!?
THERE, ON SENSEI'S FACE...
IT'S THE MOS-QUITO!!
IT'S GOING TO EAT HIM!
TCH...
I HATE THIS!! I HATE PEOPLE AND MYSELF! I CAN'T KEEP AN ASSISTANT!
I-I SHOULD JUST QUIT MANG—
TIME FOR LUNCH!

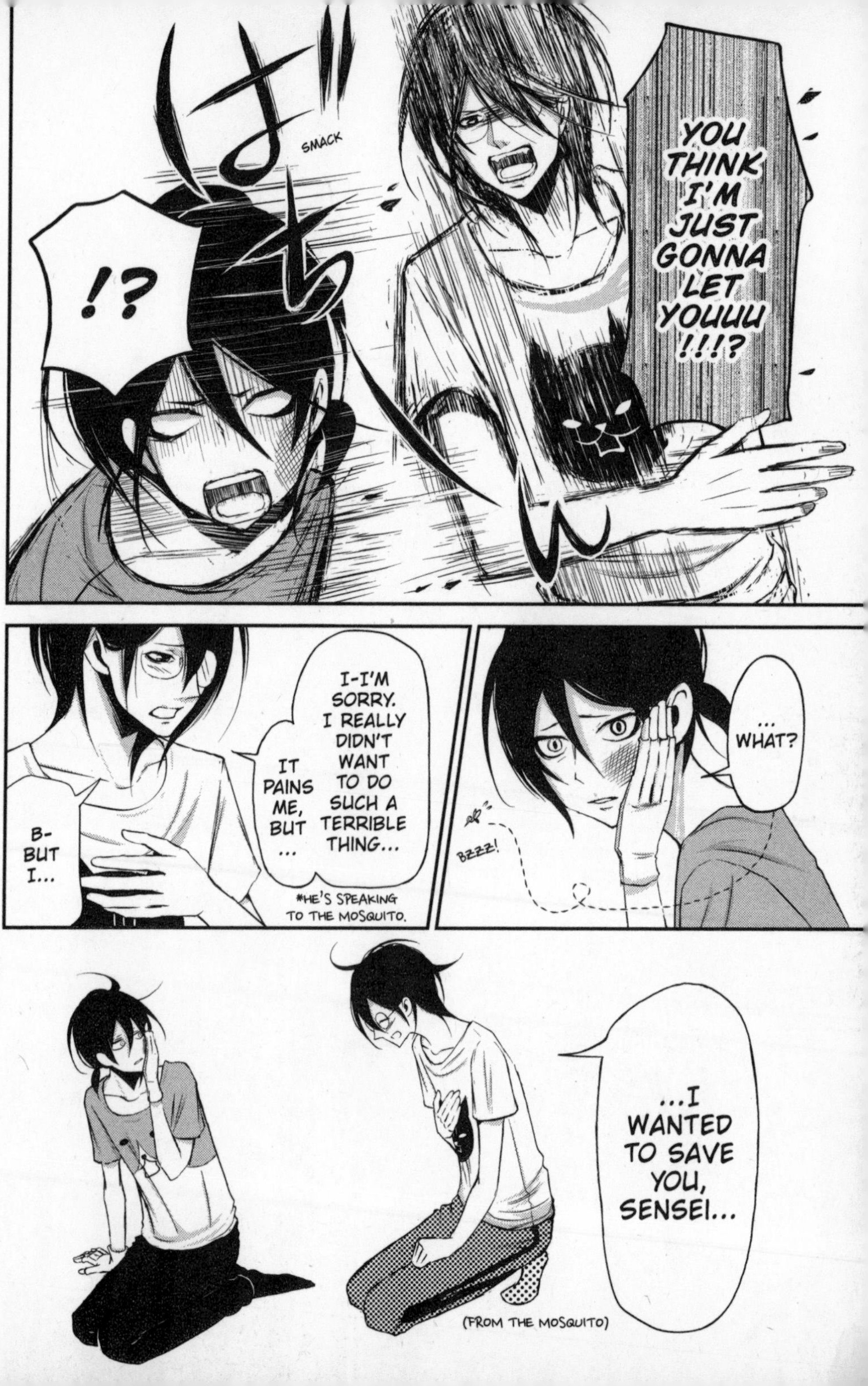
YOU THINK I'M JUST GONNA LET YOUUU!!!?
SMACK
!?
...WHAT?
BZZZ!
I-I'M SORRY. I REALLY DIDN'T WANT TO DO SUCH A TERRIBLE THING...
IT PAINS ME, BUT...
B-BUT I...
*HE'S SPEAKING TO THE MOSQUITO.
...I WANTED TO SAVE YOU, SENSEI...
(FROM THE MOSQUITO)

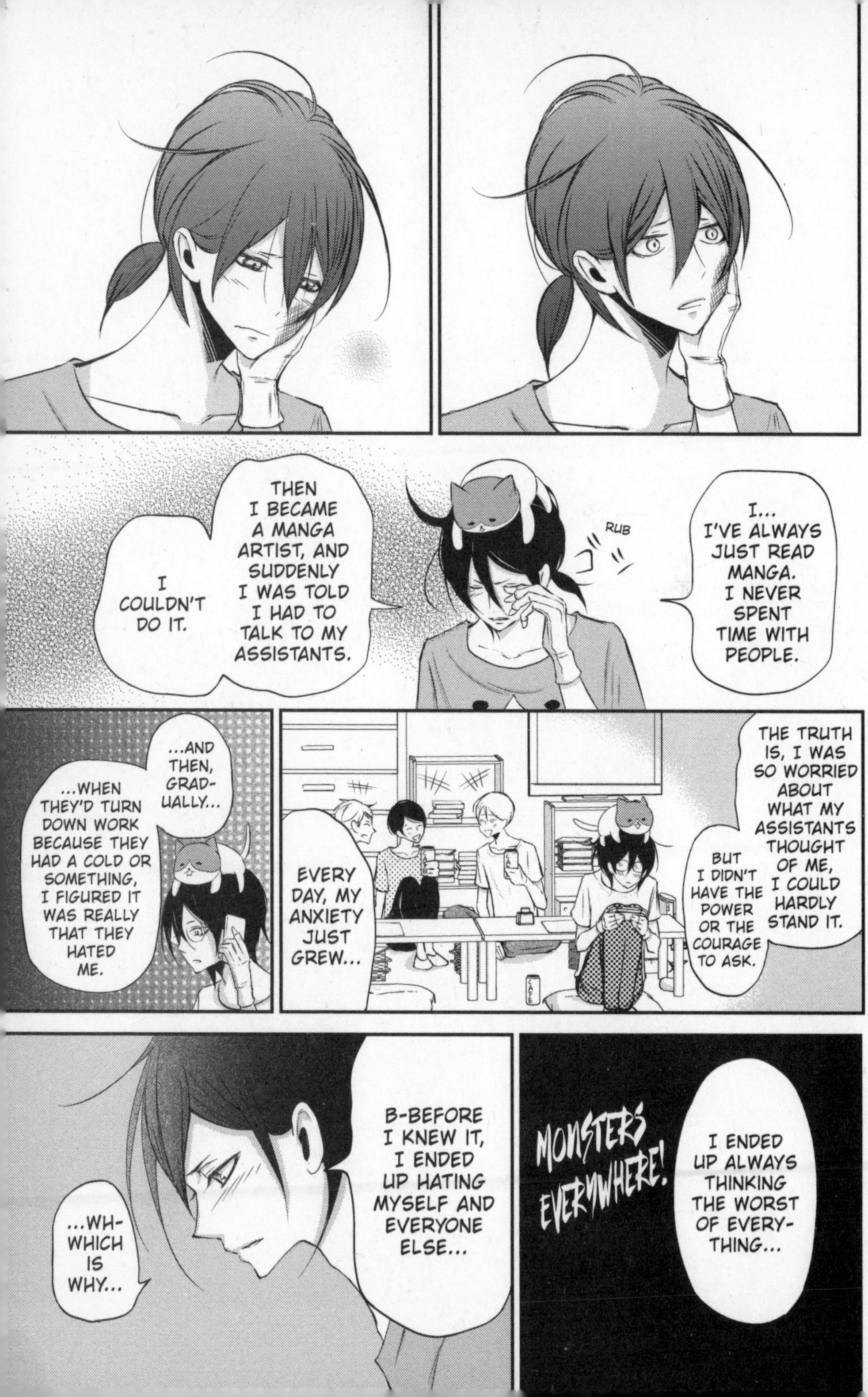
I... I'VE ALWAYS JUST READ MANGA. I NEVER SPENT TIME WITH PEOPLE.
RUB
THEN I BECAME A MANGA ARTIST, AND SUDDENLY I WAS TOLD I HAD TO TALK TO MY ASSISTANTS.
I COULDN'T DO IT.
THE TRUTH IS, I WAS SO WORRIED ABOUT WHAT MY ASSISTANTS THOUGHT OF ME, I COULD HARDLY STAND IT.
BUT I DIDN'T HAVE THE POWER OR THE COURAGE TO ASK.
EVERY DAY, MY ANXIETY JUST GREW...
...AND THEN, GRAD-UALLY...
...WHEN THEY'D TURN DOWN WORK BECAUSE THEY HAD A COLD OR SOMETHING, I FIGURED IT WAS REALLY THAT THEY HATED ME.
I ENDED UP ALWAYS THINKING THE WORST OF EVERY-THING...
MONSTERS EVERYWHERE!
B-BEFORE I KNEW IT, I ENDED UP HATING MYSELF AND EVERYONE ELSE...
...WH-WHICH IS WHY...

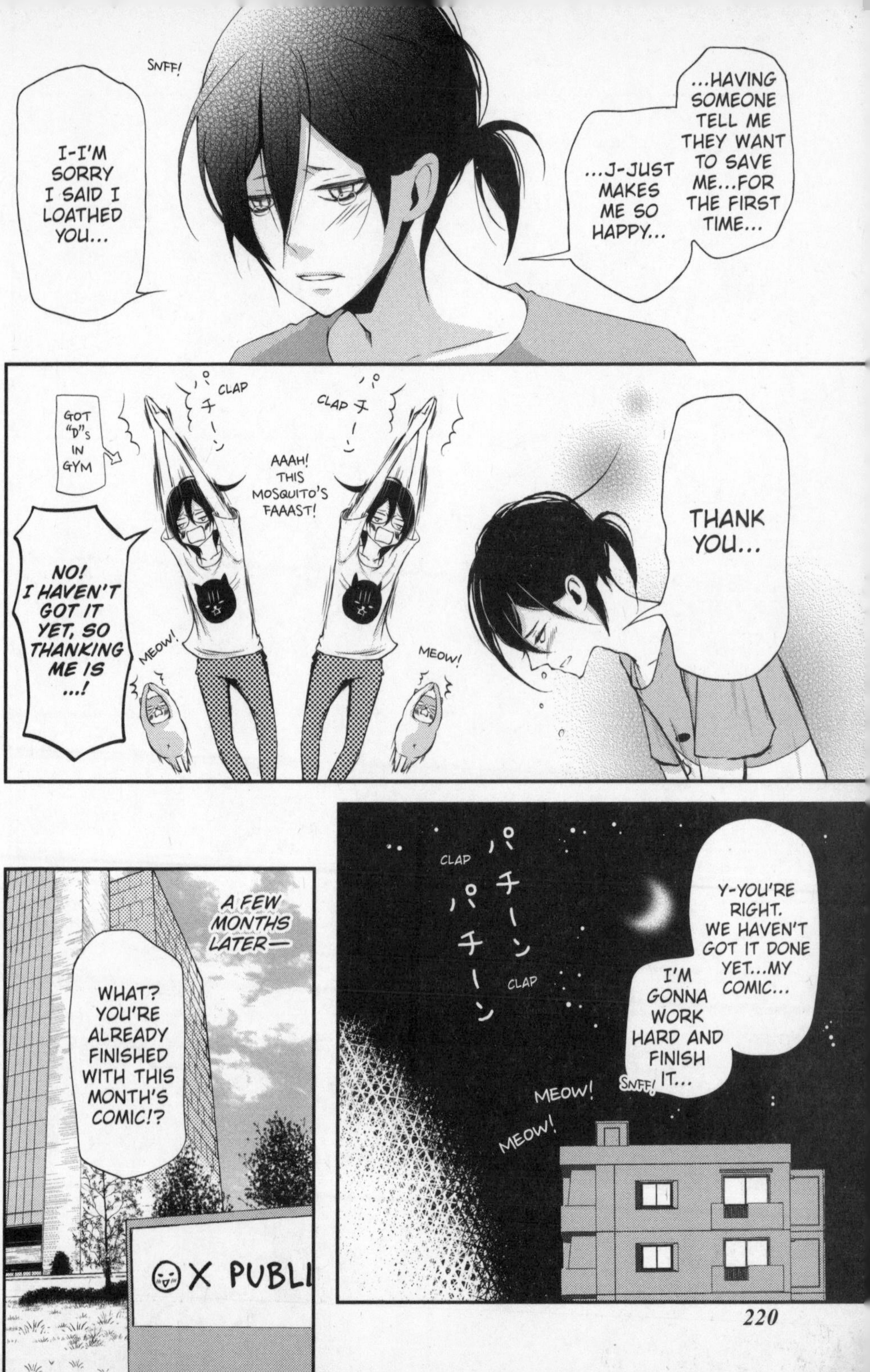
...HAVING SOMEONE TELL ME THEY WANT TO SAVE ME...FOR THE FIRST TIME...
...J-JUST MAKES ME SO HAPPY...
SNFF!
I-I'M SORRY I SAID I LOATHED YOU...
THANK YOU...
パチーン
CLAP
AAAH! THIS MOSQUITO'S FAAAST!
パチーン
CLAP
MEOW!
MEOW!
GOT "D"s IN GYM
NO! I HAVEN'T GOT IT YET, SO THANKING ME IS ...!
Y-YOU'RE RIGHT. WE HAVEN'T GOT IT DONE YET...MY COMIC...
I'M GONNA WORK HARD AND FINISH IT...
SNFF!
パチーン
CLAP
パチーン
CLAP
MEOW!
MEOW!
A FEW MONTHS LATER—
WHAT? YOU'RE ALREADY FINISHED WITH THIS MONTH'S COMIC!?
X PUBL

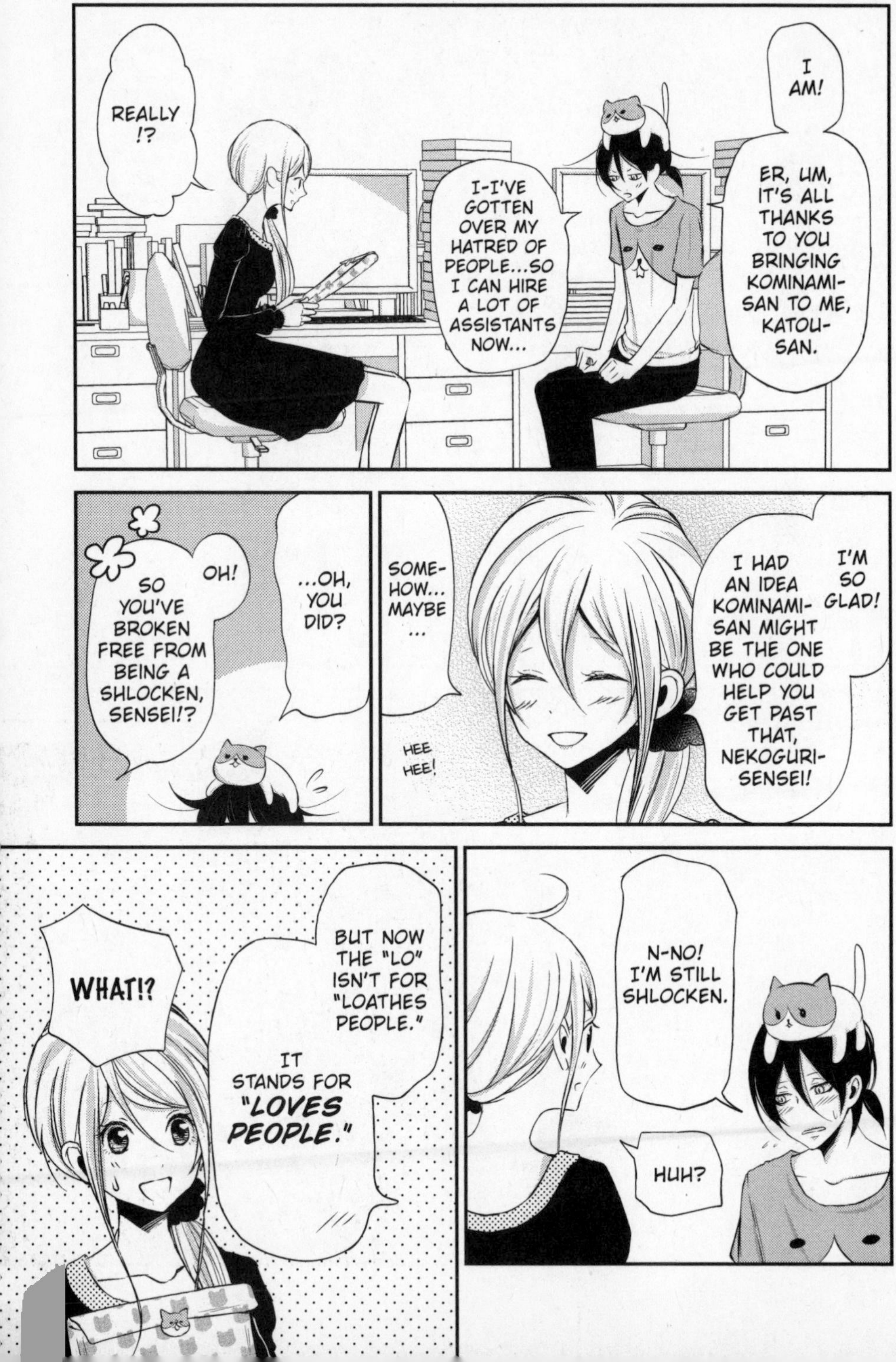
I AM!
ER, UM, IT'S ALL THANKS TO YOU BRINGING KOMINAMI-SAN TO ME, KATOU-SAN.
I-I'VE GOTTEN OVER MY HATRED OF PEOPLE...SO I CAN HIRE A LOT OF ASSISTANTS NOW...
REALLY!?
I'M SO GLAD!
I HAD AN IDEA KOMINAMI-SAN MIGHT BE THE ONE WHO COULD HELP YOU GET PAST THAT, NEKOGURI-SENSEI!
HEE HEE!
SOME-HOW... MAYBE ...
...OH, YOU DID?
OH!
SO YOU'VE BROKEN FREE FROM BEING A SHLOCKEN, SENSEI!?
N-NO! I'M STILL SHLOCKEN.
HUH?
BUT NOW THE "LO" ISN'T FOR "LOATHES PEOPLE."
IT STANDS FOR "LOVES PEOPLE."
WHAT!?

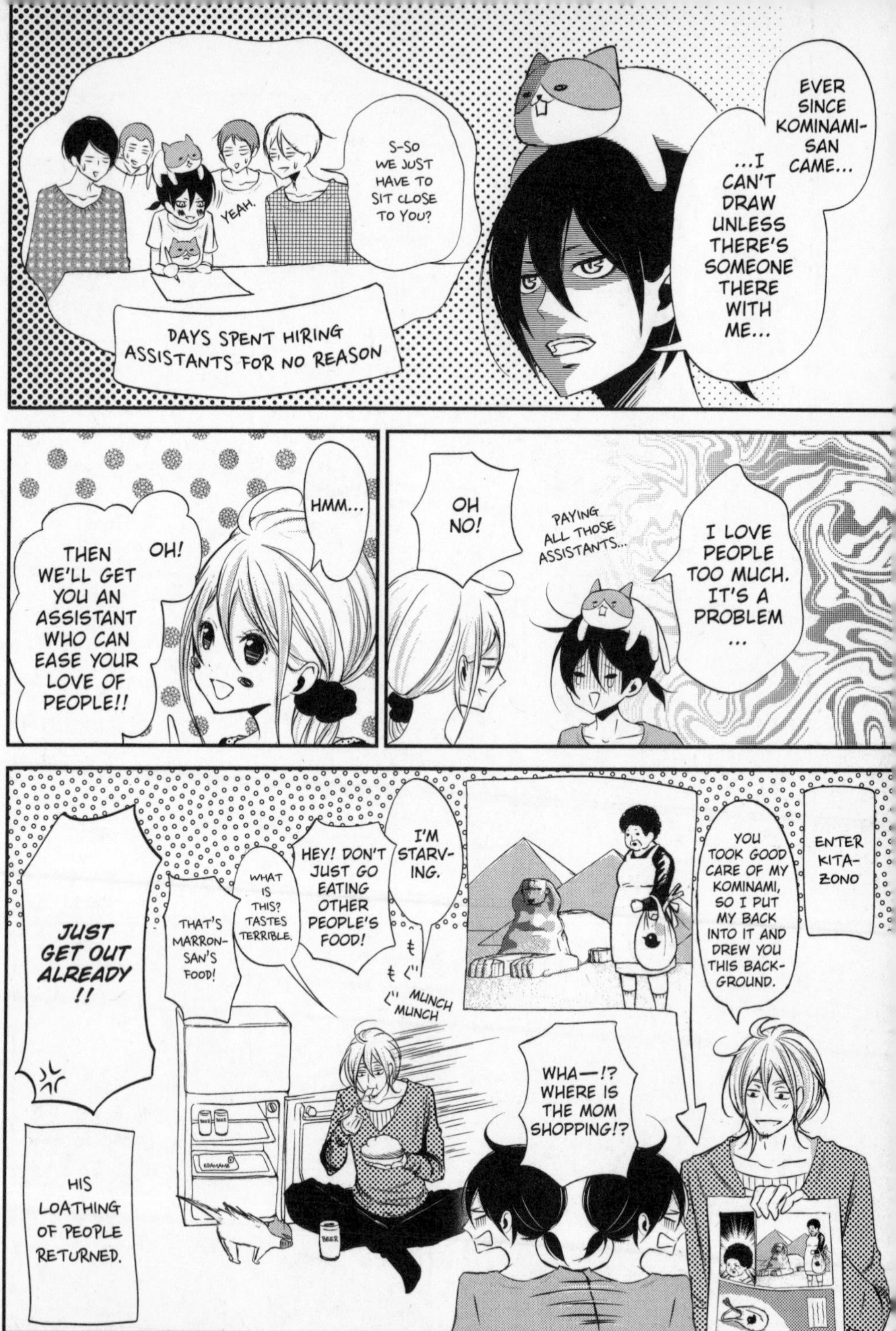
EVER SINCE KOMINAMI-SAN CAME...
...I CAN'T DRAW UNLESS THERE'S SOMEONE THERE WITH ME...
S-SO WE JUST HAVE TO SIT CLOSE TO YOU?
YEAH.
DAYS SPENT HIRING ASSISTANTS FOR NO REASON
I LOVE PEOPLE TOO MUCH. IT'S A PROBLEM...
PAYING ALL THOSE ASSISTANTS...
OH NO!
HMM...
OH!
THEN WE'LL GET YOU AN ASSISTANT WHO CAN EASE YOUR LOVE OF PEOPLE!!
ENTER KITA-ZONO
YOU TOOK GOOD CARE OF MY KOMINAMI, SO I PUT MY BACK INTO IT AND DREW YOU THIS BACK-GROUND.
WHA—!? WHERE IS THE MOM SHOPPING!?
I'M STARV-ING.
HEY! DON'T JUST GO EATING OTHER PEOPLE'S FOOD!
WHAT IS THIS? TASTES TERRIBLE.
THAT'S MARRON-SAN'S FOOD!
もぐ もぐ
MUNCH MUNCH
JUST GET OUT ALREADY!!
HIS LOATHING OF PEOPLE RETURNED.

TO BE CONTINUED

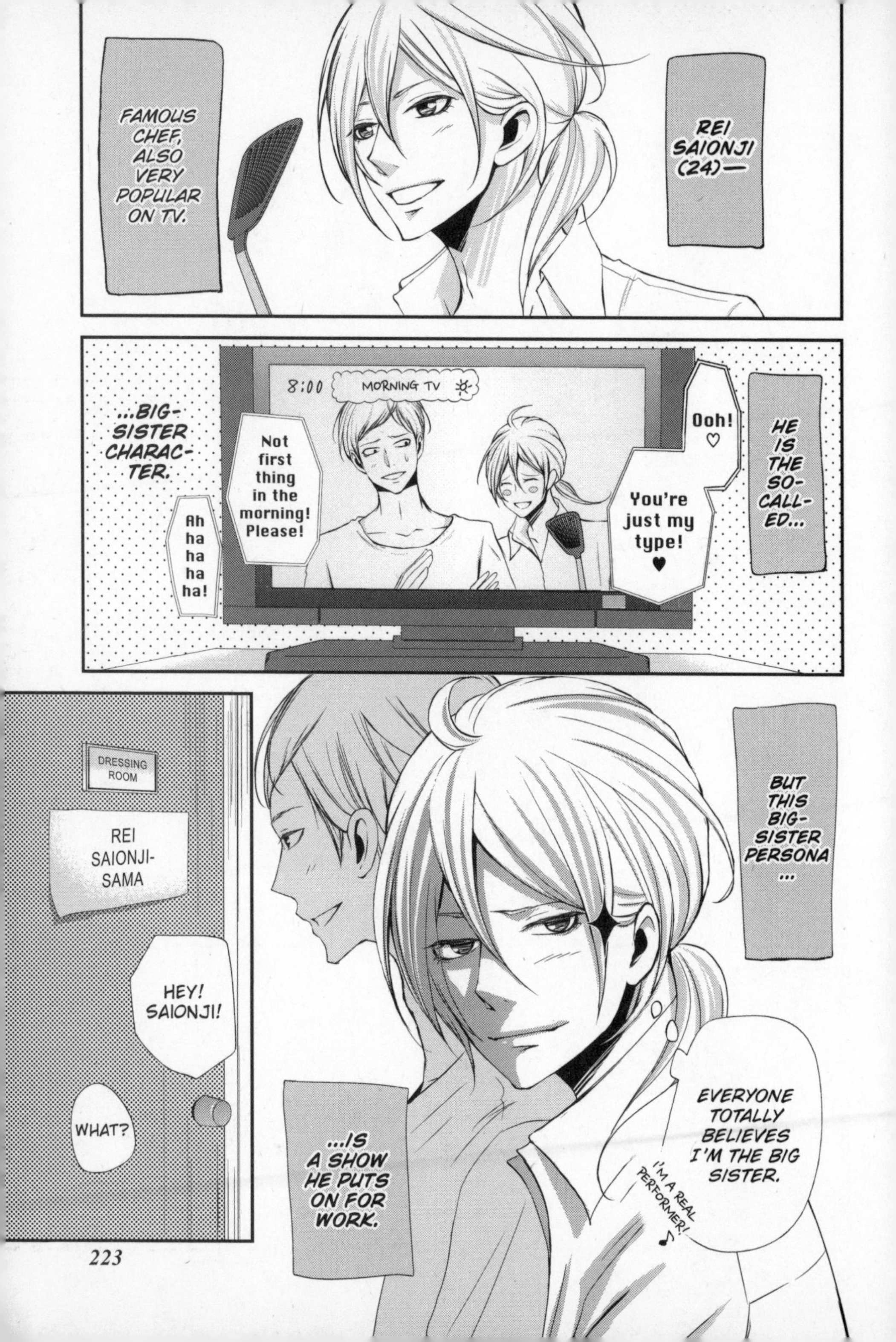

REI SAIONJI (24)—
FAMOUS CHEF, ALSO VERY POPULAR ON TV.
HE IS THE SO-CALLED...
Ooh! ♡
You're just my type! ♥
8:00 MORNING TV
Not first thing in the morning! Please!
Ah ha ha ha ha!
...BIG-SISTER CHARACTER.
BUT THIS BIG-SISTER PERSONA...
EVERYONE TOTALLY BELIEVES I'M THE BIG SISTER.
I'M A REAL PERFORMER! ♪
...IS A SHOW HE PUTS ON FOR WORK.
DRESSING ROOM
REI SAIONJI-SAMA
HEY! SAIONJI!
WHAT?

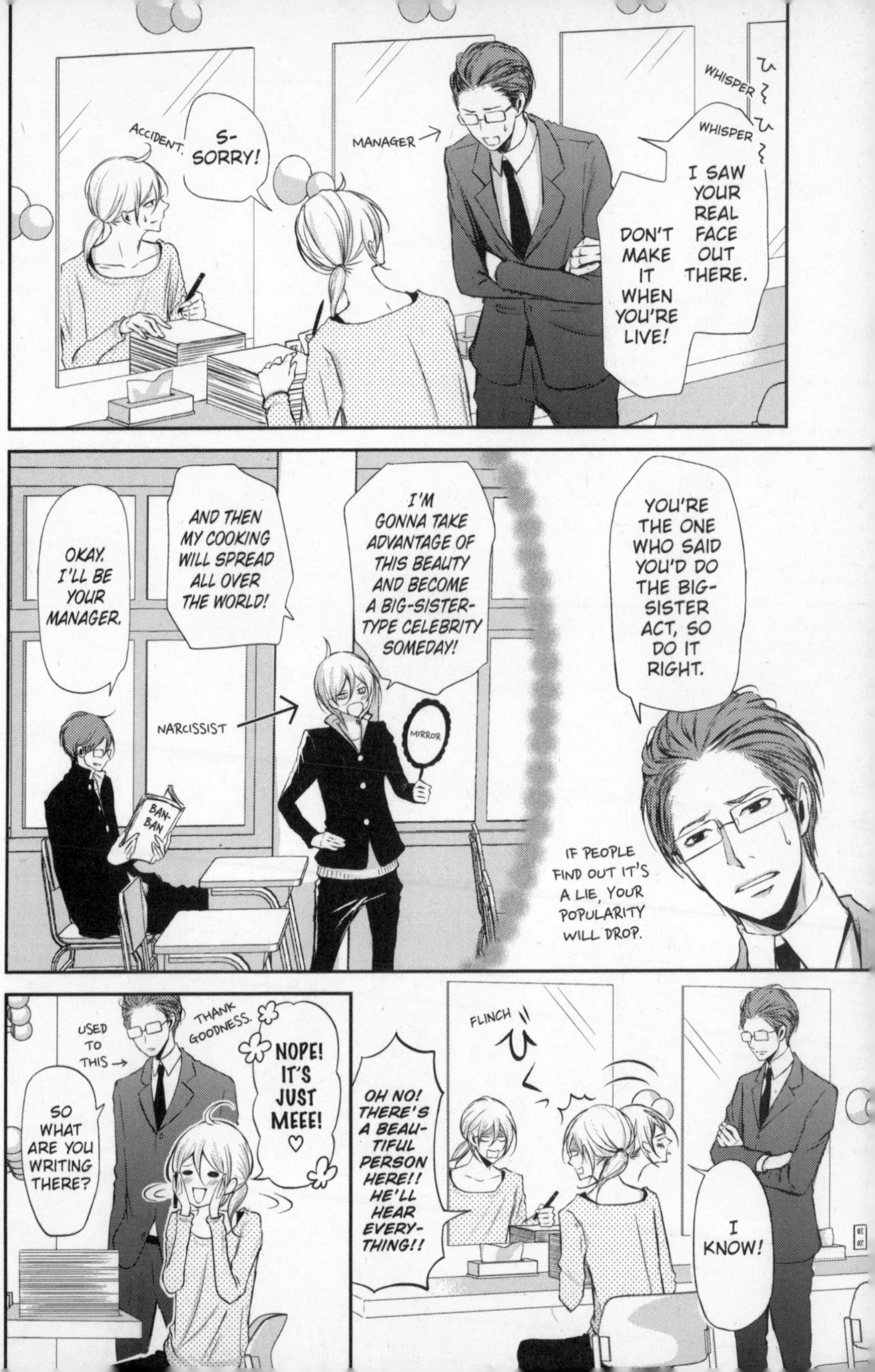
WHISPER
WHISPER
I SAW YOUR REAL FACE OUT THERE.
DON'T MAKE IT WHEN YOU'RE LIVE!
MANAGER
S-SORRY!
ACCIDENT.
YOU'RE THE ONE WHO SAID YOU'D DO THE BIG-SISTER ACT, SO DO IT RIGHT.
IF PEOPLE FIND OUT IT'S A LIE, YOUR POPULARITY WILL DROP.
I'M GONNA TAKE ADVANTAGE OF THIS BEAUTY AND BECOME A BIG-SISTER-TYPE CELEBRITY SOMEDAY!
MIRROR
NARCISSIST
AND THEN MY COOKING WILL SPREAD ALL OVER THE WORLD!
OKAY. I'LL BE YOUR MANAGER.
BAN-BAN
I KNOW!
FLINCH
OH NO! THERE'S A BEAUTIFUL PERSON HERE!! HE'LL HEAR EVERYTHING!!
NOPE! IT'S JUST MEEE! ♡
THANK GOODNESS.
USED TO THIS
SO WHAT ARE YOU WRITING THERE?

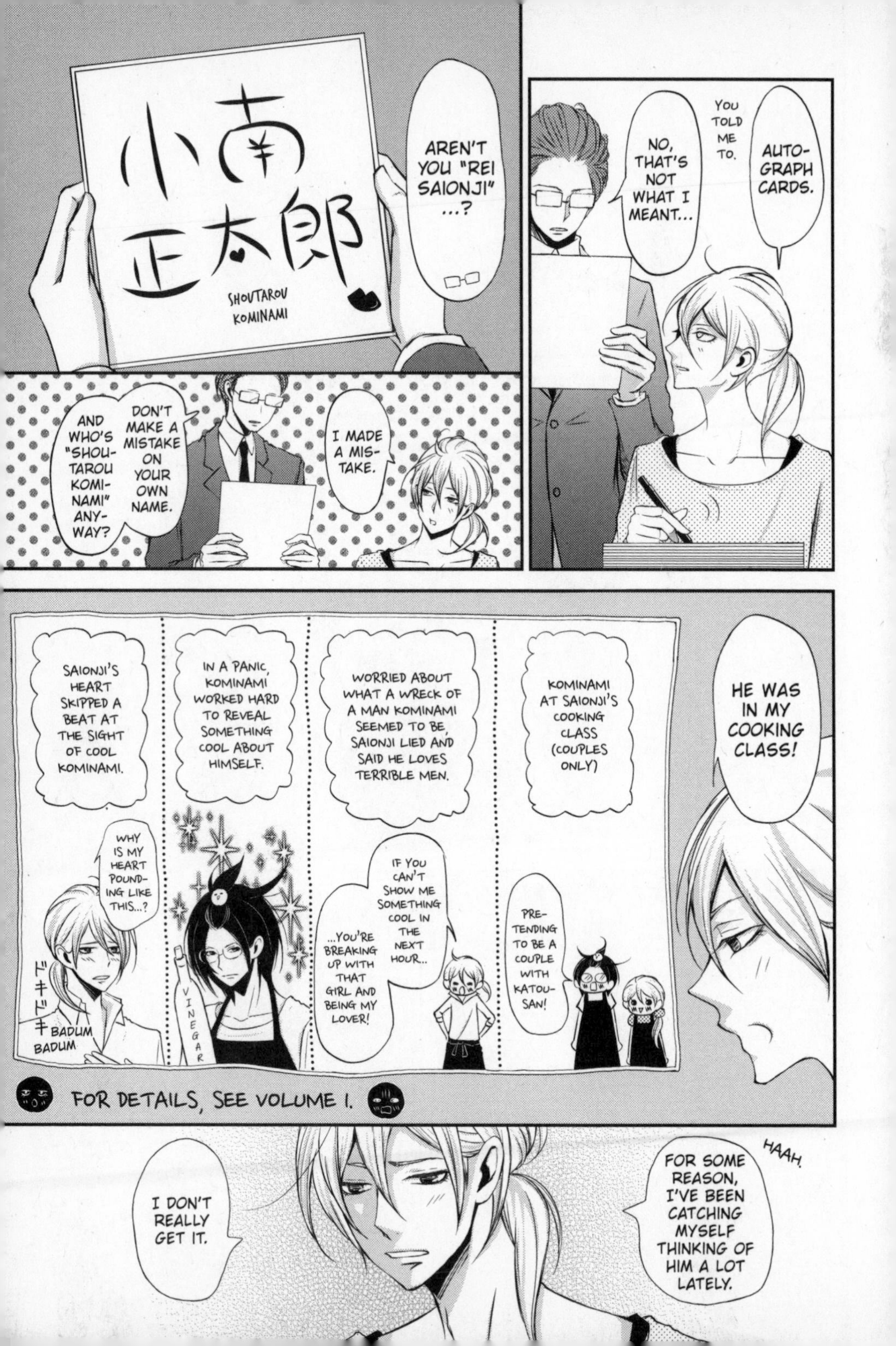
AUTO-GRAPH CARDS.
YOU TOLD ME TO.
NO, THAT'S NOT WHAT I MEANT...
小南正太郎
SHOUTAROU KOMINAMI
AREN'T YOU "REI SAIONJI" ...?
I MADE A MIS-TAKE.
DON'T MAKE A MISTAKE ON YOUR OWN NAME.
AND WHO'S "SHOU-TAROU KOMI-NAMI" ANY-WAY?
HE WAS IN MY COOKING CLASS!
KOMINAMI AT SAIONJI'S COOKING CLASS (COUPLES ONLY)
PRE-TENDING TO BE A COUPLE WITH KATOU-SAN!
WORRIED ABOUT WHAT A WRECK OF A MAN KOMINAMI SEEMED TO BE, SAIONJI LIED AND SAID HE LOVES TERRIBLE MEN.
IF YOU CAN'T SHOW ME SOMETHING COOL IN THE NEXT HOUR...
...YOU'RE BREAKING UP WITH THAT GIRL AND BEING MY LOVER!
IN A PANIC, KOMINAMI WORKED HARD TO REVEAL SOMETHING COOL ABOUT HIMSELF.
VINEGAR
SAIONJI'S HEART SKIPPED A BEAT AT THE SIGHT OF COOL KOMINAMI.
WHY IS MY HEART POUND-ING LIKE THIS...?
ドキドキ
BADUM BADUM
FOR DETAILS, SEE VOLUME 1.
HAAH.
FOR SOME REASON, I'VE BEEN CATCHING MYSELF THINKING OF HIM A LOT LATELY.
I DON'T REALLY GET IT.

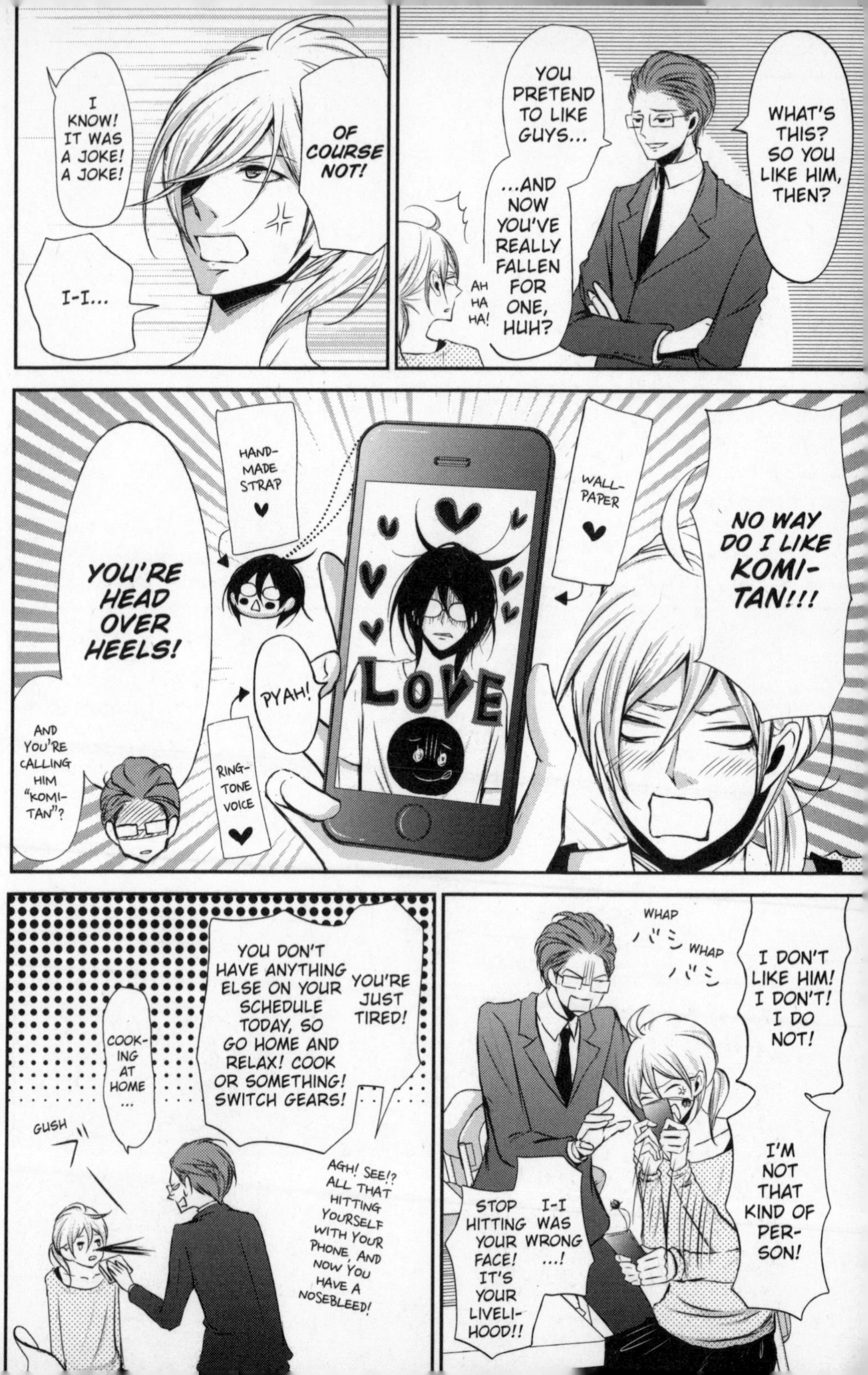
WHAT'S THIS? SO YOU LIKE HIM, THEN?
YOU PRETEND TO LIKE GUYS...
...AND NOW YOU'VE REALLY FALLEN FOR ONE, HUH?
AH HA HA!
OF COURSE NOT!
I KNOW! IT WAS A JOKE! A JOKE!
I-I...
NO WAY DO I LIKE KOMI-TAN!!!
WALL-PAPER ♥
HAND-MADE STRAP ♥
YOU'RE HEAD OVER HEELS!
LOVE
PYAH!
RING-TONE VOICE ♥
AND YOU'RE CALLING HIM "KOMI-TAN"?
I DON'T LIKE HIM! I DON'T! I DO NOT!
WHAP バシ
WHAP バシ
I'M NOT THAT KIND OF PER-SON!
I-I WAS WRONG ...!
STOP HITTING YOUR FACE! IT'S YOUR LIVELI-HOOD!!
YOU'RE JUST TIRED!
YOU DON'T HAVE ANYTHING ELSE ON YOUR SCHEDULE TODAY, SO GO HOME AND RELAX! COOK OR SOMETHING! SWITCH GEARS!
COOK-ING AT HOME ...
GUSH
AGH! SEE!? ALL THAT HITTING YOURSELF WITH YOUR PHONE, AND NOW YOU HAVE A NOSEBLEED!

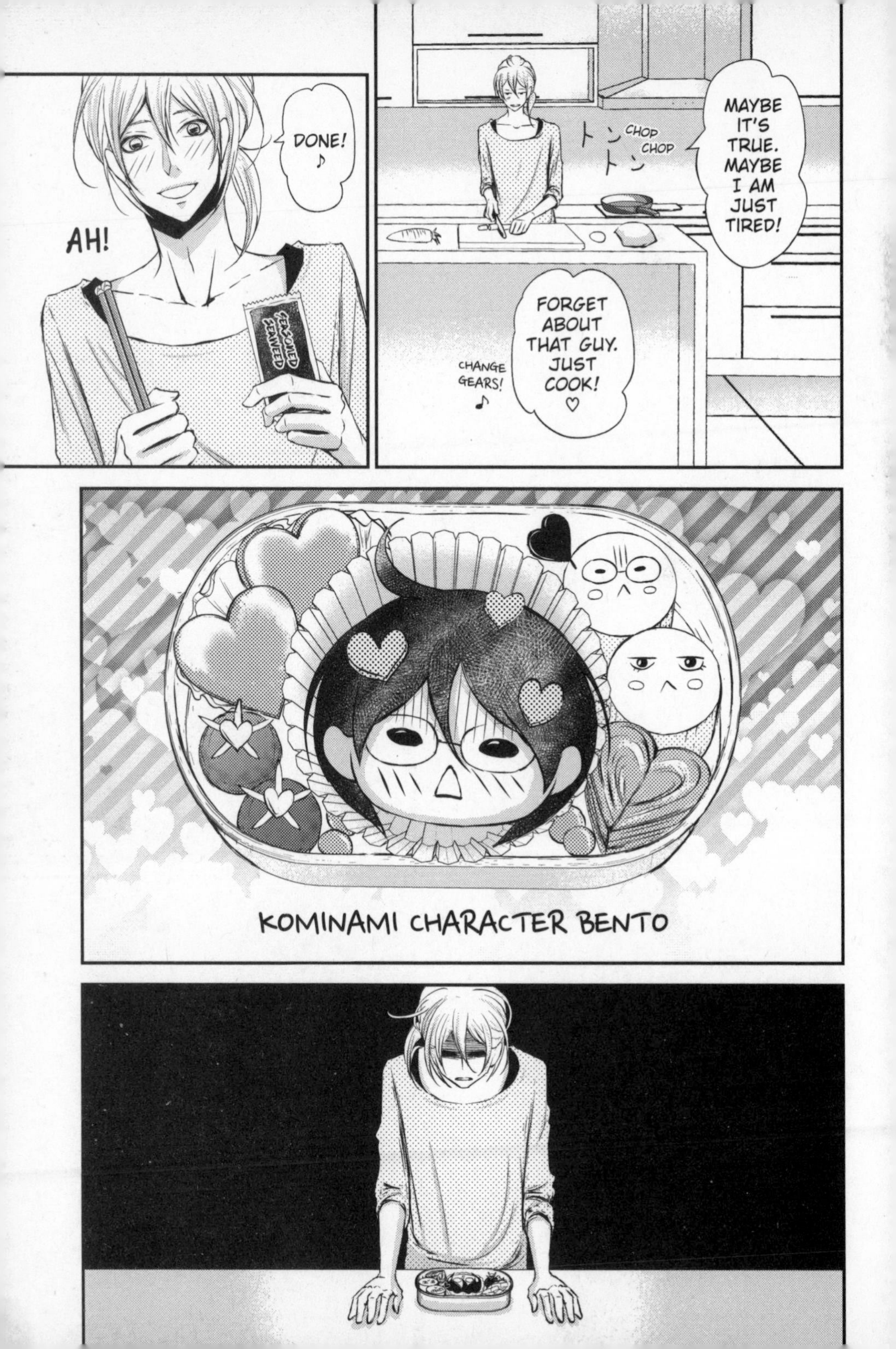
MAYBE IT'S TRUE. MAYBE I AM JUST TIRED!
トン トン
CHOP CHOP
FORGET ABOUT THAT GUY. JUST COOK! ♡
CHANGE GEARS! ♪
DONE! ♪
AH!
SEASONED SEAWEED
KOMINAMI CHARACTER BENTO

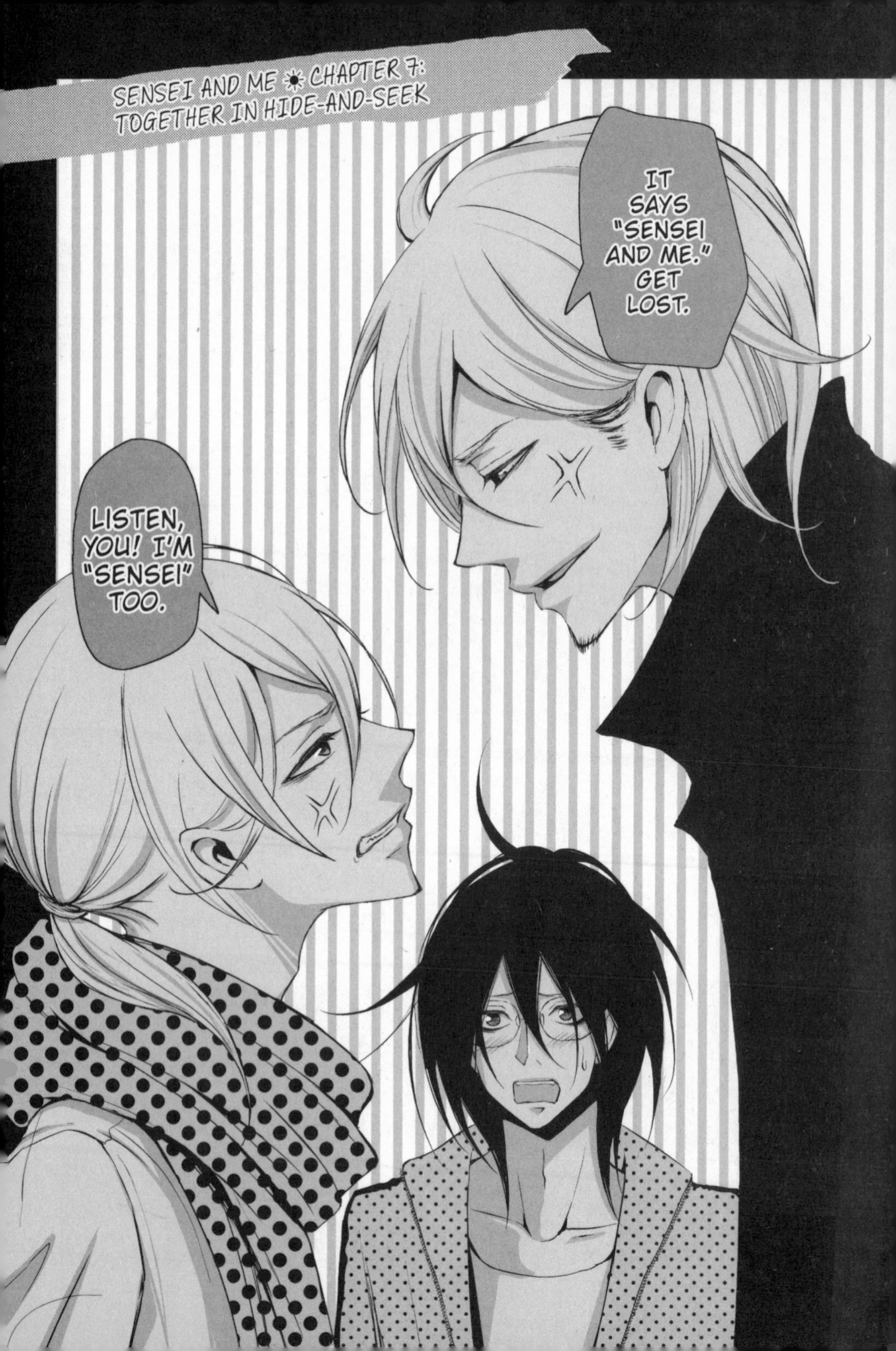
SENSEI AND ME ☀ CHAPTER 7: TOGETHER IN HIDE-AND-SEEK
IT SAYS "SENSEI AND ME." GET LOST.
LISTEN, YOU! I'M "SENSEI" TOO.

SOME-THING'S WEIRD...

A-ANYWAY, I'LL JUST GO AND SEE HIM ONE MORE TIME.

WOBBLE

WOBBLE

OH! IT'S THAT FRUITCAKE FROM TV!

REI SAIONJI COOKING CLASS
♡ PARTICIPANT REGISTRATION ♡

BOYFRIEND		
NAME	Shoutarou Kominami	
ADDRESS	#203 Tanpopo Heights 5-chome, 37-3△○, OX Ward Tokyo	

GIRLFRIEND		
NAME	Sumire Katou	
ADDRESS	2-12-9 △ Tokyo	

I'M SURE I'LL SNAP OUT OF THIS IF I DO ...!!

OH! IT IS!! EEEEE! SO PRETTY! ♡

HELLO? KOMI-NAMI? IT'S ME.

LET'S SEE. NUMBER FIVE IS...

I MEAN, IT'S NOT LOVE OR ANY-THING!

IT'S NOT GOOD TO STEAL SOMEONE...

A-AND HE'S ALREADY DATING THIS KATOU AND ALL...

MISTAKENLY BELIEVES KATOU-SAN IS KOMINAMI'S GIRLFRIEND

229

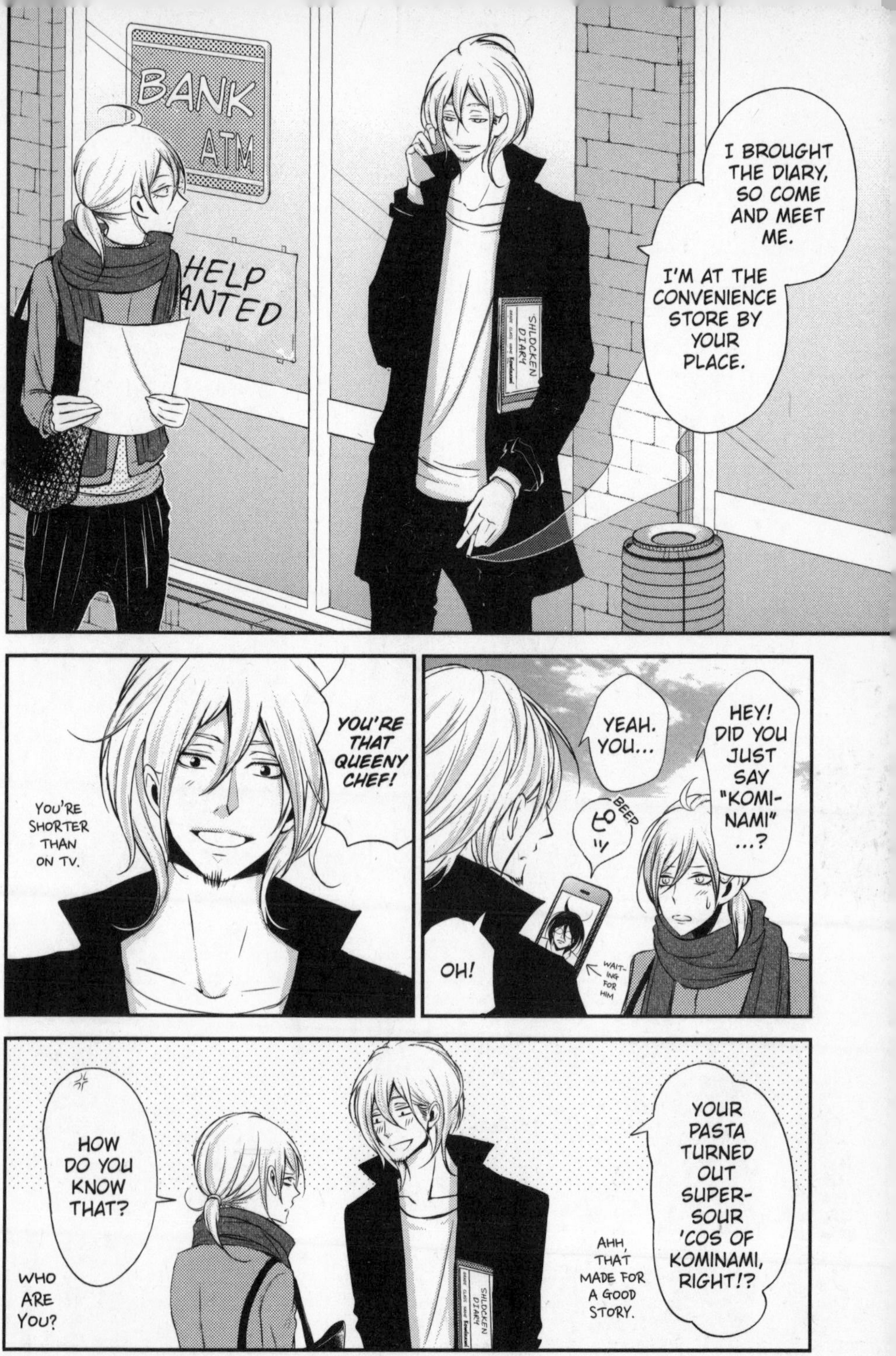
BANK ATM
HELP ANTED
SHLDCKEN DIARY
I BROUGHT THE DIARY, SO COME AND MEET ME.
I'M AT THE CONVENIENCE STORE BY YOUR PLACE.
HEY! DID YOU JUST SAY "KOMI-NAMI" ...?
YEAH. YOU...
BEEP
WAITING FOR HIM
OH!
YOU'RE THAT QUEENY CHEF!
YOU'RE SHORTER THAN ON TV.
YOUR PASTA TURNED OUT SUPER-SOUR 'COS OF KOMINAMI, RIGHT!?
AHH, THAT MADE FOR A GOOD STORY.
HOW DO YOU KNOW THAT?
WHO ARE YOU?

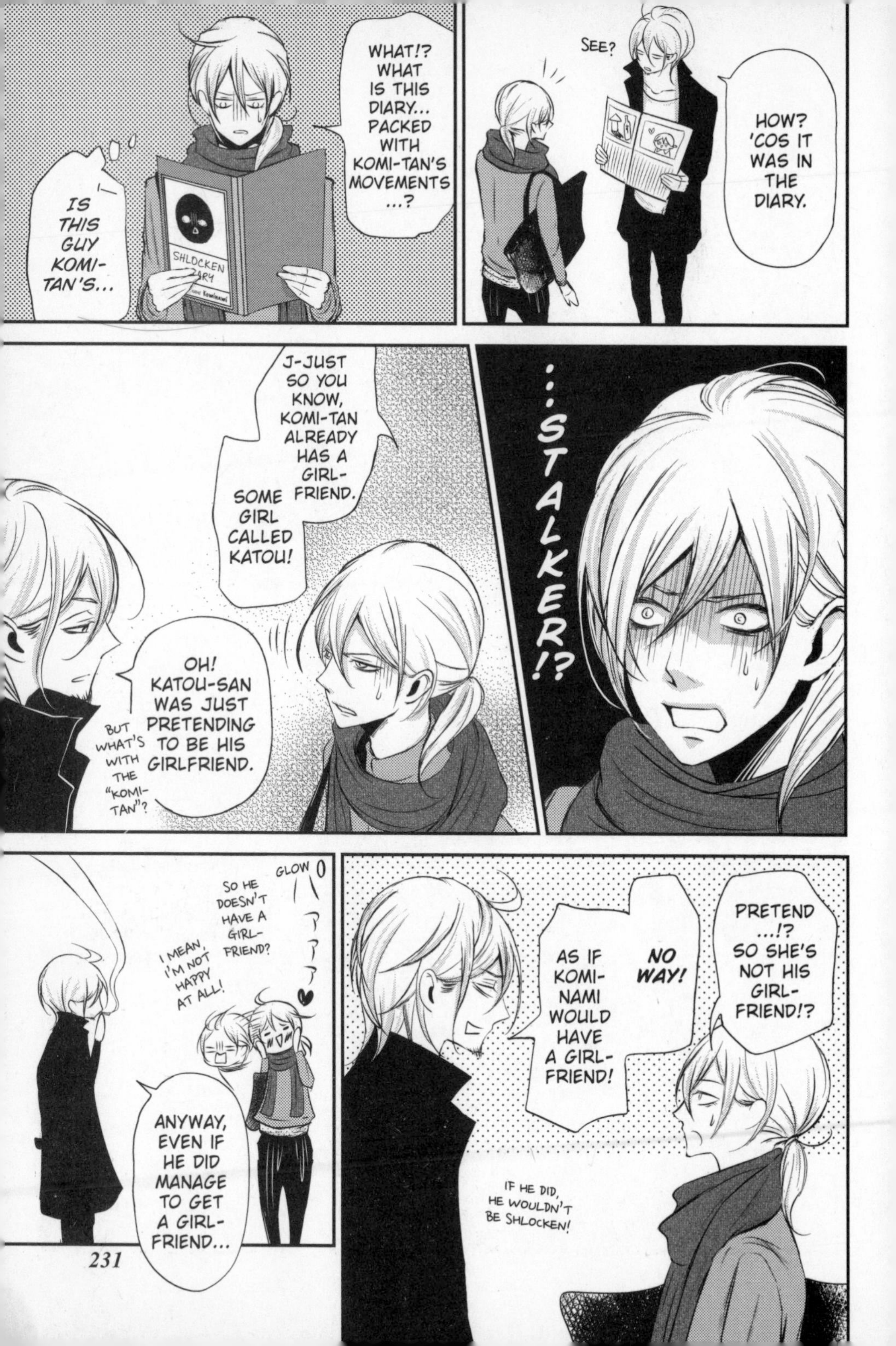
SEE?
HOW? 'COS IT WAS IN THE DIARY.
WHAT!? WHAT IS THIS DIARY... PACKED WITH KOMI-TAN'S MOVEMENTS ...?
SHLOCKEN
IS THIS GUY KOMI-TAN'S...
...STALKER!?
J-JUST SO YOU KNOW, KOMI-TAN ALREADY HAS A GIRL-FRIEND.
SOME GIRL CALLED KATOU!
OH! KATOU-SAN WAS JUST PRETENDING TO BE HIS GIRLFRIEND.
BUT WHAT'S WITH THE "KOMI-TAN"?
PRETEND ...!? SO SHE'S NOT HIS GIRL-FRIEND!?
NO WAY!
AS IF KOMI-NAMI WOULD HAVE A GIRL-FRIEND!
IF HE DID, HE WOULDN'T BE SHLOCKEN!
GLOW
SO HE DOESN'T HAVE A GIRL-FRIEND?
I MEAN, I'M NOT HAPPY AT ALL!
ANYWAY, EVEN IF HE DID MANAGE TO GET A GIRL-FRIEND...

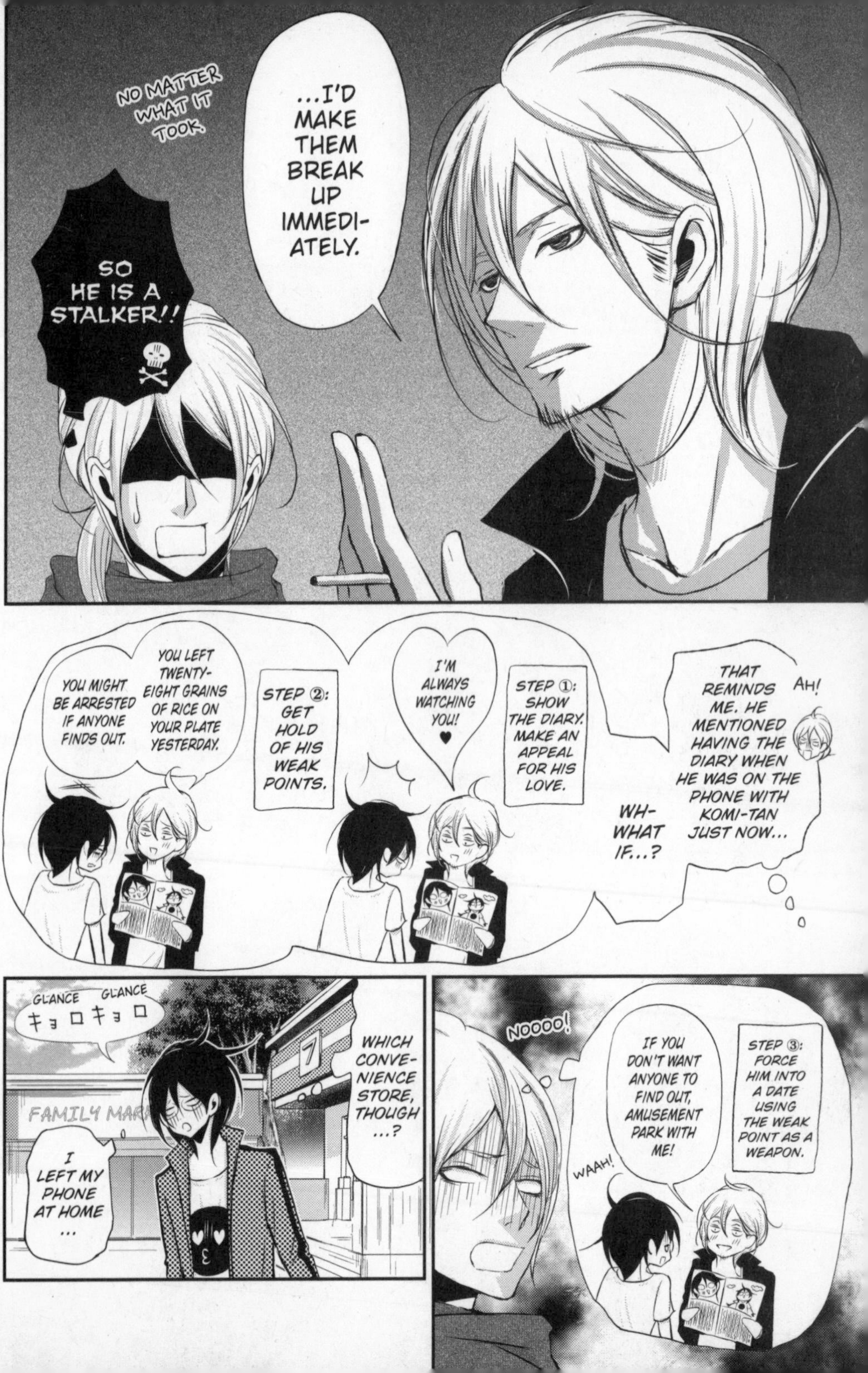
...I'D MAKE THEM BREAK UP IMMEDI-ATELY.
NO MATTER WHAT IT TOOK.
SO HE IS A STALKER!!
AH!
THAT REMINDS ME. HE MENTIONED HAVING THE DIARY WHEN HE WAS ON THE PHONE WITH KOMI-TAN JUST NOW...
WH-WHAT IF...?
STEP ①: SHOW THE DIARY. MAKE AN APPEAL FOR HIS LOVE.
I'M ALWAYS WATCHING YOU! ♥
STEP ②: GET HOLD OF HIS WEAK POINTS.
YOU LEFT TWENTY-EIGHT GRAINS OF RICE ON YOUR PLATE YESTERDAY.
YOU MIGHT BE ARRESTED IF ANYONE FINDS OUT.
STEP ③: FORCE HIM INTO A DATE USING THE WEAK POINT AS A WEAPON.
IF YOU DON'T WANT ANYONE TO FIND OUT, AMUSEMENT PARK WITH ME!
WAAH!
NOOOO!
WHICH CONVENIENCE STORE, THOUGH...?
GLANCE GLANCE
キョロキョロ
7
FAMILY MAR
I LEFT MY PHONE AT HOME...

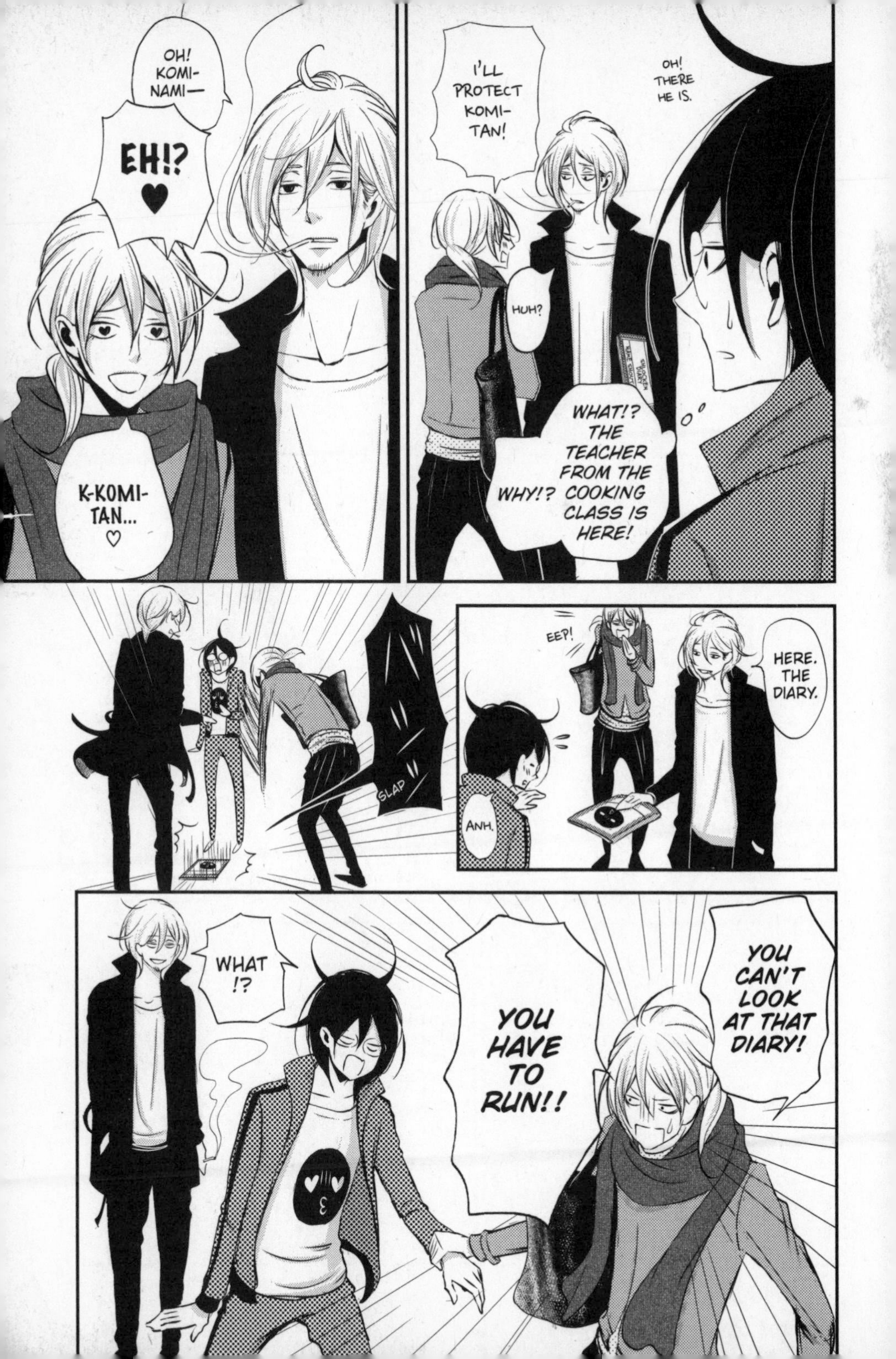
OH! THERE HE IS.
I'LL PROTECT KOMI-TAN!
HUH?
WHAT!? THE TEACHER FROM THE COOKING CLASS IS HERE!
WHY!?
OH! KOMI-NAMI—
EH!? ♥
K-KOMI-TAN... ♡
HERE. THE DIARY.
EEP!
ANH.
SLAP
YOU CAN'T LOOK AT THAT DIARY!
YOU HAVE TO RUN!!
WHAT !?

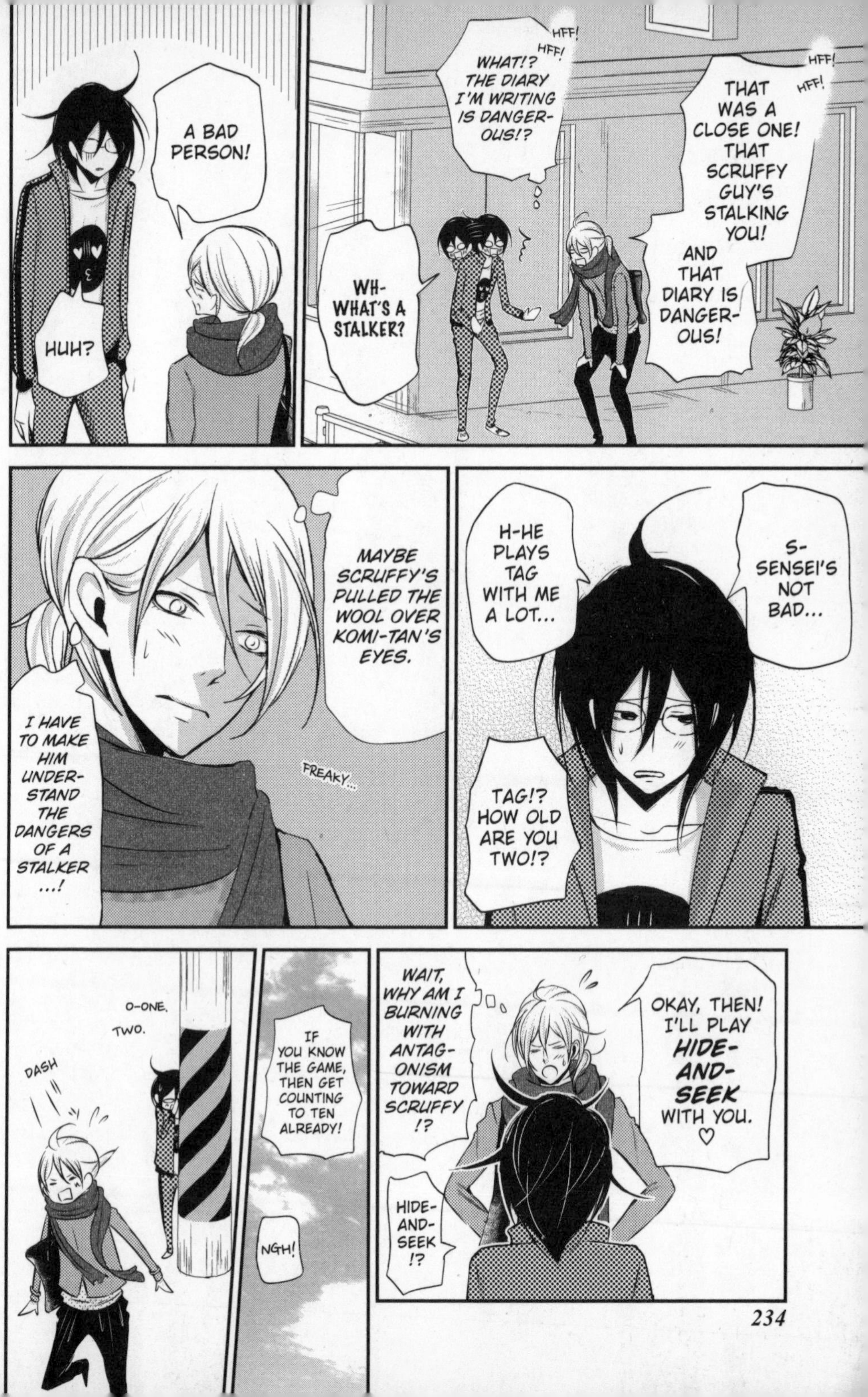
HFF!
HFF!
WHAT!? THE DIARY I'M WRITING IS DANGEROUS!?
HFF!
HFF!
THAT WAS A CLOSE ONE! THAT SCRUFFY GUY'S STALKING YOU!
AND THAT DIARY IS DANGEROUS!
WH-WHAT'S A STALKER?
A BAD PERSON!
HUH?
S-SENSEI'S NOT BAD...
H-HE PLAYS TAG WITH ME A LOT...
TAG!? HOW OLD ARE YOU TWO!?
MAYBE SCRUFFY'S PULLED THE WOOL OVER KOMI-TAN'S EYES.
I HAVE TO MAKE HIM UNDERSTAND THE DANGERS OF A STALKER ...!
FREAKY...
OKAY, THEN! I'LL PLAY HIDE-AND-SEEK WITH YOU. ♡
WAIT, WHY AM I BURNING WITH ANTAGONISM TOWARD SCRUFFY !?
HIDE-AND-SEEK !?
IF YOU KNOW THE GAME, THEN GET COUNTING TO TEN ALREADY!
NGH!
O-ONE.
TWO.
DASH

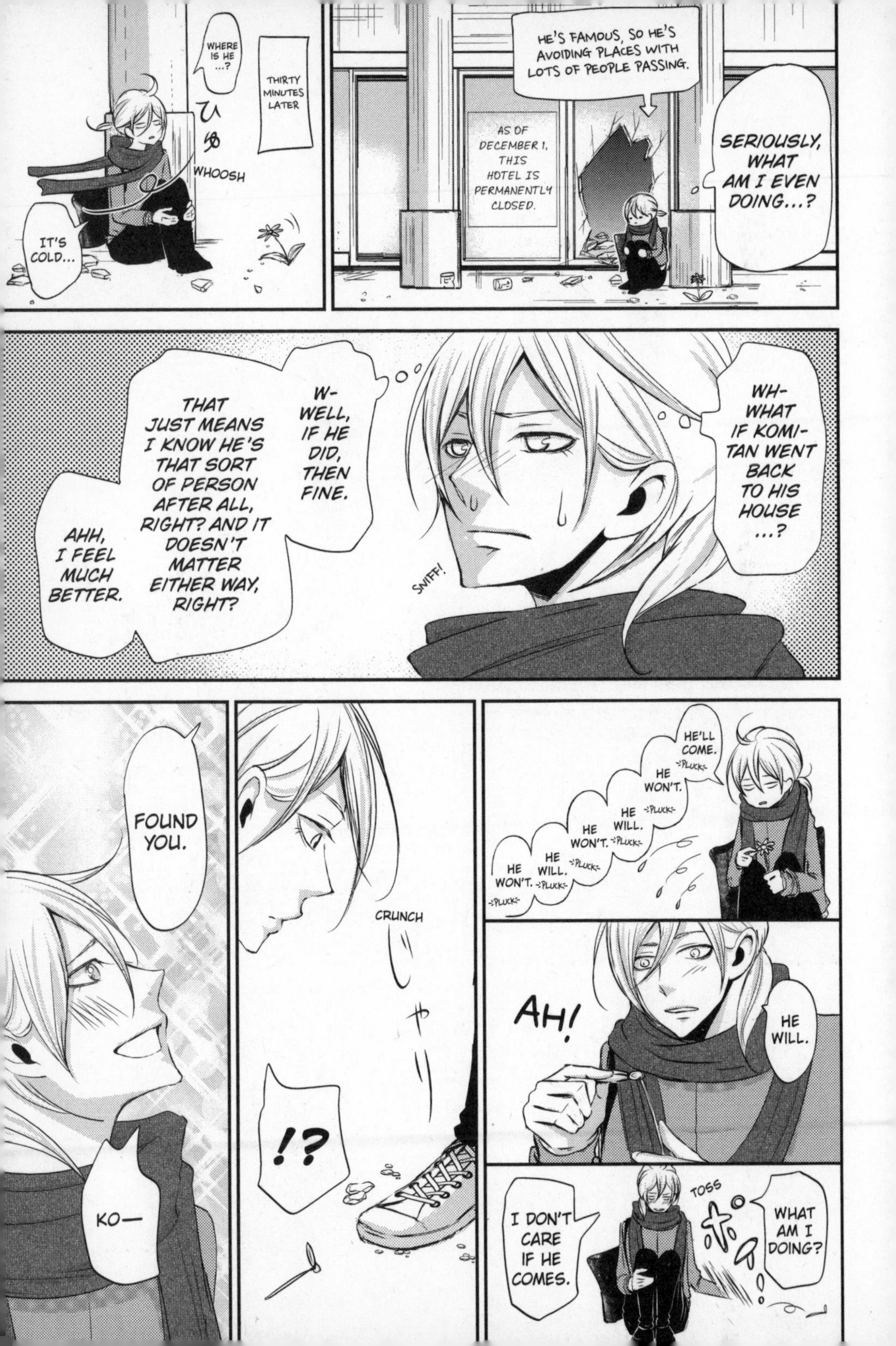
HE'S FAMOUS, SO HE'S AVOIDING PLACES WITH LOTS OF PEOPLE PASSING.
AS OF DECEMBER 1, THIS HOTEL IS PERMANENTLY CLOSED.
SERIOUSLY, WHAT AM I EVEN DOING...?
THIRTY MINUTES LATER
WHERE IS HE ...?
ひゅ
WHOOSH
IT'S COLD...
WH-WHAT IF KOMI-TAN WENT BACK TO HIS HOUSE ...?
SNIFF!
W-WELL, IF HE DID, THEN FINE.
THAT JUST MEANS I KNOW HE'S THAT SORT OF PERSON AFTER ALL, RIGHT? AND IT DOESN'T MATTER EITHER WAY, RIGHT?
AHH, I FEEL MUCH BETTER.
HE'LL COME.
PLUCK
HE WON'T.
PLUCK
HE WILL.
PLUCK
HE WON'T.
PLUCK
HE WILL.
PLUCK
HE WON'T.
PLUCK
HE WILL.
AH!
WHAT AM I DOING?
TOSS
I DON'T CARE IF HE COMES.
CRUNCH
!?
CRUNCH
FOUND YOU.
KO—

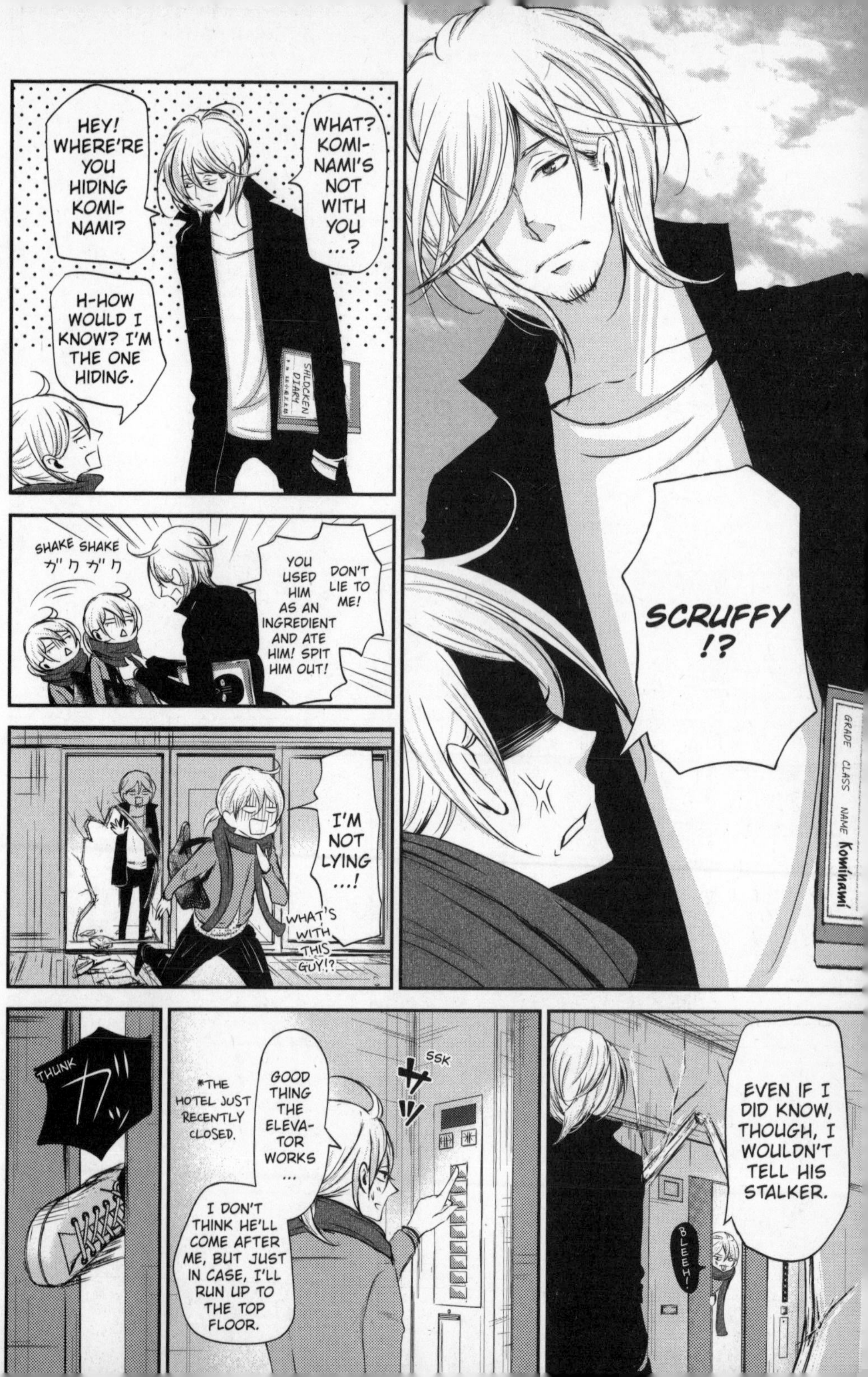
SCRUFFY !?
GRADE CLASS NAME Kominami
WHAT? KOMI-NAMI'S NOT WITH YOU ...?
HEY! WHERE'RE YOU HIDING KOMI-NAMI?
SHLOCKEN DIARY
H-HOW WOULD I KNOW? I'M THE ONE HIDING.
DON'T LIE TO ME!
YOU USED HIM AS AN INGREDIENT AND ATE HIM! SPIT HIM OUT!
SHAKE SHAKE
ガクガク
I'M NOT LYING ...!
WHAT'S WITH THIS GUY!?
EVEN IF I DID KNOW, THOUGH, I WOULDN'T TELL HIS STALKER.
BLEEH!
SSK
GOOD THING THE ELEVATOR WORKS ...
*THE HOTEL JUST RECENTLY CLOSED.
I DON'T THINK HE'LL COME AFTER ME, BUT JUST IN CASE, I'LL RUN UP TO THE TOP FLOOR.
THUNK

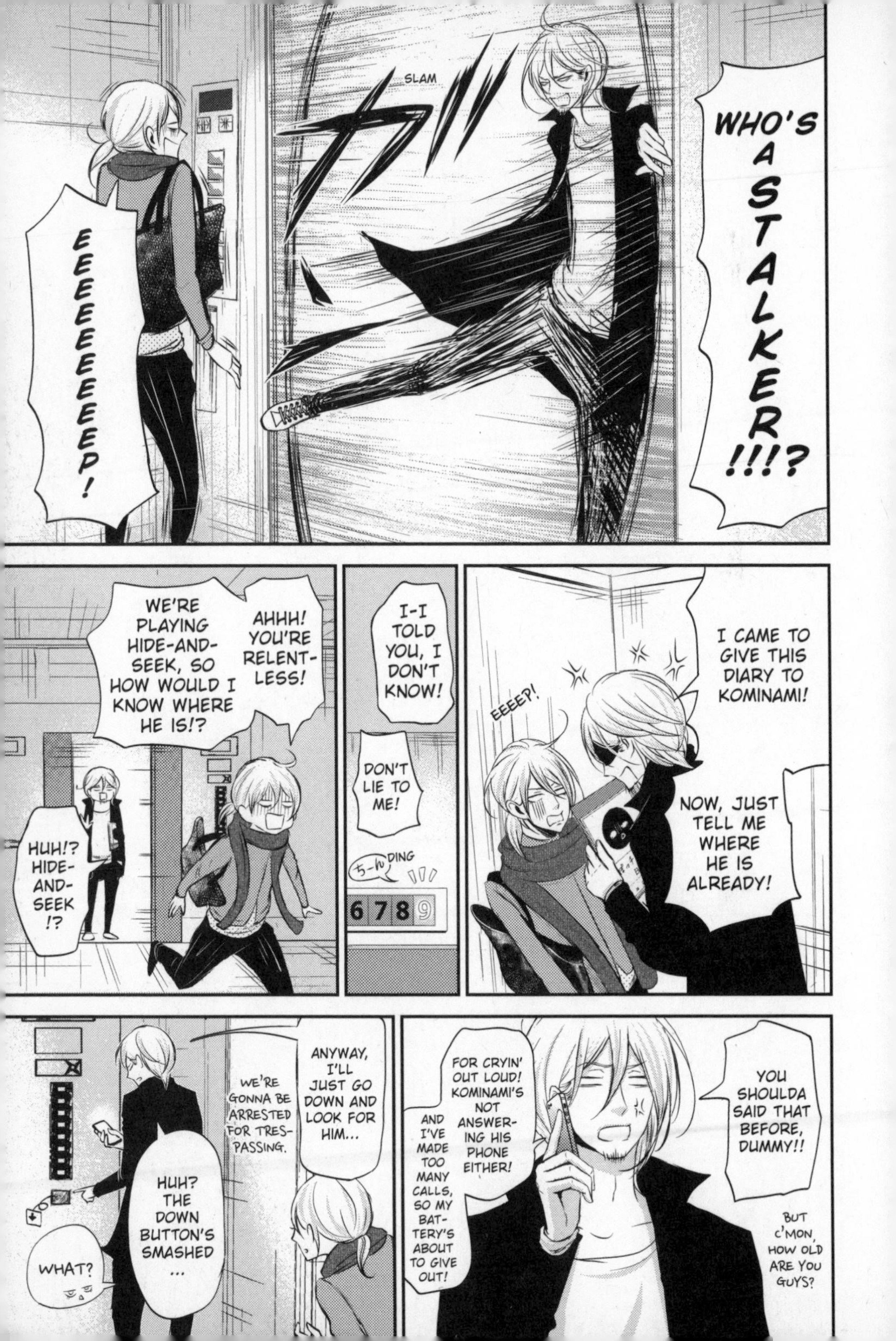
WHO'S A STALKER!!!?
SLAM
EEEEEEEEEEEP!
I CAME TO GIVE THIS DIARY TO KOMINAMI!
EEEEP!
NOW, JUST TELL ME WHERE HE IS ALREADY!
I-I TOLD YOU, I DON'T KNOW!
DON'T LIE TO ME!
ちーん DING
6789
AHHH! YOU'RE RELENT-LESS!
WE'RE PLAYING HIDE-AND-SEEK, SO HOW WOULD I KNOW WHERE HE IS!?
HUH!? HIDE-AND-SEEK!?
YOU SHOULDA SAID THAT BEFORE, DUMMY!!
FOR CRYIN' OUT LOUD! KOMINAMI'S NOT ANSWER-ING HIS PHONE EITHER!
AND I'VE MADE TOO MANY CALLS, SO MY BAT-TERY'S ABOUT TO GIVE OUT!
BUT C'MON, HOW OLD ARE YOU GUYS?
ANYWAY, I'LL JUST GO DOWN AND LOOK FOR HIM...
WE'RE GONNA BE ARRESTED FOR TRES-PASSING.
HUH? THE DOWN BUTTON'S SMASHED...
WHAT?

WELP, I GUESS IT'S THE STAIRS, THEN...
STAIRS
RATTLE RATTLE ガチャガチャ
HUH? IT'S LOCKED.
EMERGENCY EXIT
RATTLE RATTLE ガチャガチャ
HUH... THIS ONE TOO.
WELP, GUESS THAT'S THAT... I'LL CALL NISHIDA.
AH! MY BATTERY DIED.
HEY! GIMME YOUR PHONE.
IF I GOTTA ...
ゴソゴソ DIG DIG
SEASONED SEAWEED
SORRY. IT LOOKS LIKE I MISTOOK THIS SEAWEED FOR MY SMART-PHONE.
MY HEAD WAS SO FULL OF KOMI-TAN...

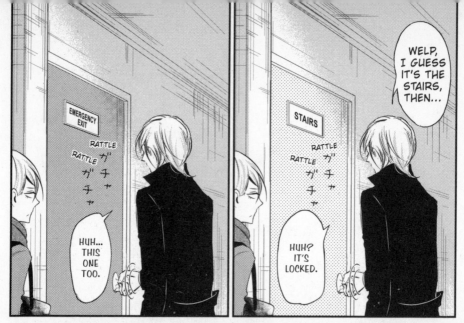

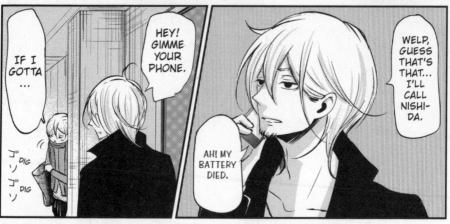

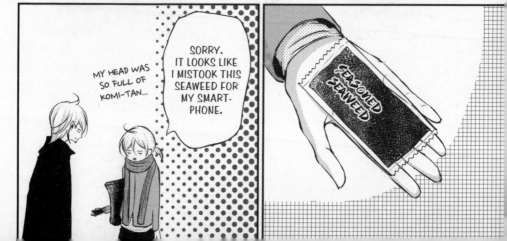

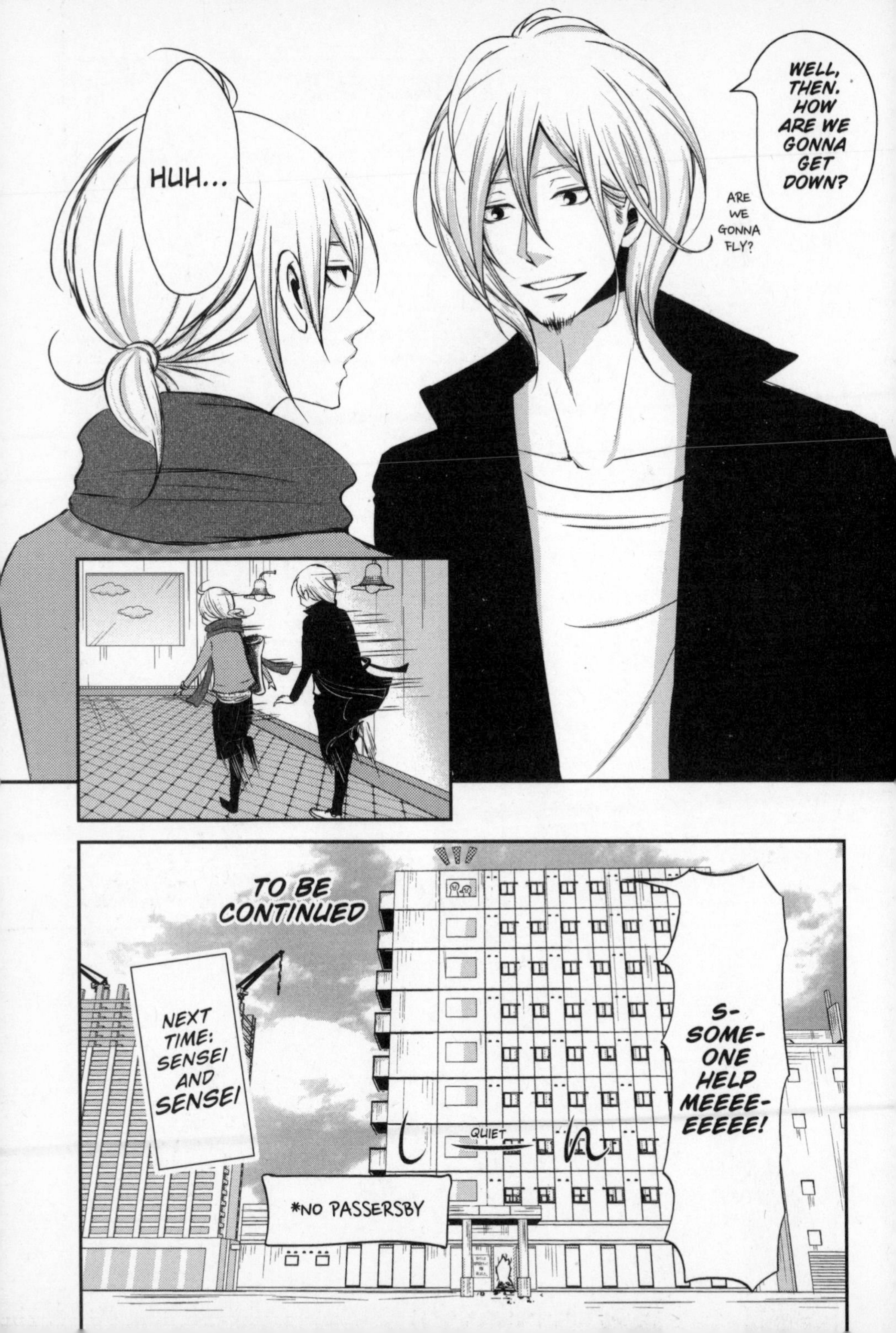
WELL, THEN. HOW ARE WE GONNA GET DOWN?
ARE WE GONNA FLY?
HUH...
S-SOMEONE HELP MEEEE-EEEEE!
QUIET
*NO PASSERSBY
TO BE CONTINUED
NEXT TIME: SENSEI AND SENSEI

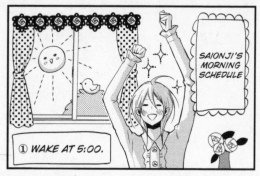

SAIONJI'S MORNING SCHEDULE
① WAKE AT 5:00.
WHO'S FAIRER, ME OR SNOW WHITE!?
MIR-ROR
② QUIZ HIS MANAGER.
...YOU. IT'S YOU.
Correct !!
MANAGER
BEEP
③ GET HUNG UP ON IN HALF ANGER.
SECOND QUES-TION!
One question a day!!
BEEP
④ GET HUNG UP ON IN FULL-BLOWN ANGER.

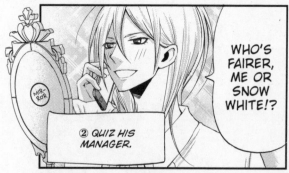

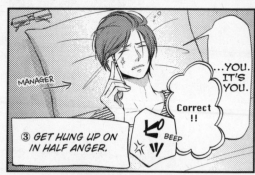

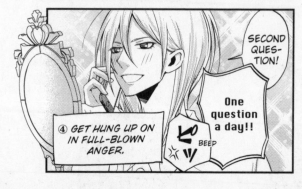

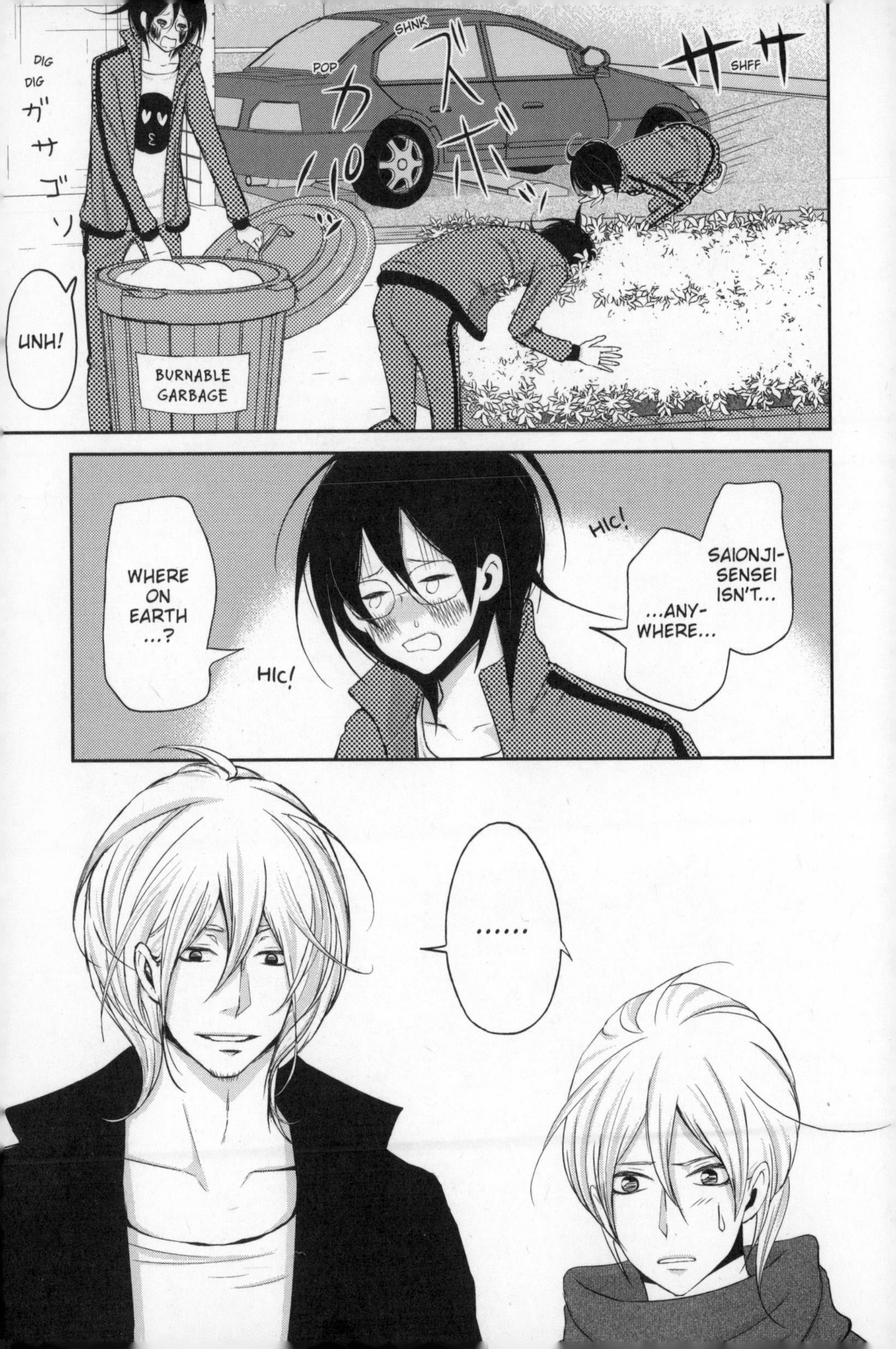
ササ
SHFF
ズボッ
SHNK
カパ
POP
BURNABLE GARBAGE
ガサゴソ
DIG DIG
UNH!
HIC!
SAIONJI-SENSEI ISN'T...
...ANY-WHERE...
HIC!
WHERE ON EARTH...?
......

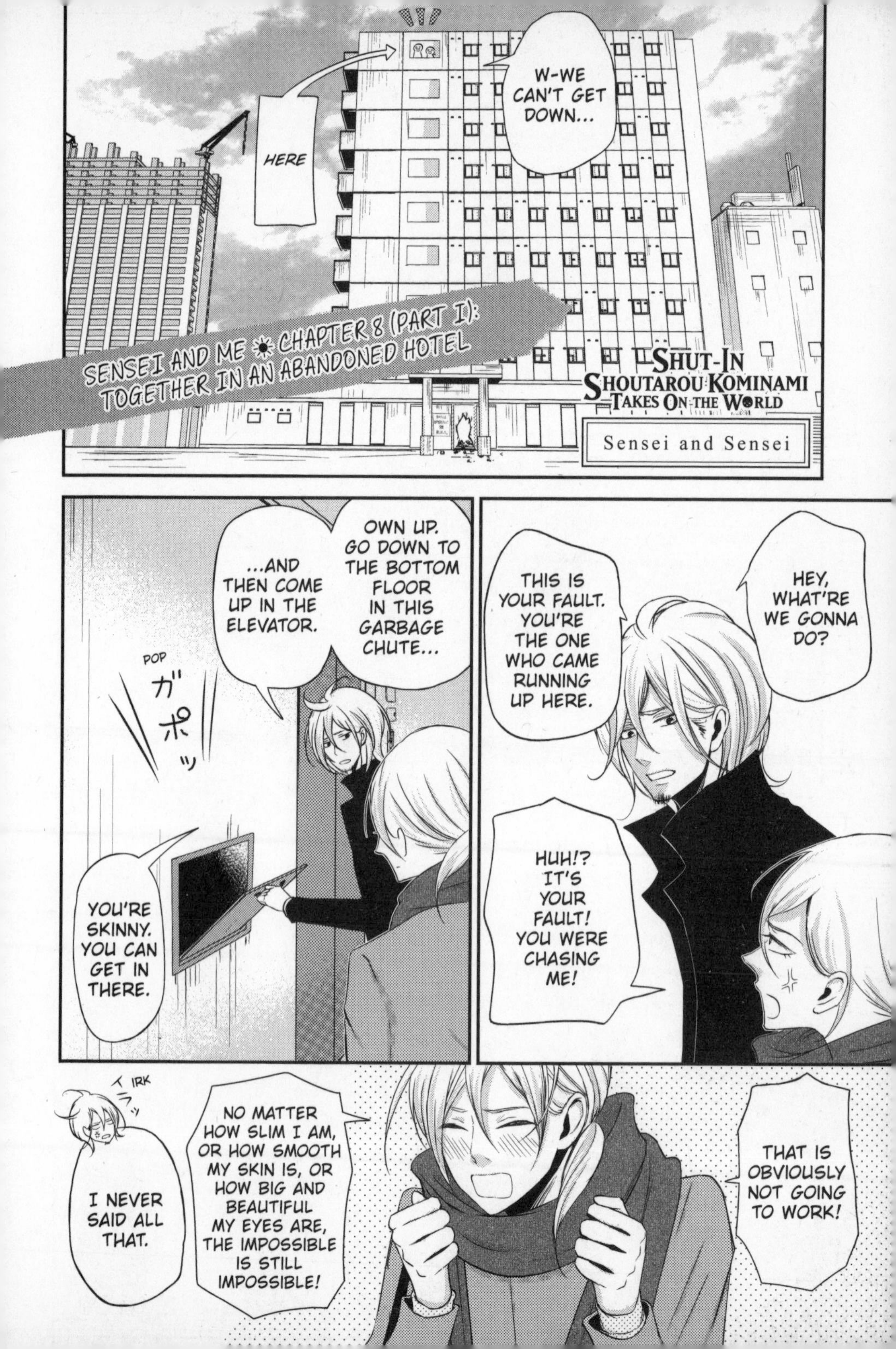
W-WE CAN'T GET DOWN...
HERE
SENSEI AND ME ☀ CHAPTER 8 (PART I): TOGETHER IN AN ABANDONED HOTEL
SHUT-IN SHOUTAROU KOMINAMI TAKES ON THE WORLD
Sensei and Sensei
HEY, WHAT'RE WE GONNA DO?
THIS IS YOUR FAULT. YOU'RE THE ONE WHO CAME RUNNING UP HERE.
HUH!? IT'S YOUR FAULT! YOU WERE CHASING ME!
OWN UP. GO DOWN TO THE BOTTOM FLOOR IN THIS GARBAGE CHUTE...
...AND THEN COME UP IN THE ELEVATOR.
ガポッ
POP
YOU'RE SKINNY. YOU CAN GET IN THERE.
THAT IS OBVIOUSLY NOT GOING TO WORK!
NO MATTER HOW SLIM I AM, OR HOW SMOOTH MY SKIN IS, OR HOW BIG AND BEAUTIFUL MY EYES ARE, THE IMPOSSIBLE IS STILL IMPOSSIBLE!
イラッ
IRK
I NEVER SAID ALL THAT.

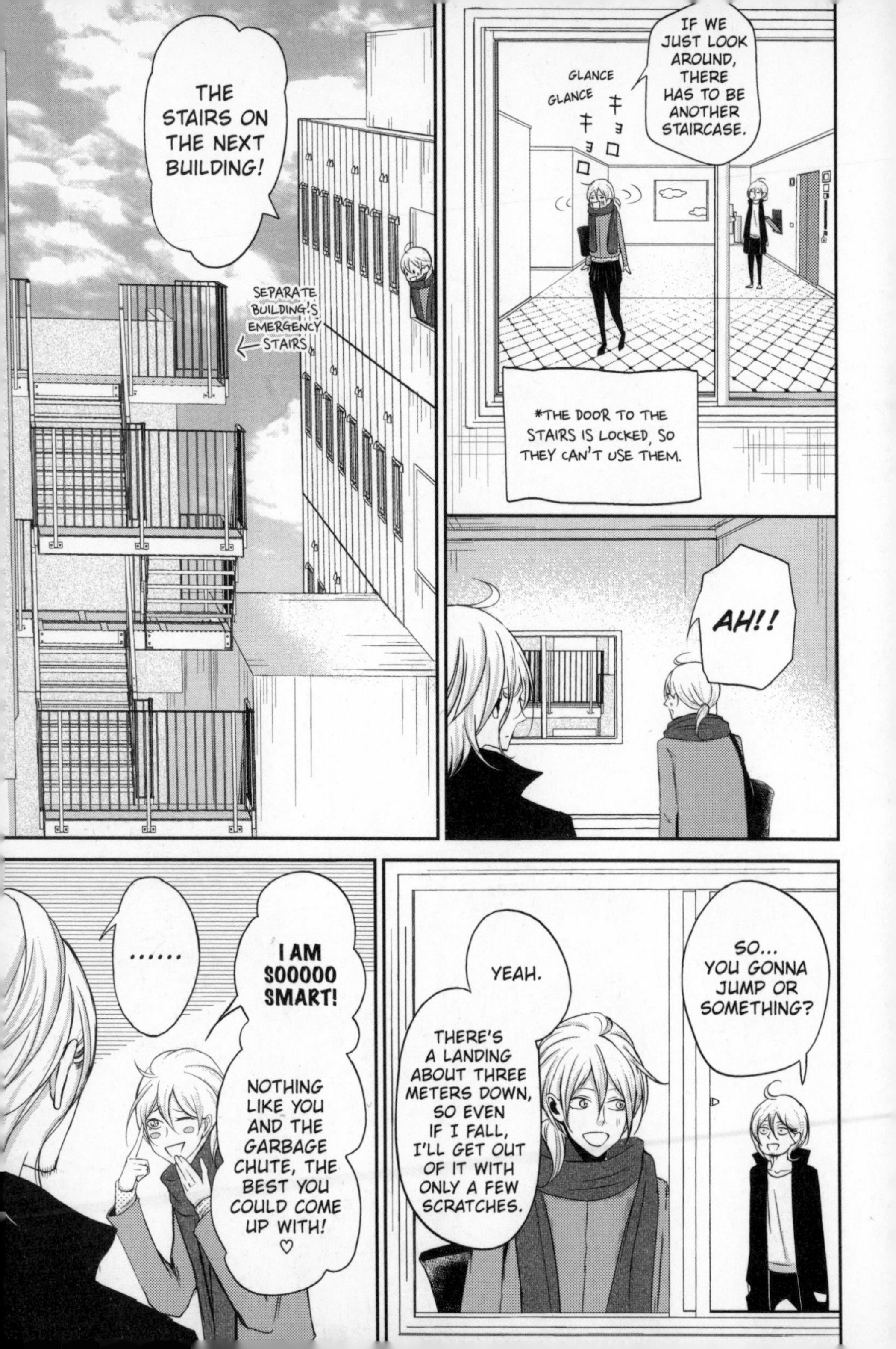

IF WE JUST LOOK AROUND, THERE HAS TO BE ANOTHER STAIRCASE.
GLANCE
GLANCE
キョロ
キョロ
*THE DOOR TO THE STAIRS IS LOCKED, SO THEY CAN'T USE THEM.
AH!!
THE STAIRS ON THE NEXT BUILDING!
SEPARATE BUILDING'S EMERGENCY STAIRS
SO... YOU GONNA JUMP OR SOMETHING?
YEAH.
THERE'S A LANDING ABOUT THREE METERS DOWN, SO EVEN IF I FALL, I'LL GET OUT OF IT WITH ONLY A FEW SCRATCHES.
I AM SOOOOO SMART!
......
NOTHING LIKE YOU AND THE GARBAGE CHUTE, THE BEST YOU COULD COME UP WITH! ♡

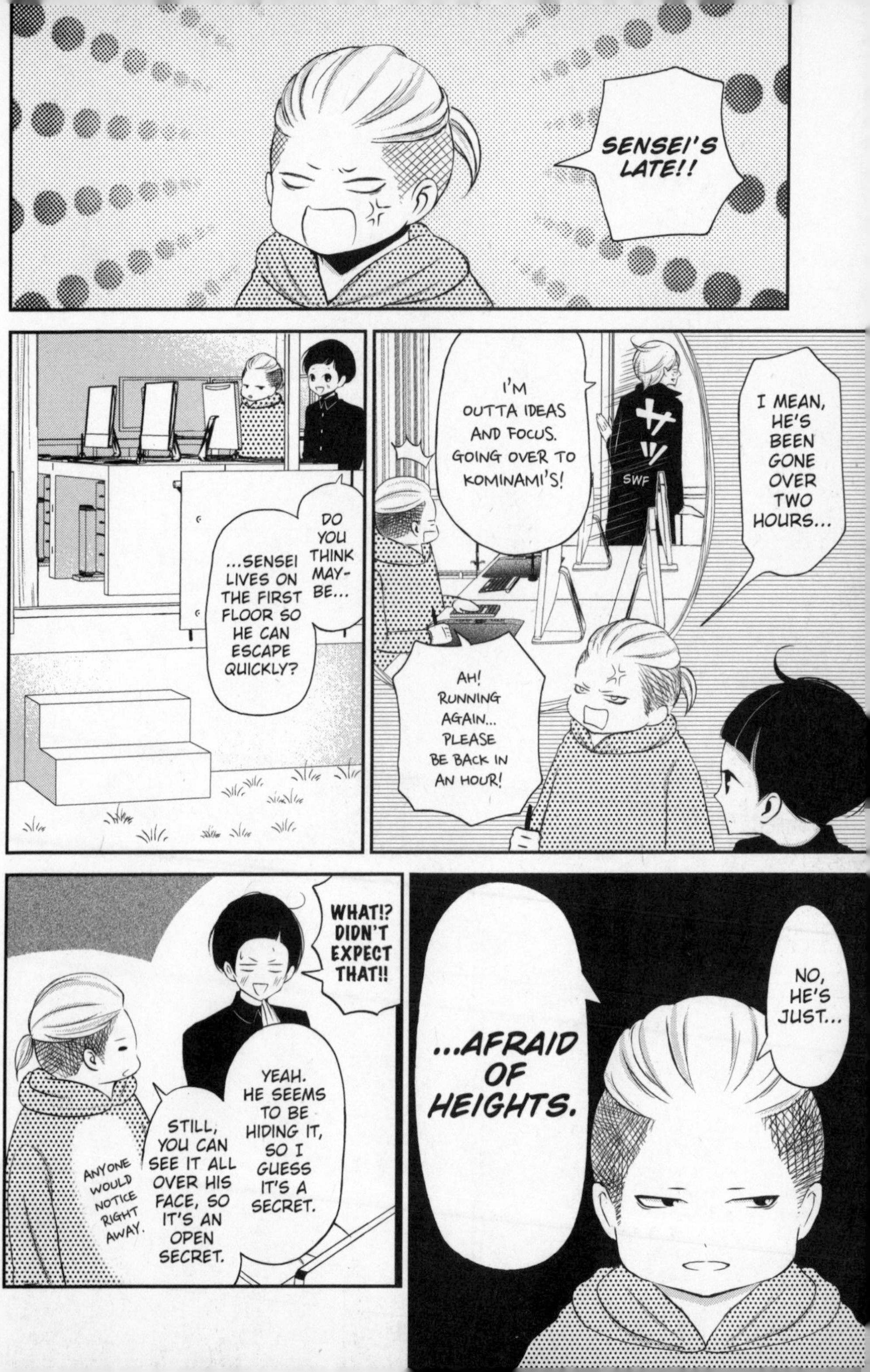
SENSEI'S LATE!!
I'M OUTTA IDEAS AND FOCUS. GOING OVER TO KOMINAMI'S!
SWF
AH! RUNNING AGAIN... PLEASE BE BACK IN AN HOUR!
I MEAN, HE'S BEEN GONE OVER TWO HOURS...
DO YOU THINK MAY-BE...
...SENSEI LIVES ON THE FIRST FLOOR SO HE CAN ESCAPE QUICKLY?
NO, HE'S JUST...
...AFRAID OF HEIGHTS.
WHAT!? DIDN'T EXPECT THAT!!
YEAH. HE SEEMS TO BE HIDING IT, SO I GUESS IT'S A SECRET.
STILL, YOU CAN SEE IT ALL OVER HIS FACE, SO IT'S AN OPEN SECRET.
ANYONE WOULD NOTICE RIGHT AWAY.

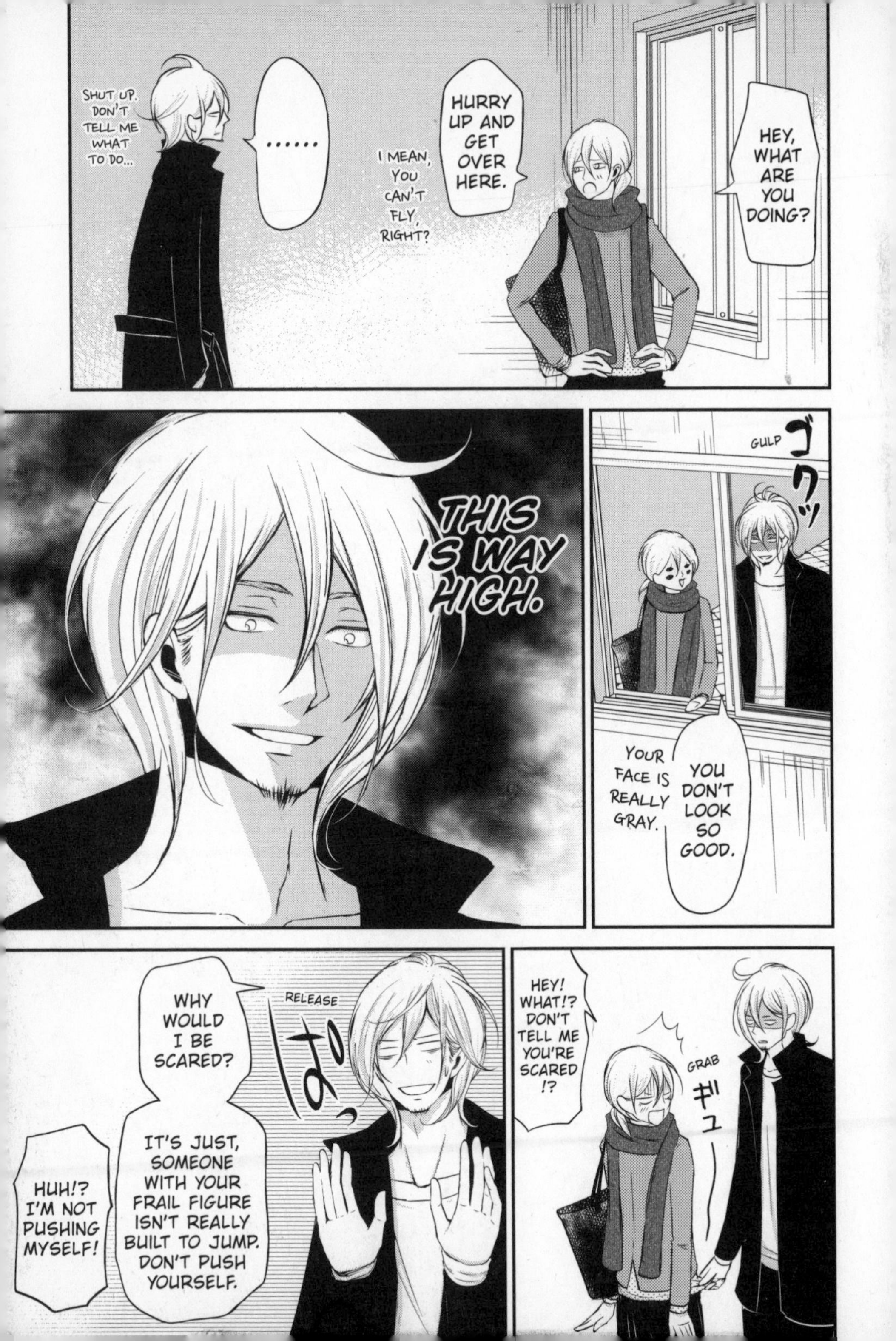
HEY, WHAT ARE YOU DOING?
HURRY UP AND GET OVER HERE.
I MEAN, YOU CAN'T FLY, RIGHT?
......
SHUT UP. DON'T TELL ME WHAT TO DO...
GULP
ゴクッ
YOU DON'T LOOK SO GOOD.
YOUR FACE IS REALLY GRAY.
THIS IS WAY HIGH.
HEY! WHAT!? DON'T TELL ME YOU'RE SCARED!?
GRAB
ギュー
WHY WOULD I BE SCARED?
RELEASE
ぱっ
IT'S JUST, SOMEONE WITH YOUR FRAIL FIGURE ISN'T REALLY BUILT TO JUMP. DON'T PUSH YOURSELF.
HUH!? I'M NOT PUSHING MYSELF!

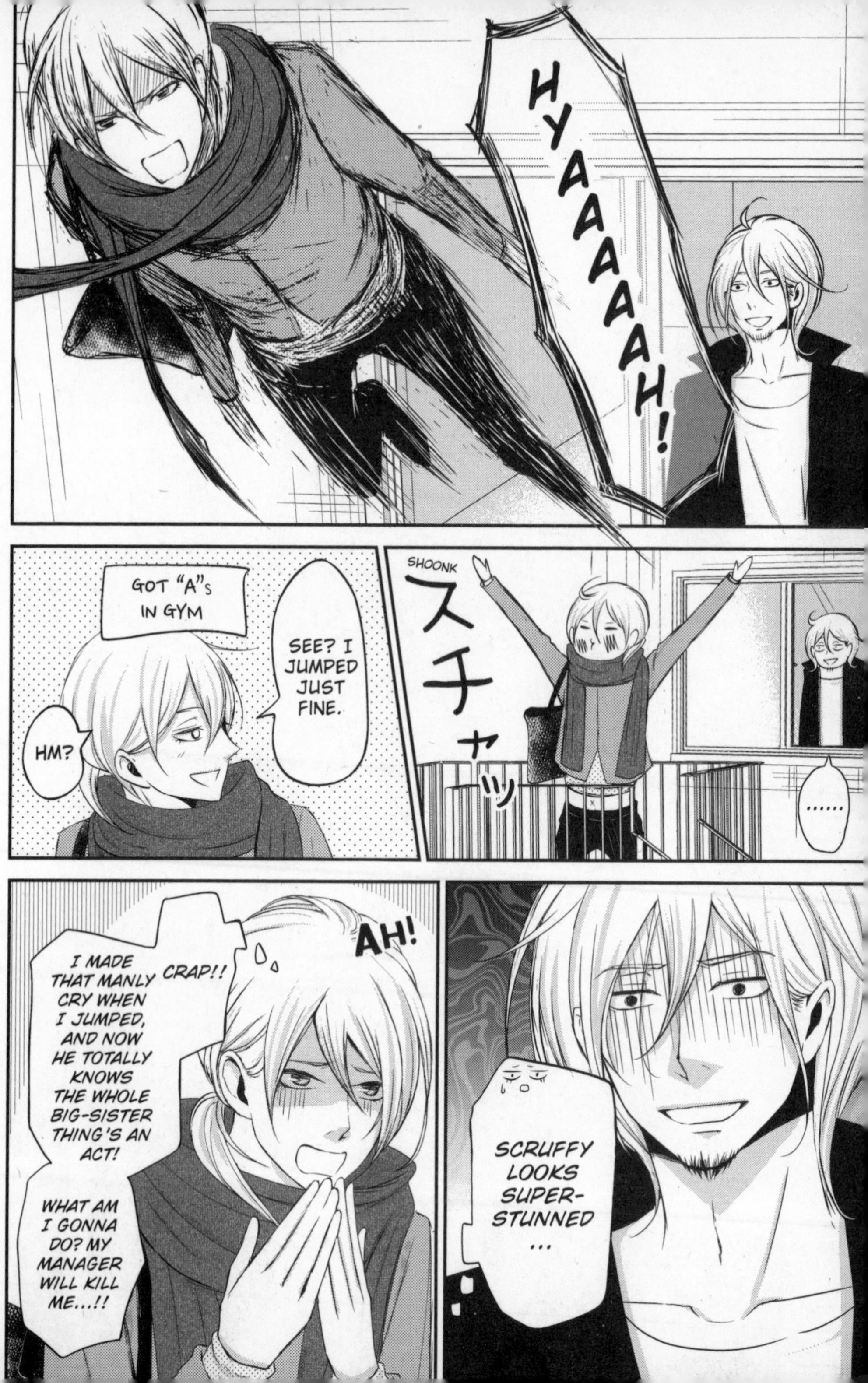
HYAAAAAH!
SHOONK
スチャッ
......
GOT "A"s IN GYM
SEE? I JUMPED JUST FINE.
HM?
SCRUFFY LOOKS SUPER-STUNNED ...
AH!
CRAP!!
I MADE THAT MANLY CRY WHEN I JUMPED, AND NOW HE TOTALLY KNOWS THE WHOLE BIG-SISTER THING'S AN ACT!
WHAT AM I GONNA DO? MY MANAGER WILL KILL ME...!!

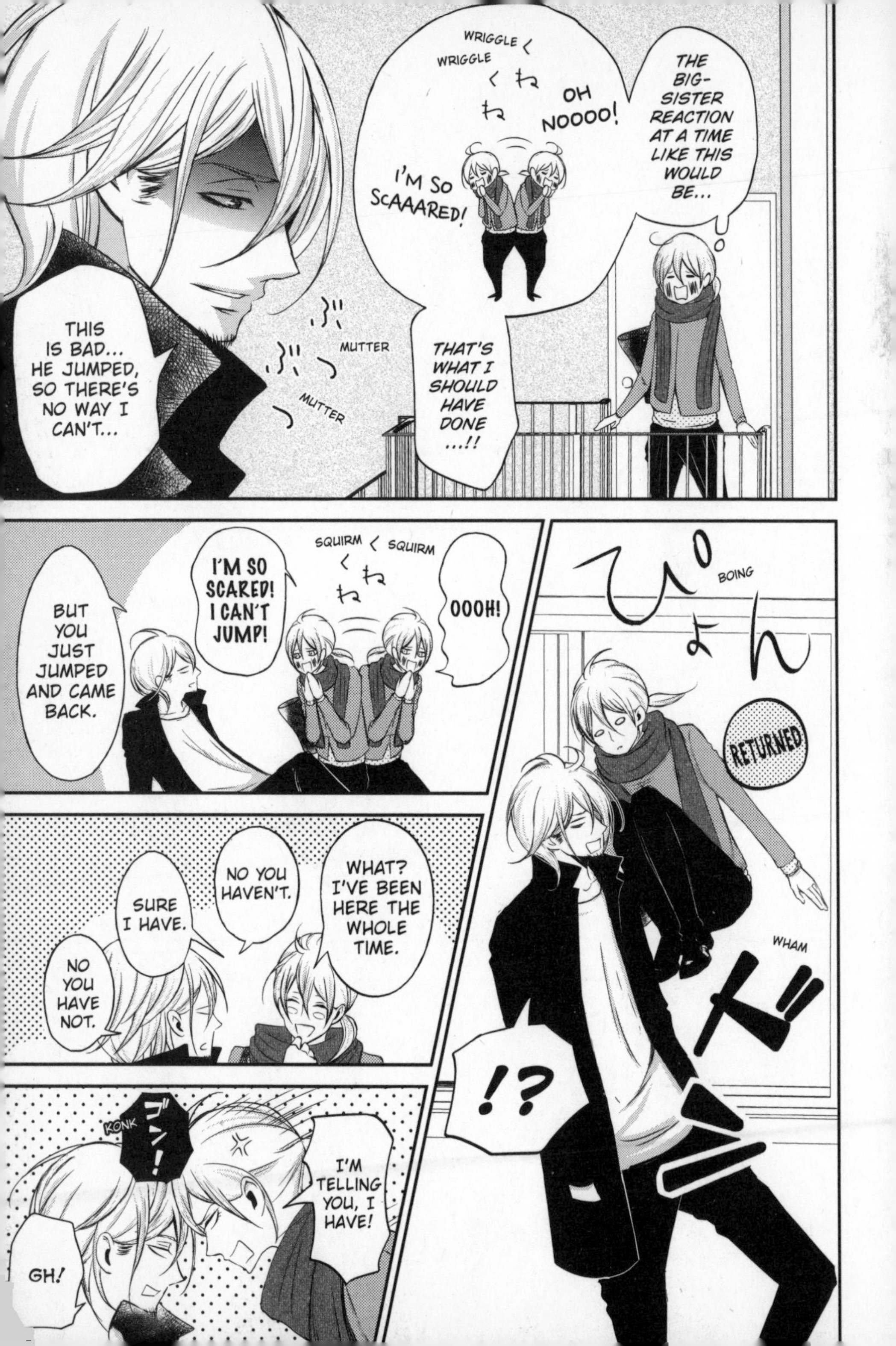
THE BIG-SISTER REACTION AT A TIME LIKE THIS WOULD BE...
WRIGGLE
WRIGGLE
OH NOOOO!
I'M SO SCAAARED!
THAT'S WHAT I SHOULD HAVE DONE ...!!
MUTTER
MUTTER
THIS IS BAD... HE JUMPED, SO THERE'S NO WAY I CAN'T...
BOING
RETURNED
WHAM
!?
OOOH!
SQUIRM
SQUIRM
I'M SO SCARED! I CAN'T JUMP!
BUT YOU JUST JUMPED AND CAME BACK.
WHAT? I'VE BEEN HERE THE WHOLE TIME.
NO YOU HAVEN'T.
SURE I HAVE.
NO YOU HAVE NOT.
I'M TELLING YOU, I HAVE!
KONK
GH!

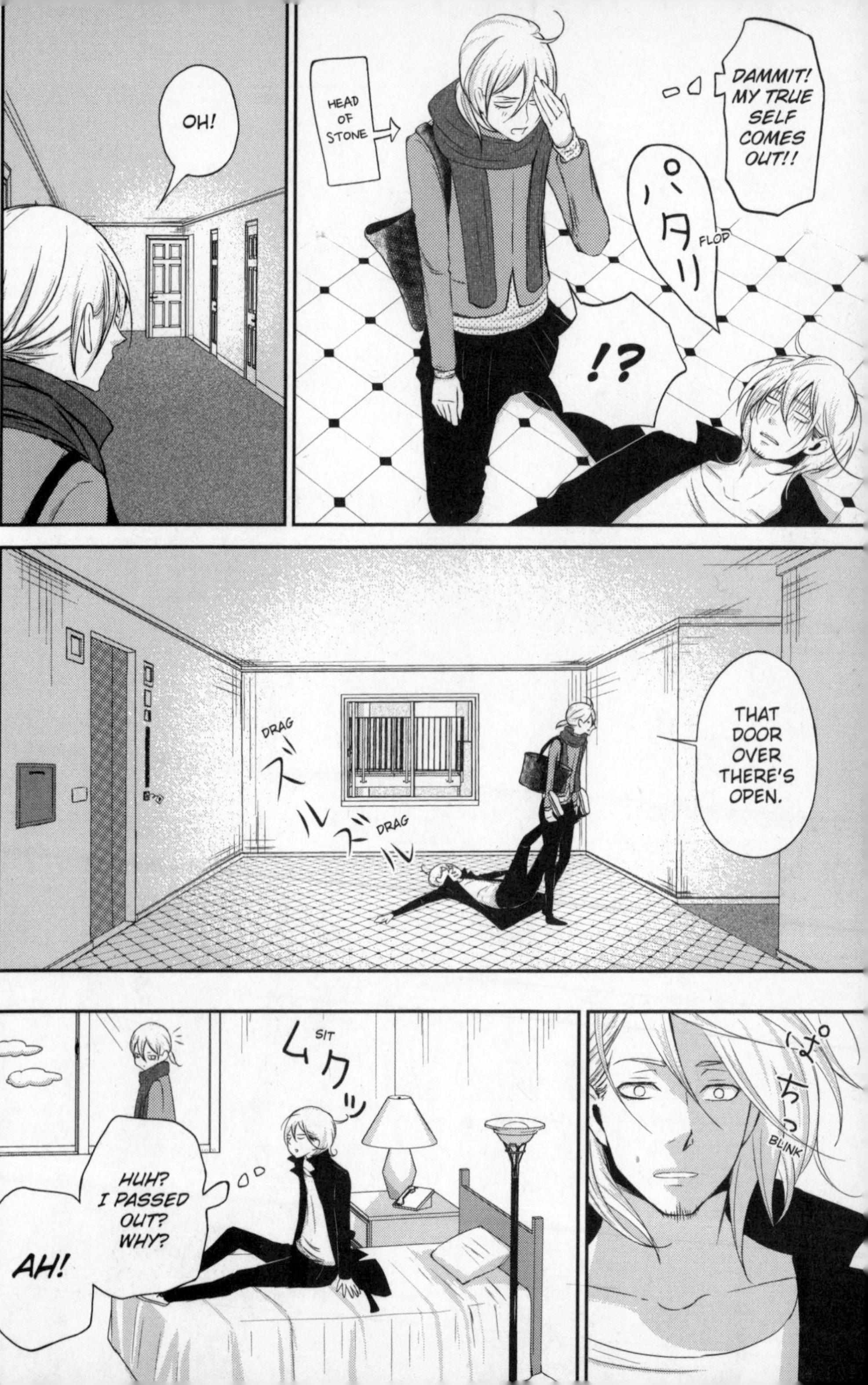
DAMMIT! MY TRUE SELF COMES OUT!!
HEAD OF STONE
パタリ
FLOP
!?
OH!
THAT DOOR OVER THERE'S OPEN.
ズルズル
DRAG
DRAG
ぱちっ
BLINK
ムクッ
SIT
HUH? I PASSED OUT? WHY?
AH!

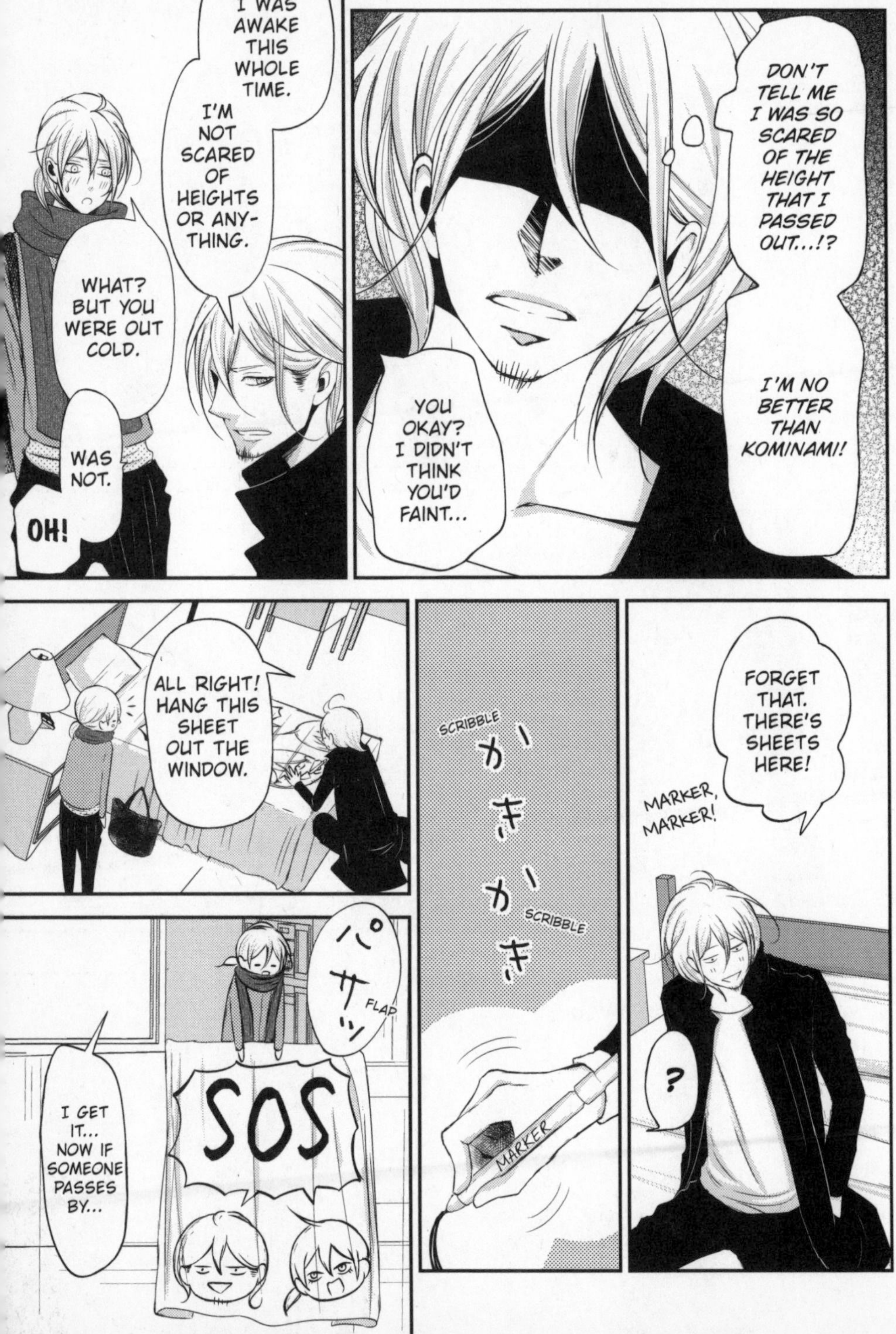
DON'T TELL ME I WAS SO SCARED OF THE HEIGHT THAT I PASSED OUT...!?
I'M NO BETTER THAN KOMINAMI!
YOU OKAY? I DIDN'T THINK YOU'D FAINT...
HUH? I WAS AWAKE THIS WHOLE TIME.
I'M NOT SCARED OF HEIGHTS OR ANYTHING.
WHAT? BUT YOU WERE OUT COLD.
WAS NOT.
OH!
FORGET THAT. THERE'S SHEETS HERE!
MARKER, MARKER!
?
かきかき
SCRIBBLE
SCRIBBLE
MARKER
ALL RIGHT! HANG THIS SHEET OUT THE WINDOW.
パサッ
FLAP
SOS
I GET IT... NOW IF SOMEONE PASSES BY...

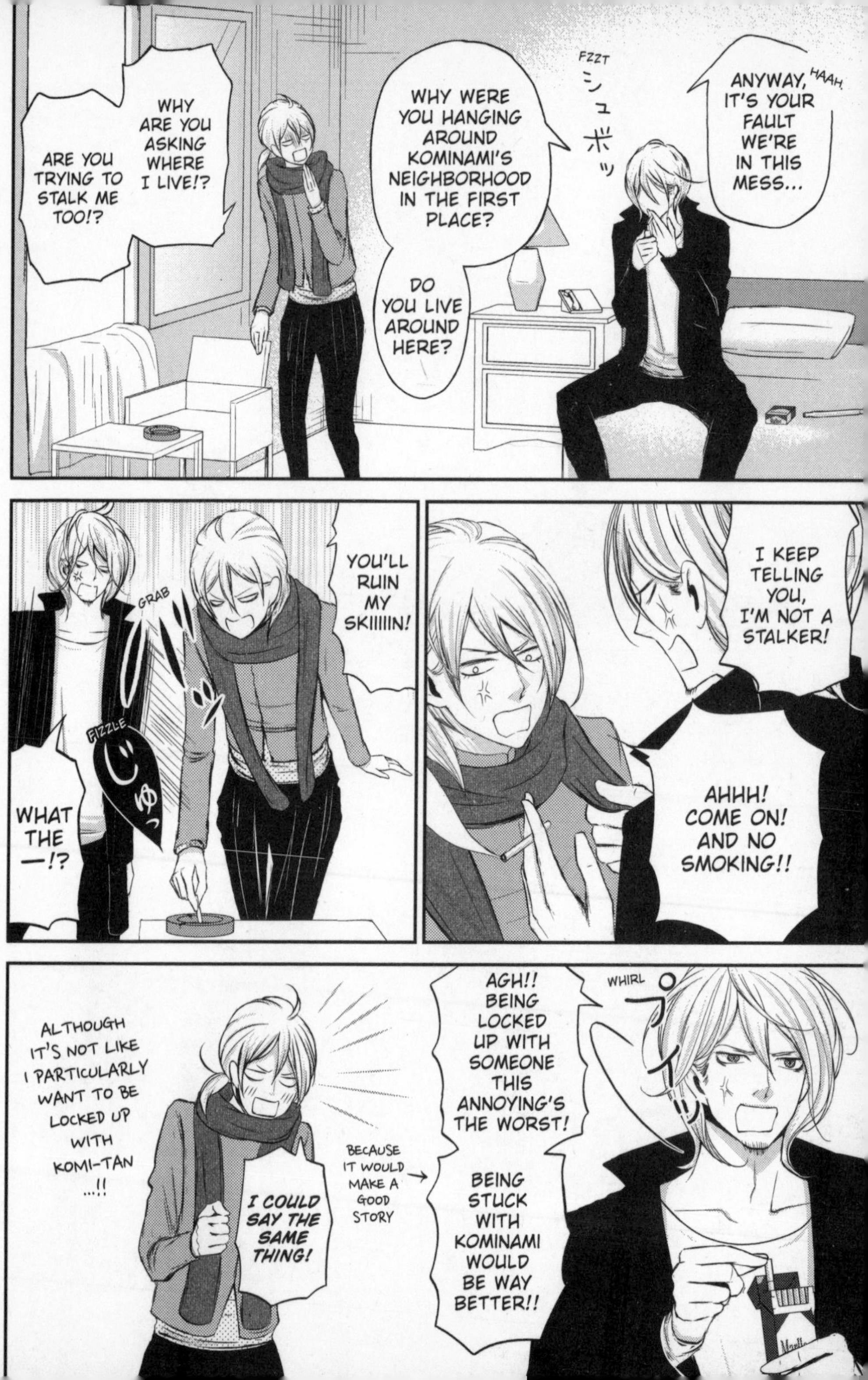
FZZT
シュボッ
HAAH.
ANYWAY, IT'S YOUR FAULT WE'RE IN THIS MESS...
WHY WERE YOU HANGING AROUND KOMINAMI'S NEIGHBORHOOD IN THE FIRST PLACE?
DO YOU LIVE AROUND HERE?
WHY ARE YOU ASKING WHERE I LIVE!?
ARE YOU TRYING TO STALK ME TOO!?
I KEEP TELLING YOU, I'M NOT A STALKER!
AHHH! COME ON! AND NO SMOKING!!
YOU'LL RUIN MY SKIIIIIN!
GRAB
FIZZLE
じゅっ
WHAT THE—!?
WHIRL
AGH!! BEING LOCKED UP WITH SOMEONE THIS ANNOYING'S THE WORST!
BEING STUCK WITH KOMINAMI WOULD BE WAY BETTER!!
BECAUSE IT WOULD MAKE A GOOD STORY
I COULD SAY THE SAME THING!
ALTHOUGH IT'S NOT LIKE I PARTICULARLY WANT TO BE LOCKED UP WITH KOMI-TAN ...!!

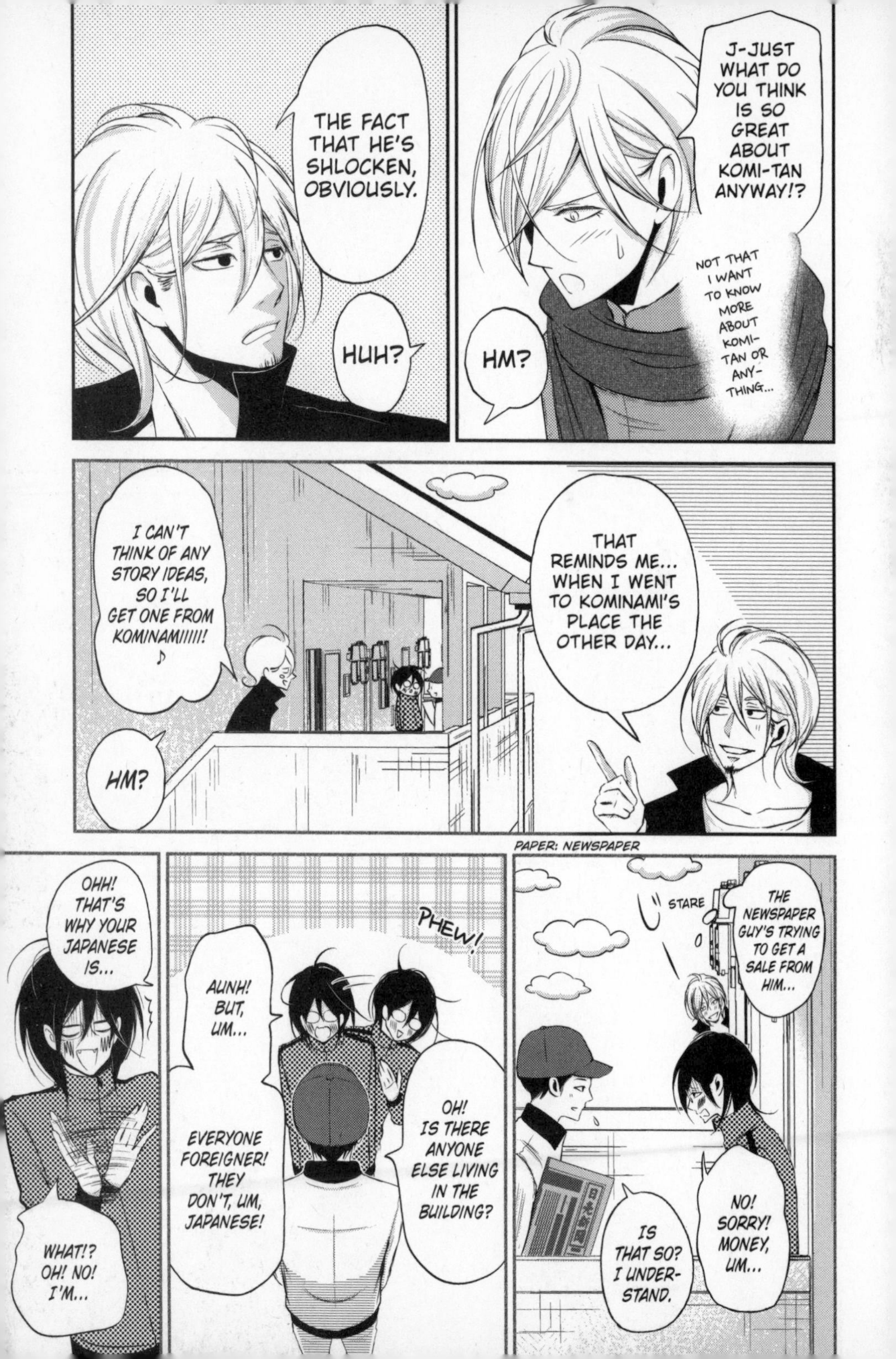
J-JUST WHAT DO YOU THINK IS SO GREAT ABOUT KOMI-TAN ANYWAY!?
NOT THAT I WANT TO KNOW MORE ABOUT KOMI-TAN OR ANY-THING...
HM?
THE FACT THAT HE'S SHLOCKEN, OBVIOUSLY.
HUH?
THAT REMINDS ME... WHEN I WENT TO KOMINAMI'S PLACE THE OTHER DAY...
I CAN'T THINK OF ANY STORY IDEAS, SO I'LL GET ONE FROM KOMINAMI!!!!!! ♪
HM?
PAPER: NEWSPAPER
THE NEWSPAPER GUY'S TRYING TO GET A SALE FROM HIM...
STARE
NO! SORRY! MONEY, UM...
IS THAT SO? I UNDER-STAND.
PHEW!
AUNH! BUT, UM...
OH! IS THERE ANYONE ELSE LIVING IN THE BUILDING?
EVERYONE FOREIGNER! THEY DON'T, UM, JAPANESE!
OHH! THAT'S WHY YOUR JAPANESE IS...
WHAT!? OH! NO! I'M...

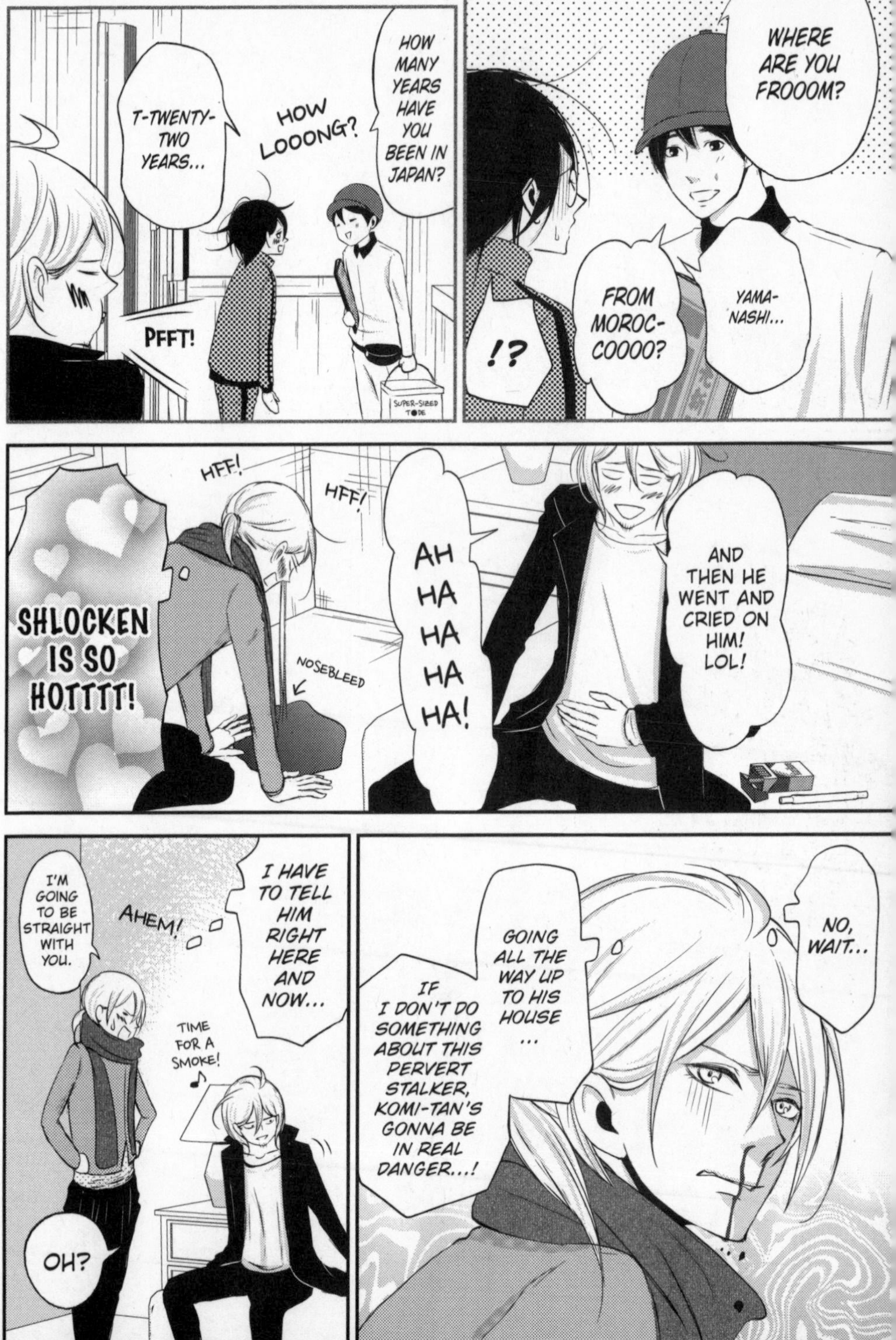
WHERE ARE YOU FROOOM?
YAMA-NASHI...
FROM MOROC-COOOO?
!?
HOW MANY YEARS HAVE YOU BEEN IN JAPAN?
HOW LOOONG?
T-TWENTY-TWO YEARS...
PFFT!
AND THEN HE WENT AND CRIED ON HIM! LOL!
AH HA HA HA HA!
HFF!
HFF!
NOSEBLEED
SHLOCKEN IS SO HOTTTT!
NO, WAIT...
GOING ALL THE WAY UP TO HIS HOUSE...
IF I DON'T DO SOMETHING ABOUT THIS PERVERT STALKER, KOMI-TAN'S GONNA BE IN REAL DANGER...!
I HAVE TO TELL HIM RIGHT HERE AND NOW...
I'M GOING TO BE STRAIGHT WITH YOU.
AHEM!
TIME FOR A SMOKE!
OH?

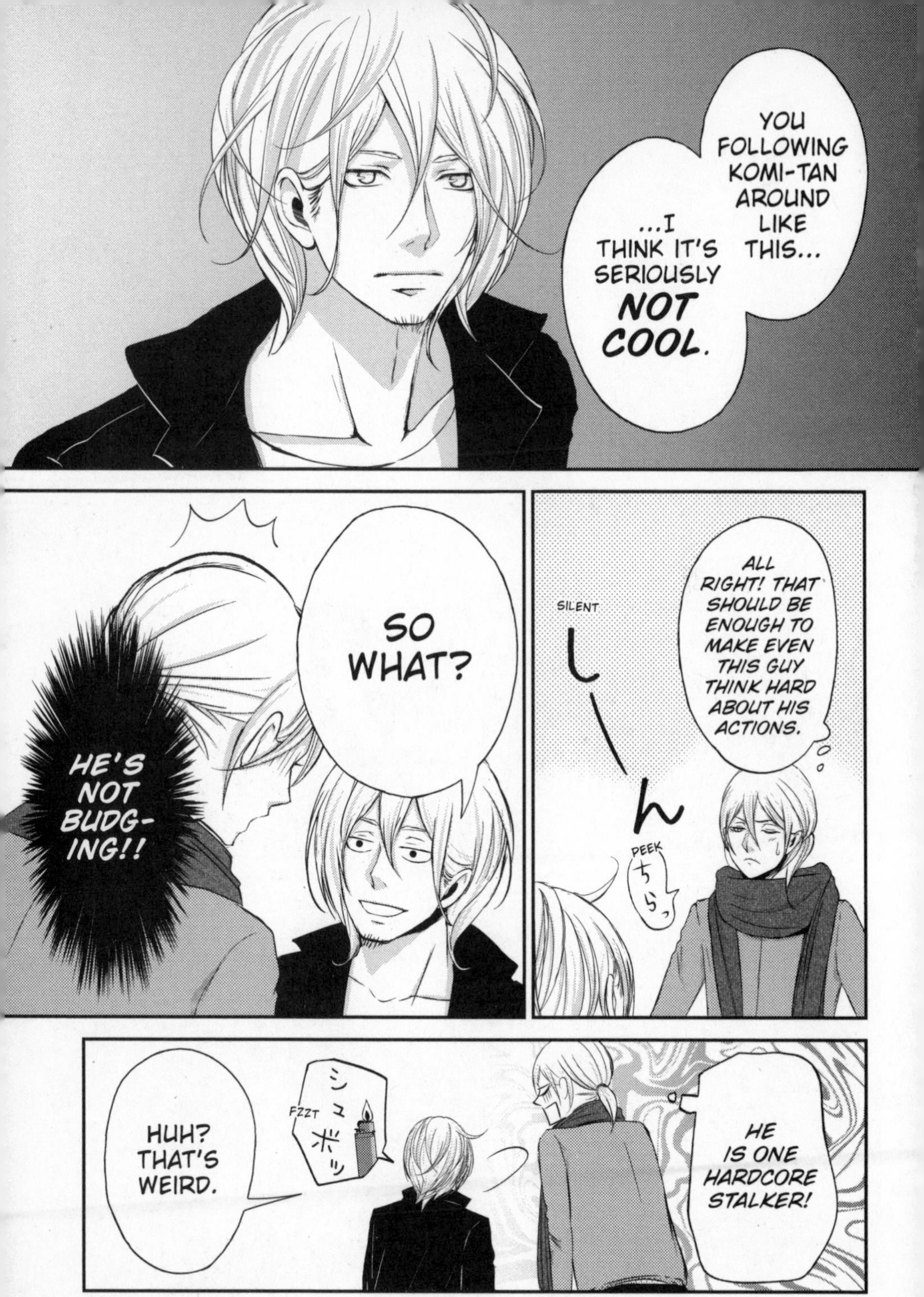
YOU FOLLOWING KOMI-TAN AROUND LIKE THIS...
...I THINK IT'S SERIOUSLY NOT COOL.
ALL RIGHT! THAT SHOULD BE ENOUGH TO MAKE EVEN THIS GUY THINK HARD ABOUT HIS ACTIONS.
SILENT
しーん
PEEK
ちらっ
SO WHAT?
HE'S NOT BUDGING!!
HE IS ONE HARDCORE STALKER!
FZZT
シュボッ
HUH? THAT'S WEIRD.

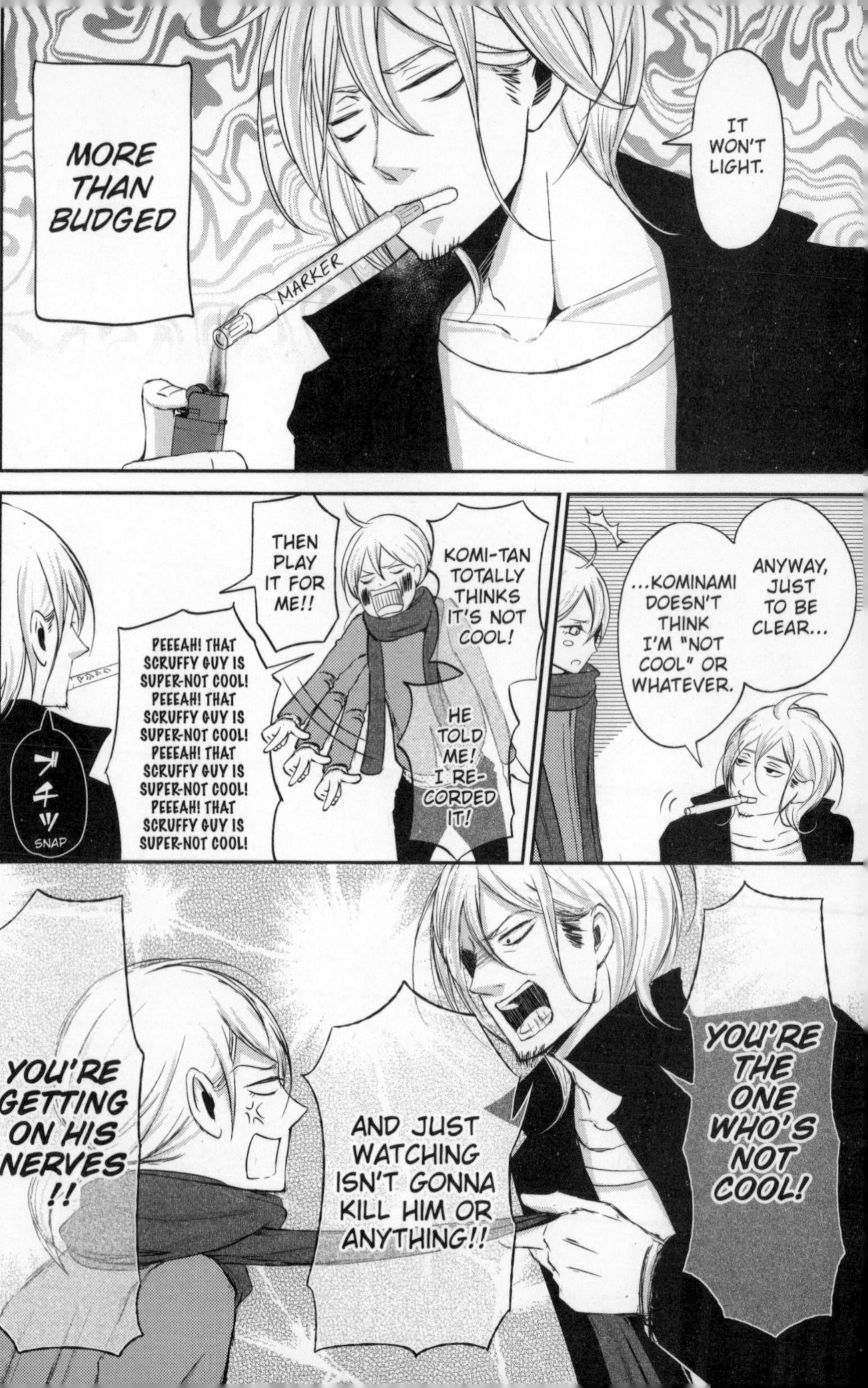
IT WON'T LIGHT.
MORE THAN BUDGED
MARKER
ANYWAY, JUST TO BE CLEAR...
...KOMINAMI DOESN'T THINK I'M "NOT COOL" OR WHATEVER.
KOMI-TAN TOTALLY THINKS IT'S NOT COOL!
HE TOLD ME! I RE-CORDED IT!
THEN PLAY IT FOR ME!!
PEEEAH! THAT SCRUFFY GUY IS SUPER-NOT COOL! PEEEAH! THAT SCRUFFY GUY IS SUPER-NOT COOL! PEEEAH! THAT SCRUFFY GUY IS SUPER-NOT COOL! PEEEAH! THAT SCRUFFY GUY IS SUPER-NOT COOL!
ブチッ
SNAP
YOU'RE THE ONE WHO'S NOT COOL!
AND JUST WATCHING ISN'T GONNA KILL HIM OR ANYTHING!!
YOU'RE GETTING ON HIS NERVES!!

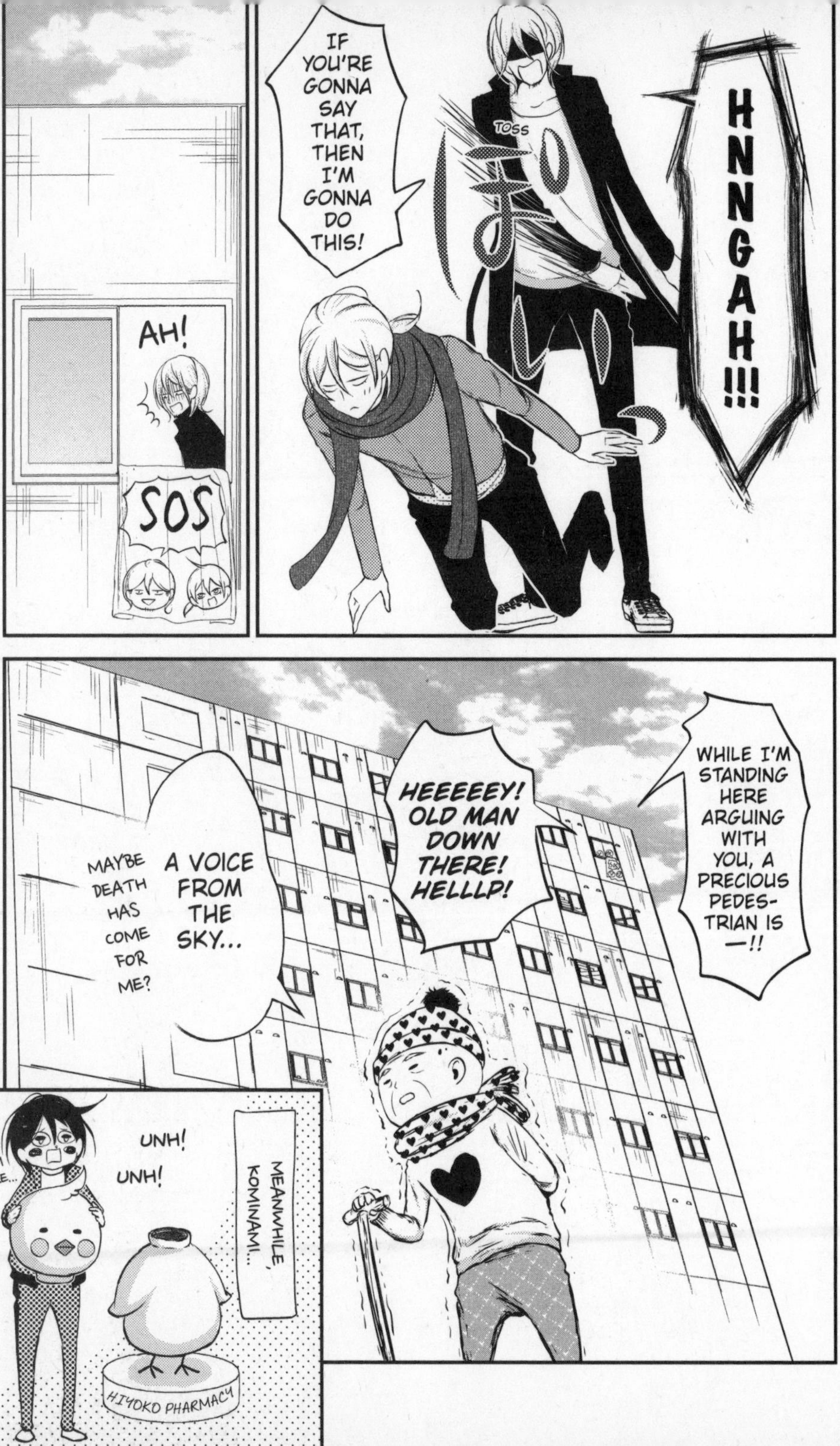
HNNGAH!!!
TOSS
IF YOU'RE GONNA SAY THAT, THEN I'M GONNA DO THIS!
AH!
SOS
WHILE I'M STANDING HERE ARGUING WITH YOU, A PRECIOUS PEDESTRIAN IS—!!
HEEEEEY! OLD MAN DOWN THERE! HELLLP!
A VOICE FROM THE SKY...
MAYBE DEATH HAS COME FOR ME?
MEANWHILE, KOMINAMI...
UNH!
UNH!
I CAN'T FIND HIM ANYWHERE...
HIYOKO PHARMACY

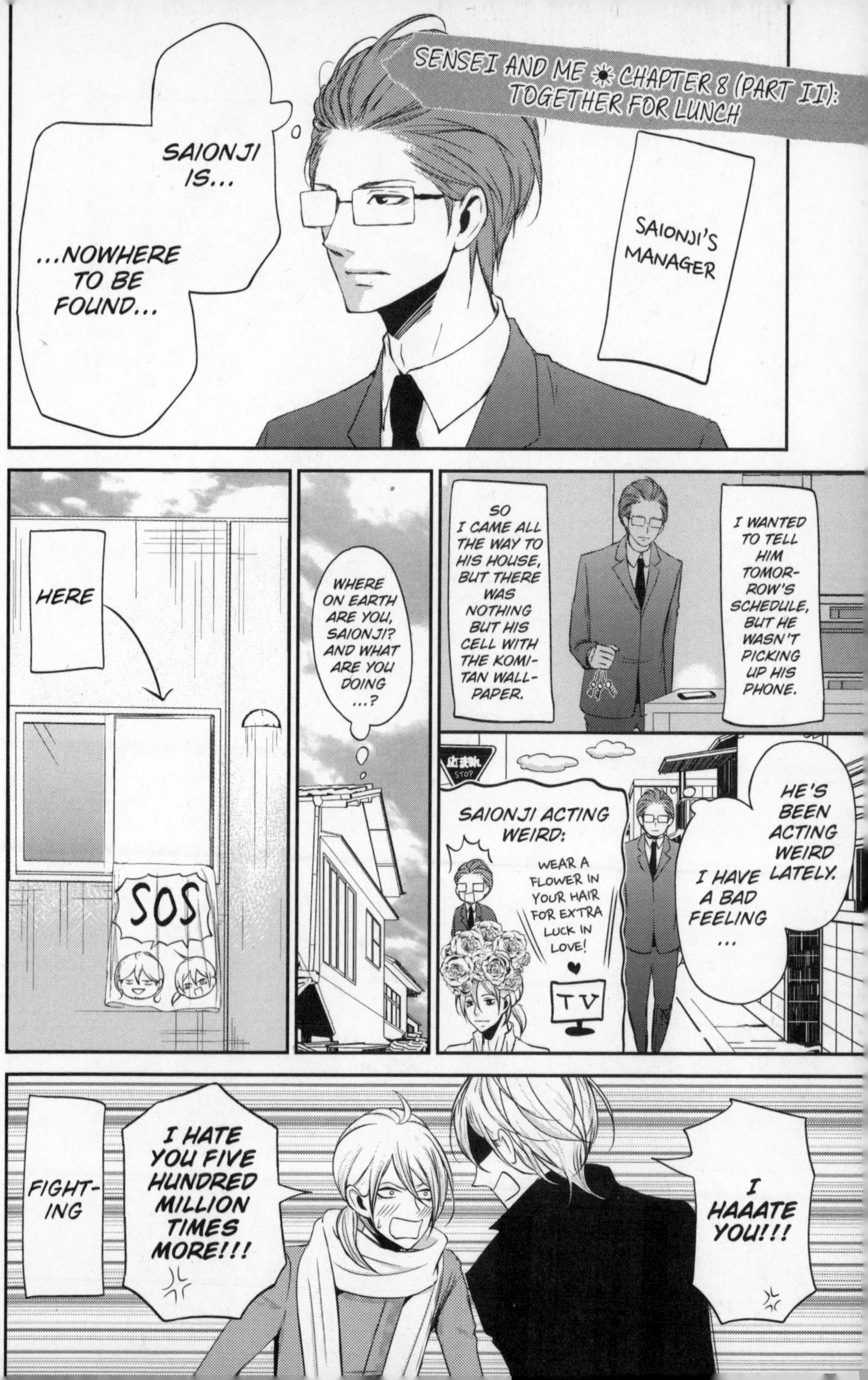
SENSEI AND ME ☀ CHAPTER 8 (PART II): TOGETHER FOR LUNCH
SAIONJI'S MANAGER
SAIONJI IS...
...NOWHERE TO BE FOUND...
I WANTED TO TELL HIM TOMORROW'S SCHEDULE, BUT HE WASN'T PICKING UP HIS PHONE.
SO I CAME ALL THE WAY TO HIS HOUSE, BUT THERE WAS NOTHING BUT HIS CELL WITH THE KOMITAN WALLPAPER.
HE'S BEEN ACTING WEIRD LATELY.
I HAVE A BAD FEELING...
SAIONJI ACTING WEIRD:
WEAR A FLOWER IN YOUR HAIR FOR EXTRA LUCK IN LOVE!
TV
STOP
WHERE ON EARTH ARE YOU, SAIONJI? AND WHAT ARE YOU DOING...?
HERE
SOS
I HAAATE YOU!!!
I HATE YOU FIVE HUNDRED MILLION TIMES MORE!!!
FIGHTING

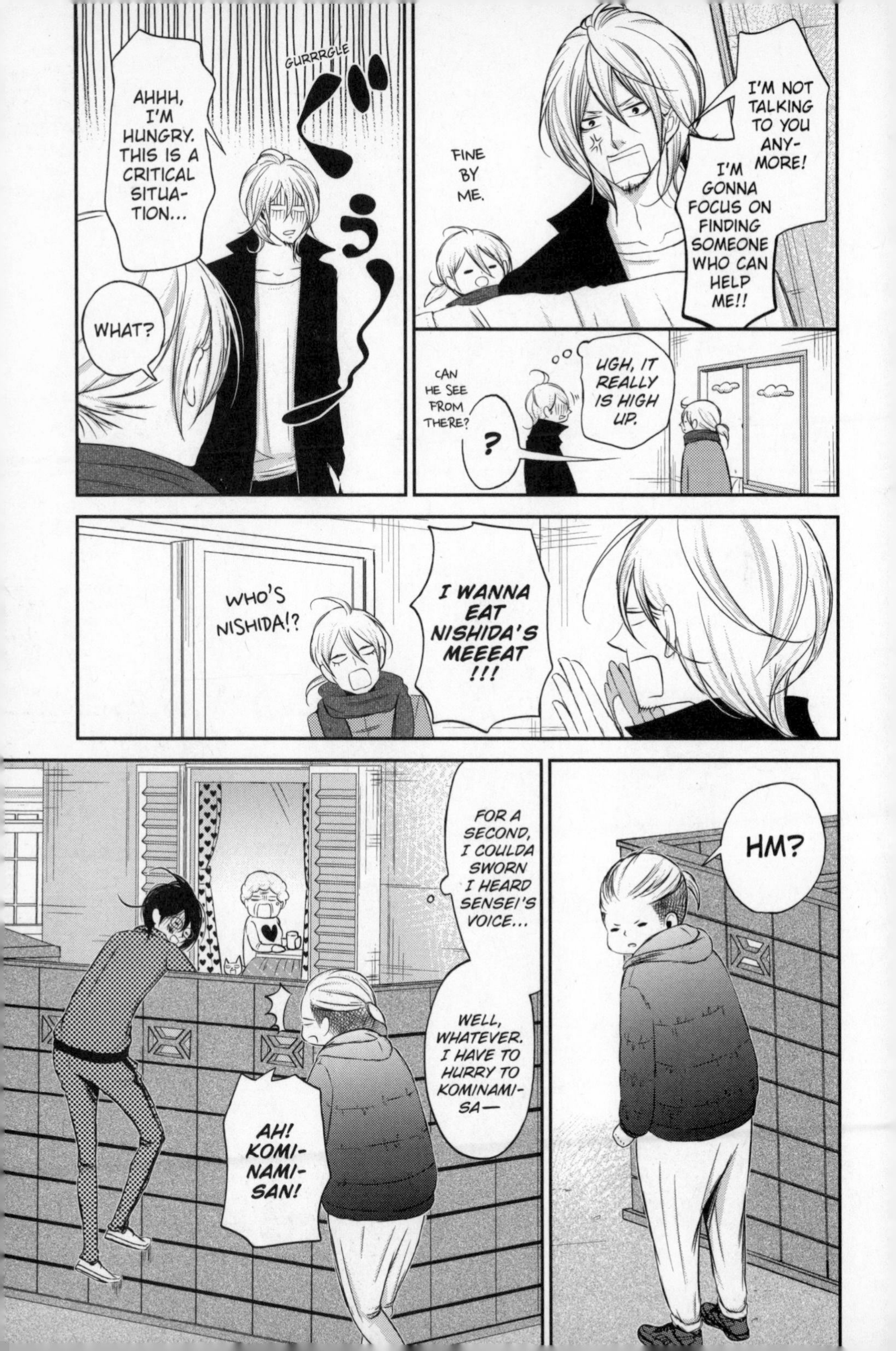
I'M NOT TALKING TO YOU ANYMORE!
I'M GONNA FOCUS ON FINDING SOMEONE WHO CAN HELP ME!!
FINE BY ME.
UGH, IT REALLY IS HIGH UP.
?
CAN HE SEE FROM THERE?
AHHH, I'M HUNGRY. THIS IS A CRITICAL SITUATION...
GURRRGLE
WHAT?
I WANNA EAT NISHIDA'S MEEEAT!!!
WHO'S NISHIDA!?
HM?
FOR A SECOND, I COULDA SWORN I HEARD SENSEI'S VOICE...
WELL, WHATEVER. I HAVE TO HURRY TO KOMINAMI-SA—
AH! KOMINAMI-SAN!

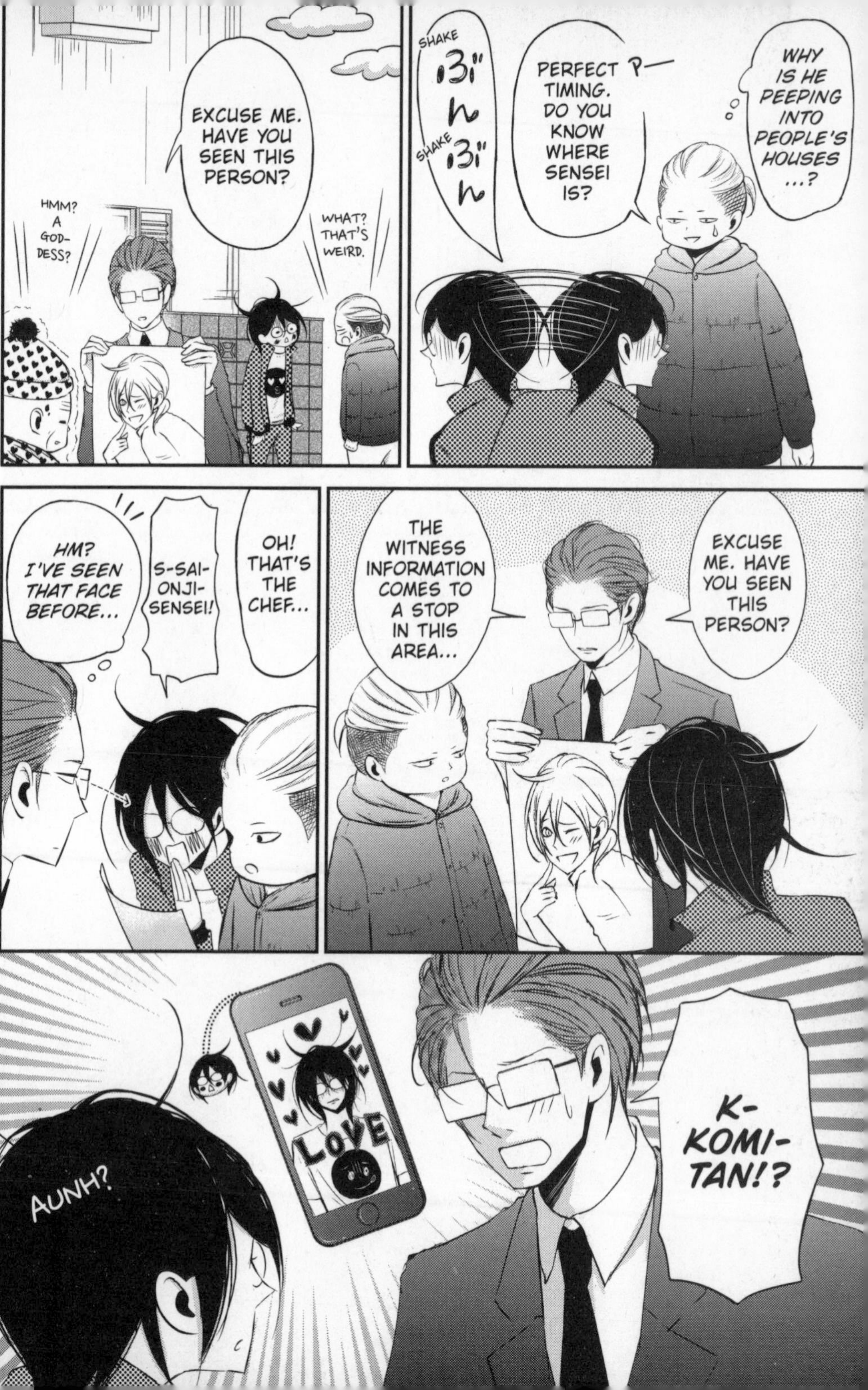
WHY IS HE PEEPING INTO PEOPLE'S HOUSES ...?
PERFECT TIMING. DO YOU KNOW WHERE SENSEI IS?
SHAKE
SHAKE
EXCUSE ME. HAVE YOU SEEN THIS PERSON?
WHAT? THAT'S WEIRD.
HMM? A GOD-DESS?
EXCUSE ME. HAVE YOU SEEN THIS PERSON?
THE WITNESS INFORMATION COMES TO A STOP IN THIS AREA...
OH! THAT'S THE CHEF...
S-SAI-ONJI-SENSEI!
HM? I'VE SEEN THAT FACE BEFORE...
K-KOMI-TAN!?
LOVE
AUNH?

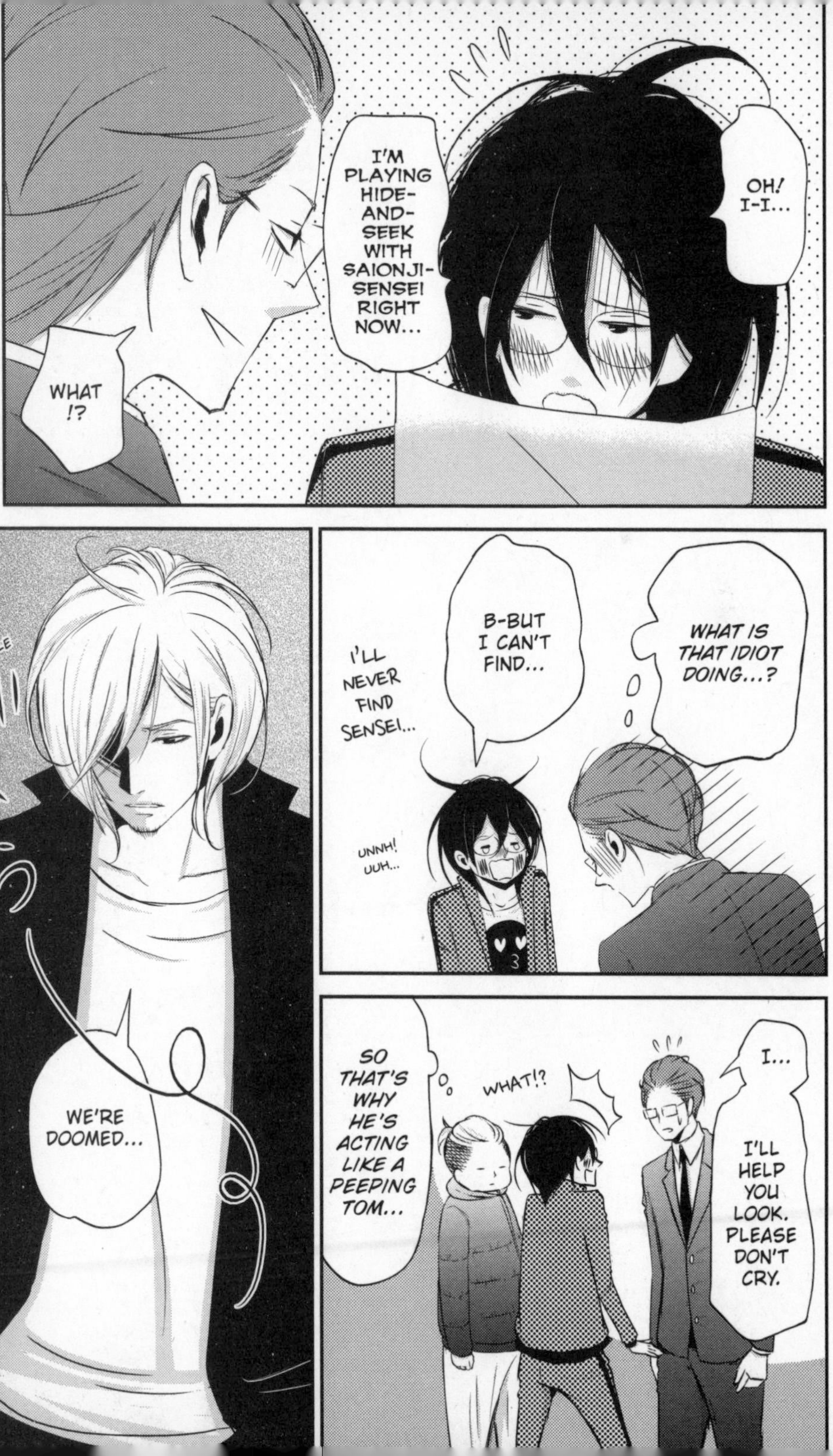

OH! I-I...
I'M PLAYING HIDE-AND-SEEK WITH SAIONJI-SENSEI RIGHT NOW...
WHAT!?
WHAT IS THAT IDIOT DOING...?
B-BUT I CAN'T FIND...
I'LL NEVER FIND SENSEI...
UNNH! UUH...
I... I'LL HELP YOU LOOK. PLEASE DON'T CRY.
WHAT!?
SO THAT'S WHY HE'S ACTING LIKE A PEEPING TOM...
GURGLE
WE'RE DOOMED...

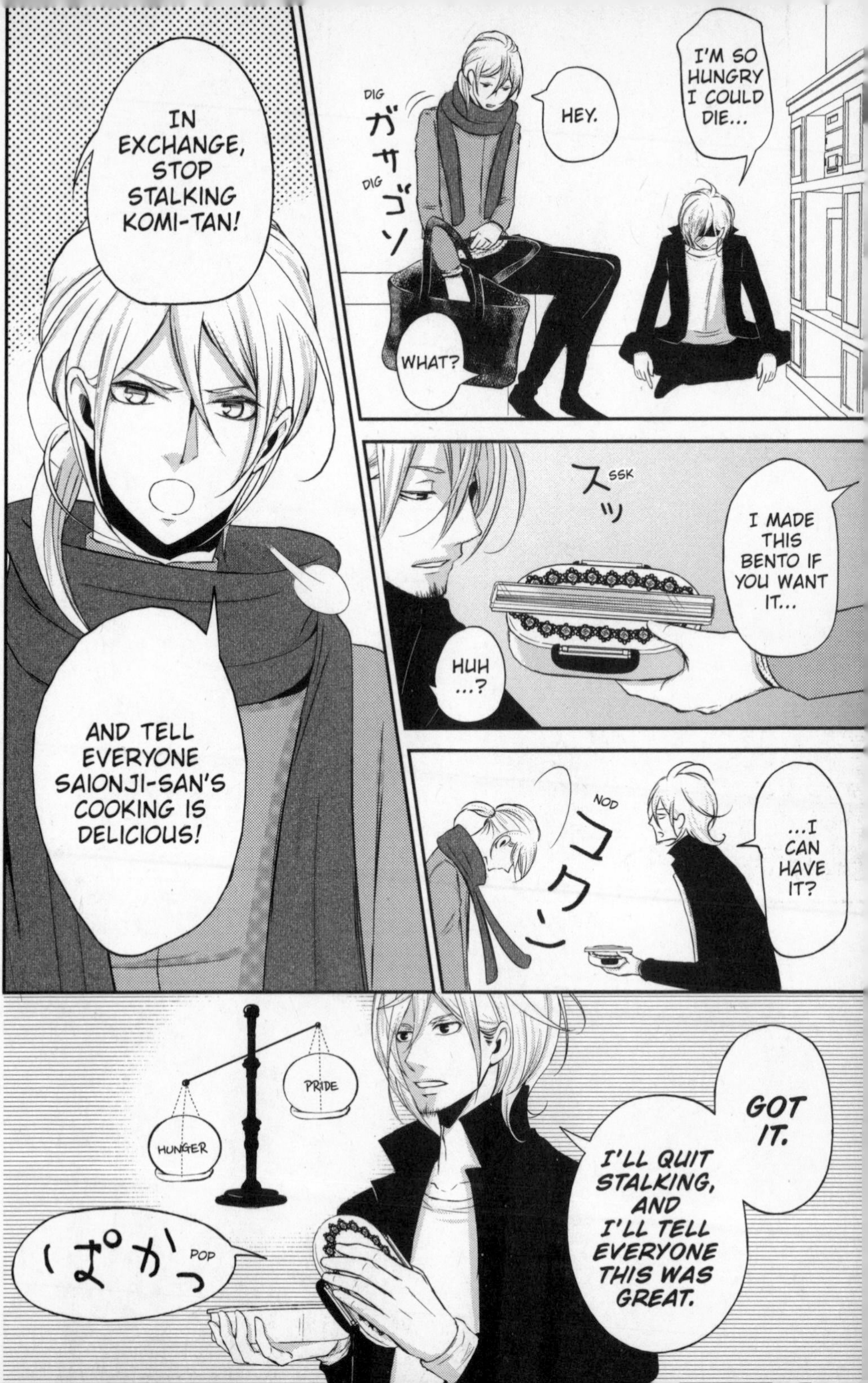
I'M SO HUNGRY I COULD DIE...
HEY.
ガサゴソ DIG DIG
WHAT?
I MADE THIS BENTO IF YOU WANT IT...
スッ SSK
HUH...?
...I CAN HAVE IT?
コクン NOD
IN EXCHANGE, STOP STALKING KOMI-TAN!
AND TELL EVERYONE SAIONJI-SAN'S COOKING IS DELICIOUS!
GOT IT.
I'LL QUIT STALKING, AND I'LL TELL EVERYONE THIS WAS GREAT.
PRIDE
HUNGER
ぱかっ POP

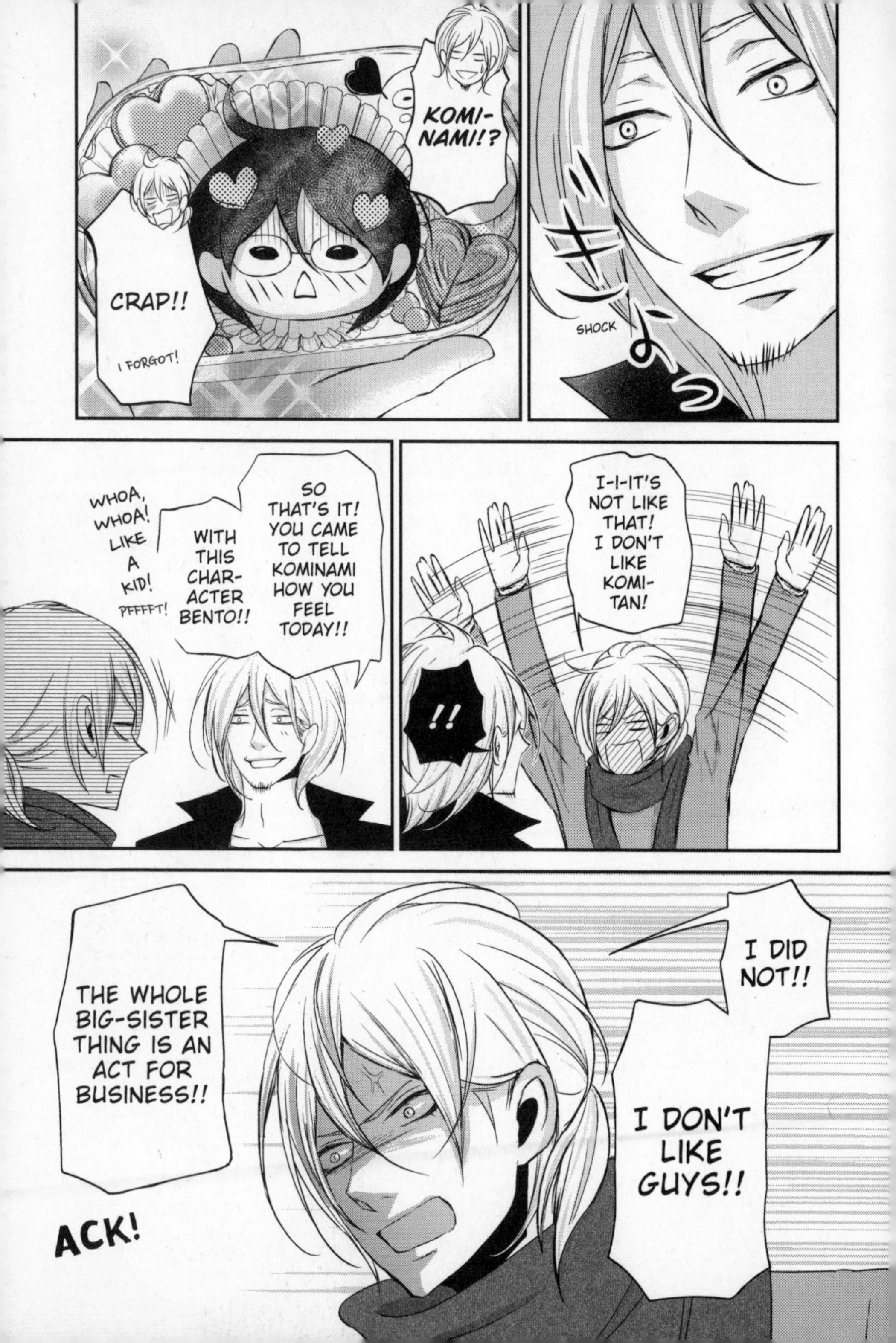
SHOCK
KOMINAMI!?
CRAP!!
I FORGOT!
I-I-IT'S NOT LIKE THAT! I DON'T LIKE KOMI-TAN!
!!
SO THAT'S IT! YOU CAME TO TELL KOMINAMI HOW YOU FEEL TODAY!!
WITH THIS CHARACTER BENTO!!
WHOA, WHOA! LIKE A KID!
PFFFFT!
I DID NOT!!
I DON'T LIKE GUYS!!
THE WHOLE BIG-SISTER THING IS AN ACT FOR BUSINESS!!
ACK!

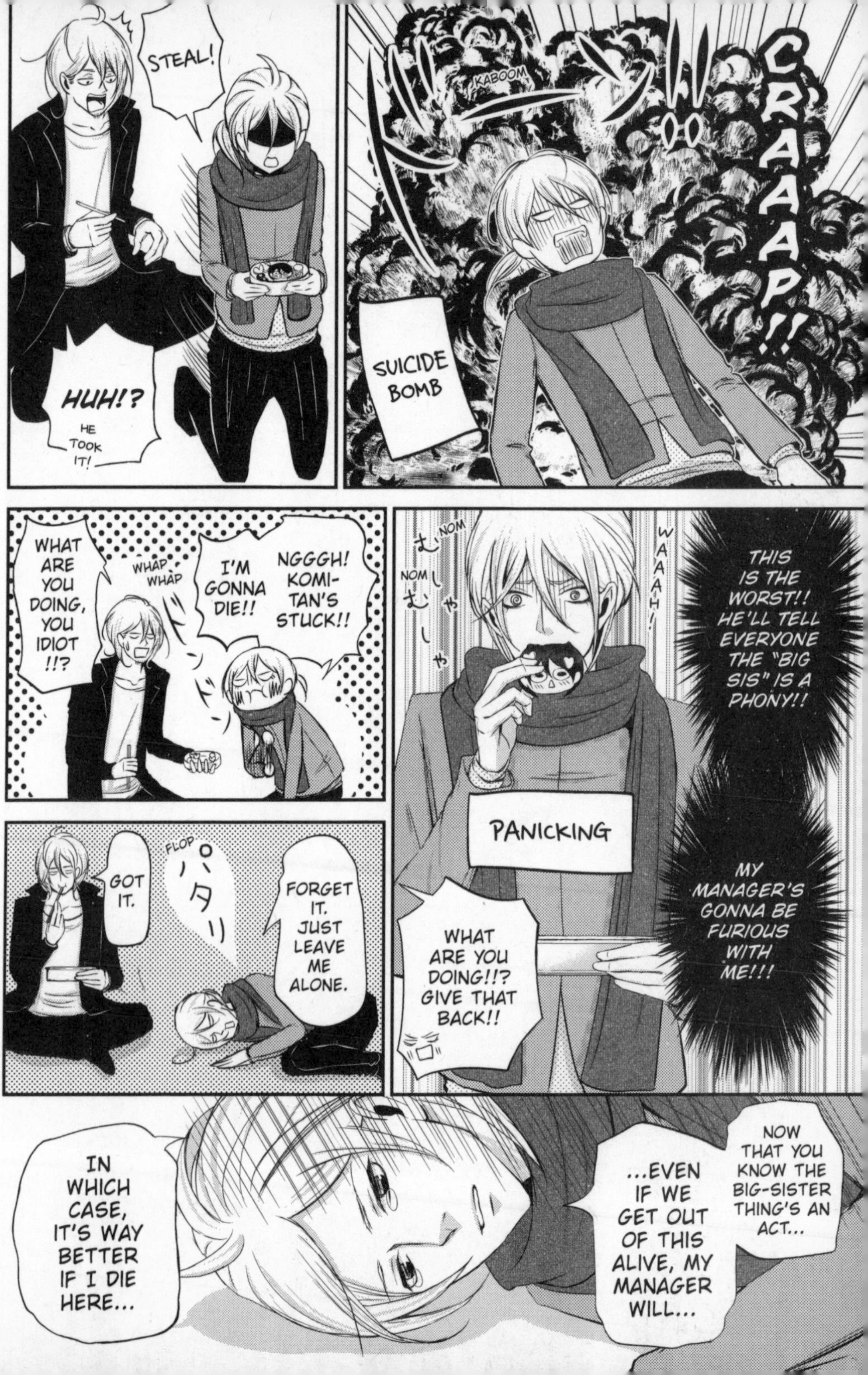
KABOOM
CRAAAP!!
SUICIDE BOMB
STEAL!
HUH!?
HE TOOK IT!
THIS IS THE WORST!! HE'LL TELL EVERYONE THE "BIG SIS" IS A PHONY!!
WAAAH!
NOM NOM
PANICKING
MY MANAGER'S GONNA BE FURIOUS WITH ME!!!
WHAT ARE YOU DOING!!? GIVE THAT BACK!!
NGGGH! KOMI-TAN'S STUCK!!
I'M GONNA DIE!!
WHAP WHAP
WHAT ARE YOU DOING, YOU IDIOT!!?
FORGET IT. JUST LEAVE ME ALONE.
FLOP
GOT IT.
NOW THAT YOU KNOW THE BIG-SISTER THING'S AN ACT...
...EVEN IF WE GET OUT OF THIS ALIVE, MY MANAGER WILL...
IN WHICH CASE, IT'S WAY BETTER IF I DIE HERE...

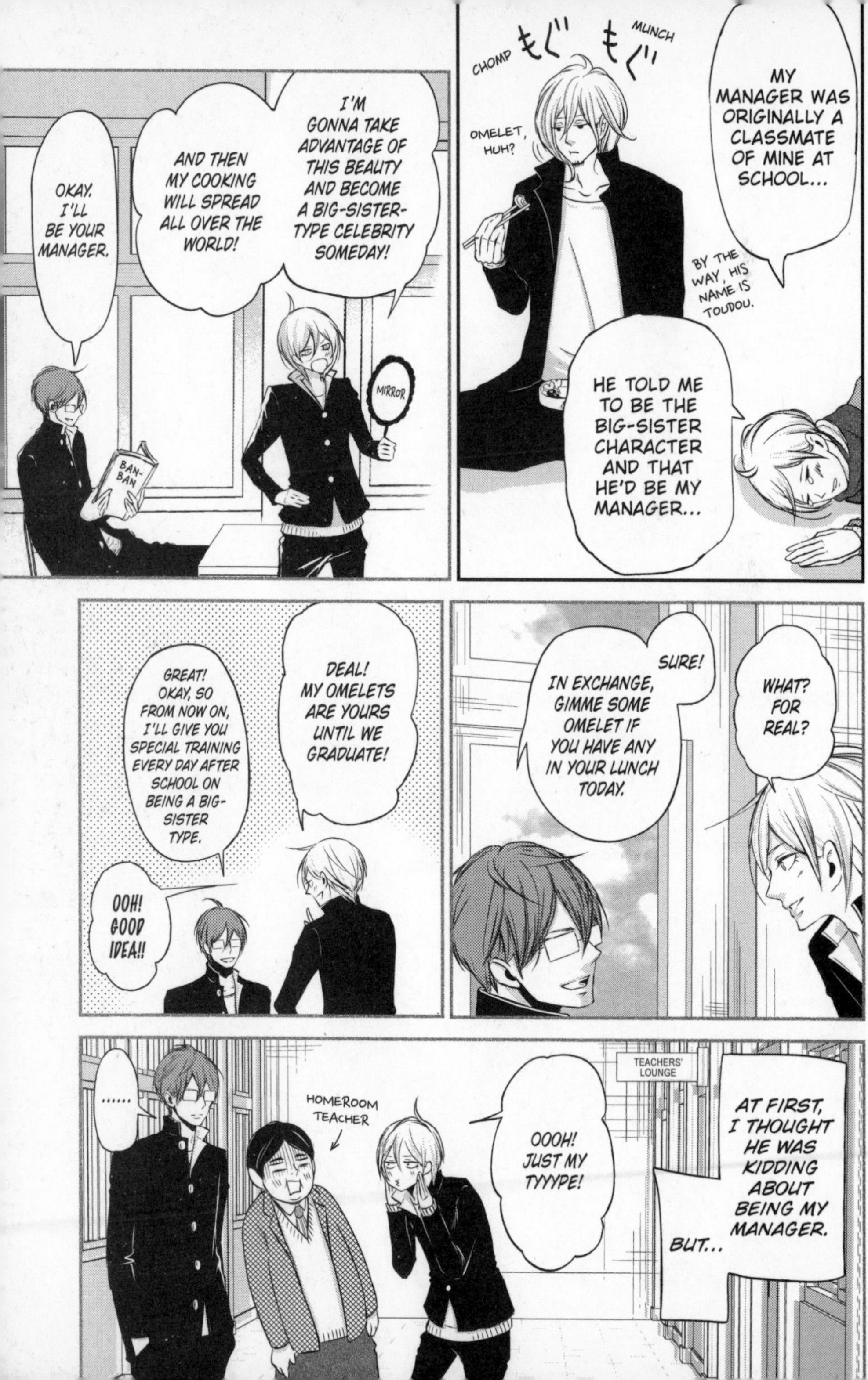
MY MANAGER WAS ORIGINALLY A CLASSMATE OF MINE AT SCHOOL...
MUNCH
もぐ もぐ
CHOMP
BY THE WAY, HIS NAME IS TOUDOU.
OMELET, HUH?
HE TOLD ME TO BE THE BIG-SISTER CHARACTER AND THAT HE'D BE MY MANAGER...
I'M GONNA TAKE ADVANTAGE OF THIS BEAUTY AND BECOME A BIG-SISTER-TYPE CELEBRITY SOMEDAY!
AND THEN MY COOKING WILL SPREAD ALL OVER THE WORLD!
OKAY. I'LL BE YOUR MANAGER.
MIRROR
BAN-BAN
WHAT? FOR REAL?
SURE! IN EXCHANGE, GIMME SOME OMELET IF YOU HAVE ANY IN YOUR LUNCH TODAY.
DEAL! MY OMELETS ARE YOURS UNTIL WE GRADUATE!
GREAT! OKAY, SO FROM NOW ON, I'LL GIVE YOU SPECIAL TRAINING EVERY DAY AFTER SCHOOL ON BEING A BIG-SISTER TYPE.
OOH! GOOD IDEA!!
AT FIRST, I THOUGHT HE WAS KIDDING ABOUT BEING MY MANAGER.
BUT...
TEACHERS' LOUNGE
OOOH! JUST MY TYYYPE!
HOMEROOM TEACHER
......

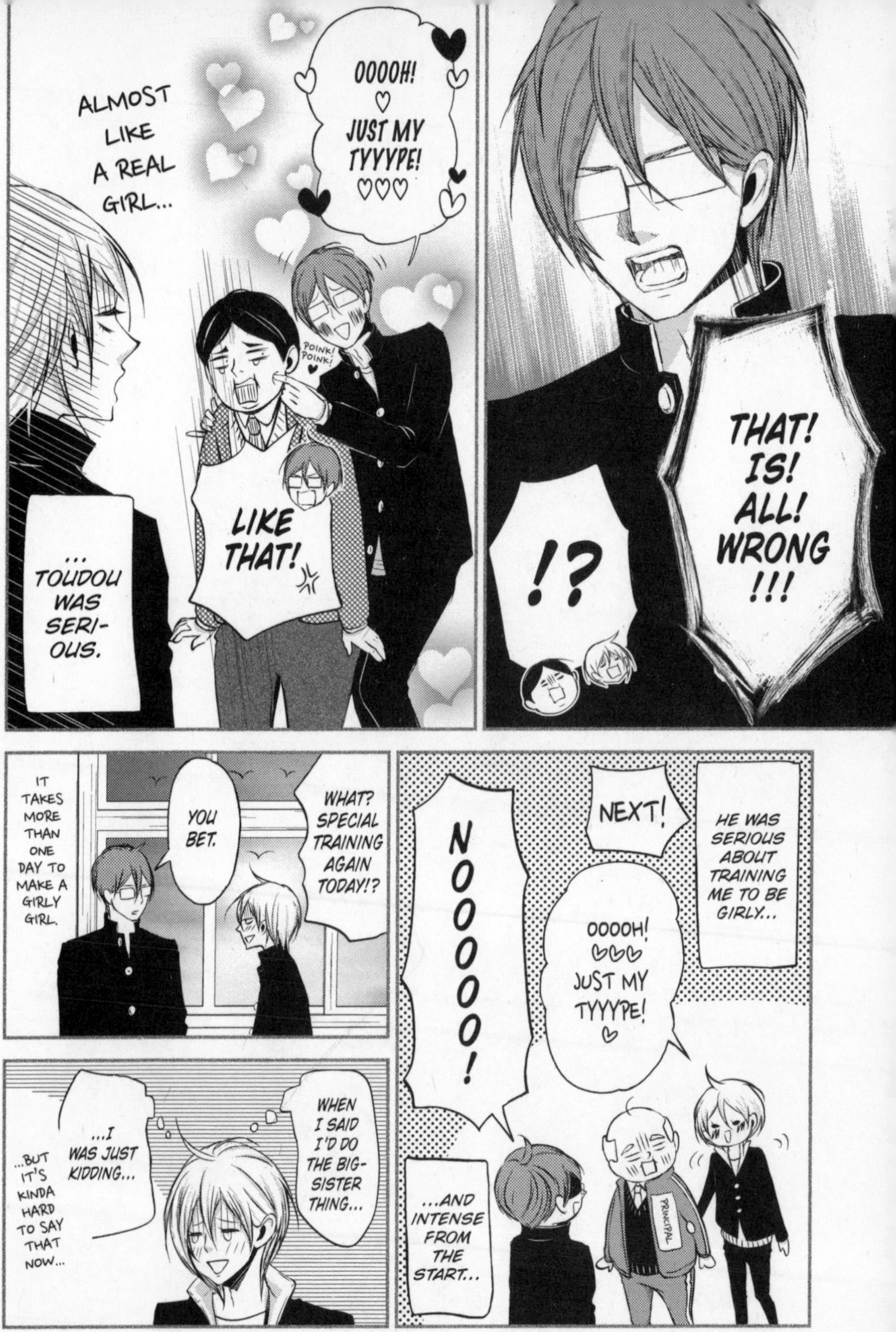
ALMOST LIKE A REAL GIRL...
OOOOH! ♡ JUST MY TYYYPE! ♡♡♡
POINK! POINK! ♥
LIKE THAT!
...TOUDOU WAS SERI-OUS.
THAT! IS! ALL! WRONG!!!
!?
WHAT? SPECIAL TRAINING AGAIN TODAY!?
YOU BET.
IT TAKES MORE THAN ONE DAY TO MAKE A GIRLY GIRL.
WHEN I SAID I'D DO THE BIG-SISTER THING...
...I WAS JUST KIDDING...
...BUT IT'S KINDA HARD TO SAY THAT NOW...
HE WAS SERIOUS ABOUT TRAINING ME TO BE GIRLY...
NEXT!
OOOOH! ♡♡♡ JUST MY TYYYPE! ♡
NOOOOOO!
...AND INTENSE FROM THE START...
PRINCIPAL

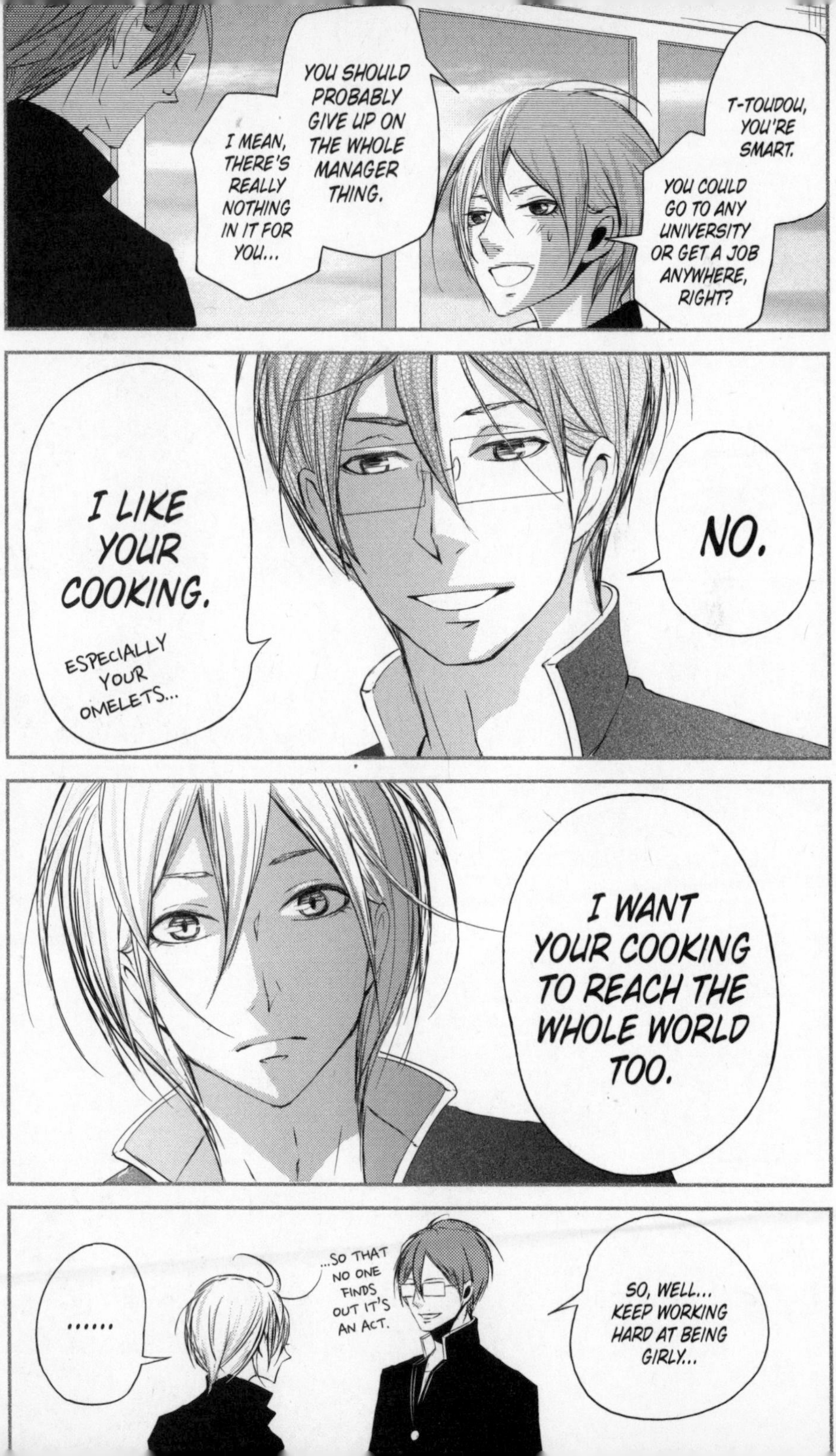
T-TOUDOU, YOU'RE SMART.
YOU COULD GO TO ANY UNIVERSITY OR GET A JOB ANYWHERE, RIGHT?
YOU SHOULD PROBABLY GIVE UP ON THE WHOLE MANAGER THING.
I MEAN, THERE'S REALLY NOTHING IN IT FOR YOU...
NO.
I LIKE YOUR COOKING.
ESPECIALLY YOUR OMELETS...
I WANT YOUR COOKING TO REACH THE WHOLE WORLD TOO.
SO, WELL... KEEP WORKING HARD AT BEING GIRLY...
...SO THAT NO ONE FINDS OUT IT'S AN ACT.
......

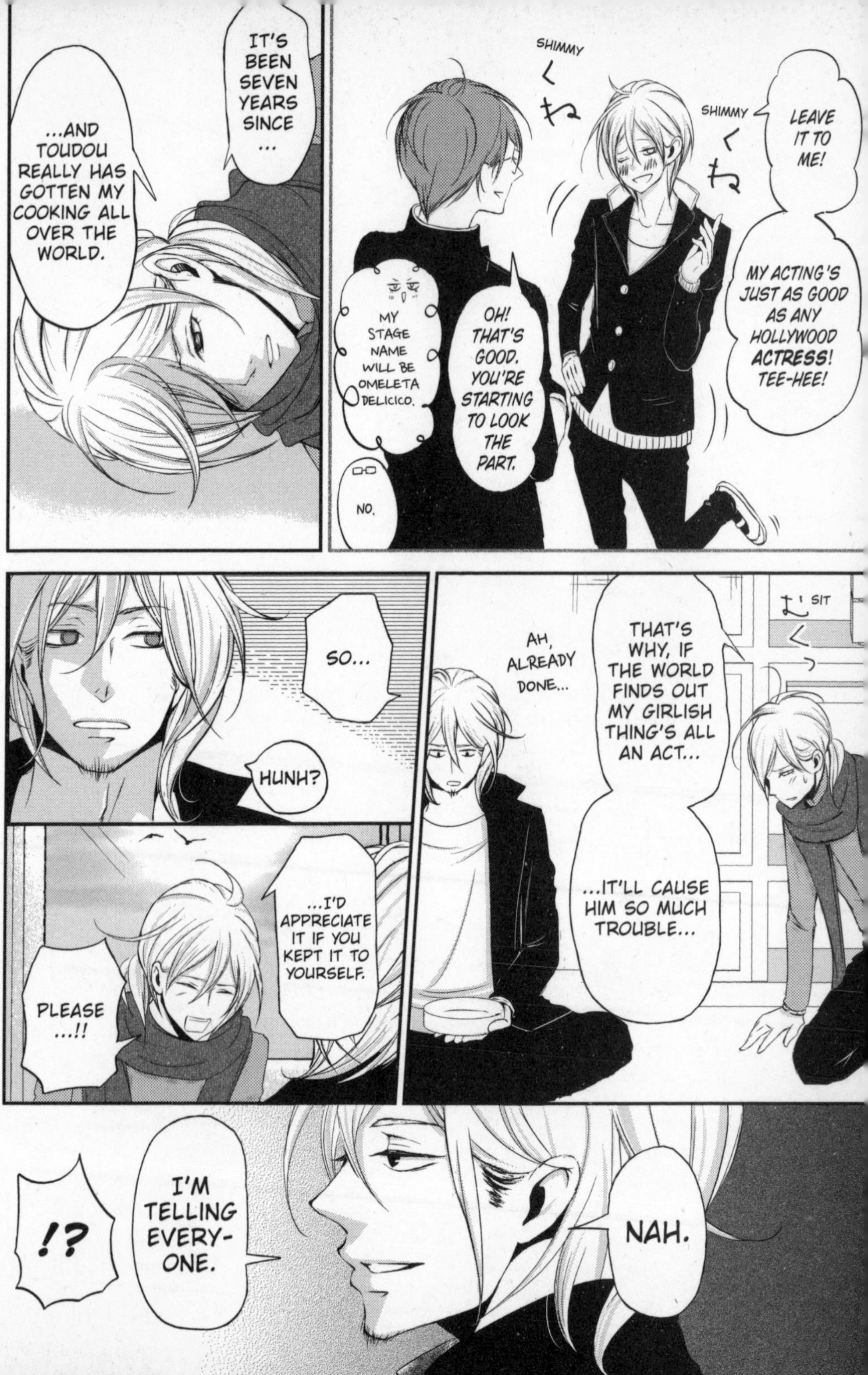
LEAVE IT TO ME!
MY ACTING'S JUST AS GOOD AS ANY HOLLYWOOD ACTRESS! TEE-HEE!
SHIMMY
SHIMMY
OH! THAT'S GOOD. YOU'RE STARTING TO LOOK THE PART.
MY STAGE NAME WILL BE OMELETA DELICICO.
NO.
IT'S BEEN SEVEN YEARS SINCE...
...AND TOUDOU REALLY HAS GOTTEN MY COOKING ALL OVER THE WORLD.
SIT
THAT'S WHY, IF THE WORLD FINDS OUT MY GIRLISH THING'S ALL AN ACT...
...IT'LL CAUSE HIM SO MUCH TROUBLE...
AH, ALREADY DONE...
SO...
HUNH?
...I'D APPRECIATE IT IF YOU KEPT IT TO YOURSELF.
PLEASE ...!!
NAH.
I'M TELLING EVERY-ONE.
!?

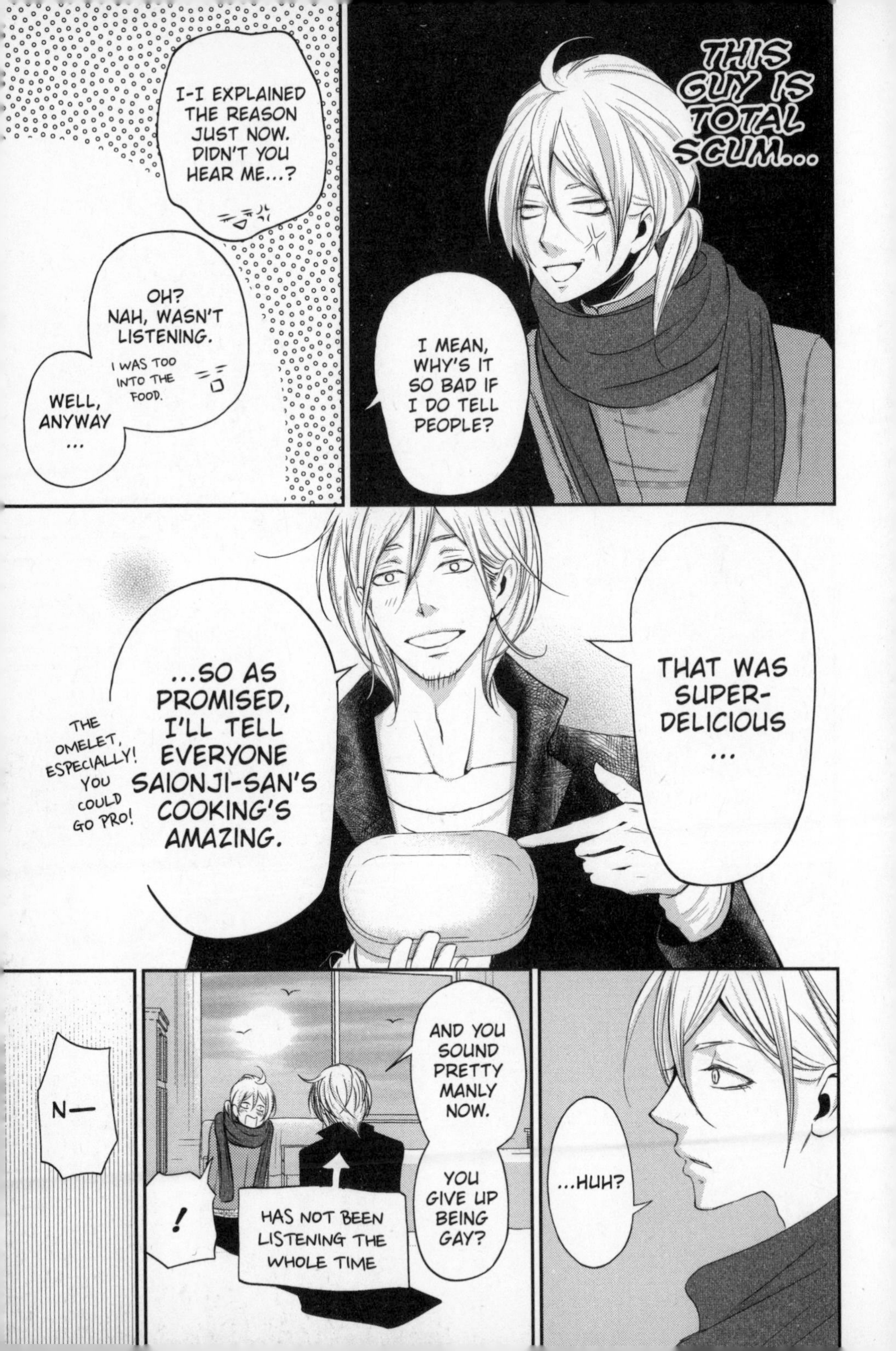
THIS GUY IS TOTAL SCUM...
I MEAN, WHY'S IT SO BAD IF I DO TELL PEOPLE?
I-I EXPLAINED THE REASON JUST NOW. DIDN'T YOU HEAR ME...?
OH? NAH, WASN'T LISTENING.
I WAS TOO INTO THE FOOD.
WELL, ANYWAY...
THAT WAS SUPER-DELICIOUS...
...SO AS PROMISED, I'LL TELL EVERYONE SAIONJI-SAN'S COOKING'S AMAZING.
THE OMELET, ESPECIALLY! YOU COULD GO PRO!
...HUH?
AND YOU SOUND PRETTY MANLY NOW.
YOU GIVE UP BEING GAY?
HAS NOT BEEN LISTENING THE WHOLE TIME
!
N—

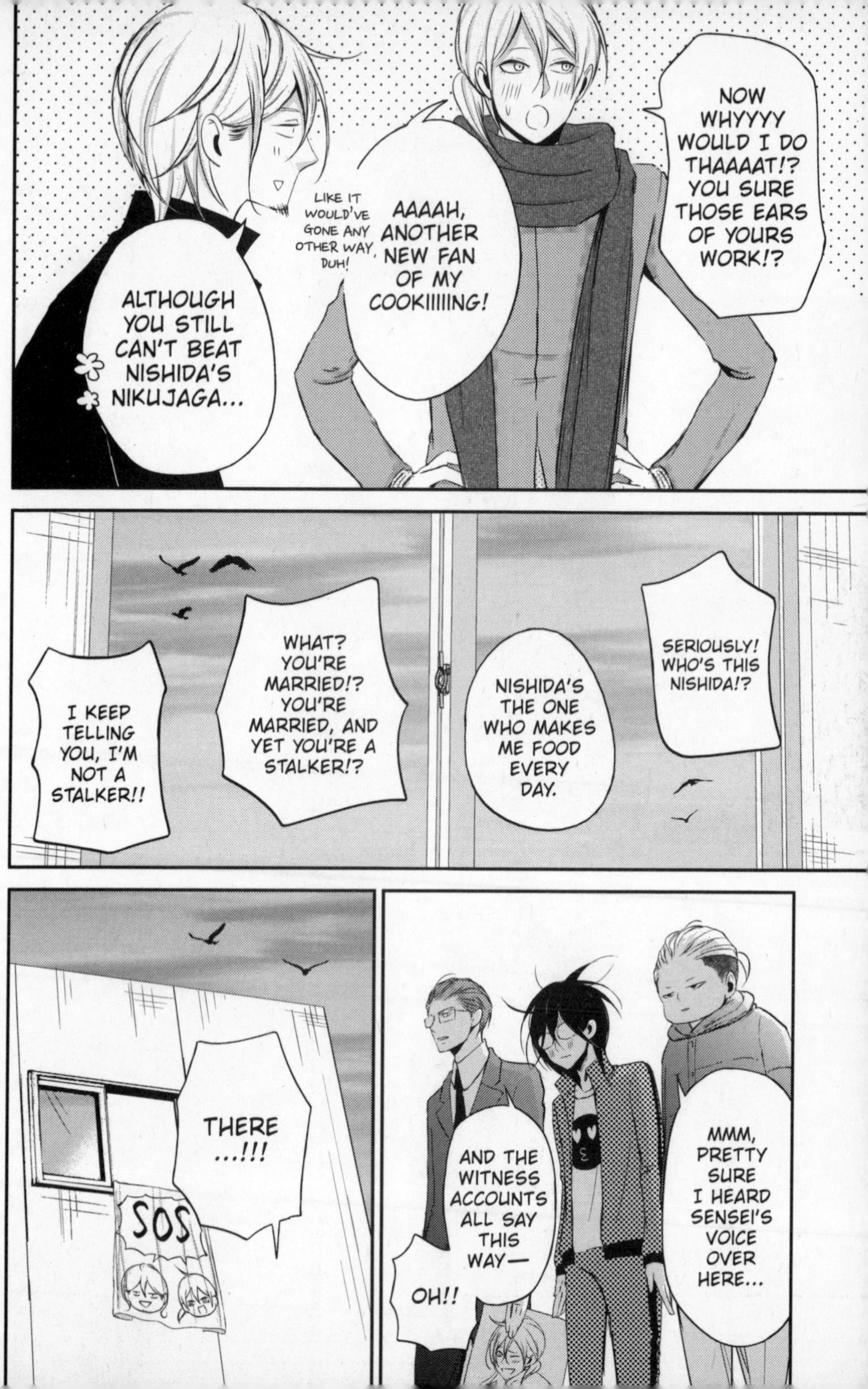
NOW WHYYYY WOULD I DO THAAAAT!? YOU SURE THOSE EARS OF YOURS WORK!?
AAAAH, ANOTHER NEW FAN OF MY COOKIIIIIING!
LIKE IT WOULD'VE GONE ANY OTHER WAY, DUH!
ALTHOUGH YOU STILL CAN'T BEAT NISHIDA'S NIKUJAGA...
SERIOUSLY! WHO'S THIS NISHIDA!?
NISHIDA'S THE ONE WHO MAKES ME FOOD EVERY DAY.
WHAT? YOU'RE MARRIED!? YOU'RE MARRIED, AND YET YOU'RE A STALKER!?
I KEEP TELLING YOU, I'M NOT A STALKER!!
MMM, PRETTY SURE I HEARD SENSEI'S VOICE OVER HERE...
AND THE WITNESS ACCOUNTS ALL SAY THIS WAY—
OH!!
THERE...!!!
SOS

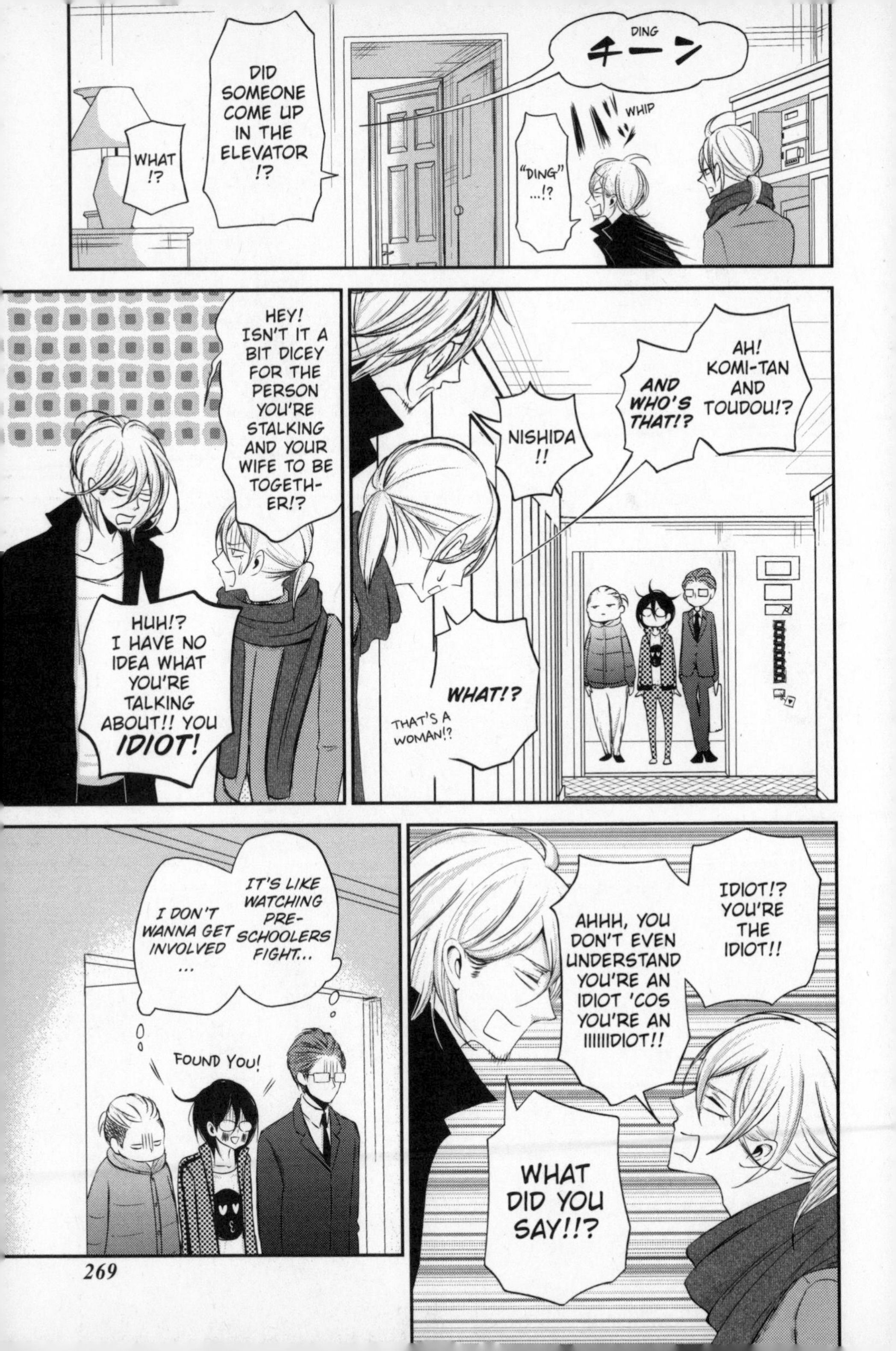
DING
チーン
WHIP
"DING" ...!?
DID SOMEONE COME UP IN THE ELEVATOR!?
WHAT!?
AH! KOMI-TAN AND TOUDOU!?
AND WHO'S THAT!?
NISHIDA!!
WHAT!?
THAT'S A WOMAN!?
HEY! ISN'T IT A BIT DICEY FOR THE PERSON YOU'RE STALKING AND YOUR WIFE TO BE TOGETH-ER!?
HUH!? I HAVE NO IDEA WHAT YOU'RE TALKING ABOUT!! YOU IDIOT!
IDIOT!? YOU'RE THE IDIOT!!
AHHH, YOU DON'T EVEN UNDERSTAND YOU'RE AN IDIOT 'COS YOU'RE AN IIIIIIDIOT!!
WHAT DID YOU SAY!!?
IT'S LIKE WATCHING PRE-SCHOOLERS FIGHT...
I DON'T WANNA GET INVOLVED ...
FOUND YOU!

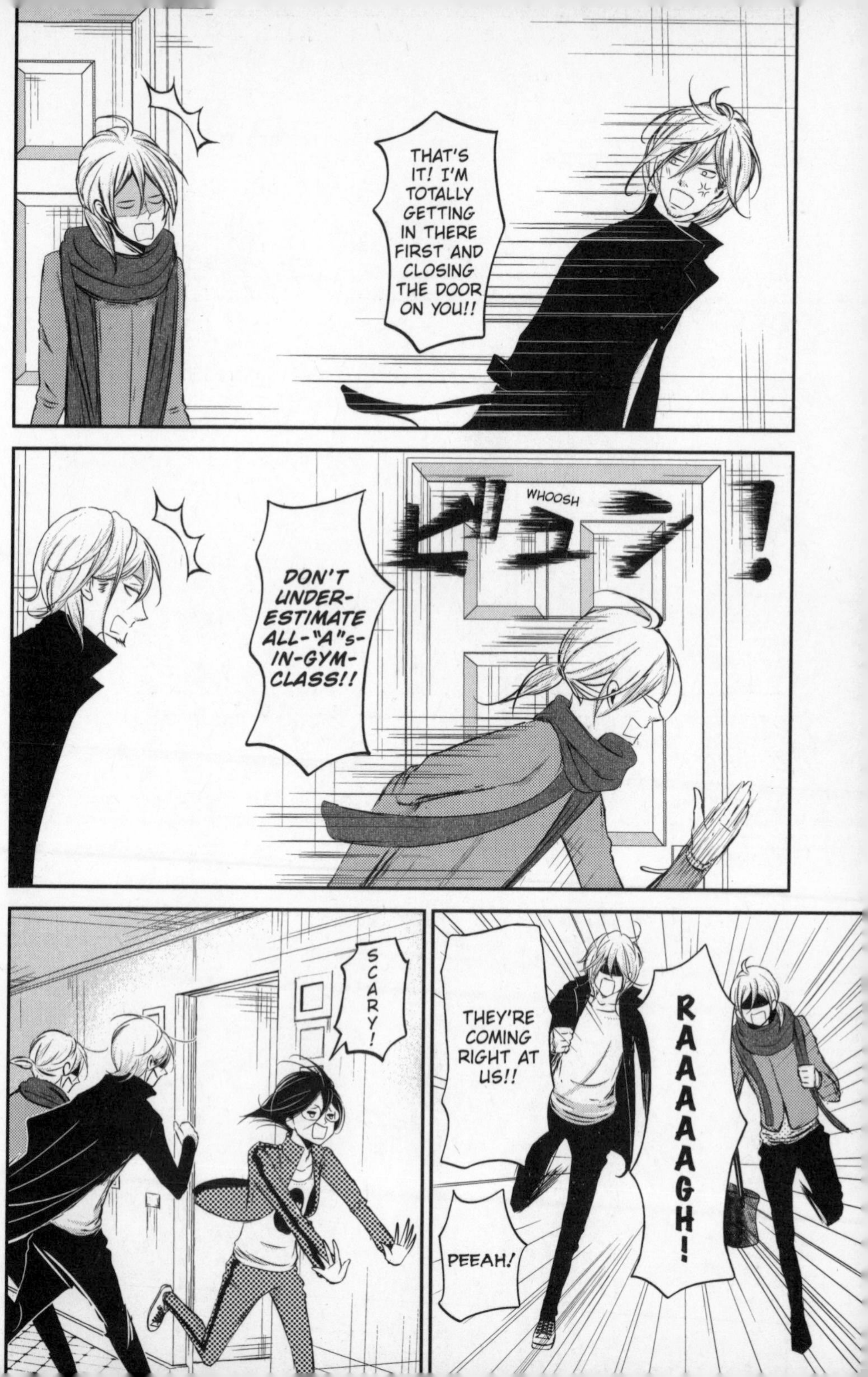
THAT'S IT! I'M TOTALLY GETTING IN THERE FIRST AND CLOSING THE DOOR ON YOU!!
WHOOSH
DON'T UNDER-ESTIMATE ALL-"A"s-IN-GYM-CLASS!!
RAAAAAGH!
THEY'RE COMING RIGHT AT US!!
PEEAH!
SCARY!

だん！ *BANG*

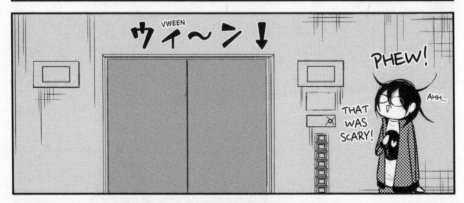

ぴしゃ！ *SHUT*

ウイ〜ン↓ *VWEEN*

PHEW!

AHH...

THAT WAS SCARY!

HUH?

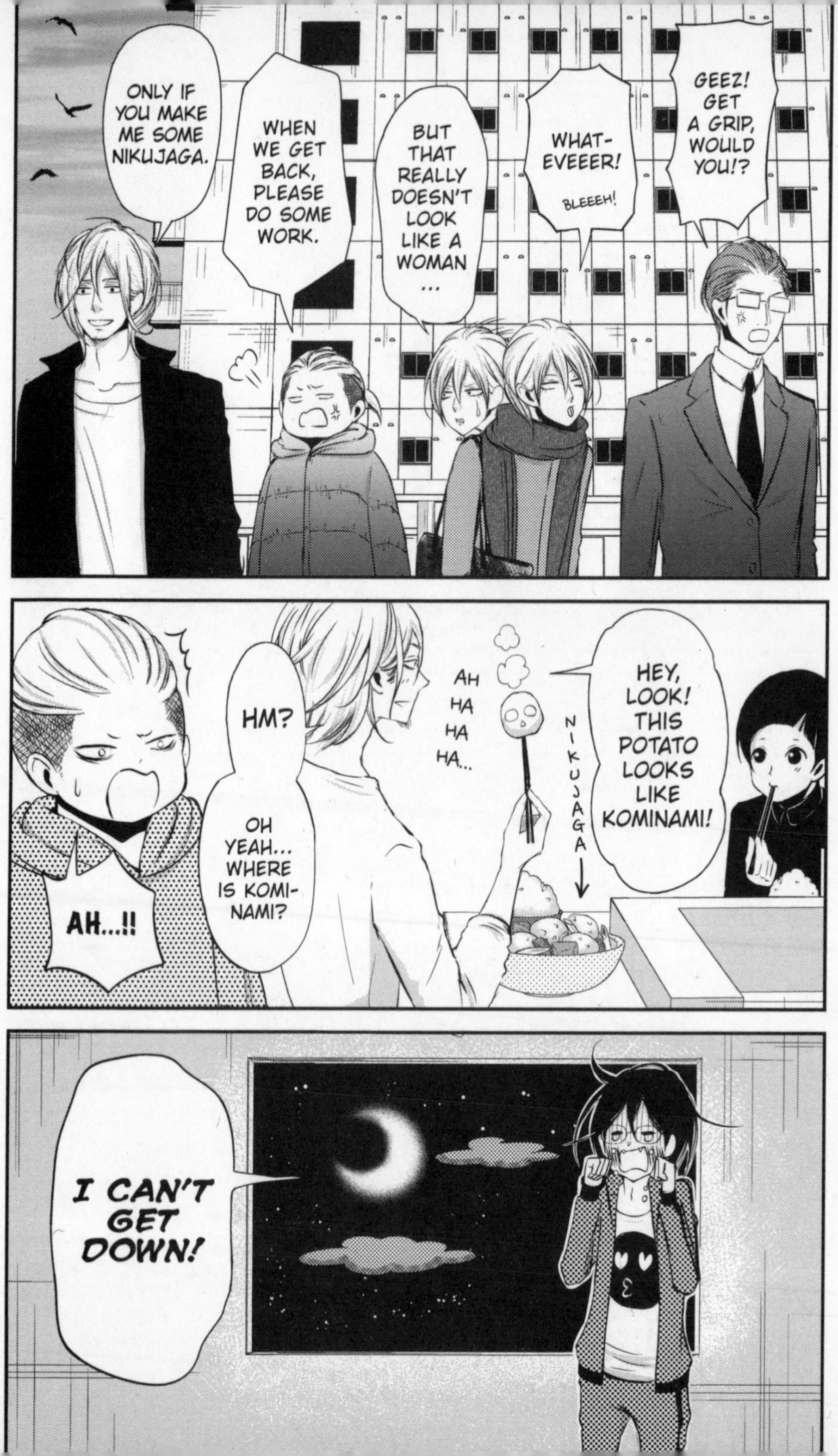
GEEZ! GET A GRIP, WOULD YOU!?
WHAT-EVEEER!
BLEEEH!
BUT THAT REALLY DOESN'T LOOK LIKE A WOMAN...
WHEN WE GET BACK, PLEASE DO SOME WORK.
ONLY IF YOU MAKE ME SOME NIKUJAGA.
HEY, LOOK! THIS POTATO LOOKS LIKE KOMINAMI!
NIKUJAGA
AH HA HA HA...
HM?
OH YEAH... WHERE IS KOMI-NAMI?
AH...!!
I CAN'T GET DOWN!

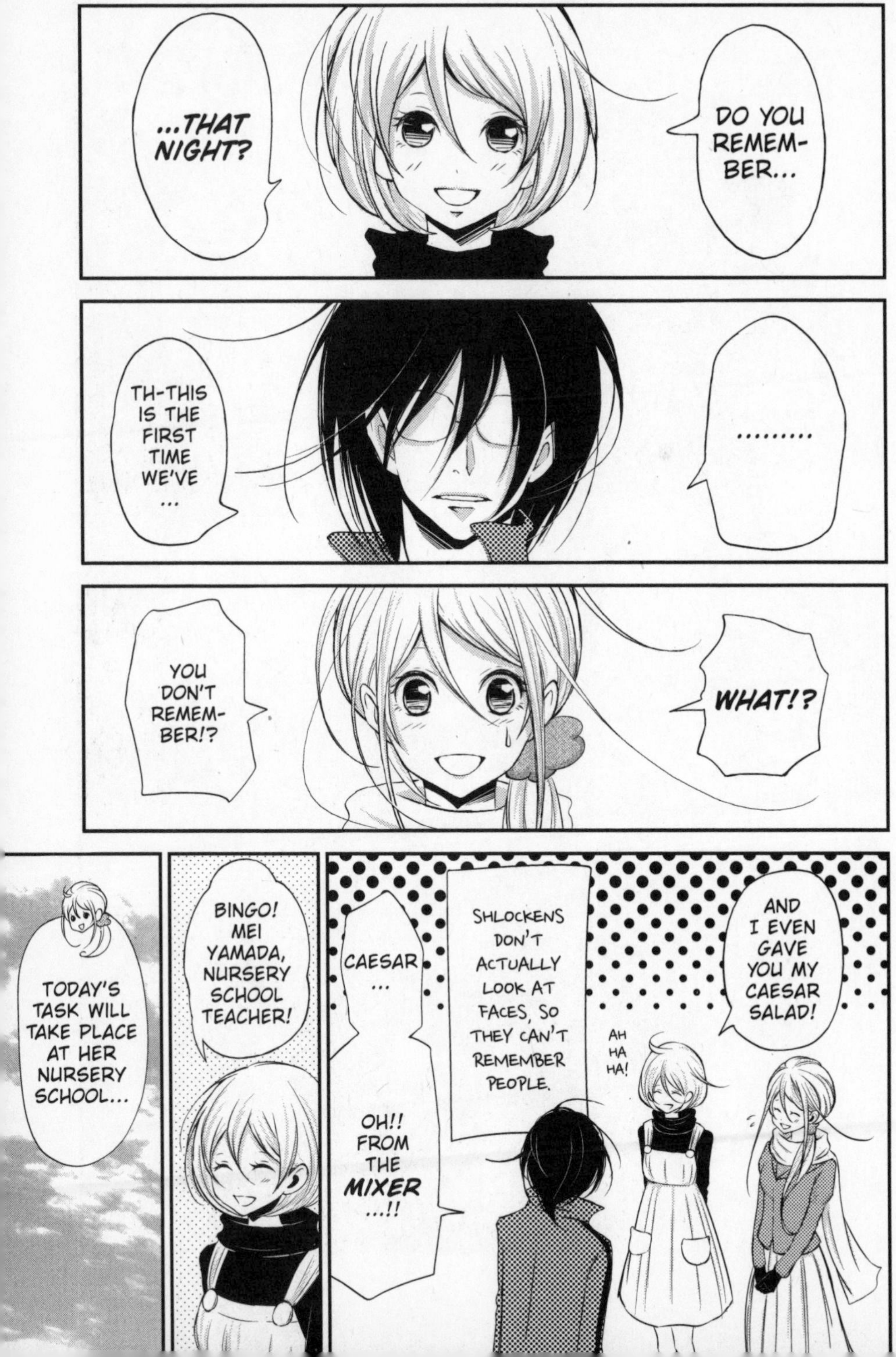
DO YOU REMEMBER-BER...
...THAT NIGHT?
....
TH-THIS IS THE FIRST TIME WE'VE ...
WHAT!?
YOU DON'T REMEMBER!?
AND I EVEN GAVE YOU MY CAESAR SALAD!
AH HA HA!
SHLOCKENS DON'T ACTUALLY LOOK AT FACES, SO THEY CAN'T REMEMBER PEOPLE.
CAESAR ...
OH!! FROM THE MIXER ...!!
BINGO! MEI YAMADA, NURSERY SCHOOL TEACHER!
TODAY'S TASK WILL TAKE PLACE AT HER NURSERY SCHOOL...

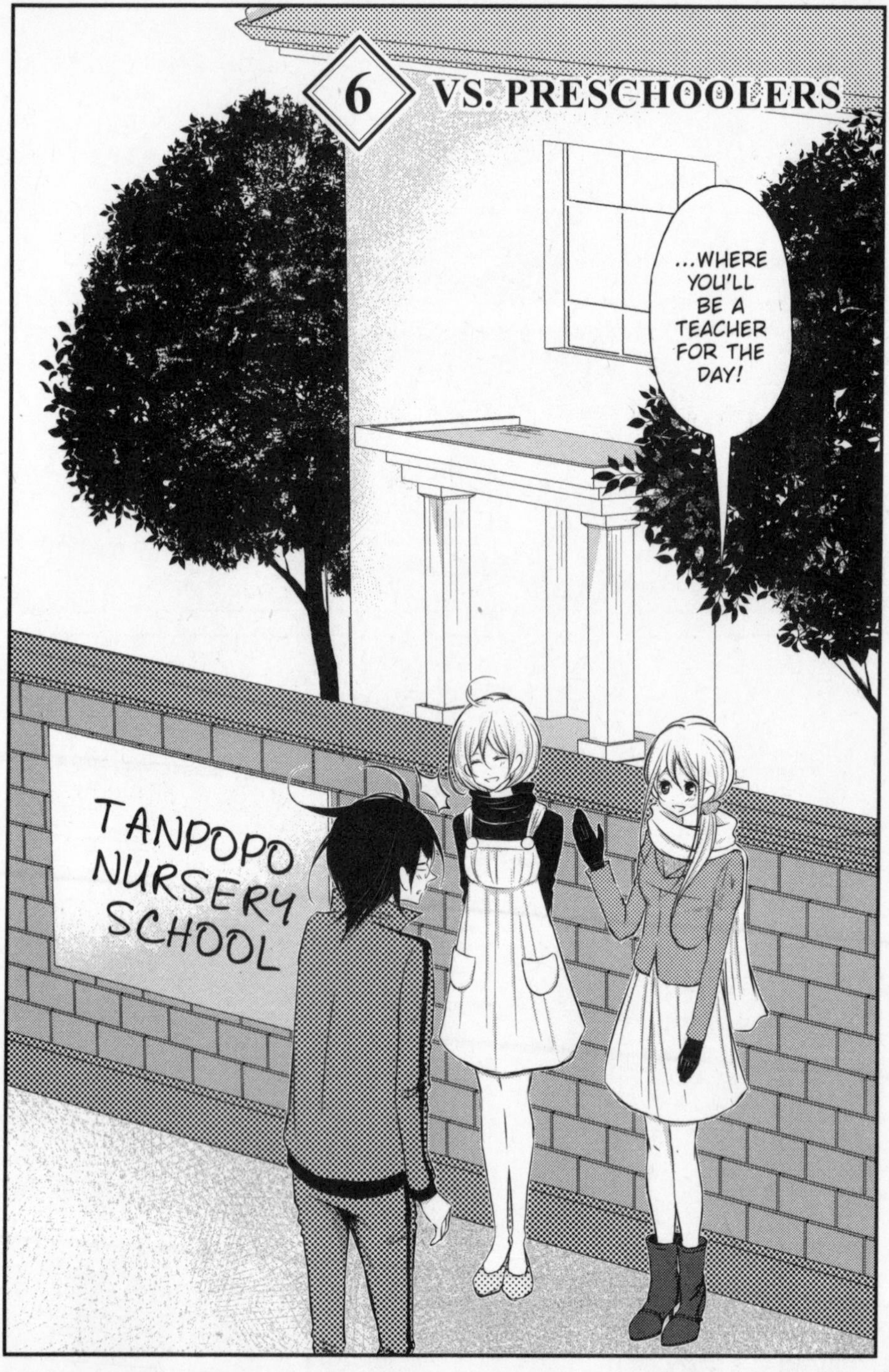
6 VS. PRESCHOOLERS
...WHERE YOU'LL BE A TEACHER FOR THE DAY!
TANPOPO NURSERY SCHOOL

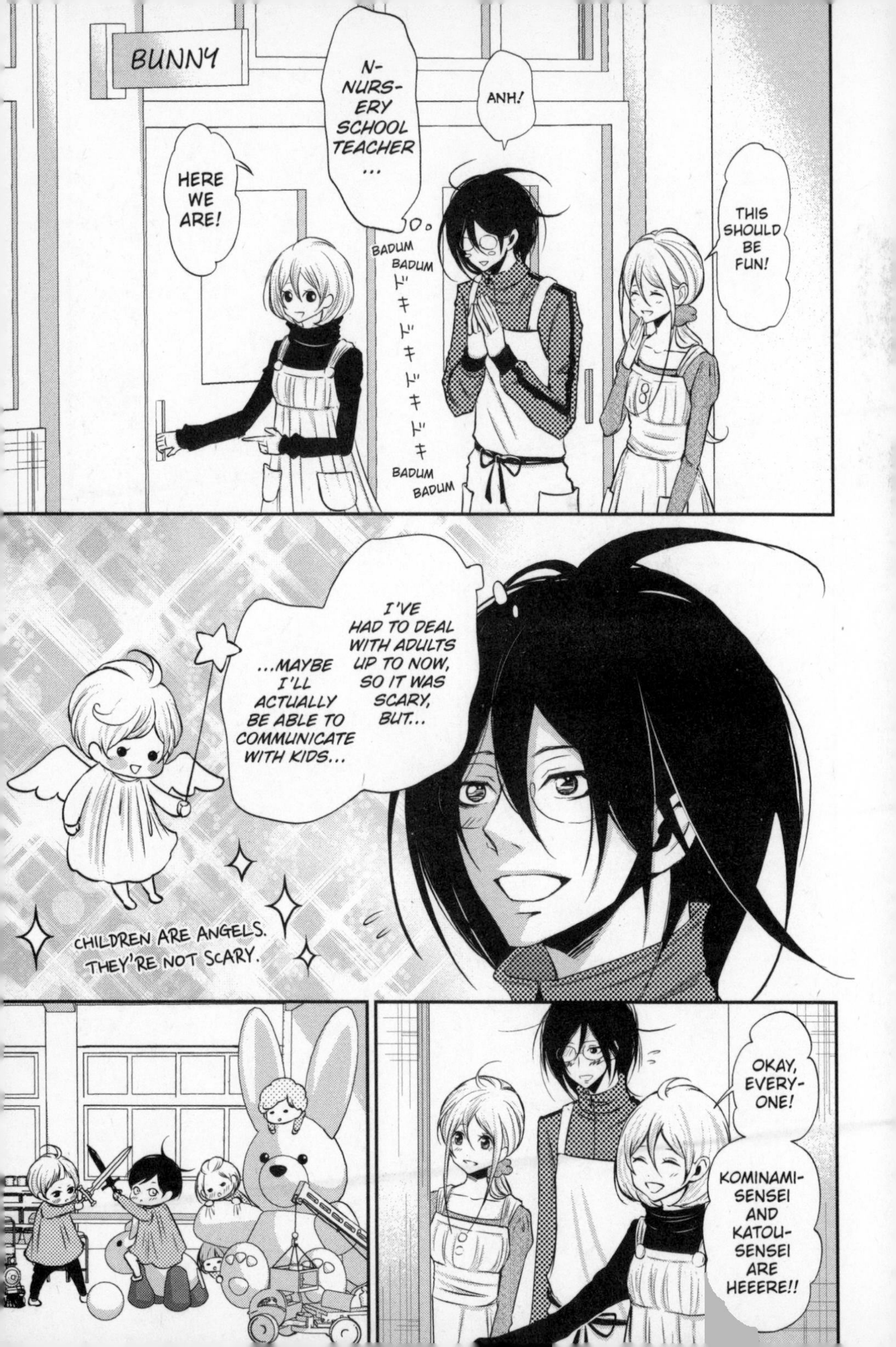
THIS SHOULD BE FUN!
ANH!
N-NURSERY SCHOOL TEACHER...
BUNNY
HERE WE ARE!
BADUM BADUM
ドキドキドキドキドキ
BADUM BADUM
I'VE HAD TO DEAL WITH ADULTS UP TO NOW, SO IT WAS SCARY, BUT...
...MAYBE I'LL ACTUALLY BE ABLE TO COMMUNICATE WITH KIDS...
CHILDREN ARE ANGELS. THEY'RE NOT SCARY.
OKAY, EVERYONE!
KOMINAMI-SENSEI AND KATOU-SENSEI ARE HEEERE!!

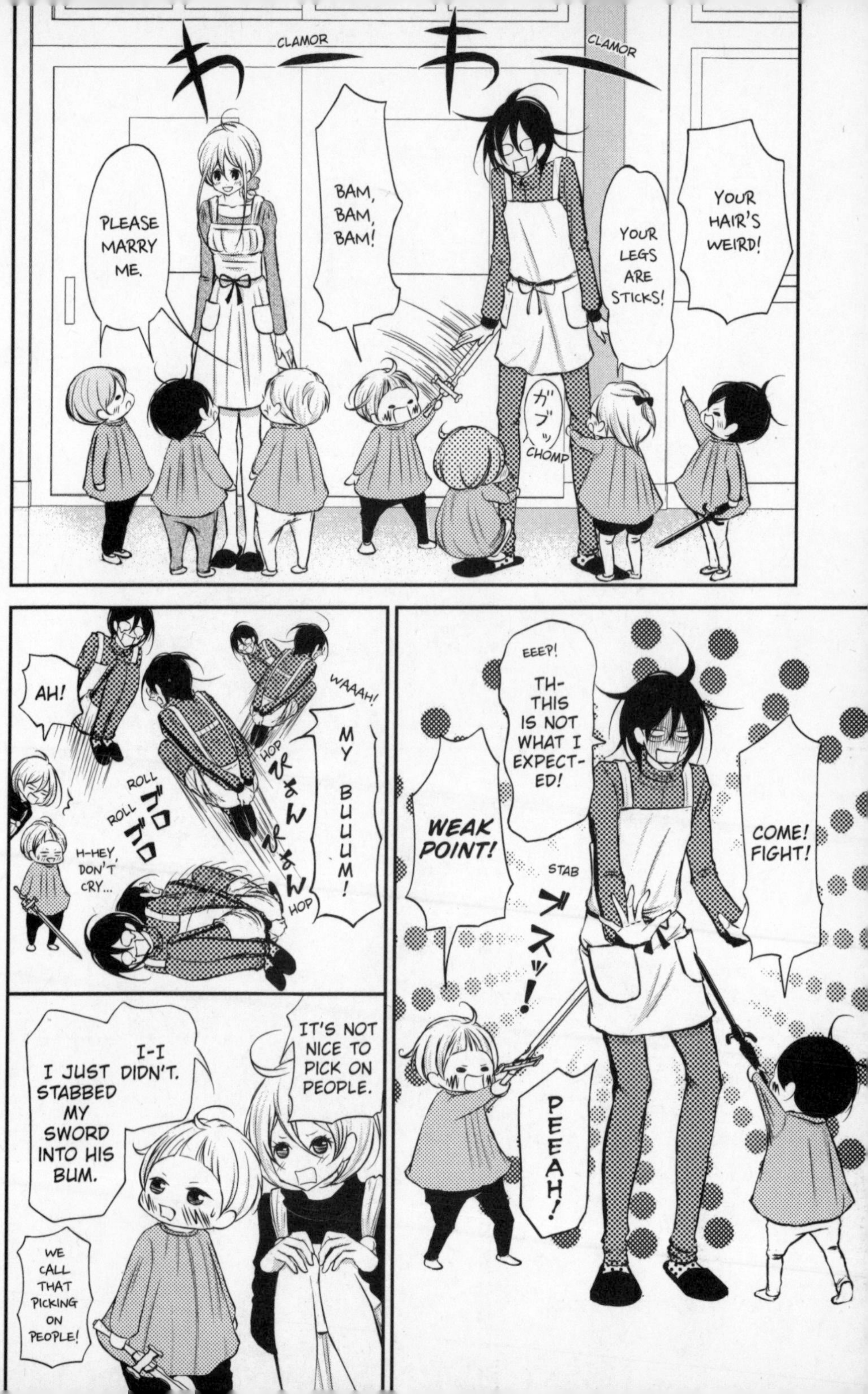
CLAMOR
CLAMOR
YOUR HAIR'S WEIRD!
YOUR LEGS ARE STICKS!
ガブッ CHOMP
BAM, BAM, BAM!
PLEASE MARRY ME.
EEEP! TH-THIS IS NOT WHAT I EXPECTED!
COME! FIGHT!
WEAK POINT!
STAB
PEEAH!
WAAAH!
MY BUUUM!
HOP HOP
ROLL ROLL
AH!
H-HEY, DON'T CRY...
IT'S NOT NICE TO PICK ON PEOPLE.
I-I DIDN'T. I JUST STABBED MY SWORD INTO HIS BUM.
WE CALL THAT PICKING ON PEOPLE!

I'M SORRY, KOMINAMI-SAN.
THIS BOY'S THE MOST MISCHIEVOUS OF THE BUNNY CLASS...
COME ON, REO-KUN! SAY YOU'RE SORRY TO KOMINAMI-SENSEI.
MY BAD, KOMINAMI.
REO! IT'S "KOMINAMI-SENSEI"!
BUT ANYONE WHO CRIES SO EASY ISN'T A GROWN-UP! HE CAN'T BE A SENSEI.
THAT'S TRUE...!
WEAK POINT!
べちっ
SMACK
PEEAH!
REO!
KYA HA HA HA HA!
THEY'RE NOT ANGELS...
ズキズキ
THROB THROB
...THEY'RE DEVILS...
SCARY...

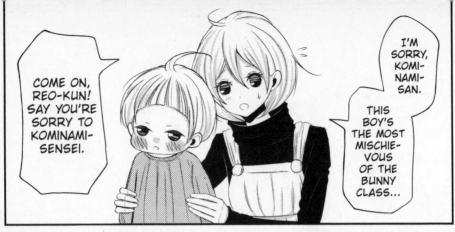

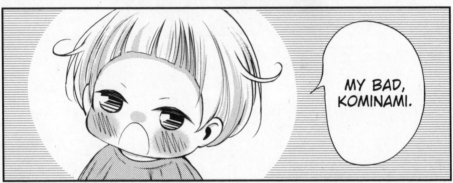

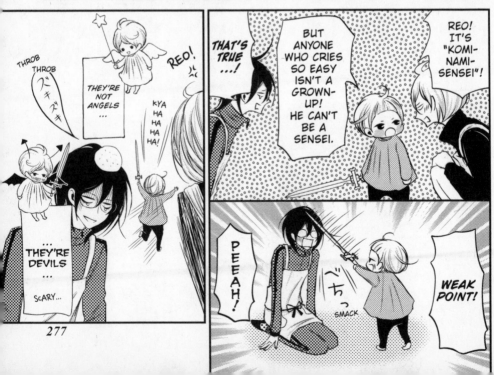

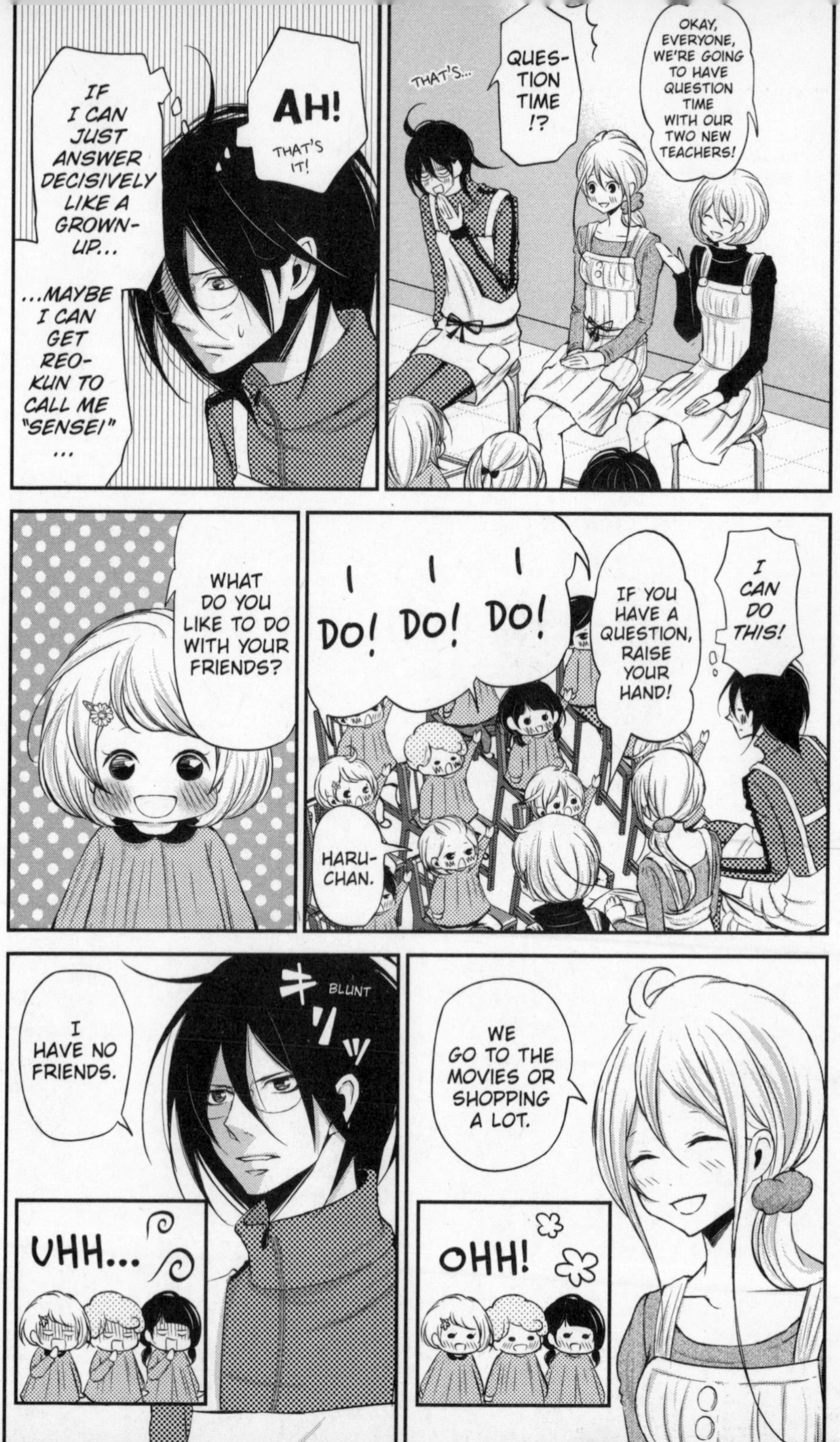

OKAY, EVERYONE, WE'RE GOING TO HAVE QUESTION TIME WITH OUR TWO NEW TEACHERS!
QUES-TION TIME !?
THAT'S...
AH!
THAT'S IT!
IF I CAN JUST ANSWER DECISIVELY LIKE A GROWN-UP...
...MAYBE I CAN GET REO-KUN TO CALL ME "SENSEI"...
I CAN DO THIS!
IF YOU HAVE A QUESTION, RAISE YOUR HAND!
I DO! I DO! I DO!
HARU-CHAN.
WHAT DO YOU LIKE TO DO WITH YOUR FRIENDS?
WE GO TO THE MOVIES OR SHOPPING A LOT.
OHH!
BLUNT
I HAVE NO FRIENDS.
UHH...

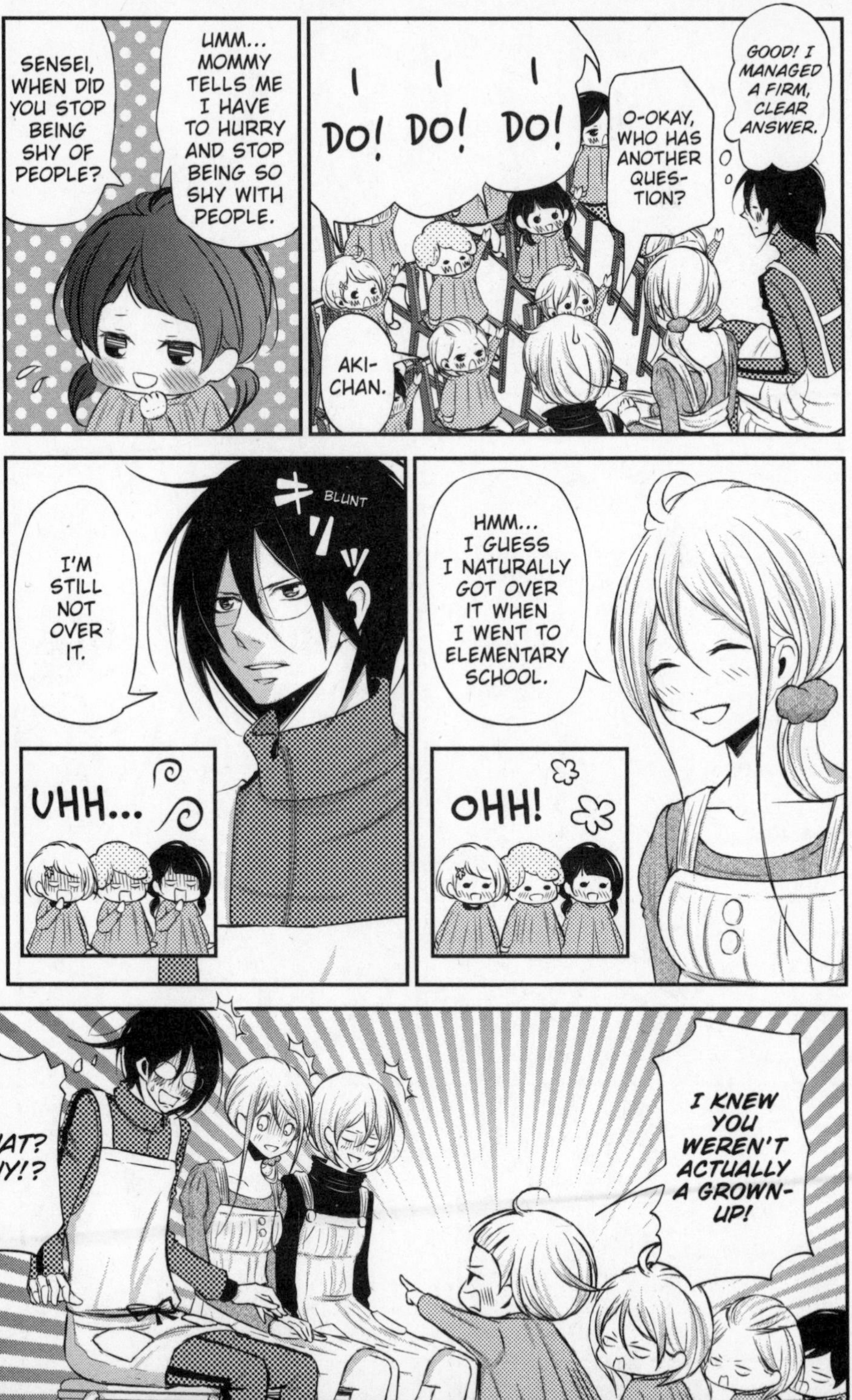
GOOD! I MANAGED A FIRM, CLEAR ANSWER.
O-OKAY, WHO HAS ANOTHER QUES-TION?
I DO! I DO! I DO!
AKI-CHAN.
UMM... MOMMY TELLS ME I HAVE TO HURRY AND STOP BEING SO SHY WITH PEOPLE.
SENSEI, WHEN DID YOU STOP BEING SHY OF PEOPLE?
HMM... I GUESS I NATURALLY GOT OVER IT WHEN I WENT TO ELEMENTARY SCHOOL.
OHH!
BLUNT
I'M STILL NOT OVER IT.
UHH...
I KNEW YOU WEREN'T ACTUALLY A GROWN-UP!
WHAT? WHY!?

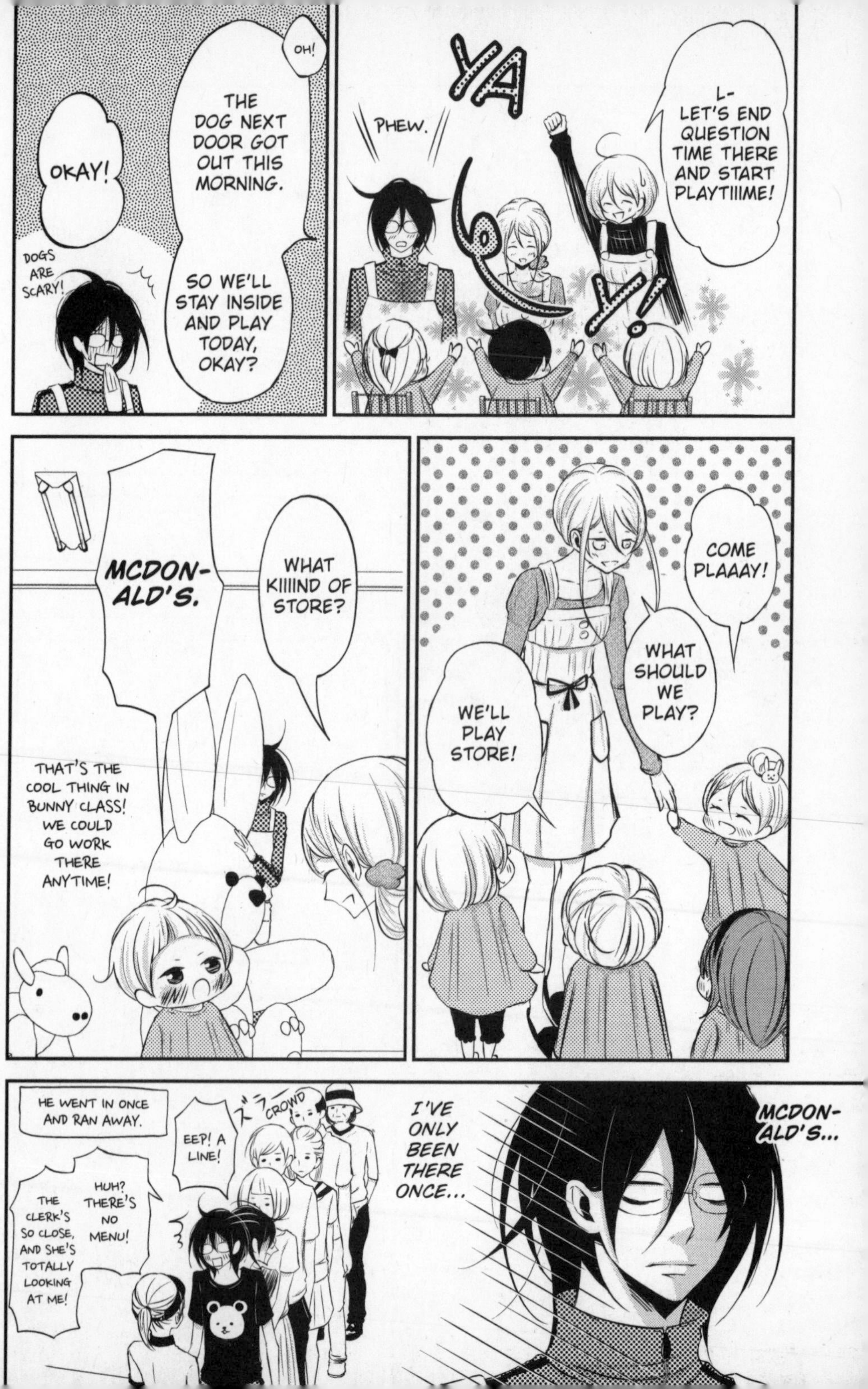
L- LET'S END QUESTION TIME THERE AND START PLAYTIIIME!
YAY!
PHEW.
OH!
THE DOG NEXT DOOR GOT OUT THIS MORNING.
SO WE'LL STAY INSIDE AND PLAY TODAY, OKAY?
OKAY!
DOGS ARE SCARY!
COME PLAAAY!
WHAT SHOULD WE PLAY?
WE'LL PLAY STORE!
WHAT KIIIIND OF STORE?
MCDON-ALD'S.
THAT'S THE COOL THING IN BUNNY CLASS! WE COULD GO WORK THERE ANYTIME!
MCDON-ALD'S...
I'VE ONLY BEEN THERE ONCE...
HE WENT IN ONCE AND RAN AWAY.
CROWD
EEP! A LINE!
HUH? THERE'S NO MENU!
THE CLERK'S SO CLOSE, AND SHE'S TOTALLY LOOKING AT ME!

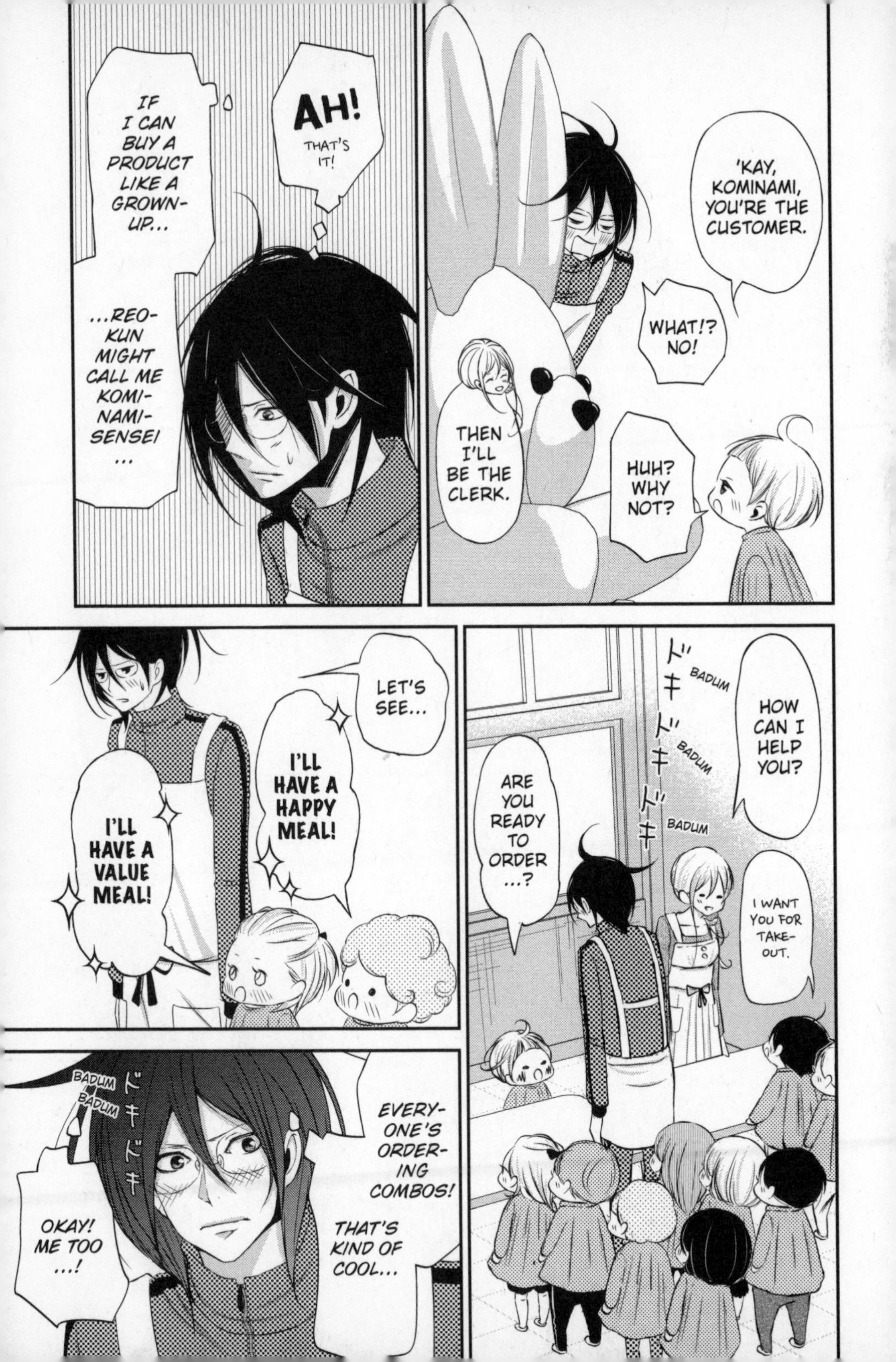

'KAY, KOMINAMI, YOU'RE THE CUSTOMER.
WHAT!? NO!
HUH? WHY NOT?
THEN I'LL BE THE CLERK.
AH!
THAT'S IT!
IF I CAN BUY A PRODUCT LIKE A GROWN-UP...
...REO-KUN MIGHT CALL ME KOMINAMI-SENSEI...
HOW CAN I HELP YOU?
ドキドキドキ
BADUM BADUM BADUM
ARE YOU READY TO ORDER...?
I WANT YOU FOR TAKE-OUT.
LET'S SEE...
I'LL HAVE A HAPPY MEAL!
I'LL HAVE A VALUE MEAL!
EVERYONE'S ORDERING COMBOS!
THAT'S KIND OF COOL...
ドキドキ
BADUM BADUM
OKAY! ME TOO...!

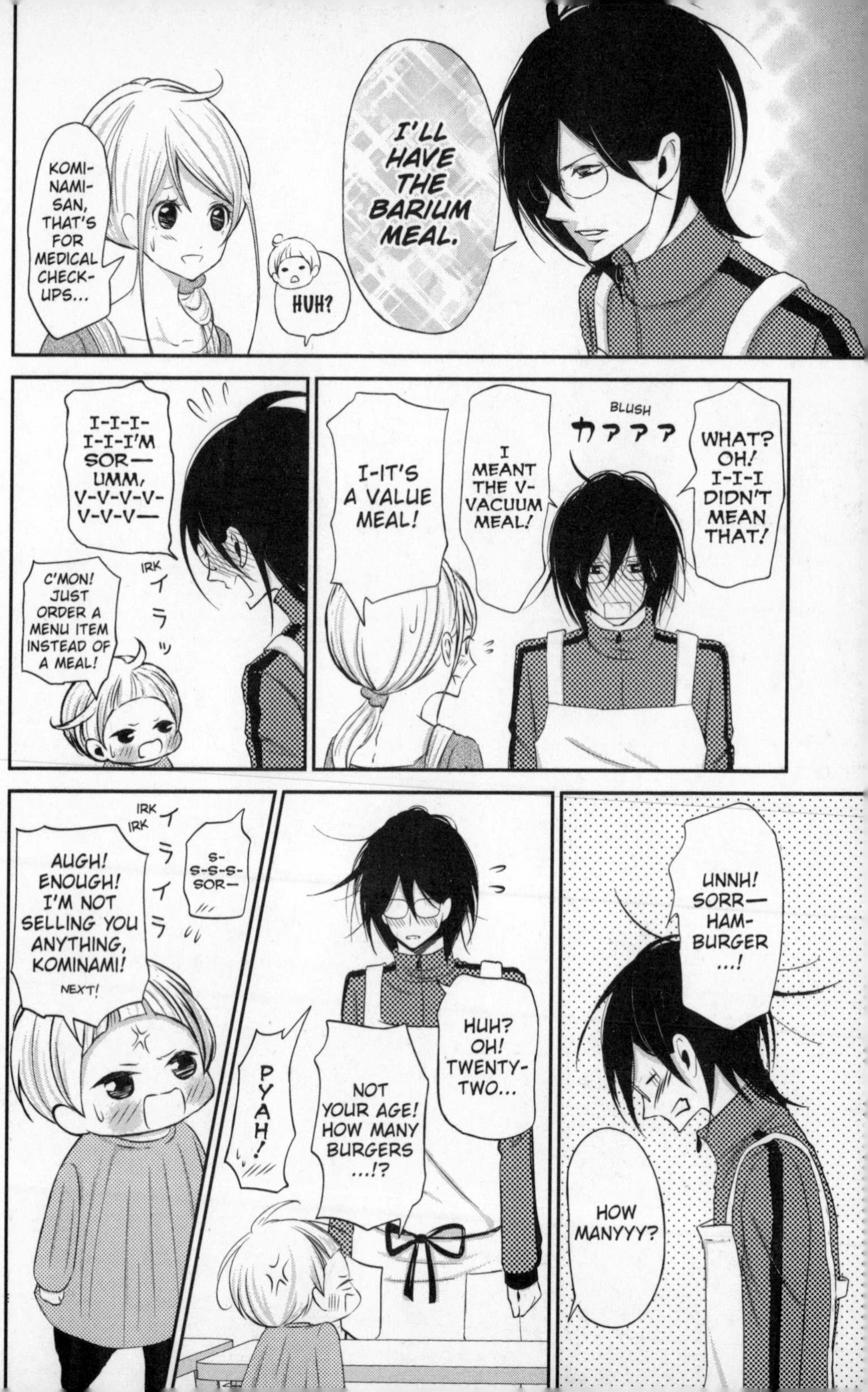
I'LL HAVE THE BARIUM MEAL.
HUH?
KOMI-NAMI-SAN, THAT'S FOR MEDICAL CHECK-UPS...
WHAT? OH! I-I-I DIDN'T MEAN THAT!
BLUSH
カアアア
I MEANT THE V-VACUUM MEAL!
I-IT'S A VALUE MEAL!
I-I-I-I-I-I'M SOR— UMM, V-V-V-V-V-V-V—
IRK
イラッ
C'MON! JUST ORDER A MENU ITEM INSTEAD OF A MEAL!
UNNH! SORR— HAM-BURGER ...!
HOW MANYYY?
HUH? OH! TWENTY-TWO...
NOT YOUR AGE! HOW MANY BURGERS ...!?
PYAH!
S-S-S-S-SOR—
IRK IRK
イライラ
AUGH! ENOUGH! I'M NOT SELLING YOU ANYTHING, KOMINAMI!
NEXT!

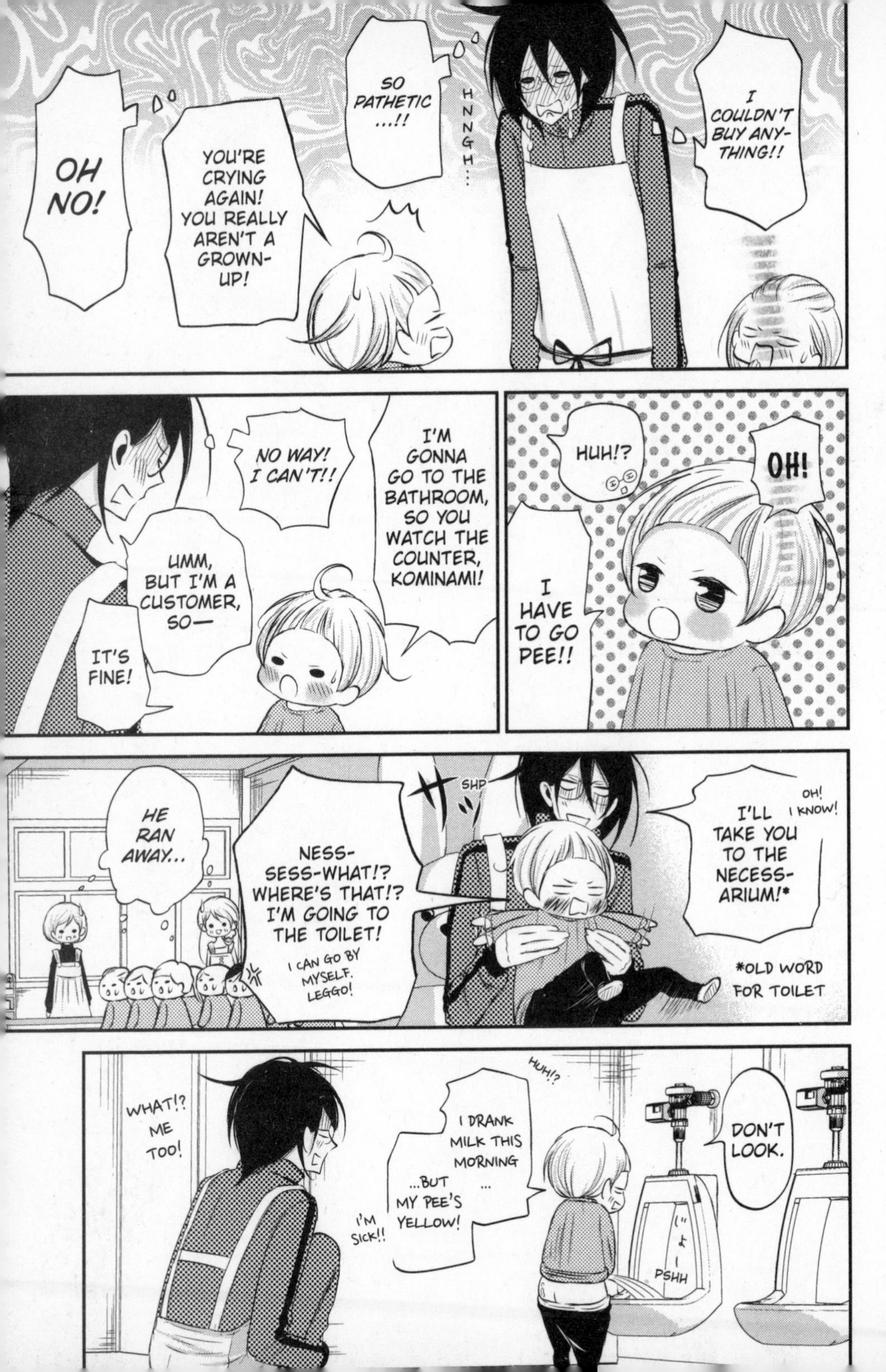
I COULDN'T BUY ANY-THING!!
HNNGH...
SO PATHETIC ...!!
YOU'RE CRYING AGAIN! YOU REALLY AREN'T A GROWN-UP!
OH NO!
OH!
HUH!?
I HAVE TO GO PEE!!
I'M GONNA GO TO THE BATHROOM, SO YOU WATCH THE COUNTER, KOMINAMI!
NO WAY! I CAN'T!!
UMM, BUT I'M A CUSTOMER, SO—
IT'S FINE!
OH! I KNOW!
I'LL TAKE YOU TO THE NECESS-ARIUM!*
*OLD WORD FOR TOILET
SHP
NESS-SESS-WHAT!? WHERE'S THAT!? I'M GOING TO THE TOILET!
I CAN GO BY MYSELF. LEGGO!
HE RAN AWAY...
DON'T LOOK.
PSHH
HUH!?
I DRANK MILK THIS MORNING ...
...BUT MY PEE'S YELLOW!
I'M SICK!!
WHAT!? ME TOO!

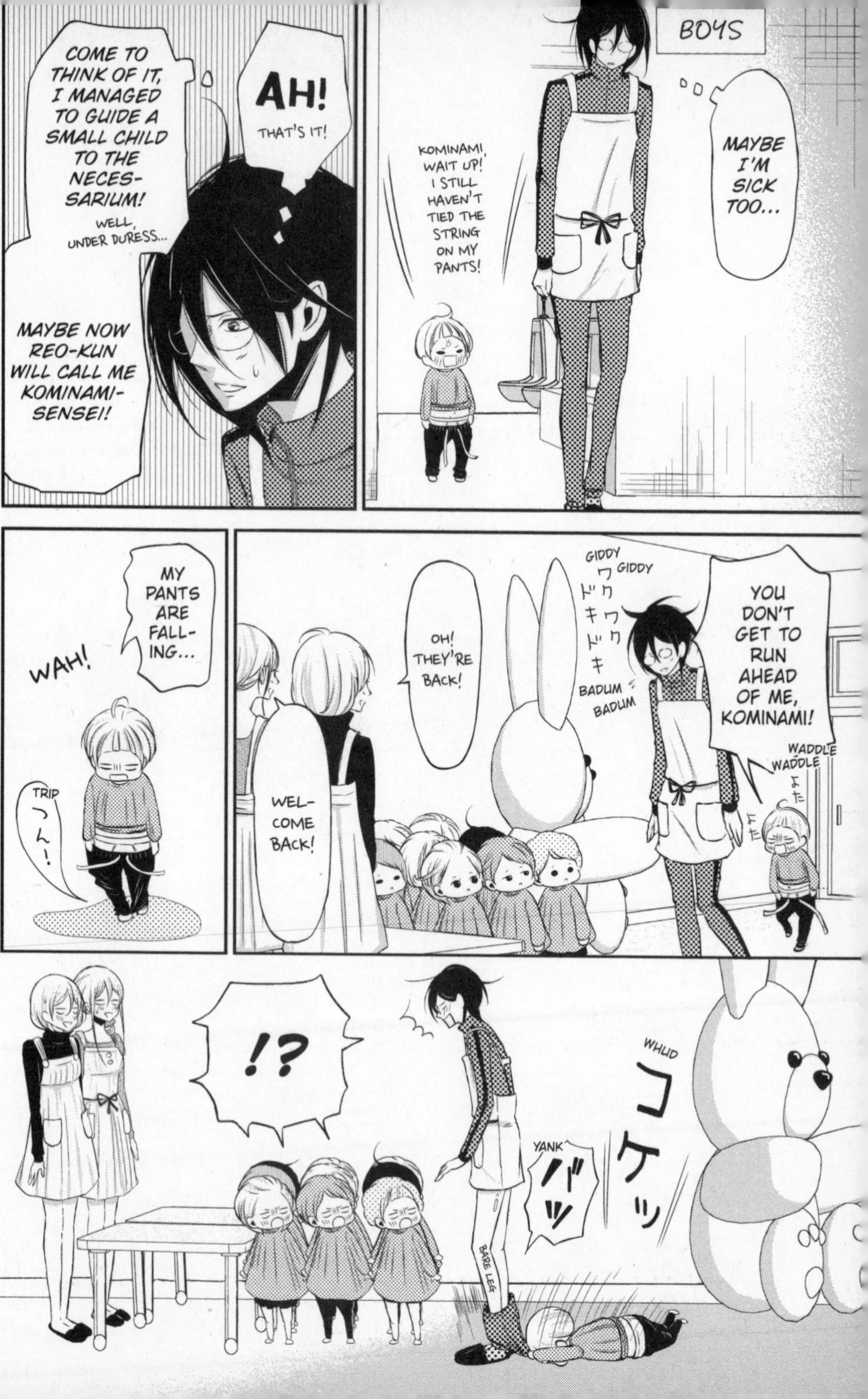

BOYS
MAYBE I'M SICK TOO...
KOMINAMI! WAIT UP! I STILL HAVEN'T TIED THE STRING ON MY PANTS!
AH!
THAT'S IT!
COME TO THINK OF IT, I MANAGED TO GUIDE A SMALL CHILD TO THE NECES-SARIUM!
WELL, UNDER DURESS...
MAYBE NOW REO-KUN WILL CALL ME KOMINAMI-SENSEI!!
YOU DON'T GET TO RUN AHEAD OF ME, KOMINAMI!
WADDLE WADDLE
よた よた
GIDDY GIDDY
ワクワク
ドキドキ
BADUM BADUM
OH! THEY'RE BACK!
WEL-COME BACK!
MY PANTS ARE FALL-ING...
WAH!
TRIP
つん!
WHUD
コケッ
YANK
バッ
BARE LEG
!?

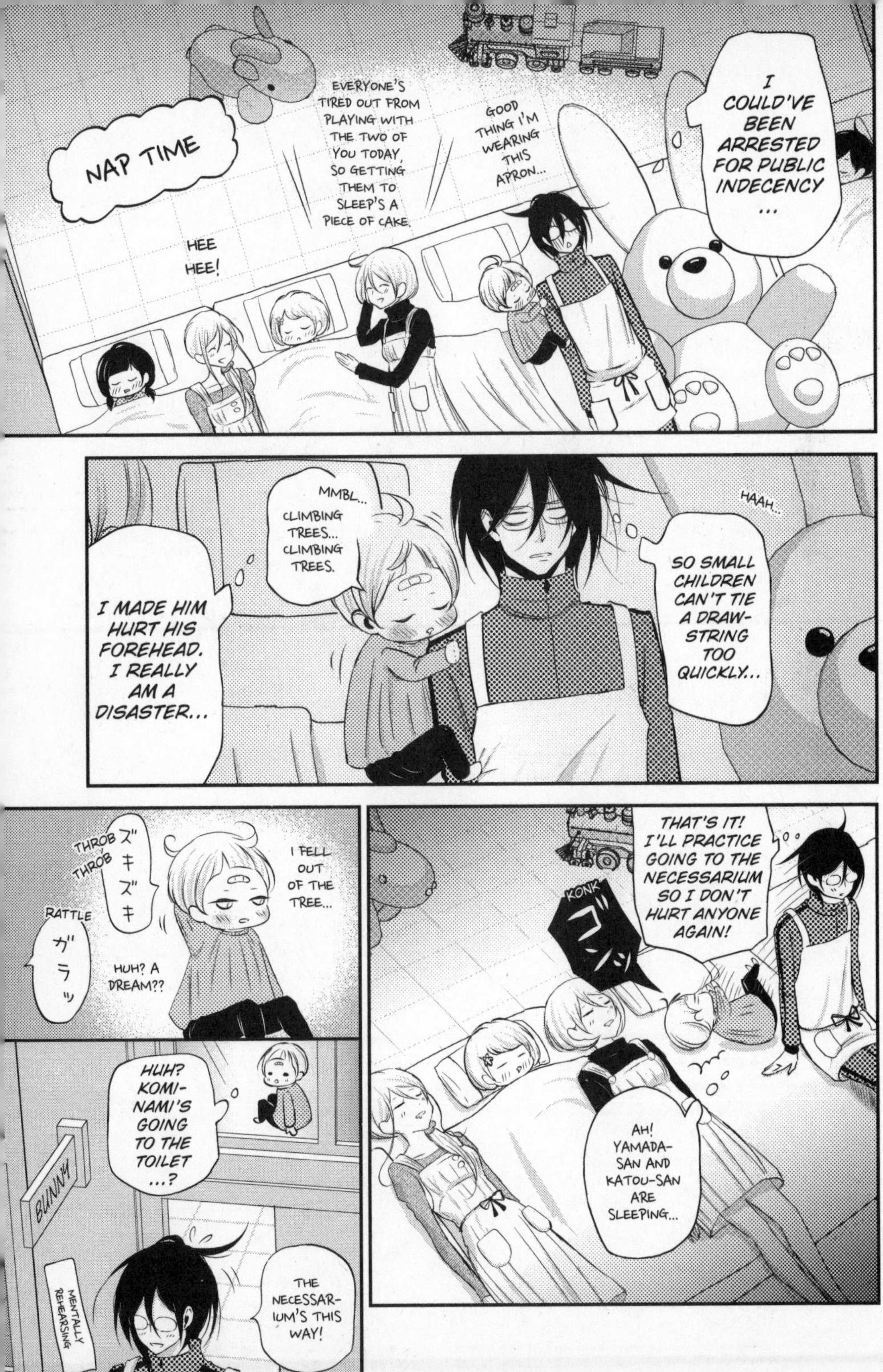
I COULD'VE BEEN ARRESTED FOR PUBLIC INDECENCY ...
GOOD THING I'M WEARING THIS APRON...
EVERYONE'S TIRED OUT FROM PLAYING WITH THE TWO OF YOU TODAY, SO GETTING THEM TO SLEEP'S A PIECE OF CAKE.
NAP TIME
HEE HEE!
HA'AH...
SO SMALL CHILDREN CAN'T TIE A DRAW-STRING TOO QUICKLY...
MMBL... CLIMBING TREES... CLIMBING TREES.
I MADE HIM HURT HIS FOREHEAD. I REALLY AM A DISASTER...
THAT'S IT! I'LL PRACTICE GOING TO THE NECESSARIUM SO I DON'T HURT ANYONE AGAIN!
KONK
AH! YAMADA-SAN AND KATOU-SAN ARE SLEEPING...
I FELL OUT OF THE TREE...
THROB THROB ズキズキ
HUH? A DREAM??
RATTLE ガラッ
HUH? KOMI-NAMI'S GOING TO THE TOILET ...?
BUNNY
THE NECESSAR-IUM'S THIS WAY!
MENTALLY REHEARSING

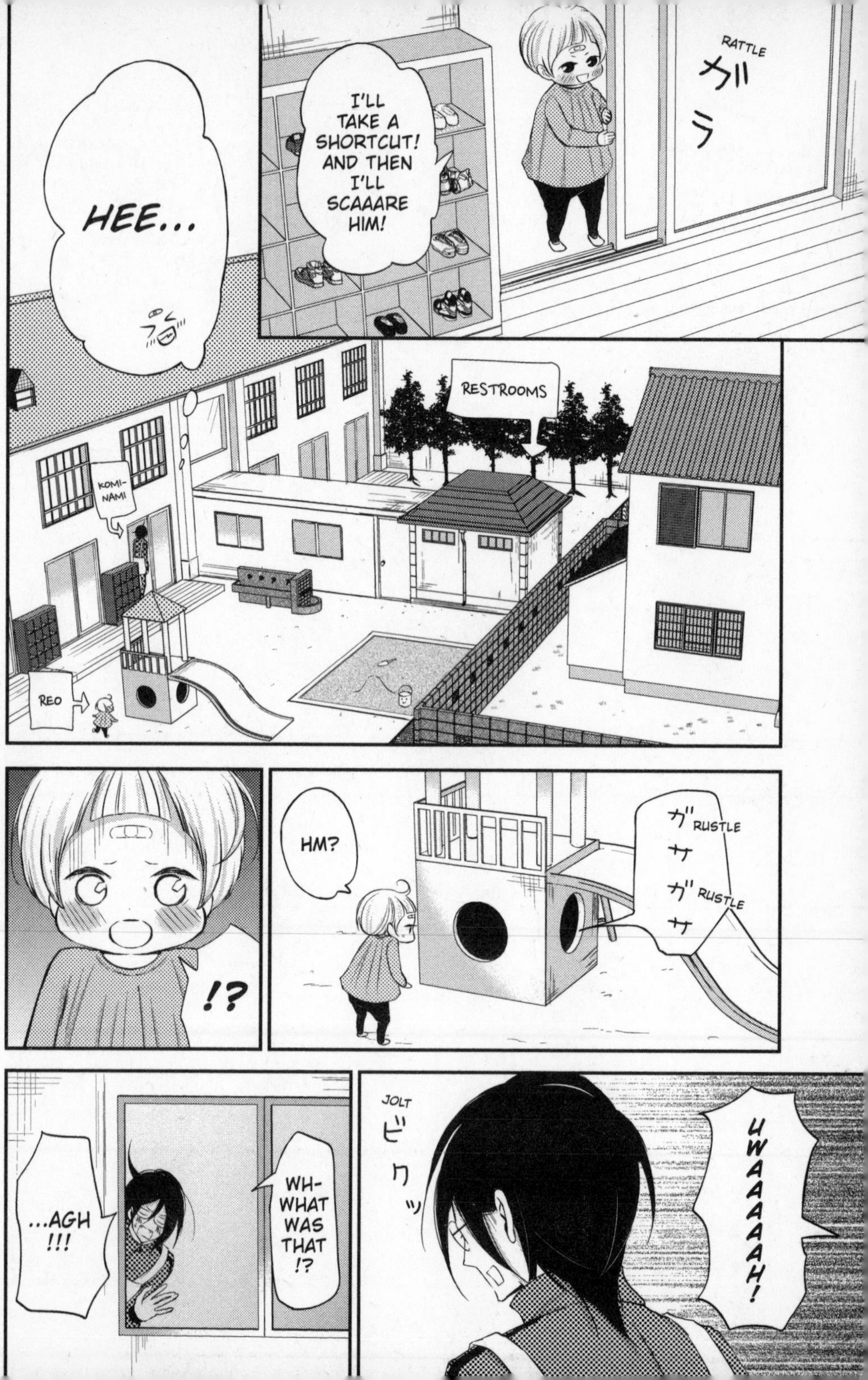
RATTLE
ガラ
I'LL TAKE A SHORTCUT! AND THEN I'LL SCAAARE HIM!
HEE...
RESTROOMS
KOMI-NAMI
REO
ガ RUSTLE
サ
ガ RUSTLE
サ
HM?
!?
UWAAAAAAH!
JOLT
ビクッ
WH-WHAT WAS THAT!?
...AGH!!!

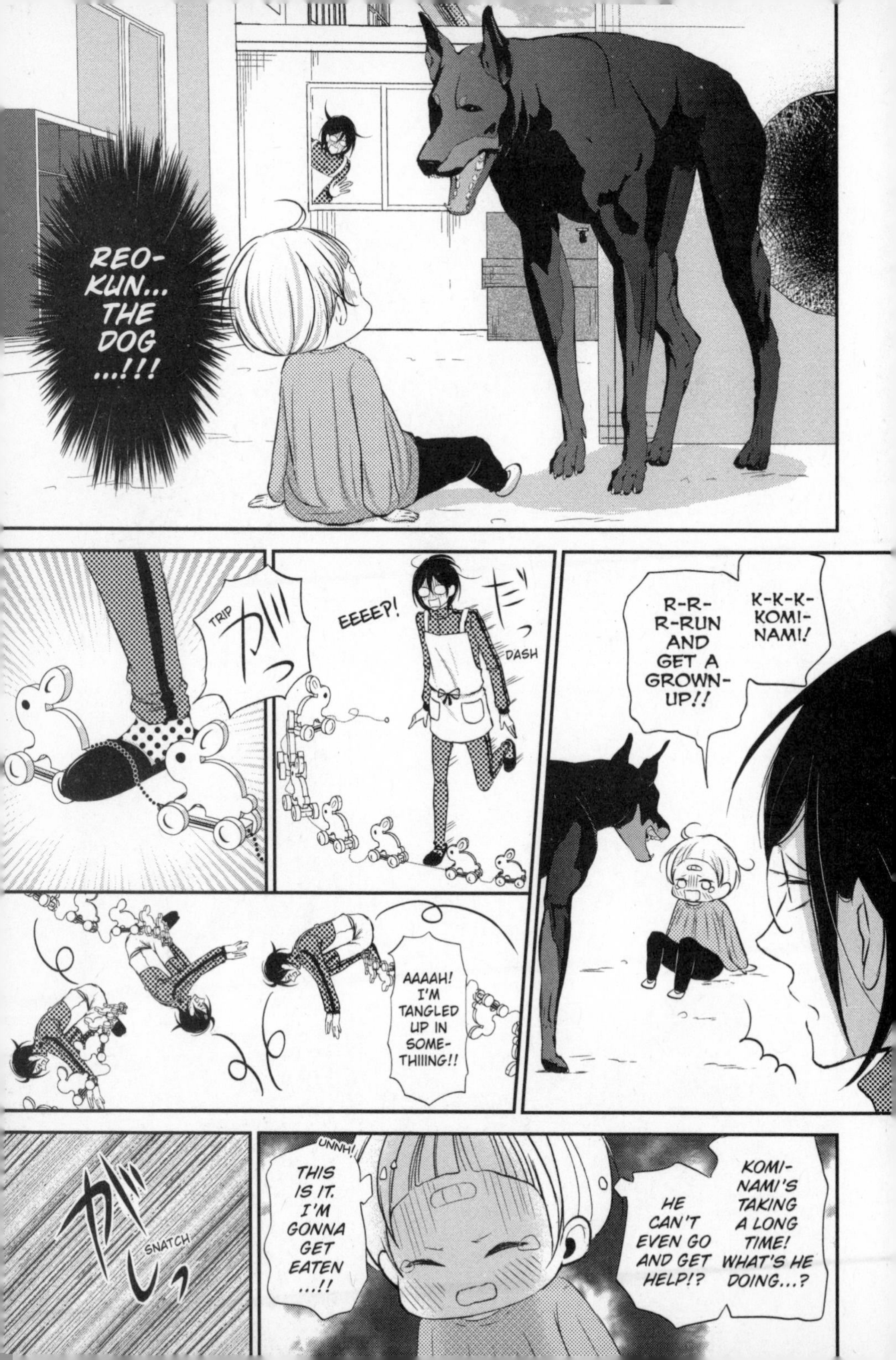
REO-KUN... THE DOG ...!!!
K-K-K-KOMI-NAMI!
R-R-R-RUN AND GET A GROWN-UP!!
EEEEP!
DASH
TRIP
AAAAH! I'M TANGLED UP IN SOME-THIIING!!
KOMI-NAMI'S TAKING A LONG TIME! WHAT'S HE DOING...?
HE CAN'T EVEN GO AND GET HELP!?
UNNH!
THIS IS IT. I'M GONNA GET EATEN ...!!
SNATCH

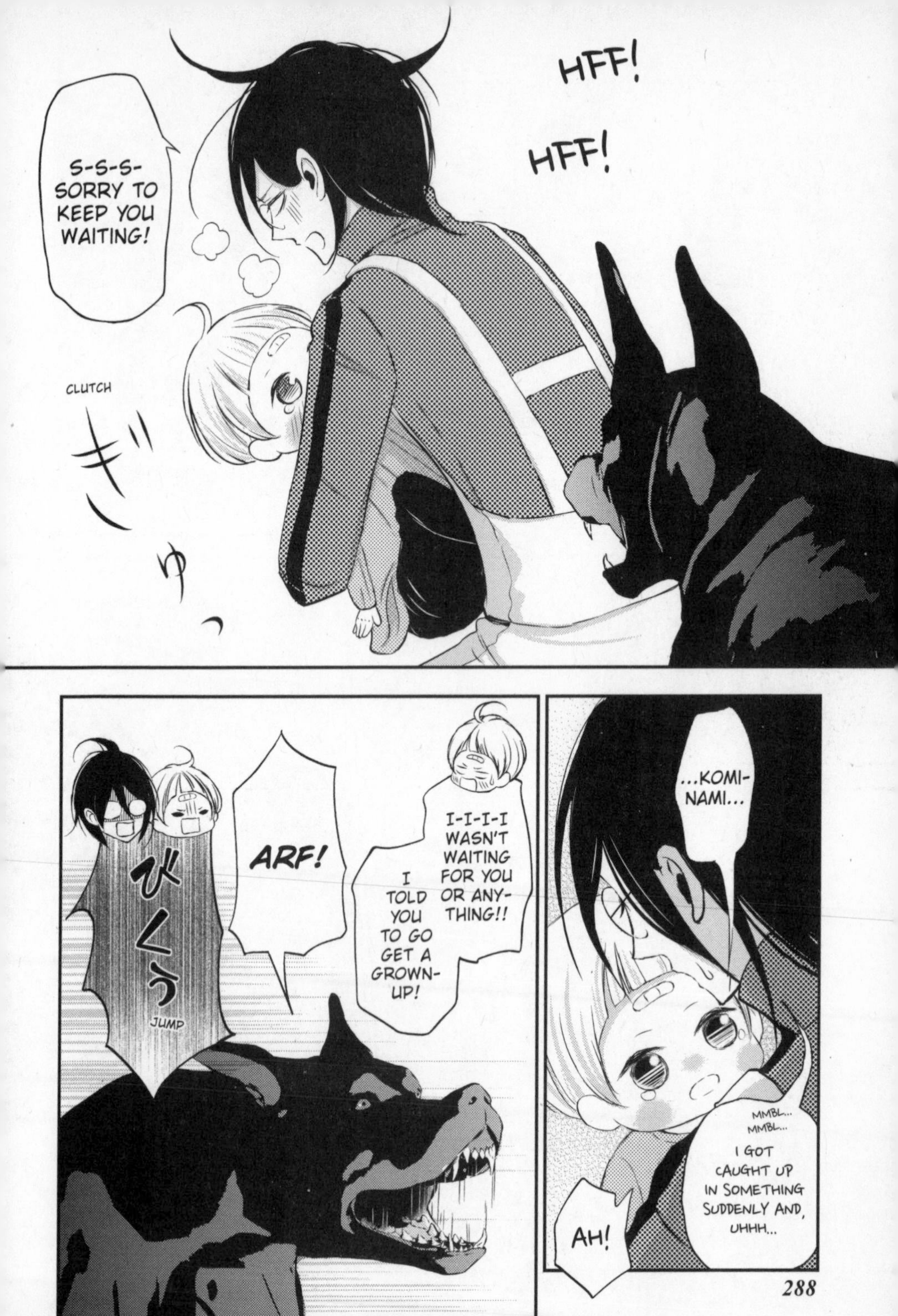
HFF!
HFF!
S-S-S-SORRY TO KEEP YOU WAITING!
CLUTCH
ぎゅっ
...KOMI-NAMI...
MMBL... MMBL...
I GOT CAUGHT UP IN SOMETHING SUDDENLY AND, UHHH...
AH!
I-I-I-I WASN'T WAITING FOR YOU OR ANY-THING!!
I TOLD YOU TO GO GET A GROWN-UP!
ARF!
びくぅ
JUMP

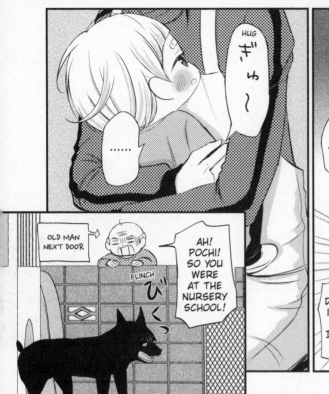

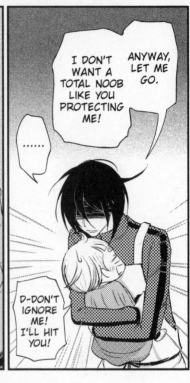

ANYWAY, LET ME GO.
I DON'T WANT A TOTAL NOOB LIKE YOU PROTECTING ME!
......
D-DON'T IGNORE ME! I'LL HIT YOU!
HUG
ぎゅ～
......
AH! POCHI! SO YOU WERE AT THE NURSERY SCHOOL!
OLD MAN NEXT DOOR
FLINCH
びくっ
I'M SORRY! I REALLY AM!
I'LL MAKE SURE TO GET A COLLAR ON HER!
SHE JUST WANTED TO GO ON THE SLIDE WITH THE WEE ONES.
COME ON! FOR REAL! LEGGO ...!
I HEAR YELLING...
SLIDE
ガラッ
MURMUR
MURMUR
ざわざわ
OH! IT'S THE DOG FROM NEXT DOOR!

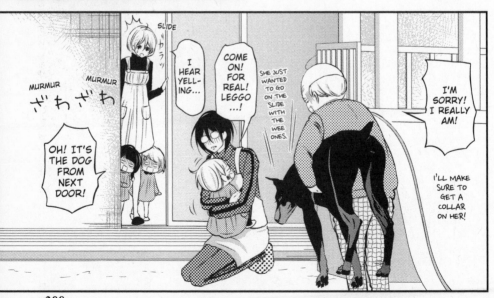

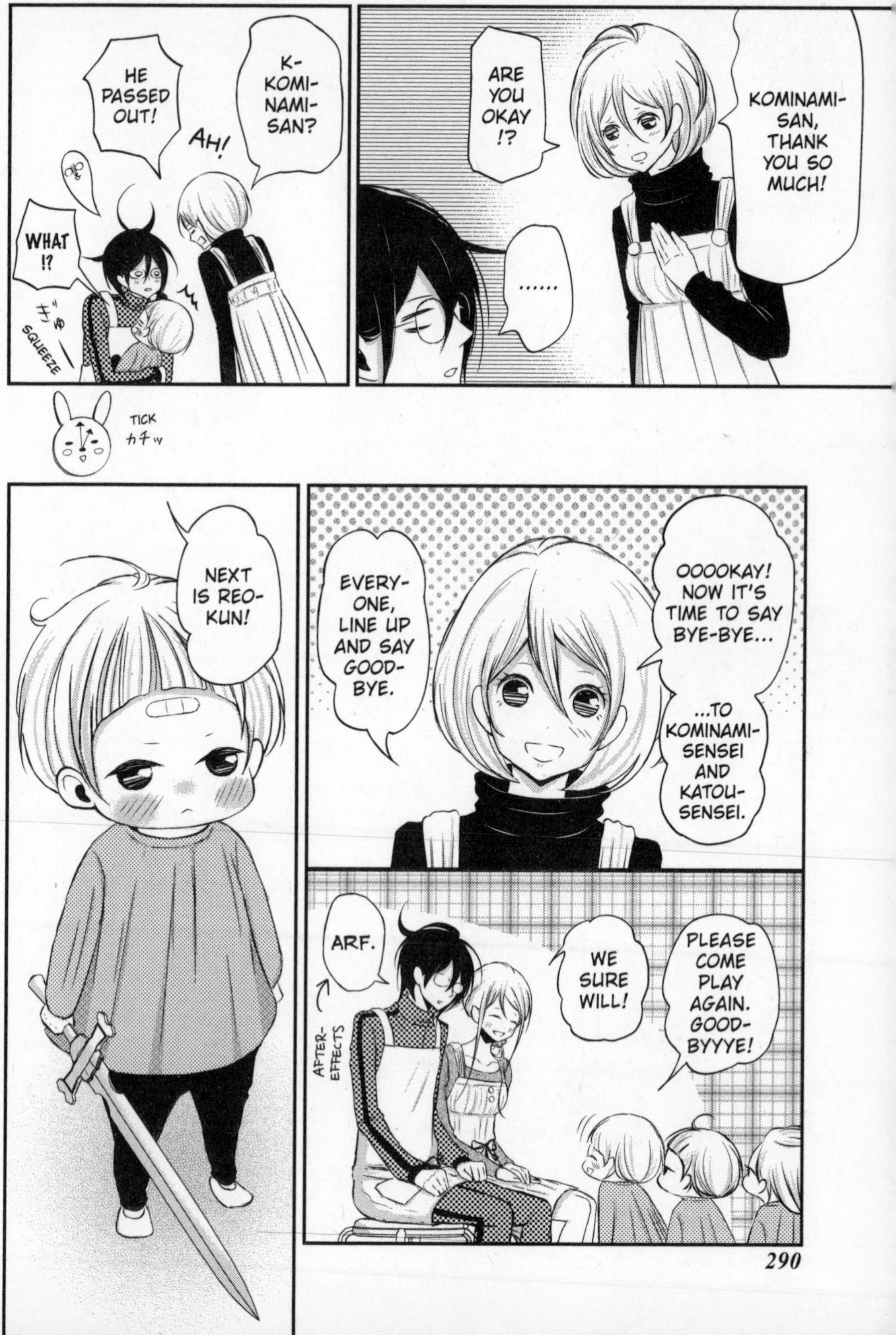
KOMINAMI-SAN, THANK YOU SO MUCH!
ARE YOU OKAY !?
......
K-KOMINAMI-SAN?
AH!
HE PASSED OUT!
WHAT !?
ぎゅ
SQUEEZE
TICK
カチッ
OOOOKAY! NOW IT'S TIME TO SAY BYE-BYE...
...TO KOMINAMI-SENSEI AND KATOU-SENSEI.
EVERY-ONE, LINE UP AND SAY GOOD-BYE.
PLEASE COME PLAY AGAIN. GOOD-BYYYE!
WE SURE WILL!
ARF.
AFTER-EFFECTS
NEXT IS REO-KUN!

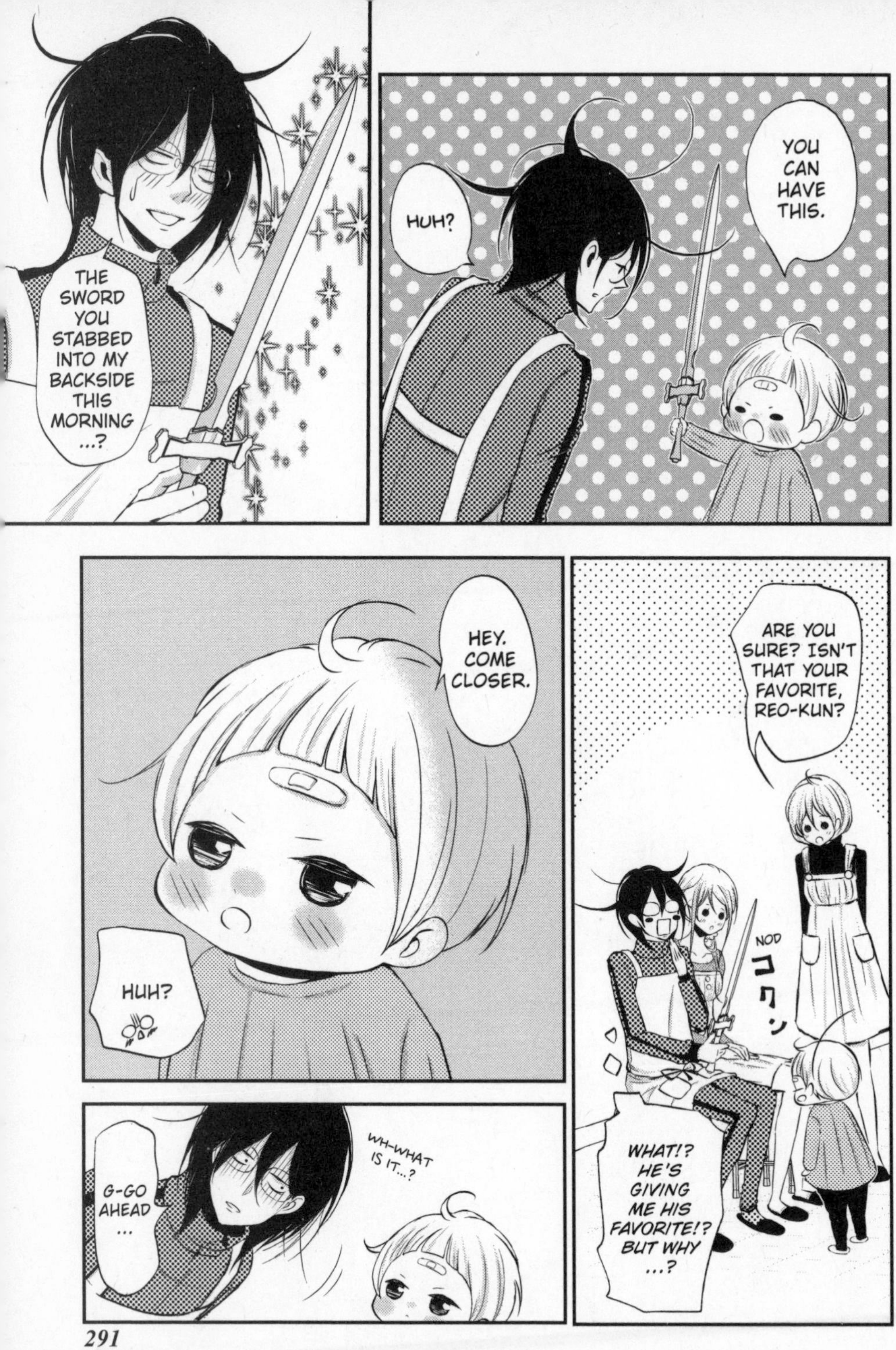
YOU CAN HAVE THIS.
HUH?
THE SWORD YOU STABBED INTO MY BACKSIDE THIS MORNING ...?
ARE YOU SURE? ISN'T THAT YOUR FAVORITE, REO-KUN?
NOD
WHAT!? HE'S GIVING ME HIS FAVORITE!? BUT WHY ...?
HEY. COME CLOSER.
HUH?
WH-WHAT IS IT...?
G-GO AHEAD ...

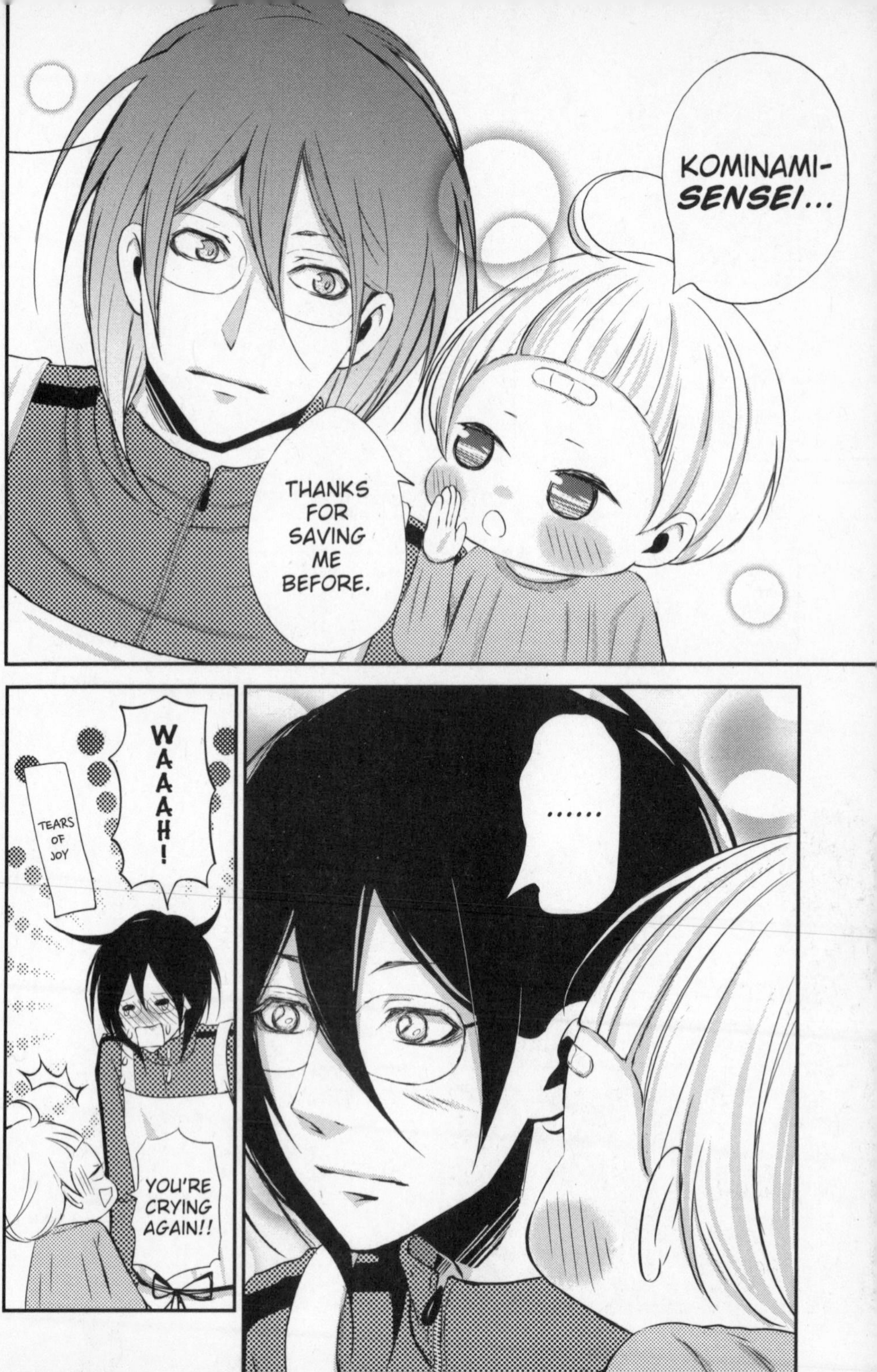
KOMINAMI-SENSEI...
THANKS FOR SAVING ME BEFORE.
......
WAAAAH!
TEARS OF JOY
YOU'RE CRYING AGAIN!!

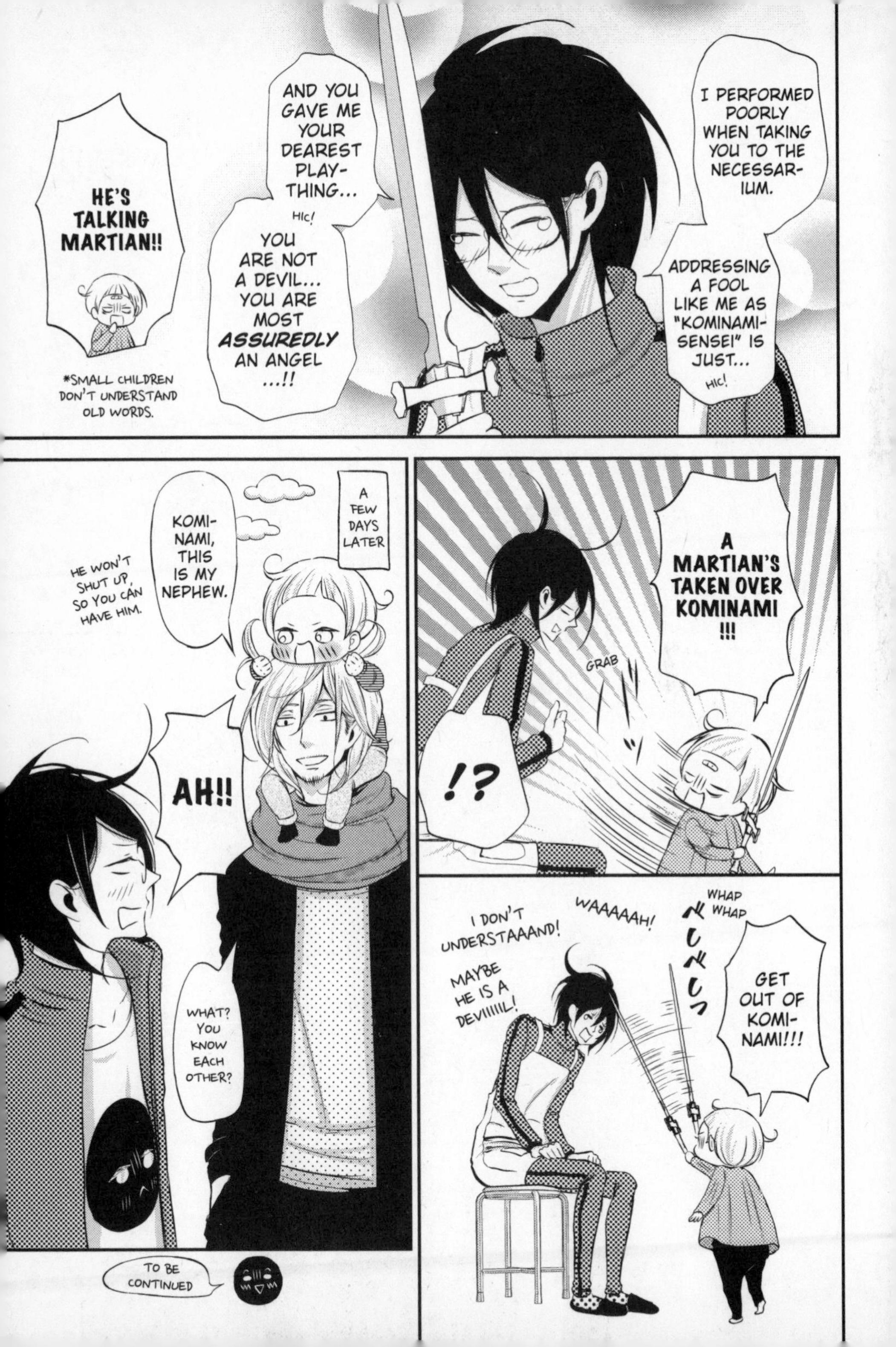
I PERFORMED POORLY WHEN TAKING YOU TO THE NECESSAR-IUM.
ADDRESSING A FOOL LIKE ME AS "KOMINAMI-SENSEI" IS JUST...
HIC!
AND YOU GAVE ME YOUR DEAREST PLAY-THING...
HIC!
YOU ARE NOT A DEVIL... YOU ARE MOST ASSUREDLY AN ANGEL ...!!
HE'S TALKING MARTIAN!!
*SMALL CHILDREN DON'T UNDERSTAND OLD WORDS.
A MARTIAN'S TAKEN OVER KOMINAMI !!!
GRAB
!?
GET OUT OF KOMI-NAMI!!!
WHAP WHAP
べしべしっ
WAAAAAH!
I DON'T UNDERSTAAAND!
MAYBE HE IS A DEVIIIIIL!
A FEW DAYS LATER
KOMI-NAMI, THIS IS MY NEPHEW.
HE WON'T SHUT UP, SO YOU CAN HAVE HIM.
AH!!
WHAT? YOU KNOW EACH OTHER?
TO BE CONTINUED

"WHAT IF EVERYONE WERE IN NURSERY SCHOOL" COMIC

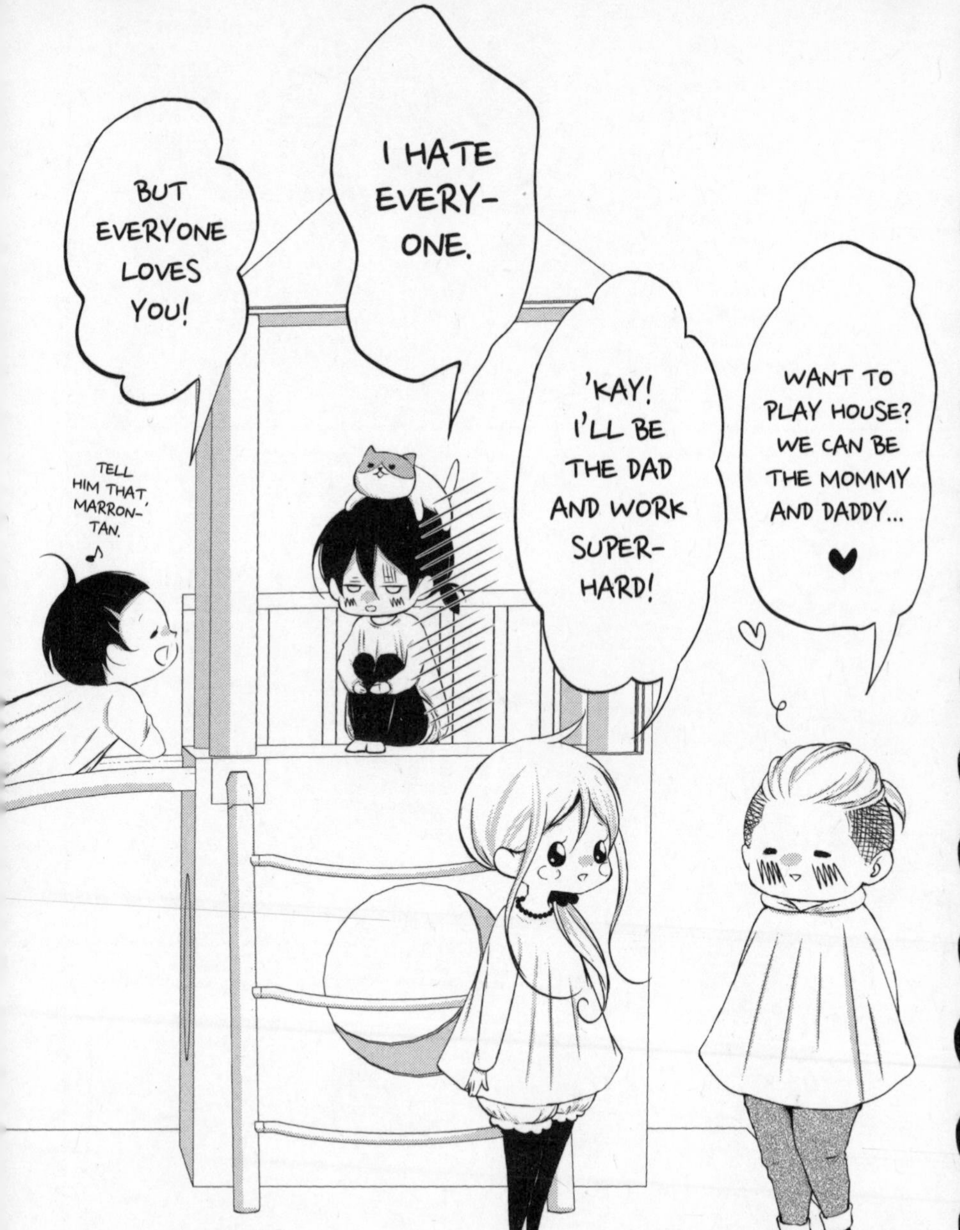
WANT TO PLAY HOUSE? WE CAN BE THE MOMMY AND DADDY... ♥
'KAY! I'LL BE THE DAD AND WORK SUPER-HARD!
I HATE EVERY-ONE.
BUT EVERYONE LOVES YOU!
TELL HIM THAT, MARRON-TAN. ♪

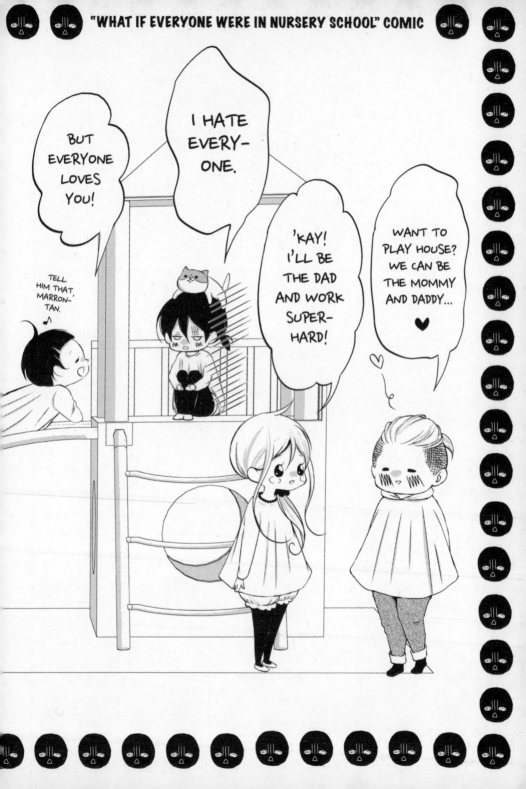

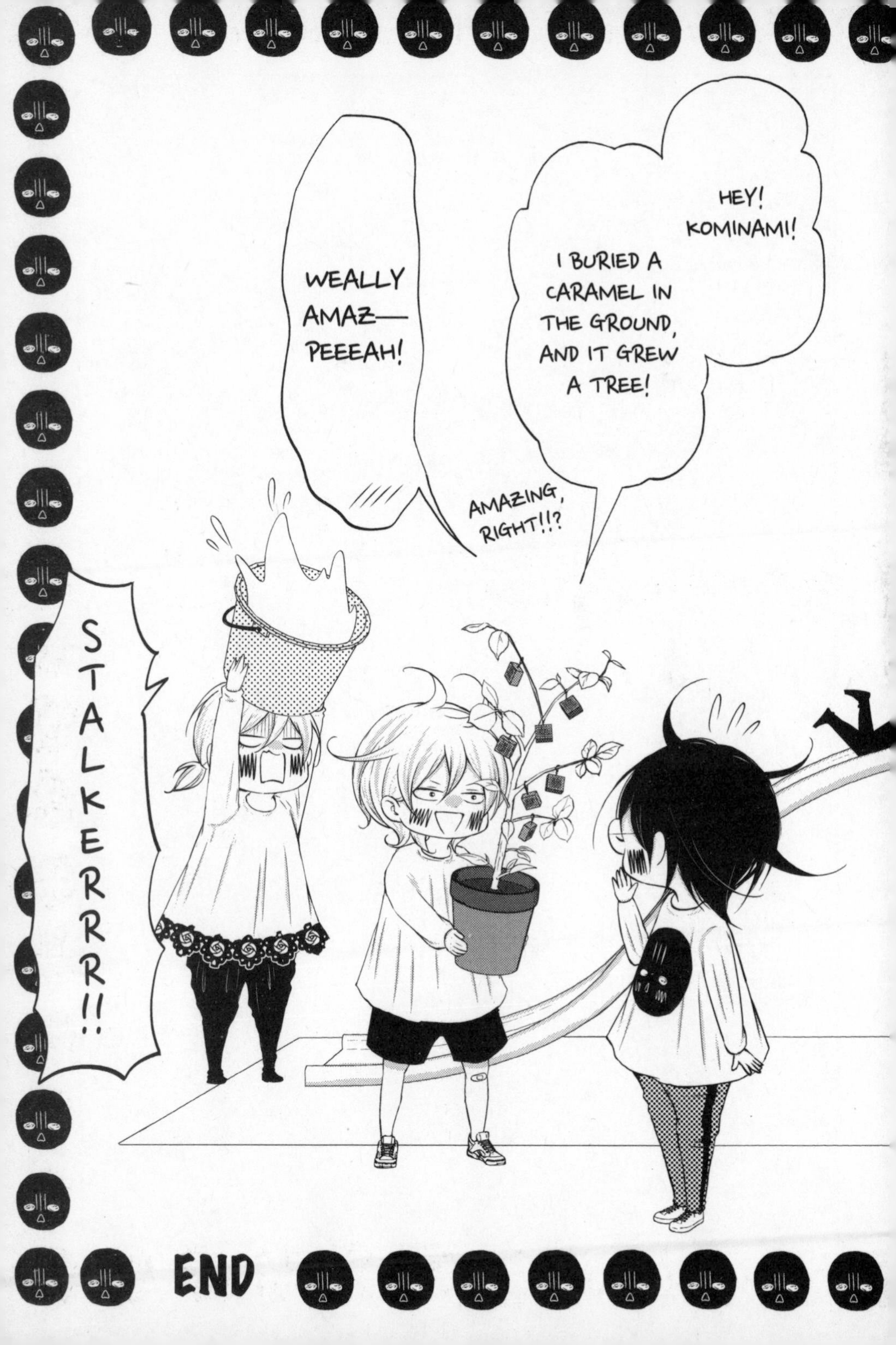
HEY! KOMINAMI!
I BURIED A CARAMEL IN THE GROUND, AND IT GREW A TREE!
AMAZING, RIGHT!!?
WEALLY AMAZ— PEEEAH!
STALKERRR!!
END

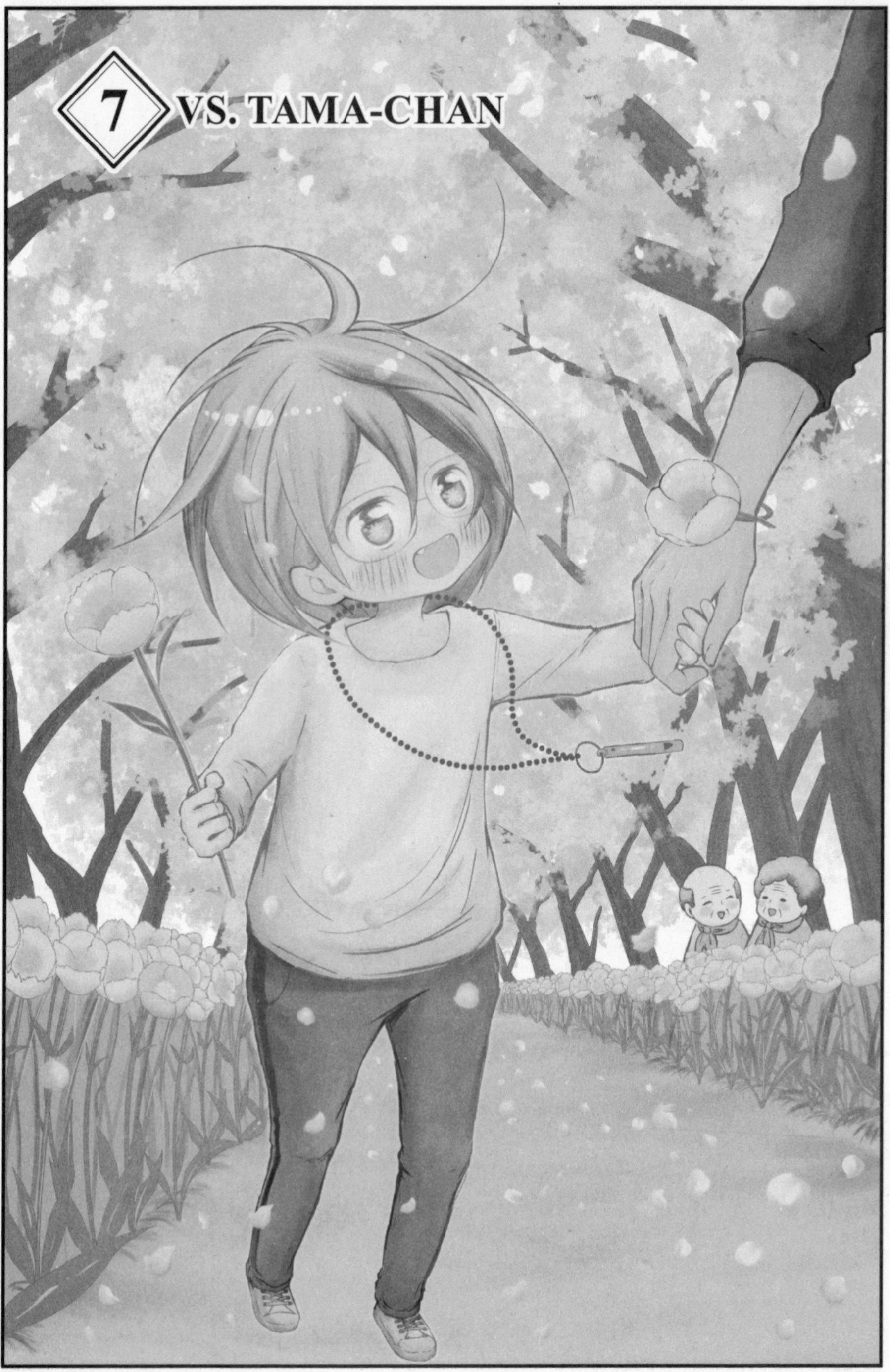
7 VS. TAMA-CHAN

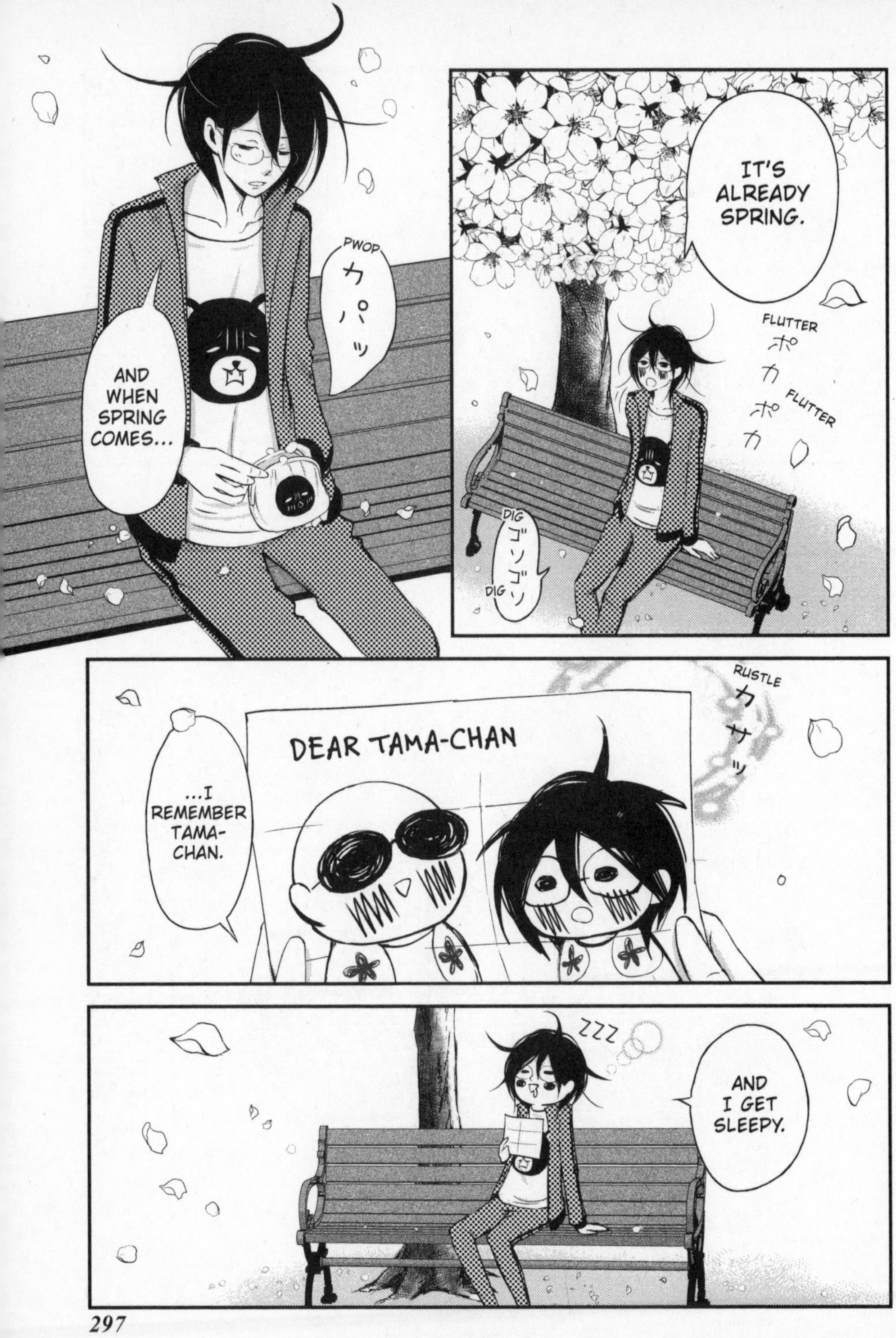
IT'S ALREADY SPRING.
FLUTTER
ポカポカ
FLUTTER
DIG
ゴソゴソ
DIG
PWOP
カパッ
AND WHEN SPRING COMES...
RUSTLE
カサッ
DEAR TAMA-CHAN
...I REMEMBER TAMA-CHAN.
ZZZ
AND I GET SLEEPY.

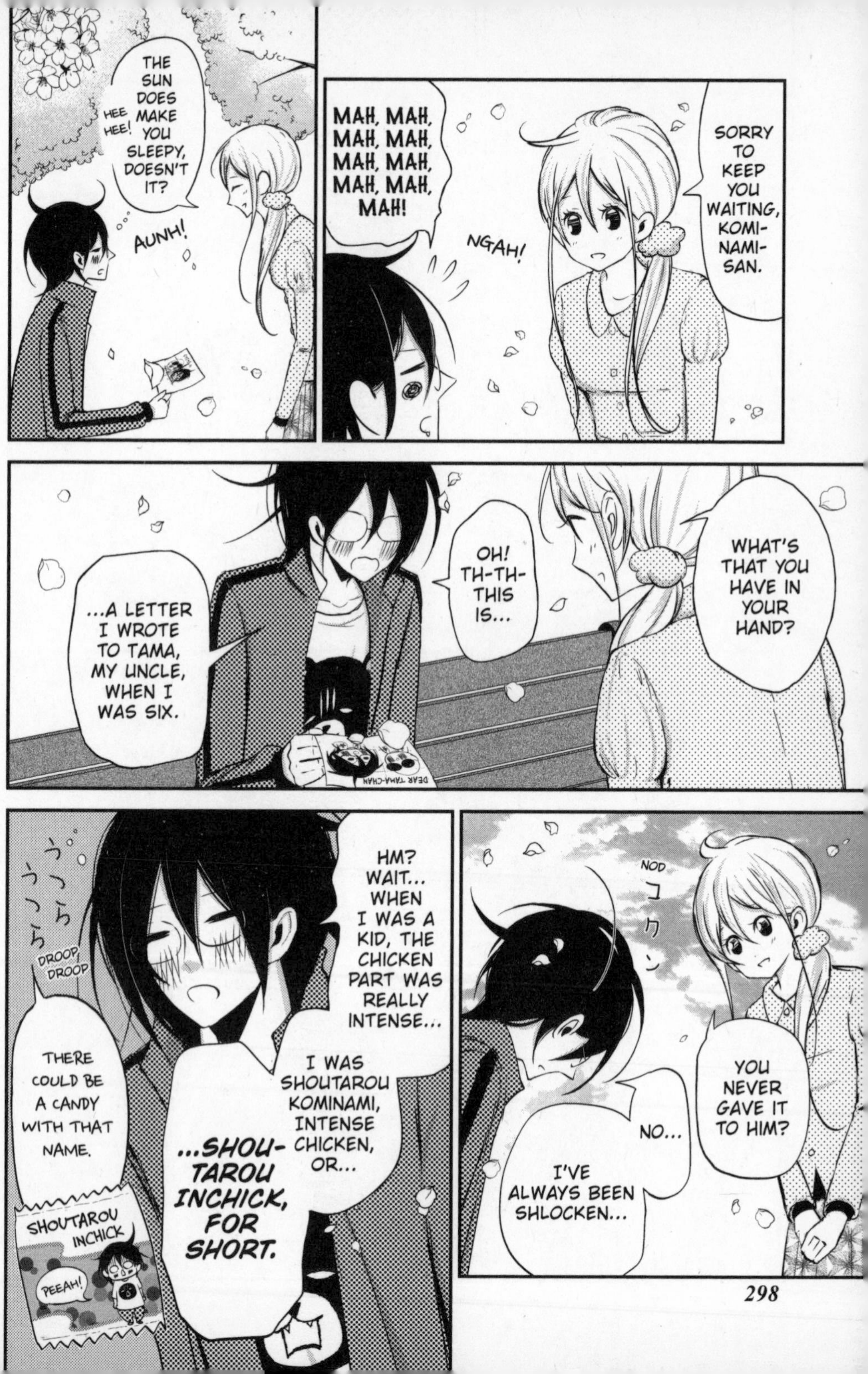
SORRY TO KEEP YOU WAITING, KOMINAMI-SAN.
NGAH!
MAH, MAH, MAH, MAH, MAH, MAH, MAH, MAH, MAH!
THE SUN DOES MAKE YOU SLEEPY, DOESN'T IT?
HEE HEE!
AUNH!
WHAT'S THAT YOU HAVE IN YOUR HAND?
OH! TH-TH-THIS IS...
...A LETTER I WROTE TO TAMA, MY UNCLE, WHEN I WAS SIX.
DEAR TAMA-CHAN
YOU NEVER GAVE IT TO HIM?
NOD
コクン
NO...
I'VE ALWAYS BEEN SHLOCKEN...
HM? WAIT... WHEN I WAS A KID, THE CHICKEN PART WAS REALLY INTENSE...
I WAS SHOUTAROU KOMINAMI, INTENSE CHICKEN, OR...
...SHOU-TAROU INCHICK, FOR SHORT.
うつらうつら
DROOP DROOP
THERE COULD BE A CANDY WITH THAT NAME.
SHOUTAROU INCHICK
PEEAH!

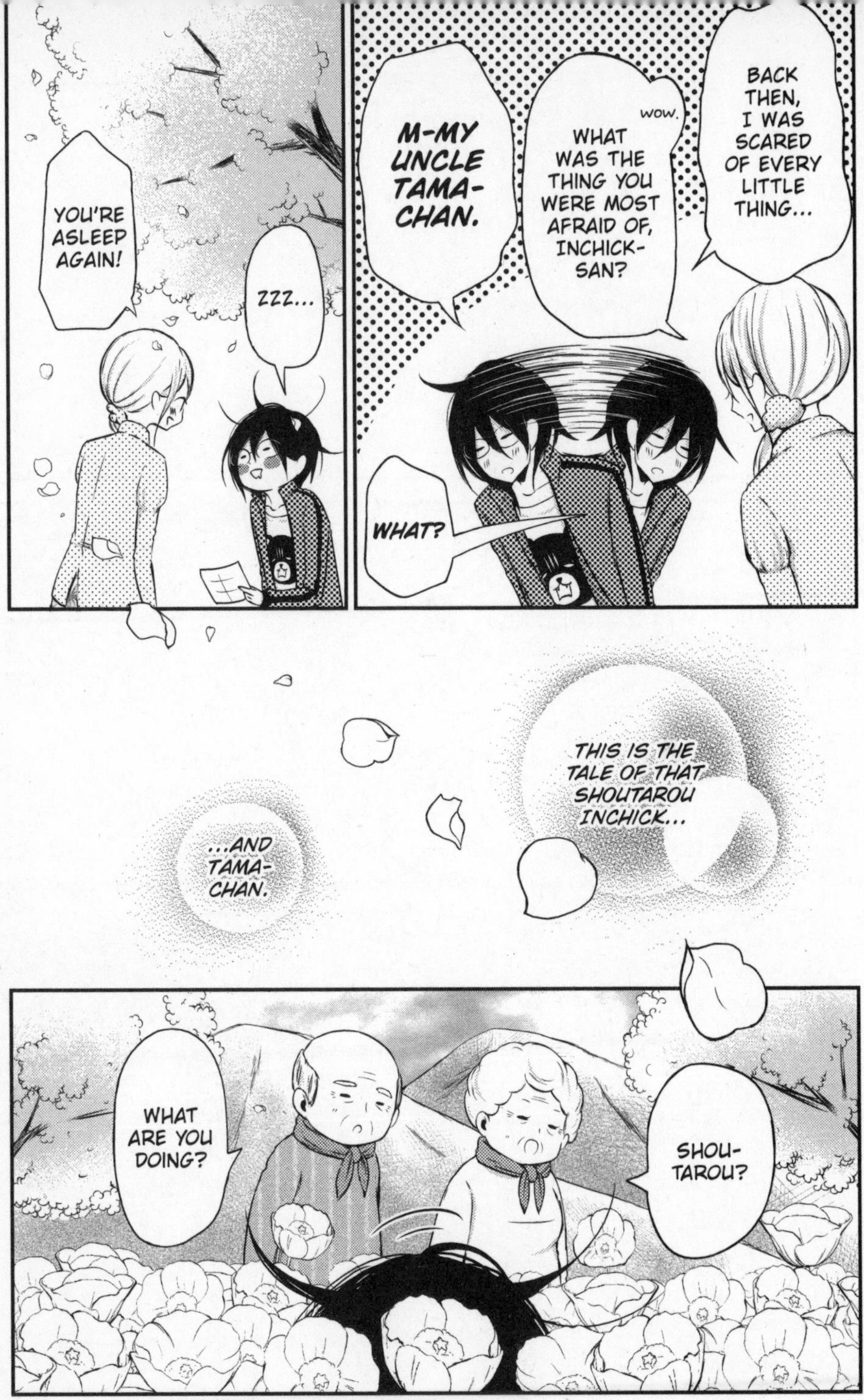
BACK THEN, I WAS SCARED OF EVERY LITTLE THING...
WOW.
WHAT WAS THE THING YOU WERE MOST AFRAID OF, INCHICK-SAN?
M-MY UNCLE TAMA-CHAN.
WHAT?
ZZZ...
YOU'RE ASLEEP AGAIN!
THIS IS THE TALE OF THAT SHOUTAROU INCHICK...
...AND TAMA-CHAN.
SHOU-TAROU?
WHAT ARE YOU DOING?

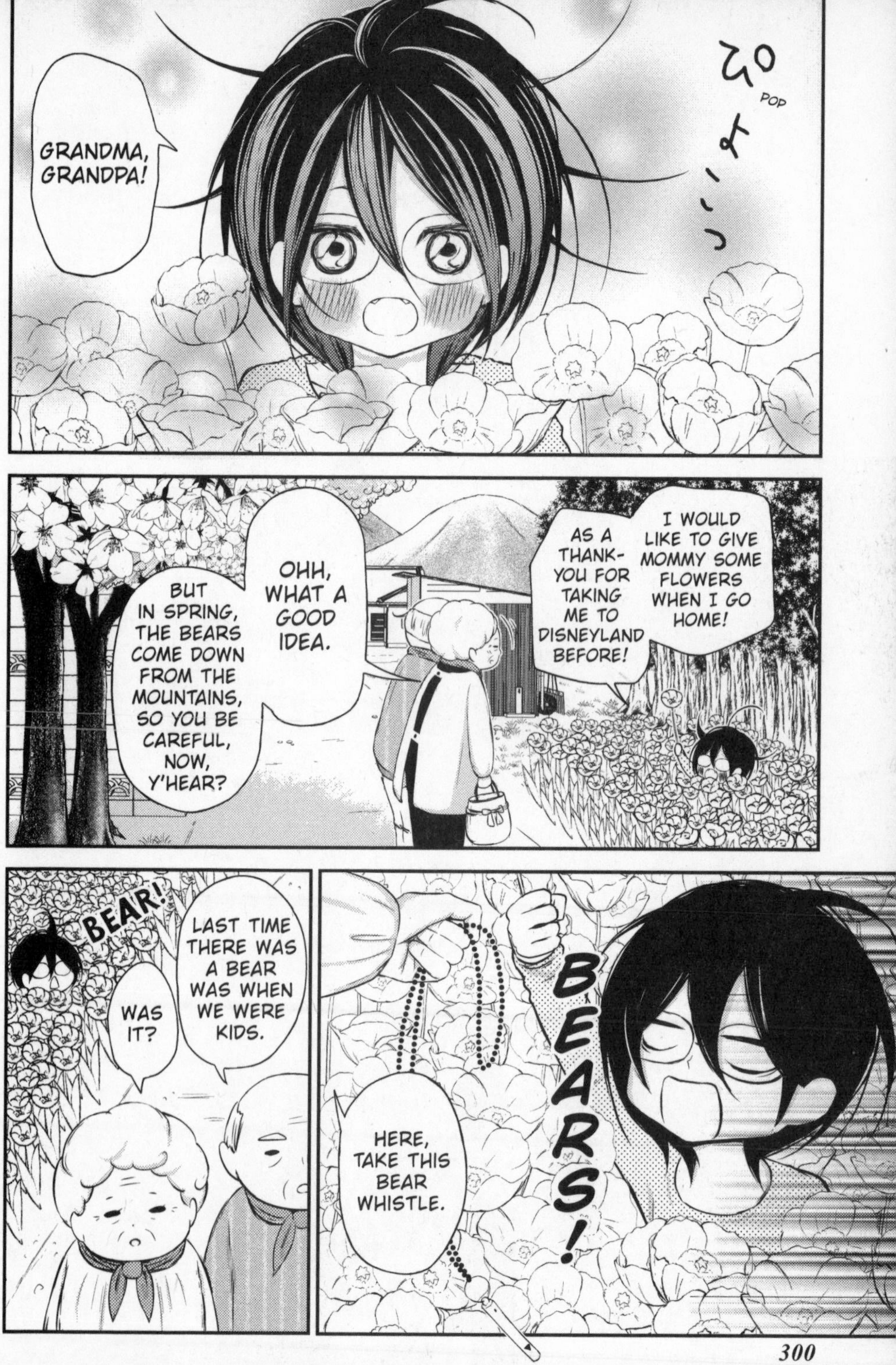
ぴょこっ
POP
GRANDMA, GRANDPA!
I WOULD LIKE TO GIVE MOMMY SOME FLOWERS WHEN I GO HOME!
AS A THANK-YOU FOR TAKING ME TO DISNEYLAND BEFORE!
OHH, WHAT A GOOD IDEA.
BUT IN SPRING, THE BEARS COME DOWN FROM THE MOUNTAINS, SO YOU BE CAREFUL, NOW, Y'HEAR?
BEARS!
HERE, TAKE THIS BEAR WHISTLE.
BEAR!
LAST TIME THERE WAS A BEAR WAS WHEN WE WERE KIDS.
WAS IT?

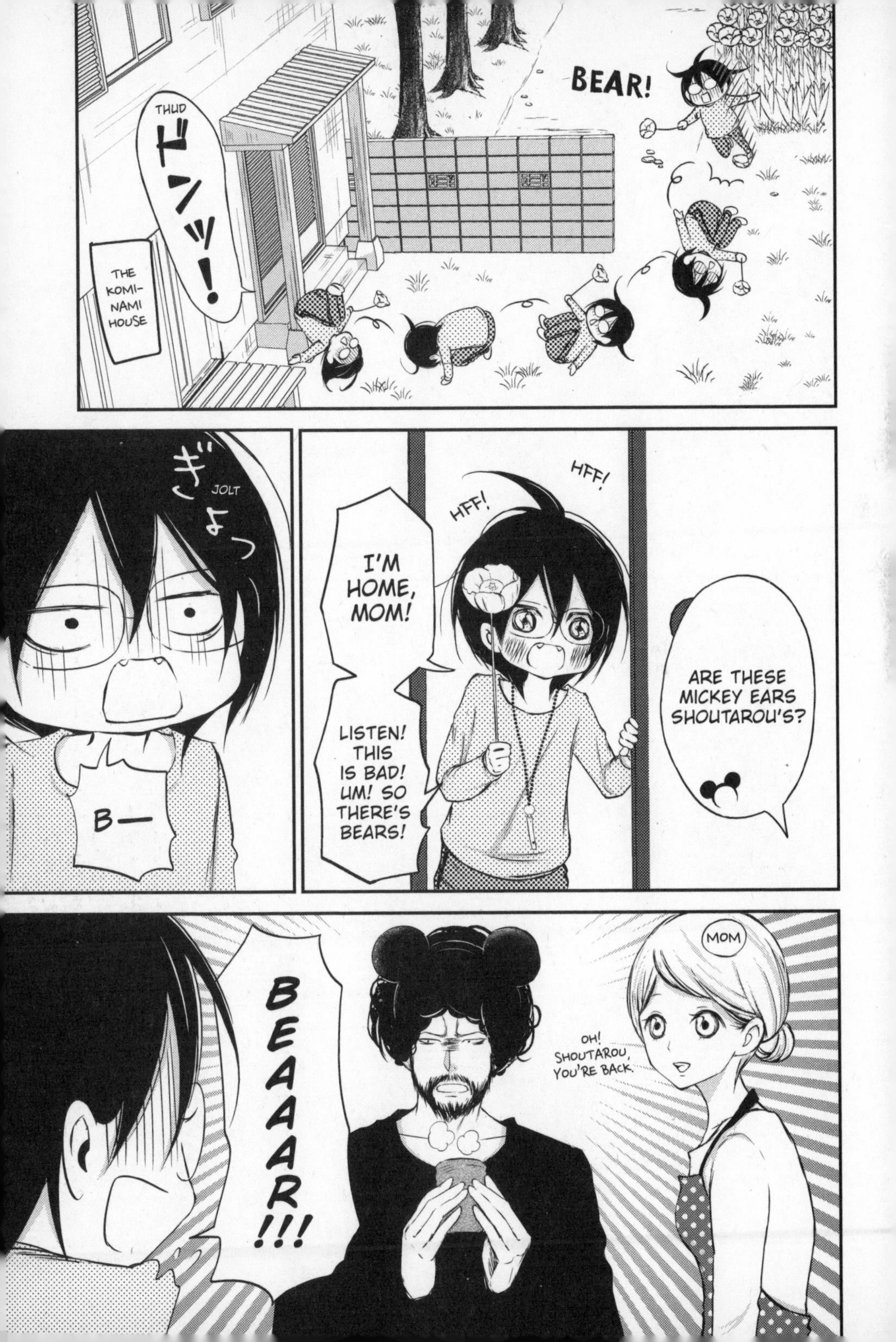
BEAR!
THUD
ドンッ!
THE KOMI-NAMI HOUSE
HFF!
HFF!
I'M HOME, MOM!
ARE THESE MICKEY EARS SHOUTAROU'S?
LISTEN! THIS IS BAD! UM! SO THERE'S BEARS!
ぎょっ
JOLT
B—
MOM
OH! SHOUTAROU, YOU'RE BACK.
BEAAAAR!!!

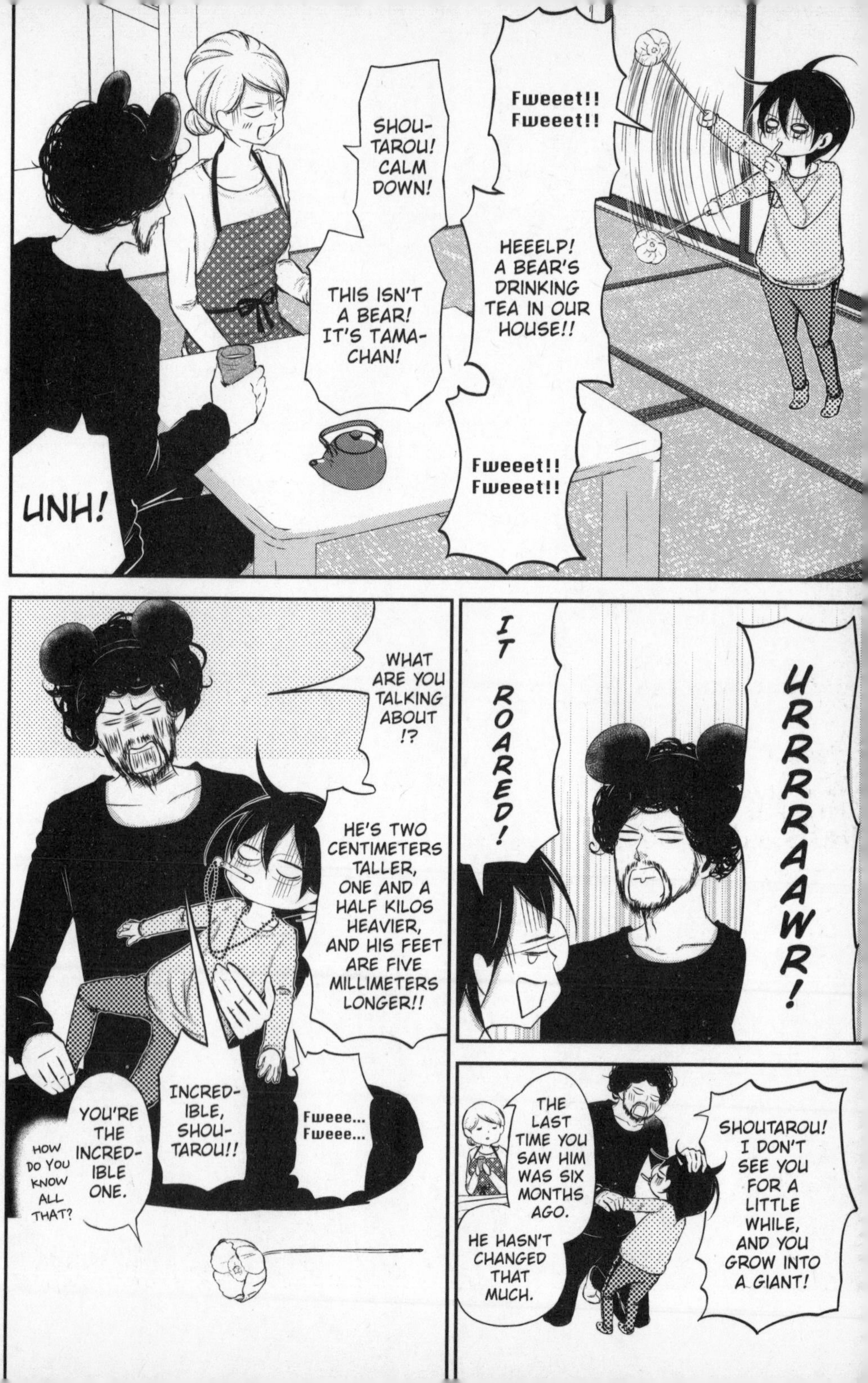
Fweeet!! Fweeet!!
SHOUTAROU! CALM DOWN!
HEEELP! A BEAR'S DRINKING TEA IN OUR HOUSE!!
THIS ISN'T A BEAR! IT'S TAMA-CHAN!
Fweeet!! Fweeet!!
UNH!
URRRRAAWR!
IT ROARED!
SHOUTAROU! I DON'T SEE YOU FOR A LITTLE WHILE, AND YOU GROW INTO A GIANT!
THE LAST TIME YOU SAW HIM WAS SIX MONTHS AGO.
HE HASN'T CHANGED THAT MUCH.
WHAT ARE YOU TALKING ABOUT!?
HE'S TWO CENTIMETERS TALLER, ONE AND A HALF KILOS HEAVIER, AND HIS FEET ARE FIVE MILLIMETERS LONGER!!
Fweee... Fweee...
INCREDIBLE, SHOUTAROU!!
YOU'RE THE INCREDIBLE ONE.
HOW DO YOU KNOW ALL THAT?

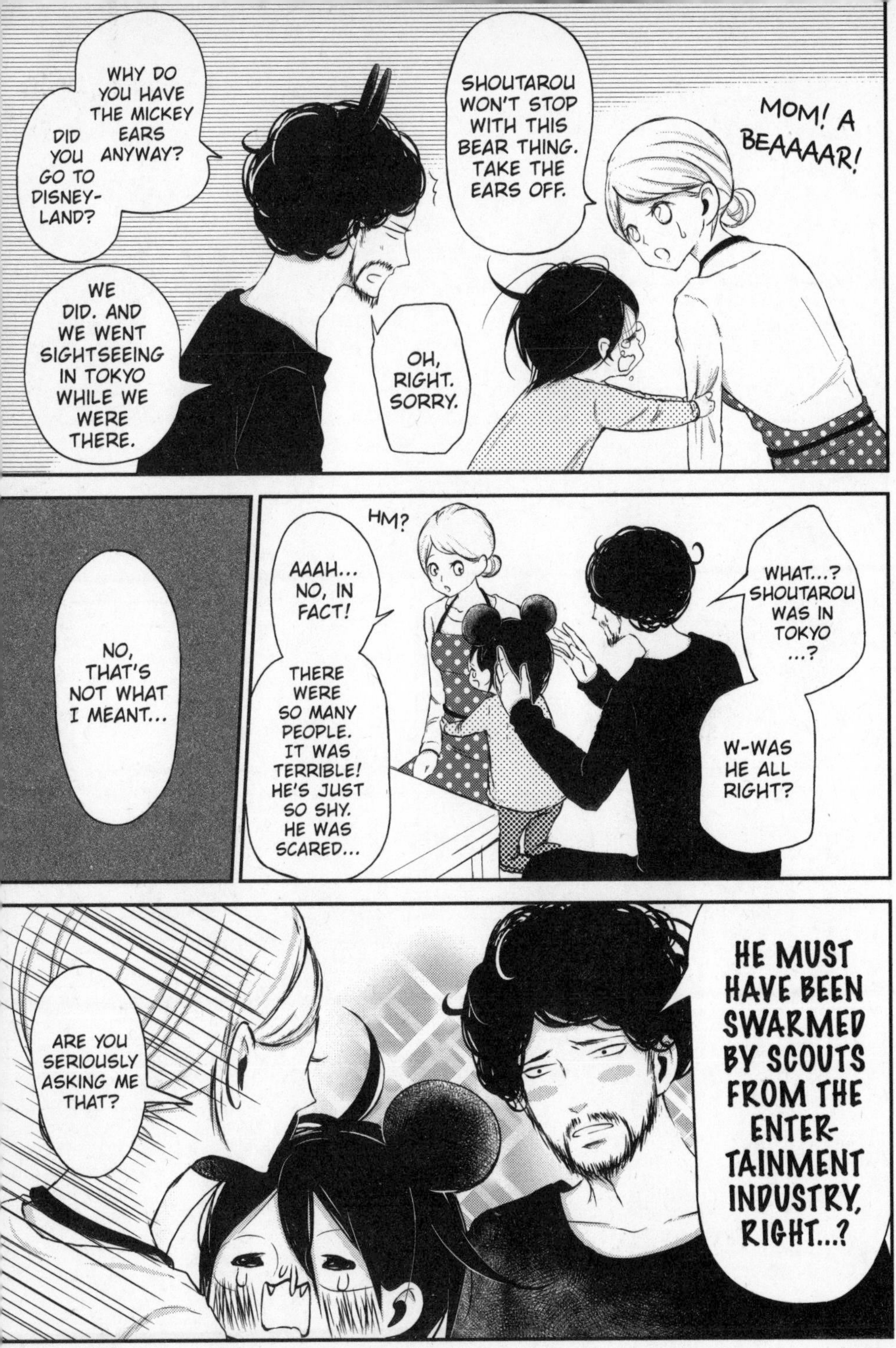
MOM! A BEAAAAR!
SHOUTAROU WON'T STOP WITH THIS BEAR THING. TAKE THE EARS OFF.
OH, RIGHT. SORRY.
WHY DO YOU HAVE THE MICKEY EARS ANYWAY?
DID YOU GO TO DISNEY-LAND?
WE DID. AND WE WENT SIGHTSEEING IN TOKYO WHILE WE WERE THERE.
WHAT...? SHOUTAROU WAS IN TOKYO ...?
HM?
AAAH... NO, IN FACT!
W-WAS HE ALL RIGHT?
THERE WERE SO MANY PEOPLE. IT WAS TERRIBLE! HE'S JUST SO SHY. HE WAS SCARED...
NO, THAT'S NOT WHAT I MEANT...
HE MUST HAVE BEEN SWARMED BY SCOUTS FROM THE ENTER-TAINMENT INDUSTRY, RIGHT...?
ARE YOU SERIOUSLY ASKING ME THAT?

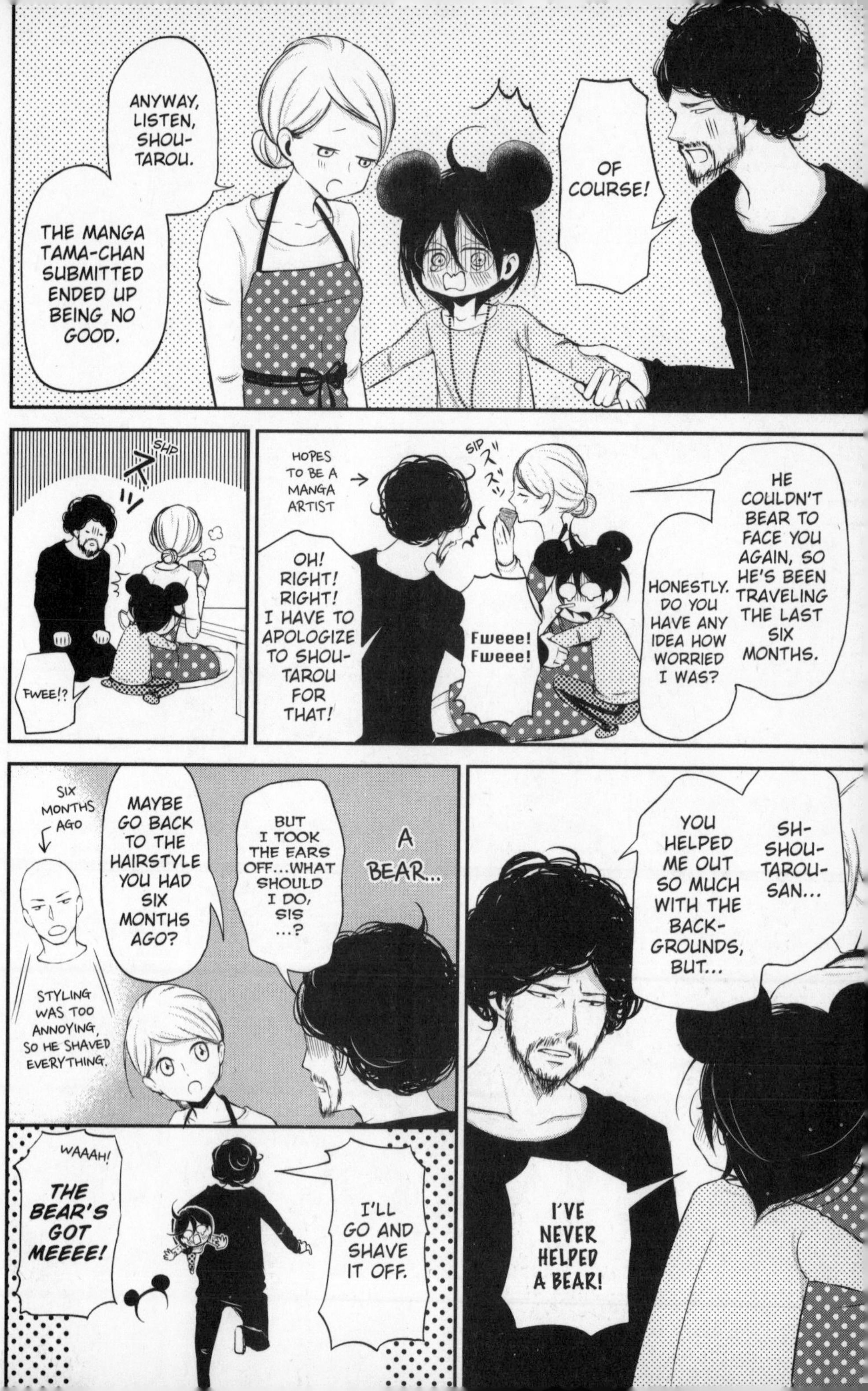
OF COURSE!
ANYWAY, LISTEN, SHOU-TAROU.
THE MANGA TAMA-CHAN SUBMITTED ENDED UP BEING NO GOOD.
HE COULDN'T BEAR TO FACE YOU AGAIN, SO HE'S BEEN TRAVELING THE LAST SIX MONTHS.
HONESTLY. DO YOU HAVE ANY IDEA HOW WORRIED I WAS?
SIP
Fweee! Fweee!
HOPES TO BE A MANGA ARTIST
OH! RIGHT! RIGHT! I HAVE TO APOLOGIZE TO SHOU-TAROU FOR THAT!
SHP
FWEE!?
SH-SHOU-TAROU-SAN...
YOU HELPED ME OUT SO MUCH WITH THE BACK-GROUNDS, BUT...
I'VE NEVER HELPED A BEAR!
A BEAR...
BUT I TOOK THE EARS OFF...WHAT SHOULD I DO, SIS ...?
MAYBE GO BACK TO THE HAIRSTYLE YOU HAD SIX MONTHS AGO?
SIX MONTHS AGO
STYLING WAS TOO ANNOYING, SO HE SHAVED EVERYTHING.
I'LL GO AND SHAVE IT OFF.
WAAAH!
THE BEAR'S GOT MEEEE!

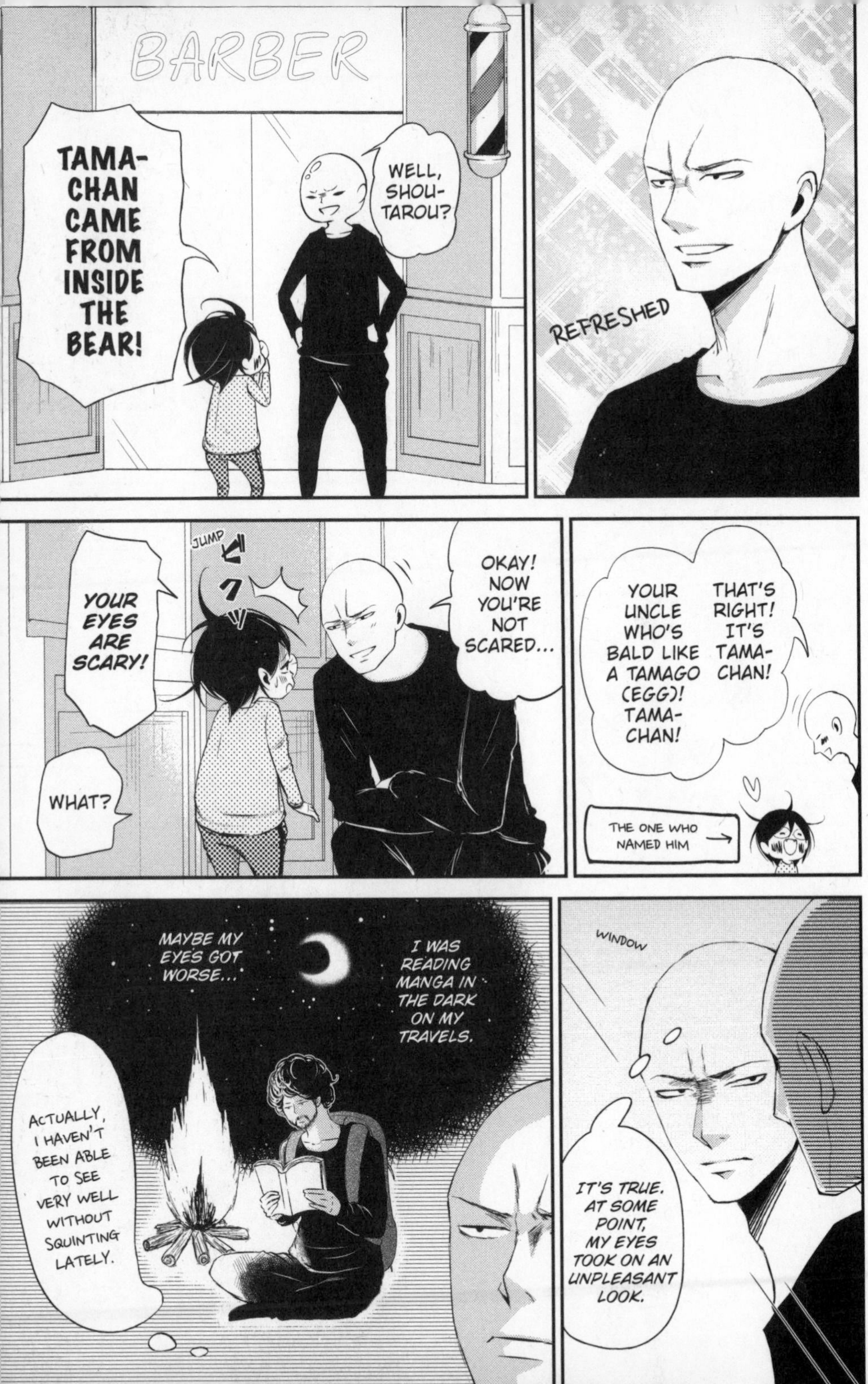
REFRESHED
BARBER
WELL, SHOU-TAROU?
TAMA-CHAN CAME FROM INSIDE THE BEAR!
THAT'S RIGHT! IT'S TAMA-CHAN!
YOUR UNCLE WHO'S BALD LIKE A TAMAGO (EGG)! TAMA-CHAN!
THE ONE WHO NAMED HIM
OKAY! NOW YOU'RE NOT SCARED...
JUMP
YOUR EYES ARE SCARY!
WHAT?
WINDOW
IT'S TRUE. AT SOME POINT, MY EYES TOOK ON AN UNPLEASANT LOOK.
I WAS READING MANGA IN THE DARK ON MY TRAVELS.
MAYBE MY EYES GOT WORSE...
ACTUALLY, I HAVEN'T BEEN ABLE TO SEE VERY WELL WITHOUT SQUINTING LATELY.

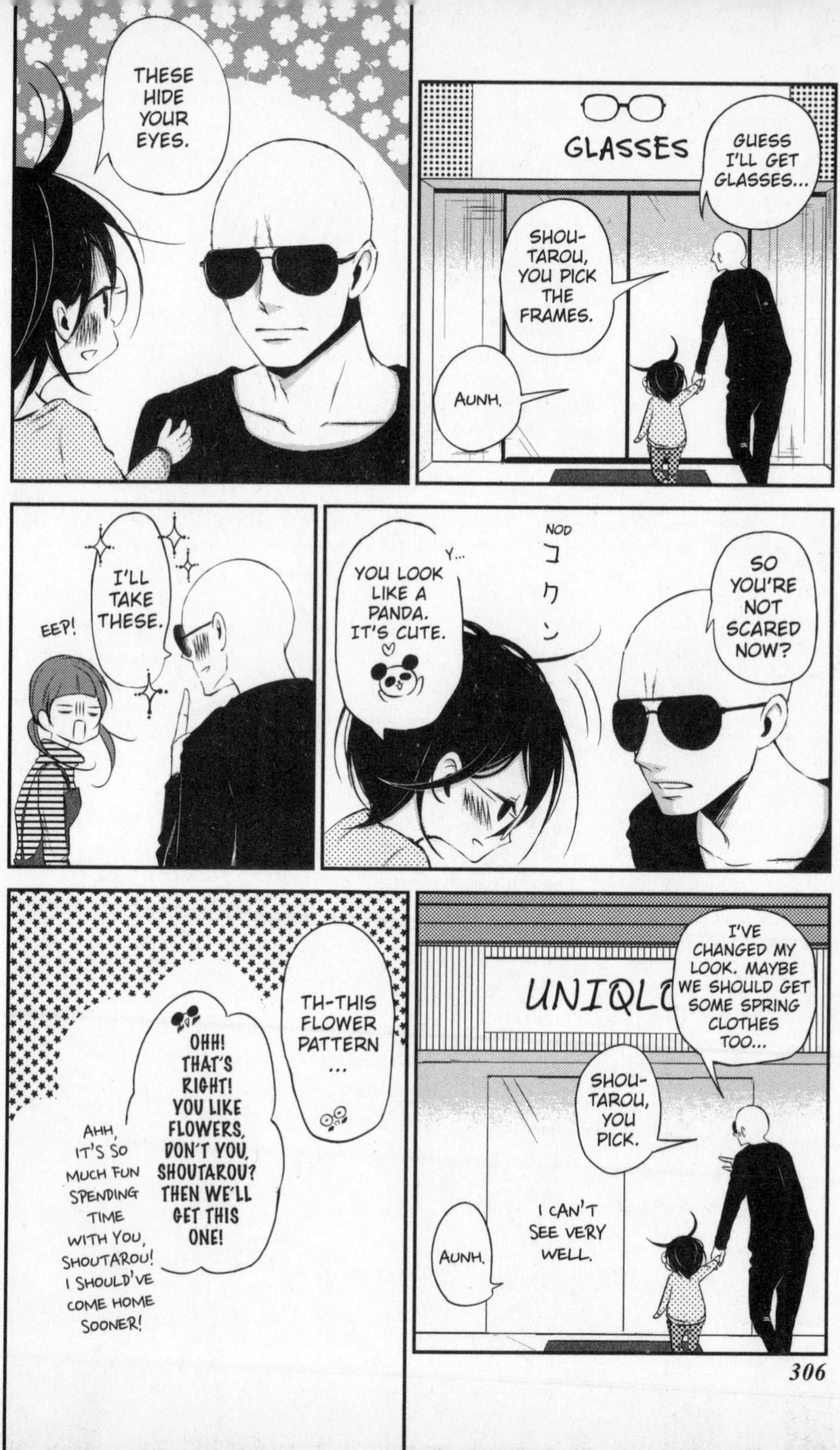
GLASSES
GUESS I'LL GET GLASSES...
SHOUTAROU, YOU PICK THE FRAMES.
AUNH.
THESE HIDE YOUR EYES.
SO YOU'RE NOT SCARED NOW?
NOD
コクン
Y...
YOU LOOK LIKE A PANDA. IT'S CUTE.
I'LL TAKE THESE.
EEP!
UNIQLO
I'VE CHANGED MY LOOK. MAYBE WE SHOULD GET SOME SPRING CLOTHES TOO...
SHOUTAROU, YOU PICK.
I CAN'T SEE VERY WELL.
AUNH.
TH-THIS FLOWER PATTERN ...
OHH! THAT'S RIGHT! YOU LIKE FLOWERS, DON'T YOU, SHOUTAROU? THEN WE'LL GET THIS ONE!
AHH, IT'S SO MUCH FUN SPENDING TIME WITH YOU, SHOUTAROU! I SHOULD'VE COME HOME SOONER!

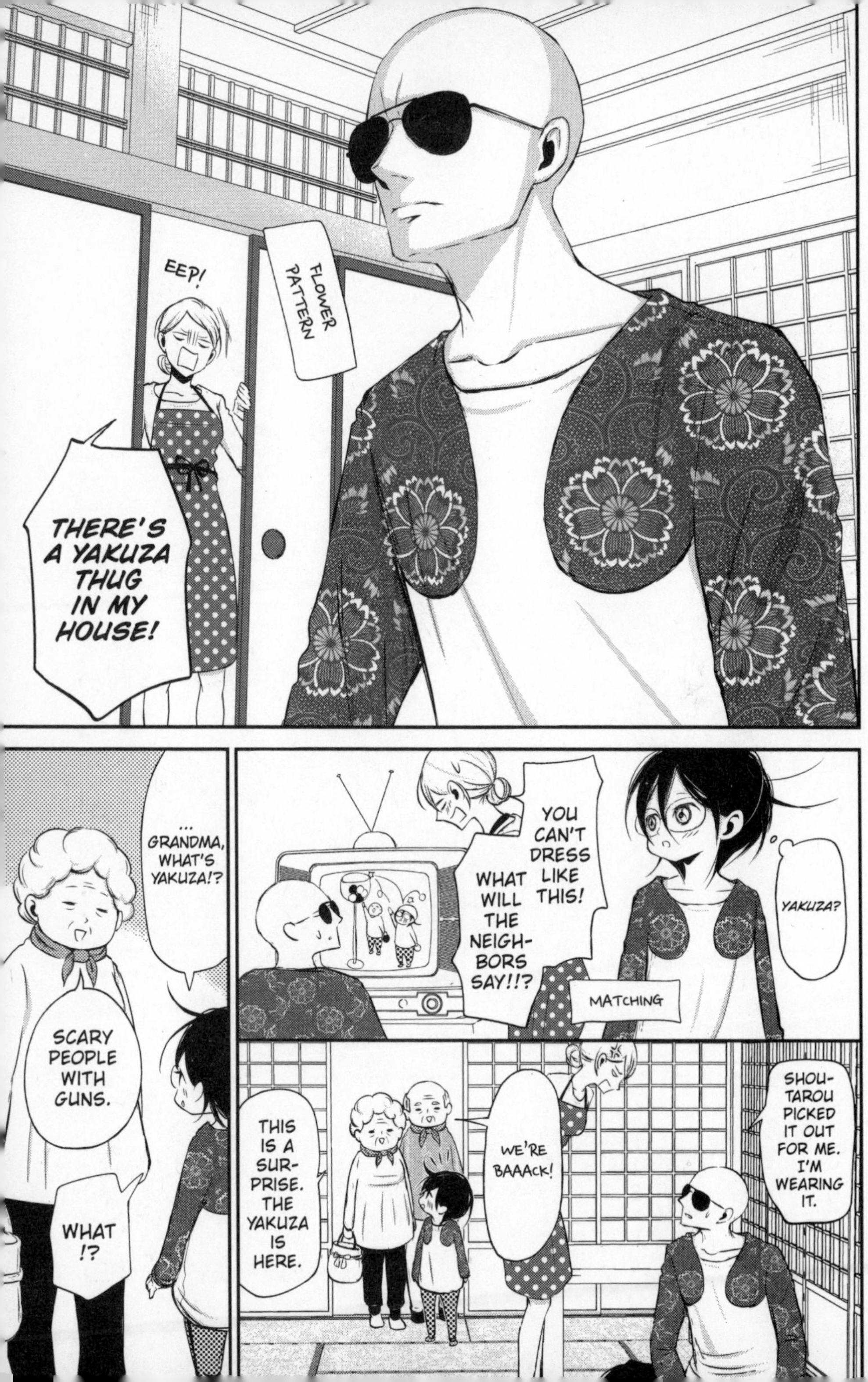
FLOWER PATTERN
EEP!
THERE'S A YAKUZA THUG IN MY HOUSE!
YAKUZA?
YOU CAN'T DRESS LIKE THIS!
WHAT WILL THE NEIGH-BORS SAY!!?
MATCHING
SHOU-TAROU PICKED IT OUT FOR ME. I'M WEARING IT.
WE'RE BAAACK!
THIS IS A SUR-PRISE. THE YAKUZA IS HERE.
... GRANDMA, WHAT'S YAKUZA!?
SCARY PEOPLE WITH GUNS.
WHAT !?

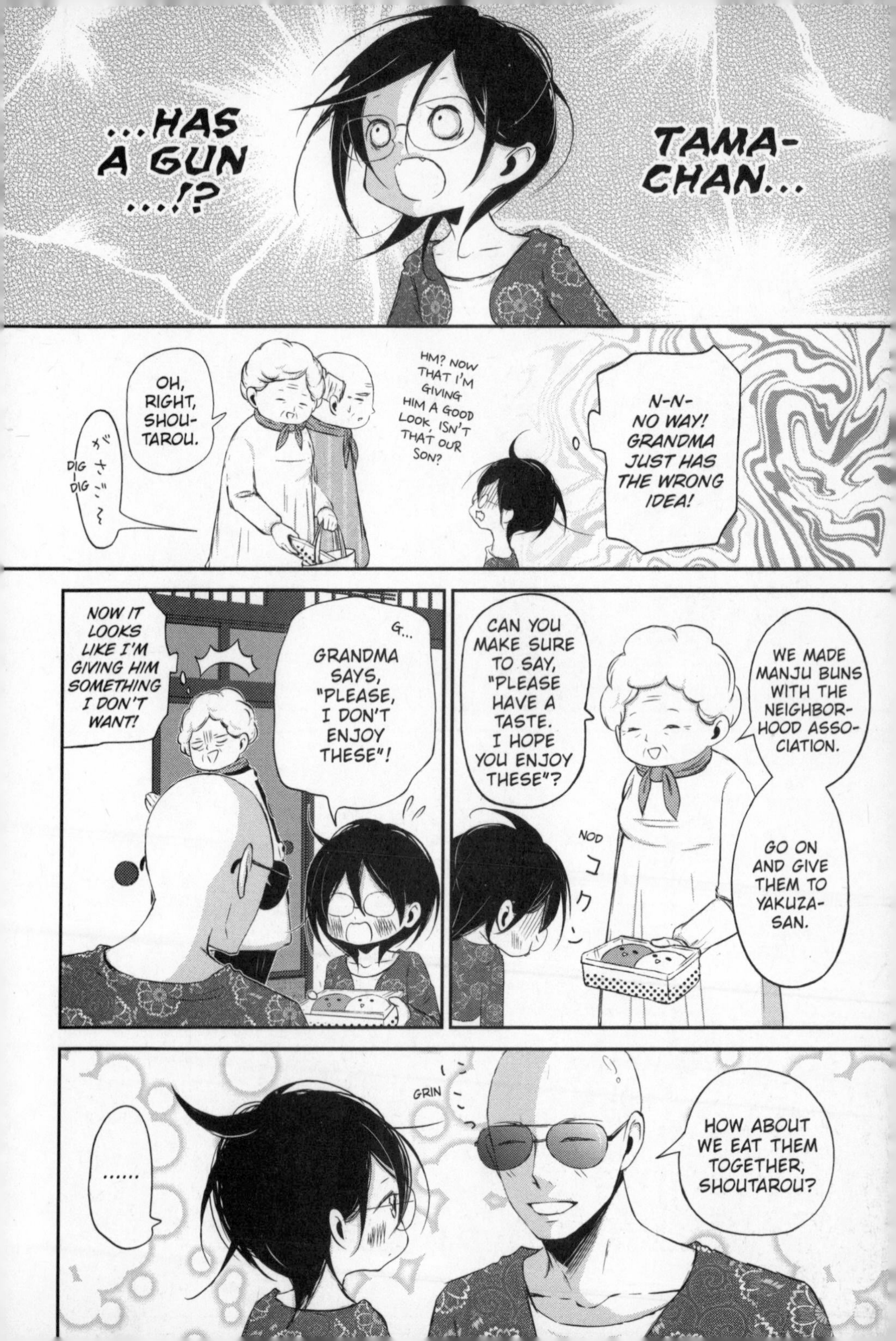
TAMA-CHAN...
...HAS A GUN ...!?
N-N-NO WAY! GRANDMA JUST HAS THE WRONG IDEA!
HM? NOW THAT I'M GIVING HIM A GOOD LOOK, ISN'T THAT OUR SON?
OH, RIGHT, SHOUTAROU.
DIG DIG
WE MADE MANJU BUNS WITH THE NEIGHBORHOOD ASSOCIATION.
GO ON AND GIVE THEM TO YAKUZA-SAN.
CAN YOU MAKE SURE TO SAY, "PLEASE HAVE A TASTE. I HOPE YOU ENJOY THESE"?
NOD
G...
GRANDMA SAYS, "PLEASE, I DON'T ENJOY THESE"!
NOW IT LOOKS LIKE I'M GIVING HIM SOMETHING I DON'T WANT!
HOW ABOUT WE EAT THEM TOGETHER, SHOUTAROU?
GRIN
......

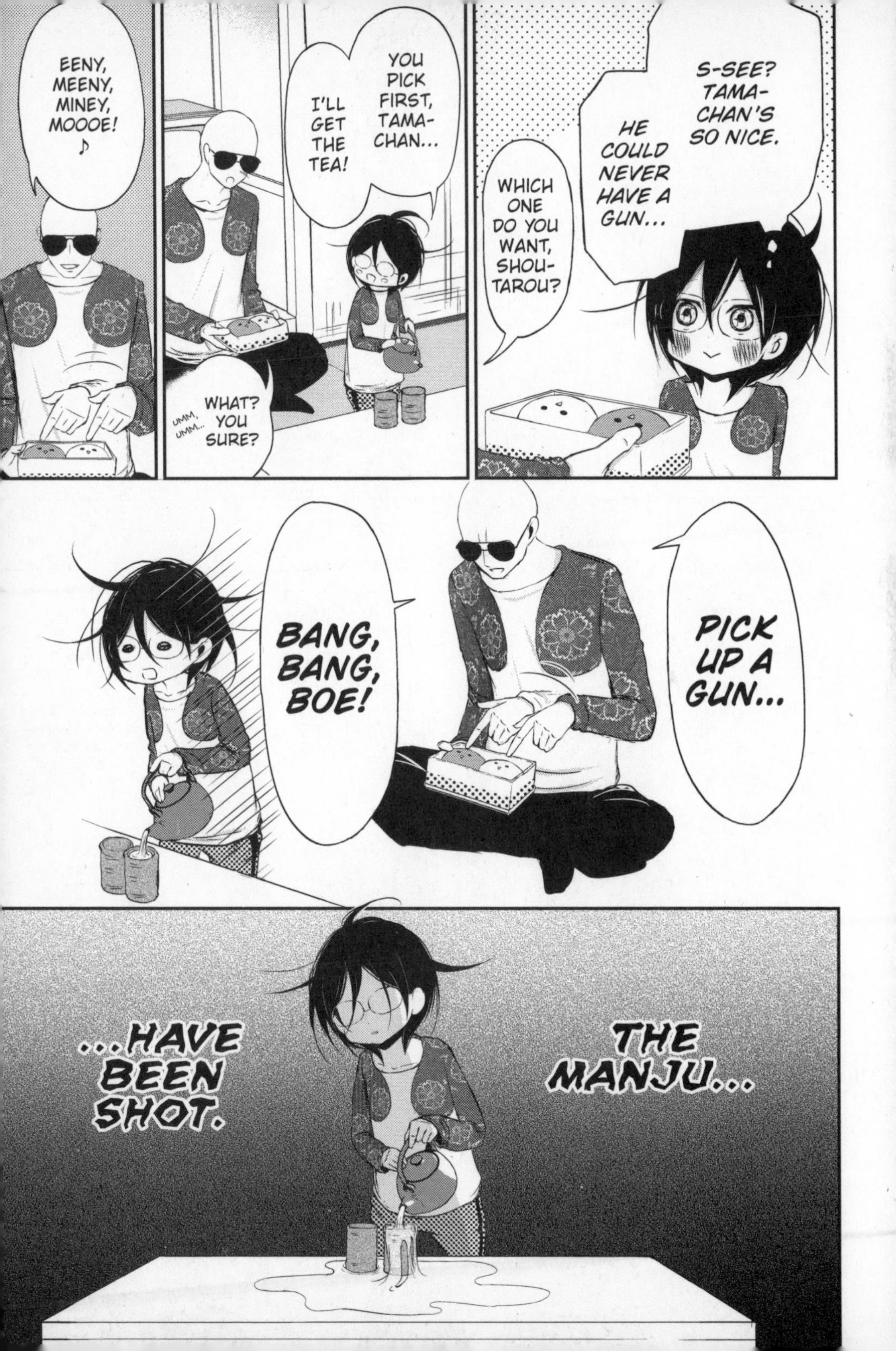
S-SEE? TAMA-CHAN'S SO NICE.
HE COULD NEVER HAVE A GUN...
WHICH ONE DO YOU WANT, SHOUTAROU?
YOU PICK FIRST, TAMA-CHAN...
I'LL GET THE TEA!
WHAT? YOU SURE?
UMM, UMM...
EENY, MEENY, MINEY, MOOOE! ♪
PICK UP A GUN...
BANG, BANG, BOE!
THE MANJU...
...HAVE BEEN SHOT.

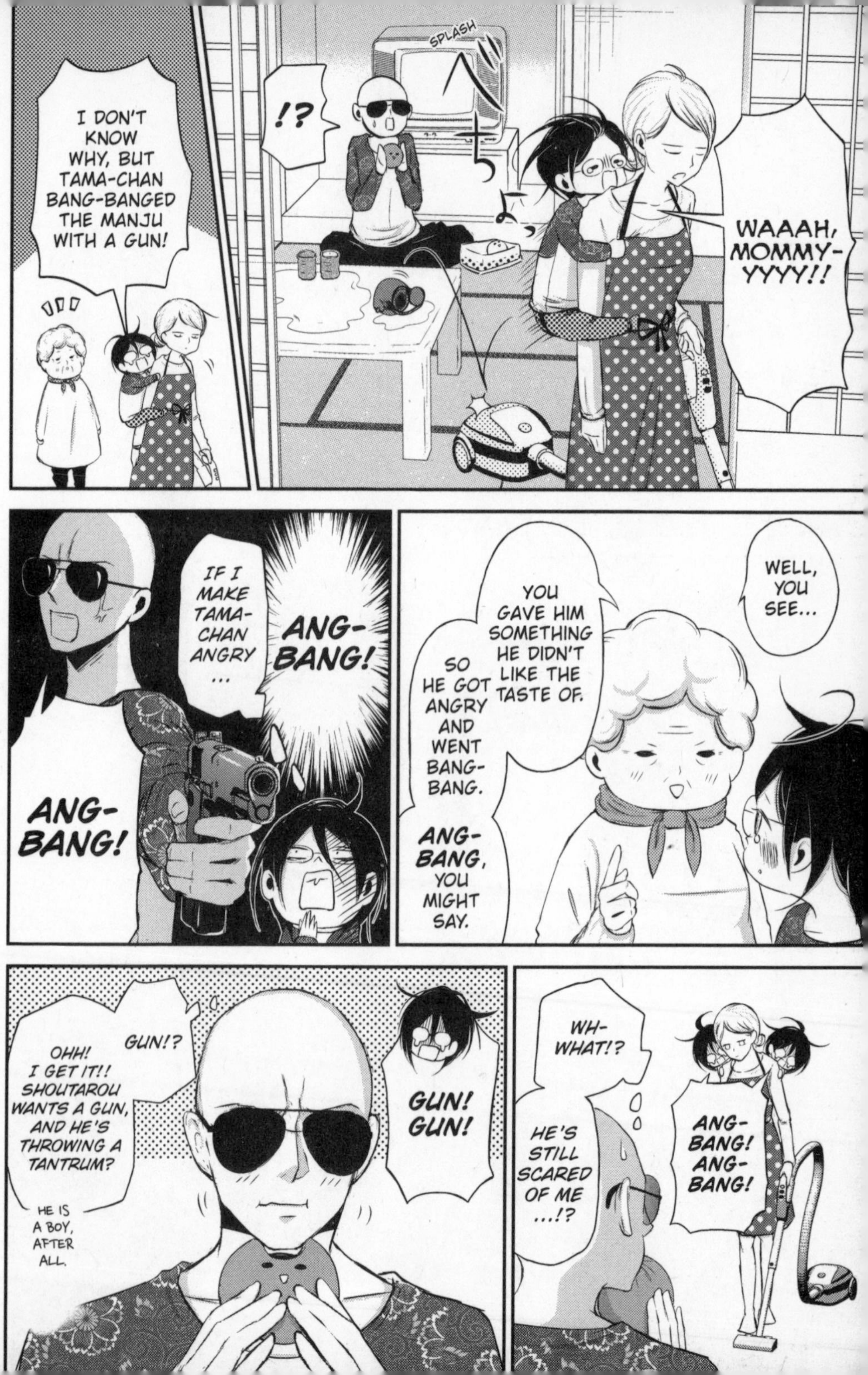
SPLASH
WAAAH, MOMMY-YYYY!!
!?
I DON'T KNOW WHY, BUT TAMA-CHAN BANG-BANGED THE MANJU WITH A GUN!
WELL, YOU SEE...
YOU GAVE HIM SOMETHING HE DIDN'T LIKE THE TASTE OF.
SO HE GOT ANGRY AND WENT BANG-BANG.
ANG-BANG, YOU MIGHT SAY.
IF I MAKE TAMA-CHAN ANGRY...
ANG-BANG!
ANG-BANG!
WH-WHAT!?
ANG-BANG! ANG-BANG!
HE'S STILL SCARED OF ME...!?
GUN!?
OHH! I GET IT!! SHOUTAROU WANTS A GUN, AND HE'S THROWING A TANTRUM?
GUN! GUN!
HE IS A BOY, AFTER ALL.

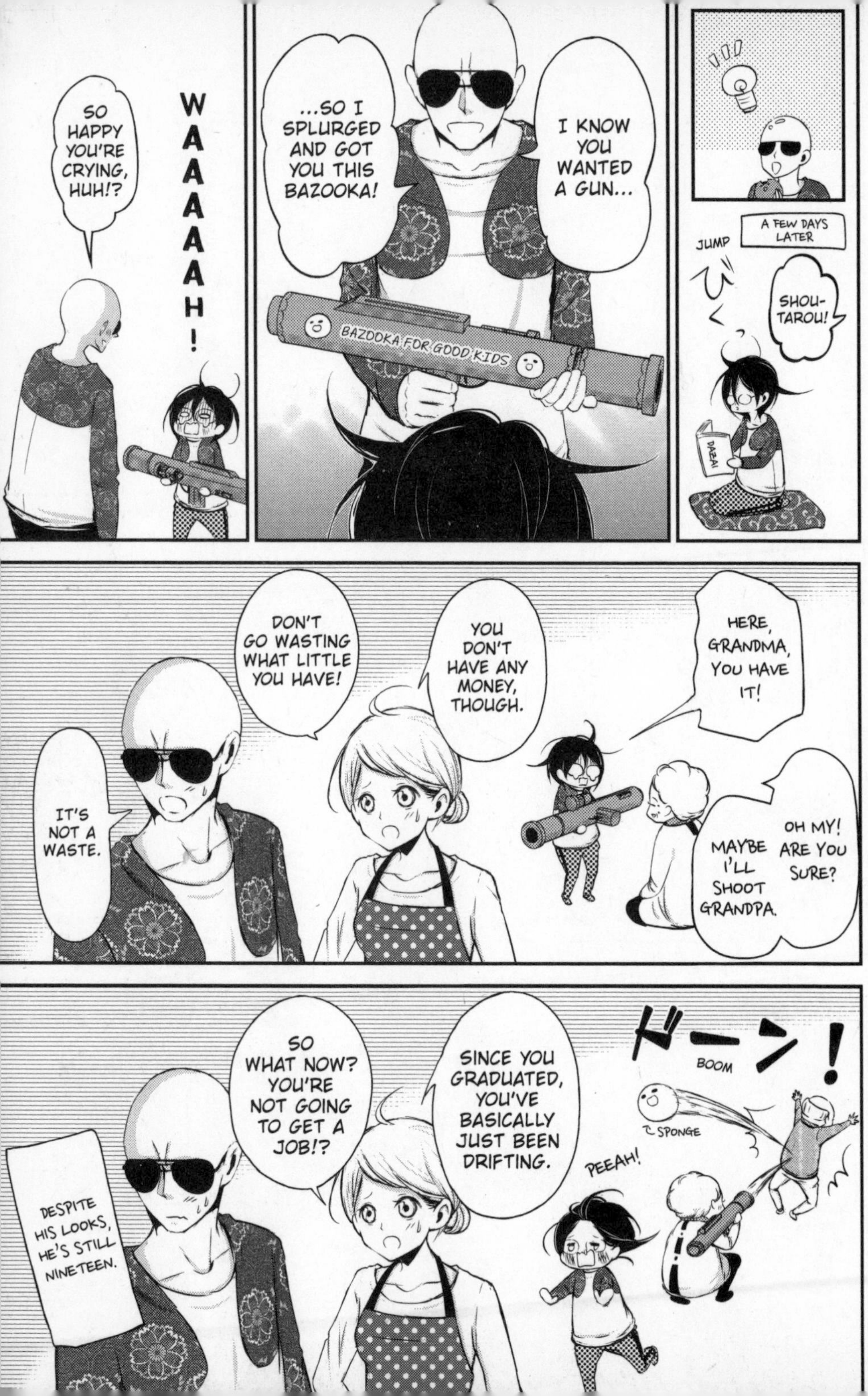

A FEW DAYS LATER
JUMP
SHOUTAROU!
DAZAI
I KNOW YOU WANTED A GUN...
...SO I SPLURGED AND GOT YOU THIS BAZOOKA!
BAZOOKA FOR GOOD KIDS
WAAAAAH!
SO HAPPY YOU'RE CRYING, HUH!?
HERE, GRANDMA, YOU HAVE IT!
OH MY! ARE YOU SURE?
MAYBE I'LL SHOOT GRANDPA.
YOU DON'T HAVE ANY MONEY, THOUGH.
DON'T GO WASTING WHAT LITTLE YOU HAVE!
IT'S NOT A WASTE.
ドーン!
BOOM
SPONGE
PEEAH!
SINCE YOU GRADUATED, YOU'VE BASICALLY JUST BEEN DRIFTING.
SO WHAT NOW? YOU'RE NOT GOING TO GET A JOB!?
DESPITE HIS LOOKS, HE'S STILL NINETEEN.

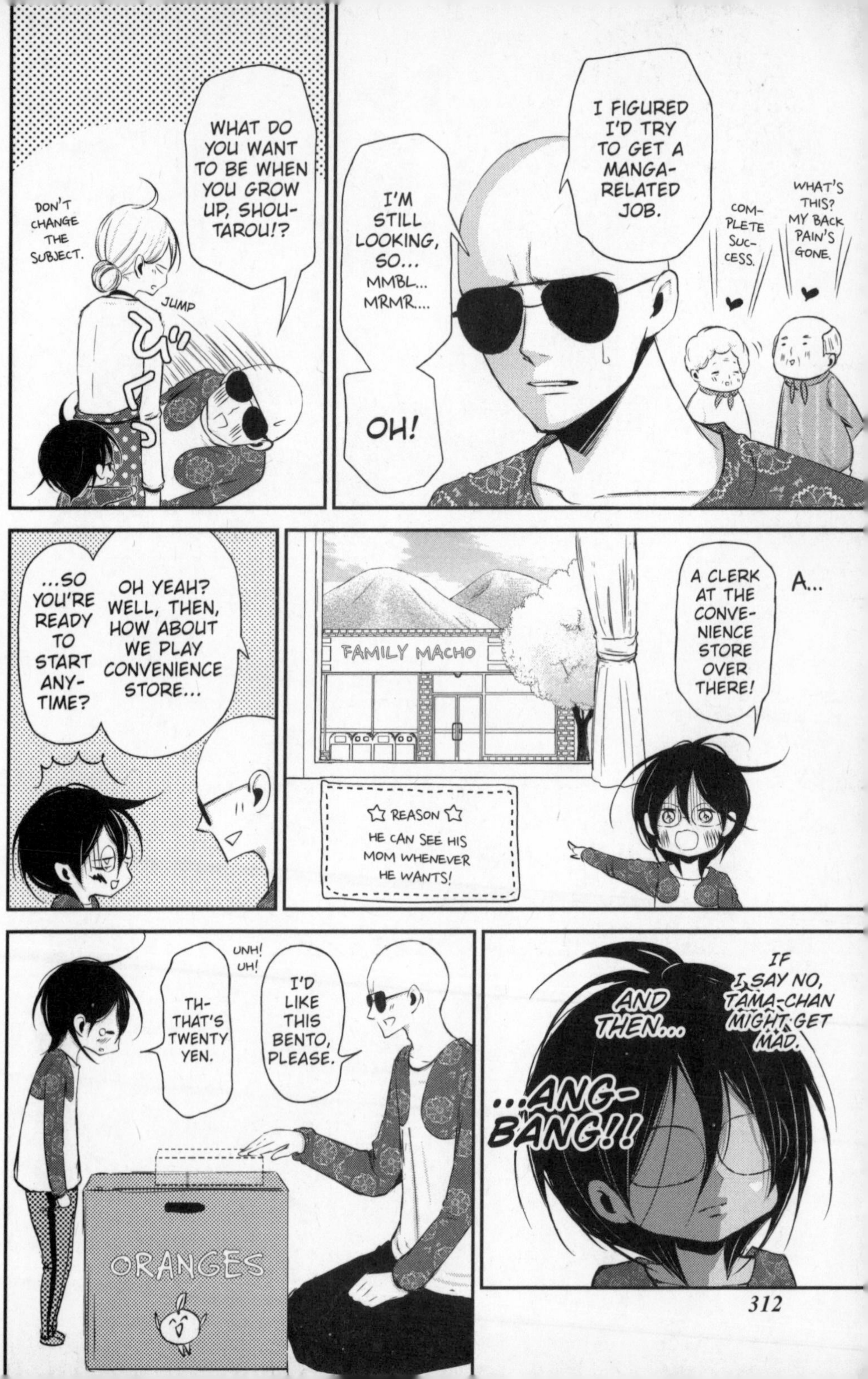
I FIGURED I'D TRY TO GET A MANGA-RELATED JOB.
WHAT'S THIS? MY BACK PAIN'S GONE.
COMPLETE SUCCESS.
I'M STILL LOOKING, SO... MMBL... MRMR...
OH!
WHAT DO YOU WANT TO BE WHEN YOU GROW UP, SHOUTAROU!?
DON'T CHANGE THE SUBJECT.
JUMP
A...
A CLERK AT THE CONVENIENCE STORE OVER THERE!
FAMILY MACHO
☆ REASON ☆ HE CAN SEE HIS MOM WHENEVER HE WANTS!
OH YEAH? WELL, THEN, HOW ABOUT WE PLAY CONVENIENCE STORE...
...SO YOU'RE READY TO START ANYTIME?
IF I SAY NO, TAMA-CHAN MIGHT GET MAD.
AND THEN...
...ANG-BANG!!
I'D LIKE THIS BENTO, PLEASE.
UNH! UH!
TH-THAT'S TWENTY YEN.
ORANGES

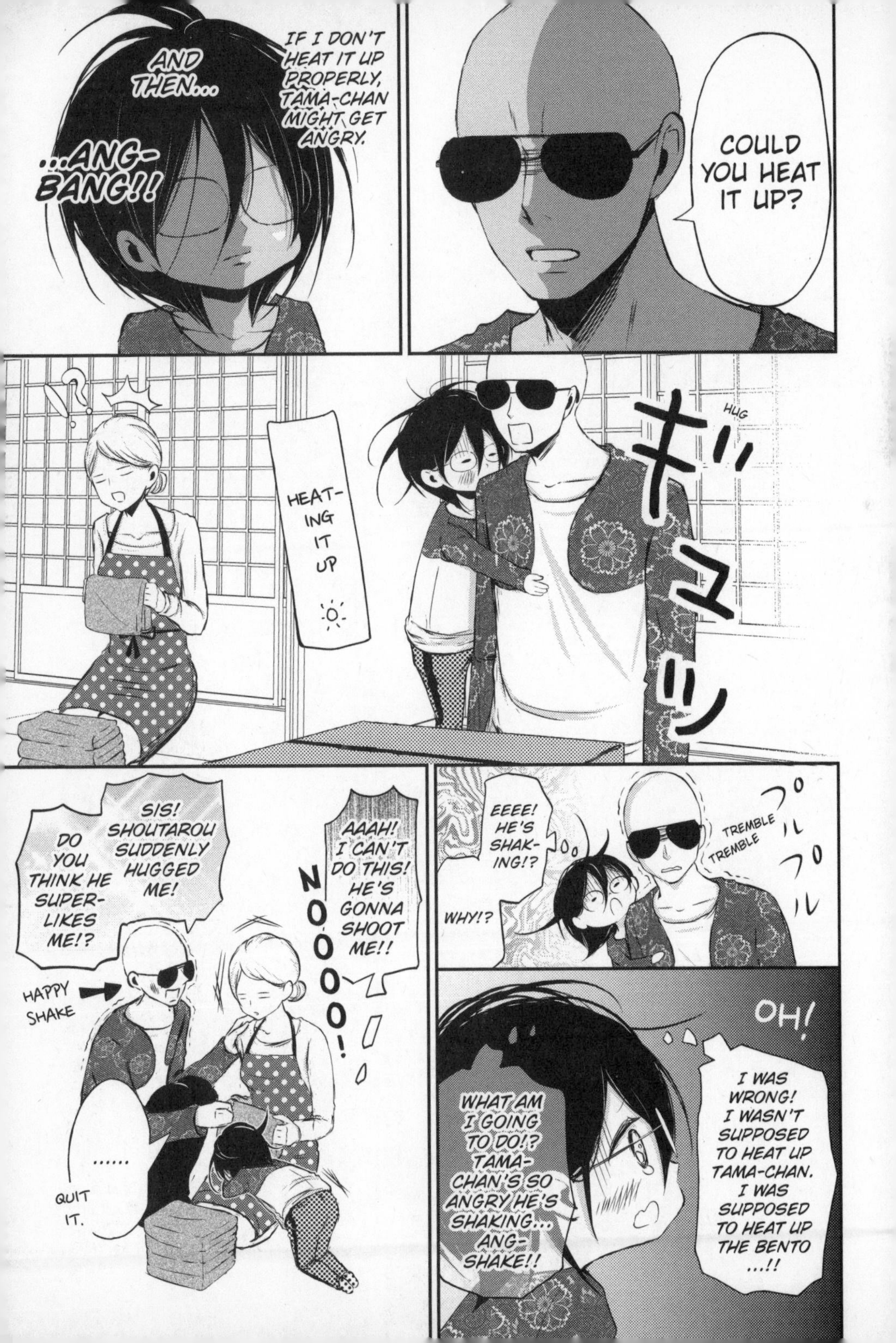
COULD YOU HEAT IT UP?
IF I DON'T HEAT IT UP PROPERLY, TAMA-CHAN MIGHT GET ANGRY.
AND THEN...
...ANG-BANG!!
ギュッ
HUG
HEAT-ING IT UP
EEEE! HE'S SHAK-ING!?
WHY!?
プルプル
TREMBLE TREMBLE
OH!
I WAS WRONG! I WASN'T SUPPOSED TO HEAT UP TAMA-CHAN. I WAS SUPPOSED TO HEAT UP THE BENTO ...!!
WHAT AM I GOING TO DO!? TAMA-CHAN'S SO ANGRY HE'S SHAKING... ANG-SHAKE!!
AAAH! I CAN'T DO THIS! HE'S GONNA SHOOT ME!!
NOOOOOO!
SIS! SHOUTAROU SUDDENLY HUGGED ME!
DO YOU THINK HE SUPER-LIKES ME!?
HAPPY SHAKE
......
QUIT IT.

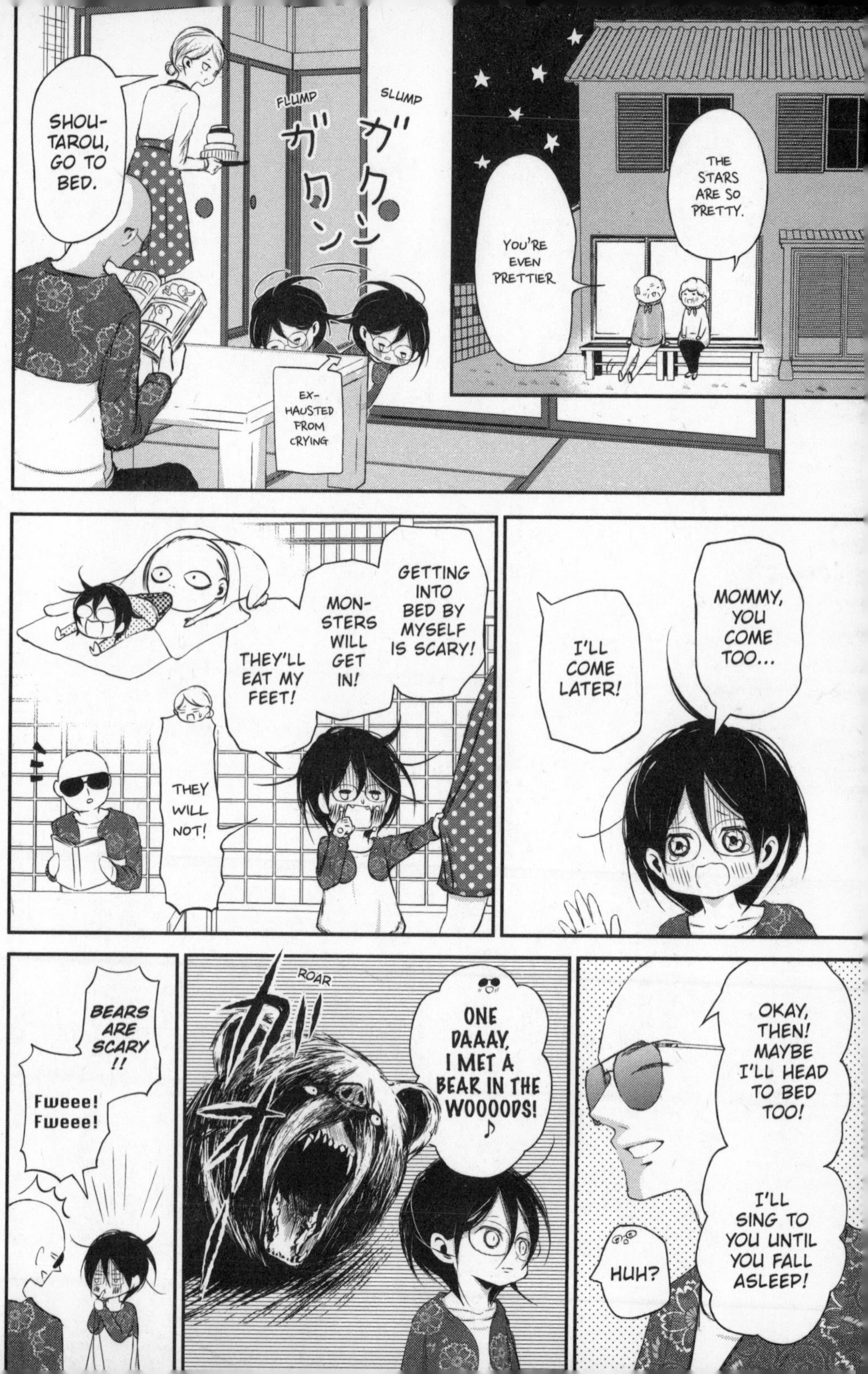
THE STARS ARE SO PRETTY.
YOU'RE EVEN PRETTIER
SLUMP
ガクン
FLUMP
ガクン
SHOU-TAROU, GO TO BED.
EX-HAUSTED FROM CRYING
MOMMY, YOU COME TOO…
I'LL COME LATER!
GETTING INTO BED BY MYSELF IS SCARY!
MONSTERS WILL GET IN!
THEY'LL EAT MY FEET!
THEY WILL NOT!
OKAY, THEN! MAYBE I'LL HEAD TO BED TOO!
I'LL SING TO YOU UNTIL YOU FALL ASLEEP!
HUH?
ONE DAAAY, I MET A BEAR IN THE WOOOODS! ♪
ROAR
BEARS ARE SCARY!!
Fweee! Fweee!

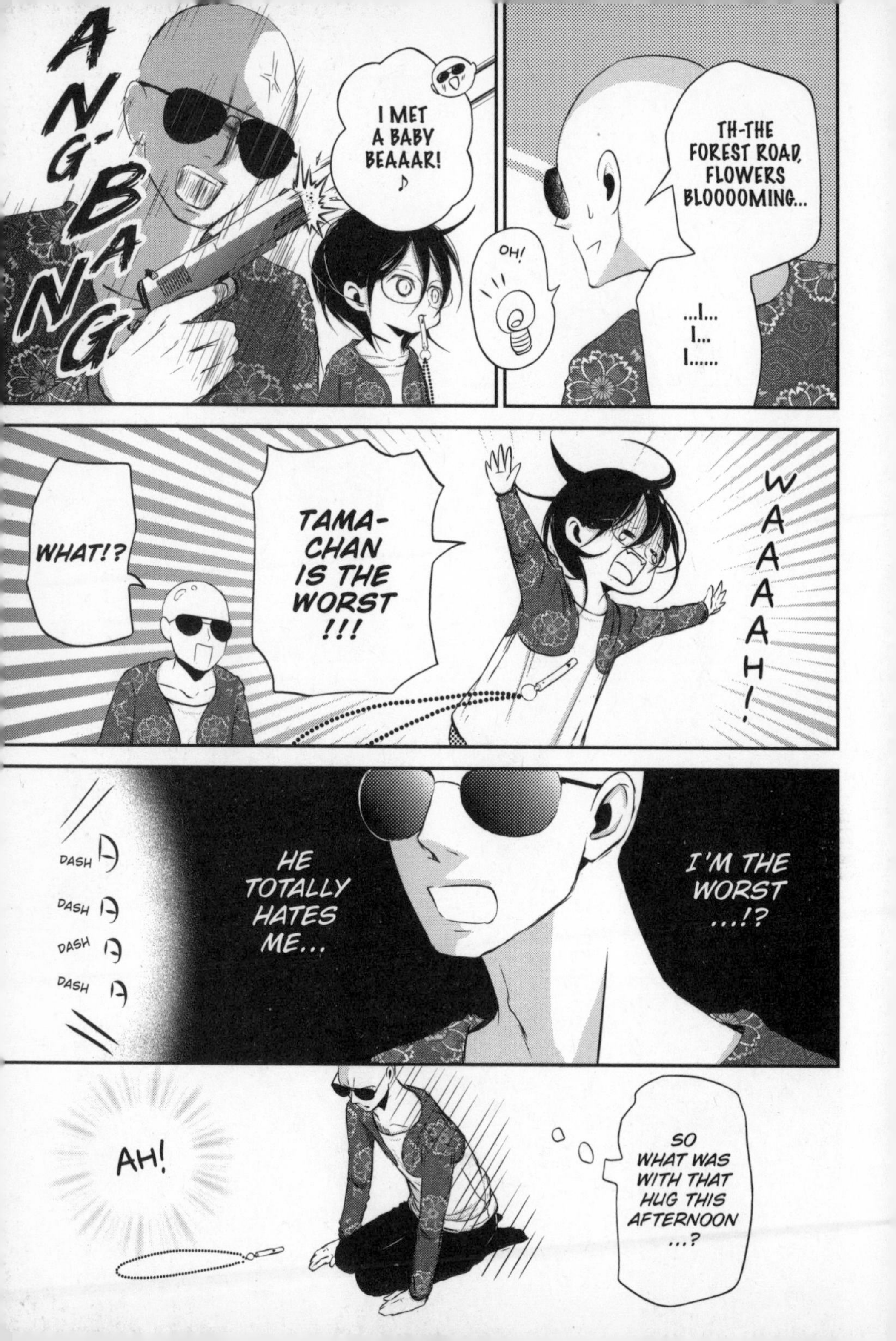

TH-THE FOREST ROAD, FLOWERS BLOOOOMING...
...I... I... I......
OH!
I MET A BABY BEAAAR! ♪
ANG-BANG
WAAAAAH!
TAMA-CHAN IS THE WORST!!!
WHAT!?
I'M THE WORST ...!?
HE TOTALLY HATES ME...
DASH
DASH
DASH
DASH
SO WHAT WAS WITH THAT HUG THIS AFTERNOON ...?
AH!

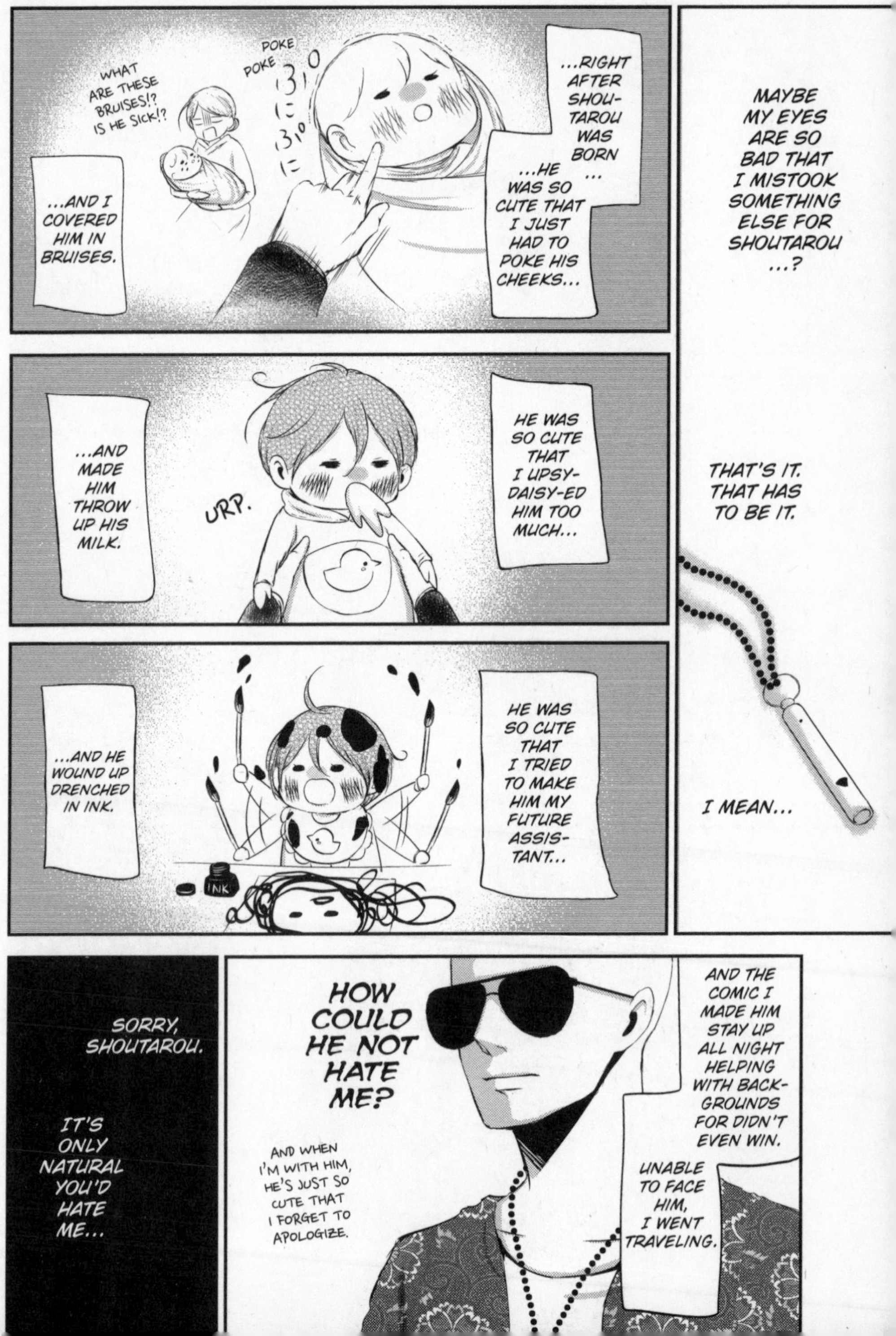
MAYBE MY EYES ARE SO BAD THAT I MISTOOK SOMETHING ELSE FOR SHOUTAROU ...?
THAT'S IT. THAT HAS TO BE IT.
I MEAN...
...RIGHT AFTER SHOU-TAROU WAS BORN ...
...HE WAS SO CUTE THAT I JUST HAD TO POKE HIS CHEEKS...
POKE POKE
WHAT ARE THESE BRUISES!? IS HE SICK!?
...AND I COVERED HIM IN BRUISES.
HE WAS SO CUTE THAT I UPSY-DAISY-ED HIM TOO MUCH...
URP.
...AND MADE HIM THROW UP HIS MILK.
HE WAS SO CUTE THAT I TRIED TO MAKE HIM MY FUTURE ASSIS-TANT...
INK
...AND HE WOUND UP DRENCHED IN INK.
AND THE COMIC I MADE HIM STAY UP ALL NIGHT HELPING WITH BACK-GROUNDS FOR DIDN'T EVEN WIN.
HOW COULD HE NOT HATE ME?
UNABLE TO FACE HIM, I WENT TRAVELING.
AND WHEN I'M WITH HIM, HE'S JUST SO CUTE THAT I FORGET TO APOLOGIZE.
SORRY, SHOUTAROU.
IT'S ONLY NATURAL YOU'D HATE ME...

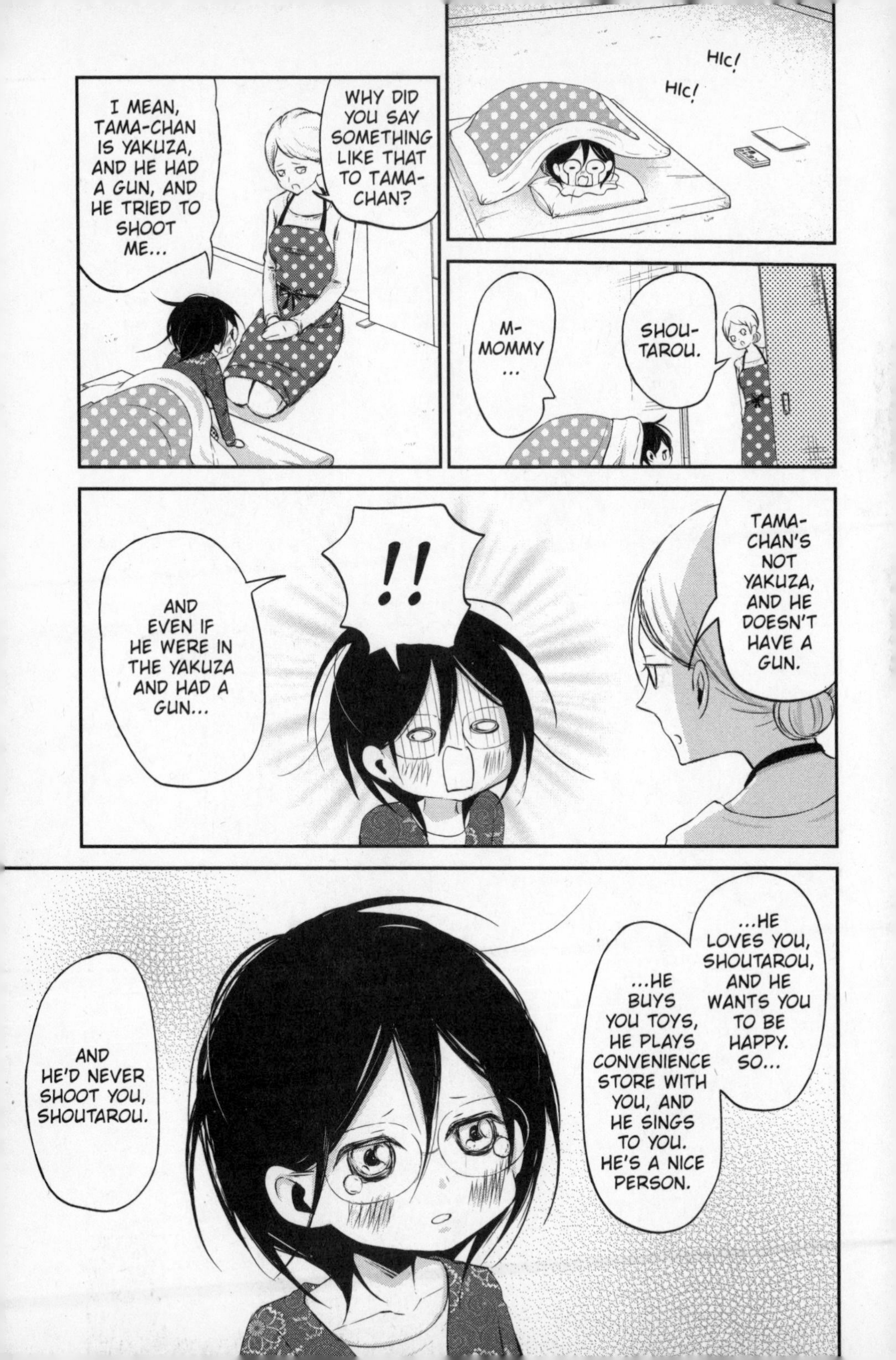
HIC!
HIC!
SHOU-TAROU.
M-MOMMY...
WHY DID YOU SAY SOMETHING LIKE THAT TO TAMA-CHAN?
I MEAN, TAMA-CHAN IS YAKUZA, AND HE HAD A GUN, AND HE TRIED TO SHOOT ME...
TAMA-CHAN'S NOT YAKUZA, AND HE DOESN'T HAVE A GUN.
!!
AND EVEN IF HE WERE IN THE YAKUZA AND HAD A GUN...
...HE LOVES YOU, SHOUTAROU, AND HE WANTS YOU TO BE HAPPY. SO...
...HE BUYS YOU TOYS, HE PLAYS CONVENIENCE STORE WITH YOU, AND HE SINGS TO YOU. HE'S A NICE PERSON.
AND HE'D NEVER SHOOT YOU, SHOUTAROU.

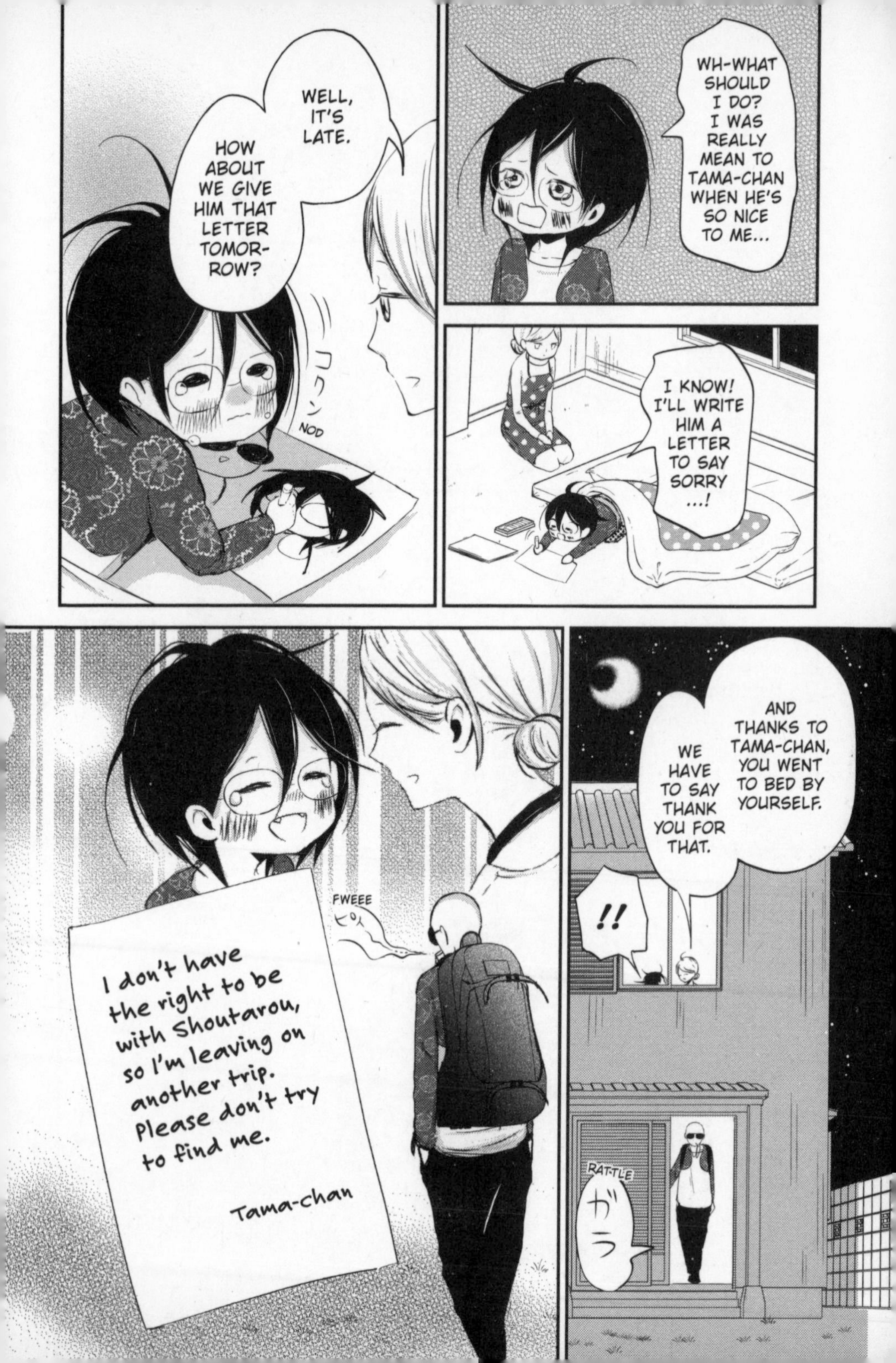
WH-WHAT SHOULD I DO? I WAS REALLY MEAN TO TAMA-CHAN WHEN HE'S SO NICE TO ME...
I KNOW! I'LL WRITE HIM A LETTER TO SAY SORRY ...!
WELL, IT'S LATE.
HOW ABOUT WE GIVE HIM THAT LETTER TOMOR-ROW?
コクン
NOD
AND THANKS TO TAMA-CHAN, YOU WENT TO BED BY YOURSELF.
WE HAVE TO SAY THANK YOU FOR THAT.
!!
RATTLE
ガラ
FWEEE
I don't have the right to be with Shoutarou, so I'm leaving on another trip. Please don't try to find me.
Tama-chan

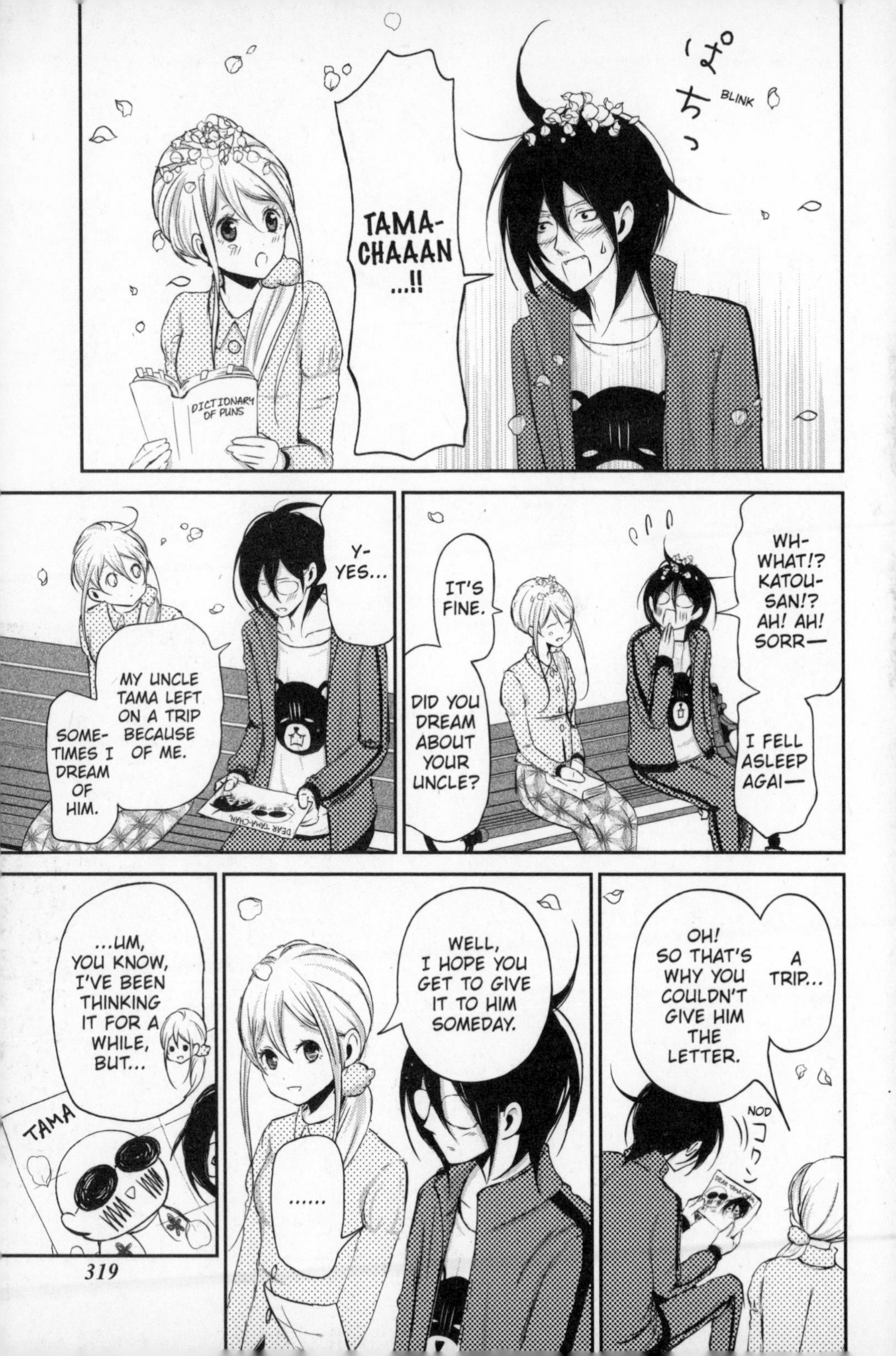
ぽちっ
BLINK
TAMA-CHAAAN...!!
DICTIONARY OF PUNS
WH- WHAT!? KATOU-SAN!? AH! AH! SORR—
I FELL ASLEEP AGAI—
IT'S FINE.
DID YOU DREAM ABOUT YOUR UNCLE?
Y- YES...
MY UNCLE TAMA LEFT ON A TRIP BECAUSE OF ME.
SOMETIMES I DREAM OF HIM.
DEAR TAMA-CHAN,
A TRIP...
OH! SO THAT'S WHY YOU COULDN'T GIVE HIM THE LETTER.
NOD
WELL, I HOPE YOU GET TO GIVE IT TO HIM SOMEDAY.
......
...UM, YOU KNOW, I'VE BEEN THINKING IT FOR A WHILE, BUT...
TAMA

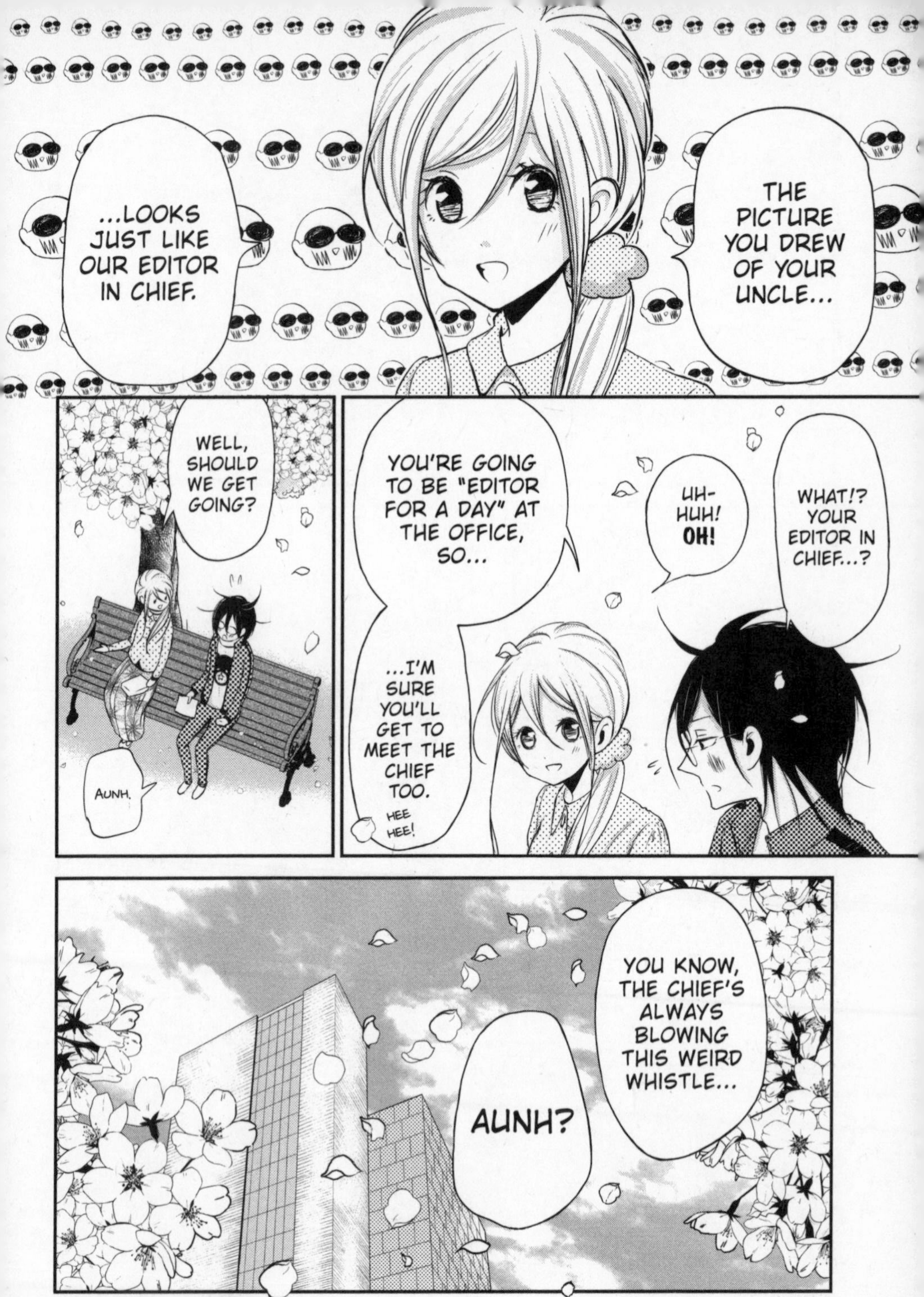
THE PICTURE YOU DREW OF YOUR UNCLE...
...LOOKS JUST LIKE OUR EDITOR IN CHIEF.
WHAT!? YOUR EDITOR IN CHIEF...?
UH-HUH! OH!
YOU'RE GOING TO BE "EDITOR FOR A DAY" AT THE OFFICE, SO...
...I'M SURE YOU'LL GET TO MEET THE CHIEF TOO.
HEE HEE!
WELL, SHOULD WE GET GOING?
AUNH.
YOU KNOW, THE CHIEF'S ALWAYS BLOWING THIS WEIRD WHISTLE...
AUNH?

TO BE CONTINUED

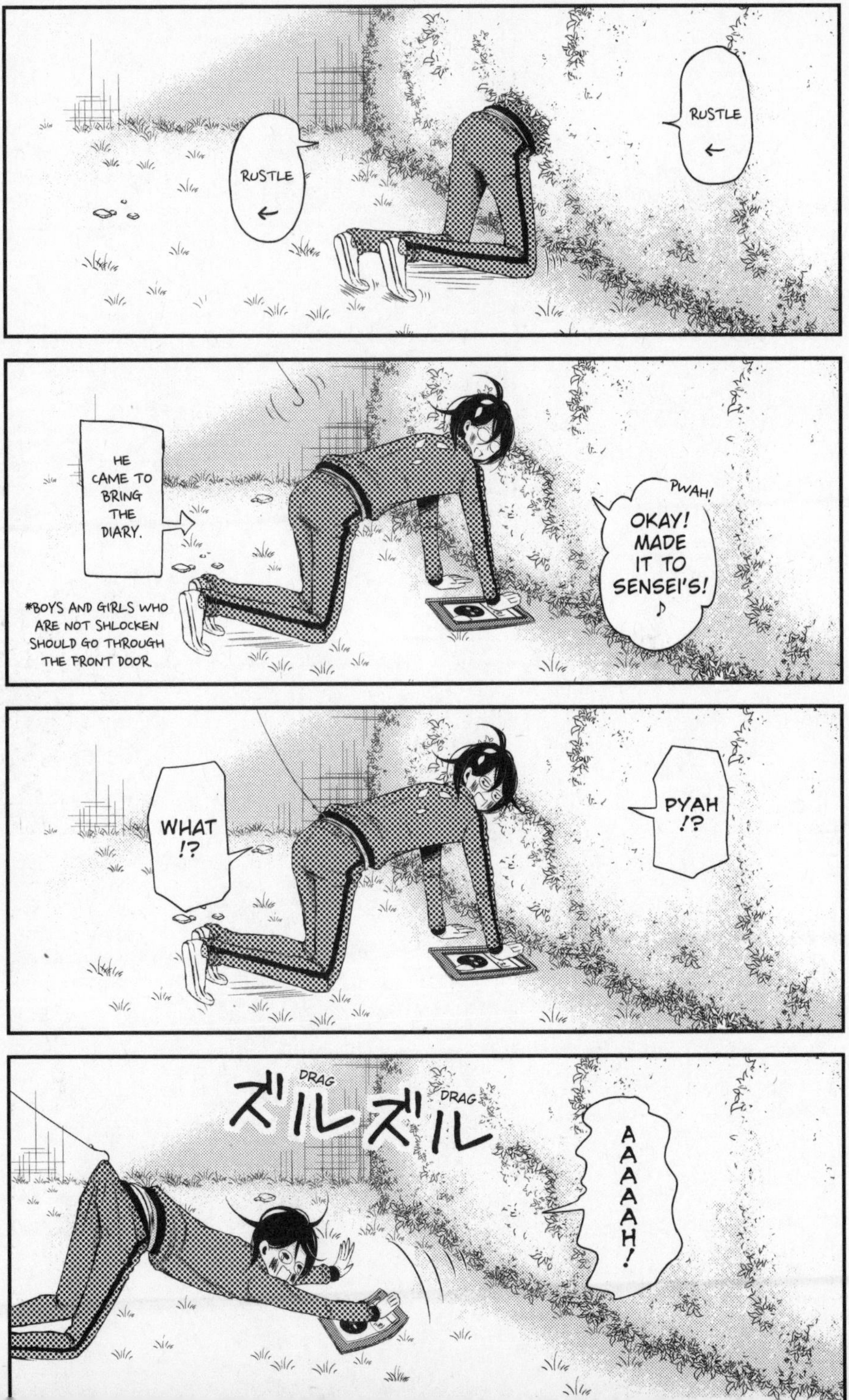
RUSTLE
RUSTLE
PWAH!
OKAY! MADE IT TO SENSEI'S! ♪
HE CAME TO BRING THE DIARY.
*BOYS AND GIRLS WHO ARE NOT SHLOCKEN SHOULD GO THROUGH THE FRONT DOOR
PYAH!?
WHAT!?
AAAAAH!
ズルズル
DRAG DRAG

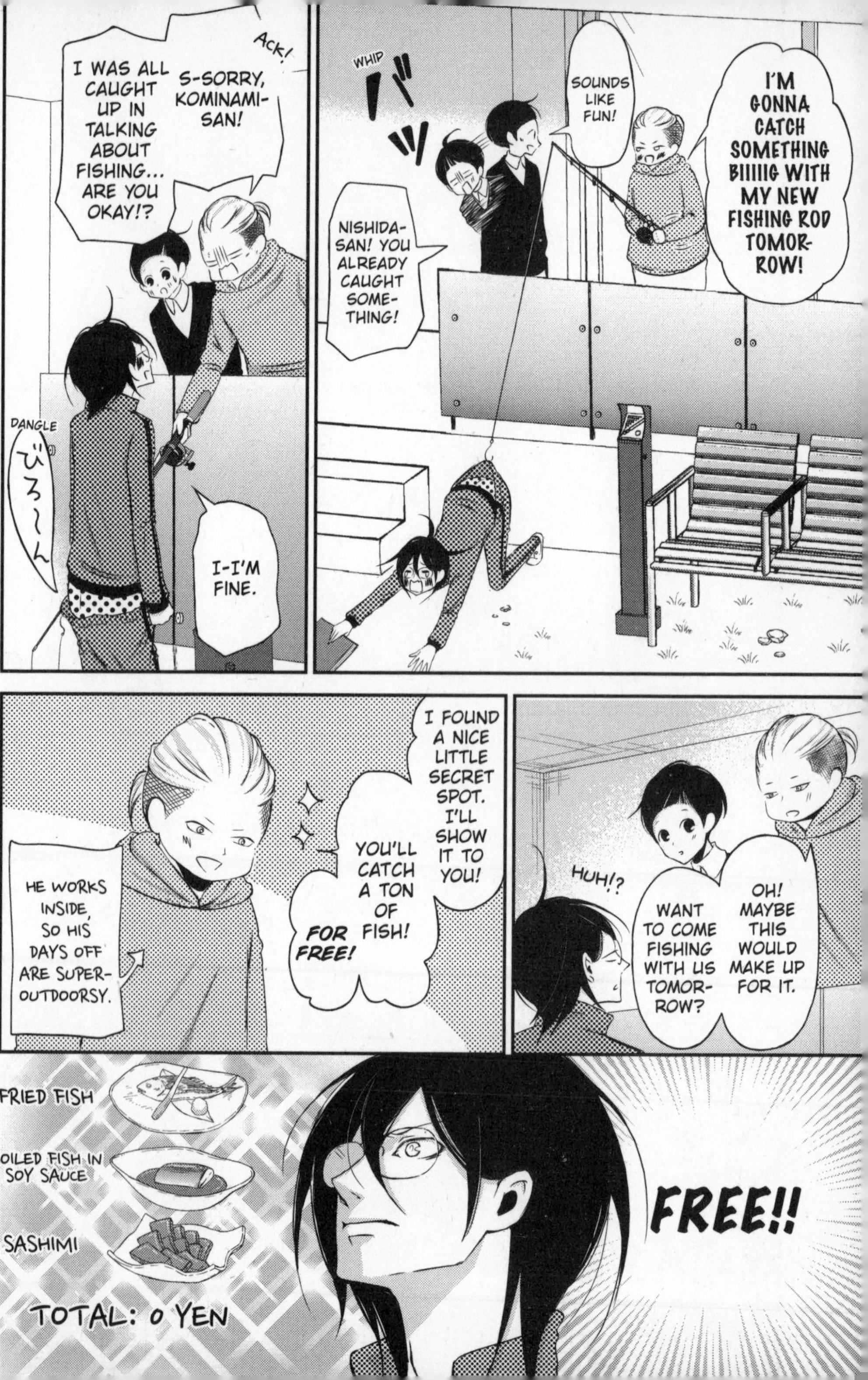
I'M GONNA CATCH SOMETHING BIIIIIG WITH MY NEW FISHING ROD TOMORROW!
SOUNDS LIKE FUN!
WHIP
バ
NISHIDA-SAN! YOU ALREADY CAUGHT SOMETHING!
ACK!
S-SORRY, KOMINAMI-SAN!
I WAS ALL CAUGHT UP IN TALKING ABOUT FISHING... ARE YOU OKAY!?
DANGLE
びろ～ん
I-I'M FINE.
OH! MAYBE THIS WOULD MAKE UP FOR IT.
WANT TO COME FISHING WITH US TOMORROW?
HUH!?
I FOUND A NICE LITTLE SECRET SPOT. I'LL SHOW IT TO YOU!
YOU'LL CATCH A TON OF FISH!
FOR FREE!
HE WORKS INSIDE, SO HIS DAYS OFF ARE SUPER-OUTDOORSY.
FREE!!
FRIED FISH
BOILED FISH IN SOY SAUCE
SASHIMI
TOTAL: 0 YEN

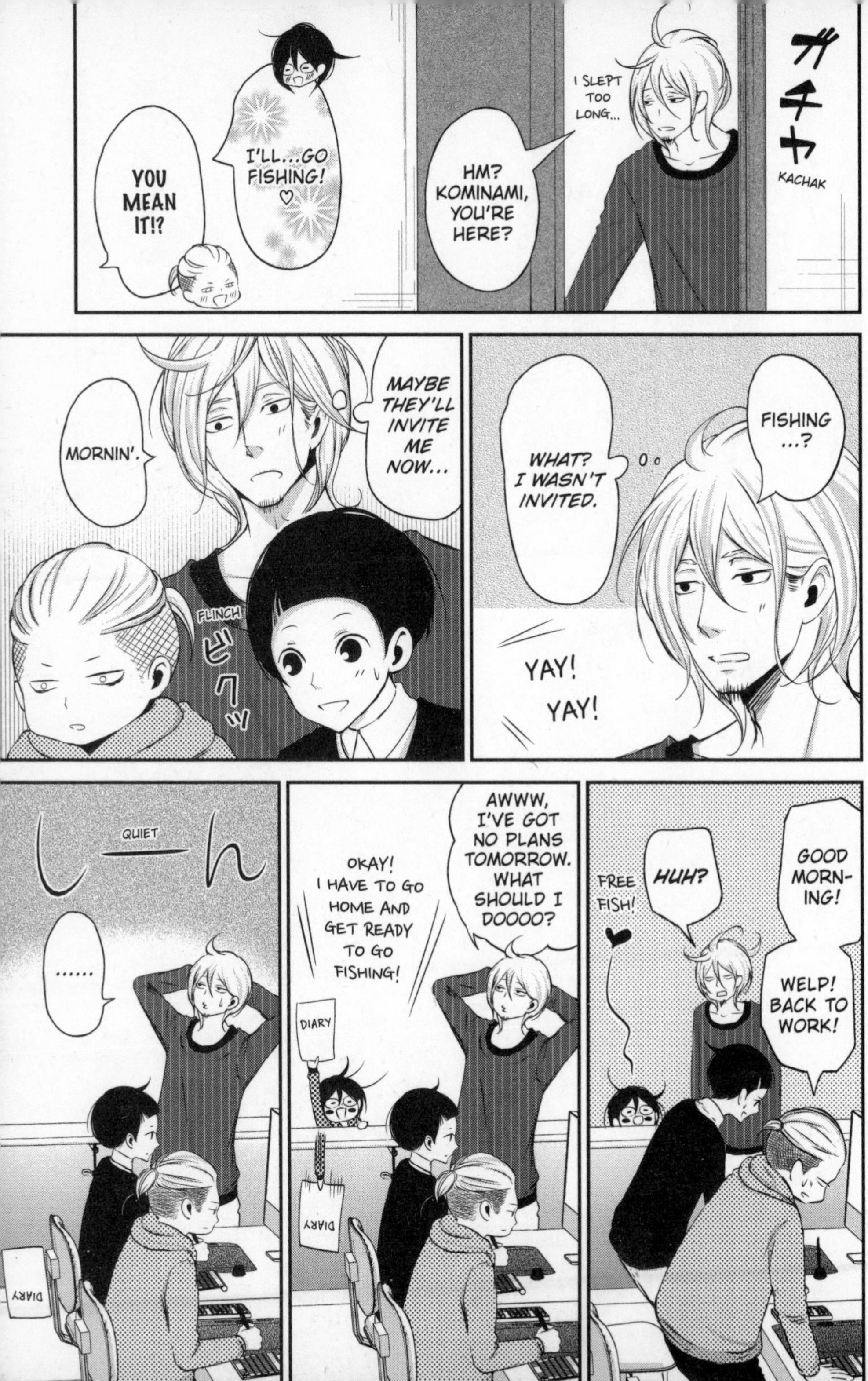
ガチャ
KACHAK
I SLEPT TOO LONG...
HM? KOMINAMI, YOU'RE HERE?
I'LL...GO FISHING! ♡
YOU MEAN IT!?
FISHING ...?
WHAT? I WASN'T INVITED.
YAY!
YAY!
MAYBE THEY'LL INVITE ME NOW...
MORNIN'.
FLINCH
ビクッ
GOOD MORNING!
WELP! BACK TO WORK!
HUH?
FREE FISH!
AWWW, I'VE GOT NO PLANS TOMORROW. WHAT SHOULD I DOOOO?
OKAY! I HAVE TO GO HOME AND GET READY TO GO FISHING!
DIARY
DIARY
QUIET
し一ん
......
DIARY

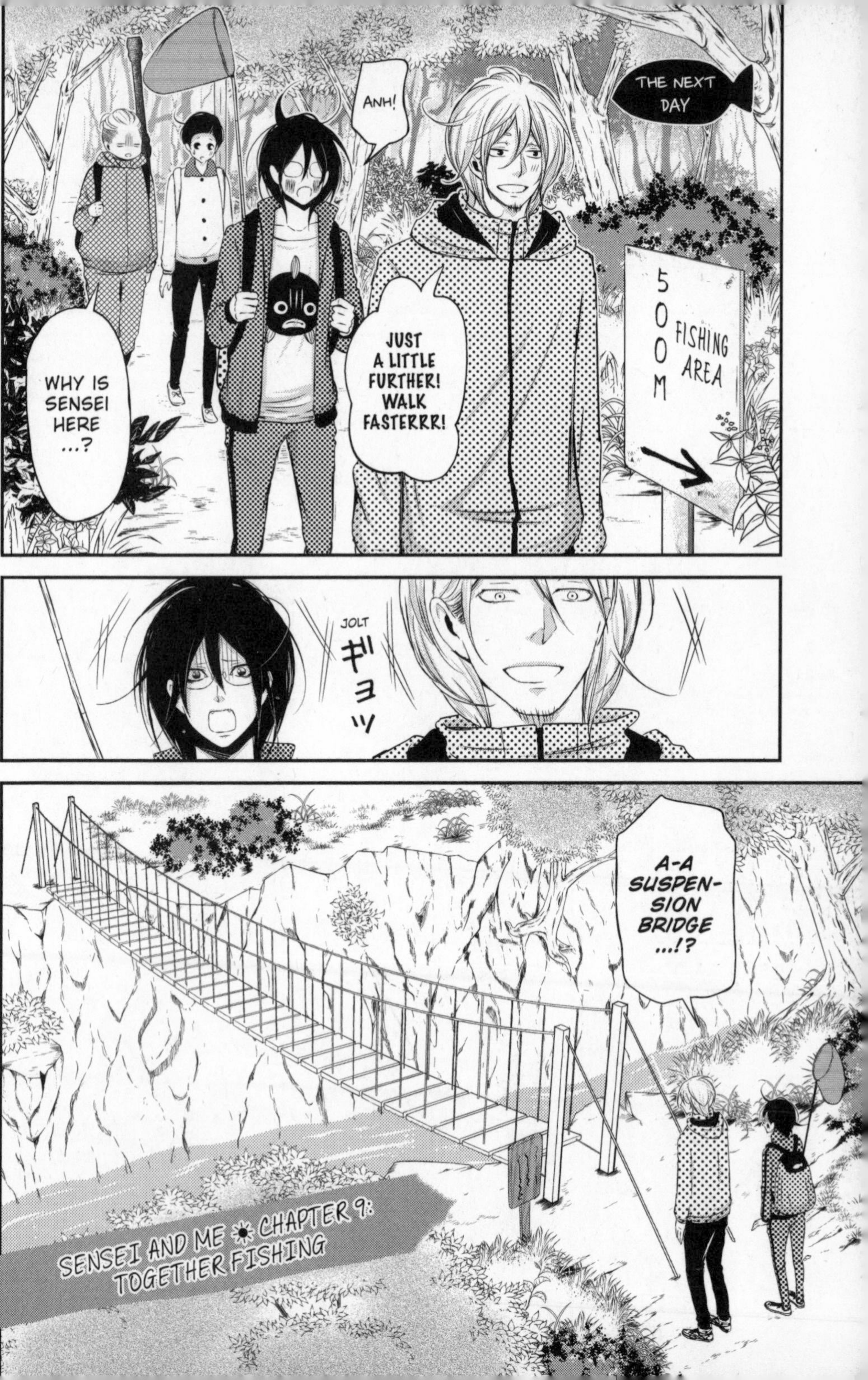
THE NEXT DAY
ANH!
JUST A LITTLE FURTHER! WALK FASTERRR!
500M FISHING AREA
WHY IS SENSEI HERE ...?
JOLT
ギョッ
A-A SUSPENSION BRIDGE ...!?
SENSEI AND ME ☀ CHAPTER 9: TOGETHER FISHING

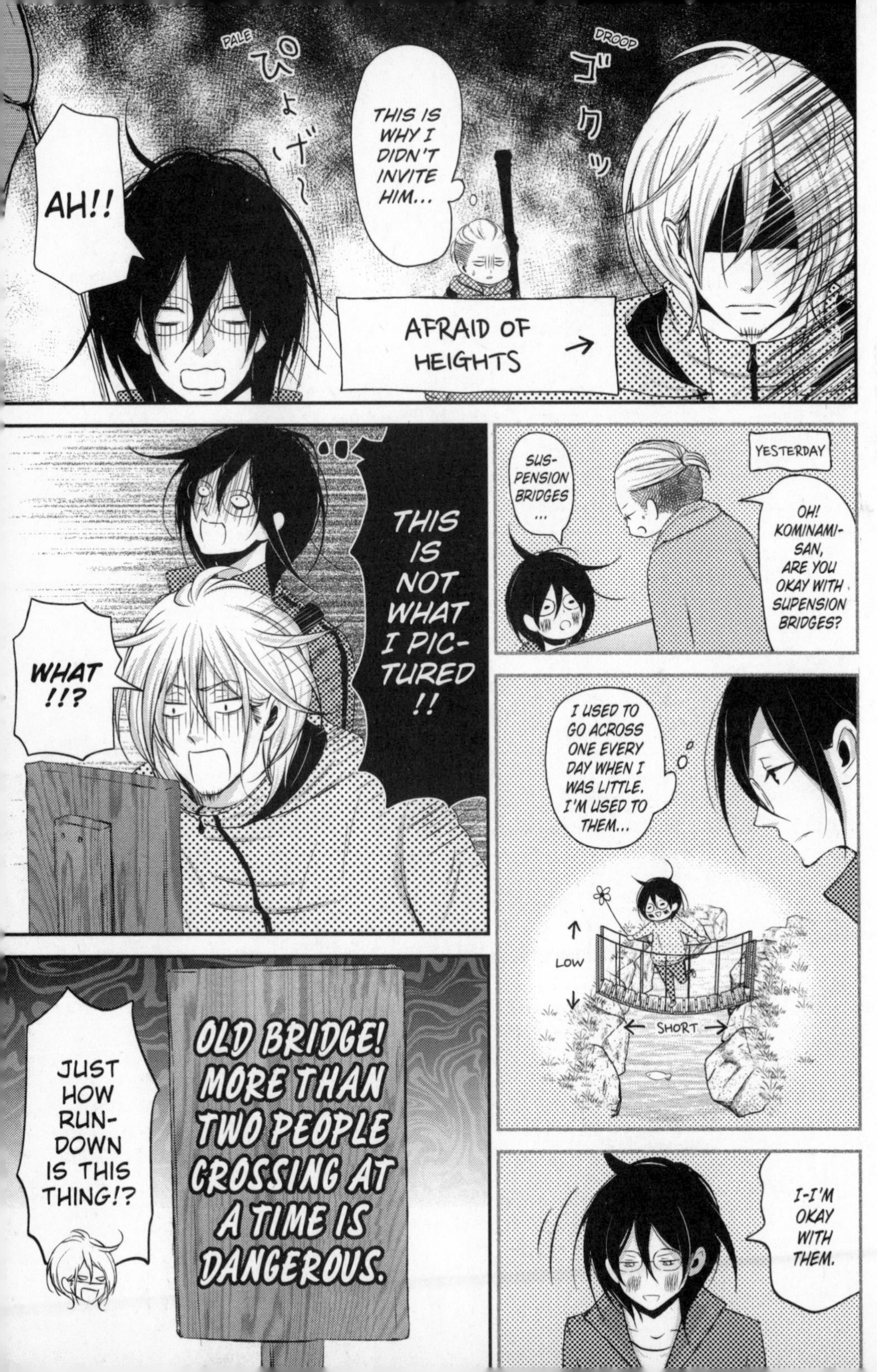
DROOP
ゴクッ
AFRAID OF HEIGHTS →
THIS IS WHY I DIDN'T INVITE HIM...
PALE
ぴょげ~
AH!!
YESTERDAY
OH! KOMINAMI-SAN, ARE YOU OKAY WITH SUPENSION BRIDGES?
SUS-PENSION BRIDGES ...
I USED TO GO ACROSS ONE EVERY DAY WHEN I WAS LITTLE. I'M USED TO THEM...
LOW
SHORT
I-I'M OKAY WITH THEM.
THIS IS NOT WHAT I PIC-TURED!!
WHAT!!?
OLD BRIDGE! MORE THAN TWO PEOPLE CROSSING AT A TIME IS DANGEROUS.
JUST HOW RUN-DOWN IS THIS THING!?

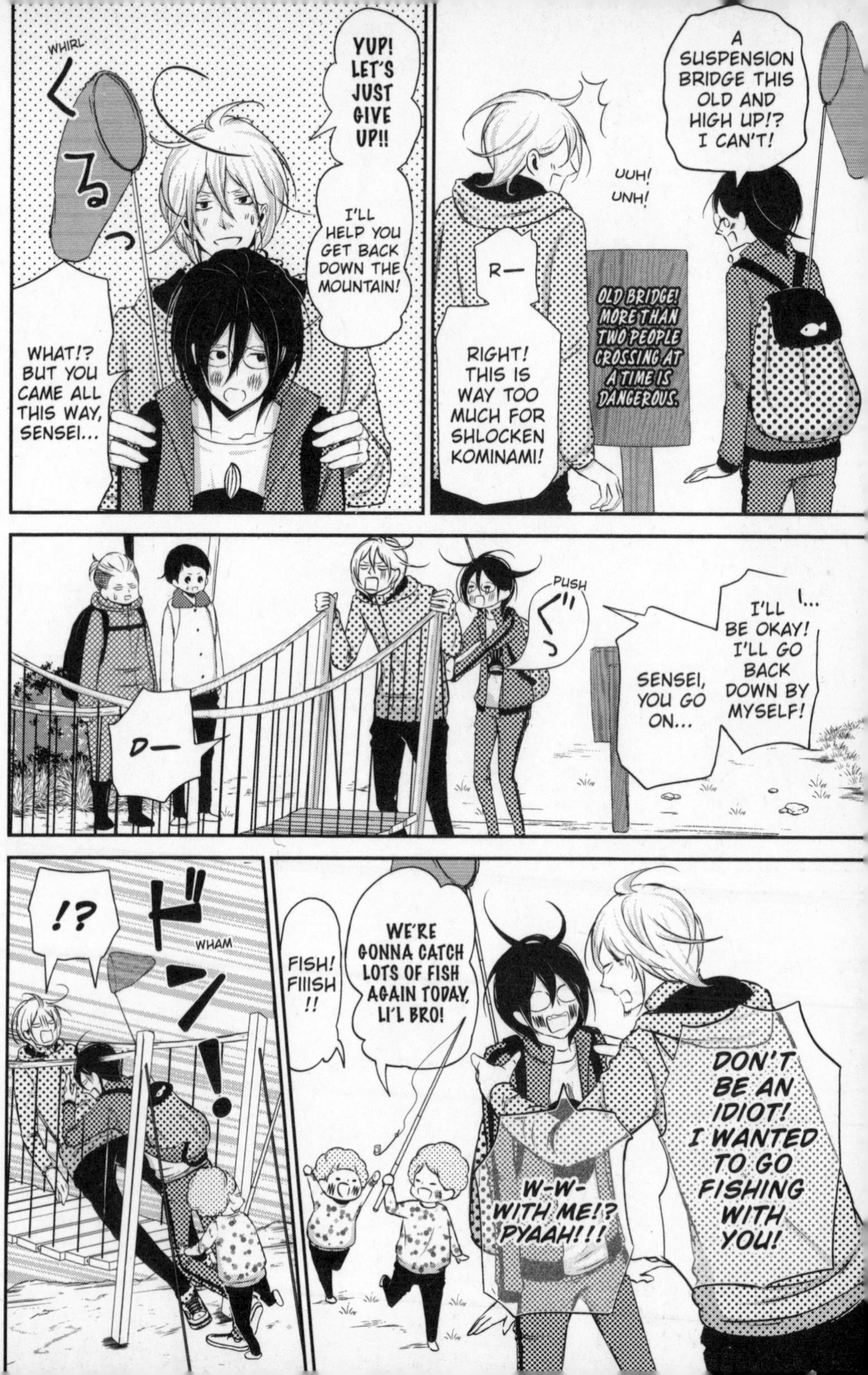
A SUSPENSION BRIDGE THIS OLD AND HIGH UP!? I CAN'T!
UUH! UNH!
R—
OLD BRIDGE! MORE THAN TWO PEOPLE CROSSING AT A TIME IS DANGEROUS.
RIGHT! THIS IS WAY TOO MUCH FOR SHLOCKEN KOMINAMI!
YUP! LET'S JUST GIVE UP!!
I'LL HELP YOU GET BACK DOWN THE MOUNTAIN!
WHIRL
WHAT!? BUT YOU CAME ALL THIS WAY, SENSEI...
I...
I'LL BE OKAY! I'LL GO BACK DOWN BY MYSELF!
SENSEI, YOU GO ON...
PUSH
D—
DON'T BE AN IDIOT! I WANTED TO GO FISHING WITH YOU!
W-W-WITH ME!? PYAAH!!!
WE'RE GONNA CATCH LOTS OF FISH AGAIN TODAY, LI'L BRO!
FISH! FIIISH!!
!?
WHAM

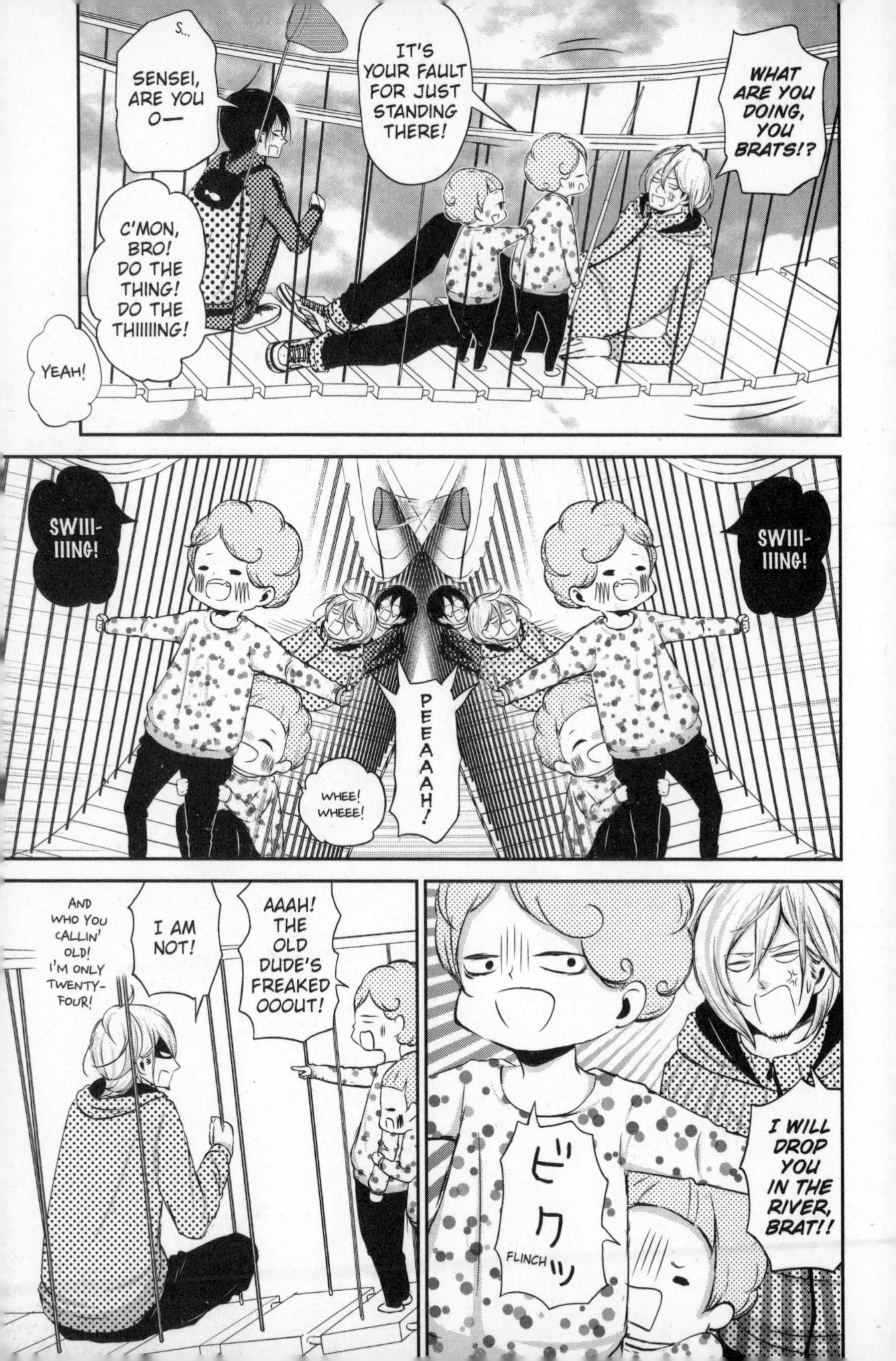
WHAT ARE YOU DOING, YOU BRATS!?
IT'S YOUR FAULT FOR JUST STANDING THERE!
S...
SENSEI, ARE YOU O—
C'MON, BRO! DO THE THING! DO THE THIIIIING!
YEAH!
SWIII-IIING!
SWIII-IIING!
PEEAAAAH!
WHEE! WHEEE!
ビクッ
FLINCH
I WILL DROP YOU IN THE RIVER, BRAT!!
AAAH! THE OLD DUDE'S FREAKED OOOUT!
I AM NOT!
AND WHO YOU CALLIN' OLD! I'M ONLY TWENTY-FOUR!

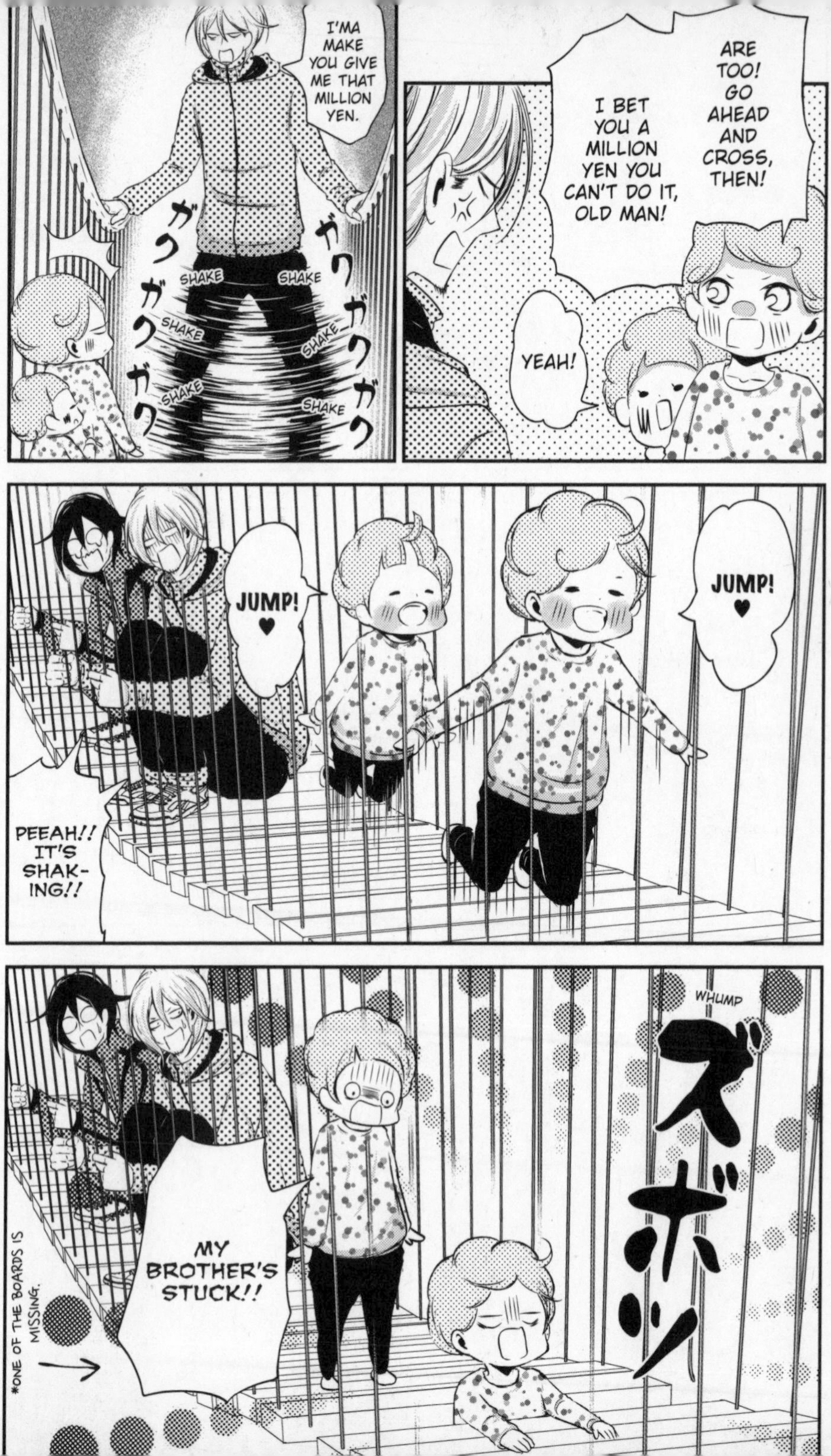
ARE TOO! GO AHEAD AND CROSS, THEN!
I BET YOU A MILLION YEN YOU CAN'T DO IT, OLD MAN!
YEAH!
I'MA MAKE YOU GIVE ME THAT MILLION YEN.
ガクガクガク
SHAKE SHAKE SHAKE
ガクガクガク
SHAKE SHAKE SHAKE
JUMP! ♥
JUMP! ♥
PEEAH!! IT'S SHAKING!!
WHUMP
ズボッ
MY BROTHER'S STUCK!!
*ONE OF THE BOARDS IS MISSING.

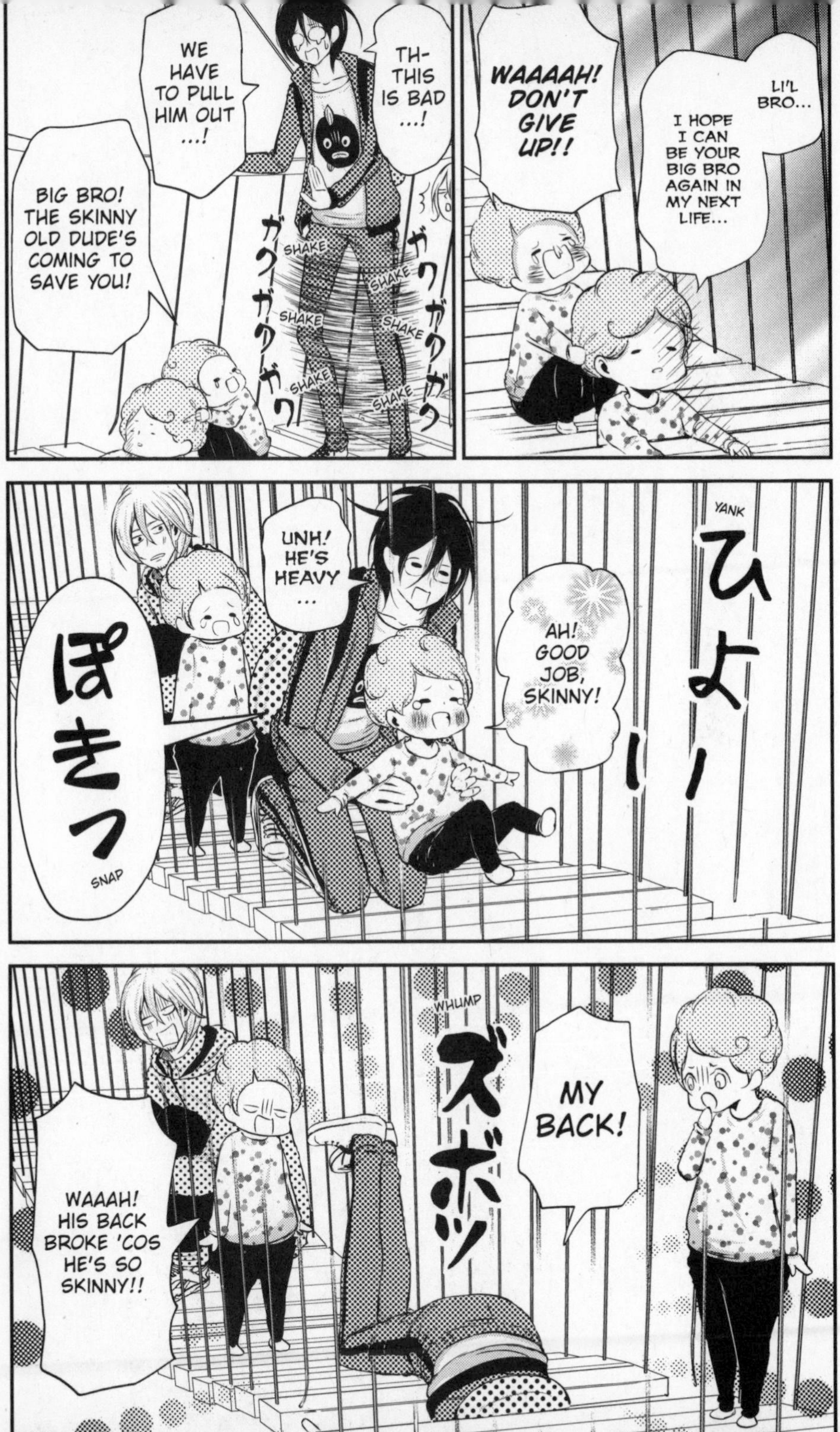
LI'L BRO...
I HOPE I CAN BE YOUR BIG BRO AGAIN IN MY NEXT LIFE...
WAAAAH! DON'T GIVE UP!!
TH-THIS IS BAD ...!
WE HAVE TO PULL HIM OUT ...!
ガクガクガクガク
SHAKE SHAKE SHAKE SHAKE SHAKE SHAKE
BIG BRO! THE SKINNY OLD DUDE'S COMING TO SAVE YOU!
YANK
ひょい
AH! GOOD JOB, SKINNY!
UNH! HE'S HEAVY ...
ぽきっ
SNAP
MY BACK!
WHUMP
ズボッ
WAAAH! HIS BACK BROKE 'COS HE'S SO SKINNY!!

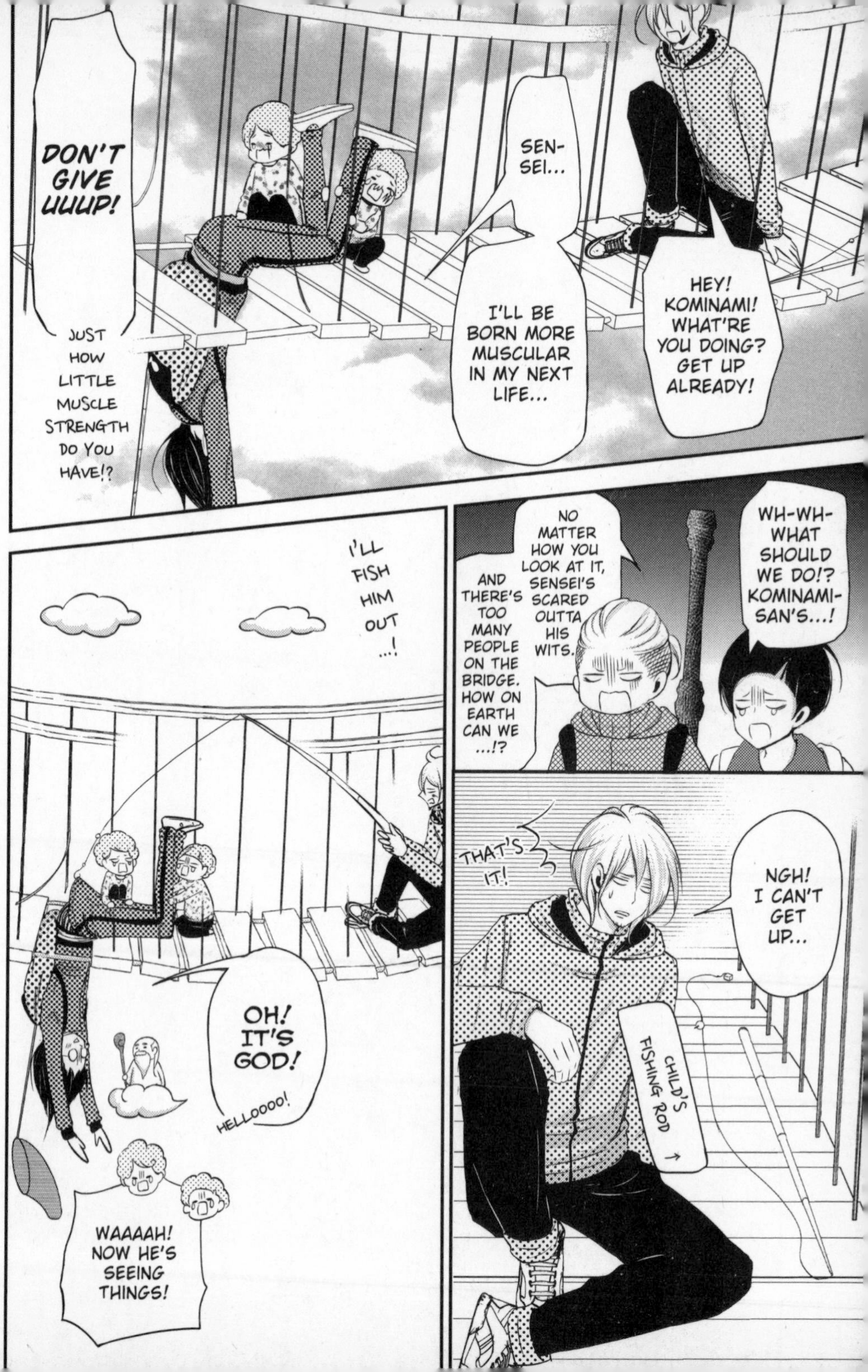
HEY! KOMINAMI! WHAT'RE YOU DOING? GET UP ALREADY!
SEN-SEI...
I'LL BE BORN MORE MUSCULAR IN MY NEXT LIFE...
DON'T GIVE UUUP!
JUST HOW LITTLE MUSCLE STRENGTH DO YOU HAVE!?
WH-WH-WHAT SHOULD WE DO!? KOMINAMI-SAN'S...!
NO MATTER HOW YOU LOOK AT IT, SENSEI'S SCARED OUTTA HIS WITS.
AND THERE'S TOO MANY PEOPLE ON THE BRIDGE. HOW ON EARTH CAN WE ...!?
NGH! I CAN'T GET UP...
THAT'S IT!
CHILD'S FISHING ROD
I'LL FISH HIM OUT ...!
OH! IT'S GOD!
HELLOOOO!
WAAAAH! NOW HE'S SEEING THINGS!

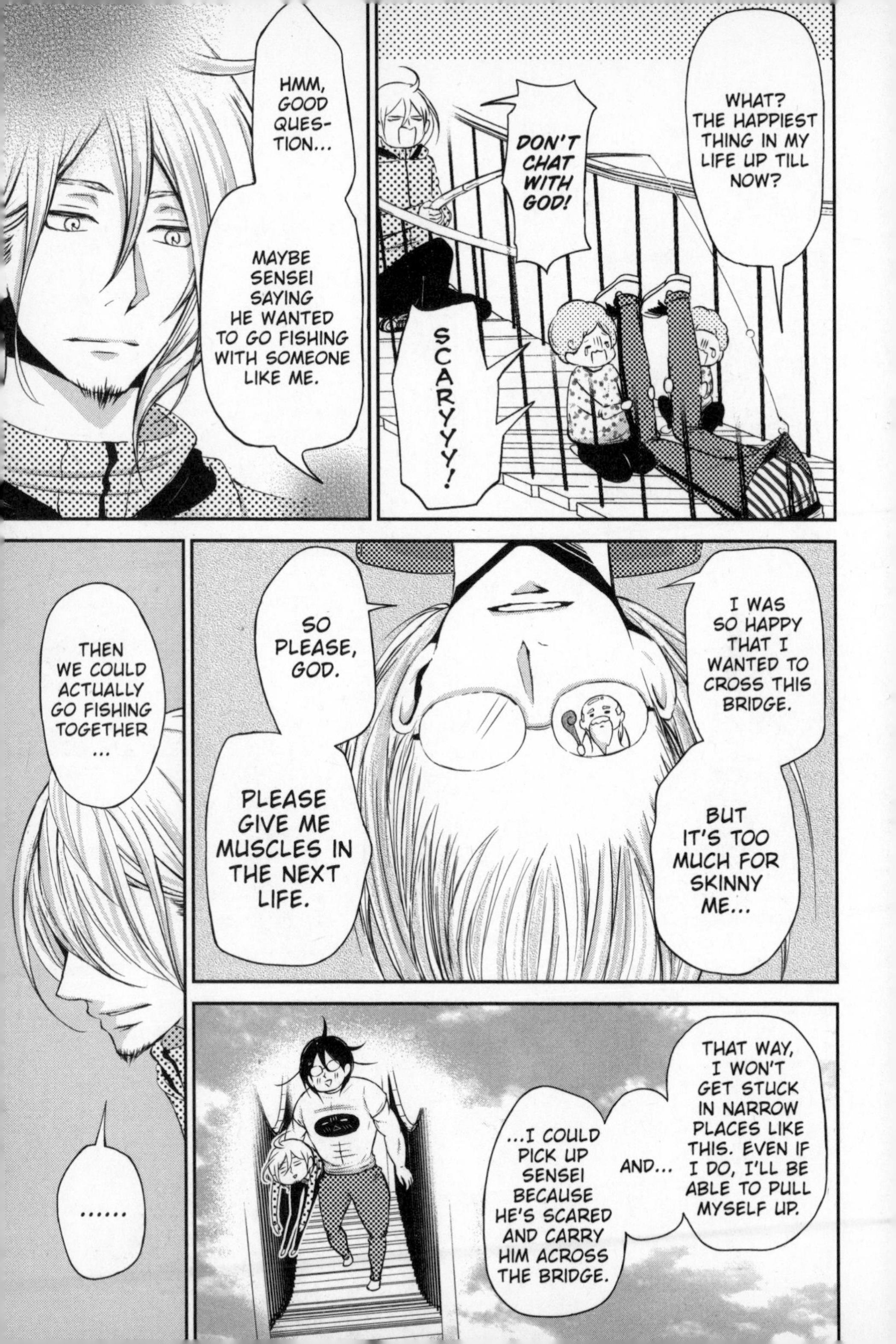
WHAT? THE HAPPIEST THING IN MY LIFE UP TILL NOW?
DON'T CHAT WITH GOD!
SCARYYY!
HMM, GOOD QUES-TION...
MAYBE SENSEI SAYING HE WANTED TO GO FISHING WITH SOMEONE LIKE ME.
I WAS SO HAPPY THAT I WANTED TO CROSS THIS BRIDGE.
BUT IT'S TOO MUCH FOR SKINNY ME...
SO PLEASE, GOD.
PLEASE GIVE ME MUSCLES IN THE NEXT LIFE.
THAT WAY, I WON'T GET STUCK IN NARROW PLACES LIKE THIS. EVEN IF I DO, I'LL BE ABLE TO PULL MYSELF UP.
AND...
...I COULD PICK UP SENSEI BECAUSE HE'S SCARED AND CARRY HIM ACROSS THE BRIDGE.
THEN WE COULD ACTUALLY GO FISHING TOGETHER ...
......

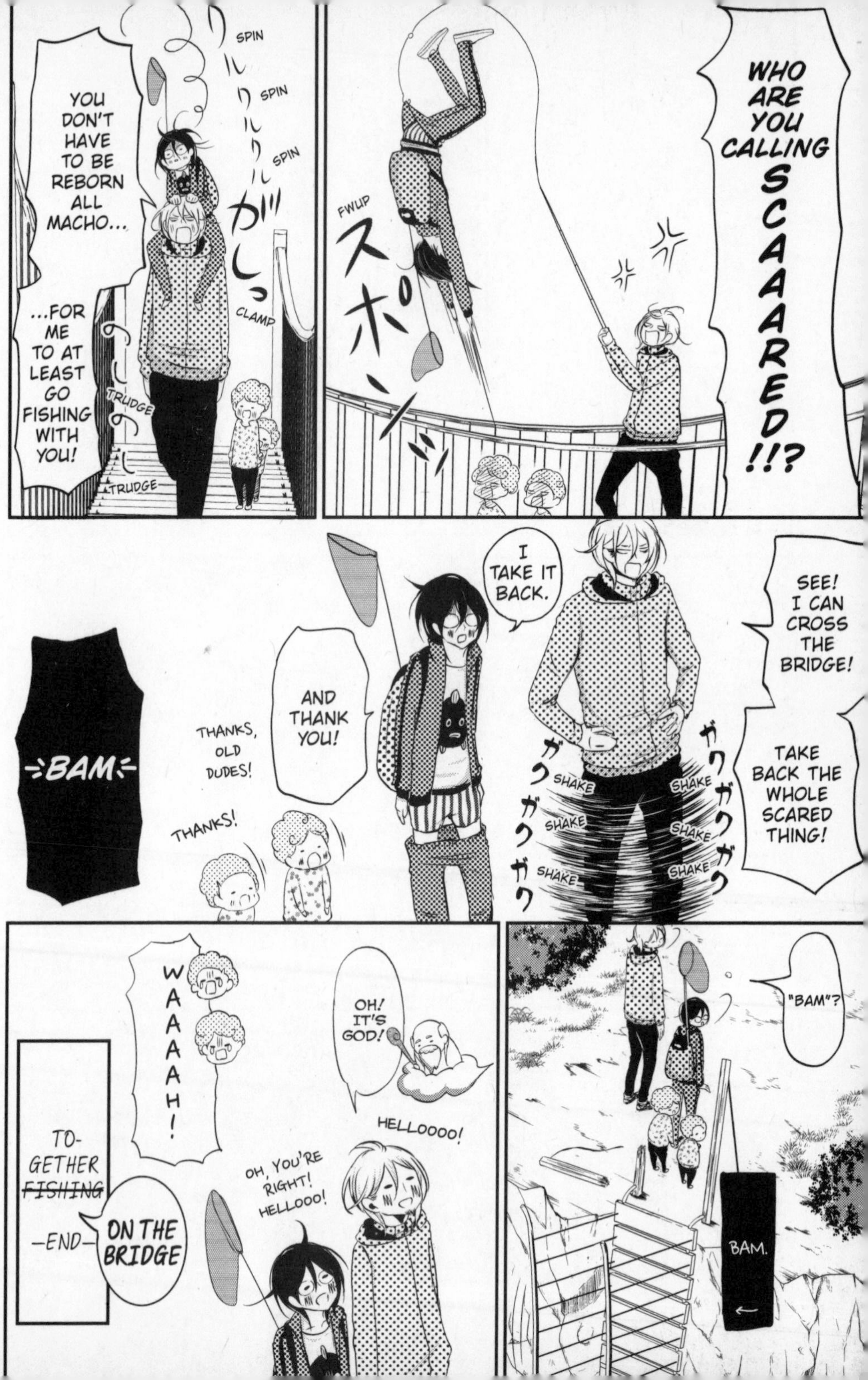
WHO ARE YOU CALLING SCAAARED!!?
FWUP
YOU DON'T HAVE TO BE REBORN ALL MACHO...
SPIN
SPIN
SPIN
CLAMP
...FOR ME TO AT LEAST GO FISHING WITH YOU!
TRUDGE
TRUDGE
SEE! I CAN CROSS THE BRIDGE!
TAKE BACK THE WHOLE SCARED THING!
SHAKE SHAKE SHAKE
SHAKE SHAKE SHAKE
I TAKE IT BACK.
AND THANK YOU!
THANKS, OLD DUDES!
THANKS!
BAM
"BAM"?
BAM. ←
OH! IT'S GOD!
WAAAAAH!
HELLOOOO!
OH, YOU'RE RIGHT! HELLOOO!
ON THE BRIDGE
TO-GETHER ~~FISHING~~
—END—

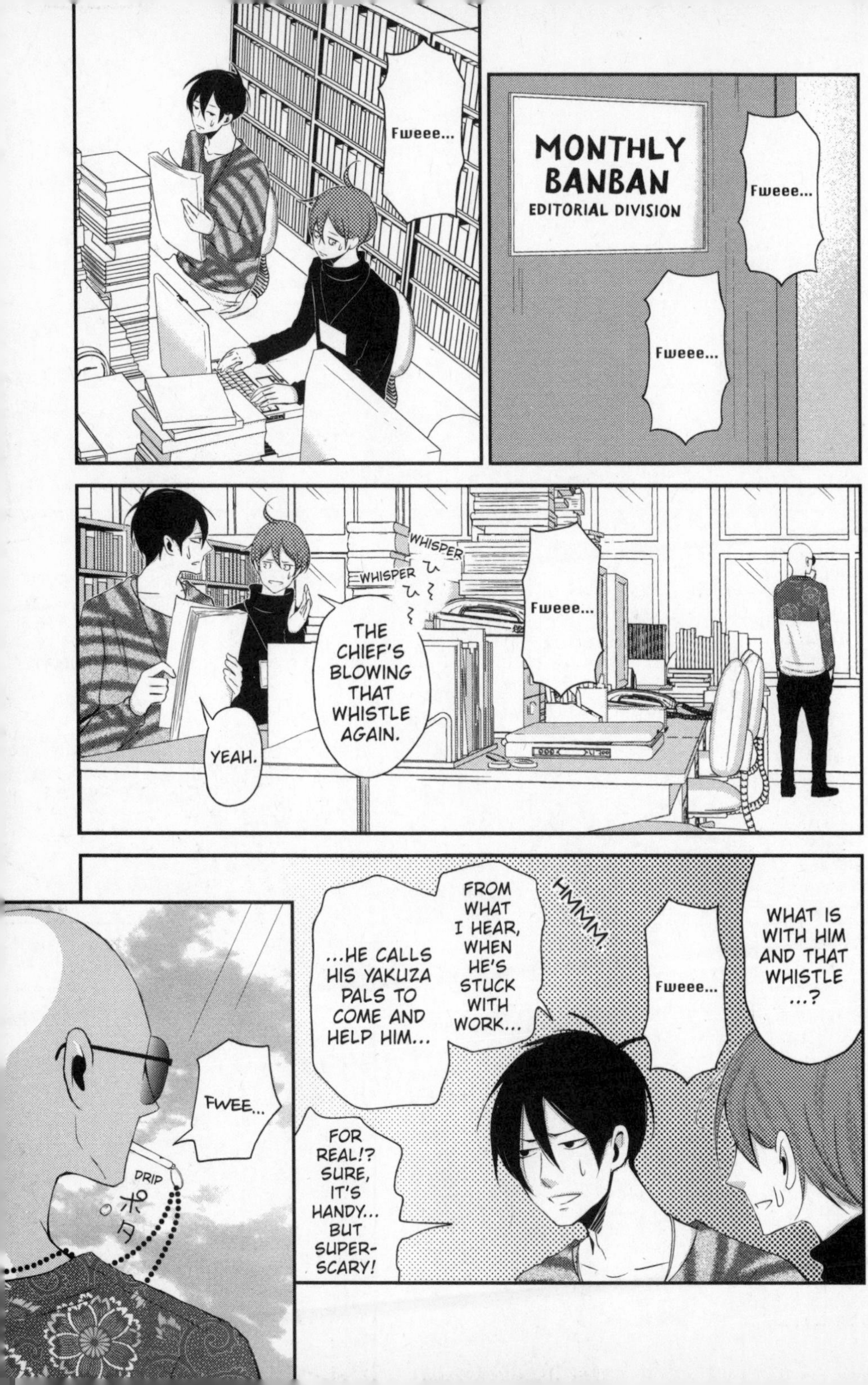
MONTHLY BANBAN EDITORIAL DIVISION
Fweee...
Fweee...
Fweee...
Fweee...
WHISPER
WHISPER
THE CHIEF'S BLOWING THAT WHISTLE AGAIN.
YEAH.
WHAT IS WITH HIM AND THAT WHISTLE ...?
Fweee...
HMMM.
FROM WHAT I HEAR, WHEN HE'S STUCK WITH WORK...
...HE CALLS HIS YAKUZA PALS TO COME AND HELP HIM...
FOR REAL!? SURE, IT'S HANDY... BUT SUPER-SCARY!
FWEE...
DRIP

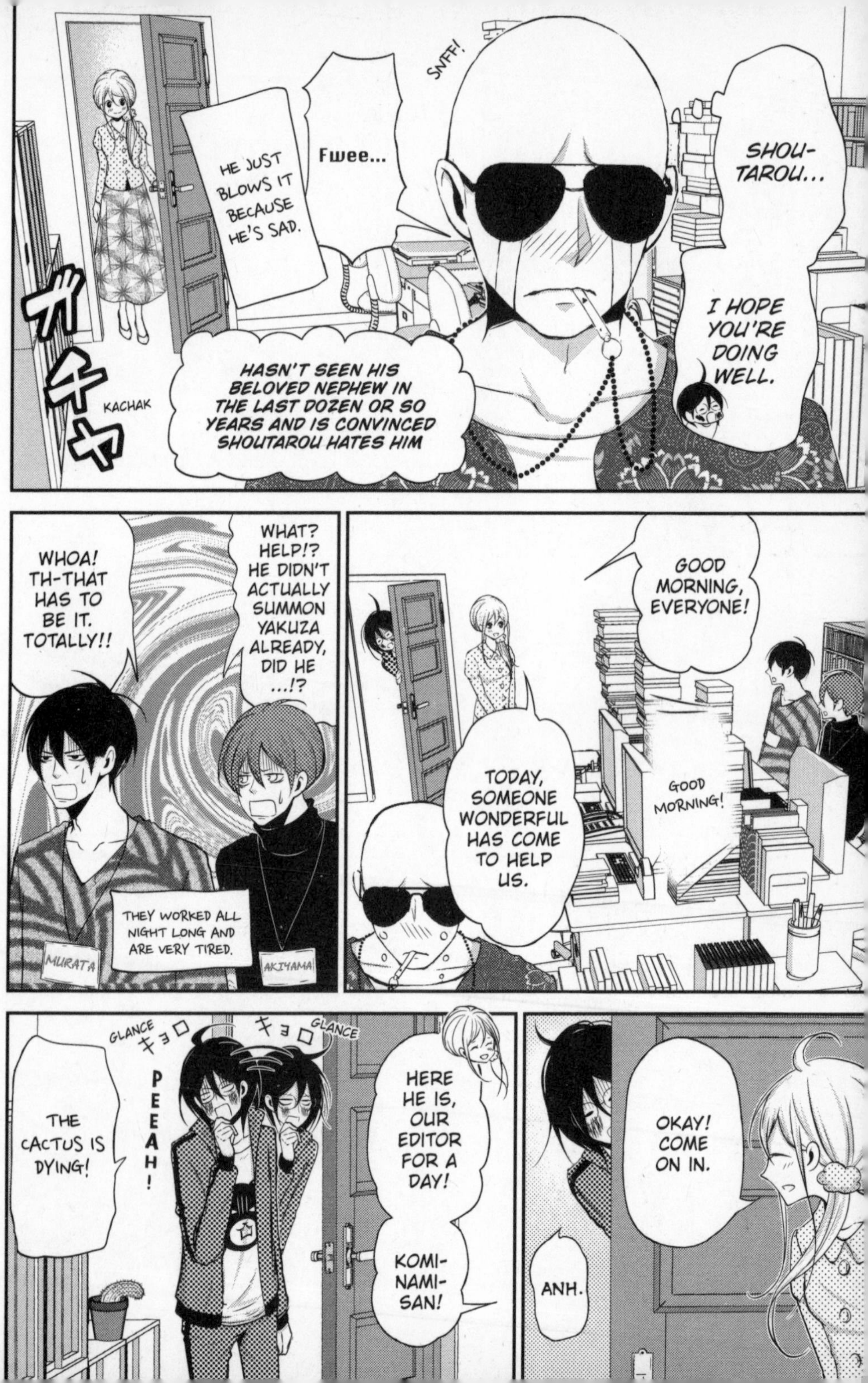
SHOU-TAROU...
I HOPE YOU'RE DOING WELL.
SNFF!
Fwee...
HE JUST BLOWS IT BECAUSE HE'S SAD.
HASN'T SEEN HIS BELOVED NEPHEW IN THE LAST DOZEN OR SO YEARS AND IS CONVINCED SHOUTAROU HATES HIM
ガチャ
KACHAK
GOOD MORNING, EVERYONE!
GOOD MORNING!
TODAY, SOMEONE WONDERFUL HAS COME TO HELP US.
WHAT? HELP!? HE DIDN'T ACTUALLY SUMMON YAKUZA ALREADY, DID HE ...!?
WHOA! TH-THAT HAS TO BE IT. TOTALLY!!
THEY WORKED ALL NIGHT LONG AND ARE VERY TIRED.
AKIYAMA
MURATA
OKAY! COME ON IN.
ANH.
HERE HE IS, OUR EDITOR FOR A DAY!
KOMI-NAMI-SAN!
キョロ GLANCE
GLANCE キョロ
PEEEAH!
THE CACTUS IS DYING!

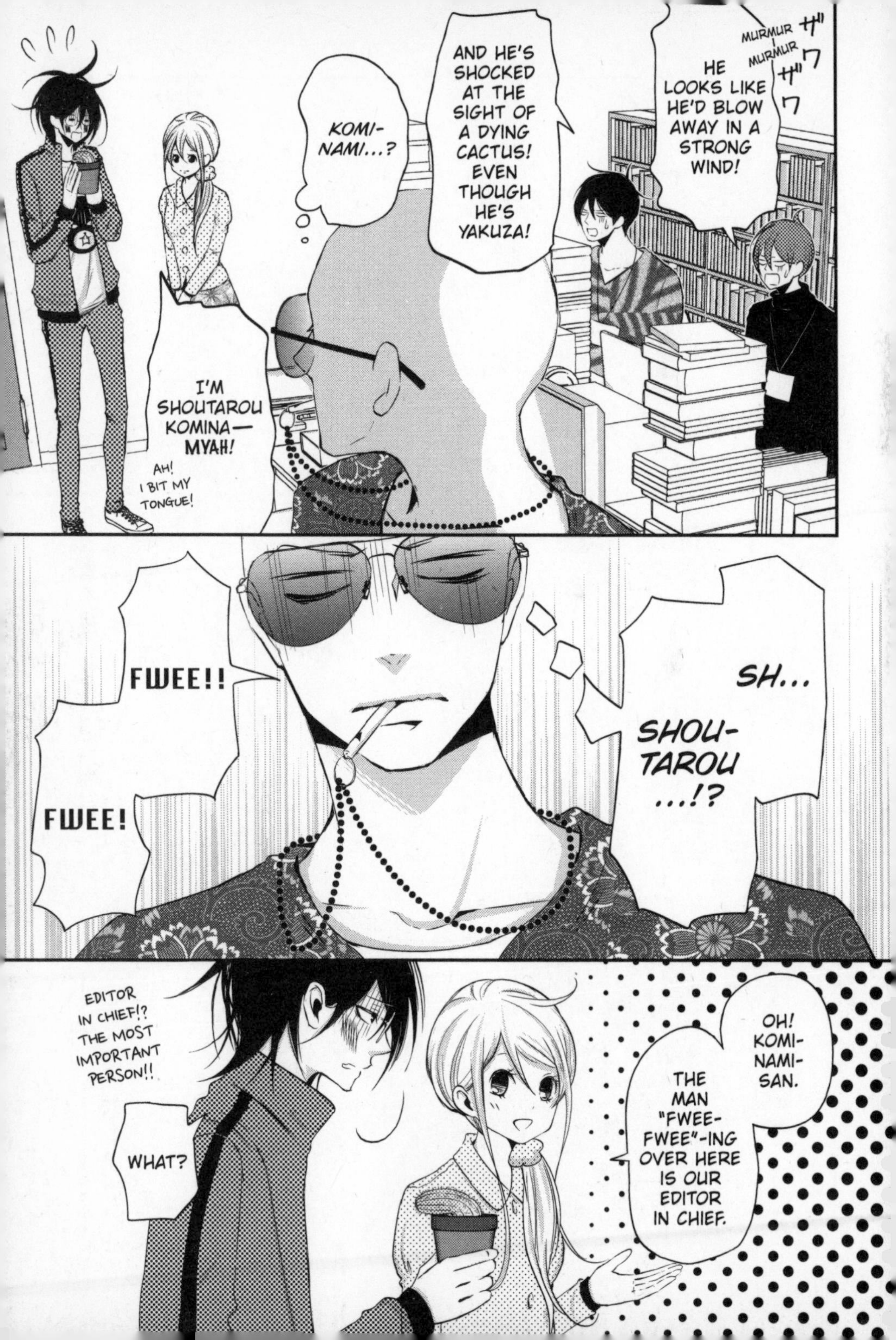
MURMUR MURMUR
ザワザワ
HE LOOKS LIKE HE'D BLOW AWAY IN A STRONG WIND!
AND HE'S SHOCKED AT THE SIGHT OF A DYING CACTUS! EVEN THOUGH HE'S YAKUZA!
KOMI-NAMI...?
I'M SHOUTAROU KOMINA—MYAH!
AH! I BIT MY TONGUE!
SH... SHOU-TAROU ...!?
FWEE!!
FWEE!
OH! KOMI-NAMI-SAN.
THE MAN "FWEE-FWEE"-ING OVER HERE IS OUR EDITOR IN CHIEF.
WHAT?
EDITOR IN CHIEF!? THE MOST IMPORTANT PERSON!!

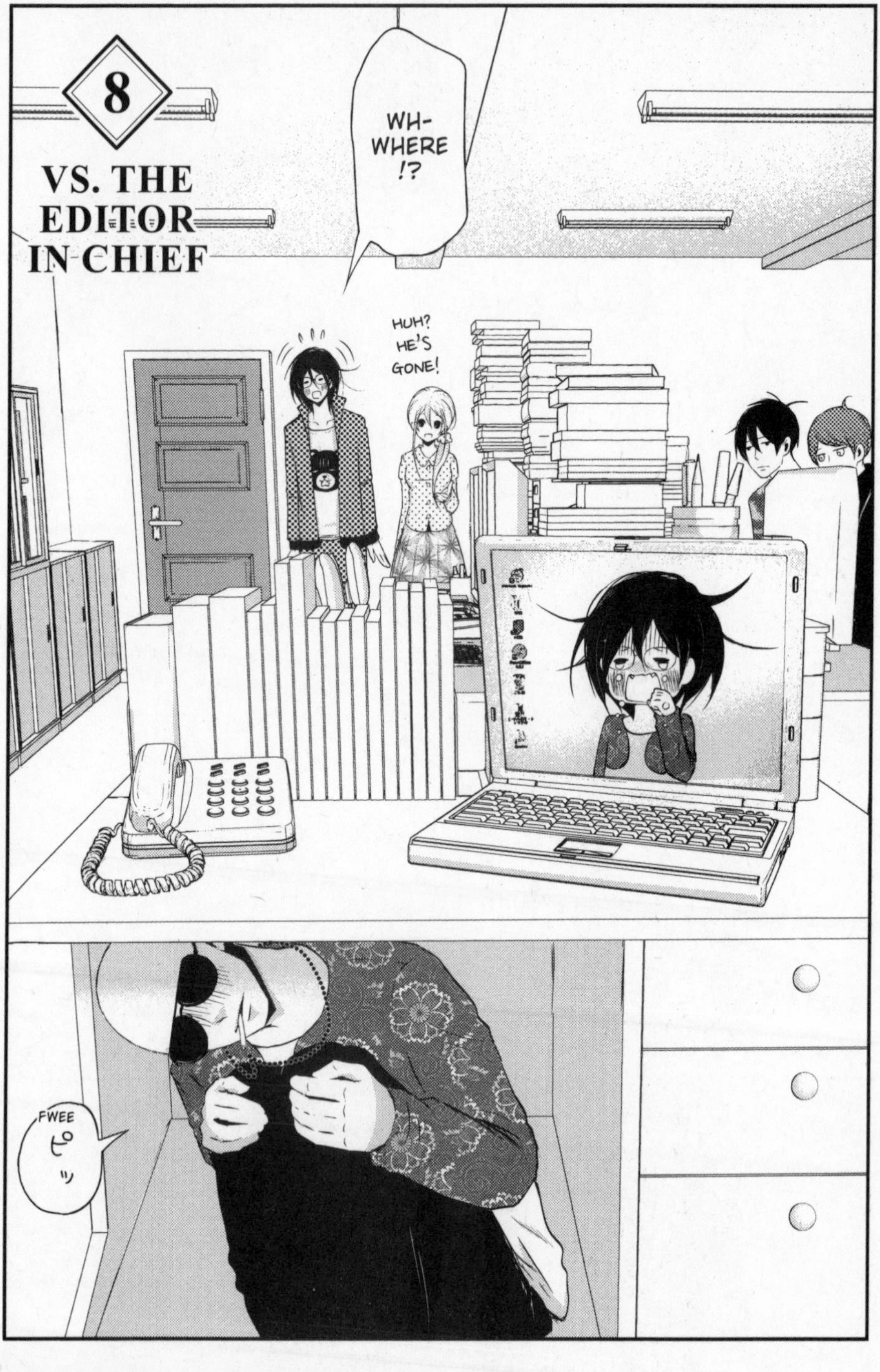
8
VS. THE EDITOR IN-CHIEF
WH- WHERE !?
HUH? HE'S GONE!
FWEE ピッ

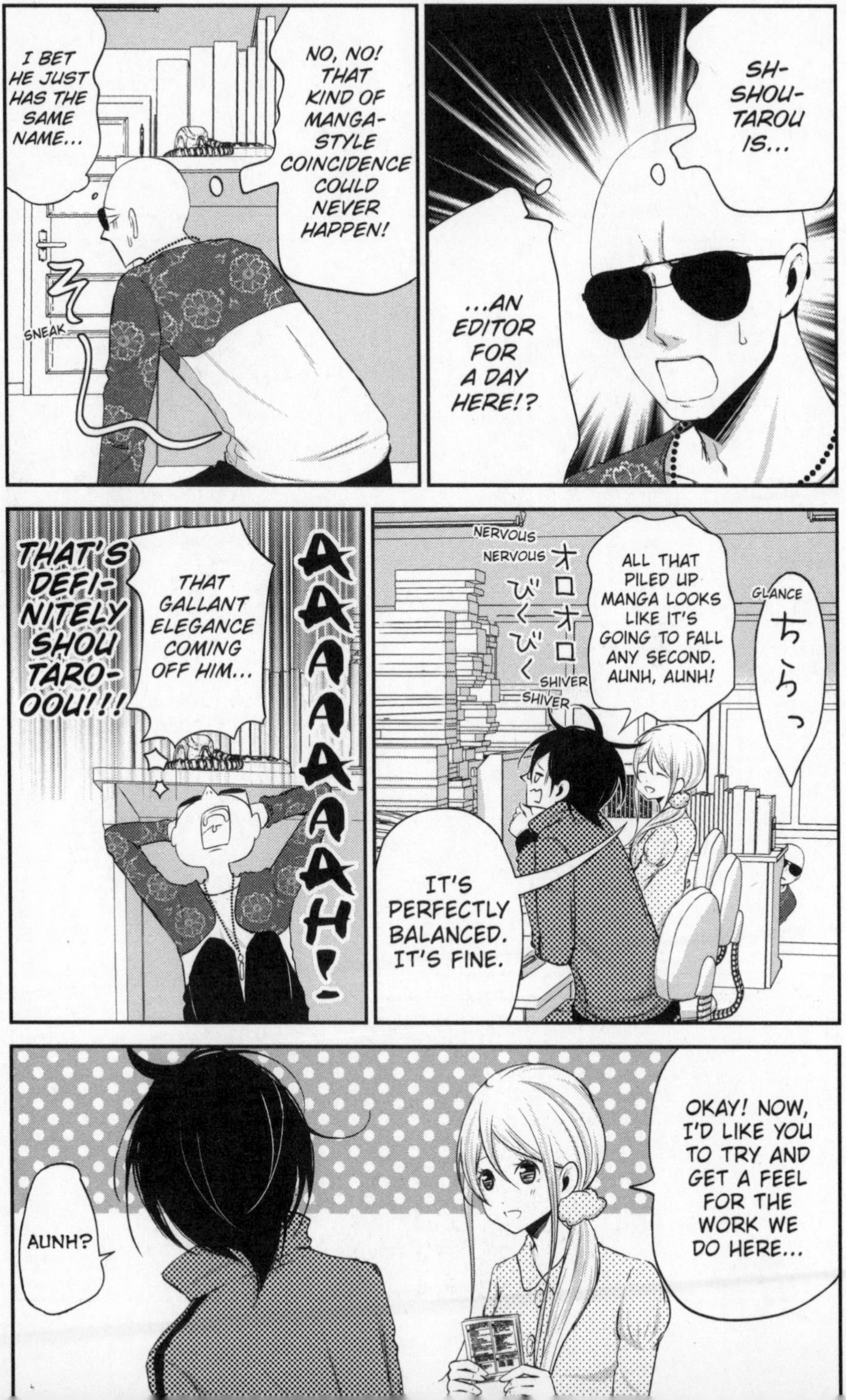
SH-SHOU-TAROU IS...
...AN EDITOR FOR A DAY HERE!?
NO, NO! THAT KIND OF MANGA-STYLE COINCIDENCE COULD NEVER HAPPEN!
I BET HE JUST HAS THE SAME NAME...
SNEAK
GLANCE
ちらっ
ALL THAT PILED UP MANGA LOOKS LIKE IT'S GOING TO FALL ANY SECOND. AUNH, AUNH!
NERVOUS NERVOUS
オロオロ
びくびく
SHIVER SHIVER
IT'S PERFECTLY BALANCED. IT'S FINE.
AAAAAAAH!
THAT GALLANT ELEGANCE COMING OFF HIM...
THAT'S DEFINITELY SHOU TAROOOU!!!
OKAY! NOW, I'D LIKE YOU TO TRY AND GET A FEEL FOR THE WORK WE DO HERE...
AUNH?

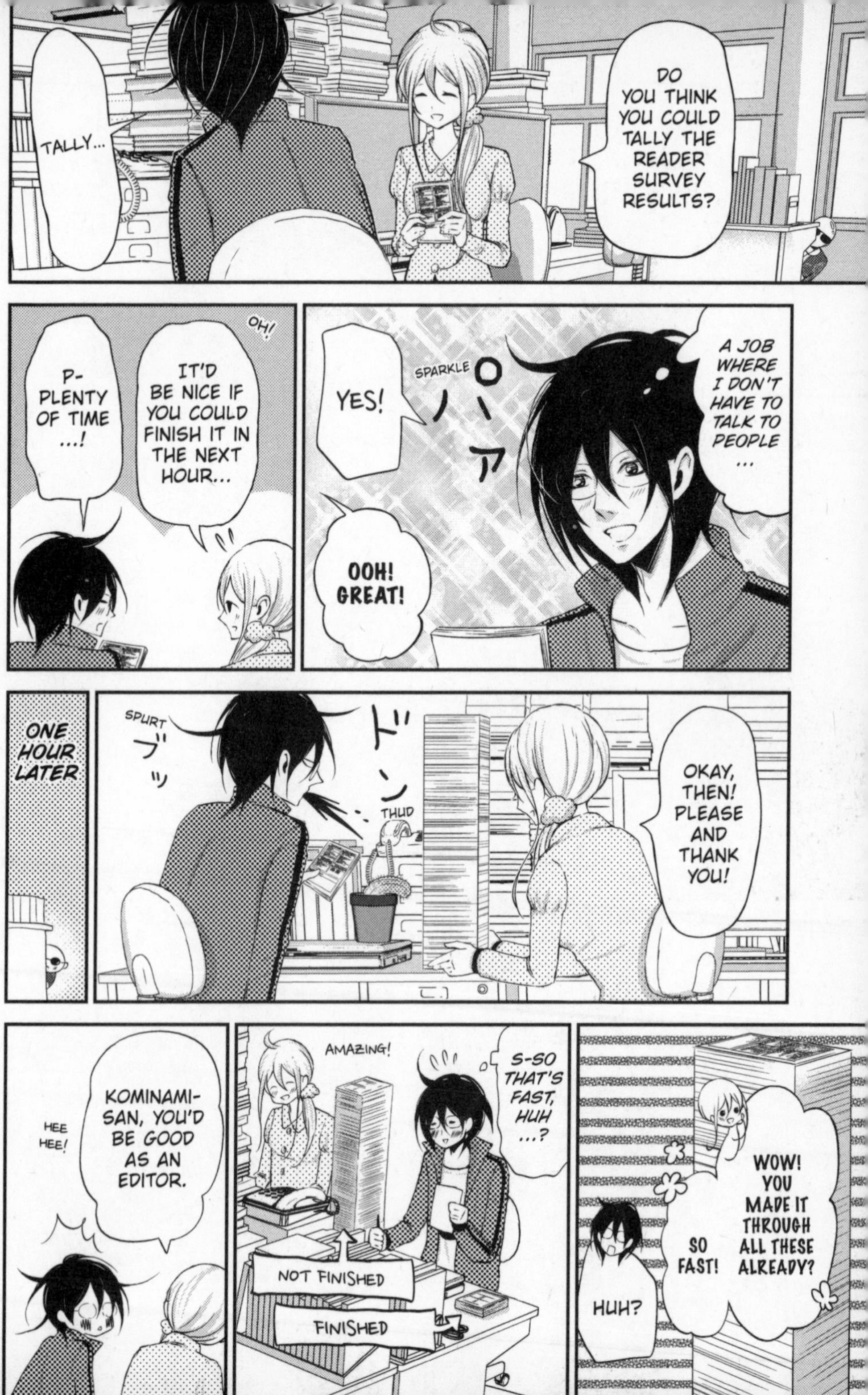
DO YOU THINK YOU COULD TALLY THE READER SURVEY RESULTS?
TALLY...
A JOB WHERE I DON'T HAVE TO TALK TO PEOPLE ...
SPARKLE
パァ
YES!
OOH! GREAT!
OH!
IT'D BE NICE IF YOU COULD FINISH IT IN THE NEXT HOUR...
P- PLENTY OF TIME ...!
OKAY, THEN! PLEASE AND THANK YOU!
ドン
THUD
SPURT
ブッ
ONE HOUR LATER
WOW! YOU MADE IT THROUGH ALL THESE ALREADY?
SO FAST!
HUH?
S-SO THAT'S FAST, HUH ...?
AMAZING!
NOT FINISHED
FINISHED
KOMINAMI-SAN, YOU'D BE GOOD AS AN EDITOR.
HEE HEE!

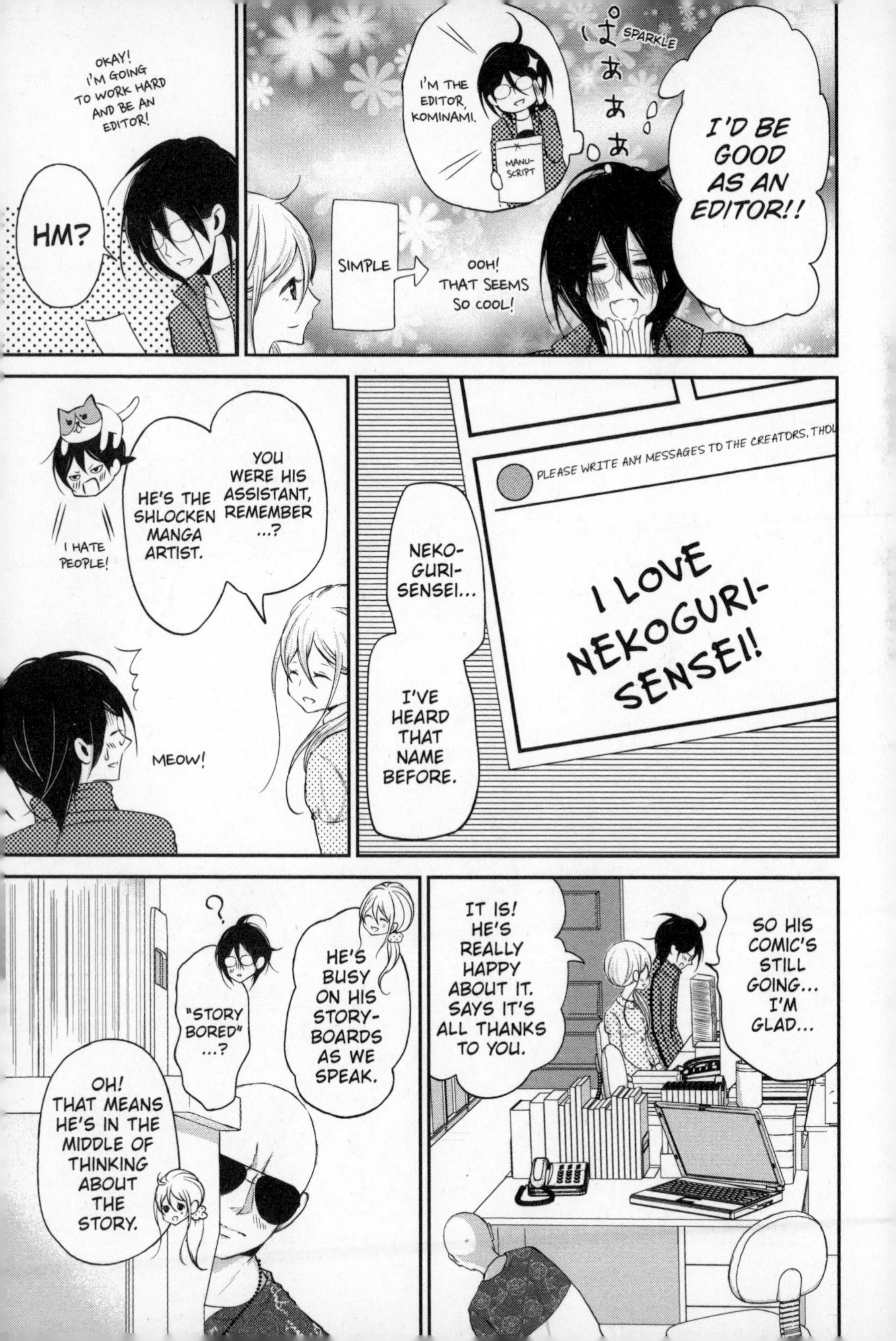
I'D BE GOOD AS AN EDITOR!!
ぱあぁぁ
SPARKLE
I'M THE EDITOR, KOMINAMI.
MANU-SCRIPT
SIMPLE
OOH! THAT SEEMS SO COOL!
OKAY! I'M GOING TO WORK HARD AND BE AN EDITOR!
HM?
PLEASE WRITE ANY MESSAGES TO THE CREATORS, THOU
I LOVE NEKOGURI-SENSEI!
NEKO-GURI-SENSEI...
I'VE HEARD THAT NAME BEFORE.
YOU WERE HIS ASSISTANT, REMEMBER ...?
HE'S THE SHLOCKEN MANGA ARTIST.
I HATE PEOPLE!
MEOW!
SO HIS COMIC'S STILL GOING... I'M GLAD...
IT IS! HE'S REALLY HAPPY ABOUT IT. SAYS IT'S ALL THANKS TO YOU.
HE'S BUSY ON HIS STORY-BOARDS AS WE SPEAK.
"STORY BORED" ...?
OH! THAT MEANS HE'S IN THE MIDDLE OF THINKING ABOUT THE STORY.

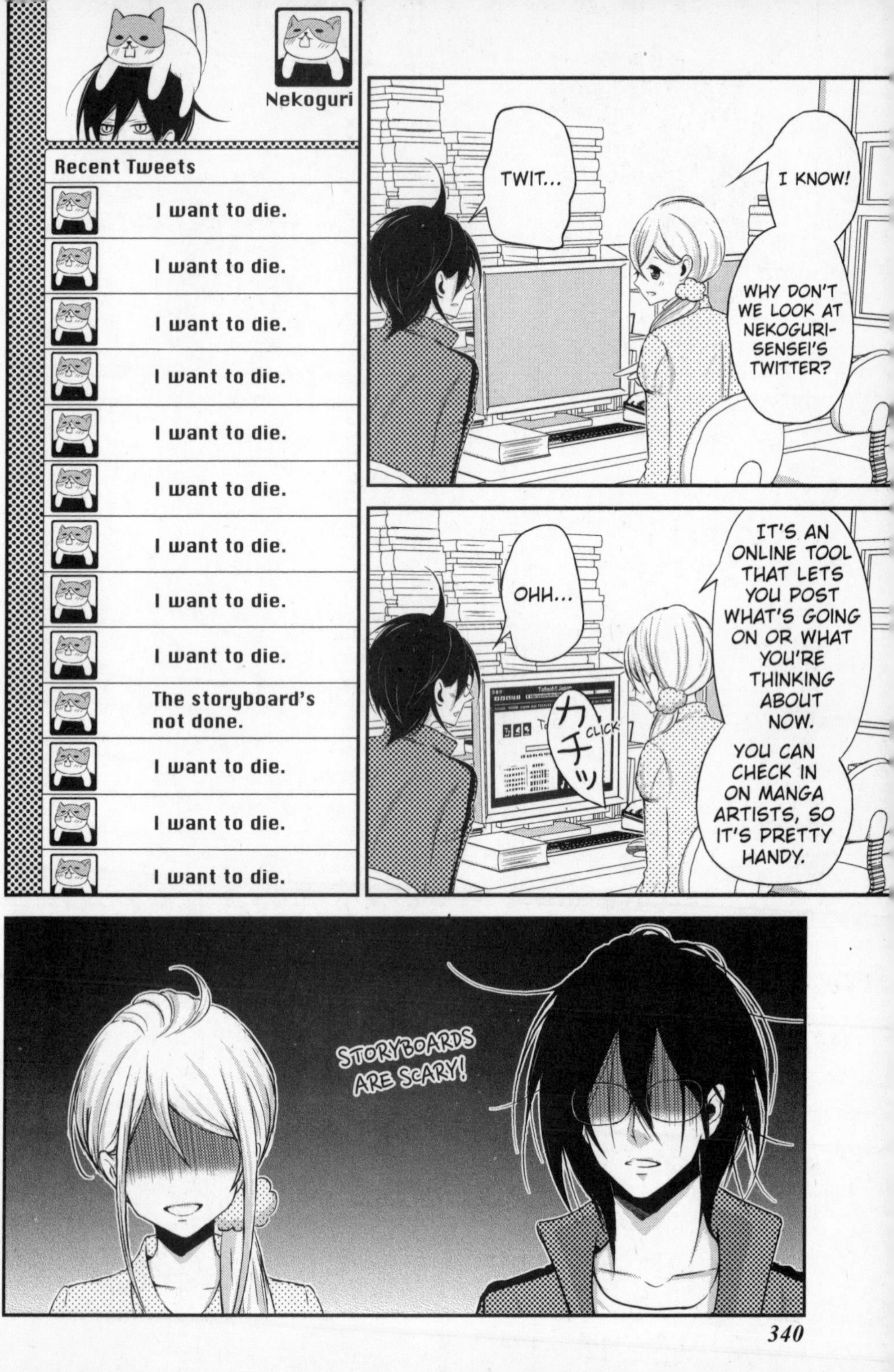
I KNOW!
WHY DON'T WE LOOK AT NEKOGURI-SENSEI'S TWITTER?
TWIT...
IT'S AN ONLINE TOOL THAT LETS YOU POST WHAT'S GOING ON OR WHAT YOU'RE THINKING ABOUT NOW.
YOU CAN CHECK IN ON MANGA ARTISTS, SO IT'S PRETTY HANDY.
カチッ
CLICK
OHH...
Nekoguri
Recent Tweets
I want to die.
I want to die.
I want to die.
I want to die.
I want to die.
I want to die.
I want to die.
I want to die.
I want to die.
The storyboard's not done.
I want to die.
I want to die.
I want to die.
STORYBOARDS ARE SCARY!

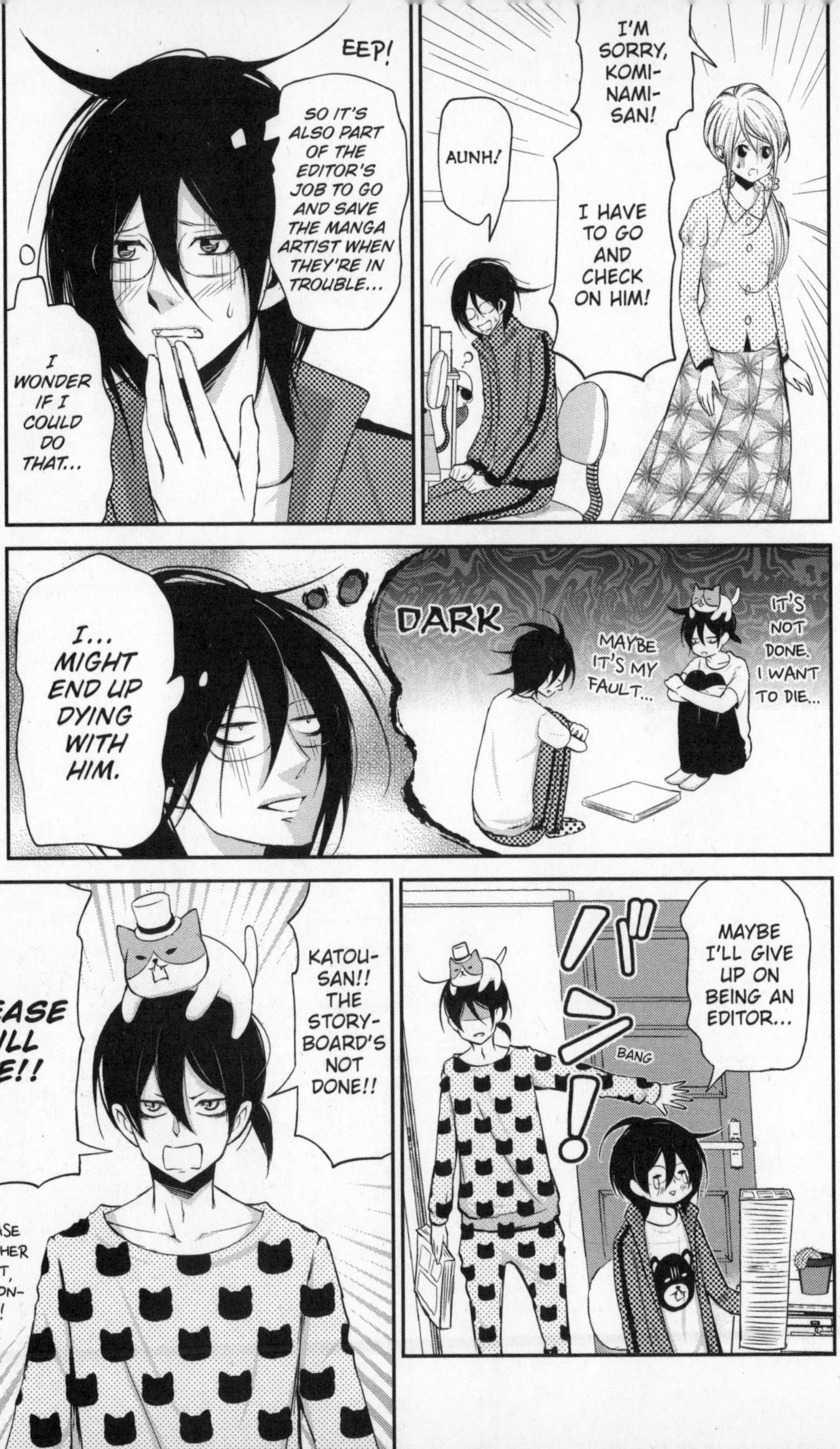

I'M SORRY, KOMI-NAMI-SAN!
I HAVE TO GO AND CHECK ON HIM!
AUNH!
EEP!
SO IT'S ALSO PART OF THE EDITOR'S JOB TO GO AND SAVE THE MANGA ARTIST WHEN THEY'RE IN TROUBLE...
I WONDER IF I COULD DO THAT...
IT'S NOT DONE. I WANT TO DIE...
MAYBE IT'S MY FAULT...
DARK
I... MIGHT END UP DYING WITH HIM.
MAYBE I'LL GIVE UP ON BEING AN EDITOR...
BANG
KATOU-SAN!! THE STORY-BOARD'S NOT DONE!!
PLEASE KILL ME!!
PLEASE TELL HER THAT, MARRON-SAN!

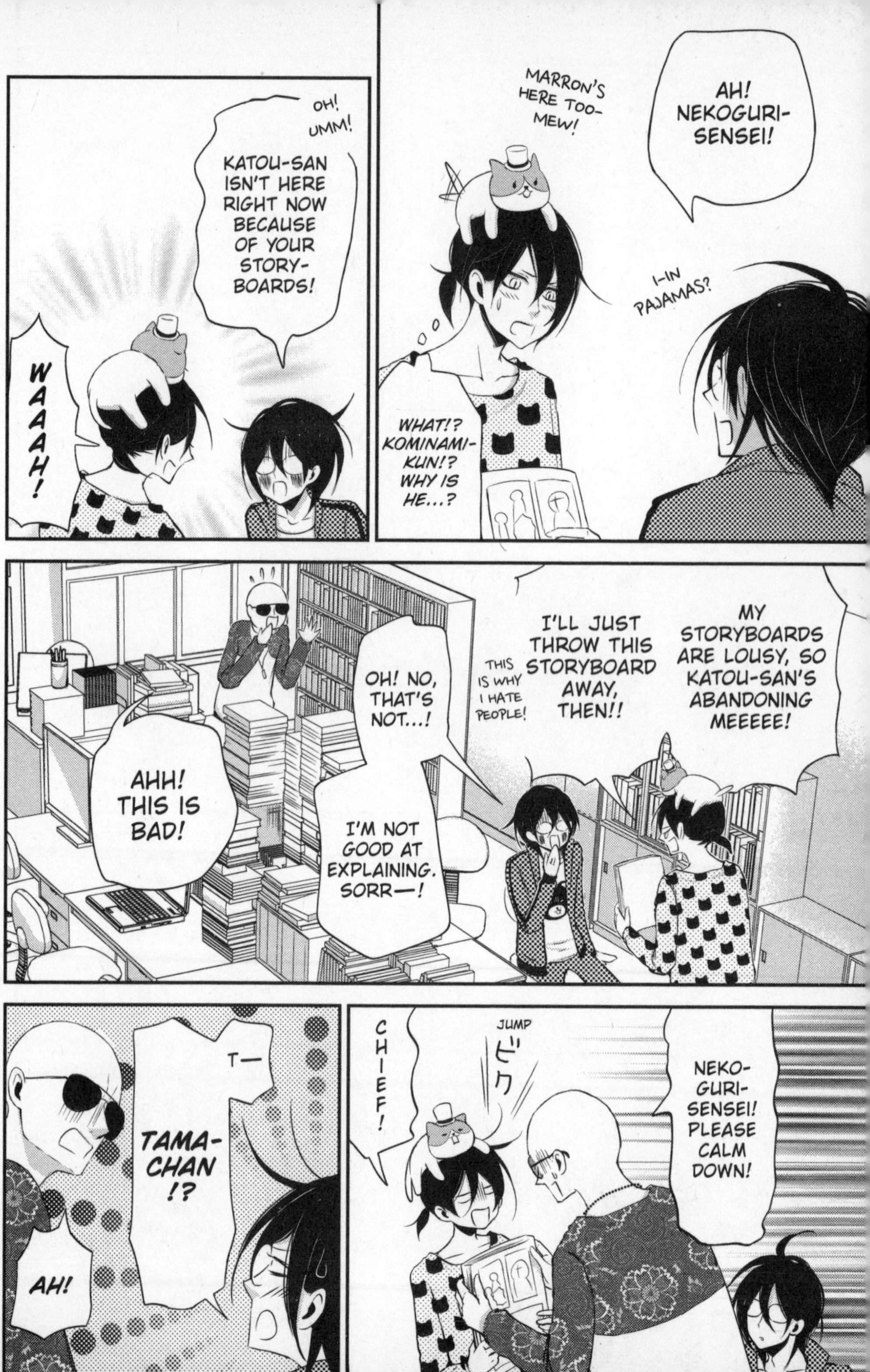
AH! NEKOGURI-SENSEI!
MARRON'S HERE TOO—MEW!
I-IN PAJAMAS?
WHAT!? KOMINAMI-KUN!? WHY IS HE...?
OH! UMM!
KATOU-SAN ISN'T HERE RIGHT NOW BECAUSE OF YOUR STORY-BOARDS!
WAAAAH!
MY STORYBOARDS ARE LOUSY, SO KATOU-SAN'S ABANDONING MEEEEE!
I'LL JUST THROW THIS STORYBOARD AWAY, THEN!!
THIS IS WHY I HATE PEOPLE!
OH! NO, THAT'S NOT...!
I'M NOT GOOD AT EXPLAINING. SORR—!
AHH! THIS IS BAD!
NEKO-GURI-SENSEI! PLEASE CALM DOWN!
JUMP
ビク
CHIEF!
T—
TAMA-CHAN!?
AH!

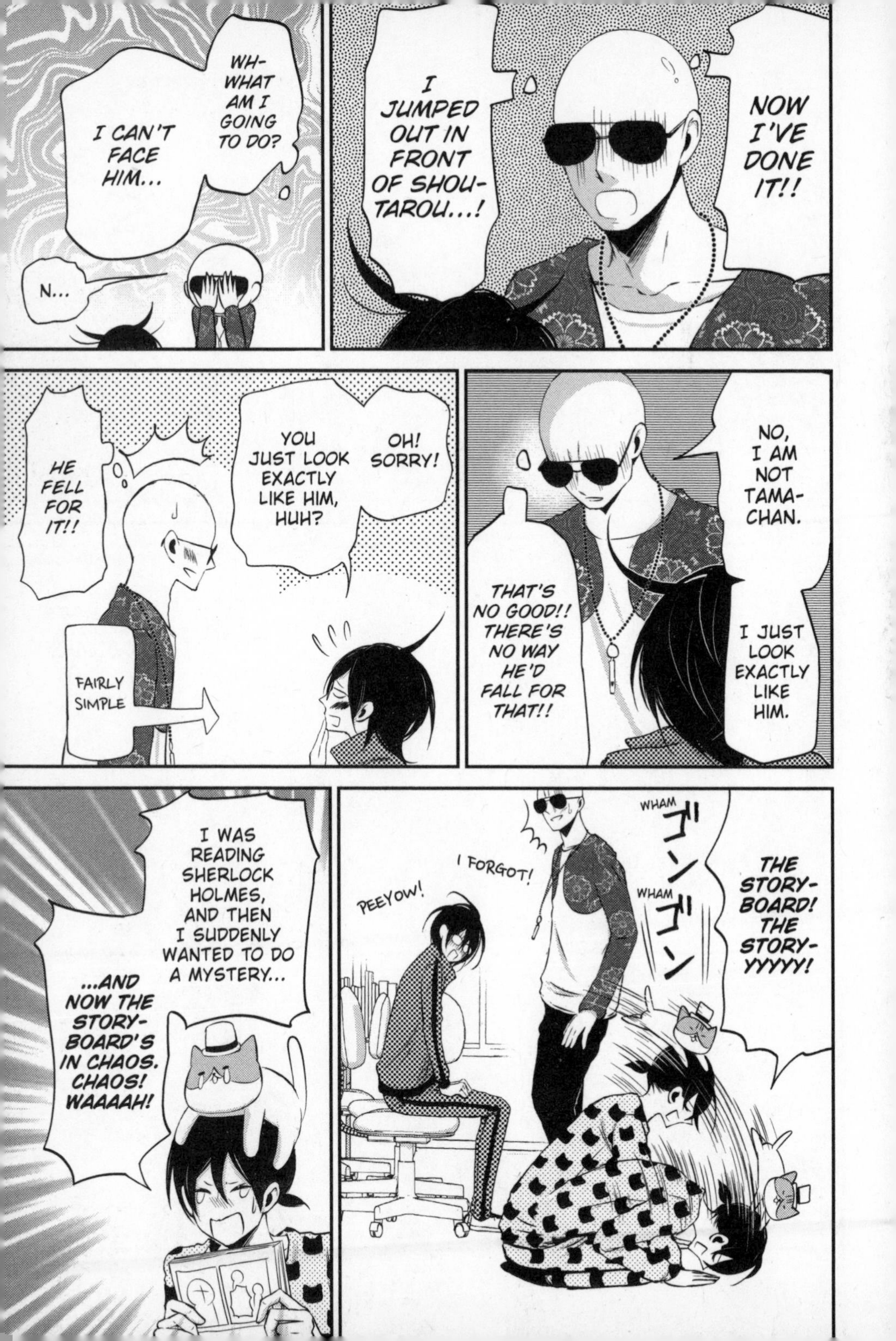
NOW I'VE DONE IT!!
I JUMPED OUT IN FRONT OF SHOUTAROU...!
WH-WHAT AM I GOING TO DO?
I CAN'T FACE HIM...
N...
NO, I AM NOT TAMA-CHAN.
I JUST LOOK EXACTLY LIKE HIM.
THAT'S NO GOOD!! THERE'S NO WAY HE'D FALL FOR THAT!!
OH! SORRY!
YOU JUST LOOK EXACTLY LIKE HIM, HUH?
HE FELL FOR IT!!
FAIRLY SIMPLE
THE STORY-BOARD! THE STORY-YYYYY!
WHAM ゴン
WHAM ゴン
I FORGOT!
PEEYOW!
I WAS READING SHERLOCK HOLMES, AND THEN I SUDDENLY WANTED TO DO A MYSTERY...
...AND NOW THE STORY-BOARD'S IN CHAOS. CHAOS! WAAAAH!

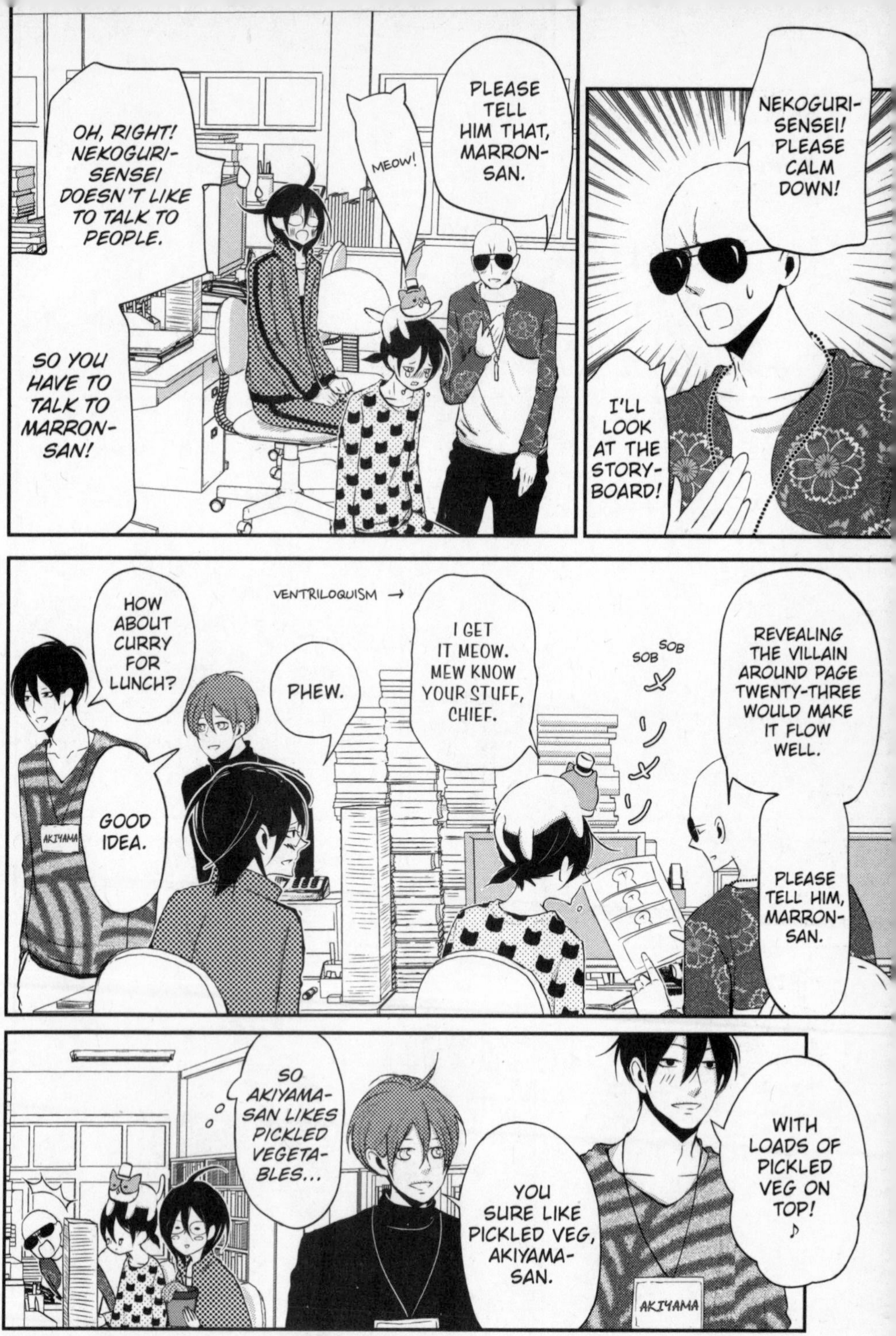
NEKOGURI-SENSEI! PLEASE CALM DOWN!
I'LL LOOK AT THE STORYBOARD!
PLEASE TELL HIM THAT, MARRON-SAN.
MEOW!
OH, RIGHT! NEKOGURI-SENSEI DOESN'T LIKE TO TALK TO PEOPLE.
SO YOU HAVE TO TALK TO MARRON-SAN!
REVEALING THE VILLAIN AROUND PAGE TWENTY-THREE WOULD MAKE IT FLOW WELL.
PLEASE TELL HIM, MARRON-SAN.
SOB SOB
I GET IT MEOW. MEW KNOW YOUR STUFF, CHIEF.
VENTRILOQUISM →
PHEW.
HOW ABOUT CURRY FOR LUNCH?
AKIYAMA
GOOD IDEA.
WITH LOADS OF PICKLED VEG ON TOP! ♪
AKIYAMA
YOU SURE LIKE PICKLED VEG, AKIYAMA-SAN.
SO AKIYAMA-SAN LIKES PICKLED VEGETA-BLES...

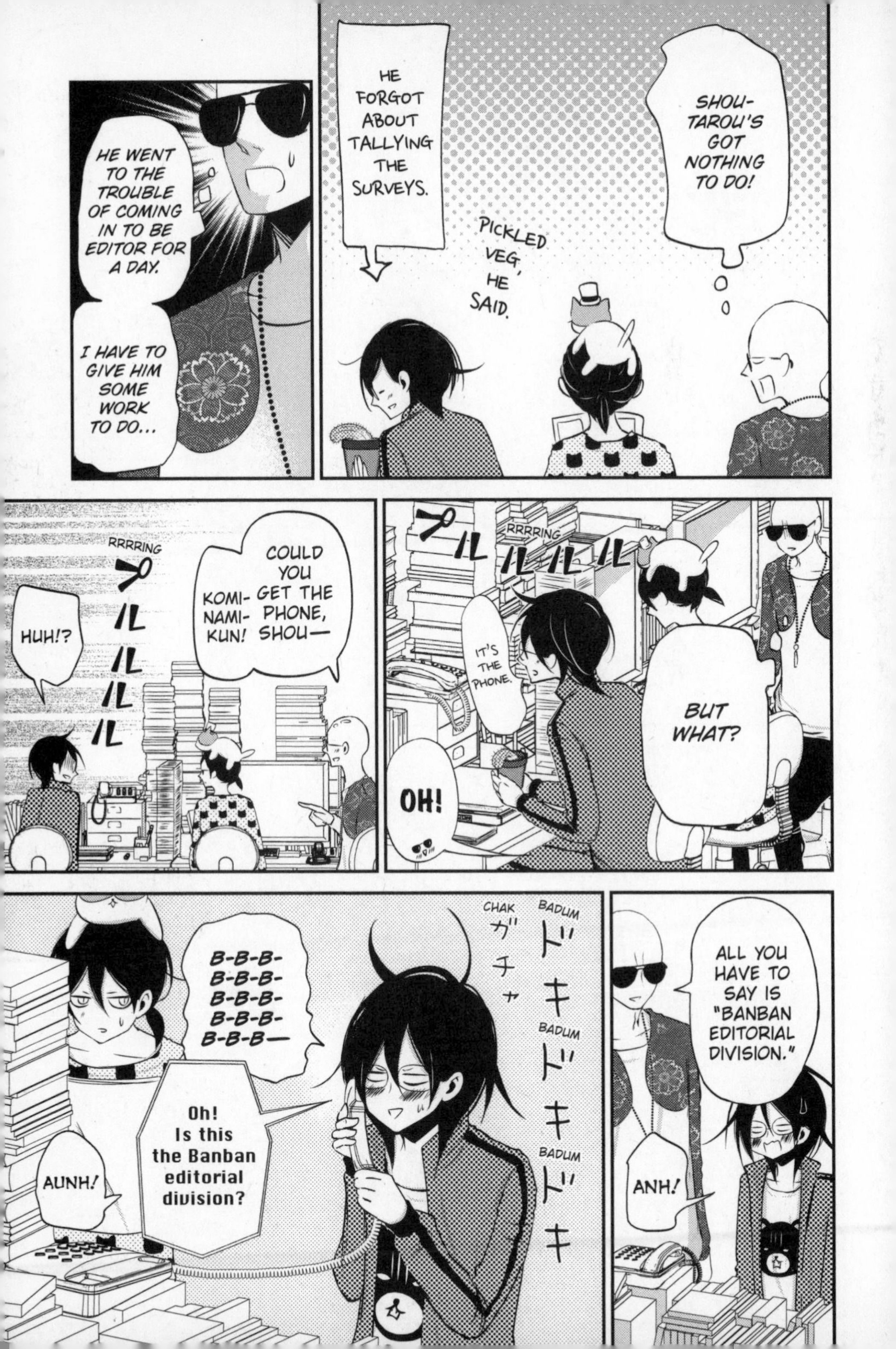
SHOU-TAROU'S GOT NOTHING TO DO!
HE FORGOT ABOUT TALLYING THE SURVEYS.
PICKLED VEG, HE SAID.
HE WENT TO THE TROUBLE OF COMING IN TO BE EDITOR FOR A DAY.
I HAVE TO GIVE HIM SOME WORK TO DO...
RRRRING
プルルルル
IT'S THE PHONE.
BUT WHAT?
OH!
COULD YOU GET THE PHONE, SHOU—
KOMI-NAMI-KUN!
RRRRING
プルルルル
HUH!?
ALL YOU HAVE TO SAY IS "BANBAN EDITORIAL DIVISION."
ANH!
BADUM
ドキ
BADUM
ドキ
BADUM
ドキ
CHAK
ガチャ
B-B-B-B-B-B-B-B-B-B-B-B-B-B-B—
Oh! Is this the Banban editorial division?
AUNH!

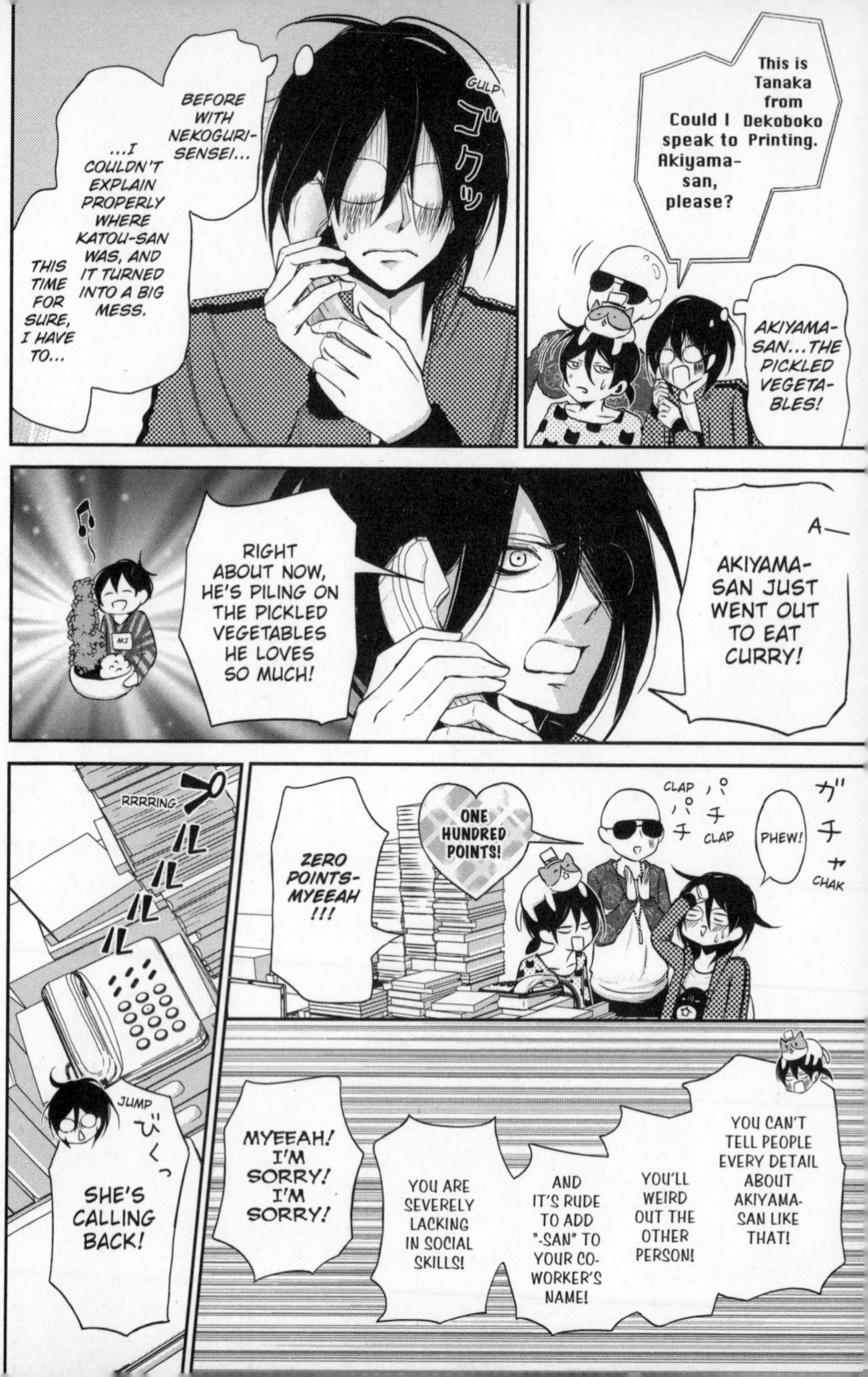

This is Tanaka from Dekoboko Printing.
Could I speak to Akiyama-san, please?
AKIYAMA-SAN...THE PICKLED VEGETABLES!
GULP
ゴクッ
BEFORE WITH NEKOGURI-SENSEI...
...I COULDN'T EXPLAIN PROPERLY WHERE KATOU-SAN WAS, AND IT TURNED INTO A BIG MESS.
THIS TIME FOR SURE, I HAVE TO...
A—
AKIYAMA-SAN JUST WENT OUT TO EAT CURRY!
RIGHT ABOUT NOW, HE'S PILING ON THE PICKLED VEGETABLES HE LOVES SO MUCH!
AKI
ガチャ
CHAK
PHEW!
パチパチ
CLAP CLAP
ONE HUNDRED POINTS!
ZERO POINTS-MYEEAH!!!
YOU CAN'T TELL PEOPLE EVERY DETAIL ABOUT AKIYAMA-SAN LIKE THAT!
YOU'LL WEIRD OUT THE OTHER PERSON!
AND IT'S RUDE TO ADD "-SAN" TO YOUR CO-WORKER'S NAME!
YOU ARE SEVERELY LACKING IN SOCIAL SKILLS!
MYEEAH! I'M SORRY! I'M SORRY!
RRRRING
プルルル
JUMP
びくっ
SHE'S CALLING BACK!

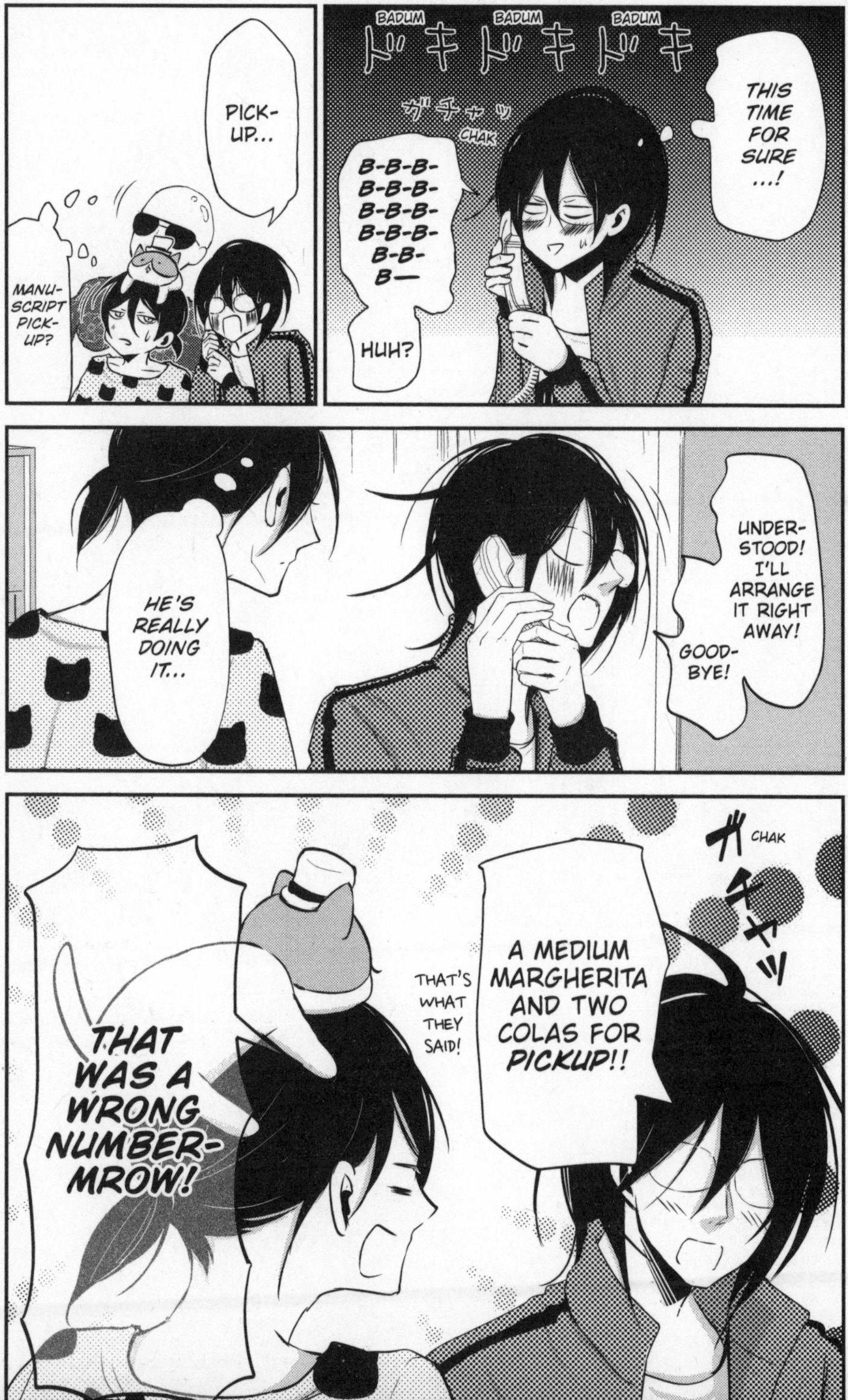
BADUM BADUM BADUM
ドキドキドキ
THIS TIME FOR SURE ...!
ガチャッ
CHAK
B-B-B-B-B-B-B-B-B-B-B-B-B-B-B—
HUH?
PICK-UP...
MANU-SCRIPT PICK-UP?
UNDERSTOOD! I'LL ARRANGE IT RIGHT AWAY!
GOOD-BYE!
HE'S REALLY DOING IT...
ガチャッ
CHAK
A MEDIUM MARGHERITA AND TWO COLAS FOR PICKUP!!
THAT'S WHAT THEY SAID!
THAT WAS A WRONG NUMBER-MROW!

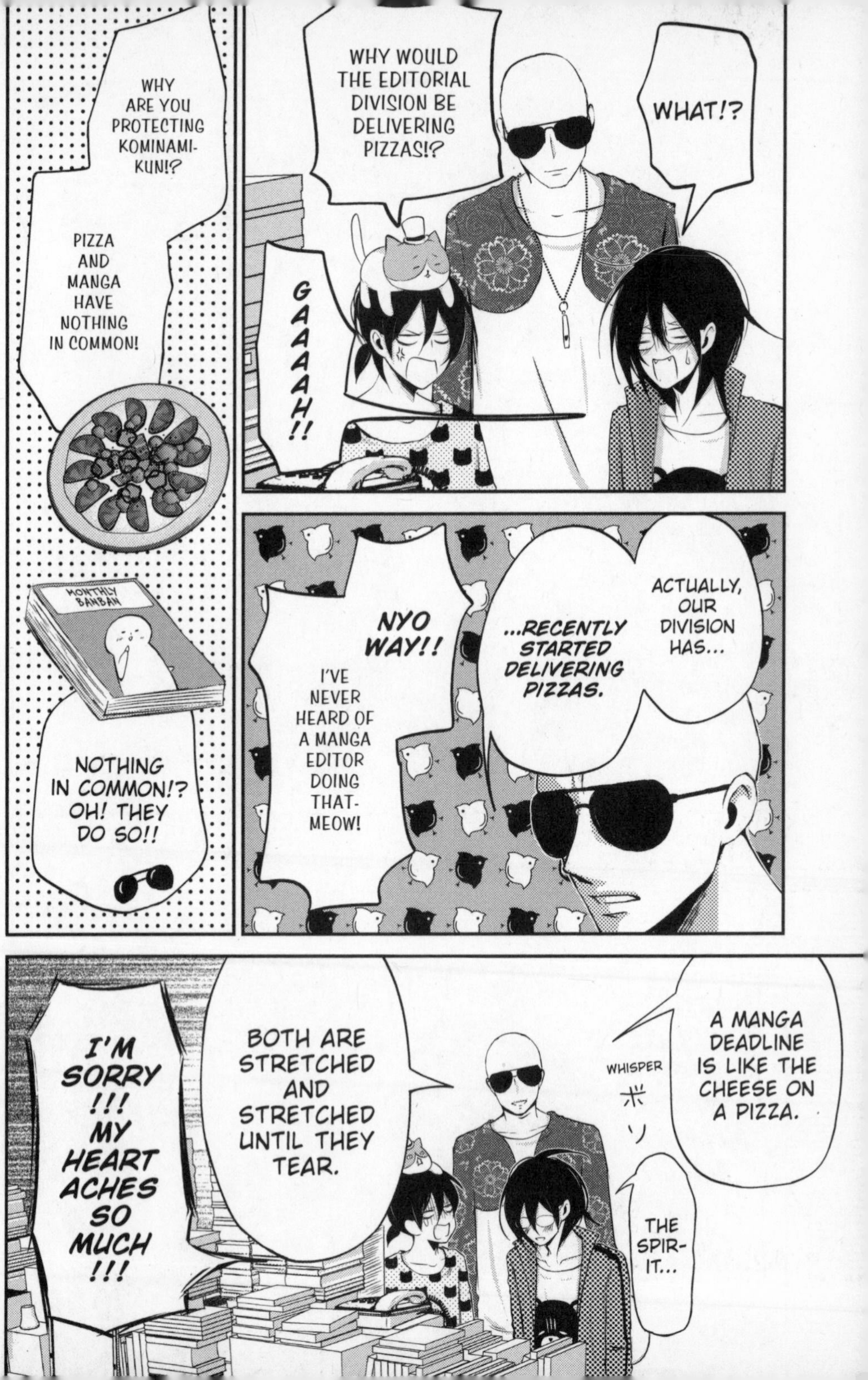
WHAT!?
WHY WOULD THE EDITORIAL DIVISION BE DELIVERING PIZZAS!?
GAAAAAH!!
ACTUALLY, OUR DIVISION HAS...
...RECENTLY STARTED DELIVERING PIZZAS.
NYO WAY!!
I'VE NEVER HEARD OF A MANGA EDITOR DOING THAT-MEOW!
WHY ARE YOU PROTECTING KOMINAMI-KUN!?
PIZZA AND MANGA HAVE NOTHING IN COMMON!
MONTHLY BANBAN
NOTHING IN COMMON!? OH! THEY DO SO!!
A MANGA DEADLINE IS LIKE THE CHEESE ON A PIZZA.
WHISPER
ボソ
THE SPIR-IT...
BOTH ARE STRETCHED AND STRETCHED UNTIL THEY TEAR.
I'M SORRY!!! MY HEART ACHES SO MUCH!!!

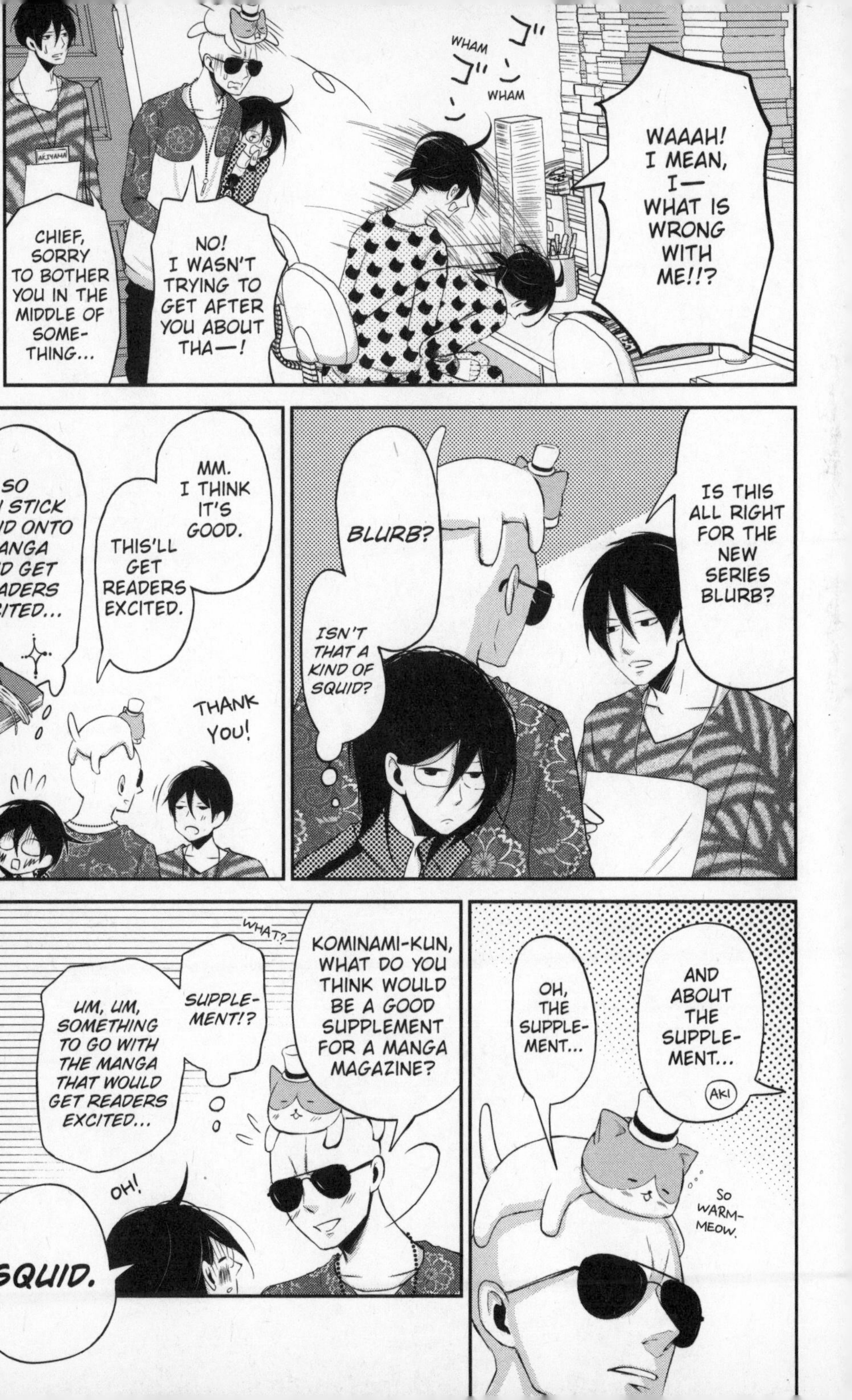

ゴン WHAM
ゴン WHAM
WAAAH! I MEAN, I— WHAT IS WRONG WITH ME!!?
NO! I WASN'T TRYING TO GET AFTER YOU ABOUT THA—!
CHIEF, SORRY TO BOTHER YOU IN THE MIDDLE OF SOME-THING...
AKIYAMA
IS THIS ALL RIGHT FOR THE NEW SERIES BLURB?
BLURB?
ISN'T THAT A KIND OF SQUID?
MM. I THINK IT'S GOOD.
THIS'LL GET READERS EXCITED.
SO YOU STICK SQUID ONTO MANGA AND GET READERS EXCITED...
THANK YOU!
AND ABOUT THE SUPPLE-MENT...
AKI
OH, THE SUPPLE-MENT...
SO WARM-MEOW.
KOMINAMI-KUN, WHAT DO YOU THINK WOULD BE A GOOD SUPPLEMENT FOR A MANGA MAGAZINE?
WHAT?
SUPPLE-MENT!?
UM, UM, SOMETHING TO GO WITH THE MANGA THAT WOULD GET READERS EXCITED...
OH!
SQUID.

THE MAGAZINE'S GONNA STINK!! PEE-MEW!

SQUID IT IS!

THE SQUID HAS FALLEN FROM MY EYYYYES!

AKIYAMA-KUN, THIS KID'S IDEAS ARE SQUID-TASTIC!

THAT'S IT! AND A SQUID COULD BE A BOOKMARK TOO!!

SQUI-IIIIID!

BLUSH BLUSH

Detective Nekoguri-mode

HMM...

WHY IS THE CHIEF SO SOFT ON KOMINAMI-KUN...?

THERE HAS TO BE SOME EXPLANATION, WATSON-KUN.

IT'S MARRON-MEOW.

OH! NEKO-GURI-SENSEI!?

OH! KATOU-SAN...

HE WASN'T THERE... I'M BACK...

ガチャ
KACHAK

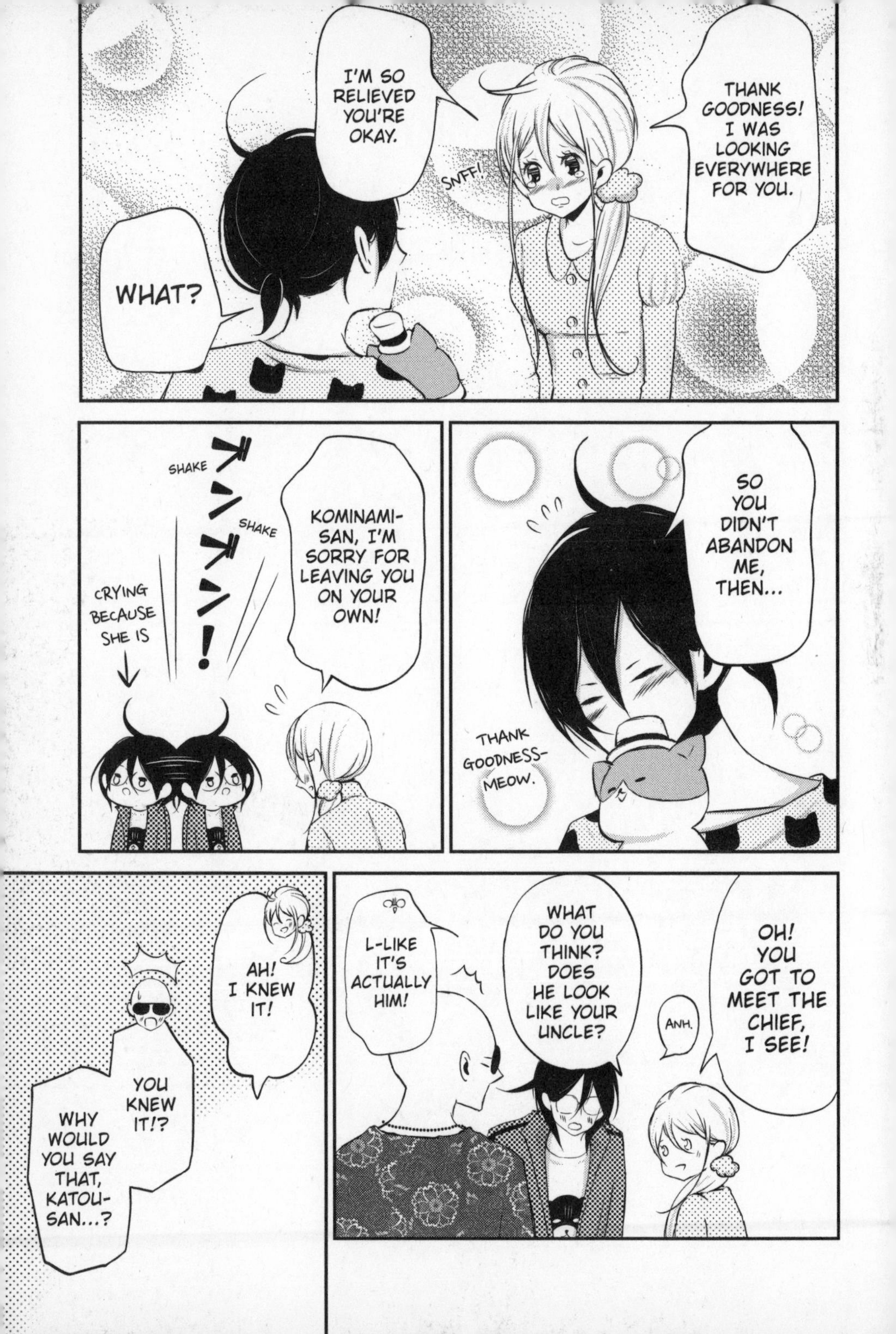
THANK GOODNESS! I WAS LOOKING EVERYWHERE FOR YOU.
SNFF!
I'M SO RELIEVED YOU'RE OKAY.
WHAT?
SO YOU DIDN'T ABANDON ME, THEN...
THANK GOODNESS-MEOW.
KOMINAMI-SAN, I'M SORRY FOR LEAVING YOU ON YOUR OWN!
SHAKE
SHAKE
CRYING BECAUSE SHE IS
OH! YOU GOT TO MEET THE CHIEF, I SEE!
ANH.
WHAT DO YOU THINK? DOES HE LOOK LIKE YOUR UNCLE?
L-LIKE IT'S ACTUALLY HIM!
AH! I KNEW IT!
YOU KNEW IT!?
WHY WOULD YOU SAY THAT, KATOU-SAN...?

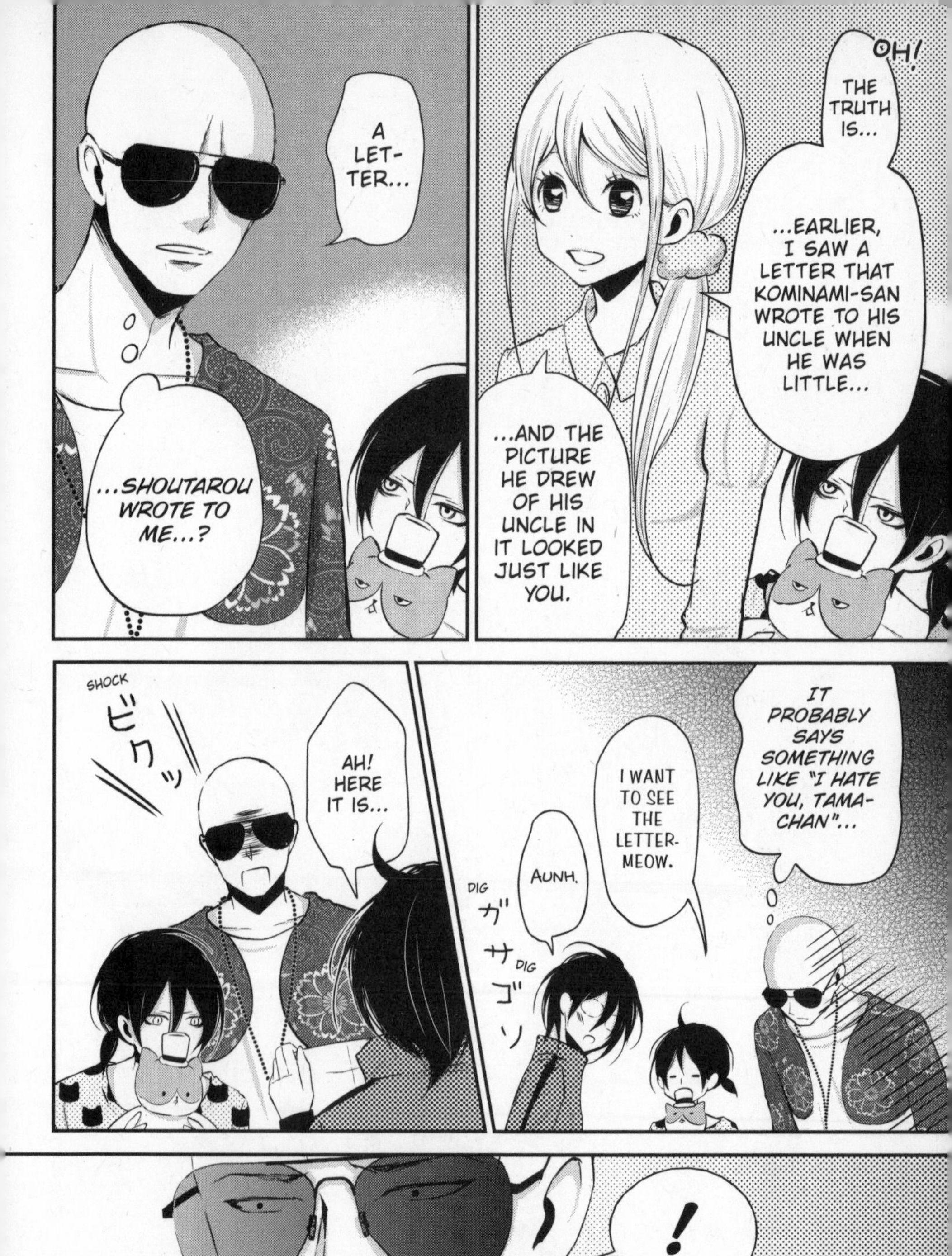
OH!
THE TRUTH IS...
...EARLIER, I SAW A LETTER THAT KOMINAMI-SAN WROTE TO HIS UNCLE WHEN HE WAS LITTLE...
...AND THE PICTURE HE DREW OF HIS UNCLE IN IT LOOKED JUST LIKE YOU.
A LETTER...
...SHOUTAROU WROTE TO ME...?
IT PROBABLY SAYS SOMETHING LIKE "I HATE YOU, TAMA-CHAN"...
I WANT TO SEE THE LETTER-MEOW.
AUNH.
DIG
ガサゴソ
DIG
SHOCK
ビクッ
AH! HERE IT IS...
!

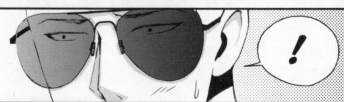

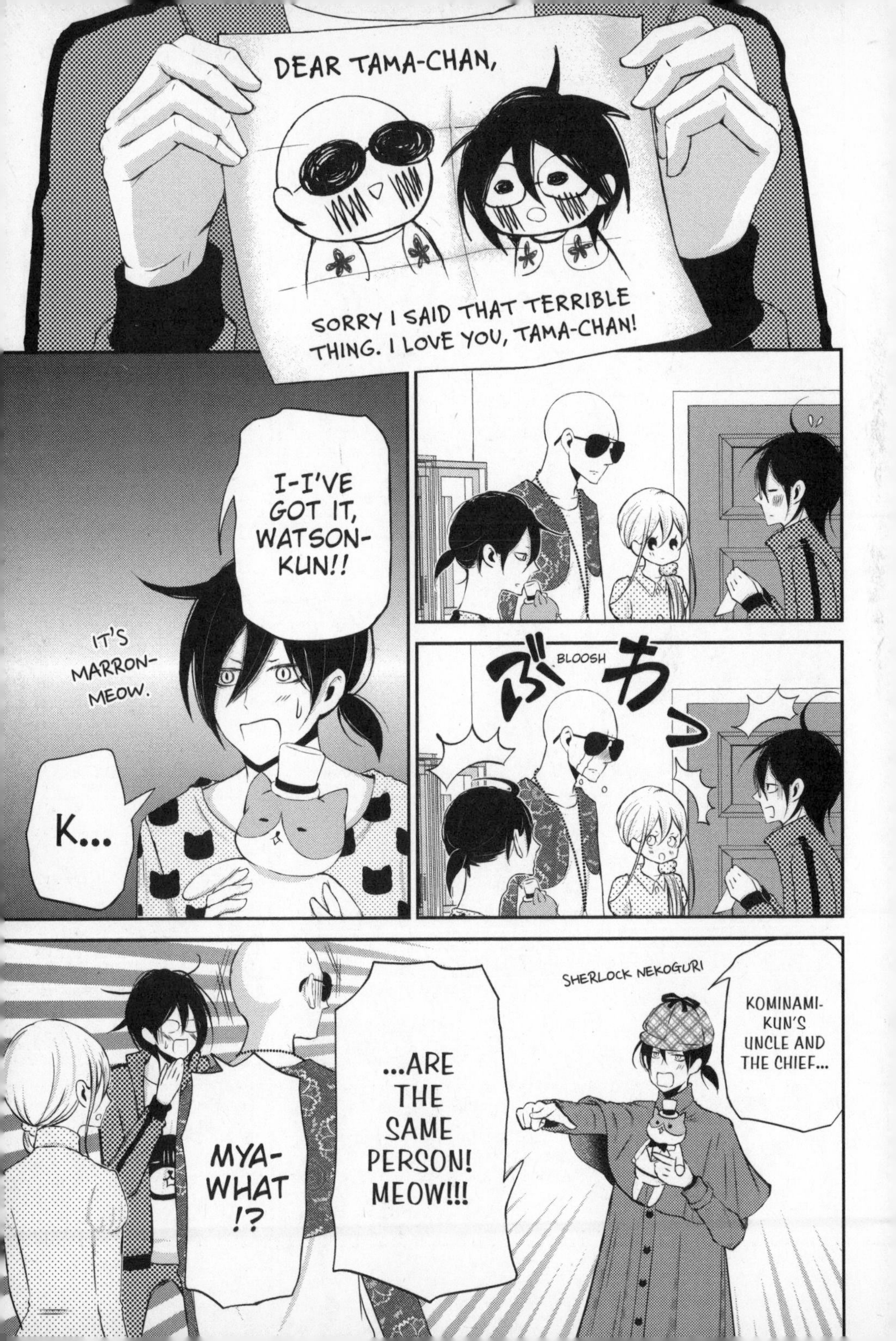
DEAR TAMA-CHAN,
SORRY I SAID THAT TERRIBLE THING. I LOVE YOU, TAMA-CHAN!
ぶわっ
BLOOSH
I-I'VE GOT IT, WATSON-KUN!!
IT'S MARRON-MEOW.
K...
KOMINAMI-KUN'S UNCLE AND THE CHIEF...
SHERLOCK NEKOGURI
...ARE THE SAME PERSON! MEOW!!!
MYA-WHAT!?

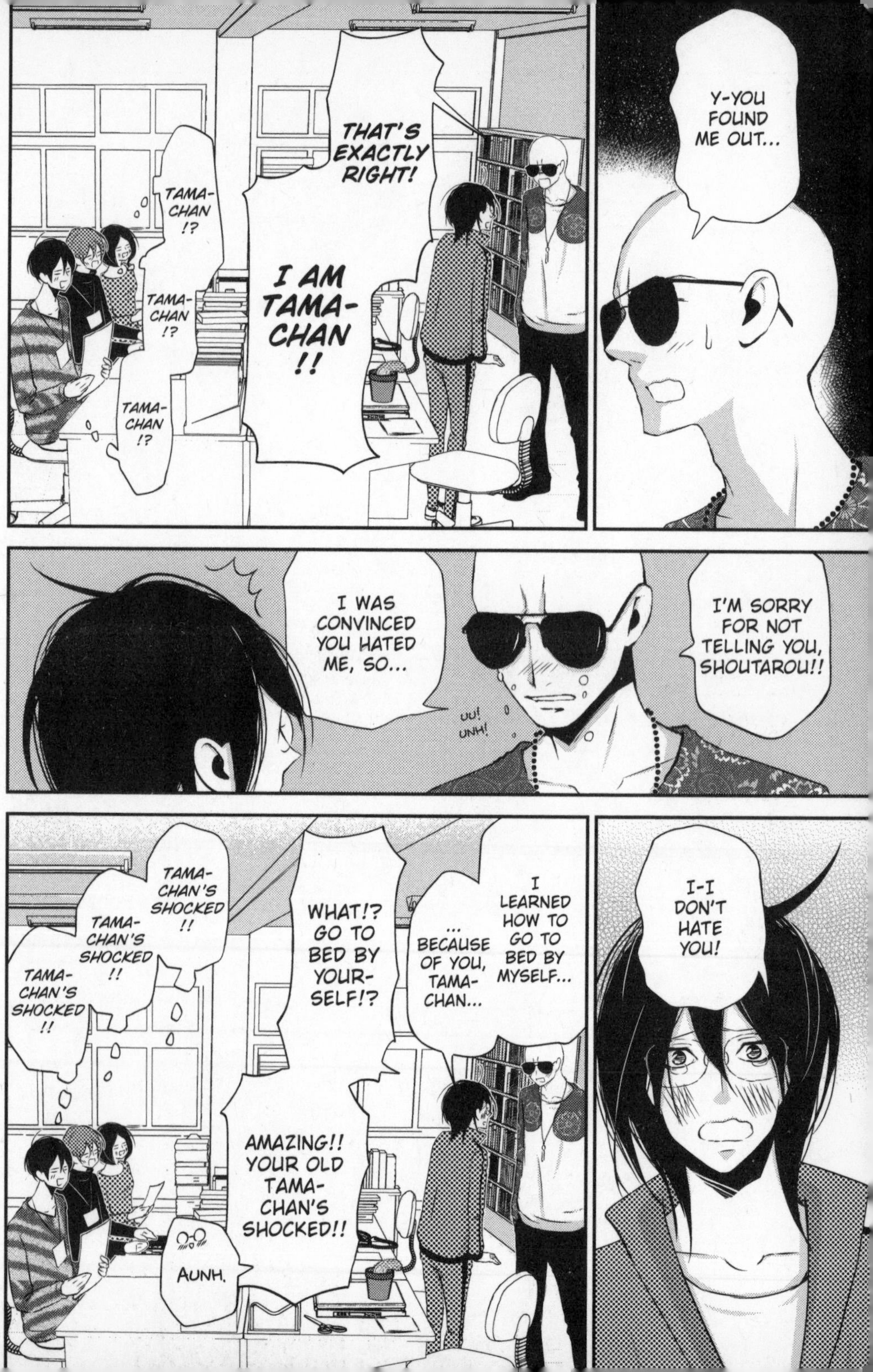
Y-YOU FOUND ME OUT...
THAT'S EXACTLY RIGHT!
I AM TAMA-CHAN!!
TAMA-CHAN!?
TAMA-CHAN!?
TAMA-CHAN!?
I'M SORRY FOR NOT TELLING YOU, SHOUTAROU!!
UU! UNH!
I WAS CONVINCED YOU HATED ME, SO...
I-I DON'T HATE YOU!
I LEARNED HOW TO GO TO BED BY MYSELF...
... BECAUSE OF YOU, TAMA-CHAN...
WHAT!? GO TO BED BY YOURSELF!?
TAMA-CHAN'S SHOCKED!!
TAMA-CHAN'S SHOCKED!!
TAMA-CHAN'S SHOCKED!!
AMAZING!! YOUR OLD TAMA-CHAN'S SHOCKED!!
AUNH.

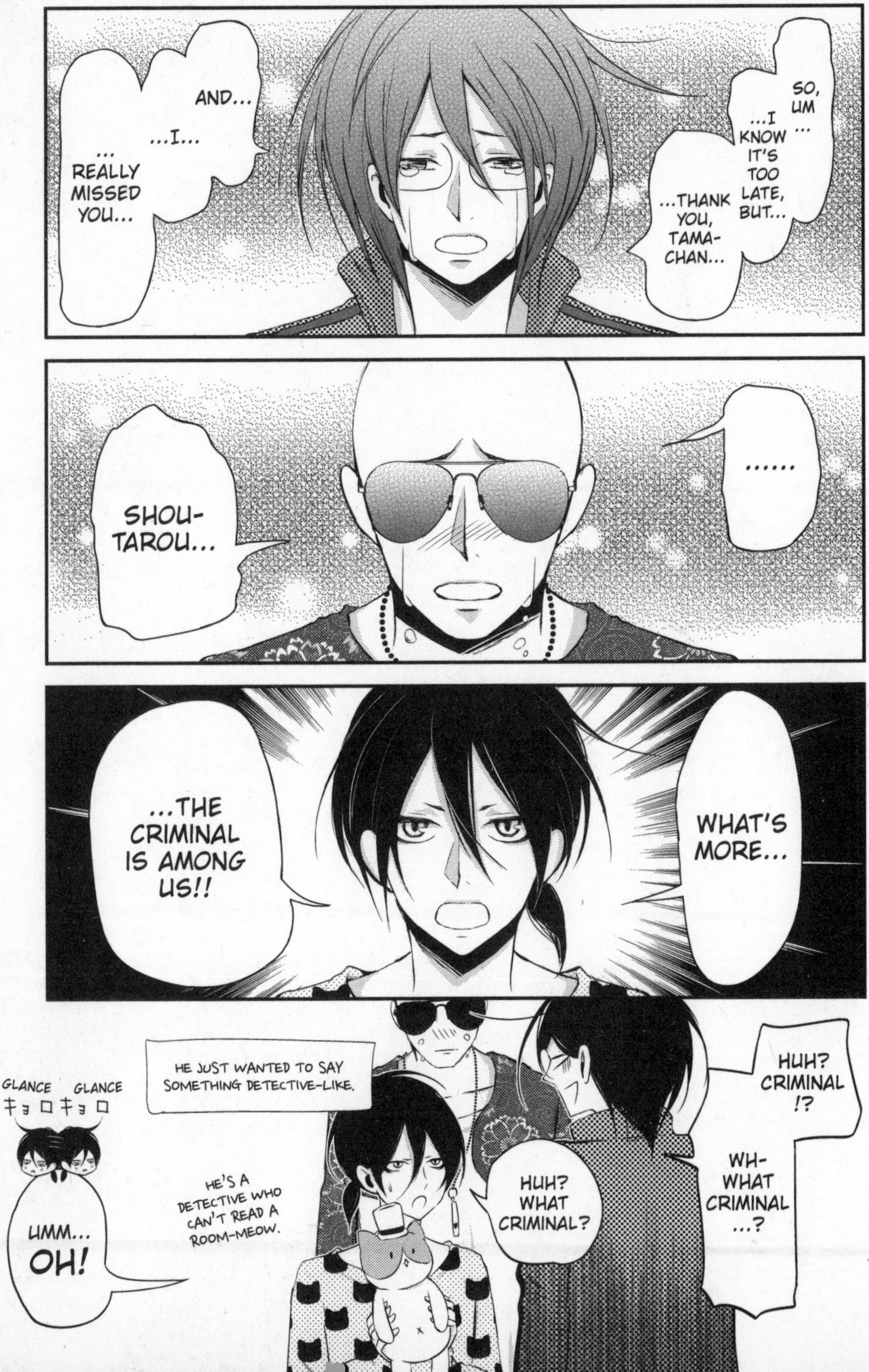
SO, UM ...
...I KNOW IT'S TOO LATE, BUT...
...THANK YOU, TAMA-CHAN...
AND...
...I...
...REALLY MISSED YOU...
......
SHOU-TAROU...
WHAT'S MORE...
...THE CRIMINAL IS AMONG US!!
HUH? CRIMINAL!?
WH-WHAT CRIMINAL...?
HE JUST WANTED TO SAY SOMETHING DETECTIVE-LIKE.
HUH? WHAT CRIMINAL?
HE'S A DETECTIVE WHO CAN'T READ A ROOM-MEOW.
GLANCE GLANCE
キョロキョロ
UMM... OH!

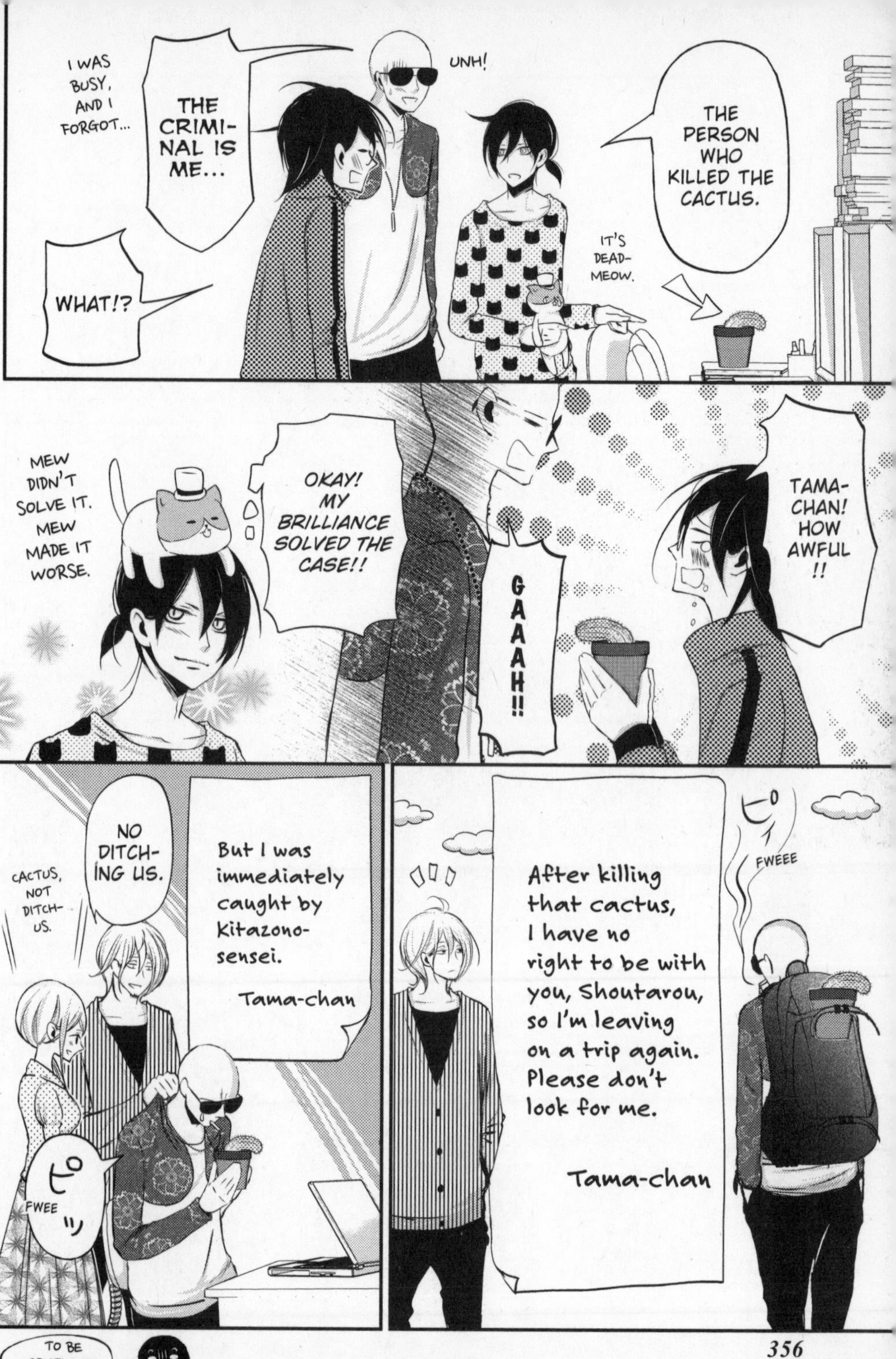
THE PERSON WHO KILLED THE CACTUS.
IT'S DEAD-MEOW.
UNH!
THE CRIMINAL IS ME...
I WAS BUSY, AND I FORGOT...
WHAT!?
TAMA-CHAN! HOW AWFUL!!
GAAAAH!!
OKAY! MY BRILLIANCE SOLVED THE CASE!!
MEW DIDN'T SOLVE IT. MEW MADE IT WORSE.
ピー
FWEEE
After killing that cactus, I have no right to be with you, Shoutarou, so I'm leaving on a trip again. Please don't look for me.
Tama-chan
But I was immediately caught by Kitazono-sensei.
Tama-chan
NO DITCHING US.
CACTUS, NOT DITCH-US.
ピッ
FWEE
TO BE CONTINUED

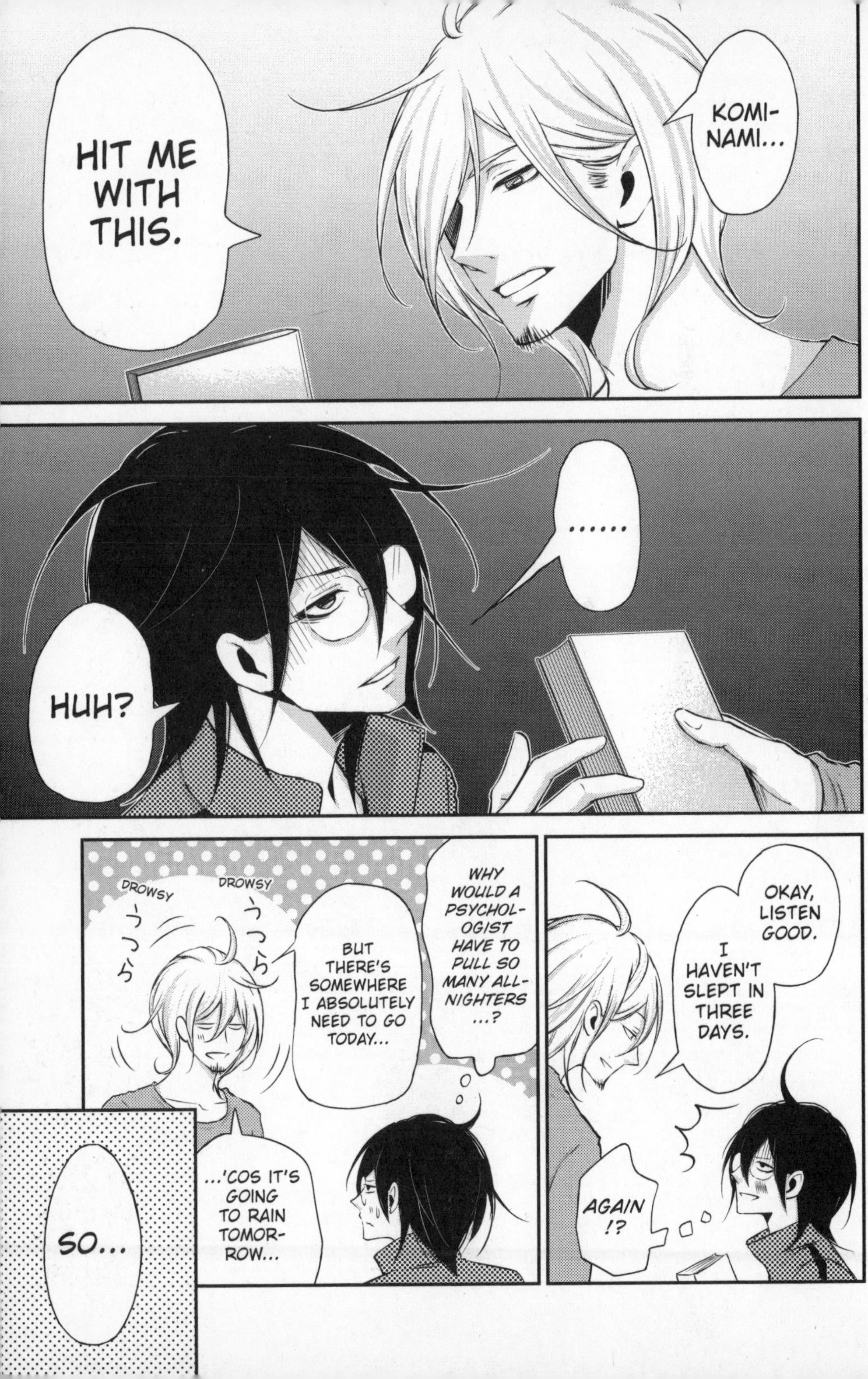
KOMI-NAMI...
HIT ME WITH THIS.
......
HUH?
OKAY, LISTEN GOOD.
I HAVEN'T SLEPT IN THREE DAYS.
AGAIN!?
WHY WOULD A PSYCHOLOGIST HAVE TO PULL SO MANY ALL-NIGHTERS...?
DROWSY
うつら
DROWSY
うつら
BUT THERE'S SOMEWHERE I ABSOLUTELY NEED TO GO TODAY...
...'COS IT'S GOING TO RAIN TOMORROW...
SO...

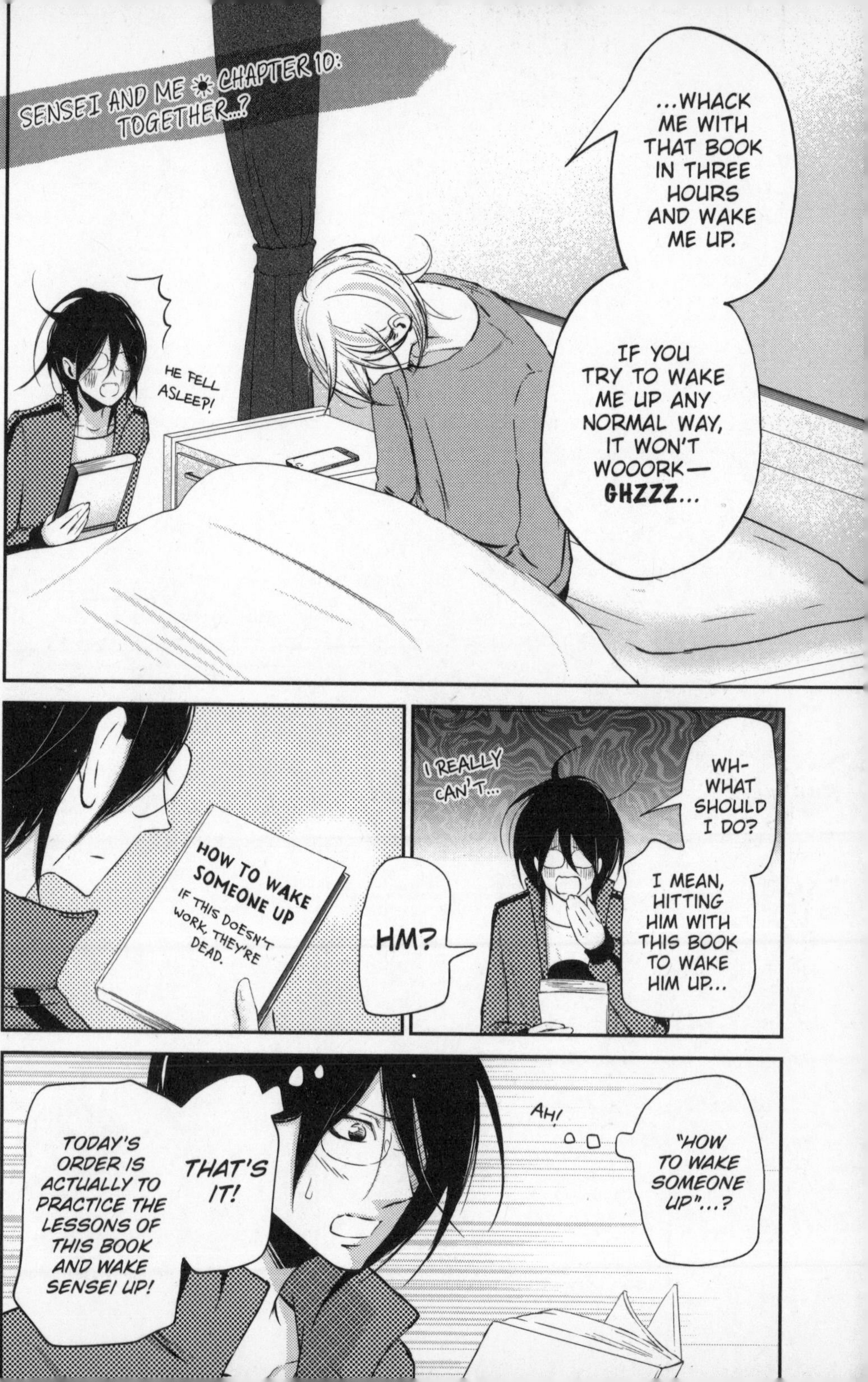
SENSEI AND ME ☀ CHAPTER 10: TOGETHER...?
...WHACK ME WITH THAT BOOK IN THREE HOURS AND WAKE ME UP.
IF YOU TRY TO WAKE ME UP ANY NORMAL WAY, IT WON'T WOOORK—GHZZZ...
HE FELL ASLEEP!
WH-WHAT SHOULD I DO?
I MEAN, HITTING HIM WITH THIS BOOK TO WAKE HIM UP...
I REALLY CAN'T...
HM?
HOW TO WAKE SOMEONE UP
IF THIS DOESN'T WORK, THEY'RE DEAD.
AH!
"HOW TO WAKE SOMEONE UP"...?
THAT'S IT!
TODAY'S ORDER IS ACTUALLY TO PRACTICE THE LESSONS OF THIS BOOK AND WAKE SENSEI UP!

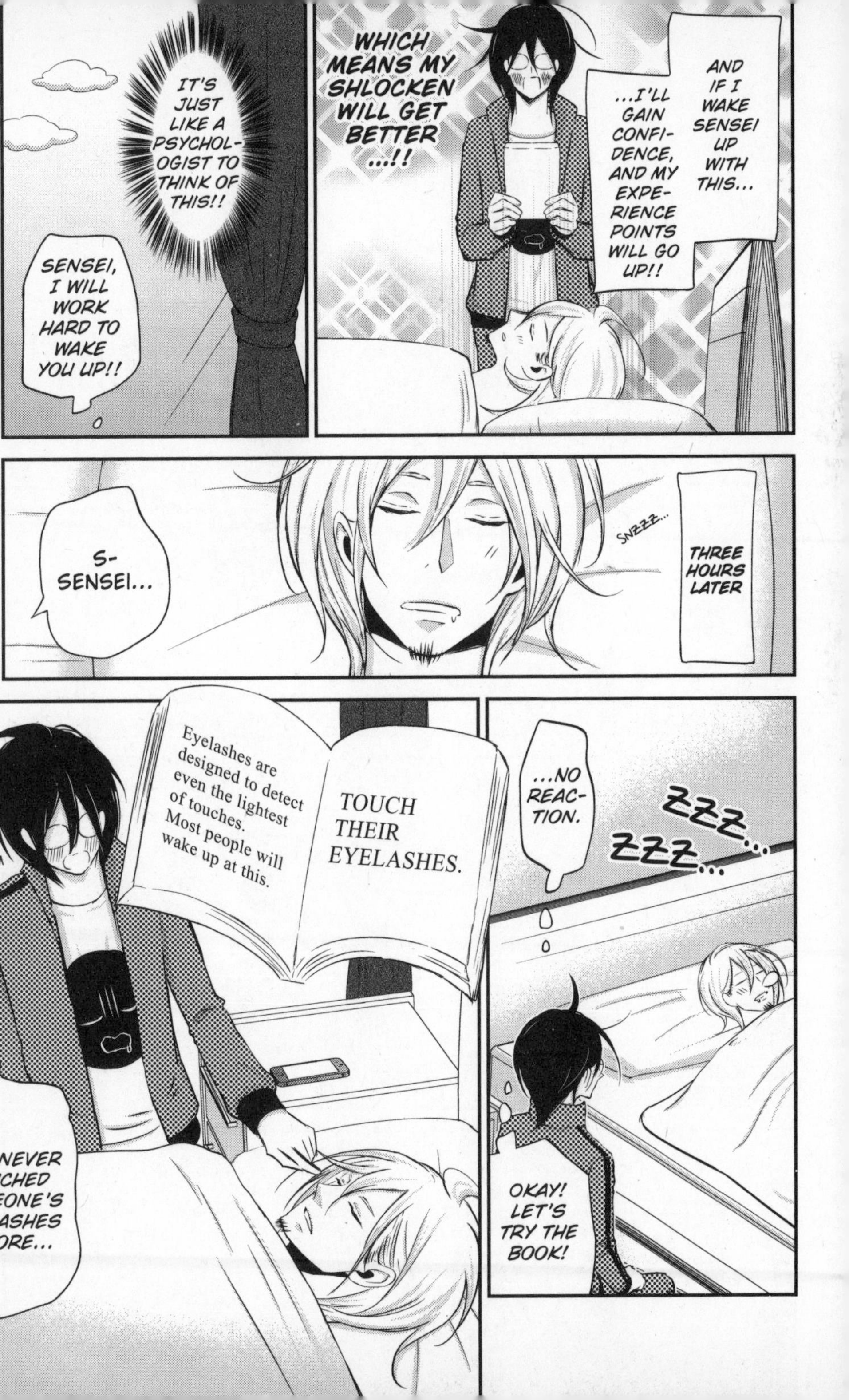
AND IF I WAKE SENSEI UP WITH THIS...
...I'LL GAIN CONFIDENCE, AND MY EXPERIENCE POINTS WILL GO UP!!
WHICH MEANS MY SHLOCKEN WILL GET BETTER ...!!
IT'S JUST LIKE A PSYCHOLOGIST TO THINK OF THIS!!
SENSEI, I WILL WORK HARD TO WAKE YOU UP!!
THREE HOURS LATER
SNZZZ...
S-SENSEI...
...NO REACTION.
ZZZ...
ZZZ...
OKAY! LET'S TRY THE BOOK!
TOUCH THEIR EYELASHES.
Eyelashes are designed to detect even the lightest of touches. Most people will wake up at this.
BADUM
ドキ
BADUM
ドキ
I'VE NEVER TOUCHED SOMEONE'S EYELASHES BEFORE...

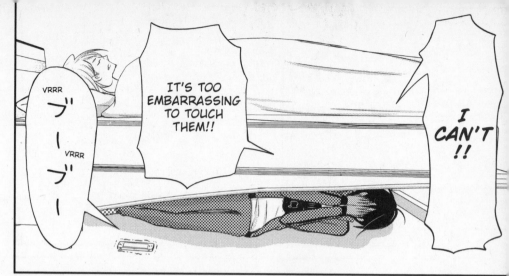

I CAN'T!!
IT'S TOO EMBARRASSING TO TOUCH THEM!!
VRRR
ブーブー
VRRR
HM?
ピッ
BEEP
HELLO? MOM?
UNDER A BED...
I HAVE TO TOUCH MY BOSS'S EYELASHES...
What kind of job do you have?
A JOB TO CURE MY SHLOCKEN—
AH!
KONK
ゴン
THAT'S IT! THIS IS MY JOB...!

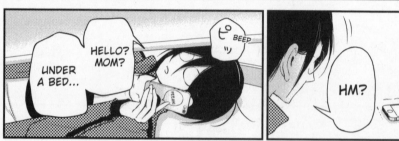

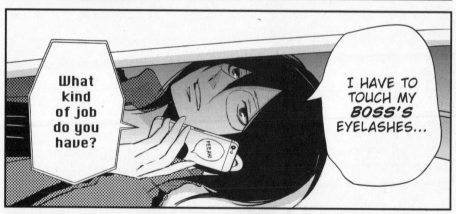

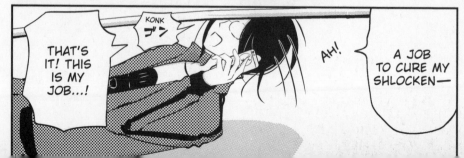

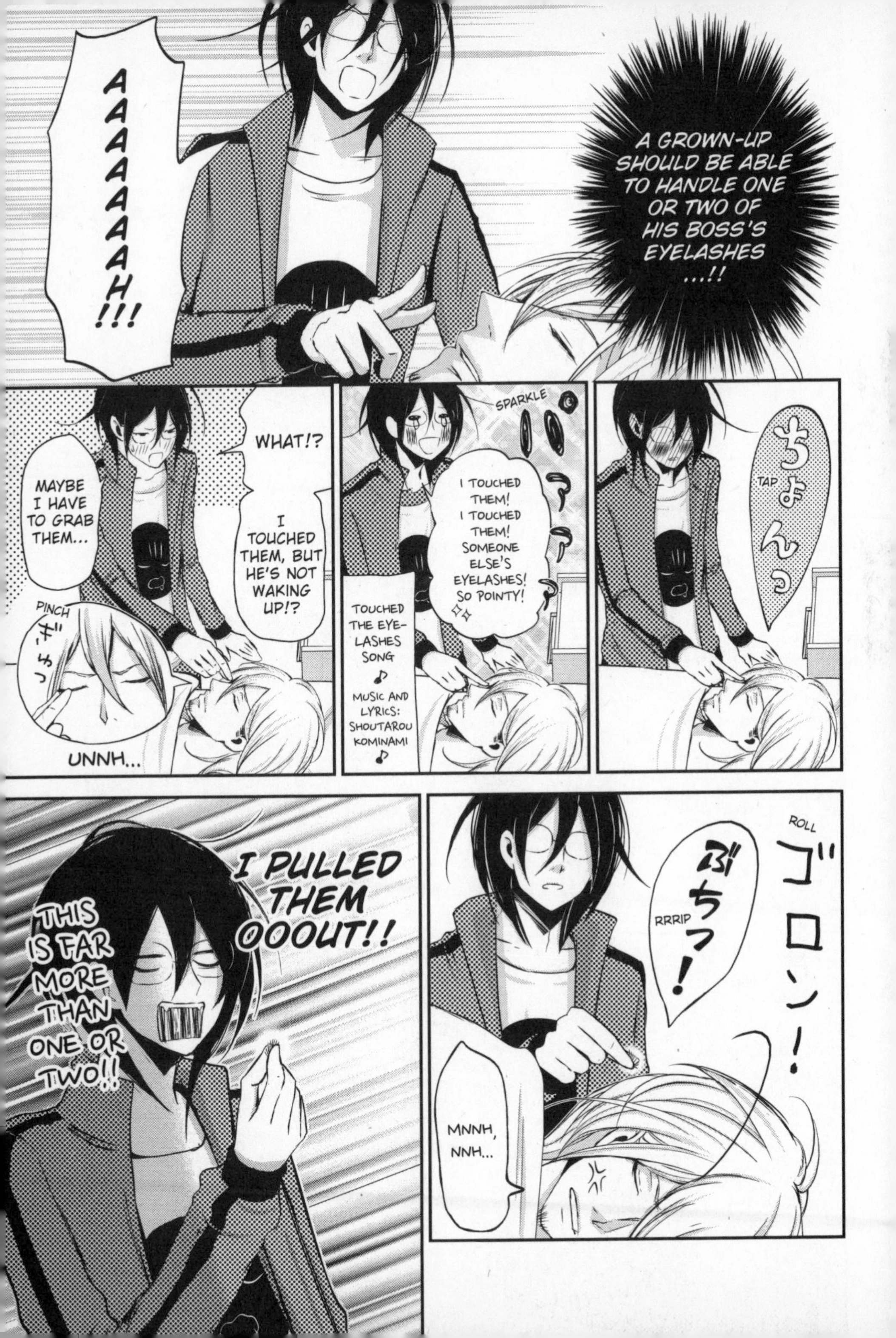
A GROWN-UP SHOULD BE ABLE TO HANDLE ONE OR TWO OF HIS BOSS'S EYELASHES ...!!
AAAAAAAAAH!!!
TAP
ちょんっ
SPARKLE
I TOUCHED THEM! I TOUCHED THEM! SOMEONE ELSE'S EYELASHES! SO POINTY!
TOUCHED THE EYE-LASHES SONG ♪ MUSIC AND LYRICS: SHOUTAROU KOMINAMI ♪
WHAT!?
I TOUCHED THEM, BUT HE'S NOT WAKING UP!?
MAYBE I HAVE TO GRAB THEM...
PINCH
UNNH...
ROLL
ゴロン！
RRRIP
ぶちっ！
MNNH, NNH...
I PULLED THEM OOOUT!!
THIS IS FAR MORE THAN ONE OR TWO!!

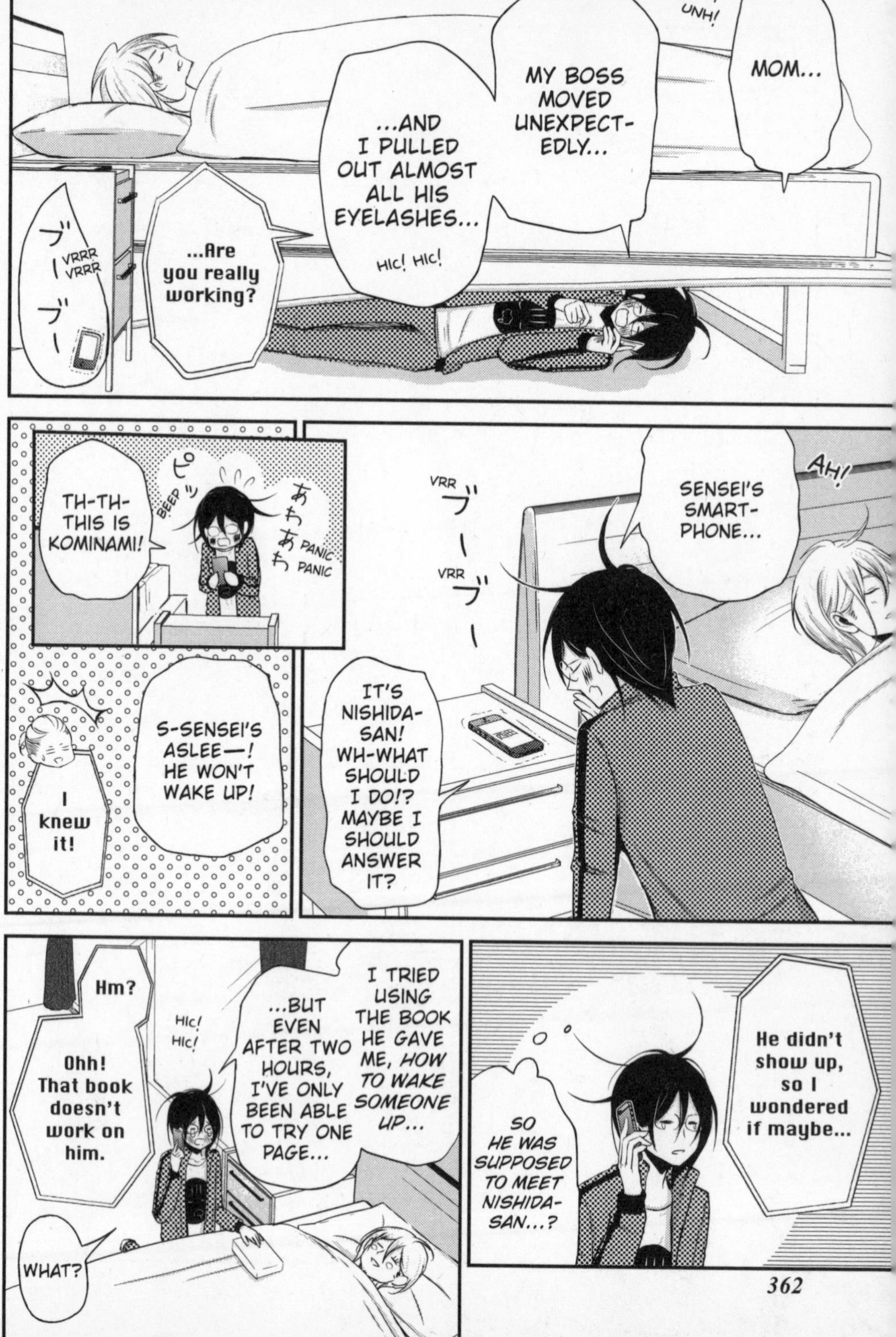
UU! UNH!
MOM...
MY BOSS MOVED UNEXPECT-EDLY...
...AND I PULLED OUT ALMOST ALL HIS EYELASHES...
HIC! HIC!
...Are you really working?
ブーブー
VRRR VRRR
AH!
SENSEI'S SMART-PHONE...
ブーブー
VRR VRR
IT'S NISHIDA-SAN! WH-WHAT SHOULD I DO!? MAYBE I SHOULD ANSWER IT?
あちあち
PANIC PANIC
ピッ
BEEP
TH-TH-THIS IS KOMINAMI!
S-SENSEI'S ASLEE—! HE WON'T WAKE UP!
I knew it!
He didn't show up, so I wondered if maybe...
SO HE WAS SUPPOSED TO MEET NISHIDA-SAN...?
I TRIED USING THE BOOK HE GAVE ME, *HOW TO WAKE SOMEONE UP*...
...BUT EVEN AFTER TWO HOURS, I'VE ONLY BEEN ABLE TO TRY ONE PAGE...
HIC! HIC!
Hm?
Ohh! That book doesn't work on him.
WHAT?

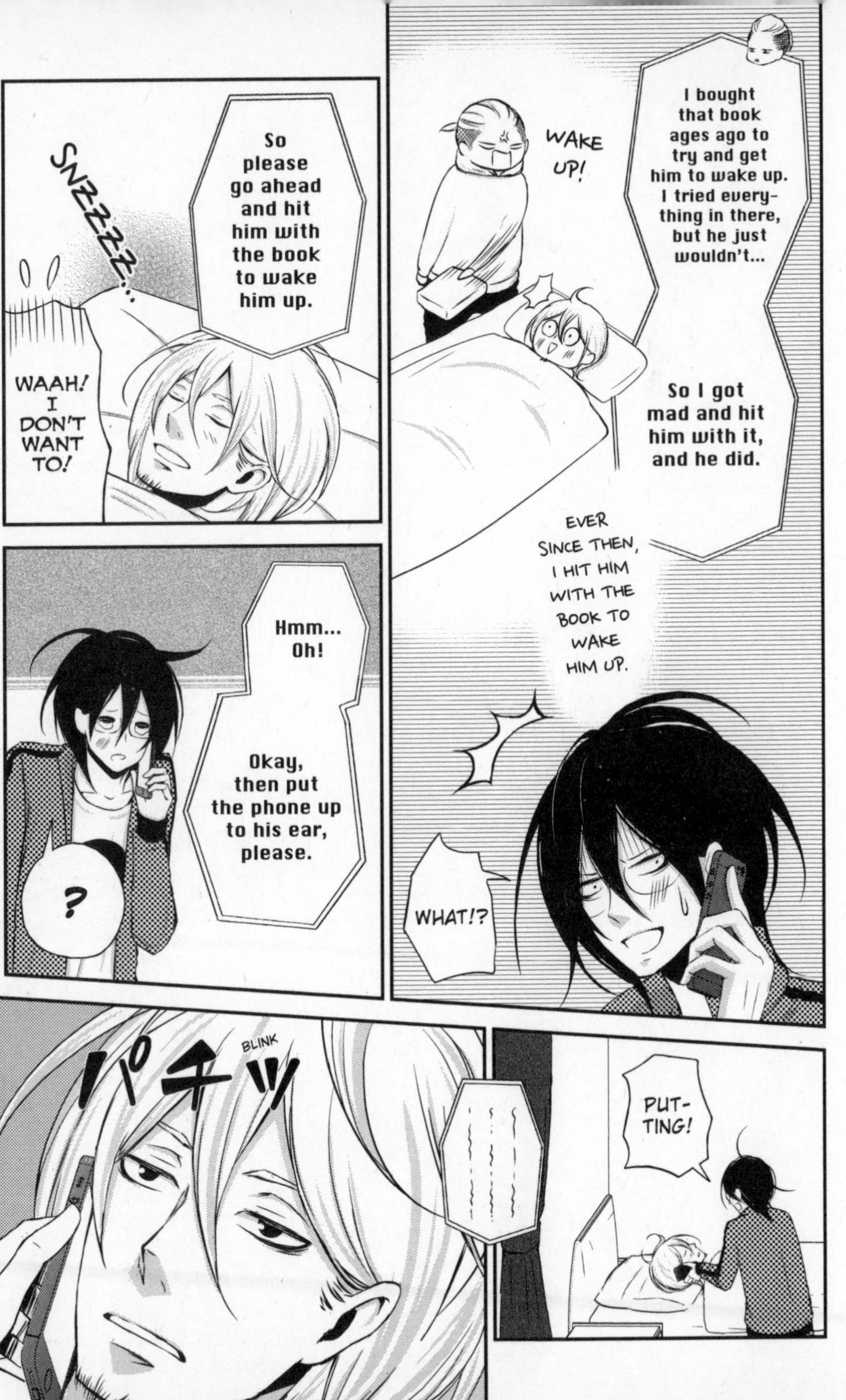
I bought that book ages ago to try and get him to wake up. I tried every-thing in there, but he just wouldn't...
WAKE UP!
So I got mad and hit him with it, and he did.
EVER SINCE THEN, I HIT HIM WITH THE BOOK TO WAKE HIM UP.
WHAT!?
So please go ahead and hit him with the book to wake him up.
SNZZZZ...
WAAH! I DON'T WANT TO!
Hmm... Oh!
Okay, then put the phone up to his ear, please.
?
PUT-TING!
BLINK
パチッ
...

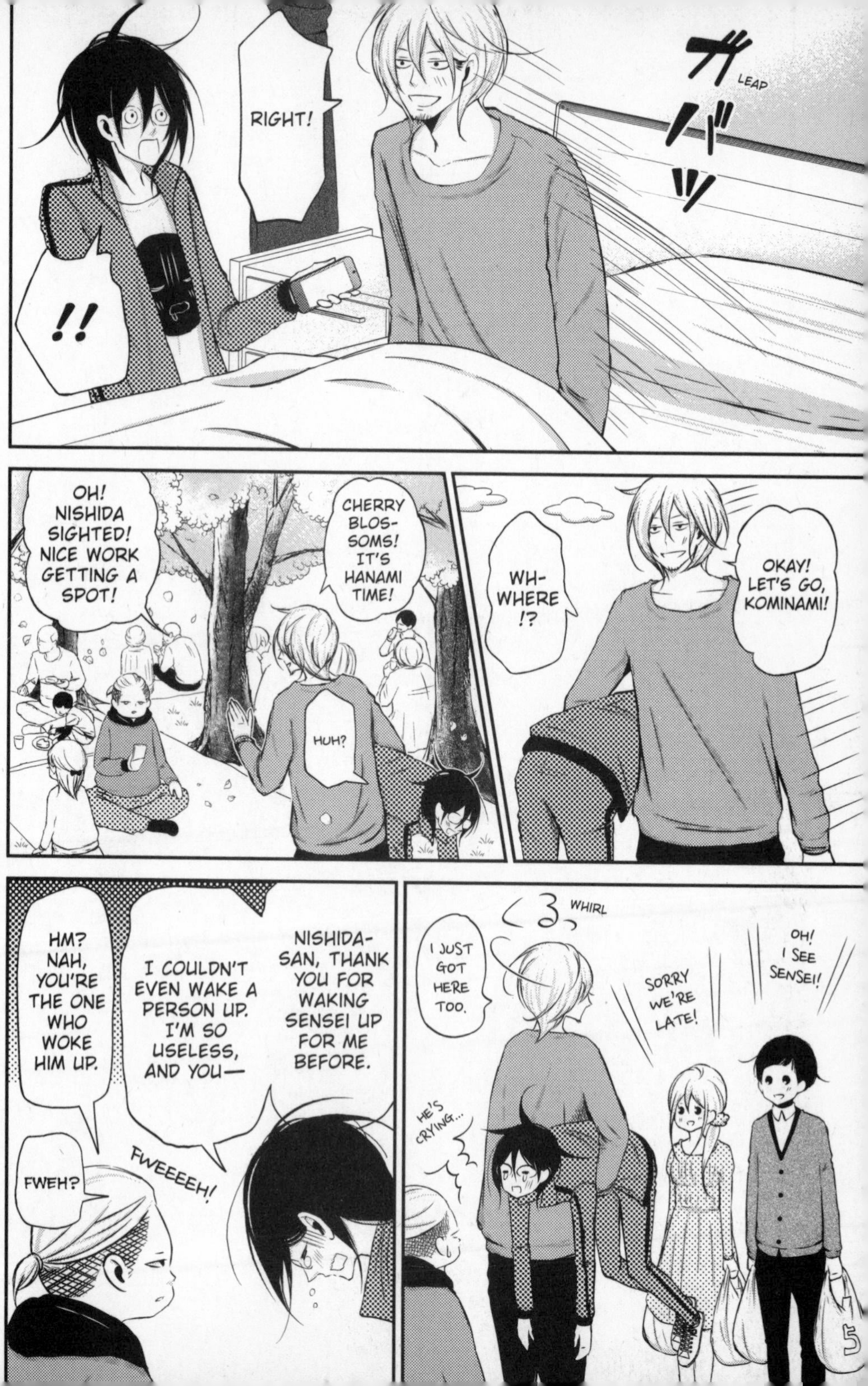
LEAP
RIGHT!
!!
OKAY! LET'S GO, KOMINAMI!
WH-WHERE !?
CHERRY BLOS-SOMS! IT'S HANAMI TIME!
OH! NISHIDA SIGHTED! NICE WORK GETTING A SPOT!
HUH?
WHIRL
OH! I SEE SENSEI!
SORRY WE'RE LATE!
I JUST GOT HERE TOO.
HE'S CRYING...
NISHIDA-SAN, THANK YOU FOR WAKING SENSEI UP FOR ME BEFORE.
I COULDN'T EVEN WAKE A PERSON UP. I'M SO USELESS, AND YOU—
HM? NAH, YOU'RE THE ONE WHO WOKE HIM UP.
FWEEEEH!
FWEH?

DECEMBER 25: SENSEI AND ME TOO.

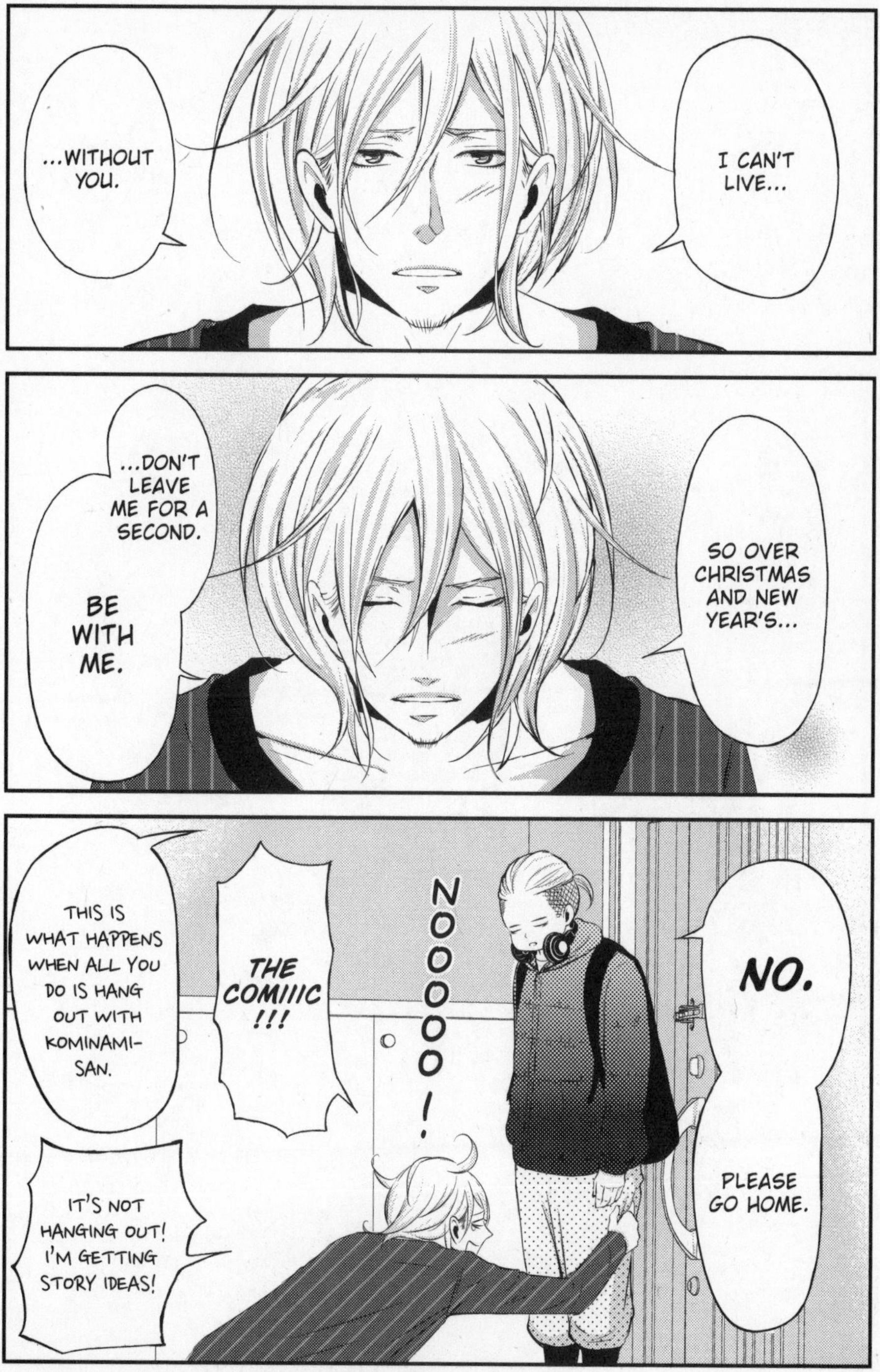
I CAN'T LIVE...
...WITHOUT YOU.
SO OVER CHRISTMAS AND NEW YEAR'S...
...DON'T LEAVE ME FOR A SECOND.
BE WITH ME.
NO.
PLEASE GO HOME.
NOOOOOO!
THE COMIIIC!!!
THIS IS WHAT HAPPENS WHEN ALL YOU DO IS HANG OUT WITH KOMINAMI-SAN.
IT'S NOT HANGING OUT! I'M GETTING STORY IDEAS!

HE FOLLOWED ME ALL THE WAY HOME. (LATER TESTIMONY FROM NISHIDA)

START NEW YEAR'S HOLIDAY WITH A SHLOCKEN

DECEMBER 24: ONLY A FEW DAYS LEFT IN THE YEAR

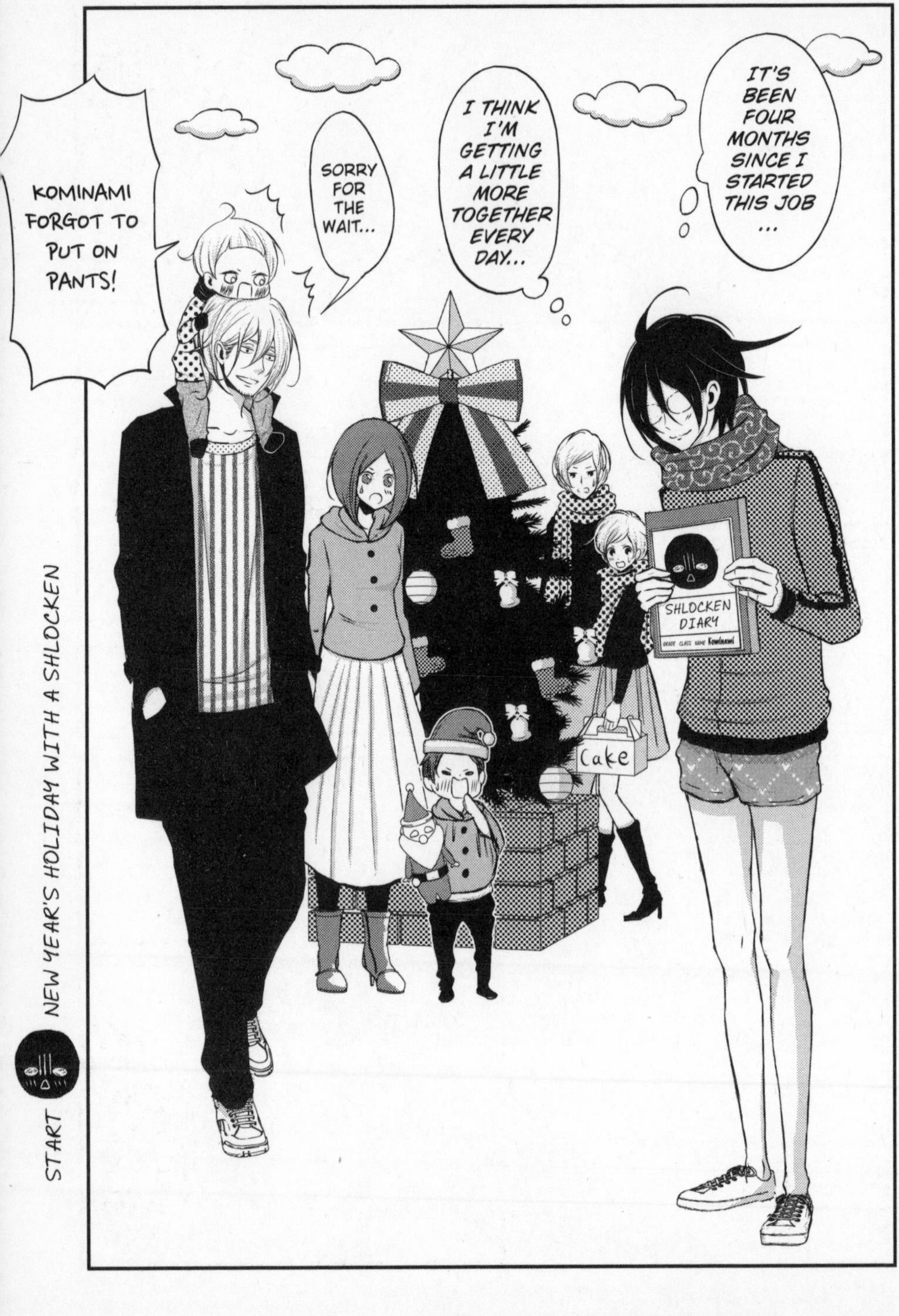
IT'S BEEN FOUR MONTHS SINCE I STARTED THIS JOB ...
I THINK I'M GETTING A LITTLE MORE TOGETHER EVERY DAY...
SORRY FOR THE WAIT...
KOMINAMI FORGOT TO PUT ON PANTS!
SHLOCKEN DIARY
Cake

THE BONUS COMIC "NEW YEAR'S HOLIDAY WITH A SHLOCKEN" STARTS ON THE NEXT PAGE!

PEEAH!

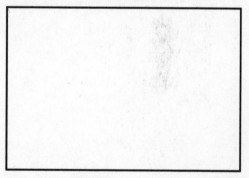

ENJOY!

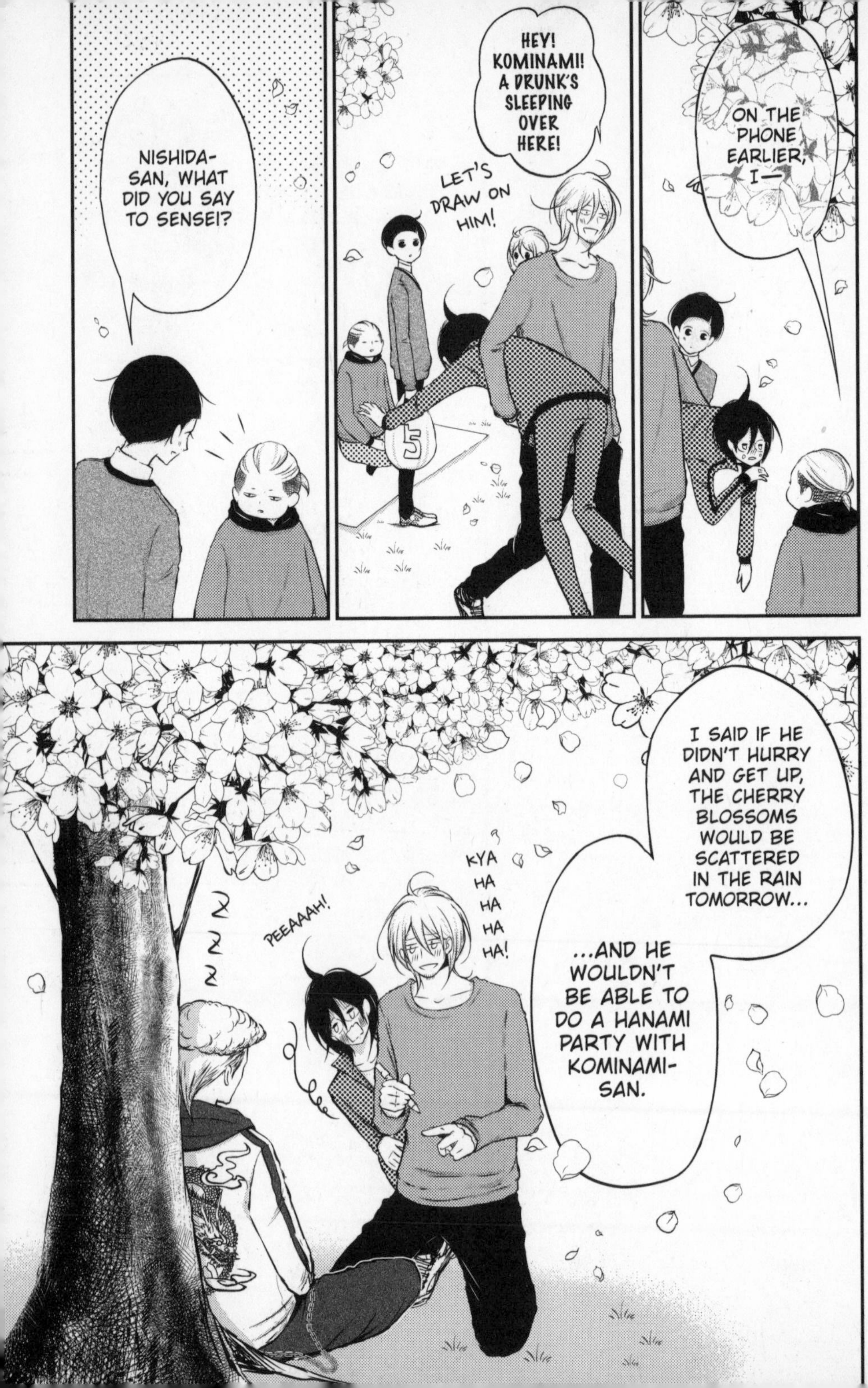
ON THE PHONE EARLIER, I—
HEY! KOMINAMI! A DRUNK'S SLEEPING OVER HERE!
LET'S DRAW ON HIM!
NISHIDA-SAN, WHAT DID YOU SAY TO SENSEI?
I SAID IF HE DIDN'T HURRY AND GET UP, THE CHERRY BLOSSOMS WOULD BE SCATTERED IN THE RAIN TOMORROW...
...AND HE WOULDN'T BE ABLE TO DO A HANAMI PARTY WITH KOMINAMI-SAN.
KYA HA HA HA HA!
PEEAAAH!
Z Z Z

DECEMBER 26: NEW YEAR'S X SAIONJI-SENSEI

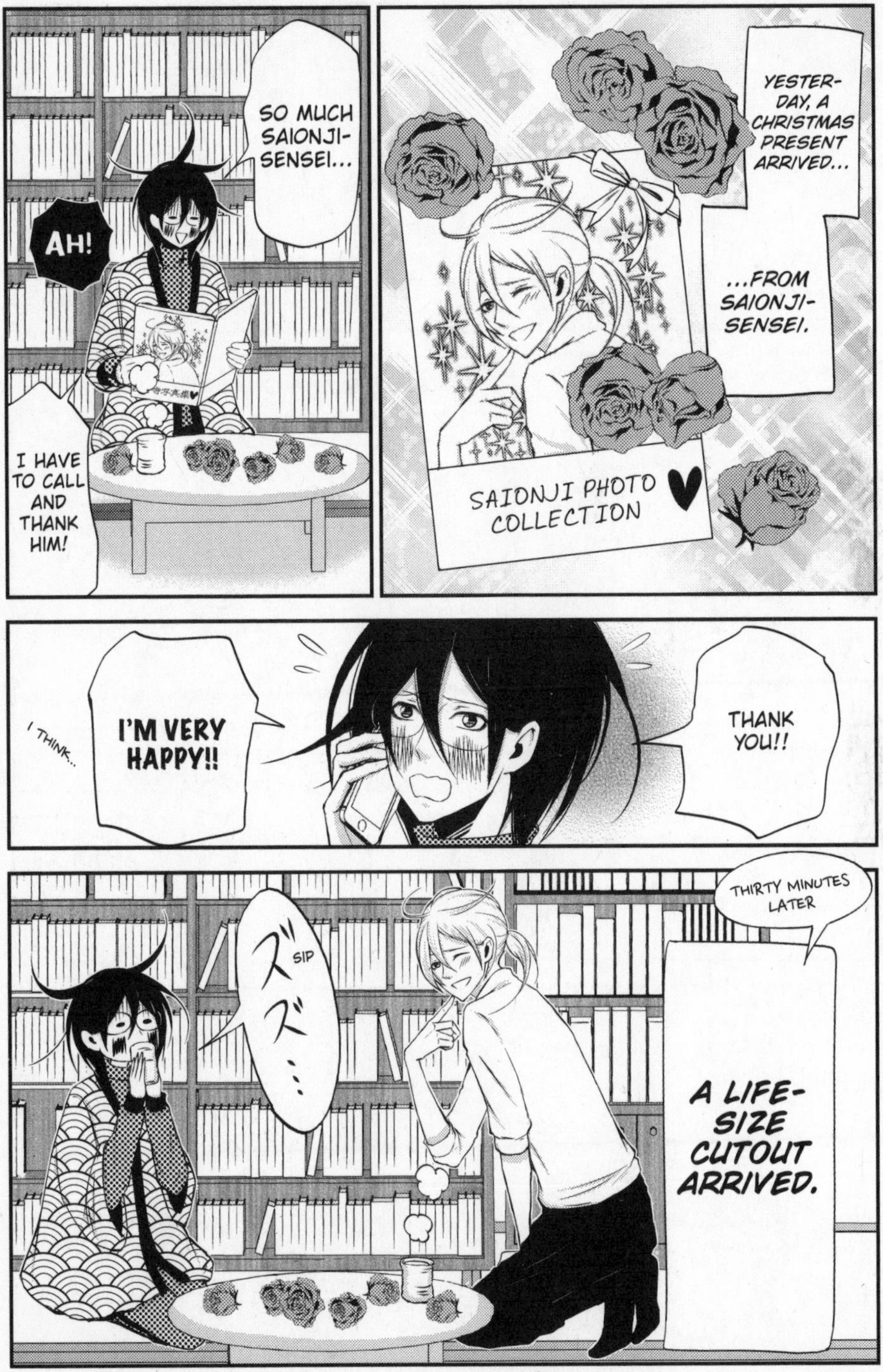
YESTER-DAY, A CHRISTMAS PRESENT ARRIVED...
...FROM SAIONJI-SENSEI.
SAIONJI PHOTO COLLECTION ♥
SO MUCH SAIONJI-SENSEI...
AH!
I HAVE TO CALL AND THANK HIM!
THANK YOU!!
I'M VERY HAPPY!!
I THINK...
THIRTY MINUTES LATER
A LIFE-SIZE CUTOUT ARRIVED.
ズズ…
SIP

THE REAL THING MIGHT ARRIVE NEXT.

DECEMBER 27: NEW YEAR'S × KATOU-SAN

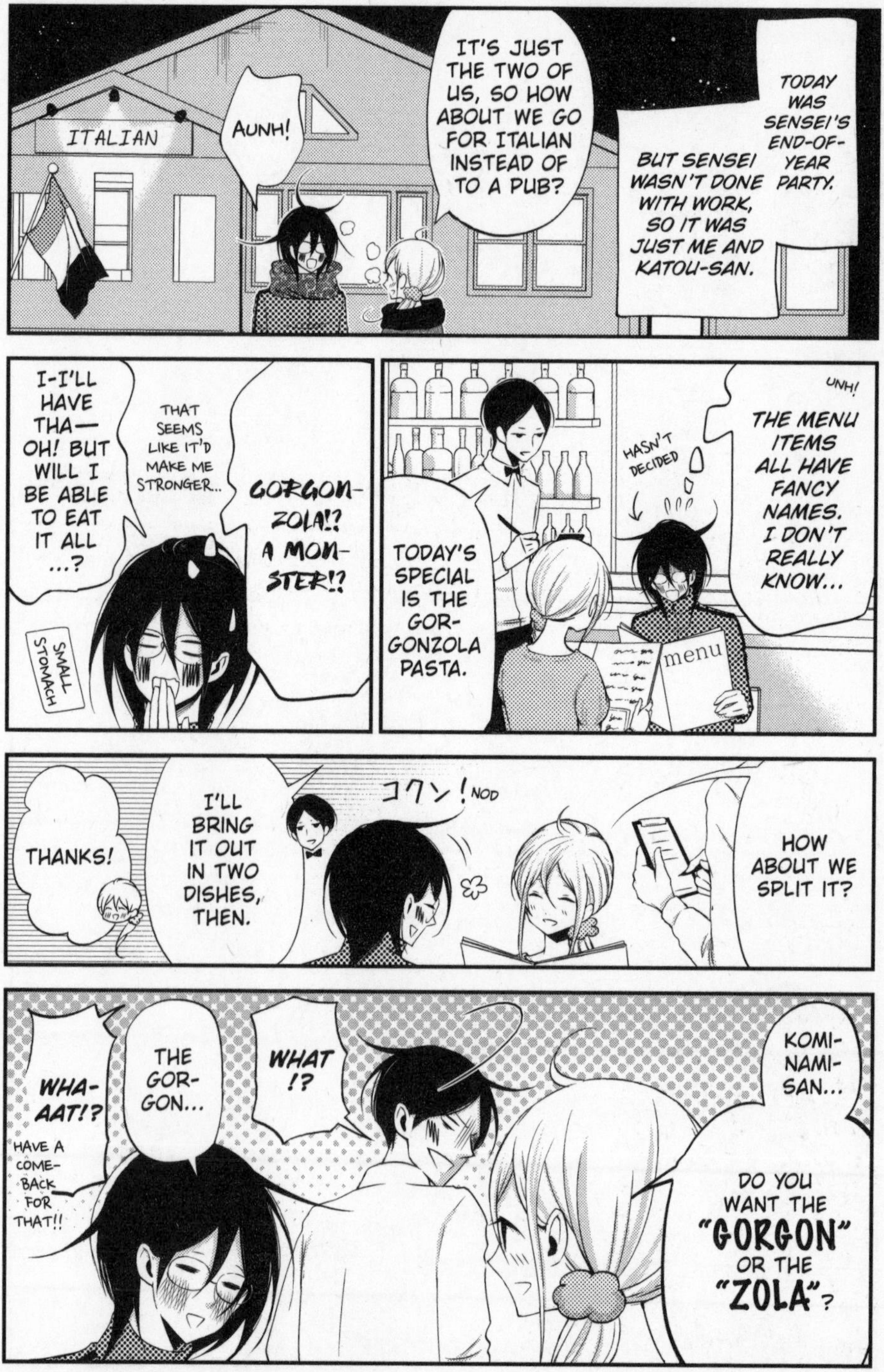

TODAY WAS SENSEI'S END-OF-YEAR PARTY.
BUT SENSEI WASN'T DONE WITH WORK, SO IT WAS JUST ME AND KATOU-SAN.
IT'S JUST THE TWO OF US, SO HOW ABOUT WE GO FOR ITALIAN INSTEAD OF TO A PUB?
AUNH!
ITALIAN
UNH!
THE MENU ITEMS ALL HAVE FANCY NAMES. I DON'T REALLY KNOW...
HASN'T DECIDED
TODAY'S SPECIAL IS THE GORGONZOLA PASTA.
GORGONZOLA!? A MONSTER!?
THAT SEEMS LIKE IT'D MAKE ME STRONGER...
I-I'LL HAVE THA— OH! BUT WILL I BE ABLE TO EAT IT ALL...?
SMALL STOMACH
HOW ABOUT WE SPLIT IT?
コクン! NOD
I'LL BRING IT OUT IN TWO DISHES, THEN.
THANKS!
KOMINAMI-SAN...
DO YOU WANT THE "GORGON" OR THE "ZOLA"?
WHAT!?
THE GORGON...
WHAAAT!?
HAVE A COMEBACK FOR THAT!!

NO COMEBACKS HERE

DECEMBER 28: NEW YEAR'S × NEKOGURI-SENSEI

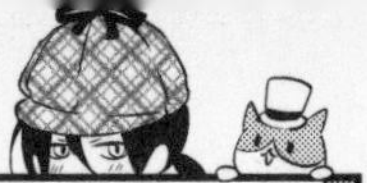

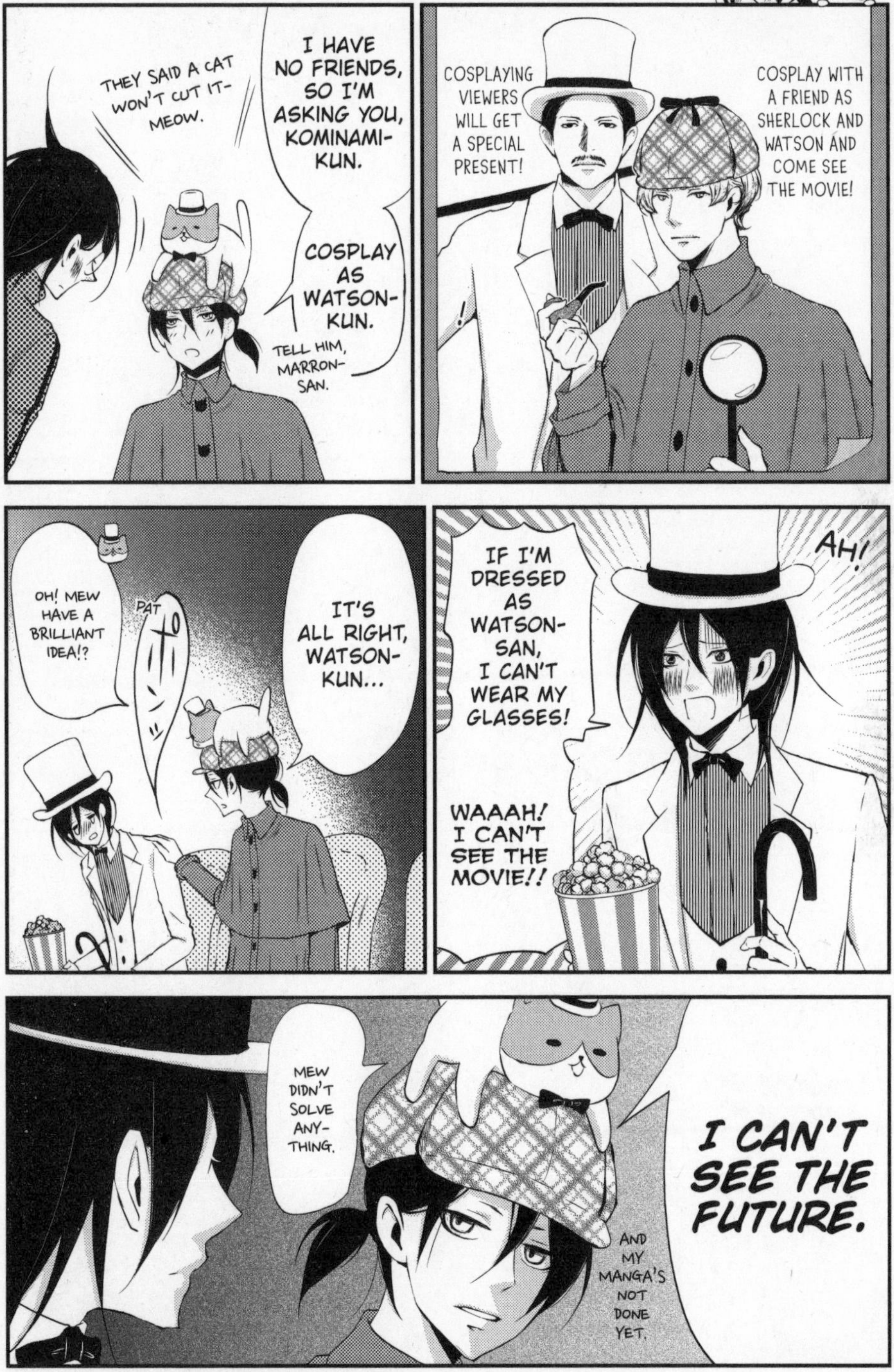
COSPLAY WITH A FRIEND AS SHERLOCK AND WATSON AND COME SEE THE MOVIE!
COSPLAYING VIEWERS WILL GET A SPECIAL PRESENT!
I HAVE NO FRIENDS, SO I'M ASKING YOU, KOMINAMI-KUN.
COSPLAY AS WATSON-KUN.
TELL HIM, MARRON-SAN.
THEY SAID A CAT WON'T CUT IT—MEOW.
AH!
IF I'M DRESSED AS WATSON-SAN, I CAN'T WEAR MY GLASSES!
WAAAH! I CAN'T SEE THE MOVIE!!
IT'S ALL RIGHT, WATSON-KUN...
PAT
OH! MEW HAVE A BRILLIANT IDEA!?
MEW DIDN'T SOLVE ANYTHING.
I CAN'T SEE THE FUTURE.
AND MY MANGA'S NOT DONE YET.

DETECTIVE OF CONFUSION

DECEMBER 29: I'VE CHANGED.

I USED TO HAVE A SHORT TEMPER.
WHAM
TCH.
WATCH WHERE YOU'RE GOING. DAMN.
NO, I WAS LOOKING.
YOU HIT ME.
BUT NOW I MAKE MY LIVING DRAWING MY BELOVED MANGA, SO...
WHAM
WHY ARE YOU EVEN OUT ON THE STREET!!?
STAY AT !!
...I HAVE A SUPER-SHORT TEMPER.

ESPECIALLY BEFORE A DEADLINE

DECEMBER 30: PAT-PAT-POKE

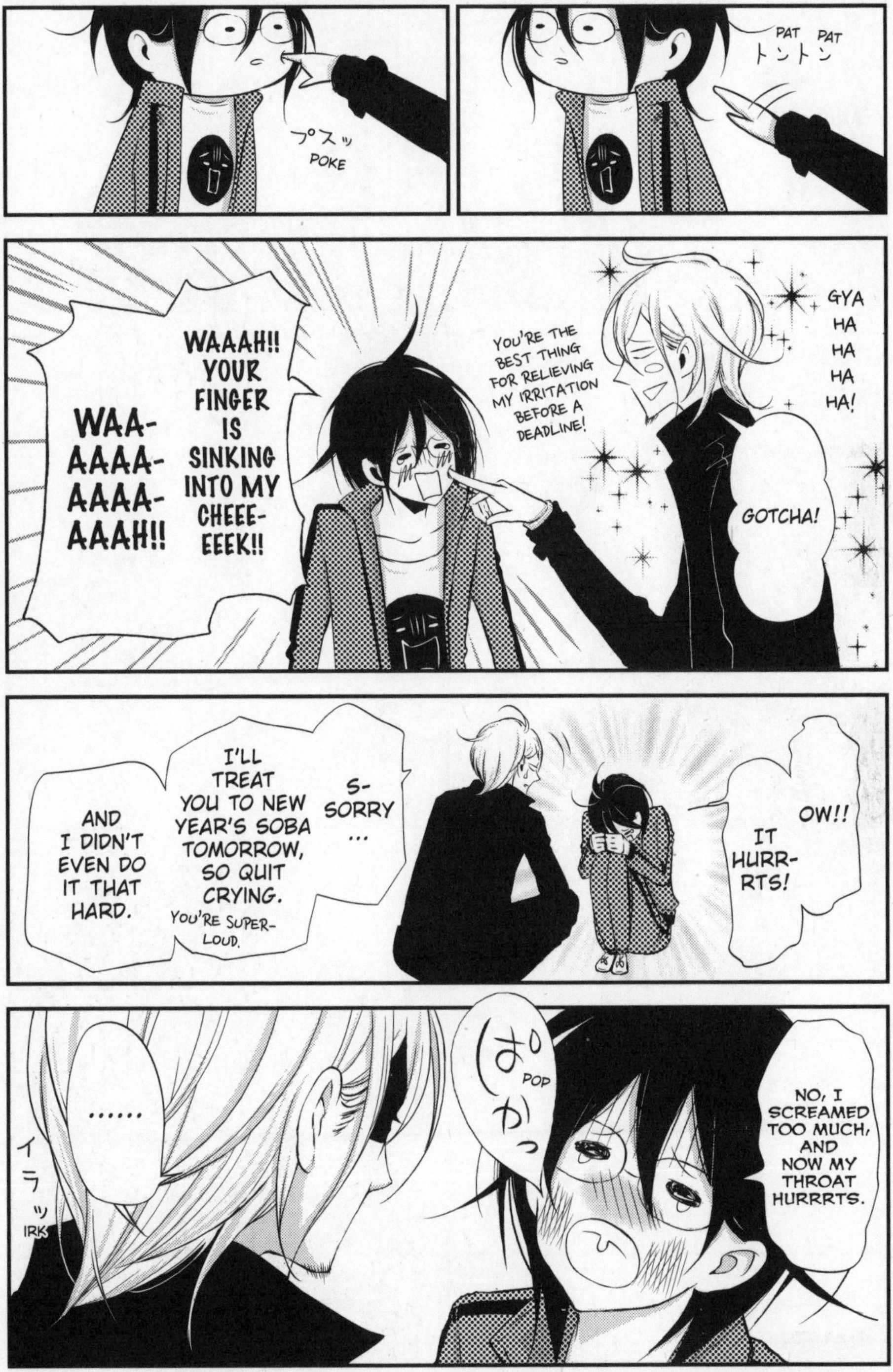
PAT PAT
トントン
プスッ
POKE
GYA HA HA HA HA!
GOTCHA!
YOU'RE THE BEST THING FOR RELIEVING MY IRRITATION BEFORE A DEADLINE!
WAAAH!! YOUR FINGER IS SINKING INTO MY CHEEE-EEEK!!
WAA-AAAA-AAAA-AAAH!!
OW!! IT HURRRTS!
S-SORRY...
I'LL TREAT YOU TO NEW YEAR'S SOBA TOMORROW, SO QUIT CRYING.
YOU'RE SUPER-LOUD.
AND I DIDN'T EVEN DO IT THAT HARD.
NO, I SCREAMED TOO MUCH, AND NOW MY THROAT HURRRTS.
ぽかっ
POP
......
イラッ
IRK

THAT WAS THE LOUDEST HE YELLED THIS YEAR.

DECEMBER 31: THE LAST TIME THIS YEAR...

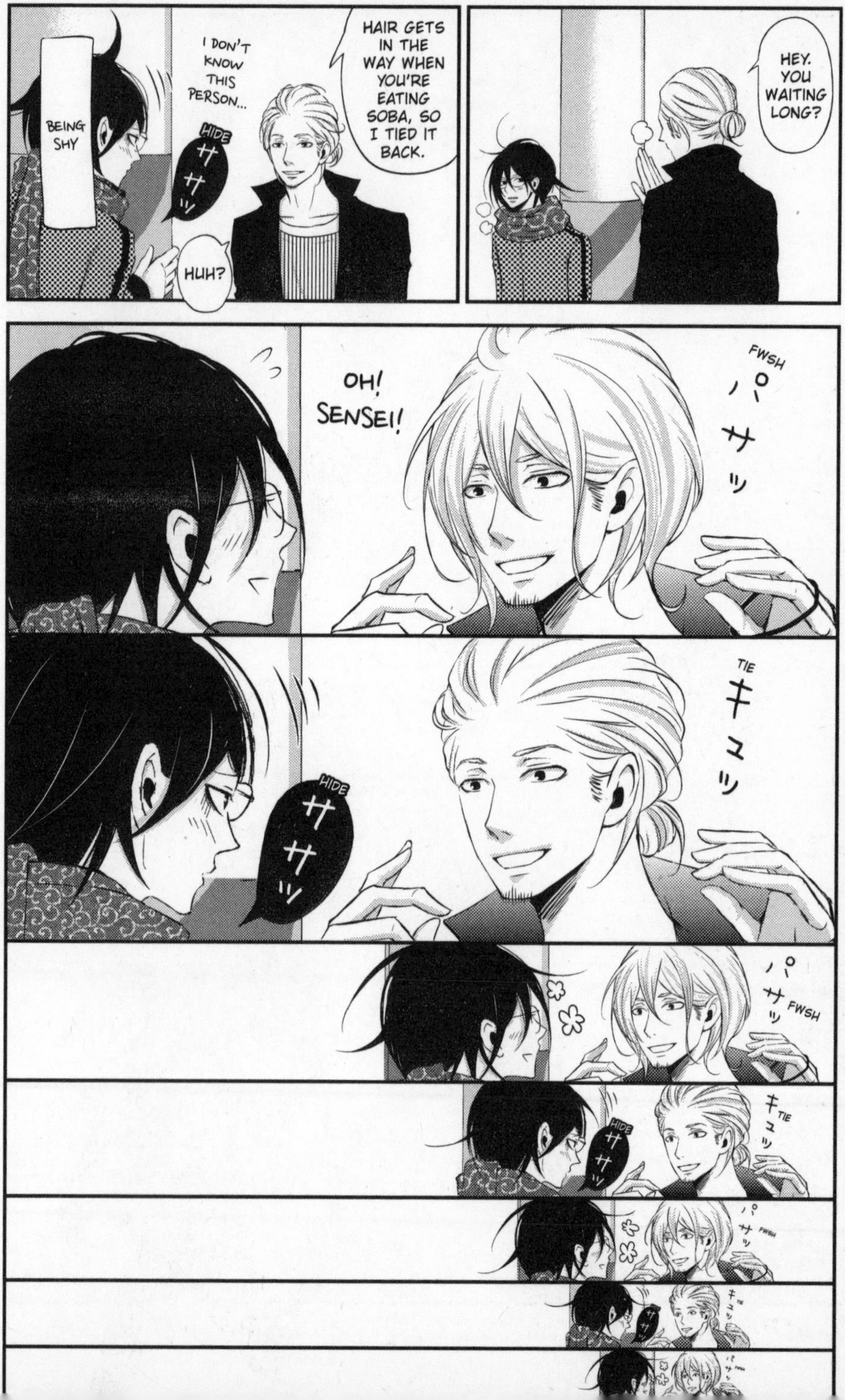
HEY. YOU WAITING LONG?
HAIR GETS IN THE WAY WHEN YOU'RE EATING SOBA, SO I TIED IT BACK.
I DON'T KNOW THIS PERSON...
BEING SHY
HIDE
HUH?
FWSH
OH! SENSEI!
TIE
HIDE
FWSH
TIE
HIDE
FWSH
TIE

THIS CONTINUED UNTIL SENSEI GOT BORED.

JANUARY 1: A TRUTH I WOULD NEVER HAVE KNOWN IF YOU WEREN'T AROUND, SENSEI.

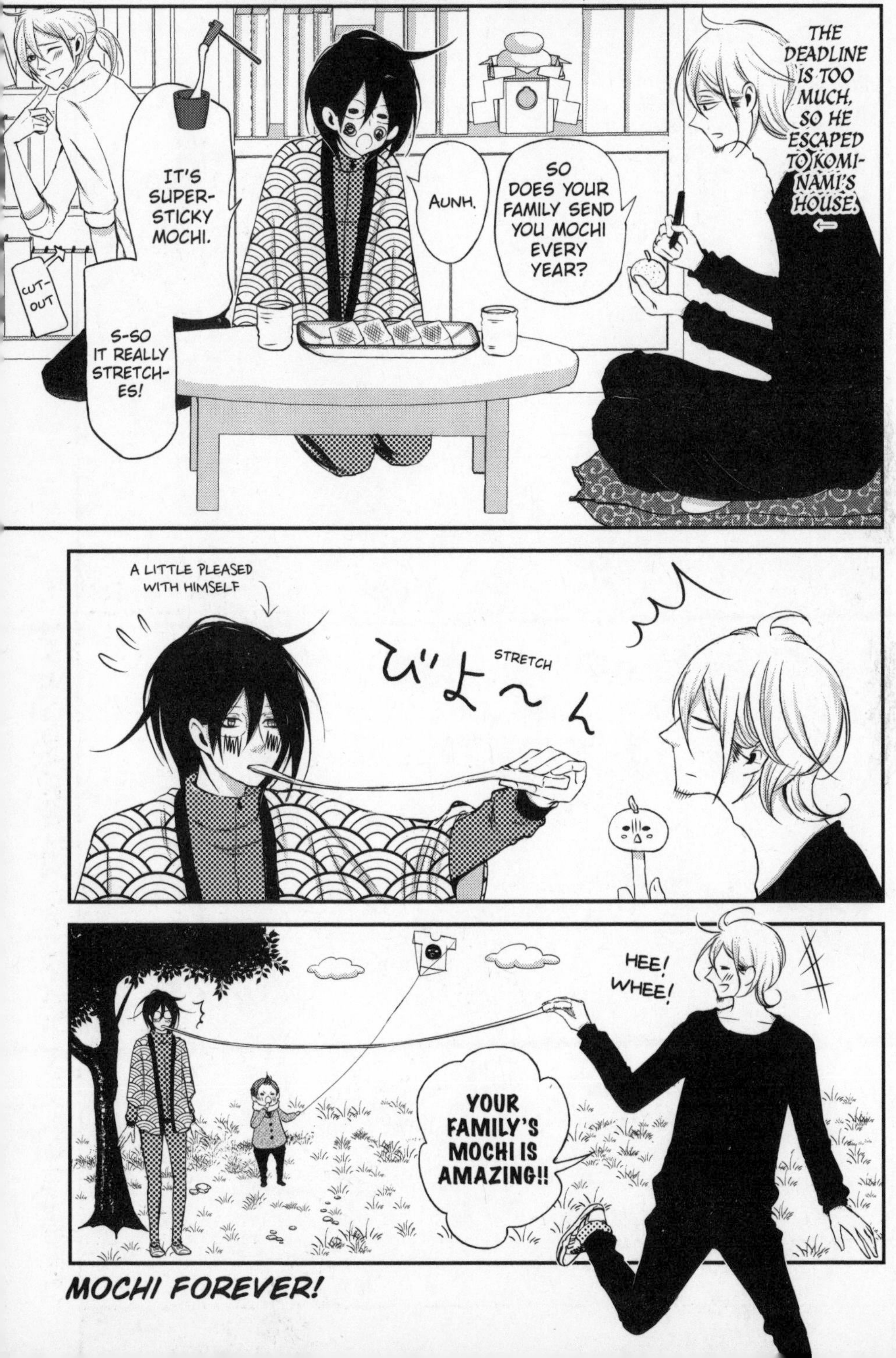

THE DEADLINE IS TOO MUCH, SO HE ESCAPED TO KOMINAMI'S HOUSE.
SO DOES YOUR FAMILY SEND YOU MOCHI EVERY YEAR?
AUNH.
IT'S SUPER-STICKY MOCHI.
S-SO IT REALLY STRETCHES!
CUT-OUT
びよ〜ん
STRETCH
A LITTLE PLEASED WITH HIMSELF
HEE! WHEE!
YOUR FAMILY'S MOCHI IS AMAZING!!

MOCHI FOREVER!

JANUARY 2: THIS YEAR...

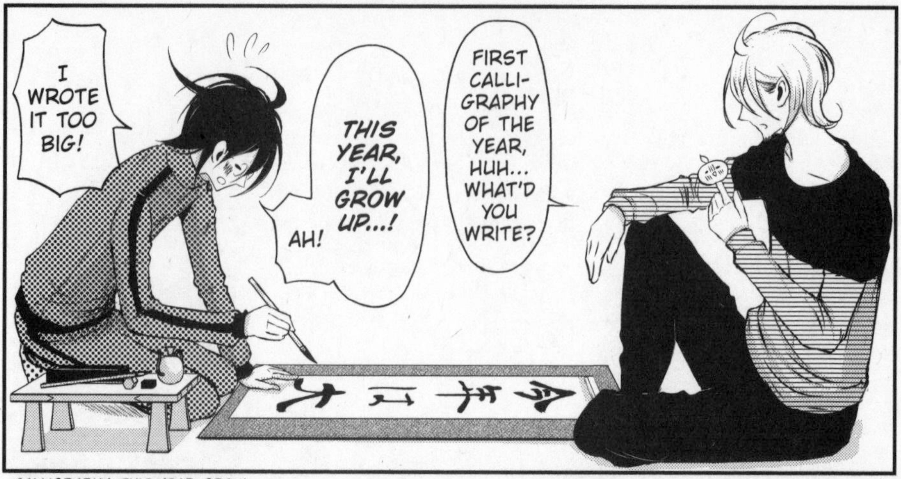
FIRST CALLIGRAPHY OF THE YEAR, HUH... WHAT'D YOU WRITE?
THIS YEAR, I'LL GROW UP...!
AH!
I WROTE IT TOO BIG!

CALLIGRAPHY: THIS YEAR, GROW

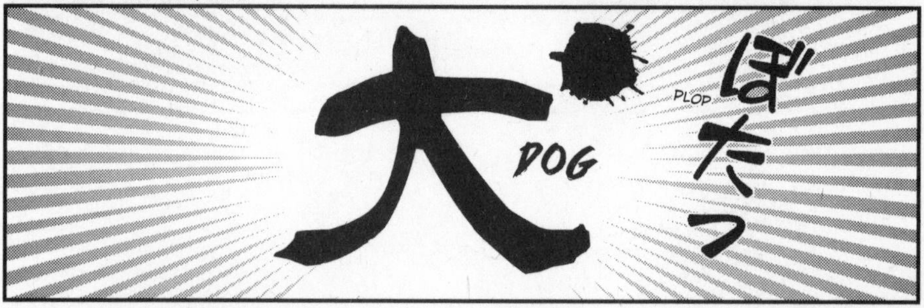
ぼたっ
PLOP
大
DOG

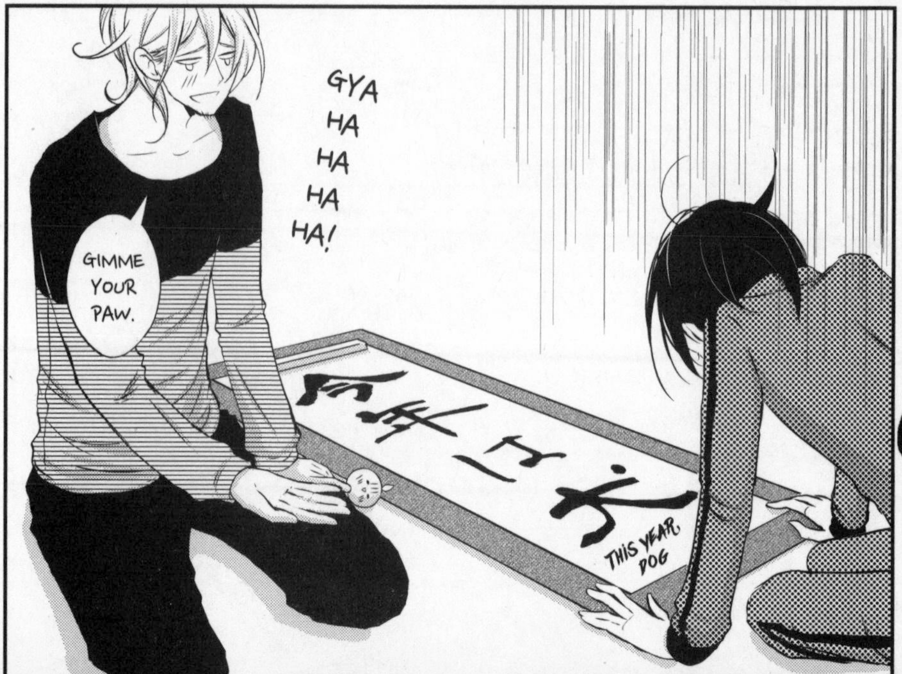
GYA HA HA HA HA!
GIMME YOUR PAW.
THIS YEAR DOG

NEW YEAR'S HOLIDAY WITH A SHLOCKEN END

TRANSLATION NOTES

Page 216
A police box is a small, neighborhood police office, usually staffed by two police officers. People in the neighborhood may go there to get directions, report local (usually minor) crimes, and turn in found items.

Page 227
A bento is a common boxed lunch. A character bento (kyaraben) is prepared so that the various foods in the lunch look like people, animals, or anime characters, among other things.

Page 242
In Japanese, the title of the "Sensei and Me" sections is "Sensei to Issho." For this chapter, the *to* is crossed out and replaced with *ga*, changing the meaning from "together with sensei" to "Sensei and Sensei."

Page 252
In Japan, household goods, such as laundry detergent, are often given as freebies for subscribing to newspapers.

Page 255
Hiyoko means "baby chick."

Page 268
Nikujaga is a beef and potato stew made using Japanese seasonings.

Page 309
Tama-chan is singing a Japanese choosing song in the vein of "Eeny, Meeny, Miny, Moe." The full song is "Which one should I choose? / We'll choose what God in heaven says / Pull out a gun / BANG! BANG! BANG!" This variant of the song is most commonly heard in the Okinawan region.

Page 346
Dekoboko means "uneven" or "rough."

Page 349
The Japanese word used for "blurb" is aori, which is a word that may also refer to a type of squid known in English as the bigfin reef squid.

Page 373
New Year's soba, or toshikoshi soba, is eaten at the end of the year as a symbolic break from the hardships of the past year because soba noodles are easier to cut than other types of noodles.

Page 375
Mochi are sticky cakes made of pounded rice and are traditionally eaten over New Year's.

Page 376
The first Chinese character, or kanji, in "grow up" differs from the character for "dog" only by a single stroke in the top right of the character. So although Shoutarou successfully writes "grow," the drop of ink lands in a place that turns the character into "dog."

I'M ON TWITTER NOW.
@ICHIKAWADAN

THANK YOU SO MUCH FOR
PICKING UP VOLUME 2.

I'VE GOTTEN SOME LOVELY
LETTERS FROM READERS, WHICH
MAKES ME SO HAPPY. I'VE READ
THEM OVER AND OVER COUNTLESS
TIMES.

I ENDED UP MEMORIZING THEM.
—DAN ICHIKAWA

SHUT-IN
SHOUTAROU KOMINAMI
TAKES ON THE WORLD

Date: 7/25   Day: F ☀

Today, I went to the beach with Sensei. I swam about
two meters. I drowned a little bit.

I'm super-tired and sleepy, but I'm working hard to stay
awake and write this diary entry on the train hom

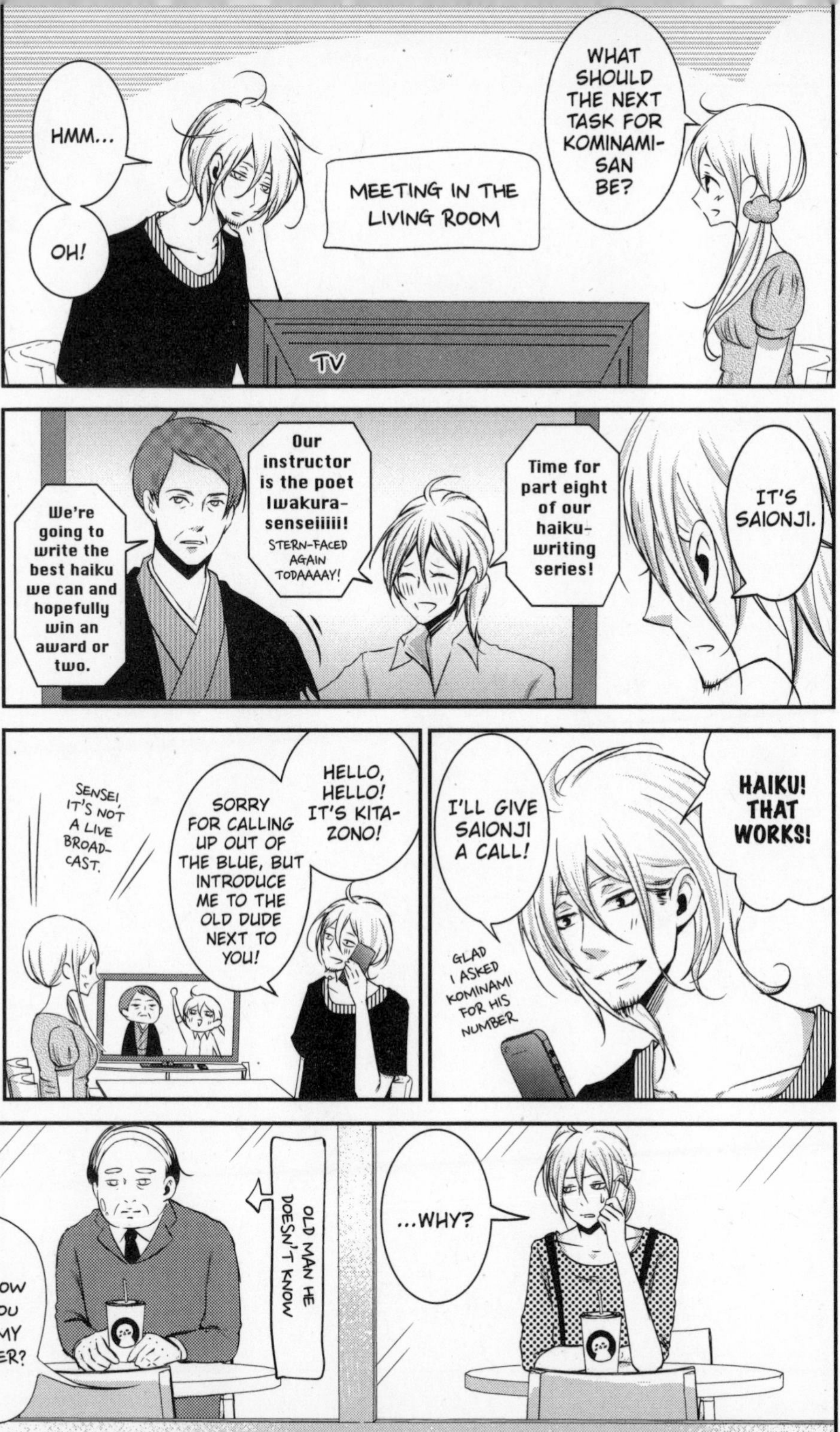
WHAT SHOULD THE NEXT TASK FOR KOMINAMI-SAN BE?
MEETING IN THE LIVING ROOM
HMM...
OH!
TV
IT'S SAIONJI.
Time for part eight of our haiku-writing series!
Our instructor is the poet Iwakura-senseiiiii!
STERN-FACED AGAIN TODAAAAY!
We're going to write the best haiku we can and hopefully win an award or two.
HAIKU! THAT WORKS!
I'LL GIVE SAIONJI A CALL!
GLAD I ASKED KOMINAMI FOR HIS NUMBER
HELLO, HELLO! IT'S KITA-ZONO!
SORRY FOR CALLING UP OUT OF THE BLUE, BUT INTRODUCE ME TO THE OLD DUDE NEXT TO YOU!
SENSEI IT'S NOT A LIVE BROADCAST.
...WHY?
OLD MAN HE DOESN'T KNOW
AND HOW DID YOU GET MY NUMBER?

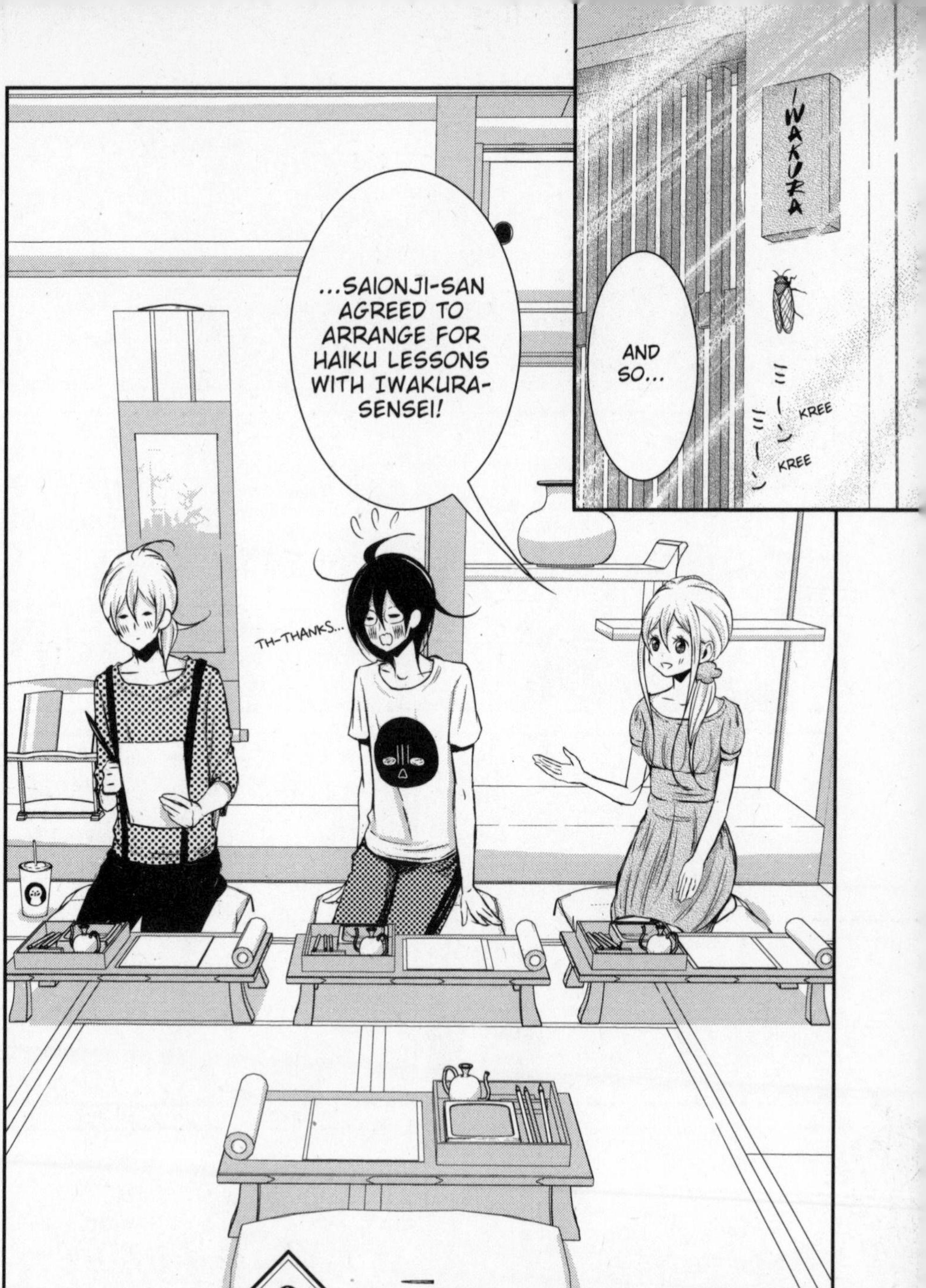
IWAKURA
AND SO...
ミーン
KREE
ミーン
KREE
...SAIONJI-SAN AGREED TO ARRANGE FOR HAIKU LESSONS WITH IWAKURA-SENSEI!
TH-THANKS...

9 VS. THE HAIKU LESSON

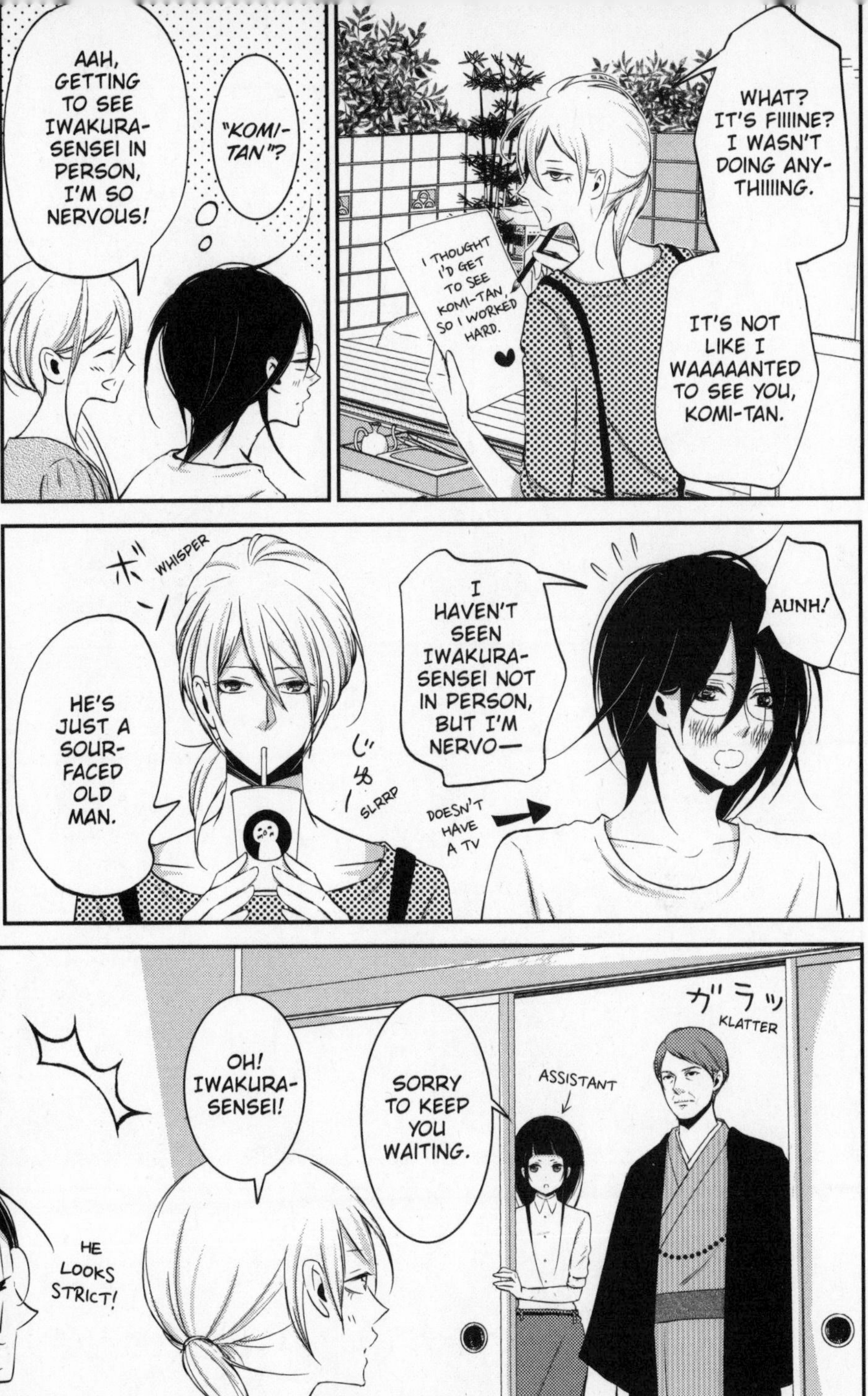
WHAT? IT'S FIIIINE? I WASN'T DOING ANY-THIIIING.
I THOUGHT I'D GET TO SEE KOMI-TAN, SO I WORKED HARD.
IT'S NOT LIKE I WAAAAANTED TO SEE YOU, KOMI-TAN.
"KOMI-TAN"?
AAH, GETTING TO SEE IWAKURA-SENSEI IN PERSON, I'M SO NERVOUS!
AUNH!
I HAVEN'T SEEN IWAKURA-SENSEI NOT IN PERSON, BUT I'M NERVO—
DOESN'T HAVE A TV
ボ
WHISPER
HE'S JUST A SOUR-FACED OLD MAN.
SLRRP
ガラッ
KLATTER
ASSISTANT
SORRY TO KEEP YOU WAITING.
OH! IWAKURA-SENSEI!
HE LOOKS STRICT!

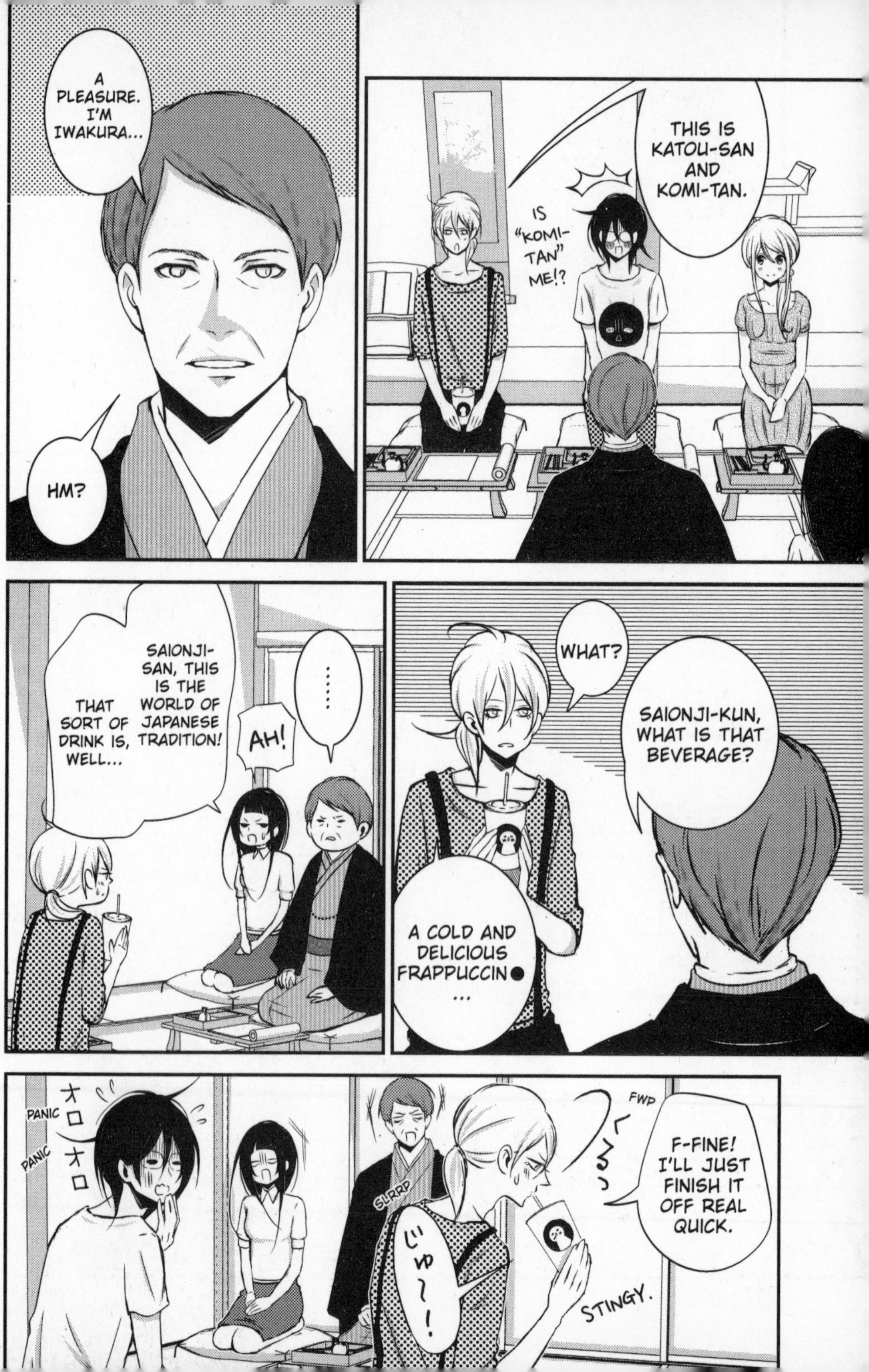
THIS IS KATOU-SAN AND KOMI-TAN.
IS "KOMI-TAN" ME!?
A PLEASURE. I'M IWAKURA...
HM?
SAIONJI-KUN, WHAT IS THAT BEVERAGE?
WHAT?
A COLD AND DELICIOUS FRAPPUCCIN● ...
......
AH!
SAIONJI-SAN, THIS IS THE WORLD OF JAPANESE TRADITION!
THAT SORT OF DRINK IS, WELL...
F-FINE! I'LL JUST FINISH IT OFF REAL QUICK.
FWP
くるっ
STINGY.
SLURRP
じゅ~!
PANIC
PANIC
オロオロ

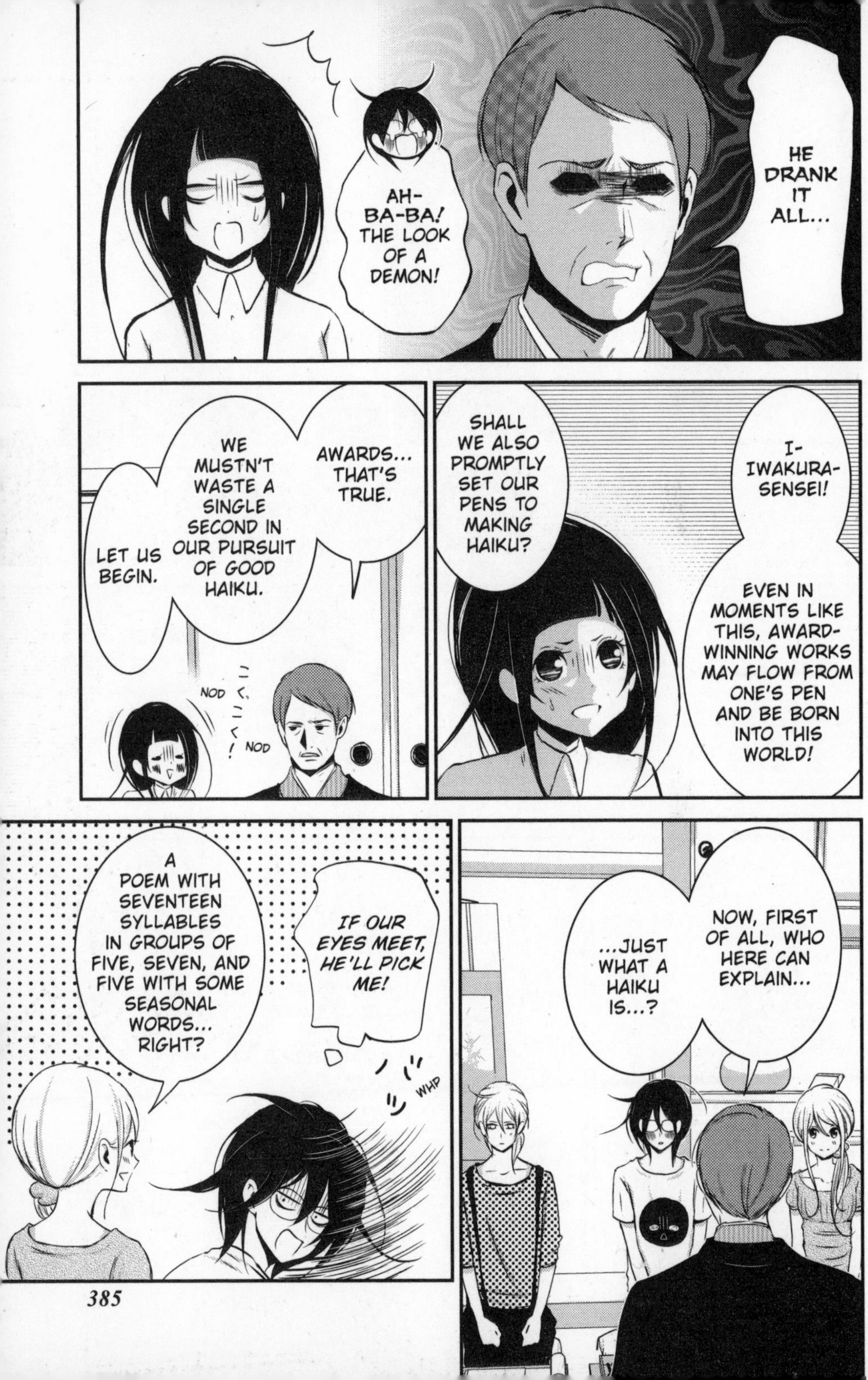
HE DRANK IT ALL...
AH-BA-BA! THE LOOK OF A DEMON!
I-IWAKURA-SENSEI!
EVEN IN MOMENTS LIKE THIS, AWARD-WINNING WORKS MAY FLOW FROM ONE'S PEN AND BE BORN INTO THIS WORLD!
SHALL WE ALSO PROMPTLY SET OUR PENS TO MAKING HAIKU?
AWARDS... THAT'S TRUE.
WE MUSTN'T WASTE A SINGLE SECOND IN OUR PURSUIT OF GOOD HAIKU.
LET US BEGIN.
NOD
NOD
NOW, FIRST OF ALL, WHO HERE CAN EXPLAIN...
...JUST WHAT A HAIKU IS...?
IF OUR EYES MEET, HE'LL PICK ME!
A POEM WITH SEVENTEEN SYLLABLES IN GROUPS OF FIVE, SEVEN, AND FIVE WITH SOME SEASONAL WORDS... RIGHT?
WHP

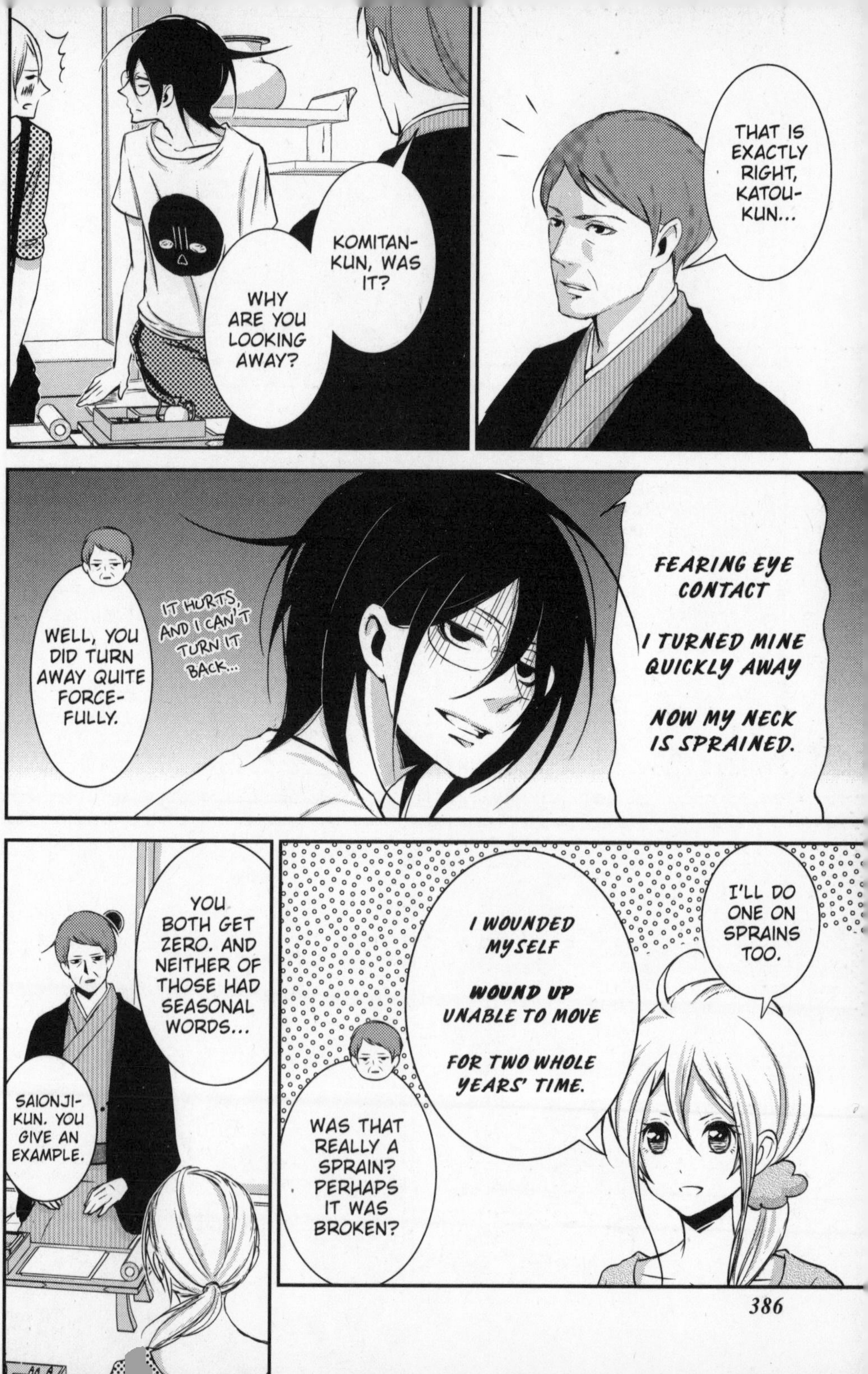
THAT IS EXACTLY RIGHT, KATOU-KUN...
KOMITAN-KUN, WAS IT?
WHY ARE YOU LOOKING AWAY?
FEARING EYE CONTACT
I TURNED MINE QUICKLY AWAY
NOW MY NECK IS SPRAINED.
IT HURTS, AND I CAN'T TURN IT BACK...
WELL, YOU DID TURN AWAY QUITE FORCE-FULLY.
I'LL DO ONE ON SPRAINS TOO.
I WOUNDED MYSELF
WOUND UP UNABLE TO MOVE
FOR TWO WHOLE YEARS' TIME.
WAS THAT REALLY A SPRAIN? PERHAPS IT WAS BROKEN?
YOU BOTH GET ZERO. AND NEITHER OF THOSE HAD SEASONAL WORDS...
SAIONJI-KUN. YOU GIVE AN EXAMPLE.

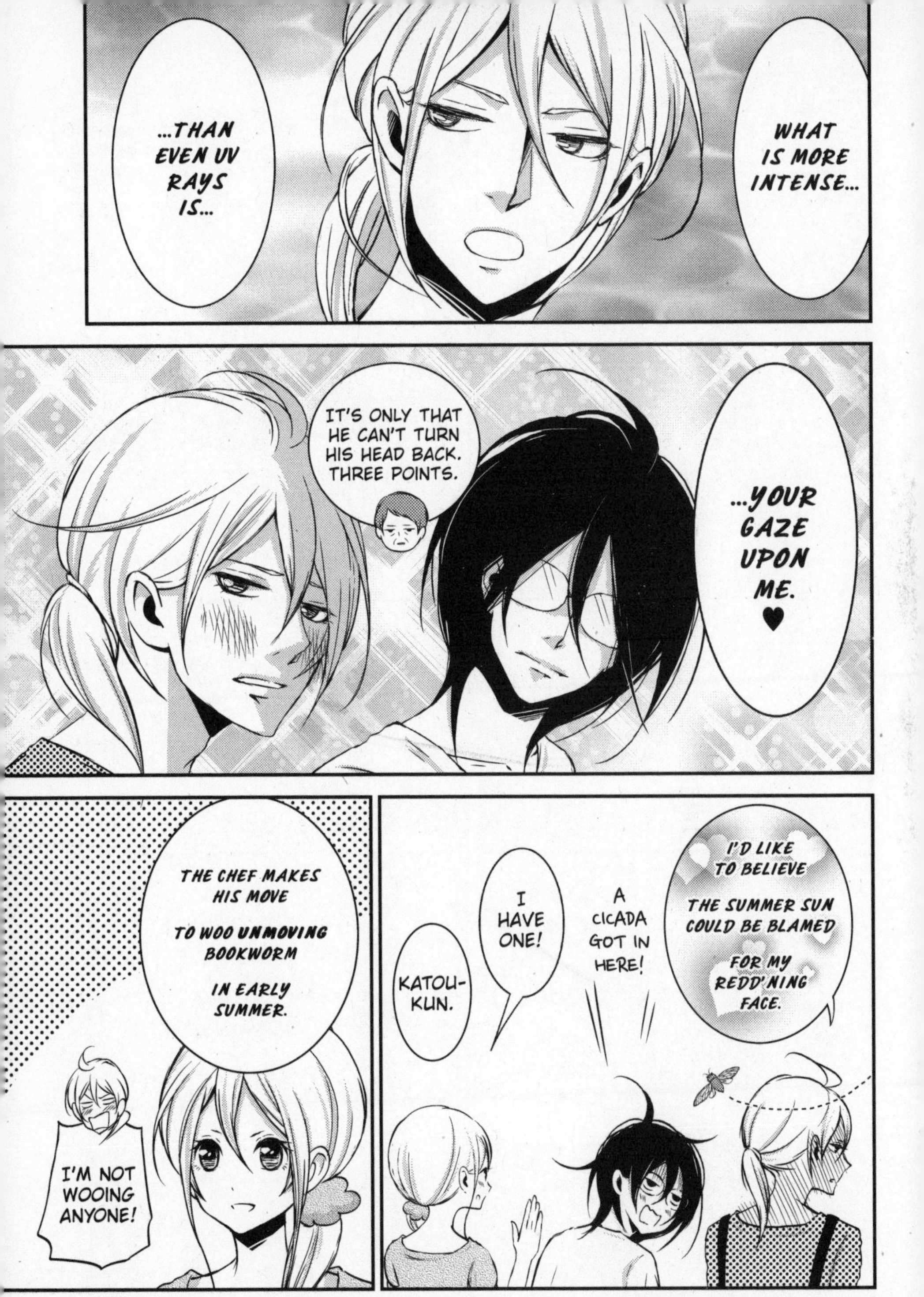
WHAT IS MORE INTENSE...
...THAN EVEN UV RAYS IS...
...YOUR GAZE UPON ME. ♥
IT'S ONLY THAT HE CAN'T TURN HIS HEAD BACK. THREE POINTS.
I'D LIKE TO BELIEVE THE SUMMER SUN COULD BE BLAMED FOR MY REDD'NING FACE.
A CICADA GOT IN HERE!
I HAVE ONE!
KATOU-KUN.
THE CHEF MAKES HIS MOVE TO WOO UNMOVING BOOKWORM IN EARLY SUMMER.
I'M NOT WOOING ANYONE!

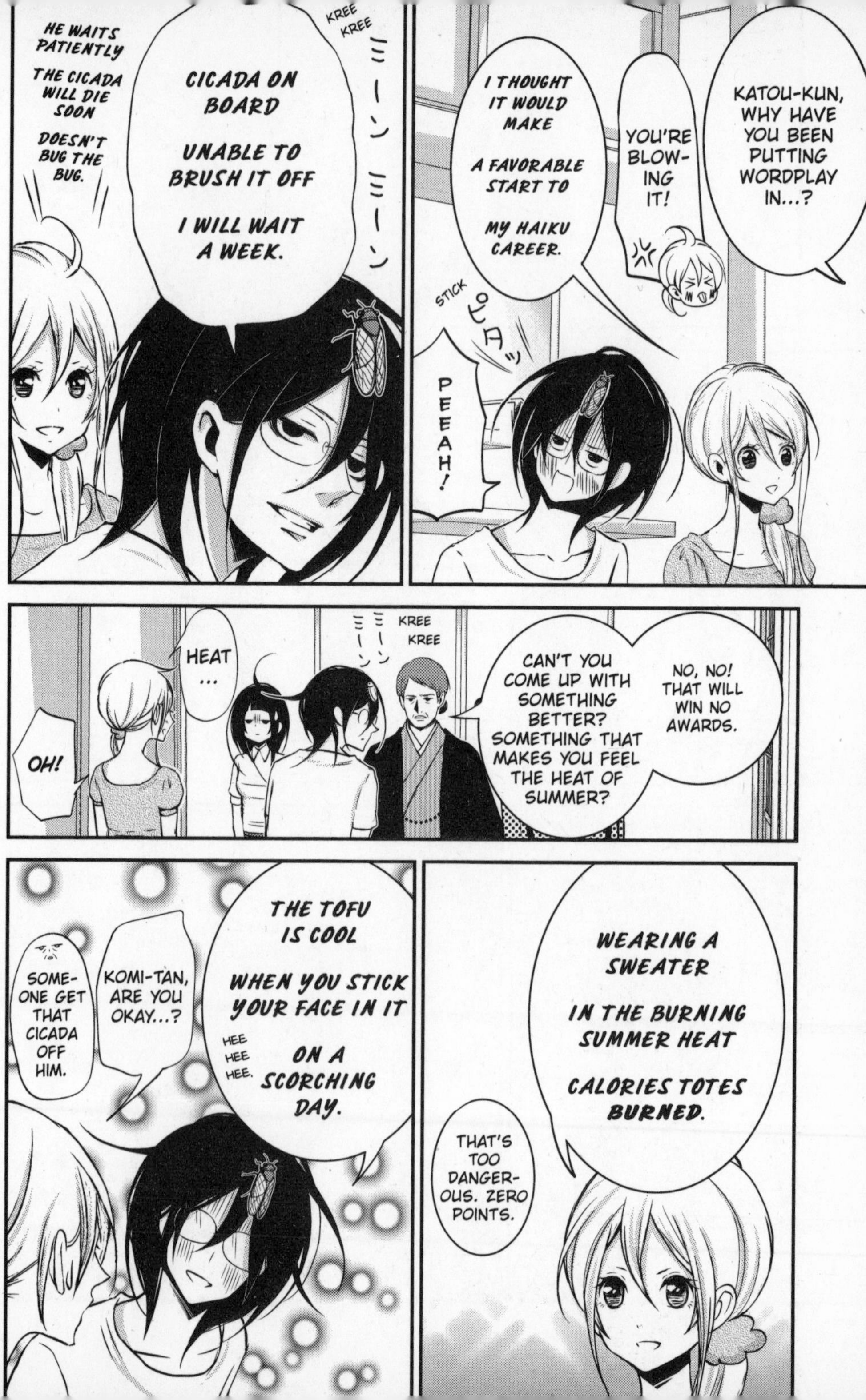
KATOU-KUN, WHY HAVE YOU BEEN PUTTING WORDPLAY IN...?
YOU'RE BLOWING IT!
I THOUGHT IT WOULD MAKE A FAVORABLE START TO MY HAIKU CAREER.
ピタッ
STICK
PEEAH!
KREE KREE
ミーン ミーン
CICADA ON BOARD
UNABLE TO BRUSH IT OFF
I WILL WAIT A WEEK.
HE WAITS PATIENTLY
THE CICADA WILL DIE SOON
DOESN'T BUG THE BUG.
NO, NO! THAT WILL WIN NO AWARDS.
CAN'T YOU COME UP WITH SOMETHING BETTER? SOMETHING THAT MAKES YOU FEEL THE HEAT OF SUMMER?
KREE KREE
ミーン ミーン
HEAT...
OH!
WEARING A SWEATER
IN THE BURNING SUMMER HEAT
CALORIES TOTES BURNED.
THAT'S TOO DANGEROUS. ZERO POINTS.
THE TOFU IS COOL
WHEN YOU STICK YOUR FACE IN IT
ON A SCORCHING DAY.
HEE HEE HEE.
KOMI-TAN, ARE YOU OKAY...?
SOMEONE GET THAT CICADA OFF HIM.

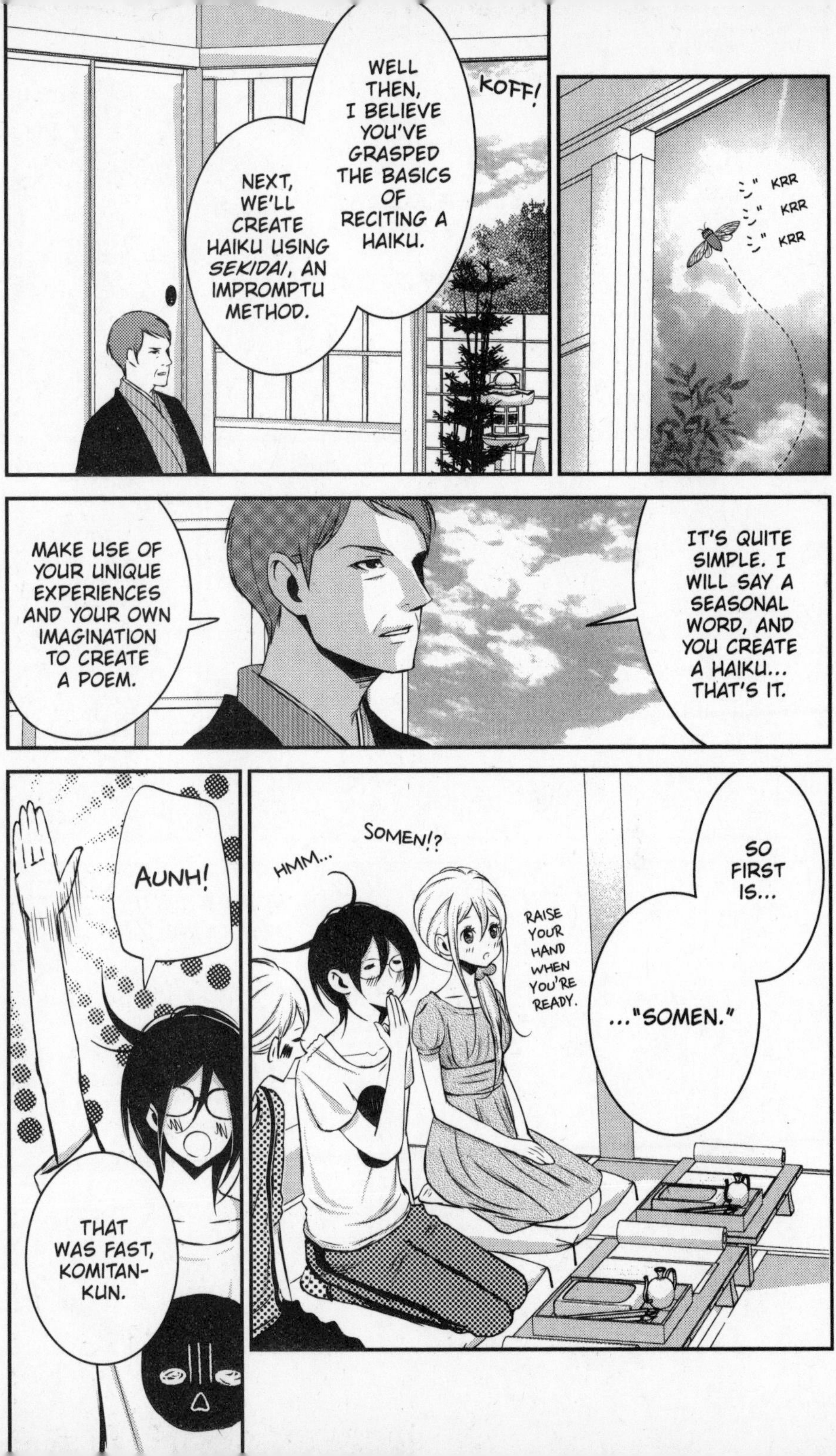

KRR
KRR
KRR
KOFF!
WELL THEN, I BELIEVE YOU'VE GRASPED THE BASICS OF RECITING A HAIKU.
NEXT, WE'LL CREATE HAIKU USING *SEKIDAI*, AN IMPROMPTU METHOD.
IT'S QUITE SIMPLE. I WILL SAY A SEASONAL WORD, AND YOU CREATE A HAIKU... THAT'S IT.
MAKE USE OF YOUR UNIQUE EXPERIENCES AND YOUR OWN IMAGINATION TO CREATE A POEM.
SO FIRST IS...
..."SOMEN."
RAISE YOUR HAND WHEN YOU'RE READY.
SOMEN!?
HMM...
AUNH!
THAT WAS FAST, KOMITAN-KUN.

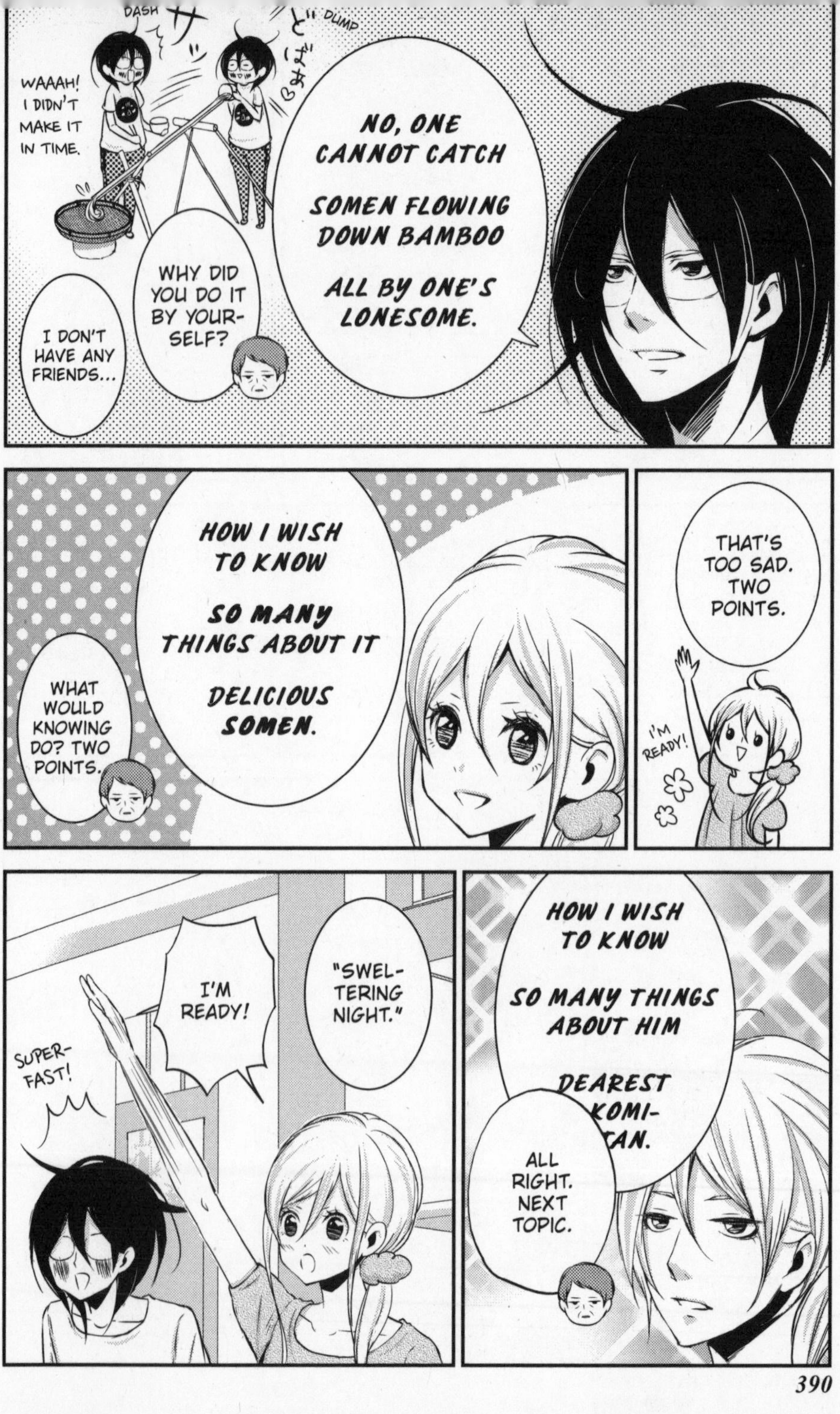
NO, ONE CANNOT CATCH SOMEN FLOWING DOWN BAMBOO ALL BY ONE'S LONESOME.
DUMP
DASH
WAAAH! I DIDN'T MAKE IT IN TIME.
WHY DID YOU DO IT BY YOUR-SELF?
I DON'T HAVE ANY FRIENDS...
THAT'S TOO SAD. TWO POINTS.
I'M READY!
HOW I WISH TO KNOW SO MANY THINGS ABOUT IT DELICIOUS SOMEN.
WHAT WOULD KNOWING DO? TWO POINTS.
HOW I WISH TO KNOW SO MANY THINGS ABOUT HIM DEAREST KOMI-TAN.
ALL RIGHT. NEXT TOPIC.
"SWEL-TERING NIGHT."
I'M READY!
SUPER-FAST!

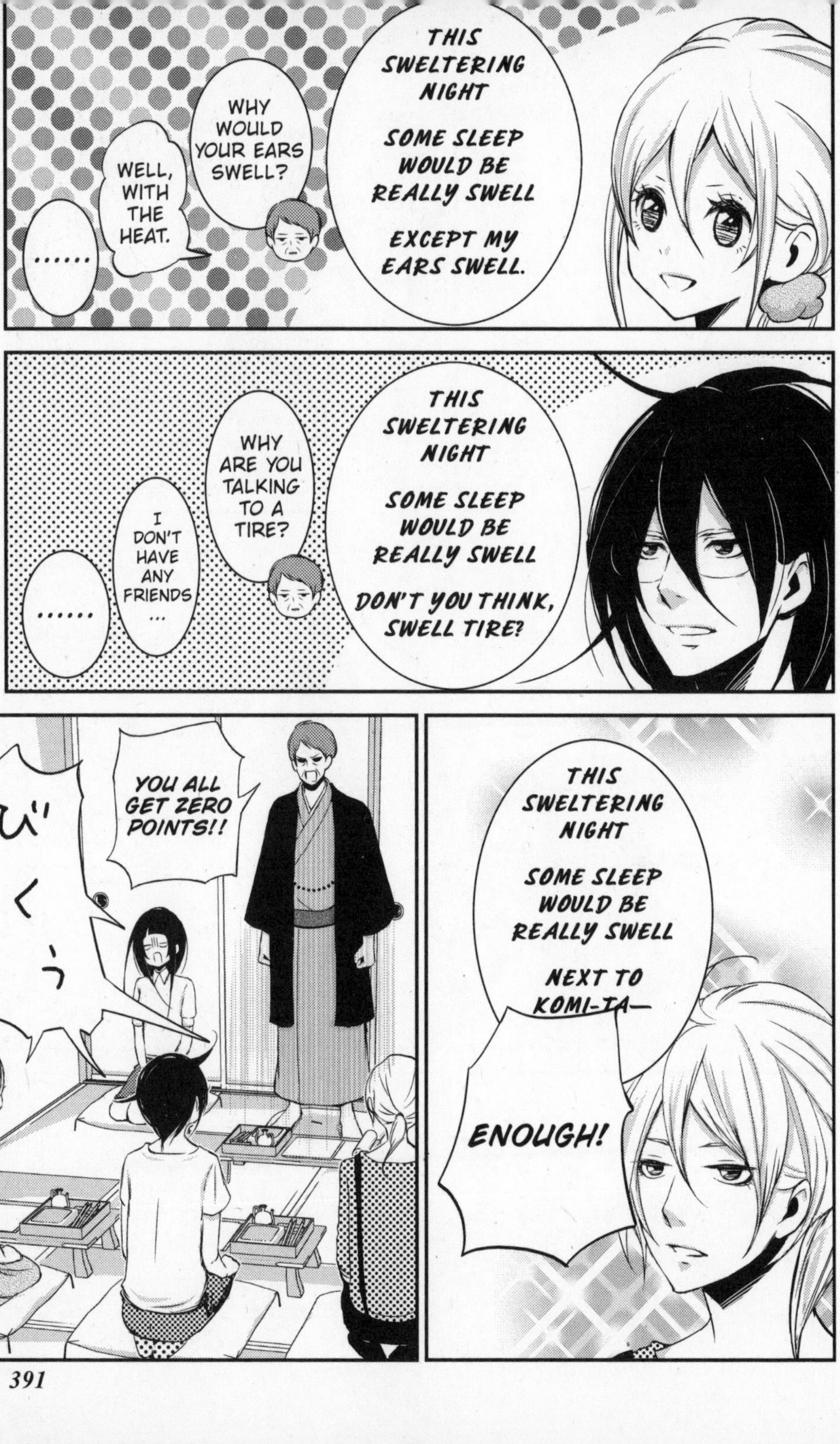
THIS SWELTERING NIGHT SOME SLEEP WOULD BE REALLY SWELL EXCEPT MY EARS SWELL.
WHY WOULD YOUR EARS SWELL?
WELL, WITH THE HEAT.
......
THIS SWELTERING NIGHT SOME SLEEP WOULD BE REALLY SWELL DON'T YOU THINK, SWELL TIRE?
WHY ARE YOU TALKING TO A TIRE?
I DON'T HAVE ANY FRIENDS ...
......
THIS SWELTERING NIGHT SOME SLEEP WOULD BE REALLY SWELL NEXT TO KOMI-TA—
ENOUGH!
YOU ALL GET ZERO POINTS!!
GULP
びくう

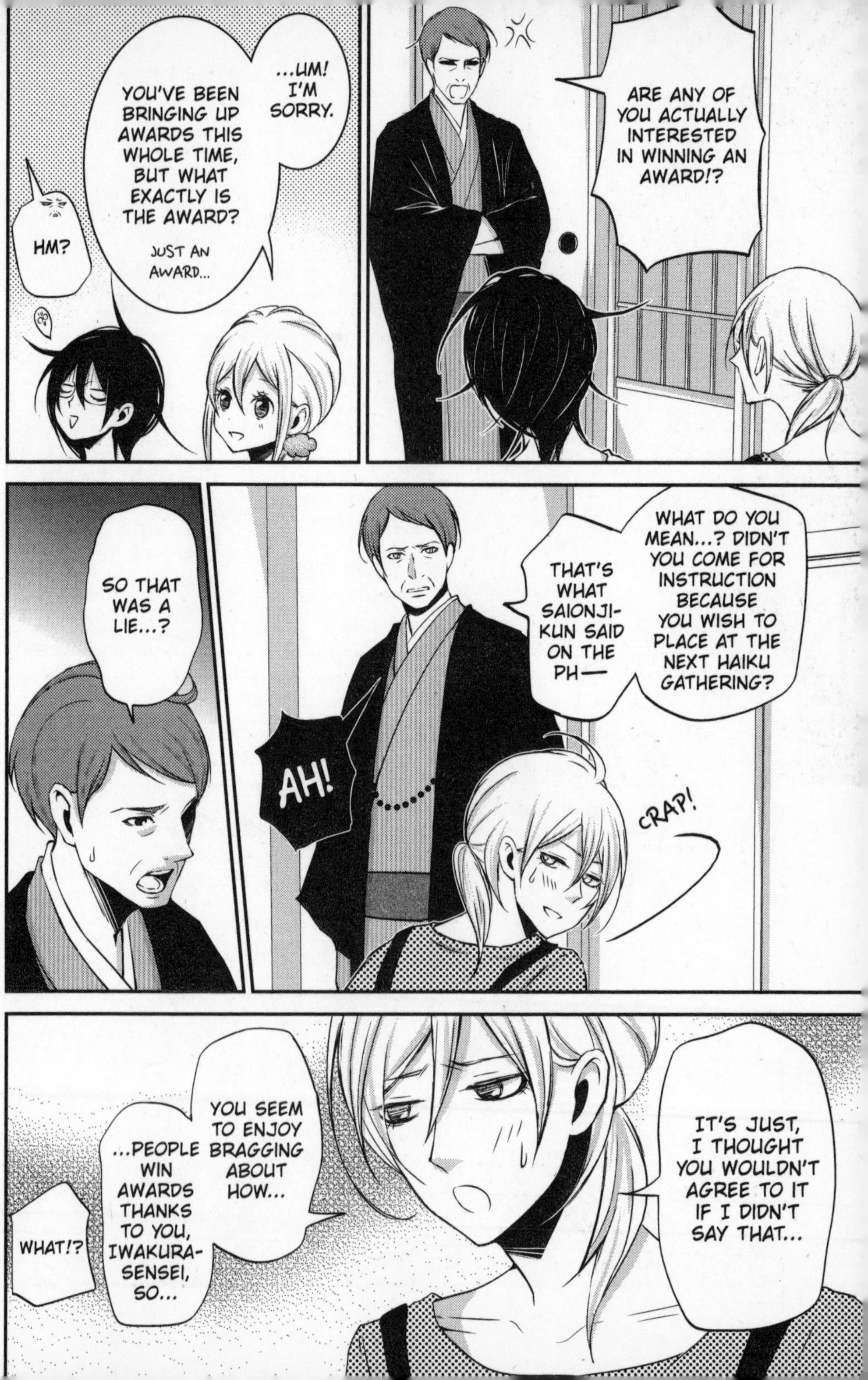
ARE ANY OF YOU ACTUALLY INTERESTED IN WINNING AN AWARD!?
...UM! I'M SORRY.
YOU'VE BEEN BRINGING UP AWARDS THIS WHOLE TIME, BUT WHAT EXACTLY IS THE AWARD?
JUST AN AWARD...
HM?
WHAT DO YOU MEAN...? DIDN'T YOU COME FOR INSTRUCTION BECAUSE YOU WISH TO PLACE AT THE NEXT HAIKU GATHERING?
THAT'S WHAT SAIONJI-KUN SAID ON THE PH—
AH!
CRAP!
SO THAT WAS A LIE...?
IT'S JUST, I THOUGHT YOU WOULDN'T AGREE TO IT IF I DIDN'T SAY THAT...
YOU SEEM TO ENJOY BRAGGING ABOUT HOW...
...PEOPLE WIN AWARDS THANKS TO YOU, IWAKURA-SENSEI, SO...
WHAT!?

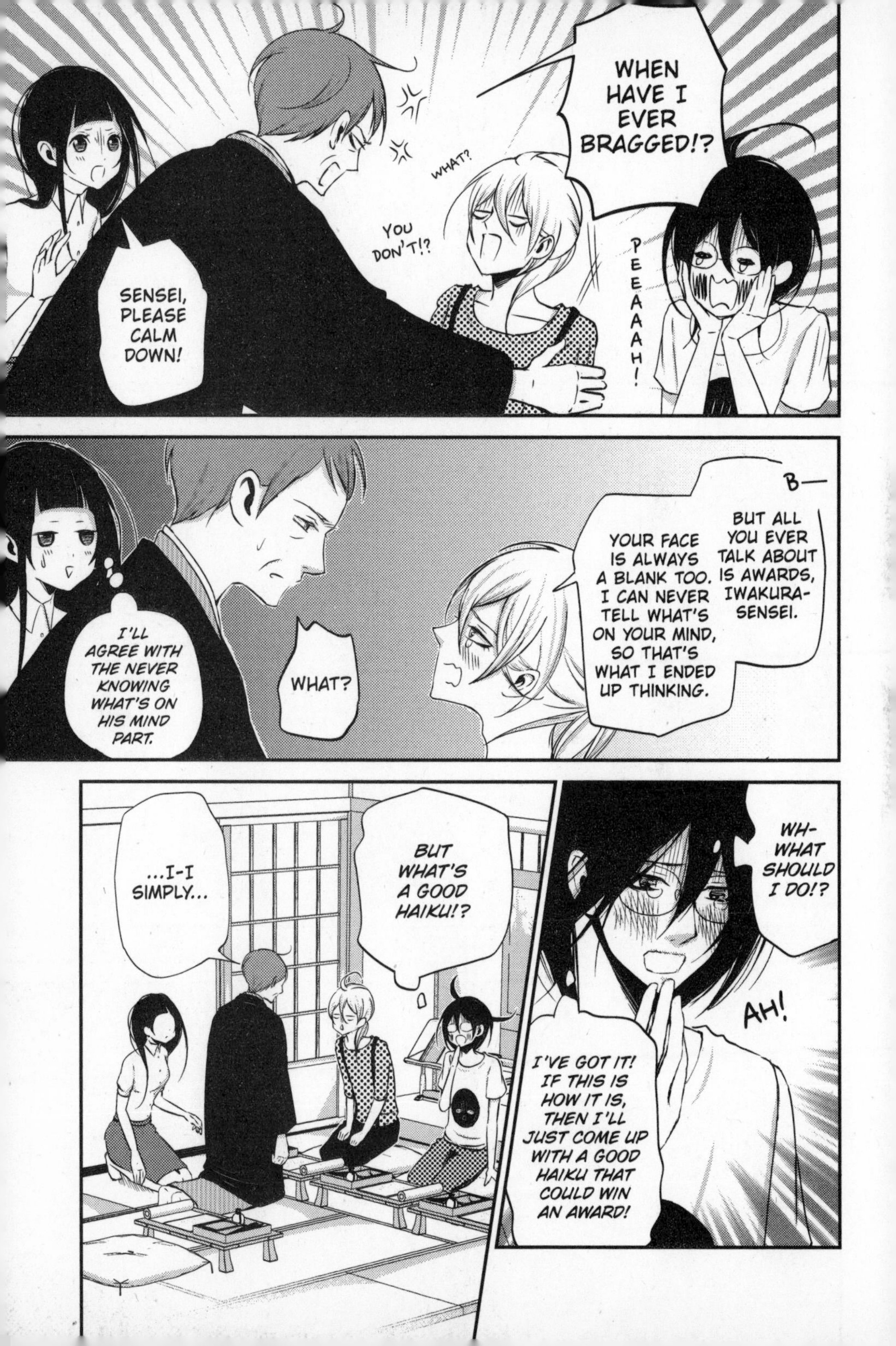
WHEN HAVE I EVER BRAGGED!?
PEEAAAH!
WHAT?
YOU DON'T!?
SENSEI, PLEASE CALM DOWN!
B—
BUT ALL YOU EVER TALK ABOUT IS AWARDS, IWAKURA-SENSEI.
YOUR FACE IS ALWAYS A BLANK TOO. I CAN NEVER TELL WHAT'S ON YOUR MIND, SO THAT'S WHAT I ENDED UP THINKING.
WHAT?
I'LL AGREE WITH THE NEVER KNOWING WHAT'S ON HIS MIND PART.
WH-WHAT SHOULD I DO!?
AH!
I'VE GOT IT! IF THIS IS HOW IT IS, THEN I'LL JUST COME UP WITH A GOOD HAIKU THAT COULD WIN AN AWARD!
BUT WHAT'S A GOOD HAIKU!?
...I-I SIMPLY...

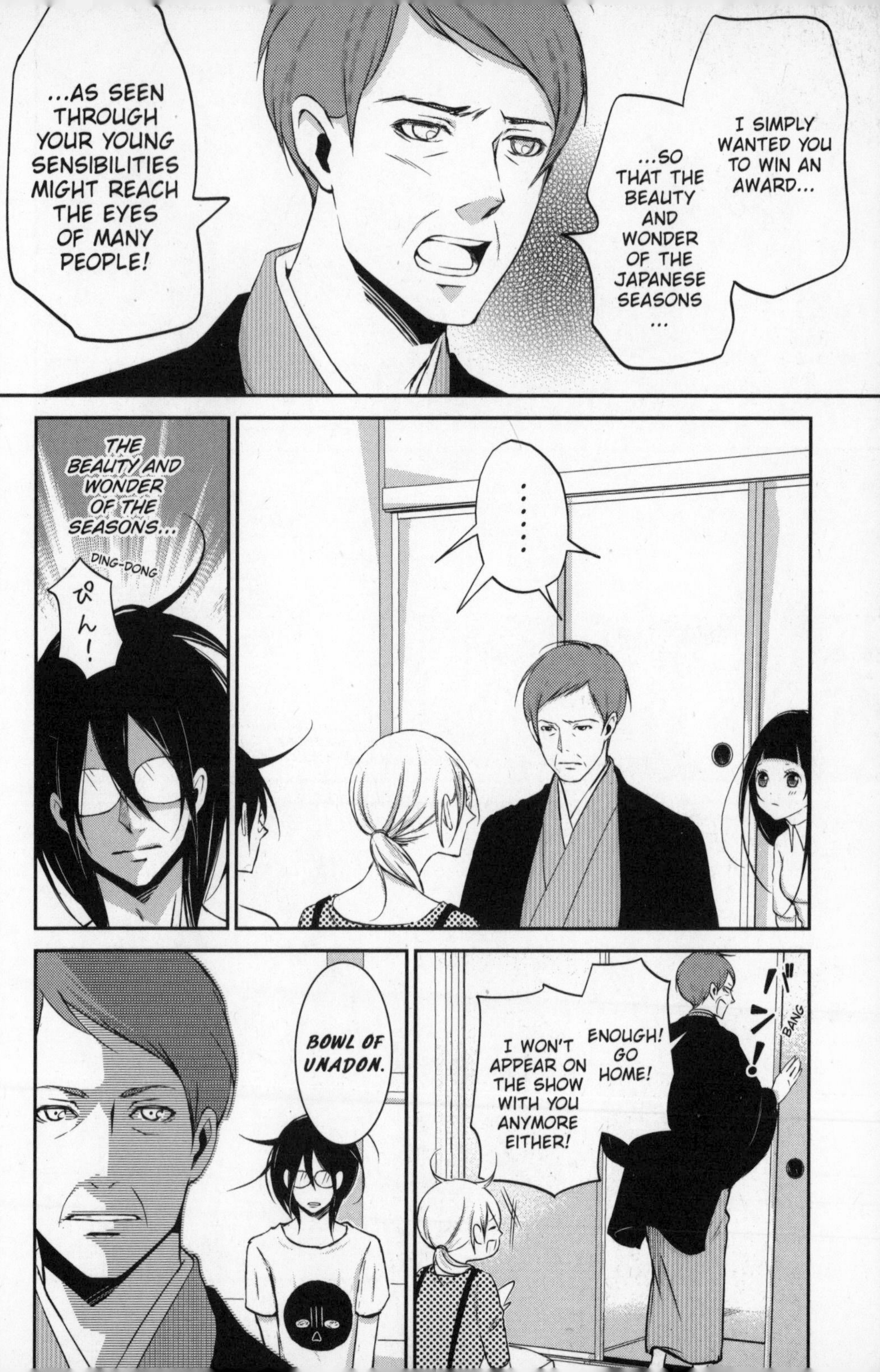

I SIMPLY WANTED YOU TO WIN AN AWARD...
...SO THAT THE BEAUTY AND WONDER OF THE JAPANESE SEASONS ...
...AS SEEN THROUGH YOUR YOUNG SENSIBILITIES MIGHT REACH THE EYES OF MANY PEOPLE!
......
THE BEAUTY AND WONDER OF THE SEASONS...
DING-DONG
ぴん!
BANG
ENOUGH! GO HOME!
I WON'T APPEAR ON THE SHOW WITH YOU ANYMORE EITHER!
BOWL OF UNADON.

SHF
スッ
YOU THREE...
YOU'VE MADE ME REMEMBER SOMETHING VERY IMPORTANT.
I APOLOGIZE FOR YELLING AT YOU.
AND THANK YOU.
KREE
ミーン
ミーン
KREE
THE HAIKU YOU HAD SUCH FUN MAKING...
BEEEAM
パァァァァ
...ALL GET ONE HUNDRED POINTS.
OH! ME TOO.
I'M SORRY I LIED.
NO, IT'S FINE. I WAS IN THE WRONG.

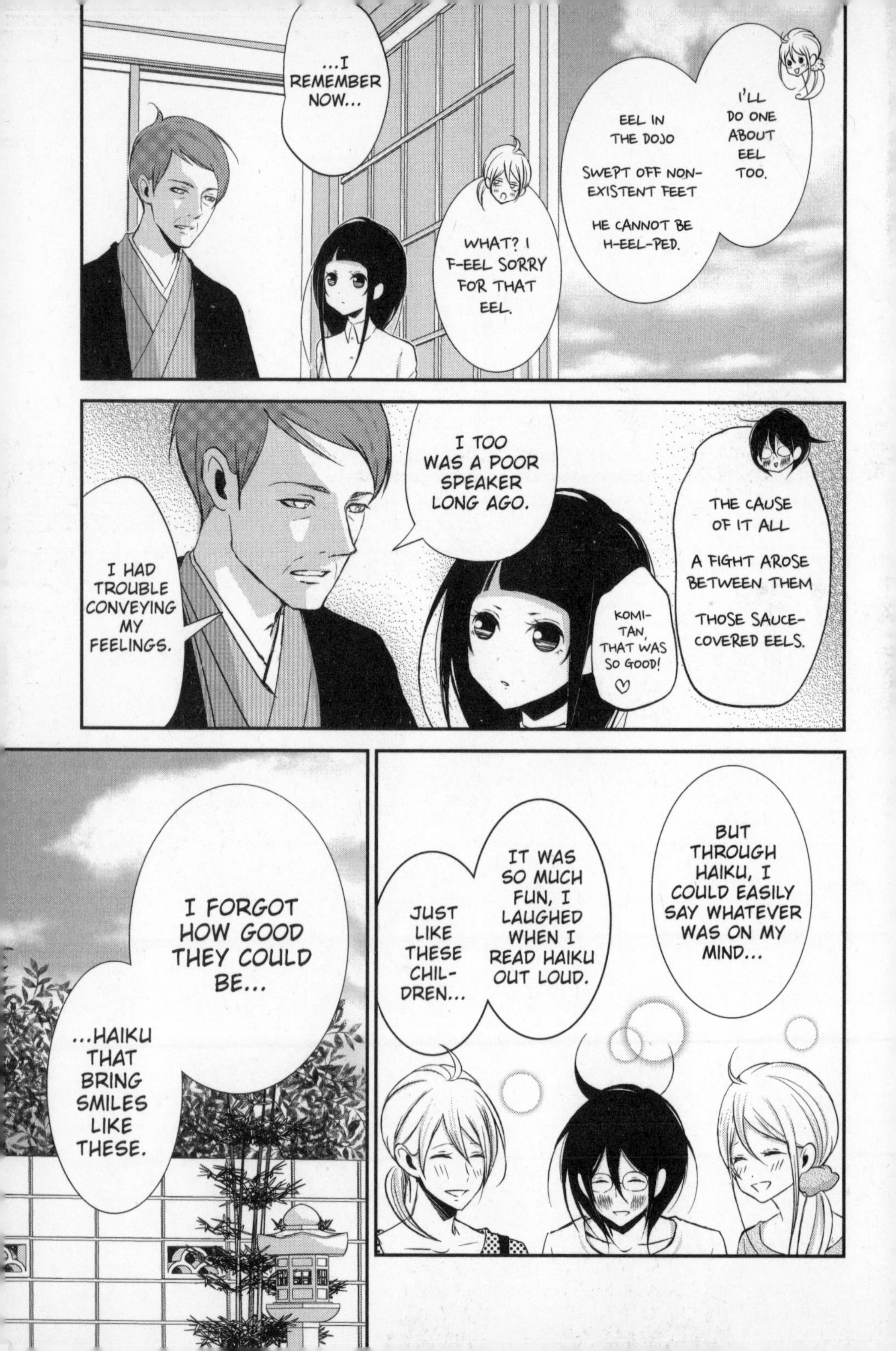
I'LL DO ONE ABOUT EEL TOO.
EEL IN THE DOJO
SWEPT OFF NON-EXISTENT FEET
HE CANNOT BE H-EEL-PED.
WHAT? I F-EEL SORRY FOR THAT EEL.
...I REMEMBER NOW...
THE CAUSE OF IT ALL
A FIGHT AROSE BETWEEN THEM
THOSE SAUCE-COVERED EELS.
KOMI-TAN, THAT WAS SO GOOD! ♡
I TOO WAS A POOR SPEAKER LONG AGO.
I HAD TROUBLE CONVEYING MY FEELINGS.
BUT THROUGH HAIKU, I COULD EASILY SAY WHATEVER WAS ON MY MIND...
IT WAS SO MUCH FUN, I LAUGHED WHEN I READ HAIKU OUT LOUD.
JUST LIKE THESE CHIL-DREN...
I FORGOT HOW GOOD THEY COULD BE...
...HAIKU THAT BRING SMILES LIKE THESE.

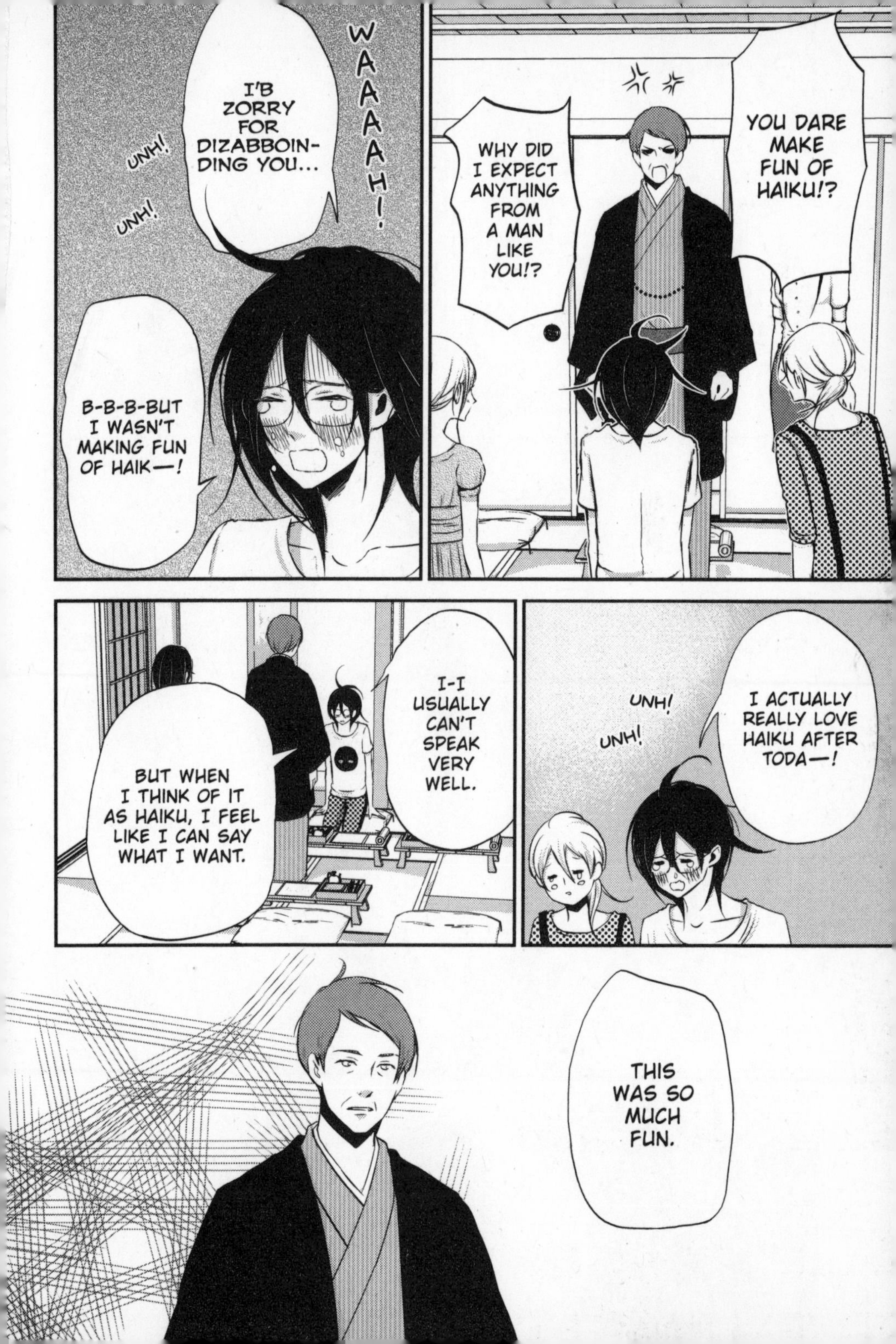
YOU DARE MAKE FUN OF HAIKU!?
WHY DID I EXPECT ANYTHING FROM A MAN LIKE YOU!?
WAAAAAH!
I'B ZORRY FOR DIZABBOIN-DING YOU...
UNH!
UNH!
B-B-B-BUT I WASN'T MAKING FUN OF HAIK—!
I ACTUALLY REALLY LOVE HAIKU AFTER TODA—!
UNH!
UNH!
I-I USUALLY CAN'T SPEAK VERY WELL.
BUT WHEN I THINK OF IT AS HAIKU, I FEEL LIKE I CAN SAY WHAT I WANT.
THIS WAS SO MUCH FUN.

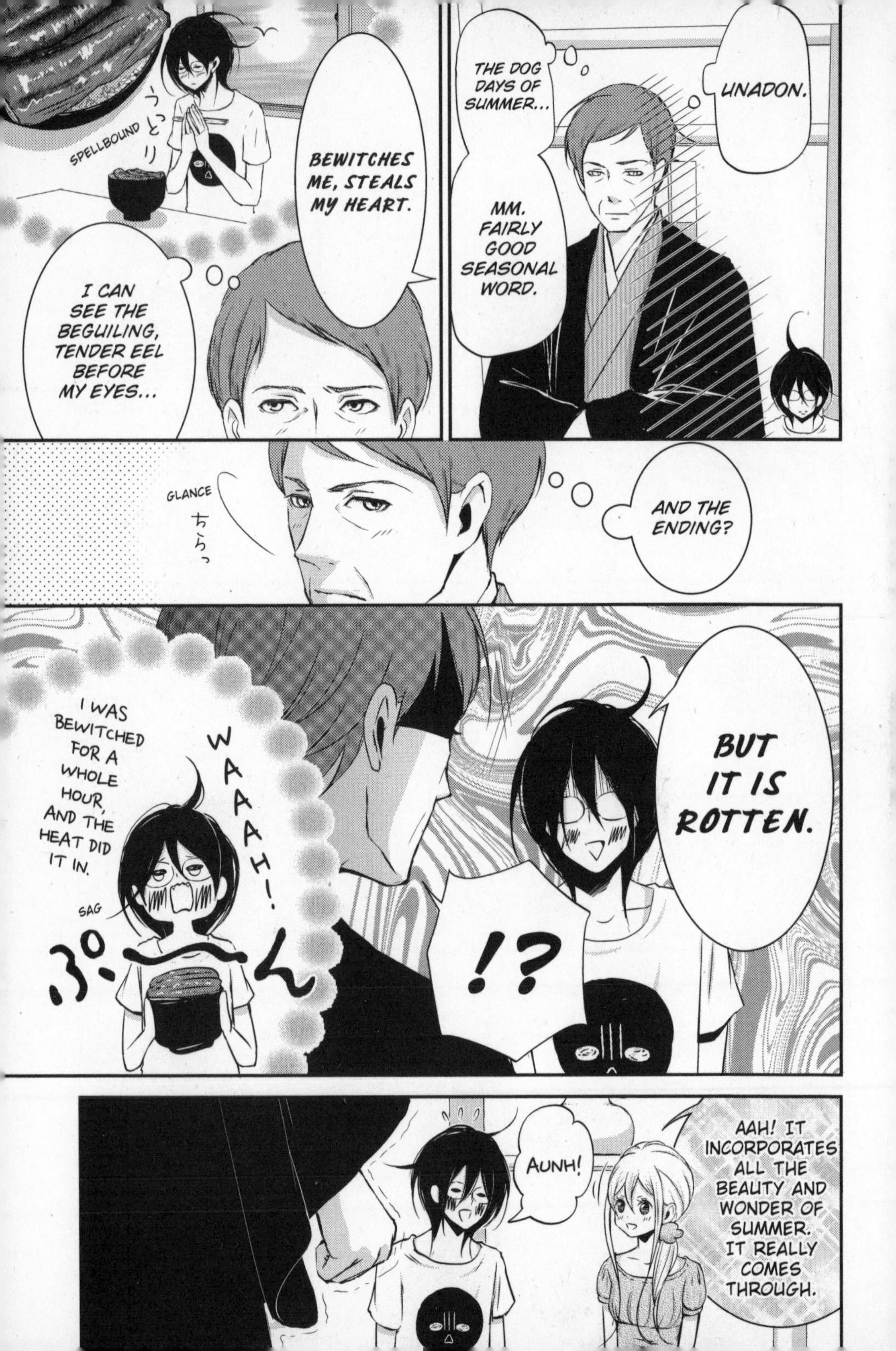
UNADON.
THE DOG DAYS OF SUMMER...
MM. FAIRLY GOOD SEASONAL WORD.
BEWITCHES ME, STEALS MY HEART.
I CAN SEE THE BEGUILING, TENDER EEL BEFORE MY EYES...
SPELLBOUND
うっとり
AND THE ENDING?
GLANCE
ちらっ
BUT IT IS ROTTEN.
!?
WAAAH!
I WAS BEWITCHED FOR A WHOLE HOUR, AND THE HEAT DID IT IN.
SAG
ぷ〜ん
AAH! IT INCORPORATES ALL THE BEAUTY AND WONDER OF SUMMER. IT REALLY COMES THROUGH.
AUNH!

AND I'M SORRY FOR SECRETLY CALLING YOU A SOUR-FACED OLD MAN.
HEH
I UNDERSTAND. I FORGIVE YOU.
IN EXCHANGE, PERHAPS I CAN ASK TO KEEP DOING THE SHOW WITH YOU?
NOD
HMM...
MAYBE I TOO WILL MAKE AN HONEST HAIKU FOR THE FIRST TIME IN A LONG TIME...
WHAT?
SENSEI'S HONEST HAIKU...
ゴクリ…
GULP
I WANTED TO SAY
GIVE ME A LITTLE SIP OF
YOUR FRAPPUCCIN●.

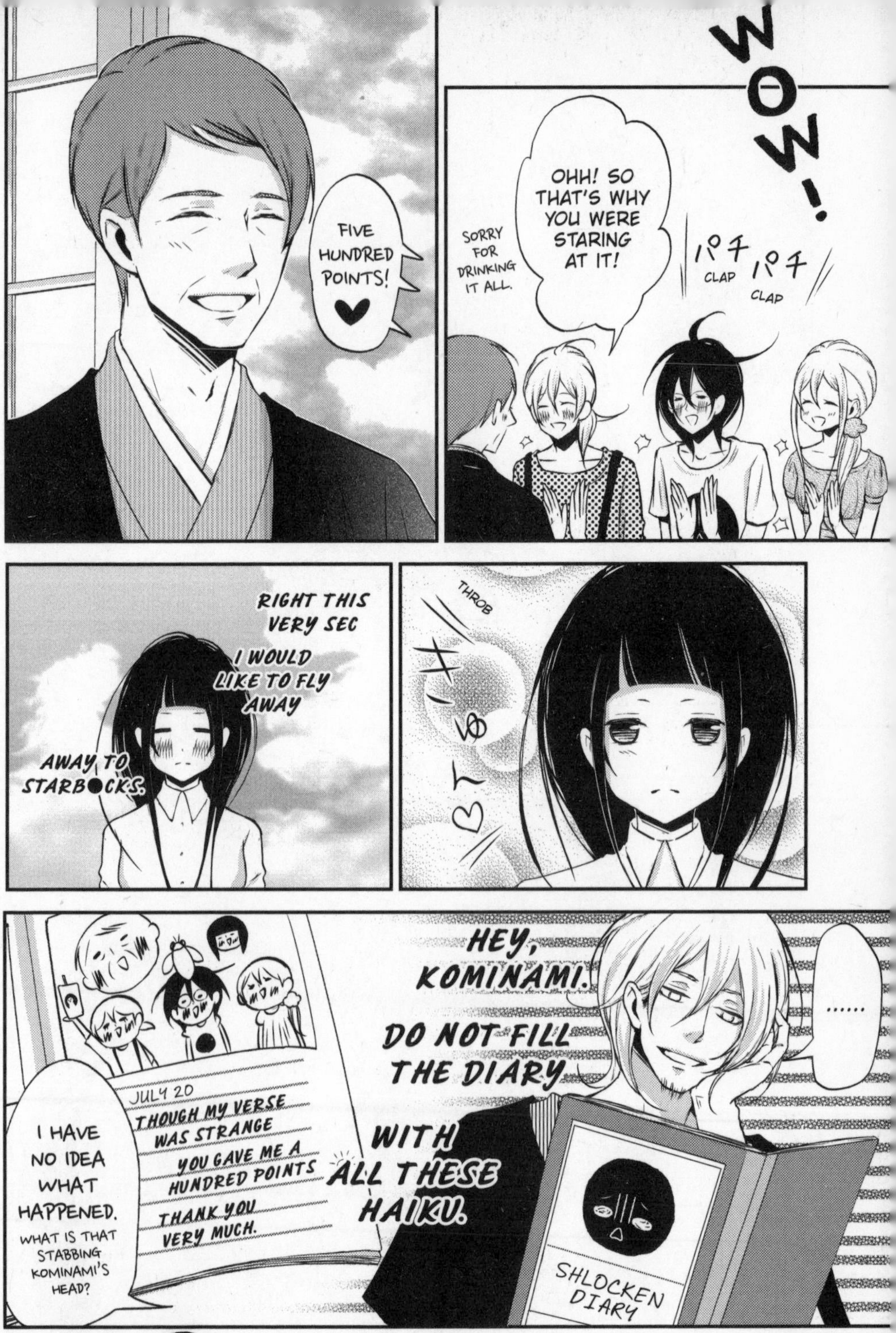
WOW!
OHH! SO THAT'S WHY YOU WERE STARING AT IT!
SORRY FOR DRINKING IT ALL.
パチ CLAP パチ CLAP
FIVE HUNDRED POINTS! ♥
THROB
RIGHT THIS VERY SEC
I WOULD LIKE TO FLY AWAY
AWAY TO STARB●CKS.
HEY, KOMINAMI.
DO NOT FILL THE DIARY
WITH ALL THESE HAIKU.
......
SHLOCKEN DIARY
JULY 20
THOUGH MY VERSE WAS STRANGE
YOU GAVE ME A HUNDRED POINTS
THANK YOU VERY MUCH.
I HAVE NO IDEA WHAT HAPPENED.
WHAT IS THAT STABBING KOMINAMI'S HEAD?

TO BE CONTINUED

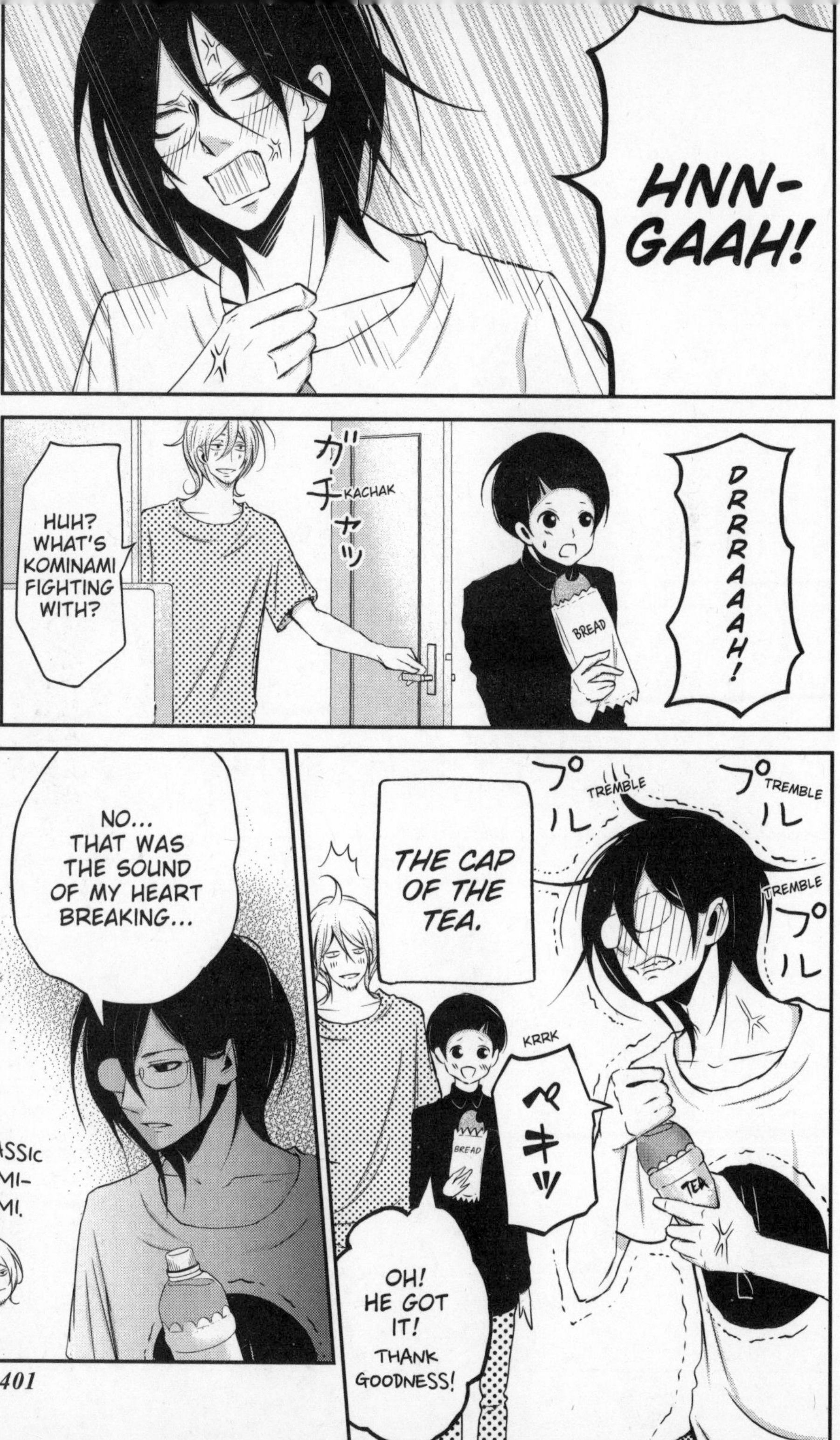
HNN-GAAH!
DRRRAAAH!
ガチャッ KACHAK
HUH? WHAT'S KOMINAMI FIGHTING WITH?
プル TREMBLE
プル TREMBLE
プル TREMBLE
THE CAP OF THE TEA.
ペキッ KRRK
OH! HE GOT IT! THANK GOODNESS!
NO... THAT WAS THE SOUND OF MY HEART BREAKING...
CLASSIC KOMI-NAMI.

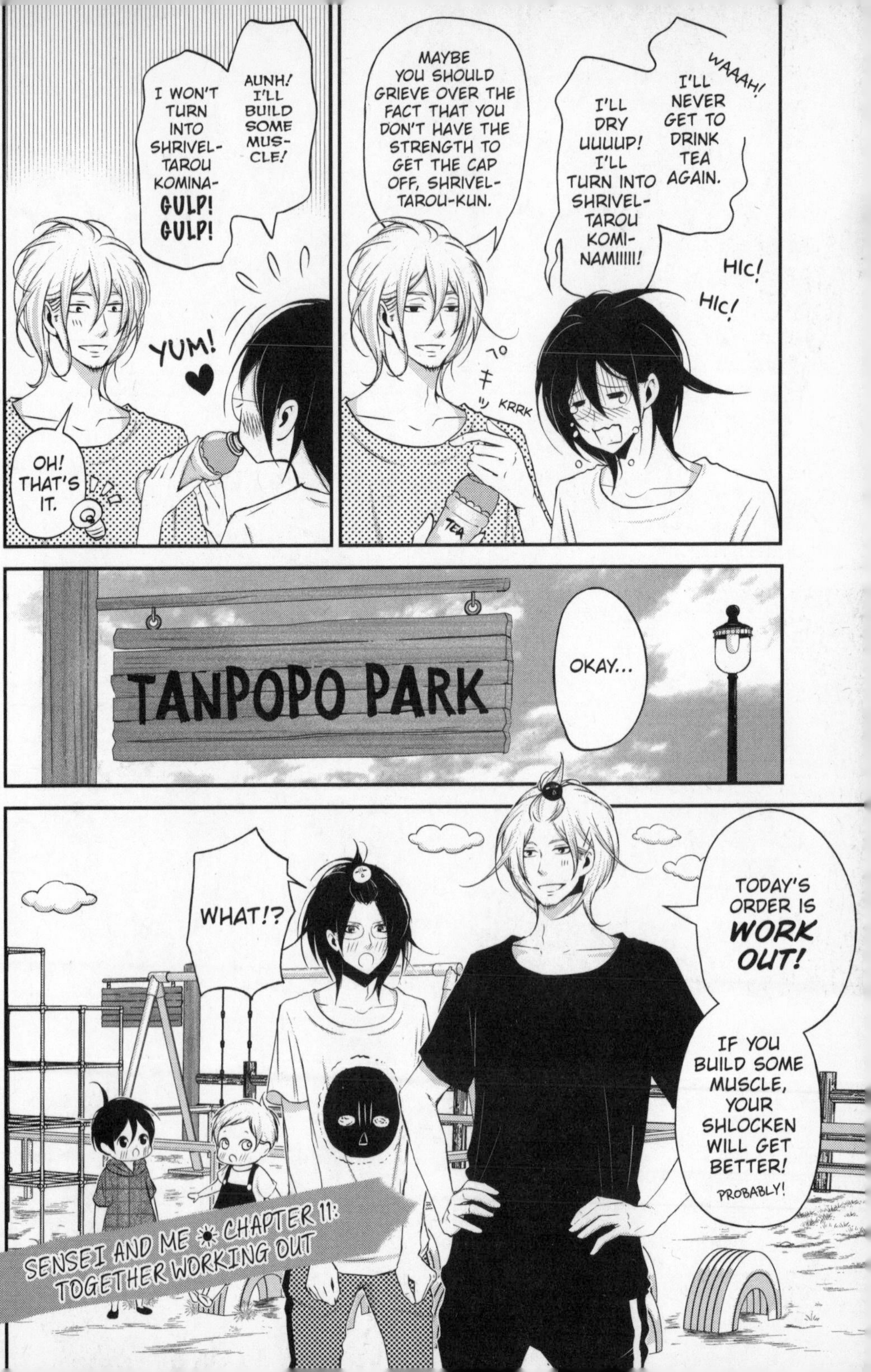
WAAAH!
I'LL NEVER GET TO DRINK TEA AGAIN.
I'LL DRY UUUUP! I'LL TURN INTO SHRIVEL-TAROU KOMI-NAMIIIIII!
HIC!
HIC!
MAYBE YOU SHOULD GRIEVE OVER THE FACT THAT YOU DON'T HAVE THE STRENGTH TO GET THE CAP OFF, SHRIVEL-TAROU-KUN.
ペキッ
KRRK
TEA
AUNH! I'LL BUILD SOME MUS-CLE!
I WON'T TURN INTO SHRIVEL-TAROU KOMINA- GULP! GULP!
YUM!
OH! THAT'S IT.
OKAY...
TANPOPO PARK
TODAY'S ORDER IS WORK OUT!
IF YOU BUILD SOME MUSCLE, YOUR SHLOCKEN WILL GET BETTER!
PROBABLY!
WHAT!?
SENSEI AND ME ☀ CHAPTER 11: TOGETHER WORKING OUT

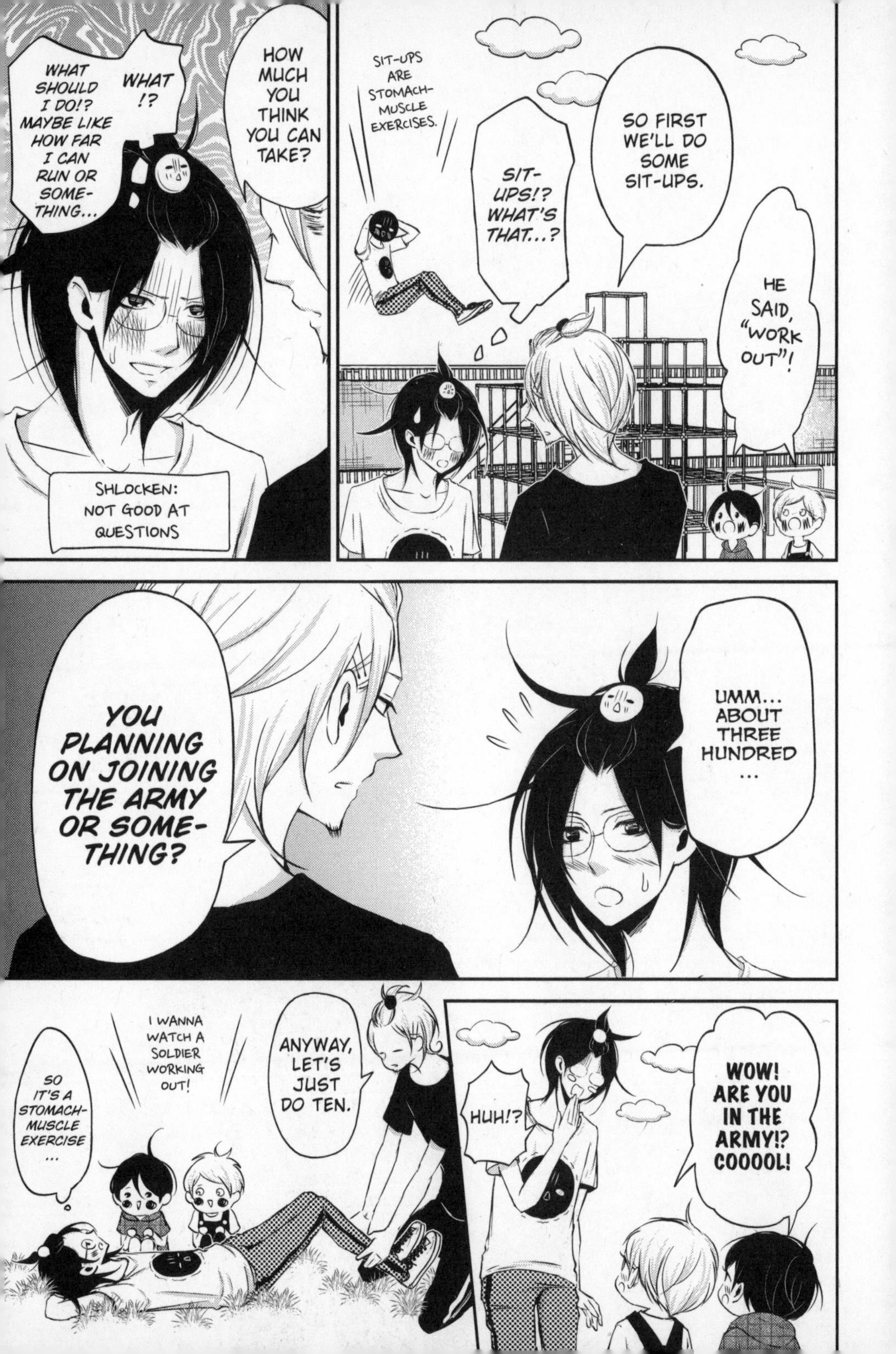
SO FIRST WE'LL DO SOME SIT-UPS.
SIT-UPS!? WHAT'S THAT...?
SIT-UPS ARE STOMACH-MUSCLE EXERCISES.
HE SAID, "WORK OUT"!
HOW MUCH YOU THINK YOU CAN TAKE?
WHAT !?
WHAT SHOULD I DO!? MAYBE LIKE HOW FAR I CAN RUN OR SOME-THING...
SHLOCKEN: NOT GOOD AT QUESTIONS
UMM... ABOUT THREE HUNDRED ...
YOU PLANNING ON JOINING THE ARMY OR SOME-THING?
WOW! ARE YOU IN THE ARMY!? COOOOL!
HUH!?
ANYWAY, LET'S JUST DO TEN.
I WANNA WATCH A SOLDIER WORKING OUT!
SO IT'S A STOMACH-MUSCLE EXERCISE ...

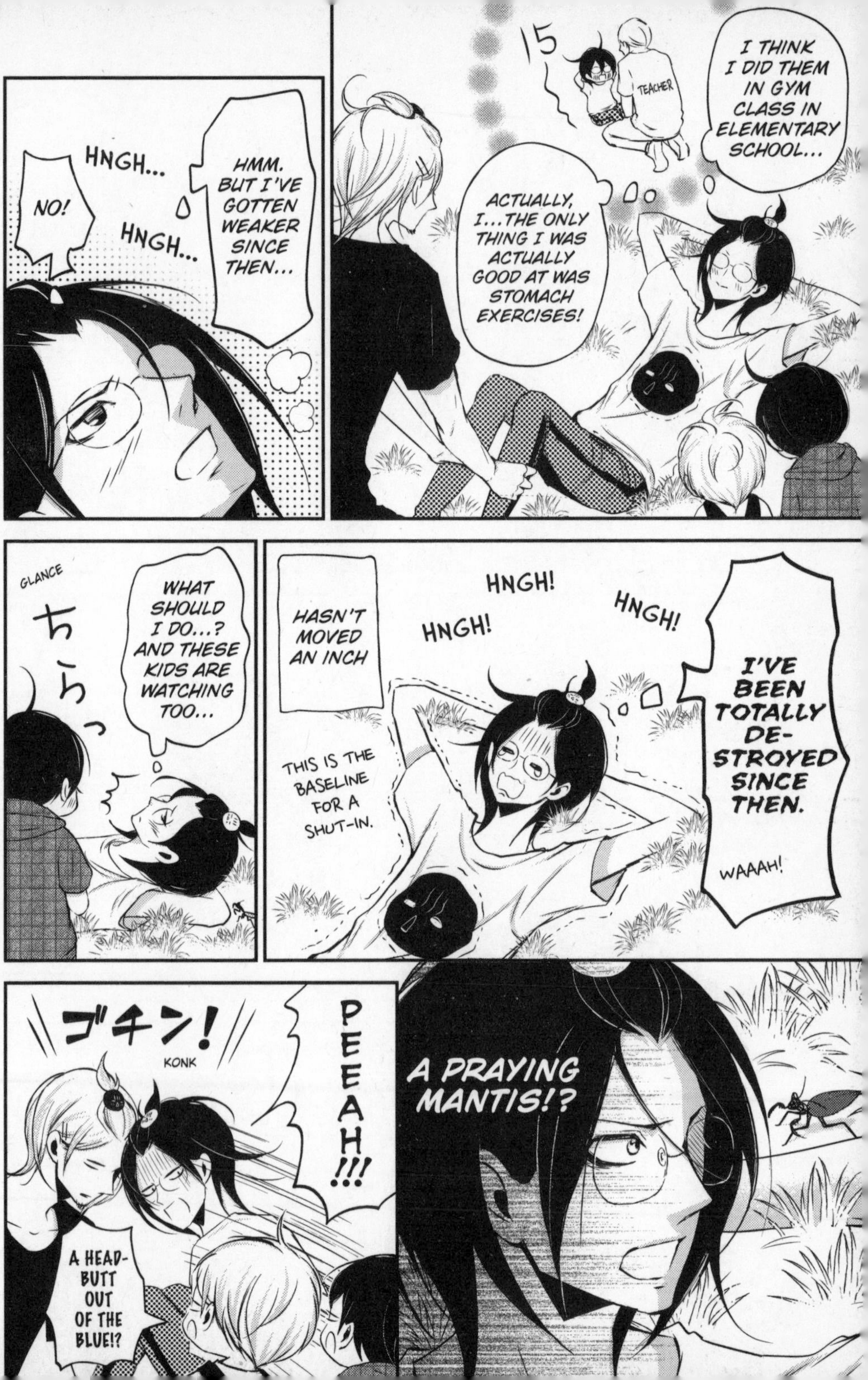
I THINK I DID THEM IN GYM CLASS IN ELEMENTARY SCHOOL...
TEACHER
ACTUALLY, I...THE ONLY THING I WAS ACTUALLY GOOD AT WAS STOMACH EXERCISES!
HMM. BUT I'VE GOTTEN WEAKER SINCE THEN...
HNGH...
HNGH...
NO!
HNGH!
HNGH!
HNGH!
I'VE BEEN TOTALLY DE-STROYED SINCE THEN.
WAAAH!
HASN'T MOVED AN INCH
THIS IS THE BASELINE FOR A SHUT-IN.
WHAT SHOULD I DO...? AND THESE KIDS ARE WATCHING TOO...
GLANCE
ちらっ
A PRAYING MANTIS!?
PEEEAH!!!
ゴチン!
KONK
A HEAD-BUTT OUT OF THE BLUE!?

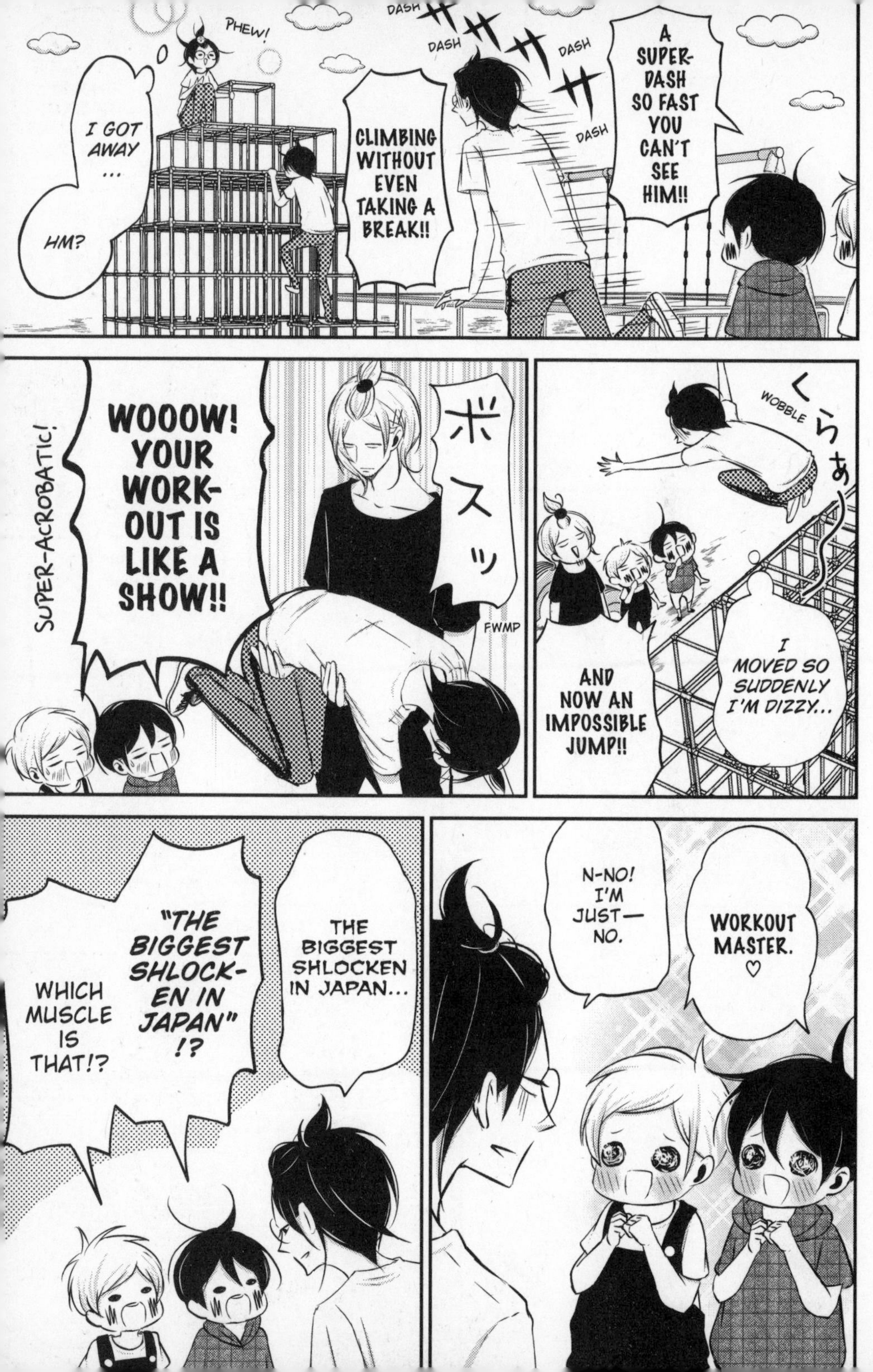
A SUPER-DASH SO FAST YOU CAN'T SEE HIM!!
DASH DASH DASH DASH
CLIMBING WITHOUT EVEN TAKING A BREAK!!
PHEW!
I GOT AWAY ...
HM?
くらぁ~
WOBBLE
I MOVED SO SUDDENLY I'M DIZZY...
AND NOW AN IMPOSSIBLE JUMP!!
ボスッ
FWMP
WOOOW! YOUR WORK-OUT IS LIKE A SHOW!!
SUPER-ACROBATIC!
WORKOUT MASTER. ♡
N-NO! I'M JUST— NO.
THE BIGGEST SHLOCKEN IN JAPAN...
"THE BIGGEST SHLOCK-EN IN JAPAN" !?
WHICH MUSCLE IS THAT!?

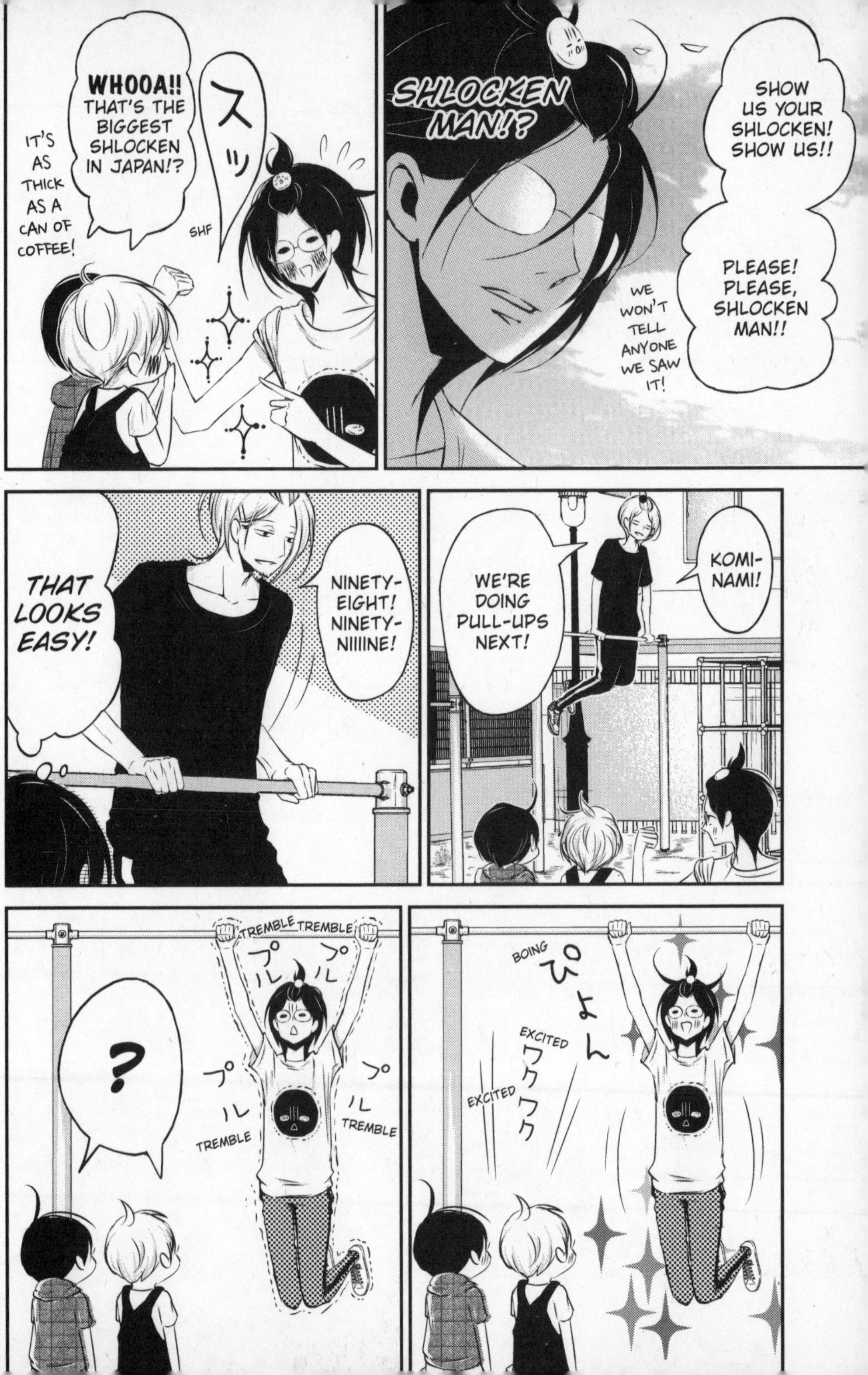
SHOW US YOUR SHLOCKEN! SHOW US!!
SHLOCKEN MAN!?
PLEASE! PLEASE, SHLOCKEN MAN!!
WE WON'T TELL ANYONE WE SAW IT!
スッ
SHF
WHOOA!! THAT'S THE BIGGEST SHLOCKEN IN JAPAN!?
IT'S AS THICK AS A CAN OF COFFEE!
KOMI-NAMI!
WE'RE DOING PULL-UPS NEXT!
NINETY-EIGHT! NINETY-NIIIINE!
THAT LOOKS EASY!
ぴょん
BOING
ワクワク
EXCITED
EXCITED
TREMBLE TREMBLE
プルプル
プルプル
TREMBLE
TREMBLE
?

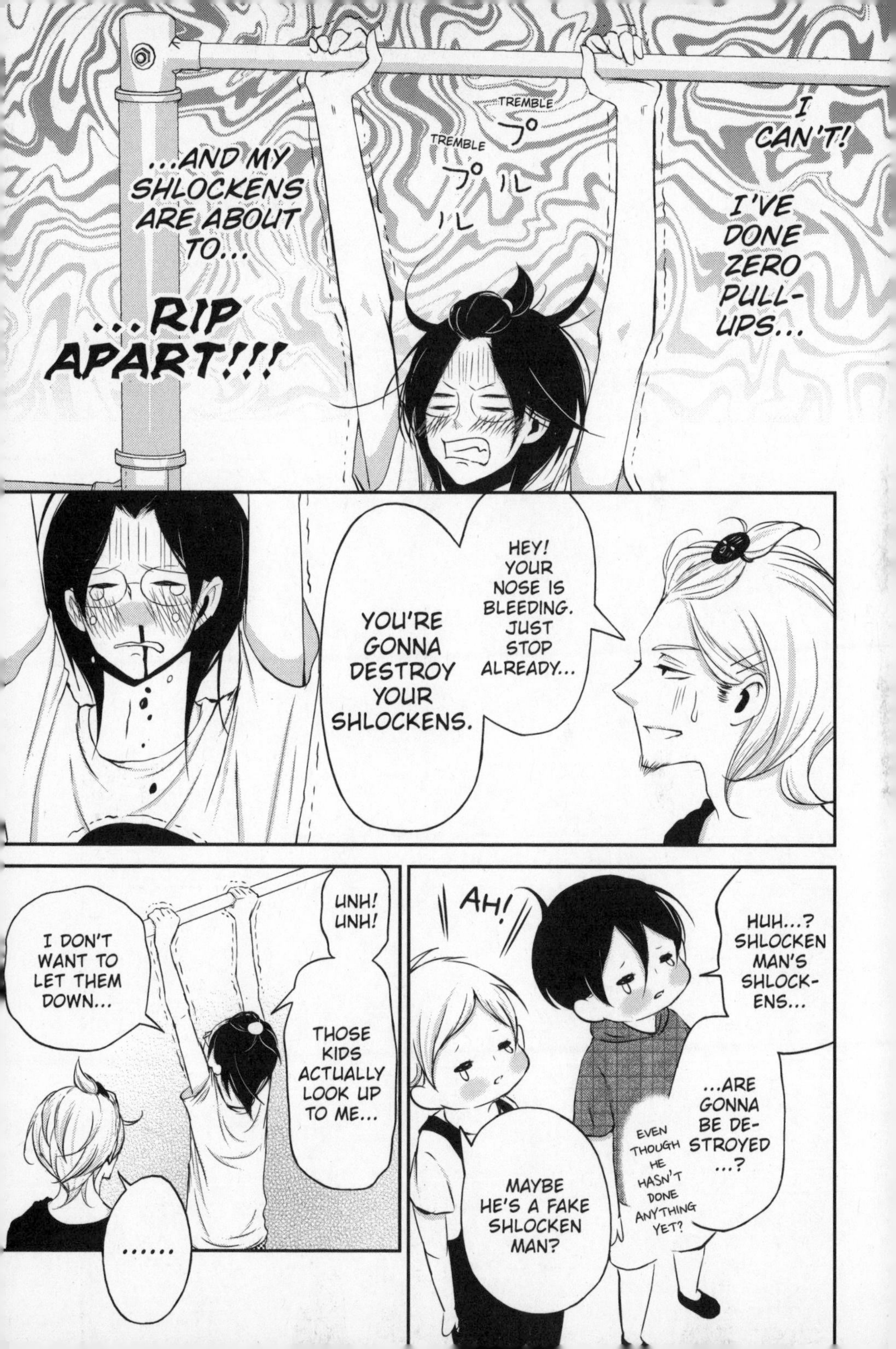
I CAN'T!
I'VE DONE ZERO PULL-UPS...
TREMBLE
TREMBLE
...AND MY SHLOCKENS ARE ABOUT TO...
...RIP APART!!!
HEY! YOUR NOSE IS BLEEDING. JUST STOP ALREADY...
YOU'RE GONNA DESTROY YOUR SHLOCKENS.
AH!
HUH...? SHLOCKEN MAN'S SHLOCK-ENS...
...ARE GONNA BE DE-STROYED ...?
EVEN THOUGH HE HASN'T DONE ANYTHING YET?
MAYBE HE'S A FAKE SHLOCKEN MAN?
UNH! UNH!
I DON'T WANT TO LET THEM DOWN...
THOSE KIDS ACTUALLY LOOK UP TO ME...
......

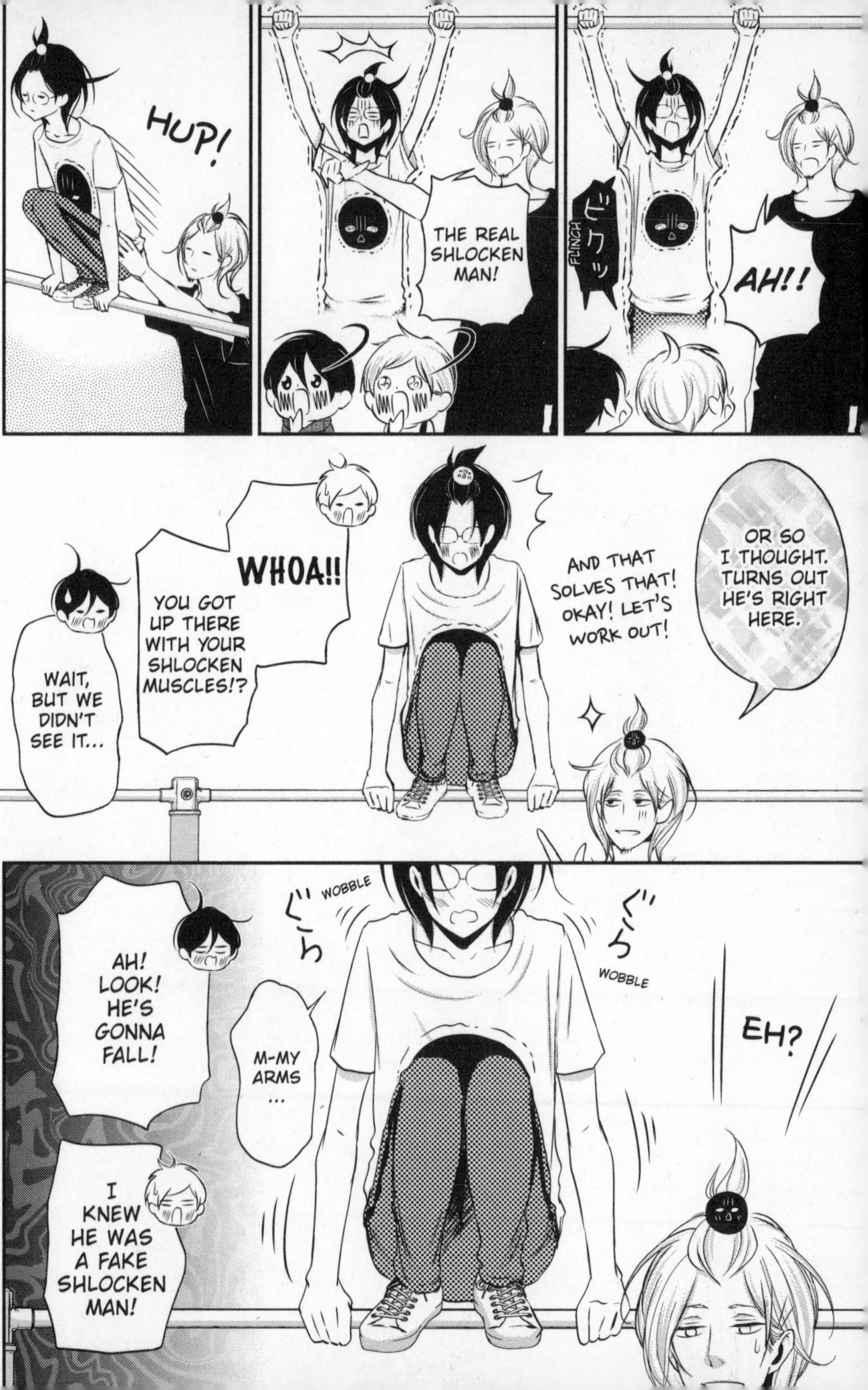

ビクッ
FLINCH
AH!!
THE REAL SHLOCKEN MAN!
HUP!
OR SO I THOUGHT. TURNS OUT HE'S RIGHT HERE.
AND THAT SOLVES THAT! OKAY! LET'S WORK OUT!
WHOA!!
YOU GOT UP THERE WITH YOUR SHLOCKEN MUSCLES!?
WAIT, BUT WE DIDN'T SEE IT...
EH?
ぐら
WOBBLE
ぐら
WOBBLE
M-MY ARMS ...
AH! LOOK! HE'S GONNA FALL!
I KNEW HE WAS A FAKE SHLOCKEN MAN!

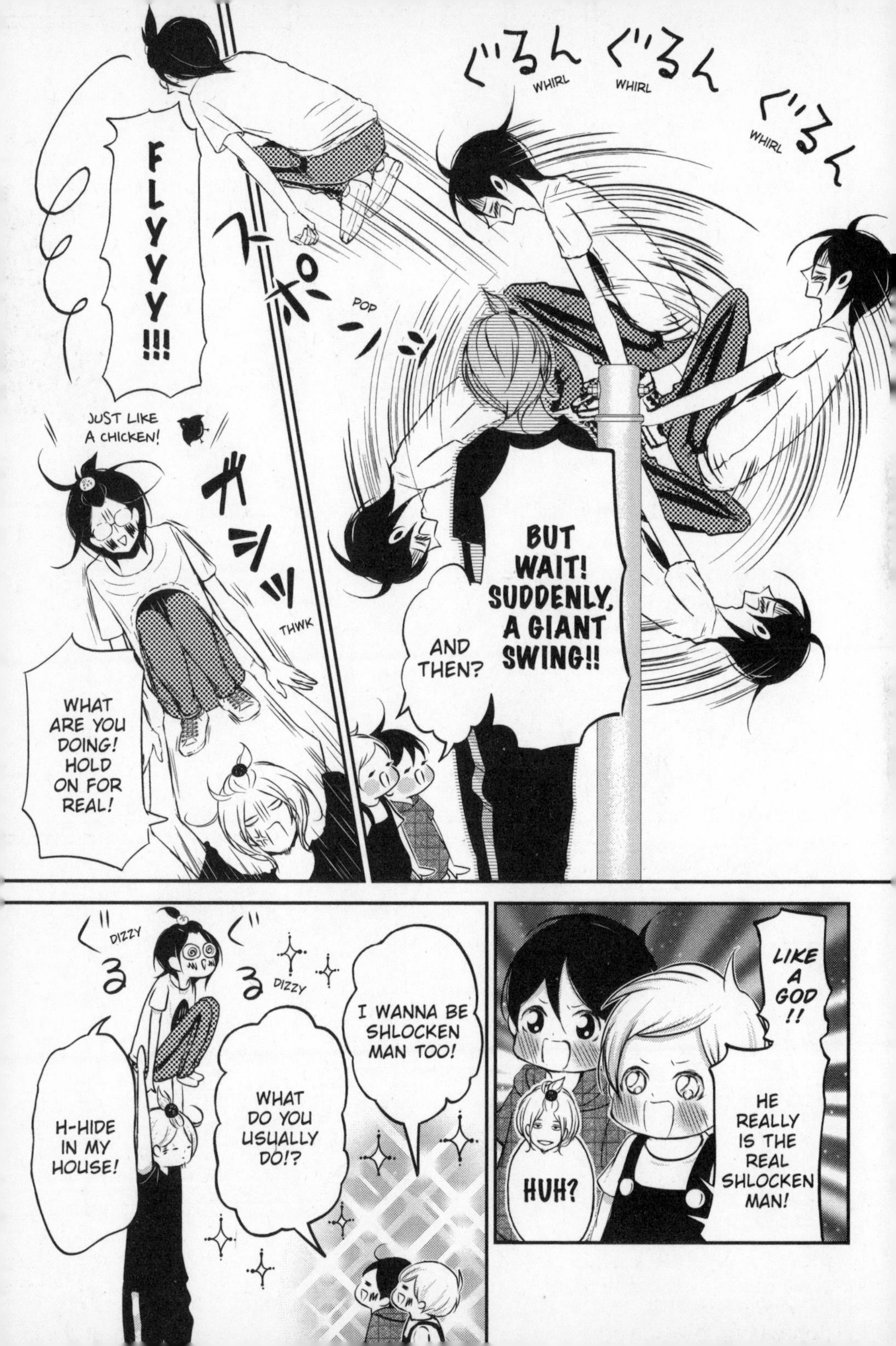

ぐるん ぐるん ぐるん
WHIRL
WHIRL
WHIRL
BUT WAIT! SUDDENLY, A GIANT SWING!!
AND THEN?
スポーン
POP
FLYYY!!!
JUST LIKE A CHICKEN!
ガシッ
THWK
WHAT ARE YOU DOING! HOLD ON FOR REAL!
LIKE A GOD!!
HE REALLY IS THE REAL SHLOCKEN MAN!
HUH?
I WANNA BE SHLOCKEN MAN TOO!
WHAT DO YOU USUALLY DO!?
ぐる
DIZZY
ぐる
DIZZY
H-HIDE IN MY HOUSE!

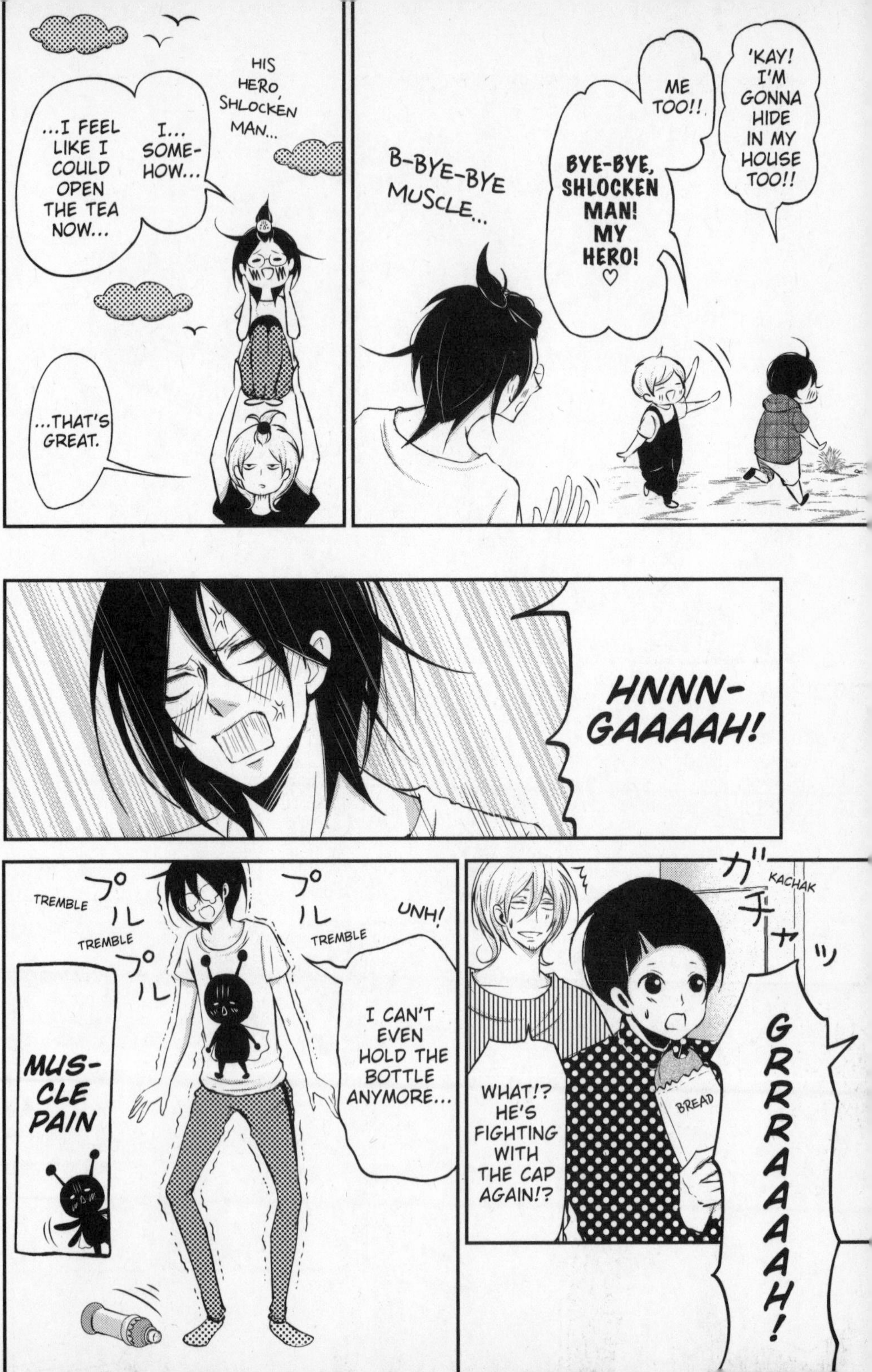
'KAY! I'M GONNA HIDE IN MY HOUSE TOO!!
ME TOO!!
BYE-BYE, SHLOCKEN MAN! MY HERO! ♡
B-BYE-BYE MUSCLE...
HIS HERO, SHLOCKEN MAN...
I... SOME-HOW...
...I FEEL LIKE I COULD OPEN THE TEA NOW...
...THAT'S GREAT.
HNNN-GAAAAH!
ガチャッ
KACHAK
GRRRAAAAAH!
WHAT!? HE'S FIGHTING WITH THE CAP AGAIN!?
BREAD
UNH!
プル TREMBLE
プル TREMBLE
プル TREMBLE
I CAN'T EVEN HOLD THE BOTTLE ANYMORE...
MUS-CLE PAIN

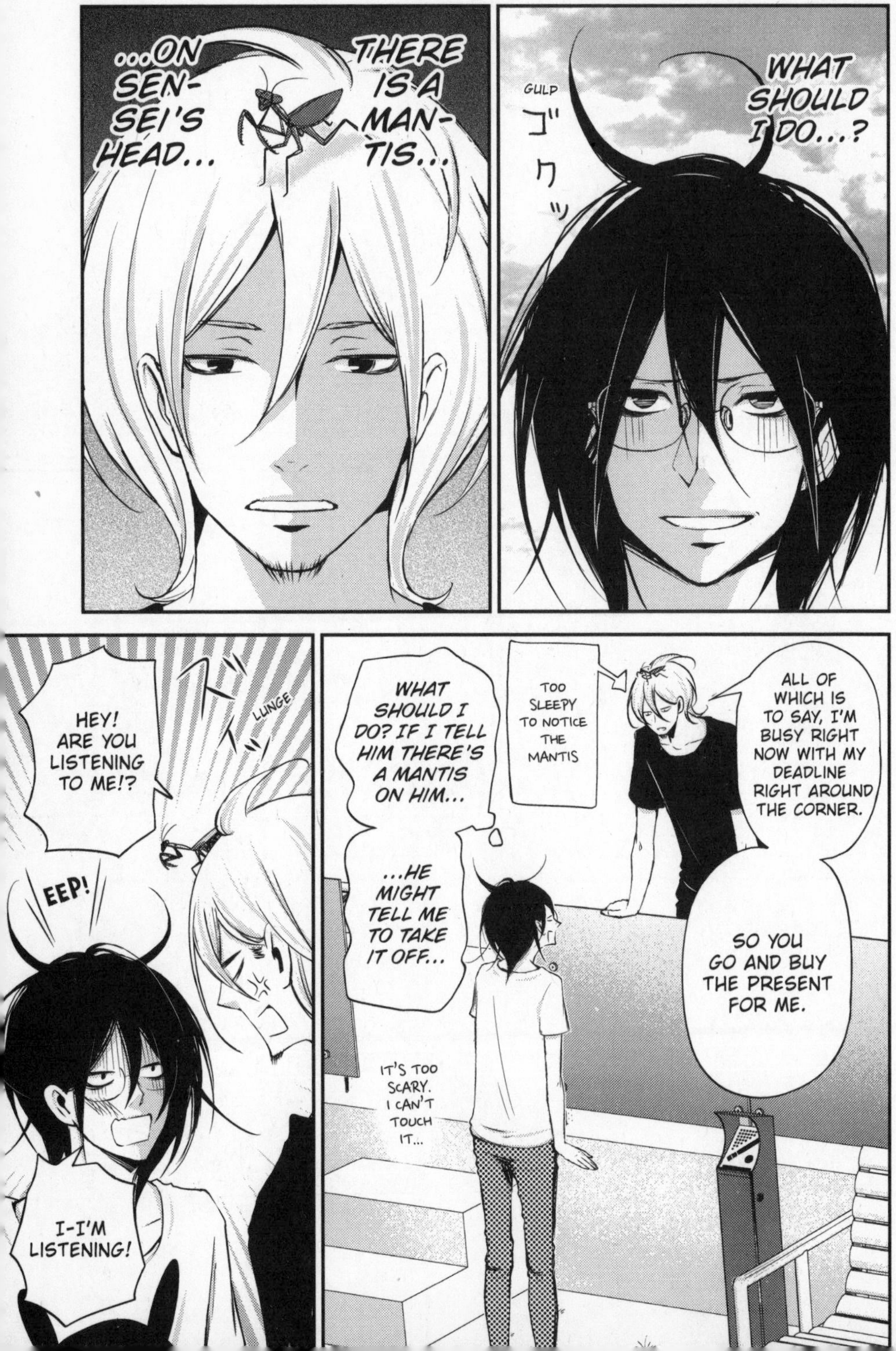
WHAT SHOULD I DO...?
GULP
ゴクッ
THERE IS A MANTIS...
...ON SEN-SEI'S HEAD...
ALL OF WHICH IS TO SAY, I'M BUSY RIGHT NOW WITH MY DEADLINE RIGHT AROUND THE CORNER.
TOO SLEEPY TO NOTICE THE MANTIS
WHAT SHOULD I DO? IF I TELL HIM THERE'S A MANTIS ON HIM...
...HE MIGHT TELL ME TO TAKE IT OFF...
SO YOU GO AND BUY THE PRESENT FOR ME.
IT'S TOO SCARY. I CAN'T TOUCH IT...
LUNGE
HEY! ARE YOU LISTENING TO ME!?
EEP!
I-I'M LISTENING!

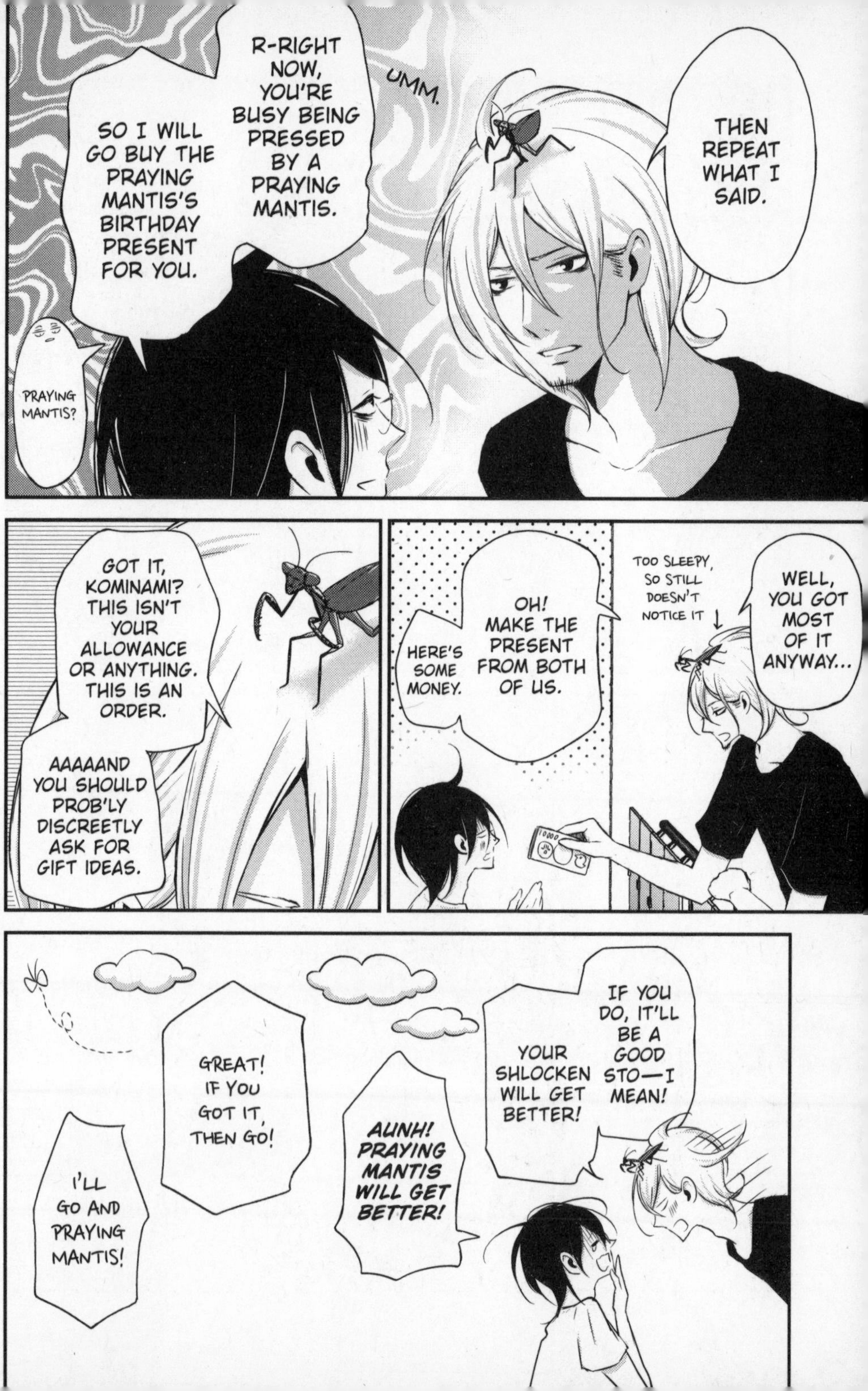
THEN REPEAT WHAT I SAID.
UMM.
R-RIGHT NOW, YOU'RE BUSY BEING PRESSED BY A PRAYING MANTIS.
SO I WILL GO BUY THE PRAYING MANTIS'S BIRTHDAY PRESENT FOR YOU.
PRAYING MANTIS?
WELL, YOU GOT MOST OF IT ANYWAY...
TOO SLEEPY, SO STILL DOESN'T NOTICE IT
OH! MAKE THE PRESENT FROM BOTH OF US.
HERE'S SOME MONEY.
GOT IT, KOMINAMI? THIS ISN'T YOUR ALLOWANCE OR ANYTHING. THIS IS AN ORDER.
AAAAAND YOU SHOULD PROB'LY DISCREETLY ASK FOR GIFT IDEAS.
IF YOU DO, IT'LL BE A GOOD STO—I MEAN!
YOUR SHLOCKEN WILL GET BETTER!
AUNH! PRAYING MANTIS WILL GET BETTER!
GREAT! IF YOU GOT IT, THEN GO!
I'LL GO AND PRAYING MANTIS!

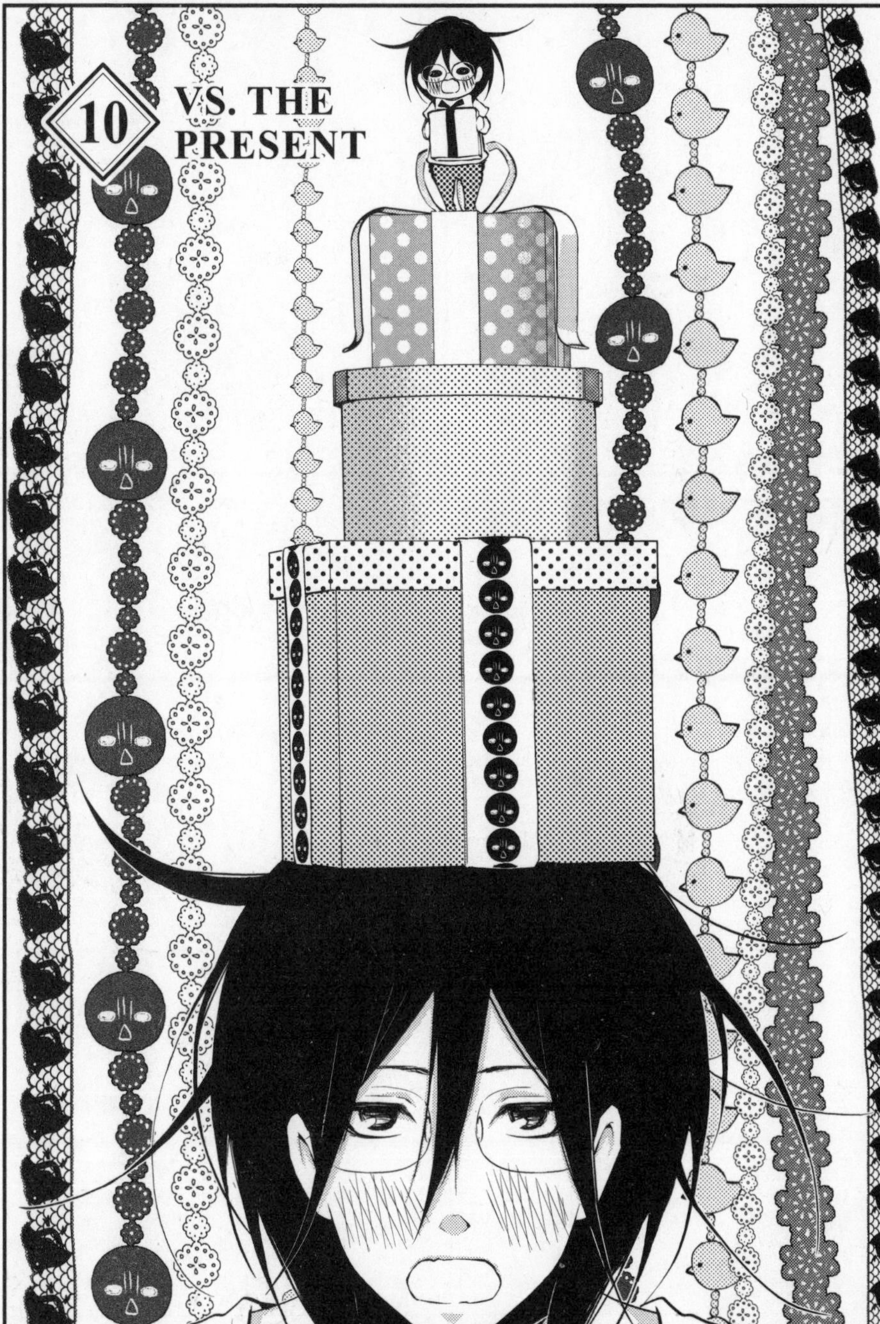
10
VS. THE
PRESENT

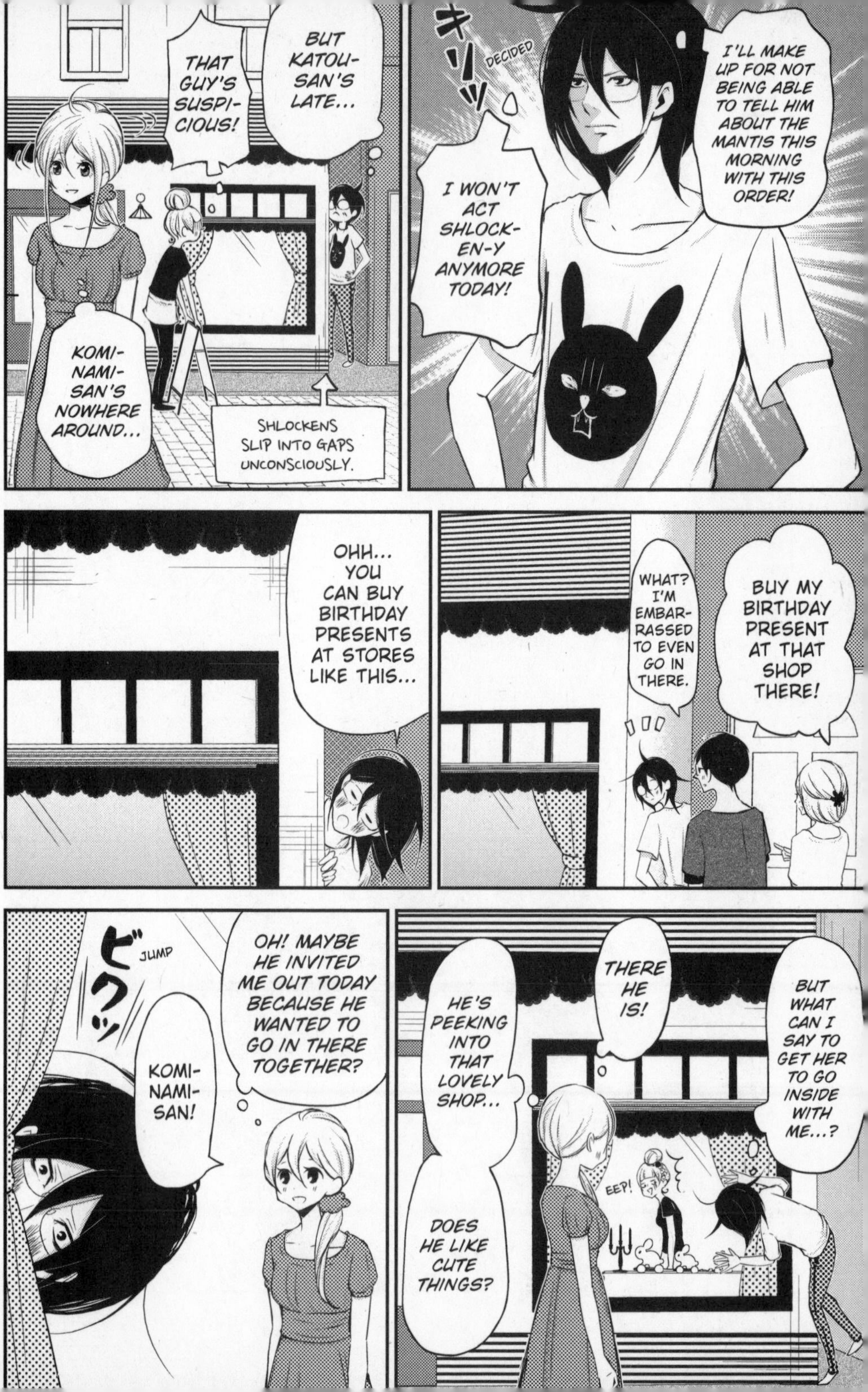
キッ
DECIDED
I'LL MAKE UP FOR NOT BEING ABLE TO TELL HIM ABOUT THE MANTIS THIS MORNING WITH THIS ORDER!
I WON'T ACT SHLOCK-EN-Y ANYMORE TODAY!
BUT KATOU-SAN'S LATE...
THAT GUY'S SUSPICIOUS!
KOMI-NAMI-SAN'S NOWHERE AROUND...
SHLOCKENS SLIP INTO GAPS UNCONSCIOUSLY.
BUY MY BIRTHDAY PRESENT AT THAT SHOP THERE!
WHAT? I'M EMBARRASSED TO EVEN GO IN THERE.
OHH... YOU CAN BUY BIRTHDAY PRESENTS AT STORES LIKE THIS...
BUT WHAT CAN I SAY TO GET HER TO GO INSIDE WITH ME...?
THERE HE IS!
HE'S PEEKING INTO THAT LOVELY SHOP...
EEP!
DOES HE LIKE CUTE THINGS?
OH! MAYBE HE INVITED ME OUT TODAY BECAUSE HE WANTED TO GO IN THERE TOGETHER?
ビクッ
JUMP
KOMI-NAMI-SAN!

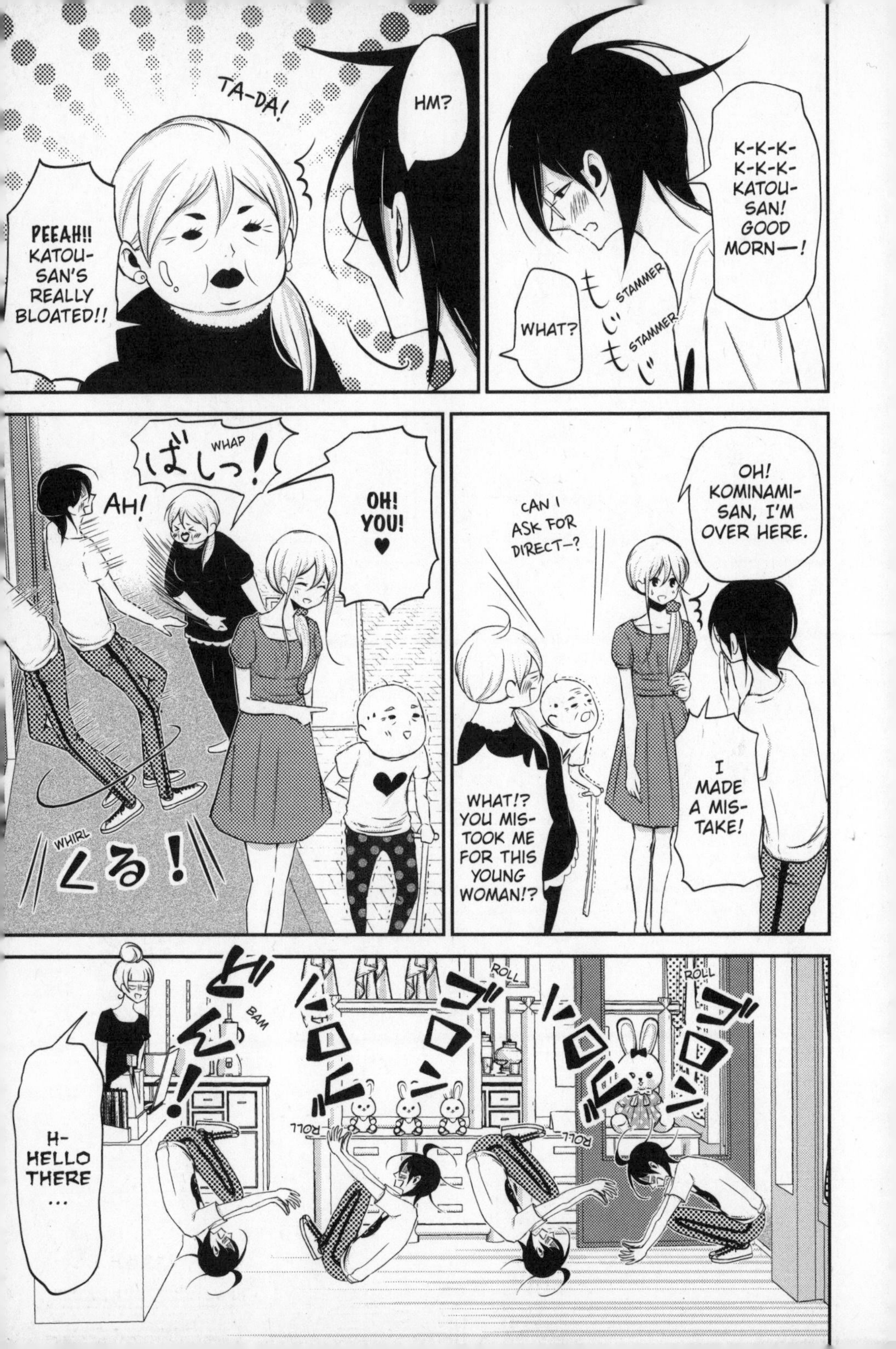
K-K-K-K-K-K-KATOU-SAN! GOOD MORN—!
もじ STAMMER
もじ STAMMER
WHAT?
HM?
TA-DA!
PEEAH!! KATOU-SAN'S REALLY BLOATED!!
OH! KOMINAMI-SAN, I'M OVER HERE.
CAN I ASK FOR DIRECT—?
I MADE A MISTAKE!
WHAT!? YOU MISTOOK ME FOR THIS YOUNG WOMAN!?
ばしっ! WHAP
OH! YOU! ♥
AH!
くる! WHIRL
ゴロン ROLL
ゴロン ROLL
ROLL
ROLL
どん! BAM
H-HELLO THERE ...

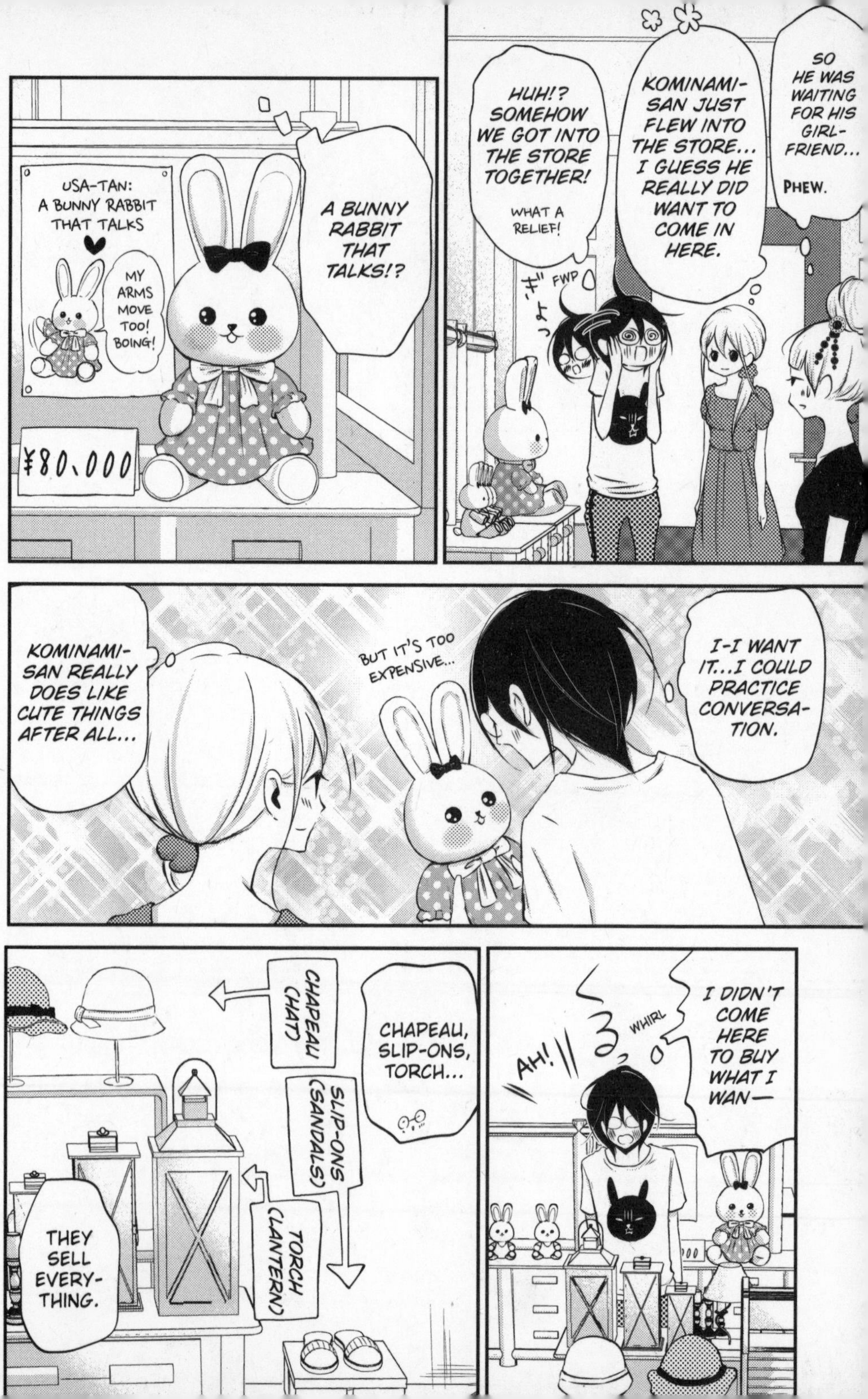
SO HE WAS WAITING FOR HIS GIRL-FRIEND... PHEW.
KOMINAMI-SAN JUST FLEW INTO THE STORE... I GUESS HE REALLY DID WANT TO COME IN HERE.
HUH!? SOMEHOW WE GOT INTO THE STORE TOGETHER!
WHAT A RELIEF!
FWP
A BUNNY RABBIT THAT TALKS!?
USA-TAN: A BUNNY RABBIT THAT TALKS
MY ARMS MOVE TOO! BOING!
¥80,000
I-I WANT IT...I COULD PRACTICE CONVERSA-TION.
BUT IT'S TOO EXPENSIVE...
KOMINAMI-SAN REALLY DOES LIKE CUTE THINGS AFTER ALL...
I DIDN'T COME HERE TO BUY WHAT I WAN—
WHIRL
AH!
CHAPEAU, SLIP-ONS, TORCH...
CHAPEAU (HAT)
SLIP-ONS (SANDALS)
TORCH (LANTERN)
THEY SELL EVERY-THING.

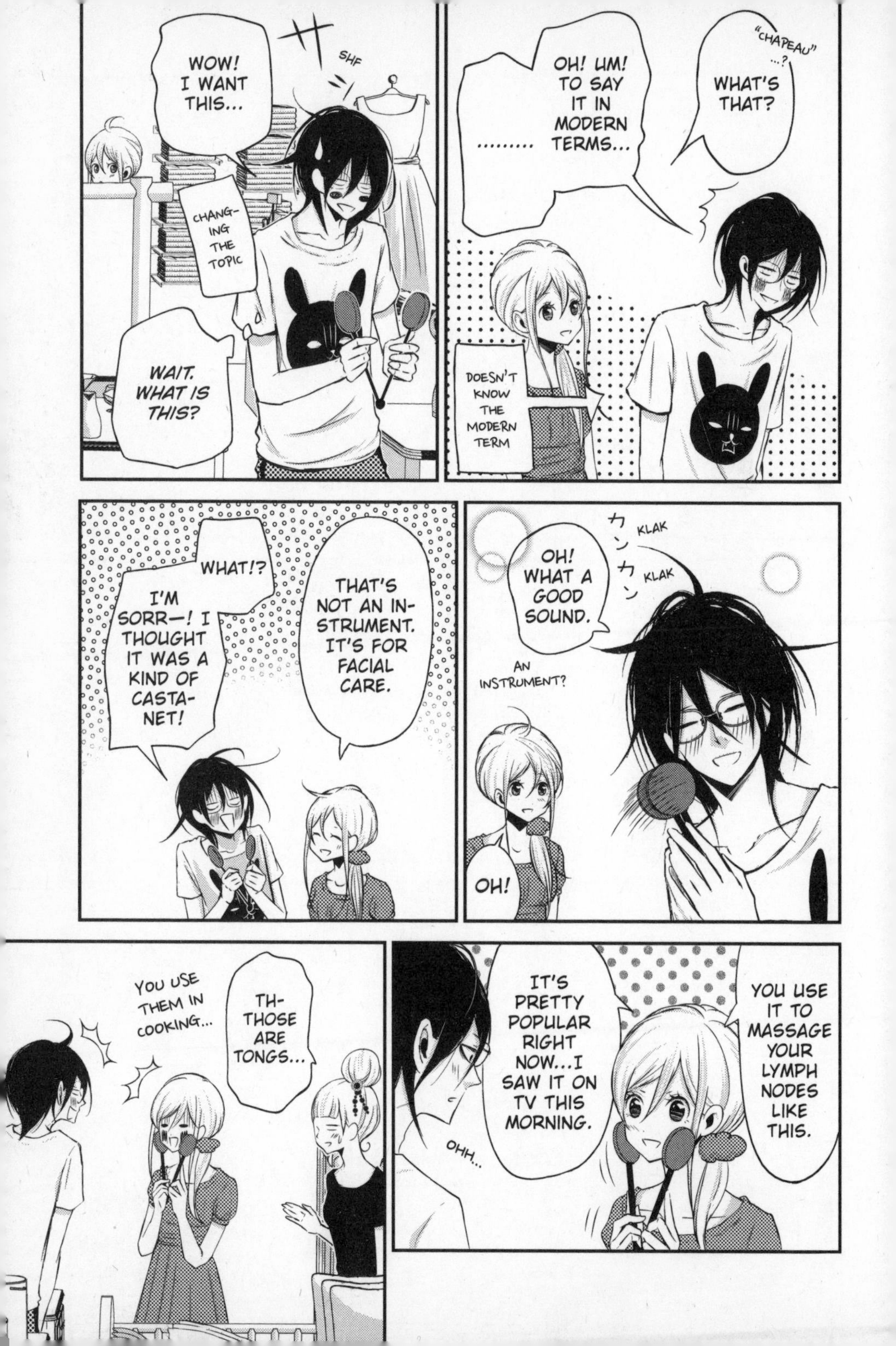
"CHAPEAU" ...?
WHAT'S THAT?
OH! UM! TO SAY IT IN MODERN TERMS...
....
DOESN'T KNOW THE MODERN TERM
WOW! I WANT THIS...
SHF
CHANGING THE TOPIC
WAIT. WHAT IS THIS?
カン KLAK
カン KLAK
OH! WHAT A GOOD SOUND.
AN INSTRUMENT?
OH!
THAT'S NOT AN INSTRUMENT. IT'S FOR FACIAL CARE.
WHAT!?
I'M SORR—! I THOUGHT IT WAS A KIND OF CASTANET!
YOU USE IT TO MASSAGE YOUR LYMPH NODES LIKE THIS.
IT'S PRETTY POPULAR RIGHT NOW...I SAW IT ON TV THIS MORNING.
OHH...
TH-THOSE ARE TONGS...
YOU USE THEM IN COOKING...

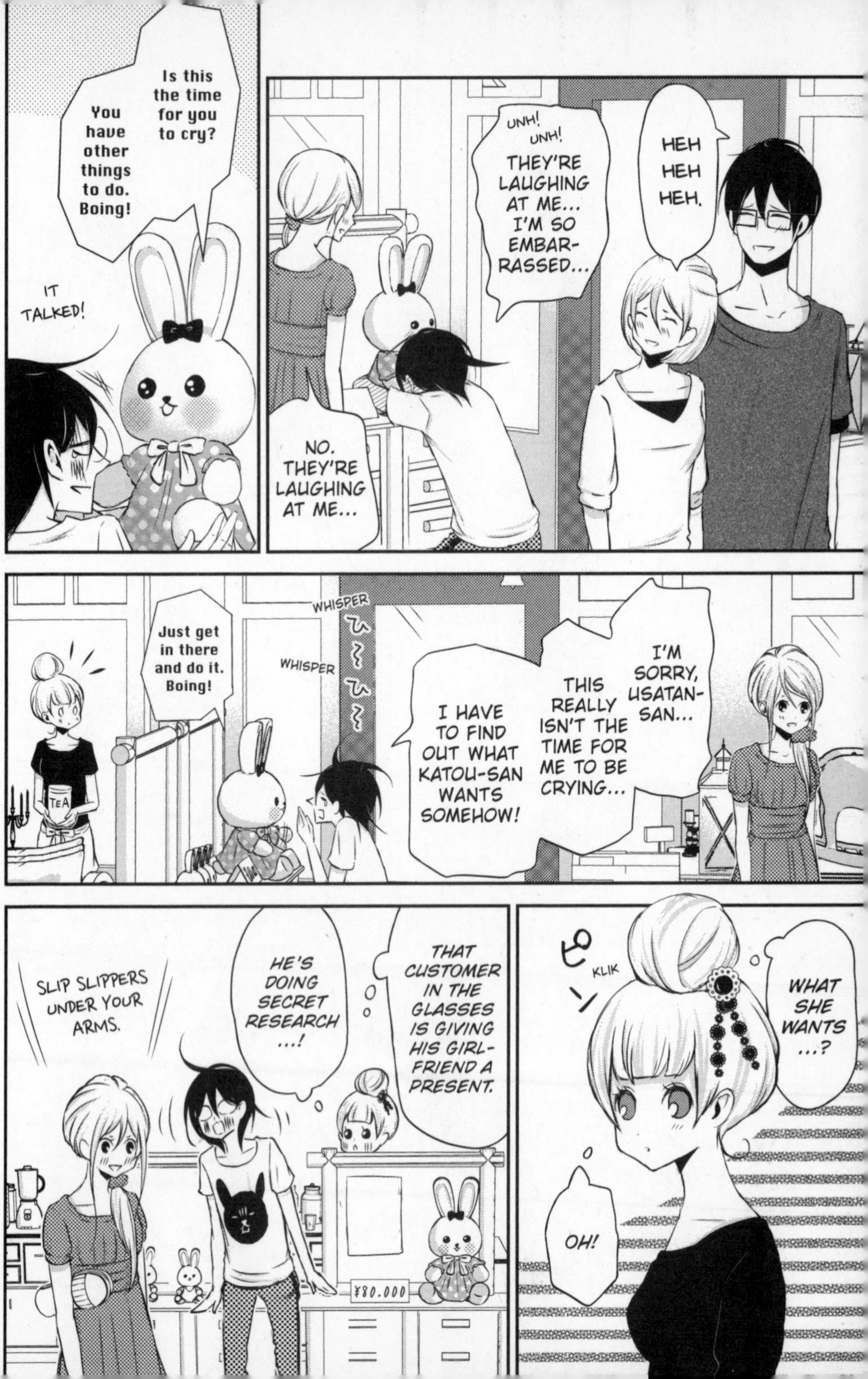
HEH HEH HEH.
UNH! UNH! THEY'RE LAUGHING AT ME... I'M SO EMBARRASSED...
NO. THEY'RE LAUGHING AT ME...
Is this the time for you to cry?
You have other things to do. Boing!
IT TALKED!
I'M SORRY, USATAN-SAN...
THIS REALLY ISN'T THE TIME FOR ME TO BE CRYING...
I HAVE TO FIND OUT WHAT KATOU-SAN WANTS SOMEHOW!
WHISPER
ひ~ひ~
WHISPER
Just get in there and do it. Boing!
TEA
WHAT SHE WANTS...?
ピン
KLIK
OH!
THAT CUSTOMER IN THE GLASSES IS GIVING HIS GIRLFRIEND A PRESENT.
HE'S DOING SECRET RESEARCH...!
SLIP SLIPPERS UNDER YOUR ARMS.
¥80.000

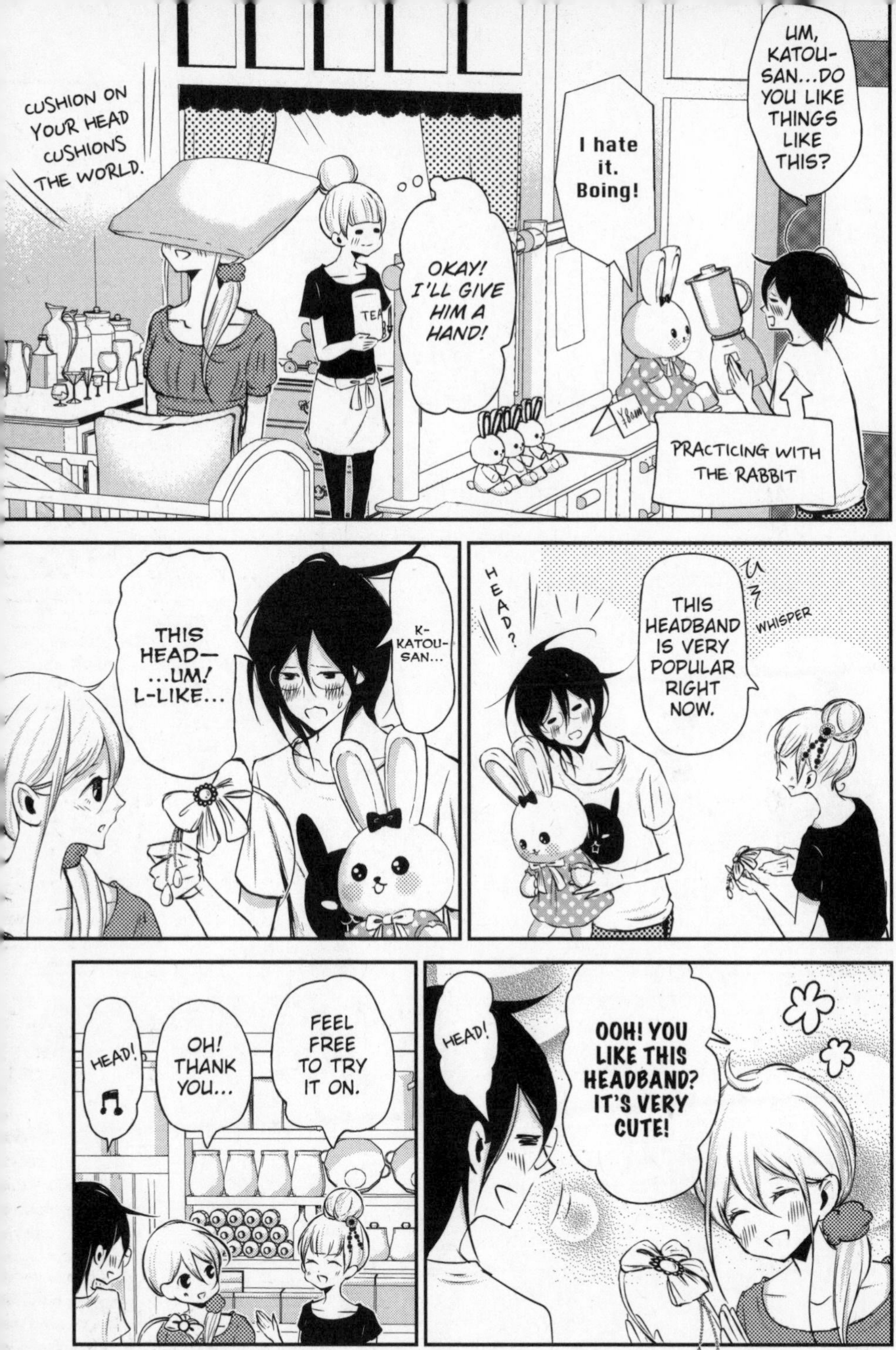
UM, KATOU-SAN...DO YOU LIKE THINGS LIKE THIS?
I hate it. Boing!
PRACTICING WITH THE RABBIT
OKAY! I'LL GIVE HIM A HAND!
CUSHION ON YOUR HEAD CUSHIONS THE WORLD.
THIS HEADBAND IS VERY POPULAR RIGHT NOW.
WHISPER
HEAD?
K-KATOU-SAN...
THIS HEAD—...UM! L-LIKE...
OOH! YOU LIKE THIS HEADBAND? IT'S VERY CUTE!
HEAD!
FEEL FREE TO TRY IT ON.
OH! THANK YOU...
HEAD! ♪

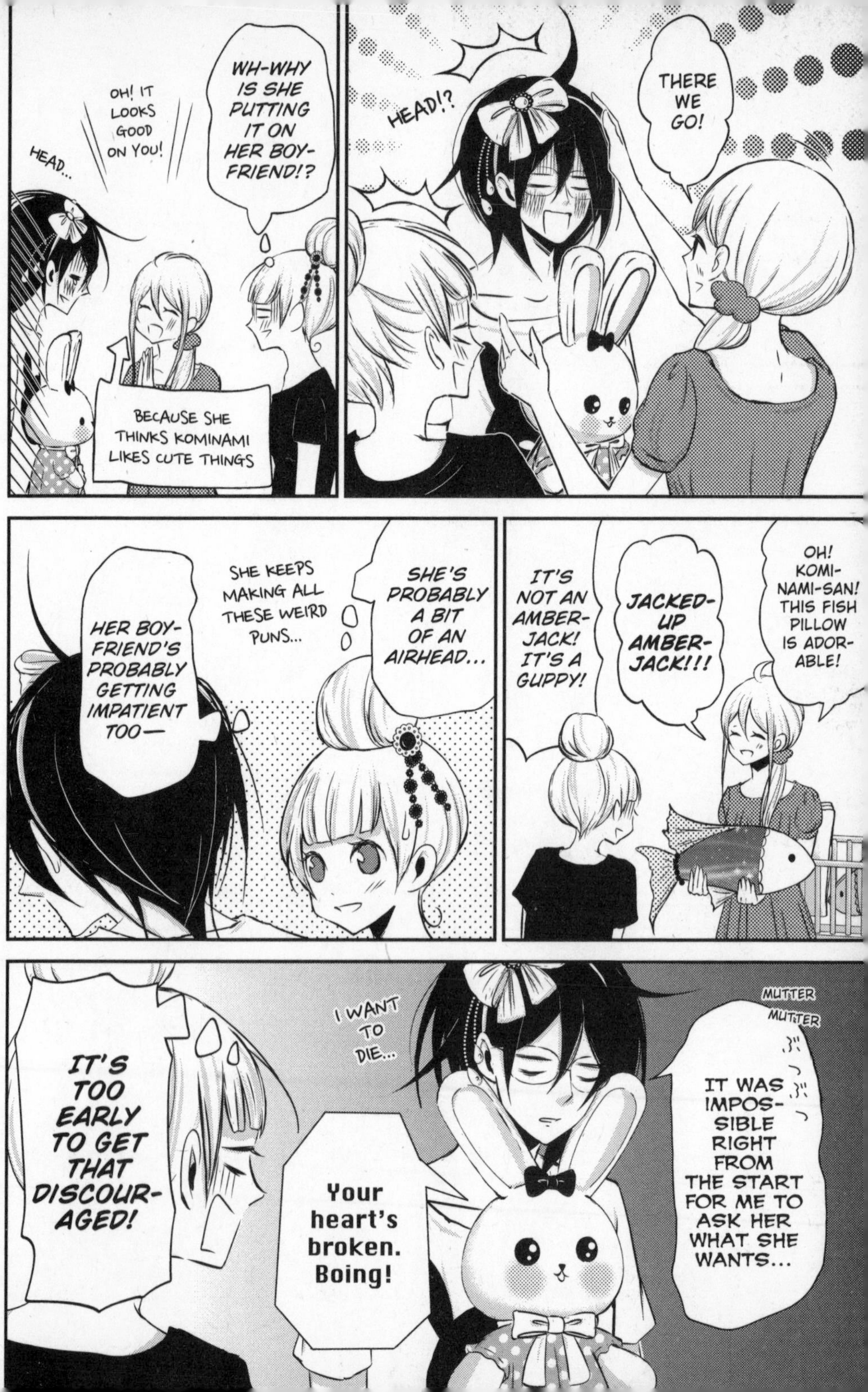
THERE WE GO!
HEAD!?
WH-WHY IS SHE PUTTING IT ON HER BOY-FRIEND!?
OH! IT LOOKS GOOD ON YOU!
HEAD...
BECAUSE SHE THINKS KOMINAMI LIKES CUTE THINGS
OH! KOMI-NAMI-SAN! THIS FISH PILLOW IS ADORABLE!
JACKED-UP AMBER-JACK!!!
IT'S NOT AN AMBER-JACK! IT'S A GUPPY!
SHE'S PROBABLY A BIT OF AN AIRHEAD...
SHE KEEPS MAKING ALL THESE WEIRD PUNS...
HER BOY-FRIEND'S PROBABLY GETTING IMPATIENT TOO—
MUTTER MUTTER
IT WAS IMPOS-SIBLE RIGHT FROM THE START FOR ME TO ASK HER WHAT SHE WANTS...
I WANT TO DIE...
Your heart's broken. Boing!
IT'S TOO EARLY TO GET THAT DISCOUR-AGED!

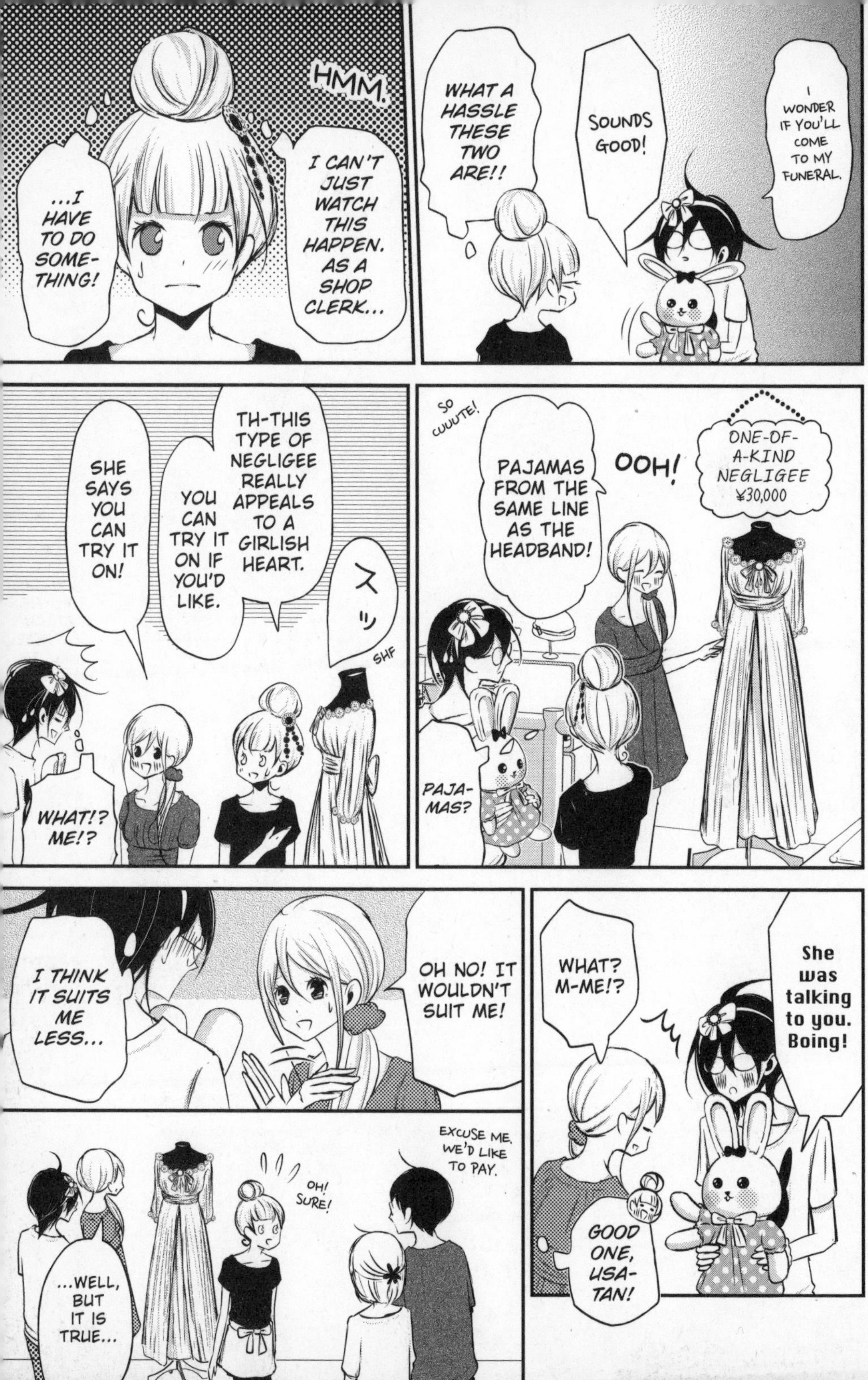
I WONDER IF YOU'LL COME TO MY FUNERAL.
SOUNDS GOOD!
WHAT A HASSLE THESE TWO ARE!!
HMM.
I CAN'T JUST WATCH THIS HAPPEN. AS A SHOP CLERK...
...I HAVE TO DO SOMETHING!
ONE-OF-A-KIND NEGLIGEE ¥30,000
OOH!
PAJAMAS FROM THE SAME LINE AS THE HEADBAND!
SO CUUUTE!
PAJAMAS?
スッ
SHF
TH-THIS TYPE OF NEGLIGEE REALLY APPEALS TO A GIRLISH HEART.
YOU CAN TRY IT ON IF YOU'D LIKE.
SHE SAYS YOU CAN TRY IT ON!
WHAT!? ME!?
She was talking to you. Boing!
WHAT? M-ME!?
GOOD ONE, USA-TAN!
OH NO! IT WOULDN'T SUIT ME!
I THINK IT SUITS ME LESS...
EXCUSE ME. WE'D LIKE TO PAY.
OH! SURE!
...WELL, BUT IT IS TRUE...

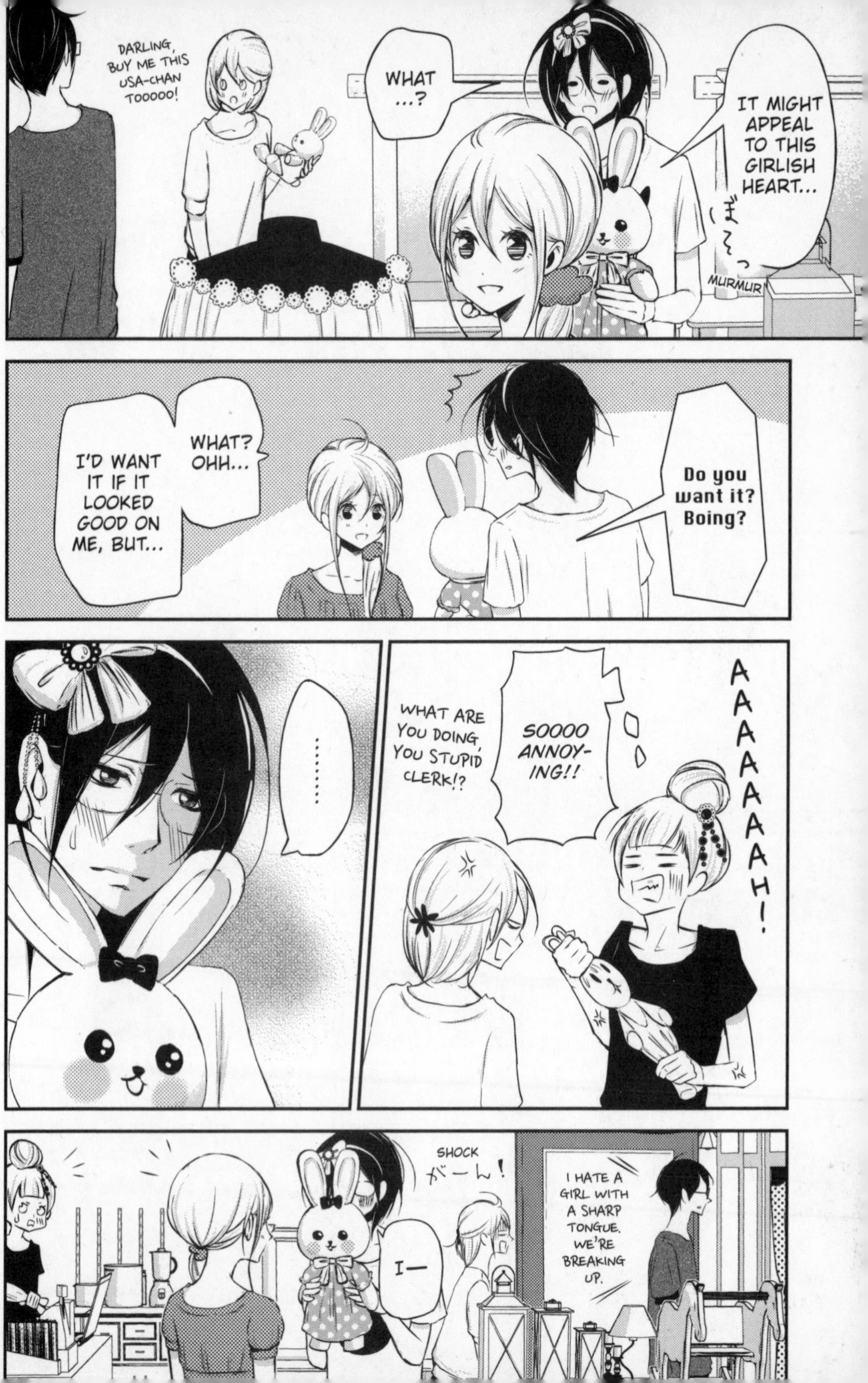
IT MIGHT APPEAL TO THIS GIRLISH HEART...
ぼそっ
MURMUR
WHAT ...?
DARLING, BUY ME THIS USA-CHAN TOOOOO!
Do you want it? Boing?
WHAT? OHH...
I'D WANT IT IF IT LOOKED GOOD ON ME, BUT...
AAAAAAAH!
SOOOO ANNOY-ING!!
WHAT ARE YOU DOING, YOU STUPID CLERK!?
......
I HATE A GIRL WITH A SHARP TONGUE. WE'RE BREAKING UP.
がーん!
SHOCK
I—

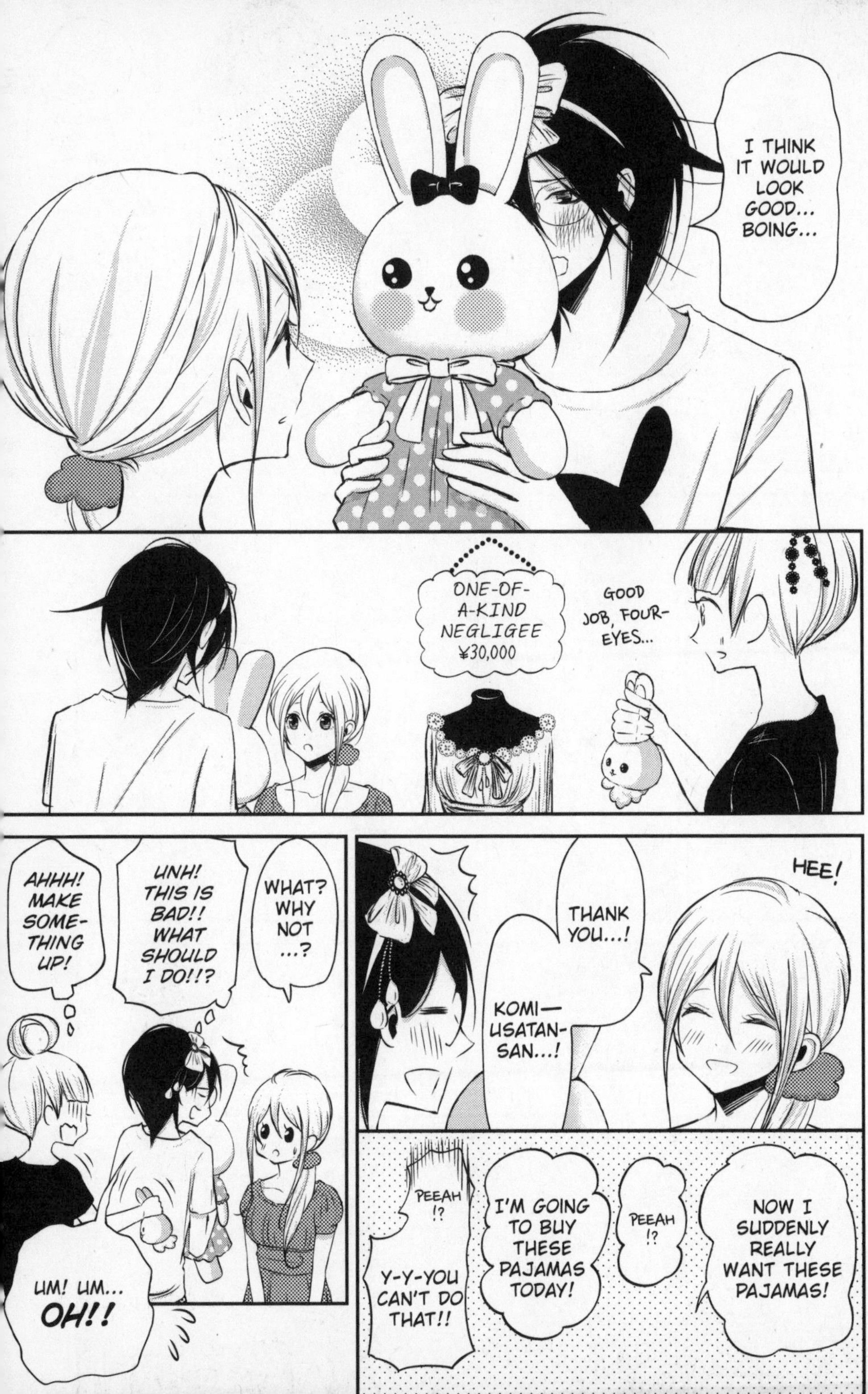
I THINK IT WOULD LOOK GOOD... BOING...
GOOD JOB, FOUR-EYES...
ONE-OF-A-KIND NEGLIGEE ¥30,000
HEE!
THANK YOU...!
KOMI-USATAN-SAN...!
NOW I SUDDENLY REALLY WANT THESE PAJAMAS!
PEEAH !?
I'M GOING TO BUY THESE PAJAMAS TODAY!
PEEAH !?
Y-Y-YOU CAN'T DO THAT!!
WHAT? WHY NOT ...?
UNH! THIS IS BAD!! WHAT SHOULD I DO!!?
AHHH! MAKE SOMETHING UP!
UM! UM... OH!!

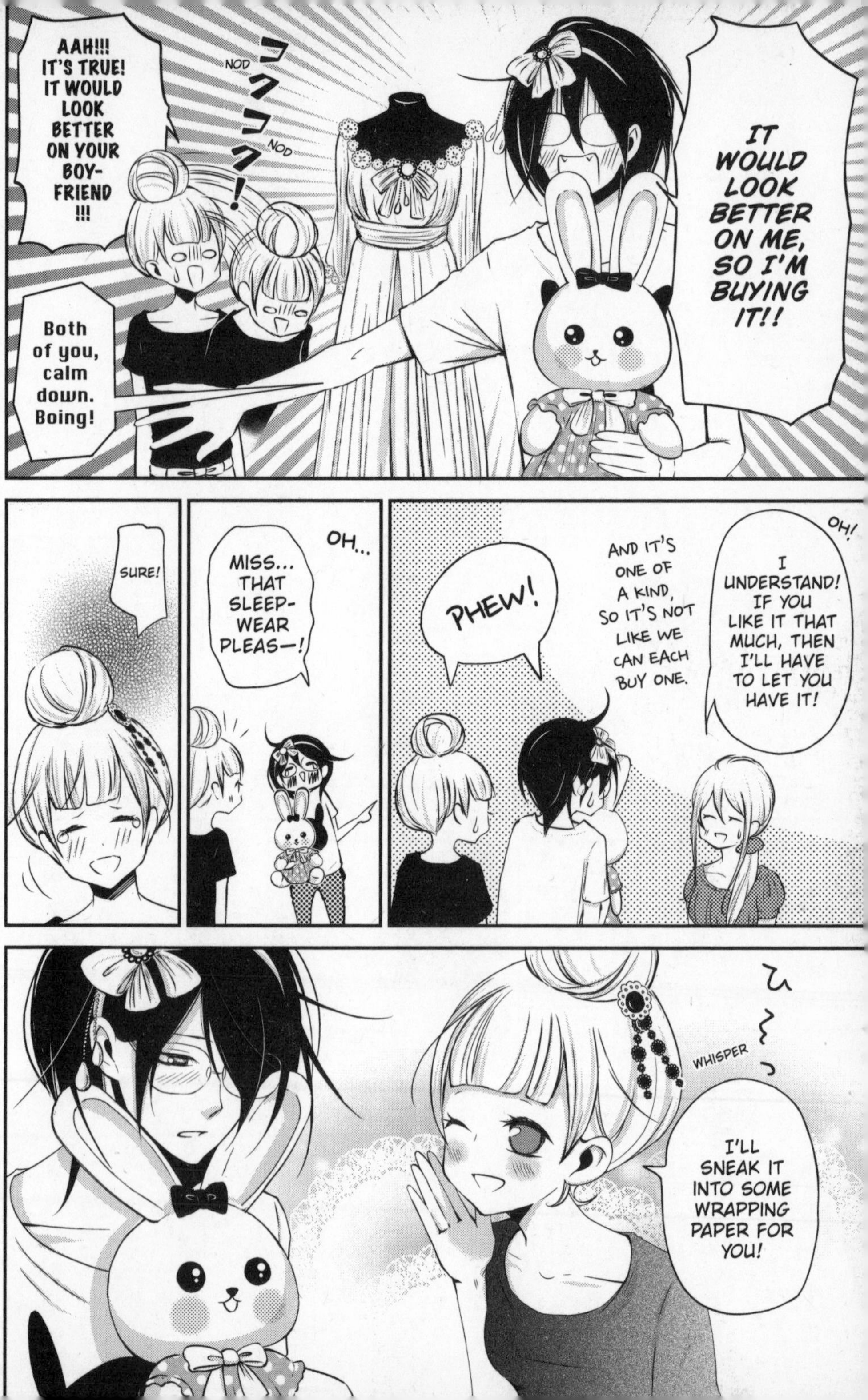
IT WOULD LOOK BETTER ON ME, SO I'M BUYING IT!!
コクコク!
NOD NOD
AAH!!! IT'S TRUE! IT WOULD LOOK BETTER ON YOUR BOY-FRIEND!!!
Both of you, calm down. Boing!
OH!
I UNDERSTAND! IF YOU LIKE IT THAT MUCH, THEN I'LL HAVE TO LET YOU HAVE IT!
AND IT'S ONE OF A KIND, SO IT'S NOT LIKE WE CAN EACH BUY ONE.
PHEW!
OH...
MISS... THAT SLEEP-WEAR PLEAS—!
SURE!
WHISPER
I'LL SNEAK IT INTO SOME WRAPPING PAPER FOR YOU!

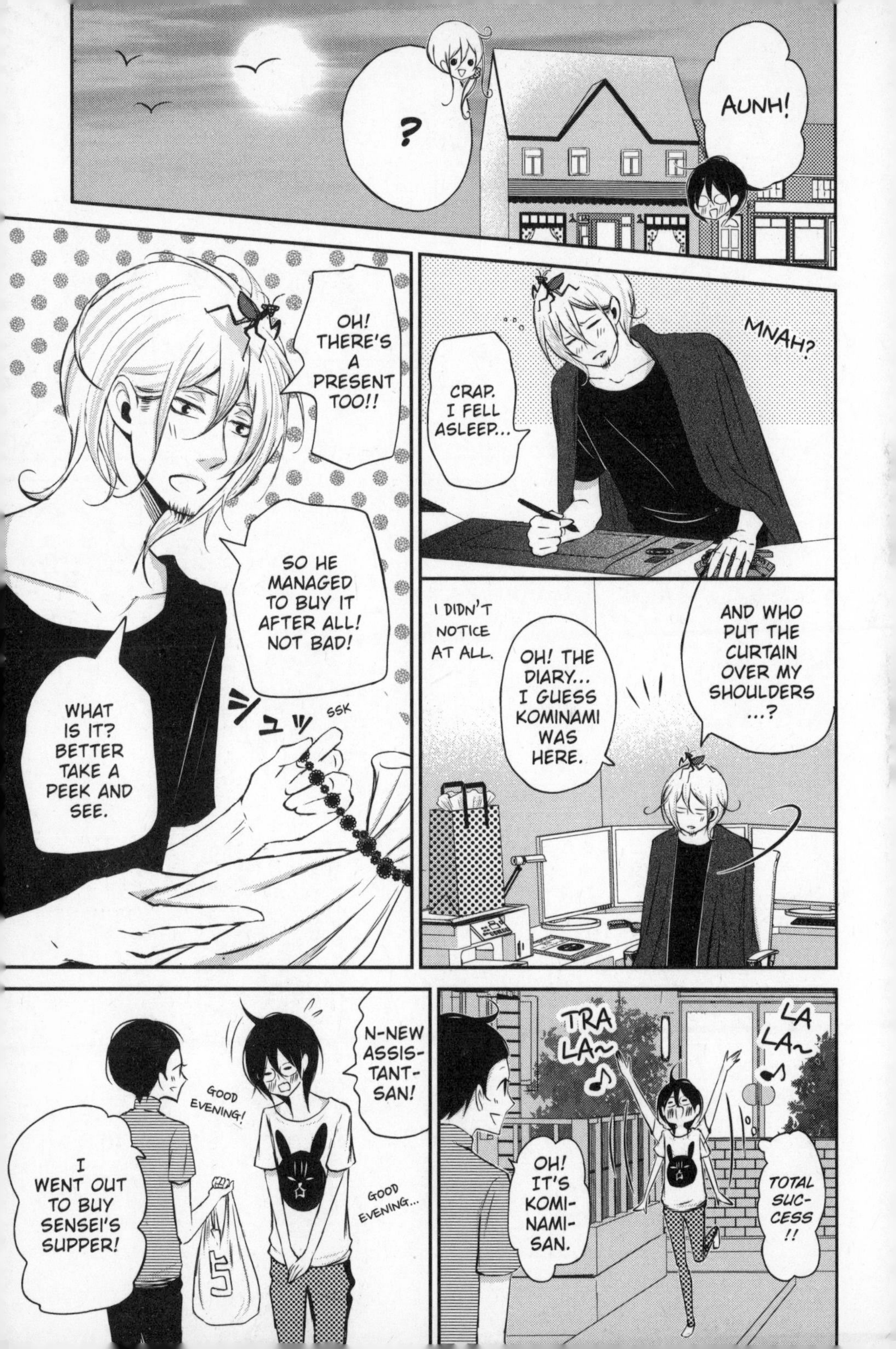
AUNH!
?
MNAH?
CRAP. I FELL ASLEEP...
AND WHO PUT THE CURTAIN OVER MY SHOULDERS ...?
OH! THE DIARY... I GUESS KOMINAMI WAS HERE.
I DIDN'T NOTICE AT ALL.
OH! THERE'S A PRESENT TOO!!
SO HE MANAGED TO BUY IT AFTER ALL! NOT BAD!
シュッ
SSK
WHAT IS IT? BETTER TAKE A PEEK AND SEE.
LA LA~
TRA LA~
TOTAL SUC-CESS!!
OH! IT'S KOMI-NAMI-SAN.
N-NEW ASSIS-TANT-SAN!
GOOD EVENING!
GOOD EVENING...
I WENT OUT TO BUY SENSEI'S SUPPER!

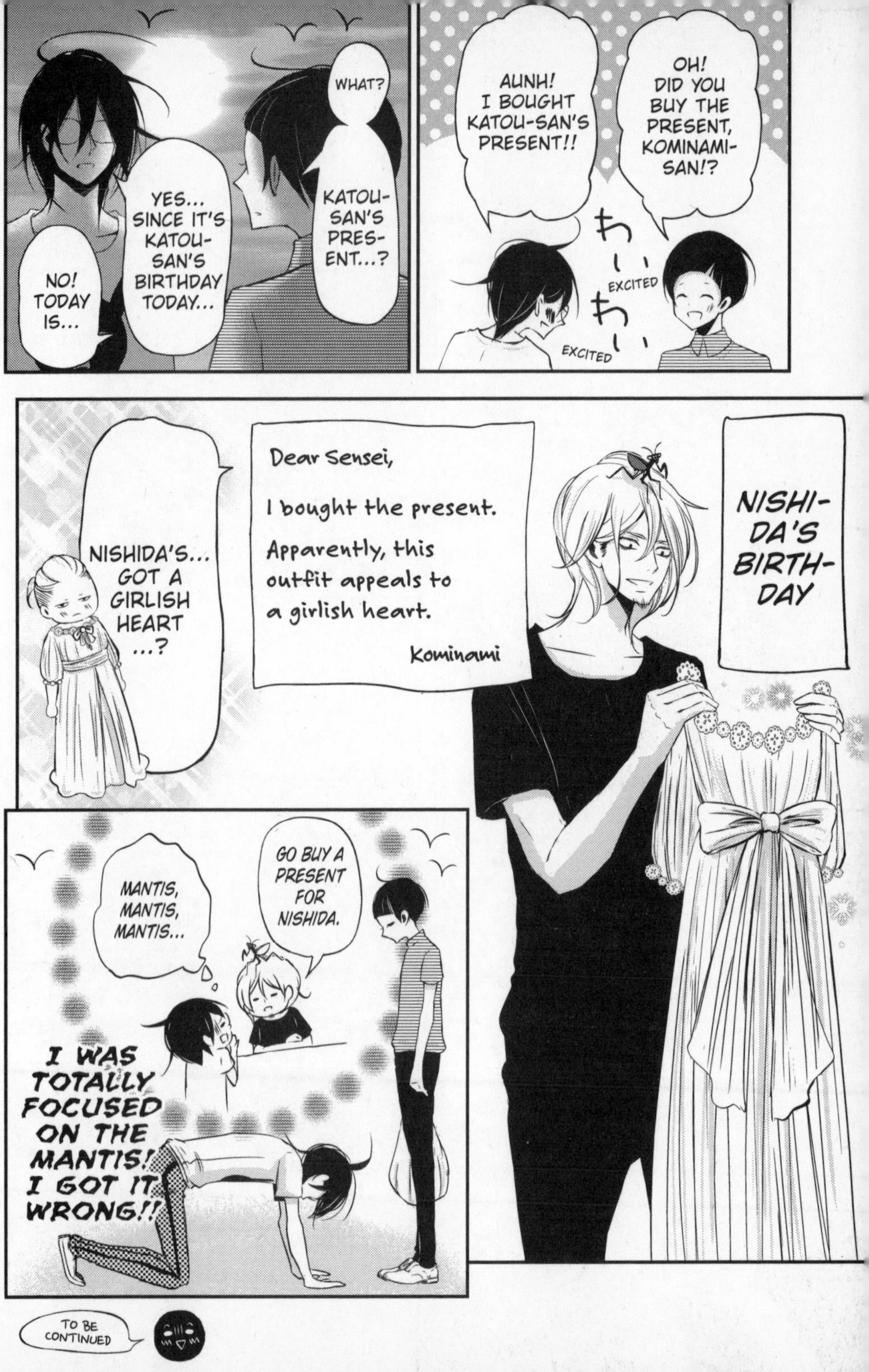
OH! DID YOU BUY THE PRESENT, KOMINAMI-SAN!?
AUNH! I BOUGHT KATOU-SAN'S PRESENT!!
わい EXCITED
わい EXCITED
WHAT?
KATOU-SAN'S PRESENT...?
YES... SINCE IT'S KATOU-SAN'S BIRTHDAY TODAY...
NO! TODAY IS...
NISHIDA'S BIRTHDAY
Dear Sensei,
I bought the present.
Apparently, this outfit appeals to a girlish heart.
Kominami
NISHIDA'S... GOT A GIRLISH HEART ...?
GO BUY A PRESENT FOR NISHIDA.
MANTIS, MANTIS, MANTIS...
I WAS TOTALLY FOCUSED ON THE MANTIS! I GOT IT WRONG!!
TO BE CONTINUED

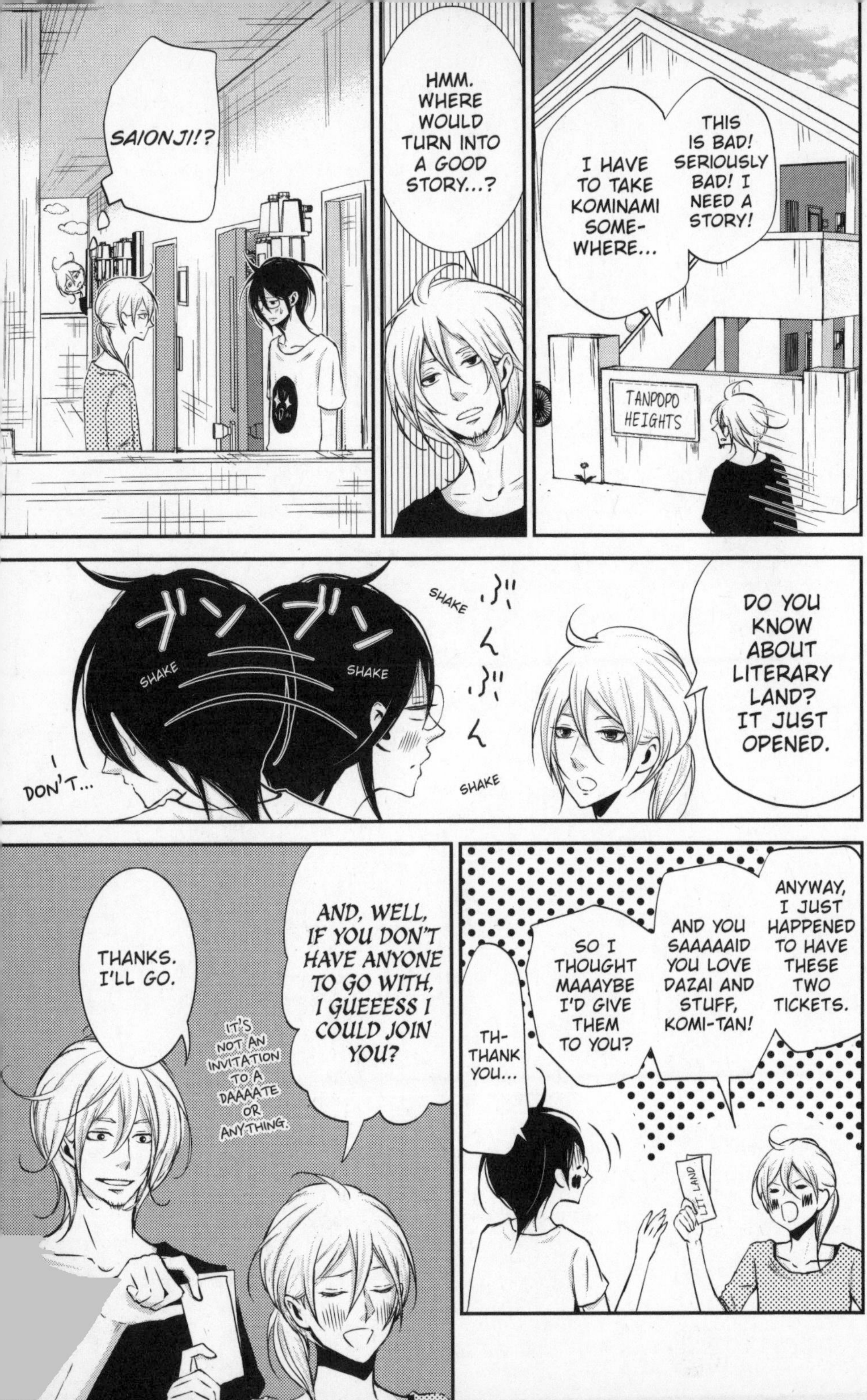
THIS IS BAD! SERIOUSLY BAD! I NEED A STORY!
I HAVE TO TAKE KOMINAMI SOMEWHERE...
TANPOPO HEIGHTS
HMM. WHERE WOULD TURN INTO A GOOD STORY...?
SAIONJI!?
DO YOU KNOW ABOUT LITERARY LAND? IT JUST OPENED.
ぶんぶん
SHAKE
SHAKE
ブンブン
SHAKE
SHAKE
I DON'T...
ANYWAY, I JUST HAPPENED TO HAVE THESE TWO TICKETS.
AND YOU SAAAAAID YOU LOVE DAZAI AND STUFF, KOMI-TAN!
SO I THOUGHT MAAAYBE I'D GIVE THEM TO YOU?
TH-THANK YOU...
LIT. LAND
AND, WELL, IF YOU DON'T HAVE ANYONE TO GO WITH, I GUEEESS I COULD JOIN YOU?
IT'S NOT AN INVITATION TO A DAAAATE OR ANYTHING.
THANKS. I'LL GO.

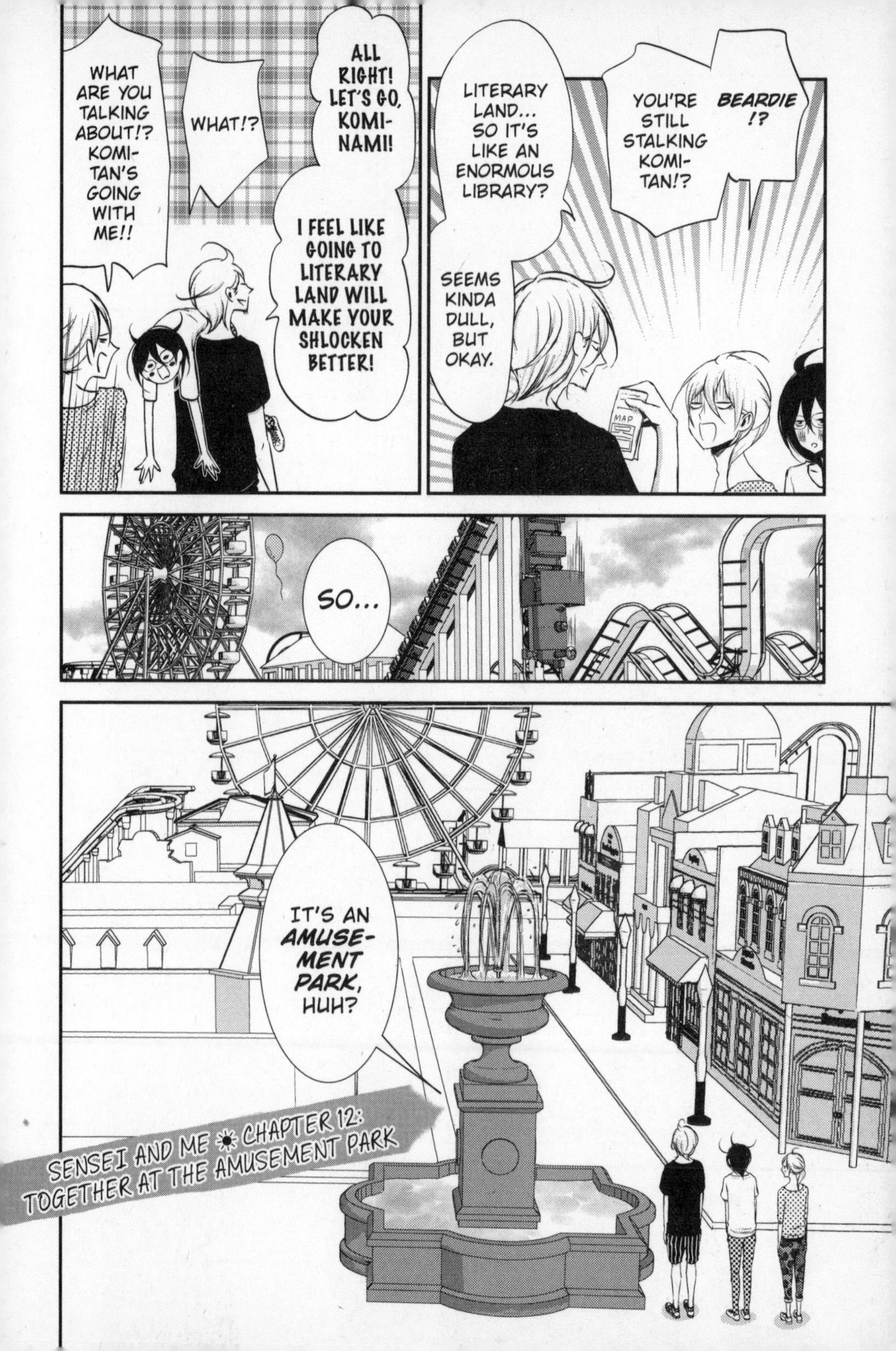
BEARDIE!?
YOU'RE STILL STALKING KOMI-TAN!?
LITERARY LAND... SO IT'S LIKE AN ENORMOUS LIBRARY?
SEEMS KINDA DULL, BUT OKAY.
ALL RIGHT! LET'S GO, KOMI-NAMI!
I FEEL LIKE GOING TO LITERARY LAND WILL MAKE YOUR SHLOCKEN BETTER!
WHAT!?
WHAT ARE YOU TALKING ABOUT!? KOMI-TAN'S GOING WITH ME!!
SO...
IT'S AN AMUSEMENT PARK, HUH?
SENSEI AND ME ☀ CHAPTER 12: TOGETHER AT THE AMUSEMENT PARK

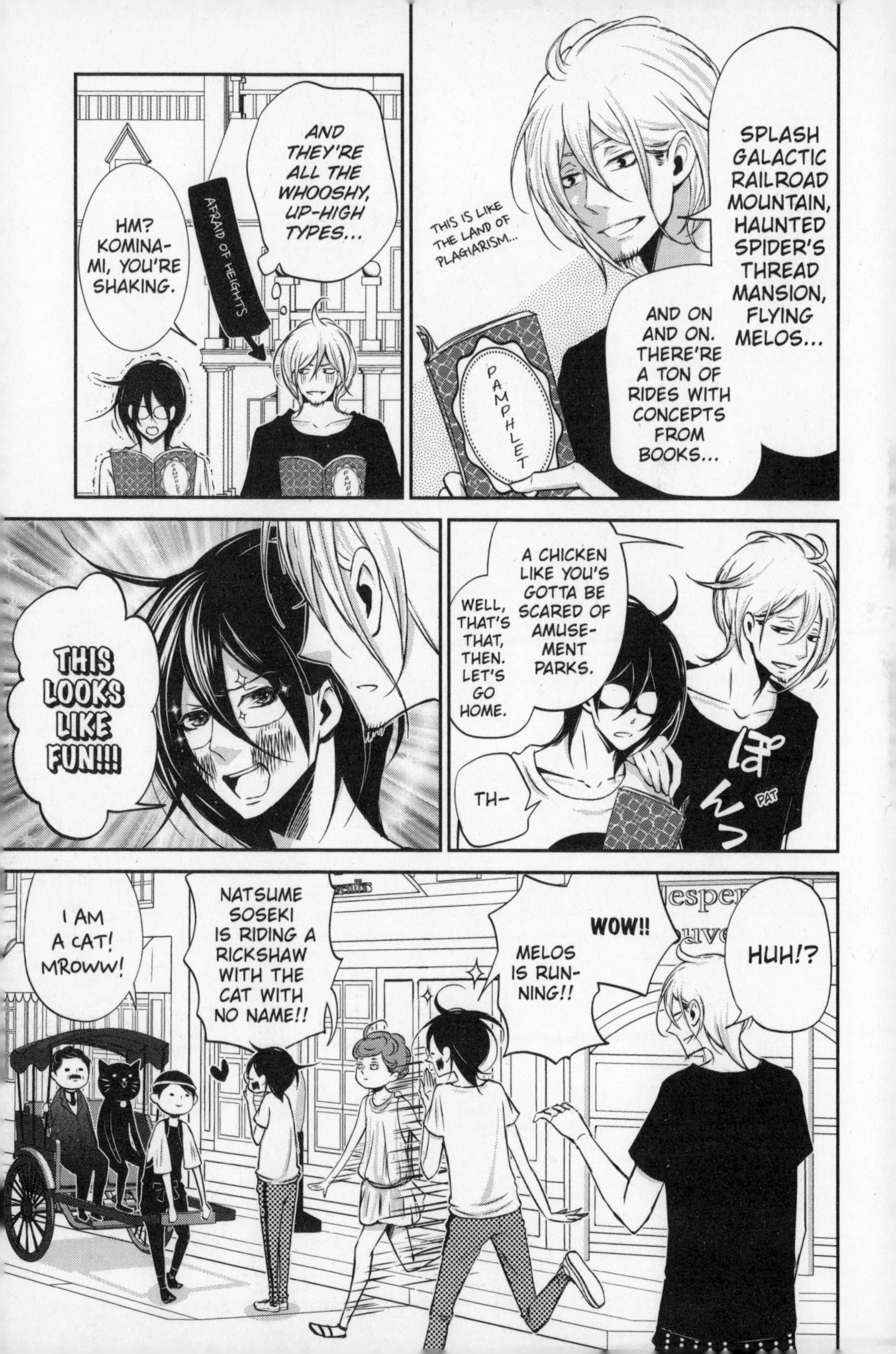
SPLASH GALACTIC RAILROAD MOUNTAIN, HAUNTED SPIDER'S THREAD MANSION, FLYING MELOS...
AND ON AND ON. THERE'RE A TON OF RIDES WITH CONCEPTS FROM BOOKS...
THIS IS LIKE THE LAND OF PLAGIARISM...
PAMPHLET
AND THEY'RE ALL THE WHOOSHY, UP-HIGH TYPES...
AFRAID OF HEIGHTS
HM? KOMINAMI, YOU'RE SHAKING.
A CHICKEN LIKE YOU'S GOTTA BE SCARED OF AMUSEMENT PARKS.
WELL, THAT'S THAT, THEN. LET'S GO HOME.
PAT
TH-
THIS LOOKS LIKE FUN!!!
HUH!?
WOW!!
MELOS IS RUNNING!!
NATSUME SOSEKI IS RIDING A RICKSHAW WITH THE CAT WITH NO NAME!!
I AM A CAT! MROWW!

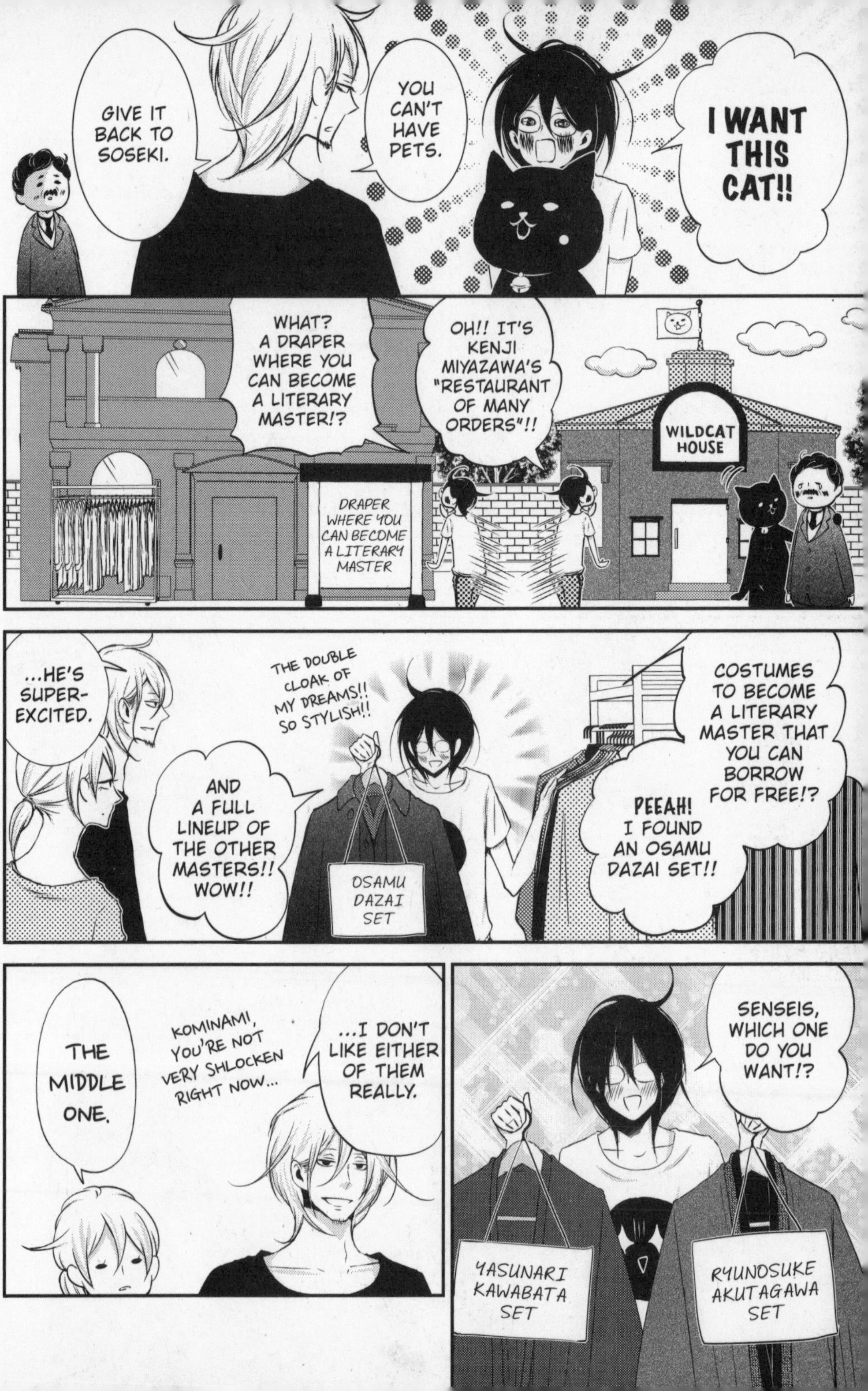
I WANT THIS CAT!!
YOU CAN'T HAVE PETS.
GIVE IT BACK TO SOSEKI.
OH!! IT'S KENJI MIYAZAWA'S "RESTAURANT OF MANY ORDERS"!!
WHAT? A DRAPER WHERE YOU CAN BECOME A LITERARY MASTER!?
WILDCAT HOUSE
DRAPER WHERE YOU CAN BECOME A LITERARY MASTER
COSTUMES TO BECOME A LITERARY MASTER THAT YOU CAN BORROW FOR FREE!?
PEEAH! I FOUND AN OSAMU DAZAI SET!!
THE DOUBLE CLOAK OF MY DREAMS!! SO STYLISH!!
...HE'S SUPER-EXCITED.
AND A FULL LINEUP OF THE OTHER MASTERS!! WOW!!
OSAMU DAZAI SET
SENSEIS, WHICH ONE DO YOU WANT!?
RYUNOSUKE AKUTAGAWA SET
YASUNARI KAWABATA SET
...I DON'T LIKE EITHER OF THEM REALLY.
KOMINAMI, YOU'RE NOT VERY SHLOCKEN RIGHT NOW...
THE MIDDLE ONE.

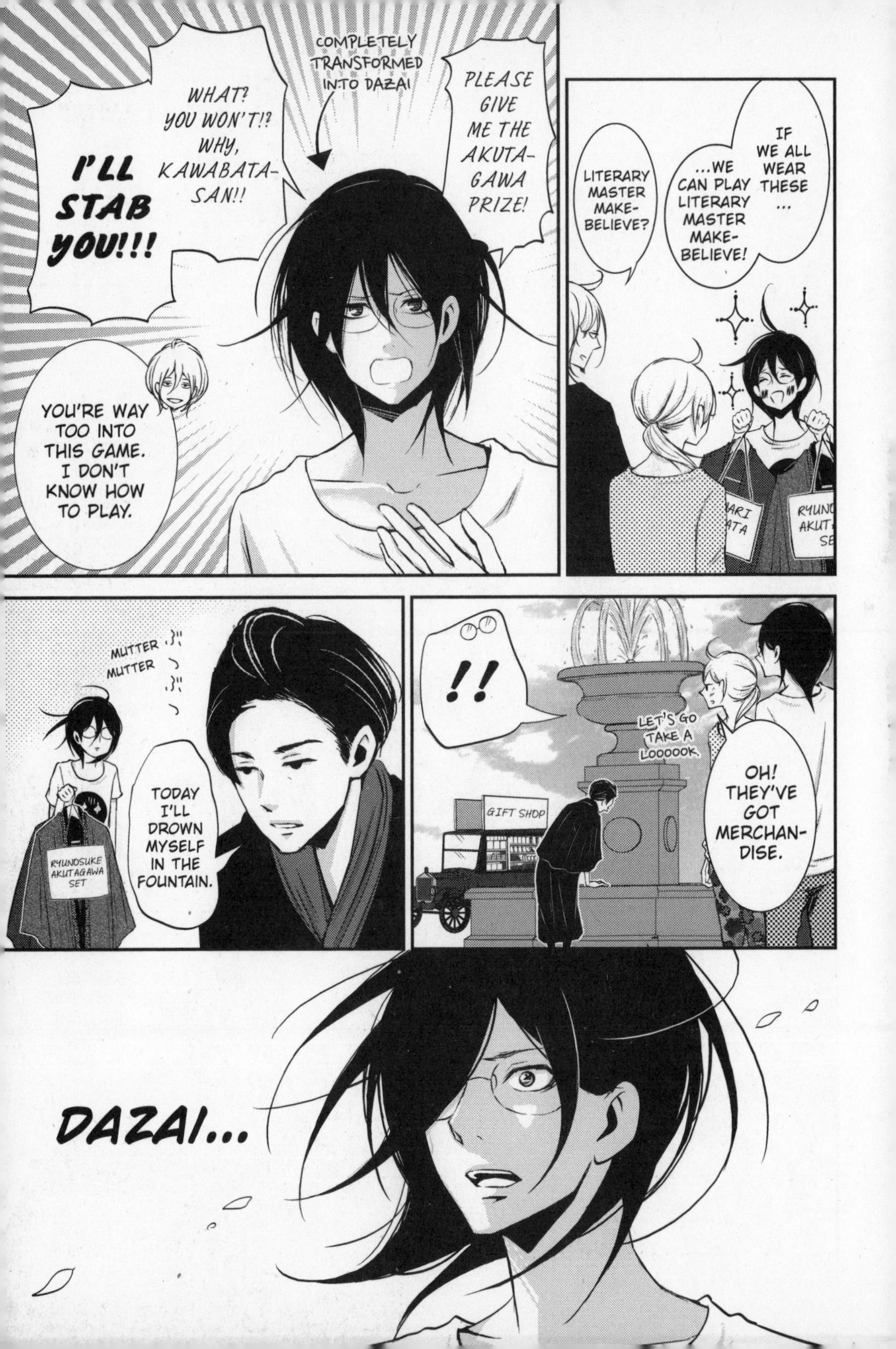
IF WE ALL WEAR THESE...
...WE CAN PLAY LITERARY MASTER MAKE-BELIEVE!
LITERARY MASTER MAKE-BELIEVE?
PLEASE GIVE ME THE AKUTAGAWA PRIZE!
COMPLETELY TRANSFORMED INTO DAZAI
WHAT? YOU WON'T!? WHY, KAWABATA-SAN!!
I'LL STAB YOU!!!
YOU'RE WAY TOO INTO THIS GAME. I DON'T KNOW HOW TO PLAY.
OH! THEY'VE GOT MERCHANDISE.
LET'S GO TAKE A LOOOOOK.
!!
GIFT SHOP
TODAY I'LL DROWN MYSELF IN THE FOUNTAIN.
MUTTER MUTTER
RYUNOSUKE AKUTAGAWA SET
DAZAI...

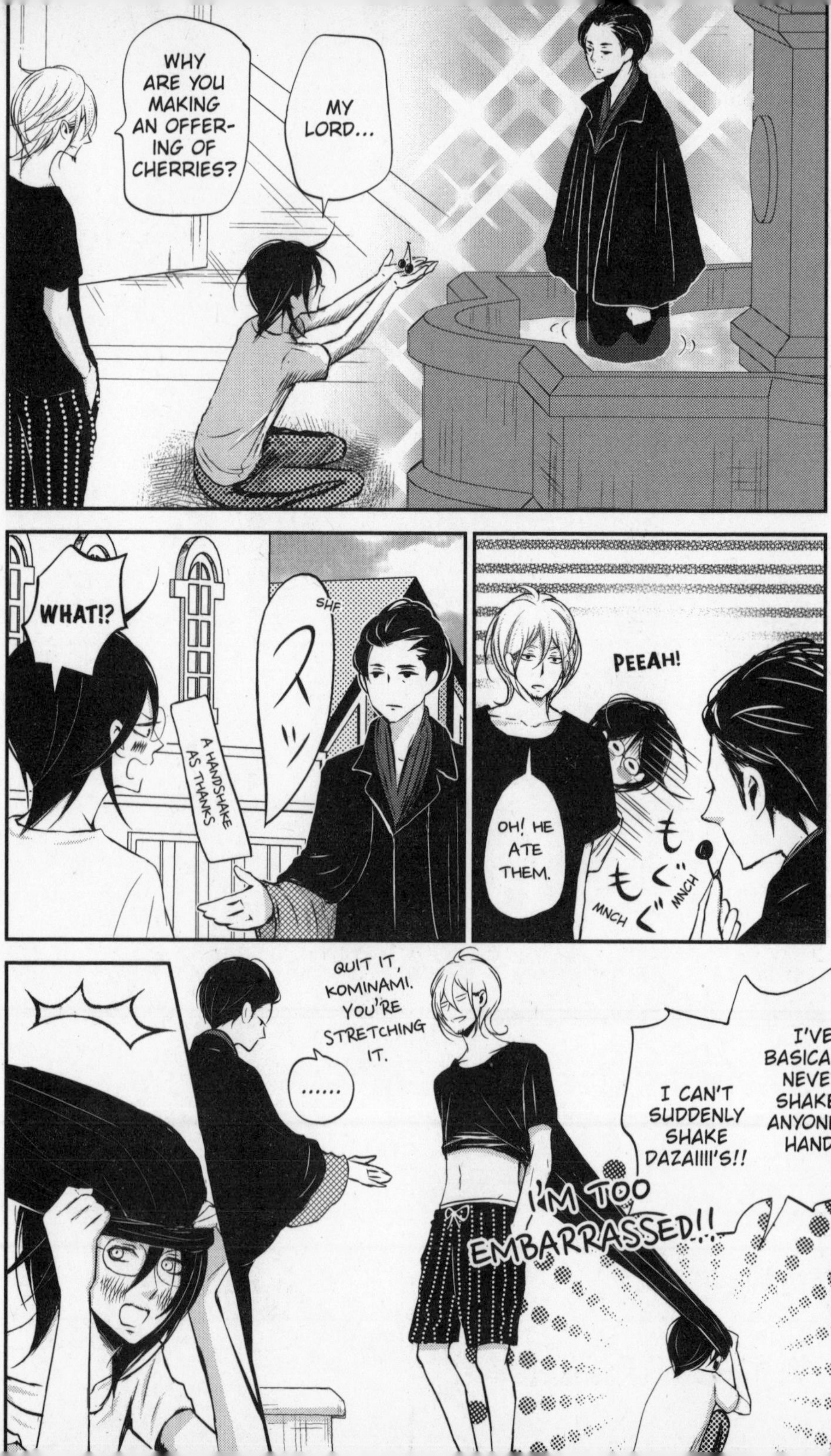
MY LORD...
WHY ARE YOU MAKING AN OFFERING OF CHERRIES?
PEEAH!
OH! HE ATE THEM.
もぐもぐ
MNCH MNCH
SHF
スッ
A HANDSHAKE AS THANKS
WHAT!?
I'VE BASICALLY NEVER SHAKEN ANYONE'S HAND.
I CAN'T SUDDENLY SHAKE DAZAIIII'S!!
I'M TOO EMBARRASSED!!
QUIT IT, KOMINAMI. YOU'RE STRETCHING IT.
....

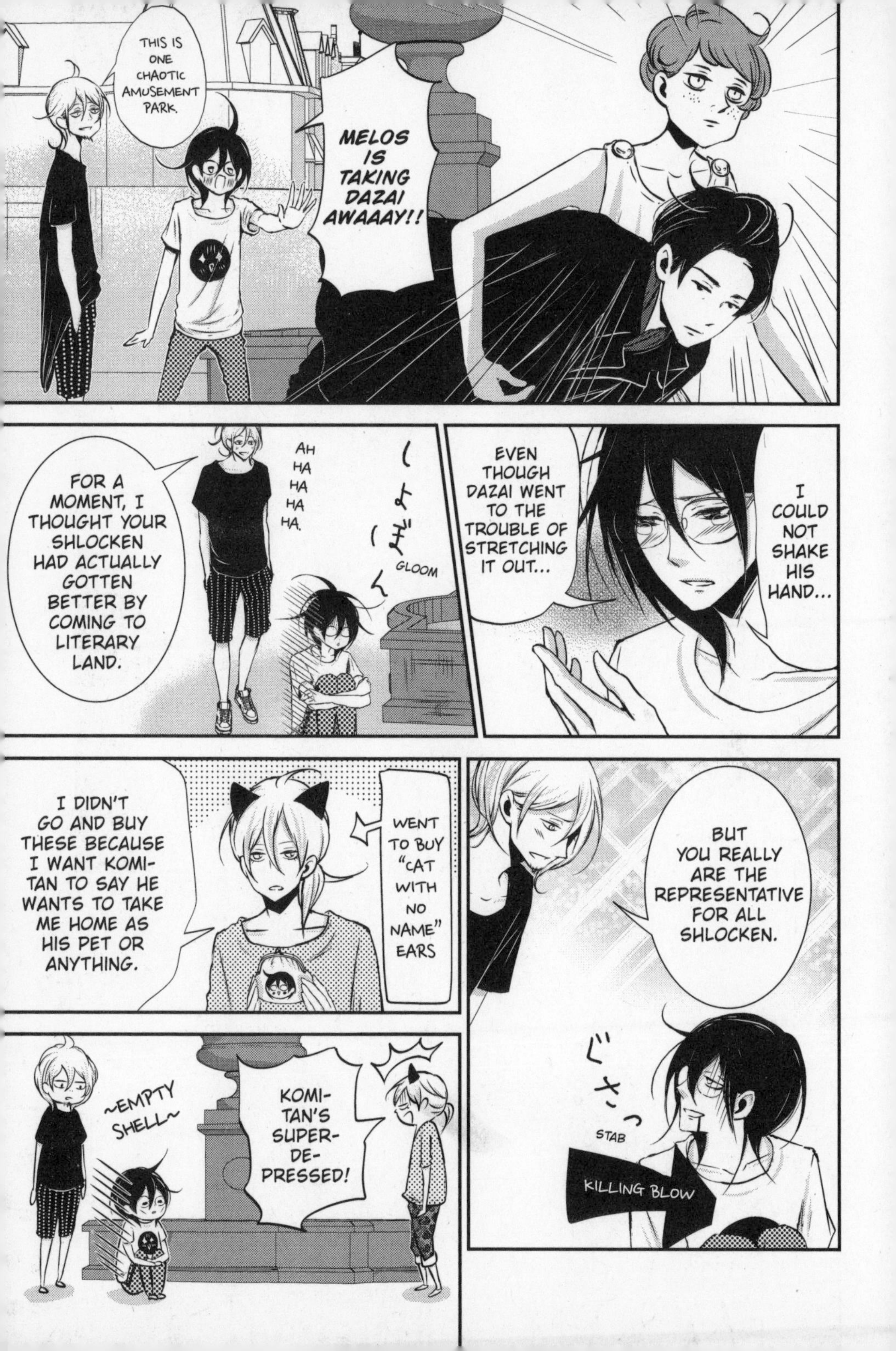
MELOS IS TAKING DAZAI AWAAAY!!
THIS IS ONE CHAOTIC AMUSEMENT PARK.
EVEN THOUGH DAZAI WENT TO THE TROUBLE OF STRETCHING IT OUT...
I COULD NOT SHAKE HIS HAND...
AH HA HA HA HA.
GLOOM
FOR A MOMENT, I THOUGHT YOUR SHLOCKEN HAD ACTUALLY GOTTEN BETTER BY COMING TO LITERARY LAND.
BUT YOU REALLY ARE THE REPRESENTATIVE FOR ALL SHLOCKEN.
STAB
KILLING BLOW
WENT TO BUY "CAT WITH NO NAME" EARS
I DIDN'T GO AND BUY THESE BECAUSE I WANT KOMI-TAN TO SAY HE WANTS TO TAKE ME HOME AS HIS PET OR ANYTHING.
KOMI-TAN'S SUPER-DEPRESSED!
~EMPTY SHELL~

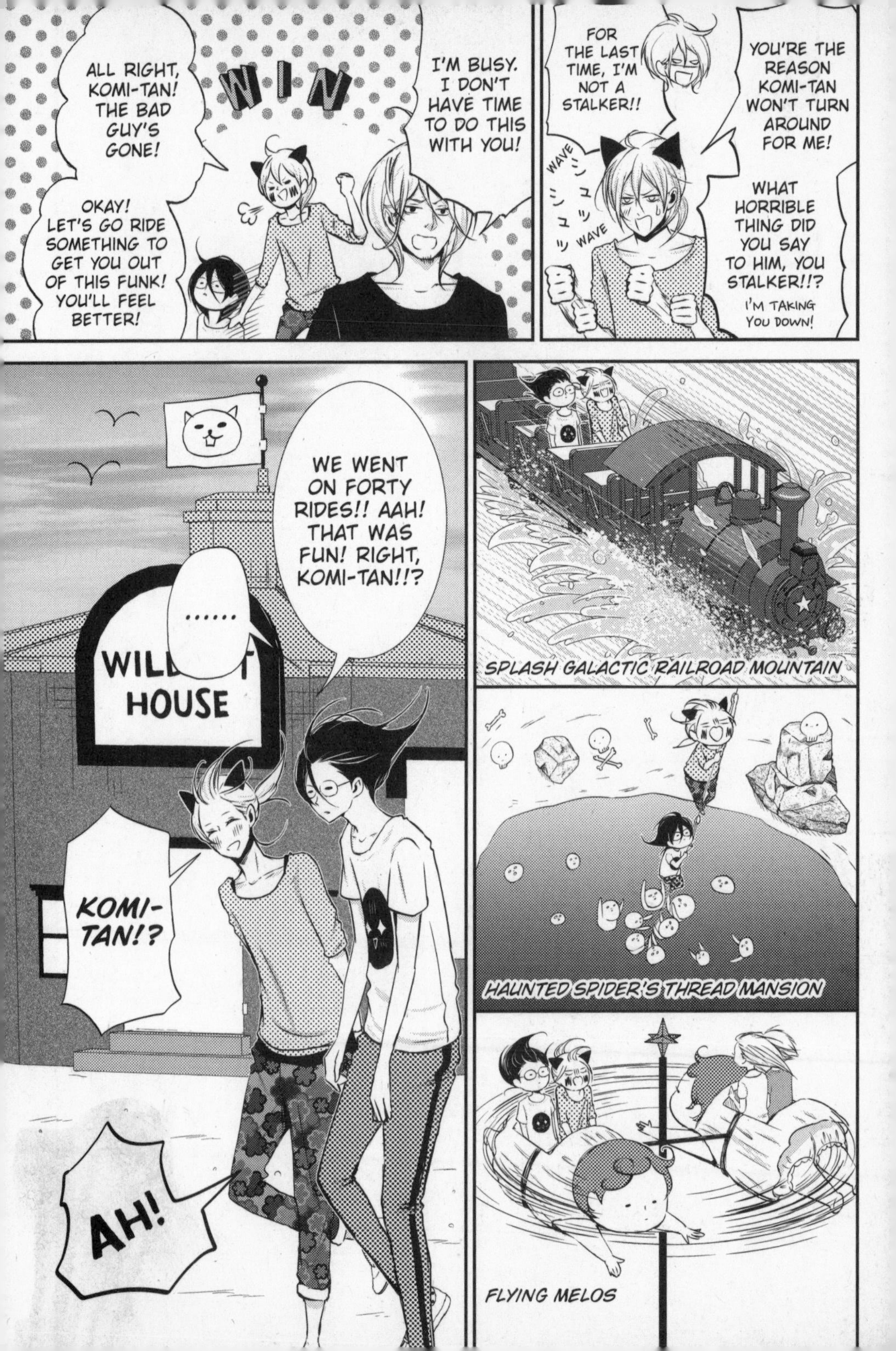
YOU'RE THE REASON KOMI-TAN WON'T TURN AROUND FOR ME!
FOR THE LAST TIME, I'M NOT A STALKER!!
WAVE シュッ
WAVE シュッ
WHAT HORRIBLE THING DID YOU SAY TO HIM, YOU STALKER!!?
I'M TAKING YOU DOWN!
I'M BUSY. I DON'T HAVE TIME TO DO THIS WITH YOU!
WIN
ALL RIGHT, KOMI-TAN! THE BAD GUY'S GONE!
OKAY! LET'S GO RIDE SOMETHING TO GET YOU OUT OF THIS FUNK! YOU'LL FEEL BETTER!
SPLASH GALACTIC RAILROAD MOUNTAIN
HAUNTED SPIDER'S THREAD MANSION
FLYING MELOS
WE WENT ON FORTY RIDES!! AAH! THAT WAS FUN! RIGHT, KOMI-TAN!!?
......
WILD T
HOUSE
KOMI-TAN!?
AH!

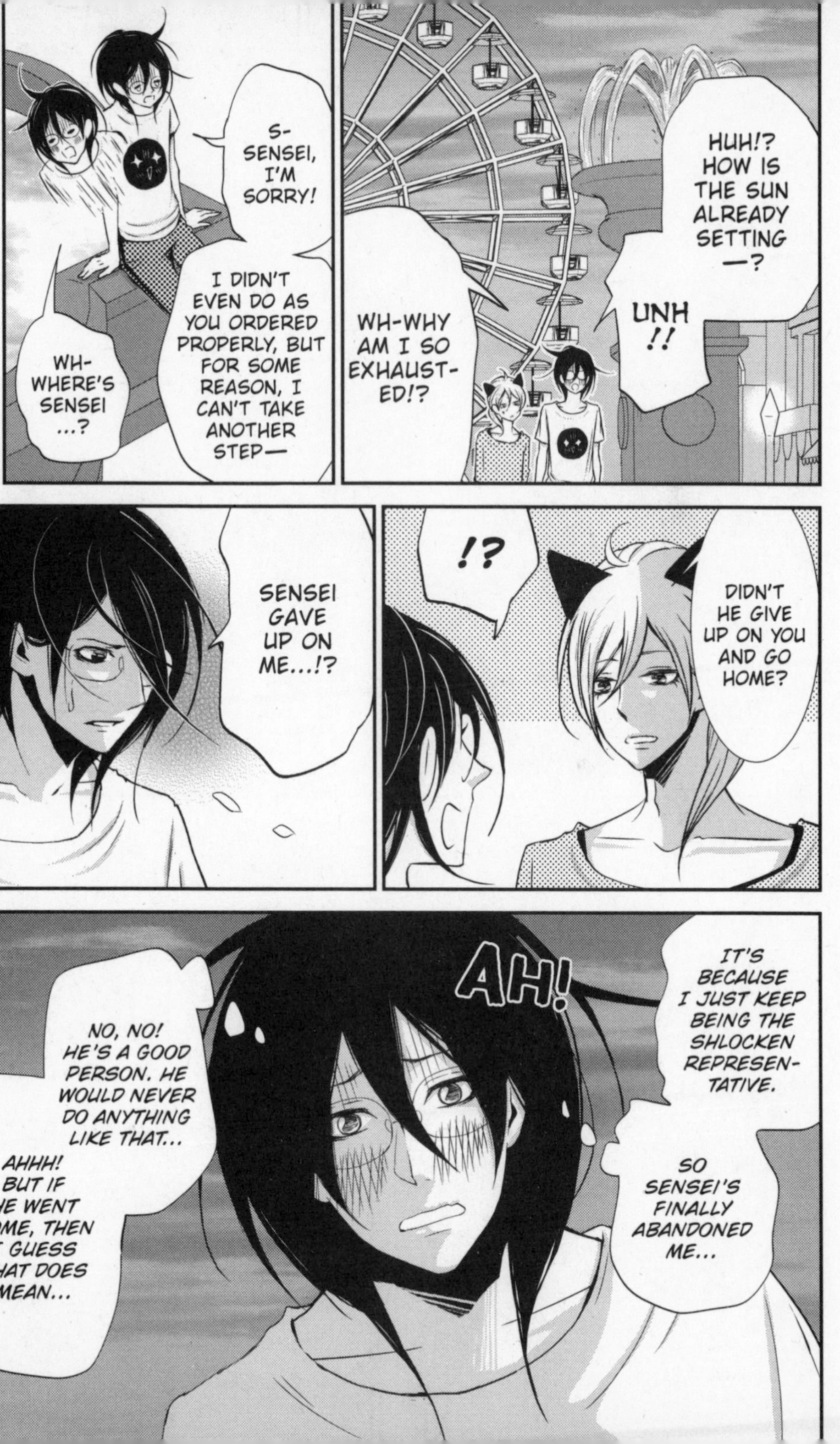
HUH!? HOW IS THE SUN ALREADY SETTING—?
UNH !!
WH-WHY AM I SO EXHAUST-ED!?
S-SENSEI, I'M SORRY!
I DIDN'T EVEN DO AS YOU ORDERED PROPERLY, BUT FOR SOME REASON, I CAN'T TAKE ANOTHER STEP—
WH-WHERE'S SENSEI ...?
DIDN'T HE GIVE UP ON YOU AND GO HOME?
!?
SENSEI GAVE UP ON ME...!?
AH!
IT'S BECAUSE I JUST KEEP BEING THE SHLOCKEN REPRESEN-TATIVE.
SO SENSEI'S FINALLY ABANDONED ME...
NO, NO! HE'S A GOOD PERSON. HE WOULD NEVER DO ANYTHING LIKE THAT...
AHHH! BUT IF HE WENT HOME, THEN I GUESS THAT DOES MEAN...

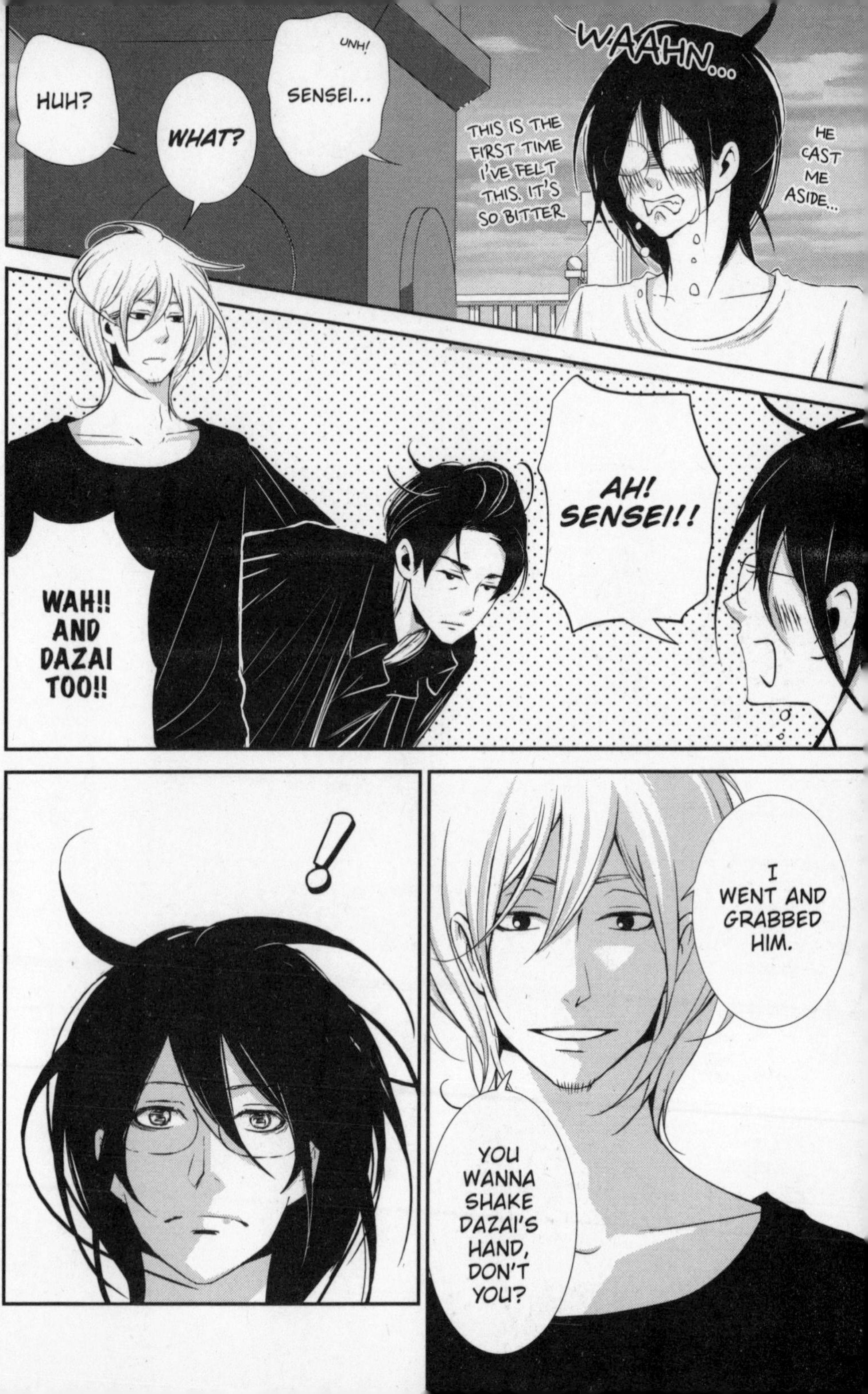

WAAHN...
HE CAST ME ASIDE...
THIS IS THE FIRST TIME I'VE FELT THIS. IT'S SO BITTER
UNH!
SENSEI...
WHAT?
HUH?
AH! SENSEI!!
WAH!! AND DAZAI TOO!!
I WENT AND GRABBED HIM.
YOU WANNA SHAKE DAZAI'S HAND, DON'T YOU?
!

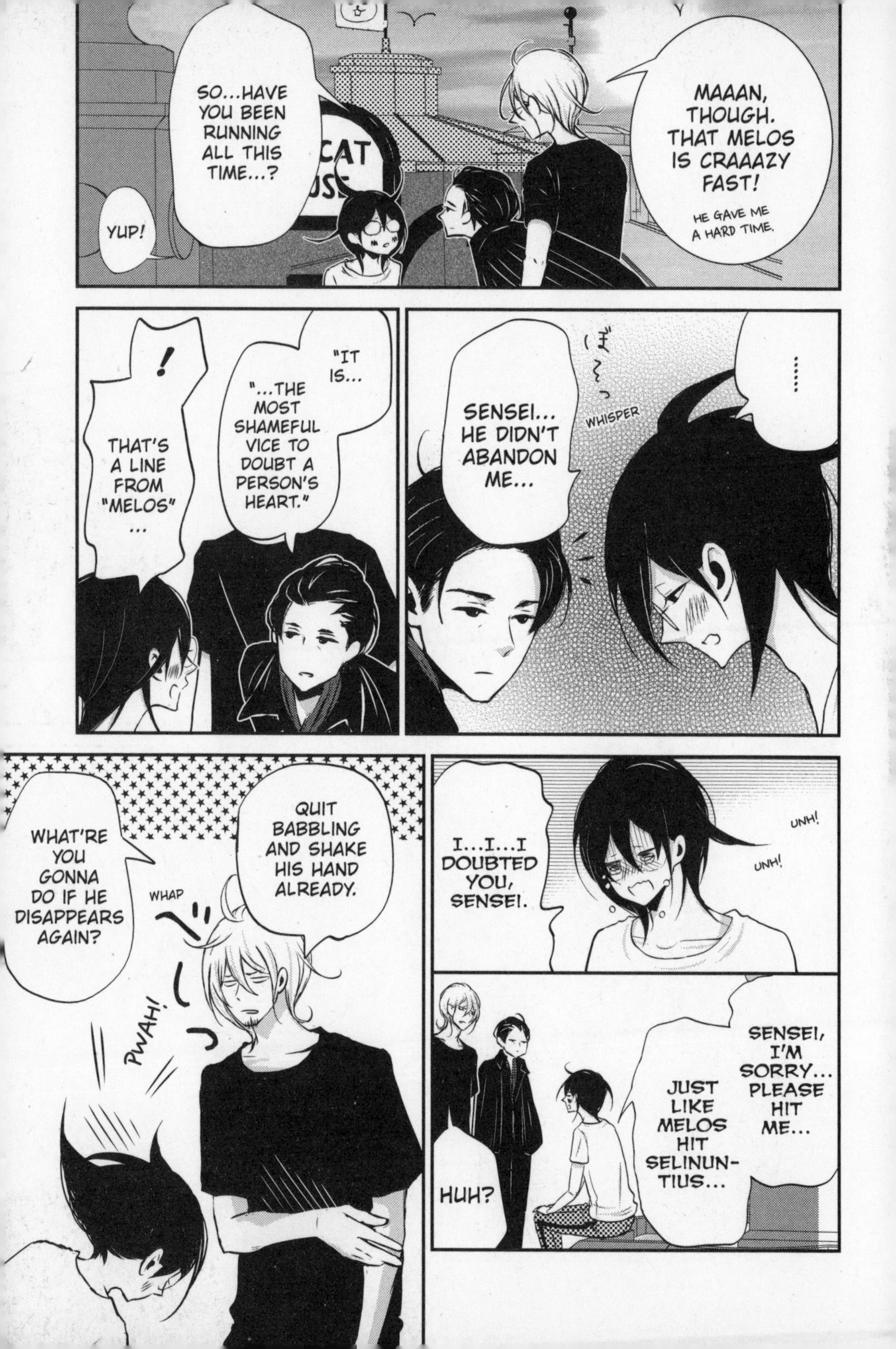
MAAAN, THOUGH. THAT MELOS IS CRAAAZY FAST!
HE GAVE ME A HARD TIME.
SO...HAVE YOU BEEN RUNNING ALL THIS TIME...?
YUP!
......
SENSEI... HE DIDN'T ABANDON ME...
WHISPER
"IT IS...
"...THE MOST SHAMEFUL VICE TO DOUBT A PERSON'S HEART."
!
THAT'S A LINE FROM "MELOS"...
UNH!
UNH!
I...I...I DOUBTED YOU, SENSEI.
SENSEI, I'M SORRY... PLEASE HIT ME...
JUST LIKE MELOS HIT SELINUNTIUS...
HUH?
QUIT BABBLING AND SHAKE HIS HAND ALREADY.
WHAP
WHAT'RE YOU GONNA DO IF HE DISAPPEARS AGAIN?
PWAH!

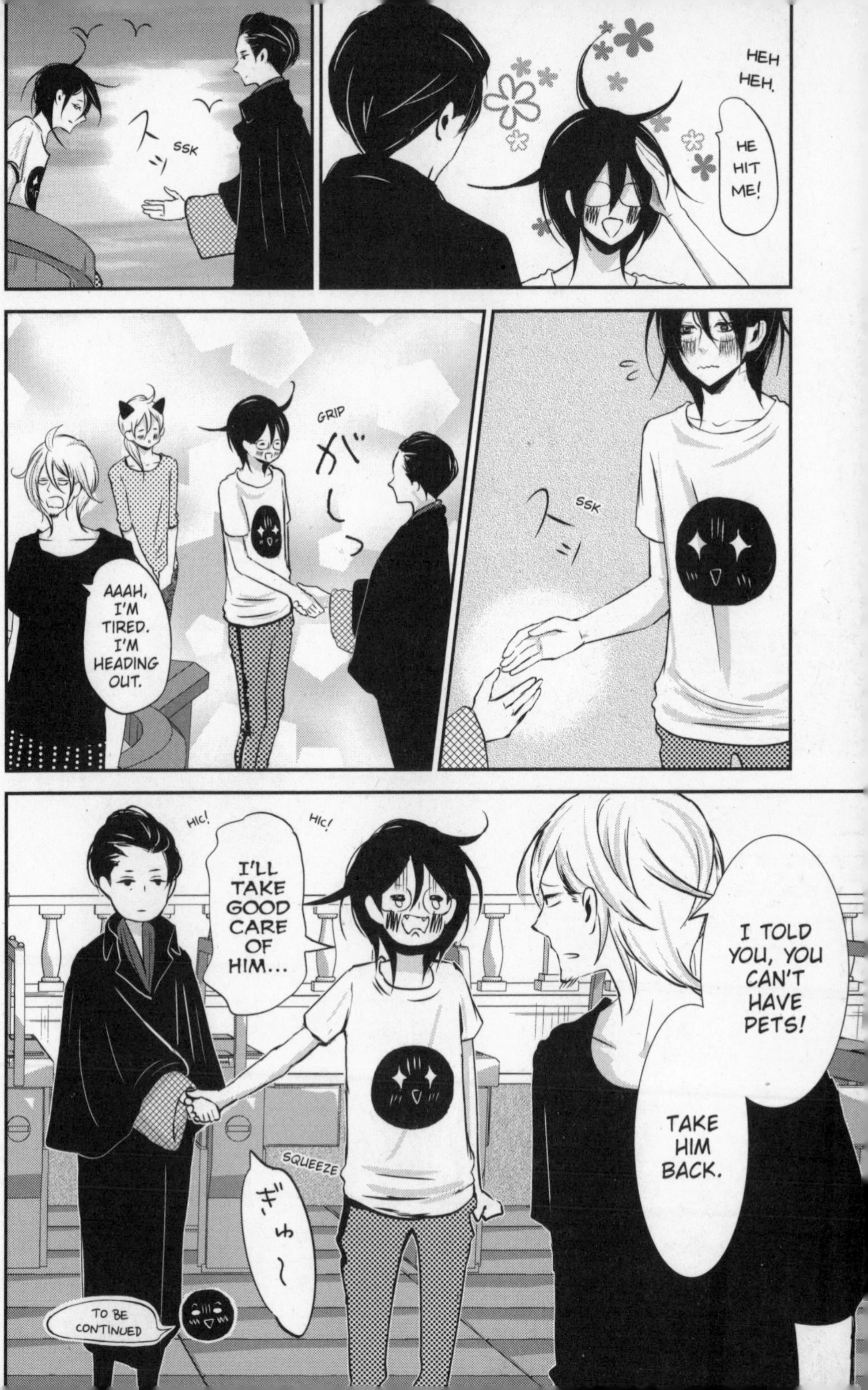
HEH HEH.
HE HIT ME!
SSK
スッ
SSK
スッ
GRIP
がしっ
AAAH, I'M TIRED. I'M HEADING OUT.
I TOLD YOU, YOU CAN'T HAVE PETS!
TAKE HIM BACK.
HIC!
HIC!
I'LL TAKE GOOD CARE OF HIM...
SQUEEZE
ぎゅ～
TO BE CONTINUED

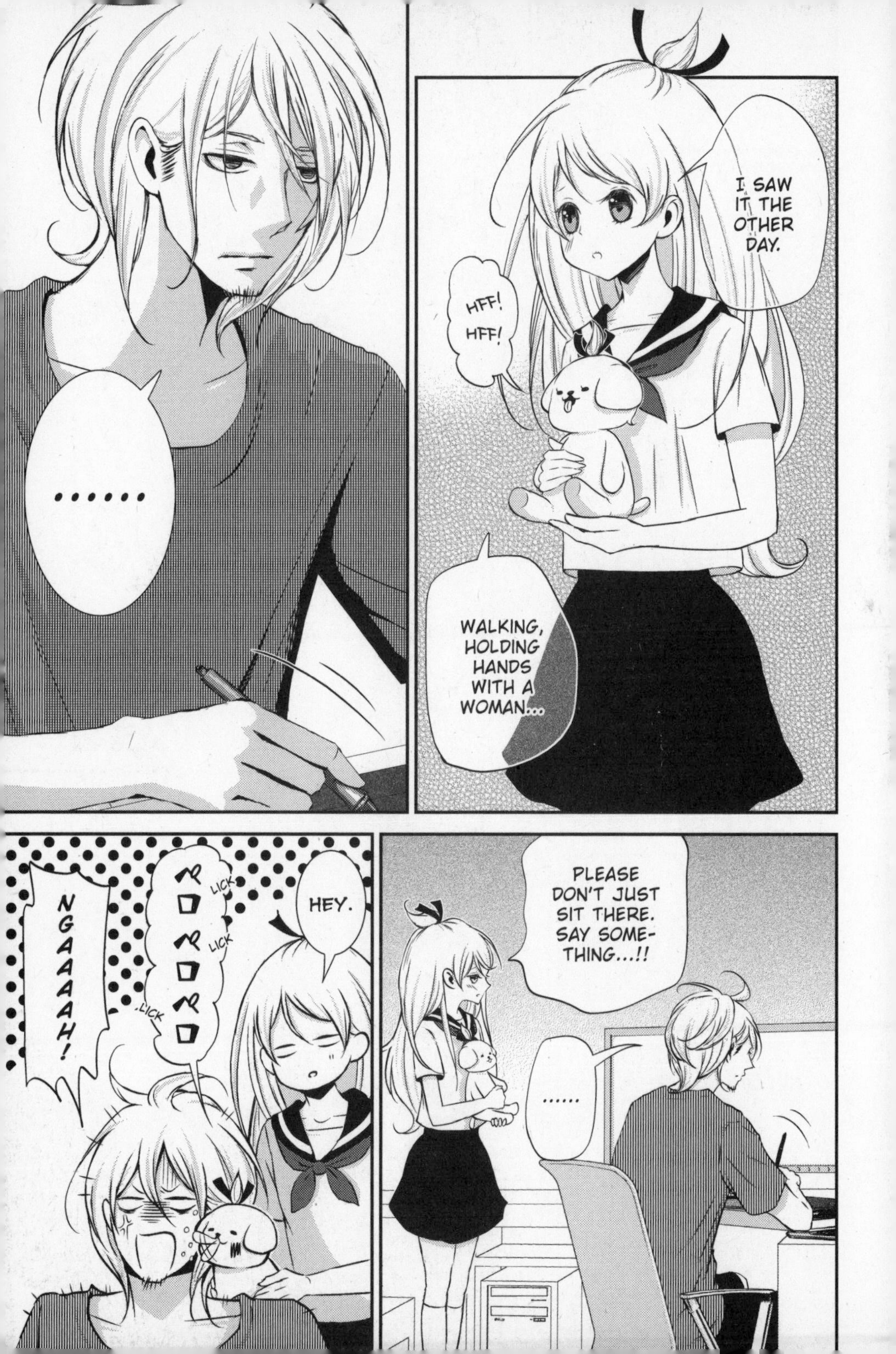
I SAW IT THE OTHER DAY.
HFF! HFF!
WALKING, HOLDING HANDS WITH A WOMAN...
......
PLEASE DON'T JUST SIT THERE. SAY SOME-THING...!!
......
HEY.
ペロペロペロ
LICK LICK LICK
NGAAAAAH!

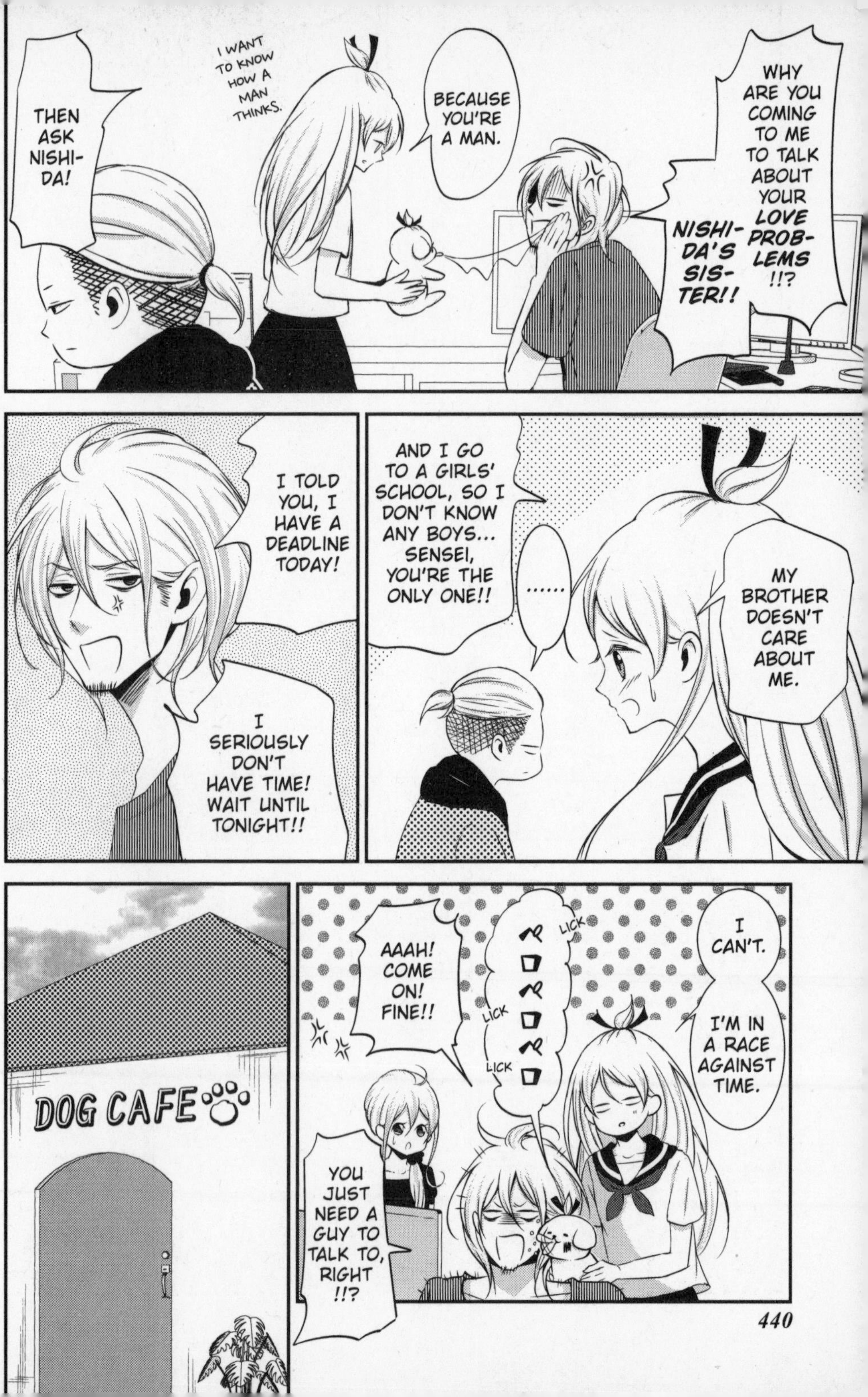

WHY ARE YOU COMING TO ME TO TALK ABOUT YOUR LOVE PROBLEMS!!?
NISHIDA'S SISTER!!
BECAUSE YOU'RE A MAN.
I WANT TO KNOW HOW A MAN THINKS.
THEN ASK NISHIDA!
MY BROTHER DOESN'T CARE ABOUT ME.
AND I GO TO A GIRLS' SCHOOL, SO I DON'T KNOW ANY BOYS... SENSEI, YOU'RE THE ONLY ONE!!
......
I TOLD YOU, I HAVE A DEADLINE TODAY!
I SERIOUSLY DON'T HAVE TIME! WAIT UNTIL TONIGHT!!
I CAN'T.
I'M IN A RACE AGAINST TIME.
ペロペロペロ
LICK
LICK
LICK
AAAH! COME ON! FINE!!
YOU JUST NEED A GUY TO TALK TO, RIGHT!!?
DOG CAFE

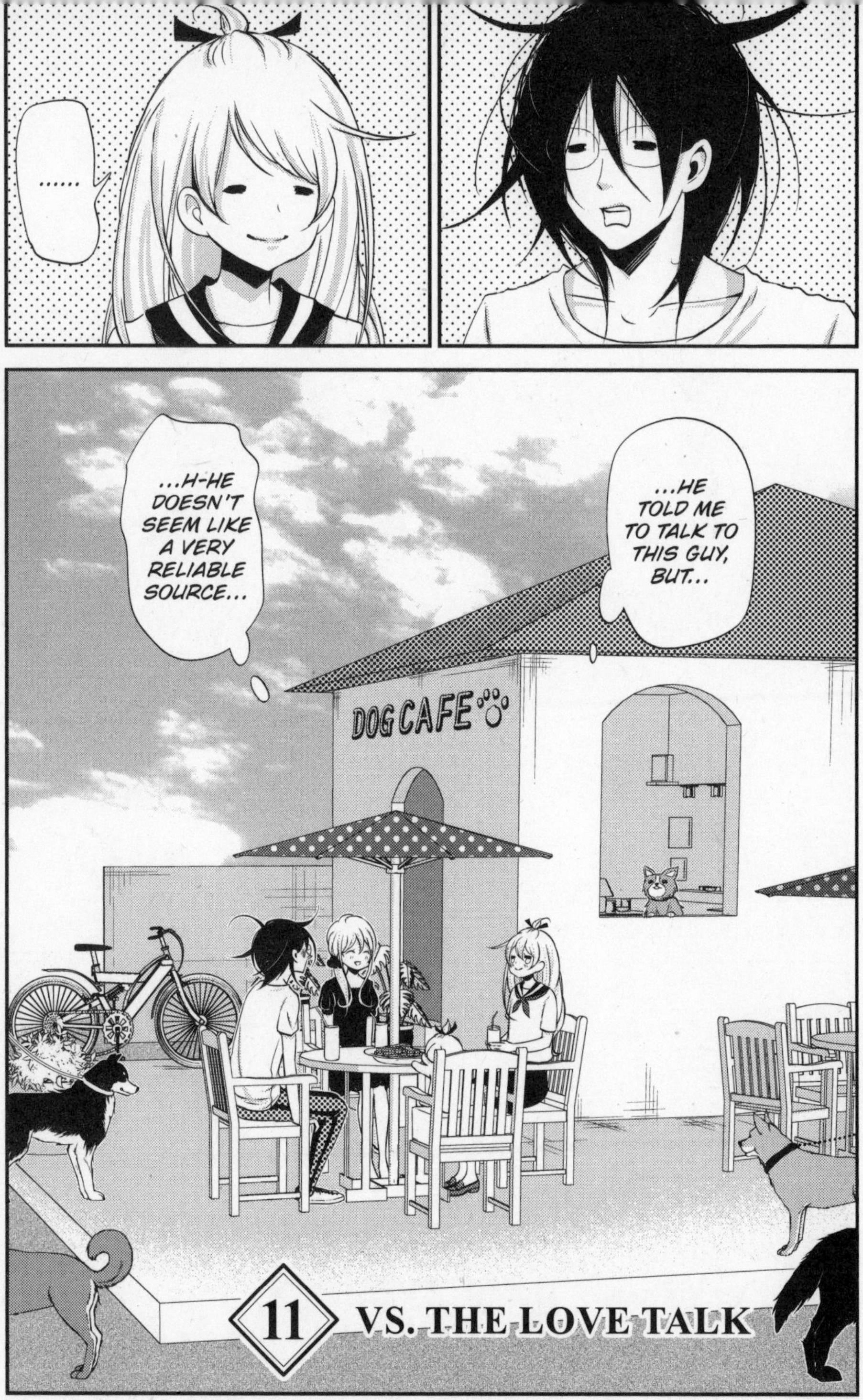
......
...HE TOLD ME TO TALK TO THIS GUY, BUT...
...H-HE DOESN'T SEEM LIKE A VERY RELIABLE SOURCE...
DOG CAFE
11 VS. THE LOVE TALK

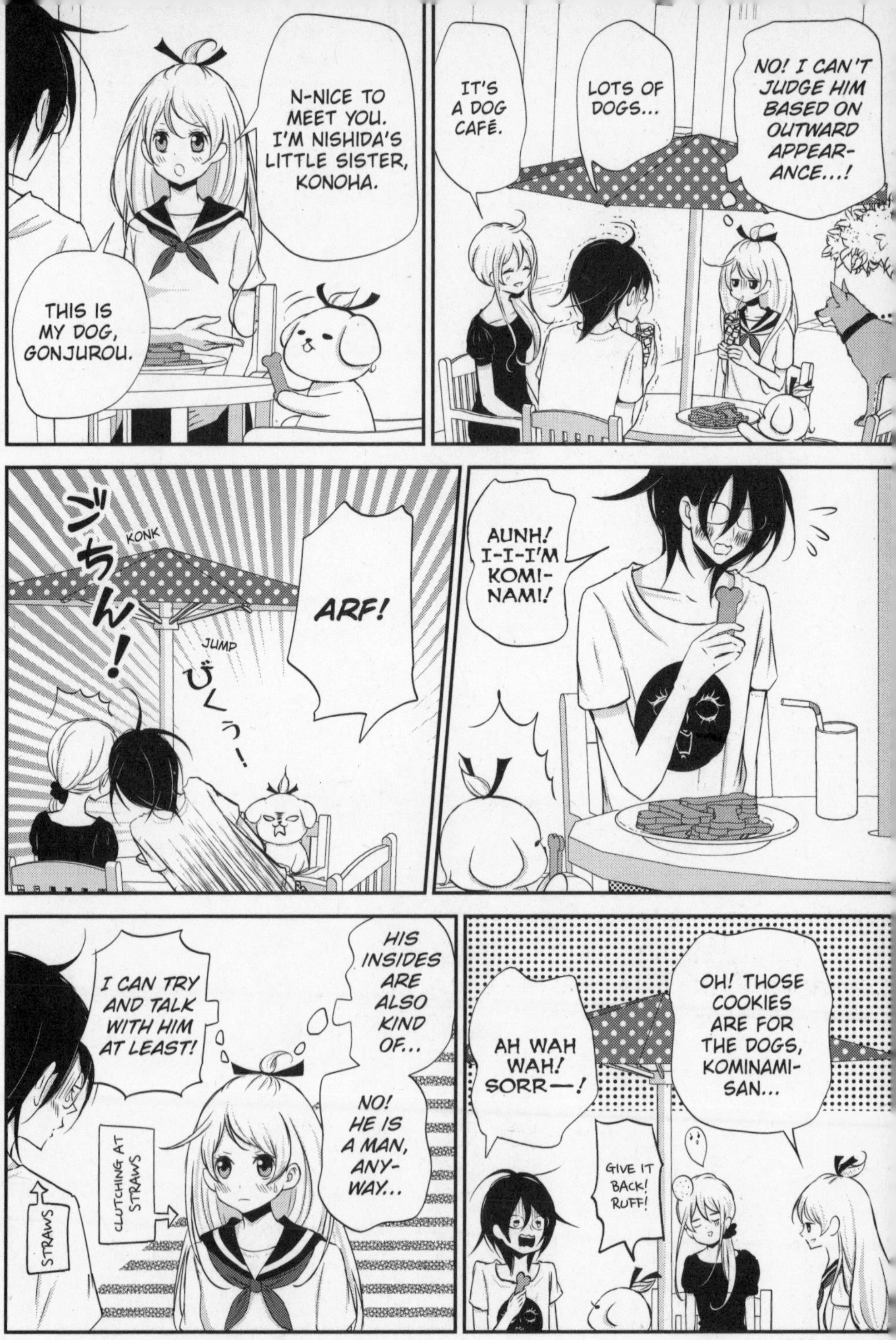
NO! I CAN'T JUDGE HIM BASED ON OUTWARD APPEARANCE...!
LOTS OF DOGS...
IT'S A DOG CAFÉ.
N-NICE TO MEET YOU. I'M NISHIDA'S LITTLE SISTER, KONOHA.
THIS IS MY DOG, GONJUROU.
AUNH! I-I-I'M KOMI-NAMI!
ARF!
ゴちん!
KONK
JUMP
びくぅ!
OH! THOSE COOKIES ARE FOR THE DOGS, KOMINAMI-SAN...
AH WAH WAH! SORR—!
GIVE IT BACK! RUFF!
HIS INSIDES ARE ALSO KIND OF...
NO! HE IS A MAN, ANYWAY...
I CAN TRY AND TALK WITH HIM AT LEAST!
CLUTCHING AT STRAWS
STRAWS

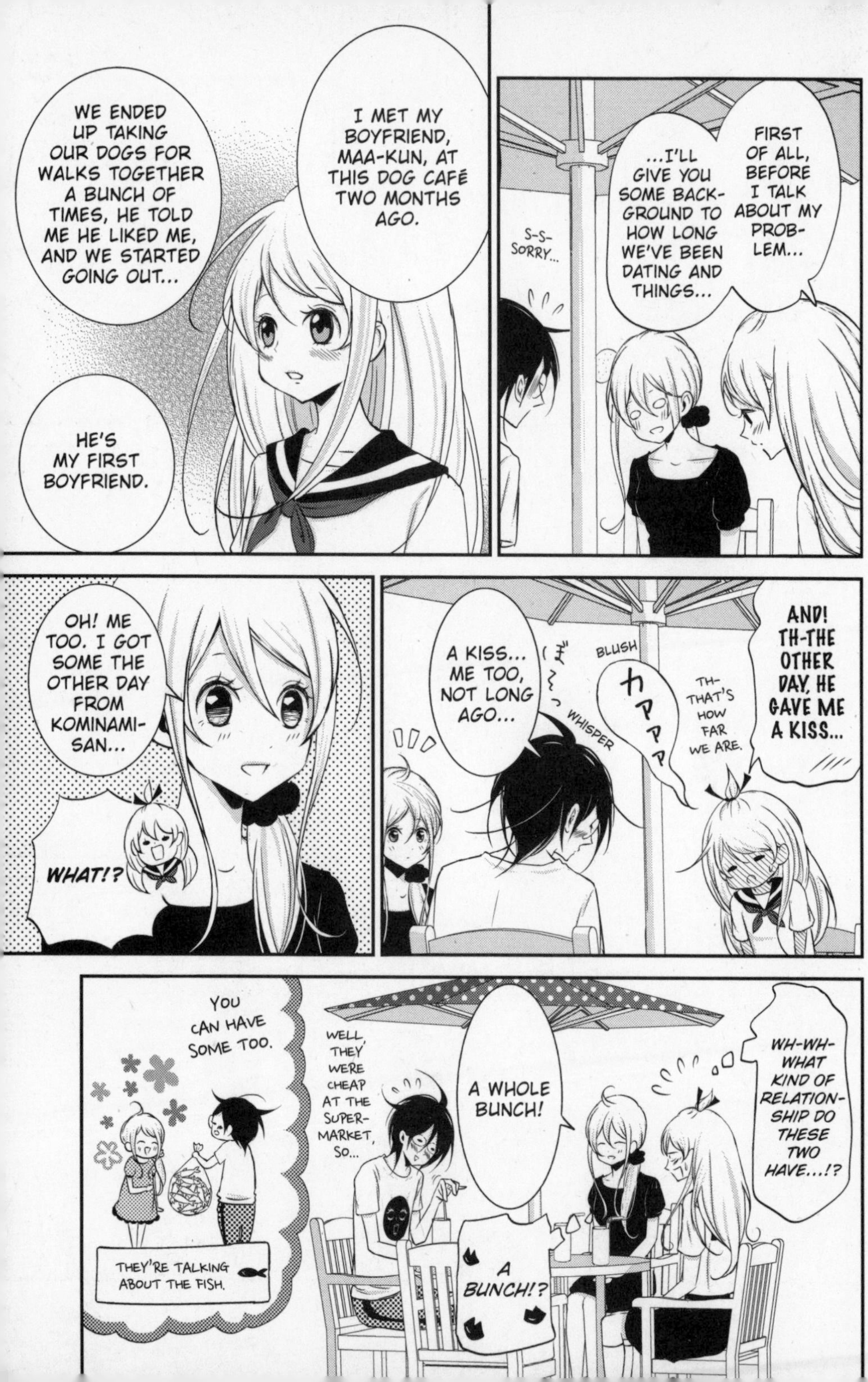
FIRST OF ALL, BEFORE I TALK ABOUT MY PROBLEM...
...I'LL GIVE YOU SOME BACKGROUND TO HOW LONG WE'VE BEEN DATING AND THINGS...
S-S-SORRY...
I MET MY BOYFRIEND, MAA-KUN, AT THIS DOG CAFÉ TWO MONTHS AGO.
WE ENDED UP TAKING OUR DOGS FOR WALKS TOGETHER A BUNCH OF TIMES, HE TOLD ME HE LIKED ME, AND WE STARTED GOING OUT...
HE'S MY FIRST BOYFRIEND.
AND! TH-THE OTHER DAY, HE GAVE ME A KISS...
TH-THAT'S HOW FAR WE ARE.
カァァ
BLUSH
A KISS... ME TOO, NOT LONG AGO...
WHISPER
OH! ME TOO. I GOT SOME THE OTHER DAY FROM KOMINAMI-SAN...
WHAT!?
WH-WH-WHAT KIND OF RELATIONSHIP DO THESE TWO HAVE...!?
A WHOLE BUNCH!
WELL, THEY WERE CHEAP AT THE SUPERMARKET, SO...
A BUNCH!?
YOU CAN HAVE SOME TOO.
THEY'RE TALKING ABOUT THE FISH.

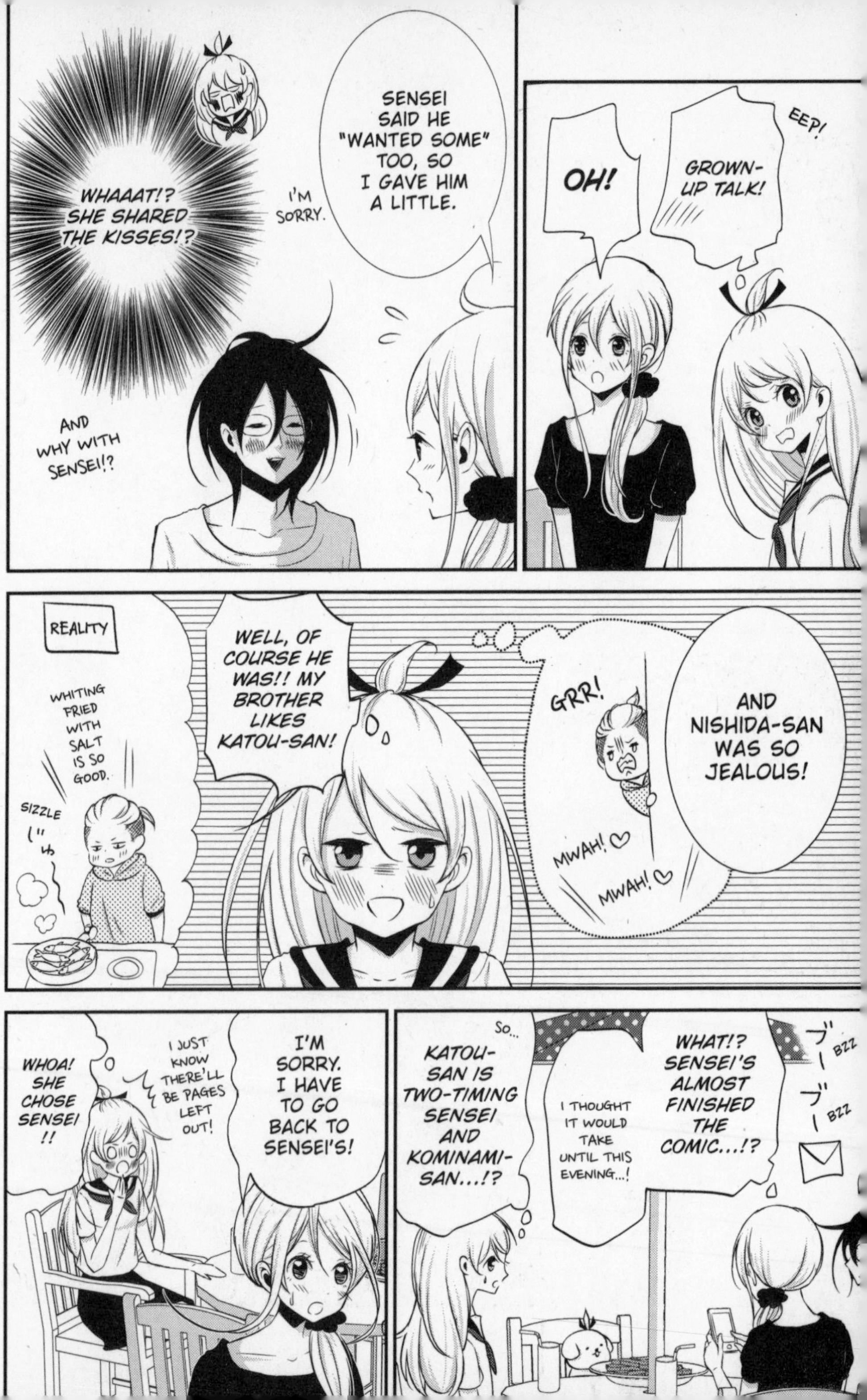
EEP!
GROWN-UP TALK!
OH!
SENSEI SAID HE "WANTED SOME" TOO, SO I GAVE HIM A LITTLE.
I'M SORRY.
WHAAAT!? SHE SHARED THE KISSES!?
AND WHY WITH SENSEI!?
AND NISHIDA-SAN WAS SO JEALOUS!
GRR!
MWAH! ♡
MWAH! ♡
WELL, OF COURSE HE WAS!! MY BROTHER LIKES KATOU-SAN!
REALITY
WHITING FRIED WITH SALT IS SO GOOD.
SIZZLE
じゅ
ブーブー
BZZ
BZZ
WHAT!? SENSEI'S ALMOST FINISHED THE COMIC...!?
I THOUGHT IT WOULD TAKE UNTIL THIS EVENING...!
So...
KATOU-SAN IS TWO-TIMING SENSEI AND KOMINAMI-SAN...!?
I'M SORRY. I HAVE TO GO BACK TO SENSEI'S!
I JUST KNOW THERE'LL BE PAGES LEFT OUT!
WHOA! SHE CHOSE SENSEI!!

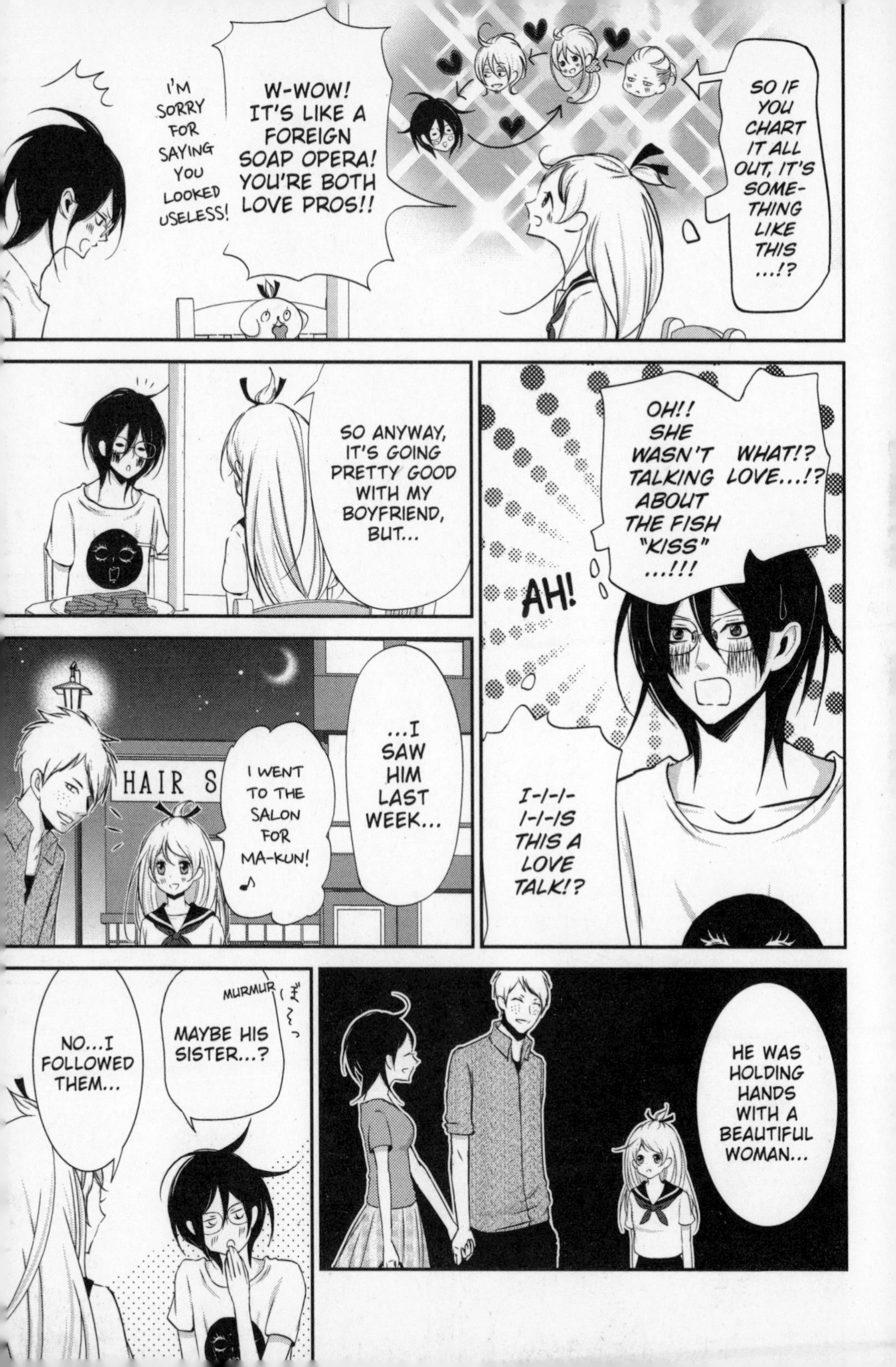
SO IF YOU CHART IT ALL OUT, IT'S SOME-THING LIKE THIS ...!?
W-WOW! IT'S LIKE A FOREIGN SOAP OPERA! YOU'RE BOTH LOVE PROS!!
I'M SORRY FOR SAYING YOU LOOKED USELESS!
WHAT!? LOVE...!?
OH!! SHE WASN'T TALKING ABOUT THE FISH "KISS" ...!!!
AH!
I-I-I-I-I-IS THIS A LOVE TALK!?
SO ANYWAY, IT'S GOING PRETTY GOOD WITH MY BOYFRIEND, BUT...
...I SAW HIM LAST WEEK...
I WENT TO THE SALON FOR MA-KUN! ♪
HAIR S
HE WAS HOLDING HANDS WITH A BEAUTIFUL WOMAN...
MURMUR
MAYBE HIS SISTER...?
NO...I FOLLOWED THEM...

...AND THEY KISSED GOOD-BYE.
HE'S CLEARLY CHEATING ON ME.
I'M NOT GOOD ENOUGH SOMEHOW, I JUST KNOW IT...
IF I DON'T DO SOME-THING, MA-KUN MIGHT LEAVE ME...
SO PLEASE TELL ME, KOMINAMI-SAN!
WHAT AM I MISSING!?
I CAN'T SEE MA-KUN UNTIL I KNOW...
OH! I'M SORRY... IT MUST SOUND CHILDISH TO A PRO LIKE YOU...
I CAN'T... A SHLOCKEN LIKE ME...
KISS
THAT SITUATION... I CAN'T EVEN IMAGINE IT...
HELP ME, DAZAI...

BUT I JUST GOT FAT AND WOUND UP LOOKING LIKE MY BROTHER...

I HAVE TRIED AND EVERY-THING... I DRANK LOTS OF MILK...

I GUESS IT'S A MATTER OF ADULT SEX APPEAL... I'M FLAT-CHESTED...

WHAAAT!?

I BASICALLY KNOW NOTHING ABOUT LOVE...

I'VE NEVER DATED ANYONE...

I-I'M SORRY. I-I—

JUMP

FISH!?

TH-THAT WAS ABOUT FISH... SORR...

B-BUT YOU SAID YOU KISSED KATOU-SAN...

It's Ma-kun ...!

!?

?

SHF

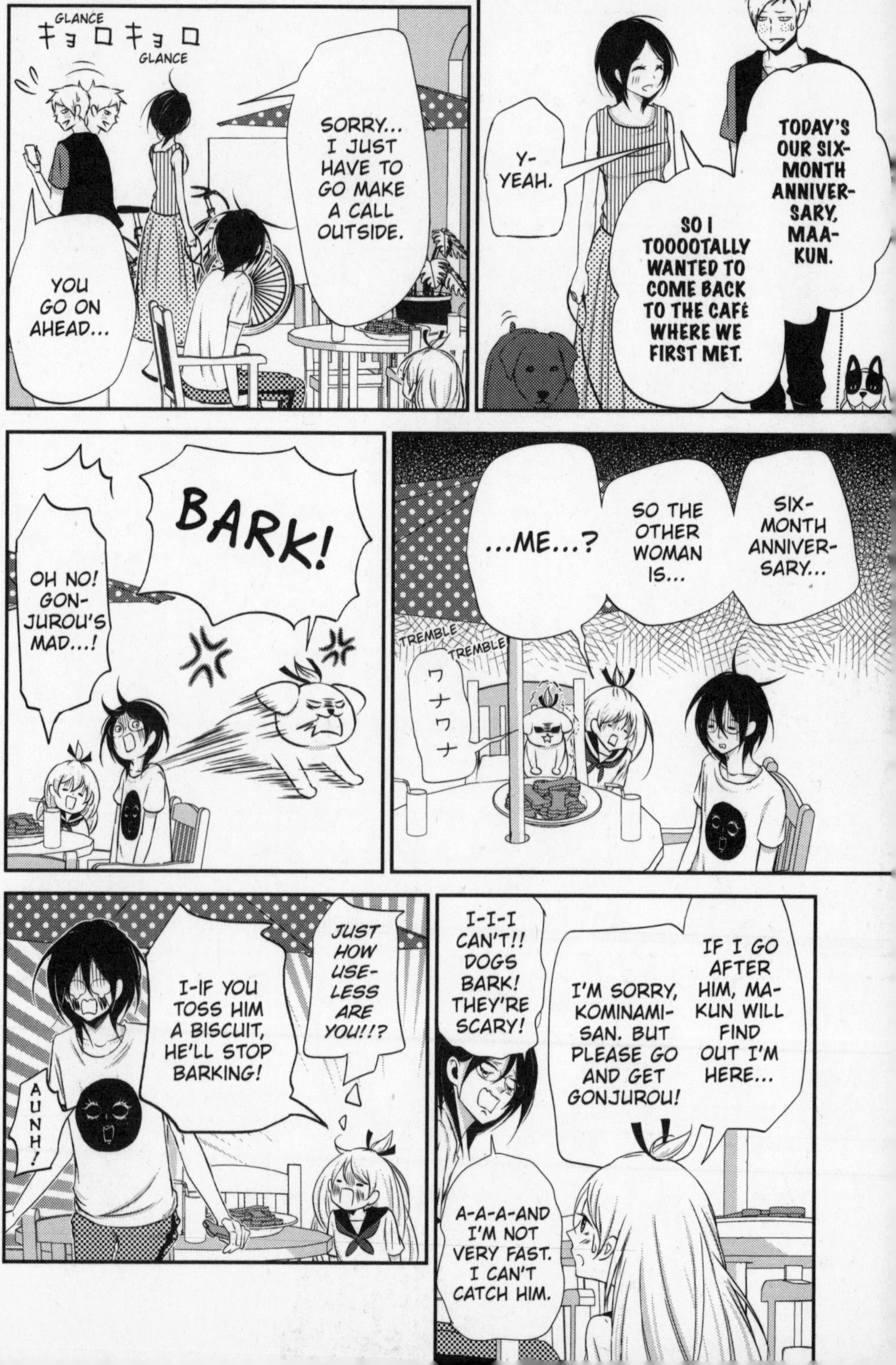
TODAY'S OUR SIX-MONTH ANNIVERSARY, MAA-KUN.
SO I TOOOOTALLY WANTED TO COME BACK TO THE CAFÉ WHERE WE FIRST MET.
Y-YEAH.
GLANCE
キョロキョロ
GLANCE
SORRY... I JUST HAVE TO GO MAKE A CALL OUTSIDE.
YOU GO ON AHEAD...
SIX-MONTH ANNIVERSARY...
SO THE OTHER WOMAN IS...
...ME...?
TREMBLE
TREMBLE
ワナワナ
BARK!
OH NO! GONJUROU'S MAD...!
IF I GO AFTER HIM, MA-KUN WILL FIND OUT I'M HERE...
I'M SORRY, KOMINAMI-SAN. BUT PLEASE GO AND GET GONJUROU!
I-I-I CAN'T!! DOGS BARK! THEY'RE SCARY!
A-A-A-AND I'M NOT VERY FAST. I CAN'T CATCH HIM.
JUST HOW USELESS ARE YOU!!?
I-IF YOU TOSS HIM A BISCUIT, HE'LL STOP BARKING!
AUNH!

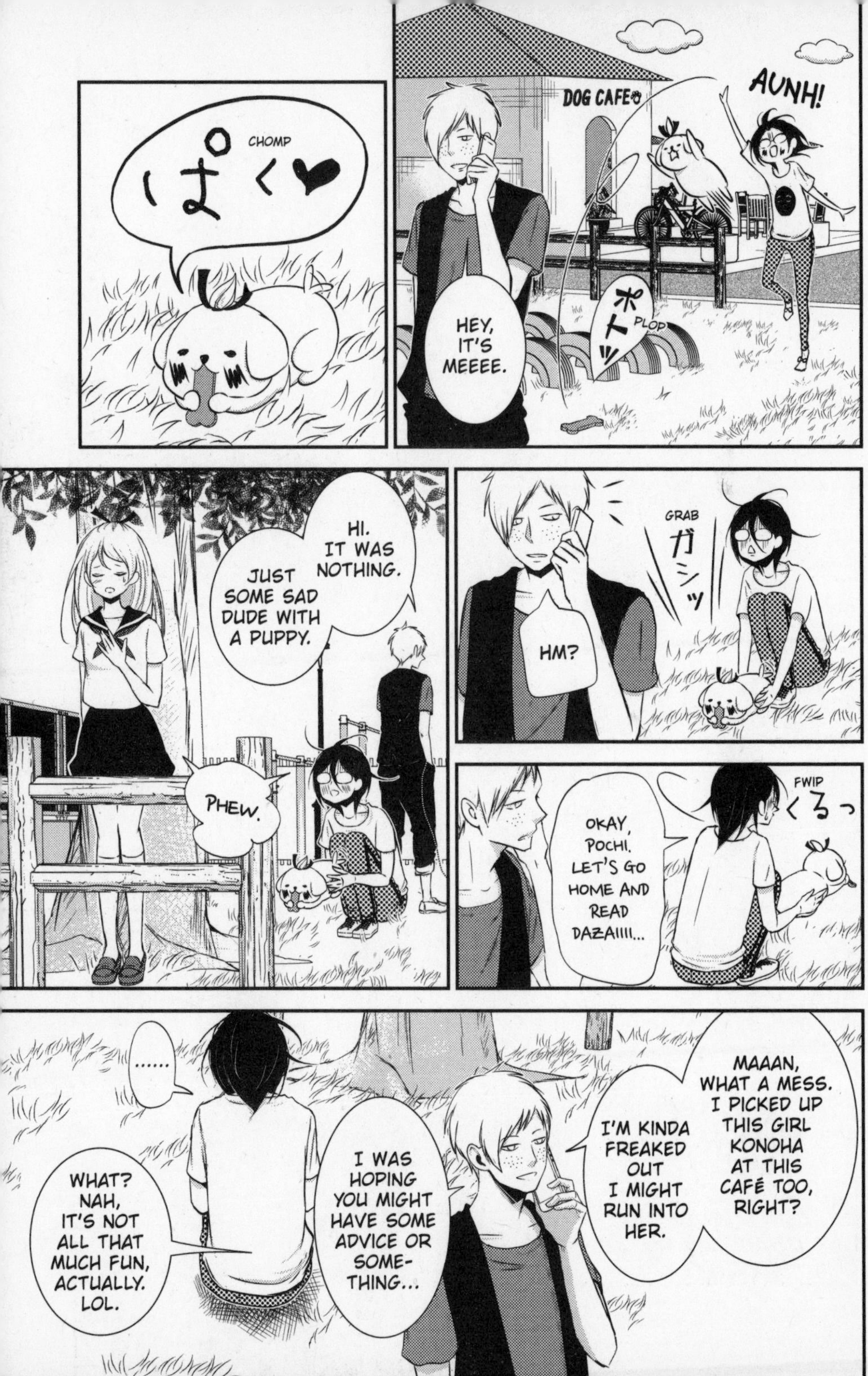

AUNH!
DOG CAFE
HEY, IT'S MEEEE.
ポトッ
PLOP
CHOMP
ぱく♥
HM?
GRAB
ガシッ
FWIP
くるっ
OKAY, POCHI. LET'S GO HOME AND READ DAZAIIII...
HI. IT WAS NOTHING.
JUST SOME SAD DUDE WITH A PUPPY.
PHEW.
MAAAN, WHAT A MESS. I PICKED UP THIS GIRL KONOHA AT THIS CAFÉ TOO, RIGHT?
I'M KINDA FREAKED OUT I MIGHT RUN INTO HER.
I WAS HOPING YOU MIGHT HAVE SOME ADVICE OR SOME-THING...
......
WHAT? NAH, IT'S NOT ALL THAT MUCH FUN, ACTUALLY. LOL.

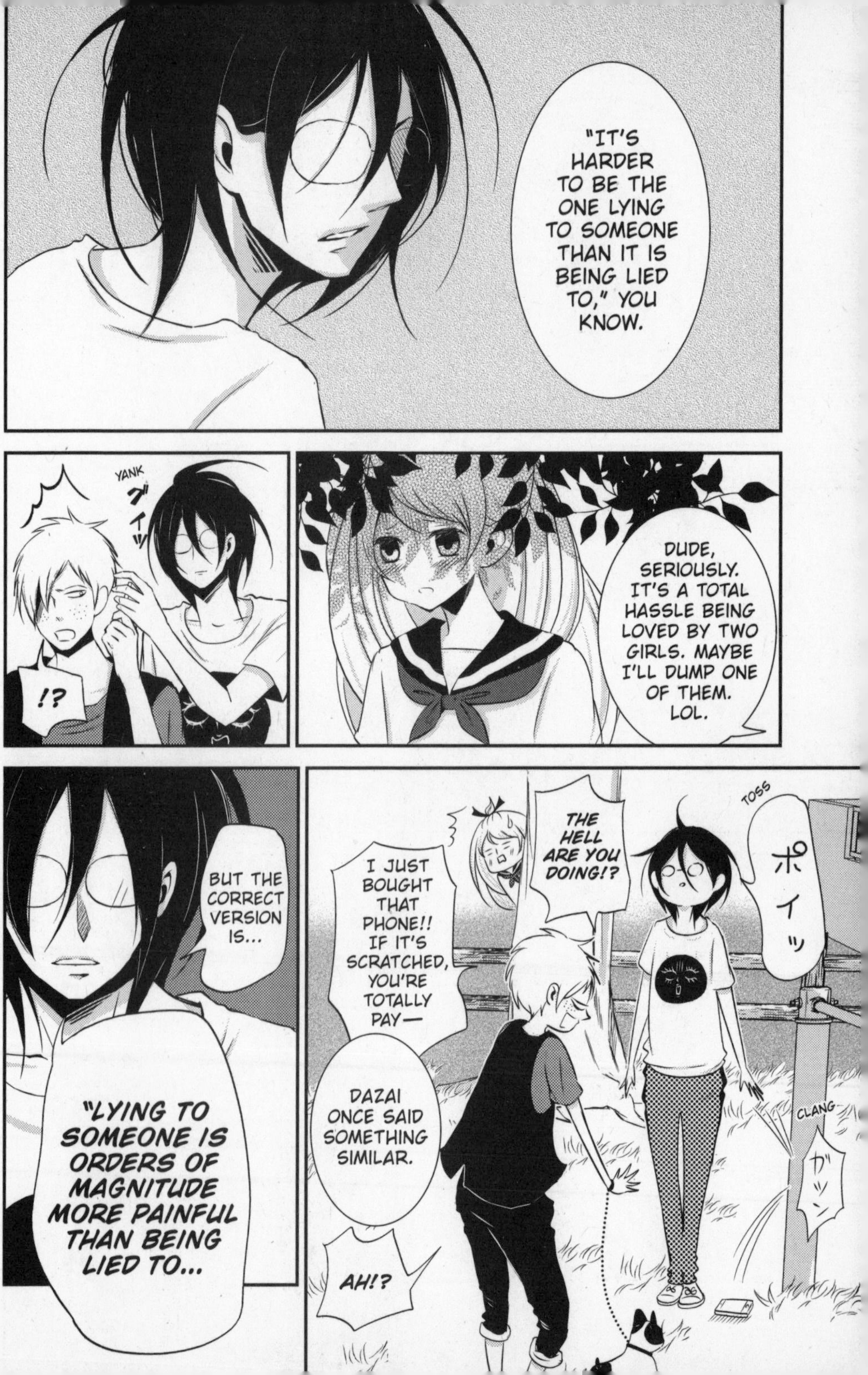

"IT'S HARDER TO BE THE ONE LYING TO SOMEONE THAN IT IS BEING LIED TO," YOU KNOW.
DUDE, SERIOUSLY. IT'S A TOTAL HASSLE BEING LOVED BY TWO GIRLS. MAYBE I'LL DUMP ONE OF THEM. LOL.
YANK
グイッ
!?
TOSS
ポイッ
THE HELL ARE YOU DOING!?
I JUST BOUGHT THAT PHONE!! IF IT'S SCRATCHED, YOU'RE TOTALLY PAY—
CLANG
ガツン
DAZAI ONCE SAID SOMETHING SIMILAR.
AH!?
BUT THE CORRECT VERSION IS...
"LYING TO SOMEONE IS ORDERS OF MAGNITUDE MORE PAINFUL THAN BEING LIED TO...

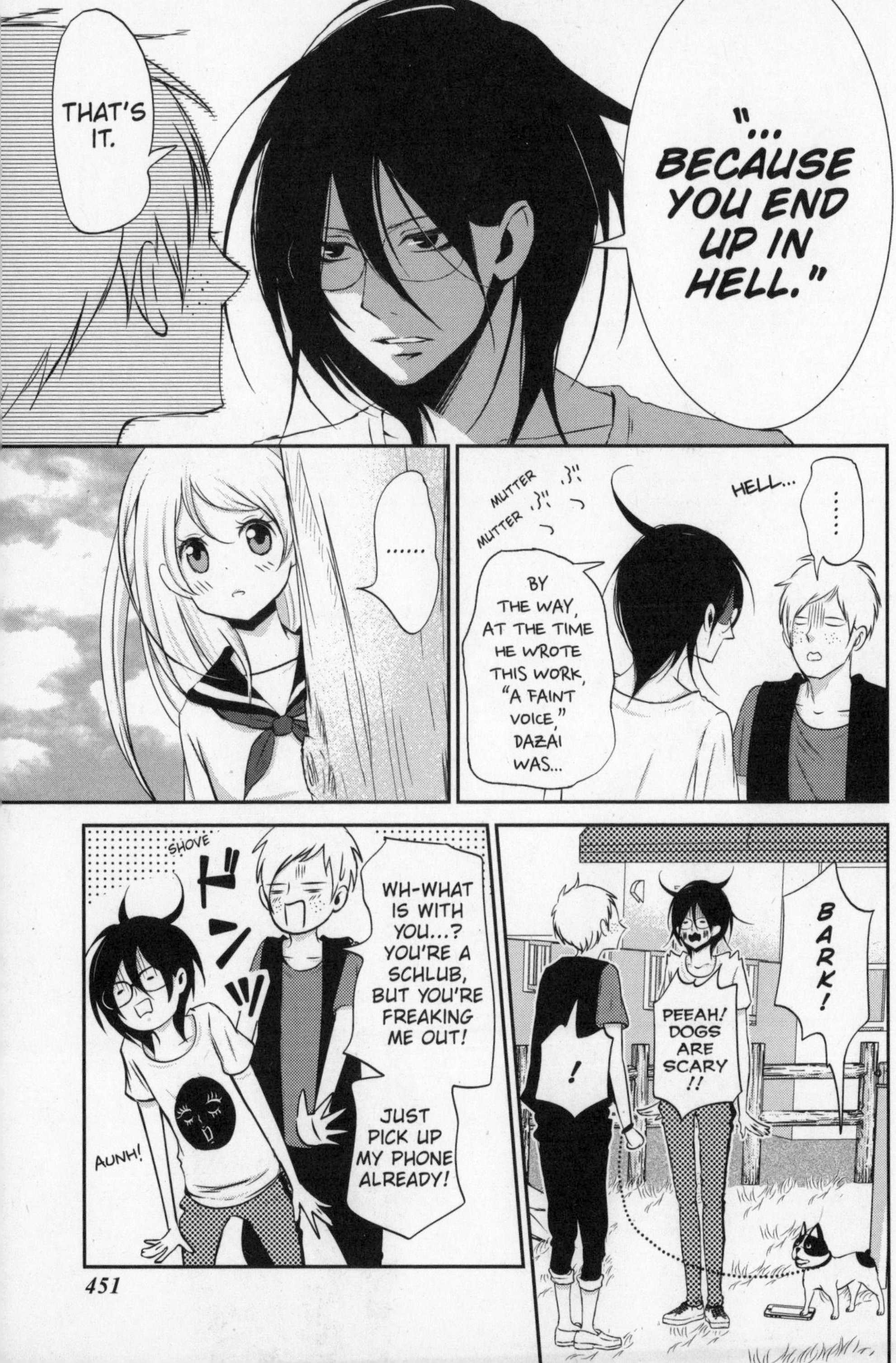
"...BECAUSE YOU END UP IN HELL."
THAT'S IT.
HELL...
......
MUTTER MUTTER
BY THE WAY, AT THE TIME HE WROTE THIS WORK, "A FAINT VOICE," DAZAI WAS...
......
BARK!
!
PEEAH! DOGS ARE SCARY!!
SHOVE
WH-WHAT IS WITH YOU...? YOU'RE A SCHLUB, BUT YOU'RE FREAKING ME OUT!
JUST PICK UP MY PHONE ALREADY!
AUNH!

I-I WON'T PICK IT UP...!
AAH!?
WHAT SHOULD I DO? KOMI-NAMI-SAN'S...
ガサッ
RUSTLE
!?
ひょいっ
YOINK
TAKE THAT. GON-JUROU'S HELL SHOWER.
BARK!
しゃーー!
PSSH
!?

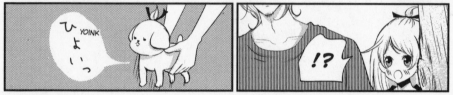

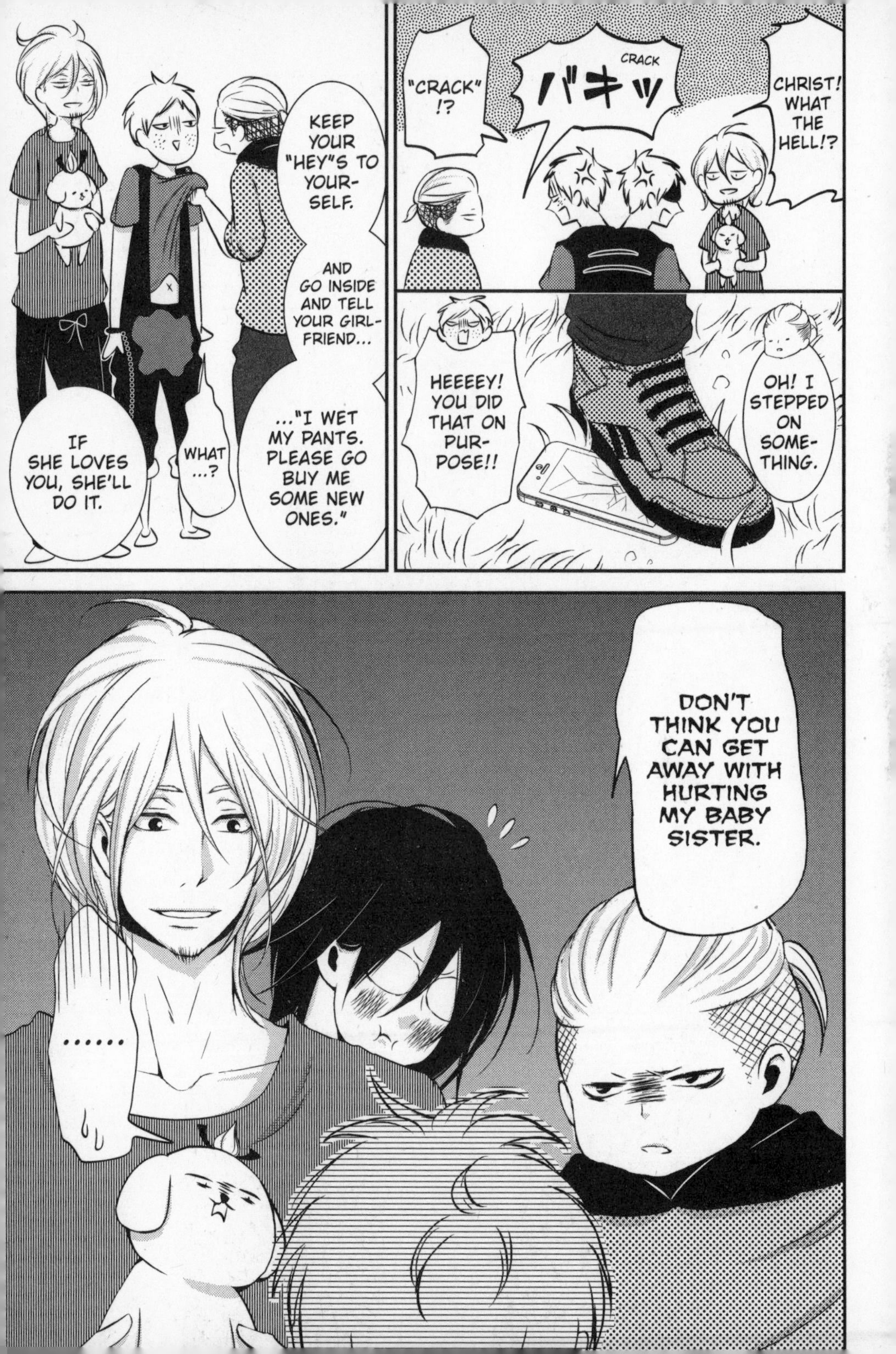
CHRIST! WHAT THE HELL!?
CRACK
バキッ
"CRACK" !?
OH! I STEPPED ON SOMETHING.
HEEEEY! YOU DID THAT ON PURPOSE!!
KEEP YOUR "HEY"S TO YOURSELF.
AND GO INSIDE AND TELL YOUR GIRLFRIEND...
..."I WET MY PANTS. PLEASE GO BUY ME SOME NEW ONES."
WHAT ...?
IF SHE LOVES YOU, SHE'LL DO IT.
DON'T THINK YOU CAN GET AWAY WITH HURTING MY BABY SISTER.
......

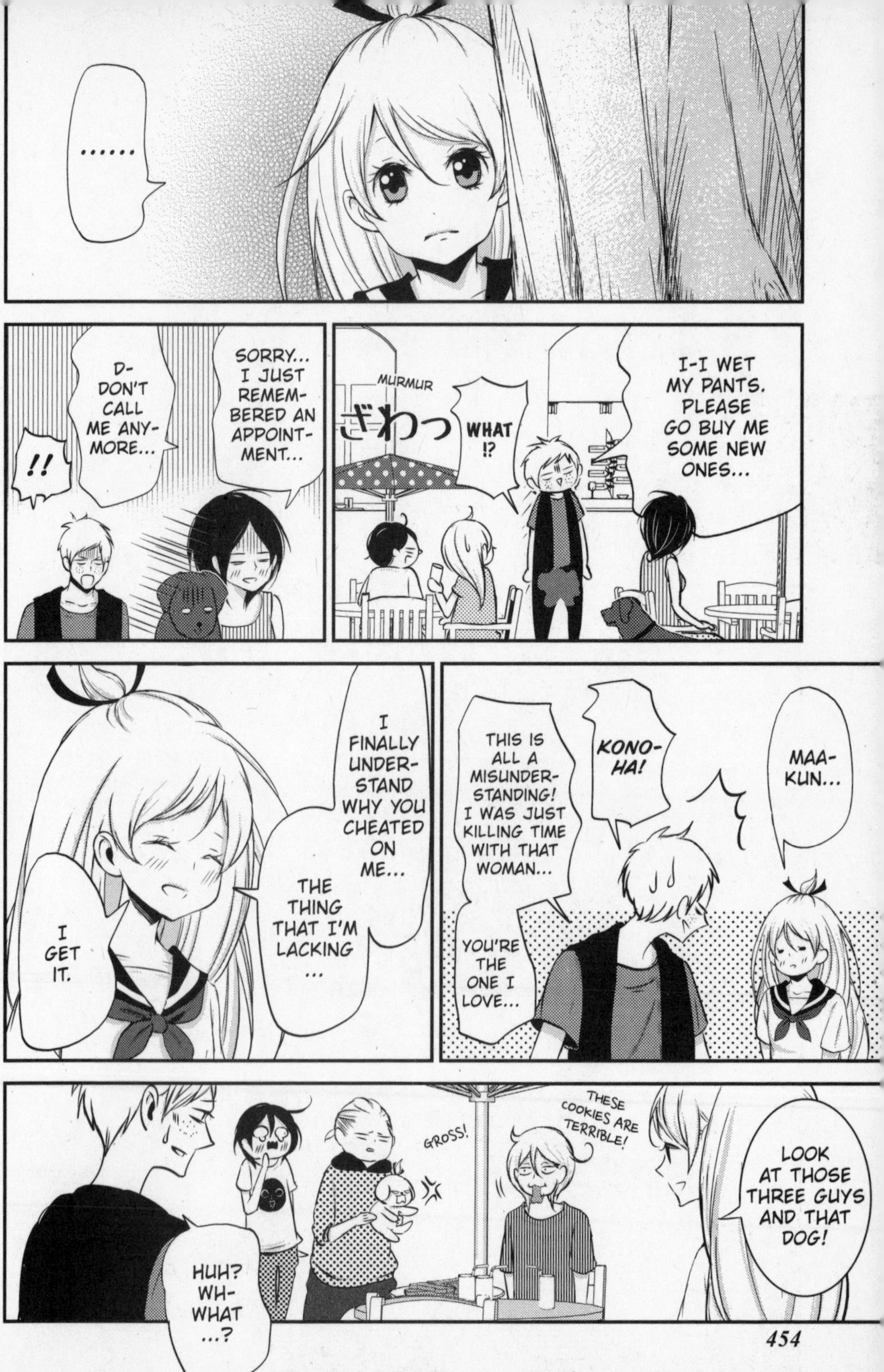
......
I-I WET MY PANTS. PLEASE GO BUY ME SOME NEW ONES...
WHAT!?
MURMUR
ざわっ
SORRY... I JUST REMEMBERED AN APPOINTMENT...
D-DON'T CALL ME ANYMORE...
!!
MAA-KUN...
KONOHA!
THIS IS ALL A MISUNDERSTANDING! I WAS JUST KILLING TIME WITH THAT WOMAN...
YOU'RE THE ONE I LOVE...
I FINALLY UNDERSTAND WHY YOU CHEATED ON ME...
THE THING THAT I'M LACKING...
I GET IT.
LOOK AT THOSE THREE GUYS AND THAT DOG!
THESE COOKIES ARE TERRIBLE!
GROSS!
HUH? WH-WHAT...?

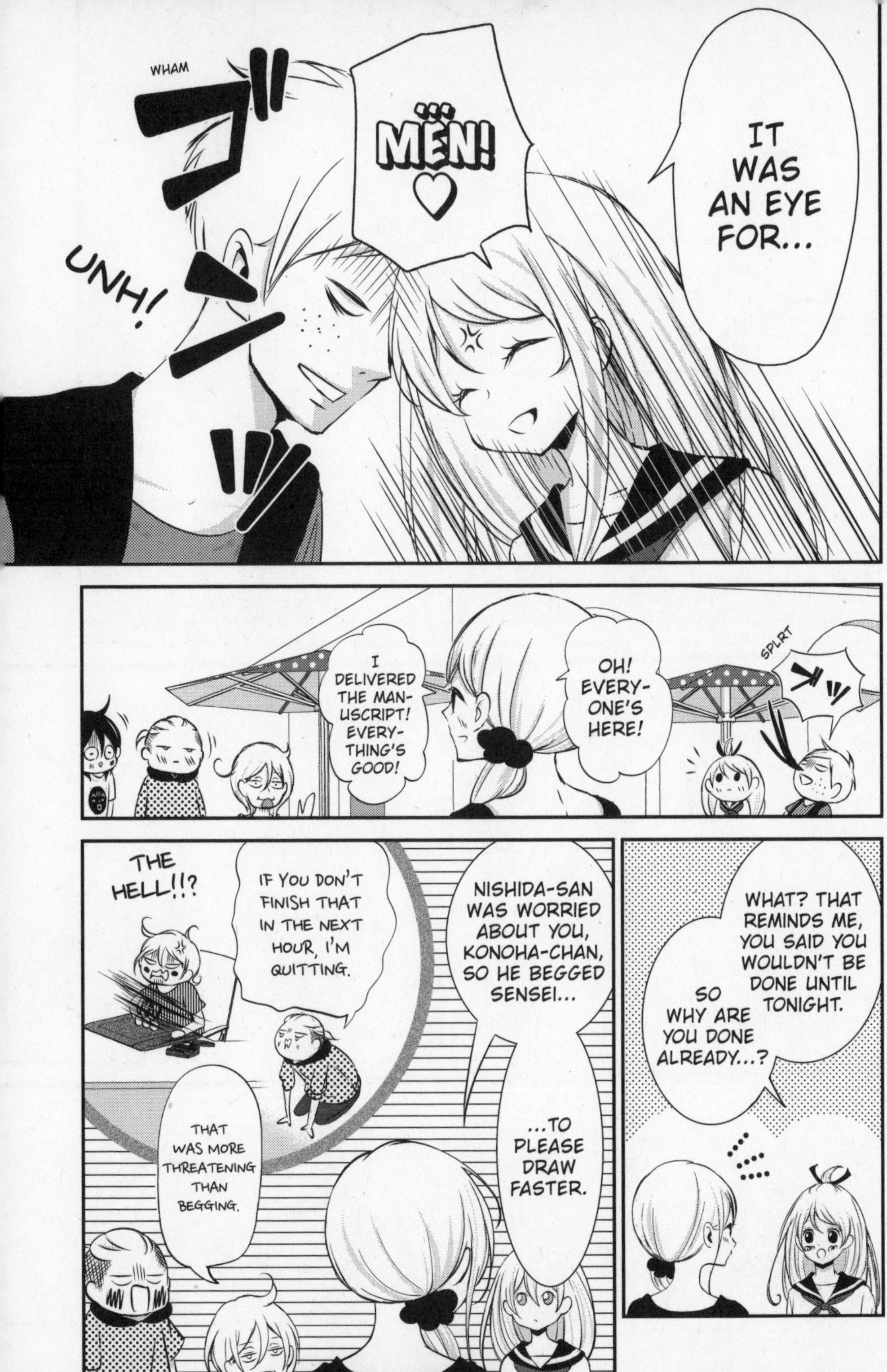
IT WAS AN EYE FOR...
...MEN! ♥
WHAM
UNH!
SPLRT
OH! EVERYONE'S HERE!
I DELIVERED THE MANUSCRIPT! EVERYTHING'S GOOD!
WHAT? THAT REMINDS ME, YOU SAID YOU WOULDN'T BE DONE UNTIL TONIGHT.
SO WHY ARE YOU DONE ALREADY...?
......
NISHIDA-SAN WAS WORRIED ABOUT YOU, KONOHA-CHAN, SO HE BEGGED SENSEI...
IF YOU DON'T FINISH THAT IN THE NEXT HOUR, I'M QUITTING.
THE HELL!!?
...TO PLEASE DRAW FASTER.
THAT WAS MORE THREATENING THAN BEGGING.

KATOU-SAN, WHY DID YOU TELL HERRR?
WHAT!? OH! I'M SORRY ...!!
TO MAKE UP FOR IT, KISS...
WHAT!?
THEY WERE SO CHEAP AT THE SUPER-MARKET !!
...OF COURSE THEY WERE.
LOL.
OOH! THOSE FISH LOOK GOOD...
BUT THOSE ARE ACTUALLY SHISHAMO.
AH HA HA!
WHAT!?
NEXT TIME, I WANT TO MAKE SURE I MEET...
... SOMEONE KIND...
...LIKE THESE MEN...!
UNNH, I'M IN HELL...
JUST LIKE DAZAI SAID!

TO BE CONTINUED

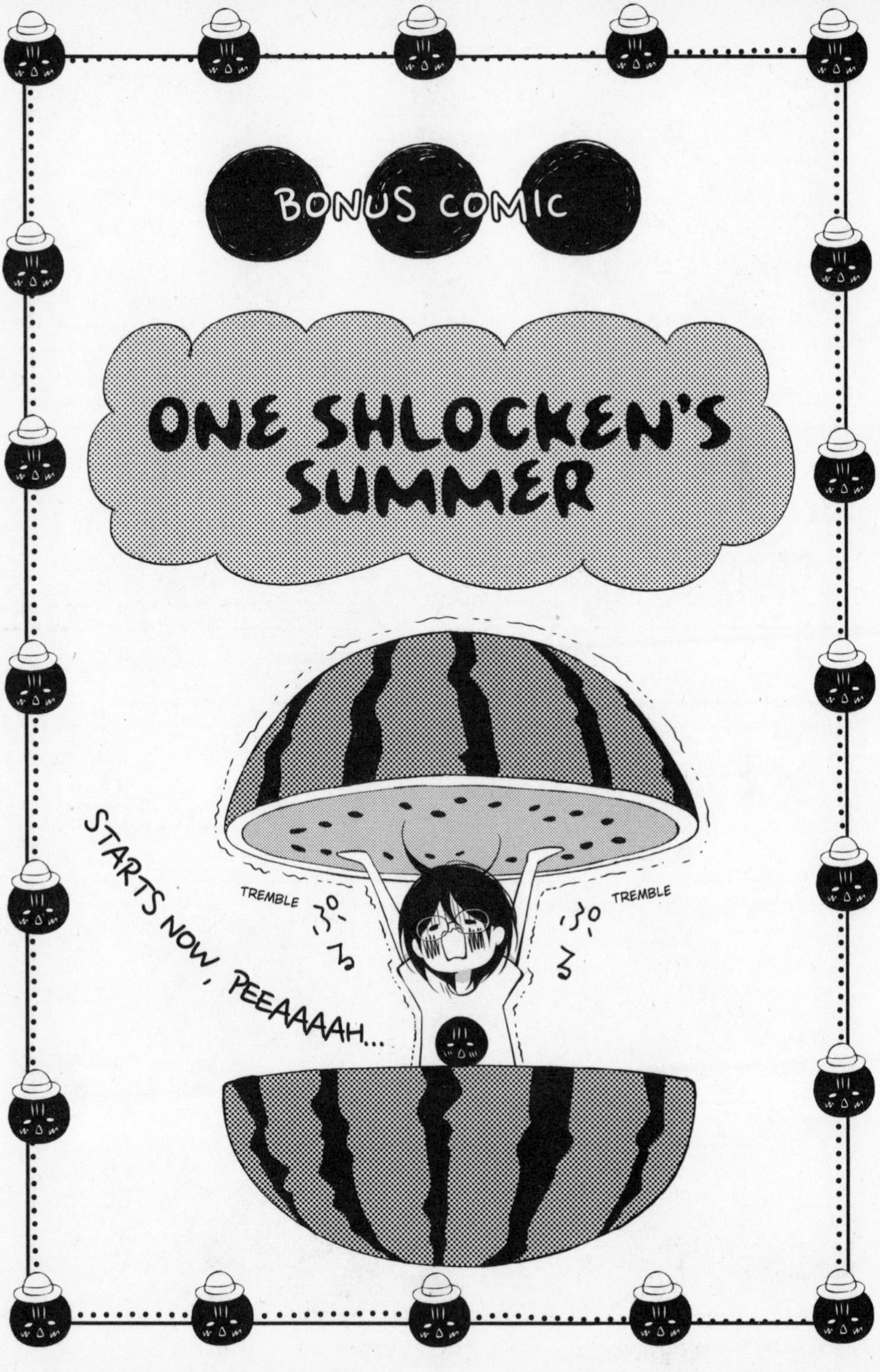
BONUS COMIC
ONE SHLOCKEN'S SUMMER
STARTS NOW, PEEAAAAH...
TREMBLE
TREMBLE

BARLEY TEA

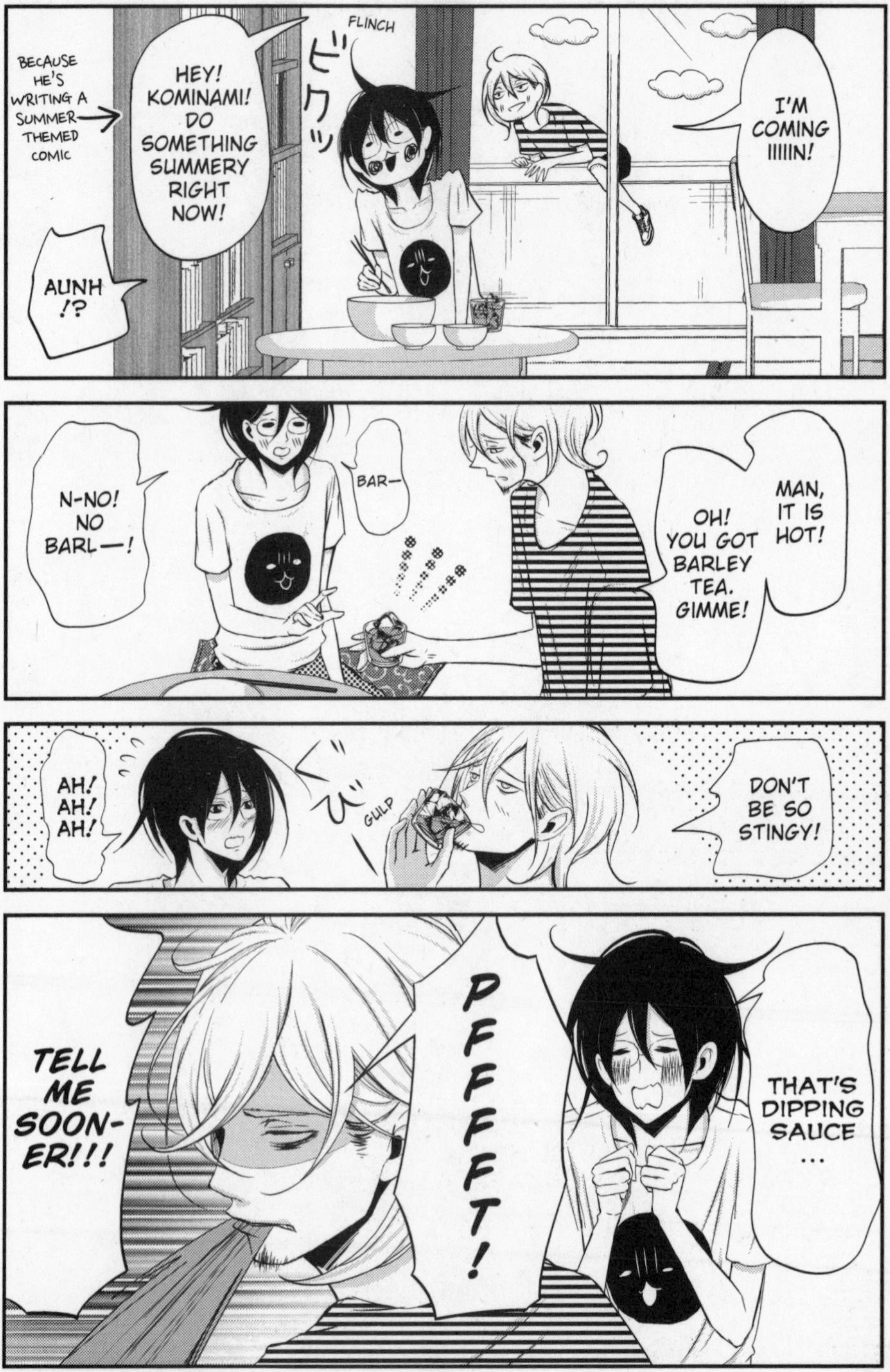
I'M COMING IIIIIN!
FLINCH
ビクッ
HEY! KOMINAMI! DO SOMETHING SUMMERY RIGHT NOW!
BECAUSE HE'S WRITING A SUMMER-THEMED COMIC
AUNH!?
MAN, IT IS HOT!
OH! YOU GOT BARLEY TEA. GIMME!
BAR—
N-NO! NO BARL—!
DON'T BE SO STINGY!
ぐび
GULP
AH! AH! AH!
THAT'S DIPPING SAUCE ...
PFFFFT!
TELL ME SOON-ER!!!

SOMETHING SUMMERY(?) HAPPENED ALMOST IMMEDIATELY.

MOVIE

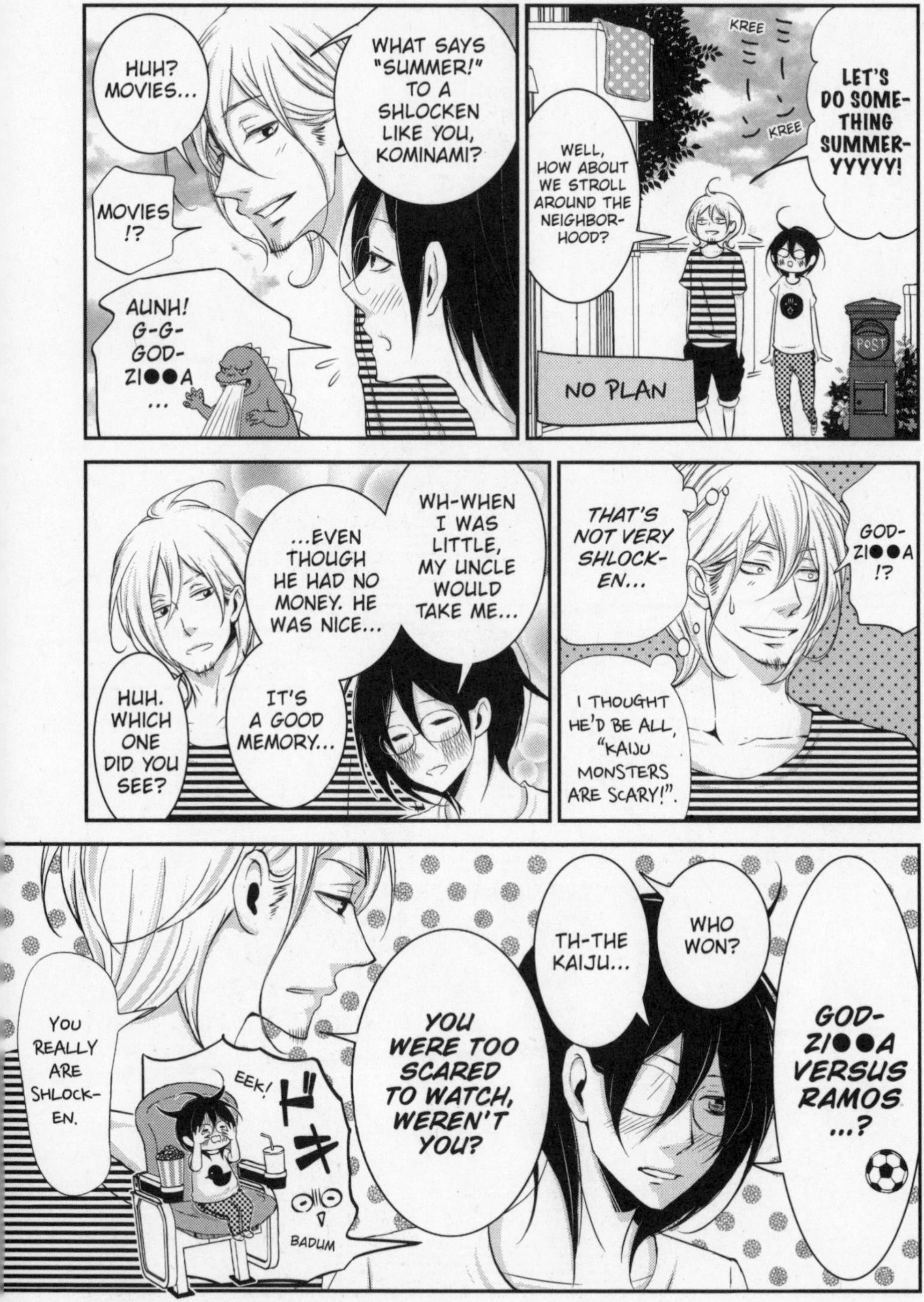
LET'S DO SOME-THING SUMMER-YYYYY!
KREE
KREE
WELL, HOW ABOUT WE STROLL AROUND THE NEIGHBOR-HOOD?
NO PLAN
WHAT SAYS "SUMMER!" TO A SHLOCKEN LIKE YOU, KOMINAMI?
HUH? MOVIES...
MOVIES!?
AUNH! G-G-GOD-ZI●●A ...
THAT'S NOT VERY SHLOCK-EN...
GOD-ZI●●A!?
I THOUGHT HE'D BE ALL, "KAIJU MONSTERS ARE SCARY!".
WH-WHEN I WAS LITTLE, MY UNCLE WOULD TAKE ME...
...EVEN THOUGH HE HAD NO MONEY. HE WAS NICE...
IT'S A GOOD MEMORY...
HUH. WHICH ONE DID YOU SEE?
GOD-ZI●●A VERSUS RAMOS ...?
WHO WON?
TH-THE KAIJU...
YOU WERE TOO SCARED TO WATCH, WEREN'T YOU?
ドキ
BADUM
EEK!
YOU REALLY ARE SHLOCK-EN.

TAMA-CHAN WAS SHOCKED.

GARIGARI-KUN

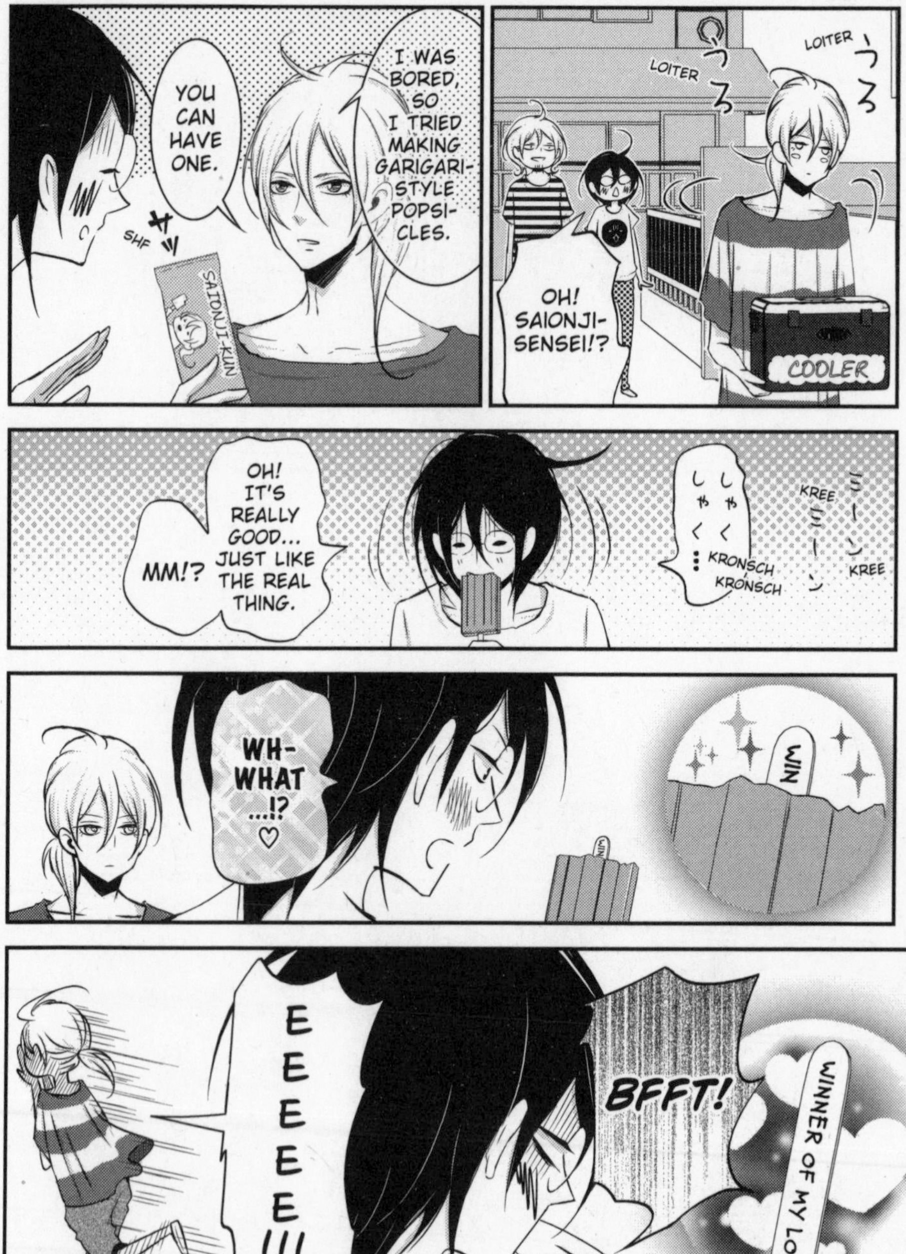

LOITER うろ
LOITER うろ
OH! SAIONJI-SENSEI!?
COOLER
I WAS BORED, SO I TRIED MAKING GARIGARI-STYLE POPSICLES.
YOU CAN HAVE ONE.
SHF サッ
SAIONJI-KUN
ミーンミーン
KREE KREE
しゃくしゃく…
KRONSCH KRONSCH
OH! IT'S REALLY GOOD... JUST LIKE THE REAL THING.
MM!?
WIN
WH-WHAT ...!? ♡
WIN
WINNER OF MY LOVE
BFFT!
EEEEE!!!
WINNER OF MY LOVE

THE PRIZE IS MEEE?

FUR

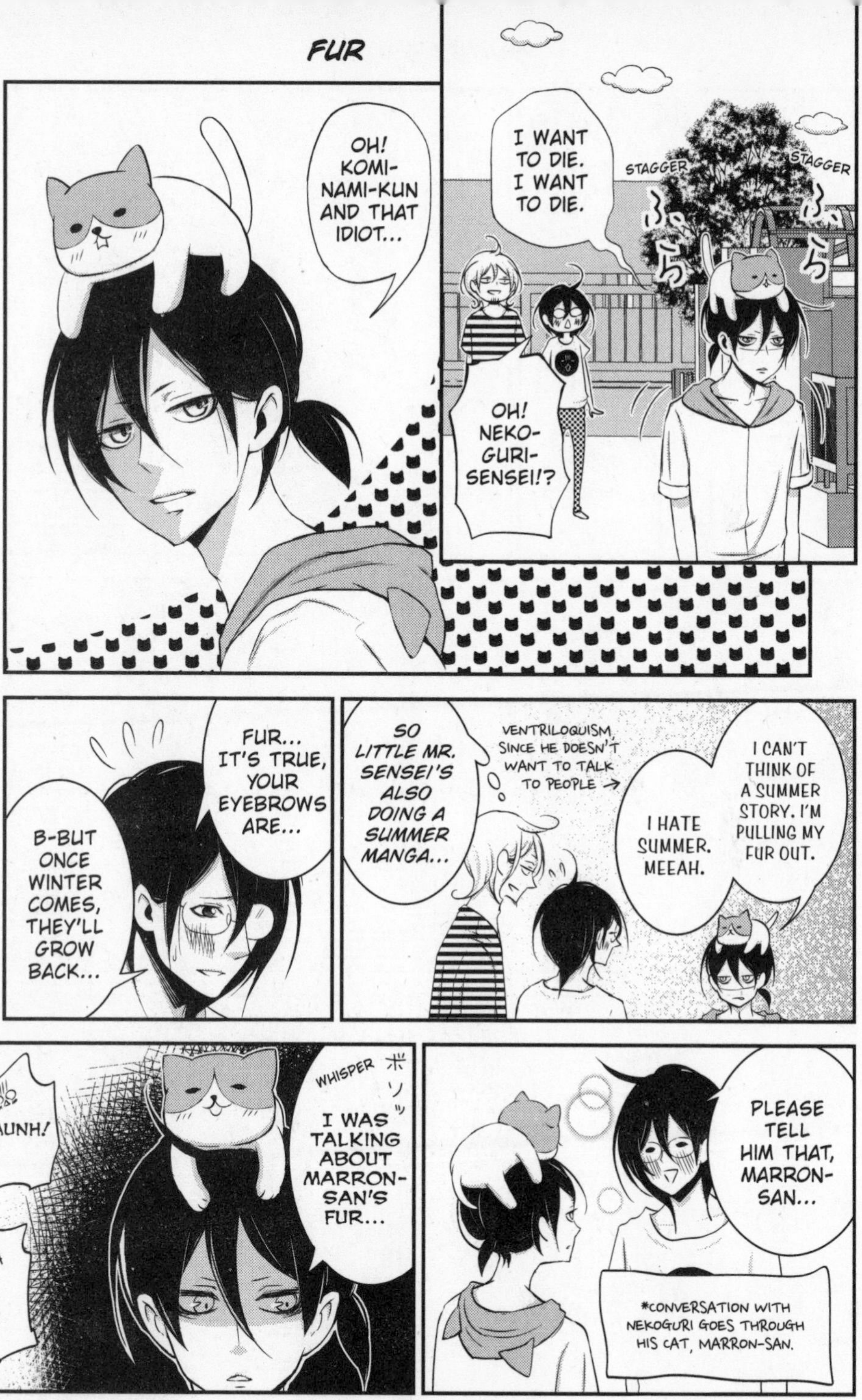

I WANT TO DIE. I WANT TO DIE.
STAGGER
ふら
STAGGER
ふら
OH! NEKO-GURI-SENSEI!?
OH! KOMI-NAMI-KUN AND THAT IDIOT...
I CAN'T THINK OF A SUMMER STORY. I'M PULLING MY FUR OUT.
I HATE SUMMER. MEEAH.
VENTRILOQUISM, SINCE HE DOESN'T WANT TO TALK TO PEOPLE →
SO LITTLE MR. SENSEI'S ALSO DOING A SUMMER MANGA...
FUR... IT'S TRUE, YOUR EYEBROWS ARE...
B-BUT ONCE WINTER COMES, THEY'LL GROW BACK...
PLEASE TELL HIM THAT, MARRON-SAN...
*CONVERSATION WITH NEKOGURI GOES THROUGH HIS CAT, MARRON-SAN.
WHISPER
ボソッ
I WAS TALKING ABOUT MARRON-SAN'S FUR...
AUNH!
KYA HA HA HA!

EYEBROWS DON'T GROW BACK! MROW!

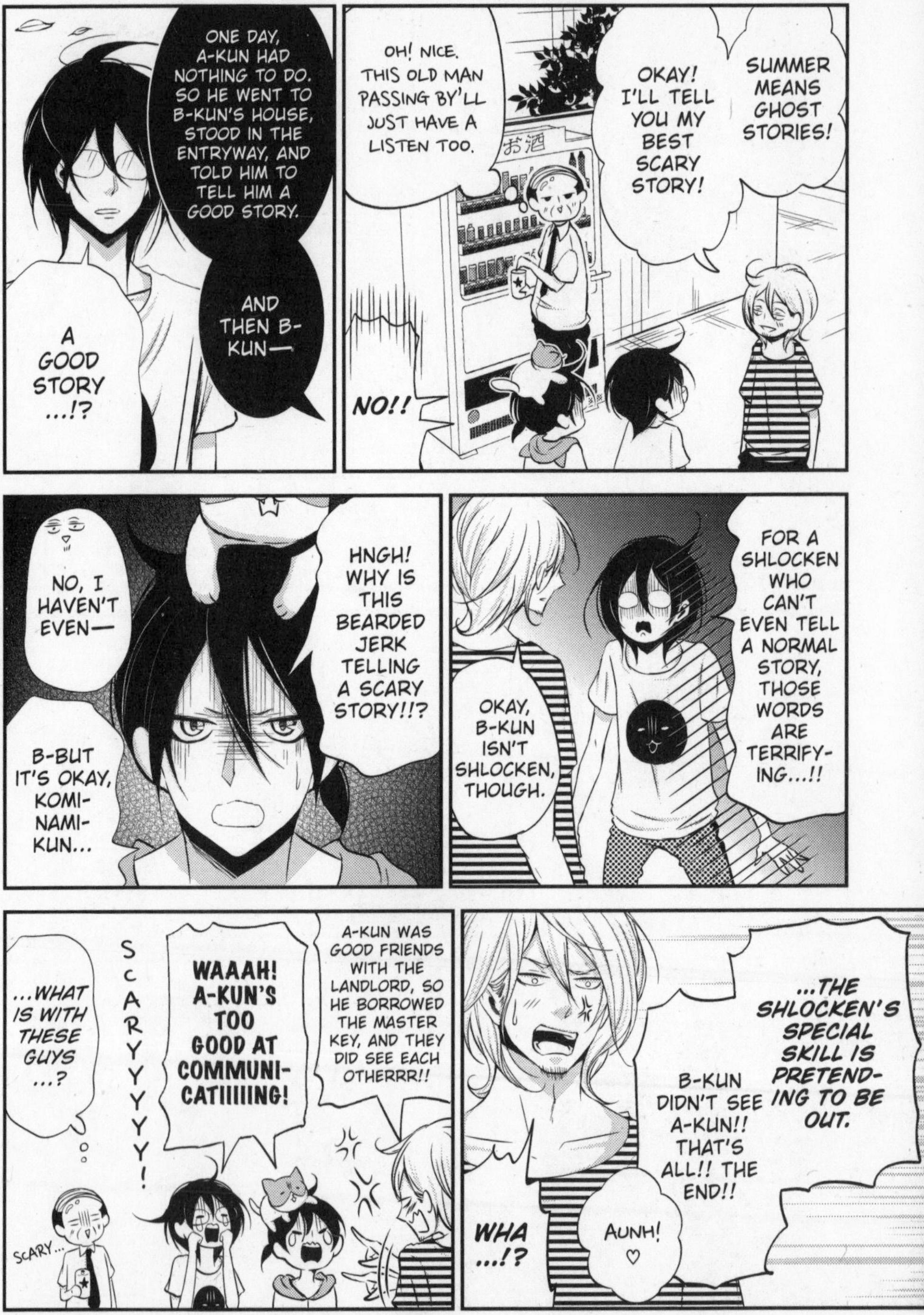
SUMMER MEANS GHOST STORIES!
OKAY! I'LL TELL YOU MY BEST SCARY STORY!
お酒
OH! NICE. THIS OLD MAN PASSING BY'LL JUST HAVE A LISTEN TOO.
NO!!
ONE DAY, A-KUN HAD NOTHING TO DO. SO HE WENT TO B-KUN'S HOUSE, STOOD IN THE ENTRYWAY, AND TOLD HIM TO TELL HIM A GOOD STORY.
AND THEN B-KUN—
A GOOD STORY ...!?
FOR A SHLOCKEN WHO CAN'T EVEN TELL A NORMAL STORY, THOSE WORDS ARE TERRIFYING...!!
OKAY, B-KUN ISN'T SHLOCKEN, THOUGH.
HNGH! WHY IS THIS BEARDED JERK TELLING A SCARY STORY!!?
NO, I HAVEN'T EVEN—
B-BUT IT'S OKAY, KOMINAMI-KUN...
...THE SHLOCKEN'S SPECIAL SKILL IS PRETENDING TO BE OUT.
B-KUN DIDN'T SEE A-KUN!! THAT'S ALL!! THE END!!
AUNH! ♡
WHA ...!?
A-KUN WAS GOOD FRIENDS WITH THE LANDLORD, SO HE BORROWED THE MASTER KEY, AND THEY DID SEE EACH OTHERRR!!
WAAAH! A-KUN'S TOO GOOD AT COMMUNICATIIIIING!
SCARYYYYY!
...WHAT IS WITH THESE GUYS ...?
SCARY...

I WANT TO KNOW THE REST OF HIS BEST SCARY STORY...

BEER GARDEN

SUMMER MEANS BEER GARDENS!!
FIDGET FIDGET
I'VE NEVER HAD ANY FRIENDS, SO I'VE NEVER BEEN TO ONE BEFORE...
NOT THAT YOU TWO ARE MY FRIENDS, BUT STILL...
WHOA! NEKO-GURI-SENSEI'S A LITTLE EXCITED.
I'M SORRY. WE CAN'T SERVE JUNIOR HIGH STUDENTS ...
STAFF
TWENTY-FIVE!? I AM SO SORRY!
DRIVER'S LICENSE
THIS IS WHY I HATE PEOPLE...
AAAH! BEER IS DELICIOUS OUTSIDE!
SOMEHOW I FEEL LIKE I COULD DRAW A SUMMER MANGA NOW...!!
ME TOO!
TH-THAT'S GREAT!
WAIT. SENSEI TOO...? MANGA ...?
OH! NO, UHH... OH!! YOUR SUMMER HOLIDAY STARTS TOMORROW, KOMINAMI!!
WHAT!? ♡
YAY!! I'M GONNA SHUT MYSELF UP IN MY HOOOUSE!!
OOLONG TEA
THE NEXT DAY...
KOMI-NAMI, WE'RE GOING TO THE BEACH.
HUH!? BUT SUMMER VACA-TION...
IT'S SUMMER VACATION, WHICH MEANS YOU GO AND HANG OUT!
NO SHUT-IN TIME

AND THIS BRINGS US TO PAGE 4.

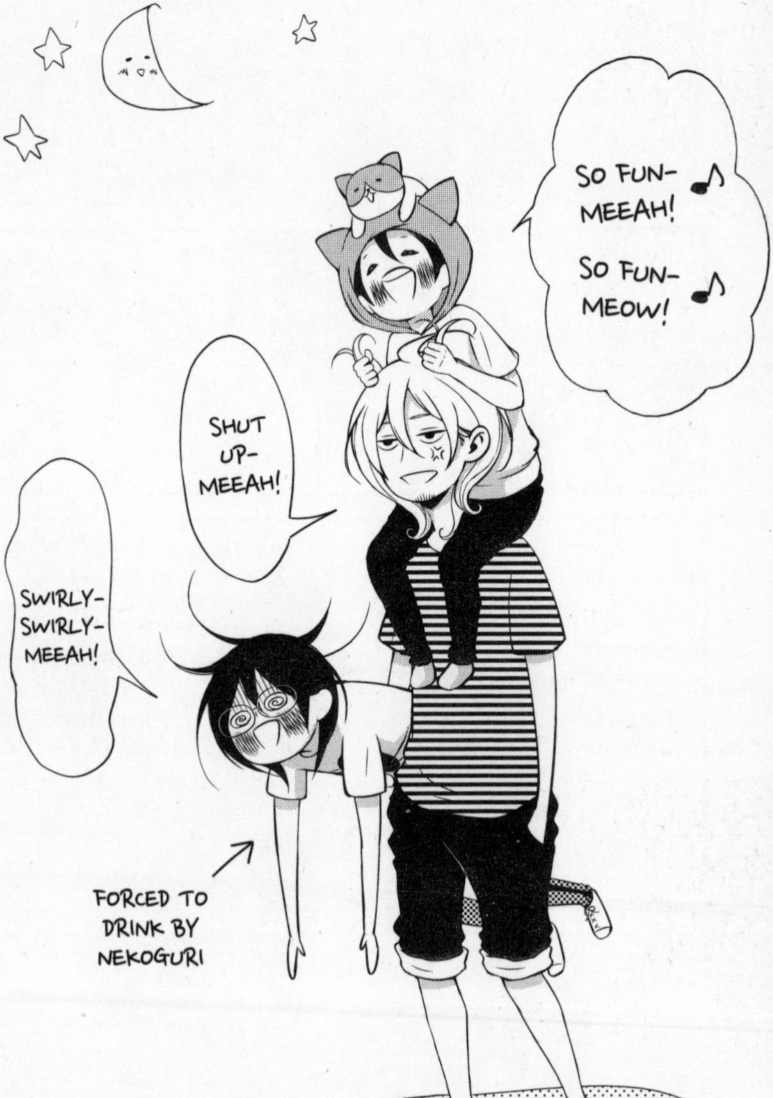
SO FUN-MEEAH! ♪ SO FUN-MEOW! ♪
SHUT UP-MEEAH!
SWIRLY-SWIRLY-MEEAH!
FORCED TO DRINK BY NEKOGURI

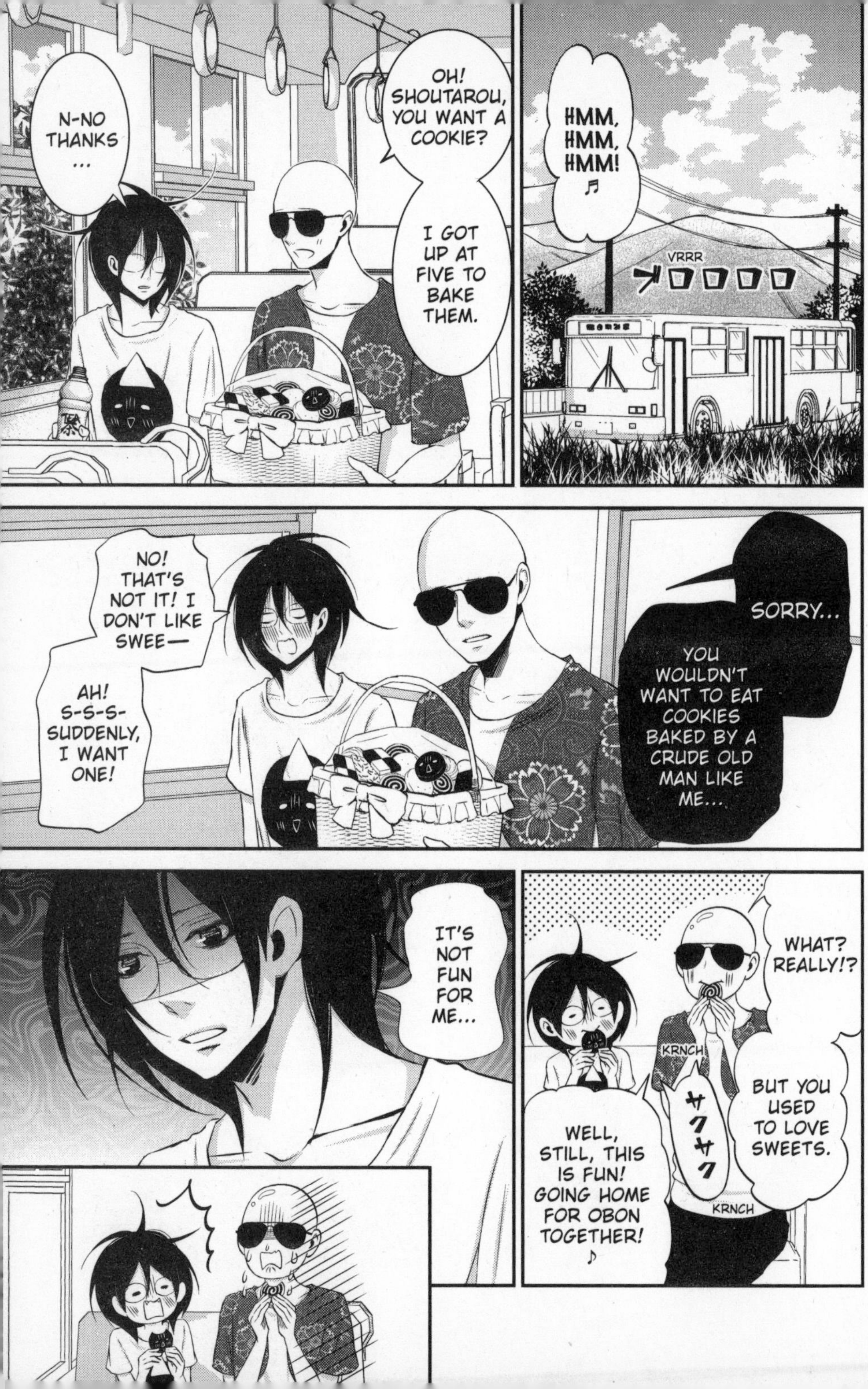

HMM, HMM, HMM! ♪
VRRR
ブロロロロ
OH! SHOUTAROU, YOU WANT A COOKIE?
I GOT UP AT FIVE TO BAKE THEM.
N-NO THANKS ...
SORRY...
YOU WOULDN'T WANT TO EAT COOKIES BAKED BY A CRUDE OLD MAN LIKE ME...
NO! THAT'S NOT IT! I DON'T LIKE SWEE—
AH! S-S-S-SUDDENLY, I WANT ONE!
WHAT? REALLY!?
BUT YOU USED TO LOVE SWEETS.
KRNCH
サクサク
KRNCH
WELL, STILL, THIS IS FUN! GOING HOME FOR OBON TOGETHER! ♪
IT'S NOT FUN FOR ME...

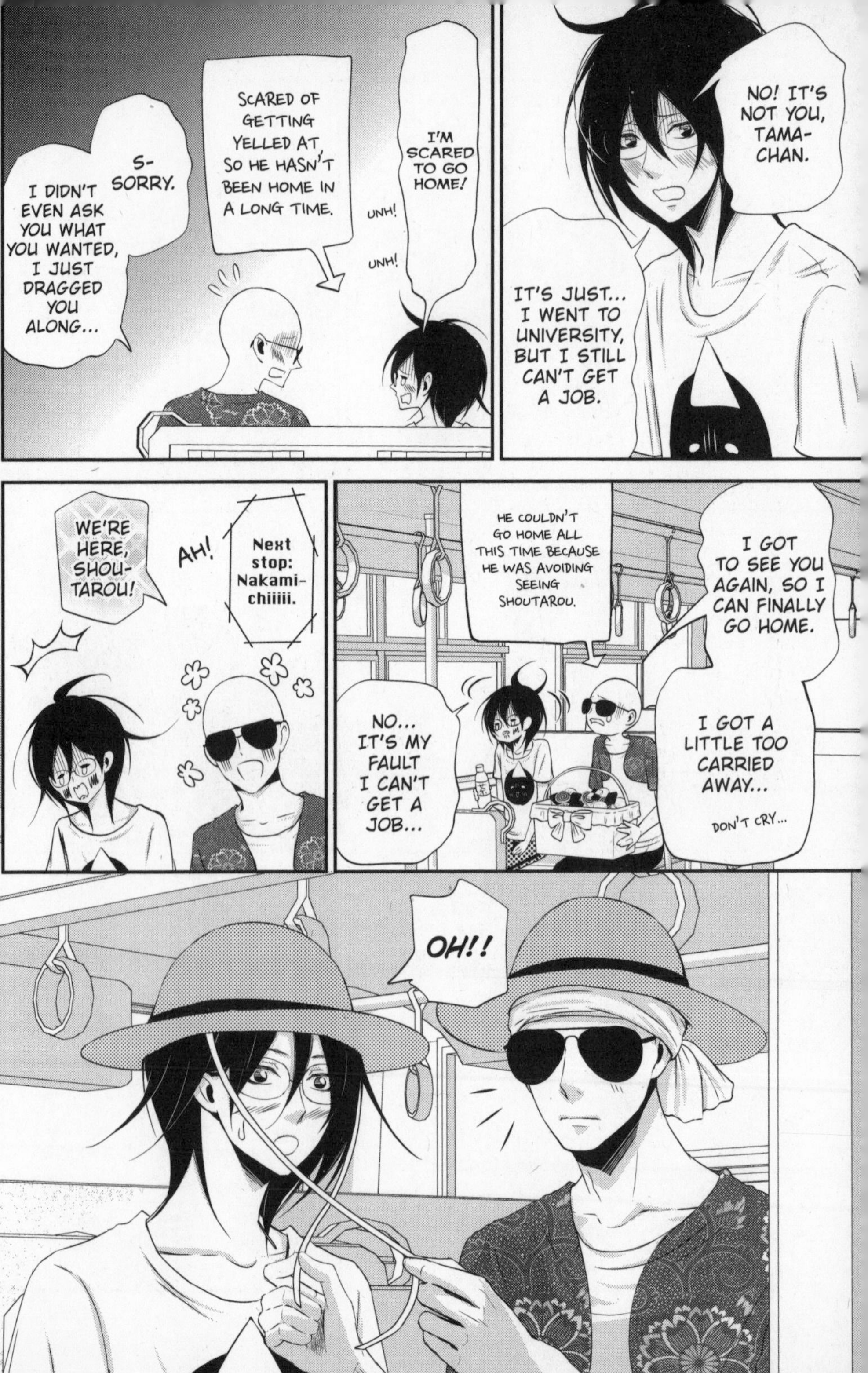
NO! IT'S NOT YOU, TAMA-CHAN.
IT'S JUST... I WENT TO UNIVERSITY, BUT I STILL CAN'T GET A JOB.
I'M SCARED TO GO HOME!
UNH!
UNH!
SCARED OF GETTING YELLED AT, SO HE HASN'T BEEN HOME IN A LONG TIME.
S-SORRY.
I DIDN'T EVEN ASK YOU WHAT YOU WANTED, I JUST DRAGGED YOU ALONG...
I GOT TO SEE YOU AGAIN, SO I CAN FINALLY GO HOME.
HE COULDN'T GO HOME ALL THIS TIME BECAUSE HE WAS AVOIDING SEEING SHOUTAROU.
I GOT A LITTLE TOO CARRIED AWAY...
DON'T CRY...
NO... IT'S MY FAULT I CAN'T GET A JOB...
Next stop: Nakamichiiiii.
AH!
WE'RE HERE, SHOUTAROU!
OH!!

12 VS. THE HOMECOMING

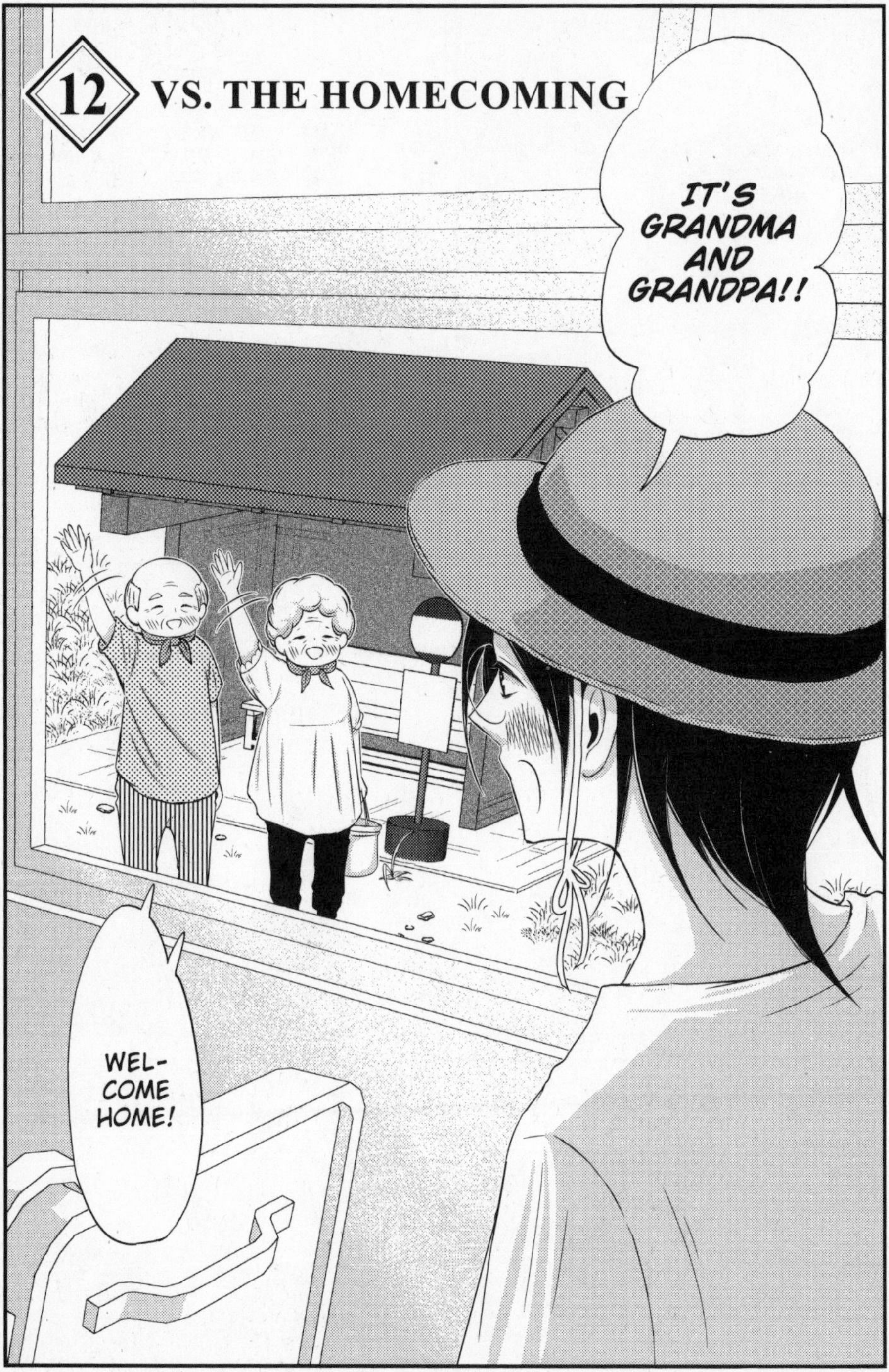
IT'S GRANDMA AND GRANDPA!!
WEL-COME HOME!

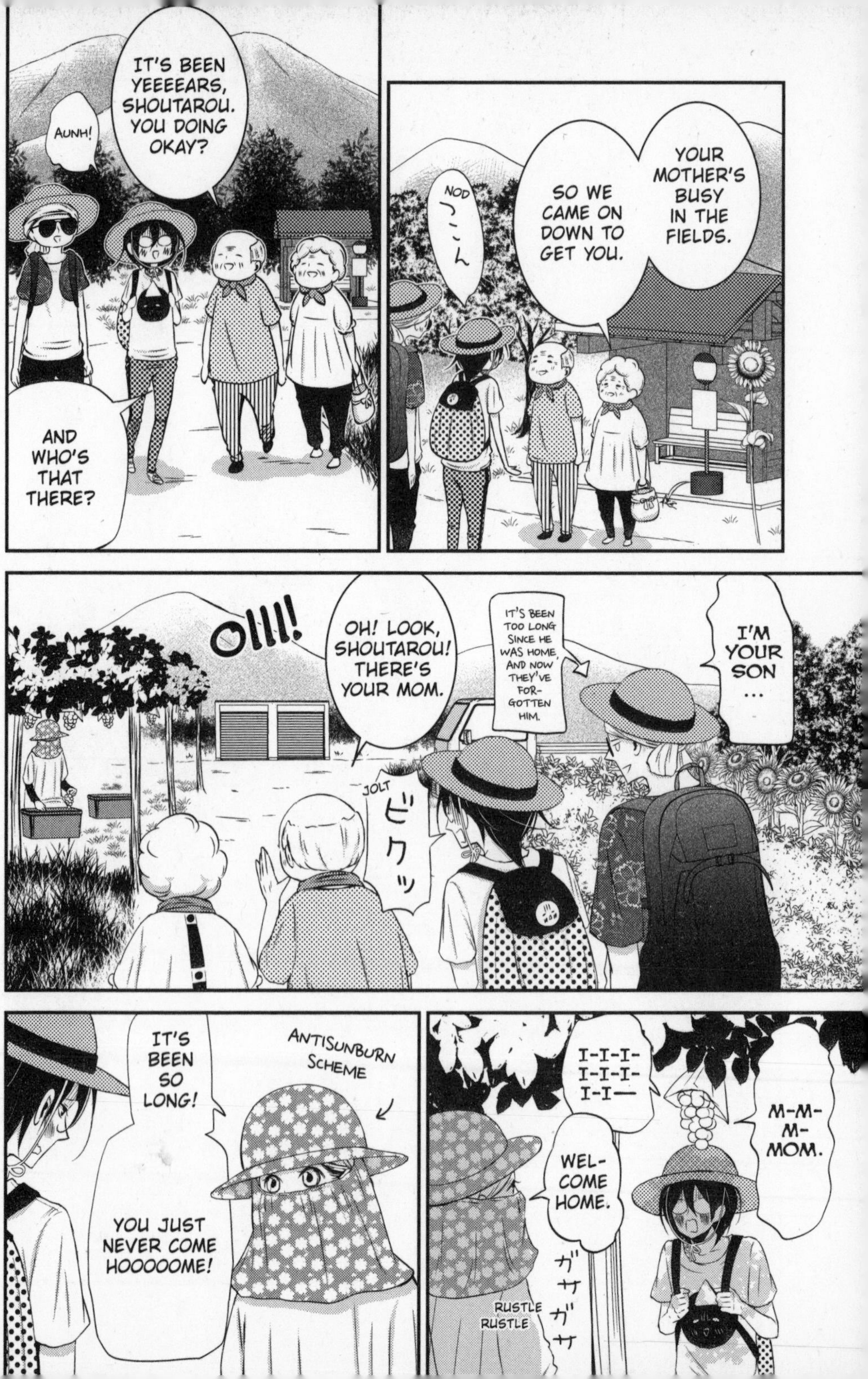
YOUR MOTHER'S BUSY IN THE FIELDS.
SO WE CAME ON DOWN TO GET YOU.
NOD
こくん
IT'S BEEN YEEEEARS, SHOUTAROU. YOU DOING OKAY?
AUNH!
AND WHO'S THAT THERE?
I'M YOUR SON ...
IT'S BEEN TOO LONG SINCE HE WAS HOME, AND NOW THEY'VE FOR-GOTTEN HIM.
OH! LOOK, SHOUTAROU! THERE'S YOUR MOM.
OIII!
JOLT
ビクッ
M-M-M-MOM.
I-I-I-I-I-I-I-I—
WEL-COME HOME.
RUSTLE RUSTLE
ガサガサ
IT'S BEEN SO LONG!
ANTISUNBURN SCHEME
YOU JUST NEVER COME HOOOOOME!

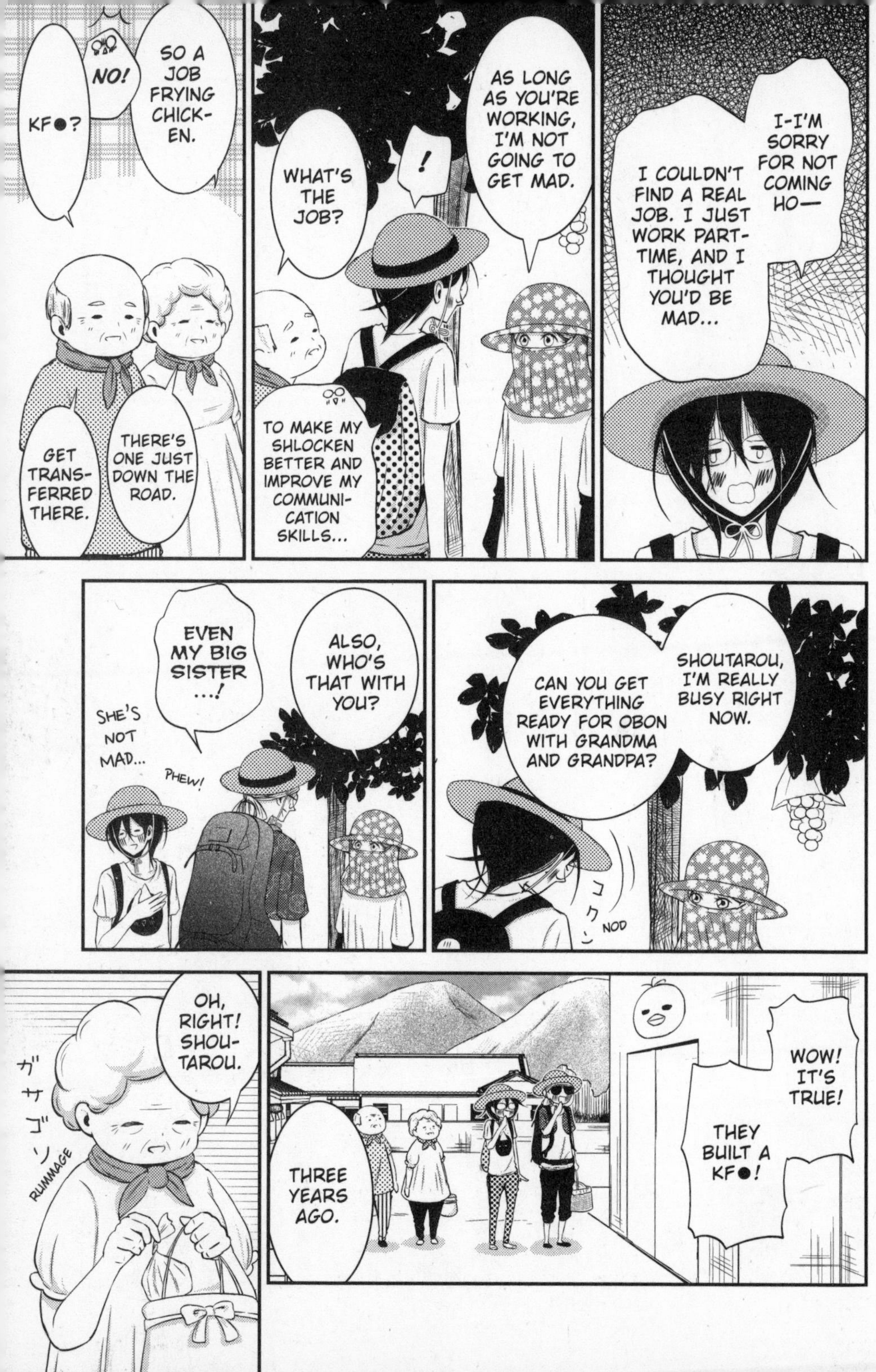
I-I'M SORRY FOR NOT COMING HO—
I COULDN'T FIND A REAL JOB. I JUST WORK PART-TIME, AND I THOUGHT YOU'D BE MAD...
AS LONG AS YOU'RE WORKING, I'M NOT GOING TO GET MAD.
!
WHAT'S THE JOB?
TO MAKE MY SHLOCKEN BETTER AND IMPROVE MY COMMUNICATION SKILLS...
SO A JOB FRYING CHICKEN.
NO!
KF●?
THERE'S ONE JUST DOWN THE ROAD.
GET TRANSFERRED THERE.
SHOUTAROU, I'M REALLY BUSY RIGHT NOW.
CAN YOU GET EVERYTHING READY FOR OBON WITH GRANDMA AND GRANDPA?
コクン
NOD
ALSO, WHO'S THAT WITH YOU?
EVEN MY BIG SISTER ...!
SHE'S NOT MAD...
PHEW!
WOW! IT'S TRUE!
THEY BUILT A KF●!
THREE YEARS AGO.
OH, RIGHT! SHOUTAROU.
ガサゴソ
RUMMAGE

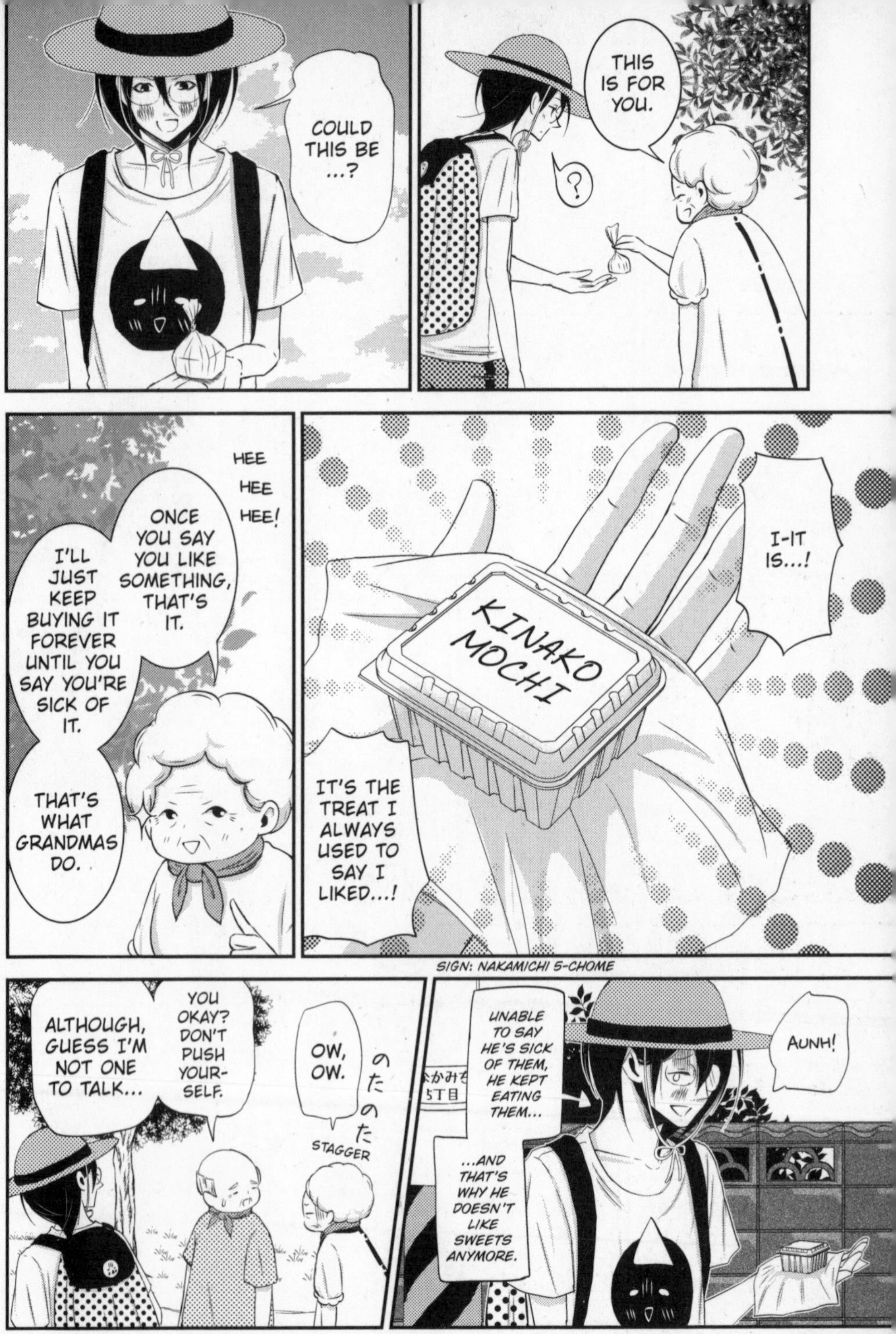
THIS IS FOR YOU.
?
COULD THIS BE ...?
I-IT IS...!
KINAKO MOCHI
IT'S THE TREAT I ALWAYS USED TO SAY I LIKED...!
HEE HEE HEE!
ONCE YOU SAY YOU LIKE SOMETHING, THAT'S IT.
I'LL JUST KEEP BUYING IT FOREVER UNTIL YOU SAY YOU'RE SICK OF IT.
THAT'S WHAT GRANDMAS DO.
SIGN: NAKAMICHI 5-CHOME
AUNH!
UNABLE TO SAY HE'S SICK OF THEM, HE KEPT EATING THEM...
...AND THAT'S WHY HE DOESN'T LIKE SWEETS ANYMORE.
のたのた
STAGGER
OW, OW.
YOU OKAY? DON'T PUSH YOURSELF.
ALTHOUGH, GUESS I'M NOT ONE TO TALK...

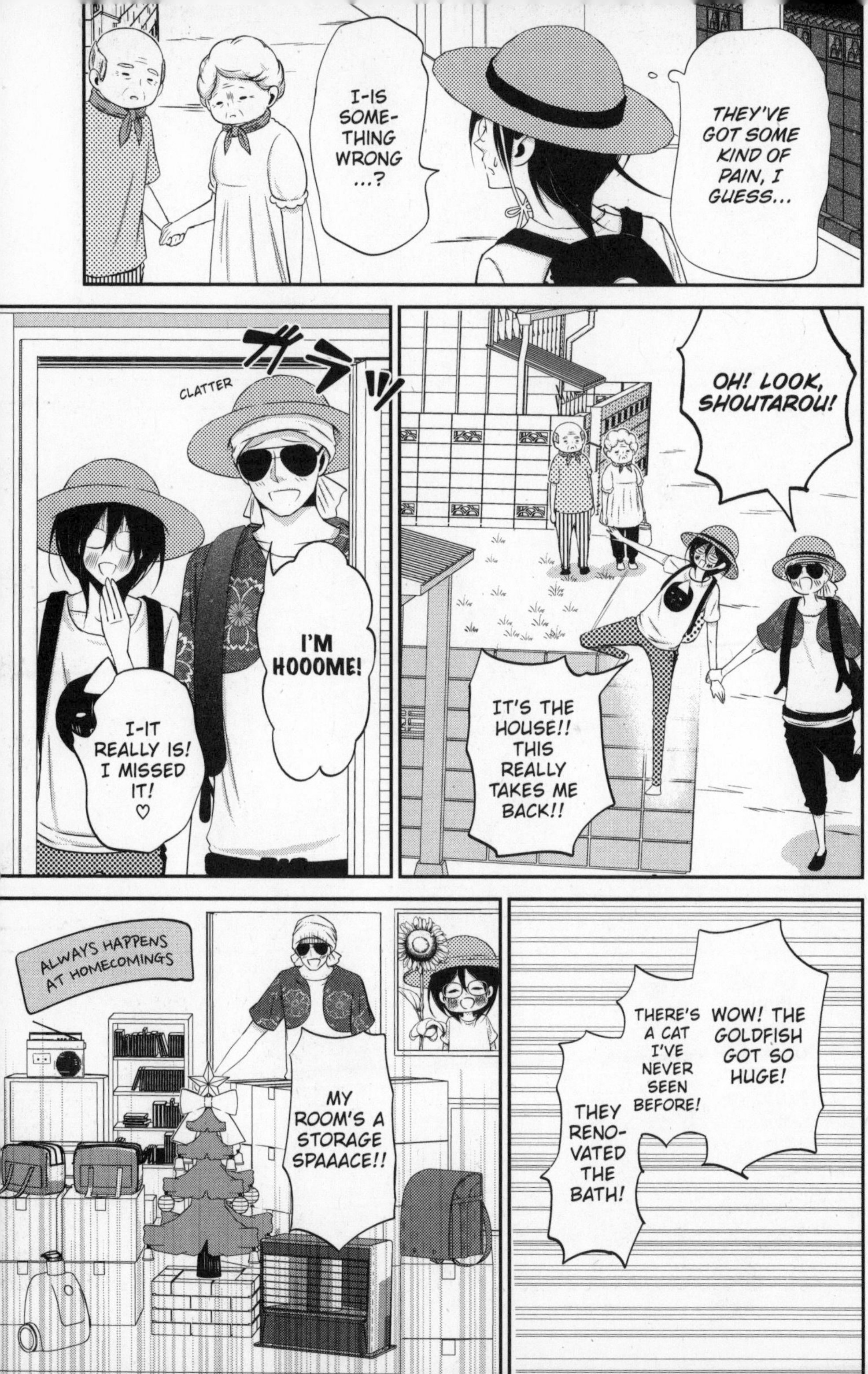
THEY'VE GOT SOME KIND OF PAIN, I GUESS...
I-IS SOME-THING WRONG ...?
OH! LOOK, SHOUTAROU!
IT'S THE HOUSE!! THIS REALLY TAKES ME BACK!!
ガラッ
CLATTER
I'M HOOOME!
I-IT REALLY IS! I MISSED IT! ♡
WOW! THE GOLDFISH GOT SO HUGE!
THERE'S A CAT I'VE NEVER SEEN BEFORE!
THEY RENO-VATED THE BATH!
ALWAYS HAPPENS AT HOMECOMINGS
MY ROOM'S A STORAGE SPAAACE!!

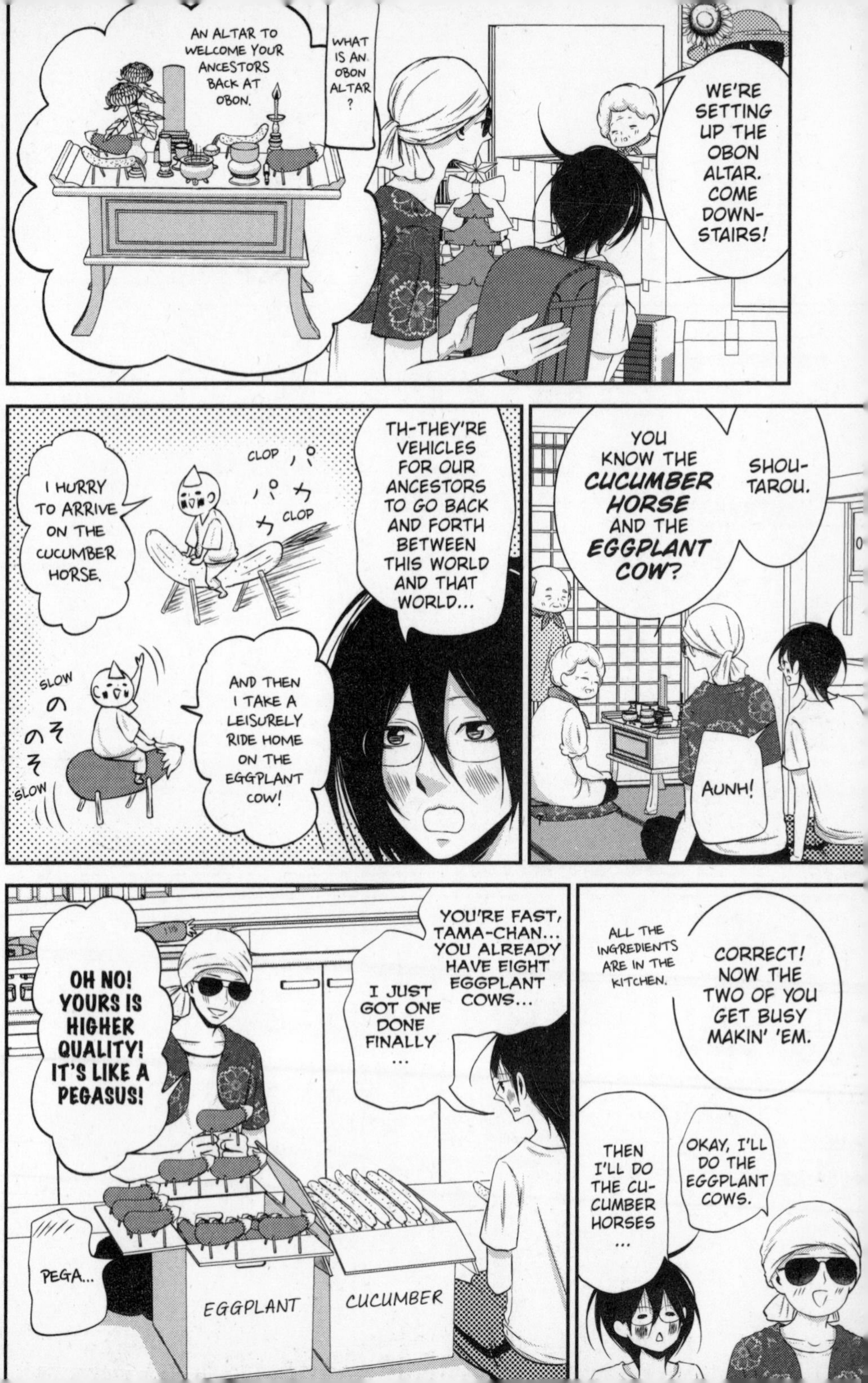
WE'RE SETTING UP THE OBON ALTAR. COME DOWN-STAIRS!
WHAT IS AN OBON ALTAR?
AN ALTAR TO WELCOME YOUR ANCESTORS BACK AT OBON.
SHOU-TAROU.
YOU KNOW THE CUCUMBER HORSE AND THE EGGPLANT COW?
AUNH!
TH-THEY'RE VEHICLES FOR OUR ANCESTORS TO GO BACK AND FORTH BETWEEN THIS WORLD AND THAT WORLD...
CLOP パカ
パカ CLOP
I HURRY TO ARRIVE ON THE CUCUMBER HORSE.
AND THEN I TAKE A LEISURELY RIDE HOME ON THE EGGPLANT COW!
SLOW のそ
のそ SLOW
CORRECT! NOW THE TWO OF YOU GET BUSY MAKIN' 'EM.
ALL THE INGREDIENTS ARE IN THE KITCHEN.
OKAY, I'LL DO THE EGGPLANT COWS.
THEN I'LL DO THE CU-CUMBER HORSES...
YOU'RE FAST, TAMA-CHAN... YOU ALREADY HAVE EIGHT EGGPLANT COWS...
I JUST GOT ONE DONE FINALLY...
OH NO! YOURS IS HIGHER QUALITY! IT'S LIKE A PEGASUS!
PEGA...
EGGPLANT
CUCUMBER

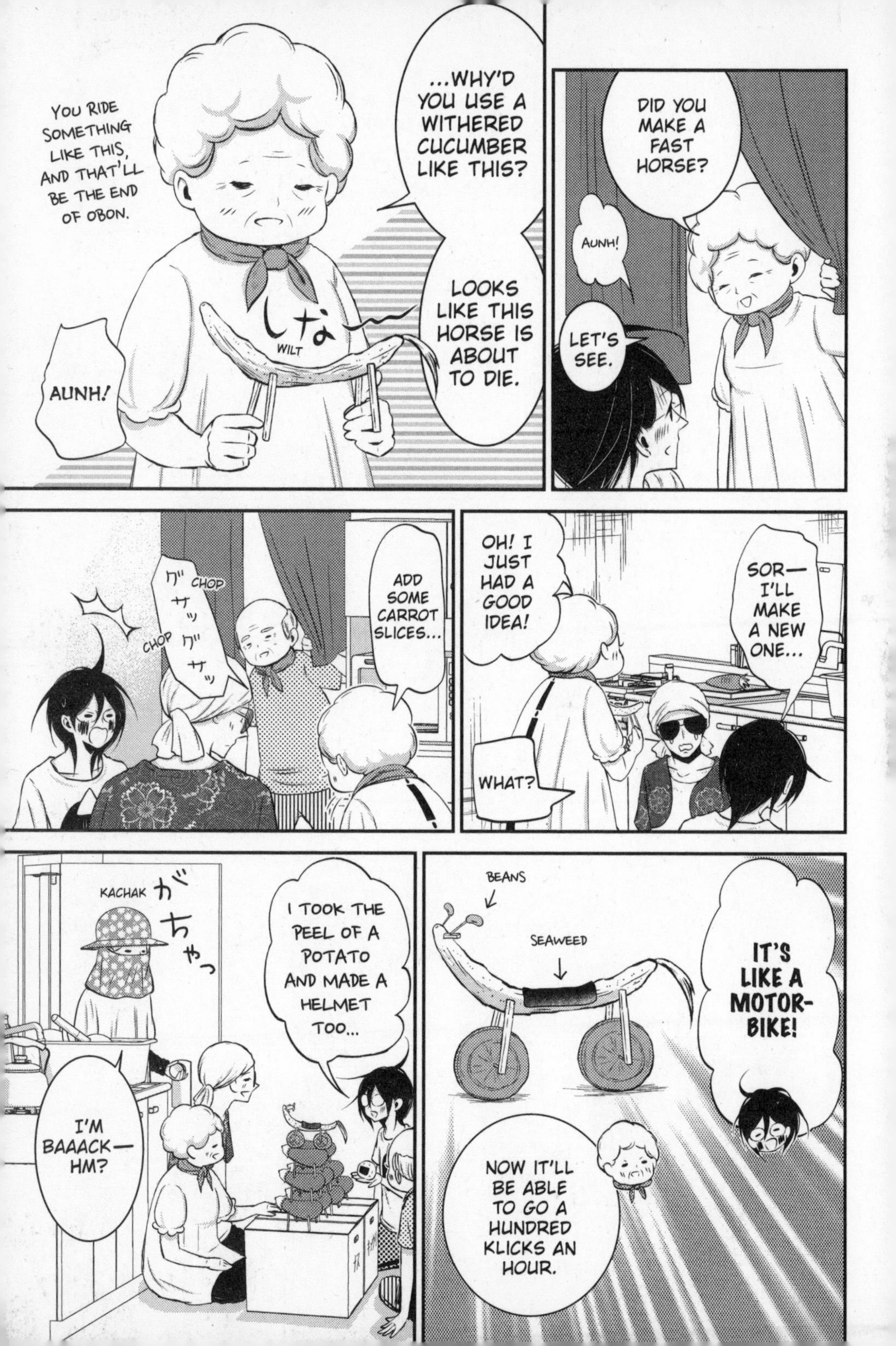
DID YOU MAKE A FAST HORSE?
AUNH!
LET'S SEE.
...WHY'D YOU USE A WITHERED CUCUMBER LIKE THIS?
LOOKS LIKE THIS HORSE IS ABOUT TO DIE.
しな〜
WILT
YOU RIDE SOMETHING LIKE THIS, AND THAT'LL BE THE END OF OBON.
AUNH!
SOR— I'LL MAKE A NEW ONE...
OH! I JUST HAD A GOOD IDEA!
WHAT?
ADD SOME CARROT SLICES...
グサッ CHOP
グサッ CHOP
IT'S LIKE A MOTOR-BIKE!
BEANS
SEAWEED
NOW IT'LL BE ABLE TO GO A HUNDRED KLICKS AN HOUR.
I TOOK THE PEEL OF A POTATO AND MADE A HELMET TOO...
がちゃっ KACHAK
I'M BAAACK—HM?

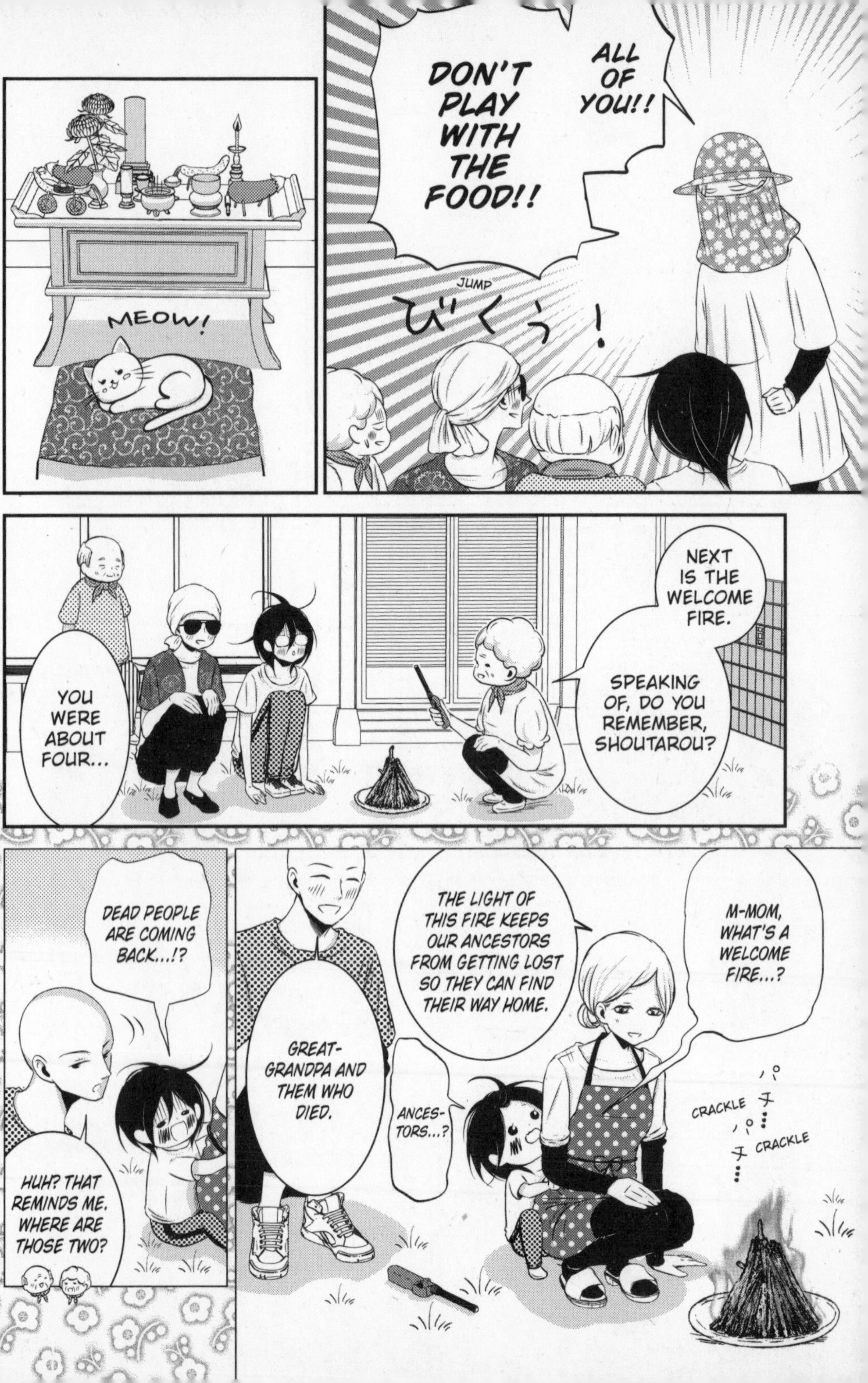
ALL OF YOU!!
DON'T PLAY WITH THE FOOD!!
JUMP
びくぅ！
MEOW!
NEXT IS THE WELCOME FIRE.
SPEAKING OF, DO YOU REMEMBER, SHOUTAROU?
YOU WERE ABOUT FOUR...
M-MOM, WHAT'S A WELCOME FIRE...?
CRACKLE
パチ… パチ…
CRACKLE
THE LIGHT OF THIS FIRE KEEPS OUR ANCESTORS FROM GETTING LOST SO THEY CAN FIND THEIR WAY HOME.
ANCES-TORS...?
GREAT-GRANDPA AND THEM WHO DIED.
DEAD PEOPLE ARE COMING BACK...!?
HUH? THAT REMINDS ME. WHERE ARE THOSE TWO?

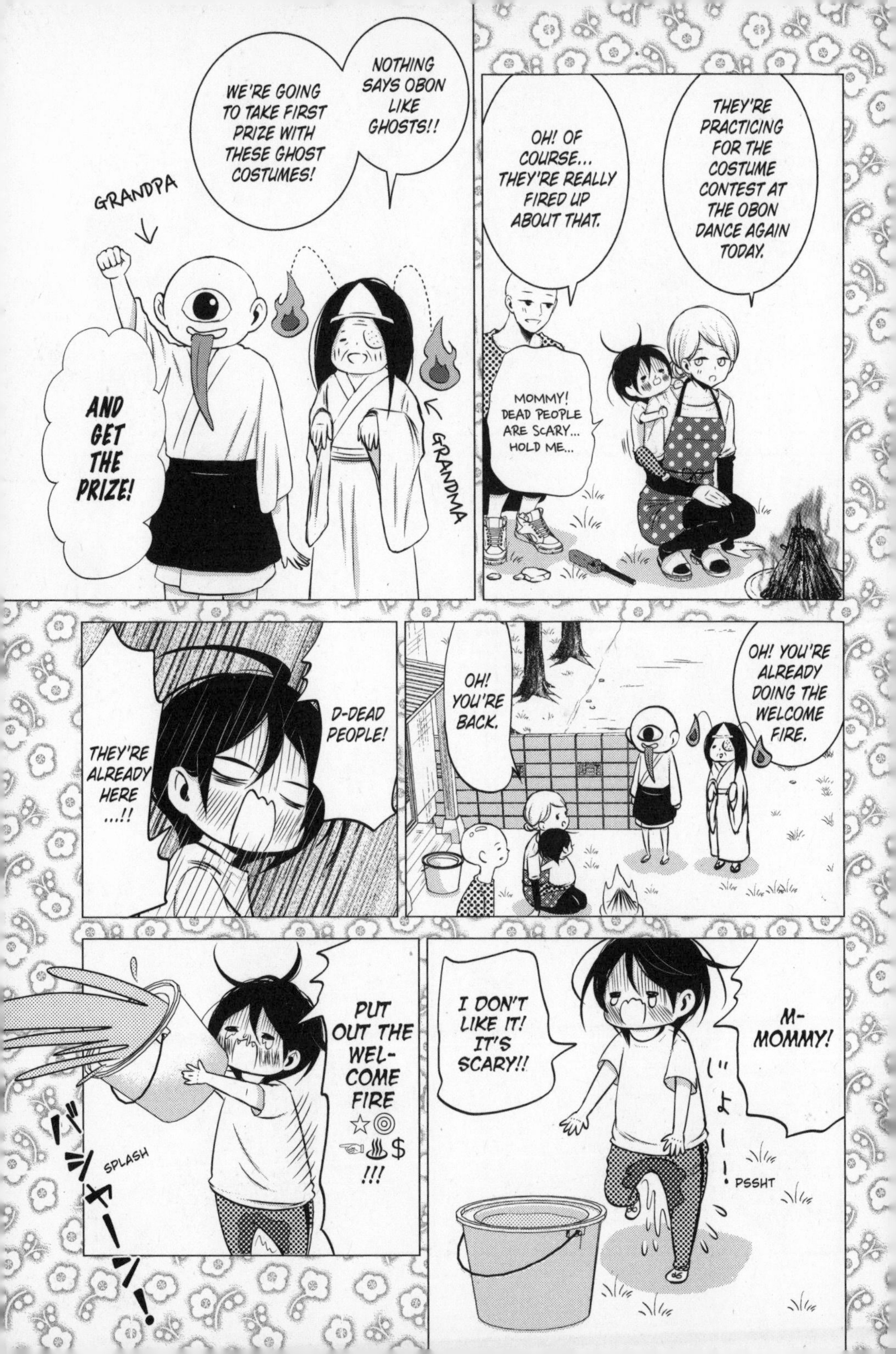

THEY'RE PRACTICING FOR THE COSTUME CONTEST AT THE OBON DANCE AGAIN TODAY.
OH! OF COURSE... THEY'RE REALLY FIRED UP ABOUT THAT.
MOMMY! DEAD PEOPLE ARE SCARY... HOLD ME...
NOTHING SAYS OBON LIKE GHOSTS!!
WE'RE GOING TO TAKE FIRST PRIZE WITH THESE GHOST COSTUMES!
GRANDPA
AND GET THE PRIZE!
GRANDMA
OH! YOU'RE ALREADY DOING THE WELCOME FIRE.
OH! YOU'RE BACK.
D-DEAD PEOPLE!
THEY'RE ALREADY HERE ...!!
M-MOMMY!
I DON'T LIKE IT! IT'S SCARY!!
PSSHT
PUT OUT THE WEL-COME FIRE ☆◎☜♨$!!!
SPLASH

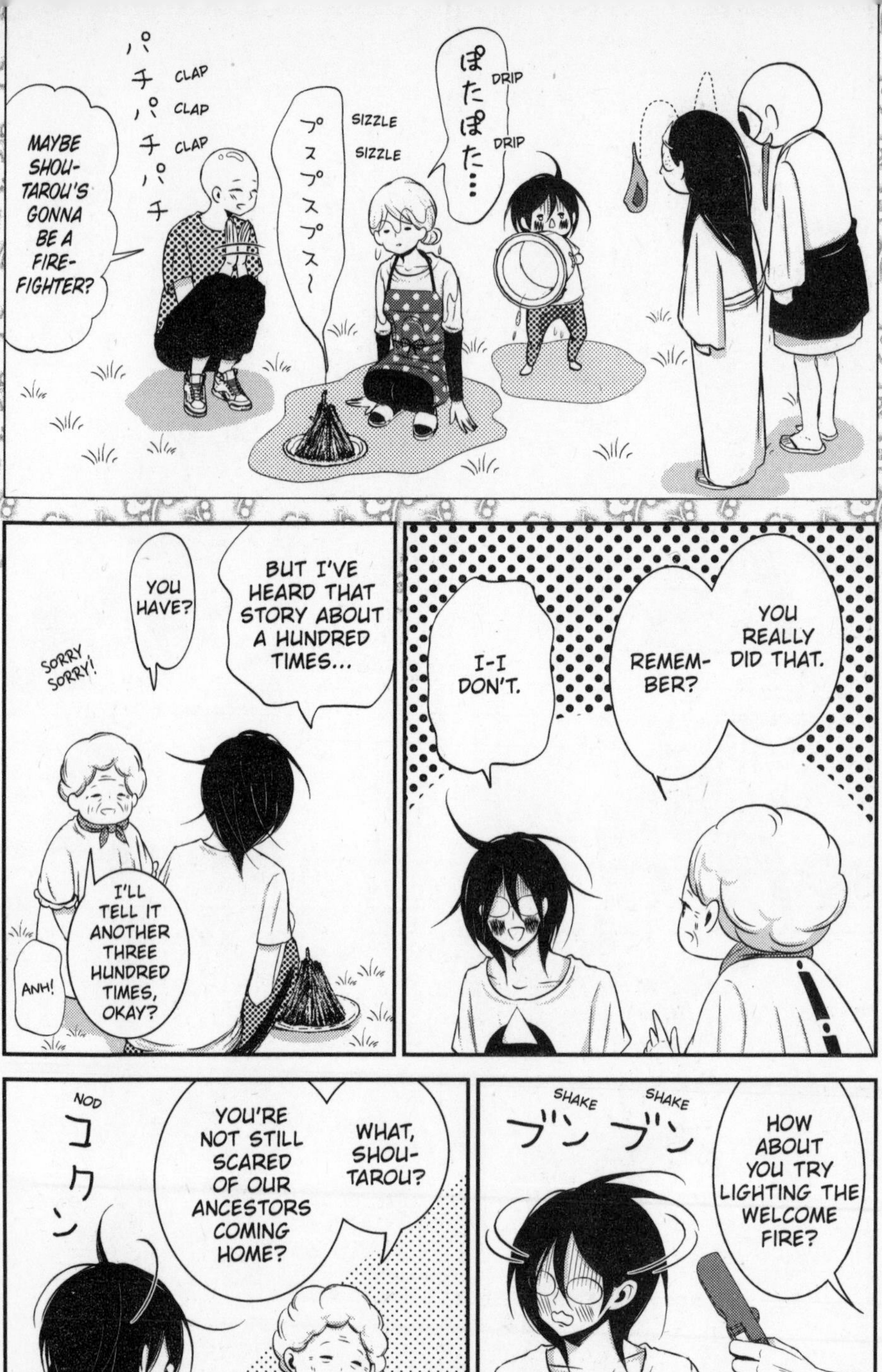
ぽたぽた…
DRIP DRIP
プスプス～
SIZZLE SIZZLE
パチパチパチ
CLAP CLAP CLAP
MAYBE SHOU-TAROU'S GONNA BE A FIRE-FIGHTER?
YOU REALLY DID THAT.
REMEM-BER?
I-I DON'T.
BUT I'VE HEARD THAT STORY ABOUT A HUNDRED TIMES...
YOU HAVE?
SORRY SORRY!
I'LL TELL IT ANOTHER THREE HUNDRED TIMES, OKAY?
ANH!
HOW ABOUT YOU TRY LIGHTING THE WELCOME FIRE?
ブンブン
SHAKE SHAKE
WHAT, SHOU-TAROU?
YOU'RE NOT STILL SCARED OF OUR ANCESTORS COMING HOME?
コクン
NOD

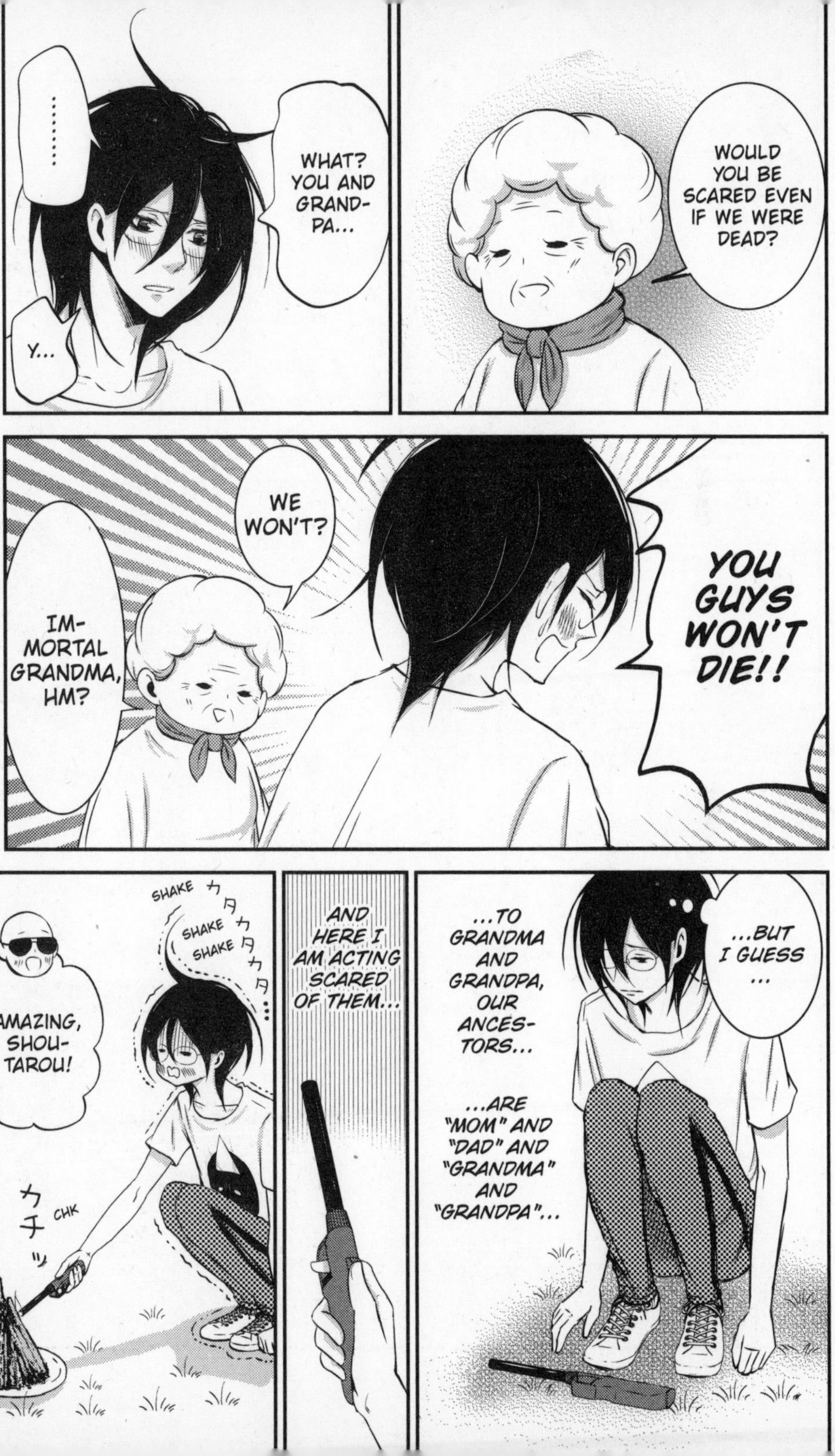
WOULD YOU BE SCARED EVEN IF WE WERE DEAD?
WHAT? YOU AND GRAND-PA...
......
Y...
YOU GUYS WON'T DIE!!
WE WON'T?
IM-MORTAL GRANDMA, HM?
...BUT I GUESS ...
...TO GRANDMA AND GRANDPA, OUR ANCES-TORS...
...ARE "MOM" AND "DAD" AND "GRANDMA" AND "GRANDPA"...
AND HERE I AM ACTING SCARED OF THEM...
SHAKE SHAKE SHAKE
カタカタカタ
AMAZING, SHOU-TAROU!
カチッ
CHK

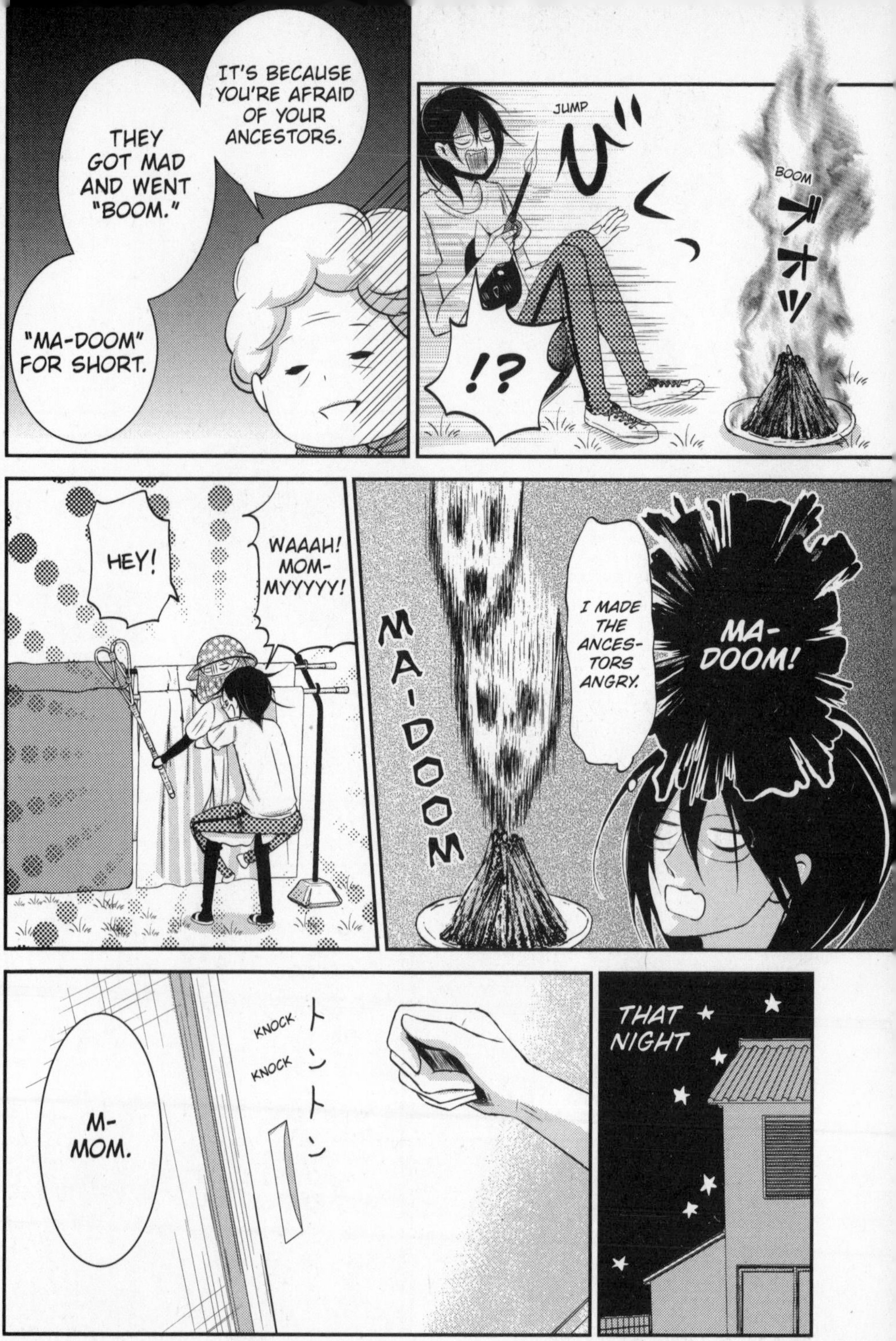
JUMP
びくっ
BOOM
ボオッ
!?
IT'S BECAUSE YOU'RE AFRAID OF YOUR ANCESTORS.
THEY GOT MAD AND WENT "BOOM."
"MA-DOOM" FOR SHORT.
MA-DOOM!
I MADE THE ANCES-TORS ANGRY.
MA-DOOM
WAAAH! MOM-MYYYYY!
HEY!
THAT NIGHT
KNOCK KNOCK
トントン
M-MOM.

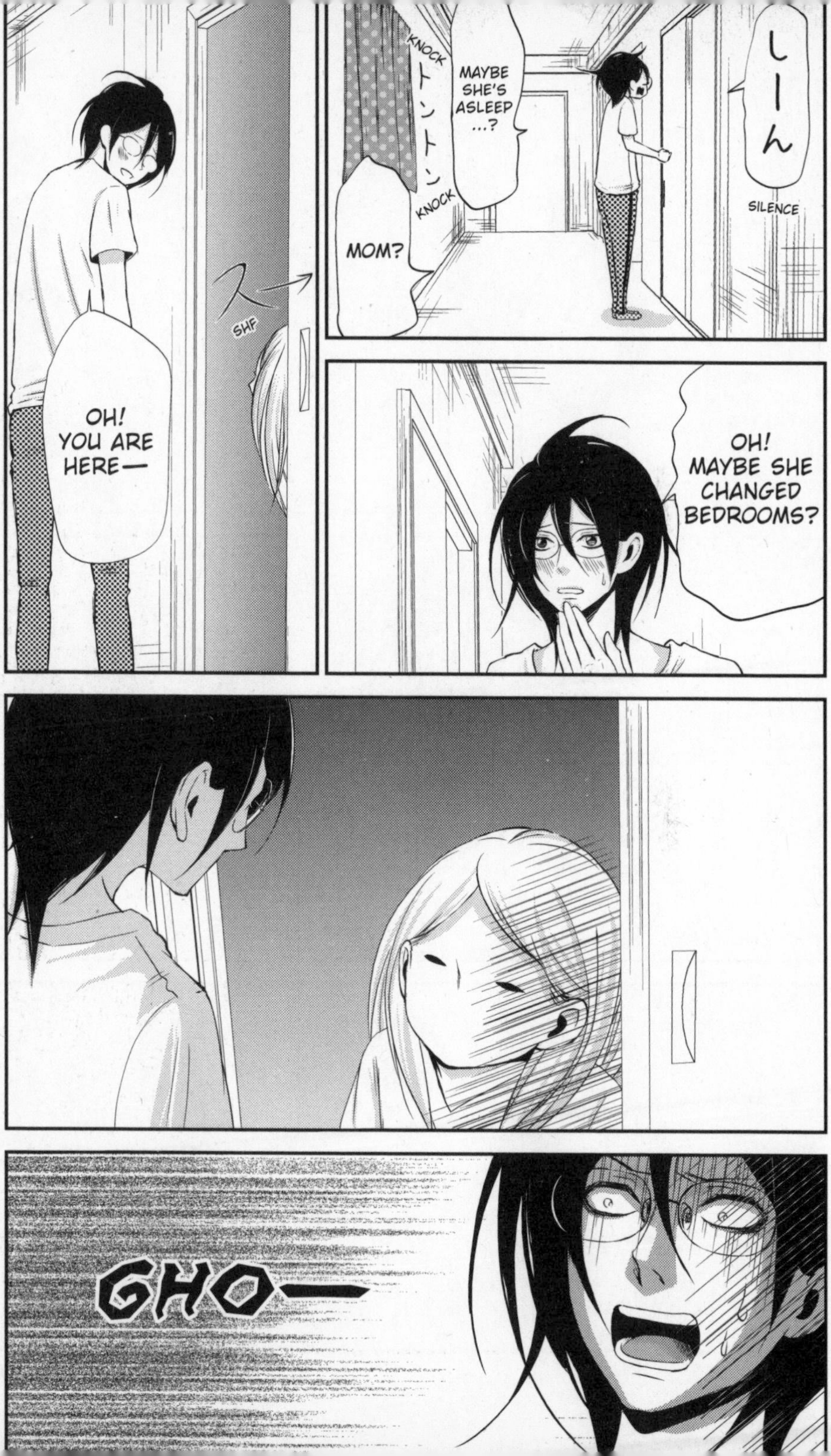
しーん
SILENCE
MAYBE SHE'S ASLEEP …?
KNOCK トントン KNOCK
MOM?
OH! MAYBE SHE CHANGED BEDROOMS?
ス
SHF
OH! YOU ARE HERE—
GHO—

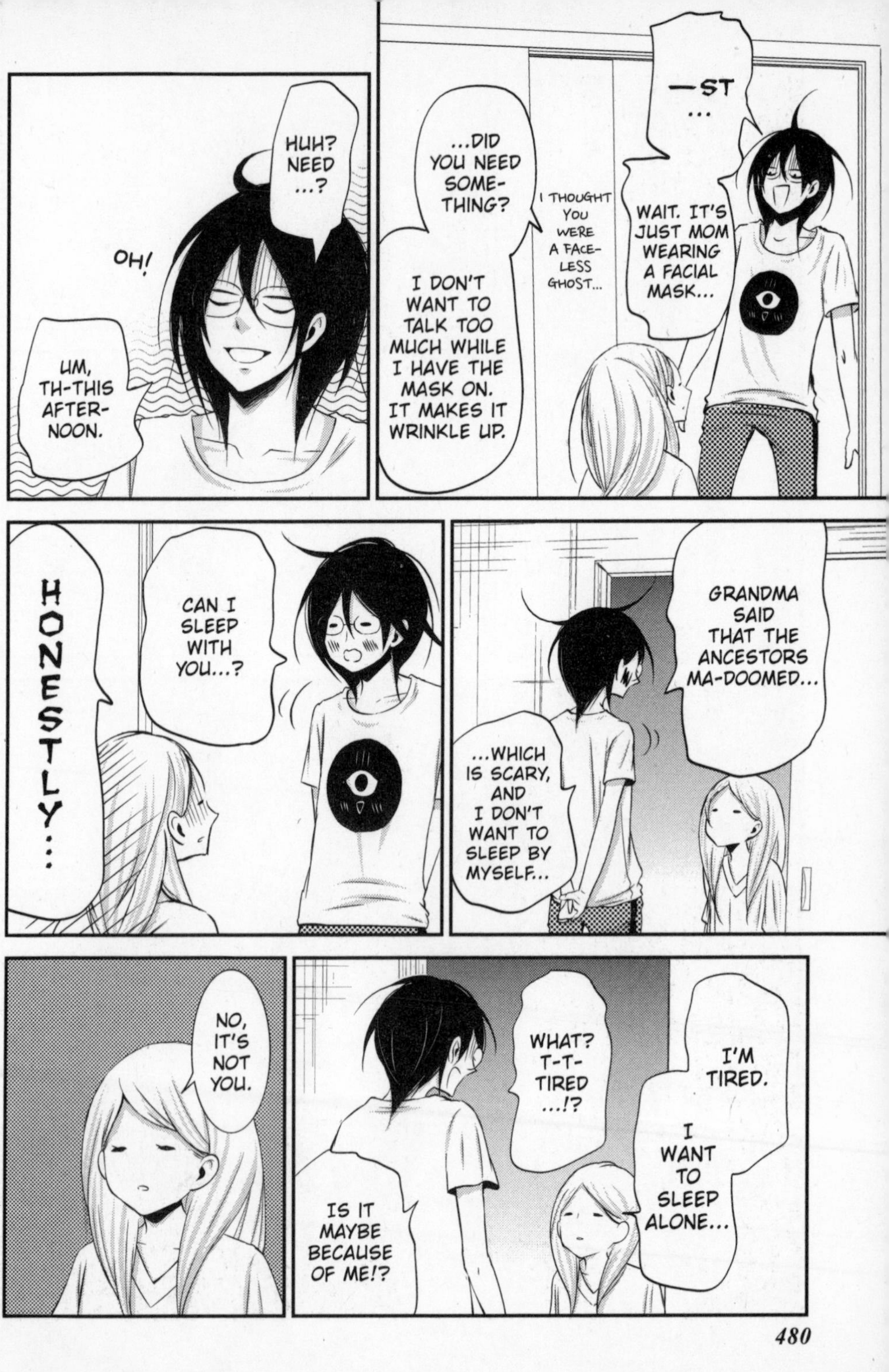
—ST ...
WAIT. IT'S JUST MOM WEARING A FACIAL MASK...
I THOUGHT YOU WERE A FACE-LESS GHOST...
...DID YOU NEED SOME-THING?
I DON'T WANT TO TALK TOO MUCH WHILE I HAVE THE MASK ON. IT MAKES IT WRINKLE UP.
HUH? NEED ...?
OH!
UM, TH-THIS AFTER-NOON.
GRANDMA SAID THAT THE ANCESTORS MA-DOOMED...
...WHICH IS SCARY, AND I DON'T WANT TO SLEEP BY MYSELF...
CAN I SLEEP WITH YOU...?
HONESTLY...
I'M TIRED.
I WANT TO SLEEP ALONE...
WHAT? T-T-TIRED ...!?
IS IT MAYBE BECAUSE OF ME!?
NO, IT'S NOT YOU.

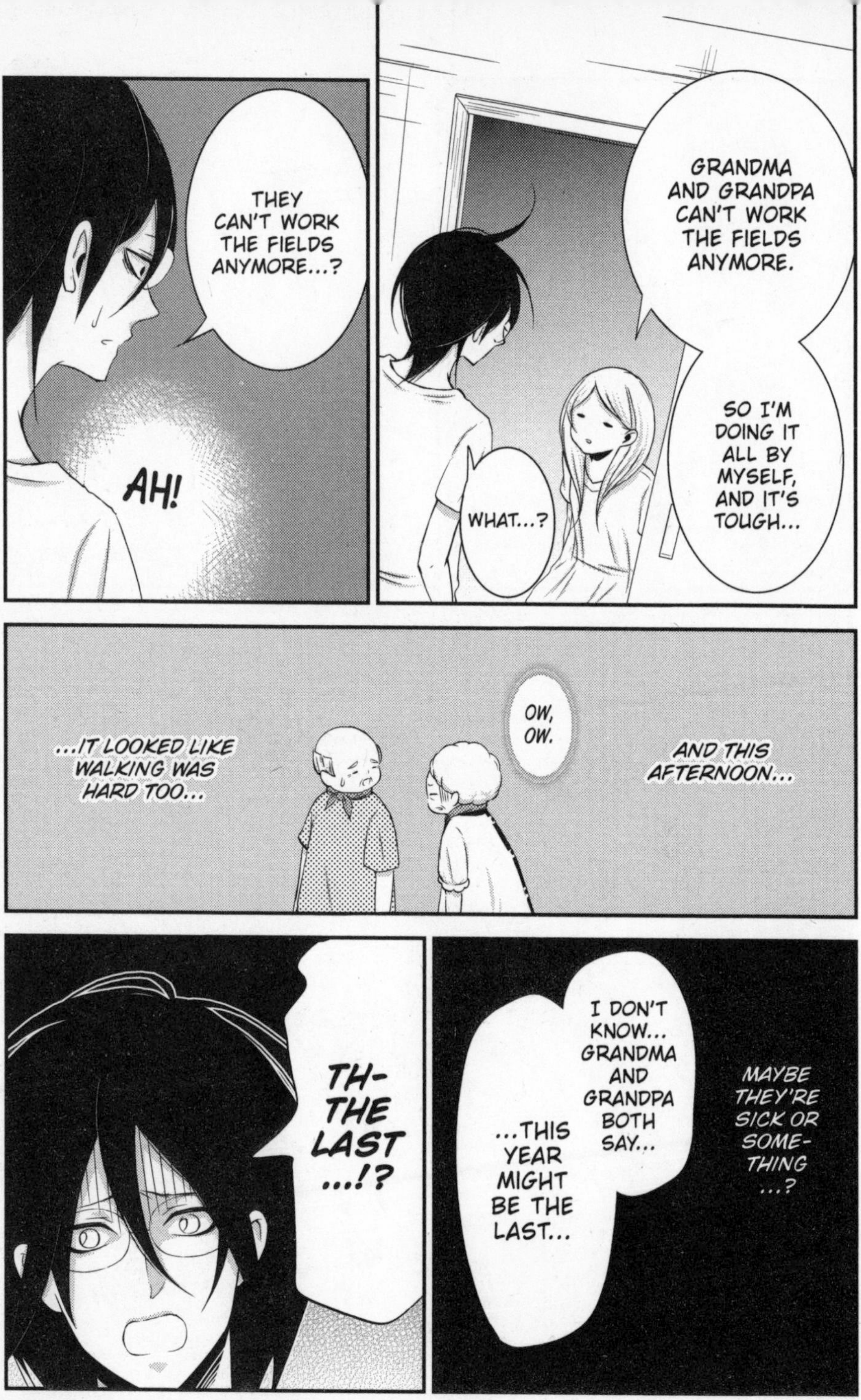
GRANDMA AND GRANDPA CAN'T WORK THE FIELDS ANYMORE.
SO I'M DOING IT ALL BY MYSELF, AND IT'S TOUGH...
WHAT...?
THEY CAN'T WORK THE FIELDS ANYMORE...?
AH!
AND THIS AFTERNOON...
OW, OW.
...IT LOOKED LIKE WALKING WAS HARD TOO...
MAYBE THEY'RE SICK OR SOME-THING...?
I DON'T KNOW... GRANDMA AND GRANDPA BOTH SAY...
...THIS YEAR MIGHT BE THE LAST...
TH-THE LAST...!?

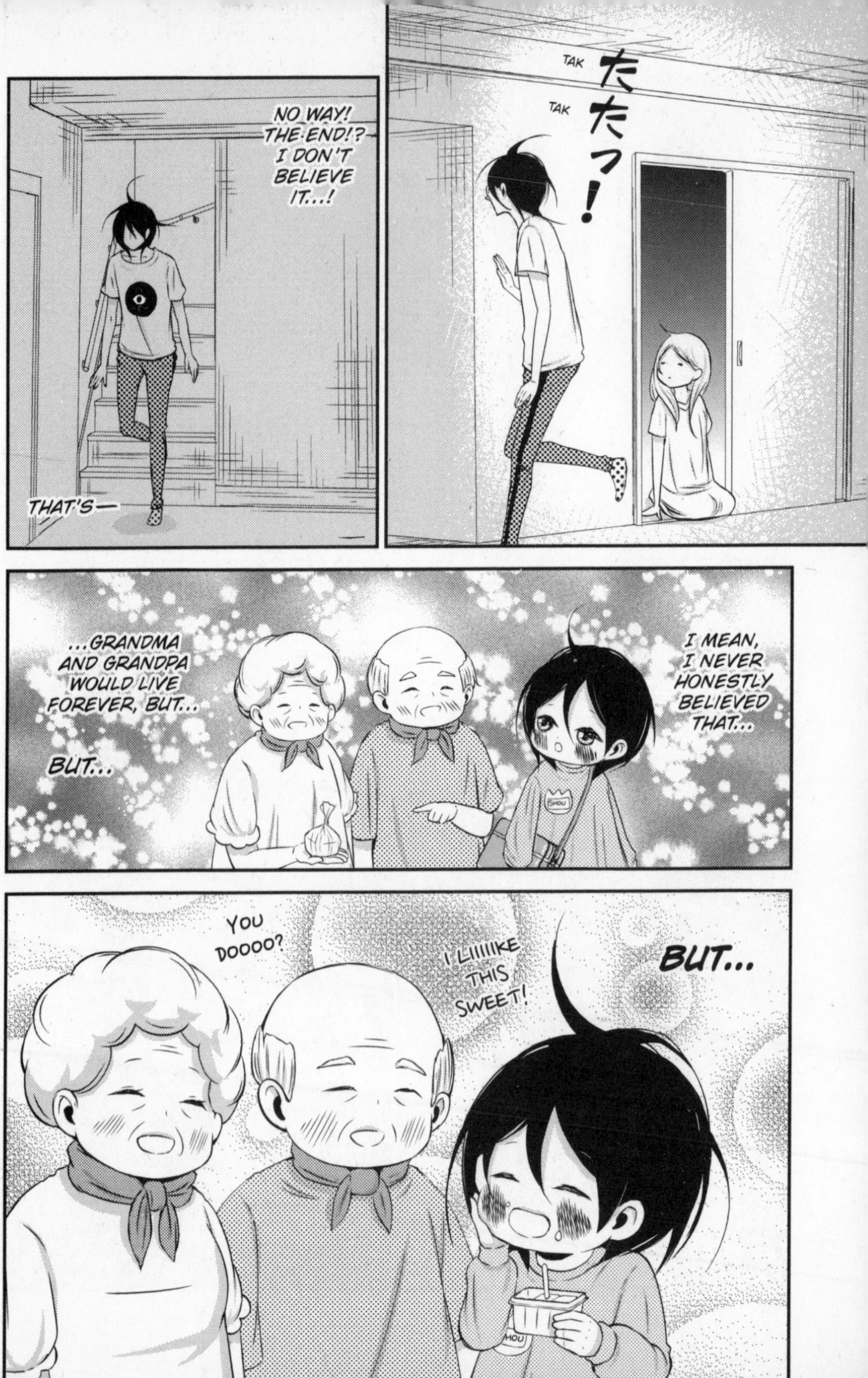
TAK
TAK
たたっ!
NO WAY! THE END!? I DON'T BELIEVE IT...!
THAT'S—
I MEAN, I NEVER HONESTLY BELIEVED THAT...
...GRANDMA AND GRANDPA WOULD LIVE FOREVER, BUT...
BUT...
BUT...
I LIIIIIKE THIS SWEET!
YOU DOOOO?

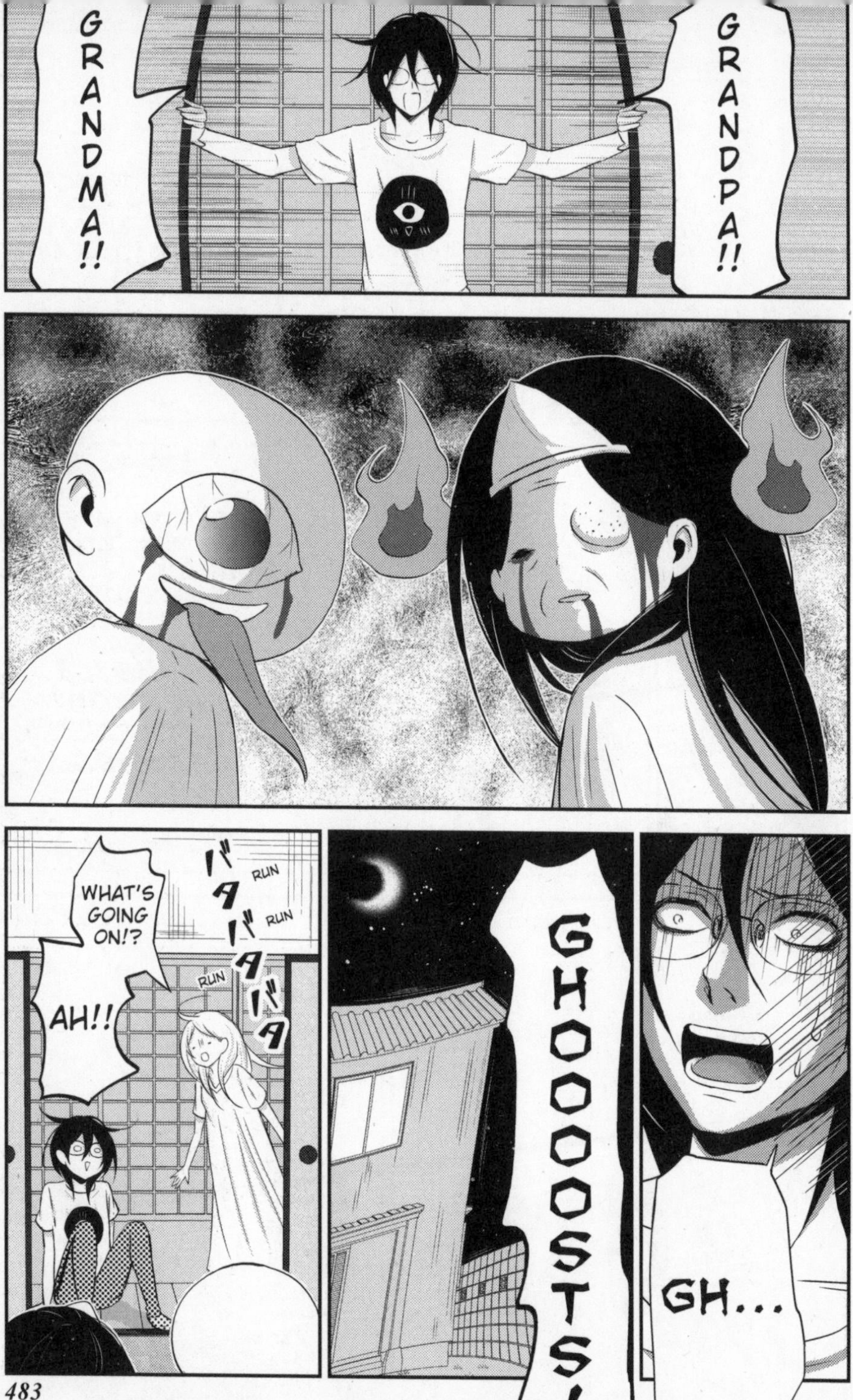
GRANDPA!!
GRANDMA!!
GH...
GHOOOOOSTS!
バタバタバタ
RUN
RUN
RUN
WHAT'S GOING ON!?
AH!!

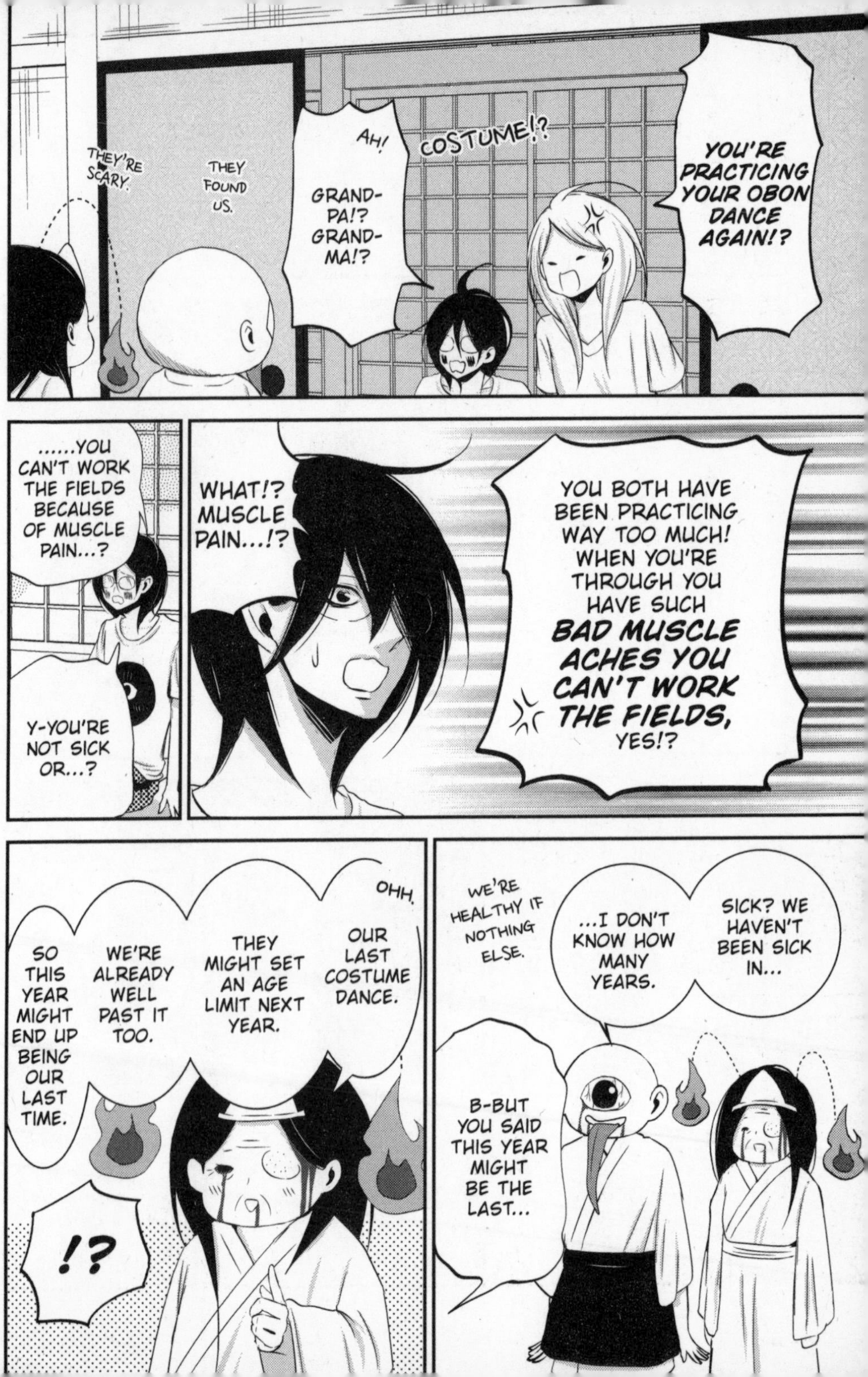
YOU'RE PRACTICING YOUR OBON DANCE AGAIN!?
COSTUME!?
AH!
GRANDPA!? GRANDMA!?
THEY FOUND US.
THEY'RE SCARY.
YOU BOTH HAVE BEEN PRACTICING WAY TOO MUCH! WHEN YOU'RE THROUGH YOU HAVE SUCH BAD MUSCLE ACHES YOU CAN'T WORK THE FIELDS, YES!?
WHAT!? MUSCLE PAIN...!?
......YOU CAN'T WORK THE FIELDS BECAUSE OF MUSCLE PAIN...?
Y-YOU'RE NOT SICK OR...?
SICK? WE HAVEN'T BEEN SICK IN...
...I DON'T KNOW HOW MANY YEARS.
WE'RE HEALTHY IF NOTHING ELSE.
B-BUT YOU SAID THIS YEAR MIGHT BE THE LAST...
OHH.
OUR LAST COSTUME DANCE.
THEY MIGHT SET AN AGE LIMIT NEXT YEAR.
WE'RE ALREADY WELL PAST IT TOO.
SO THIS YEAR MIGHT END UP BEING OUR LAST TIME.
!?

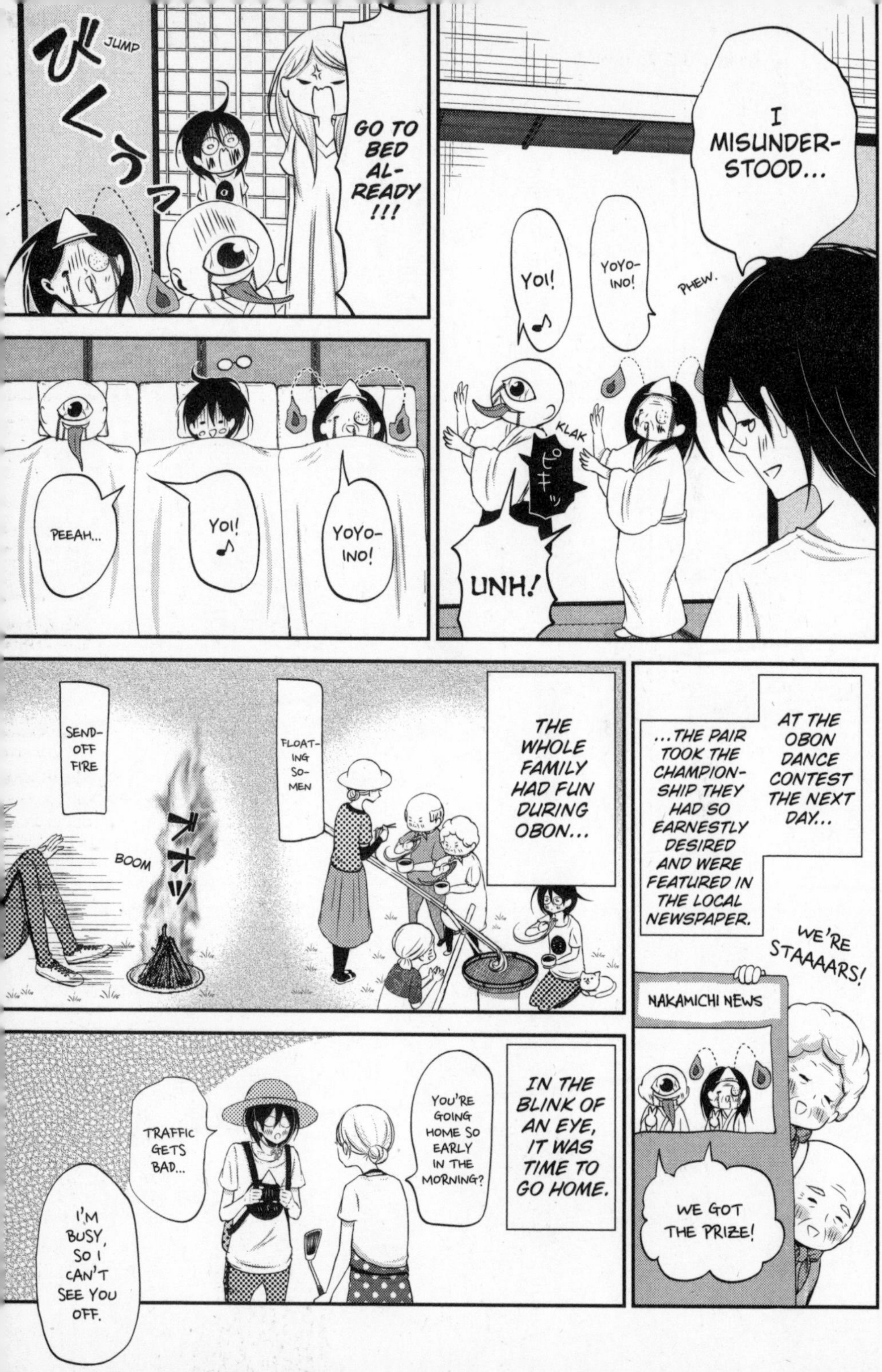
I MISUNDER-STOOD...
PHEW.
YOYO-INO!
YOI! ♪
KLAK
ピキッ
UNH!
GO TO BED AL-READY!!!
びくぅ
JUMP
YOYO-INO!
YOI! ♪
PEEAH...
AT THE OBON DANCE CONTEST THE NEXT DAY...
...THE PAIR TOOK THE CHAMPION-SHIP THEY HAD SO EARNESTLY DESIRED AND WERE FEATURED IN THE LOCAL NEWSPAPER.
WE'RE STAAAARS!
NAKAMICHI NEWS
WE GOT THE PRIZE!
THE WHOLE FAMILY HAD FUN DURING OBON...
FLOATING SO-MEN
SEND-OFF FIRE
BOOM
IN THE BLINK OF AN EYE, IT WAS TIME TO GO HOME.
YOU'RE GOING HOME SO EARLY IN THE MORNING?
TRAFFIC GETS BAD...
I'M BUSY, SO I CAN'T SEE YOU OFF.

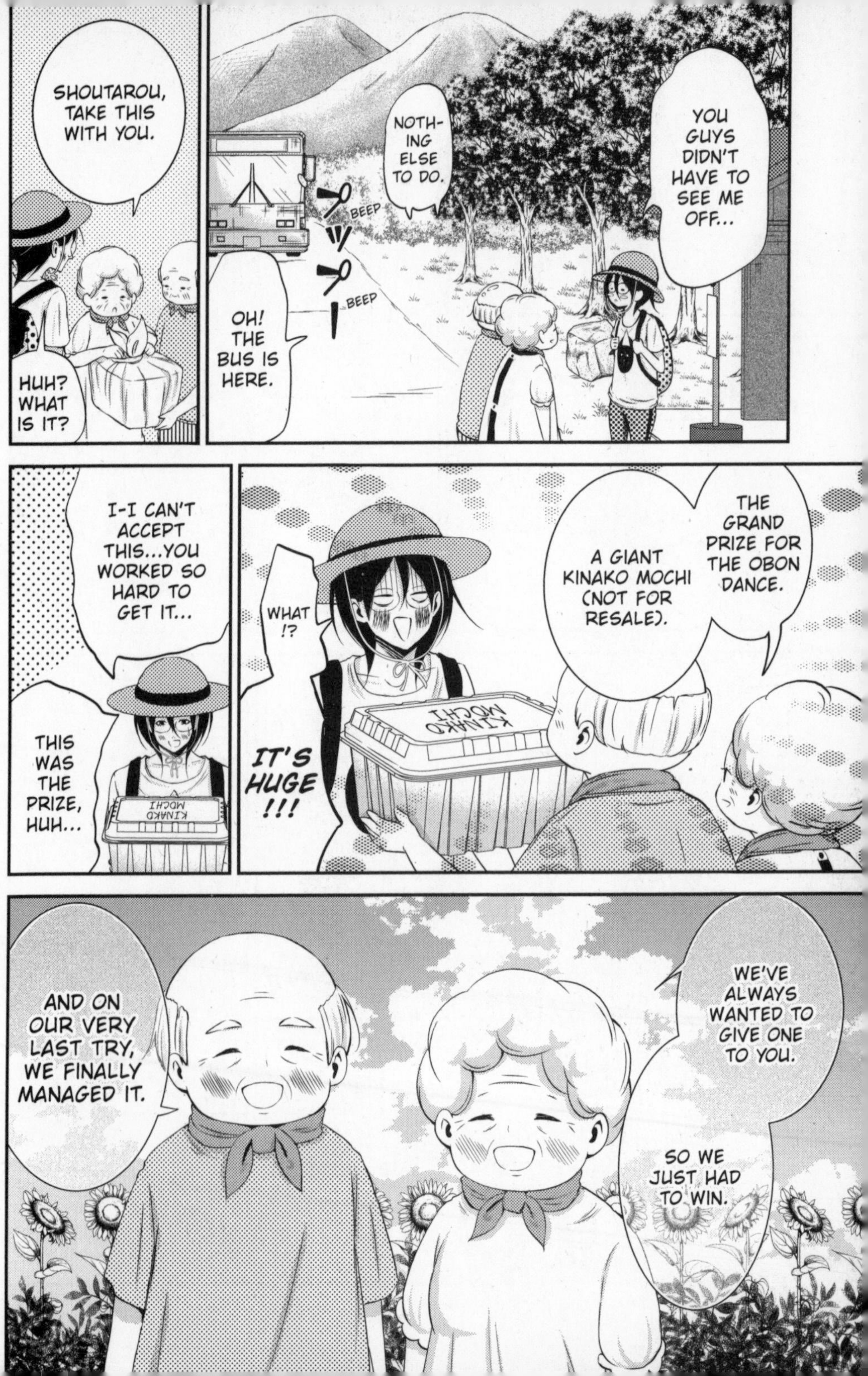
YOU GUYS DIDN'T HAVE TO SEE ME OFF...
NOTHING ELSE TO DO.
BEEP
BEEP
OH! THE BUS IS HERE.
SHOUTAROU, TAKE THIS WITH YOU.
HUH? WHAT IS IT?
THE GRAND PRIZE FOR THE OBON DANCE.
A GIANT KINAKO MOCHI (NOT FOR RESALE).
WHAT!?
KINAKO MOCHI
IT'S HUGE!!!
I-I CAN'T ACCEPT THIS...YOU WORKED SO HARD TO GET IT...
THIS WAS THE PRIZE, HUH...
KINAKO MOCHI
WE'VE ALWAYS WANTED TO GIVE ONE TO YOU.
SO WE JUST HAD TO WIN.
AND ON OUR VERY LAST TRY, WE FINALLY MANAGED IT.

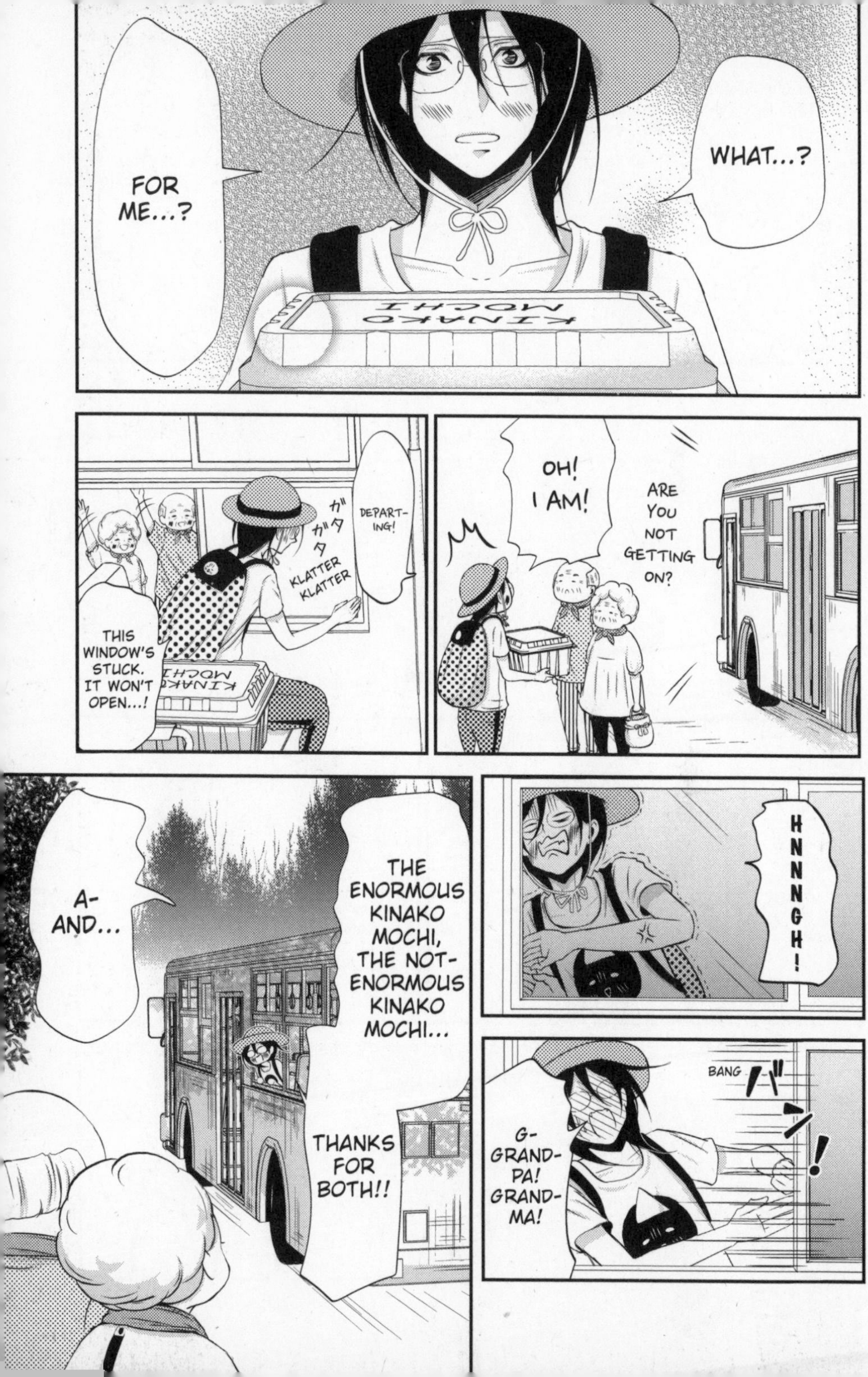
WHAT...?
FOR ME...?
KINAKO MOCHI
ARE YOU NOT GETTING ON?
OH! I AM!
DEPART-ING!
ガタガタ
KLATTER KLATTER
THIS WINDOW'S STUCK. IT WON'T OPEN...!
KINAKO MOCHI
HNNNGH!
BANG
G-GRANDPA! GRANDMA!
THE ENORMOUS KINAKO MOCHI, THE NOT-ENORMOUS KINAKO MOCHI...
A-AND...
THANKS FOR BOTH!!

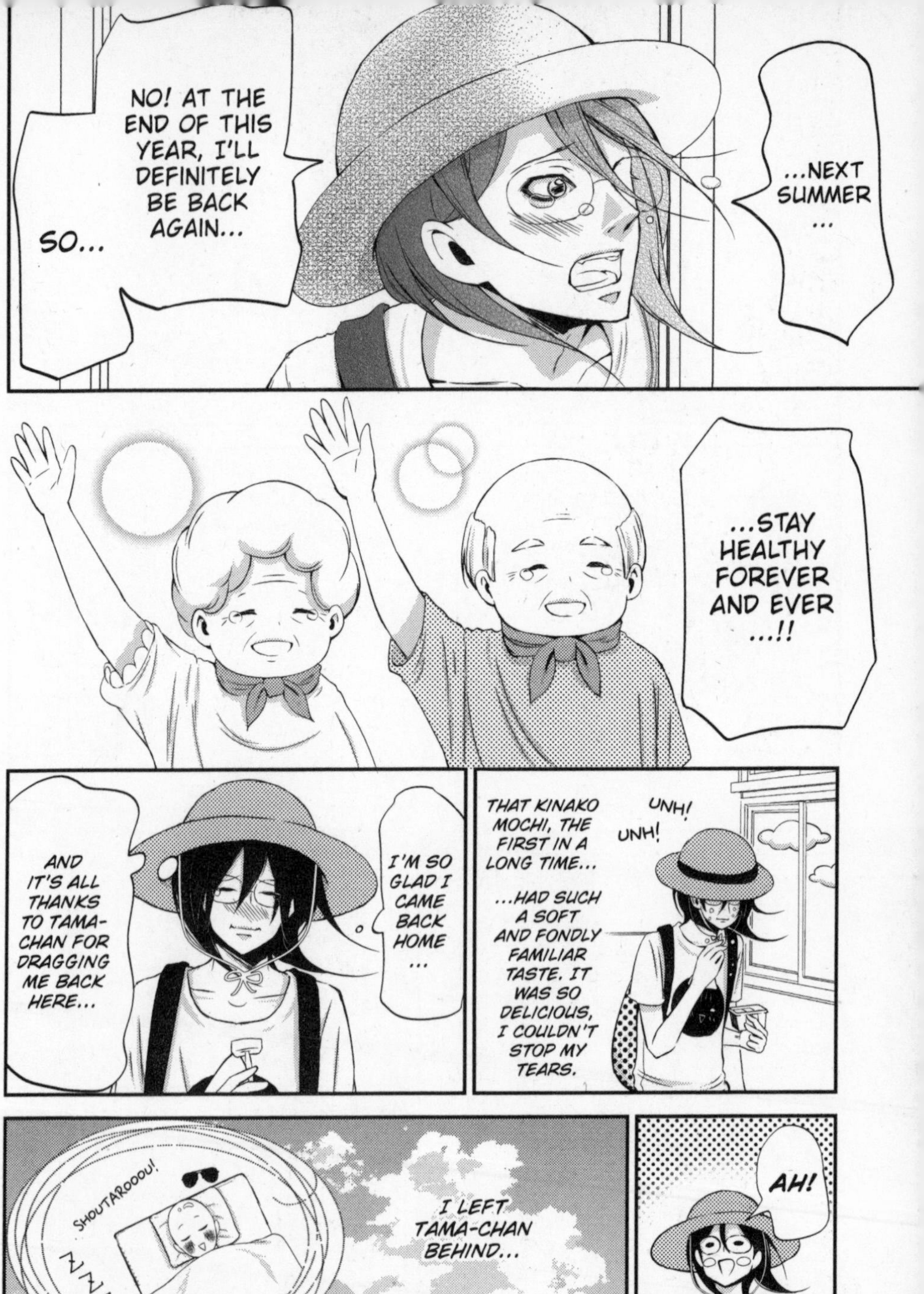
...NEXT SUMMER ...
NO! AT THE END OF THIS YEAR, I'LL DEFINITELY BE BACK AGAIN...
SO...
...STAY HEALTHY FOREVER AND EVER ...!!
UNH!
UNH!
THAT KINAKO MOCHI, THE FIRST IN A LONG TIME...
...HAD SUCH A SOFT AND FONDLY FAMILIAR TASTE. IT WAS SO DELICIOUS, I COULDN'T STOP MY TEARS.
I'M SO GLAD I CAME BACK HOME ...
AND IT'S ALL THANKS TO TAMA-CHAN FOR DRAGGING ME BACK HERE...
AH!
I LEFT TAMA-CHAN BEHIND...
SHOUTAROOOU!

TO BE CONTINUED

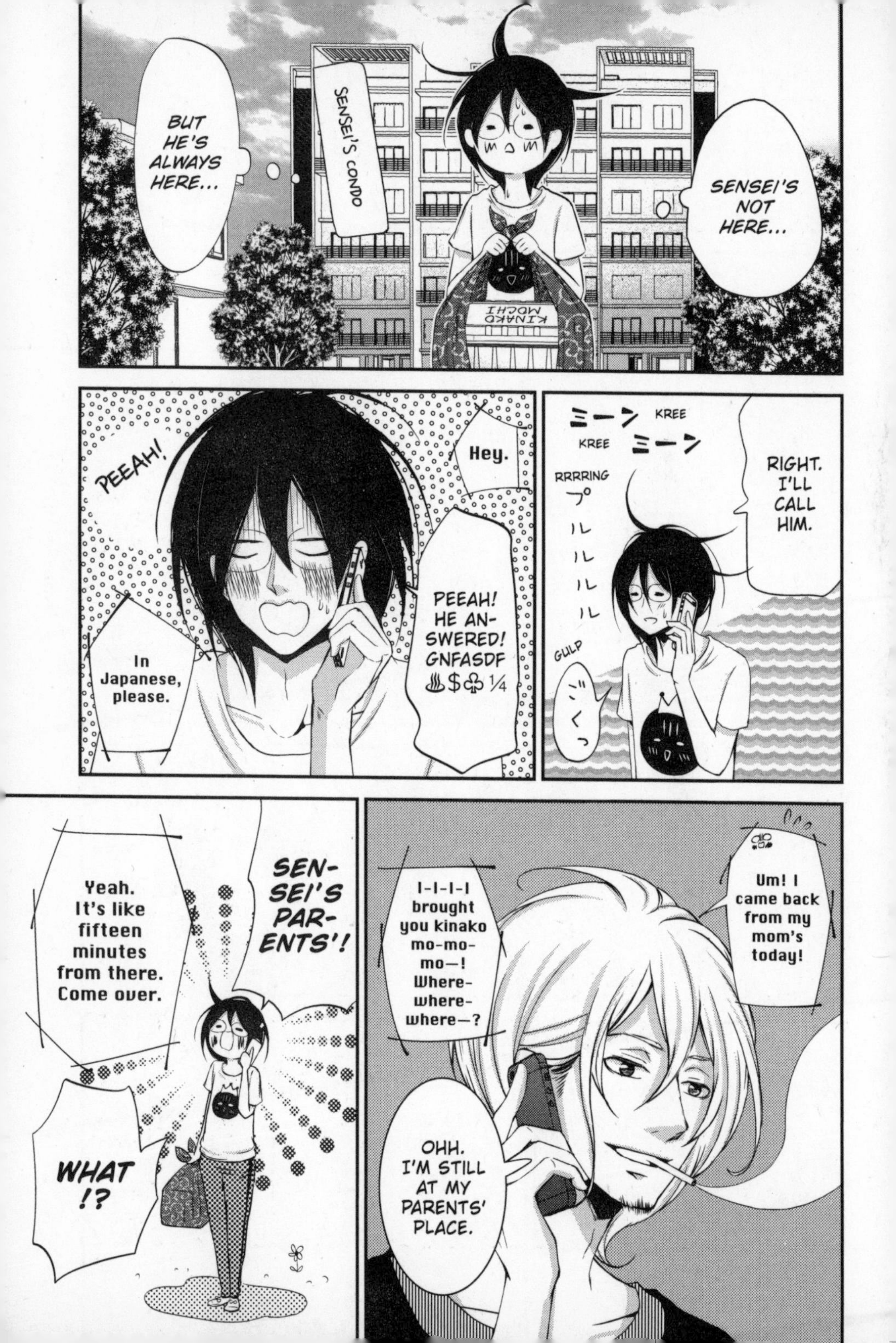
SENSEI'S NOT HERE...
SENSEI'S CONDO
BUT HE'S ALWAYS HERE...
KINAKO MOCHI
ミーン
KREE
KREE
ミーン
RIGHT. I'LL CALL HIM.
RRRRING
プルルルル
GULP
ごくっ
Hey.
PEEAH!
PEEAH! HE ANSWERED! GNFASDF ♨$♣¼
In Japanese, please.
Um! I came back from my mom's today!
I-I-I-I brought you kinako mo-mo-mo—! Where-where-where—?
OHH. I'M STILL AT MY PARENTS' PLACE.
SENSEI'S PARENTS'!
Yeah. It's like fifteen minutes from there. Come over.
WHAT!?

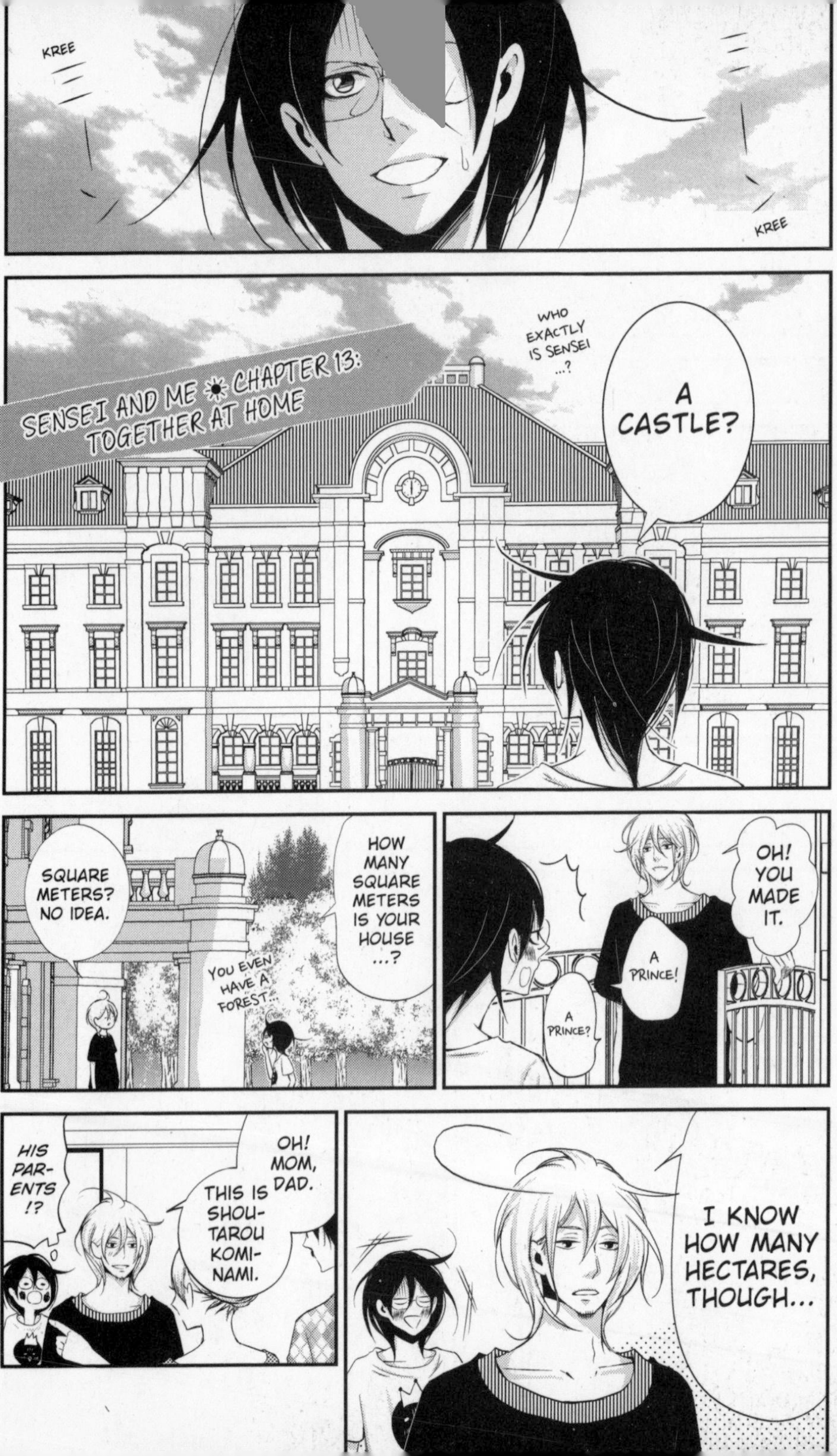
KREE
KREE
A CASTLE?
WHO EXACTLY IS SENSEI ...?
SENSEI AND ME ☀ CHAPTER 13: TOGETHER AT HOME
OH! YOU MADE IT.
A PRINCE!
A PRINCE?
HOW MANY SQUARE METERS IS YOUR HOUSE ...?
YOU EVEN HAVE A FOREST...
SQUARE METERS? NO IDEA.
I KNOW HOW MANY HECTARES, THOUGH...
OH! MOM, DAD.
THIS IS SHOU-TAROU KOMI-NAMI.
HIS PAR-ENTS !?

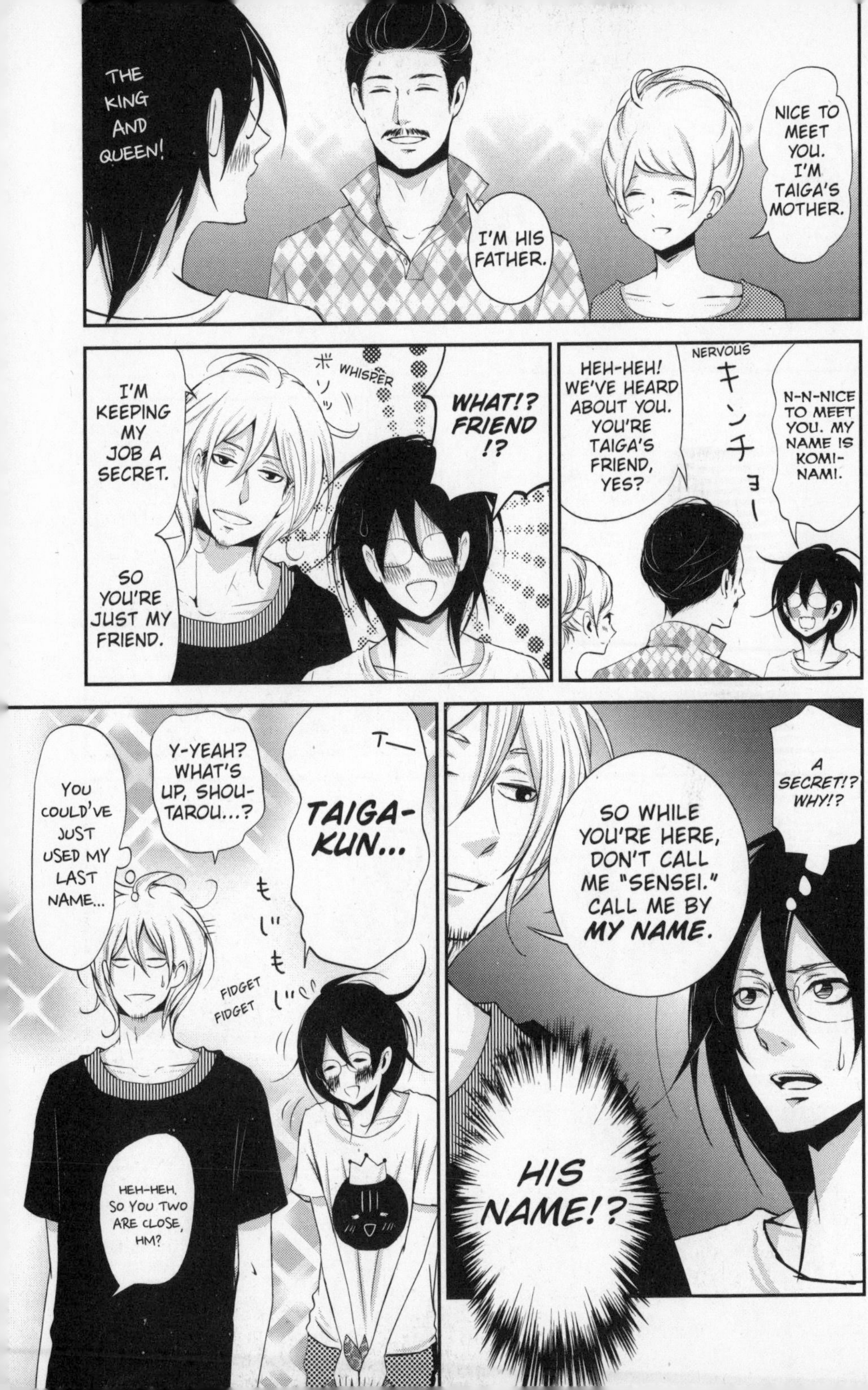
NICE TO MEET YOU. I'M TAIGA'S MOTHER.
I'M HIS FATHER.
THE KING AND QUEEN!
N-N-NICE TO MEET YOU. MY NAME IS KOMI-NAMI.
NERVOUS
キンチョー
HEH-HEH! WE'VE HEARD ABOUT YOU. YOU'RE TAIGA'S FRIEND, YES?
WHAT!? FRIEND!?
ボソッ
WHISPER
I'M KEEPING MY JOB A SECRET.
SO YOU'RE JUST MY FRIEND.
A SECRET!? WHY!?
SO WHILE YOU'RE HERE, DON'T CALL ME "SENSEI." CALL ME BY MY NAME.
HIS NAME!?
T—
TAIGA-KUN...
Y-YEAH? WHAT'S UP, SHOU-TAROU...?
You could've just used my last name...
もじもじ
FIDGET FIDGET
HEH-HEH. SO YOU TWO ARE CLOSE, HM?

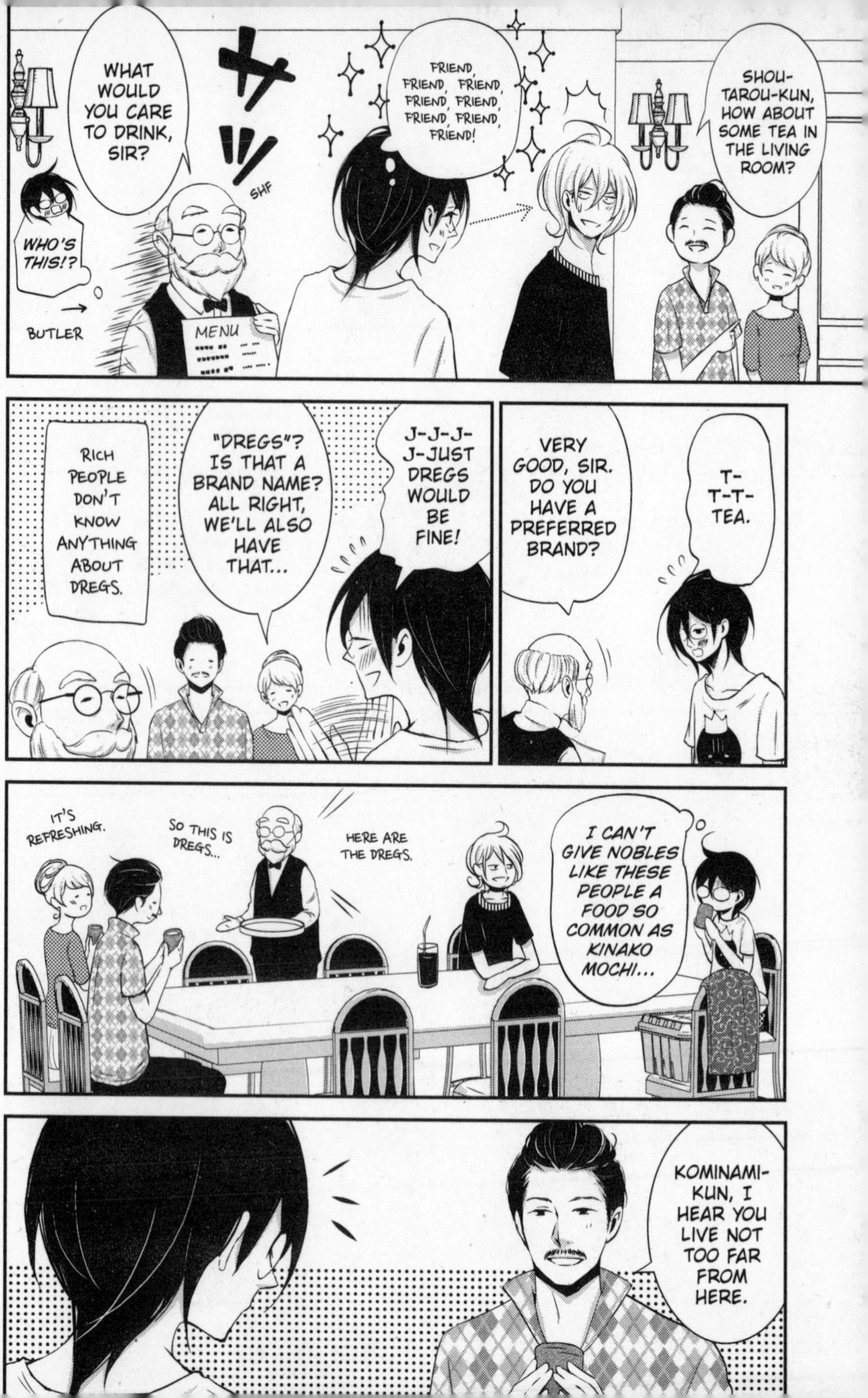
SHOU-TAROU-KUN, HOW ABOUT SOME TEA IN THE LIVING ROOM?
FRIEND, FRIEND, FRIEND, FRIEND, FRIEND, FRIEND, FRIEND, FRIEND!
サッ
SHF
WHAT WOULD YOU CARE TO DRINK, SIR?
WHO'S THIS!?
BUTLER
MENU
T-T-T-TEA.
VERY GOOD, SIR. DO YOU HAVE A PREFERRED BRAND?
J-J-J-J-JUST DREGS WOULD BE FINE!
"DREGS"? IS THAT A BRAND NAME? ALL RIGHT, WE'LL ALSO HAVE THAT...
RICH PEOPLE DON'T KNOW ANYTHING ABOUT DREGS.
I CAN'T GIVE NOBLES LIKE THESE PEOPLE A FOOD SO COMMON AS KINAKO MOCHI...
HERE ARE THE DREGS.
SO THIS IS DREGS...
IT'S REFRESHING.
KOMINAMI-KUN, I HEAR YOU LIVE NOT TOO FAR FROM HERE.

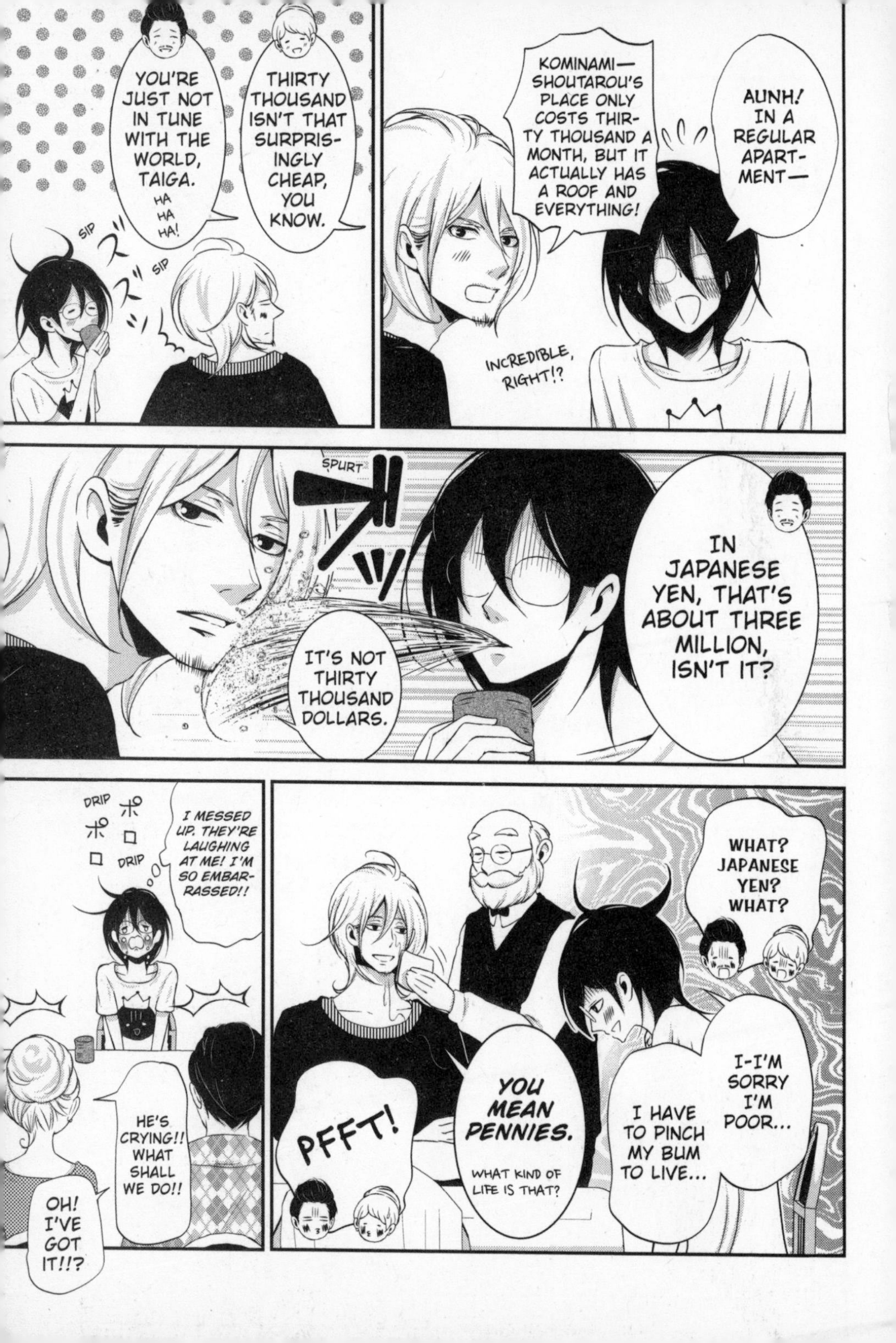
AUNH! IN A REGULAR APARTMENT—
KOMINAMI—SHOUTAROU'S PLACE ONLY COSTS THIRTY THOUSAND A MONTH, BUT IT ACTUALLY HAS A ROOF AND EVERYTHING!
INCREDIBLE, RIGHT!?
THIRTY THOUSAND ISN'T THAT SURPRISINGLY CHEAP, YOU KNOW.
YOU'RE JUST NOT IN TUNE WITH THE WORLD, TAIGA.
HA HA HA!
SIP
ズズ
SIP
SPURT
IN JAPANESE YEN, THAT'S ABOUT THREE MILLION, ISN'T IT?
IT'S NOT THIRTY THOUSAND DOLLARS.
WHAT? JAPANESE YEN? WHAT?
I-I'M SORRY I'M POOR...
I HAVE TO PINCH MY BUM TO LIVE...
YOU MEAN PENNIES.
WHAT KIND OF LIFE IS THAT?
PFFT!
I MESSED UP. THEY'RE LAUGHING AT ME! I'M SO EMBARRASSED!!
DRIP
ポロ
DRIP
ポロ
HE'S CRYING!! WHAT SHALL WE DO!!
OH! I'VE GOT IT!!?

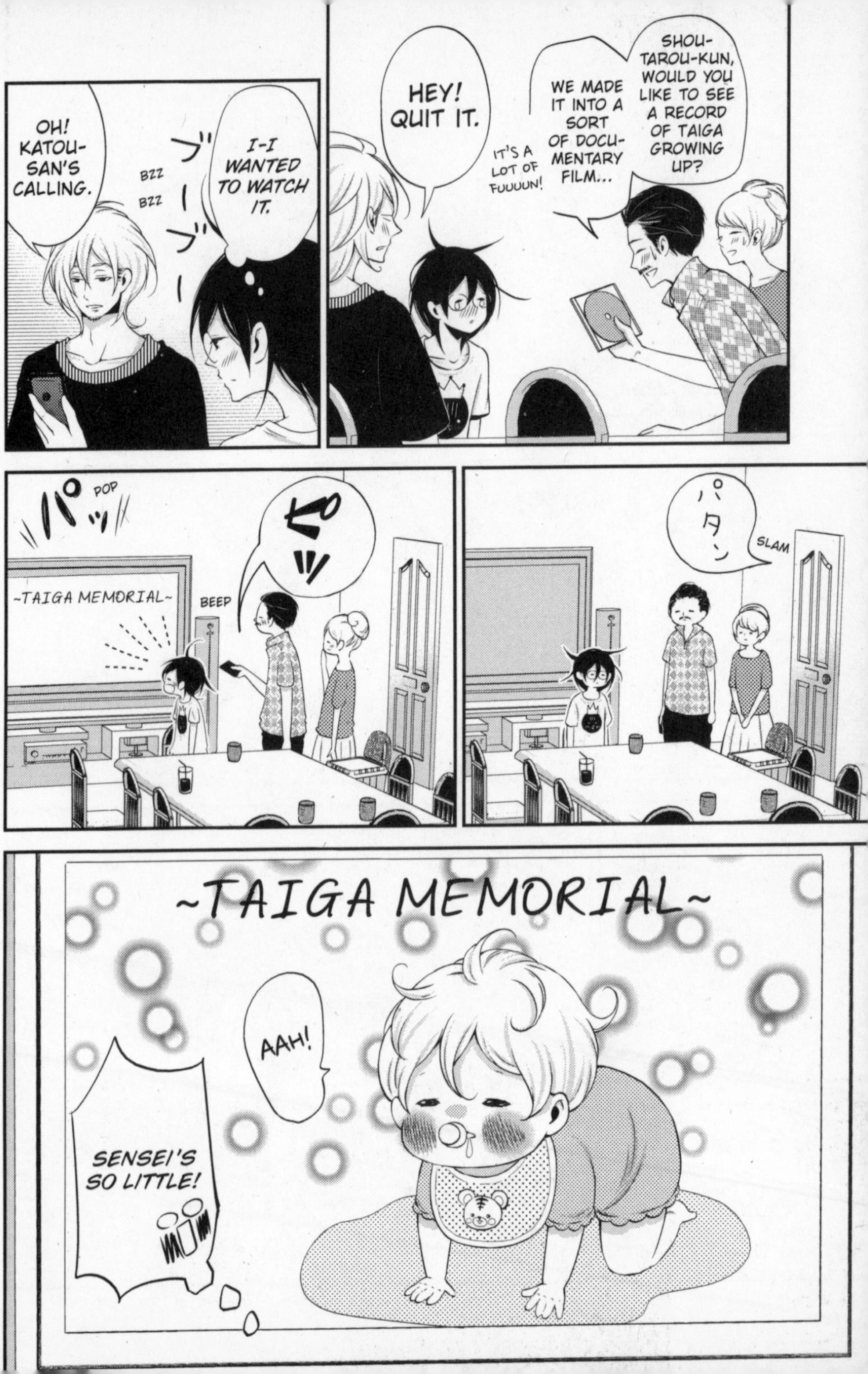
SHOU-TAROU-KUN, WOULD YOU LIKE TO SEE A RECORD OF TAIGA GROWING UP?
WE MADE IT INTO A SORT OF DOCU-MENTARY FILM...
IT'S A LOT OF FUUUUN!
HEY! QUIT IT.
I-I WANTED TO WATCH IT.
ブーブー
BZZ BZZ
OH! KATOU-SAN'S CALLING.
パタン
SLAM
ピッ
BEEP
パッ
POP
~TAIGA MEMORIAL~
~TAIGA MEMORIAL~
AAH!
SENSEI'S SO LITTLE!

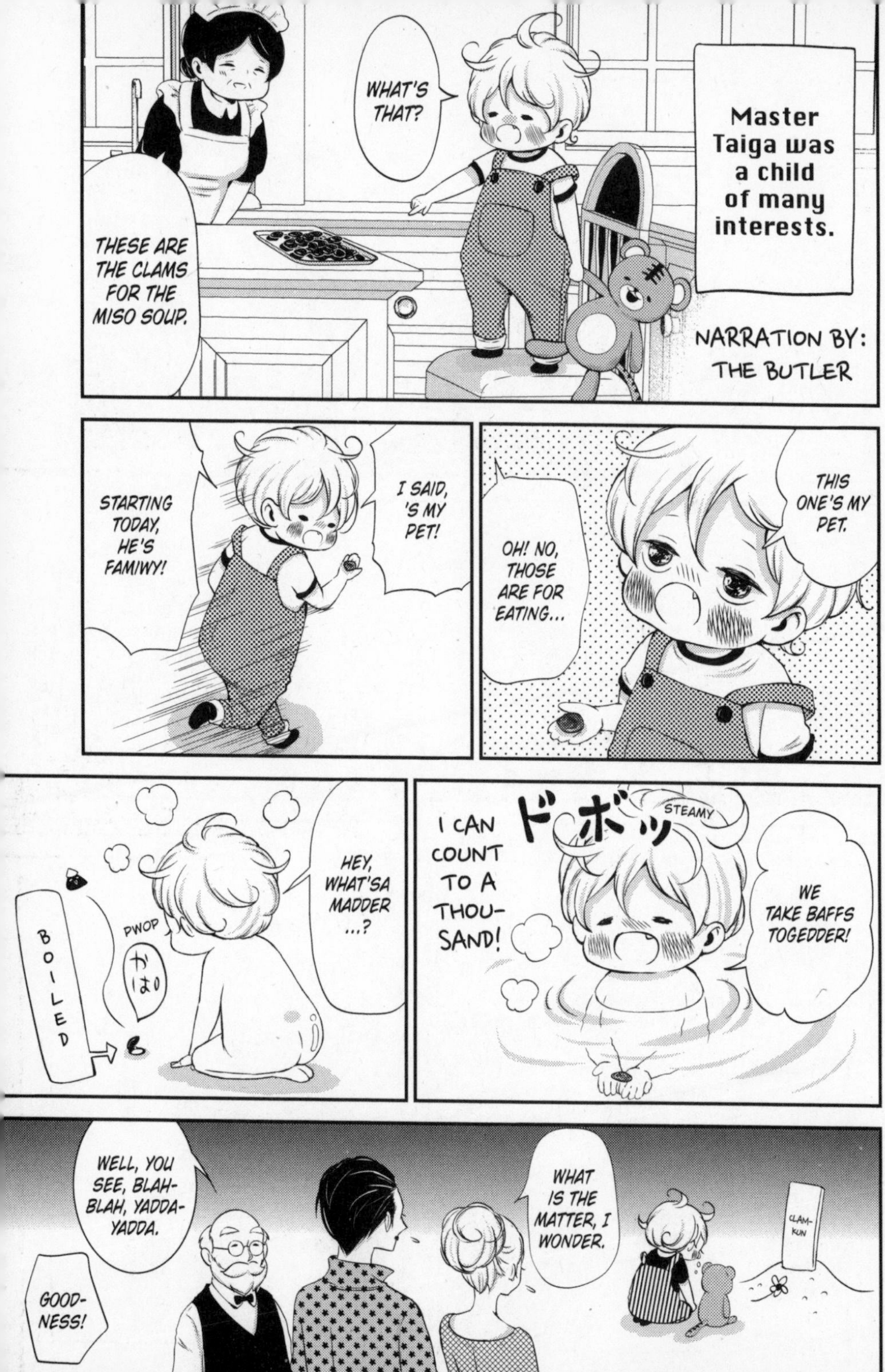
Master Taiga was a child of many interests.
NARRATION BY: THE BUTLER
WHAT'S THAT?
THESE ARE THE CLAMS FOR THE MISO SOUP.
THIS ONE'S MY PET.
OH! NO, THOSE ARE FOR EATING...
I SAID, 'S MY PET!
STARTING TODAY, HE'S FAMIWY!
WE TAKE BAFFS TOGEDDER!
STEAMY
ドボッ
I CAN COUNT TO A THOU-SAND!
HEY, WHAT'SA MADDER ...?
PWOP
がはっ
BOILED
CLAM-KUN
WHAT IS THE MATTER, I WONDER.
WELL, YOU SEE, BLAH-BLAH, YADDA-YADDA.
GOOD-NESS!

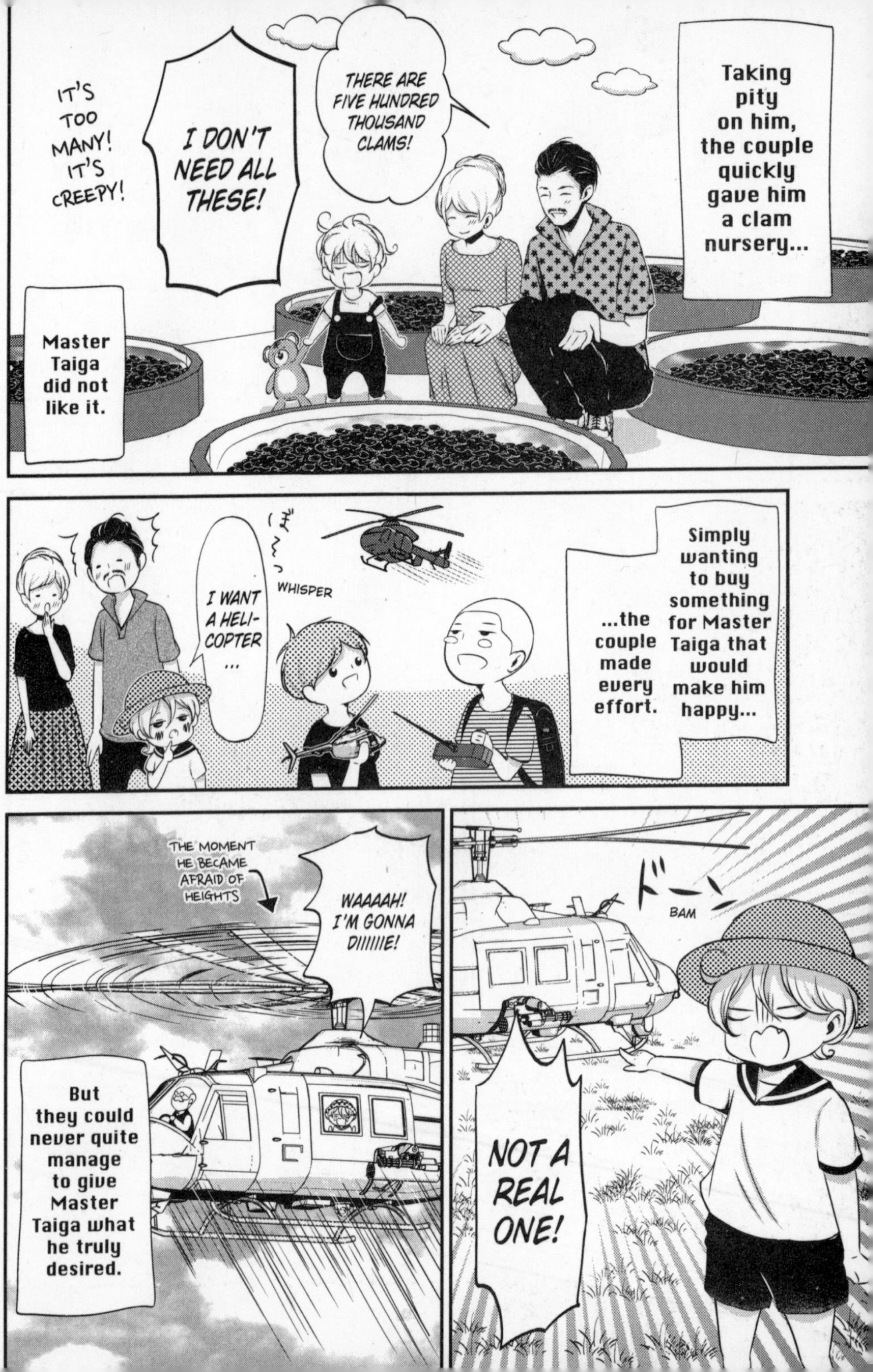
Taking pity on him, the couple quickly gave him a clam nursery...
THERE ARE FIVE HUNDRED THOUSAND CLAMS!
I DON'T NEED ALL THESE!
IT'S TOO MANY! IT'S CREEPY!
Master Taiga did not like it.
Simply wanting to buy something for Master Taiga that would make him happy...
...the couple made every effort.
WHISPER
I WANT A HELI-COPTER ...
ドーン
BAM
NOT A REAL ONE!
WAAAAH! I'M GONNA DIIIIIIE!
THE MOMENT HE BECAME AFRAID OF HEIGHTS
But they could never quite manage to give Master Taiga what he truly desired.

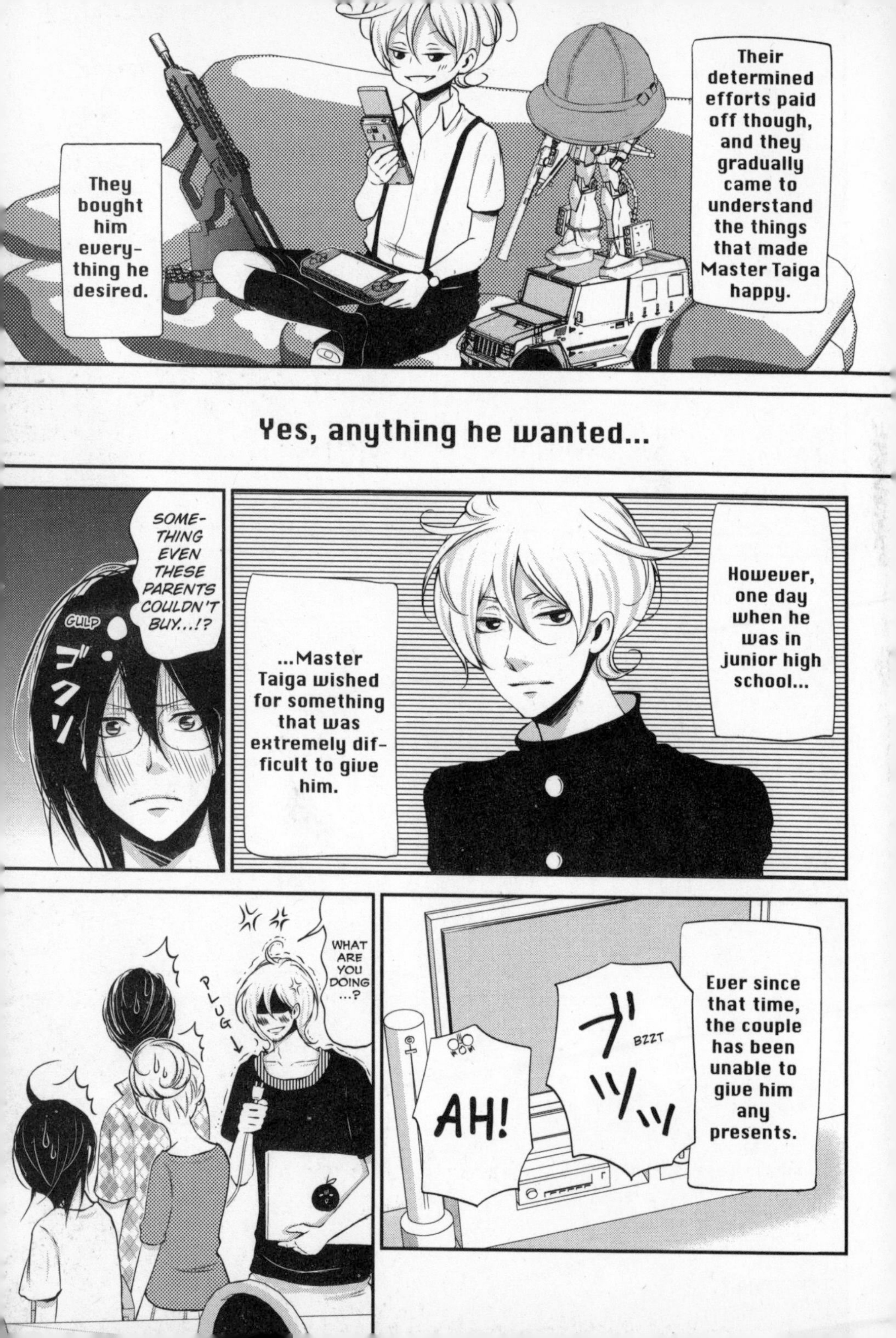
Their determined efforts paid off though, and they gradually came to understand the things that made Master Taiga happy.
They bought him every-thing he desired.
Yes, anything he wanted...
However, one day when he was in junior high school...
...Master Taiga wished for something that was extremely dif-ficult to give him.
SOME-THING EVEN THESE PARENTS COULDN'T BUY...!?
GULP
Ever since that time, the couple has been unable to give him any presents.
BZZT
AH!
WHAT ARE YOU DOING...?
PLUG

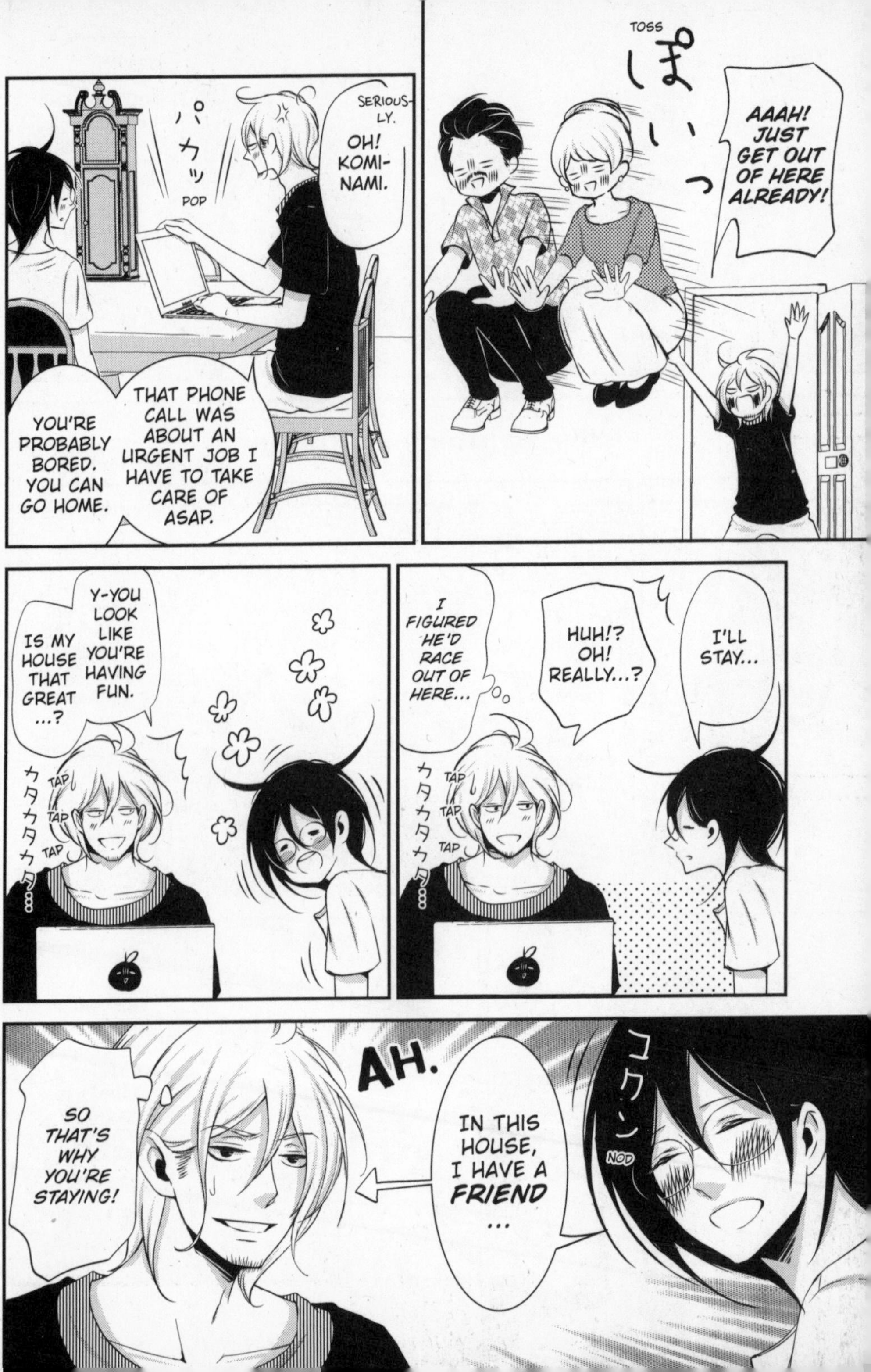
TOSS
ぽいっ
AAAH! JUST GET OUT OF HERE ALREADY!
SERIOUSLY.
OH! KOMINAMI.
パカッ
POP
THAT PHONE CALL WAS ABOUT AN URGENT JOB I HAVE TO TAKE CARE OF ASAP.
YOU'RE PROBABLY BORED. YOU CAN GO HOME.
I'LL STAY...
HUH!? OH! REALLY...?
I FIGURED HE'D RACE OUT OF HERE...
カタカタカタ...
TAP TAP TAP
Y-YOU LOOK LIKE YOU'RE HAVING FUN.
IS MY HOUSE THAT GREAT ...?
カタカタカタ...
TAP TAP TAP
コクン
NOD
IN THIS HOUSE, I HAVE A FRIEND ...
AH.
SO THAT'S WHY YOU'RE STAYING!

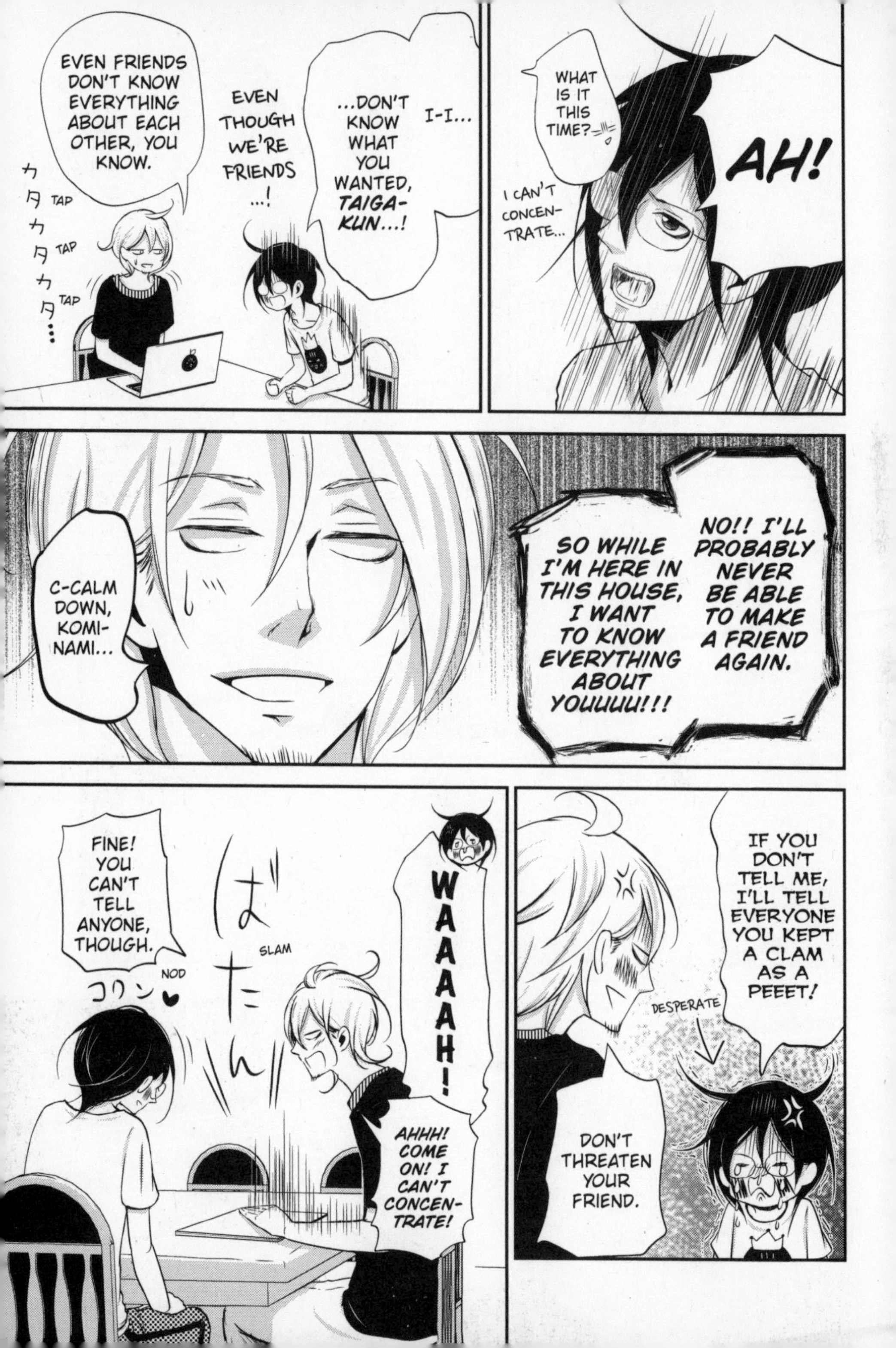
WHAT IS IT THIS TIME?
AH!
I CAN'T CONCENTRATE...
I-I...
...DON'T KNOW WHAT YOU WANTED, TAIGA-KUN...!
EVEN THOUGH WE'RE FRIENDS...!
EVEN FRIENDS DON'T KNOW EVERYTHING ABOUT EACH OTHER, YOU KNOW.
カタカタカタ…
TAP TAP TAP
NO!! I'LL PROBABLY NEVER BE ABLE TO MAKE A FRIEND AGAIN.
SO WHILE I'M HERE IN THIS HOUSE, I WANT TO KNOW EVERYTHING ABOUT YOUUUUU!!!
C-CALM DOWN, KOMINAMI...
IF YOU DON'T TELL ME, I'LL TELL EVERYONE YOU KEPT A CLAM AS A PEEET!
DESPERATE
DON'T THREATEN YOUR FRIEND.
WAAAAAH!
AHHH! COME ON! I CAN'T CONCENTRATE!
ばたん
SLAM
FINE! YOU CAN'T TELL ANYONE, THOUGH.
コクン
NOD

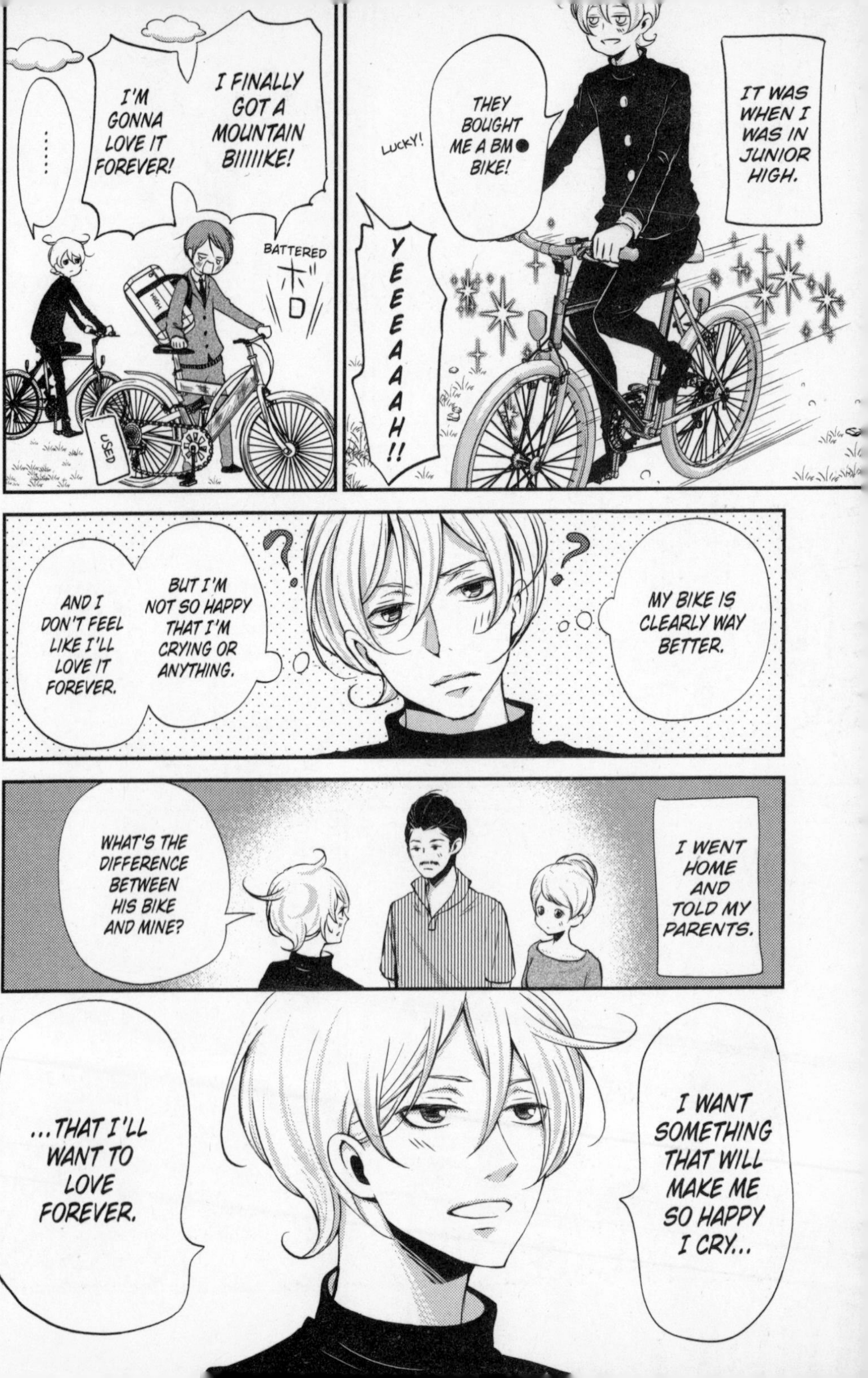
IT WAS WHEN I WAS IN JUNIOR HIGH.
THEY BOUGHT ME A BM● BIKE!
LUCKY!
YEEEAAAAH!!
I FINALLY GOT A MOUNTAIN BIIIIIKE!
I'M GONNA LOVE IT FOREVER!
BATTERED
USED
......
MY BIKE IS CLEARLY WAY BETTER.
BUT I'M NOT SO HAPPY THAT I'M CRYING OR ANYTHING.
AND I DON'T FEEL LIKE I'LL LOVE IT FOREVER.
I WENT HOME AND TOLD MY PARENTS.
WHAT'S THE DIFFERENCE BETWEEN HIS BIKE AND MINE?
I WANT SOMETHING THAT WILL MAKE ME SO HAPPY I CRY...
...THAT I'LL WANT TO LOVE FOREVER.

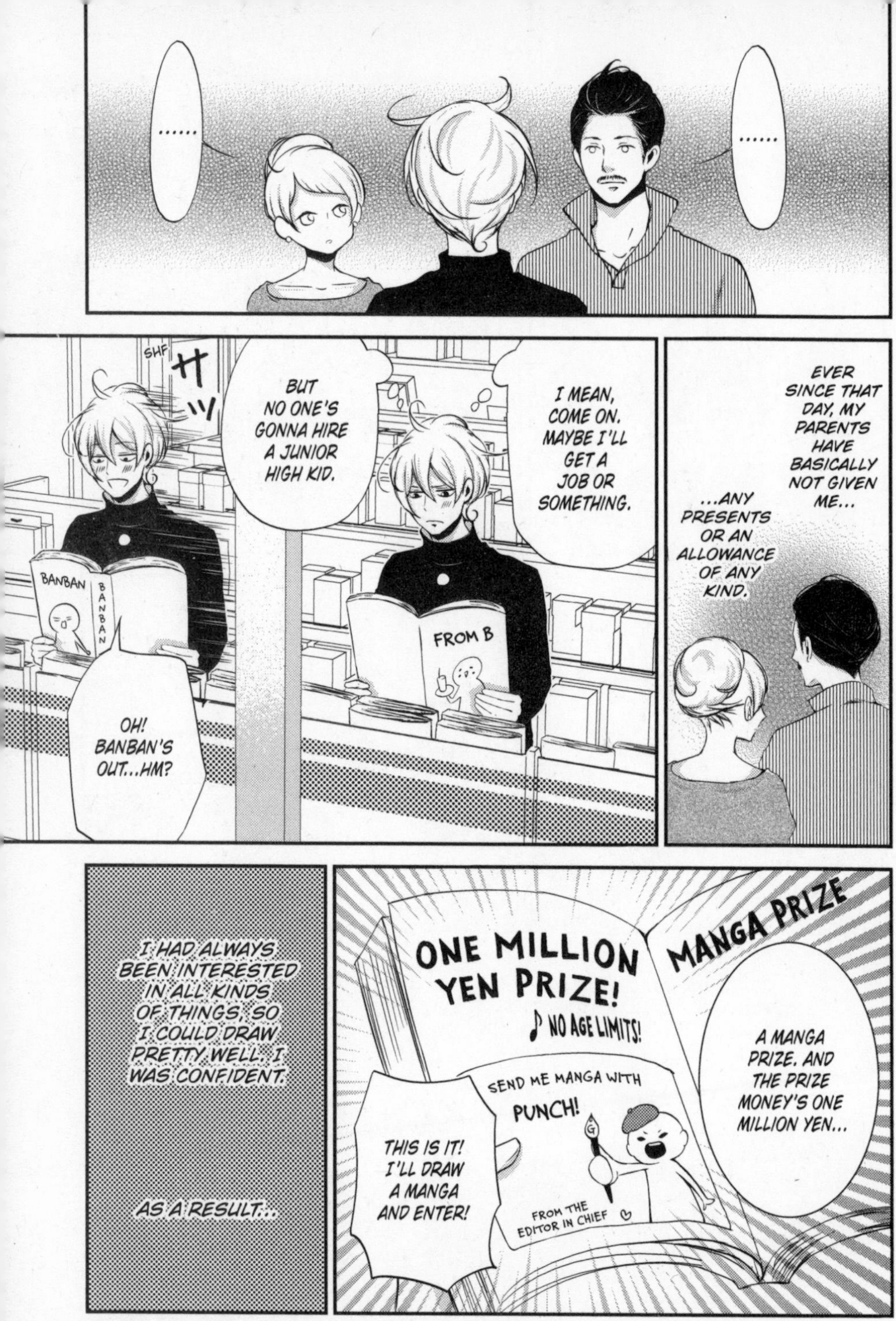
……
……
EVER SINCE THAT DAY, MY PARENTS HAVE BASICALLY NOT GIVEN ME…
…ANY PRESENTS OR AN ALLOWANCE OF ANY KIND.
I MEAN, COME ON. MAYBE I'LL GET A JOB OR SOMETHING.
BUT NO ONE'S GONNA HIRE A JUNIOR HIGH KID.
FROM B
SHF
ッ
BANBAN
BANBAN
OH! BANBAN'S OUT…HM?
MANGA PRIZE
ONE MILLION YEN PRIZE!
♪ NO AGE LIMITS!
A MANGA PRIZE. AND THE PRIZE MONEY'S ONE MILLION YEN…
SEND ME MANGA WITH PUNCH!
FROM THE EDITOR IN CHIEF
THIS IS IT! I'LL DRAW A MANGA AND ENTER!
I HAD ALWAYS BEEN INTERESTED IN ALL KINDS OF THINGS, SO I COULD DRAW PRETTY WELL. I WAS CONFIDENT.
AS A RESULT…

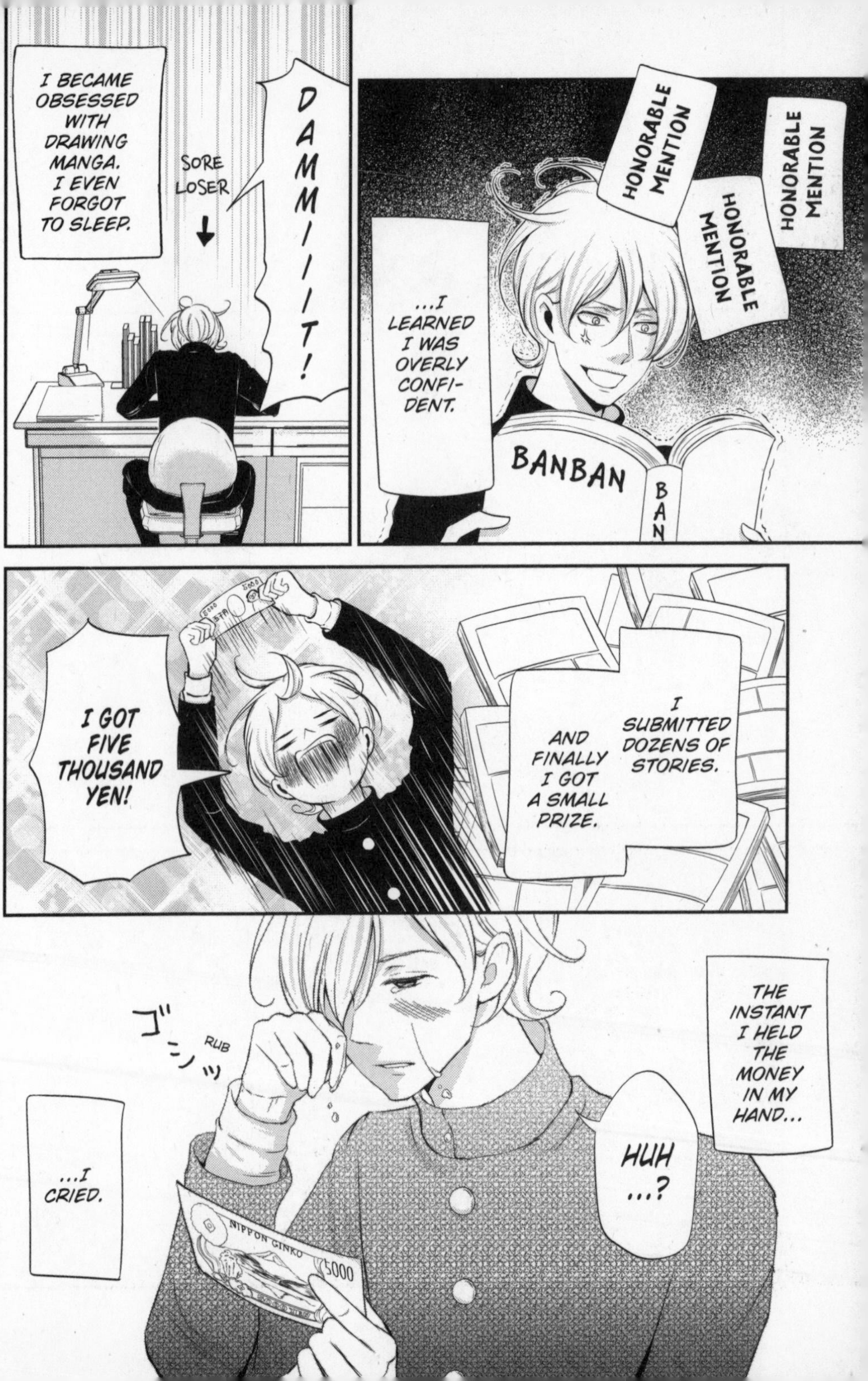

HONORABLE MENTION
HONORABLE MENTION
HONORABLE MENTION
...I LEARNED I WAS OVERLY CONFI-DENT.
BANBAN
BAN
I BECAME OBSESSED WITH DRAWING MANGA. I EVEN FORGOT TO SLEEP.
DAMMIIIIT!
SORE LOSER
I SUBMITTED DOZENS OF STORIES.
AND FINALLY I GOT A SMALL PRIZE.
I GOT FIVE THOUSAND YEN!
THE INSTANT I HELD THE MONEY IN MY HAND...
HUH...?
ゴシッ
RUB
...I CRIED.
NIPPON GINKO
5000

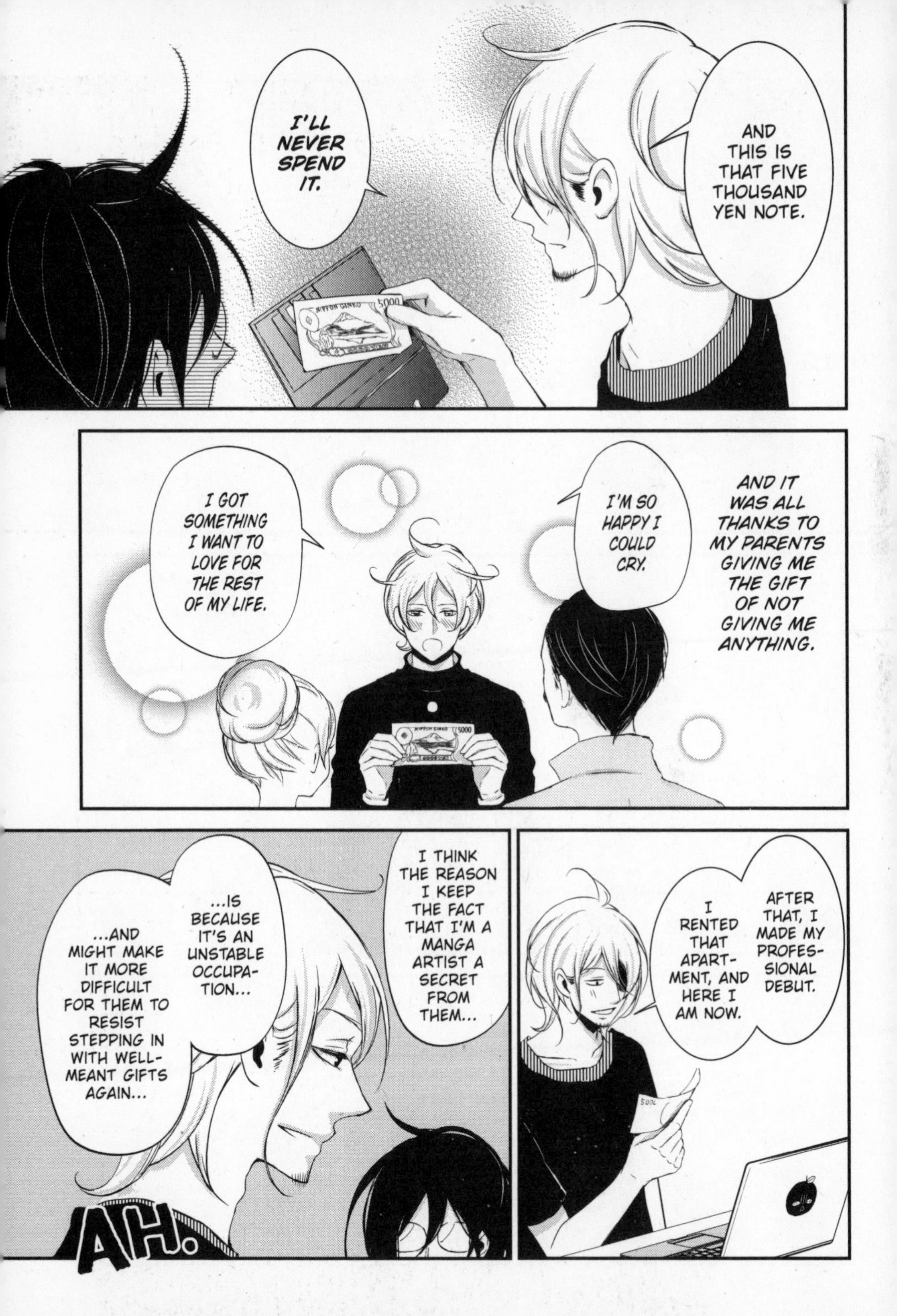
AND THIS IS THAT FIVE THOUSAND YEN NOTE.
I'LL NEVER SPEND IT.
AND IT WAS ALL THANKS TO MY PARENTS GIVING ME THE GIFT OF NOT GIVING ME ANYTHING.
I'M SO HAPPY I COULD CRY.
I GOT SOMETHING I WANT TO LOVE FOR THE REST OF MY LIFE.
AFTER THAT, I MADE MY PROFESSIONAL DEBUT.
I RENTED THAT APARTMENT, AND HERE I AM NOW.
I THINK THE REASON I KEEP THE FACT THAT I'M A MANGA ARTIST A SECRET FROM THEM...
...IS BECAUSE IT'S AN UNSTABLE OCCUPATION...
...AND MIGHT MAKE IT MORE DIFFICULT FOR THEM TO RESIST STEPPING IN WITH WELL-MEANT GIFTS AGAIN...
AH.

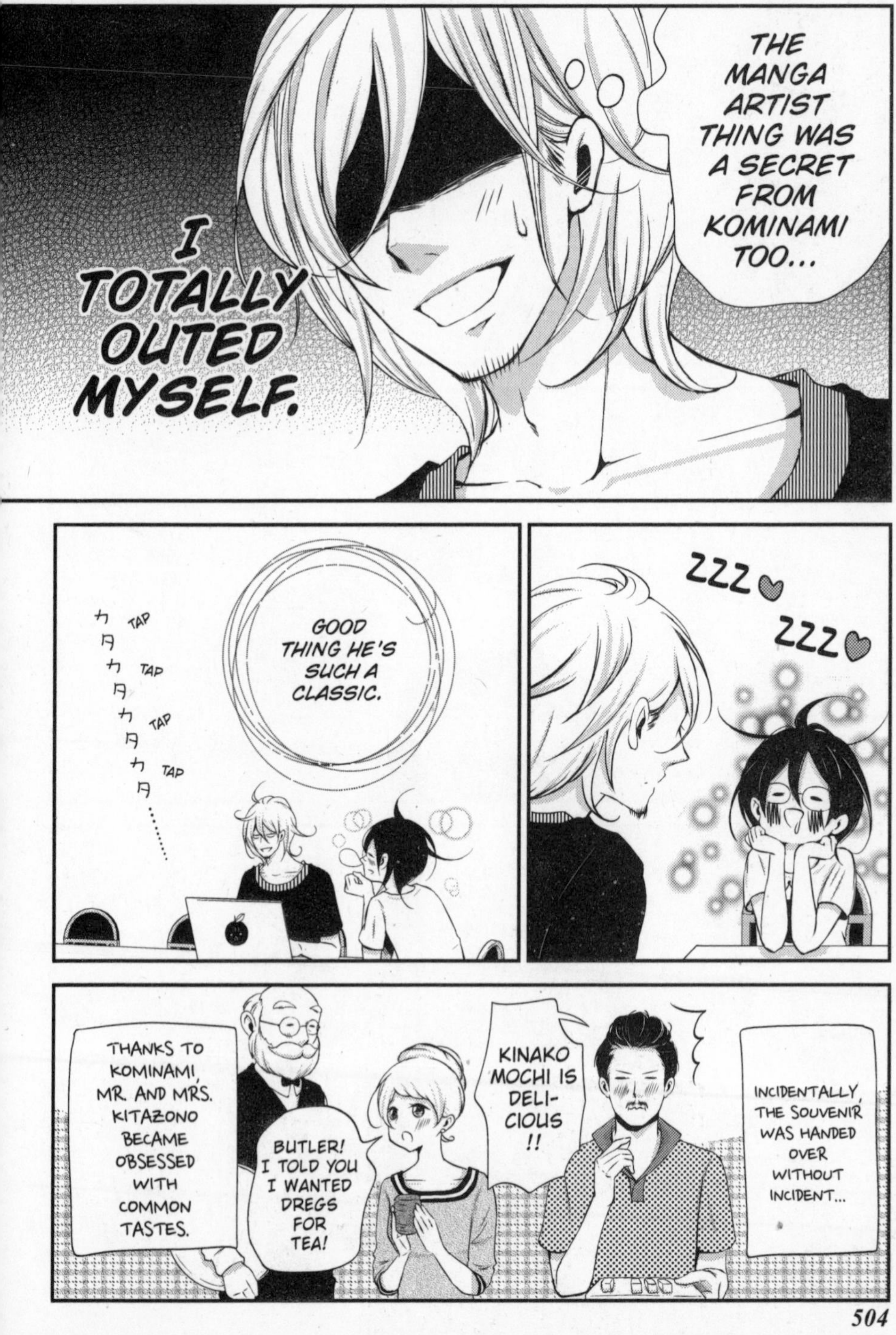
THE MANGA ARTIST THING WAS A SECRET FROM KOMINAMI TOO...
I TOTALLY OUTED MYSELF.
ZZZ
ZZZ
GOOD THING HE'S SUCH A CLASSIC.
カタ TAP
カタ TAP
カタ TAP
カタ TAP
......
INCIDENTALLY, THE SOUVENIR WAS HANDED OVER WITHOUT INCIDENT...
KINAKO MOCHI IS DELI-CIOUS!!
BUTLER! I TOLD YOU I WANTED DREGS FOR TEA!
THANKS TO KOMINAMI, MR. AND MRS. KITAZONO BECAME OBSESSED WITH COMMON TASTES.

YOU STILL HAVE A HUNDRED SHIKISHI TO SIGN FOR THE READER PRESENTS.

I'M GONNA JUMP IN THE BATH AND HIT THE HAAAAY!

AAAH! I FINALLY FINISHED THE MANGAAAA!

SUN	MON	TUE	WED	THU	FRI	
		2	3	4	5	
	9	10	11	12	13	
15	16	17	18	19	2	
22	23	24	25	26		
9	30					

30 —DEJECTION —SHIKISHI —DEADLINE

AH! VOLUME FIFTEEN OF DEJEC-TION MAN GOES ON SALE TODAY!

SHI-KISHI...

HIS WEAPON, A BEAN SPROUT! HIS BRAINS, NATTO!

DEJECTION MAN, BORN FROM A SOYBEAN!

DEJECTION!

UH, NO! I STILL HAVE WORK TO DO.

SENSEI, YOU LIKE DEJECTION MAN?

IT'S POPULAR WITH ELEMENTARY KIDS, RIGHT?

OF COURSE NOT.

HUH?

I GOTTA DRAW THE SHIKISHI.

NISHIDA, GO TO THE BOOKSTORE AND BUY IT.

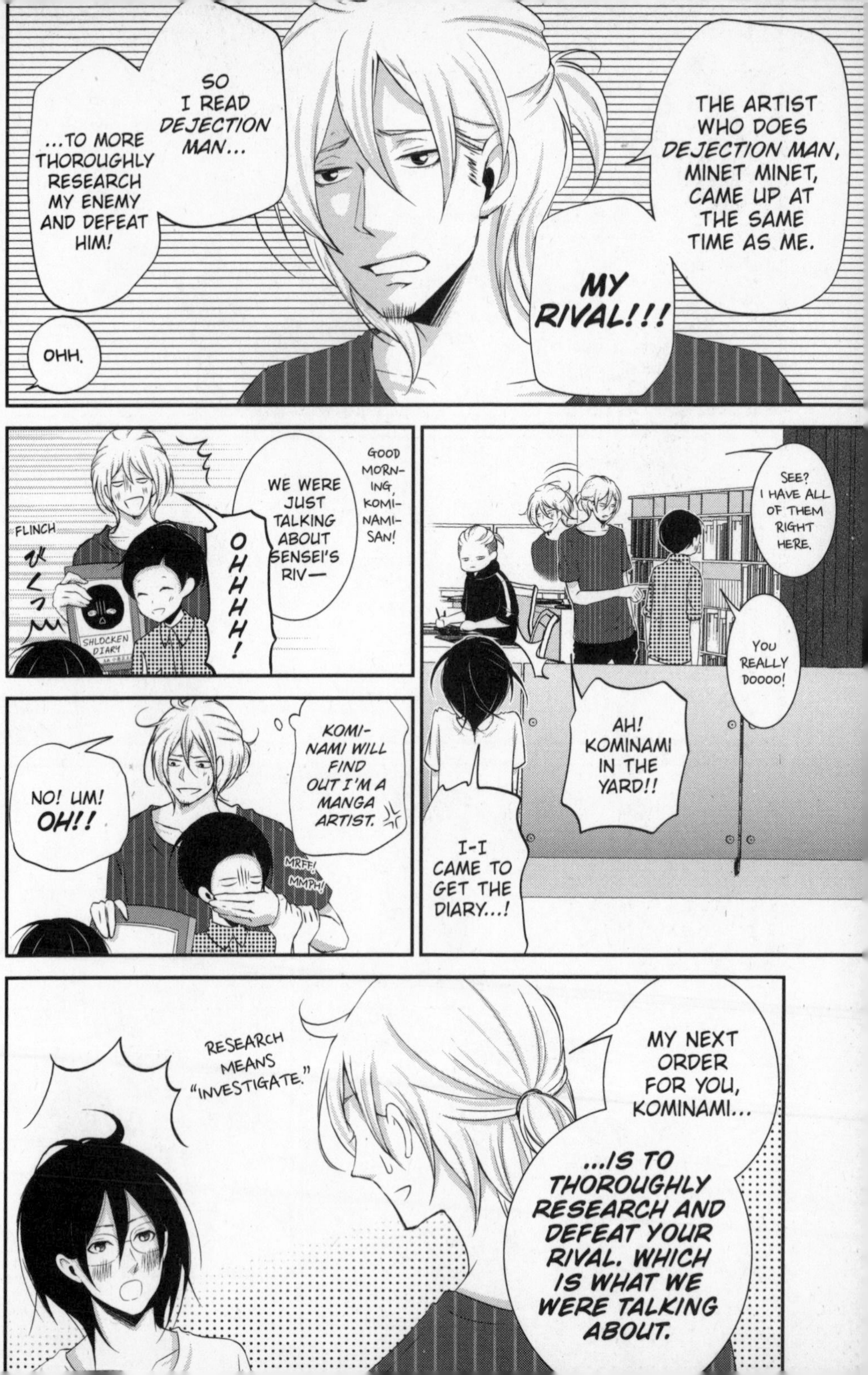
THE ARTIST WHO DOES DEJECTION MAN, MINET MINET, CAME UP AT THE SAME TIME AS ME.
MY RIVAL!!!
SO I READ DEJECTION MAN...
...TO MORE THOROUGHLY RESEARCH MY ENEMY AND DEFEAT HIM!
OHH.
SEE? I HAVE ALL OF THEM RIGHT HERE.
YOU REALLY DOOOO!
AH! KOMINAMI IN THE YARD!!
I-I CAME TO GET THE DIARY...!
GOOD MORNING, KOMINAMI-SAN!
WE WERE JUST TALKING ABOUT SENSEI'S RIV—
OHHHH!
FLINCH
SHLOCKEN DIARY
KOMINAMI WILL FIND OUT I'M A MANGA ARTIST.
NO! UM! OH!!
MRFF! MMPH!
MY NEXT ORDER FOR YOU, KOMINAMI...
...IS TO THOROUGHLY RESEARCH AND DEFEAT YOUR RIVAL. WHICH IS WHAT WE WERE TALKING ABOUT.
RESEARCH MEANS "INVESTIGATE."

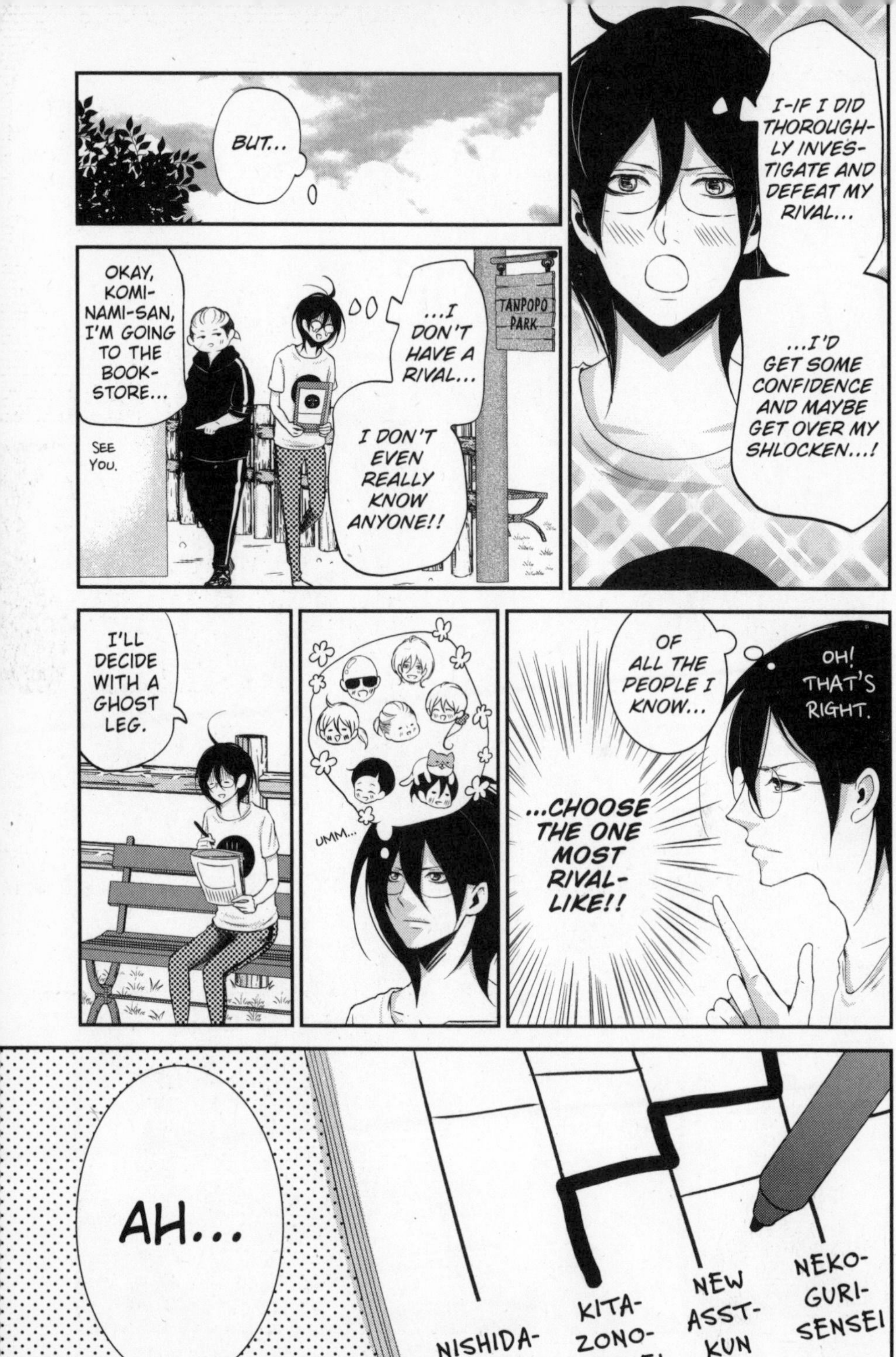
I-IF I DID THOROUGHLY INVESTIGATE AND DEFEAT MY RIVAL...
...I'D GET SOME CONFIDENCE AND MAYBE GET OVER MY SHLOCKEN...!
BUT...
...I DON'T HAVE A RIVAL...
I DON'T EVEN REALLY KNOW ANYONE!!
TANPOPO PARK
OKAY, KOMINAMI-SAN, I'M GOING TO THE BOOKSTORE...
SEE YOU.
OH! THAT'S RIGHT.
OF ALL THE PEOPLE I KNOW...
...CHOOSE THE ONE MOST RIVAL-LIKE!!
UMM...
I'LL DECIDE WITH A GHOST LEG.
NEKO-GURI-SENSEI
NEW ASST-KUN
KITA-ZONO-SENSEI
NISHIDA-SAN
AH...

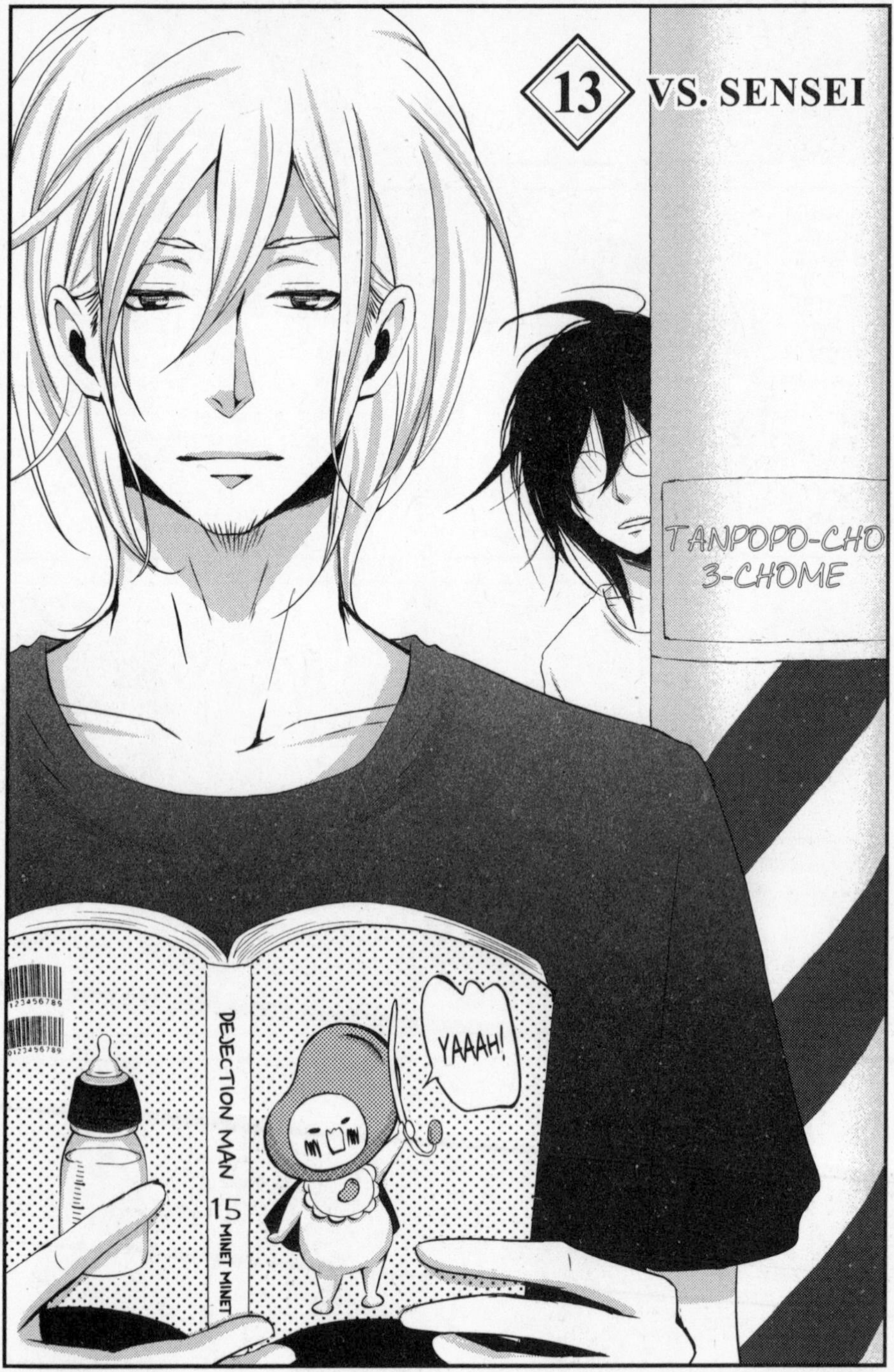
13 VS. SENSEI
TANPOPO-CHO 3-CHOME
DEJECTION MAN 15 MINET MINET
YAAAH!

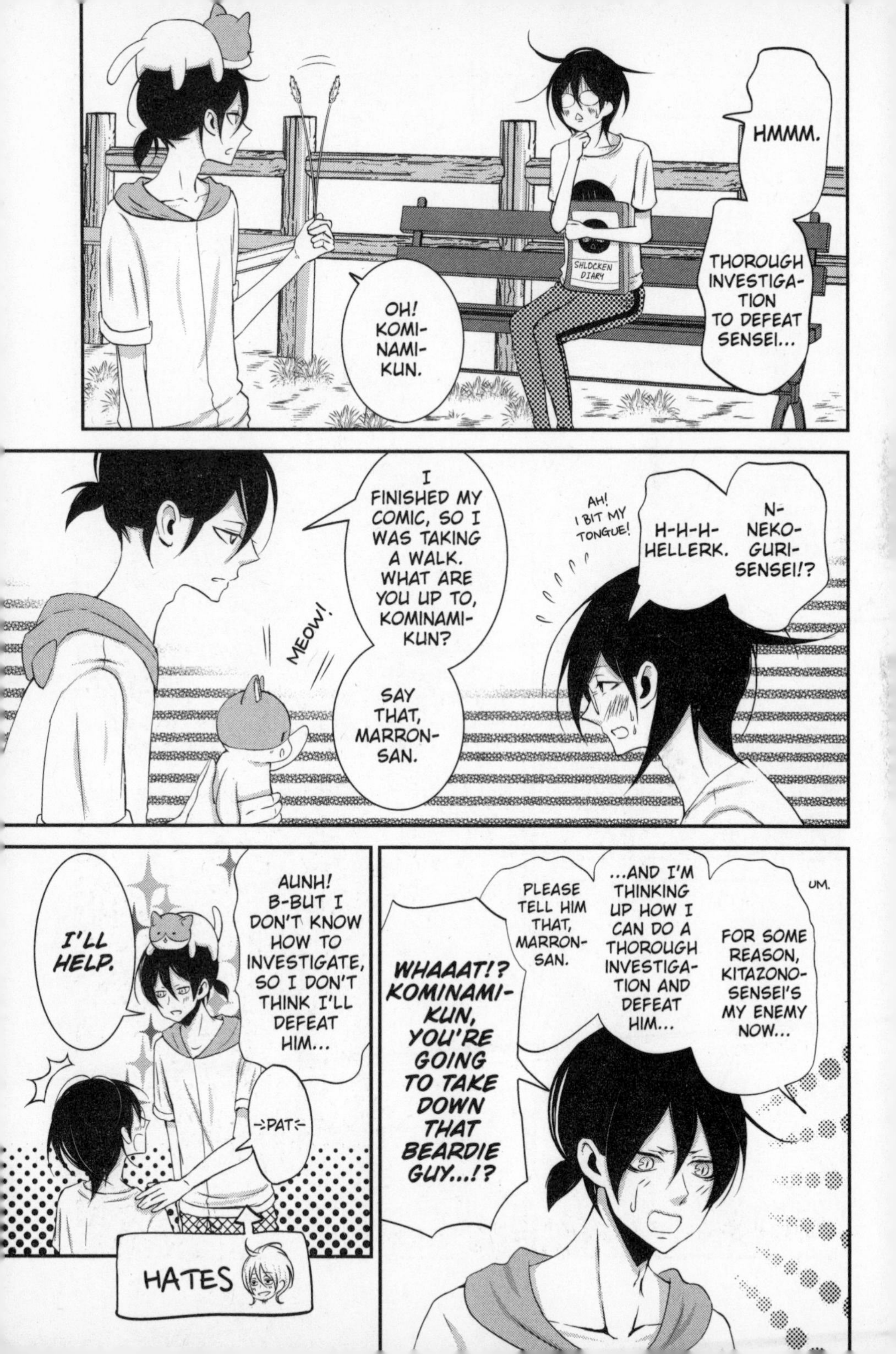
HMMM.
THOROUGH INVESTIGATION TO DEFEAT SENSEI...
OH! KOMINAMI-KUN.
N-NEKOGURI-SENSEI!?
H-H-H-HELLERK.
AH! I BIT MY TONGUE!
I FINISHED MY COMIC, SO I WAS TAKING A WALK. WHAT ARE YOU UP TO, KOMINAMI-KUN?
SAY THAT, MARRON-SAN.
MEOW!
UM.
FOR SOME REASON, KITAZONO-SENSEI'S MY ENEMY NOW...
...AND I'M THINKING UP HOW I CAN DO A THOROUGH INVESTIGATION AND DEFEAT HIM...
PLEASE TELL HIM THAT, MARRON-SAN.
WHAAAT!? KOMINAMI-KUN, YOU'RE GOING TO TAKE DOWN THAT BEARDIE GUY...!?
AUNH! B-BUT I DON'T KNOW HOW TO INVESTIGATE, SO I DON'T THINK I'LL DEFEAT HIM...
I'LL HELP.
PAT
HATES

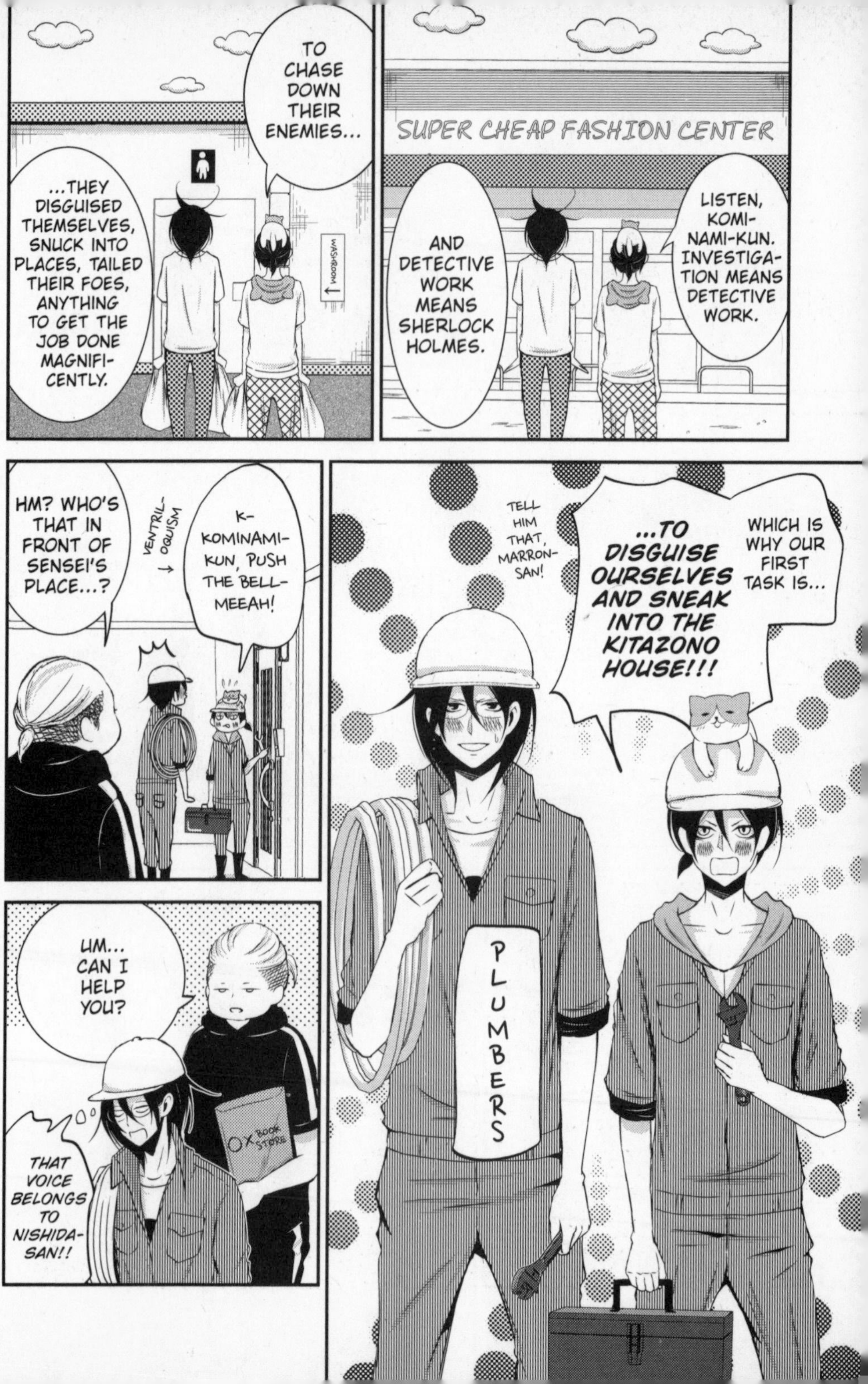
SUPER CHEAP FASHION CENTER
LISTEN, KOMI-NAMI-KUN. INVESTIGATION MEANS DETECTIVE WORK.
AND DETECTIVE WORK MEANS SHERLOCK HOLMES.
TO CHASE DOWN THEIR ENEMIES...
WASHROOM
...THEY DISGUISED THEMSELVES, SNUCK INTO PLACES, TAILED THEIR FOES, ANYTHING TO GET THE JOB DONE MAGNIFI-CENTLY.
WHICH IS WHY OUR FIRST TASK IS...
...TO DISGUISE OURSELVES AND SNEAK INTO THE KITAZONO HOUSE!!!
TELL HIM THAT, MARRON-SAN!
PLUMBERS
K-KOMINAMI-KUN, PUSH THE BELL-MEEAH!
VENTRIL-OQUISM
HM? WHO'S THAT IN FRONT OF SENSEI'S PLACE...?
UM... CAN I HELP YOU?
OX BOOK STORE
THAT VOICE BELONGS TO NISHIDA-SAN!!

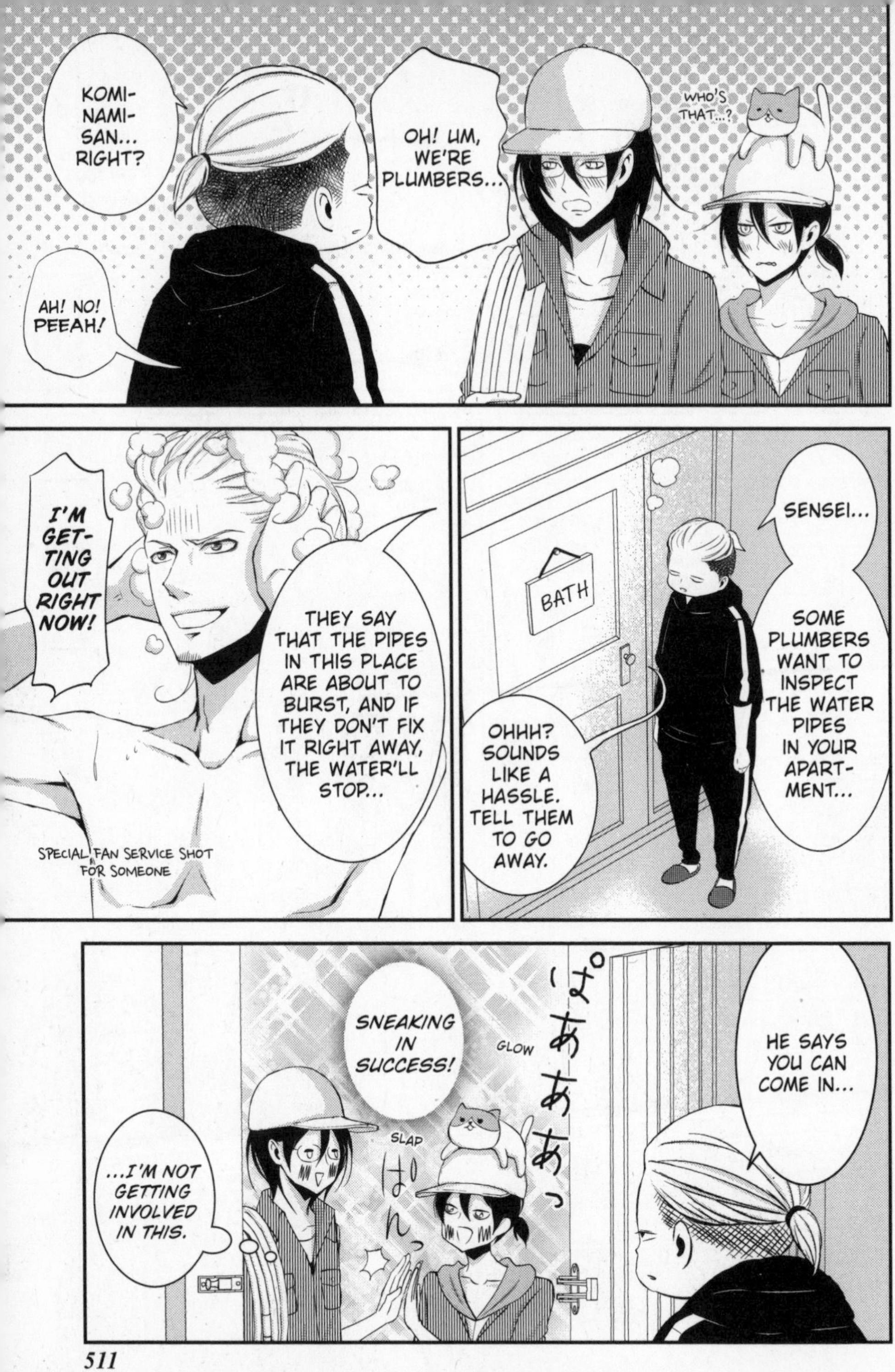
WHO'S THAT...?
OH! UM, WE'RE PLUMBERS...
KOMI-NAMI-SAN... RIGHT?
AH! NO! PEEAH!
SENSEI...
SOME PLUMBERS WANT TO INSPECT THE WATER PIPES IN YOUR APART-MENT...
BATH
OHHH? SOUNDS LIKE A HASSLE. TELL THEM TO GO AWAY.
THEY SAY THAT THE PIPES IN THIS PLACE ARE ABOUT TO BURST, AND IF THEY DON'T FIX IT RIGHT AWAY, THE WATER'LL STOP...
I'M GET-TING OUT RIGHT NOW!
SPECIAL FAN SERVICE SHOT FOR SOMEONE
HE SAYS YOU CAN COME IN...
ぱあああっ
GLOW
SNEAKING IN SUCCESS!
SLAP
ぱんっ
...I'M NOT GETTING INVOLVED IN THIS.

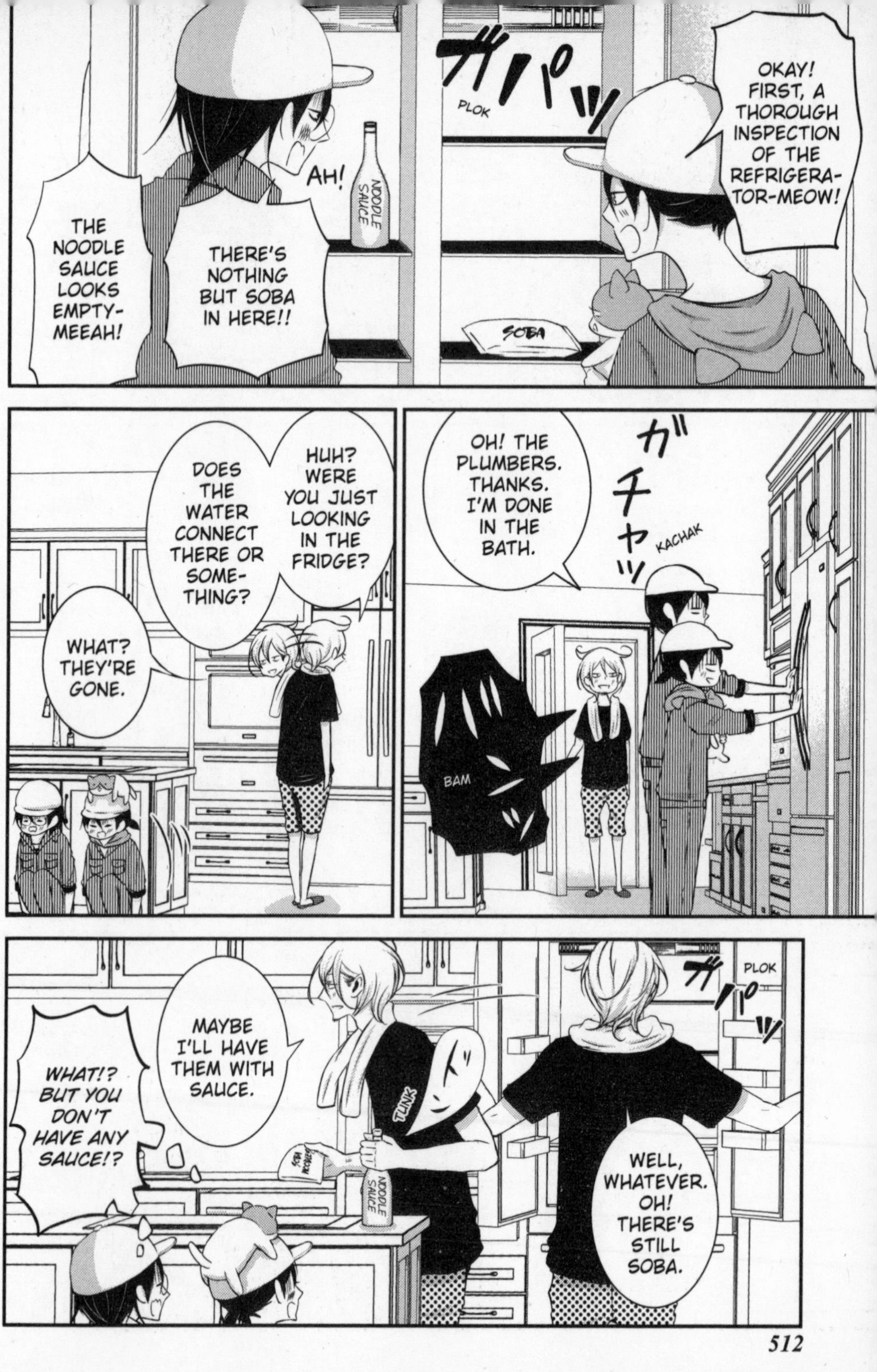
OKAY! FIRST, A THOROUGH INSPECTION OF THE REFRIGERATOR-MEOW!
PLOK
SOBA
NOODLE SAUCE
AH!
THERE'S NOTHING BUT SOBA IN HERE!!
THE NOODLE SAUCE LOOKS EMPTY-MEEAH!
KACHAK
OH! THE PLUMBERS. THANKS. I'M DONE IN THE BATH.
BAM
HUH? WERE YOU JUST LOOKING IN THE FRIDGE?
DOES THE WATER CONNECT THERE OR SOMETHING?
WHAT? THEY'RE GONE.
PLOK
WELL, WHATEVER. OH! THERE'S STILL SOBA.
TUNK
NOODLE SAUCE
MAYBE I'LL HAVE THEM WITH SAUCE.
WHAT!? BUT YOU DON'T HAVE ANY SAUCE!?

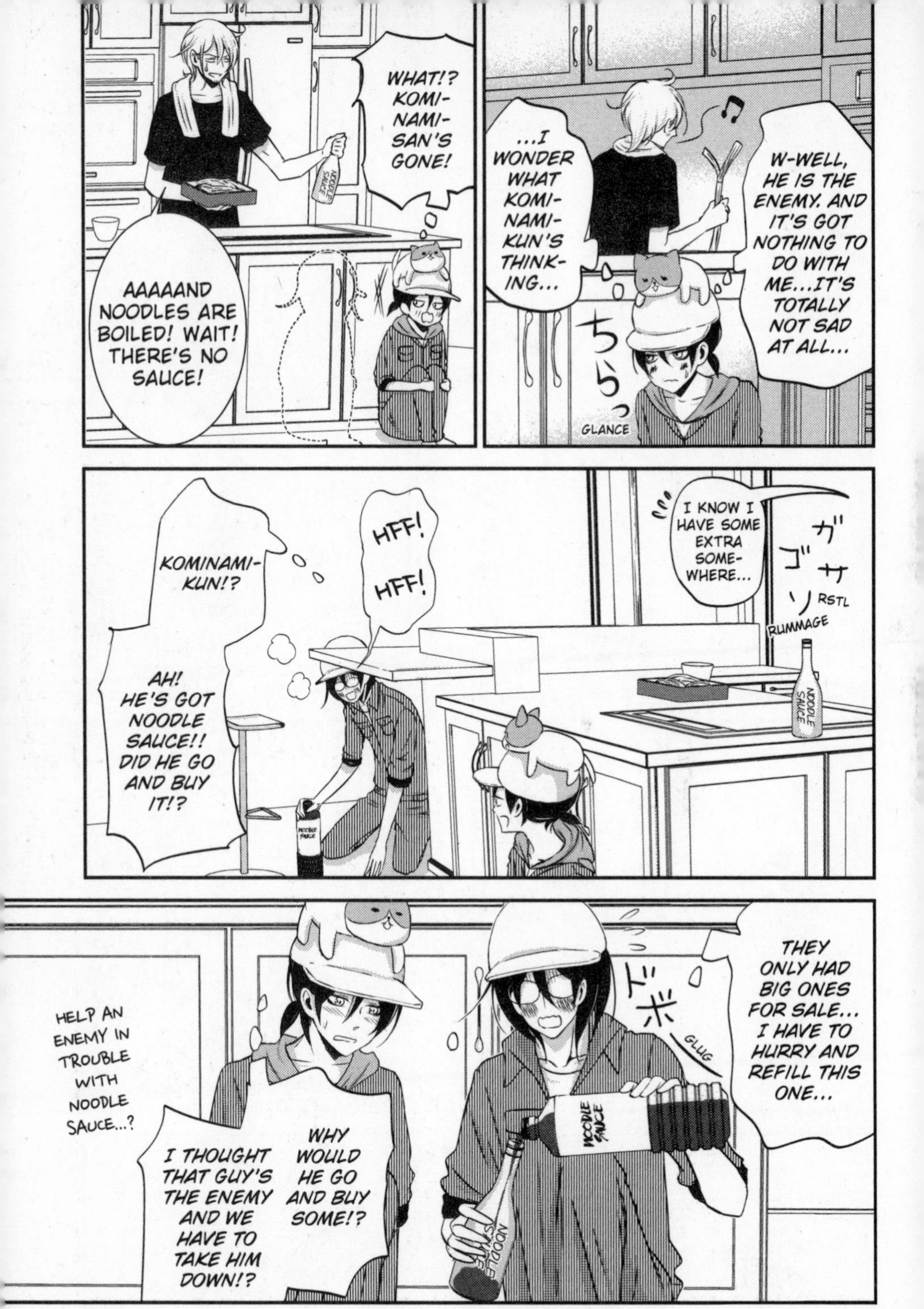
W-WELL, HE IS THE ENEMY. AND IT'S GOT NOTHING TO DO WITH ME...IT'S TOTALLY NOT SAD AT ALL...
...I WONDER WHAT KOMINAMI-KUN'S THINKING...
ちらっ
GLANCE
WHAT!? KOMINAMI-SAN'S GONE!
AAAAAND NOODLES ARE BOILED! WAIT! THERE'S NO SAUCE!
NOODLE SAUCE
ガサゴソ
RSTL
RUMMAGE
I KNOW I HAVE SOME EXTRA SOMEWHERE...
NOODLE SAUCE
HFF! HFF!
KOMINAMI-KUN!?
AH! HE'S GOT NOODLE SAUCE!! DID HE GO AND BUY IT!?
THEY ONLY HAD BIG ONES FOR SALE... I HAVE TO HURRY AND REFILL THIS ONE...
ドボ
GLUG
NOODLE SAUCE
WHY WOULD HE GO AND BUY SOME!?
I THOUGHT THAT GUY'S THE ENEMY AND WE HAVE TO TAKE HIM DOWN!?
HELP AN ENEMY IN TROUBLE WITH NOODLE SAUCE...?

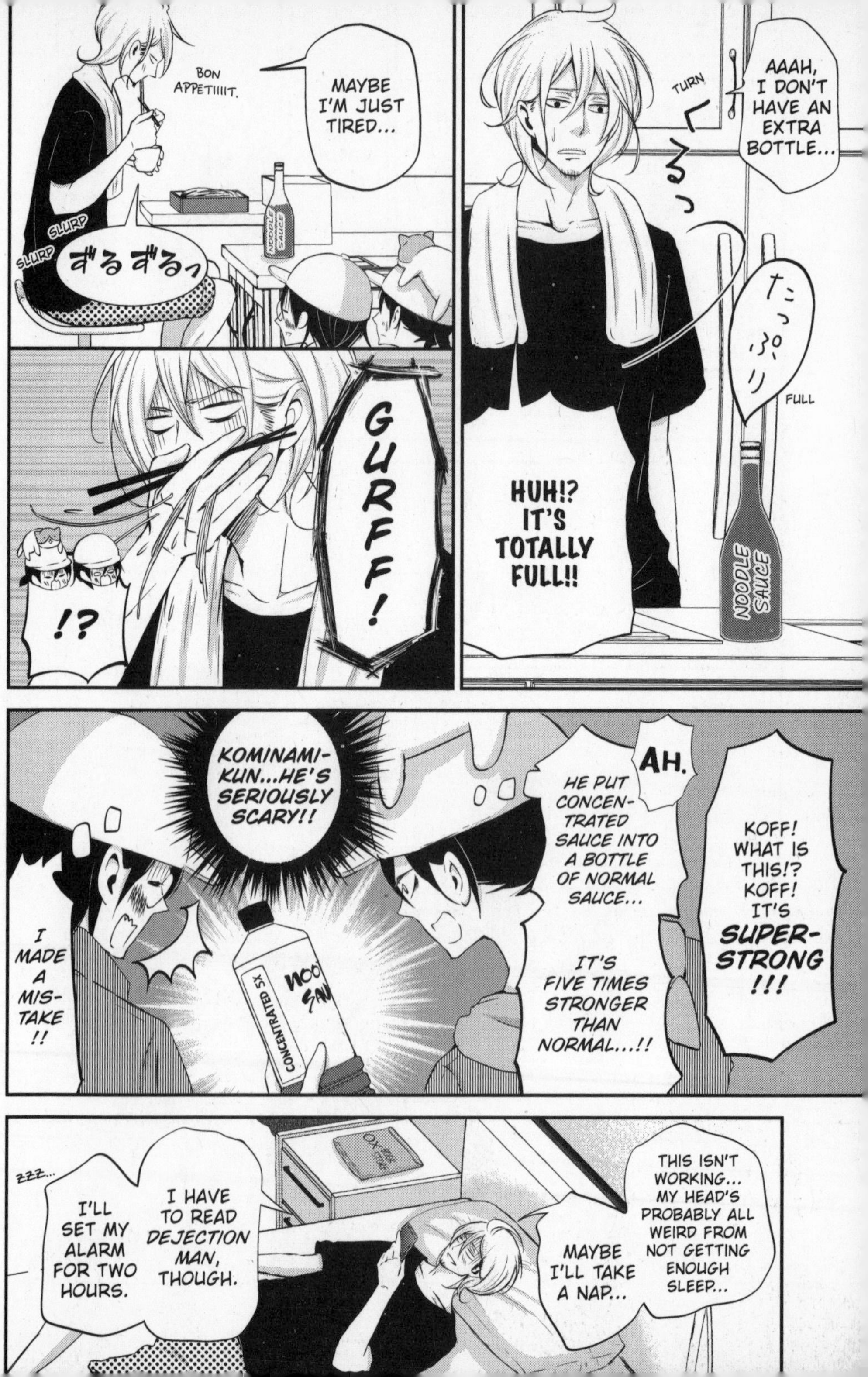
AAAH, I DON'T HAVE AN EXTRA BOTTLE...
TURN
くるっ
たっぷり
FULL
HUH!? IT'S TOTALLY FULL!!
NOODLE SAUCE
BON APPETIIIIT.
MAYBE I'M JUST TIRED...
NOODLE SAUCE
SLURP
SLURP
ずるずるっ
GURFF!
!?
KOFF! WHAT IS THIS!? KOFF! IT'S SUPER-STRONG!!!
AH.
HE PUT CONCENTRATED SAUCE INTO A BOTTLE OF NORMAL SAUCE...
IT'S FIVE TIMES STRONGER THAN NORMAL...!!
KOMINAMI-KUN...HE'S SERIOUSLY SCARY!!
I MADE A MIS-TAKE!!
CONCENTRATED 5X
THIS ISN'T WORKING... MY HEAD'S PROBABLY ALL WEIRD FROM NOT GETTING ENOUGH SLEEP...
MAYBE I'LL TAKE A NAP...
I HAVE TO READ DEJECTION MAN, THOUGH.
I'LL SET MY ALARM FOR TWO HOURS.
ZZZ...

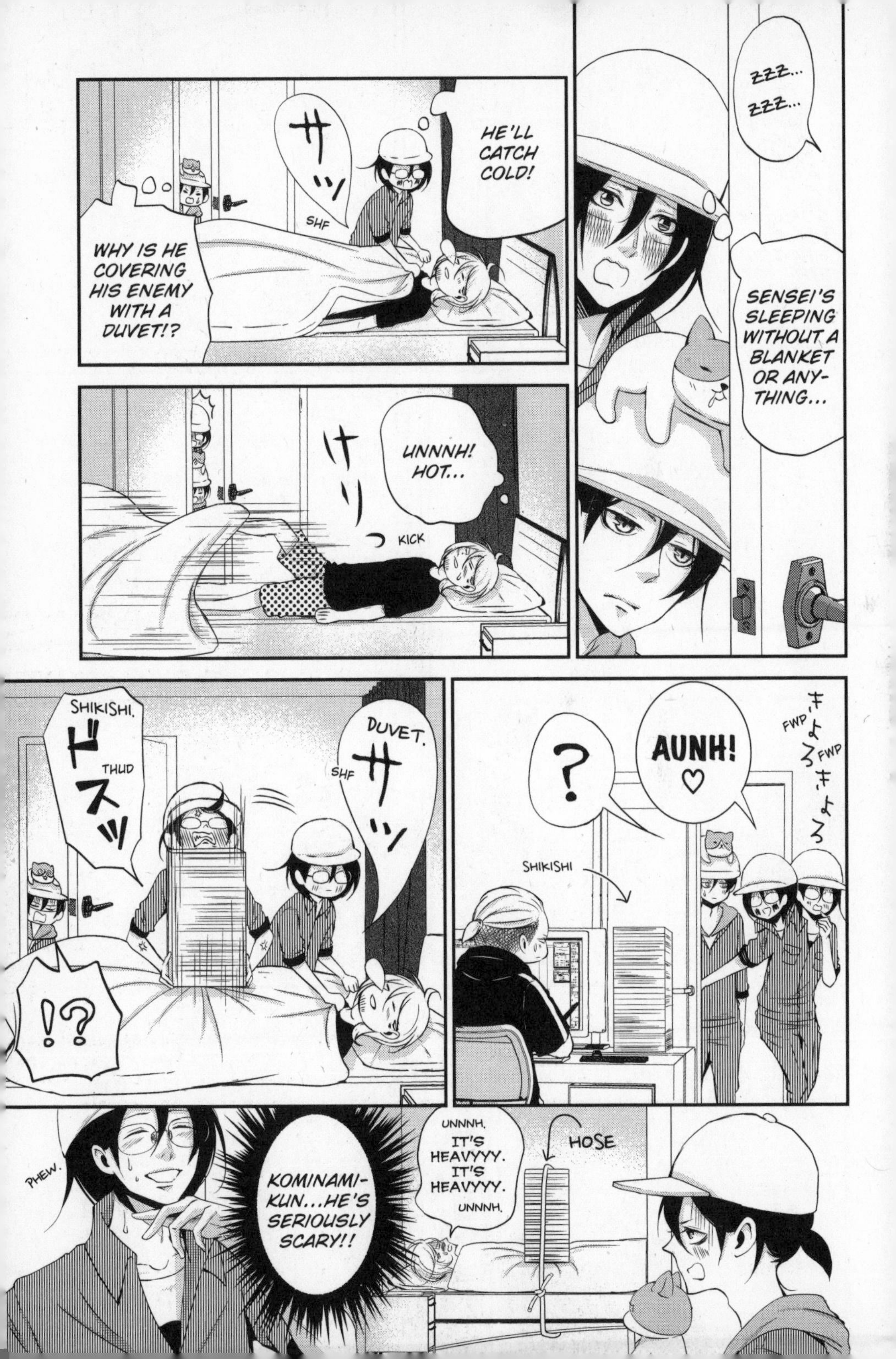

ZZZ...
ZZZ...
SENSEI'S SLEEPING WITHOUT A BLANKET OR ANY-THING...
HE'LL CATCH COLD!
サッ
SHF
WHY IS HE COVERING HIS ENEMY WITH A DUVET!?
UNNNH! HOT...
けりっ
KICK
AUNH! ♡
?
きょろきょろ
FWP FWP
SHIKISHI
DUVET.
サッ
SHF
SHIKISHI.
ドスッ
THUD
!?
HOSE
UNNNH. IT'S HEAVYYY. IT'S HEAVYYY. UNNNH.
KOMINAMI-KUN...HE'S SERIOUSLY SCARY!!
PHEW.

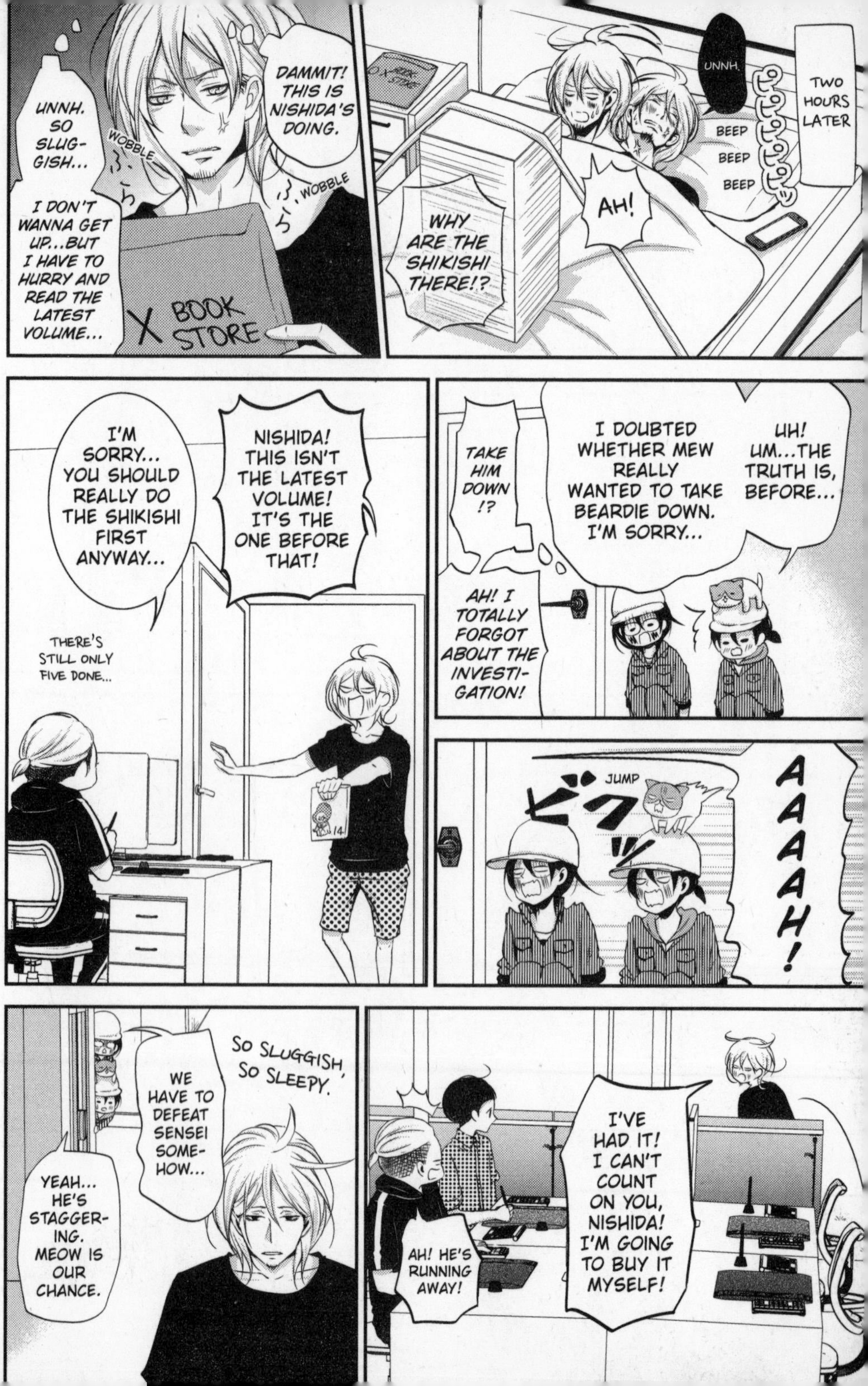
TWO HOURS LATER
UNNH.
ピピピピピッ
BEEP
BEEP
BEEP
AH!
WHY ARE THE SHIKISHI THERE!?
DAMMIT! THIS IS NISHIDA'S DOING.
UNNH. SO SLUGGISH...
WOBBLE
WOBBLE
I DON'T WANNA GET UP...BUT I HAVE TO HURRY AND READ THE LATEST VOLUME...
X BOOK STORE
UH! UM...THE TRUTH IS, BEFORE...
I DOUBTED WHETHER MEW REALLY WANTED TO TAKE BEARDIE DOWN. I'M SORRY...
TAKE HIM DOWN!?
AH! I TOTALLY FORGOT ABOUT THE INVESTIGATION!
AAAAAH!
JUMP
ビク
NISHIDA! THIS ISN'T THE LATEST VOLUME! IT'S THE ONE BEFORE THAT!
I'M SORRY... YOU SHOULD REALLY DO THE SHIKISHI FIRST ANYWAY...
THERE'S STILL ONLY FIVE DONE...
14
I'VE HAD IT! I CAN'T COUNT ON YOU, NISHIDA! I'M GOING TO BUY IT MYSELF!
AH! HE'S RUNNING AWAY!
SO SLUGGISH, SO SLEEPY.
WE HAVE TO DEFEAT SENSEI SOMEHOW...
YEAH... HE'S STAGGERING. MEOW IS OUR CHANCE.

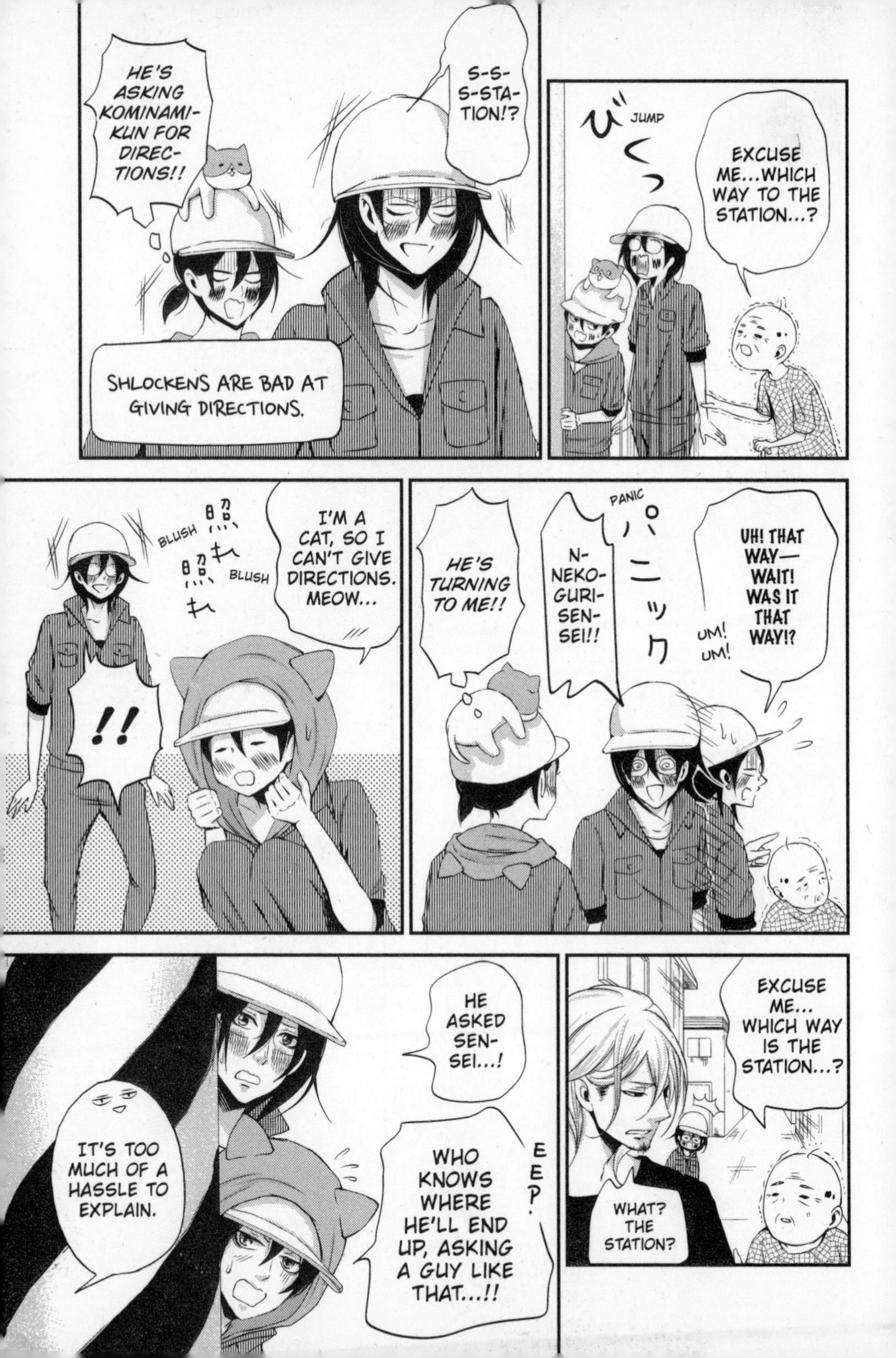
EXCUSE ME...WHICH WAY TO THE STATION...?
びくっ JUMP
S-S-S-STATION!?
HE'S ASKING KOMINAMI-KUN FOR DIRECTIONS!!
SHLOCKENS ARE BAD AT GIVING DIRECTIONS.
UH! THAT WAY—WAIT! WAS IT THAT WAY!?
UM! UM!
パニック PANIC
N-NEKOGURI-SENSEI!!
HE'S TURNING TO ME!!
I'M A CAT, SO I CAN'T GIVE DIRECTIONS. MEOW...
照れ BLUSH
照れ BLUSH
!!
EXCUSE ME... WHICH WAY IS THE STATION...?
WHAT? THE STATION?
HE ASKED SENSEI...!
EEP!
WHO KNOWS WHERE HE'LL END UP, ASKING A GUY LIKE THAT...!!
IT'S TOO MUCH OF A HASSLE TO EXPLAIN.

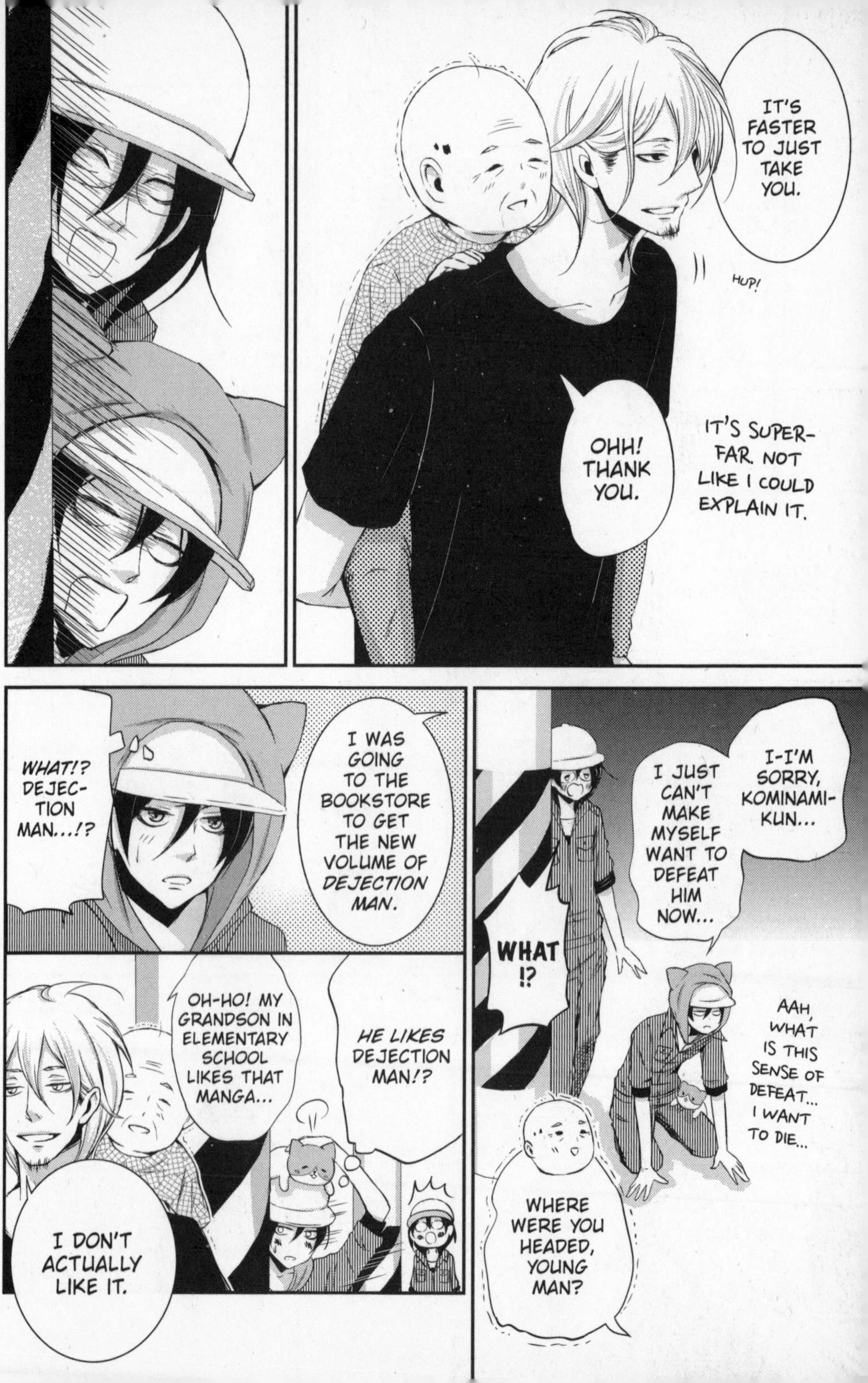
IT'S FASTER TO JUST TAKE YOU.
HUP!
OHH! THANK YOU.
IT'S SUPER-FAR. NOT LIKE I COULD EXPLAIN IT.
I-I'M SORRY, KOMINAMI-KUN...
I JUST CAN'T MAKE MYSELF WANT TO DEFEAT HIM NOW...
WHAT!?
AAH, WHAT IS THIS SENSE OF DEFEAT... I WANT TO DIE...
WHERE WERE YOU HEADED, YOUNG MAN?
I WAS GOING TO THE BOOKSTORE TO GET THE NEW VOLUME OF DEJECTION MAN.
WHAT!? DEJECTION MAN...!?
HE LIKES DEJECTION MAN!?
OH-HO! MY GRANDSON IN ELEMENTARY SCHOOL LIKES THAT MANGA...
I DON'T ACTUALLY LIKE IT.

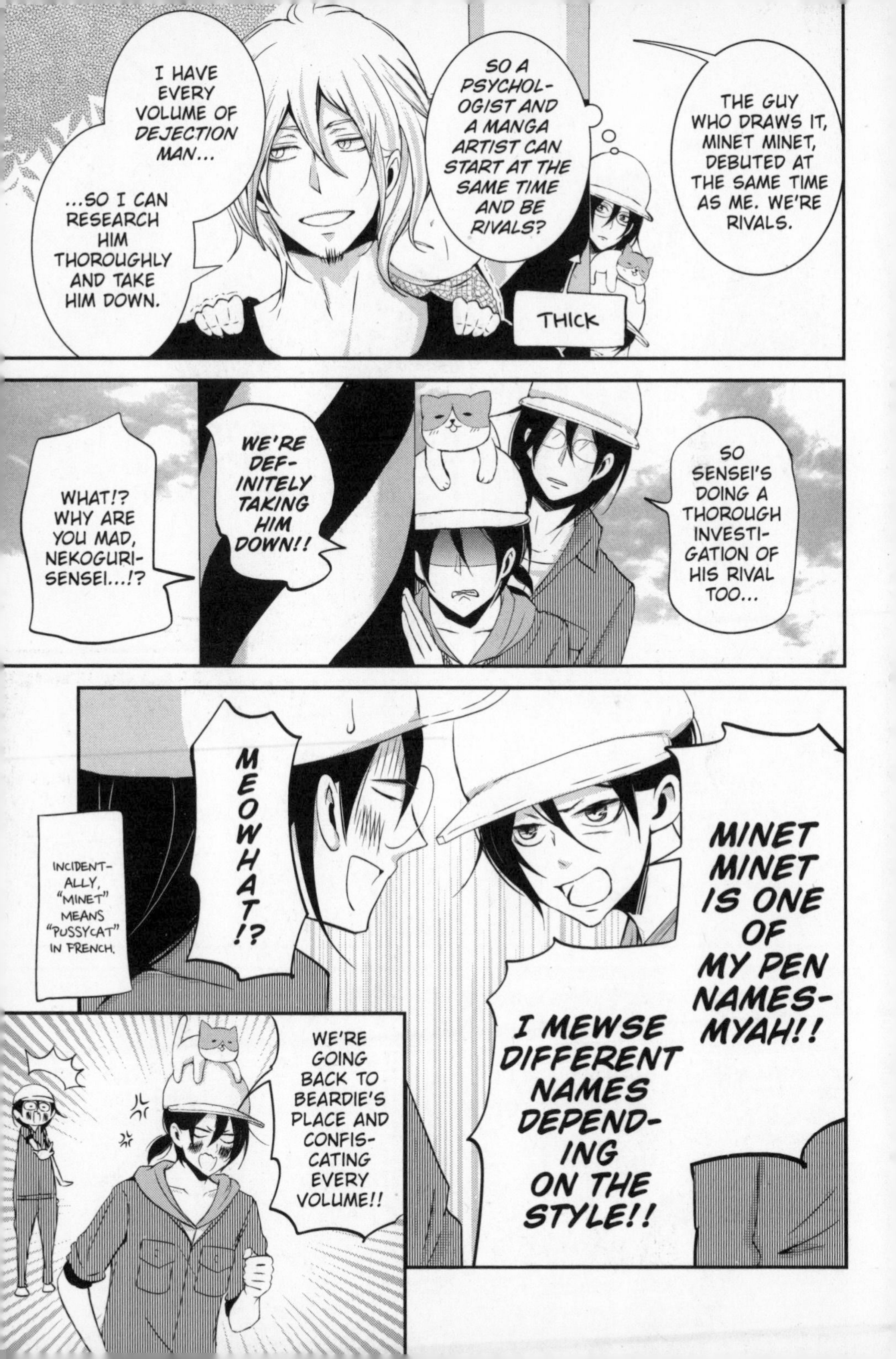
THE GUY WHO DRAWS IT, MINET MINET, DEBUTED AT THE SAME TIME AS ME. WE'RE RIVALS.
SO A PSYCHOLOGIST AND A MANGA ARTIST CAN START AT THE SAME TIME AND BE RIVALS?
THICK
I HAVE EVERY VOLUME OF DEJECTION MAN...
...SO I CAN RESEARCH HIM THOROUGHLY AND TAKE HIM DOWN.
SO SENSEI'S DOING A THOROUGH INVESTIGATION OF HIS RIVAL TOO...
WE'RE DEFINITELY TAKING HIM DOWN!!
WHAT!? WHY ARE YOU MAD, NEKOGURI-SENSEI...!?
MINET MINET IS ONE OF MY PEN NAMES-MYAH!!
I MEWSE DIFFERENT NAMES DEPENDING ON THE STYLE!!
MEOWHAT!?
INCIDENTALLY, "MINET" MEANS "PUSSYCAT" IN FRENCH.
WE'RE GOING BACK TO BEARDIE'S PLACE AND CONFISCATING EVERY VOLUME!!

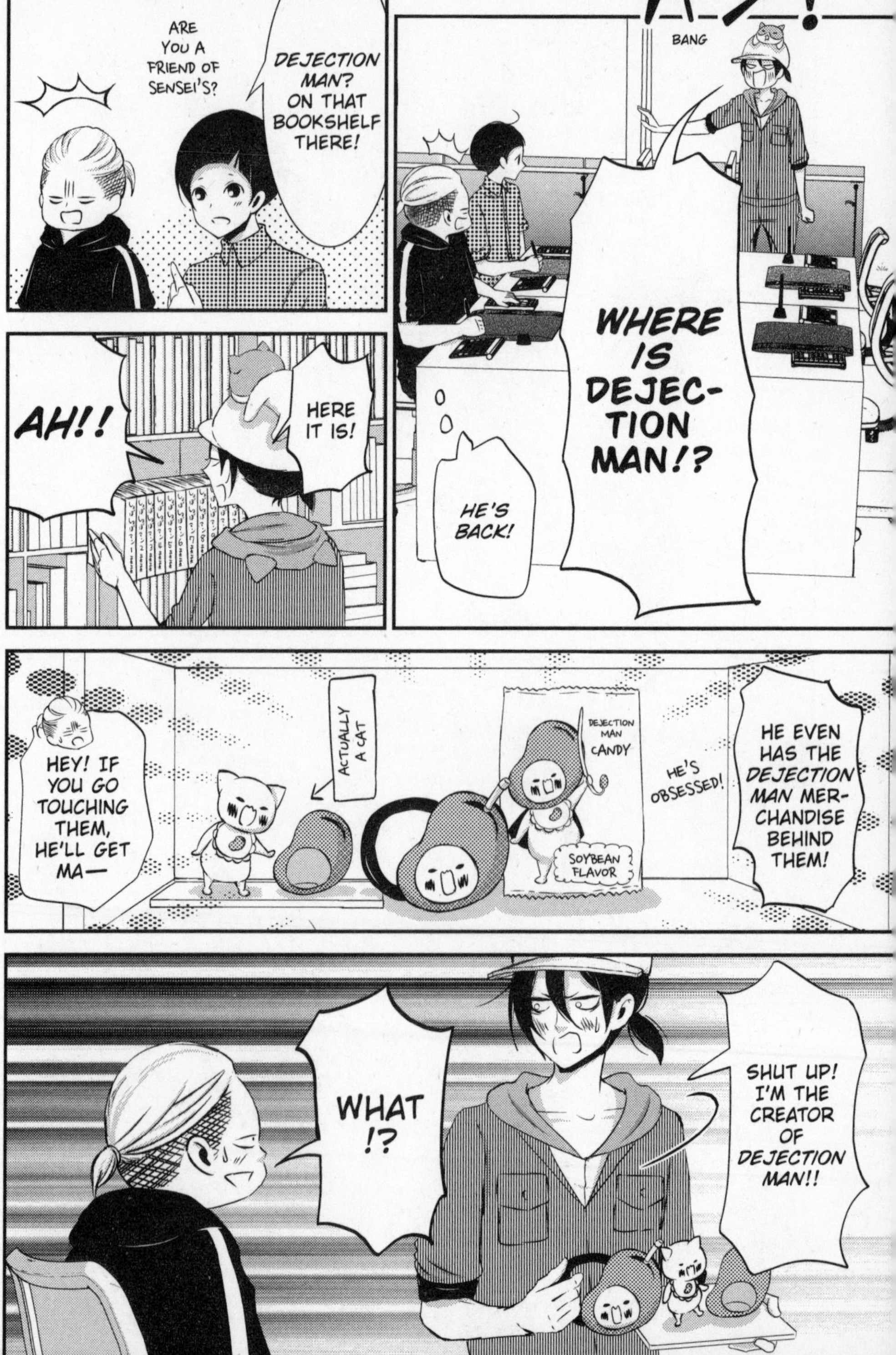
バン!
BANG
WHERE IS DEJECTION-MAN!?
HE'S BACK!
DEJECTION MAN? ON THAT BOOKSHELF THERE!
ARE YOU A FRIEND OF SENSEI'S?
HERE IT IS!
AH!!
HE EVEN HAS THE DEJECTION MAN MERCHANDISE BEHIND THEM!
HE'S OBSESSED!
DEJECTION MAN CANDY
SOYBEAN FLAVOR
ACTUALLY A CAT
HEY! IF YOU GO TOUCHING THEM, HE'LL GET MA—
SHUT UP! I'M THE CREATOR OF DEJECTION MAN!!
WHAT!?

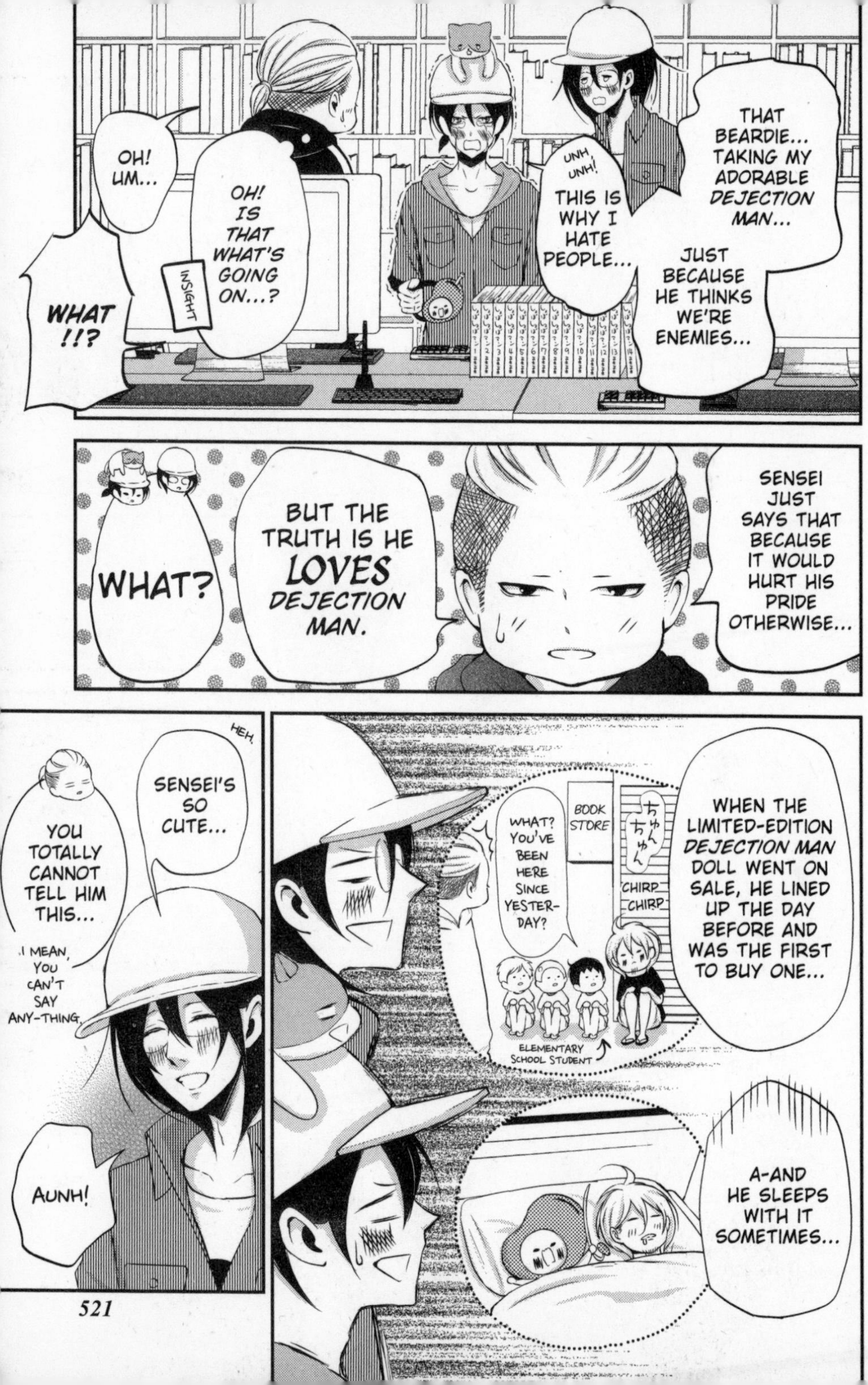

THAT BEARDIE... TAKING MY ADORABLE *DEJECTION MAN*...
JUST BECAUSE HE THINKS WE'RE ENEMIES...
UNH UNH!
THIS IS WHY I HATE PEOPLE...
OH! IS THAT WHAT'S GOING ON...?
INSIGHT
OH! UM...
WHAT!!?
SENSEI JUST SAYS THAT BECAUSE IT WOULD HURT HIS PRIDE OTHERWISE...
BUT THE TRUTH IS HE **LOVES** *DEJECTION MAN*.
WHAT?
WHEN THE LIMITED-EDITION *DEJECTION MAN* DOLL WENT ON SALE, HE LINED UP THE DAY BEFORE AND WAS THE FIRST TO BUY ONE...
ちゅんちゅん
CHIRP CHIRP
BOOK STORE
WHAT? YOU'VE BEEN HERE SINCE YESTER-DAY?
ELEMENTARY SCHOOL STUDENT
A-AND HE SLEEPS WITH IT SOMETIMES...
HEH.
SENSEI'S SO CUTE...
YOU TOTALLY CANNOT TELL HIM THIS...
I MEAN, YOU CAN'T SAY ANY-THING.
AUNH!

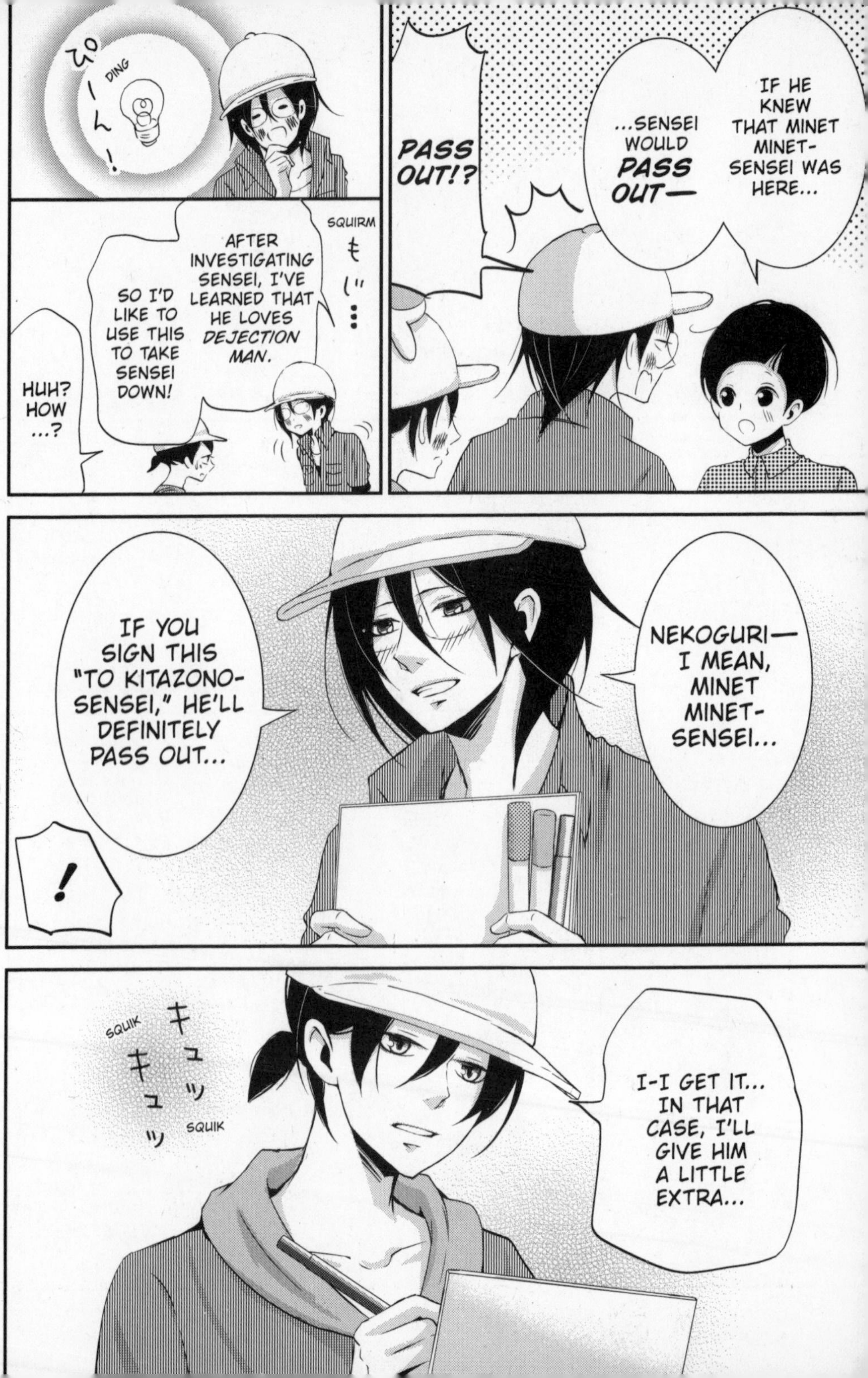
IF HE KNEW THAT MINET MINET-SENSEI WAS HERE...
...SENSEI WOULD PASS OUT—
PASS OUT!?
ぴーん!
DING
もじ…
SQUIRM
AFTER INVESTIGATING SENSEI, I'VE LEARNED THAT HE LOVES DEJECTION MAN.
SO I'D LIKE TO USE THIS TO TAKE SENSEI DOWN!
HUH? HOW ...?
NEKOGURI— I MEAN, MINET MINET-SENSEI...
IF YOU SIGN THIS "TO KITAZONO-SENSEI," HE'LL DEFINITELY PASS OUT...
!
I-I GET IT... IN THAT CASE, I'LL GIVE HIM A LITTLE EXTRA...
キュッ
SQUIK
キュッ
SQUIK

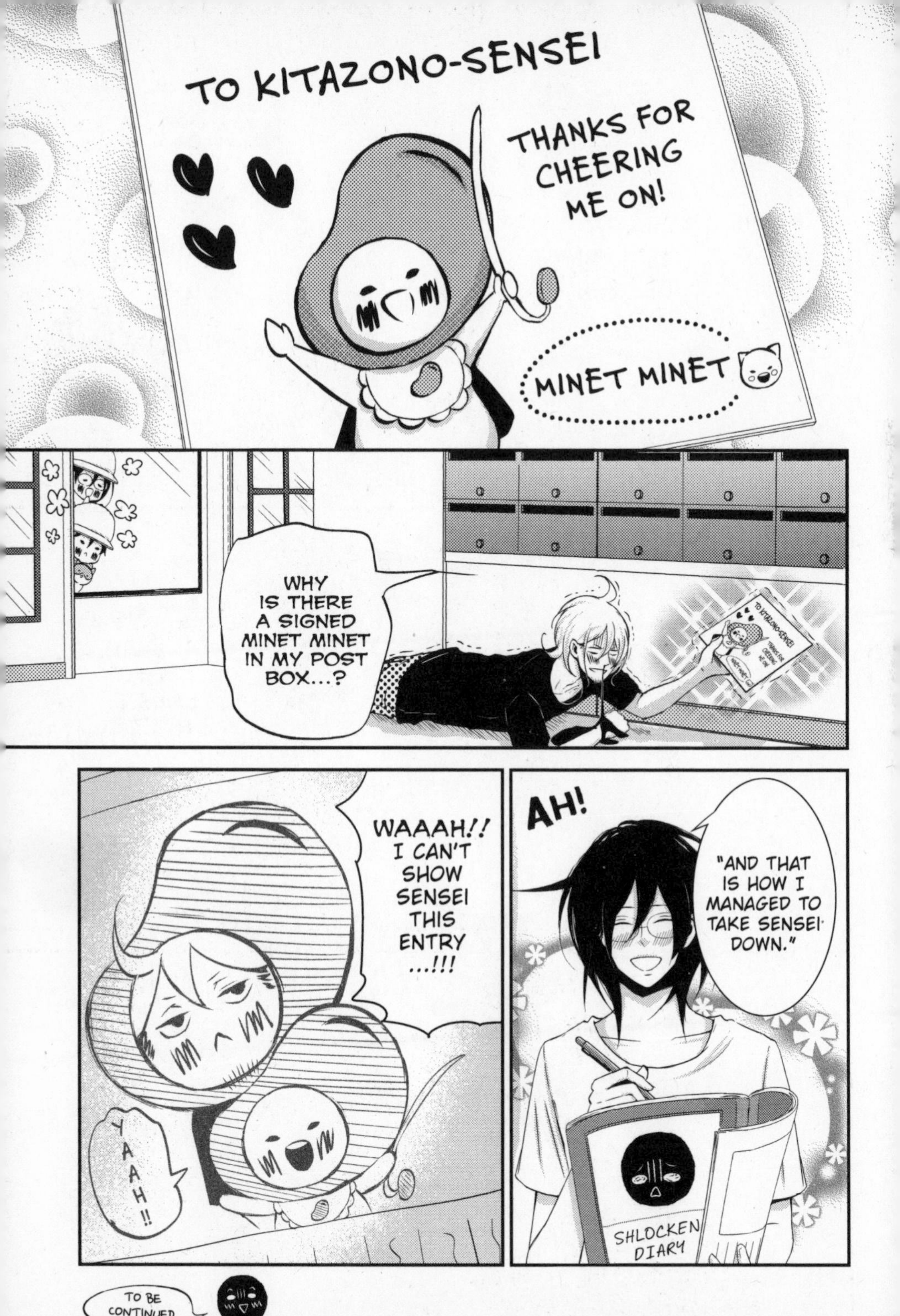
TO KITAZONO-SENSEI
THANKS FOR CHEERING ME ON!
MINET MINET
WHY IS THERE A SIGNED MINET MINET IN MY POST BOX...?
AH!
"AND THAT IS HOW I MANAGED TO TAKE SENSEI DOWN."
SHLOCKEN DIARY
WAAAH!! I CAN'T SHOW SENSEI THIS ENTRY ...!!!
YAAAH!!
TO BE CONTINUED

DEJECTION MAN VS. SHLOCKEN MAN

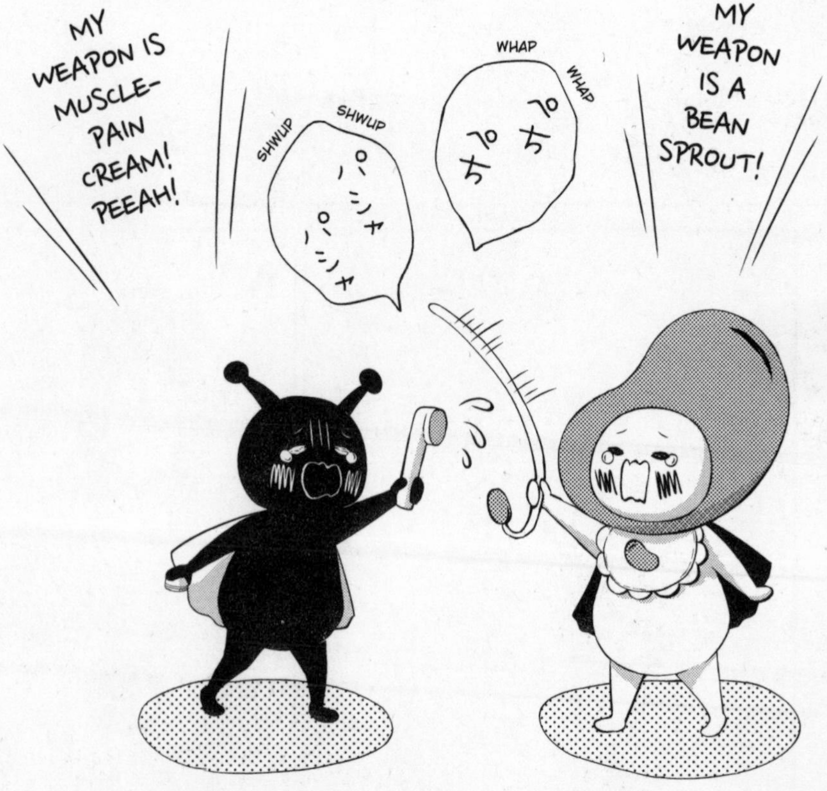
MY WEAPON IS A BEAN SPROUT!
WHAP
WHAP
SHWUP
SHWUP
MY WEAPON IS MUSCLE-PAIN CREAM! PEEAH!

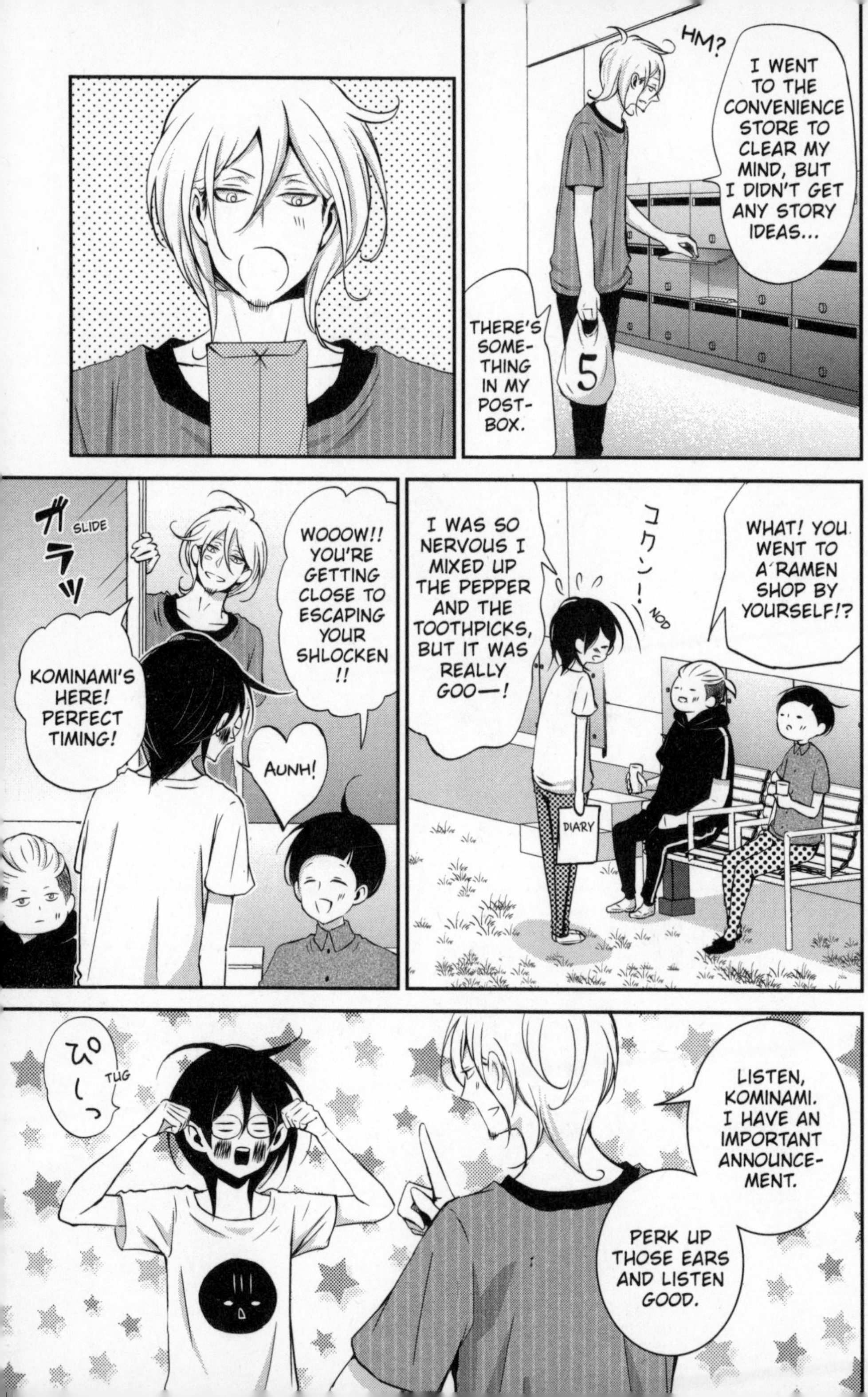
HM?
I WENT TO THE CONVENIENCE STORE TO CLEAR MY MIND, BUT I DIDN'T GET ANY STORY IDEAS...
THERE'S SOME-THING IN MY POST-BOX.
5
WHAT! YOU WENT TO A RAMEN SHOP BY YOURSELF!?
コクン!
NOD
I WAS SO NERVOUS I MIXED UP THE PEPPER AND THE TOOTHPICKS, BUT IT WAS REALLY GOO—!
DIARY
WOOOW!! YOU'RE GETTING CLOSE TO ESCAPING YOUR SHLOCKEN!!
ガラッ
SLIDE
KOMINAMI'S HERE! PERFECT TIMING!
AUNH!
LISTEN, KOMINAMI. I HAVE AN IMPORTANT ANNOUNCE-MENT.
PERK UP THOSE EARS AND LISTEN GOOD.
ぴしっ
TUG

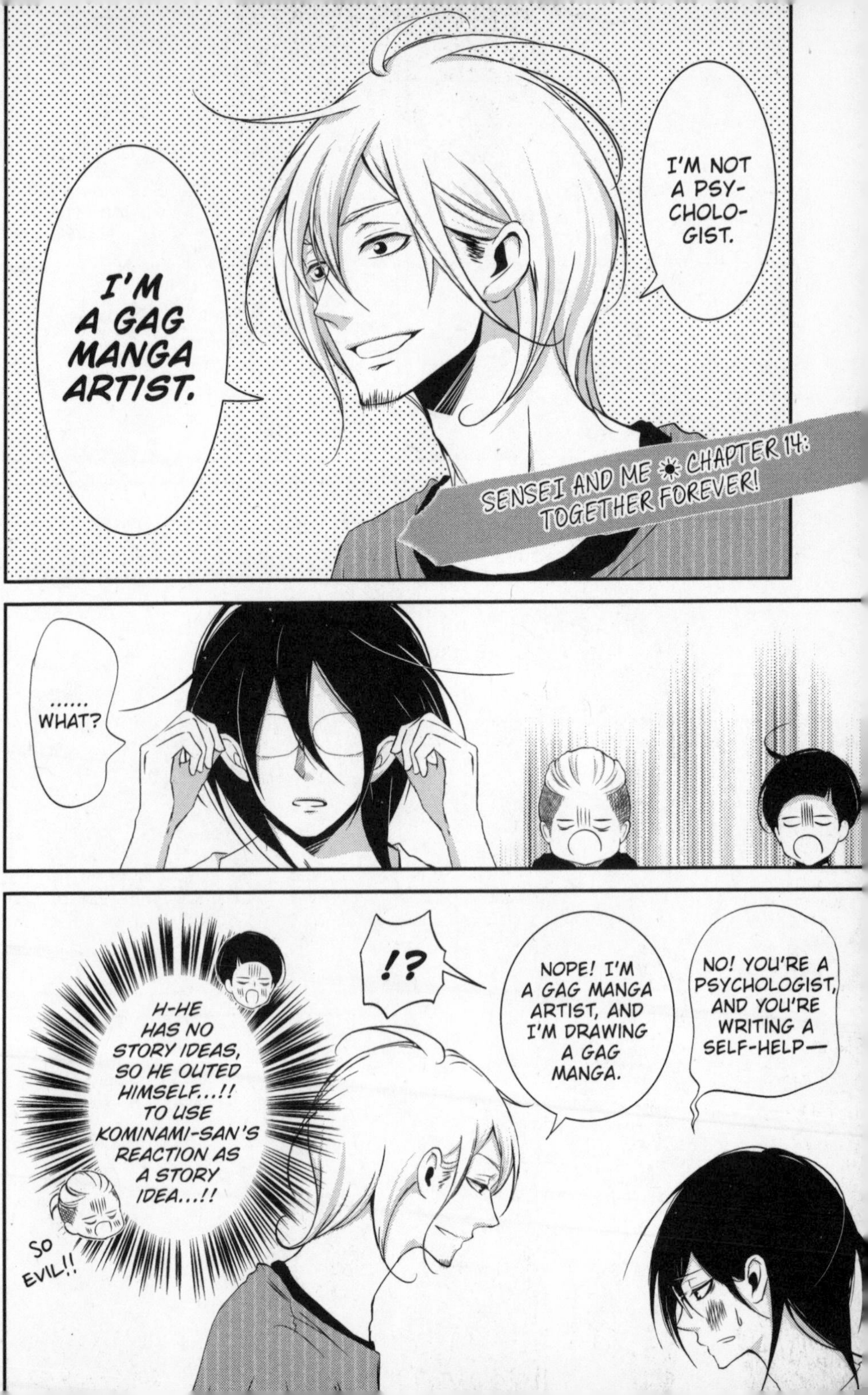
I'M NOT A PSYCHOLOGIST.
I'M A GAG MANGA ARTIST.
SENSEI AND ME ☀ CHAPTER 14: TOGETHER FOREVER!
...... WHAT?
NO! YOU'RE A PSYCHOLOGIST, AND YOU'RE WRITING A SELF-HELP—
NOPE! I'M A GAG MANGA ARTIST, AND I'M DRAWING A GAG MANGA.
!?
H-HE HAS NO STORY IDEAS, SO HE OUTED HIMSELF...!! TO USE KOMINAMI-SAN'S REACTION AS A STORY IDEA...!!
SO EVIL!!

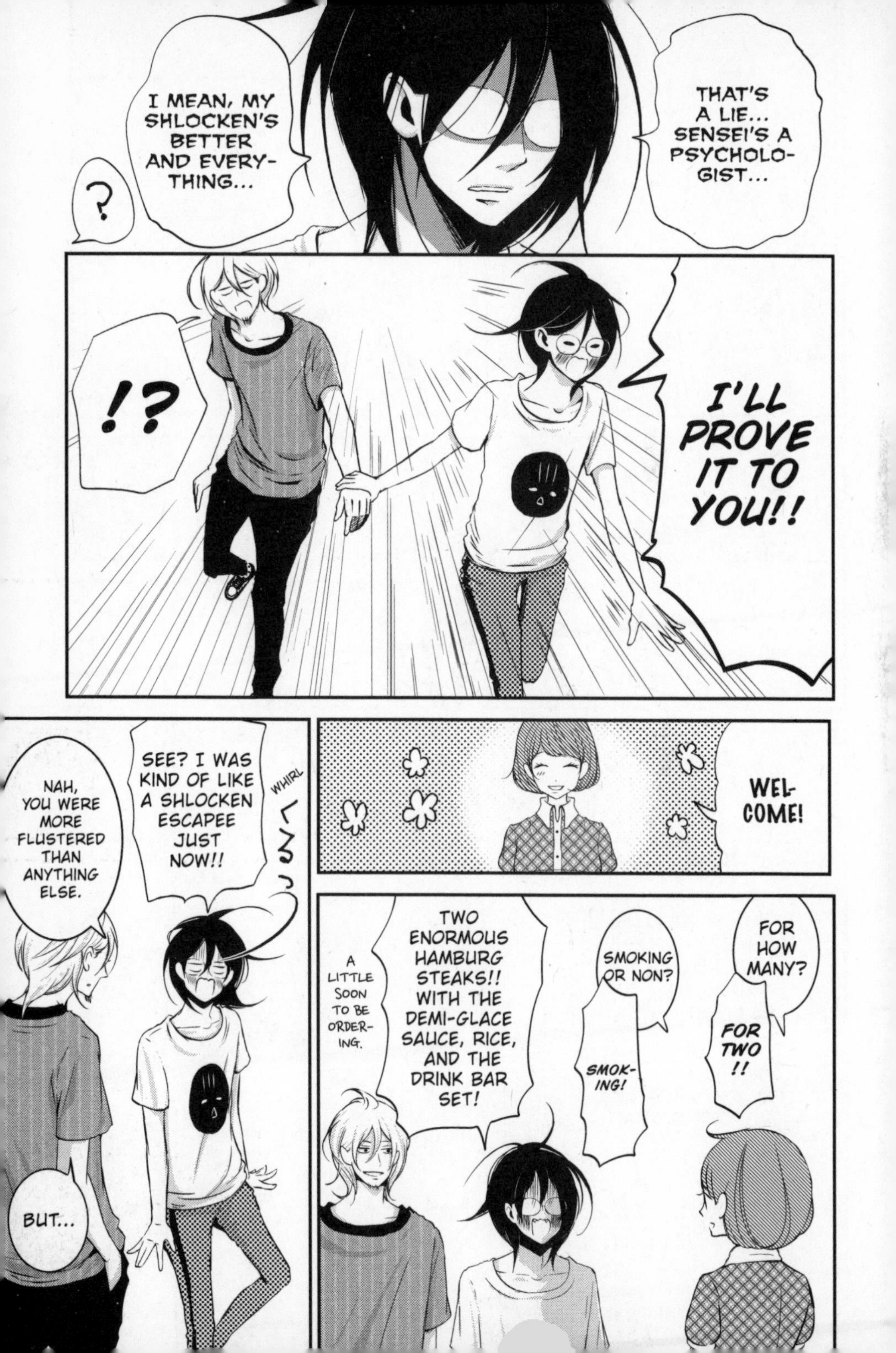

THAT'S A LIE... SENSEI'S A PSYCHOLO-GIST...
I MEAN, MY SHLOCKEN'S BETTER AND EVERY-THING...
?
I'LL PROVE IT TO YOU!!
!?
WEL-COME!
FOR HOW MANY?
FOR TWO!!
SMOKING OR NON?
SMOK-ING!
TWO ENORMOUS HAMBURG STEAKS!! WITH THE DEMI-GLACE SAUCE, RICE, AND THE DRINK BAR SET!
A LITTLE SOON TO BE ORDER-ING.
SEE? I WAS KIND OF LIKE A SHLOCKEN ESCAPEE JUST NOW!!
WHIRL
NAH, YOU WERE MORE FLUSTERED THAN ANYTHING ELSE.
BUT...

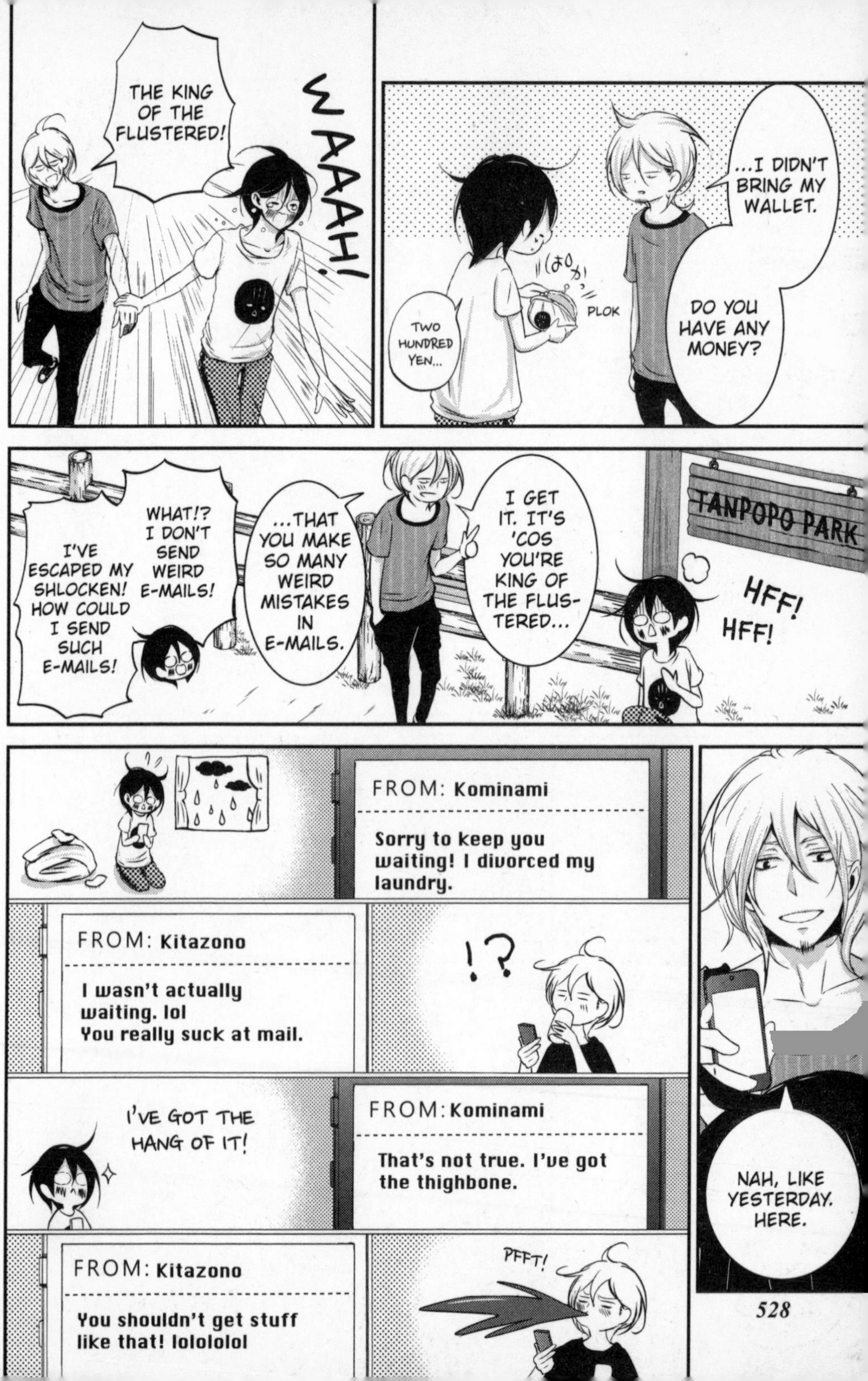

...I DIDN'T BRING MY WALLET.
DO YOU HAVE ANY MONEY?
PLOK
TWO HUNDRED YEN...
WAAAH!
THE KING OF THE FLUSTERED!
TANPOPO PARK
I GET IT. IT'S 'COS YOU'RE KING OF THE FLUSTERED...
HFF! HFF!
...THAT YOU MAKE SO MANY WEIRD MISTAKES IN E-MAILS.
WHAT!? I DON'T SEND WEIRD E-MAILS!
I'VE ESCAPED MY SHLOCKEN! HOW COULD I SEND SUCH E-MAILS!
NAH, LIKE YESTERDAY. HERE.
FROM: Kominami
Sorry to keep you waiting! I divorced my laundry.
!?
FROM: Kitazono
I wasn't actually waiting. lol
You really suck at mail.
FROM: Kominami
That's not true. I've got the thighbone.
I'VE GOT THE HANG OF IT!
PFFT!
FROM: Kitazono
You shouldn't get stuff like that! lololol

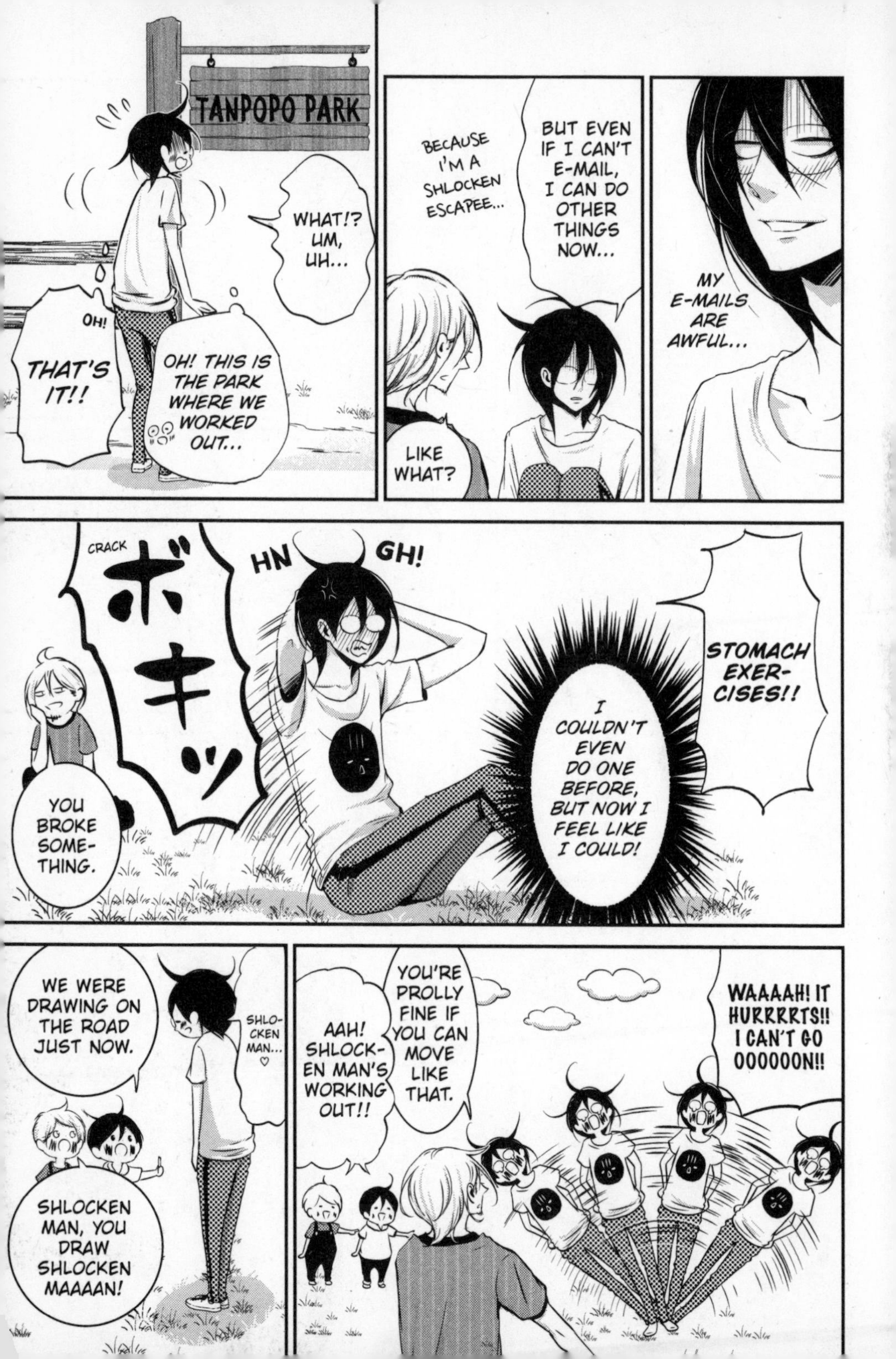
MY E-MAILS ARE AWFUL...
BUT EVEN IF I CAN'T E-MAIL, I CAN DO OTHER THINGS NOW...
BECAUSE I'M A SHLOCKEN ESCAPEE...
LIKE WHAT?
TANPOPO PARK
WHAT!? UM, UH...
OH! THIS IS THE PARK WHERE WE WORKED OUT...
OH! THAT'S IT!!
STOMACH EXER-CISES!!
I COULDN'T EVEN DO ONE BEFORE, BUT NOW I FEEL LIKE I COULD!
HN GH!
ボキッ
CRACK
YOU BROKE SOME-THING.
WAAAAH! IT HURRRRTS!! I CAN'T GO OOOOOON!!
YOU'RE PROLLY FINE IF YOU CAN MOVE LIKE THAT.
AAH! SHLOCK-EN MAN'S WORKING OUT!!
SHLO-CKEN MAN... ♡
WE WERE DRAWING ON THE ROAD JUST NOW.
SHLOCKEN MAN, YOU DRAW SHLOCKEN MAAAAN!

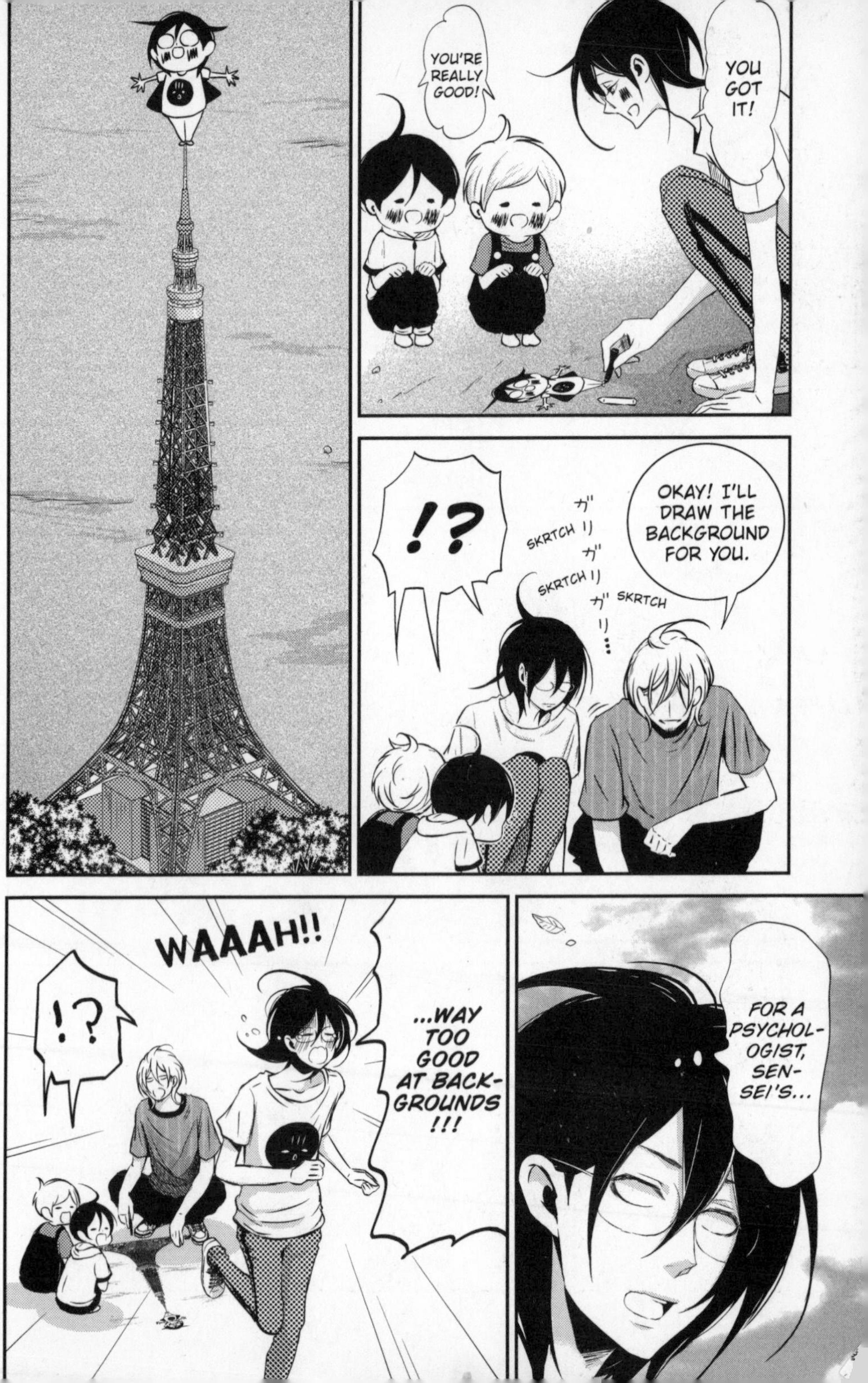
YOU GOT IT!
YOU'RE REALLY GOOD!
OKAY! I'LL DRAW THE BACKGROUND FOR YOU.
ガリ SKRTCH
ガリ SKRTCH
ガリ… SKRTCH
!?
FOR A PSYCHOL-OGIST, SEN-SEI'S...
...WAY TOO GOOD AT BACK-GROUNDS!!!
WAAAH!!
!?

ズボッ
SHLPP
SENSEI'S A MANGA ARTIST!!!
ふんが
ふんが
FUME
FUME
GOT YOU.
HE GOT ME!
KOMINAMI, YOU HAVE TO LISTEN ALL THE WAY TO THE END.
I WON'T!!
BAD LITTLE BOYS WHO DON'T LISTEN GET EATEN UP BY DEMONS.
OKAY, I'LL LISTEN!!
OKAY, READY?
IT'S TRUE THAT I AM A GAG MANGA ARTIST.
BUT...
?
RUSTLE

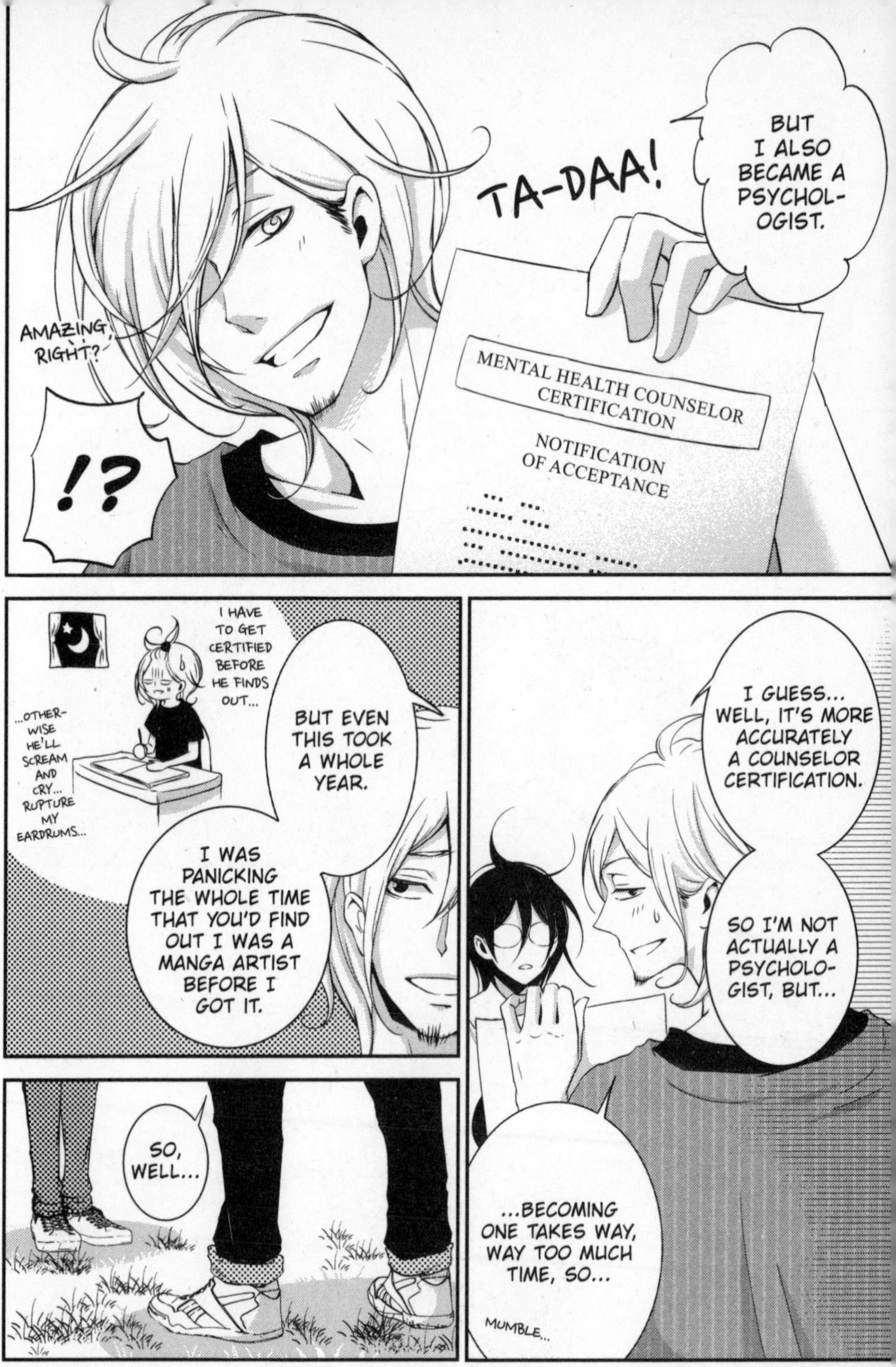
BUT I ALSO BECAME A PSYCHOLOGIST.
TA-DAA!
MENTAL HEALTH COUNSELOR CERTIFICATION
NOTIFICATION OF ACCEPTANCE
AMAZING, RIGHT?
!?
I GUESS... WELL, IT'S MORE ACCURATELY A COUNSELOR CERTIFICATION.
SO I'M NOT ACTUALLY A PSYCHOLOGIST, BUT...
...BECOMING ONE TAKES WAY, WAY TOO MUCH TIME, SO...
MUMBLE...
BUT EVEN THIS TOOK A WHOLE YEAR.
I HAVE TO GET CERTIFIED BEFORE HE FINDS OUT...
...OTHERWISE HE'LL SCREAM AND CRY... RUPTURE MY EARDRUMS...
I WAS PANICKING THE WHOLE TIME THAT YOU'D FIND OUT I WAS A MANGA ARTIST BEFORE I GOT IT.
SO, WELL...

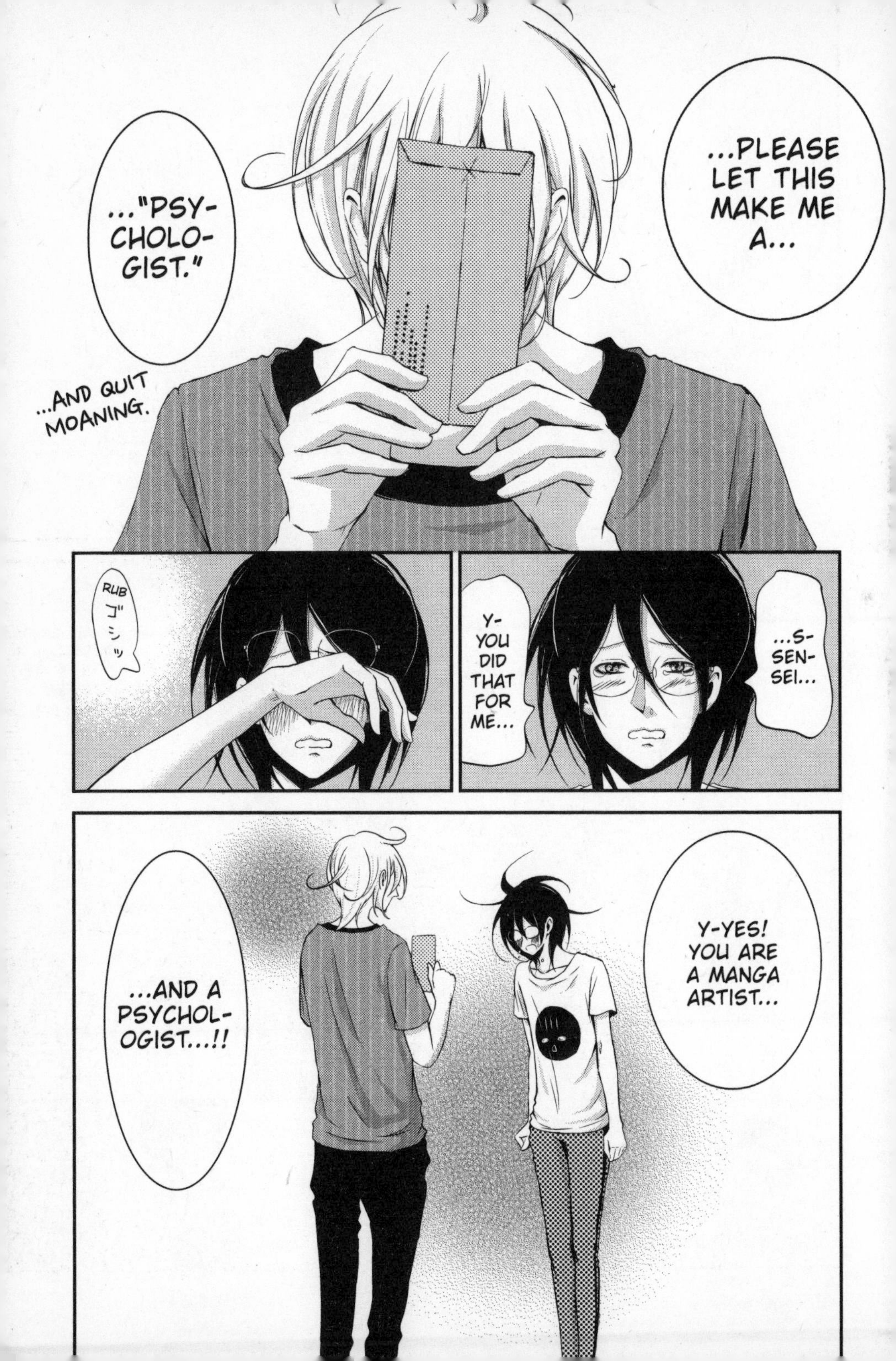
...PLEASE LET THIS MAKE ME A...
..."PSY-CHOLO-GIST."
...AND QUIT MOANING.
...S-SEN-SEI...
Y-YOU DID THAT FOR ME...
RUB ゴシッ
Y-YES! YOU ARE A MANGA ARTIST...
...AND A PSYCHOL-OGIST...!!

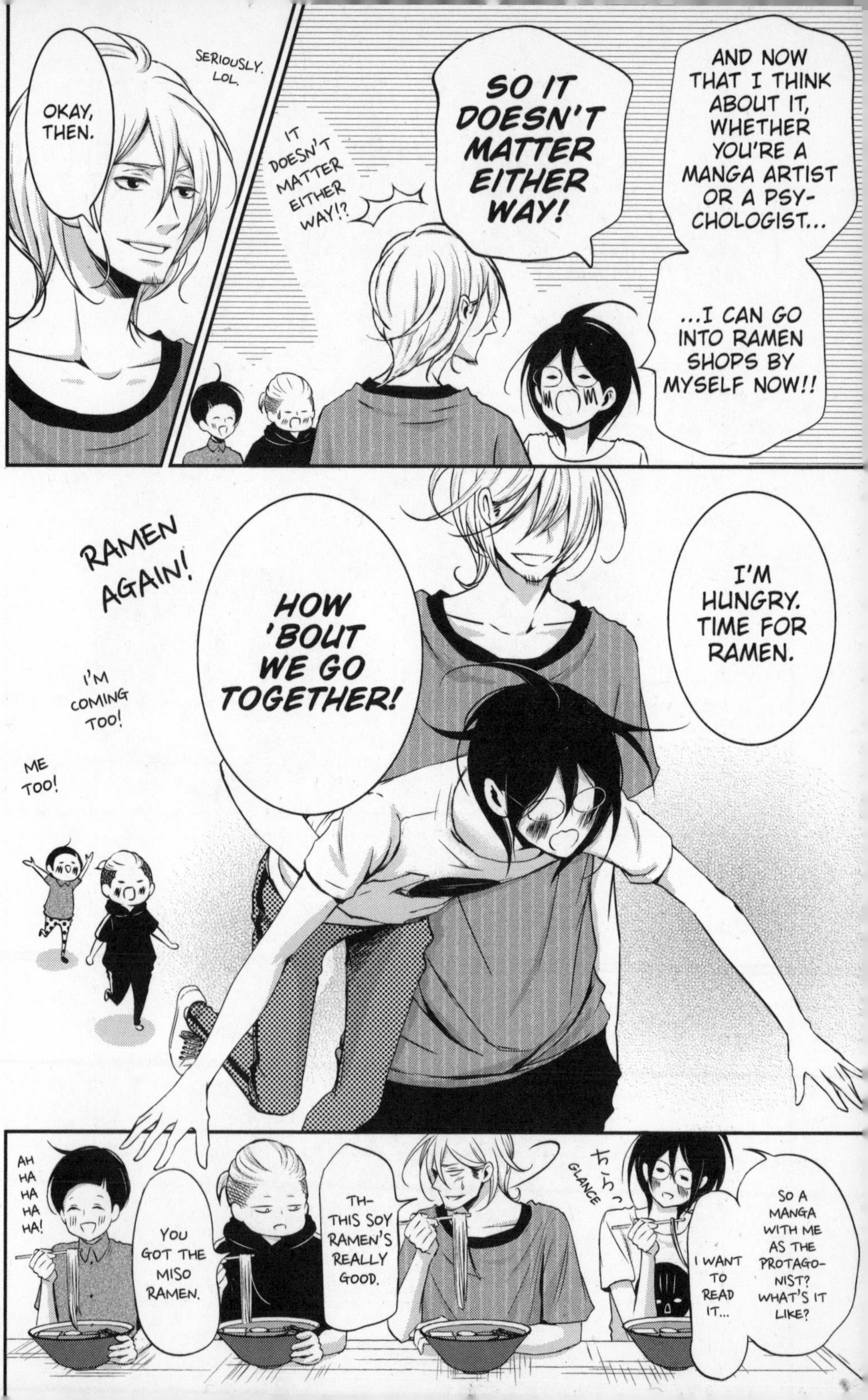

AND NOW THAT I THINK ABOUT IT, WHETHER YOU'RE A MANGA ARTIST OR A PSY-CHOLOGIST...
...I CAN GO INTO RAMEN SHOPS BY MYSELF NOW!!
SO IT DOESN'T MATTER EITHER WAY!
IT DOESN'T MATTER EITHER WAY!?
SERIOUSLY. LOL.
OKAY, THEN.
I'M HUNGRY. TIME FOR RAMEN.
HOW 'BOUT WE GO TOGETHER!
RAMEN AGAIN!
I'M COMING TOO!
ME TOO!
SO A MANGA WITH ME AS THE PROTAGO-NIST? WHAT'S IT LIKE?
I WANT TO READ IT...
GLANCE
TH- THIS SOY RAMEN'S REALLY GOOD.
YOU GOT THE MISO RAMEN.
AH HA HA HA HA!

パカッ
POP
THE BONUS COMIC "SHLOCKEN VS. XX" STARTS ON THE NEXT PAGE!
SHUT
パタン！
PWOK
ぱこっ
ENJOY!

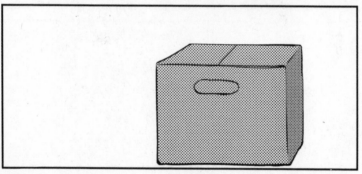

Shlocken vs. the Dog

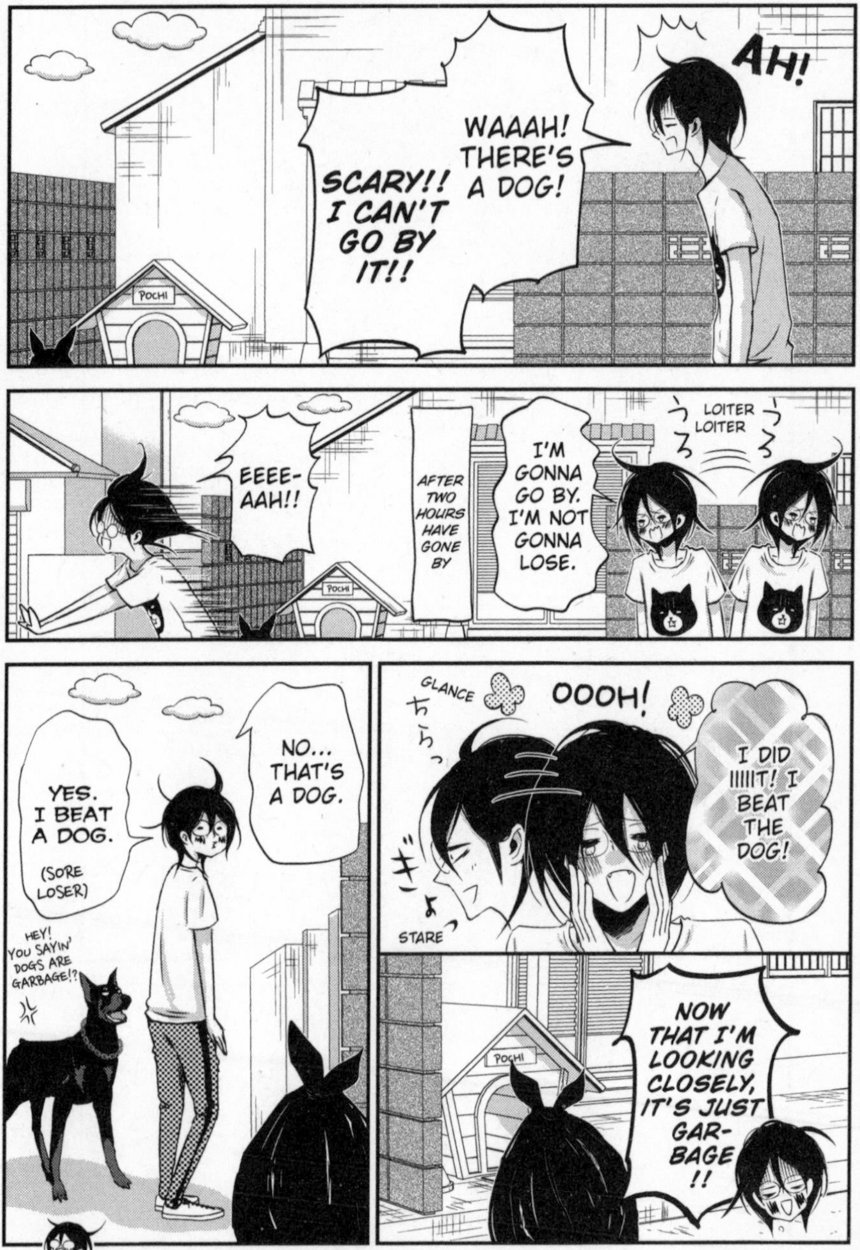
AH!
WAAAH! THERE'S A DOG!
SCARY!! I CAN'T GO BY IT!!
POCHI
LOITER LOITER
I'M GONNA GO BY. I'M NOT GONNA LOSE.
AFTER TWO HOURS HAVE GONE BY
EEEE-AAH!!
POCHI
OOOH!
I DID IIIIIT! I BEAT THE DOG!
GLANCE
STARE
NOW THAT I'M LOOKING CLOSELY, IT'S JUST GAR-BAGE!!
POCHI
NO... THAT'S A DOG.
YES. I BEAT A DOG.
(SORE LOSER)
HEY! YOU SAYIN' DOGS ARE GARBAGE!?
PEEAAAAAAAAH!

Shlocken vs. the Tissue Guy

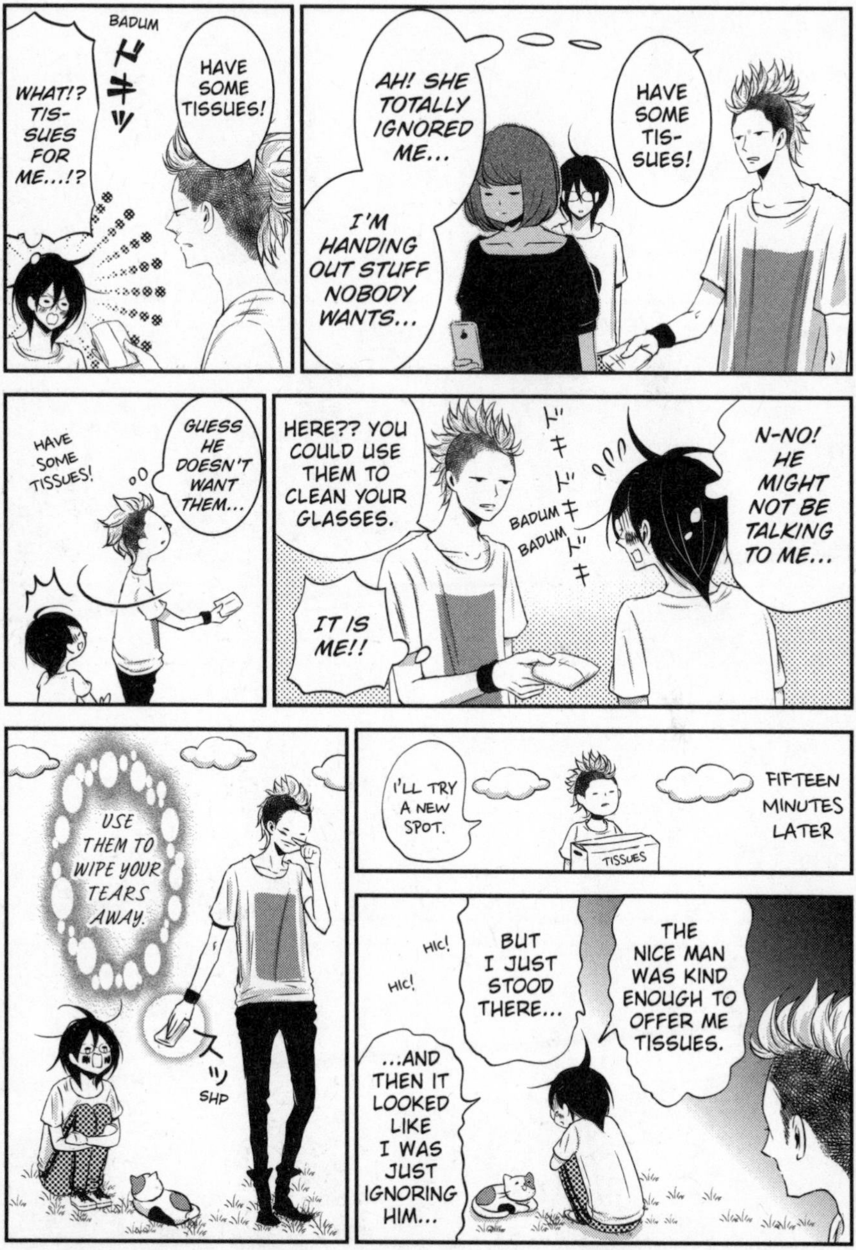
HAVE SOME TIS- SUES!
AH! SHE TOTALLY IGNORED ME...
I'M HANDING OUT STUFF NOBODY WANTS...
HAVE SOME TISSUES!
BADUM
ドキッ
WHAT!? TIS- SUES FOR ME...!?
N-NO! HE MIGHT NOT BE TALKING TO ME...
ドキドキ
BADUM BADUM
HERE?? YOU COULD USE THEM TO CLEAN YOUR GLASSES.
IT IS ME!!
GUESS HE DOESN'T WANT THEM...
HAVE SOME TISSUES!
FIFTEEN MINUTES LATER
I'LL TRY A NEW SPOT.
TISSUES
THE NICE MAN WAS KIND ENOUGH TO OFFER ME TISSUES.
BUT I JUST STOOD THERE...
HIC!
HIC!
...AND THEN IT LOOKED LIKE I WAS JUST IGNORING HIM...
USE THEM TO WIPE YOUR TEARS AWAY.
スッ
SHP

HEARTS CONNECTED BY TISSUES♡

Shlocken vs. Shiritori

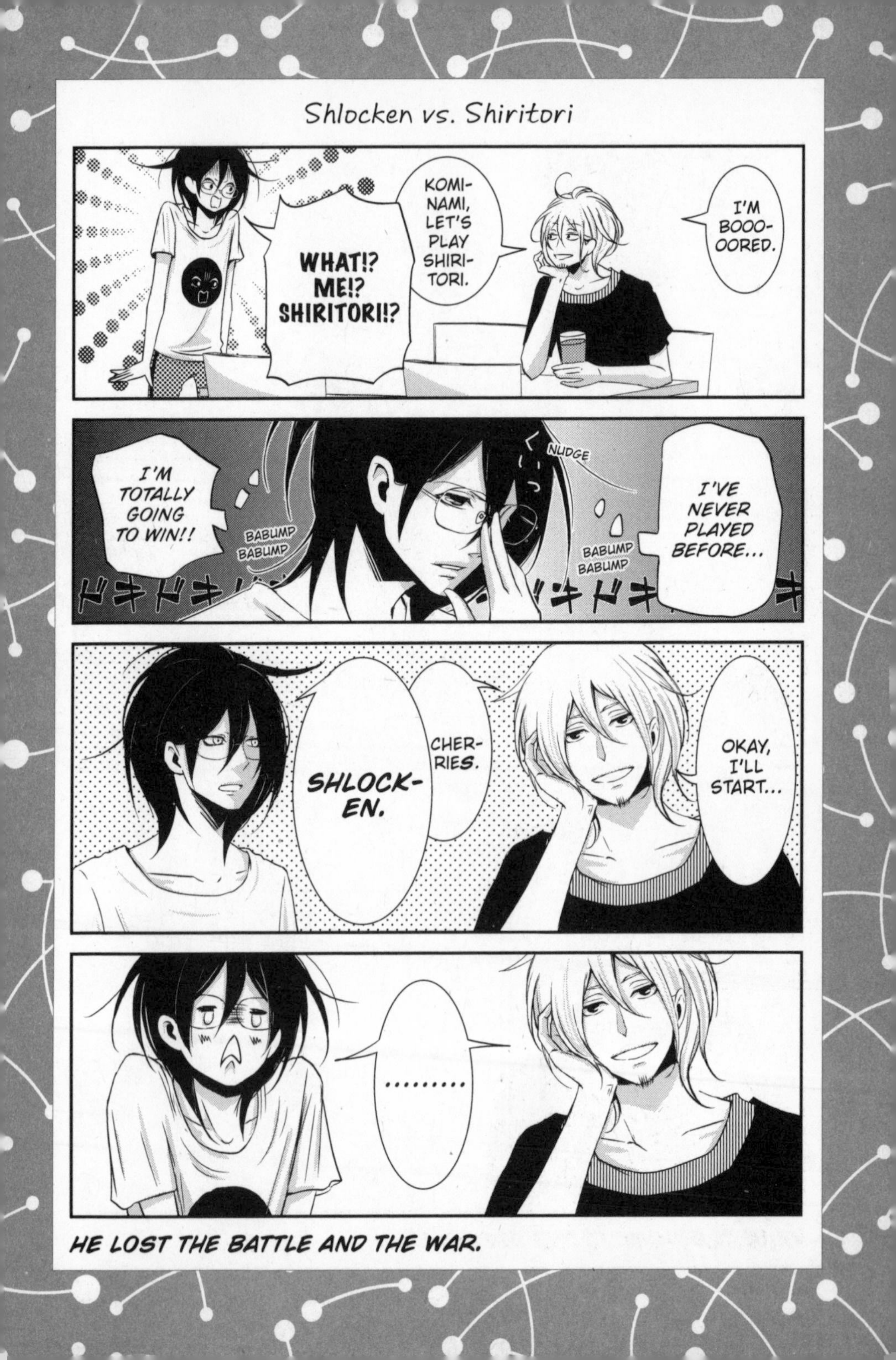
I'M BOOOO-OORED.
KOMI-NAMI, LET'S PLAY SHIRI-TORI.
WHAT!? ME!? SHIRITORI!?
NUDGE
I'VE NEVER PLAYED BEFORE...
BABUMP BABUMP
I'M TOTALLY GOING TO WIN!!
BABUMP BABUMP
OKAY, I'LL START...
CHER-RIES.
SHLOCK-EN.
....

HE LOST THE BATTLE AND THE WAR.

Shlocken vs. the Kanji Test

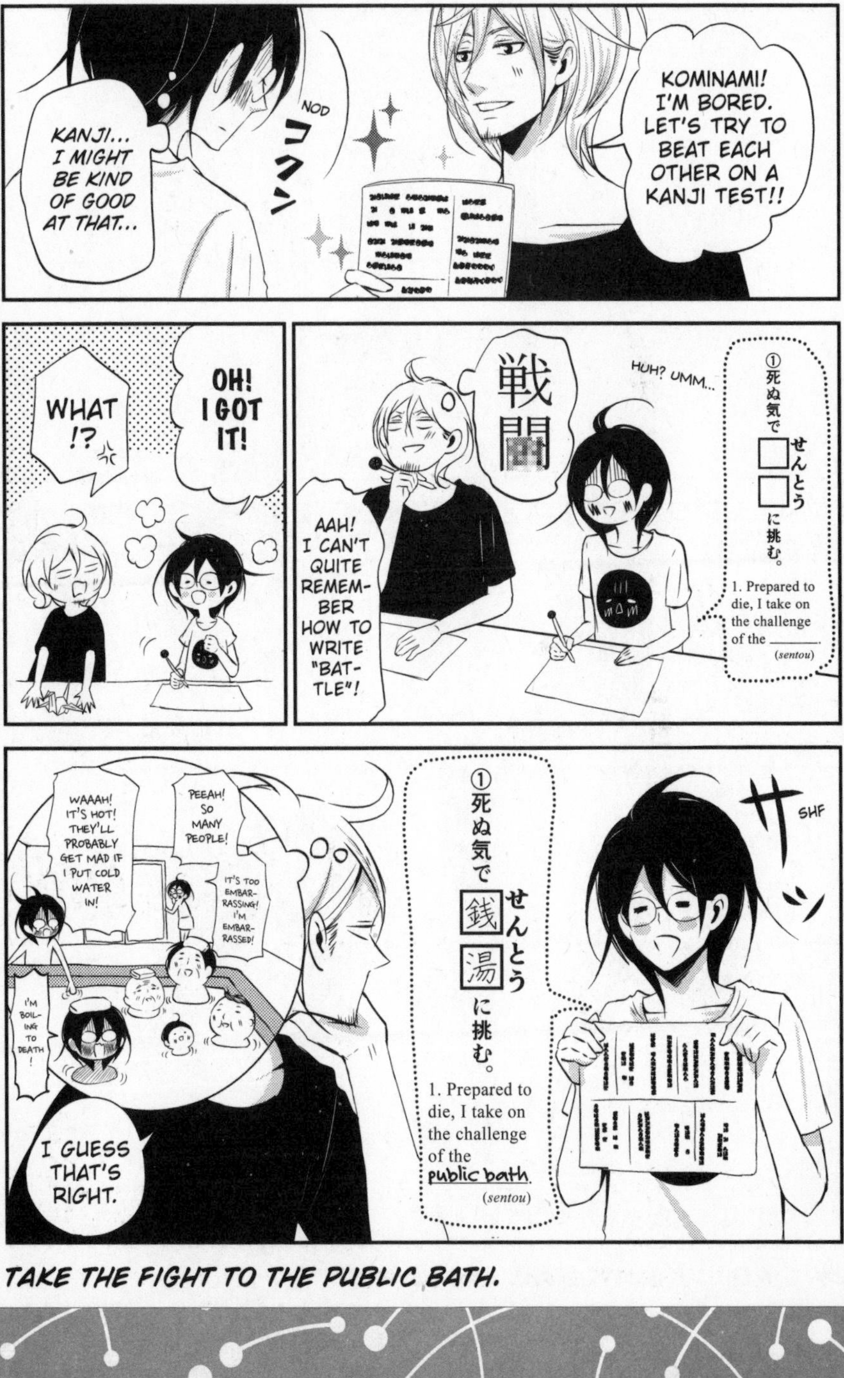
KOMINAMI! I'M BORED. LET'S TRY TO BEAT EACH OTHER ON A KANJI TEST!!
NOD
コクン
KANJI... I MIGHT BE KIND OF GOOD AT THAT...
①死ぬ気で□□せんとうに挑む。
1. Prepared to die, I take on the challenge of the ______. (sentou)
HUH? UMM...
戦闘
AAH! I CAN'T QUITE REMEMBER HOW TO WRITE "BATTLE"!
OH! I GOT IT!
WHAT!?
①死ぬ気で銭湯せんとうに挑む。
1. Prepared to die, I take on the challenge of the public bath. (sentou)
サッ
SHF
PEEAH! SO MANY PEOPLE!
WAAAH! IT'S HOT! THEY'LL PROBABLY GET MAD IF I PUT COLD WATER IN!
IT'S TOO EMBARRASSING! I'M EMBARRASSED!
I'M BOILING TO DEATH!
I GUESS THAT'S RIGHT.

TAKE THE FIGHT TO THE PUBLIC BATH.

Shlocken vs. the Famous Saying

BOOK OF GENESIS
OSAMU DAZAI
BOOK OF GENESIS
Osamu Dazai
"Love is a word."
DAZAI...
WHEN PEOPLE HEAR THIS WONDERFUL WORD, THEY REALLY DO WANT TO TELL SOMEONE...
DID YOU KNOW LOVE IS A WORD?
...THERE'S NO REASON A POTATO WOULD KNOW THAT.

BUT HIS COMMUNICATION SKILLS AREN'T UP TO IT.

14

VS. THE END

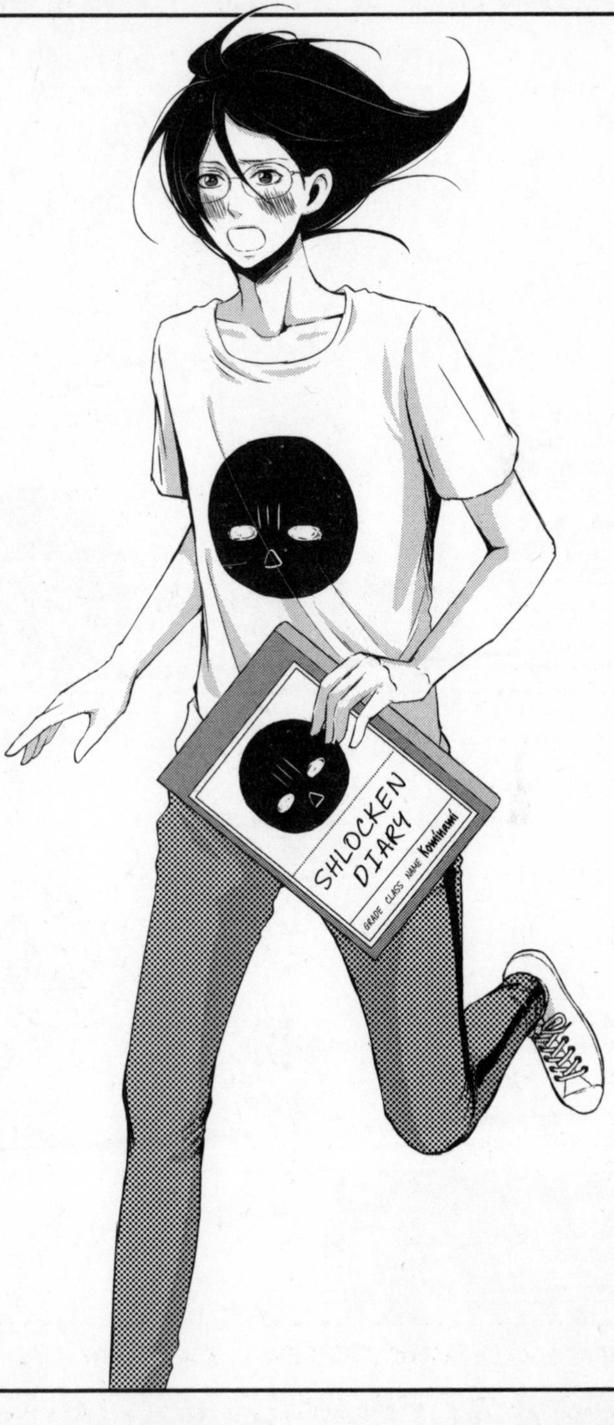
SHLOCKEN DIARY
GRADE CLASS NAME Kominami

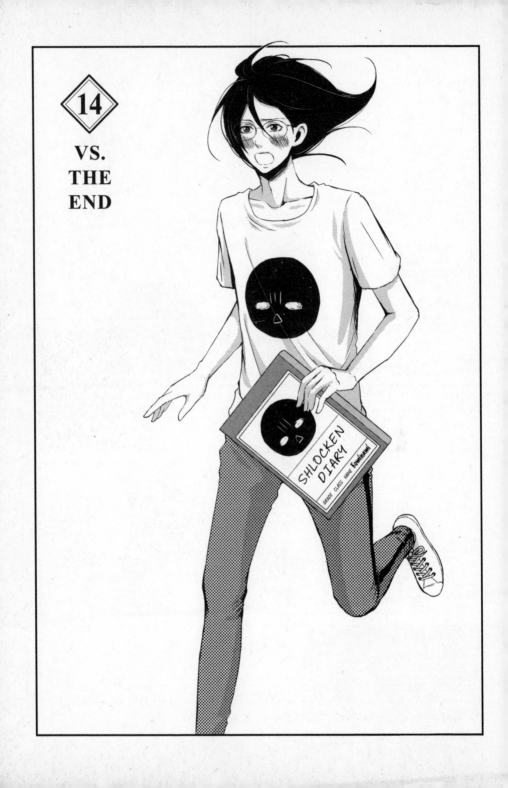

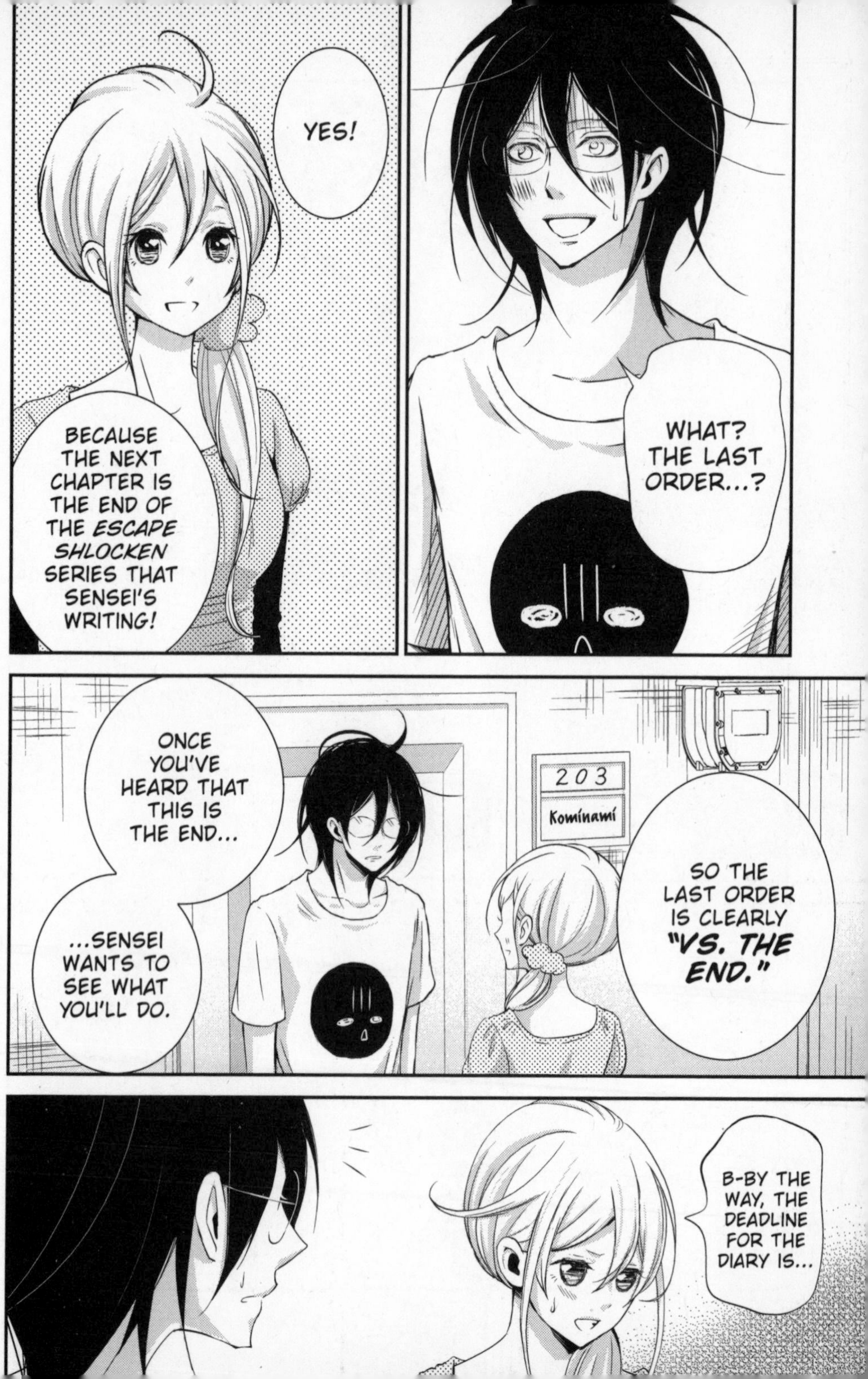
WHAT? THE LAST ORDER...?
YES!
BECAUSE THE NEXT CHAPTER IS THE END OF THE *ESCAPE SHLOCKEN* SERIES THAT SENSEI'S WRITING!
203
Kominami
SO THE LAST ORDER IS CLEARLY ***"VS. THE END."***
ONCE YOU'VE HEARD THAT THIS IS THE END...
...SENSEI WANTS TO SEE WHAT YOU'LL DO.
B-BY THE WAY, THE DEADLINE FOR THE DIARY IS...

REASON ↓

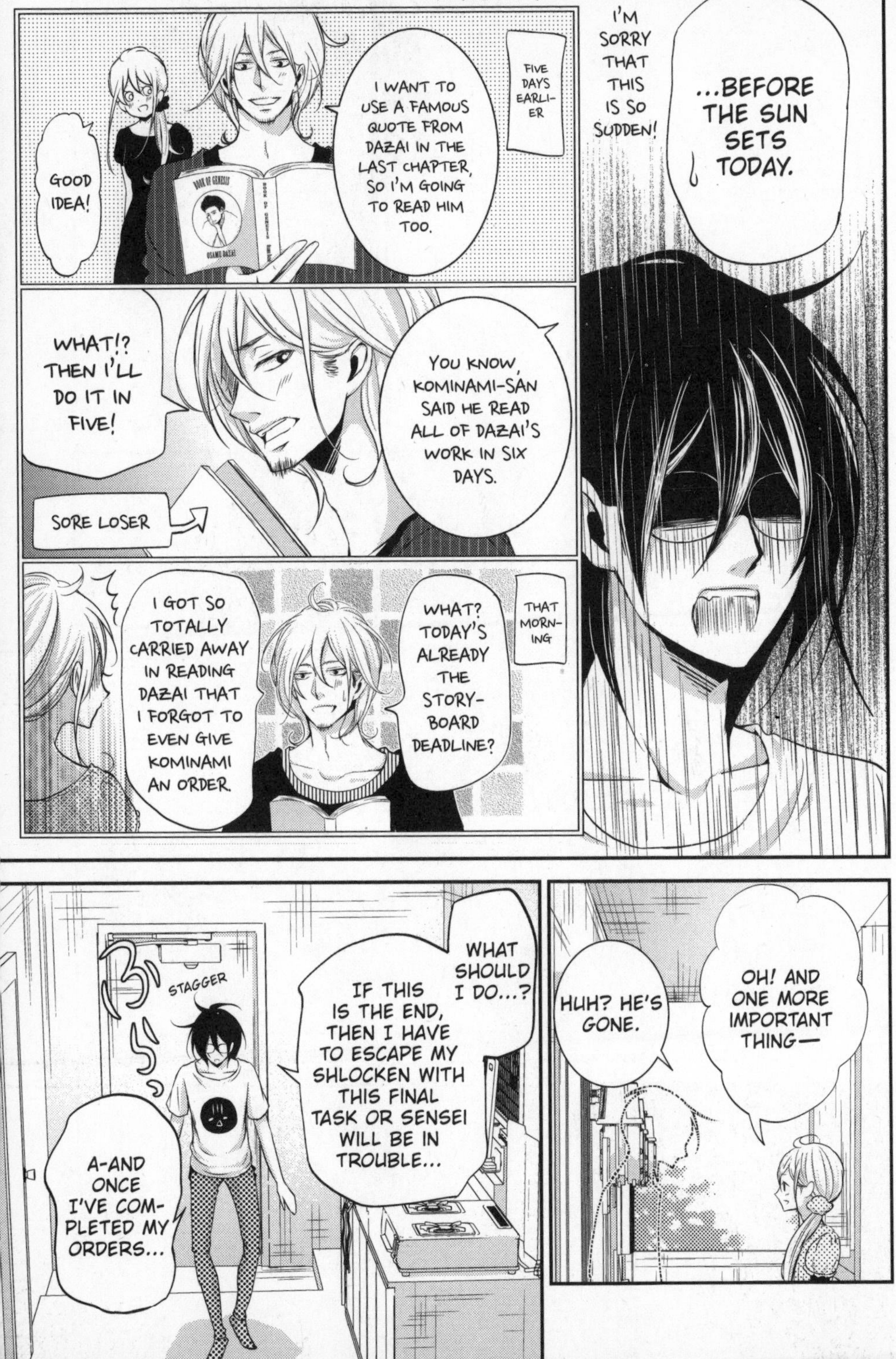
...BEFORE THE SUN SETS TODAY.
I'M SORRY THAT THIS IS SO SUDDEN!
FIVE DAYS EARLIER
I WANT TO USE A FAMOUS QUOTE FROM DAZAI IN THE LAST CHAPTER, SO I'M GOING TO READ HIM TOO.
GOOD IDEA!
BOOK OF GENESIS
OSAMU DAZAI
YOU KNOW, KOMINAMI-SAN SAID HE READ ALL OF DAZAI'S WORK IN SIX DAYS.
WHAT!? THEN I'LL DO IT IN FIVE!
SORE LOSER
THAT MORNING
WHAT? TODAY'S ALREADY THE STORY-BOARD DEADLINE?
I GOT SO TOTALLY CARRIED AWAY IN READING DAZAI THAT I FORGOT TO EVEN GIVE KOMINAMI AN ORDER.
OH! AND ONE MORE IMPORTANT THING—
HUH? HE'S GONE.
WHAT SHOULD I DO...?
IF THIS IS THE END, THEN I HAVE TO ESCAPE MY SHLOCKEN WITH THIS FINAL TASK OR SENSEI WILL BE IN TROUBLE...
STAGGER
A-AND ONCE I'VE COM-PLETED MY ORDERS...

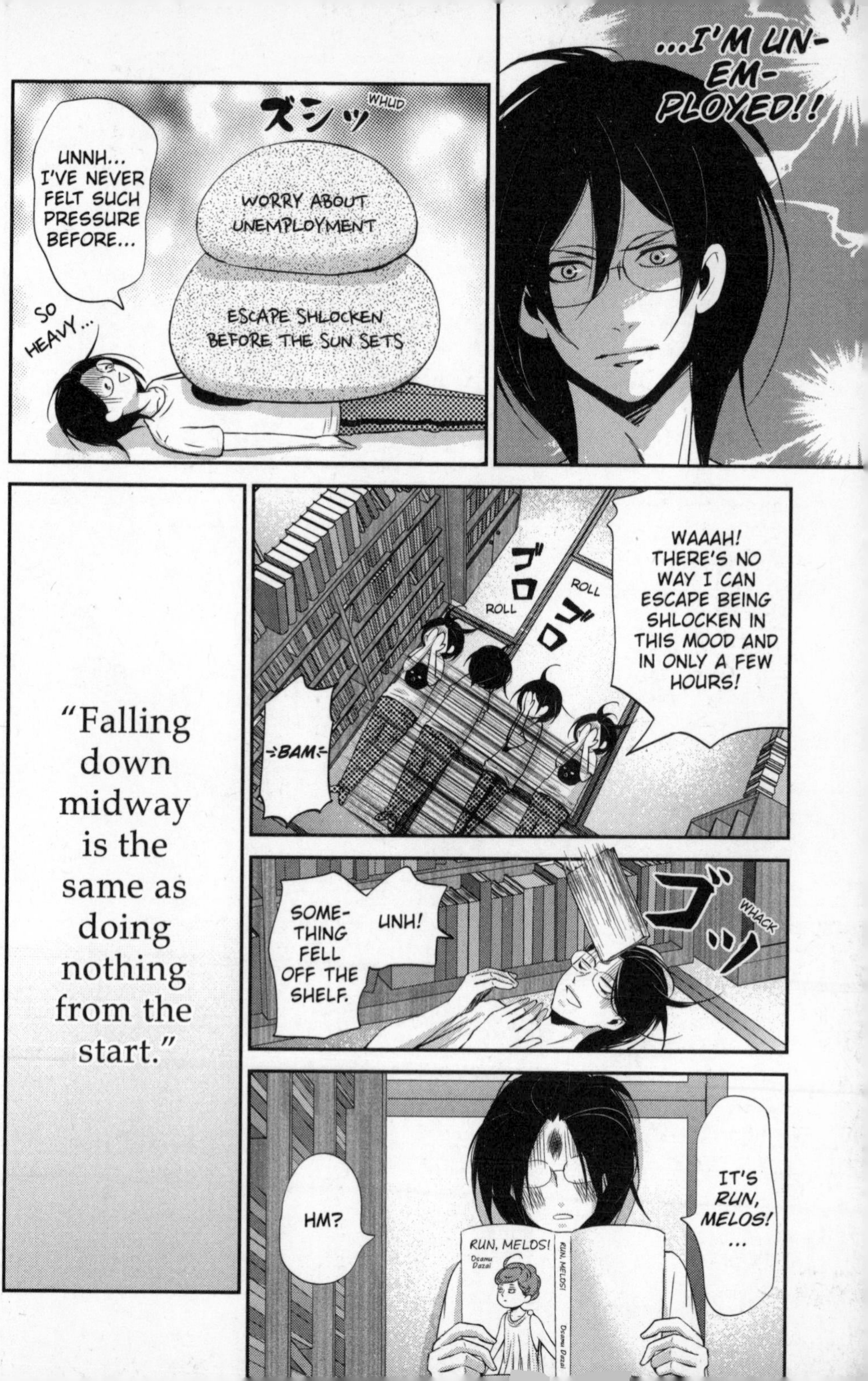
...I'M UN-EM-PLOYED!!
ズシッ WHUD
WORRY ABOUT UNEMPLOYMENT
UNNH... I'VE NEVER FELT SUCH PRESSURE BEFORE...
ESCAPE SHLOCKEN BEFORE THE SUN SETS
SO HEAVY...
WAAAH! THERE'S NO WAY I CAN ESCAPE BEING SHLOCKEN IN THIS MOOD AND IN ONLY A FEW HOURS!
ゴロ ROLL
ゴロ ROLL
BAM
ゴッ WHACK
UNH!
SOME-THING FELL OFF THE SHELF.
IT'S RUN, MELOS! ...
HM?
RUN, MELOS! Osamu Dazai
RUN, MELOS! Osamu Dazai
"Falling down midway is the same as doing nothing from the start."

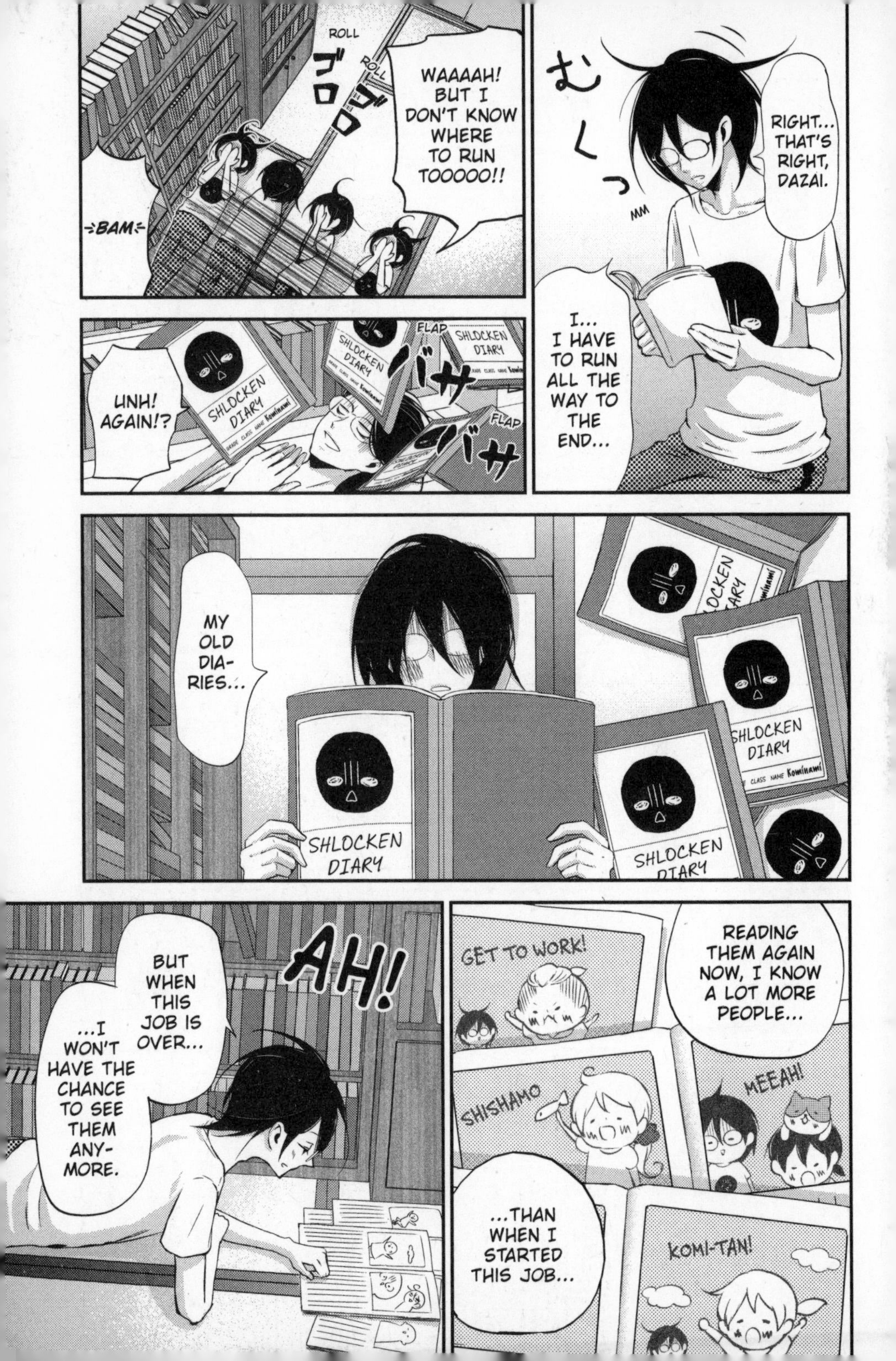
むくっ
MM
RIGHT... THAT'S RIGHT, DAZAI.
I... I HAVE TO RUN ALL THE WAY TO THE END...
ROLL ROLL
ゴロゴロ
WAAAAH! BUT I DON'T KNOW WHERE TO RUN TOOOOO!!
BAM
FLAP
バサ
FLAP
バサ
SHLOCKEN DIARY
UNH! AGAIN!?
MY OLD DIA-RIES...
SHLOCKEN DIARY
READING THEM AGAIN NOW, I KNOW A LOT MORE PEOPLE...
GET TO WORK!
MEEAH!
SHISHAMO
...THAN WHEN I STARTED THIS JOB...
KOMI-TAN!
AH!
BUT WHEN THIS JOB IS OVER...
...I WON'T HAVE THE CHANCE TO SEE THEM ANY-MORE.

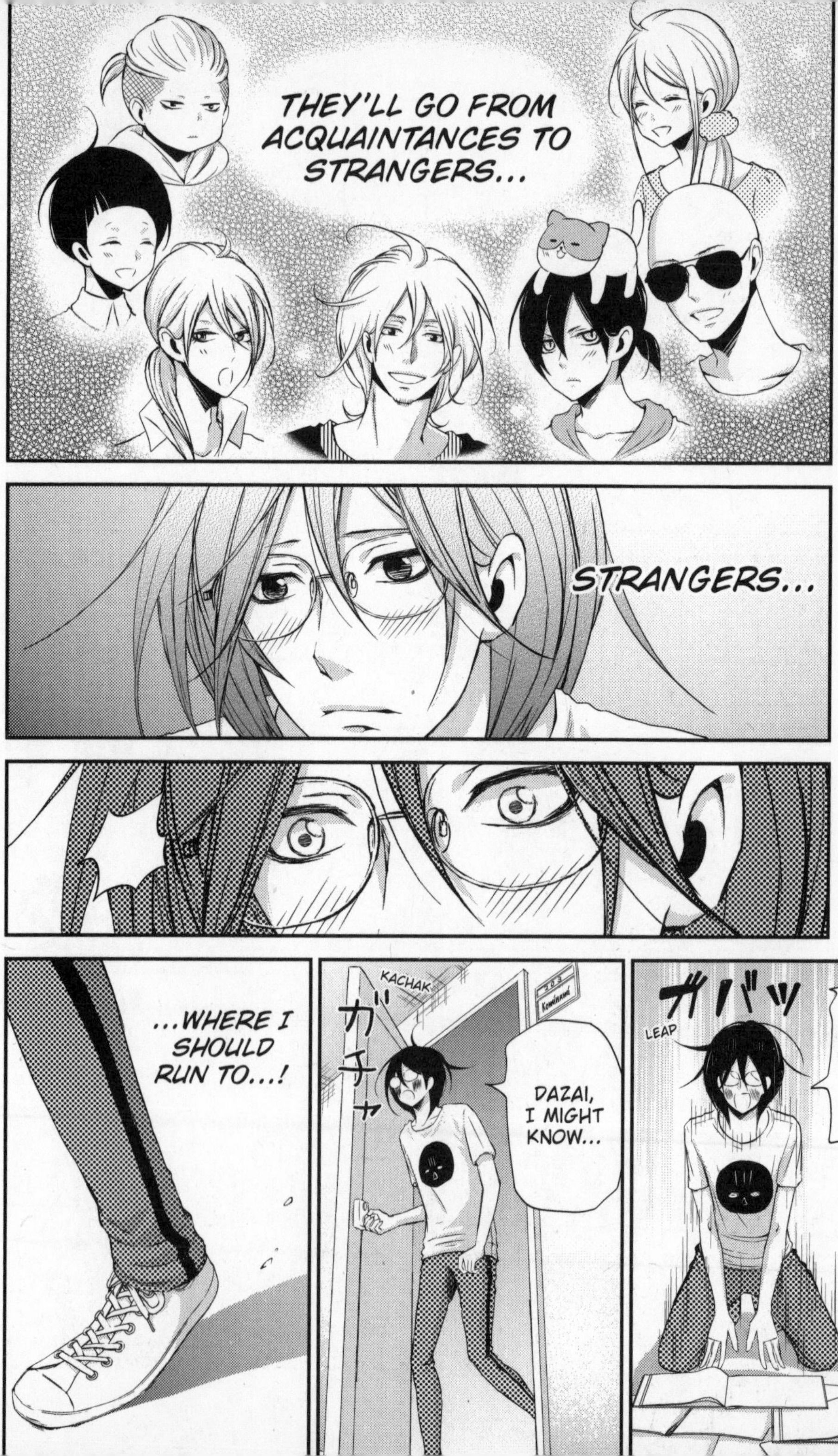
THEY'LL GO FROM ACQUAINTANCES TO STRANGERS...
STRANGERS...
ガバッ
LEAP
THAT'S IT!
ガチャ
KACHAK
DAZAI, I MIGHT KNOW...
...WHERE I SHOULD RUN TO...!

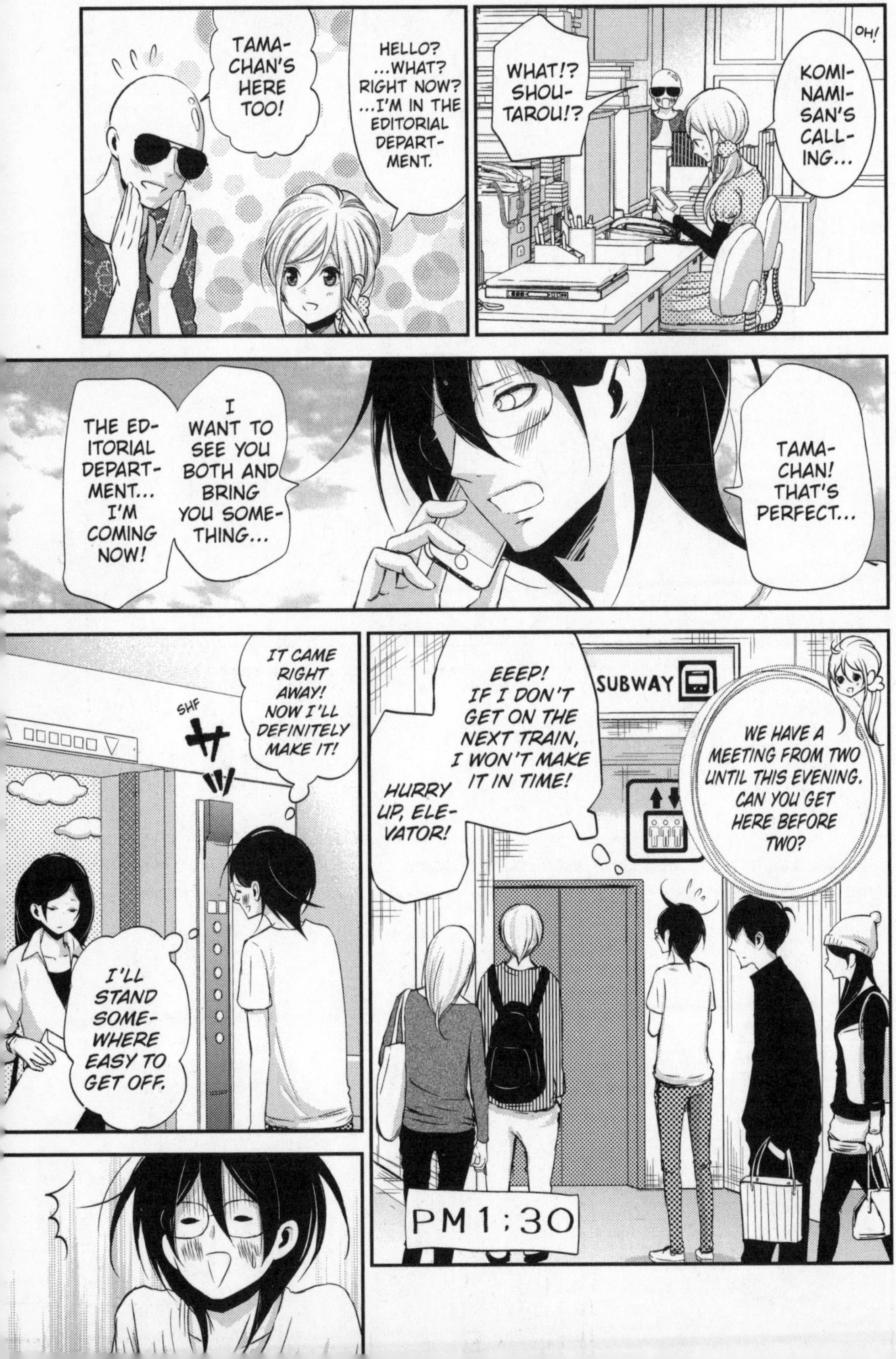
OH!
KOMI-NAMI-SAN'S CALLING...
WHAT!? SHOUTAROU!?
HELLO? ...WHAT? RIGHT NOW? ...I'M IN THE EDITORIAL DEPARTMENT.
TAMA-CHAN'S HERE TOO!
TAMA-CHAN! THAT'S PERFECT...
I WANT TO SEE YOU BOTH AND BRING YOU SOMETHING...
THE EDITORIAL DEPARTMENT... I'M COMING NOW!
SUBWAY
WE HAVE A MEETING FROM TWO UNTIL THIS EVENING. CAN YOU GET HERE BEFORE TWO?
EEEP! IF I DON'T GET ON THE NEXT TRAIN, I WON'T MAKE IT IN TIME!
HURRY UP, ELEVATOR!
PM1:30
IT CAME RIGHT AWAY! NOW I'LL DEFINITELY MAKE IT!
SHF
I'LL STAND SOMEWHERE EASY TO GET OFF.

IN THIS POSITION, I HAVE TO BE IN CHARGE OF PRESSING THE BUTTONS!
AH! HOLD THE DOORS!
IT WOULD BE TERRIBLE IF THE DOOR CLOSED NOW.
PUNCH, PUNCH, PUNCH THE "OPEN" BUTTON!
がしゃんっ!
WHUK
がしゃんっ!
WHUK
がしゃんっ!
WHUK
!?
THE BUTTON ISN'T WORKING!! PUNCH, PUNCH, PUNCH, PUNCH!!
がしゃんっ!
WHUK
がしゃんっ!
WHUK
PFFT! UM...YOU'RE PRESSING THE "CLOSE" BUTTON. PFFT!
WHUK
がしゃんっ!
I AM SO SORRY! I'M REALLY SORRY!
HEE HEE.

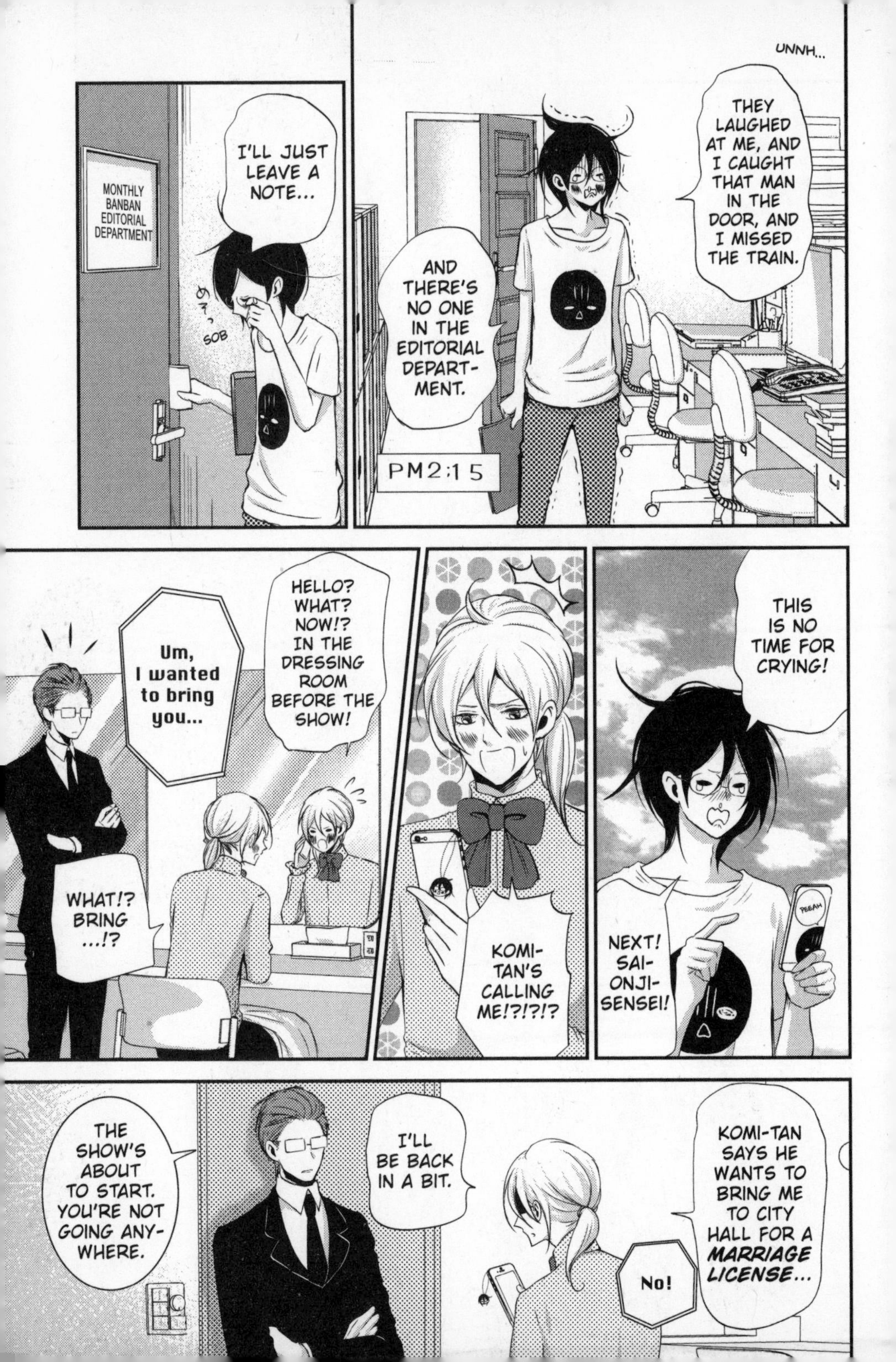
UNNH...
THEY LAUGHED AT ME, AND I CAUGHT THAT MAN IN THE DOOR, AND I MISSED THE TRAIN.
AND THERE'S NO ONE IN THE EDITORIAL DEPARTMENT.
PM2:15
MONTHLY BANBAN EDITORIAL DEPARTMENT
I'LL JUST LEAVE A NOTE...
SOB
THIS IS NO TIME FOR CRYING!
NEXT! SAI-ONJI-SENSEI!
KOMI-TAN'S CALLING ME!?!?!?
HELLO? WHAT? NOW!? IN THE DRESSING ROOM BEFORE THE SHOW!
Um, I wanted to bring you...
WHAT!? BRING ...!?
KOMI-TAN SAYS HE WANTS TO BRING ME TO CITY HALL FOR A *MARRIAGE LICENSE*...
No!
I'LL BE BACK IN A BIT.
THE SHOW'S ABOUT TO START. YOU'RE NOT GOING ANY-WHERE.

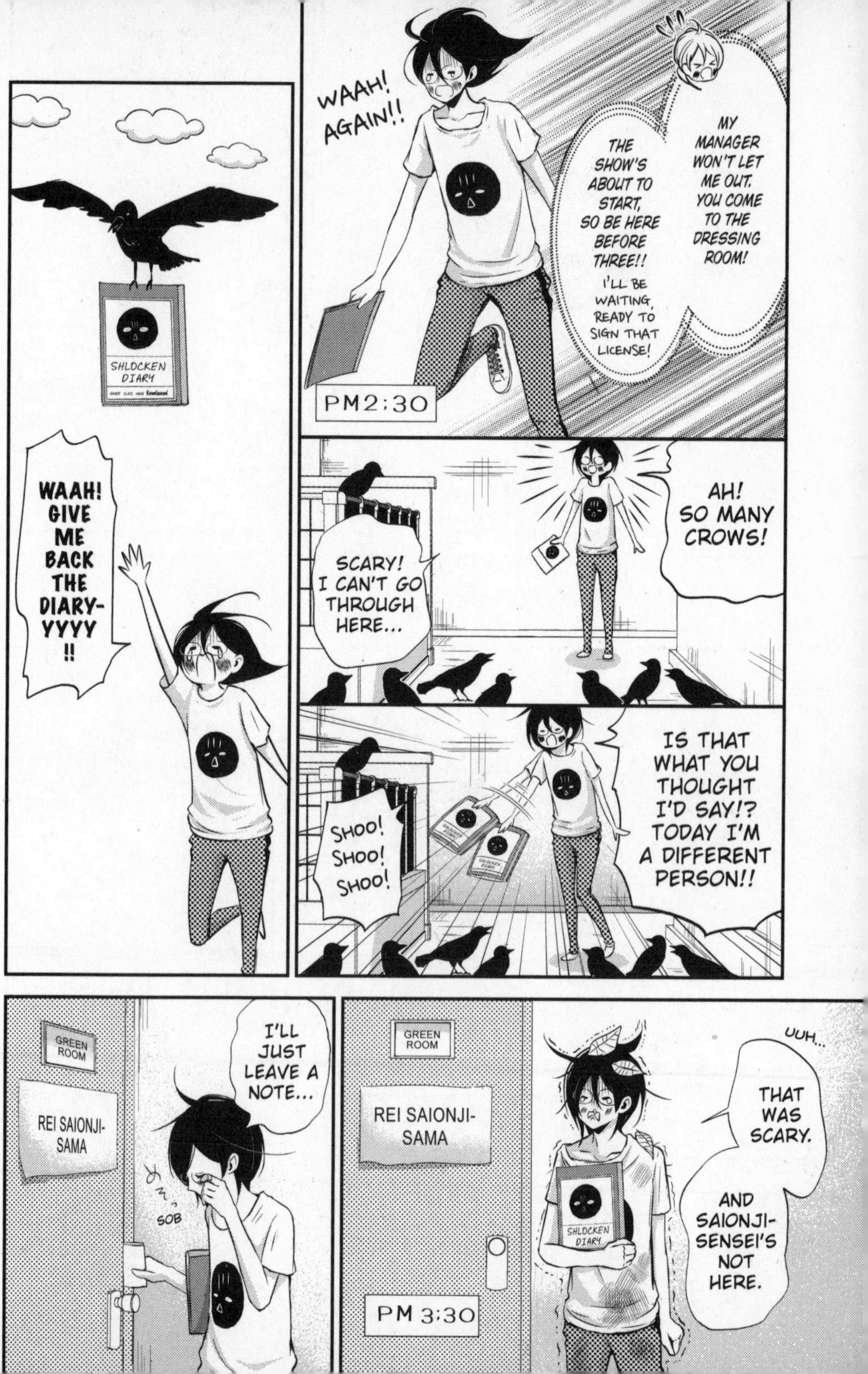
MY MANAGER WON'T LET ME OUT. YOU COME TO THE DRESSING ROOM!
THE SHOW'S ABOUT TO START, SO BE HERE BEFORE THREE!!
I'LL BE WAITING, READY TO SIGN THAT LICENSE!
WAAH! AGAIN!!
PM2:30
AH! SO MANY CROWS!
SCARY! I CAN'T GO THROUGH HERE...
IS THAT WHAT YOU THOUGHT I'D SAY!? TODAY I'M A DIFFERENT PERSON!!
SHOO! SHOO! SHOO!
SHLOCKEN DIARY
WAAH! GIVE ME BACK THE DIARY-YYYY!!
GREEN ROOM
REI SAIONJI-SAMA
UUH...
THAT WAS SCARY.
AND SAIONJI-SENSEI'S NOT HERE.
SHLOCKEN DIARY
PM 3:30
I'LL JUST LEAVE A NOTE...
GREEN ROOM
REI SAIONJI-SAMA
SOB

PEEAH!
NEXT! NEKO-GURI-SENSEI!
OH! NEKOGURI-SENSEI HATES THE PHONE. HE ONLY TOLD ME HIS E-MAIL ADDRESS!
PANIC あせ
PANIC あせ
SHLOCKEN DIARY
UMM, "ARE YOU AT HOME?"
WAAAH! I CAN'T TYPE!!
Aye aye annihilate awfulawfatea cccccccct now hung?
AH! I SENT IT!!
EEEP!
THIS MAIL IS TERRIFY-ING!!
WH-WHO SENT THIS!?
I'LL NEVER FORGIVE THEM!
POKE つん
POKE つん
WAAAH!
THE BATTERY ON MY PHONE DIED! I'LL JUST GO OVER THERE!!
PANIC パニック

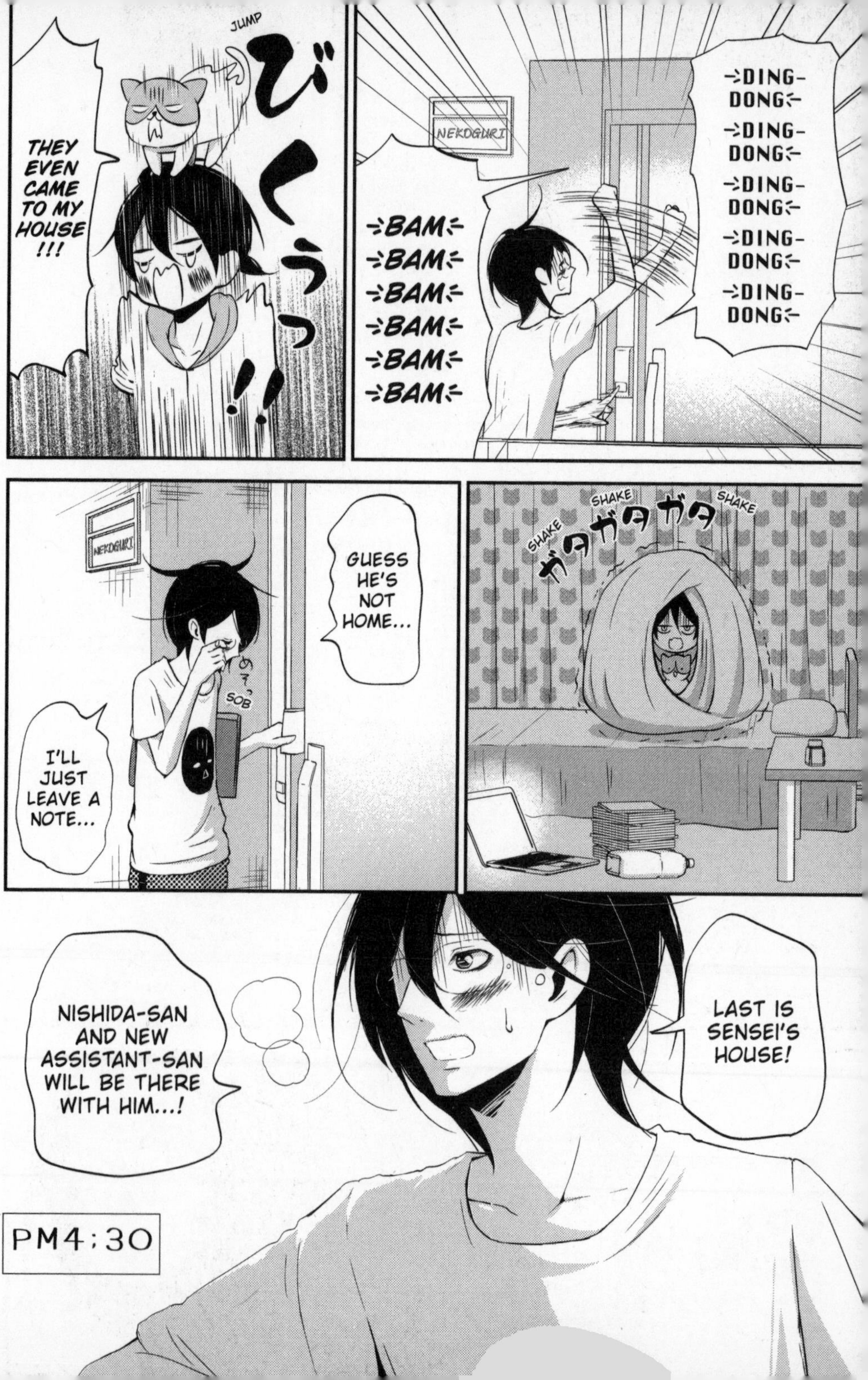
NEKOGURI
⇒DING-DONG⇐ ⇒DING-DONG⇐ ⇒DING-DONG⇐ ⇒DING-DONG⇐ ⇒DING-DONG⇐
⇒BAM⇐ ⇒BAM⇐ ⇒BAM⇐ ⇒BAM⇐ ⇒BAM⇐ ⇒BAM⇐
JUMP
びくぅっ!!
THEY EVEN CAME TO MY HOUSE!!!
SHAKE SHAKE SHAKE
ガタガタガタ
NEKOGURI
GUESS HE'S NOT HOME...
SOB
I'LL JUST LEAVE A NOTE...
LAST IS SENSEI'S HOUSE!
NISHIDA-SAN AND NEW ASSISTANT-SAN WILL BE THERE WITH HIM...!
PM4:30

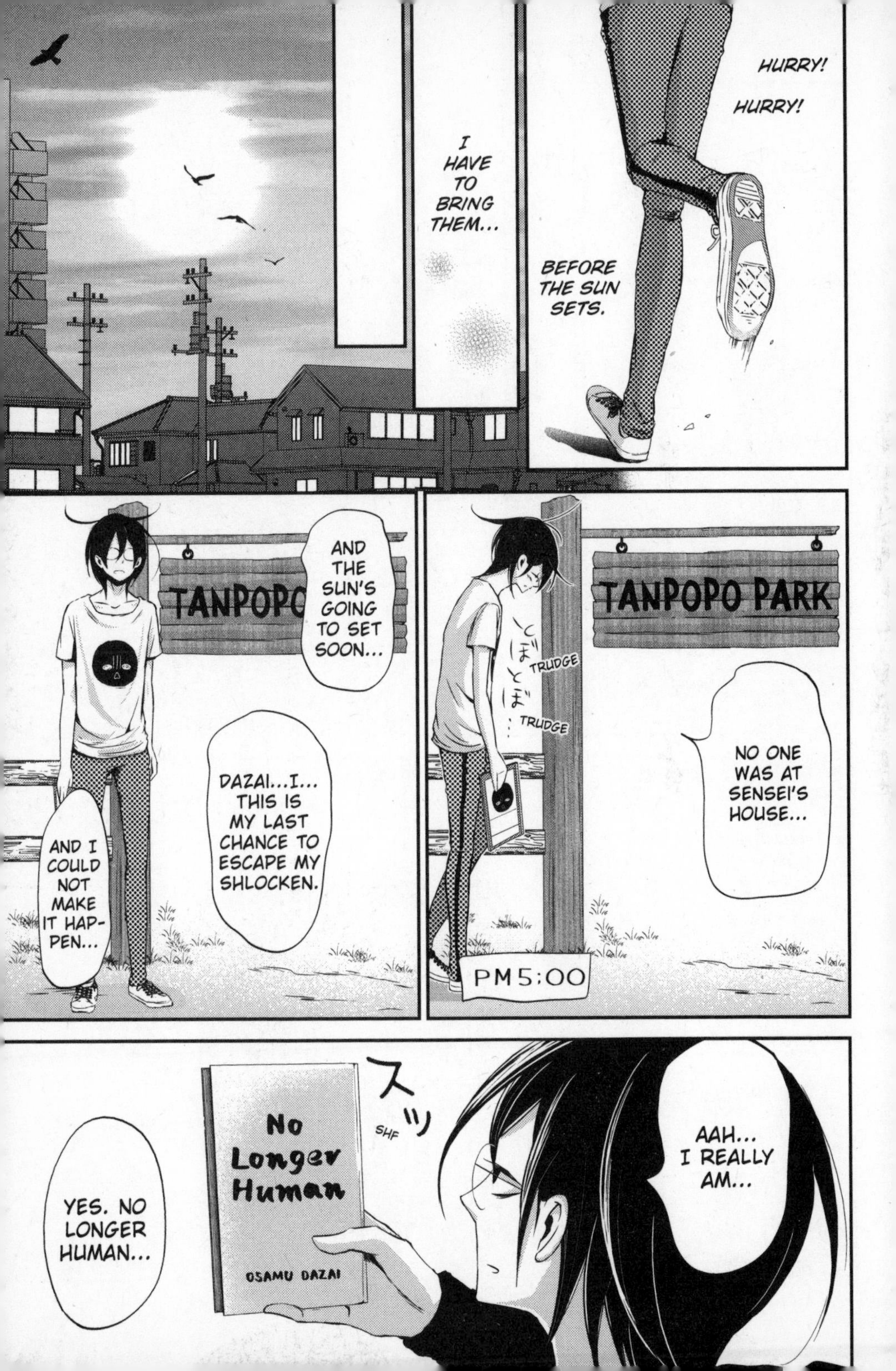
HURRY!
HURRY!
BEFORE THE SUN SETS.
I HAVE TO BRING THEM...
TANPOPO PARK
とぼとぼ
TRUDGE
TRUDGE
NO ONE WAS AT SENSEI'S HOUSE...
PM5:00
TANPOPO
AND THE SUN'S GOING TO SET SOON...
DAZAI...I... THIS IS MY LAST CHANCE TO ESCAPE MY SHLOCKEN.
AND I COULD NOT MAKE IT HAP-PEN...
AAH... I REALLY AM...
スッ
SHF
No Longer Human
OSAMU DAZAI
YES. NO LONGER HUMAN...

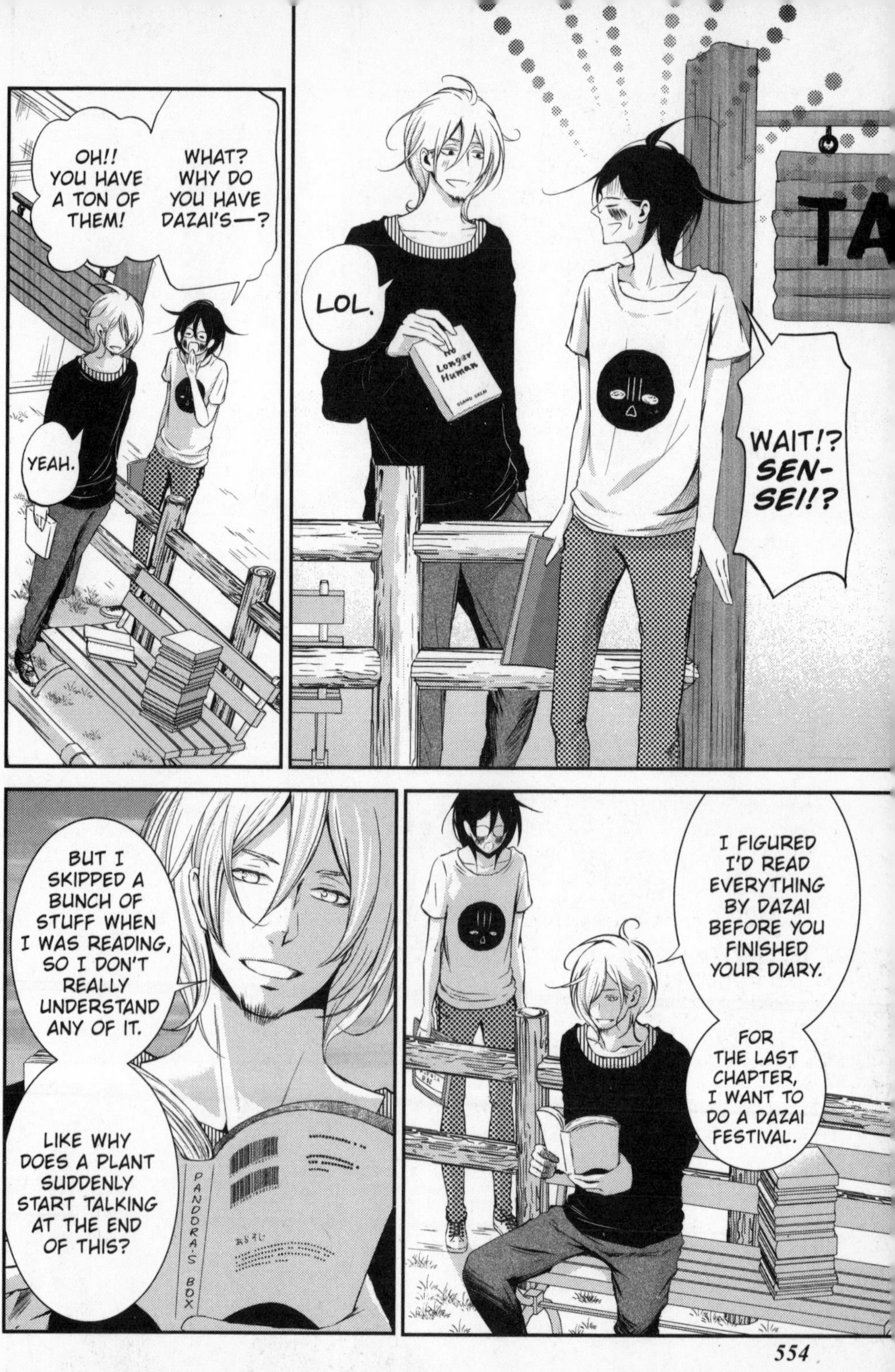
TA
WAIT!? SEN-SEI!?
LOL.
No Longer Human
WHAT? WHY DO YOU HAVE DAZAI'S—?
OH!! YOU HAVE A TON OF THEM!
YEAH.
I FIGURED I'D READ EVERYTHING BY DAZAI BEFORE YOU FINISHED YOUR DIARY.
FOR THE LAST CHAPTER, I WANT TO DO A DAZAI FESTIVAL.
BUT I SKIPPED A BUNCH OF STUFF WHEN I WAS READING, SO I DON'T REALLY UNDERSTAND ANY OF IT.
LIKE WHY DOES A PLANT SUDDENLY START TALKING AT THE END OF THIS?
PANDORA'S BOX

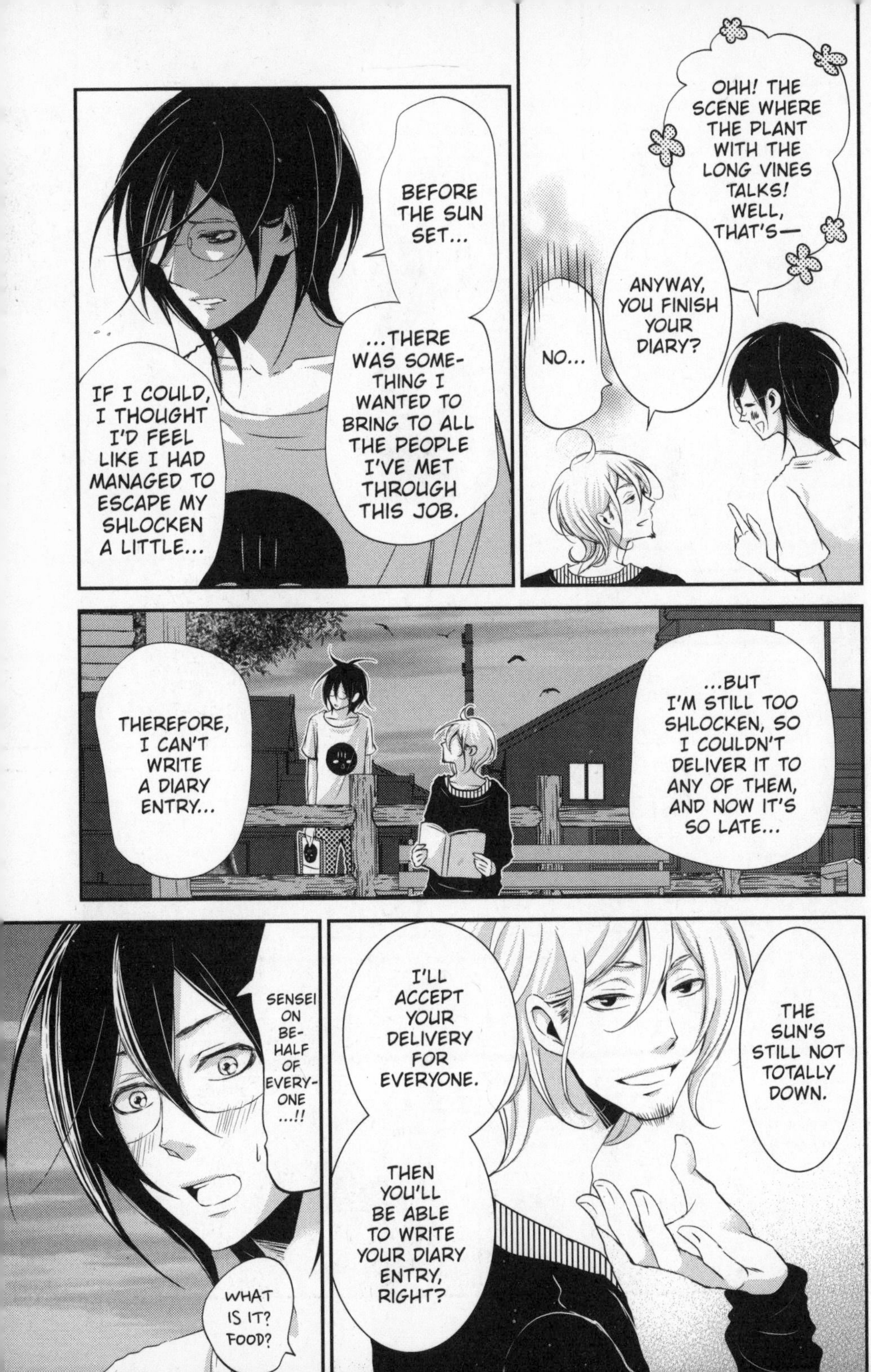
OHH! THE SCENE WHERE THE PLANT WITH THE LONG VINES TALKS! WELL, THAT'S—
ANYWAY, YOU FINISH YOUR DIARY?
NO...
BEFORE THE SUN SET...
...THERE WAS SOME-THING I WANTED TO BRING TO ALL THE PEOPLE I'VE MET THROUGH THIS JOB.
IF I COULD, I THOUGHT I'D FEEL LIKE I HAD MANAGED TO ESCAPE MY SHLOCKEN A LITTLE...
...BUT I'M STILL TOO SHLOCKEN, SO I COULDN'T DELIVER IT TO ANY OF THEM, AND NOW IT'S SO LATE...
THEREFORE, I CAN'T WRITE A DIARY ENTRY...
THE SUN'S STILL NOT TOTALLY DOWN.
I'LL ACCEPT YOUR DELIVERY FOR EVERYONE.
THEN YOU'LL BE ABLE TO WRITE YOUR DIARY ENTRY, RIGHT?
SENSEI ON BE-HALF OF EVERY-ONE ...!!
WHAT IS IT? FOOD?

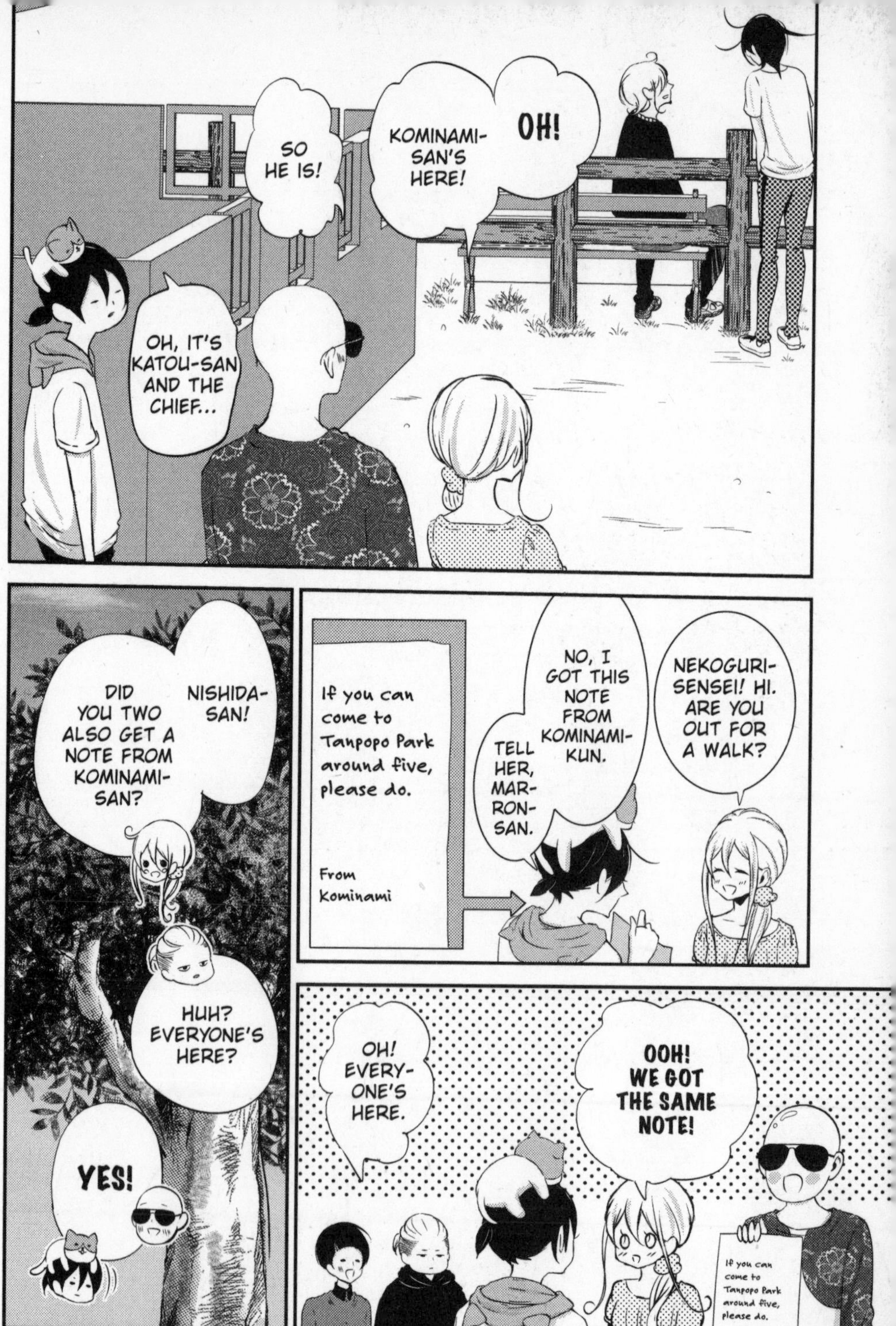
OH!
KOMINAMI-SAN'S HERE!
SO HE IS!
OH, IT'S KATOU-SAN AND THE CHIEF...
NEKOGURI-SENSEI! HI. ARE YOU OUT FOR A WALK?
NO, I GOT THIS NOTE FROM KOMINAMI-KUN.
TELL HER, MARRON-SAN.
If you can come to Tanpopo Park around five, please do.
From Kominami
OOH! WE GOT THE SAME NOTE!
OH! EVERYONE'S HERE.
If you can come to Tanpopo Park around five, please do.
NISHIDA-SAN!
DID YOU TWO ALSO GET A NOTE FROM KOMINAMI-SAN?
HUH? EVERYONE'S HERE?
YES!

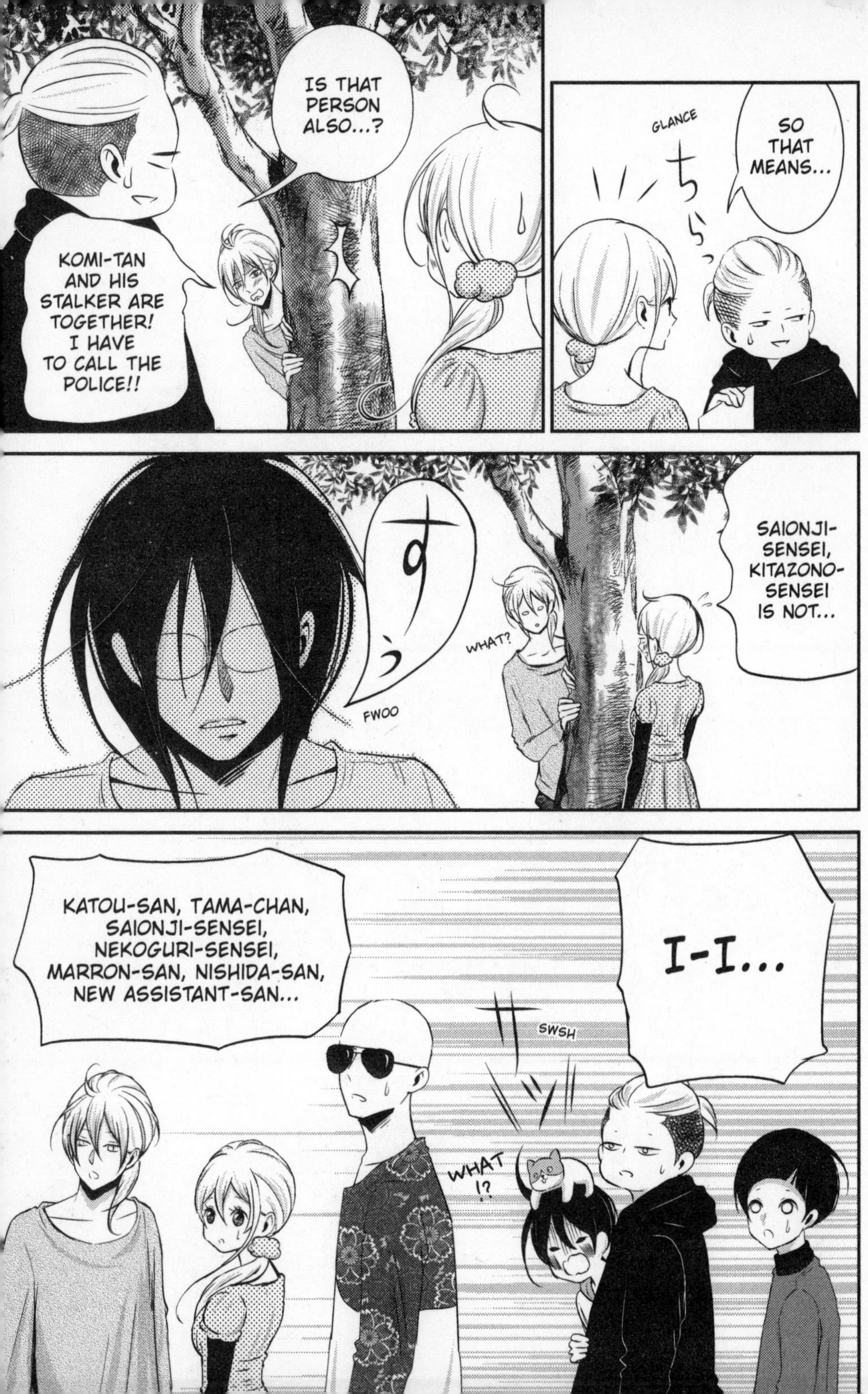

SO THAT MEANS...
GLANCE
ちらっ
IS THAT PERSON ALSO...?
KOMI-TAN AND HIS STALKER ARE TOGETHER! I HAVE TO CALL THE POLICE!!
SAIONJI-SENSEI, KITAZONO-SENSEI IS NOT...
WHAT?
すぅ
FWOO
I-I...
KATOU-SAN, TAMA-CHAN, SAIONJI-SENSEI, NEKOGURI-SENSEI, MARRON-SAN, NISHIDA-SAN, NEW ASSISTANT-SAN...
SWSH
WHAT!?

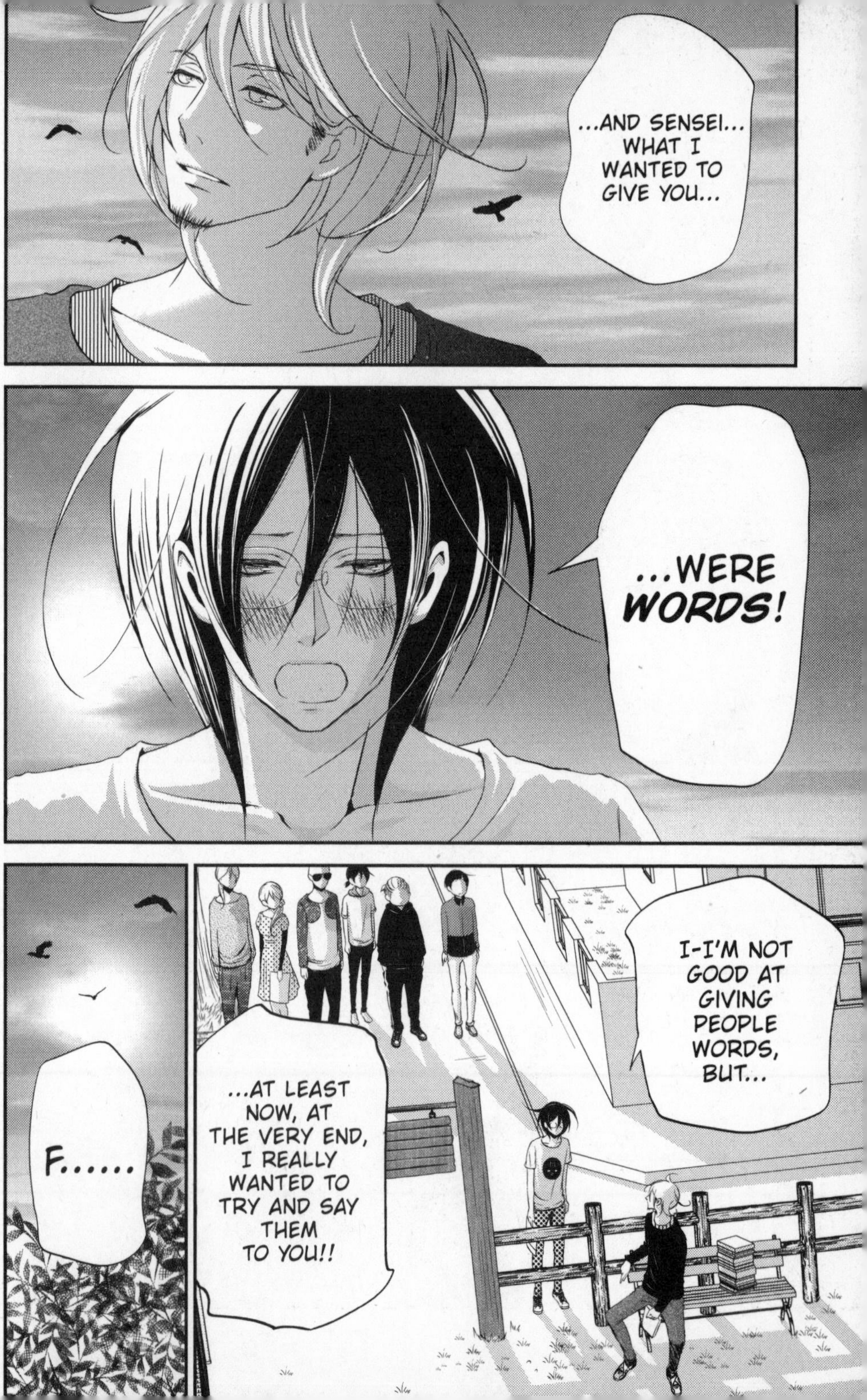
...AND SENSEI... WHAT I WANTED TO GIVE YOU...
...WERE WORDS!
I-I'M NOT GOOD AT GIVING PEOPLE WORDS, BUT...
...AT LEAST NOW, AT THE VERY END, I REALLY WANTED TO TRY AND SAY THEM TO YOU!!
F......

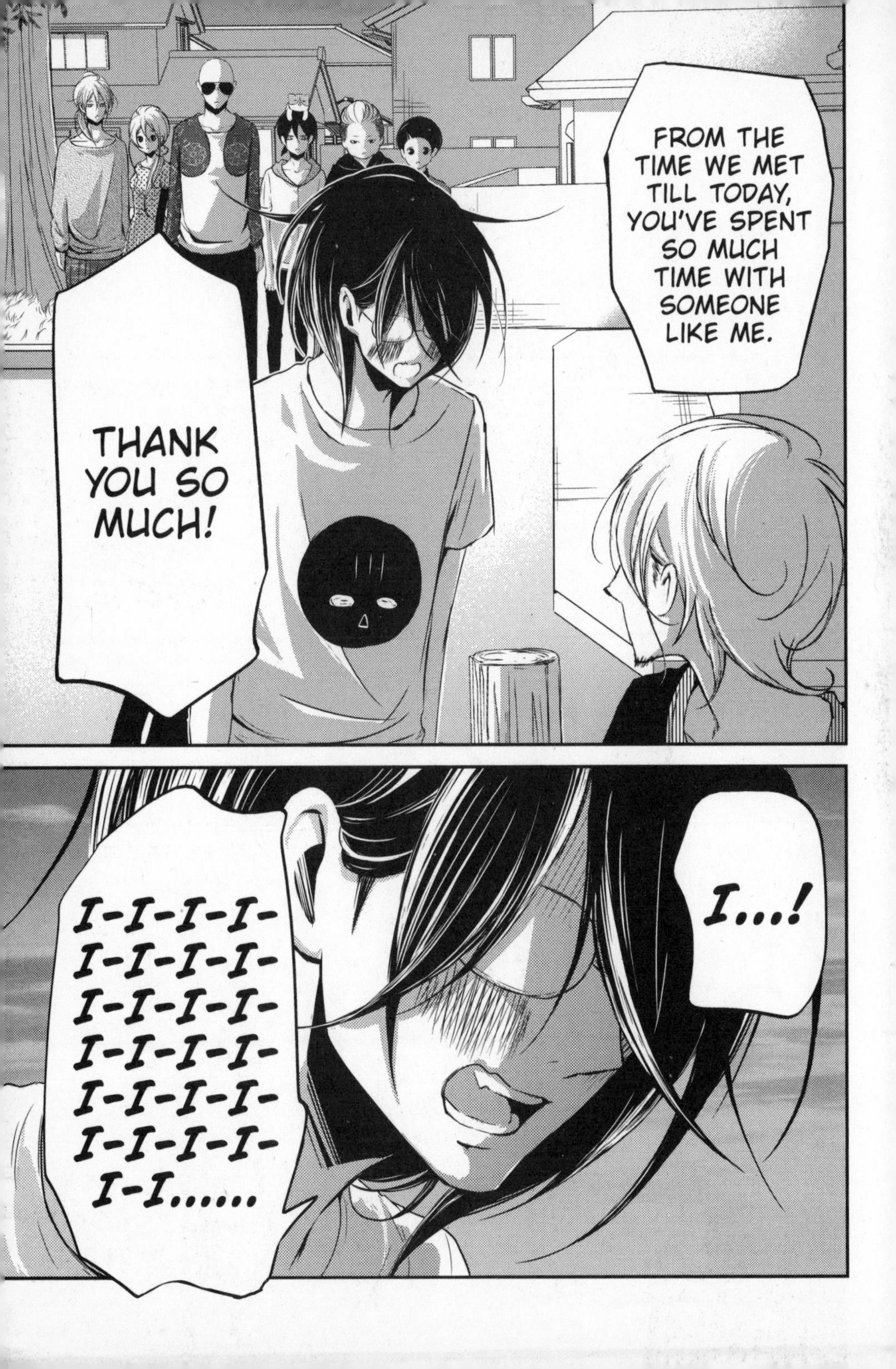
FROM THE TIME WE MET TILL TODAY, YOU'VE SPENT SO MUCH TIME WITH SOMEONE LIKE ME.
THANK YOU SO MUCH!
I...!
I-I-I-I-I-I-I-I-I-I-I-I-I-I-I-I-I-I-I-I-I-I-I-I-I-I......

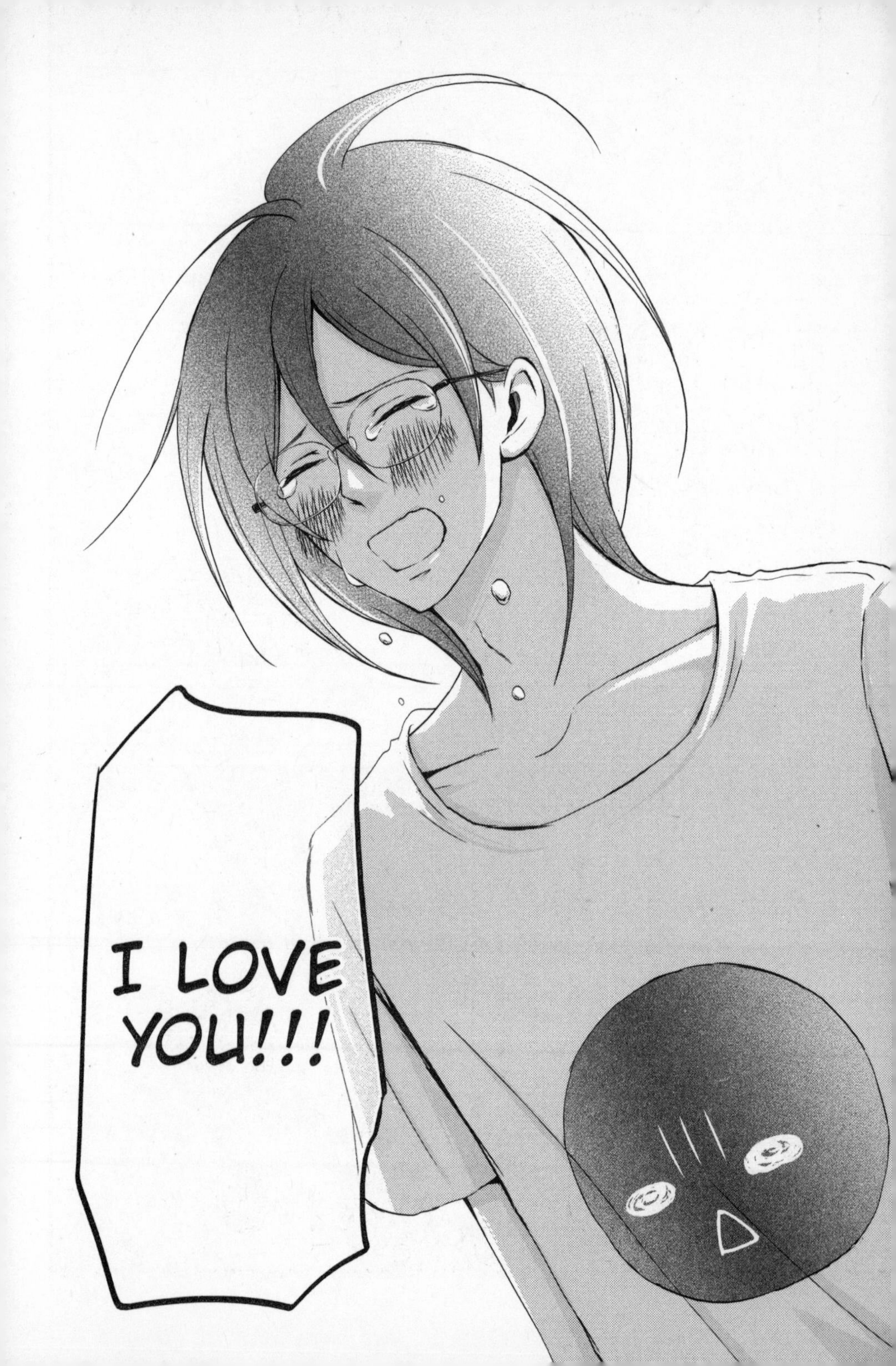
I LOVE YOU!!!

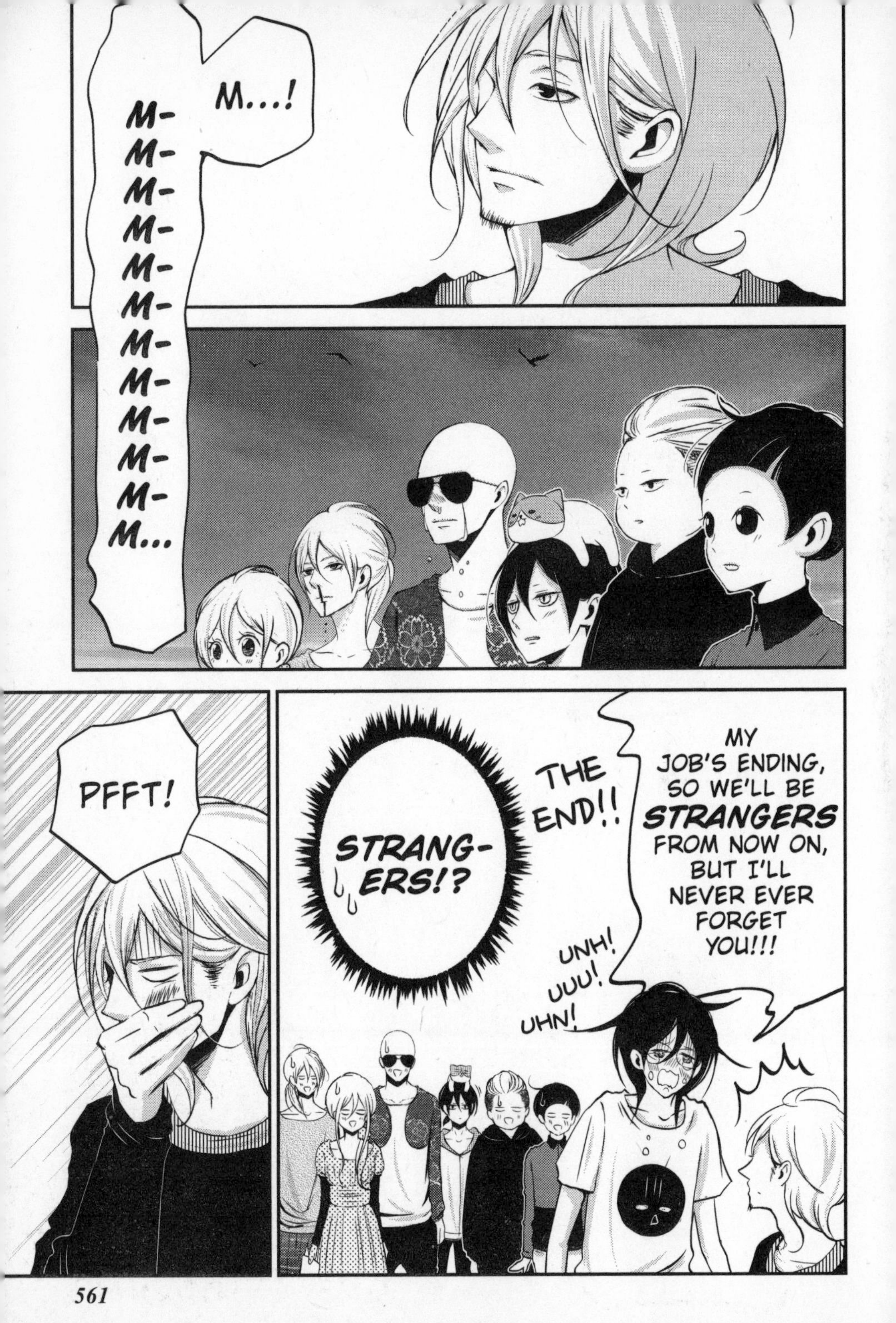
M...!
M-M-M-M-M-M-M-M-M-M-M-M...
MY JOB'S ENDING, SO WE'LL BE STRANGERS FROM NOW ON, BUT I'LL NEVER EVER FORGET YOU!!!
THE END!!
STRANG-ERS!?
UNH! UUU! UHN!
PFFT!

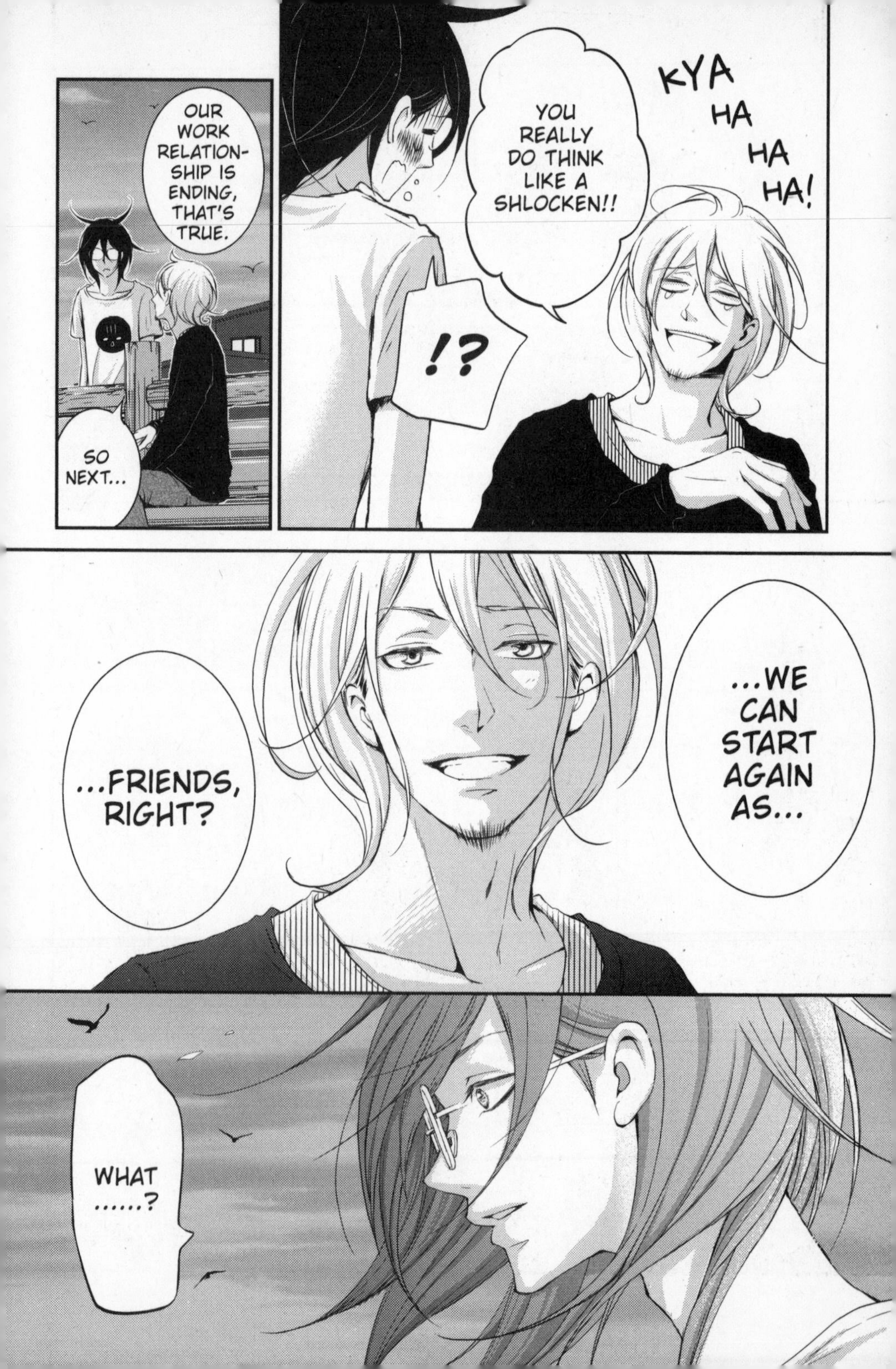
KYA HA HA HA!
YOU REALLY DO THINK LIKE A SHLOCKEN!!
!?
OUR WORK RELATIONSHIP IS ENDING, THAT'S TRUE.
SO NEXT...
...WE CAN START AGAIN AS...
...FRIENDS, RIGHT?
WHAT......?

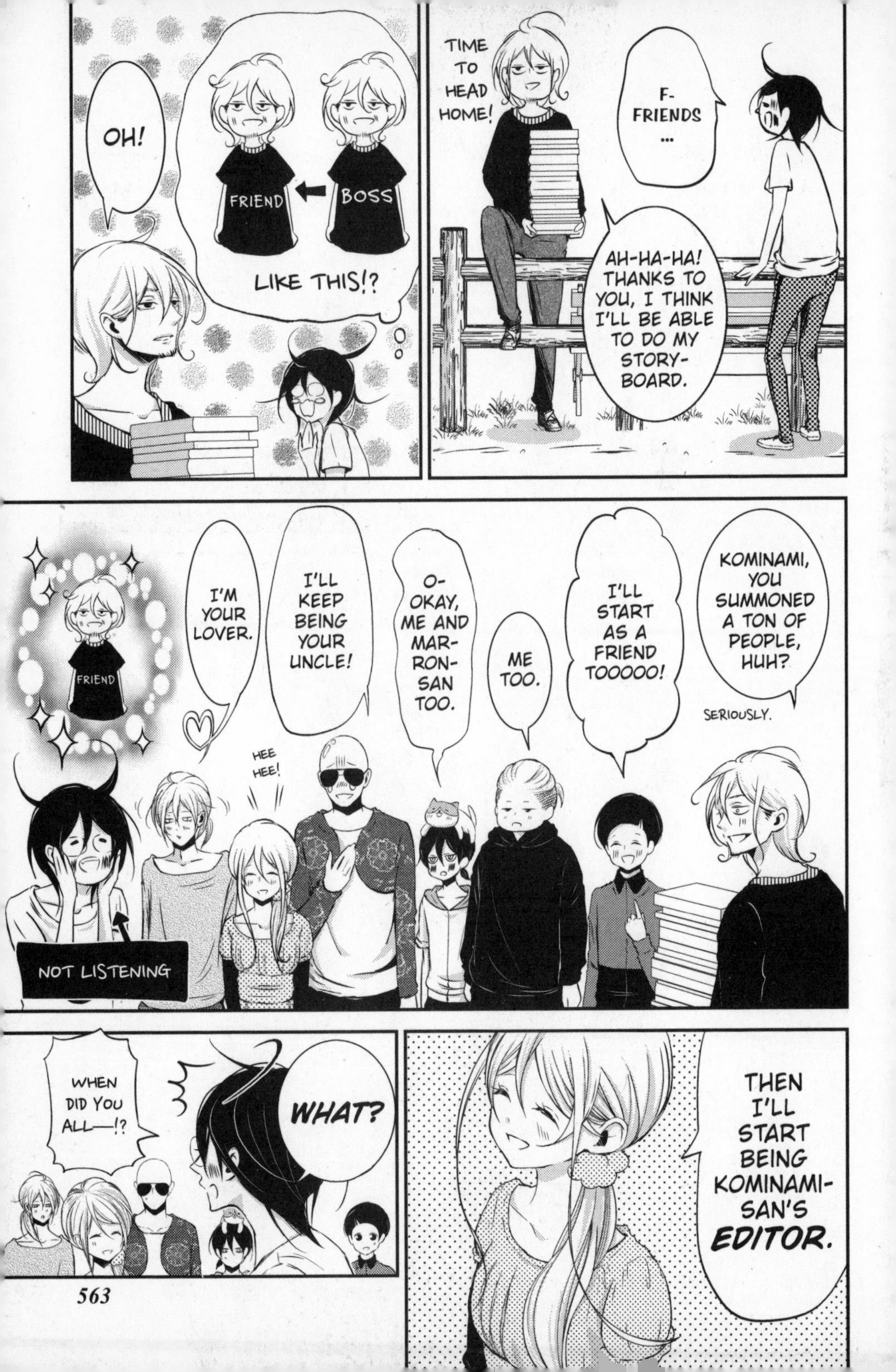
F-FRIENDS...
TIME TO HEAD HOME!
AH-HA-HA! THANKS TO YOU, I THINK I'LL BE ABLE TO DO MY STORYBOARD.
OH!
BOSS
FRIEND
LIKE THIS!?
KOMINAMI, YOU SUMMONED A TON OF PEOPLE, HUH?
SERIOUSLY.
I'LL START AS A FRIEND TOOOOO!
ME TOO.
O-OKAY, ME AND MARRON-SAN TOO.
HEE HEE!
I'LL KEEP BEING YOUR UNCLE!
I'M YOUR LOVER.
FRIEND
NOT LISTENING
THEN I'LL START BEING KOMINAMI-SAN'S **EDITOR**.
WHAT?
WHEN DID YOU ALL—!?

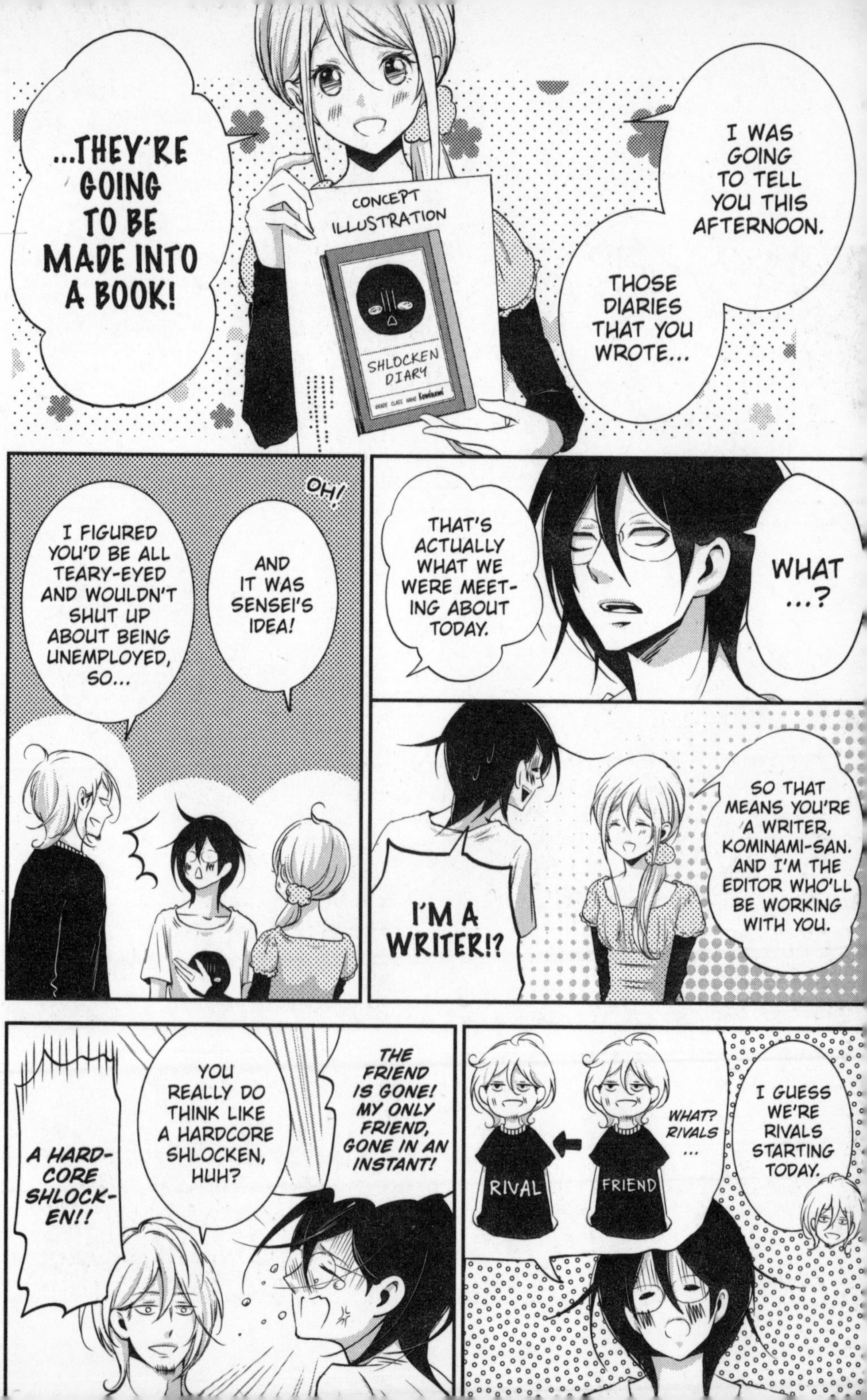
I WAS GOING TO TELL YOU THIS AFTERNOON.
THOSE DIARIES THAT YOU WROTE...
CONCEPT ILLUSTRATION
SHLOCKEN DIARY
GRADE CLASS NAME Kominami
...THEY'RE GOING TO BE MADE INTO A BOOK!
WHAT ...?
THAT'S ACTUALLY WHAT WE WERE MEET-ING ABOUT TODAY.
SO THAT MEANS YOU'RE A WRITER, KOMINAMI-SAN. AND I'M THE EDITOR WHO'LL BE WORKING WITH YOU.
I'M A WRITER!?
OH!
AND IT WAS SENSEI'S IDEA!
I FIGURED YOU'D BE ALL TEARY-EYED AND WOULDN'T SHUT UP ABOUT BEING UNEMPLOYED, SO...
I GUESS WE'RE RIVALS STARTING TODAY.
WHAT? RIVALS ...
FRIEND
RIVAL
THE FRIEND IS GONE! MY ONLY FRIEND, GONE IN AN INSTANT!
YOU REALLY DO THINK LIKE A HARDCORE SHLOCKEN, HUH?
A HARD-CORE SHLOCK-EN!!

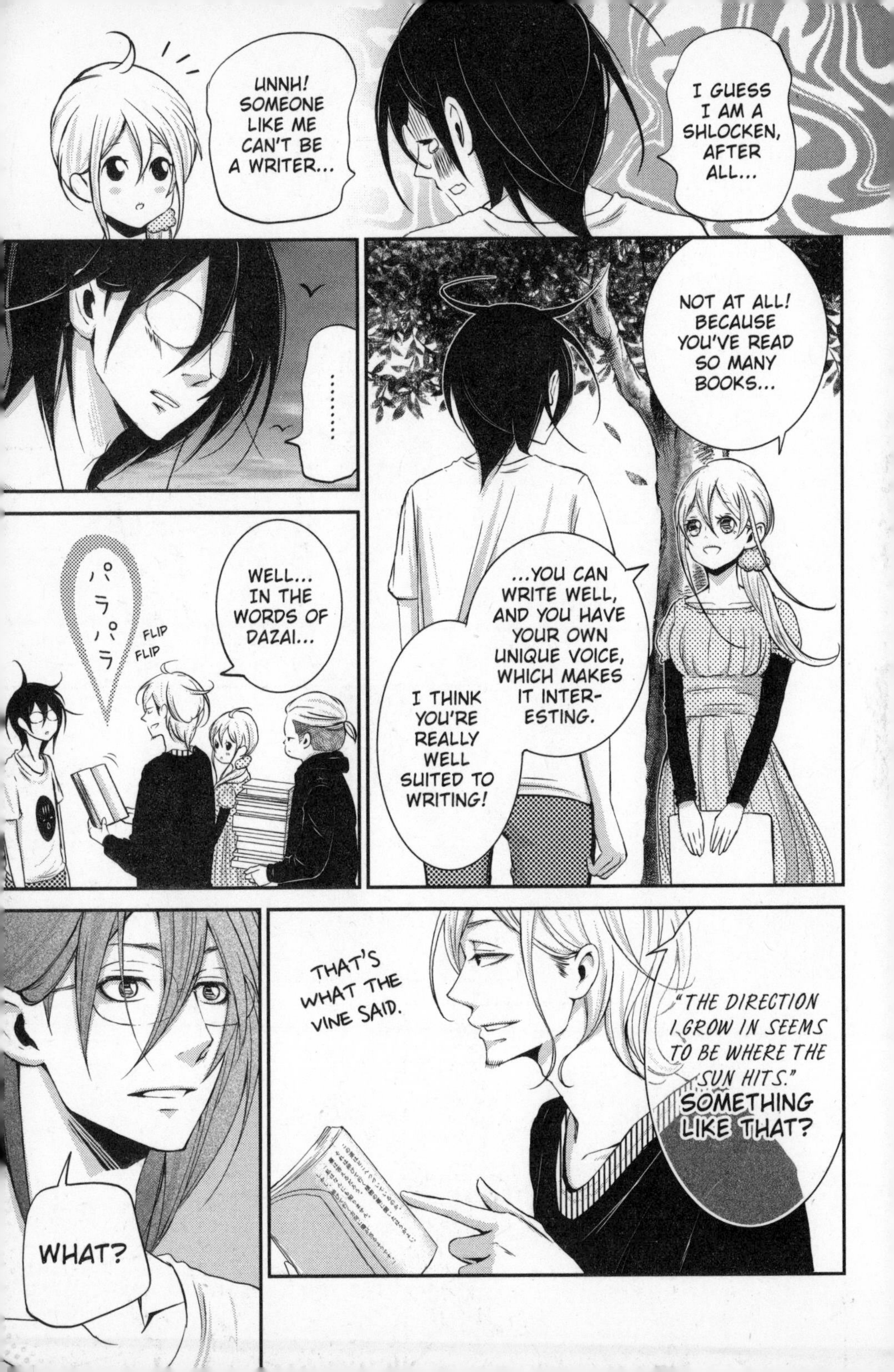
I GUESS I AM A SHLOCKEN, AFTER ALL...
UNNH! SOMEONE LIKE ME CAN'T BE A WRITER...
NOT AT ALL! BECAUSE YOU'VE READ SO MANY BOOKS...
...YOU CAN WRITE WELL, AND YOU HAVE YOUR OWN UNIQUE VOICE, WHICH MAKES IT INTER-ESTING.
I THINK YOU'RE REALLY WELL SUITED TO WRITING!
......
WELL... IN THE WORDS OF DAZAI...
パラパラ
FLIP FLIP
"THE DIRECTION I GROW IN SEEMS TO BE WHERE THE SUN HITS." SOMETHING LIKE THAT?
THAT'S WHAT THE VINE SAID.
WHAT?

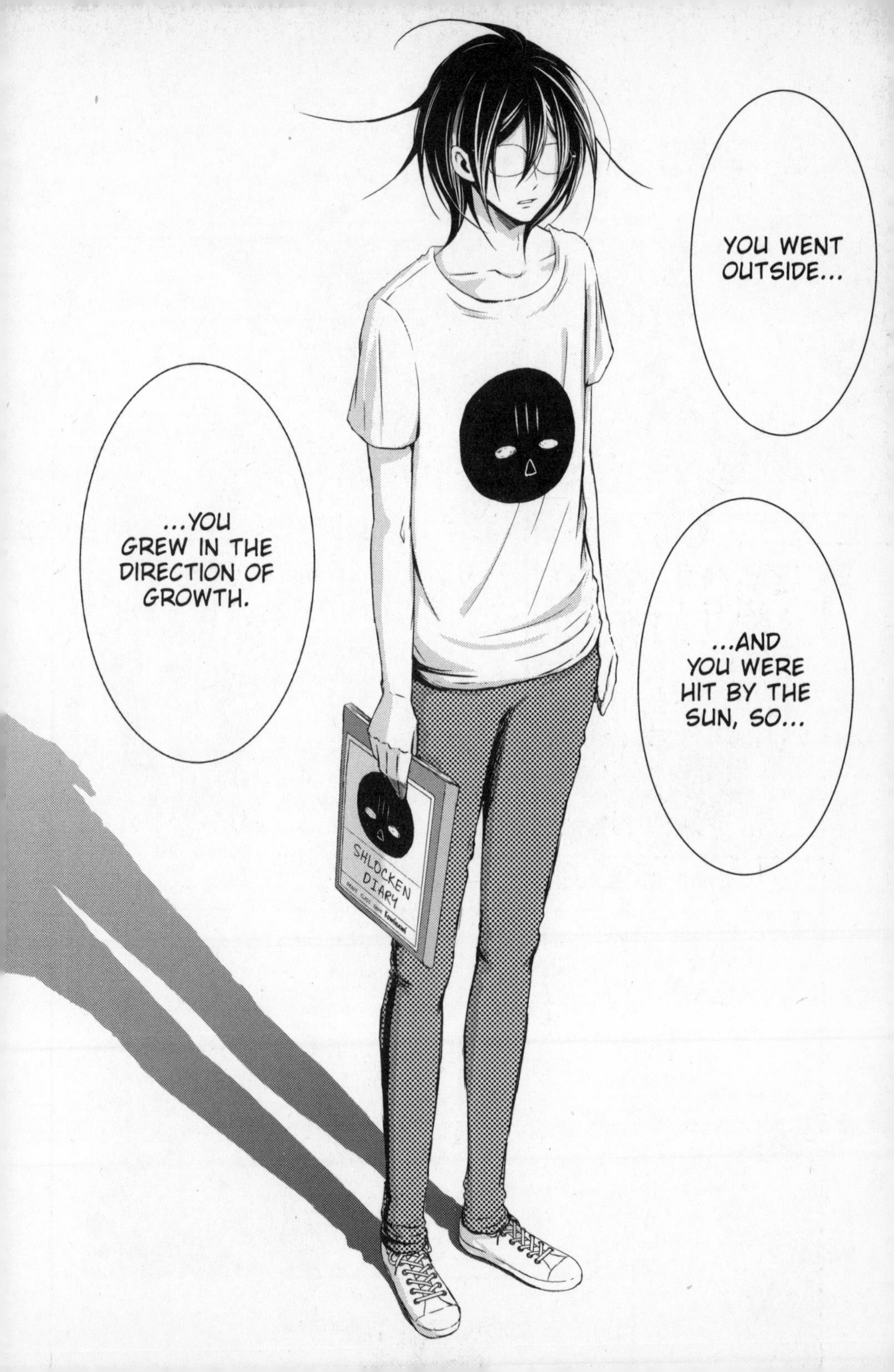
YOU WENT OUTSIDE...
...AND YOU WERE HIT BY THE SUN, SO...
...YOU GREW IN THE DIRECTION OF GROWTH.
SHLOCKEN DIARY

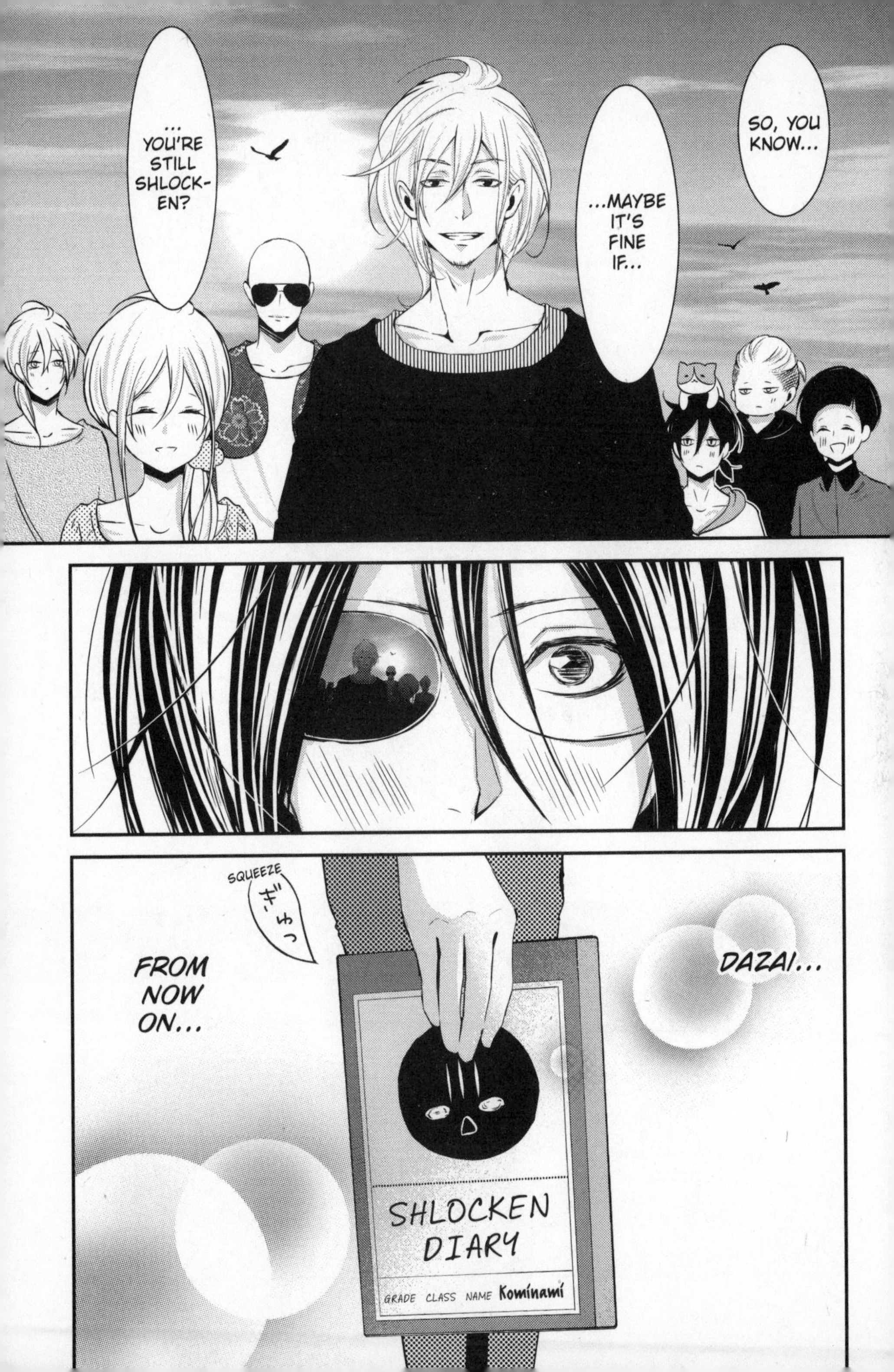
SO, YOU KNOW...
...MAYBE IT'S FINE IF...
...YOU'RE STILL SHLOCKEN?
DAZAI...
SQUEEZE
ぎゅっ
FROM NOW ON...
SHLOCKEN DIARY
GRADE CLASS NAME Kominami

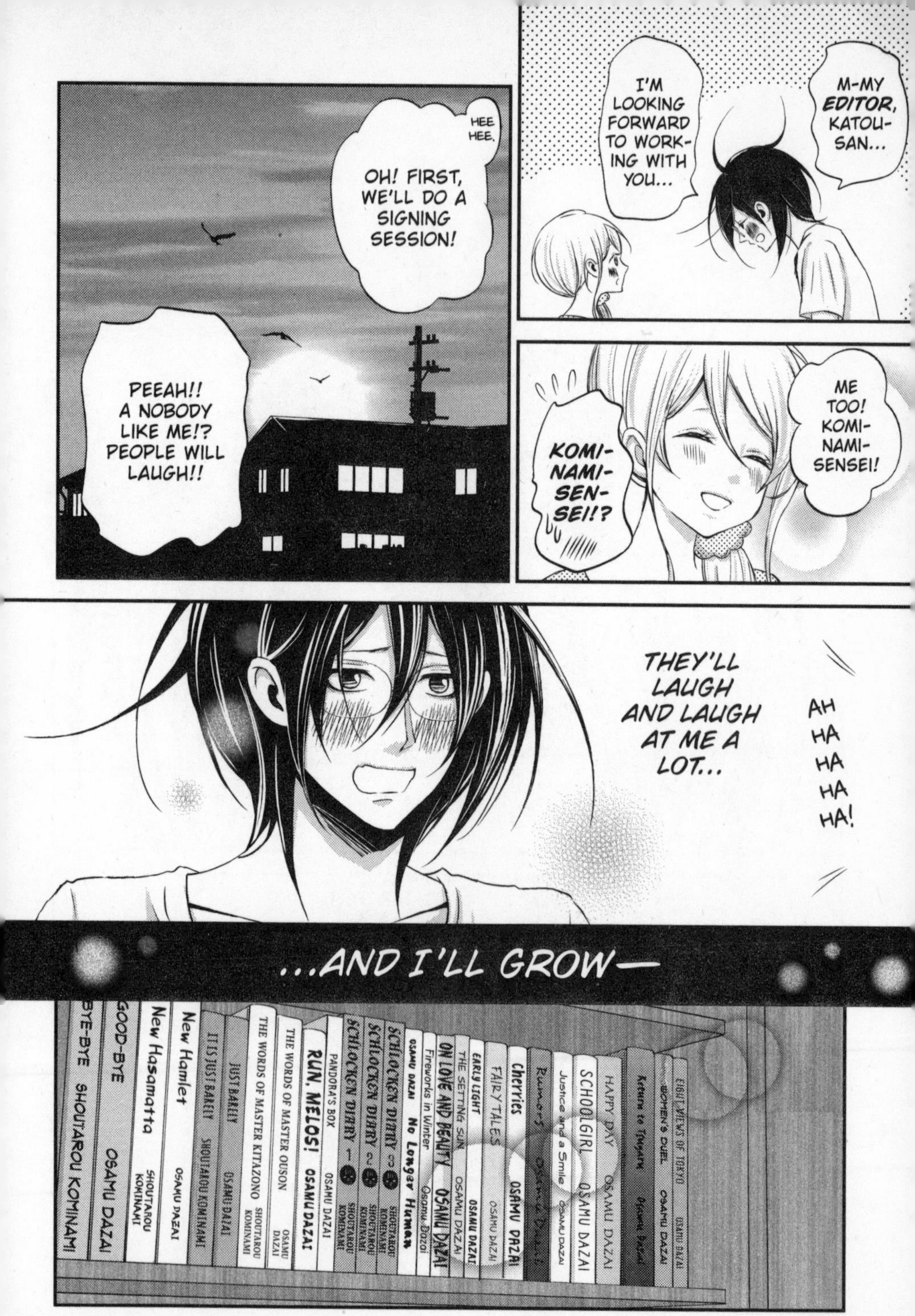
M-MY EDITOR, KATOU-SAN...
I'M LOOKING FORWARD TO WORKING WITH YOU...
ME TOO! KOMI-NAMI-SENSEI!
KOMI-NAMI-SEN-SEI!?
HEE HEE.
OH! FIRST, WE'LL DO A SIGNING SESSION!
PEEAH!! A NOBODY LIKE ME!? PEOPLE WILL LAUGH!!
AH HA HA HA HA!
THEY'LL LAUGH AND LAUGH AT ME A LOT...
...AND I'LL GROW—
EIGHT VIEWS OF TOKYO OSAMU DAZAI
WOMEN'S DUEL OSAMU DAZAI
Return to Tsugaru Osamu Dazai
HAPPY DAY OSAMU DAZAI
SCHOOLGIRL OSAMU DAZAI
Justice and a Smile OSAMU DAZAI
Rumors
Cherries OSAMU DAZAI
FAIRY TALES OSAMU DAZAI
EARLY LIGHT OSAMU DAZAI
THE SETTING SUN OSAMU DAZAI
ON LOVE AND BEAUTY OSAMU DAZAI
Fireworks in Winter Osamu Dazai
OSAMU DAZAI No Longer Human
SCHLOCKEN DIARY 3 SHOUTAROU KOMINAMI
SCHLOCKEN DIARY 2 SHOUTAROU KOMINAMI
SCHLOCKEN DIARY 1 SHOUTAROU KOMINAMI
PANDORA'S BOX OSAMU DAZAI
RUN, MELOS! OSAMU DAZAI
THE WORDS OF MASTER OUSON OSAMU DAZAI
THE WORDS OF MASTER KITAZONO SHOUTAROU KOMINAMI
JUST BARELY OSAMU DAZAI
IT IS JUST BARELY SHOUTAROU KOMINAMI
New Hamlet OSAMU DAZAI
New Hasamatta SHOUTAROU KOMINAMI
GOOD-BYE OSAMU DAZAI
BYE-BYE SHOUTAROU KOMINAMI

SHLOCKEN
DIARY

GRADE CLASS NAME Kominami

THE END

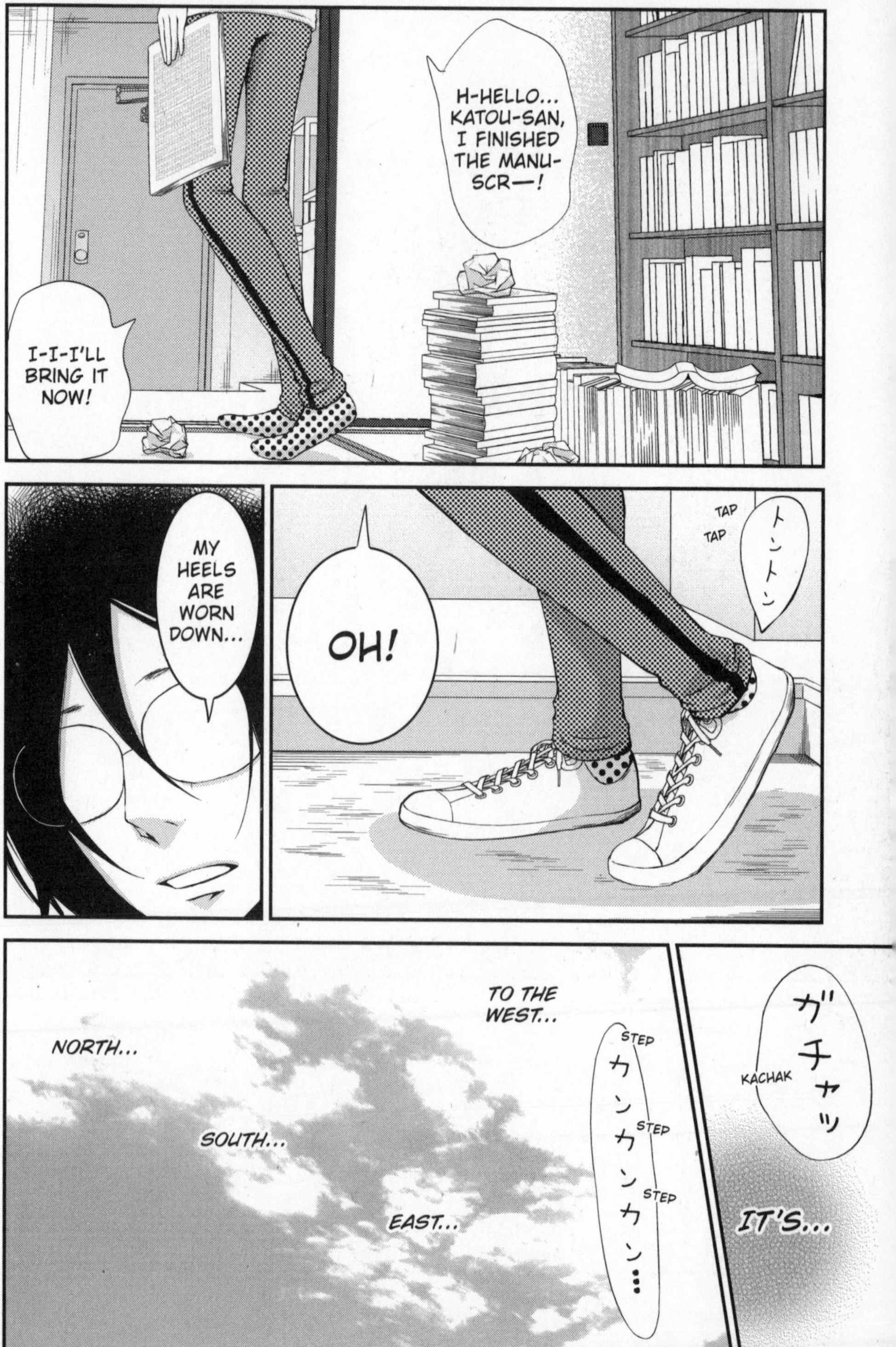
H-HELLO... KATOU-SAN, I FINISHED THE MANU-SCR—!
I-I-I'LL BRING IT NOW!
トントン
TAP TAP
OH!
MY HEELS ARE WORN DOWN...
ガチャッ
KACHAK
IT'S...
カンカンカン...
STEP STEP STEP
TO THE WEST...
NORTH...
SOUTH...
EAST...

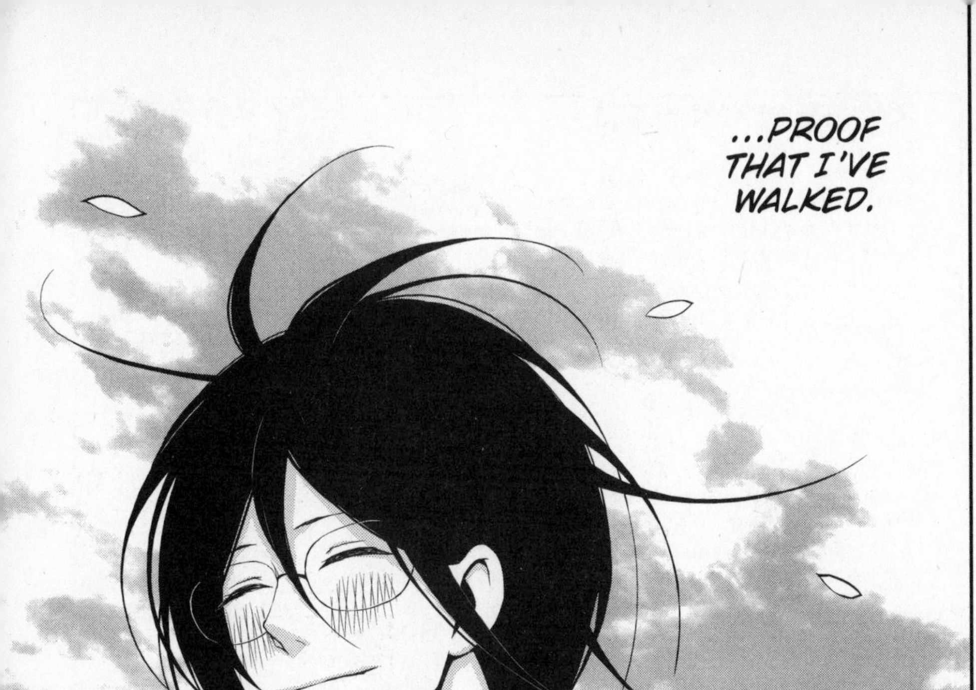
...PROOF
THAT I'VE
WALKED.

PAPER: THE STORY OF WHEN A DIGICAM WAS NOT A CARAMEL, SHOUTAROU KOMINAMI

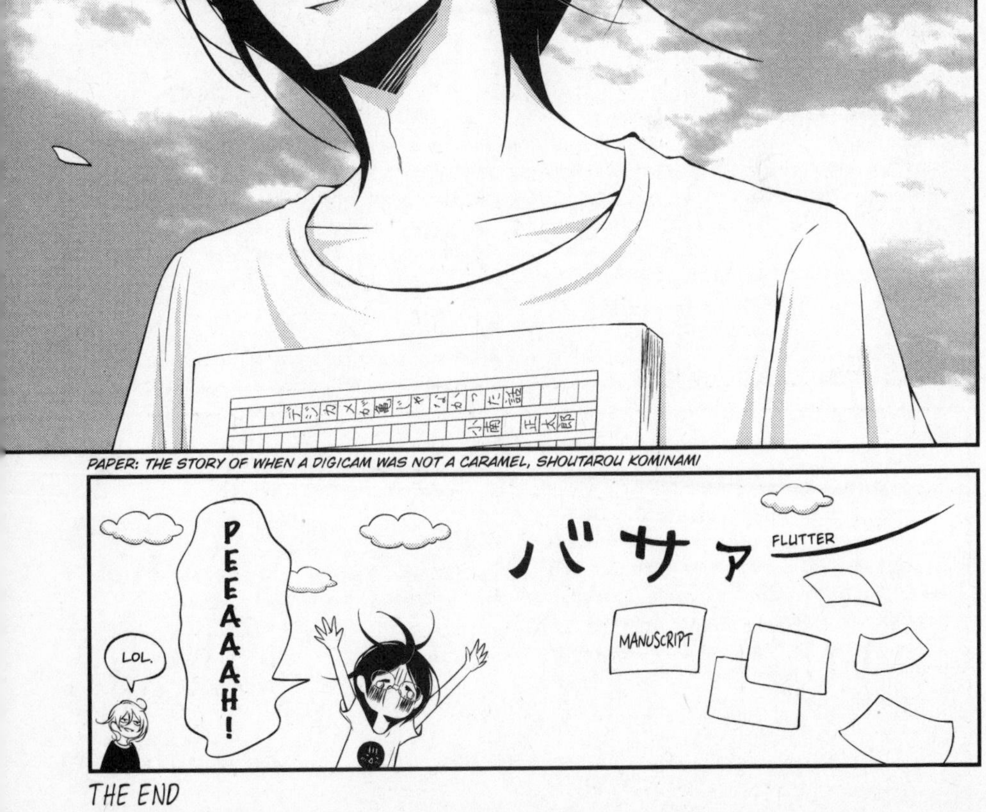
バサァ
FLUTTER
MANUSCRIPT
PEEAAAH!
LOL.

THE END

TRANSLATION NOTES

Page 387
Katou's haiku here uses the phrase *dokushoka*, which means "bookworm" in the first instance and incorporates portions of the words "seduce" and "early summer" in the second instance.

Page 389
Somen are very thin noodles generally served cold in the summertime.

Page 390
The specific dish Kominami is referring to here is *nagashi somen*. The somen noodles are sent flowing down a cold-water flume through an open length of bamboo, and people pick it out with chopsticks as it flows by.

Page 390
Katou's play on words in Japanese is between somen (the noodles) and somen ("surface area"). More literally, her haiku is "I'd like to know the total surface area of somen."

Page 391
Katou uses a homophone for "sweltering night" in each line of her haiku. More literally, her haiku is "The sweltering night / But I want to sleep / I massage my ear."

Page 394
Unadon is a dish consisting of eel on top of rice. It is also a typical summer food.

Page 406
Canned coffee is typically about half the size of a can of soda.

Page 429
Night on the Galactic Railroad is a classic Japanese novel by Kenji Miyazawa. "The Spider's Thread" is a famous short story by Ryunosuke Akutagawa. "Run, Melos!" is a famous short story by Osamu Dazai. Natsume Soseki was an important Japanese writer who penned many classic books, including *I Am a Cat* and *Kokoro*. "The cat with no name" here refers to the titular cat of *I Am a Cat*.

Page 430
Yasunari Kawabata was the first Japanese author to win the Nobel Prize in Literature.

Page 431
The Akutagawa Prize, named after famed writer Ryunosuke Akutagawa, is one of Japan's most prestigious literary awards.

Page 443
The word for "Japanese whiting" is the same as "kiss" in Japanese (*kisu*).

Page 459
The last name of Ruy Ramos, who played and coached professional soccer in Japan beginning in 1977, is spelled with the same characters as the famed Godzilla character Mothra but in a different order (*ramosu* vs. *mosura*).

Page 460
Garigari-kun is a popular popsicle brand that has crunchy bits of flavored ice in it.

Page 465
Obon is a time in the summer when Japanese people return to their hometowns to honor their ancestors by performing various rites to welcome the visiting spirits and maintain the graves of those passed, as well as to gather at local festivals and dances.

Page 470
Kinako is a powder made of roasted soybeans often used as a topping for sweets.

Page 485
Yoyoinoyoi is a nonsense word called out rhythmically during Obon dances.

Page 501
The *from B* magazine is a parody of the job-hunting magazine and website *from A*.

Page 505
Shikishi are stiff boards often used by fans getting autographs or drawings from celebrities.

Page 507
A ghost leg is a ladderlike chart commonly used in Japan to make random choices.

Page 537
Small packets of tissues are often handed out in front of stations and other public places as a form of advertising.

Page 539
Written Japanese utilizes borrowed Chinese characters, or kanji, that help distinguish homophones from one another. In this case, "public bath" is a homophone for "fight" or "battle." Kominami has mistakenly chosen the kanji for the former to complete his test.

Page 566
The books on Shoutarou's shelf now include some of his own, many of which are parodies of Osamu Dazai's titles.

Page 569
The original title of Shoutarou's manuscript is *The Story of When a Digital Camera Was Not a Turtle*, which plays on the words *digikame*, a Japanese portmanteau of "digital camera," and *kame*, which means "turtle."

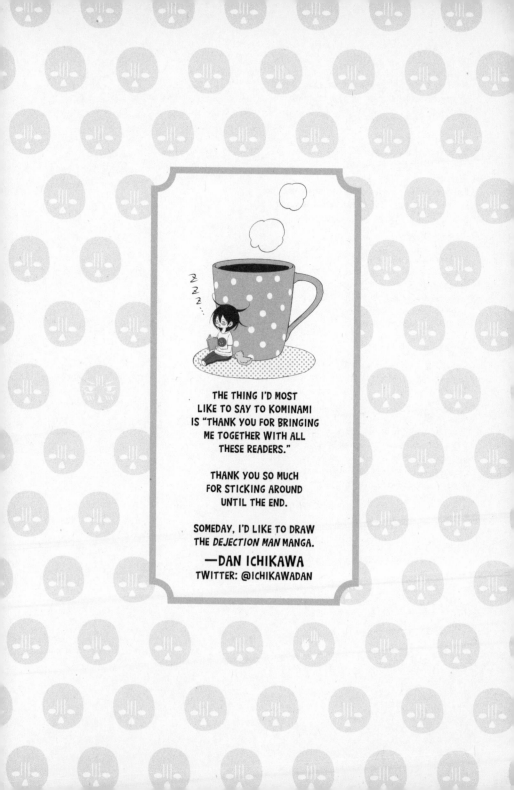

THE THING I'D MOST
LIKE TO SAY TO KOMINAMI
IS "THANK YOU FOR BRINGING
ME TOGETHER WITH ALL
THESE READERS."

THANK YOU SO MUCH
FOR STICKING AROUND
UNTIL THE END.

SOMEDAY, I'D LIKE TO DRAW
THE *DEJECTION MAN* MANGA.

—DAN ICHIKAWA
TWITTER: @ICHIKAWADAN

SHUT-IN
SHOUTAROU KOMINAMI
TAKES ON THE WORLD

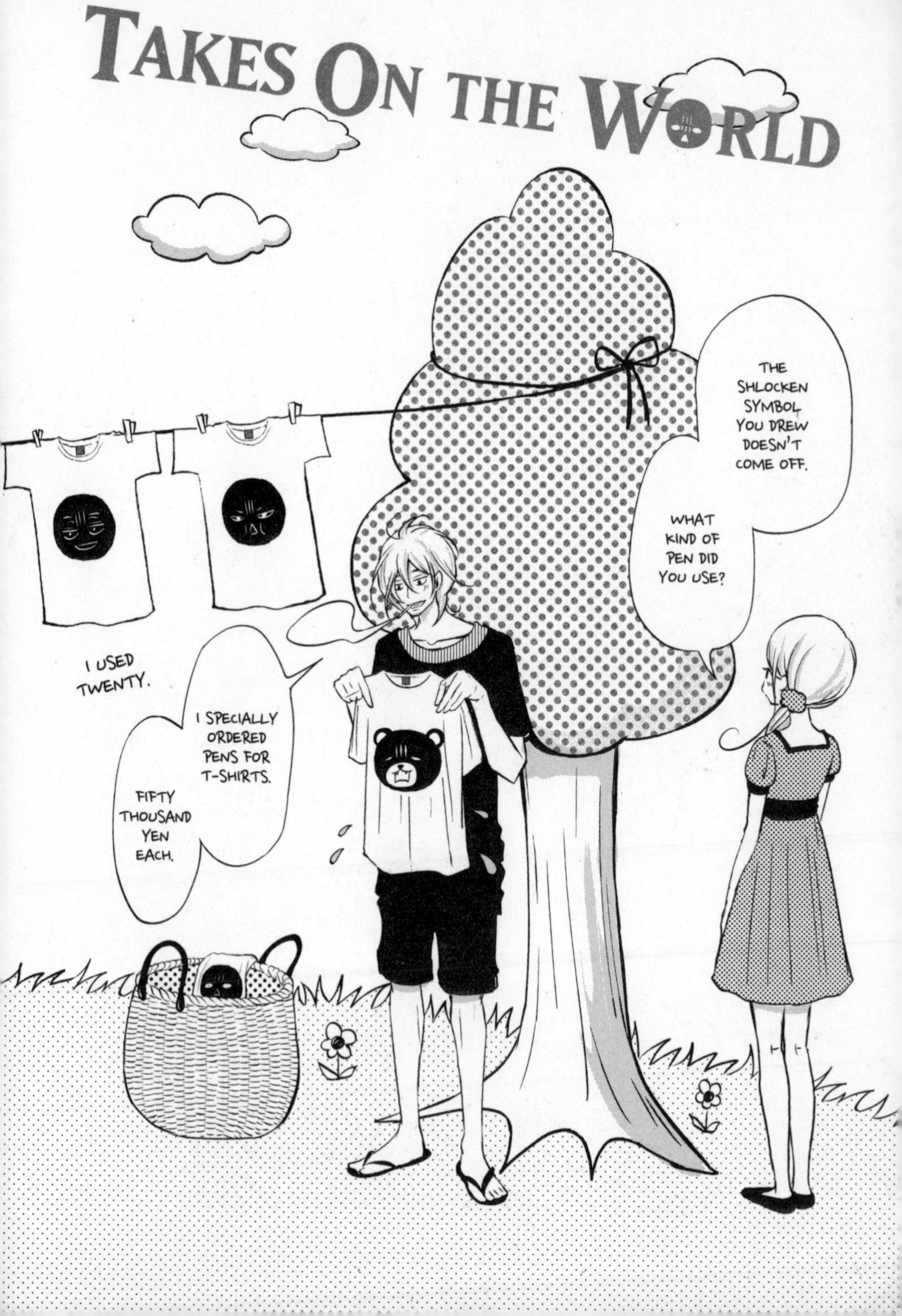
TAKES ON THE WORLD
THE SHLOCKEN SYMBOL YOU DREW DOESN'T COME OFF.
WHAT KIND OF PEN DID YOU USE?
I SPECIALLY ORDERED PENS FOR T-SHIRTS.
FIFTY THOUSAND YEN EACH.
I USED TWENTY.

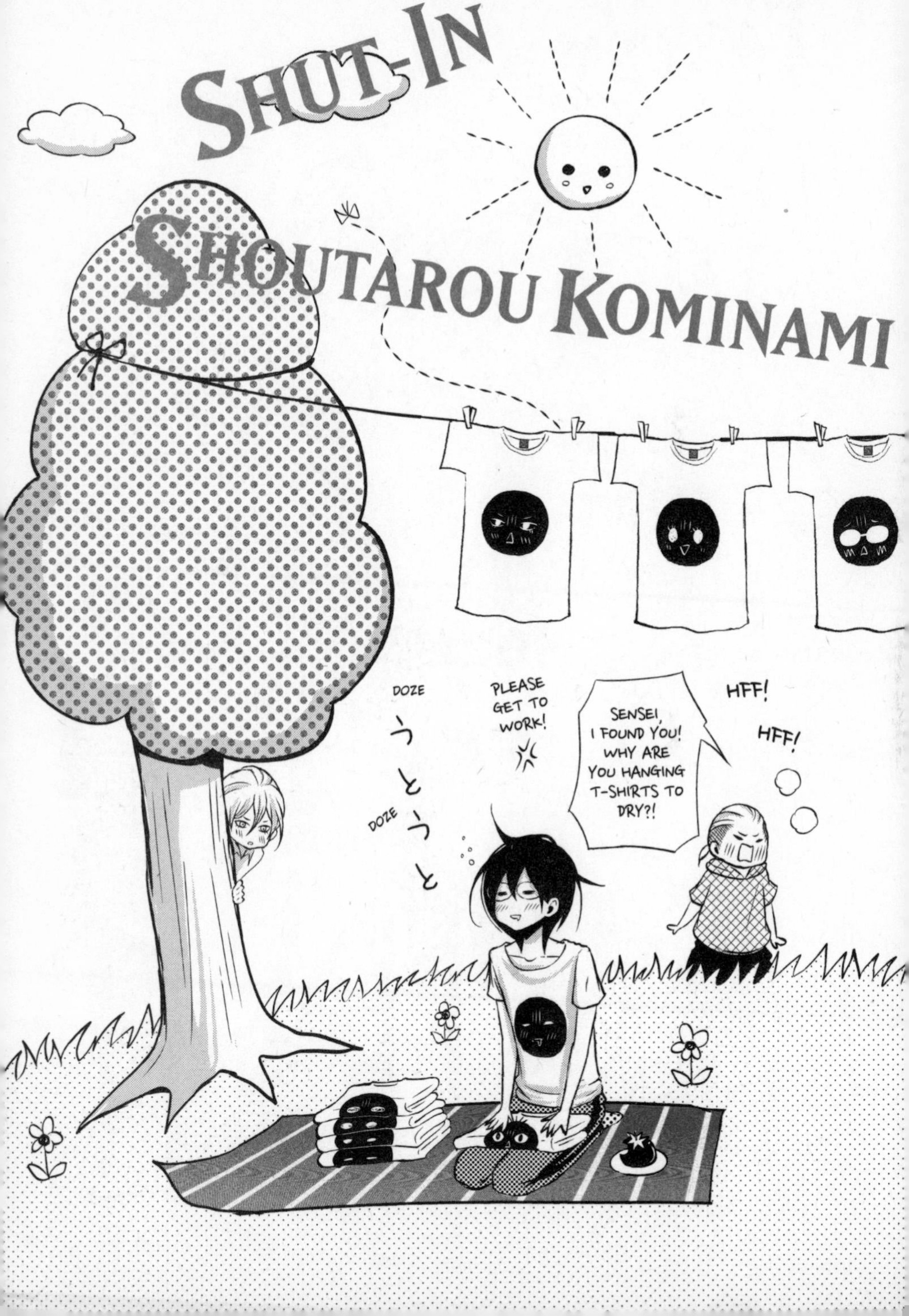
SHUT-IN SHOUTAROU KOMINAMI
HFF!
HFF!
SENSEI, I FOUND YOU! WHY ARE YOU HANGING T-SHIRTS TO DRY?!
PLEASE GET TO WORK!
DOZE
うと
DOZE
うと

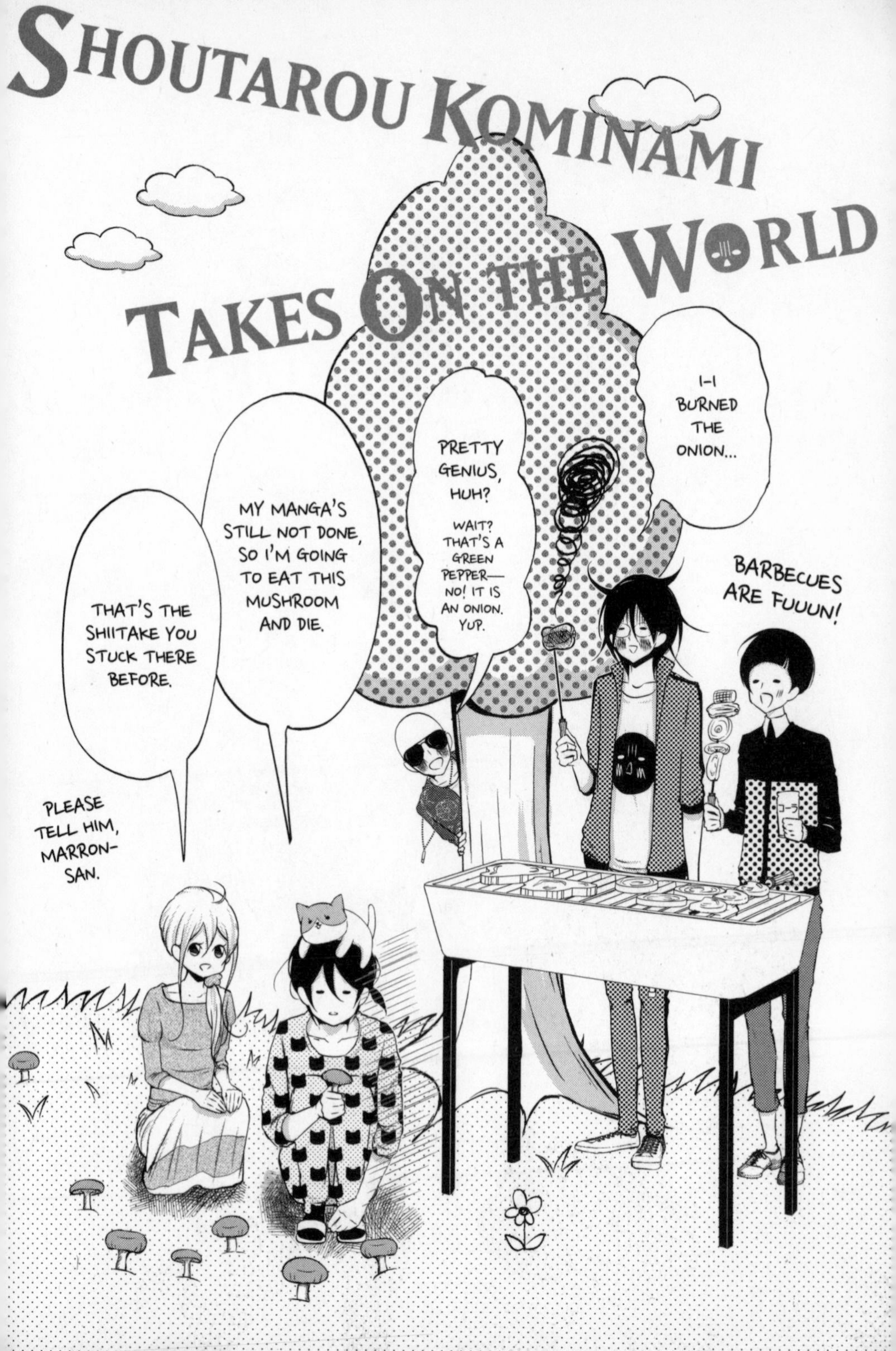
SHOUTAROU KOMINAMI TAKES ON THE WORLD
I-I BURNED THE ONION...
BARBECUES ARE FUUUN!
コーラ
PRETTY GENIUS, HUH?
WAIT? THAT'S A GREEN PEPPER— NO! IT IS AN ONION. YUP.
MY MANGA'S STILL NOT DONE, SO I'M GOING TO EAT THIS MUSHROOM AND DIE.
THAT'S THE SHIITAKE YOU STUCK THERE BEFORE.
PLEASE TELL HIM, MARRON-SAN.

SHUT-IN

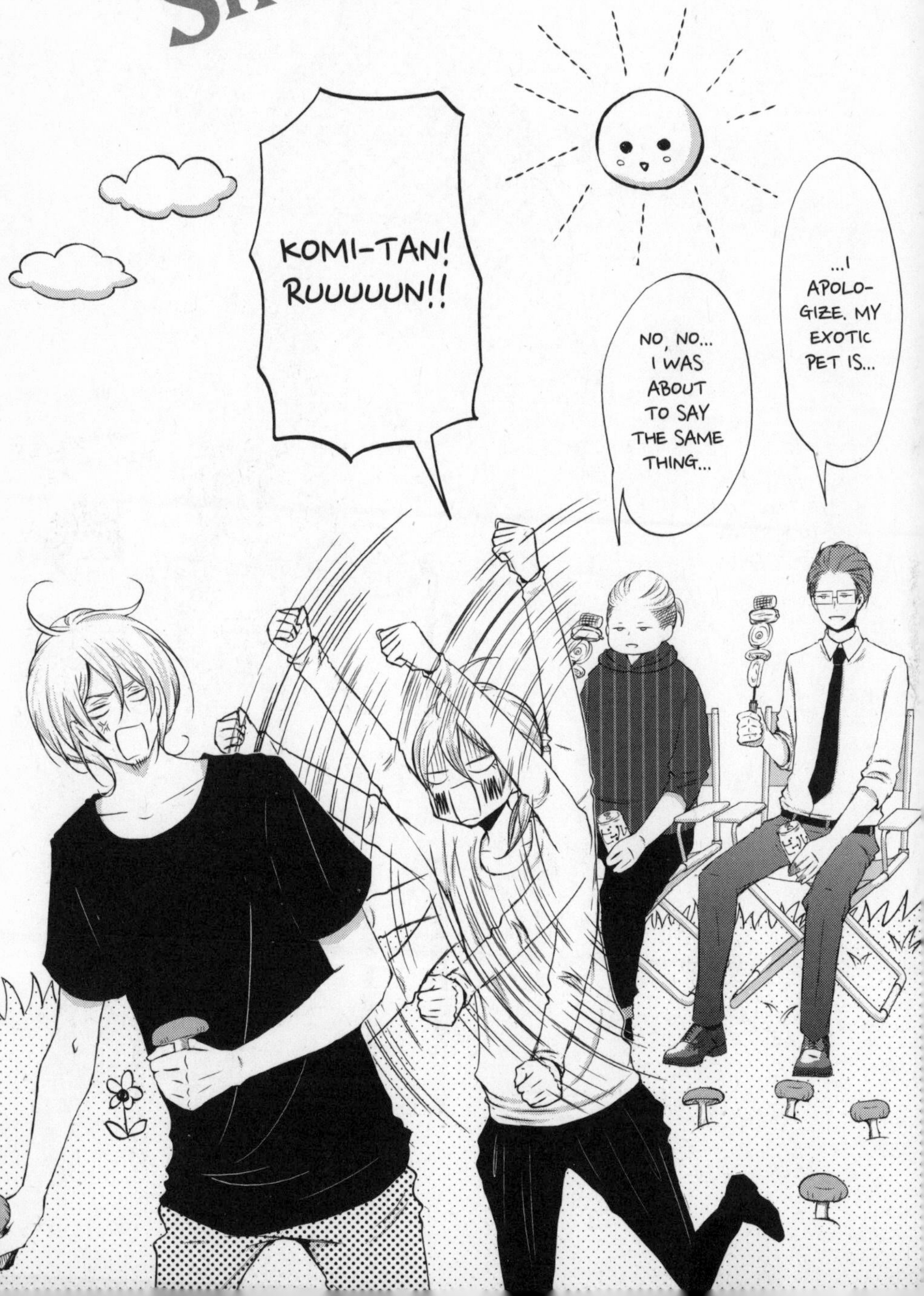
...I APOLOGIZE. MY EXOTIC PET IS...
NO, NO... I WAS ABOUT TO SAY THE SAME THING...
KOMI-TAN! RUUUUUN!!

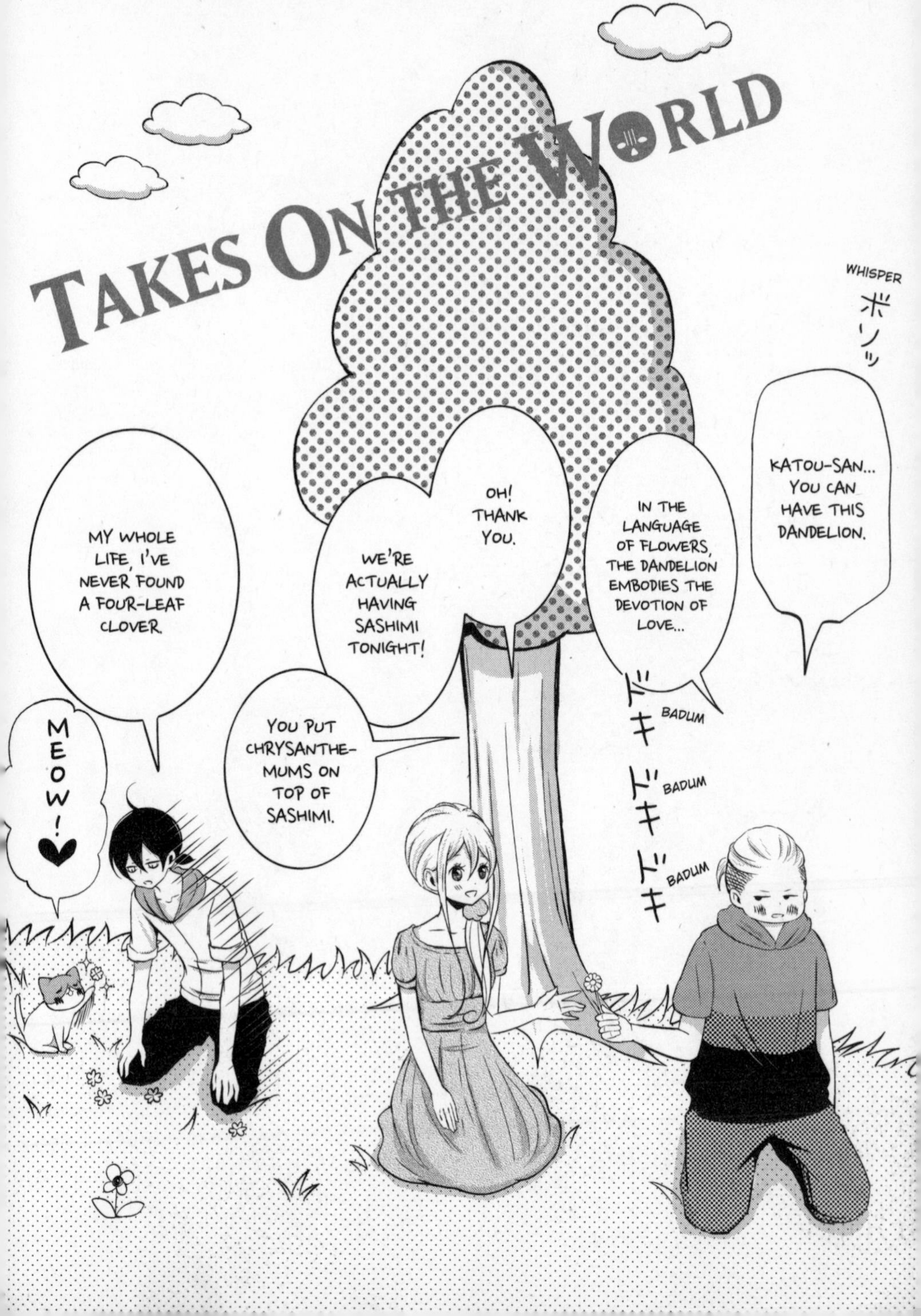
TAKES ON THE WORLD
WHISPER
ボソッ
KATOU-SAN... YOU CAN HAVE THIS DANDELION.
IN THE LANGUAGE OF FLOWERS, THE DANDELION EMBODIES THE DEVOTION OF LOVE...
ドキ BADUM
ドキ BADUM
ドキ BADUM
OH! THANK YOU.
WE'RE ACTUALLY HAVING SASHIMI TONIGHT!
YOU PUT CHRYSANTHE-MUMS ON TOP OF SASHIMI.
MY WHOLE LIFE, I'VE NEVER FOUND A FOUR-LEAF CLOVER.
MEOW! ♥

SHUT-IN SHOUTAROU KOMINAMI
SMOOCH! ♥
PYEAH! ///
LOL.
KOMI-TAN! I BROUGHT A WEAPON!
DAZAI

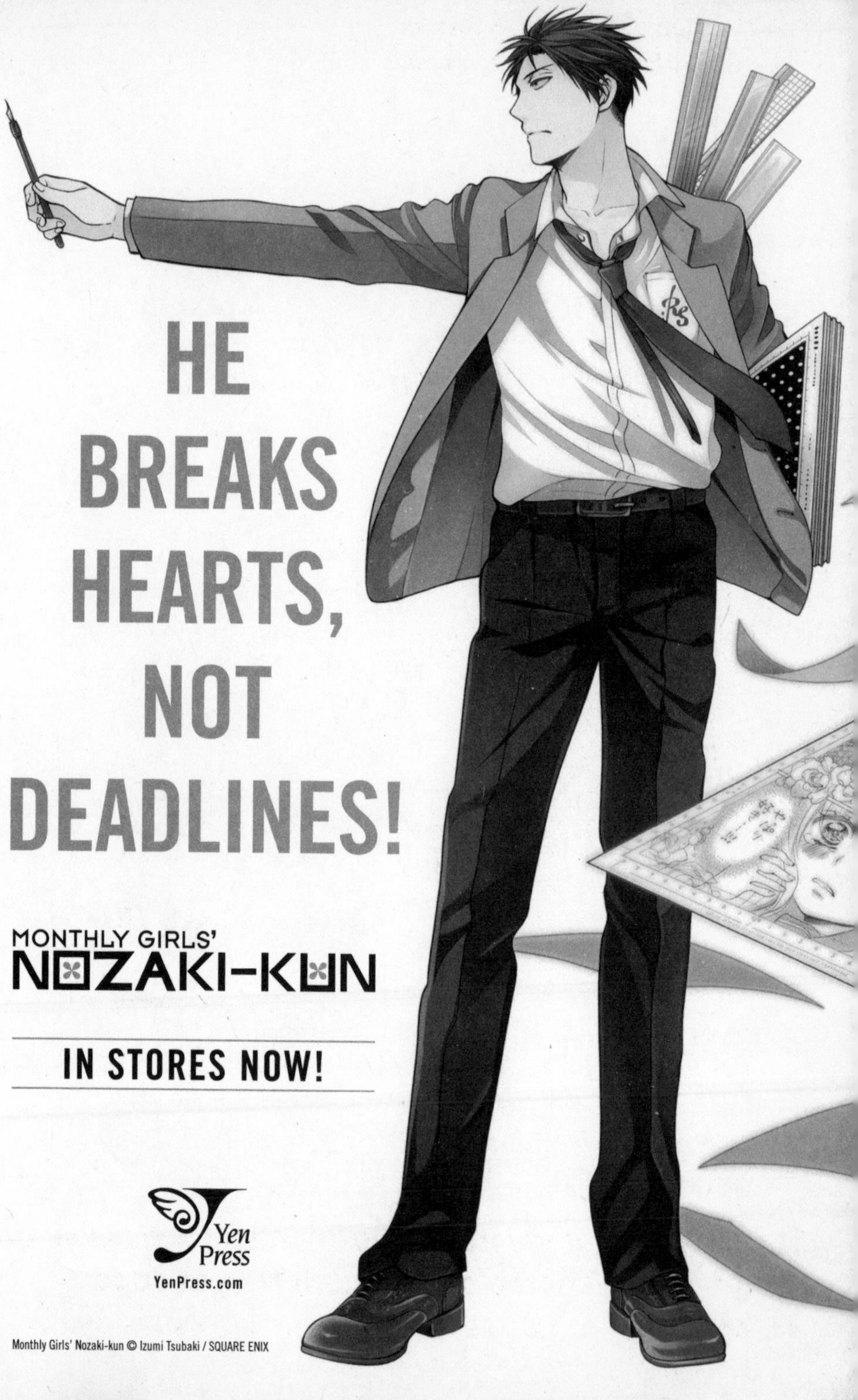
HE
BREAKS
HEARTS,
NOT
DEADLINES!
MONTHLY GIRLS'
NOZAKI-KUN
IN STORES NOW!
Yen Press
YenPress.com
Monthly Girls' Nozaki-kun © Izumi Tsubaki / SQUARE ENIX

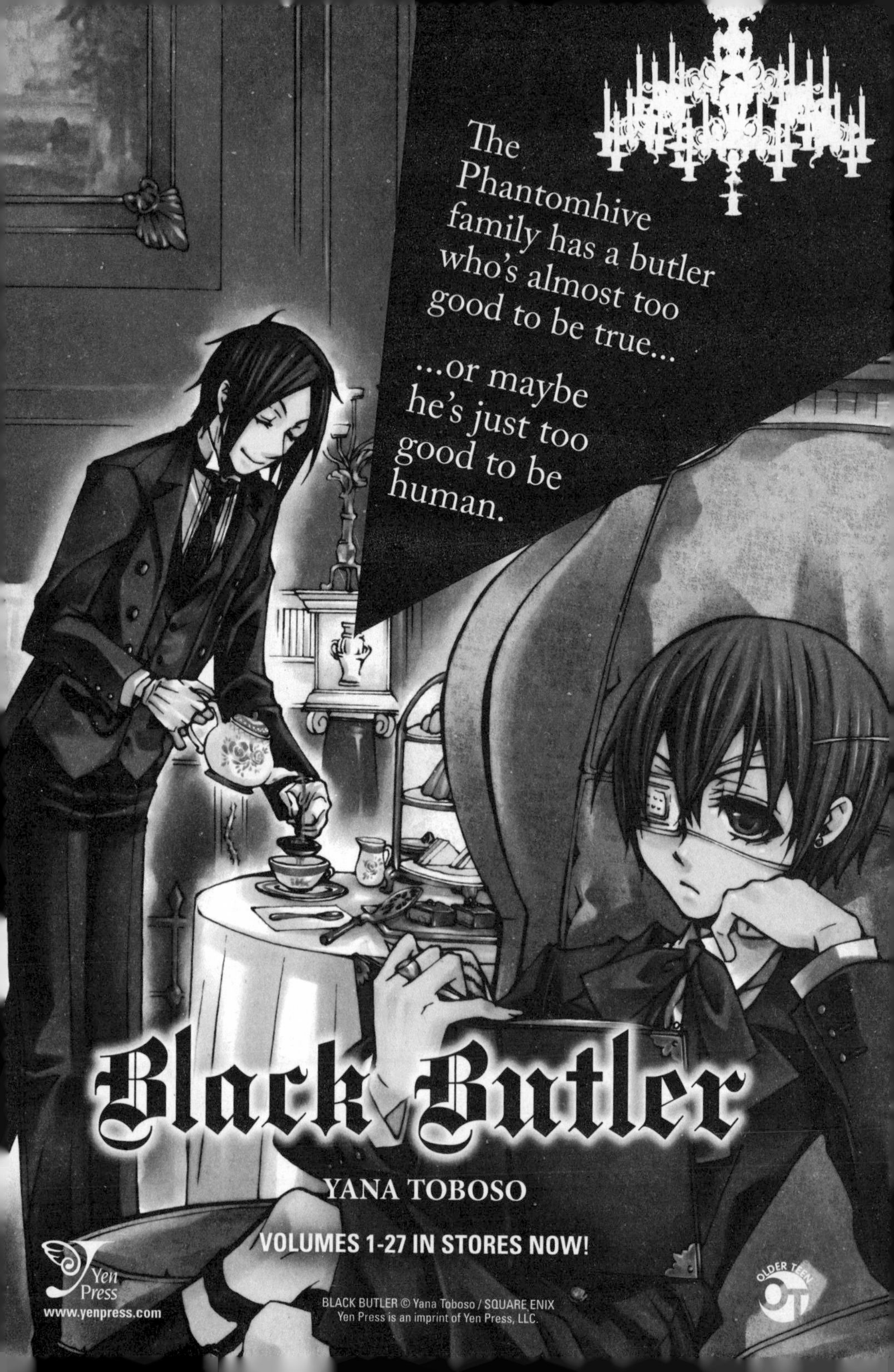

The Phantomhive family has a butler who's almost too good to be true...
...or maybe he's just too good to be human.
Black Butler
YANA TOBOSO
VOLUMES 1-27 IN STORES NOW!
Yen Press
www.yenpress.com
BLACK BUTLER © Yana Toboso / SQUARE ENIX
Yen Press is an imprint of Yen Press, LLC.
OLDER TEEN
OT

WELCOME TO IKEBUKUR
WHERE TOKYO'S WIL
CHARACTERS GATHE

BOY WHO
ABOUT T

NAIVE
TALKE

A SHUT-IN
QUESTIONA

E MOST
MAN IN

E "HEADLES
TCH-BLAC

AS THEIR PATHS CROSS, THIS ECCENTRIC
WEAVES A TWISTED, CRACKED LOVE STO

AVAILABLE NOW

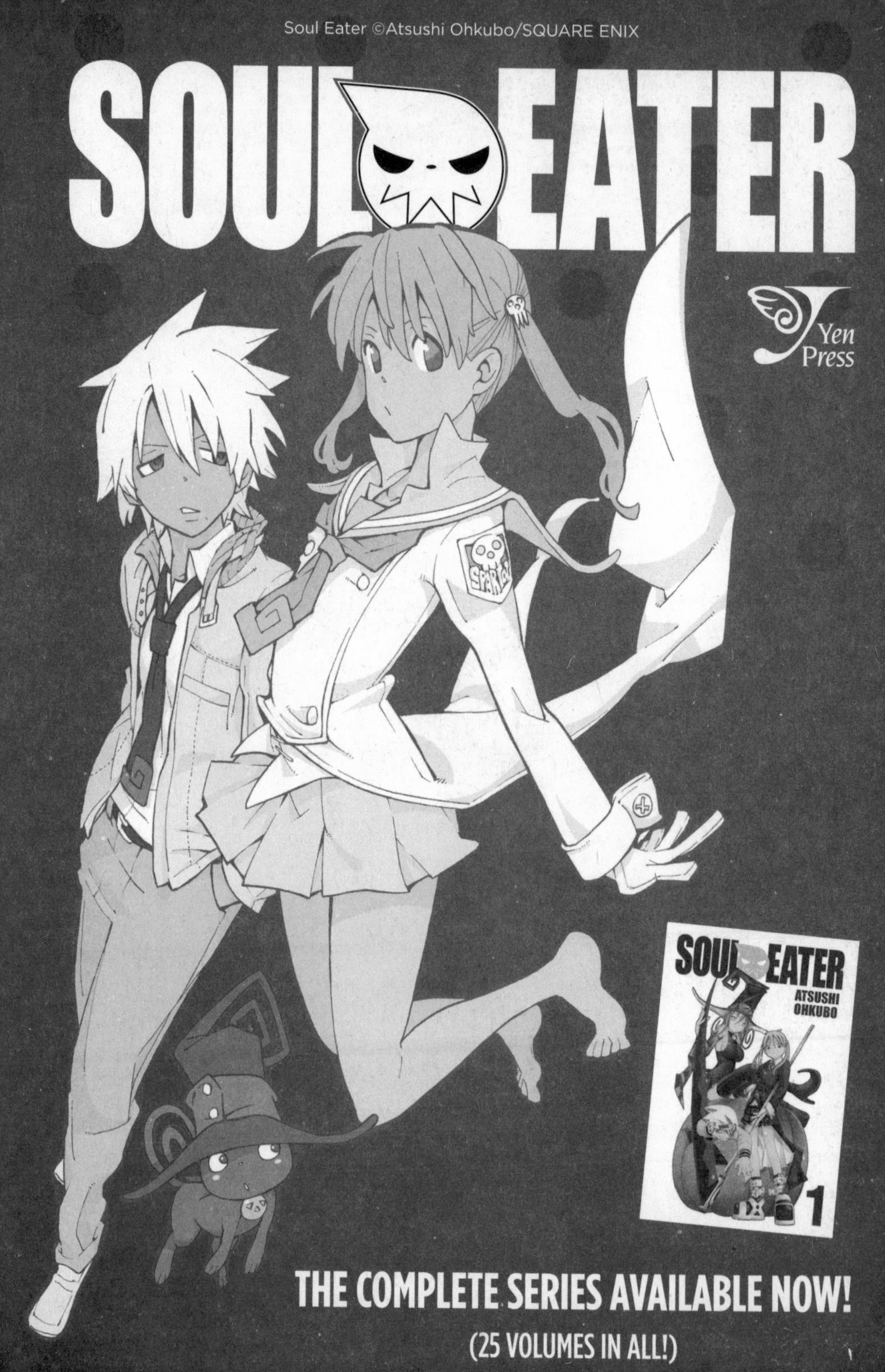
Soul Eater ©Atsushi Ohkubo/SQUARE ENIX
SOUL EATER
Yen Press
SOUL EATER
ATSUSHI OHKUBO
1
THE COMPLETE SERIES AVAILABLE NOW!
(25 VOLUMES IN ALL!)

THE BEAT OF THE SOUL CONTINUES...

VOL. 1 - 5 AVAILABLE NOW!

SHUT-IN SHOUTAROU KOMINAMI TAKES ON THE W●RLD

DAN ICHIKAWA

Translation: Jocelyne Allen   Lettering: Erin Hickman

SHUT-IN SHOUTAROU KOMINAMI TAKES ON THE WORLD, Vols. 1, 2, 3
©2013, 2014 Dan Ichikawa/SQUARE ENIX CO., LTD. First published in Japan in 2013, 2014 by SQUARE ENIX CO., LTD. English translation rights arranged with SQUARE ENIX CO., LTD. and Yen Press, LLC through Tuttle-Mori Agency, Inc., Tokyo.

English translation © 2015 by SQUARE ENIX CO., LTD.

Yen Press
1290 Avenue of the Americas
New York, NY 10104

Visit us at yenpress.com
facebook.com/yenpress
twitter.com/yenpress
yenpress.tumblr.com
instagram.com/yenpress

First Yen Press Print Edition: January 2019
The volumes in this omnibus were originally published as ebooks in September 2015 by Yen Press.

Yen Press is an imprint of Yen Press, LLC.
The Yen Press name and logo are trademarks of Yen Press, LLC.

Library of Congress Control Number: 2018958635

ISBN: 978-1-9753-8367-1

10 9 8 7 6 5 4 3 2 1

WOR

Printed in the United States of America